THE EXPOSITOR'S BIBLE COMMENTARY

THE EXPOSITOR'S BIBLE COMMENTARY

with

The New International Version
of
The Holy Bible

IN TWELVE VOLUMES

VOLUME 7
(DANIEL–MINOR PROPHETS)

Regency
Reference Library
Zondervan Publishing House
Grand Rapids, Michigan

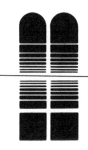

THE EXPOSITOR'S BIBLE COMMENTARY, VOLUME 7

Requests for information should be addressed to:
Zondervan Publishing House
Academic and Professional Books
Grand Rapids, Michigan 49530

Library of Congress Cataloging in Publication Data (Revised)
(Revised for volume 7)

Main entry under title:
The Expositor's Bible commentary

Vol. 7 published by Regency Reference Library.
Includes bibliographies.
CONTENTS: v. 1. Introductory articles.—
—v. 7. Daniel-Malachi—[etc.]—v. 12. Hebrews-Revelation.
1. Bible—Commentaries. I. Gaebelein, Frank Ely,
1899- II. Douglas, James Dixon. III. Bible
English. New International. 1976.
BS491.2E96 220.6 76-41334
ISBN 0-310-36490-6 (v. 7)

Printed in the United States of America

93 94 95 / DH / 11

This edition is printed on acid-free paper and meets the American National Standards Institute Z39.48 standard.

CONTENTS

CONTRIBUTORS TO VOLUME 7

Daniel: *Gleason L. Archer, Jr.*
A.B., A.M., Ph.D. Harvard University; LL.B., Suffolk Law School; B.D., Princeton Theological Seminary.
Professor of Old Testament and Semitics, Trinity Evangelical Divinity School.

Hosea: *Leon J. Wood*
A.B., Calvin College; Th.B., Th.M., Calvin Theological Seminary; Ph.D., Michigan State University.
Formerly Dean and Professor of Old Testament, Grand Rapids Baptist Bible Seminary. Deceased.

Joel: *Richard D. Patterson*
A.B., Wheaton College; M.Div., Los Angeles Baptist Theological Seminary; Th.M., Talbot Theological Seminary; M.A., Ph.D., U.C.L.A.
Chairman, Department of Biblical Studies, Liberty Baptist College.

Amos, Micah: *Thomas Edward McComiskey*
B.A., The King's College; M.Div., Faith Theological Seminary; Th.M., Westminster Theological Seminary; M.A., Ph.D., Brandeis University.
Professor of Old Testament and Semitic Languages, Trinity Evangelical Divinity School.

Obadiah, Nahum, Habakkuk: *Carl E. Armerding*
A.B., Gordon College; B.D., Trinity Evangelical Divinity School; M.A., Ph.D., Brandeis University; Post Doctoral Fellow, Hebrew Union College, Jerusalem.
Principal and Professor of Old Testament, Regent College.

Jonah: *H. L. Ellison*
B.A., B.D., Kings College, London.
Formerly Lecturer at London Bible College, Cambridge University, and Moorlands Bible College; missionary to Jews in Poland. Deceased.

Zephaniah: *Larry Lee Walker*
B.D., Northern Baptist Theological Seminary; M.A., Wheaton College Graduate School; Ph.D., Dropsie College.
Professor of Old Testament and Hebrew, Mid-America Baptist Theological Seminary.

Haggai, Malachi: *Robert L. Alden*
B.A., Barrington College; B.D., Westminster Theological Seminary; Ph.D., Hebrew Union College.
Professor of Old Testament, Denver Seminary.

Zechariah: *Kenneth L. Barker*
B.A., Northwestern College; Th.M., Dallas Theological Seminary; Ph.D., The Dropsie College for Hebrew and Cognate Learning.
Executive Secretary, NIV Committee on Bible Translation; Director, Bible Translation Department, International Bible Society.

PREFACE

The title of this work defines its purpose. Written primarily by expositors for expositors, it aims to provide preachers, teachers, and students of the Bible with a new and comprehensive commentary on the books of the Old and New Testaments. Its stance is that of a scholarly evangelicalism committed to the divine inspiration, complete trustworthiness, and full authority of the Bible. Its seventy-eight contributors come from the United States, Canada, England, Scotland, Australia, New Zealand, and Switzerland, and from various religious groups, including Anglican, Baptist, Brethren, Free, Independent, Methodist, Nazarene, Presbyterian, and Reformed churches. Most of them teach at colleges, universities, or theological seminaries.

No book has been more closely studied over a longer period of time than the Bible. From the Midrashic commentaries going back to the period of Ezra, through parts of the Dead Sea Scrolls and the Patristic literature, and on to the present, the Scriptures have been expounded. Indeed, there have been times when, as in the Reformation and on occasions since then, exposition has been at the cutting edge of Christian advance. Luther was a powerful exegete, and Calvin is still called "the prince of expositors."

Their successors have been many. And now, when the outburst of new translations and their unparalleled circulation have expanded the readership of the Bible, the need for exposition takes on fresh urgency.

Not that God's Word can ever become captive to its expositors. Among all other books, it stands first in its combination of perspicuity and profundity. Though a child can be made "wise for salvation" by believing its witness to Christ, the greatest mind cannot plumb the depths of its truth (2 Tim. 3:15; Rom. 11:33). As Gregory the Great said, "Holy Scripture is a stream of running water, where alike the elephant may swim, and the lamb walk." So, because of the inexhaustible nature of Scripture, the task of opening up its meaning is still a perennial obligation of biblical scholarship.

How that task is done inevitably reflects the outlook of those engaged in it. Every Bible scholar has presuppositions. To this neither the editors of these volumes nor the contributors to them are exceptions. They share a common commitment to the supernatural Christianity set forth in the inspired Word. Their purpose is not to supplant the many valuable commentaries that have preceded this work and from which both the editors and contributors have learned. It is rather to draw on the resources of contemporary evangelical scholarship in producing a new reference work for understanding the Scriptures.

A commentary that will continue to be useful through the years should handle contemporary trends in biblical studies in such a way as to avoid becoming outdated when critical fashions change. Biblical criticism is not in itself inadmissable, as some have mistakenly thought. When scholars investigate the authorship, date, literary characteristics, and purpose of a biblical document, they are practicing biblical criticism. So also when, in order to ascertain as nearly as possible the original form of the text, they deal with variant readings, scribal errors, emendations, and other phenomena in the manuscripts. To do these things is essential to responsible exegesis and exposition. And always there is the need to distinguish hypothesis from fact, conjecture from truth.

The chief principle of interpretation followed in this commentary is the grammatico-historical one—namely, that the primary aim of the exegete is to make clear the meaning of the text at the time and in the circumstances of its writing. This endeavor to understand what in the first instance the inspired writers actually said must not be confused with an inflexible literalism. Scripture makes lavish use of symbols and figures of speech; great portions of it are poetical. Yet when it speaks in this way, it speaks no less truly than it does in its historical and doctrinal portions. To understand its message requires attention to matters of grammar and syntax, word meanings, idioms, and literary forms—all in relation to the historical and cultural setting of the text.

The contributors to this work necessarily reflect varying convictions. In certain controversial matters the policy is that of clear statement of the contributors' own views followed by fair presentation of other ones. The treatment of eschatology, though it reflects differences of interpretation, is consistent with a general premillennial position. (Not all contributors, however, are premillennial.) But prophecy is more than prediction, and so this commentary gives due recognition to the major lode of godly social concern in the prophetic writings.

THE EXPOSITOR'S BIBLE COMMENTARY is presented as a scholarly work, though not primarily one of technical criticism. In its main portion, the Exposition, and in Volume 1 (General and Special Articles), all Semitic and Greek words are transliterated and the English equivalents given. As for the Notes, here Semitic and Greek characters are used but always with transliterations and English meanings, so that this portion of the commentary will be as accessible as possible to readers unacquainted with the original languages.

It is the conviction of the general editor, shared by his colleagues in the Zondervan editorial department, that in writing about the Bible, lucidity is not incompatible with scholarship. They are therefore endeavoring to make this a clear and understandable work.

The translation used in it is the New International Version (North American Edition). To the International Bible Society thanks are due for permission to use this most recent of the major Bible translations. It was chosen because of the clarity and beauty of its style and its faithfulness to the original texts.

To the associate editor, Richard P. Polcyn, and to the contributing editors—Dr. Walter C. Kaiser, Jr., Dr. Bruce K. Waltke, and Dr. Ralph H. Alexander for the Old Testament, and Dr. James Montgomery Boice and Dr. Merrill C. Tenney for the New Testament—the general editor expresses his gratitude for their unfailing cooperation and their generosity in advising him out of their expert scholarship. And to the many other contributors he is indebted for their invaluable part in this work. Finally, he owes a special debt of gratitude to Dr. Robert K. DeVries, publisher, The Zondervan Corporation, and Miss Elizabeth Brown, secretary, for their assistance and encouragement.

Whatever else it is—the greatest and most beautiful of books, the primary source of law and morality, the fountain of wisdom, and the infallible guide to life—the Bible is above all the inspired witness to Jesus Christ. May this work fulfill its function of expounding the Scriptures with grace and clarity, so that its users may find that both Old and New Testaments do indeed lead to our Lord Jesus Christ, who alone could say, "I have come that they may have life, and have it to the full" (John 10:10).

FRANK E. GAEBELEIN

ABBREVIATIONS

A. General Abbreviations

A	Codex Alexandrinus
Akkad.	Akkadian
א	Codex Sinaiticus
Ap. Lit.	Apocalyptic Literature
Apoc.	Apocrypha
Aq.	Aquila's Greek Translation of the Old Testament
Arab.	Arabic
Aram.	Aramaic
b	Babylonian Gemara
B	Codex Vaticanus
C	Codex Ephraemi Syri
c.	*circa*, about
cf.	*confer*, compare
ch., chs.	chapter, chapters
cod., codd.	codex, codices
contra	in contrast to
D	Codex Bezae
DSS	Dead Sea Scrolls (see E.)
ed., edd.	edited, edition, editor; editions
e.g.	*exempli gratia*, for example
Egyp.	Egyptian
et al.	*et alii*, and others
EV	English Versions of the Bible
fem.	feminine
ff.	following (verses, pages, etc.)
fl.	flourished
ft.	foot, feet
gen.	genitive
Gr.	Greek
Heb.	Hebrew
Hitt.	Hittite
ibid.	*ibidem*, in the same place
id.	*idem*, the same
i.e.	*id est*, that is
impf.	imperfect
infra.	below
in loc.	*in loco*, in the place cited
j	Jerusalem or Palestinian Gemara
Lat.	Latin
LL.	Late Latin
LXX	Septuagint
M	Mishnah
masc.	masculine
mg.	margin
Mid	Midrash
MS(S)	manuscript(s)
MT	Masoretic text
n.	note
n.d.	no date
Nestle	Nestle (ed.) *Novum Testamentum Graece*
no.	number
NT	New Testament
obs.	obsolete
OL	Old Latin
OS	Old Syriac
OT	Old Testament
p., pp.	page, pages
par.	paragraph
Pers.	Persian
Pesh.	Peshitta
Phoen.	Phoenician
pl.	plural
Pseudep.	Pseudepigrapha
Q	Quelle ("Sayings" source in the Gospels)
qt.	quoted by
q.v.	*quod vide*, which see
R	Rabbah
rev.	revised, reviser, revision
Rom.	Roman
RVm	Revised Version margin
Samar.	Samaritan recension
SCM	Student Christian Movement Press
Sem.	Semitic
sing.	singular
SPCK	Society for the Promotion of Christian Knowledge
Sumer.	Sumerian
s.v.	*sub verbo*, under the word
Syr.	Syriac
Symm.	Symmachus
T	Talmud
Targ.	Targum
Theod.	Theodotion
TR	Textus Receptus
tr.	translation, translator, translated
UBS	Tha United Bible Societies' Greek Text
Ugar.	Ugaritic
u.s.	*ut supra*, as above
v., vv.	verse, verses
viz.	*videlicet*, namely
vol.	volume
vs.	versus
Vul.	Vulgate
WH	Westcott and Hort, *The New Testament in Greek*

B. Abbreviations for Modern Translations and Paraphrases

AmT	Smith and Goodspeed, *The Complete Bible, An American Translation*
ASV	American Standard Version, American Revised Version (1901)
Beck	Beck, *The New Testament in the Language of Today*
BV	Berkeley Version (The Modern Language Bible)
JB	The Jerusalem Bible
JPS	*Jewish Publication Society Version of the Old Testament*
KJV	King James Version
Knox	R.G. Knox, *The Holy Bible: A Translation from the Latin Vulgate in the Light of the Hebrew and Greek Original*
LB	The Living Bible
Mof	J. Moffatt, *A New Translation of the Bible*
NAB	The New American Bible
NASB	New American Standard Bible
NEB	The New English Bible
NIV	The New International Version
Ph	J. B. Phillips *The New Testament in Modern English*
RSV	Revised Standard Version
RV	Revised Version — 1881–1885
TCNT	Twentieth Century New Testament
TEV	Today's English Version
Wey	*Weymouth's New Testament in Modern Speech*
Wms	C. B. Williams, *The New Testament: A Translation in the Language of the People*

C. Abbreviations for Periodicals and Reference Works

AASOR	*Annual of the American Schools of Oriental Research*
AB	*Anchor Bible*
AIs	de Vaux: *Ancient Israel*
AJA	*American Journal of Archaeology*
AJSL	*American Journal of Semitic Languages and Literatures*
AJT	*American Journal of Theology*
Alf	Alford: *Greek Testament Commentary*
ANEA	*Ancient Near Eastern Archaeology*
ANET	Pritchard: *Ancient Near Eastern Texts*
ANF	Roberts and Donaldson: *The Ante-Nicene Fathers*
ANT	M. R. James: *The Apocryphal New Testament*
A-S	Abbot-Smith: *Manual Greek Lexicon of the New Testament*
AThR	*Anglican Theological Review*
BA	*Biblical Archaeologist*
BAG	Bauer, Arndt, and Gingrich: *Greek-English Lexicon of the New Testament*
BAGD	Bauer, Arndt, Gingrich, and Danker: *Greek-English Lexicon of the New Testament* 2nd edition
BASOR	*Bulletin of the American Schools of Oriental Research*
BC	Foakes-Jackson and Lake: *The Beginnings of Christianity*
BDB	Brown, Driver, and Briggs: *Hebrew-English Lexicon of the Old Testament*
BDF	Blass, Debrunner, and Funk: *A Greek Grammar of the New Testament and Other Early Christian Literature*
BDT	Harrison: *Baker's Dictionary of Theology*
Beng.	Bengel's *Gnomon*
BETS	*Bulletin of the Evangelical Theological Society*
BH	*Biblia Hebraica*
BHS	*Biblia Hebraica Stuttgartensia*
BJRL	*Bulletin of the John Rylands Library*
BS	*Bibliotheca Sacra*
BT	*Babylonian Talmud*
BTh	*Biblical Theology*
BW	*Biblical World*
CAH	*Cambridge Ancient History*
CanJTh	*Canadian Journal of Theology*
CBQ	*Catholic Biblical Quarterly*
CBSC	*Cambridge Bible for Schools and Colleges*
CE	*Catholic Encyclopedia*
CGT	*Cambridge Greek Testament*

CHS Lange: *Commentary on the Holy Scriptures*
ChT *Christianity Today*
DDB *Davis' Dictionary of the Bible*
Deiss BS Deissmann: *Bible Studies*
Deiss LAE Deissmann: *Light From the Ancient East*
DNTT *Dictionary of New Testament Theology*
EBC *The Expositor's Bible Commentary*
EBi *Encyclopaedia Biblica*
EBr *Encyclopaedia Britannica*
EDB *Encyclopedic Dictionary of the Bible*
EGT Nicoll: *Expositor's Greek Testament*
EQ *Evangelical Quarterly*
ET *Evangelische Theologie*
ExB *The Expositor's Bible*
Exp *The Expositor*
ExpT *The Expository Times*
FLAP Finegan: *Light From the Ancient Past*
GKC Gesenius, Kautzsch, Cowley, *Hebrew Grammar*, 2nd Eng. ed.
GR *Gordon Review*
HBD *Harper's Bible Dictionary*
HDAC Hastings: *Dictionary of the Apostolic Church*
HDB Hastings: *Dictionary of the Bible*
HDBrev. Hastings: *Dictionary of the Bible*, one-vol. rev. by Grant and Rowley
HDCG Hastings: *Dictionary of Christ and the Gospels*
HERE Hastings: *Encyclopedia of Religion and Ethics*
HGEOTP Heidel: *The Gilgamesh Epic and Old Testament Parallels*
HJP Schurer: *A History of the Jewish People in the Time of Christ*
HR Hatch and Redpath: *Concordance to the Septuagint*
HTR *Harvard Theological Review*
HUCA *Hebrew Union College Annual*
IB *The Interpreter's Bible*
ICC *International Critical Commentary*
IDB *The Interpreter's Dictionary of the Bible*
IEJ *Israel Exploration Journal*
Int *Interpretation*
INT E. Harrison: *Introduction to the New Testament*
IOT R. K. Harrison: *Introduction to the Old Testament*
ISBE *The International Standard Bible Encyclopedia*
ITQ *Irish Theological Quarterly*
JAAR *Journal of American Academy of Religion*
JAOS *Journal of American Oriental Society*
JBL *Journal of Biblical Literature*
JE *Jewish Encyclopedia*
JETS *Journal of Evangelical Theological Society*
JFB Jamieson, Fausset, and Brown: *Commentary on the Old and New Testament*
JNES *Journal of Near Eastern Studies*
Jos. Antiq. Josephus: *The Antiquities of the Jews*
Jos. War Josephus: *The Jewish War*
JQR *Jewish Quarterly Review*
JR *Journal of Religion*
JSJ *Journal for the Study of Judaism in the Persian, Hellenistic and Roman Periods*
JSOR *Journal of the Society of Oriental Research*
JSS *Journal of Semitic Studies*
JT *Jerusalem Talmud*
JTS *Journal of Theological Studies*
KAHL Kenyon: *Archaeology in the Holy Land*
KB Koehler-Baumgartner: *Lexicon in Veteris Testament Libros*
KD Keil and Delitzsch: *Commentary on the Old Testament*
LSJ Liddell, Scott, Jones: *Greek-English Lexicon*
LTJM Edersheim: *The Life and Times of Jesus the Messiah*
MM Moulton and Milligan: *The Vocabulary of the Greek Testament*
MNT Moffatt: *New Testament Commentary*

MST	McClintock and Strong: *Cyclopedia of Biblical, Theological, and Ecclesiastical Literature*
NBC	Davidson, Kevan, and Stibbs: *The New Bible Commentary*, 1st ed.
NBCrev.	Guthrie and Motyer: *The New Bible Commentary*, rev. ed.
NBD	J. D. Douglas: *The New Bible Dictionary*
NCB	*New Century Bible*
NCE	*New Catholic Encyclopedia*
NIC	*New International Commentary*
NIDCC	Douglas: *The New International Dictionary of the Christian Church*
NovTest	*Novum Testamentum*
NSI	Cooke: *Handbook of North Semitic Inscriptions*
NTS	*New Testament Studies*
ODCC	*The Oxford Dictionary of the Christian Church*, rev. ed.
Peake	Black and Rowley: *Peake's Commentary on the Bible*
PEQ	*Palestine Exploration Quarterly*
PNF1	P. Schaff: *The Nicene and Post-Nicene Fathers* (1st series)
PNF2	P. Schaff and H. Wace: *The Nicene and Post-Nicene Fathers* (2nd series)
PTR	*Princeton Theological Review*
RB	*Revue Biblique*
RHG	Robertson's *Grammar of the Greek New Testament in the Light of Historical Research*
RTWB	Richardson: *A Theological Wordbook of the Bible*
SBK	Strack and Billerbeck: *Kommentar zum Neuen Testament aus Talmud und Midrash*
SHERK	*The New Schaff-Herzog Encyclopedia of Religious Knowledge*
SJT	*Scottish Journal of Theology*
SOT	Girdlestone: *Synonyms of Old Testament*
SOTI	Archer: *A Survey of Old Testament Introduction*
ST	*Studia Theologica*
TCERK	Loetscher: *The Twentieth Century Encyclopedia of Religious Knowledge*
TDNT	Kittel: *Theological Dictionary of the New Testament*
TDOT	*Theological Dictionary of the Old Testament*
THAT	*Theologisches Handbuch zum Alten Testament*
ThT	*Theology Today*
TNTC	*Tyndale New Testament Commentaries*
Trench	Trench: *Synonyms of the New Testament*
TWOT	*Theological Wordbook of the Old Testament*
UBD	*Unger's Bible Dictionary*
UT	Gordon: *Ugaritic Textbook*
VB	Allmen: *Vocabulary of the Bible*
VetTest	*Vetus Testamentum*
Vincent	Vincent: *Word-Pictures in the New Testament*
WBC	*Wycliffe Bible Commentary*
WBE	*Wycliffe Bible Encyclopedia*
WC	*Westminster Commentaries*
WesBC	*Wesleyan Bible Commentaries*
WTJ	*Westminster Theological Journal*
ZAW	*Zeitschrift für die alttestamentliche Wissenschaft*
ZNW	*Zeitschrift für die neutestamentliche Wissenschaft*
ZPBD	*The Zondervan Pictorial Bible Dictionary*
ZPEB	*The Zondervan Pictorial Encyclopedia of the Bible*
ZWT	*Zeitschrift für wissenschaftliche Theologie*

D. Abbreviations for Books of the Bible, the Apocrypha, and the Pseudepigrapha

OLD TESTAMENT

Gen	2 Chron	Dan
Exod	Ezra	Hos
Lev	Neh	Joel
Num	Esth	Amos
Deut	Job	Obad
Josh	Ps(Pss)	Jonah
Judg	Prov	Mic
Ruth	Eccl	Nah
1 Sam	S of Songs	Hab
2 Sam	Isa	Zeph
1 Kings	Jer	Hag
2 Kings	Lam	Zech
1 Chron	Ezek	Mal

NEW TESTAMENT

Matt	1 Tim
Mark	2 Tim
Luke	Titus
John	Philem
Acts	Heb
Rom	James
1 Cor	1 Peter
2 Cor	2 Peter
Gal	1 John
Eph	2 John
Phil	3 John
Col	Jude
1 Thess	Rev
2 Thess	

APOCRYPHA

1 Esd	1 Esdras
2 Esd	2 Esdras
Tobit	Tobit
Jud	Judith
Add Esth	Additions to Esther
Wisd Sol	Wisdom of Solomon
Ecclus	Ecclesiasticus (Wisdom of Jesus the Son of Sirach)
Baruch	Baruch
Ep Jer	Epistle of Jeremy
S Th Ch	Song of the Three Child (or Young Men)
Sus	Susanna
Bel	Bel and the Dragon
Pr Man	Prayer of Manasseh
1 Macc	1 Maccabees
2 Macc	2 Maccabees

PSEUDEPIGRAPHA

As Moses	Assumption of Moses
2 Baruch	Syriac Apocalypse of Baruch
3 Baruch	Greek Apocalypse of Baruch
1 Enoch	Ethiopic Book of Enoch
2 Enoch	Slavonic Book of Enoch
3 Enoch	Hebrew Book of Enoch
4 Ezra	4 Ezra
JA	Joseph and Asenath
Jub	Book of Jubilees
L Aristeas	Letter of Aristeas
Life AE	Life of Adam and Eve
Liv Proph	Lives of the Prophets
MA Isa	Martyrdom and Ascension of Isaiah
3 Macc	3 Maccabees
4 Macc	4 Maccabees
Odes Sol	Odes of Solomon
P Jer	Paralipomena of Jeremiah
Pirke Aboth	Pirke Aboth
Ps 151	Psalm 151
Pss Sol	Psalms of Solomon
Sib Oracles	Sibylline Oracles
Story Ah	Story of Ahikar
T Abram	Testament of Abraham
T Adam	Testament of Adam
T Benjamin	Testament of Benjamin
T Dan	Testament of Dan
T Gad	Testament of Gad
T Job	Testament of Job
T Jos	Testament of Joseph
T Levi	Testament of Levi
T Naph	Testament of Naphtali
T 12 Pat	Testaments of the Twe Patriarchs
Zad Frag	Zadokite Fragments

E. Abbreviations of Names of Dead Sea Scrolls and Related Texts

CD	Cairo (Genizah text of the) Damascus (Document)
DSS	Dead Sea Scrolls
Hev	Nahal Hever texts
Mas	Masada Texts
Mird	Khirbet mird texts
Mur	Wadi Murabba'at texts
P	Pesher (commentary)
Q	Qumran
1Q, 2Q, etc.	Numbered caves of Qumran, yielding written material; followed by abbreviation of biblical or apocryphal book.
QL	Qumran Literature
1QapGen	Genesis Apocryphon of Qumran Cave 1
1QH	*Hodayot* (Thanksgiving Hymns) from Qumran Cave 1
1QIsa a,b	First or second copy of Isaiah from Qumran Cave 1
1QpHab	Pesher on Habakkuk from Qumran Cave 1
1QM	*Milhamah* (War Scroll)
1QpMic	Pesher on portions of Micah from Qumran Cave 1
1QS	*Serek Hayyahad* (Rule of the Community, Manual of Discipline)

1QSa	Appendix A (Rule of the Congregation) to 1Qs
1QSb	Appendix B (Blessings) to 1QS
3Q15	Copper Scroll from Qumran Cave 3
4QExod a	Exodus Scroll, exemplar "a" from Qumran Cave 4
4QFlor	Florilegium (or Eschatological Midrashim) from Qumran Cave 4
4Qmess ar	Aramaic "Messianic" text from Qumran Cave 4
4QpNah	Pesher on portions of Nahum from Qumran Cave 4
4QPrNab	Prayer of Nabonidus from Qumran Cave 4
4QpPs37	Pesher on portions of Psalm 37 from Qumran Cave 4
4QTest	Testimonia text from Qumran Cave 4
4QTLevi	Testament of Levi from Qumran Cave 4
4QPhyl	Phylacteries from Qumran Cave 4
11QMelch	Melchizedek text from Qumran Cave 11
11QtgJob	Targum of Job from Qumran Cave 11

TRANSLITERATIONS

Hebrew

א = ʼ	ד = ḏ	י = y	ס = s	ר = r
בּ = b	ה = h	כּ = k	ע = ʻ	שׂ = ś
ב = ḇ	ו = w	ך כ = ḵ	פּ = p	שׁ = š
גּ = g	ז = z	ל = l	ף פ = p̄	תּ = t
ג = ḡ	ח = ḥ	ם מ = m	ץ צ = ṣ	ת = ṯ
דּ = d	ט = ṭ	ן נ = n	ק = q	

◌ָ(ה) = â (h)	◌ָ = ā	◌ַ = a	◌ֲ = ^{a}
◌ֵי = ê	◌ֵ = ē	◌ֶ = e	◌ֱ = ^{e}
◌ִי = î	◌ֹ = ō	◌ִ = i	◌ְ = ^{e} (if vocal)
וֹ = ô		◌ָ = o	◌ֳ = ^{o}
וּ = û		◌ֻ = u	

Aramaic

ʼ b g d h w z ḥ ṭ y k l m n s ʻ p ṣ q r ś š t

Arabic

ʼ b t ṯ ǧ ḥ ḫ d ḏ r z s š ṣ ḍ ṭ ẓ ʻ ǵ f q k l m n h w y

Ugaritic

ʼ b g d ḏ h w z ḥ ḫ ṭ ẓ y k l m n s s̀ ʻ ǵ ṗ ṣ q r š t ṯ

Greek

α — *a*	π — *p*	αἰ — *ai*
β — *b*	ρ — *r*	αὐ — *au*
γ — *g*	σ,ς — *s*	εἰ — *ei*
δ — *d*	τ — *t*	εὐ — *eu*
ε — *e*	υ — *y*	ηὐ — *ēu*
ζ — *z*	φ — *ph*	οἰ — *oi*
η — *ē*	χ — *ch*	οὐ — *ou*
θ — *th*	ψ — *ps*	υἱ — *hui*
ι — *i*	ω — *ō*	
κ — *k*		ῥ — *rh*
λ — *l*	γγ — *ng*	῾ — *h*
μ — *m*	γκ — *nk*	
ν — *n*	γξ — *nx*	ᾳ — *ā*
ξ — *x*	γχ — *nch*	ῃ — *ē*
ο — *o*		ῳ — *ō*

DANIEL

Gleason L. Archer, Jr.

DANIEL

Introduction

1. Purpose

Apart from Lamentations, Daniel is the shortest book of the Major Prophets. Yet it is one of the most important pieces of OT prophetic literature and perhaps the most frequently studied of the sixteen Major and Minor prophets. Its narrative portions, with their excitement and suspense, and its prophecies, with their wide scope and fascinating detail, have engaged the attention of readers down through the years. In NT prophecy Daniel is referred to more than any other OT book. Moreover, it contains more fulfilled prophecies than any other book in the Bible.

The reason for the extraordinary qualities of Daniel lies in the historical situation that faced God's people after the Fall of Jerusalem and their deportation into exile in Babylonia. Despite decades of solemn warning by Isaiah, Micah, Jeremiah, and many other faithful prophets, the people's flagrant apostasy and immorality—described in 2 Chronicles 36:16: "They mocked God's messengers, despised his words and scoffed at his prophets until the wrath of the LORD was aroused against his people and there was no remedy"—brought about the total destruction of Jerusalem and the temple, a destruction that God had warned his people about ever since the time of Moses (cf. Deut 28:64; 29:28). The covenant people had at last been expelled from their Promised Land and their Holy City and were condemned to captivity and enslavement in a foreign land.

From the viewpoint of a human observer, it seemed that the religion of the Hebrews had been completely discredited. Their God, Yahweh, had apparently shown himself inferior in power to the mighty gods of Assyria and Babylon; for he seemed unable to deliver his people from the worshipers of Asshur, Bel, and Nebo. When they leveled Yahweh's temple to the ground and burned its ruins, the Babylonian troops served notice to all the world that their gods were mightier than Yahweh, no matter what titles the Hebrews gave him. Ethical monotheism was exposed to universal scorn as an empty fraud. Therefore, it was essential at this time in Israel's history for God to display his power in such a way as to prove that he was the one true God (in contrast to the false gods of the heathen) and the sovereign

Lord of history. So he showed his power by a series of miracles that vindicated biblical monotheism over against its detractors and convinced the supreme rulers of Babylon and Persia that Yahweh was the greatest power both on earth and in heaven. As God found it necessary in the days of Moses to display his redemptive power in the Ten Plagues and the crossing of the Red Sea in order to deliver Israel from idolatry and spiritual cowardice, so he acted during the disgrace and humiliation of the Babylonian exile. Indeed, it was essential for him to prove by his miraculous acts that he had allowed his people to go into captivity in 587 B.C., not through weakness, but rather to maintain his integrity as a holy God, who carries out his covenant promises both for good and for ill according to the response of his people. So the whole narrative in Daniel relates a series of contests between false gods of human invention and the one true sovereign Lord and Creator of heaven and earth.

2. Authorship and Date

The clear testimony of the book itself is that Daniel was the author. Chapter 8 begins with an affirmation of Daniel's authorship: "I Daniel" (cf. also 9:2, 20; 10:2). It is conceivable that a close friend or colleague of the prophet might have composed the earlier chapters since they refer to Daniel in the third person except where he is directly quoted. But careful examination shows that the author usually writes about himself in the third person, as was the custom among ancient authors of historical memoirs. Even the Decalogue in Exodus 20 shows an easy shift from the first to the third person when the speaker unmistakably refers to himself: "I am the LORD your God, who [first person] brought you out of Egypt" (v.2). But in v.7 Yahweh speaks of himself in the third person: "The LORD will not hold anyone guiltless who misuses his name."[1]

No one disputes Xenophon's authorship of the *Anabasis*, even though he always referred to himself in the third person. The same is true of Caesar's *Gallic Wars*. The only notable exception to this rule in the narrative literature of the OT seems to be Nehemiah, whose memoirs are in the form of a personal diary. But in general it was apparently considered bad taste for a writer to speak of himself in the first person—a practice that smacked of the boastfulness of the Assyrian and Persian rulers.

There can be no question that Jesus believed in Daniel's authorship of the book bearing his name, for in Matthew 24:15 Jesus referred to " 'the abomination that causes desolation,' spoken of through [*dia*] the prophet Daniel." Since *dia* with the genitive case is used to express agency, this commits Christ—if his words are correctly reported here and in Mark 13:14—to Daniel's authorship of the predictions of the latter-day "abomination" (cf. Dan 9:27; 11:31; 12:11).[2]

---

[1]Notice that the fourth commandment (Exod 20:8–11) also speaks of Yahweh entirely in the third person. The rest of the Decalogue does not refer to God directly; so there is no choice to be made between the first and third person. But notice that v.19 reaffirms that Yahweh spoke all Ten Commandments directly to the people and that they heard him address them. "Speak to us yourself," they said to Moses, "and we will listen. But do not have God speak to us or we will die."

[2]Actually, these three passages vary slightly in wording, especially in the Hebrew. Literally, Dan 9:27 reads: "And he shall confirm a covenant with the many for one week [of years]; but [at] the middle of the week, he will make blood sacrifice and meal offering to cease, and on the wing he will set up an

Some commentators discount this testimony as a mere accommodation to a popular view in the first century. But the Gospels clearly show that Jesus stood decisively and unambiguously against prevailing popular opinion whenever it was in error. Thus he declared, "You have heard that it was said to the people. . . . But I tell you, Do not swear at all" (Matt 5:33–34). Again, in Matthew 5:38–39 he said, "You have heard that it was said, 'Eye for eye, and tooth for tooth.' . . . But I tell you, Do not resist an evil person." Many of Jesus' teachings were in serious conflict with popular views, not simply with casuistic interpretations of the Pharisees (cf. Matt 15:11–20; 19:9; John 8:24, 44). Therefore, it would have been completely out of character for Jesus to have espoused a theory of authorship he knew to be false, simply to avoid a negative response in the minds of his hearers.

It is significant that Ezekiel (14:14, 20) respectfully referred to his contemporary Daniel by quoting God as saying, "Even if these three men—Noah, Daniel and Job—were in it [i.e., a rebellious land], they could save only themselves." Some writers argue that this "Daniel" could not refer to Ezekiel's contemporary but to the old Canaanite hero Dan'el, whose story is in the Ugaritic legend of Aqhat, who must have been nearly contemporary with Job. But a careful reading of the Aqhat epic reveals that Dan'el, the father of Aqhat, was a dedicated idol-worshiper, occupied with blood sacrifices to El, Baal, and other pagan gods for weeks at a time. They depict him as getting so drunk at one of his banquets that he could not walk home. He uttered vengeful curses against the eagle or vulture that killed his son and finally split open the belly of the bird that ate Aqhat's body, killed it, and put a curse on the entire City of Vultures. The next seven years he spent weeping and mourning for his dead son and finally induced his daughter to murder a warrior named Yatpan, implicated in the death of Aqhat seven years before.

It is difficult to see in all this a moral and spiritual superiority that would impress Ezekiel (to say nothing of Yahweh, whom he quotes) as putting Dan'el on a level with Noah and Job. As to the grouping of these three, it is significant that Noah lived a good fifteen hundred years or more before Job, and Job about fifteen hundred years before Daniel, Ezekiel's contemporary. What God seems to be saying, therefore, in Ezekiel 14:14, 20 is that even though outstanding heroes of faith—like Noah at the beginning of postdiluvial history and Job in the Patriarchal Age in the middle of the second millennium—were to combine with godly, gifted Daniel to intercede for apostate Judah, their most earnest intercession would not avail to turn back God's penal judgment against his faithless people. Therefore, we conclude that the Ezekiel references (including another one in 28:3) strongly support the authenticity of Daniel as Ezekiel's contemporary.

Some have made an issue of the variation in spelling as between Ezekiel's D-N-'-L and Daniel's D-N-Y-'-L, but this is a common type of variant and of very minor importance; in all probability the name was pronounced the same, whether or not

---

abomination that causes desolation." The Hebrew for "abomination that causes desolation" is *šiqqûṣîm m^{e}šōmēm* and the Greek (LXX, Theod.) is *bdelygma tōn erēmōseōn*.

Dan 11:31 literally reads: "And they shall defile the sanctuary and the stronghold and shall remove the continual burnt offering and shall set up the abomination that appalls, makes desolate." The Hebrew for "abomination that appalls" is *haššiqqûṣ m^{e}šômēm* and the Greek is *bdelygma erēmōseōs* (LXX) and *bdelygma ēphanismenon* (Theod.).

Finally Dan 12:11 literally reads: "And from the time that the continual burnt offering is removed until the setting up of the abomination that appalls, makes desolate." The Hebrew for "abomination that appalls" is *šiqqûṣ šōmēm* and the Greek is *to bdelygma tēs erēmōseōs* (Theod. omits the *to*).

the yod (*y*) was inserted as a vowel-letter before the aleph (') thus indicating the suffix pronoun "my" ("God is my Judge"). Significantly, even back in 2400 B.C. the Ebla records show an abundance of names with this same suffix, e.g., *Ṭū-bī-Da-lu* ("Dalu is my goodness"), *Ṭū-bī-ZI-KIR* ("ZI-KIR is my goodness") (I.J. Gelb, "Thoughts About Ibla," *Syro-Mesopotamian Studies* 1, no. 1 [May 1977]: 20). So, also, *Dānī'ēl* means "God is my Judge."

As to the date of the composition of Daniel, the narrative of the prophet's earliest experiences begins with his capture as a hostage by Nebuchadnezzar back in 605–604 B.C. and according to 1:21 continues certainly till the first year of Cyrus (c. 537 B.C.), in relation to his public service, and to the third year of Cyrus (535 B.C.), in relation to his prophetic ministry (Dan 10:1). Daniel seems to have revised and completed his memoirs during his retirement sometime about 532 or 530 B.C., when he would have been close to ninety years old (assuming his birth c. 620 B.C.). The appearance of Persian-derived governmental terms, even in the earlier chapters composed in Aramaic, strongly suggests that these chapters were given their final form after Persian had become the official language of government.

3. Languages

Like Ezra, which has four chapters in Aramaic, the text of Daniel is in two languages: Hebrew (chs. 1, 8–12) and Aramaic (chs. 2–7). As we shall see later on, the linguistic evidence from the Qumran documents decisively favors a pre-second-century date for both languages Daniel used. It strongly suggests an interval of centuries before the 160s B.C. in order to account for the much older morphology, grammar, and syntax of Daniel's text, by comparison with the Genesis Apocryphon and the sectarian documents composed in the second century B.C.

But why was the book written in two languages? And what criterion did the author follow in putting half his material into Aramaic and the other half into Hebrew? A careful study of the subject matter yields fairly obvious answers: The Aramaic chapters deal with matters pertaining to the entire citizenry of the Babylonian and the Persian empires, whereas the other six chapters relate to peculiarly Jewish concerns and God's special plans for the future of his covenant people. It would seem to follow that the Aramaic chapters (2–7) were in some sense made available to the Gentile public, since Aramaic was the lingua franca of the period of the Babylonian and Persian empires during the sixth and fifth centuries B.C.

4. Canonicity

It is axiomatic among critics who rule out supernaturalism that Daniel's successful predictions of events leading up to the reign of Antiochus Epiphanes (175–164 B.C.) can be accounted for only by assuming that some unknown pseudepigrapher wrote this book so as to make it seem an authentic sixth-century prophecy. The purpose for doing this would have been to demonstrate the sovereign power of Yahweh to deliver his people from danger and bondage even in the face of impossible odds. Thus the patriotic elements among the Jewish population of Palestine would be encouraged to join the Maccabees in their heroic efforts to achieve independence. Because of the eventual success of the Maccabean revolt resulting in the establishment of a sovereign state of Israel, the Book of Daniel might very soon have achieved canonical status in the eyes of the rebels who had thrown off the Seleucid yoke. The discovery of several fragments of a second-century MS of Daniel in Qumran Cave 1 strongly suggests that it was counted by Jewish believers as one of the inspired, authoritative books of Holy Scripture.

If, on the other hand, the historic, linguistic, and hermeneutical evidence points to a late sixth-century date—as it certainly does—then we should regard Daniel as having been inherently canonical from the very time it was first written (as was true of all other books of the Bible) and as having achieved recognition by God's people as the inspired word of God quite soon after its publication. It certainly would have found a ready reception among the exiles who returned to Judea under Zerubbabel, because it would have encouraged them to trust in God's continuing providence in their behalf during the discouragements of those early years of recolonization. Among the Qumran sectarians, the Book of Daniel enjoyed a very high place. They quoted it often and relied on it as they eagerly looked for signs of the coming of the Messiah. Much of their eschatological expectation was derived from Daniel's predictive chapters describing the final struggle between the forces of good and evil. In their "War of the Sons of Light against the Sons of Darkness," columns 1 and 15–19 are written in the mood of Daniel 11:40–12:3 (cf. G. Vermes, *The Dead Sea Scrolls in English* [Baltimore: Penguin, 1968], p. 122). Whether the War Scroll is second century or first, it testifies to the special esteem in which Daniel was held by the Qumran sectarians.

Exponents of the Maccabean date hypothesis (see Special Problems) point out that in the MT Daniel was assigned to the category of the Writings rather than to the Prophets. Even though Daniel is included among the Major Prophets by the LXX and the other early versions, some critics argue that the Masoretes could not have considered Daniel to have been a true, accredited prophet, or they would have included his book within the Latter Prophets in their canon. Furthermore, say these critics, the book itself must have been composed after the prophetic canon was pretty well established by the Jewish authorities, i.e., about 200 B.C. So the book must have been written after 200 B.C.

These deductions are unjustified because they are based on a series of unproved and unprovable assumptions. If the various prophetic books were truly inspired of God at the time of their writing, they must have been inherently canonical from their earliest publication. The frequent quotations of earlier prophets by the later ones (cf. SOTIrev., p. 351; IOT, p. 796) are clear indications that they were so regarded by the believing community back in the preexilic period. The arbitrary supposition of a 200 B.C. canonization is totally without documentary proof of any kind and is largely the result of circular reasoning on the part of modern critics themselves.

As for the placement of Daniel in the Masoretic arrangement of the canon, this is completely without evidential force. Writing in the late first century A.D., Josephus made the following statement concerning the Hebrew canon (*Contra Apion* I, 38–39 [8]): "We do not possess myriads of inconsistent books, conflicting with each other. Our books, those which are justly accredited, are but two and twenty, and contain the record of all time." He then broke these twenty-two books down into three categories: five books of Moses (i.e., the Pentateuch), thirteen books of the Prophets, and the remaining four books that "embrace hymns to God and counsels for men for the conduct of life." The four books of poetry and wisdom were unquestionably Psalms, Job, Proverbs, and Ecclesiastes. These four constituted the entire third division of the canon—the Writings—in Josephus's day, rather than the thirteen assigned to it by the Masoretes of the late first millennium A.D.

As for the thirteen books of the Prophets, as recognized in the first century A.D., they were apparently the Former Prophets, including Joshua, Judges-Ruth, the two books of Samuel, the two books of Kings, the two books of Chronicles, Isaiah, Jeremiah-Lamentations, Ezekiel, Daniel (which were classified by the second century B.C. LXX as Major Prophets), the Twelve Minor Prophets as one volume (since they could all be included in one large scroll), Song of Solomon, Ezra-Nehemiah, and Esther. There is no possibility that Josephus could have regarded Daniel as belonging to the Writings. Very clearly he included it among the Prophets, along with Solomon's prophetic parable of love (S of Songs) and the exilic and postexilic books of history, all of which were composed from a prophetic perspective. Therefore, we are forced to conclude that the Masoretic division of the canon, coming as it did six or seven centuries after Flavius Josephus, has no bearing whatever on the date of Daniel's composition or on its status as a truly prophetic work.

5. Theological Values

The principal theological emphasis in Daniel is the absolute sovereignty of Yahweh, the God of Israel. At a time when it seemed to all the world that his cause was lost and that the gods of the heathen had triumphed, causing his temple to be burned to the ground, it pleased the Lord strikingly and unmistakably to display his omnipotence. The theme running through the whole book is that the fortunes of kings and the affairs of men are subject to God's decrees, and that he is able to accomplish his will despite the most determined opposition of the mightiest potentates on earth.

The miracles recorded in chapters 1–6 demonstrate God's sovereignty on behalf of his saints. The surpassing health of Daniel and his three companions after ten days of a simple vegetable diet (ch. 1); the miraculous disclosure to Daniel of the contents of Nebuchadnezzar's dream (ch. 2); the amazing deliverance of Daniel's three friends from the fiery furnace (ch. 3); the previous warning to Nebuchadnezzar of seven years of dehumanizing insanity because of his overweening pride (ch. 4); the terrifying prediction inscribed on the banquet wall of Belshazzar, followed by a speedy fulfillment of the same (ch. 5); and Daniel's deliverance from the lions' den all clearly show that the Lord God of Israel was in charge of the tide of human affairs and was perfectly able to deliver his people from pagan oppression during their captivity.

A second theological emphasis in Daniel is the mighty power of prayer. Neither Daniel nor his three companions held back from asking the Lord to deliver them from life-threatening dangers and impossible dilemmas. In chapter 2 Daniel did not hesitate to declare to Arioch, the king's commander, that he would correctly recall Nebuchadnezzar's dream and interpret its meaning. In chapter 3 Shadrach, Meshach, and Abednego did not shrink back from the prospect of a swift and horrible death in the terrible furnace, for they were certain that their God was able to save them from perishing in its heat. Their total commitment to sacrifice their lives for the Lord's cause (v.18) furnishes the firmest basis for effectual prayer.

Even more impressive was Daniel's intense and persistent prayer on behalf of his captive nation as he claimed God's promise to restore his people to their ancestral land at the end of seventy years (9:2–19; cf. 10:12–14). The third and major deportation to Babylon had taken place in 586 B.C., only fifty-two years earlier, when Daniel urgently brought this matter before the Lord. But Daniel was not content to wait for an additional eighteen years or more. He wanted to personally witness the restoration before he died, and sixty-seven years had elapsed since the captivity had begun in 605 B.C. Daniel therefore stormed the throne of God, as it were, so that the restoration of the remnant might take place in the seventieth year after his own exile. By that time he would have been a good eighty-six years old. So the Lord saw fit, in answer to Daniel's importunity, to grant him this boon by the earliest possible reckoning of the seventy-year span—even though the restoration of the temple did not occur till 516 (Ezra 6:15), or seventy years after the Solomonic temple had been destroyed (2 Chron 36:19).

A third theological emphasis of Daniel is the long-range purview of God's program of redemption. His marvelous plan of the ages is set forth on a scale almost as grandiose as that in Isaiah. Both works display the irresistible providence of almighty God's sovereign purpose to redeem his people through his divine-human Messiah, the Lord Jesus Christ. While Isaiah sets forth most clearly the substitutionary Atonement as God's means of salvation, Daniel predicts the precise year of Christ's appearance and the beginning of his ministry in A.D. 27 (cf. Dan 9:25–26). But even beyond this point, Daniel was given the revelation of the eschatological Seventieth Week (9:26b–27), which we still eagerly look forward to, expecting the rapture of the church and the second coming of the Lord, with his triumph over the rebellious powers of earth at Armageddon (11:36–12:12).

Lastly, underlying the entire scenario in Daniel is the indomitable grace of God. Even though Abraham's descendants would fall into apostasy and betray their trust, it was the Lord's unchangeable purpose to fulfill his promise to Abraham that he would "surely become a great and powerful nation, and all nations on earth will be blessed through him" (Gen 18:18). God was determined that a remnant of true believers would remain faithful and present his saving truth to the Gentiles. Despite periods of rebellion and moral declension during the times of the judges, the united monarchy, and the divided monarchy, a core of followers would remain true and keep alive the testimony of a holy people. Even after the sternest warnings of the prophets had been disregarded and severe judgment of near total destruction had overtaken the nation in 587 B.C., the Lord was merciful and gracious to his people during their exile. Isaiah, Micah, and Ezekiel foresaw the return of the remnant at the end of their chastisement; but it was Daniel, living with the exiled nation through its captivity, who witnessed their release under Cyrus, to set up the second commonwealth back in the Promised Land. God never abandoned his people to the full consequences of their sin, but in loving-kindness he subjected them to an ordeal that purged them of idolatry. Then, hearing their cry of repentance, he allowed them to return to their homeland, thus setting the stage for the coming of the Messiah. The Book of Daniel thus sets forth the pattern of God's preserving grace that characterizes the NT as well, that "God's gifts and his call are irrevocable" (Rom 11:29). And even though in the NT age Israel as a nation has experienced hardening of the heart, yet after the full number of Gentile believers (the larger "Israel" of the church age) has been redeemed, "the deliverer will come from Zion; he will turn godlessness away from Jacob" (Rom 1:25–26).

6. New Testament Usage

a. *Direct Quotations*

The actual number of passages in Daniel that are quoted in the NT is not particularly impressive. The twenty-sixth edition of the Aland-Nestle Greek NT lists five (pp. 766–67).

Daniel 3:6 contains the phrase "[they] will immediately be thrown into a blazing furnace" (referring to those who failed to bow to Nebuchadnezzar's image), which occurs in Matthew 13:42, 50, where it describes the eternal torment of those who die in unbelief.

Daniel 7:13 is the main source of the title Son of Man, which the Lord Jesus applied to himself throughout his earthly ministry. This verse is quoted or alluded to no less than six times in the NT (Matt 24:30; 26:64; Mark 13:26; 14:62; Luke 21:27; 22:69; cf. Rev 1:7).

Daniel 9:27 contains the phrase *šiqqûṣîm mešōmēm* ("abomination that causes desolation"), which appears as *haššiqqûṣ mešômēm* ("the abomination that causes desolation") in 11:31 and as *šiqqûṣ šōmēm* ("the abomination that causes desolation") in 12:11. In the Olivet Discourse (Matt 24:15; Mark 13:14) Christ refers to " 'the abomination that causes desolation' [*to bdelygma tēs erēmōseōs*], spoken of through the prophet Daniel." Jesus interpreted this as referring to an event in the end time, during the Tribulation—an image of the cult of Antichrist, perhaps.

b. *Allusions*

The influence of Daniel on the NT is not restricted to direct quotes alone. Much of what is recorded as history or prophecy in Daniel reappears in prophetic passages of the Gospels, the Epistles, and Revelation.

In Matthew 24, v.15 refers to the "abomination that causes desolation," which has just been discussed. Verse 21 states that there will be "great distress unequaled from the beginning of the world until now" which reflects Daniel 12:1: "There will be a time of distress, such as has not happened from the beginning of nations until then." Verse 30 speaks of "the sign of the Son of Man" that "will appear in the sky," conceivably reflecting Daniel 7:13, which speaks of the "son of man, coming with the clouds of heaven," though the scene in Daniel is hardly the rapture of the church, which appears to be alluded to here in v.30. There is an equally debatable motif in v.31, which speaks of Christ's sending forth his angels to "gather his elect from the four winds, from one end of the heavens to the other." This may have a connection with Daniel 7:2, which refers to the "four winds of heaven" that were "churning up the great sea." Daniel 7:3 speaks of the four beasts as coming up from the sea. Unquestionably the scene is different in these two passages and the events described are distinct.

First Thessalonians 4:17 refers to the saints being caught up "in the clouds to meet the Lord in the air," another reference to clouds as the setting for the coming of the Lord Jesus. In Daniel 7:13, however, the Lord appears before the Ancient of Days rather than before the raptured saints. In 2 Thessalonians 2:3–4 there is a clear connection with the evil king of Daniel 7:25. Paul depicted him as "the man of lawlessness [*anomias*] . . . the man doomed to destruction [*apōleias*]. He opposes and exalts himself over everything that is called God or is worshiped and even sets himself up in God's temple, proclaiming himself to be God." This probably reflects Daniel 11:36: "The king will do as he pleases. He will exalt and magnify himself above every god and will say unheard-of things against the God of gods."

Daniel's influence is principally seen in the Book of Revelation. The risen Christ is described in Revelation 1:14: "His head and hair were white like wool, as white as snow, and his eyes were like blazing fire." Daniel 7:9 describes the Ancient of Days: "His clothing was as white as snow; the hair of his head white like wool." Compare Daniel 10:6, which describes the interpreting angel: "His eyes like flaming torches, his arms and legs like the gleam of burnished bronze, and his voice like the sound of a multitude." Revelation 1:15 describes Christ as having "feet like bronze glowing in a furnace, and his voice was like the sound of rushing waters."

Revelation 1:17 says of John: "I fell at his [Christ's] feet as though dead. Then he placed his right hand on me and said, 'Do not be afraid.'" This reflects Daniel 8:17–18. At the angelic appearance Daniel "fell prostrate." He said, "I was in deep sleep, with my face to the ground. Then he touched me and raised me to my feet."

Revelation 2:10 warns the church of Smyrna: "You will suffer persecution for ten days." This is slightly reminiscent of Daniel 1:12: "Please test your servants for ten days."

Revelation 4:2 states that there "was a throne in heaven with someone sitting on it." Verse 9 adds, "The living creatures give glory, honor and thanks to him who sits on the throne and who lives for ever and ever." Compare Daniel 7:9: "As I looked, thrones were set in place, and the Ancient of Days took his seat" (cf. 4:34; 12:7).

In Revelation 5:1, John says, "I saw in the right hand of him who sat on the throne a scroll with writing on both sides and sealed with seven seals." In Daniel 12:4, Daniel is told to "close up and seal the words of this scroll until the time of the end." In Revelation it is a book of judgment on the dead, but in Daniel it is primarily a record of the prophetic visions granted to Daniel.

In Revelation 5:6 John says, "I saw a Lamb, looking as if it had been slain. . . . He had seven horns and seven eyes, which are the seven spirits of God sent out into all the earth." In Daniel 8:3, Daniel says, "I . . . looked up, and there before me was a ram with two horns, standing beside the canal." This ram represented the Medo-Persian Empire rather than the Christ-Lamb, but the imagery is similar.

In the praise of Christ in Revelation 5:9, we read, "You purchased men for God from every tribe and language and people and nation." In Daniel 3:4 the king's herald proclaims, "O peoples, nations and men of every language." Again, in 5:19 we read of "all the peoples and nations and men of every language."

Revelation 5:11 describes the angelic court of heaven "numbering thousands upon thousands, and ten thousand times ten thousand." Compare Daniel 7:10: "Thousands upon thousands attended him; ten thousand times ten thousand stood before him."

Revelation 9:20 describes the response of the rebellious world toward God's judgments: "They did not stop worshiping demons, and the idols of gold, silver, bronze, stone and wood—idols that cannot see or hear or walk." Compare Daniel 5:23, where Belshazzar and his guests are condemned by Daniel: "You praised the gods of silver and gold, of bronze, iron, wood and stone, which cannot see or hear or understand."

Revelation 10:5–6 records: "Then the angel . . . raised his right hand to heaven. And he swore by him who lives for ever and ever, who created the heavens. Daniel 12:7 describes the angel as a "man clothed in linen" who lifted his right hand and his left hand toward heaven, and . . . [swore] by him who lives forever, saying, 'It will be for a time, times and half a time.' "

Revelation 11:3 quotes the Lord as saying, "My two witnesses . . . will prophesy for 1,260 days, clothed in sackcloth." Compare the time span in Daniel 7:25, which speaks of the little horn who will "oppress his saints. . . . The saints will be handed over to him for a time, times and half a time." The term for time (*z*ᵉ*mān*) is clearly equivalent to a "year" in this passage; and three and a half years comes out to about 1,283 days, a bit in excess of 1,260.

Revelation 12:3 portrays a great red dragon "with seven heads and ten horns and seven crowns on his heads." Compare Daniel 7:7, which refers to the fourth beast as "different from all the former beasts, and it had ten horns."

Revelation 12:4 relates how the dragon's tail "swept a third of the stars out of the sky and flung them to the earth." Daniel 8:10 describes the little horn as growing up to "the host of heavens, and it threw some of the starry host down to the earth and trampled on them."

Revelation 13:1 is a further reference to the eschatological beast "coming out of the sea. He had ten horns and seven heads." Verse 2 continues, "The beast I saw resembled a leopard, and had feet like those of a bear and a mouth like that of a lion." This seems to be a composite of the beasts representing the successive empires of Babylon, Persia, and Greece described in Daniel 7:3–6.

In Daniel 7:8, Daniel is given this information about the Antichrist in his guise as the little horn: "This horn had eyes like the eyes of a man and a mouth that spoke boastfully." Revelation 13:5 says of the great dragon, "The beast was given a mouth to utter proud words and blasphemies and to exercise his authority for forty-two months." Compare Daniel 11:36: "The king will do as he pleases. He will exalt and magnify himself above every god and will say unheard-of things against the God of gods."

Revelation 13:11 quotes John as saying, "I saw another beast, coming out of the earth. He had two horns like a lamb, and he spoke like a dragon." Compare the symbol of the Medo-Persian Empire in Daniel 8:3: "A ram with two horns, standing beside the canal."

Revelation 20:4 sets forth the final judgment of God: "I saw thrones on which were seated those who had been given authority to judge." A similar scene is found in Daniel 7:9: "As I looked, thrones were set in place, and the Ancient of Days took his seat. His clothing was as white as snow; the hair of his head was white like wool."

So far as the judgment scene is concerned, there is a further parallel between Revelation 20:12—"And I saw the dead, great and small, standing before the throne, and books were opened. Another book was opened, which is the book of life"—and Daniel 7:10—"The court was seated, and the books were opened."

From the passages cited, we see that the principal passages and motifs from the Book of Daniel that are reflected or enlarged on in the NT largely relate to end-time events and personages.

7. Special Problems

The Maccabean date hypothesis, a widely held theory of the origin and date of the Book of Daniel, was originally advanced by the third-century A.D. Neoplatonic philosopher Porphyrius of Tyre. According to the relation of his opinions by Jerome (who spent much of his commentary on Daniel refuting Porphyry's arguments), Porphyry contended that the remarkably accurate "predictions" contained in Daniel (esp. ch. 11) were the result of a pious fraud, perpetrated by some zealous propagandist of the Maccabean movement, who wished to encourage a spirit of heroism among the Jewish patriots resisting Antiochus IV. The discomfiture of Nebuchadnezzar and Belshazzar as related in Daniel were intended to be prophetic of the defeats and downfall of the hated Epiphanes.

Following Jerome's refutation of Porphyry, he was more or less dismissed by Christian scholarship as a mere pagan detractor who had allowed a naturalistic bias to warp his judgment. But during the time of the Enlightenment in the eighteenth century, all supernatural elements in Scripture came under suspicion; and Porphyry's theory received increasing support from J.D. Michaelis (1771), J.G. Eichhorn (1780), L. Berthold (1806), F. Bleek (1822), and many others after them. They all agreed that every accurate prediction in Daniel was written after it had already been fulfilled (a *vaticinium ex eventu*) and therefore in the period of the Maccabean revolt (168–165 B.C.). Also some of them were inclined to question the unity of the book on the ground of internal evidence and language differences; certain portions of the book—particularly the narratives in chapters 2–6—were thought to come from third-century authors or even earlier. Essentially the same position is maintained even to this day by liberal scholars throughout Christendom. In fact, they consider the Maccabean date of Daniel one of the most assured results of modern scholarship. Yet the fact remains that the objective data, when fairly and impartially considered, provide overwhelming evidence against a second-century date for the composition and strongly favor its authenticity as a genuine work of the sixth-century Daniel.

a. *Alleged historical inaccuracies*

Advocates of the Maccabean date hypothesis argue that the text of Daniel contains such flagrant inaccuracies as to be explicable only on the basis of a garbled and confused notion of the conditions obtaining in the sixth century B.C. A romancer living four centuries later than the events might easily have become so confused as to fall into the historical blunders that distinguish this book. The historical errors usually alleged are five in number.

1) *The wrong date for Nebuchadnezzar's invasion*

Daniel 1:1 states that Nebuchadnezzar's first invasion of Judah and siege of Jerusalem took place in the third year of Jehoiakim, whereas Jeremiah 46:2 dates the first year of Nebuchadnezzar in the fourth year of Jehoiakim. This objection was raised before modern scholarship understood the complexity of ancient Near-Eastern dating systems. We now know that in Judah the non–accession-year system was followed, whereby the calendar year in which a new king acceded to the throne was reckoned as the first year of his reign (which in the case of Jehoiakim would have been 608 B.C.). But in the northern kingdom (which, of course, came to an end in 722 B.C.) and in Babylon, the accession-year system prevailed. According to this reckoning, the year when the new king came to power would be called simply his accession year. The first year of his reign would not begin until the commencement of the next calendar year. Thus, by the Babylonian reckoning, Jehoiakim's first year was 607; therefore Nebuchadnezzar's invasion in 605 was Jehoiakim's third year. Who can fault Daniel, living in Babylon, for following the Babylonian reckoning? Therefore this argument turns out to be not only worthless but a confirmation that the author of Daniel wrote from a Babylonian perspective.

2) *"Chaldeans" as a class of soothsayers*

Quite consistently the "Chaldeans" appear in the narrative of Daniel as a class of soothsayer priests. Such a usage would have been unthinkable back in the days of the Chaldean (Babylonian) Empire, when "Chaldean" was used as the term for the master race that ruled the entire domain of Nebuchadnezzar, who was himself a Chaldean. But in Daniel 2 the name appears two or three times as the designation of a class of astrologers or soothsayers, along with other professional classes of "wise men." The same usage occurs in 4:7; 5:7, 11. It is therefore alleged that such a misunderstanding of the historical use of *kaśdîm* (2:2) or *kaśdāy'ē* (2:5, 10) can only be accounted for as the result of a garbled legendary tradition that grew up long after the fall of the Chaldean Empire. But this interpretation contains a fatal flaw: *kaśdāy'ē* is also used in its ethnic sense in the text of Daniel. In 3:8 the accusation against Daniel's three compatriots was brought by certain "Chaldean men" (*gub̲rîn kaśdā'în;* NIV, "astrologers"), who were obviously high government officials rather than soothsayers; BDB (p. 1098) classifies this occurrence as "*Chaldean* by race." The second instance is beyond dispute an ethnic use: "That very night Belshazzar, king of the Babylonians [*k̲aśdāy'ā,* lit., 'Chaldeans'] was slain" (Dan 5:30). There is no possible way to reconcile this ethnic use of "Chaldean" with the theory of a garbled tradition that misunderstood "Chaldean" as designating a class of astrologer-priests rather than as a race of conquerors. So this critical theory must be discarded because of its inherent self-contradiction.

What, then, is the explanation of the two different uses of the term *kaśdāy* (pl. *kaśdā'în*)? The answer is found in the occurrence of two homonyms, one of which is the ethnic designation *kašdu* (as it was spelled in Babylonian cuneiform) and the other is a *kaš-du,* which resulted from a modification of an earlier *kal-du*. The Babylonian term *kal-du* was used of a class of astrologer-priests, as the carryover of the Sumerian title *gal-du,* which meant, literally, "master builder." (*Gal* means "great" in Sumerian and *du.a* means "builder.") As the astrologer drew squares on his diagram of the stars on his clay tablet, his chart would resemble the ground plan of a house as drawn by an architect. Thus it was from the use of such charts in working out horoscopes and predictions that these astrologer-priests came to be known to the Sumerians as "master builders." *Gal-du.a* passed into Akkadian as *kal-du*. But in the development of the Babylonian dialect of Akkadian, it became customary for sibilants to change to an *l* before a dental; thus the preposition *ultu* ("out of") developed from an earlier *ištu;* the verb form *ašṭur* ("I wrote") was altered to *alṭur*.

The last stage in the process took place in the time of the Neo-Babylonian Empire, when there was a systematic movement back to the classical Babylonian of a thousand years before. As a consequence many of the *lt, ld, lṭ* clusters were changed back to the original sibilants (*s* or *š*) before the dental consonant. But in this process a few cases occurred where an original *l* before a dental was unhistorically changed to a sibilant, by a false analogy. Such seems to be the explanation for *kal-du* being altered to *kaš-du* in the case of this professional term. The result was a pair of homonyms, having the same sound but entirely different meanings. This explanation, so ably set forth by Robert Dick Wilson (*Studies in Daniel*), furnishes a satisfactory solution to the problem of diverse usage of *kašdîn*. In this connection it should be noted that the Greeks became acquainted with the Chaldeans back in the days when the shift from *šd* to *ld* had taken place, for their historians always refer to them as *chaldaioi*, never as *chasdaioi*.

3) *The legendary account of Nebuchadnezzar's madness*

Critics who assume that nothing ever happens uniquely in history but that all true occurrences must be repetitive in nature—so that scientists may properly observe them—find great difficulty in accepting the historicity of the account in Daniel 4 of Nebuchadnezzar's seven years of madness (boanthropy). During this period he roamed the fields as a beast, imagining that he was an ox (4:33)—till finally his sanity returned to him, and he thanked the God of Daniel for his deliverance. As a matter of fact, we have no Babylonian record of any governmental activity at all on Nebuchadnezzar's part between 582 and 575; so it may well be that this was the approximate period of his madness.

Recent years have seen much discussion of a fragmentary "Prayer of Nabonidus" found in Qumran Cave 4 that bears some resemblances to Daniel 4, for it concerns a grievously sick Chaldean king who was finally cured through some Jewish exorcist. The king then acknowledged the impotence of all his heathen idols and gave glory to the God of the Hebrews (J.T. Milik, *Revue Biblique* [1956]: pl. 1). A translation of this fragment appears in Vermes (*Dead Sea Scrolls*, p. 229). Critical scholars immediately concluded that this was an earlier form of the "legend" of Nebuchadnezzar's insanity and that it was only later transferred from Nabonidus to his predecessor. But this theory runs into great difficulties when carefully examined.

1. The Prayer of Nabonidus reads far more like a late and garbled legend than does Daniel 4; it fails to name his Jewish healer and also lacks the fullness of detail the Daniel account has.
2. Nabonidus's affliction is "an evil ulcer," much more like Hezekiah's illness (Isa 38:21) than the boanthropy of Nebuchadnezzar, and far less of a humiliation to a king's pride.
3. The only resemblance between the two afflictions is that each lasted seven years.
4. The agent of healing was a nameless Jewish "exorcist" rather than a prominent official like Daniel; furthermore, Daniel 4:34 implies that no human agent was involved in Nebuchadnezzar's recovery; the full seven years the Lord had promised for his punishment had elapsed. Nor is there mention of any special prayer or action by Daniel; the text simply says, "At the end of that time, I, Nebuchadnezzar, raised my eyes toward heaven, and my sanity was restored."
5. Many words or phrases in The Prayer of Nabonidus have been supplied by the modern editor on a conjectural basis, and some of these support the alleged similarity between the Nebuchadnezzar account and that of Nabonidus somewhat more clearly than the surviving text does. (Harrison [IOT, pp. 1118–19] has an excellent discussion of the Nabonidus prayer, which he adjudges to be legendary and haggadic.)

4) *"King" Belshazzar and his relationship to Nabonidus*

During the last century, it was customary for late-date advocates to assume that Daniel's mention of Belshazzar was completely unhistorical since extrabiblical historical sources refer to Nabonidus as the final king of the Babylonian Empire. After the discovery of oath tablets in Neo-Babylonian cuneiform dating from the twelfth year of Nabonidus (543 B.C.) and associating Belshazzar, his son, with him on an equal footing (cf. Dougherty, p. 96), it became startlingly apparent that the writer of Daniel was much more accurately informed about the history of the 540s in Babylonia than Herodotus was in 450 B.C. Thus the argument based on the silence of extrabiblical Greek sources concerning Belshazzar not only collapsed but turned out to be a powerful argument in favor of a sixth-century date for the writing of the book.

There remained, however, just one possible inaccuracy to which the rationalist critics still pointed—viz., that Belshazzar was the son of Nabonidus, whereas the queen mother (Dan 5:11) and Daniel himself (5:18) declared that Belshazzar was the son of Nebuchadnezzar. But it should be understood that *'āḇ* ("father") was also used in both Hebrew and Aramaic to refer to a grandfather (Gen 28:13; 32:9) or even to a great grandfather (1 Kings 15:10–13). So the probabilities are that Nabonidus, wishing to secure his position as the usurping king of Babylon, married one of Nebuchadnezzar's daughters who had previously been married to Neriglissar (who reigned from 560 till his death in 556). If so, then Belshazzar was in fact Nebuchadnezzar's grandson. Therefore, if the queen had meant to cite Nebuchadnezzar as her son's grandfather, there was no other term for her to use than *'āḇ* or *'abbā'*.

Moreover, the ancient Semitic languages termed any predecessor in office as the "father" of his immediate or mediate successor. Thus it was with Jehu the son of Jehoshaphat, the son of Nimshi, who assassinated Omri's grandson Joram and then exterminated the entire family of Omri, the father of Ahab. Yet the Black Obelisk inscription of Shalmaneser III refers to Jehu as *mār Ḫumri* ("son of Omri"). Similar usage obtained in Egyptian also, for in the Westcar Papyrus (dating from the Hyksos period) King Neb-ka of the Third Dynasty is referred to as the "father" (*i-t*) of King Khufu of the Fourth Dynasty, a full century later. Even if Belshazzar had not been a direct descendant of Nebuchadnezzar, he would still have been in this sense Belshazzar's "father." Therefore, the writer of Daniel cannot be charged with historical inaccuracy for referring to Nebuchadnezzar as Belshazzar's father.

5) *The "legendary" Darius the Mede*

After the overthrow of Belshazzar, the first ruler mentioned as taking over the government in Babylon was Darius the Mede (5:30). Actually, it was Cyrus the Great of Persia who toppled Babylon, and there was no Darius on the throne till 522 B.C.—Darius the son of Hystaspes, who belonged to a collateral Persian line related to Cyrus himself. Therefore we are faced, claim the late-date advocates, with a gross historical blunder on the part of the Maccabean romancer who wrote Daniel. He supposed that it was the Medes who captured Babylon, rather than the Persians, and that their king was named Darius, the son of Ahasuerus, a Mede (9:1).

Further examination of the internal and external evidence shows the hopelessness of this theory. Consider the following points:

1. Darius the Mede was sixty-two (5:31) when he assumed the throne, whereas Darius the Persian—who was third successor to Cyrus rather than his predecessor—was in his early twenties when he assassinated the imposter Gaumata in 522.

2. The author of Daniel believed that Belshazzar was conquered by a coalition of Medes and Persians; in Daniel 5:28 the whole point of the wordplay is that the

Persians were about to take over the kingdom directly from the Babylonians: "*Peres:* Your kingdom is divided [*p*[e]*rîsat*, from the verb *p*[e]*rās*, "separate"] and given to the Medes and Persians [*pārās*]" (5:28). It is quite apparent that only the Persians fit into this wordplay (P-R-S are the three consonants involved in all three: *PeReS*, *P*[e]*RîSat*, *PāRāS*). The reason the Medes are mentioned first in the phrase "the Medes and Persians" here is that historically the Persians had earlier been subject to the Medes, until Cyrus defeated his uncle King Astyages of the Median Empire, back in 550.

3. It is impossible to suppose that a Jewish writer in the second century B.C. who had any acquaintance with Hellenistic culture and historiography could have fallen into such gross confusion about the career of Cyrus and the fall of Babylon as the late-date theory demands. Herodotus (1.191) states that it was Cyrus, in command of a combined Medo-Persian army, who captured Babylon by the stratagem of diverting the channel of the Euphrates and slipping into the city at night by means of the riverbed. His work was published in the middle of the fifth century B.C. Writing in the early fourth century, Xenophon related in his *Cyropaedia* (7.20) how Cyrus engineered the surprise attack through the skillful leadership of his generals Gadatas and Gobryas and thereby took control of all Babylon.

Herodotus wrote in the Ionic dialect, which may not have been as well known to the Greek-speaking Orientals of the Seleucid Empire as the regular Attic was. But there is no question that Xenophon, who wrote in the clearest and simplest Attic Greek, was widely known throughout the entire Near East during the Hellenistic period. So far as the early second century B.C. was concerned, Greek culture and literature had become so pervasive that large numbers of the younger generation became sufficiently Hellenized to demand the erection of gymnasia and the other trappings of Hellenic urbanization; and they cordially cooperated with the policies of Antiochus Epiphanes in suppressing their Jewish traditions and beliefs. Such was the situation in Jerusalem as depicted in the opening chapter of 1 Maccabees, composed in the second century B.C. In the late first century A.D., the Jewish historian Flavius Josephus related (Antiq. X, 245–49 [xi.4]) how Baltasar (as he calls Belshazzar) at the end of a seventeen-year reign perished in the capture of Babylon by "Cyrus, the king of Persia," who captured the city through his "kinsman," Darius, the son of "Astyages"—though he "had another name among the Greeks"—and was already sixty-two years of age at the time.

All these historians, despite minor variations in detail, agree that Babylon fell to the united forces of the Medes and Persians under the command of Cyrus. These authors were well known to the Greek-speaking Jews of Judea. Thus there would have been no possibility of second-century Jews crediting any account that presented the conquest of Babylon as an achievement of the Medes acting independently of the Persians prior to the supremacy of Cyrus the Great.

This brings us to the question of the identification of Darius the Mede. If he was not an earlier, independent Median monarch, who was he? How could a Mede have assumed the throne after a combined Medo-Persian army had captured Babylon? The answer is found in Cyrus's well-known practice of promoting goodwill and loyalty on the part of the Medes by choosing the ablest of them to high office in the newly constituted Medo-Persian Empire. According to Herodotus (1.127) it was a Median general named Harpagus who encouraged young Cyrus to revolt against his grandfather Astyages, king of Media. Even after he had defeated and captured Astyages, Cyrus treated him with respect and even made him satrap of Barcania or

Hyrcania (according to Ctesias, at least). The Median capital, Ecbatana, was taken over by Cyrus as administrative head of the new empire. R. Ghirshman (*Iran* [Baltimore: Pelican, 1954], p. 129) states, "The Median officials, in association with a number of Persians, were kept at their posts, and the change in the seat of power took place so discreetly that for the western peoples, the Persian was still the Median kingdom." This was certainly the case so far as Herodotus and Xenophon were concerned. They often refer to the officials and the armies of Darius and Xerxes as "Medes" in alternation with the term "Persians."

The *Encyclopaedia Britannica* article on "Media" (1969 ed., 15:68) remarks, "In the new empire they [the Medes] retained a prominent position; in honor and war they stood next to the Persians . . . many noble Medes were employed as officials, satraps and generals." It would not, therefore, be surprising for Cyrus to appoint as viceroy over the newly conquered Babylonian domain a trusted lieutenant who was a Mede. If some other section of his frontier needed his personal attention—whether in the north against the Scythians or in the northeast against the Parthians—it was highly expedient for him to turn over the administration of the new Babylonian conquests to a trusted lieutenant for a year or two, till Cyrus himself could get back to Babylon and assume the throne there with due ceremony. This viceroy was given the title of *Dār ᵉyāwēš*, which apparently meant "The Royal One," from *dara* (which is attested in Avestan Persian as a term for "king").

Do we have any inscriptional evidence for this Darius (*Dārᵉyāwēš*)? Not under that name, perhaps. But we certainly do have frequent references to a general named Gubaru (quite distinct from the Ugbaru of Gutium who lived only a few weeks after the capture of Babylon in 539). A Gubaru appears as the governor of Babylonia and of Ebir-nāri (the western domains under Chaldean sovereignty) in tablets dated from the fourth to the eighth year of Cyrus (535–532 B.C.) and even as late as the fifth year of Cambyses (525 B.C.). It seems altogether probable that during the transitional period of 539–538 he was appointed as viceroy over Babylonia, for the purpose of bringing it into full submission and cooperation with the Medo-Persian Empire, of which it had now become a part.

It would seem that Gubaru was of Median extraction, the son of an Ahasuerus (or Xerxes) who is otherwise unknown. It also appears that he was sixty-two when "made ruler" (*homlaḵ*) (9:1). *Homlaḵ* is a causative passive that strongly suggests that he was appointed king by some higher authority. In corroboration of Gubaru's appointive status, 5:31 speaks of him as having "received" (*qabbēl;* NIV, "took over") the "kingdom" (*malḵûṯā'*), rather than winning it by personal conquest. This is important because it strongly militates against an alternative suggestion made by D.J. Wiseman and others—namely, that this "Darius" was none other than Cyrus himself, who of course had a Median mother, Mandanē, and grandfather, Astyages. But even if we grant the improbable—that the Persian who overthrew the Median government would have styled himself a *Mede*, as Darius did in 5:31 and 9:1, and that the son of Cambyses would have called himself "son of Xerxes"—nevertheless this hypothesis leaves us no way of making sense of *homlaḵ*. Who could have appointed Cyrus king when he himself was already the supreme authority in the entire Middle East?

That Gubaru was given the title of *Dār ᵉyāwēš* ("Darius") and was so referred to rather than as Gubaru during his occupancy of the throne is no more surprising than that Eliakim the son of Josiah received the throne name of "Jehoiakim" and was always so referred to thereafter (2 Kings 23:34), or that Mattaniah son of Josiah should have been renamed "Zedekiah" when he was appointed to the throne of Judah by Nebuchadnezzar (2 Kings 24:17). After all, we should take note of the fact that even the later Darius, son of Hystaspes (*Wištāspa*), bore the personal name of *Spantadāta* (cf. F.W. König, *Relief und Inschrift des Königs Dareios I* [Leiden: Brill, 1938], p. 1). In his case, too, it would appear that *Dār ᵉyāwēš* was a title later assumed after coronation—just as every Roman emperor took the title of Augustus or Caesar Augustus after the decease of the original Augustus in A.D. 14. Even in his case, "Augustus" ("the Revered One") was an honorific title granted to Octavian by the Roman Senate. As W.F. Albright commented ("The Date and Personality of the Chronicler," JBL 40 [1922]:11, n.2):

> It seems to me highly probable that Gobryas [the Greek spelling of Gubaru] did actually assume the royal dignity along with the name 'Darius,' perhaps an old Iranian royal title, while Cyrus was absent on a European campaign. . . . After the cuneiform elucidation of the Belshazzar mystery . . . the vindication of Darius the Mede for history was to be expected. . . . We may safely expect the Babylonian Jewish author to be acquainted with the main facts of Neo-Babylonian history.

Some have asked whether a viceroy over a portion of the Persian Empire would have ventured to issue a decree to the inhabitants "in all the earth" (6:25, KJV), regarding the deference to be paid to Darius alone. But we should understand that the Aramaic *'ar'ā*, like its Hebrew cognate *'ereṣ*, may mean "land" rather than "earth" in its largest sense (cf. 2:35; 4:20). In this case "throughout the land" (NIV) would of course refer only to the erstwhile domains of Nebuchadnezzar. On no account could it have included Egypt, Greece, or India (all of which were well known to the sixth-century Persian world). In all probability the language of this decree was a time-honored formula—reflecting the Akkadian phrase *śar kiššati* ("king of the universe"), which was as old as Hammurabi, if not older.

6) *Remarkable knowledge for a Maccabean author*

From the Greek and Roman historians, we learn that from Persian times Susa, or Shushan, was the capital of the province of Susiana; and Elam was restricted to the territory east of the Eulaeus River. Nevertheless we now know from cuneiform records that Shushan was part of the territory of Elam back in Chaldean times and before. It is very striking that Daniel 8:2 refers to "Susa in the province of Elam"—an item of information scarcely accessible to a second-century B.C. author.

A very interesting testimony along this line comes from R.H. Pfeiffer (*Introduction to the Old Testament* [New York: Harper, 1941], pp. 758–59), who advocates the late date of Daniel:

> Only two details of his [i.e., the author of Daniel] are genuinely historical and, being ignored by Hebrew and Greek historians, would seem to be an echo of Babylonian writings. We shall presumably never know how our author learned that the new Babylon was the creation of Nebuchadnezzar (4:30), as the excavations have proved (see R. Koldewey, *Excavations at Babylon*, 1915) and that Belshazzar, mentioned only in Babylonian records, in Daniel, and in Bar. 1:11, which is based on Daniel, was functioning as king when Cyrus took Babylon in 538 (ch. 5).

Pfeiffer could not explain such knowledge, on the basis of the Maccabean date hypothesis. Neither can anyone else—on that basis.

b. *Composite authorship theory*

Not all liberal scholarship has found the 165 B.C. date for the Book of Daniel entirely satisfactory. The Hebrew chapters containing specific predictions of the events leading up to the persecutions of Antiochus must, of course, have been contemporary with the events themselves, since genuine predictive prophecy in Scripture requires belief in a personal God who inspires his prophets accurately to foretell the future. But there are some things in the first six or seven chapters of the book that are thought to point to third or even late fourth-century B.C. conditions.

Gustav Hoelscher, in his 1919 publication *Die Entstehung des Buches Daniel*, pointed out that the portrait of Nebuchadnezzar presents on the whole a far more enlightened and tolerant attitude toward the Hebrew faith than that of Antiochus Epiphanes, who tried to stamp it out altogether. Martin Noth, in his *Zur Komposition des Buches Daniel* (1926), went so far as to date chapters 2 and 7 from the time of Alexander the Great (336–323 B.C.), at least in their original form. He felt that the legends of chapters 1–6 were collected and reworked some time during the third century. H.L. Ginsburg (*Studies in Daniel* [New York: Jewish Theological Seminary of America, 1948], pp. 5–30) isolated no less than six different authors who contributed to the corpus of Daniel: (1) chapters 1–6 were composed between 292 and 261 B.C.; (2) chapter 2 was later subjected to reworking and insertions of various sorts between 246 and 220 B.C.; (3) chapter 7 came from a different Maccabean author than the one who (4) composed chapters 10–12; (5) chapter 8 was written by a third Maccabean author between 166 and 165 B.C.; and (6) chapter 9 came from a period slightly later than 165 B.C. (Observe that Ginsburg dated only the first two sources in the third century; the rest were all contemporaries of the Maccabean revolt.)

In general, all these advocates of the diverse authorship of Daniel tried to establish the most likely historical setting for these supposed contributors and argued on somewhat subjective grounds. Nevertheless, they did serve notice of the fact that a Maccabean setting did not really explain all the tendencies and factors discoverable in the first six or seven chapters of the book. They prompted H.H. Rowley ("The Unity of the Book of Daniel," HUCA 23 [January 1950]) to concede that some of the material found in chapters 1–6 may have gone back to oral traditions from an earlier century. Still he vigorously maintained that the final form of composition as we have it dates only to the Maccabean period and that the literary evidence is all in favor of unity. In this refutation of multiple authorship, Rowley occupied highly defensible ground. But in regard to the period of composition, he was led by his antisupernaturalistic stance into a biased handling of the historical and linguistic evidence, as we shall presently see.

1) *Linguistic arguments*

a) *Alleged Greek loan words*

In earlier days the critical scholars used to argue that *kārôz* (3:4) was a loan word from the Greek *kēryx* ("herald"), but this view (expressed in BDB, p. 1097) has been abandoned since *khrausa* ("caller") has been found in Old Persian (KB, p. 1087) and perhaps comes originally from Hurrian *kirezzi* ("proclamation") (so K.A.

Kitchen, *Ancient Orient and Old Testament* [Chicago: InterVarsity, 1966], p. 144). C.C. Torrey and A. Cowley identified *piṯgām* ("word," "account," "report") in 3:16; 4:17 [14MT] as a Greek derivative. This, however, has been universally given up since E.Y. Kutscher in *Kedem* (2.74) published a leather scroll of Arsames dating from 410 B.C., in which *piṯgām* appears. It probably came from the Old Persian *pratigama*, which compounded *prati* ("to," "forth") with *gama* ("go," "proceed"), therefore meaning "communication," "order."

It is now pretty well agreed that there are but three words in the Aramaic of Daniel that have undoubtedly been borrowed from Greek. All of them are names of musical instruments: *qayṯ*^{e}*rōs*, derived from *kitharis* ("lyre," "zither"); *p*^{e}*santērîn*, from *psaltērion* ("trigon"); and *sûmpōn*^{e}*yāh*, from *symphōnia* ("harmony," "bagpipe"). These all occur in a list of instruments played by the royal symphony orchestra in Daniel 3:5, 10, 15.

How could such words have been part of the vocabulary of sixth-century B.C. Aramaic in Babylon? Very easily, for the inscriptions of Sargon II (722–705) back in the Assyrian period refer to Greek captives from Cyprus and Ionia sold into slavery. Some of them may well have been musicians who played these instruments. The celebrated poet Alcaeus of Lesbos (c. 600 B.C.) refers to his brother Antimenidas as serving in the Babylonian army. E.F. Weidner ("Jojachin König von Juda," *Mélanges Syriens* 2 [1939]: 923–35) published some Neo-Babylonian ration tablets listing supplies for Ionian carpenters, shipbuilders, and others, along with musicians from Ashkelon. It is therefore evident that Greek mercenaries and slaves served in the Babylonian and Assyrian periods, some of whom were undoubtedly versed in Greek music and musical instruments. It is no more surprising that Greek names for these instruments were borrowed by Aramaic than that "piano" and "viola" were borrowed into our language from Italian.

On the other hand, it is inconceivable that Greek terms for government and administration would not have been adopted into Aramaic by the second century B.C. if Greek had indeed been the language of government for over 160 years (between 332 and 167 B.C.). It is evident that the language of Daniel was a lingua franca that readily absorbed foreign terms in precisely this area. There are approximately fifteen Persian derivatives pertaining to government and administration that appear in the Aramaic chapters of Daniel.[3] Even the Hebrew chapters contain Persian words like *'appeḏen* ("palace" [11:45], from *apadāna*), *part*^{e}*mîm* ("noblemen" [1:3], from *fratama*), *paṯbag̱* ("king's portion" [1:5], from *patibaga*).[3]

---

[3]The other certain or suspected loan words from Persian, in the order of their appearance in Daniel, are as follows:

2:5—*'azdā'* ("sure," "assured"), from *azda* ("decided," "assured")
2:5—*haddām* ("limb," "member"), from *handāma* (Avestan) ("member")
2:9—*dāṯ* ("law"), from *dāta* ("law")
2:18—*rāz* ("secret"), from *rāz* (Pehlevi) ("secret")
3:2—*'*^{a}*ḥašdarp*^{e}*nayyā'* ("satraps"), from *kshatrapāwan* ("realm protectors," "satraps")
3:2—*'*^{a}*ḏargāzar* ("adviser"), from *andarzaghar* (Av.) ("counsel-giver")
3:2—*g*^{e}*ḏāḇ*^{e}*rayyā*, ("treasurers"), from *ganzavar* (Pehl.) ("treasurer")
3:2—*d*^{e}*ṯāḇ*^{e}*rayyā'* ("judge"), from *dātabara* ("law-bearer," "judge")
3:2—*tiptāyē'* ("magistrates"), from *adipati* ("overchief")
3:5—*sabb*^{e}*ḵā'* ("trigon"[?], a musical instrument), from Persian?
3:21—*sarbāl* ("trousers"), from *shirwāl* (Modern Persian for "trousers")
3:21—*paṭṭîš* ("shirt," "tunic"), from *patyuša* (M. Pers. for "garment")
5:5—*neḇraštā'* ("lampstand"), from *nibrās* (M. Pers. for "lampstand")

All this points unquestionably to composition in the Persian period (c. 530 B.C.). But it renders a later date in the post-Alexandrian period linguistically impossible.[4]

A second line of evidence is found in the translation errors committed by the LXX of Daniel, which was written in the second century B.C., in Maccabean or Hasmonean times. If Daniel itself had been composed in second-century Aramaic, as the late-date theory maintains, then there should have been no difficulty in rendering any of the technical terms into Greek. But even in the single verse of Daniel 3:2, we find that the LXX translates *'ᵃḏargāzᵉrayyā'* ("counselors") by *hypatous* ("magnates"); *gᵉḏāḇᵉrayyā'* ("treasurers") by *dioikētas* ("administrators"); and *tiptāyē'* or *dᵉṯāḇᵉrayyā'* ("magistrates," "judges") by the vague, general phrase *tous ep' exousiōn* ("those in authority"). It is impossible to explain how within a few decades after the alleged composition of Daniel in the 160s B.C., the meaning of these terms could have been so completely forgotten by the Alexandrian Jews who composed the LXX that they did not know how to translate them correctly (cf. Wiseman, *Problems in Daniel*, p. 43).

5:7—*hamnîḵā'* ("necklace"), from *hamyān* (M. Pers.) (diminutive: *hamyānak*, "small belt")

6:3—*sāraḵ* ("chief," "overseer"), perhaps from *sār* ("prince") which probably would have entered Persian from Semitic, but cf. also the Arabic *shārikun* ("partner," "companion [viz., of the king]").

7:15—*niḏneh* ("sheath," "body"), cf. Sanskrit *nidhāna* ("receptacle"), which raises the possibility of a Persian cognate (since Persian is related to Sanskrit).

[4]In this connection it is interesting to observe that the discovery and publication of the Elephantine Papyri by Sayce and Cowley in 1906 (*Aramaic Papyri Discovered at Assuan* [London]) and by Sachau in Leipzig (1911) provided considerable embarrassment to the Maccabean date hypothesis. Containing about ninety documents of varying length (including a large fragment of a literary work, "The Words of Aḥikar," and an Aramaic rendition of the Behistun Rock inscription of Darius I), these late fifth-century Aramaic documents bore a marked resemblance to the Aramaic chapters of Ezra (4–7) and also to the six Aramaic chapters of Daniel. This imperiled the theory of a second-century date for Daniel and compelled critics like H.H. Rowley to set up special criteria for dating on the basis of the Persian loan words discoverable in the Elephantine material. In *The Aramaic of the Old Testament*, Rowley pointed out that of the "twenty" (there are actually only nineteen) Persian loan words in Daniel, thirteen are attested in the Targums (composed in first century B.C. and later). Yet of the twenty-six Persian derivatives in the Elephantine documents, only two occur in the Targums. On this basis he reasoned (p. 139) that "in this matter, therefore, Biblical Aramaic . . . stands very much nearer to the Targums than do the Papyri." (In the Aramaic of Ezra, there are thirteen certain borrowings of this type—Rowley found only nine—of which five appear in the Targums.) By this statistical count Rowley felt he had salvaged a second-century date for Daniel, even though it belonged to the same general class of *Reichsaramäisch* ("Imperial Aramaic") as did the Papyri.

This entire line of argument has been brilliantly dismantled by Kitchen in *Problems in Daniel* (pp. 36–44). He points out that in the fifth- and sixth-century documents in Imperial Aramaic, nearly half of Daniel's Persian derivatives appear. In the Elephantine Papyri we find *piṯgām, 'azdā', zēn, tiptāyē'*, *gizbār*, and *rāz;* in the sixth-century treasury orders at Persepolis (via Elamite) we find *'ᵃḥašdarpān* and *dāṯ*. In other words, nearly half of the Persian-derived words in Daniel are attested for the fifth and sixth centuries B.C. Of these eight, four or five happen to occur in the Targums as well. By Rowley's criterion these too would "stand nearer to the Targums," but since they are found in fifth- or sixth-century documents, they cannot be found datable to a later century. Therefore Rowley's criterion leads to false results and must be discarded. Kitchen remarks (*Problems in Daniel*, p. 37): "The plain fact is that all of these eight or nine words came into Aramaic (and Akkadian and Elamite) in the sixth-fifth centuries B.C., and some of them happened to be retained four centuries later. The occurrence of four or five of them in both Persian imperial documents and Targums merely leaves the date of Daniel's Aramaic where it was before: in the sixth to second centuries B.C." He then goes on to point out that in the case of Ezra, three-fourths of the thirteen Persian loan words are attested in the fifth-sixth century documents, which certainly argues for an early date for Ezra. But of the nine words in this category, four occur in the Targums. "In other words, again, half of the words are 'early' only, and half both early and late, with the same result as in Daniel, i.e., sixth-fifth to second centuries for scope in dating" (ibid., p. 38).

b) *The Aramaic of Daniel*

The Maccabean date hypothesis was propounded long before the discovery of the Genesis Apocryphon from Qumran Cave 1. Before the publication of this scroll, there was no Palestinian Aramaic document extant from the third or second century B.C.; and it was therefore theoretically possible to date the Aramaic of Daniel as coming from the 160s B.C. But with the publication and linguistic analysis of the Apocryphon (which is a sort of midrash for Genesis), it has become apparent that Daniel is composed in a type of centuries-earlier Aramaic. A full discussion of this evidence appears in my article "The Aramaic of the Genesis Apocryphon." The Apocryphon was probably composed (according to its editors, N. Avigad and Y. Yadin) in the third century B.C., even though this copy dates from the first century B.C. Yet linguistic analysis indicates that in morphology, vocabulary, and syntax, the Apocryphon shows a considerably later stage of the Aramaic language than do the Aramaic chapters of Daniel.[5]

As for the characteristic word-order, the Apocryphon tends to follow the normal sequence of Northwest Semitic—verb first, followed by subject, then object—in the characteristic structure of the clause. Beyond question this was the normal practice of Western Aramaic used in Palestine during the Maccabean period. But the Aramaic of Daniel shows a marked tendency for the verb to be deferred till a later position in the clause, often even after the noun object—somewhat like the word order of Akkadian (Babylonian and Assyrian) as used in Babylonia from the time of Sargon of Agade (twenty-fourth cent. B.C.) onward. On the basis of the word order alone, it is safe to conclude that Daniel could not have been composed in Palestine (as the Maccabean hypothesis demands) but in the eastern sector of the Fertile Crescent, in all probability in Babylon itself. The above-mentioned article contains several pages that should prove quite conclusively to any scholar that the second-century date and Palestinian provenance of the Book of Daniel cannot be upheld any longer without violence being done to the science of linguistics.

c) *The Hebrew of Daniel*

As a follow-up to his study "The Aramaic of the Genesis Apocryphon," this commentator conducted a similar linguistic comparison between the Hebrew chapters of Daniel (1, 8–12) and the second-century B.C. Hebrew prose of 1QS and 1QM, the two foremost documents composed for the Essenes of Qumran. This twelve-page study (cf. "The Hebrew of Daniel" in Skilton, ed., *The Law and the Prophets*, pp. 470–81) contains a very large number of examples of later Hebrew morphology, syntax, and vocabulary appearing in 1QS and 1QM as contrasted with Daniel.[6]

---

[5]The Apocryphon uses *hā* for the third feminine singular suffix (hitherto regarded as Targumic) instead of Daniel's *ah;* for the third feminine singular perfect of the lamed-aleph verb, it uses *iyat* rather than the earlier *āt* used by Daniel and Ezra. It occasionally uses a *mif'ōl* pattern for the Pe'al infinitive (e.g., mišbōq, "to leave") rather than the earlier *mif'al* used invariably in Daniel. The third masculine plural suffix appears as *ôn* (Talmudic and Midrashic!) rather than the earlier *hôn* or *hôm* used by Ezra and Daniel. As for adverbs, the Apocryphon uses *kamān* for "how great," rather than *k^emā'*, the earlier form used in Daniel, likewise, *tammān* for "there" rather than *tammā*.

[6]Morphological examples are, first of all, an Aramaic-type third singular masculine suffix after a plural noun, such as *yômôy* instead of the regular *yāmāyw* ("his days") used by Daniel. Similarly, the Aramaic-type *'^alēhôn* ("upon them") in 1QS 3:25 instead of the earlier *'^alēhem* invariably used in Daniel. As for the masculine plural nouns, at least twenty-five times the Aramaic *în* is used in place of the Hebrew *îm* in the

For further examples, the reader is referred to the article mentioned above. But the evidence cited is enough to demonstrate that, from the standpoint of linguistic science, there is no possibility that the text of Daniel could have been composed as late as the Maccabean uprising, and that there is every likelihood that the Aramaic comes from the same period, if not a century earlier, than the Aramaic of the Elephantine Papyri and of Ezra, which are admittedly fifth-century productions. It goes without saying that if the predictions concerning the period of Antiochus III and Antiochus IV (222–164 B.C.) are composed in language antedating the second-century and third-century B.C., then the whole effort to explain Daniel as a *vaticinium ex eventu* must be abandoned. We are still faced with the phenomenon of fulfilled prophecy, even as regards Antiochus Epiphanes.

2) *Alleged prophecy after the event*

In the preceding paragraphs we have seen that the linguistic evidence from Qumran makes the rationalistic explanation for Daniel no longer tenable. It is difficult to see how any scholar can defend this view and maintain intellectual respectability. We now proceed to two areas of internal evidence that completely rule out the Maccabean hypothesis as a credible explanation for the origin of Daniel.

a) *Daniel's fourth kingdom*

The identification of the fourth kingdom of Nebuchadnezzar's dream in chapter 2 is absolutely crucial for the Maccabean date hypothesis. If the "romance" about Daniel was composed in the 160s B.C., then the latest vista in the prophet's predictive vision would have to be the Greek Empire, established by Alexander the Great and then subdivided into the Ptolemaic, Seleucid, Thracian, and Macedonian domains. Vital to this theory, then, is the proposition that the Maccabean author, confused and ill-informed as to the historical situation in the sixth century, supposed incorrectly (1) that it was the Medes and the Medes alone who overthrew the Chaldean Empire in 539; (2) that Darius the Mede was ruler in his own right and sovereign over the entire Middle East and the Near East as well; and (3) that, even though his reign lasted less than two years, his "empire" was put on the same level with the Babylonian Empire, which endured for 67 years, and the Persian Empire, which lasted for over 200 years, and the Greek Empire, which had been going on for over 160 years by the time of the Maccabees. The supposed Median stage could have lasted no more than a year and a half, according to the author of Daniel

---

eleven columns of 1QS. Daniel has only one such example—*hayyāmîn* ("the days"), in 12:13. Already the later first plural pronoun *'ānû* is beginning to show up in sectarian Hebrew (1QS 1:25 and 1QM 3:6), but never in Daniel or, indeed, in the rest of the OT (except for a Kethiv reading in Jer 42:6).

So far as verb inflection is concerned, the sectarians occasionally omit the initial *h* of the Niphal and Hiphil infinitives; e.g., *liyyāḥēḏ* (1QS 1:8; 3:7) instead of *l^{e}hiyyāḥēḏ* ("to be united"); *laqrîḇ* instead of *l^{e}haqrîḇ* ("to bring near"; 1QS 8:9); *liṯyassēr* (1QS 9:11) is used for the Hithpael *l^{e}hiṯyassēr* ("to be disciplined"). Daniel's Hebrew always retains the *h*. The Qumran documents often use the preposition *l^{e}* ("to") as a locution for the imperfect tense, even where a plural subject is intended. Thus we find *lah^{a}ḇînām* ("they shall give them understanding") instead of *yāḇînûm;* in 1QS 1:7 *l^{e}lamm^{e}ḏēhû* is used instead of *y^{e}lamm^{e}dûhû* ("they shall teach him"). In 1QM 14:14 we have *ûl^{e}hārîm l^{e}ḵāh* for *w^{e}ṯārîm l^{e}ḵā* ("and you raise up to you")—followed by *l^{e}hašpîl* for *tašpîl* ("you cast down"). This construction is never met with in the Hebrew of Daniel, but it had evidently become quite common by the second century B.C.

himself, since he never spoke of a later date than the "first year of Darius son of Xerxes" (9:1). The extremely brief and ephemeral character of this supposed "empire" is a very telling argument in its disfavor. It looks like a desperate evasion of the obvious inference from the text that the four empires represented the series: Chaldean, Medo-Persian, Greek, and Roman.

A second consideration militating against the theory of an earlier, independent Median kingdom prior to and separate from the Persian is found in the wordplay associated with the handwriting on the wall of Belshazzar's banqueting hall. The third word of this announcement of doom was *parsîn* (5:25), which was interpreted by Daniel himself in the singular form *p*^{e}*rēs*. Daniel 5:28 derives from *p*^{e}*rēs* (which may have appeared to mean "division into two" or "half shekel") the verb *p*^{e}*rîsaṯ* ("is divided") and the noun *pārās* ("Persians"). The only possible inference is that the author who wrote these words believed that imperial power was taken from the Babylonians under Belshazzar and given over directly and immediately to the Persians, who at the time of the capture of Babylon were already merged with the Medes in a single domain: "Your kingdom is divided and given to the Medes and Persians." The triliteral *p-r-s* is involved in the linkage of a triple wordplay, and there can be no legitimate alternative to the proposition that the author—whoever he was and whenever he wrote—believed that the second empire was the Medo-Persian, not the Median alone. This carries with it the fatal consequence that the third empire was Greek, not Persian, and that the fourth empire must have been one that superseded and overcame the Greek one and turned out to be the Roman Empire, which took over the Near East in the first century B.C., a century later than the death of Antiochus Epiphanes.

Third, the symbolism of chapter 7 and chapter 8 points unmistakably to the identification of the second kingdom as Medo-Persian and the third as Greek. In chapter 7, v.4 introduces the Babylonian power in the form of a lion; concerning this there is no dispute. The second power is a bear (v.5), reclining with one side higher than the other (suggesting the predominance of the Persians over the Medes), and devouring meat from three ribs of his prey. The three ribs correspond to the three major conquests of the Medo-Persian federation: (1) Lydia, captured around 740 B.C.; (2) Babylon, captured in 539 B.C.; (3) Egypt, annexed by Cambyses around 525 B.C. No such three-stage conquest can be associated with the career of the Median Empire, from Cyaxeres to Astyages, and so this symbolism does not fit. The third beast is the four-winged leopard (v.6) with four heads. This calls to mind the rapid conquest of the Persian Empire by Alexander the Great (334–330 B.C.) and the division of his domains into four subdivisions after his death: the Seleucid, the Ptolemaic, the Thrace-Asia Minor domain of Lysimachus, and the Macedonian-Greco merger maintained by Antipater and his son Cassander. The fourth beast (v.7) was more fearsome than all the preceding, with ten horns and large iron teeth. As such it appropriately symbolized that widespread power of Rome, with the same number of horns as the toes of the feet of Nebuchadnezzar's dream-image in chapter 2. The ten horns appear to refer to an end-time revival of the Roman Empire, out of which the final Antichrist, or Beast, will arise to assume tyrannical authority over the world. This eschatological world-dictator is symbolized by a little horn that grows into prominence after uprooting three of the original ten horns. Here, then, the little horn emerges from the fourth kingdom.

In chapter 8 the little horn grows out of the four large horns of the goat (v.8) who had overcome the two-horned ram of Medo-Persia, one of whose horns was larger than the other. This little horn has mistakenly been equated by exponents of the Maccabean hypothesis with the little horn of chapter 7. In both cases the "horn" begins small but rises to prominence and uses his power as a tyrant, speaking blasphemously against God. Both little horns suspend worship at the Jerusalem temple and replace it with a Hitler-like idolatry (cf. 8:11 with 7:8; 9:27). On the other hand, the tyrant in chapter 8 is from the third kingdom and the one in chapter 7 from the fourth kingdom. The only way to harmonize these two is to see in the little horn of chapter 8 the type (Antiochus Epiphanes) and in the little horn of chapter 7 the antitype (the Beast, or Antichrist, of the last days who figures so prominently in Rev 13). So interpreted, the problems are solved in regard to interpretation and the fulfillment of prophecy. Antiochus, the type, made a supreme effort to stamp out the true faith during the 160s B.C.; the eschatological antitype, the "beast" (Rev 13), will make another determined attempt to do the same in the last days.

b) *The prophecy of the Seventy Weeks*

In our discussion of Daniel 9, we will devote much attention to the prediction of the Seventy Weeks, set forth in Daniel 9:24–27. Here we simply point out that the term "weeks" (rendered in NIV as "sevens") is *šāḇûʿîm*, from *šāḇûaʿ*, which always takes a feminine plural, *šeḇuʿôṯ*, when it means a seven of days, namely, a "week." The masculine plural here probably indicates that the word is meant as a heptad (so BDB, pp. 988–89) of years.

The figure 70 corresponds to the 70 years of the Babylonian captivity, but this predictive number adds up to 70 times 7, or 490 years. It appears, however, from 9:25 that at first only 7 plus 62 are being discussed, and so it is at the end of 483 years that the "Anointed One" will appear. The *terminus a quo* for this 483-year period is stated in 9:25 to be the issuing of a "decree to restore and rebuild Jerusalem"; the *terminus ad quem* is to be the coming of the "Anointed One" (*māšîaḥ nāgîḏ*, lit., "Messiah Prince").

As the exegesis in the commentary will show, the above-mentioned decree was probably that of Artaxerxes I in 457 B.C., issued to Ezra in connection with his return to Palestine. While he did not actually accomplish the rebuilding of the walls of Jerusalem, he was evidently given royal permission to do so (Ezra 9:9), if he could find sufficient resources and support to carry through with it (hence Nehemiah's great disappointment in 445 B.C., when he found out that the project had not been accomplished [Neh 1:3–4]). Reckoning, then, from 457 B.C., we come out to A.D. 26 as the full number of 483 years—with one more gained as we pass directly from 1 B.C. to A.D. 1. This results in the precise date of A.D. 27 for Christ's appearance as Messiah of Israel. If he was crucified in A.D. 30, as is generally believed, and if his ministry lasted for three years, then A.D. 27 would be the accurate date of fulfillment of this remarkable prophecy.

For this amazing pattern of prediction and fulfillment, there can be no successful answer on the part of critics who espouse the Maccabean date hypothesis. There is no evading the conclusion that the prophecies of the Book of Daniel were inspired by the same God who later fulfilled them, or who will fulfill them in the last days, which are destined to close our present era with the final great conflict of Armageddon and the second coming of our Lord Jesus Christ.

6. Bibliography

Commentaries

Aalders, G.C. *Daniel*. Koorte Verklaring Series. The Netherlands: Kampen, 1965.
Baldwin, Joyce. *Daniel: An Introduction and Commentary*. Wheaton: InterVarsity, 1978.
Boutflower, Charles. *In and Around the Book of Daniel*. Grand Rapids: Zondervan, 1963.
Culver, Robert D. *Daniel and the Latter Days*. Chicago: Moody, 1954.
DeHaan, M.R. *Daniel the Prophet*. Grand Rapids: Zondervan, 1947.
Driver, S.R. *The Book of Daniel*. CBCS. Cambridge: University Press, 1900.
Ford, Desmond. *Daniel*. Nashville: Southern Publishing House, 1978.
Gaebelein, Arno C. *The Prophet Daniel*. New York: Our Hope, 1911.
Hammer, Raymond. *The Book of Daniel*. CBCS. Cambridge: University Press, 1976.
Ironside, H.A. *Lectures on Daniel the Prophet*. Neptune, N.J.: Loizeaux, 1920.
Jerome. *Commentary on Daniel*. Translated by G.L. Archer. Grand Rapids: Baker, 1958.
Kelly, William. *Lectures on the Book of Daniel*. London: G. Morrish, 1881.
Leupold, H.C. *Exposition of Daniel*. 1949. Reprint ed. Grand Rapids: Baker, 1969.
Montgomery, J.A. *A Critical and Exegetical Commentary on the Book of Daniel*. ICC. New York: Scribner's, 1927.
Porteous, N.W. *Daniel: A Commentary*. Philadelphia: Westminster, 1965.
Pusey, E.B. *Daniel the Prophet*. New York: Funk & Wagnalls, 1891.
Strauss, Lehman. *The Prophecies of Daniel*. Neptune, N.J.: Loizeaux, 1965.
Talbot, Louis T. *The Prophecies of Daniel*. 3d ed. Wheaton: Van Kampen, 1954.
Walvoord, John F. *Daniel: The Key to Prophetic Revelation*. Chicago: Moody, 1971.
Wood, Leon. *A Commentary on Daniel*. Grand Rapids: Zondervan, 1973.
Wright, Charles H.H. *Daniel and His Prophecies*. London: Williams & Norgate, 1906.
Young, E.J. *The Prophecy of Daniel*. Grand Rapids: Eerdmans, 1949.

Special Studies

Anderson, Robert. *The Coming Prince*. London: Hodder & Stoughton, 1895.
Barton, G.A. *Archaeology and the Bible*. 7th ed. Philadelphia: American Sunday School Union, 1937.
Borgognini Duca, F. *Le LXX Settimane di Daniele e le Date Messianiche*. Padova, 1951.
Charles, R.H. *Apocrypha and Pseudepigrapha of the Old Testament in English*. 2 vols. Oxford: Clarendon, 1913.
Cross, Frank M. *The Ancient Library of Qumran and Modern Biblical Studies*. Garden City, N.Y.: Doubleday, 1958.
Dougherty, R.P. *Nabonidus and Belshazzar*. Yale Oriental Series. New Haven: Yale University Press, 1929.
Finegan, Jack. *Handbook of Biblical Chronology*. Princeton, N.J.: Princeton University Press, 1964.
Herodotus. *History*. Translated by G. Rawlinson. New York: Tudor, 1934.
Kromminga, D.H. *The Millennium*. Grand Rapids: Eerdmans, 1948.
Mauro, Philip. *The Seventy Weeks and the Great Tribulation*. Boston: Scripture Truth, 1923.
McClain, Alva J. *Daniel's Prophecy of the Seventy Weeks*. Grand Rapids: Zondervan, 1940.
Merrill, E.H. *An Historical Survey of the Old Testament*. Nutley, N.J.: Craig, 1966.
Payne, J.B. *The Theology of the Older Testament*. Grand Rapids: Zondervan, 1962.
———. *Encyclopedia of Biblical Prophecy*. New York: Harper & Row, 1973.
Pentecost, J.D. *Prophecy for Today*. Grand Rapids: Zondervan, 1961.
Peters, G.N.H. *The Theocratic Kingdom*. 3 vols. Grand Rapids: Kregel, 1952.
Pritchard, J.B., ed. *Ancient Near Eastern Texts Relating to the Old Testament*. 3d ed. Princeton, N.J.: University Press, 1969.

Rowley, H.H. *The Aramaic of the Old Testament*. Oxford: Clarendon, 1929.
______. *Darius the Mede and the Four Empires in the Book of Daniel*. Cardiff: University of Wales, 1935.
Schultz, S.J. *The Old Testament Speaks*. New York: Harper & Row, 1970.
Thomas, D.W. *Archaeology and Old Testament Study*. Oxford: Clarendon, 1967.
Unger, M.F. *Introductory Guide to the Old Testament*. Grand Rapids: Zondervan, 1952.
Urquhart, John. *The Wonders of Prophecy*. London: Pickering & Inglis, 1939.
Whitcomb, John C. *Darius the Mede*. Grand Rapids: Eerdmans, 1959.
Wilson, Robert Dick. *The Aramaic of Daniel*. New York: Scribner's, 1912.
______. *Studies in the Book of Daniel*. New York: Putnam's Sons, 1917.
______. *Studies in the Book of Daniel: Second Series*. New York: Revell, 1938.
Wiseman, D.J. *The Chronicles of the Chaldean Kings*. London: Trustees of the British Museum, 1956.
______ et al. *Notes on Some Problems in the Book of Daniel*. London: Tyndale, 1965.
Yamauchi, E.M. *Greece and Babylon*. Grand Rapids: Baker, 1967.

Articles

Archer, G.L. "The Aramaic of the Genesis Apocryphon Compared with the Aramaic of Daniel." *New Perspectives on the Old Testament*. Edited by J.B. Payne. Waco: Word, 1970, pp. 160–69.
______. "The Hebrew of Daniel Compared with the Qumran Sectarian Documents." *The Law and the Prophets*. Edited by J. Skilton. Nutley, N.J.: Presbyterian and Reformed, 1974.
Young, E.J. "Daniel." *New Bible Commentary: Revised*. Edited by D. Guthrie et al. London: InterVarsity, 1970.

9. Outline

I. The Selection and Preparation of God's Special Servants (1:1–21)
   1. The First Hostages of the Babylonian Captivity (1:1–2)
   2. Nebuchadnezzar's Training Program (1:3–7)
   3. The First Demonstration of Faith (1:8–16)
   4. The Excellence of God's Special Servants (1:17–21)

II. Nebuchadnezzar's First Dream: God's Plan for the Ages (2:1–49)
   1. The Babylonian Wise Men's Impotence (2:1–13)
   2. Daniel's Intercession and Offer (2:14–23)
   3. Daniel's Recitation of the King's Dream (2:24–35)
   4. Daniel's Interpretation of the King's Dream (2:36–47)
   5. The Promotion of Daniel and His Comrades (2:48–49)

III. The Golden Image and the Fiery Furnace (3:1–30)
   1. The Erection of the Image (3:1–3)
   2. The Institution of State Religion (3:4–7)
   3. The Accusation and Trial of God's Faithful Witnesses (3:8–18)
   4. The Sentence Imposed and Executed (3:19–23)
   5. The Deliverance and the Fourth Man (3:24–27)
   6. Nebuchadnezzar's Second Submission to God (3:28–30)

IV. Nebuchadnezzar's Second Dream and Humiliation (4:1–37)
   1. The Circumstances of the Second Dream (4:1–7)
   2. The Description of the Dream (4:8–18)
   3. Daniel's Interpretation and Warning (4:19–27)
   4. The King's Punishment (4:28–33)
   5. The King's Repentance (4:34–37)

V. Belshazzar's Feast (5:1–31)
   1. The Profanation of the Holy Vessels (5:1–4)
   2. The Handwriting on the Wall (5:5–9)
   3. The Queen Mother's Recommendation (5:10–16)
   4. Daniel's Interpretation (5:17–28)
   5. Daniel's Honor and Belshazzar's Demise (5:29–31)

VI. Daniel and the Lions' Den (6:1–28)
   1. The Conspiracy Against Daniel (6:1–9)
   2. Daniel's Detection, Trial, and Sentence (6:10–17)
   3. Daniel's Deliverance and His Foes' Punishment (6:18–24)
   4. Darius's Testimony to God's Sovereignty (6:25–28)

VII. The Triumph of the Son of Man (7:1–28)
   1. The Four Beasts and the Succession of Empires (7:1–8)
   2. The Kingdom of God and the Enthroned Messiah (7:9–14)
   3. The Vision Interpreted by the Angel (7:15–28)

VIII. The Grecian Conquest of Persia and the Tyranny of Antiochus Epiphanes (8:1–27)

1. The Vision of the Ram, the He-Goat, and the Little Horn (8:1–12)
2. Gabriel's Interpretation of the Vision (8:13–27)

IX. The Vision of the Seventy Weeks (9:1–27)
1. Daniel's Great Prayer (9:1–19)
2. The Divine Answer: Seventy Heptads of Years (9:20–27)

X. The Triumph of Persistent Prayer (10:1–21)
1. Daniel's Disturbing Vision and Prayerful Concern (10:1–3)
2. God's Delayed Messenger (10:4–14)
3. The Angel's Encouragement (10:15–21)

XI. Tribulation Under Antiochus and Under Antichrist (11:1–45)
1. From the Persian Empire to the Death of Alexander (11:1–4)
2. The Wars Between the Ptolemies and the Seleucids (11:5–20)
3. The Great Persecution Under Antiochus Epiphanes (11:21–35)
4. The Latter-Day Counterpart Persecution (11:36–39)
5. The Triumph and Fall of Antichrist (11:40–45)

XII. The Great Tribulation and the Final Triumph of God's People (12:1–13)
1. The Great Tribulation (12:1)
2. The Resurrection and Judgment (12:2–3)
3. The Sealed Prophecies (12:4)
4. The Prediction of the Three and One-Half Years (12:5–7)
5. The Final Commission to Daniel (12:8–13)

Text and Exposition

I. The Selection and Preparation of God's Special Servants (1:1–21)

1. *The First Hostages of the Babylonian Captivity*

1:1–2

> [1]In the third year of the reign of Jehoiakim king of Judah, Nebuchadnezzar king of Babylon came to Jerusalem and besieged it. [2]And the Lord delivered Jehoiakim king of Judah into his hand, along with some of the articles from the temple of God. These he carried off to the temple of his god in Babylonia and put in the treasure house of his god.

1 This 605 B.C. expedition was the first of three major invasions of Palestine by Nebuchadnezzar son of Nabopolassar, the king of Babylon. The second occurred in 597 B.C., when Jehoiachin, the son of Jehoiakim, was compelled by the Chaldeans to surrender Jerusalem (2 Kings 24:10–14) and go into captivity with all his princes and leaders, the flower of his army, and all the skilled craftsmen in his capital—including some of the priests, like young Ezekiel. The third and final captivity took place after the storming of Jerusalem in 587 B.C., when all the people of Judah that had not escaped to the hills and joined the guerillas were taken into captivity in Babylonia.

Note that it is important to keep these stages of the Captivity in mind when computing the seventy years of exile announced by Jeremiah 29:10; the interval between the first deportation in 605 B.C., in which Daniel himself was involved, and 536 B.C., when the first returnees under Zerubbabel once more set up an altar in Jerusalem, amounted to seventy years. Likewise, the interval between the destruction of the first temple by Nebuzaradan in 586 and the completion of the second temple by Zerubbabel in 516 was about seventy years.

The date of the first invasion in 605 B.C. (which has been verified by Wiseman, *Chaldean Kings*, pp. 25, 46–47, 66–69) is here given as the "third" year of the reign of Jehoiakim. This follows Babylonian practice, which reckoned the first regnal year as beginning on the first of Nisan following the year of accession to the throne. Thus Nebuchadnezzar's first regnal year was computed as commencing in Nisan (April) of 604, even though he had already been crowned in Tishri (September) of 605.

Jehoiakim began his reign in 608, as an appointee of Necho king of Egypt, who officially changed his name from Eliakim ("El will establish") to Jehoiakim ("Yahweh will establish"). Necho then invested him as vassal king under Egyptian authority sometime in the fall of 609, after his brother Jehoahaz had ruled for the three months following the death of their father, Josiah. At the Battle of Megiddo, Josiah had made a vain attempt to halt the progress of Necho northward as he went to join his Assyrian allies at Haran. If, then, Jehoiakim's first regnal year began in Nisan 608, the Battle of Carchemish, in which Nebuchadnezzar defeated the Assyrian-Egyptian coalition in June 605, would have taken place in Jehoiakim's third regnal year, according to the Babylonian reckoning; and Nebuchadnezzar's subsequent advance on Jerusalem (prior to Nisan 604) would have fallen in the same year.

The Jewish calendar, however, began the civil New Year on the first of Tishri (the seventh month), rather than the first of Nisan (the first month of their religious year), and reckoned regnal years accordingly. So if Jehoiakim was first appointed king in the late fall of 609, his first regnal year must have begun in Tishri 608. Therefore Tishri 605 would have marked the beginning of his fourth regnal year, and Nebuchadnezzar apparently did not reach Jerusalem in his mopping-up operations after the victory at Carchemish till November or December of 605. It is only natural, therefore, that Jeremiah (25:1; 46:2) would refer to this event as taking place in the fourth year of Jehoiakim. Hence there is no discrepancy whatever between the two reckonings, and the often-repeated argument (based on these reckonings) against the historical trustworthiness of Daniel is worthless.

2 From the very beginning of this record, it is made clear that Nebuchadnezzar's success was not through his prowess alone; it was the work of the one true God (Yahweh of hosts), who brought about the complete collapse of the Judean monarchy and the deportation of the people of Jerusalem into exile. Thus the theme of God's absolute sovereignty is here implied. It continues to dominate the entire Book of Daniel, along with the accompanying theme of God's unwavering purpose to bring his people back to repentance through disciplinary suffering, so equipping them spiritually for restoration to the Land of Promise. The divine motive behind all this dreadful humiliation, suffering, and loss was redemptive and altogether in harmony with God's promises given to the generation of Moses (Lev 26; Deut 28; cf. also 2 Chron 36:14–21). Precisely because it was Yahweh who gave over the Jews into Nebuchadnezzar's power, it was Yahweh's hand that could again snatch them away from their foreign bondage, once they were ready to renew their covenant fellowship with him and carry out their part in his program of redemption.

Notes

1 נְבוּכַדְנֶאצַּר (*N*^{e}*b̲ûk̲ad̲ne'ṣṣar*, "Nebuchadnezzar") is the form that is given in Daniel (as well as 2 Kings, Chron, Ezra, Neh, and Esth), whereas נְבוּכַדְרֶאצַּר (*N*^{e}*b̲ûk̲ad̲re'ṣṣar*, "Nebuchadrezzar") appears in Jeremiah (except ch. 28) and in Ezekiel. The Akkadian original was *Nabu-kudurri-uṣur* ("Nebo, protect my boundary!"). Therefore the spelling with the *r* is more accurate. But quite frequently these two sounds (*n* and *r*) were confused in Aramaic, especially after dentals (cf. Aram. תְּרֵין [*t*^{e}*rên*, "two"] instead of the etymologically correct תְּנֵין [*t*^{e}*nên*]); so the tendency was to replace the *r* by an *n* after the dental *d*. But it is not clear why Jeremiah in the Palestinian West and Ezekiel in the Babylonian East should have both preferred to adhere to the original *r*.

2 Although NIV has rendered אֱלֹהָיו (*'*^{e}*lōhāyw*) as singular—"his god"—it may have been intended as a plural (which it is in form) since Nebuchadnezzar was a polytheist.

2. *Nebuchadnezzar's Training Program*

1:3–7

3 Then the king ordered Ashpenaz, chief of his court officials, to bring in some of
the Israelites from the royal family and the nobility— 4 young men without any
physical defect, handsome, showing aptitude for every kind of learning, well informed, quick to understand, and qualified to serve in the king's palace. He was

to teach them the language and literature of the Babylonians. [5]The king assigned them a daily amount of food and wine from the king's table. They were to be trained for three years, and after that they were to enter the king's service.

[6]Among these were some from Judah: Daniel, Hananiah, Mishael and Azariah. [7]The chief official gave them new names: to Daniel, the name Belteshazzar; to Hananiah, Shadrach; to Mishael, Meshach; and to Azariah, Abednego.

3–5 Somewhat like Alexander the Great at a later time, Nebuchadnezzar adopted an enlightened policy of enlisting the most promising young men of his new empire into government service, whatever their nationality. Rather than reserving leadership for the Chaldeans alone, or even for the ethnic Babylonians whose cultural traditions reached back to the age of Hammurabi, Nebuchadnezzar resolved to pool the best brains and abilities discoverable in the ranks of the nations he had conquered. Since the hostages from Judah included the finest of the royalty and nobility, it was reasonable to open up special opportunities for gifted young Jews at the royal academy in Babylon. The court official named Ashpenaz was put in charge of these students, once they had qualified.

As to the etymology of "Ashpenaz" (v.3), there is no clear connection with Old Persian, though the Pahlevi *aspanj* ("guest-friend") may furnish a clue. This derivation, however, is by no means certain; and it is a bit unlikely that so responsible an official would have borne a Persian name, or even have been of Median background. (The difference between Persian and Median was apparently only a matter of dialect, so far as we know. Still it is conceivable that Nebuchadnezzar, with his concern for enlisting the best talents of his subject peoples, might have appointed a Mede to this responsible post. Certainly it was true that the Babylonians and Medes still maintained cordial and respectful relations with each other as erstwhile allies in the overthrow of Nineveh back in 612 B.C. Whatever his national origin, however, it was clearly Ashpenaz's responsibility to watch over the physical as well as intellectual development of the scholarship students in the Royal Academy. He had recruited them personally, selecting those of most promising appearance and intelligence from the ranks of the nobility and royalty of each subject nation.

At this point, Ashpenaz's title, "chief of his court officials" (*raḇ sārîsāyw*), requires comment. Was Ashpenaz a eunuch? The term *sārîs* was—at least sometimes—understood as denoting castration or natural impotence; it is so used in Isaiah 56:3 ("I am only a dry tree"), in Jeremiah 38:7 (Zedekiah's Ethiopian eunuch), and in Persia as reflected in Esther 2:3. But etymologically the word *sārîs* is derived from the Akkadian *ša rēši šarri* ("he who is of the king's head") and therefore had no original connotation of sexual impotence. In Genesis 39:1 the commander of Pharaoh's bodyguard, Potiphar, is described as *seris par'ōh* ("one of Pharaoh's officials"), and it was his wife who vainly enticed Joseph to sin. A castrated or impotent man would hardly have a wife. Nevertheless, eunuchs were valued officials in a king's harem precisely because they were incapable of having sexual relations.

Verses 3–4 do not tell us how many other Jewish youths were accepted as students in the Royal Academy besides Daniel and his three friends. Possibly there were several others. Only these four, however, had the courage to observe the dietary laws of the Torah (cf. Lev 11; Deut 14), which forbade Jews to eat unclean foods. Probably most of the meat items on the menu were taken from animals sacrificed to the patron gods of Babylon (Marduk, Nebo, and Ishtar, for example), and no doubt the wine from the king's table (v.5) had first been part of the libation to these deities. Therefore even those portions of food and drink not inherently unclean had been tainted by contact with pagan cultic usage.

At the very beginning of their career in a three-year program, the young Yahweh worshipers were faced with a clearcut issue of obedience and faith. They were doubtless subjected to intense social pressure from their classmates and teachers to do what everyone else was doing. They might have argued with themselves about the apparent folly of letting a ceremonial quibble destroy their chances of attaining high positions in the government. Should they not accept the royal diet and thus avoid giving needless offense to their classmates or to the officials of the king himself? Worldly wisdom pointed in that direction. By their compliance they would please everybody. But they would not please God, to whom they were surrendered body and soul. So at the start of their career, they faced squarely their priorities and determined to trust God to see them through the perils of noncompliance and possible forfeiture of all that they had gained. By their early refusal to disobey God, they prepared themselves for future greatness as true witnesses for the one true God in the midst of a degenerate pagan culture. It is significant that precisely in the matter of forbidden food, in which Satan successfully tripped up Adam and Eve, these four Hebrew youths passed their first test with flying colors.

6–7 The names of the four Hebrew youths were (1) Daniel (*Dānîyē'l*, "My Judge is El [God]"), who was assigned the Babylonian name Belteshazzar (*Bēlṭ^{e}ša'ṣṣar*);[7] (2) Hananiah (*Ḥ^{a}nanyāh*, "Yahweh has shown grace"), who was renamed Shadrach (*Šaḏraḵ*, which probably is *Shudur-Aku*, "The Command of Aku," a Sumerian or Elamite moon-god); (3) Mishael (*Mîšā'ēl*, "Who is what God is?") was assigned the pagan equivalent Meshach (*Mêšāḵ*, from *Mī-ša-Aku*, "Who is what Aku is?"); and (4) Azariah (*'^{a}zaryāh*, "Yahweh has helped") was called Abednego (*'^{a}ḇēḏ n^{e}gô*, the first part of which means "servant of," and Nego is obviously a god's name, very close to Nebo in sound, yet for some unknown reason *g* is substituted for *b*). (Incidentally, Abednego also occurs in the Elephantine Papyri of the fifth century B.C.)

Obviously, pagan theophoric names like these must have been assigned arbitrarily to these four Israelite students without any consultation with them, since the new names contained the names of false gods. Yet observe that even later Jewish exiles of the stature of Zerubbabel ("The seed of Babylon") and Shenazzar (*Sin-ab-uṣur*, "Sin [the moon-god] protect the father!") of the Davidic royal line seem to have adopted Babylonian names like this quite voluntarily, though these too might conceivably have been imposed by the Chaldean government during the Exile.

These four godly youths, then, were committed to a demanding and many-faceted course of study (v.4), comprising all the language and literature of the Chaldeans. This must have included not only a mastery of spoken Chaldean (which may originally have been a northeastern Arabian dialect, perhaps mingled with Aramaic, though we have no written documents in the ancestral language of the Chaldeans and can only conjecture about this) but also of Akkadian, the official, literary language of Babylon from the days of Hammurabi and before. In addition to the renewed interest in classical Akkadian, abundantly attested in many documents from Nebuchadnezzar's reign, there must also have been extensive study in the non-Semitic language of ancient Sumeria, from which Akkadian borrowed its entire writing system and many of its religious terms. Babylonian religion had always required a thorough knowledge of Sumerian literature—religious, magical, astrological, and scientific. Daniel and his three friends were subjected to a very rigorous and demanding curriculum, requiring their full attention as they mastered the important documents written in cuneiform Akkadian and Sumerian and contained in the central imperial library in Babylon. Thus they prepared themselves for the final examinations in "all kinds of literature and learning" (v.17).

Here it is appropriate to ask how likely it would be for a Maccabean Jewish writer to fabricate a legend that his shining model of heroic commitment to the Hebrew faith would have received a pagan education for service in a pagan caste. The only reasonable explanation for this is that it really happened that way in actual history.

Notes

7 בֵּלְטְשַׁאצַּר (*Bēlṭ^{e}šaʾṣṣar*) derives from the Akkadian *Balaṭ-su-uṣur*, possibly shortened from *Nabu-balaṭsu-uṣur* ("Nebo, protect his life!" cf. 4:8, where Nebuchadnezzar says, "Belteshazzar, after the name of my god"—and presumably "his god" was Nebo). P.R. Berger, however, in "Der Zyroš-Zylinder," *Zeitschrift für Assyriologie* 64 (1975): 224–34, suggests *Bēlet-shar-uṣur* ("Lady, protect the king"); *Shādurāku* ("I am very fearful," namely, of God); *Mēšāku* ("I am of little account"); and, for Abednego, *Arad-Nabu* ("Servant of the Shining One," involving a play on the name of the god Nebo). Yet the nontheophorous character of these names and their contemptuous meaning—at least in the case of Shadrach and Meshach—seem most unlikely in this setting.

3. *The First Demonstration of Faith*

1:8–16

[8]But Daniel resolved not to defile himself with the royal food and wine, and he asked the chief official for permission not to defile himself this way. [9]Now God had caused the official to show favor and sympathy to Daniel, [10]but the official told Daniel, "I am afraid of my lord the king, who has assigned your food and drink. Why should he see you looking worse than the other young men your age? The king would then have my head because of you."

[11]Daniel then said to the guard whom the chief official had appointed over Daniel, Hananiah, Mishael and Azariah, [12]"Please test your servants for ten days: Give us nothing but vegetables to eat and water to drink. [13]Then compare our appearance with that of the young men who eat the royal food, and treat your servants in accordance with what you see." [14]So he agreed to this and tested them for ten days.

[15]At the end of the ten days they looked healthier and better nourished than any of the young men who ate the royal food. [16]So the guard took away their choice food and the wine they were to drink and gave them vegetables instead.

8 Evidently Daniel himself was the leader and chief spokesman for the four young Hebrew believers. The record suggests that he was the first to make up his mind (*wayyāśem ʿal-libbô*, lit., "and he placed on his heart"; NIV, "but Daniel resolved") to refuse the food from the king's table and then to communicate his settled resolve to the other three. What he sought to avoid was being "defiled" (*lōʾ-yitgāʾāl*, lit., "that he might not defile himself") by contact with unclean meats—or even clean meats that had become contaminated with heathen worship. Rather than break faith with God, Daniel was willing to risk expulsion from the Royal Academy with the disgrace and danger that entailed. His priorities were firm.

9–16 It is highly significant that Daniel enjoyed good rapport with his "guard" (*melṣar*, "guardian," "overseer"), according to v.11—and even with Ashpenaz himself, the "chief official" (*śar hassārîsîm*) who was in charge of the whole academy (v.9). He had found "favor" (*ḥeseḏ* implies a love or loyalty based on a relationship of mutual commitment) and "sympathy" (*raḥᵃmîm*) with Ashpenaz (v.9) and felt he could confide in him. Like Joseph son of Jacob, who had commended himself to Potiphar and to the warden of his prison, Daniel must have shown an attitude of sincere good will and faithfulness to duty toward those over him. So he did not hesitate to ask Ashpenaz (v.11) to exempt the four young Hebrews from the royal diet. Daniel proposed that they be given "vegetables" (*zērōʿîm*, "herbs" or "garden plants" raised from cultivated seed) to eat and "water to drink" (v.12). In answer to the objection that this would lead to malnutrition of the Jewish students and punishment or even death for Ashpenaz (v.10), Daniel proposed that Ashpenaz see whether after a ten-day testing period, all four of them would look healthier than any of the other students (v.13). Such reversal of the laws of nutrition would require a miracle. Yet Ashpenaz was willing to take the risk (v.14). This was the first-recorded exercise of faith on Daniel's part, and it served to prepare him for the even greater testings that were to follow. It proved completely successful; and at the end of the ten days the four Israelites looked healthier and handsomer than all their classmates (v.15). No further objection, therefore, could be raised against their continuing on this simple diet (v.16).

4. *The Excellence of God's Special Servants*

1:17–21

[17]To these four young men God gave knowledge and understanding of all kinds of literature and learning. And Daniel could understand visions and dreams of all kinds.

[18]At the end of the time set by the king to bring them in, the chief official presented them to Nebuchadnezzar. [19]The king talked with them, and he found none equal to Daniel, Hananiah, Mishael and Azariah; so they entered the king's service. [20]In every matter of wisdom and understanding about which the king questioned them, he found them ten times better than all the magicians and enchanters in his whole kingdom.

[21]And Daniel remained there until the first year of King Cyrus.

17 This verse makes it clear that Daniel and his friends were granted special intellectual ability by the Lord, not because of their diet, but because of his approval of their faith and commitment to his word. Not only did they master every branch of Akkadian and Sumerian scholarship, but they—or at least Daniel himself—even mastered oneiromancy (the interpretation of dreams), in which Joseph had excelled in the court of Egypt.

18–20 When the time for the final examinations came (v.18), Ashpenaz was proud to present his students before Nebuchadnezzar himself, who apparently was in charge of the oral exams (v.19). And out of the entire group of brilliant young men, the king found that the four highest were Belteshazzar, Shadrach, Meshach, and Abednego.

So impressed was the king with them that he decided to give them responsible posts in his government. His good judgment was soon vindicated by their performance in comparison with previous appointees. Indeed, they turned out to be superior to all the other government officials and, in particular, "ten times better than all the magicians and enchanters in his whole kingdom" (v.20).

But what about the involvement of these four faithful Hebrews in the occult arts? The term for "magicians" (v.20) is *ḥarṭummîm;* a *ḥarṭōm* was probably a diviner, one who used some sort of inscribed chart or magical design (possibly imposed on a chart of the stars) in order to arrive at an answer to questions put to him. "Enchanters" (*'aššāp̱îm*) is derived from the Akkadian *ašipum* ("soothsayer"). Observe in this connection that the text does not state that the four Hebrews actually engaged in the practice of divination or conjuration themselves, which would doubtless have been forbidden them (cf. Deut 18:10–12). It simply states that they attained *ḥok̠maṯ bînāh* (lit., "the wisdom of understanding"; NIV, "wisdom and understanding"). This implies that in the attainment of results, the securing of a knowledge of the future or of what would be the best decision to make on the part of the government in view of unknown future contingencies, or the like, Daniel and his three colleagues far excelled the professional heathen diviners and conjurers.

Examples of Daniel's superiority appear in chapter 2, where he alone could reconstruct Nebuchadnezzar's dream about the fourfold image; chapter 4, where he alone could interpret the warning dream of the felled tree; and chapter 5, where he alone could interpret the mysterious handwriting on the wall. In none of these instances is there any indication that Daniel resorted to occult practices; he simply went to God directly in prayer, and God revealed the answer to him. Nevertheless Daniel was at least "ten times better" than all the pagan magicians and conjurers in the realm, who for all their incantations and sorceries could not come up with the answer the king was looking for.

21 This verse gives us a significant fact about the length of Daniel's career in public service—viz., he continued "until the first year of King Cyrus." Since Babylon fell before the Persian onslaught in 539 B.C., the first year of Cyrus might be computed as 539–538. But since we are informed by 5:31 that the rule of Babylonia was at first entrusted to Darius the Mede by King Cyrus, and since Daniel 9 is dated in the "first year" of that Darius (9:1), it is fair to assume that Darius remained as titular king till 538 or 537. If so, the "first year" of Cyrus as king of Babylon (doubtless a formal coronation ceremony took place in 537) would have been 537–536 B.C., which was probably the year when the forty-two thousand Jews returned to Palestine under Zerubbabel and Jeshua. If Daniel was put into the Royal Academy for three years, his first government appointment might have been around 601 B.C. Thus his whole term of service (with, apparently, a temporary retirement during the reign of Belshazzar) would have been about sixty-five years (601–536 B.C.). (It may have been that Daniel and his three comrades were taken as hostages to Babylon two or three years after the original invasion. D.J. Wiseman suggests 602 as a likely date for this [cf. *Bibliotheca Orientalis* 34 (1977): 336]. If so, Daniel would not have been through with his training till 599 or 598. However, this would furnish a problem to reconcile with the date of Nebuchadnezzar's dream in the *second* year of his reign [Dan 2:1].) Daniel's retirement must have taken place some years before his death, for he spoke of receiving his revelations in "the third year of Cyrus" (10:1), or two years after his retirement.

Notes

20 חָכְמָה (*ḥoḵmāh*, "wisdom") comes from a root that in Arabic means "legal judgment" or "the exercise of government"; it may also refer to a wise and capable physician. In Hebrew it combines the idea of knowledge arrived at through accurate discernment and the ability or skill to apply that knowledge effectively to the task to be done or the decision to be made. It certainly involves an understanding of the world and of life in general, but is always viewed with relation to God himself, the Creator, Designer, and Governor, who imparts meaning and value to all he has fashioned and to all the laws that govern the physical universe and the moral one as well. But the emphasis of *ḥoḵmāh* is primarily moral and practical and leads to a proper and successful adaptation of what we know to what we have to do. It involves a well-ordered and purposeful way of life and cultivates the art of using the right means to achieve one's ends. The classical Greek philosopher was motivated by intellectual curiosity; his pursuit of σοφία (*sophia*, "wisdom") was directed toward discovering the primal origins and the impersonal laws of cause and effect that would explain the phenomena of the world around him. But for the most part, the Greek philosopher was interested in acquiring a mastery of this theory that would lead to greater personal success and a fuller exploitation of the resources of nature and of mathematics and physics. But the Hebrew *ḥoḵmāh* was primarily concerned with living responsibly before God and coping successfully with every problem or task confronting him as a servant of God. Especially in the matter of prudence in business and in the area of human relations (the aspect most frequent in Proverbs), the *ḥoḵmāh* that proceeded from the fear of the Lord played a decisive role. In the management of armies in time of war or the administration of government in time of peace—i.e., the knowledge of the right thing to do under the circumstances—or for wise policies to follow in dealing with men, *ḥoḵmāh* was essential.

בִּינָה (*bînāh*, "understanding") is a term that emphasizes the power of discernment, the ability to distinguish between appearance and reality, between the false and the true, between the evil and the good. It implies a kind of perceptiveness that can see through any deception or specious appearance and grasp the issue in its proper light. In the administration of the affairs of a great empire, King Nebuchadnezzar felt a special need for advisors who possessed this kind of discernment and could warn him against ill-considered measures that might turn out badly.

That חַרְטֻמִּים (*ḥarṭummîm*, "magicians") were diviners using charts assumes the derivation of this term from חֶרֶט (*ḥereṭ*, "stylus"). Another explanation, favored more recently by Stricker, takes note of the fact that *ḥarṭummîm* are mentioned prominently in Exod 7–9, where the Egyptian "diviners" confront Moses, and derives the word from the Egyptian *ḥry-tp*, which allegedly means "soothsayer priest." Although the Egyptian lexicons define it as a general word for overseer, chieftain, or governor, literally it means "he who is over the head of," and as such could mean a head priest, or someone of that sort. There are, however, both phonetic and semantic objections to this etymology. It is most unlikely that the Egyptian *t* could be represented by a Hebrew or an Aramaic *ṭ* (tet) rather than a *t* (taw), and it is difficult to explain how the Egyptian *p* could have come out as a final *m*. Some feel that the Akkadian *lú ḫarṭibi* ("dream interpreters") comes also from the same Egyptian term (cf. J. Vergote, *Joseph en Egypte* [Louvain: Publications Universitaires, 1959], pp. 80–94, 209).

The Akkadian *ašipum* (underlying *aššapîm*, "enchanters") was equivalent to the Sumerian *išib* (written LU_2.ENIM.ENIM ["man of words, commands"]). It certainly involved the use of uttered spells or potent combinations of words or phrases thought to possess the ability to accomplish desired magical results.

II. Nebuchadnezzar's First Dream: God's Plan for the Ages (2:1–49)

1. *The Babylonian Wise Men's Impotence*

2:1–13

[1]In the second year of his reign, Nebuchadnezzar had dreams; his mind was troubled and he could not sleep. [2]So the king summoned the magicians, enchanters, sorcerers and astrologers to tell him what he had dreamed. When they came in and stood before the king, [3]he said to them, "I have had a dream that troubles me and I want to know what it means."

[4]Then the astrologers answered the king in Aramaic, "O king, live forever! Tell your servants the dream, and we will interpret it."

[5]The king replied to the astrologers, "This is what I have firmly decided: If you do not tell me what my dream was and interpret it, I will have you cut into pieces and your houses turned into piles of rubble. [6]But if you tell me the dream and explain it, you will receive from me gifts and rewards and great honor. So tell me the dream and interpret it for me."

[7]Once more they replied, "Let the king tell his servants the dream, and we will interpret it."

[8]Then the king answered, "I am certain that you are trying to gain time, because you realize that this is what I have firmly decided: [9]If you do not tell me the dream, there is just one penalty for you. You have conspired to tell me misleading and wicked things, hoping the situation will change. So then, tell me the dream, and I will know that you can interpret it for me."

[10]The astrologers answered the king, "There is not a man on earth who can do what the king asks! No king, however great and mighty, has ever asked such a thing of any magician or enchanter or astrologer. [11]What the king asks is too difficult. No one can reveal it to the king except the gods, and they do not live among men."

[12]This made the king so angry and furious that he ordered the execution of all the wise men of Babylon. [13]So the decree was issued to put the wise men to death, and men were sent to look for Daniel and his friends to put them to death.

1–3 This remarkable dream, with its disclosure of God's plan for the ages till the final triumph of Christ, was granted Nebuchadnezzar in the second year of his reign (v.1)—i.e., between April 603 and March 602 B.C. He was convinced that it contained a message of utmost importance and was not, like most dreams, a passing fancy. So being greatly in need of the help of his experts in oneiromancy, he turned in vain to them to reconstruct the dream itself (v.2) and then to tell him its significance (v.3). It is not quite clear why Nebuchadnezzar refused to describe the dream, for he apparently retained a sufficient recollection of it so that he could later certify the correctness of Daniel's reconstruction of it. The KJV suggests that the king had actually forgotten its contents, rendering *millᵉṯā' minnî 'azdā'* as "The thing is gone from me" (v.5), which identifies *'azdā'* as equivalent to *'āzᵉlā'* (Pe'al part. fem. from *'ᵃzal*, "depart"). But this involves amending a *d* to an *l* (or else assuming the later Jewish Aramaic *'ᵃzad* ["be cut off," "go apart"; cf. Marcus Jastrow, *A Dictionary of the Targumim, the Talmud Babli and Yerushali, and the Midrashic Literature*, 2 vols. [New York: Pardes, 1950, s.v.]) and also repointing the initial short *a* to be a long *a*. It is far more likely that *'azdā'* is a loan word from the Persian *azdā* ("a notice, promulgation") and that this clause means "The word [*millᵉṯā*,] has been promulgated by me" (Montgomery; KB).

Notice that in addition to the other classes of wise men (the magicians or diviners

—*ḥarṭummîm;* the enchanters or conjurers—*'aššāp̱îm*), the "sorcerers" (*m^e^ḵašš^e^p̱îm*) are mentioned, in addition to the "Chaldeans" (*kaśdîm;* NIV, "astrologers"). *M^e^ḵašš^e^p̱îm* comes from the Piel of *kāšap̱* and means "to practice sorcery" (or witchcraft). Like *'aššāp̱,* it is a loan word from Akkadian: in this case *kišpu* ("sorcery"), which renders a Sumerian logogram composed of a sign for dead or death inside a mouth, strongly suggesting necromancy as the original idea.

As for *kaśdîm,* it has already been discussed in the Introduction. It seems to have been derived from an original *kaldu* in Akkadian, which was by false analogy with the ethnic term *kaldu* ("Chaldean") archaized back into *kasdu*. But actually *kaldu* was a loan word from a Sumerian GAL.DU ("master-builder"), a term applied to a special class of astrologer-soothsayers. It was this fourth class of wise men who acted as spokesmen for the whole group to the king. After he had told them why he summoned them, namely, his disturbing dream, they encouraged him to tell them what the dream was (v.3).

At v.4 there is a transition from Hebrew (which has been used from 1:1 to 2:3) to Aramaic, prefaced by the statement that the wise men spoke Aramaic with the king. This does not necessarily mean that they had previously been speaking in some other language, though they might have been conversing in Neo-Babylonian Akkadian, in which most of Nebuchadnezzar's inscriptions were written; here it may only emphasize that the exact words of the magicians are given in the Aramaic language they habitually employed. If some of them did not know Neo-Babylonian, Aramaic—the lingua franca used all over the Middle and Near East for international business and diplomacy—was the most convenient language. The Book of Daniel continues to use Aramaic rather than Hebrew from 2:4 to the very end of chapter 7 (cf. Introduction: Language). These chapters deal with matters of empire-wide concern. But in chapters 8–12 the language reverts to Hebrew because in them the center of attention is on the future destiny of the Jews.

It may have been that the first seven chapters (or at least chs. 2–7) were actually written by Daniel before he saw the vision of chapters 8–12 and that these earlier chapters even became available for Gentile scrutiny, as well as for the captive Jews themselves, who by this time knew Aramaic.

4–6 In their respectful reply to the king, the soothsayers used the customary salutation addressed to sovereigns: "Live forever!" (*l^e^'āl^e^mîn ḥ^e^yî,* lit., "To the ages live!"). This expression did not necessarily imply an expectation that the potentate would never die; it was rather an emphatic way of expressing the same idea as "Long live the king!" This represented a wish or hope that the king would live on from one age to another, with no foreseeable termination by death. This formula was very rarely used in earlier history (apparently it was only Bathsheba who so addressed her son King Solomon [1 Kings 1:31]: *Y^e^ḥî hammeleḵ . . . l^e^'ōlām* ["May the king live forever!"]). But by the sixth century it had become a customary greeting addressed to rulers by their subjects.

The soothsayers responded naturally to their sovereign, urging him to divulge his dream to them so that they might study and interpret it (v.4). But their reasonable request was met with a surprising rejection (v.5). Apparently Nebuchadnezzar had already decided on an unheard of test of their magical abilities to interpret his dream. Before they explained its meaning, they would have to give its contents. He apparently reasoned that, if they had the powers of divination they claimed, they ought to be able to relate what he had dreamed—for surely their gods would know this and be able to pass it on to their devotees. If, however, he simply related the dream to them at first, then they might come up with some purely human and essentially worthless conjecture. He was interested, not in speculation, but in supernatural disclosure.

To his stringent demand, Nebuchadnezzar added a gruesome threat. If they failed to reconstruct his dream (and he held all wise men responsible), he would conclude that they were all charlatans and deserved death for all the years they had deceived him into thinking they really had occult powers (v.5). Nor would theirs be routine executions, but their arms and legs would be tied to four powerful trees, temporarily roped together at the top. When these ropes were cut, the victim would suddenly be torn apart into four pieces. At least this is one way of understanding the expression *haddāmîn tiṯʿaḇeḏûn* ("you shall be made into limbs"). Yet most commentators understand this to mean hacking the body to pieces with swords or axes (NIV, "have you cut to pieces"; cf. Ezek 16:40; 23:47, where Chaldeans cut up their victims with swords), though no verb for "cutting" is used here, nor is there any mention of a cutting instrument. Not only would the charlatans be torn (or hacked) to pieces, their homes and estates would be utterly destroyed and left as refuse heaps. On the other hand, if they should succeed in divining his dream, Nebuchadnezzar promised them wealth and honor far beyond what they already had (v.6).

7–9 But no matter how terrible the threats of punishment or how strong the inducements of reward, the "wise men" were powerless. They could only beg the king to change his mind and divulge his dream (v.7). This only enraged him still further. He accused them of stalling for time—as indeed they were—and of trying to find a way out of their dilemma (v.8). But no prevarication ("misleading and wicked things," NIV) would help them, nor could they look for any unexpected turn of events to extricate them (v.9). (The word NIV renders "situation" [*ʿiddānāʾ*] usually signifies "appointed time," "occasion," "opportunity," something like the Greek *kairos*, which appears so often in the NT.)

10–13 In a last effort to avoid death, the wise men insisted that the king's demand was completely unreasonable (v.10), not only because it was beyond all human capacity, but because it had never been made by any other ruler in human history. He was asking them to do what only the immortal gods could do (v.11). The wise men seemed to imply that it was impossible—or at least out of the question—that the all-knowing gods in heaven would reveal such knowledge even to their most-gifted soothsayers.

This defense failed to convince the king. He concluded that his wise men were liars and deserved the penalty he had announced. So he issued a warrant for the arrest and execution of all the wise men (v.12), even those who had not been present when he spoke with their leaders. This, of course, included the four young Hebrews (v.13).

Notes

---

1 It should be noted that the Babylonian method of accession-year dating made 602 B.C. (the spring of 602) the end of Nebuchadnezzar's second regnal year, even though he may have

captured Daniel and his three companions in the Palestinian campaign of 605 and had them enrolled in the royal academy before that year was out. Thus 602 would have been their third year of schooling, even though it was his second full year of reign.

---

2. *Daniel's Intercession and Offer*

2:14–23

14When Arioch, the commander of the king's guard, had gone out to put to death the wise men of Babylon, Daniel spoke to him with wisdom and tact. 15He asked the king's officer, "Why did the king issue such a harsh decree?" Arioch then explained the matter to Daniel. 16At this, Daniel went in to the king and asked for time, so that he might interpret the dream for him.

17Then Daniel returned to his house and explained the matter to his friends Hananiah, Mishael and Azariah. 18He urged them to plead for mercy from the God of heaven concerning this mystery, so that he and his friends might not be executed with the rest of the wise men of Babylon. 19During the night the mystery was revealed to Daniel in a vision. Then Daniel praised the God of heaven 20and said:

"Praise be to the name of God for ever and ever;
wisdom and power are his.
21He changes times and seasons;
he sets up kings and deposes them.
He gives wisdom to the wise.
and knowledge to the discerning.
22He reveals deep and hidden things;
he knows what lies in darkness,
and light dwells with him.
23I thank and praise you, O God of my fathers:
You have given me wisdom and power,
you have made known to me what we asked of you,
you have made known to us the dream of the king."

14–16 The captain of the royal bodyguard was Arioch (v.14). (This name had been borne in Abraham's time by a king of Ellasar, an ally of Kedorlaomer [Gen 14:1]; it appears also as *Arriwuk* in the Mari correspondence and as *Ariuki* in the Nuzi documents.) When Arioch came to Daniel's quarters to take him to death row, he told Daniel why all the wise men had been condemned (v.15). Then, at Daniel's request, the captain took him in before Nebuchadnezzar himself, so as to secure a stay of execution till Daniel had an opportunity to consult his God about the mysterious dream (v.16). The stage was now set to show the reality, wisdom, and power of the one true God—Yahweh—as over against the inarticulate and impotent imaginary gods the magicians worshiped. It is the same general theme that dominates the remainder of the book and serves to remind the Hebrew nation that despite their own failure, collapse, and banishment into exile, the God of Israel remains as omnipotent as he ever was in the days of Moses and that his covenantal love remains as steadfast toward the seed of Abraham as it ever had been.

As for Daniel, he knew beyond doubt that in this deadly emergency he was to trust himself to the faithfulness of his God, the one who could do the impossible. Never before had an interpreter of dreams—not even Joseph in Egypt—been required to reconstruct the dream itself. But Daniel had confidence that Yahweh could even do this unprecedented miracle and do it for his own glory. The pagan wise men had confessed that only deity could comply with the king's request. Nebuchadnezzar and all Babylon were therefore to be confronted with unanswerable proof that only Israel's God was real, sovereign, and limitless in his power.

17–23 Because for Daniel the demonstration of God's glory took precedence over his own safety, Daniel was confident that God would answer his prayer. But he also realized that the effectiveness of prayer may be heightened when believers unite in common supplication. So he gathered his three companions in a concert of prayer (v.17), that they might "plead for mercy [*raḥ^{a}mîn*] from the God of heaven concerning this mystery [*rāz*]" (v.18). There is no account given of Daniel's actual prayer nor of how the Lord answered him, though the latter is implied in Daniel's words (vv.27–35) to the king. But vv.20–23, voicing Daniel's gratitude, serve as a ringing manifesto of biblical faith over against the pretensions of pagan pride. Though the Babylonians may have vanquished God's people and dragged them into bondage after burning their temple, yet it was the God of Israel who was absolute sovereign in heaven and on earth.

Observe the emphasis on two of God's attributes (v.20): "power" (*g^{e}ḇûrṯā'*, which originally meant manly strength, from *geber*, "man") and "wisdom" (*ḥoḵm^{e}ṯā'*). His power is then illustrated by his complete control over the events of history, particularly in bringing about the reversals of fortune that give history its unpredictability (v.21a). "He changes [*m^{e}hašnē'*, from š^{e}nā', 'be different'; hence, 'make different,' 'alter'] the times [*'iddānayyā'*, from the same 'iddān discussed at v.9] and seasons [*zimnayyā'*, from *z^{e}man*, a length or interval of time]." In other words, God determines when in history events are to take place and how long each process or phase in history is to endure. Thus Yahweh not only decreed the fall and destruction of Jerusalem in 587 B.C.—an event future for Daniel in 602 B.C.—but also the exact number of years the captivity would last (cf. 9:2). The rulers of earth may imagine they have attained power by their own might, but it is only by God's choice that they are permitted their transient authority. At any time he may remove them from their thrones and set up others in their place (v.21a).

Next (v.21b) Daniel turned to another divine attribute—God's wisdom. Whatever wisdom the wise of this world have attained has come from God, whether or not they recognize this. Humans are prone to swell with pride over their growing understanding of nature and its laws, when only by God's gifts do they achieve anything. Moreover (v.22), even the cleverest minds will never understand certain areas of mystery and foreknowledge—namely, "the deep and hidden things" and that which "lies in darkness." The bafflement of the pagan wise men in Nebuchadnezzar's court illustrates this. All their knowledge could not deliver them from imminent death. So the great existential questions of life and death continue to be insoluble to the worldly wise. Without divine revelation, there is only conjecture and subjective opinion. Only in Yahweh, the God of Scripture, is ultimate truth to be found: "light dwells with him."

In v.23 Daniel closed his thanksgiving on a joyous note. In a remarkable display of faith, he assumed in advance that the knowledge he had received was absolutely accurate, even before he told it to Nebuchadnezzar. Most believers seldom have the faith to thank God in advance for his answers to prayer. But Daniel was no ordinary believer. He gladly gave God all the glory for the superhuman "wisdom" and "power" he was about to display as the interpreter of the king's dream. He also acknowledged that this revelation had been granted in response to the collective prayers in which his four companions had joined him: "You have made known to *me* what *we* asked of you" (italics mine).

3. *Daniel's Recitation of the King's Dream*

2:24–35

24Then Daniel went to Arioch, whom the king had appointed to execute the wise men of Babylon, and said to him, "Do not execute the wise men of Babylon. Take me to the king, and I will interpret his dream for him."

25Arioch took Daniel to the king at once and said, "I have found a man among the exiles from Judah who can tell the king what his dream means."

26The king asked Daniel (also called Belteshazzar), "Are you able to tell me what I saw in my dream and interpret it?"

27Daniel replied, "No wise man, enchanter, magician or diviner can explain to the king the mystery he has asked about, 28but there is a God in heaven who reveals mysteries. He has shown King Nebuchadnezzar what will happen in days to come. Your dream and the visions that passed through your mind as you lay on your bed are these:

29"As you were lying there, O king, your mind turned to things to come, and the revealer of mysteries showed you what is going to happen. 30As for me, this mystery has been revealed to me, not because I have greater wisdom than other living men, but so that you, O king, may know the interpretation and that you may understand what went through your mind.

31"You looked, O king, and there before you stood a large statue—an enormous, dazzling statue, awesome in appearance. 32The head of the statue was made of pure gold, its chest and arms of silver, its belly and thighs of bronze, 33its legs of iron, its feet partly of iron and partly of baked clay. 34While you were watching, a rock was cut out, but not by human hands. It struck the statue on its feet of iron and clay and smashed them. 35Then the iron, the clay, the bronze, the silver and the gold were broken to pieces at the same time and became like chaff on a threshing floor in the summer. The wind swept them away without leaving a trace. But the rock that struck the statue became a huge mountain and filled the whole earth.

24–25 Observe how Arioch, who had been appointed to execute the wise men (v.24), claimed a measure of credit for himself in having discovered Daniel. After having been assured by Daniel that he had the answer, Arioch hurried to tell Nebuchadnezzar: "I have found a man . . . who can tell the king what his dream means" (v.25). Arioch may not have known that Daniel had already asked the king for a stay of execution, unless v.16 merely implies a request with Nebuchadnezzar through a secretary—or else Arioch may simply have forgotten this. At any rate, his attempt to enhance his standing through Daniel's success shows his complete confidence in Daniel's ability to recall the details of the dream.

26–30 As Nebuchadnezzar half-incredulously asked Daniel whether he could actually describe his dream (v.26), Daniel used to the full his opportunity to witness to Yahweh's unique power to reveal what the false gods of the pagan seers could not tell them—viz., the substance and meaning of the dream (vv.27–30). As he spoke of their inability to unravel the mystery (v.27), Daniel implied the worthlessness of their theology—indeed, of polytheism in general. That he alone, as Yahweh's spokesman, had the answer points unmistakably to the reality of the God of the Hebrews (v.28). "But there is a God in heaven who reveals mysteries," in contrast to all the imaginary gods of the heathen who are helpless to reveal anything. "He has shown King Nebuchadnezzar what will happen in days to come" (*bᵉ'aḥᵃrîṯ* *yômayyā'*, lit., "in the end of the days," a phrase generally pointing to the times of the Messiah, when human history will be brought to its close; cf. Notes). Then, having explained his ability to do what none of the others could do—all because of his wonderful God—Daniel told Nebuchadnezzar what he had seen in his dream.

In v.29 Daniel reminded the king of the train of thought that had preceded his dream: "As you were lying there, O king, your mind turned to things to come." So he implied that Yahweh had graciously taken note of the king's statesmanlike concern and had granted him a full answer to his inquiry (v.30). Again Daniel disclaimed any personal ability in transmitting this revelation but openly and publicly gave God all the glory.

31–35 Daniel next disclosed the main theme of the dream—the colossal image (v.31) composed of four different metals: the head of gold (v.32), the breast and arms of silver, the belly and thighs of bronze, and the legs of iron (v.33), with their oddly constructed feet of iron mingled with clay. This composite statue was then reduced to powder by a huge stone (v.34), and the powder was blown away by the wind (v.35). Where the image had stood, the rock grew to the size of a huge mountain that filled the whole scene. To his astonishment, Nebuchadnezzar recognized the accuracy of every detail of Daniel's description. He must have been leaning forward to hear the explanation from what he now knew to be a spokesman from God.

Notes

---

28 The expression בְּאַחֲרִית יוֹמַיָּא (*b^e'aḥ^{a}rîṯ yômayyā'*, "in days to come") in Hebrew—הימים באחרית (*b^e'aḥ^{a}rîṯ hayyāmîm*, "in days to come")—first appears in Gen 49:1, where Jacob foretold the lot of the Twelve Tribes after their conquest of Canaan some four centuries later. In Deut 4:30 it refers to the period of Israel's return to God after adversity, in 31:29 of the period of Israel's future rebellion. In Isa 2:2 it points forward to the establishment of the millennial kingdom, in Ezek 38:16 to the eschatological war of Gog against restored Israel. Here (Dan 2:28) it seems to refer to all the coming events subsequent to the lifetime of Nebuchadnezzar and including the final establishment of the fifth kingdom (the Millennial Age). The other occurrence in Dan 10:14 seems to include both the "Proto-Tribulation" under Antiochus Epiphanes in the second century B.C. and the antitypical Great Tribulation under the Beast in the last days. So far as NT usage is concerned, Peter in his Pentecost sermon in Acts 2:17 referred Joel 2:28–32 to the "last days" (ἐν ταῖς ἐσχάταις ἡμέραις, *en tais eschatais hēmerais*) and evidently included the whole post-Crucifixion period, from the establishment of the NT church to the second coming of Christ. In Heb 1:2, the phrase ἐπ' ἐσχάτου τῶν ἡμερῶν τούτων (*ep eschatou tōn hēmerōn toutōn*, "in these last days") occurs with evident reference to the church age, but without any specific *terminus ad quem*.

---

4. *Daniel's Interpretation of the King's Dream*

2:36–47

36"This was the dream, and now we will interpret it to the king. 37You, O king, are the king of kings. The God of heaven has given you dominion and power and might and glory; 38in your hands he has placed mankind and the beasts of the

field and the birds of the air. Wherever they live, he has made you ruler over them
all. You are that head of gold.
39"After you, another kingdom will rise, inferior to yours. Next, a third kingdom,
one of bronze, will rule over the whole earth. 40Finally, there will be a fourth
kingdom, strong as iron—for iron breaks and smashes everything—and as iron
breaks things to pieces, so it will crush and break all the others. 41Just as you saw
that the feet and toes were partly of baked clay and partly of iron, so this will be
a divided kingdom; yet it will have some of the strength of iron in it, even as you
saw iron mixed with clay. 42As the toes were partly iron and partly clay, so this
kingdom will be partly strong and partly brittle. 43And just as you saw the iron
mixed with baked clay, so the people will be a mixture and will not remain united,
any more than iron mixes with clay.
44"In the time of those kings, the God of heaven will set up a kingdom that will
never be destroyed, nor will it be left to another people. It will crush all those
kingdoms and bring them to an end, but it will endure forever. 45This is the meaning of the vision of the rock cut out of a mountain, but not by human hands—a
rock that broke the iron, the bronze, the clay, the silver and the gold to pieces.
"The great God has shown the king what will take place in the future. The
dream is true and the interpretation is trustworthy."
46Then King Nebuchadnezzar fell prostrate before Daniel and paid him honor
and ordered that an offering and incense be presented to him. 47The king said to
Daniel, "Surely your God is the God of gods and the Lord of kings and a revealer
of mysteries, for you were able to reveal this mystery."

This section presents the foreordained succession of world powers that are to dominate the Near East till the final victory of the Messiah in the last days. See the Introduction (pp. 24–26) for the varying identifications of these successive empires. It is thus unnecessary to repeat the evidence against identifying the third empire with Persia and the fourth with Greece. In the following discussion, the tradition in the church that the third is Greek and the fourth Roman will be assumed.

36–38 Verses 37–38 identify the golden head of the dream-image with Nebuchadnezzar and the Babylonian Empire. The head comes first in the explanation (rather than the feet) probably because "head" (*rēʾšāh*) is often used to mean "beginning" (at least in the form of the Heb. cognate *rōʾš*); from this root the regular word for "beginning" (*rēʾšîṯ*) is derived. For a despot like Nebuchadnezzar, his government was the ideal type and was therefore esteemed as highly as gold. He exercised unrestricted authority over life and death throughout all Babylon. His word was law; no prior written law could challenge his will (v.38). Yet Daniel was careful to remind him that even this autocracy of his was under the almighty God. For only by his sufferance could Nebuchadnezzar continue to draw breath; only by God's decree could he exercise political power: "You . . . are the king of kings" (v.36). "The God of heaven has given you dominion and power and might and glory," Daniel declared (v.37).

The first of the four world-empires, then, was the Neo-Babylonian Empire of the Chaldeans that Nebuchadnezzar, whose reign began in 605 B.C., was to rule over for about forty more years—till 562 or 560 B.C. But his empire did not last more than twenty-one years after his death. His son Evil-Merodach (Amel-Marduk in Akkad.) reigned two years only (560–558, or else 562–560, according to another reckoning). Neriglissar (or *Nergal-shar-uṣur*) reigned four years (560–556) and Labashi-Marduk only one (556). Nabonidus engineered a *coup d'etat* in 555 and ruled till Babylon fell to the Persians in 539.

39 Daniel turned next to the other empires. About the second one (represented by silver) he said little except that it was "inferior" (*'ᵃra' minnāḵ*, lit., "beneath you") to Babylon. From Nebuchadnezzar's standpoint the restriction on the monarch's authority to annul a law once he had made it (6:12) was less desirable than his own unfettered power. The silver empire was to be Medo-Persia, which began with Cyrus the Great, who conquered Babylon in 539 and died ten years later. His older son, Cambyses, conquered Egypt but died in 523 or 522. After a brief reign by an upstart claiming to be Cyrus's younger son, Darius son of Hystaspes deposed and assassinated him and established a new dynasty. Darius brought the Persian Empire to its zenith of power but left unsettled the question of the Greeks in his western border, even though he did conquer Thrace. Xerxes (485–464) his son, in his abortive invasion of 480–479, failed to conquer the Greeks. Nor did his successor Artaxerxes I (464–424) do this but rather contented himself with intrigue by setting the Greek city-states against one another. Later Persian emperors—Darius II (423–404); Artaxerxes II (404–359); Artaxerxes III (359–338); Arses (338–336); and Darius III (336–331)—declined still further in power. This silver empire was supreme in the Near and Middle East for about two centuries.

As for the third empire (represented by bronze), it was even less desirable from Nebuchadnezzar's standpoint; though Greece was to "rule over the whole earth," its political tradition was more republican than its predecessor. The bronze empire was the Greco-Macedonian Empire established by Alexander the Great, who began his invasion of Persia in 334, crushed its last resistance in 331, and established a realm extending from the border of Yugoslavia to beyond the Indus Valley in India—the largest empire of ancient times. After his death in 323, Alexander's territory soon split up into four smaller realms, ruled over by his former generals (Antipater in Macedon-Greece, Lysimachus in Thrace-Asia Minor, Seleucus in Asia, and Ptolemy in Egypt, Cyrenaica, and Palestine). This situation crystallized after the Battle of Ipsus in 301, when the final attempt to maintain a unified empire was crushed through the defeat of the imperial regent Antigonus. The eastern sections of the Seleucid realm revolted from the central authority at Antioch and were gradually absorbed by the Parthians as far westward as Mesopotamia. But the remainder of the former Greek Empire was annexed by Rome after Antiochus the Great was defeated at Magnesia in 190 B.C. Macedon was annexed by Rome in 168, Greece was permanently subdued in 146, the Seleucid domains west of the Tigris were annexed by Pompey the Great in 63 B.C., and Egypt was reduced to a Roman province after the Battle of Actium in 31 B.C. Thus the bronze kingdom lasted for about 260 or 300 years before it was supplanted by the fourth kingdom prefigured in Nebuchadnezzar's dream-image.

40–43 Verse 40 describes this fourth empire, symbolized by the legs of iron. From a despotic standpoint, the Roman Republic was of far less value than gold, silver, or bronze; yet iron was most suited to crush opposing powers. Iron connotes toughness and ruthlessness and describes the Roman Empire that reached its widest extent under the reign of Trajan (98–117 A.D.), who occupied Rumania and much of Assyria for at least a few brief years.

Verse 41 deals with a later phase or outgrowth of this fourth empire, symbolized by the feet and ten toes—made up of iron and earthenware, a fragile base for the huge monument. The text clearly implies that this final phase will be marked by some sort of federation rather than by a powerful single realm. The iron may possibly represent the influence of the old Roman culture and tradition, and the pottery may represent the inherent weakness in a socialist society based on relativism in morality and philosophy. Out of this mixture of iron and clay come weakness and confusion, pointing to the approaching day of doom. Within the scope of v.43 are disunity, class struggle, and even civil war, resulting from the failure of a hopelessly divided society to achieve an integrated world-order. The iron and pottery may coexist, but they cannot combine into a strong and durable world-order.

An alternative view of the identity of the fourth empire has been proposed by Otto Zoeckler in his commentary on Daniel (CHS). Identifying the third empire as that of Alexander the Great, he took the fourth empire of Nebuchadnezzar's dream image to be that of the Seleucids—one of the four divisions Alexander's empire was partitioned into (that of Seleucus I, c. 311 B.C.). This would mean that the third kingdom (that of Alexander) lasted only eleven or twelve years, with an additional twelve years during which Perdiccas and Antigonus tried vainly to maintain the unity of the empire. Thus it was from this fourth or Seleucid empire (ignoring the other three realms that continued their existence alongside the Seleucids) that the little horn, Antiochus IV, emerged. But such an identification of the fourth empire can hardly be reconciled with the description of the fourth kingdom (cf. 7:7) as greater and stronger than the third. Could one segment of Alexander's empire be considered more extensive than his entire realm? Or could its power be considered more formidable than that of Alexander himself—Alexander who never lost a battle? This theory cannot be taken seriously.

44–45a These verses present the final scene. The rock cut from a mountain (v.45a), the rock that becomes the fifth kingdom, rolls down from a mountain and smashes against the brittle feet of the great image and topples it over. It then reduces the entire monument—including its four metals—to dust, which the wind sweeps away (v.35), after which the rock becomes a mountain (kingdom) that fills the earth. In contrast to the limited number of centuries the four man-made empires lasted, this fifth God-established kingdom is destined to endure forever (v.44)—a realm never to be destroyed. Not only Daniel 7, but parallel passages leave us in no doubt that this fifth realm is the kingdom of God, ruled over by Christ and enduring eternally, even after its earthly, millennial phase is over.

45b–47 Daniel closed his interpretation of the dream by assuring Nebuchadnezzar (v.45b) that it was divinely inspired and absolutely trustworthy. Thus the God of heaven had graciously granted the king the knowledge of the future he had asked for. The baffling mystery had at last been unraveled by the spokesman of the one true God. The king could only acknowledge Yahweh as "God of gods" (i.e., the Supreme God), the absolute sovereign over all the powers of heaven (even including the king's own patron gods, Marduk and Nabu), and "Lord of kings" on earth, the true Lord of history (v.47). Moreover, the king acknowledged Yahweh's supremacy in wisdom as being alone able to reveal the mysteries of the future, something no pagan god could do.

In token of his submission to Daniel's God, Nebuchadnezzar then bowed before Daniel (v.46) and offered incense to him as if he were Deity. What a remarkable scene! The despot who but an hour before had ordered the execution of all his wise men was prostrating himself before this foreign captive from a third-rate subject nation! Even though he opposed the wisdom of the Chaldeans, this absurd monotheist (Daniel) had somehow found the right answer. Surely, therefore, his God was worthy of honor above all the other deities, who had completely failed to reveal the dream. The king's praise to the Lord does not necessarily mean that he doubted the existence of other gods, much less that he had experienced any sort of conversion.

Notes

44 Rather striking is the reference to the unity of the four-part image in vv.34–35; it is described as still composed of the four different metal sections at the time it is destroyed by the "rock cut out of a mountain, but not by human hands" (v.45). This seems to imply that in its essential posture of self-will, self-aggrandizement, and defiance of the one true God, the composite image represents a sustained revolt of organized human society and government against the Lord. In this sense, then, Babylon set the tone of hubris and oppressive cruelty that characterized all her successors to world power. This may shed some light on the prominence of Babylon as a symbol of human materialism, religious apostasy, and revolt in the last days, as described in the lament: "Fallen is Babylon the Great!" (Rev 18:2). The dirge in Rev 18:2–20 may be intended to celebrate the destruction of the depraved, humanistic government to make way for God's effective rule on the earth.

45a For the following information, I am indebted to Bruce Waltke of Regent College. Morris Jastrow (*The Religion of Babylonia and Assyria* [Boston: Athenaeum, 1898], p. 614) states, "According to Babylonian notions . . . the earth is pictured as a huge mountain." Morris Forbridge (*Studies in Biblical and Semitic Symbolism* [New York: Ktav, 1970], pp. 180–81) points out that "Jensen has shown that the Babylonians regarded the earth as a huge mountain. In fact, the earth was actually called E-kur, 'Mountain House.'" Ford cites these and other sources to furnish the best explanation for v.36. He also has a fine discussion of "the rock" on pp. 86–87.

5. *The Promotion of Daniel and His Comrades*

2:48–49

48Then the king placed Daniel in a high position and lavished many gifts on him. He made him ruler over the entire province of Babylon and placed him in charge of all its wise men. 49Moreover, at Daniel's request the king appointed Shadrach, Meschach and Abednego administrators over the province of Babylon, while Daniel himself remained at the royal court.

48 Since Daniel had so decisively proved himself a true prophet with access to the great God he worshiped, it was only logical for Nebuchadnezzar to put him in charge of all the diviners at the court of Babylon. Hence he officially became "ruler" (*raḇ-signîn*, lit., "chief of appointed officials"; the word *s^e gan* is from Akkad. *šaknu*, "appointed one") over the whole bureau of "wise men." It was also understandable that the king fulfilled his original promise (2:6) and loaded him with gifts and royal honors. But that he went on to appoint Daniel civil governor of the entire capital province of Babylon—a post of highest importance in the political structure—was indeed noteworthy. Normally this position would be reserved for a Chaldean nobleman, a member, like Nebuchadnezzar, of the master race. For a Jew from the Captivity to be so honored was unprecedented and shows how deeply his intelligence and integrity had impressed the king.

49 Daniel's loyalty to his three comrades was shown by his request that they too might be given high appointments. Of course, it strengthened Daniel's hand to have his three trusted friends help him in his administrative duties.

III. The Golden Image and the Fiery Furnace (3:1–30)

1. *The Erection of the Image*

3:1–3

[1]King Nebuchadnezzar made an image of gold, ninety feet high and nine feet wide, and set it up on the plain of Dura in the province of Babylon. [2]He then summoned the satraps, prefects, governors, advisers, treasurers, judges, magistrates and all the other provincial officials to come to the dedication of the image he had set up. [3]So the satraps, prefects, governors, advisers, treasurers, judges, magistrates and all the other provincial officials assembled for the dedication of the image that King Nebuchadnezzar had set up, and they stood before it.

Despite Yahweh's warning through the dream and interpretation that he would judge and destroy the idol-worshiping empires, Nebuchadnezzar forgot his new religious insights and proceeded to force on all his subjects—even the Yahweh-worshiping Jews—the worship of the patron god of the Chaldean government. This not only indicates the superficial nature of his earlier confession of Yahweh as "God of gods and Lord of kings" (2:47), but it also suggests an egotism tending toward megalomania. Yet we cannot be certain why he took this extraordinary step. He may have felt, like many pagans, that multiple loyalties were permissible in worshiping the gods. He may have seen no more conflict between worshiping several different deities than between serving a local government and the central government. In any event, he laid down no requirement for his subjects to renounce or to cease private worship of their own personal gods; he simply demanded complete loyalty to the state, as represented by this public ceremony of prostration before his patron god (presumably Nabu). Failure to do this would not only amount to impiety and irreligion, it would also be treason.

1 Moreover, Nebuchadnezzar had the statue made of gold (i.e., covered with gold leaf). Actually, there was not enough gold in all Babylonia to make a statue so large of solid gold. The erecting of the golden image undoubtedly reflected the symbolism of the dream-image in which the head of gold represented Babylonia. Perhaps Nebuchadnezzar was motivated by a desire to fulfill the type. As to whom the statue represented, it seems doubtful that it was the king himself (as some have suggested). We have no evidence that statues of a Mesopotamian ruler were ever worshiped as divine during the ruler's lifetime. Such practices may have been followed in the Egypt of Ramses II (though we have no decisive proof of this) but hardly in the Sumerian, Babylonian, or Assyrian empires. It is far more likely that the statue represented Nebuchadnezzar's patron god, Nebo (or Nabu). Prostration before Nebo would amount to a pledge of allegiance to his viceroy, *Nabu-kudurri-uṣur,* i.e., Nebuchadnezzar.

2 From the king's standpoint, no reasonable man could refuse to give this token of loyalty to his sovereign and his government. The fairly recent date of the establishment of the Babylonian Empire as the successor to Assyria (at least in its southern half) made it appropriate for Nebuchadnezzar to assemble all the local and provincial leaders from every part of his domain and, in essence, exact from them a solemn oath of loyalty, certified with a religious sanction by this ceremony of adoration of Babylon's god. But if any officials refused to comply, they were to be immediately executed in the superheated furnace erected nearby.

3 The titles of the various ranks of government officials give an impression of a well-organized bureaucracy. The following are listed: (1) "the satraps" (*'*^{a}*ḥašdarp*^{e}*nayyā'*, from Old Pers. *khshatrapāwan,* "realm protector"), who apparently were in charge of fairly large satrapies; (2) "prefects" (*signayyā'*, from *s*^{e}*gan,* presumably borrowed from Akkad. *šaknu,* "one who is appointed"), possibly military commanders (as KD suggests) but more likely lieutenant governors of some sort; (3) "governors" (*paḥ*^{a}*wāṯā'*, pl. of *peḥāh,* derived from Akkad. *bēl piḥāti,* "lord of an administrative district"), indicating leaders of smaller territories like the postexilic province of Judea, which (cf. Mal. 1:8) was administered by a *pe̱ḥāh̠;* (4) "advisers" (*'*^{a}*ḏargāz*^{e}*rayyā'*, plural of '^{a}dargāzar, probably derived from Pers. *andarzaghar,* "counsel-giver"); (5) "treasurers" (*g*^{e}*ḏāb*^{e}*rayyā'*, from *ganzabara,* inferrable from the Pahlevi *ganzavar,* "treasurer" or "treasure-bearer"); (6) "judges" (*d*^{e}*ṯāb*^{e}*rayyā'*, from Old Pers. *dātabara,* lit., "law-bearer"); (7) "magistrates" (a conjectural rendering of *tiptāyē'*, which may have been derived from an Old Pers. *adipati,* lit., "over-chief"); and (8) "provincial officials" (*šilṭōnê,* from *š*^{e}*liṭ,* "to have dominion over"), a general term for a governmental executive.

Observe that five of these titles are apparently of Iranian origin, even though the scene for this episode is early in the reign of Nebuchadnezzar (the Median tongue might conceivably have contributed some loan words even back around 600 B.C.). We must conclude, therefore, that Daniel 3, in its final form at least, must have been composed after the rise of the Persian Empire (in 539); and the terms used must have replaced those that were actually employed in Aramaic around the turn of the century. This agrees perfectly with the supposition that Daniel finished this book for publication around 532 B.C., when the new Persian titles would have been current in the metropolis of Babylon.

At the same time it should be pointed out that by the second century B.C. (the Maccabean period), some of these Persian loan words had become obsolete and could no longer be correctly translated, at least by the Alexandrian Jews (see Introduction, pp. 20–22, for a discussion of this). This can only mean that chapter 3 of Daniel must have been composed long enough before the second century for these words to have been forgotten—which might well have happened after a composition date in the 530s (cf. Wiseman, *Problems in Daniel,* p. 43).

2. *The Institution of State Religion*

3:4–7

[4]Then the herald loudly proclaimed, "This is what you are commanded to do, O peoples, nations and men of every language: [5]As soon as you hear the sound of

the horn, flute, zither, lyre, harp, pipes and all kinds of music, you must fall down and worship the image of gold that King Nebuchadnezzar has set up. [6]Whoever does not fall down and worship will immediately be thrown into a blazing furnace."

[7]Therefore, as soon as they heard the sound of the horn, flute, zither, lyre, harp and all kinds of music, all the peoples, nations and men of every language fell down and worshiped the image of gold that King Nebuchadnezzar had set up.

4–7 In order to furnish a proper musical setting for the ceremony of worshiping the image, Nebuchadnezzar enlisted the services of the royal musicians, who played all the instruments then in use. (cf. Notes). The six instruments listed in v.5 did not exhaust the list of different instruments, for "all kinds of music" implies that there may have been a good many others besides. It was this orchestra that was to give the signal for all the assembled throng to bow down and worship the golden statue, as a solemn declaration of their commitment to the Babylonian government and their willingness to incur divine wrath if they should ever break their oath of fealty. Nearby the furnace was roaring (v.6)—a grim reminder of the dreadful alternative to compliance. The official leadership of every nation and district under Nebuchadnezzar's rule had to join in this act of worship on pain of death. Needless to say, there was universal compliance when the music struck up (v.7), and all the foreheads in the great multitude touched the ground at the same moment—except for three men.

Notes

---

5 The musical instruments listed are (1) קַרְנָא (*qarnā'*, "horn" or "trumpet"), probably made originally from a cow's horn, though by this time it was more likely fashioned from silver; (2) מַשְׁרֹקִיתָא (*mašrōqîṯā'*, "flute"), from the root שְׁרַק (*šᵉraq*,"to whistle"); (3) קַיְתְרוֹס (*qay tᵉrôs*, "zither," "lyre," probably borrowed from the Gr. *κιθάρις*, *kitharis*), an instrument probably available on Near Eastern markets as early as the Assyrian period; (4) סַבְּכָא (*sabbᵉḵā'*, "trigon" or "triangular lyre"; NIV, "lyre"), possibly related to *sibbeḵā'* ("hairnet" or "thicket," cf. Heb. שְׂבָכָה [*śᵉbāḵāh*, "net" or "window-grating"]); (5) פְּסַנְתֵּרִין (*pᵉsantērîn*, "psaltery" or "harp"), apparently derived from *ψαλτήριον* (*psaltērion*), another stringed instrument, somewhat triangular in shape, with strings passing under the sounding board rather than over it (again, a type of instrument probably sold by Greek merchants in the Near East as early as Assyrian times); (6) סוּמְפֹּנְיָה (*sûmpōnᵉyāh*, "pipes," "bagpipe," or "Pan's pipes"), a wind instrument having at least two pipes with finger stops for note differentiation (derived from Gr. *συμφωνία* [*symphōnia*, "harmony," "bagpipe," or "Pan's pipes], a distinctive type of instrument that would have retained its Greek name even after becoming current in the Near East and Mesopotamia.

6 Bruce Waltke, in a personal letter of 7 June 1979, pointed out some parallels between Dan 3 and Rev 13: "Rev. 13:11–18 uses elements of this chapter. The final 'Babylonian' dictator will attempt to enforce idolatrous worship on all, imposing a death penalty for non-conformity, and he will use the number six in connection with that worship. Here too the saints are called upon by faith to resist the idolatrous worship and even risk death, in order that they may be delivered from eternal death (Rev. 14:9–11)."

---

3. *The Accusation and Trial of God's Faithful Witnesses*

3:8–18

8At this time some astrologers came forward and denounced the Jews. 9They said to King Nebuchadnezzar, "O king, live forever! 10You have issued a decree, O king, that everyone who hears the sound of the horn, flute, zither, lyre, harp, pipes and all kinds of music must fall down and worship the image of gold, 11and that whoever does not fall down and worship will be thrown into a blazing furnace. 12But there are some Jews whom you have set over the affairs of the province of Babylon—Shadrach, Meshach and Abednego—who pay no attention to you, O king. They neither serve your gods nor worship the image of gold you have set up."

13Furious with rage, Nebuchadnezzar summoned Shadrach, Meshach and Abednego. So these men were brought before the king, 14and Nebuchadnezzar said to them, "Is it true, Shadrach, Meshach and Abednego, that you do not serve my gods or worship the image of gold I have set up? 15Now when you hear the sound of the horn, flute, zither, lyre, harp, pipes and all kinds of music, if you are ready to fall down and worship the image I made, very good. But if you do not worship it, you will be thrown immediately into a blazing furnace. Then what god will be able to rescue you from my hand?"

16Shadrach, Meshach and Abednego replied to the king, "O Nebuchadnezzar, we do not need to defend ourselves before you in this matter. 17If we are thrown into the blazing furnace, the God we serve is able to save us from it, and he will rescue us from your hand, O king. 18But even if he does not, we want you to know, O king, that we will not serve your gods or worship the image of gold you have set up."

The three who refused to acknowledge the golden image were Shadrach, Meshach, and Abednego, the close companions of that newly promoted high official Belteshazzar. Those stubborn fools were disobeying the royal decree! They knew that everyone was supposed to conform to it. With death staring them in the face, how could they think of disobeying? Didn't they know that everyone was watching them and that they could not possibly escape the fiery furnace? How could they think of giving up their high office, the royal favor, and even their lives for the sake of their eccentric religious beliefs?

8–12 After the public worship, some malicious men (v.8) were only too glad to report to the king about the disobedience of Shadrach, Meshach, and Abednego. These informers are called "Chaldeans" (NIV mg.). Unlike chapter 2, chapter 4 does not introduce "Chaldeans" as one of a long list of soothsayers and sages. Here they approached the king as members of the master race (*gubrîn* [untr. in NIV] is used only of men of importance and high standing in the community, and *gubrîn kasdā'în* [NIV, "some astrologers"] therefore implies Chaldean nobles rather than a class of mere astrologers or soothsayers). This heightens the appropriateness of their reference to Daniel's three Hebrew associates in government service as Jewish magnates (*gubrîn yehûdā'în*, v.12; NIV, "some Jews"), with a contemptuous emphasis on their despised nationality quite akin to the derogatory tone assumed by King Darius's officials in 6:13 as they labeled Daniel "one of the exiles from Judah." These factors compelled even the lexicographers of BDB, committed though they were to the Maccabean date hypothesis, to recognize that *kaśdāy* was here used ethically rather than as a term for astrologer-priests.

With a show of zeal for the king, the Chaldeans quoted his edict word for word (vv.10–11) and then related how these three recalcitrant Jews had dared (v.12) to "pay no attention to" (*la̱'-śāmû ʿalāyk̲ ṯeʿēm*, lit., "They have not paid regard to you") the express command of "King Nebuchadnezzar" (v.9); they had refused to bow down and worship the golden image!

13–15 Nebuchadnezzar's response was all the Chaldeans could have hoped for. He became furious and ordered the offenders to be brought before him (v.13). He could not understand that they had defied him, after his many favors and in the face of such a dreadful penalty. Half incredulously he stared at them and asked whether they really had disobeyed his decree (v.14). Then, controlling his anger momentarily, he stopped questioning them and magnanimously gave them an opportunity to save themselves. He would order the musicians to play again so the three men might prove their loyalty and obedience by worshiping the image then and there (v.15).

But Shadrach, Meshach, and Abednego loved Yahweh more than life itself. Not only had they learned to recite the Shema—"Hear, O Israel: The LORD our God, the LORD is one. Love the LORD your God with all your heart and with all your soul and with all your strength" (Deut 6:4–5)—but they made it the center of their lives. For them the will and glory of Yahweh meant more than fame, position, or security. Loving him with all their heart, they were ready to lay down their lives for him. Such was the logic of genuine faith, somewhat as Paul the apostle was later to say: "However, I consider my life worth nothing to me, if only I may finish the race and complete the task the Lord Jesus has given me—the task of testifying to the gospel of God's grace" (Acts 20:24). So these three refused to plead with Nebuchadnezzar to make an exception of them.

16–18 "O Nebuchadnezzar," the three said, "we do not need to defend ourselves before you in this matter [*piṯgām*, which could also mean 'decree,' 'message,' or 'affair']." The Aramaic word order of v.16 places an emphasis on the pronoun "we," implying that it is the Lord himself who will deal with this king who thinks he is sovereign on earth.

The next statement of the three men has been variously interpreted. Its opening clause is usually rendered thus: "If it be so, our God . . . is able" (v.17). (NIV has "If we are thrown, . . . the God we serve is able.") But a more appropriate rendering in this context would be "If our God exists [*hēn 'îṯay 'elāhānā'*, in which *'îṯay*, like its Heb. cognate *yēš*, means 'there is' or 'there exists'], whom we worship, he is able to deliver us from the furnace of burning fire; and from your hand, O king, he shall deliver." Nebuchadnezzar had made the mistake of defying Yahweh, saying, "Then what god will be able to rescue you from my hand?" (v.15). Like Sennacherib, who had derided Hezekiah's trust in God by boasting that none of the gods of the other nations had ever been able to save their people from the might of Assyria (2 Kings 18:33), Nebuchadnezzar had converted his confrontation with men into a contest with the Lord God Almighty. Nebuchadnezzar's doom and fall were sure, even though he had earlier served God's purpose as a scourge to chasten God's apostate people (Jer 27:6–8). Ungratefully he had scoffed at the very God who had granted him success in battle; therefore he was to undergo one humiliation after another, till he groveled in the dust before Israel's God.

But the heroism of the three men went even further as they declared, "But even if he does not [deliver us], we want you to know, O king, that we will not serve your gods, or worship the image of gold you have set up" (v.18). They were ready to be burned up in the fiery furnace rather than betray the God they had totally surrendered their lives to. Scripture contains few more heroic words than "But even if he does not."

Concerning this confrontation between Nebuchadnezzar and the three Hebrews, Ford (p. 107) says:

> The courteous but determined refusal of the Hebrews should be carefully observed. They had obeyed "the powers that be" as far as conscience permitted. They journeyed to the Plain of Dura. And right at the point where conscience shouted, "No further!" they rejected the temptation to be arrogant in their nonconformity. As Daniel before them had been courteous in his request to follow his convictions, so these three verbally acknowledge Nebuchadnezzar as king, while committing their ultimate allegiance to the King of kings alone. (cf. Acts 5:29; Mat. 22:21.).

Before passing on to v.19, we need to face the puzzling question of why Daniel did not join his three companions in disobeying the king's decree. Several answers may be given.

1. Since Daniel is not mentioned in this chapter, he may have been absent from Babylon at the time, perhaps on government business in some other part of the kingdom.

2. He may have been closeted with other members of the king's cabinet, working on legislative or military plans.

3. He may have been (as Wood, p. 78, suggests) too ill to attend the public ceremony; we know from 8:27 that sickness occasionally interfered with his carrying on with government business (cf. also 7:28; 10:8).

4. It may simply have been assumed that as the king's vizier (prime minister, for his responsibilities amounted to that high status; cf. 2:48), he was not required to make public demonstration of his loyalty by worshiping the image of his god. After all, there is no indication that Nebuchadnezzar himself bowed down to the image. It may have been that he simply sat on his royal dais surveying the scene, with his closest friends and advisers at his side.

5. It is true that Daniel's office as ruler over the capital province of Babylon (2:48) was not specifically listed in the seven categories of public officials (cf. 3:3, though, of course, the rulers of subordinate provinces were required to be on hand); and none of the "wise men" (*ḥakkîmayyā'*), over whom Daniel had been made chief, were included in the call for this public ceremony. As a type of accredited clergy serving under the state, they may have been exempted from this act of allegiance; their religious commitment would be presumed to be beyond question. In other words, Daniel did not belong to any of the special groups of jurists, advisors, financial experts, or political leaders included in the terms of the call.

6. Perhaps Daniel's reputation as a diviner was so formidable that even the jealous Chaldeans did not dare attack him before the king.

Ford (p. 108) makes the following observation: "Had the story been the invention that many have suggested; had it originated in the days of the Maccabees to nerve the faithful against Gentile oppression, it is unlikely that the chief hero would have been omitted. Reality transcends fiction, and the very 'incompleteness' of this account testifies to its fidelity." It is hard to see how the force of this deduction can be successfully evaded. There is no psychological reason for an idealizing romancer to leave Daniel out of this exciting episode. The only way to account for this omission is that in point of fact he was not personally in attendance at this important function.

4. *The Sentence Imposed and Executed*

3:19–23

> [19]Then Nebuchadnezzar was furious with Shadrach, Meshach and Abednego, and his attitude toward them changed. He ordered the furnace heated seven times hotter than usual [20]and commanded some of the strongest soldiers in his army to tie up Shadrach, Meshach and Abednego and throw them into the blazing furnace. [21]So these men, wearing their robes, trousers, turbans and other clothes, were bound and thrown into the blazing furnace. [22]The king's command was so urgent and the furnace so hot that the flames of the fire killed the soldiers who took up Shadrach, Meshach and Abednego, [23]and these three men, firmly tied, fell into the blazing furnace.

19–23 Having been publicly defied in the name of the God of the Hebrews, Nebuchadnezzar had no recourse but to order the immediate execution of the three young Hebrews. In his rage (v.19), he went to absurd lengths, as if he were dealing with asbestos figures rather than flesh-and-blood men. No mere mortal could have survived an instant in the huge furnace, but the king insisted that additional bellows be inserted under the blazing coals and that it be heated to maximum intensity. So fierce was the fire that even to come near it was fatal (v.22). Equally absurd was Nebuchadnezzar's command for the three to be fully dressed with their hats on (v.21) so as to make sure the flames would envelop them. Finally, they were "firmly tied" (v.23) and thrown like logs into the furnace. In his fury Nebuchadnezzar had thought of everything.

Apparently there was no door or screen to hide the inside of the furnace from view. Judging from bas-reliefs, it would seem that Mesopotamian smelting furnaces tended to be like an old-fashioned glass milk-bottle in shape, with a large opening for the insertion of the ore to be smelted and a smaller aperture at ground level for the admission of wood and charcoal to furnish the heat. There must have been two or more smaller holes at this same level to permit the insertion of pipes connected with large bellows, when it was desired to raise the temperature beyond what the flue or chimney would produce. Undoubtedly the furnace itself was fashioned of very thick adobe, resistant to intense heat. The large upper door was probably raised above the level of the fire bed so that the metal smelted from the ore would spill on the ground in case the crucibles were upset. So the text says (v.23) that the three "fell down" (*n*ᵉ*palû*) into the fire. Apart from the swirling flames and smoke, then, they were quite visible to an outside observer, though, like the king, he would have to stand at a distance.

5. *The Deliverance and the Fourth Man*

3:24–27

> [24]Then King Nebuchadnezzar leaped to his feet in amazement and asked his advisers, "Weren't there three men that we tied up and threw into the fire?"
>
> They replied, "Certainly, O king."
>
> [25]He said, Look! I see four men walking around in the fire, unbound and unharmed, and the fourth looks like a son of the gods."
>
> [26]Nebuchadnezzar then approached the opening of the blazing furnace and

shouted, "Shadrach, Meshach and Abednego, servants of the Most High God, come out! Come here!"

So Shadrach, Meshach and Abednego came out of the fire, [27]and the satraps, prefects, governors and royal advisers crowded around them. They saw that the fire had not harmed their bodies, nor was a hair of their heads singed; their robes were not scorched, and there was no smell of fire on them.

24–27 The dumbfounded Nebuchadnezzar saw the Hebrews walking upright in the flames without their bonds (v.24). Even more astounding, he saw a fourth person walking with them (v.25). Where had he come from? After his officials confirmed the king's impression that only three men had been thrown into the furnace, he described the fourth one resembling deity—i.e., "like a son of gods" (*wᵉrēwēh dî rᵉbîʿāyā' dāmēh lᵉbar-'ᵉlāhîn*, lit., "and the appearance of the fourth resembles a son of gods"). Pagan that he was, Nebuchadnezzar probably meant the plural absolute ending *în* as an indefinite plural rather than equivalent to the Hebrew *'ᵉlōhîm* (which is often taken as a singular, when referring to the one true God). All four persons in the furnace were walking around freely (v.25). The blazing fire had no effect on them. Nebuchadnezzar stood face to face with a sheer miracle. Their divine companion in the flames had delivered Shadrach, Meshach, and Abednego from all harm.

Coming as near to the furnace as possible, Nebuchadnezzar shouted above the roar of the furnace (v.26). So the three climbed out—but not the fourth, who had apparently disappeared—and allowed themselves to be inspected by the king and his officials. To their amazement, neither the clothing nor the bodies of the three Hebrews showed any marks of the fire (v.27). Their clothes did not even smell of fire. Only their bonds were gone. Their God had indeed been able to deliver them from the fiery furnace, just as they had affirmed (v.17). Yahweh had triumphed over the tryant who had defied him.

6. *Nebuchadnezzar's Second Submission to God*

3:28–30

[28]Then Nebuchadnezzar said, "Praise be to the God of Shadrach, Meshach and Abednego, who has sent his angel and rescued his servants! They trusted in him and defied the king's command and were willing to give up their lives rather than serve or worship any god except their own God. [29]Therefore I decree that the people of any nation or language who say anything against the God of Shadrach, Meshach and Abednego be cut into pieces and their houses be turned into piles of rubble, for no other god can save in this way."

[30]Then the king promoted Shadrach, Meshach and Abednego in the province of Babylon.

28–30 Before such an awesome display of God's power, Nebuchadnezzar could only acknowledge his defeat. He had come up against the God he had challenged (v.15): "Then what god will be able to rescue you from my hand?" He hastened to praise Yahweh (v.28) and thereby confess his admiration for the courage and fidelity of the three Hebrews, who had been willing to die rather than worship any god but Yahweh.

To make amends Nebuchadnezzar decreed death and destruction for saying anything against the God of Israel (v.29). Then Nebuchadnezzar promoted Shadrach,

Meshach, and Abednego to a higher office in Babylon (v.30). It would be interesting to know what happened to the great idol on the Plain of Dura; presumably it was stripped of its golden covering and left to decay.

A significant fact in the subsequent history of the Jews is that the sublime courage of the three Hebrews and their faith in Yahweh greatly encouraged the Jewish patriots at the time of the Maccabean revolt, whose leaders emulated it in their own struggle against Antiochus Epiphanes. First Maccabees 2:59 tells how the dying Mattathias of Modin recalled the heroism of David and Elijah and said, "Hananiah, Azariah, and Mishael believed and were saved out of the flame." His words show his conviction of the historicity of Daniel 3. In the NT Hebrews 11:34 refers to Daniel 3: "[They] quenched the fury of the flames"—an allusion that appears in a long list of the heroes of the faith. Obviously the author of Hebrews believed that the events in Daniel 3 took place in the sixth century B.C. exactly as they are related.

IV. Nebuchadnezzar's Second Dream and Humiliation (4:1–37)

1. *The Circumstances of the Second Dream*

4:1–7

1King Nebuchadnezzar,
To the peoples, nations and men of every language, who live in all the world:

May you prosper greatly!

2It is my pleasure to tell you about the miraculous signs and wonders that the Most High God has performed for me.

3How great are his signs,
how mighty his wonders!
His kingdom is an eternal kingdom;
his dominion endures from generation to generation.

4I, Nebuchadnezzar, was at home in my palace, contented and prosperous. 5I
had a dream that made me afraid. As I was laying in my bed, the images and
visions that passed through my mind terrified me. 6So I commanded that all the
wise men of Babylon be brought before me to interpret the dream for me. 7When
the magicians, enchanters, astrologers and diviners came, I told them the dream,
but they could not interpret it for me.

1–2 For some strange reason the MT joins the first three verses of this chapter to the end of chapter 3, as if connecting it with the episode of the fiery furnace rather than with the dream in chapter 4. But it is very evident that these verses (1–3) furnish an appropriate introduction to the narrative about to follow. Thus the Masoretic division is unjustified. Verse 3 obviously serves with v.37 as an envelope enclosing the narrative in the chapter.

Verse 1, a proclamation issued by Nebuchadnezzar, introduces the chapter. Perhaps Daniel in his capacity of vizier framed the wording of the decree. Nevertheless, the feature that makes this chapter unique is that it is the only chapter in Scripture composed under the authority of a pagan. To be sure, Nebuchadnezzar spoke as one intellectually convinced of the sovereignty and omniscience of the one true God; yet he can hardly be said to have had a genuine heart conversion, however intellectually convinced he may have been.

At this point, a summary of Nebuchadnezzar's experience of God may be in order. From Daniel's interpretation of the dream about the great image that portrayed the world empires, he learned that the God of the Hebrews was all powerful and all wise and could reveal mysteries no other god could make known. From the deliverance of Shadrach, Meshach, and Abednego, he learned that Yahweh was Lord of nature and history and could by his miracle-working power override the will of the mightiest earthly potentates and deliver his servants from death. But it was not till his humiliation to the state of a beast of the field that Nebuchadnezzar really understood his weakness and folly before the almighty Lord of the Hebrews. At last he realized his utter dependence on Yahweh for his reason, his power, and his very life. He saw that he was but an instrument in the hands of the omnipotent God, the true Sovereign of the universe who ordered all history by his own decree. Thus the king of what was then the world's greatest empire had to come to terms with the main teaching of the Book of Daniel—the absolute sovereignty of God and his faithfulness to his covenant people.

Hence Nebuchadnezzar published a decree (vv.1–3) to show his gratitude to the Lord for delivering him from insanity and restoring him to his throne. He wanted every person in his empire to share this knowledge and join him in giving glory to the God of heaven. In his decree and under his own name, he frankly confessed his own hubris in arrogating to himself the glory for what the grace and power of God had done for him. After the opening formula of blessing on his subjects—"May you prosper greatly!" (lit., "May your peace [or 'welfare'] abound!"), a formula that shows awareness of his responsibility as God's instrument on their behalf to further their prosperity and security—he proceeded to exalt the miracle-working power and eternal sovereignty of Yahweh, the God of Israel. In so doing Nebuchadnezzar made it clear that he was a firsthand witness of this wonder-working power and that he had experienced its effects in his own life (v.2). He now realized the transience and uncertainty of even the greatest human potentate compared with the eternal sovereignty of the Lord God Almighty.

3 "How great are his signs [*'āṯôhî*, cognate with Heb. *'ôṯôṯ*, 'attesting miracles,' natural phenomena that because of their magnitude or timing decisively evidence God's intervention in judgment or redemption], how mighty his wonders [*timhôhî*, supernatural manifestations of divine intervention in the course of nature, cognate with Heb. *tāmah*, 'be astounded,' 'dumbfounded']!" In other words, what Nebuchadnezzar had experienced—both in connection with his warning dream (explained by God's inspired interpreter, Daniel) and in regard to its pride-shattering fulfillment, his seven years of bestial insanity—served to convince him that God alone is the source of power, both in the realm of nature and in all human affairs, and that neither he nor any other ruler possessed any authority except by God's permission. Furthermore, that in contrast to the transient regions of human rulers, the unlimited authority of God as Sovereign of the universe goes on forever and forever.

4–5 These verses (which appear in the MT as 4:1–2) relate the setting for the narrative—the apparent security and prosperity of the king after vanquishing all his enemies. (Among these were the Egyptians under Hophra [Egyp. *Waḥ-ib-Ra'*, Gr. *Apriēs*] in 588–587 B.C. [cf. 2 Kings 24:7] and Nebuchadnezzar's destruction of Jerusalem in 587–586.) Presumably the events in chapter 4 took place some eight or nine years before the end of the siege of Tyre in 573. (H.W.F. Saggs, *The Greatness*

That Was Babylon [New York: Mentor, 1968], p. 148, estimates that the siege ended in 571 B.C.; See Ezek 26:7, which foretold this major effort against the Phoenician capital.) This would allow for a seven-year interval of mental illness, during which no major military operations were undertaken—say from 582 to 575. Perhaps it was in 583 that Nebuchadnezzar had his dream, with its sinister warning.

6–7 Following his procedure of many years before (cf. 2:2), the king sent for his council of diviners (v.6), including the astrologer-priests (here "Chaldeans" [*kaśdāyē'*] must be used of the soothsayers rather than in its ethnic sense). But on this occasion (v.7) he even told them the substance of the dream (rather than compelling them to guess what it was; cf. ch. 2). Yet they could not come up with any interpretation of what he had seen. So once more he turned to the one true expert, Daniel the seer.

2. *The Description of the Dream*

4:8–18

[8]Finally, Daniel came into my presence and I told him the dream. (He is called Belteshazzar, after the name of my god, and the spirit of the holy gods is in him.)

[9]I said, "Belteshazzar, chief of the magicians, I know that the spirit of the holy gods is in you, and no mystery is too difficult for you. Here is my dream; interpret it for me. [10]These are the visions I saw while lying in my bed: I looked, and there before me stood a tree in the middle of the land. Its height was enormous. [11]The tree grew large and strong and its top touched the sky; it was visible to the ends of the earth. [12]Its leaves were beautiful, its fruit abundant, and on it was food for all. Under it the beasts of the field found shelter, and the birds of the air lived in its branches; from it every creature was fed.

[13]"In the visions I saw while lying in my bed, I looked, and there before me was a messenger, a holy one, coming down from heaven. [14]He called in a loud voice: 'Cut down the tree and trim off its branches; strip off its leaves and scatter its fruit. Let the animals flee from under it and the birds from its branches. [15]But let the stump and its roots, bound with iron and bronze, remain in the ground, in the grass of the field.

" 'Let him be drenched with the dew of heaven, and let him live with the animals among the plants of the earth. [16]Let his mind be changed from that of a man and let him be given the mind of an animal, till seven times pass by for him.

[17]" 'The decision is announced by messengers, the holy ones declare the verdict, so that the living may know that the Most High is sovereign over the kingdoms of men and gives them to anyone he wishes and sets over them the lowliest of men.'

[18]"This is the dream that I, King Nebuchadnezzar, had. Now, Belteshazzar, tell me what it means, for none of the wise men in my kingdom can interpret it for me. But you can, because the spirit of the holy gods is in you."

8 Here Daniel is called by his official court name, "Belteshazzar" (*Bēlṭ^{e}ša'ṣṣar* [Akkad. *Balaṭsu-uṣur*], "Protect his life"). The fact that the king described this as "according to the name of my god" may perhaps indicate that even this was an abbreviated form of Bel-belteshazzar (Akkad. *Bēl-balaṭsu-uṣụr*, "Bel, protect his life") or even Nebu-belteshazzar (Akkad. *Nabu-balaṭsu-uṣur*, "Nebo, protect his life")—if by "his god" the king referred to the god whose name began his own, *Nebu*-chadnezzar. He then added that in contrast to the other soothsayers in his court, Daniel was truly inspired by God (or the gods): "The spirit of the holy gods is in him." (That this *'^{e}lāhîn*, ["gods"] is meant as a true plural—rather than a plural of majesty—is shown by the plural form of the adjective *qaddîšîn* accompanying it.) Daniel had demonstrated real communication with the high God far transcending the merely human wisdom of the rest of the diviners (ch. 2).

9–12 The king next began to tell Daniel his dream (v.9), the main subject of which was the growth of a mighty tree (v.10). Verses 11–12 describe how it grew to a great height and dominated the landscape for many miles. Its lush foliage and abundant fruit attracted many birds to its branches and four-footed beasts to its shade. And for them all, it provided shelter and nourishment.

13–16 Suddenly this happy scene was disturbed. An angel descended from heaven (v.13) and pronounced judgment on the tree, ordering it to be chopped down, its branches lopped off, and its foliage stripped away (v.14). The term for "angel" (*'îr*) is peculiar; it means "watchman" and comes from the verb meaning "be wakeful," "be on the watch." This is the only biblical occurrence of the word, though it later appears in the Genesis Apocryphon from Qumran Cave 1, where it is used as a term for an angel. From v.17 we infer that this particular class of angels (if a special class is intended) has some involvement with executing the judgmental decrees of God, including their official pronouncement to mankind. The secondary result of the felling of the tree was the scattering of the birds and beasts that were dependent on it. Only the stump of the tree was spared (v.15). It was to be encircled with bands of iron and bronze and to remain in the grassy meadow.

At this point (v.16) the symbolism emerges as the angelic watchman declared that the mind of the stump was to be changed from that of a man to that of a brute beast. The word for "mind" is *l^eḇaḇ* (lit., "heart," a term that in Scripture refers to the inner self as the seat of moral reflection, choice of the will, and pattern of behavior). It includes not only the mental processes but also the feelings, affections, and emotions, along with all the motivational factors leading to decisions and responses to life situations. The person this tree stump represented was to be transformed into an animal. Verse 16 states that the duration of this bestial condition was seven *'iddānîn* ("appointed times," "seasons"), which in this instance undoubtedly refers to years (NIV mg.; cf. 7:25).

17–18 Verse 17 adds that the reason for this sentence decreed by Heaven is that the full sovereignty of the "Most High" (*'illāy'ā*—equivalent to the Heb. *'elyôn*) might be demonstrated before all the world, and that men might realize that human rulers exercise authority only by the permission of God, not because they are masters of their fate or captains of their soul. Moreover, as Daniel had already declared (2:21), it is God who, in the light of the moral condition of the people to be ruled over, chooses who is to wear the crown and sometimes selects the humblest and lowliest. (This thought is found as early as Job 5:11: "The lowly he sets on high," and also in Hannah's song of praise in 1 Samuel 2:7–8: "He humbles and exalts. . . . He lifts the needy; . . . he seats them with princes and has them inherit a throne of honor.")

The portrayal of man in his pride as a lofty tree is a familiar OT symbol: "The LORD Almighty has a day in store for all the proud and lofty . . . (and they will be humbled), for all the cedars of Lebanon, tall and lofty, and all the oaks of Bashan" (Isa 2:12–13; cf. Isa 10:34). In 587 B.C., just a few years before Nebuchadnezzar had this dream, Ezekiel had used a similar figure in describing the pride and fall of Assyria (Ezek 31:3–17). So firmly was this tree symbolism rooted in Hebrew tradition that it is difficult to imagine how a Hebrew soothsayer could have failed to fathom the symbolic meaning of the dream—though the pagan seers Nebuchadnezzar first consulted might not have known such clear parallels. But more than likely they were simply reluctant to voice any interpretation adverse to the king; so they chose to remain silent. The king, therefore, had to appeal to Daniel for the interpretation (v.18). In doing so, he showed his confidence in Daniel by saying, "But you can, because the spirit of the holy gods is in you." Thus the honor of Daniel's God was at stake, and he was bound to reveal the true interpretation.

3. *Daniel's Interpretation and Warning*

4:19–27

[19]Then Daniel (also called Belteshazzar) was greatly perplexed for a time, and his thoughts terrified him. So the king said, "Belteshazzar, do not let the dream or its meaning alarm you."

Belteshazzar answered, "My lord, if only the dream applied to your enemies and its meaning to your adversaries! [20]The tree you saw, which grew large and strong, with its top touching the sky, visible to the whole earth, [21]with beautiful leaves and abundant fruit, providing food for all, giving shelter to the beasts of the field, and having nesting places in its branches for the birds of the air—[22]you, O king, are that tree! You have become great and strong; your greatness has grown until it reaches the sky, and your dominion extends to distant parts of the earth.

[23]"You, O king, saw a messenger, a holy one, coming down from heaven and saying, 'Cut down the tree and destroy it, but leave the stump, bound with iron and bronze, in the grass of the field, while its roots remain in the ground. Let him be drenched with the dew of heaven; let him live like the wild animals, until seven times pass by for him.'

[24]"This is the interpretation, O king, and this is the decree the Most High has issued against my lord the king: [25]You will be driven away from people and will live with the wild animals; you will eat grass like cattle and be drenched with the dew of heaven. Seven times will pass by for you until you acknowledge that the Most High is sovereign over the kingdoms of men and gives them to anyone he wishes. [26]The command to leave the stump of the tree with its roots means that your kingdom will be restored to you when you acknowledge that Heaven rules. [27]Therefore, O king, be pleased to accept my advice: Renounce your sins by doing what is right, and your wickedness by being kind to the oppressed. It may be that then your prosperity will continue."

19a Interpreting the dream was no easy assignment for Daniel. He well knew what the dream meant but could hardly bring himself to reveal it to Nebuchadnezzar. Daniel's loyalty to him—whom he had served so long and well and who had always shown Daniel kindness, even when Judah was being deported from her land of promise—was genuine. His sympathy for Nebuchadnezzar caused Daniel to shrink from announcing the king's coming degradation. It was a while before he could bring himself to speak (the Aramaic literally says, "He was stupified for one hour"—but the word for "hour" [*šā'āh*] does not necessarily mean anything more definite than "a time"). At the king's insistence, however, Daniel finally began to speak.

19b–22 First Daniel voiced the fruitless wish that the dream might apply to Nebuchadnezzar's worst enemies. Then he went on to interpret the dream feature by feature. The mighty tree represented Nebuchadnezzar in all his military success and genius in organizing an empire stretching from the border of Egypt to Elam on the east (vv.20–22).

The phrase "distant parts of the earth" in v.22 raises the question of the meaning of "earth," a word whose scope always depends on its context. Here it seems to refer to the farthest reaches of the Semitic world as established by the earliest empires of Hammurabi's Babylon and the eighth-century Assyrian rulers. Undoubtedly the regions of Media to the northeast and of Elam, Persia, and India were well known to the Near East as totally distinct cultures from those of Mesopotamia and points west. But in designating the extent of empire in the Mesopotamian orbit, the custom of defining the limits of civilization as extending only to the borders of Elam was at least as early as the Third Dynasty of Ur. Back in the Sumerian period, King Amar-Enzu referred to himself as *lugal dubdalimmubak* ("king of the Four Quarters" of the earth) in his dedicatory building inscriptions, even though his empire was far more circumscribed than Nebuchadnezzar's.

23–27 In vv.23–26 Daniel came to the heart of the warning contained in the dream—viz., that Nebuchadnezzar was going to lose not only his power to rule but even his sanity as well. He was going to be reduced to the mentality of a beast of the field, unable to be cared for within a sanitarium or even a cage. For seven years he was going to be fed on the grass of the meadow like a bull in a herd of cattle. This prolonged humiliation would teach him to respect God's sovereignty over the affairs of men and to realize that he, like all earthly rulers, held authority only by permission of the Almighty in heaven above. In other words, Nebuchadnezzar had to learn that the one true God, whom Daniel served, was the one he himself was answerable to. He had to learn that he was only a frail, temporary instrument in the hands of Yahweh, to whom he owed all glory and praise for all his power.

In the excavation of Qumran Cave 4 in 1952, an Aramaic fragment of a prayer of thanksgiving attributed to Nabonidus was discovered. The translation by Milik into French is approximately as follows: "The words of the prayer which Nabunai(d), king of Assyria and Babylon, the great king, prayed when he was smitten with an unpleasant skin-disease by the ordinance of God Most High in the city of Teima: 'I was smitten with an unpleasant skin-disease for seven years. . . . But when I confessed my sins and my faults, he granted me a (favorable) verdict. And there was a Jew from . . ., and he wrote and told (me) to give honor . . . to the name of God Most High' " (this conjectural translation, dependent on several restorations of missing letters, was published by J.T. Milik in *Revue Biblique*, 63 (1956): 408; cf. Saggs, *Babylon*, p. 154, for the English version above).

When this fragment was first published, many critics assumed that it represented an earlier form of the story of Nebuchadnezzar in Daniel 4, which by a later tradition mistakenly attributed the experience to the most famous of the Chaldean kings rather than the last of them. On the contrary, a careful examination of the Nabonidus fragment shows that it is far more likely to have been a late, garbled tradition of the illness of Nebuchadnezzar himself, if indeed it does not represent a later illness that actually befell Nabonidus personally (whose ten years of confinement to the North Arabian city of Teima [Teman] may have been partly occasioned by illness.

The differences between the details of Nebuchadnezzar's experience and the Nabonidus prayer are striking: (1) Nabonidus's skin disease was far less serious than Nebuchadnezzar's insanity; (2) the locus of the narrative in Daniel 4 is apparently at or near Babylon rather than down in Teima; (3) the Jewish counselor, unnamed, is said to have written a letter to Nabonidus rather than advising him personally; and (4) the scope of Nabonidus's authority is said to have included "Assyria," an unhistorical feature never included in the Daniel account, but very likely a late, intertestamental, legendary feature. We can only conclude that it is the Nabonidus fragment that is late and legendary, and that it affords no ground for skepticism as to the historicity of Daniel 4, except for those whose bias against supernaturalism hinders objective evaluation of the evidence.

Verse 26 closes the interpretation with the prediction that the surviving tree stump signifies that Nebuchadnezzar will be preserved during his seven years of dementia for an ultimate restoration to his throne. In the ordinary course of events, any monarch suffering from insanity for such a prolonged period would have been deposed and replaced by his legal successor. But in this case, apparently no outstandingly capable regent could be found; and even the crown prince, Evil-Merodach (Amel-Marduk), was unsuitable for supreme responsibility at this time (c. 582). Either he was too young or else did not show enough ability to rule permanently. At any rate, the unlikely promise of God that the throne would be restored to Nebuchadnezzar after the termination of his insanity was fulfilled.

Still the prospect of the seven years of insanity was a terrible one. So Daniel closed his interpretation with an earnest admonition for Nebuchadnezzar to defer the evil day by immediately amending his life (v.27). That is to say, if Nebuchadnezzar would abjure his despotism—with its assumption that whatever he wanted was ipso facto morally justified—and recognize that he was subject to God's moral law and responsible to him for good government, then the threatened discipline might be deferred.

Daniel needed real courage to inform his royal master that his rule was marred by the sin of oppression and callousness toward the poor and disadvantaged among his people. Daniel's candor might have cost him his high office or even his life. But apparently Nebuchadnezzar was so intimidated by the dream as to feel that he had better do everything possible to placate the displeasure of the Almighty. Specifically Daniel urged Nebuchadnezzar to adopt two new policies: (1) to reexamine his conduct in the light of the moral law (understanding it as binding on him as on his subjects, even though as their sovereign he was immune to prosecution); (2) to show a new sensitivity to the plight of the poor in his empire, protecting them instead of allowing the rich to exploit and oppress them. Nothing is said about Nebuchadnezzar's response; the chapter does not aim to enhance his glory but only that of Yahweh. But the one-year delay in the judgment on him implies he made some effort to follow Daniel's recommendation.

4. *The King's Punishment*

4:28–33

28All this happened to King Nebuchadnezzar. 29Twelve months later, as the
king was walking on the roof of the royal palace of Babylon, 30he said, "Is not this
the great Babylon I have built as the royal residence, by my mighty power and for
the glory of my majesty?"
31The words were still on his lips when a voice came from heaven, "This is
what is decreed for you, King Nebuchadnezzar: Your royal authority has been
taken from you. 32You will be driven away from people and will live with the wild
animals; you will eat grass like cattle. Seven times will pass by for you until you

acknowledge that the Most High is sovereign over the kingdoms of men and gives them to anyone he wishes."

[33]Immediately what had been said about Nebuchadnezzar was fulfilled. He was driven away from people and ate grass like cattle. His body was drenched with the dew of heaven until his hair grew like the feathers of an eagle and his nails like the claws of a bird.

28–30 The sin at the root of Nebuchadnezzar's tyranny was not, however, touched by his attempts to amend his ways. Though eager to avoid judgment, he still retained his pride, taking to himself all the credit for the remarkable achievements he really owed to God's grace (v.30). Perhaps he refrained from boasting during his reprieve (v.29), but he never realized his indebtedness to God for all his blessings and his dependence on him for all his power. He retained a profound admiration for what he had done in beautifying his capital. In fact, his works there were most impressive. The celebrated Ishtar Gate (excavated by Robert Koldewey and the Deutsche Orientgesellschaft c. 1900) seems to have been erected by him, along with the enameled-brick facing, displaying a procession of dragons and bulls. The East India House Inscription, now in London, refers to about twenty temples he rebuilt or refurbished in Babylon and Borsippa, and also to a vast system of fortifications and large shipping docks (cf. Ira M. Price, *The Dramatic Story of Old Testament History* [Philadelphia: Revell, 1925], p. 356).

On one of his inscriptions, Nebuchadnezzar boasted, "The fortifications of Esagila [the temple of Marduk] and Babylon I strengthened, and established the name of my reign forever" (cf. George A. Barton, *Archaeology and the Bible* [Philadelphia: American Sunday School Union, 1916], p. 479). To this inscription he appended a prayer to Marduk: "O Marduk, lord of the gods, my divine creator, may my deeds find favor before thee . . . Thou art indeed my deliverer and my help, O Marduk; by thy faithful word which does not change, may my weapons advance, be sharp and be stronger than the weapons of the foe!" At the time of his enthronement, he had composed a hymn that included this humble petition to Marduk: "I am the prince who obeys thee, the creation of thy hand. Thou art my creator, and the sovereignty over the hosts of men thou hast entrusted to me. According to thy mercy, O lord, which thou hast extended over all of them, incline unto compassion thine exalted power, and set the fear of thy godhead in my heart. Grant that which may seem good unto thee" (Cuneiform Inscriptions of Western Asia, vol. 1, pl. 53). Nevertheless this official expression of deference to the patron deity of Babylon had in it a large measure of the pride of one who by his own achievements deserved the special favor of Heaven. Moreover it was devoid of any appreciation of Yahweh, the one true God, who had so marvelously revealed himself to Nebuchadnezzar (cf. chs. 2–3).

31–32 After boasting that he had built Babylon the Great as a residence for himself by his own power (v.30), Nebuchadnezzar heard an unexpected word from Yahweh (v.31). Because of his ingratitude he was going to experience the full weight of God's wrath and the fulfillment of the punishment threatened in his fateful dream: "Your royal authority has been taken from you. You will be driven away from people and will live with the wild animals" (vv.31–32). Then followed the prediction that this degradation would last seven years (*'iddānîn*), at the end of which he would recognize the truth that God alone is Sovereign over heaven and earth and bestows power on whomever he chooses. What he should have learned from his vision of the great image and from the deliverance of the three Hebrews from the fiery furnace would be indelibly impressed on him.

33 This verse describes the wretchedness of Nebuchadnezzar's condition—abhorred and despised even by his lowliest subjects, reduced to the state of a grazing beast in a field. Physically he became like the brute beast he imagined himself to be, as his skin toughened into hide through constant exposure to outdoor weather at all seasons. (The temperature in modern Iraq ranges from a high of 110 or 120 degrees Fahrenheit in summer—usually with high humidity—to a low of well below freezing in winter.) Most particularly the hair of his head and his body, becoming matted and coarse, looked like eagle feathers; his fingernails and toenails, never cut, became like claws. So the boasting king, a victim of what is known as boanthropy, sank to a subhuman level.

Notes

---

33 R.K. Harrison (IOT, pp. 1115–17) has a helpful discussion of boanthropy in the light of modern medicine.

---

5. *The King's Repentance*

4:34–37

34 At the end of that time, I, Nebuchadnezzar, raised my eyes toward heaven, and my sanity was restored. Then I praised the Most High; I honored and glorified him who lives forever.

His dominion is an eternal dominion;
  his kingdom endures from generation to generation.
35 All the peoples of the earth
  are regarded as nothing.
He does as he pleases
  with the powers of heaven
  and the peoples of the earth.
No one can hold back his hand
  or say to him: "What have you done?"

36 At the same time that my sanity was restored, my honor and splendor were returned to me for the glory of my kingdom. My advisers and nobles sought me out, and I was restored to my throne and became even greater than before.
37 Now, I, Nebuchadnezzar, praise and exalt and glorify the King of heaven, because everything he does is right and all his ways are just. And those who walk in pride he is able to humble.

34–35 Finally, at the end of Nebuchadnezzar's seven years of dementia (v.34), the Lord fulfilled his promise to restore the reason of the humiliated king. By a miracle of divine grace, his brain was suddenly healed and his reason returned. He knew what had happened to him and remembered Daniel's warning and prediction. Honestly and without resentment toward God, Nebuchadnezzar faced the meaning of his chastisement and realized that everything Daniel had told him about the Lord was true. Overwhelmed by this demonstration of Yahweh's limitless power, Nebuchadnezzar prostrated himself before the Ruler of earth and heaven. For at last he knew his powerlessness before the Almighty and his dependence on him for everything.

Nebuchadnezzar's first response to God for restoring his sanity was to praise, honor, and glorify him as the eternal, omnipotent Sovereign over the whole universe. He now was ready to give God all the glory for everything he had achieved as king of the Chaldeans and the rebuilder of Babylon.

Nebuchadnezzar next exalted God. First of all, he acknowledged God's unending existence and everlasting power as Ruler of the universe—"I honored and glorified him who lives forever"—in contrast to man in his creaturely frailty. Perhaps Nebuchadnezzar was beginning to realize that only by submitting to God's program and entering into personal fellowship with him could his own life find true meaning.

Second, Nebuchadnezzar honored God as the Ruler whose kingdom, unlike all human empires, would never end. As the dream-image (ch. 2) had taught him, even the mightiest and strongest realms would have their day and then perish. The only enduring kingdom was that of God, the ultimate source of authority and power for all human rulers, who by his own sovereign will controls history. "His kingdom endures [lit., 'is'] from generation to generation."

Third, Nebuchadnezzar acknowledged that despite all his boasted progress, man is as nothing before God (v.35). Apart from God, humanity is devoid of value or meaning and "regarded as nothing" (*kᵉlā' ḥᵃšîḇîn*—from *ḥᵃšaḇ*, "reckon," "esteem"). At last Nebuchadnezzar had learned the utter dependence of the creature on the Creator.

Fourth, Nebuchadnezzar saw that in his absolute sovereignty God is beyond the control of any of his creatures and accountable to none of them for anything he chooses to do. The pot cannot ask the Potter, "What have you done?" (cf. Rom 9:20). The wisdom and holiness of the Almighty so far surpass the comprehension of mankind as to render presumptuous any criticism of God's providences in managing his world.

36–37 Now that he had, at least in some basic form, begun to fear the Lord, Nebuchadnezzar had found the clue to wisdom—an inestimable benefit of his seven-year chastisement. It qualified him for renewed leadership (v.36). The patience of his loyal subjects in caring for their demented and tortured monarch was at last rewarded. No other leader had qualified to succeed him during the long interval. None could command the loyalty of the troops he had so often led to victory. That Nebuchadnezzar had gotten back his reason electrified the court and the army commanders, and they thronged to congratulate him and once more hail him as their sovereign. "I was restored to my throne and became even greater than before" was his grateful testimony. The "head of gold" (2:38) had bowed in humble submission to the God of Daniel (v.37).

This tremendously important principle had to be established in the minds of the captive Jews, serving out their years of bondage in Babylonia. They might well have wondered whether the God of Abraham, Moses, and Elijah was truly alive and able to stand before the triumphant Gentile nations that had reduced his holy city, Jerusalem, to rubble and his holy temple to ashes. It would have been easy for them to conclude, as all the pagan observers assumed, that the Hebrew nation had been so completely crushed and uprooted from their native land because their God was too weak to defend them from the might of the gods of Babylon: Marduk, Nebo, and Bel. True, the warnings in Leviticus 26 and Deuteronomy 28 back in Moses' day had been very clear that Yahweh would cast his people out of the Land of Promise should they ever prove unfaithful. But now they needed some definite demonstration that their Lord was the true and living God and that all the gods of the pagans were only idols. They needed a series of striking miracles to sustain their flagging faith and renew their waning courage as they waited for their deliverance from exile. The captive Jews needed to know that even the apparently limitless power of Nebuchadnezzar was under the control of the Lord God Almighty, who still cared for them and had a great future for them in their land. Therefore, each episode recorded in the first six chapters concludes with a triumphant demonstration of God's sovereignty and faithfulness and his ability to crush the pride of unconverted mankind.

Notes

34 Hebrew and Aramaic occasionally use the verb ברך (Heb. *bārak̲;* Aram. *b*^{e}*rak̲*, "bless"; NIV, "praised") of an inferior toward a superior in a special sense—viz., to acclaim that superior, or God himself, as the source of favor and power and to praise and adore Him accordingly (cf. Ps 103:1–2).

V. Belshazzar's Feast (5:1–31)

1. *The Profanation of the Holy Vessels*

5:1–4

> [1]King Belshazzar gave a great banquet for a thousand of his nobles and drank wine with them. [2]While Belshazzar was drinking his wine, he gave orders to bring in the gold and silver goblets that Nebuchadnezzar his father had taken from the temple in Jerusalem, so that the king and his nobles, his wives and concubines might drink from them. [3]So they brought in the gold goblets that had been taken from the temple of God in Jerusalem, and the king and his nobles, his wives and his concubines drank from them. [4]As they drank the wine, they praised the gods of gold and silver, of bronze, iron, wood and stone.

As background for this episode, a survey of the highlights of Babylonian history after the time of chapter 4 (c. 570 B.C.) will be helpful.

Excursus

Nebuchadnezzar had died in 563, succeeded by his son Evil-Merodach (Akkad. *Amel-Marduk*, "man of Marduk"), who released the captive Jewish king, Jehoiachin, from prison and gave him an honorable place at the court (2 Kings 25:27–30). But two years later Evil-Merodach was assassinated by his brother-in-law, General Neriglissar (Akkad. *Nergal-shar-uṣur*, "Nergal, protect the king!"), who had served under Nebuchadnezzar when Jerusalem was destroyed (587–586

B.C.). Neriglissar died just four years later (556), and his son Labashi-marduk, who succeeded him, was murdered nine months later (556). This revolt placed its leader Nabonidus (Akkad. *Nabu-na'id*, "Nebo is exalted") on the throne. He does not seem to have been related to the royal house by blood but apparently married a daughter of Nebuchadnezzar in order to legitimize his seizure of the throne. He may have been a member of the wealthy merchant class, therefore being cordially supported by the commercial leaders. A devoted worshiper of the moon-god, Sin (Sumerian Nanna), he was the son of a high priestess belonging to his cult. Intensely interested in the history of Mesopotamia, he seems to have collected a museum of artifacts from earlier ages, consisting partly of dedicatory and building inscriptions of bygone dynasties and partly of early statues taken from various temples throughout his dominions. After securing firm control of Haran, he restored the great temple of the moon-god there and also contributed to the temple of Nanna in Ur. For commercial and military advantage, he devoted much attention to North Arabia and Edom, which he conquered in 552. During the last ten years of his life, he seems to have spent most of his time in Teima, an important Edomite or North Arabian capital (possibly for reasons of health), and left the central administration to the charge of his son Belshazzar in Babylon itself—the situation still obtaining during this final year of the Chaldean Empire, 539 B.C.

Back in the 550s Nabonidus apparently supported the revolt of Cyrus of Anshan against his father-in-law, Astyages, king of Media. But after Cyrus had taken over the control of the Medo-Persian domains and attained astonishing success against the Lydian kingdom in Asia Minor, it was inevitable that Cyrus would look south toward Mesopotamia for his next conquest, especially since Nabonidus had been an ally of King Croesus of Lydia. The Medo-Persian forces soon vanquished the Babylonian troops near Opis. The Nabonidus-Cyrus Chronicle, according to a corrected reading in ANET 305–6 states: "In the month of Tashritu, when Cyrus attacked the army of Akkad in Opis on the Tigris, the inhabitants of Akkad revolted, but he (*Nabonidus*) massacred the confused inhabitants. The 15th day, Sippar was seized without battle. Nabonidus fled. The 16th day, Gobryas (*Ugbaru*), the governor of Gutium and the army of Cyrus entered Babylon without battle." Apparently Nabonidus had commanded the troops in the field, while Belshazzar headed the defense of Babylon itself. Meeting with reverses, Nabonidus retreated south toward his salient at Tema (or Teima), leaving the Persians free access to the capital. Concerning this same campaign, Herodotus reported (1.190–91): "A battle was fought at a short distance from the city, in which the Babylonians were defeated by the Persian king, whereupon they withdrew within their defences. Here they shut themselves up and made light of his seige, having laid in a store of provisions for many years in preparation against this attack."

Babylon was considered impregnable because of its magnificent fortifications. Earlier in the same book Herodotus described it as 120 stadia square, surrounded by a large moat, and defended by a wall 50 royal cubits wide and 200 royal cubits high (about 330 ft.), with 100 strongly fortified gates. As we shall see, the Persian troops could breach the walls of the city only by a surprise strategem. Later on, in the reign of Darius I (522–486), Herodotus said that young Darius was compelled to subdue the Babylonians, who did not recognize his claim to the throne. Since Cyrus had never dismantled Babylon's fortifications, the besiegers faced essentially the same problem as in 539. "The Babylonians, however, cared not a whit for his [Darius's] siege. Mounting upon the battlements that crowned their walls, they insulted and jeered at Darius and his mighty host. One even shouted to them and said, 'Why do you sit there, Persians? Why don't you go back to your homes? Till mules foal you will not take our city.' "

This same attitude may have characterized the defenders in Belshazzar's day, especially since the city had not been stormed by invaders in over a thousand years. At any rate, these besieged Babylonians were completely unconcerned about the enemy forces encamped outside their walls. If the Nabonidus-Cyrus Chronicle is correct about the fall of the city taking place on 16 Tishri, then Belshazzar's feast must have taken place on 15 Tishri (sometime in September) 539. Whether it was the young king's birthday, or whether it was some major event in the Babylonian religious calendar, Daniel did not say. But all the leaders of government, society, the armed forces, and the priests were there—along with the king's wives and concubines.

Unknown to them, Cyrus's resourceful commander, Ugbaru (referred to in the Chronicle as governor of Gutium), had diverted the waters of the Euphrates to an old channel dug by a previous ruler (Queen Nitocris, according to Herodotus 1.184), suddenly reducing the water level well below the river-gates. Before long the Persian besiegers would come wading in at night and clamber up the river-bank walls before the guards knew what was happening.

1–4 Belshazzar the king was presiding over the state banquet for a thousand of his nobles (v.1). The time had come for offering toasts and pouring out libations to the gods of Babylon. In his drunken bravado he thought of a novel way of entertaining his guests. What about those beautiful golden goblets and bowls from Solomon's temple (v.2)? Why not use them? After all, they had been fashioned for a defeated god named Yahweh, worshiped by the captive people of Judah. No sooner said than it was done (v.3). The sacred vessels, laid away for forty-seven years, were brought to the banquet hall. Belshazzar began to regale his guests by taunting Yahweh, whose reputation Nebuchadnezzar's decrees had established a few decades before, and by praising Marduk, Bel, Nebo, Ishtar, and the other gods (v.4). He drank from the holy vessels and his guests followed suit. Once again an arrogant Babylonian monarch defied the Lord God of Israel. The pagan gods are described as "the gods of gold and silver, of bronze, iron, wood and stone," because to the Hebrew monotheist these materials were all the substance the pagan gods had; except as products of pagan imagination, they had no genuine being. The stage was set for the one true God to intervene.

2. *The Handwriting on the Wall*

5:5–9

5Suddenly the fingers of a human hand appeared and wrote on the plaster of the wall, near the lampstand in the royal palace. The king watched the hand as it wrote. 6His face turned pale and he was so frightened that his knees knocked together and his legs gave way.

7The king called out for the enchanters, astrologers and diviners to be brought and said to these wise men of Babylon, "Whoever reads this writing and tells me what it means will be clothed in purple and have a gold chain placed around his neck, and he will be made the third highest ruler in the kingdom."

8Then all the king's wise men came in, but they could not read the writing or tell the king what it meant. 9So King Belshazzar became even more terrified and his face grew more pale. His nobles were baffled.

5 This intervention came without trumpet blasts, thundering voices from heaven, or earthquakes. Suddenly the fingers of a hand appeared on the palace wall and, before the wine-reddened eyes of the king, began writing just four words (v.25), the first two of them identical. Then, just as suddenly as it had appeared, the hand vanished, leaving only the blazing letters on the wall.

6 Immediately the revelry was stilled. What on earth did this handwriting mean? In great alarm the drunken Belshazzar stared at the words, his face ashen and his knees knocking together (v.6). The musicians put aside their instruments, the dancing girls stood motionless, and the waiters stopped short, as they all gazed at the words on the wall.

7–9 The king sent for his wise men and ordered them to unravel the message (v.7). Whether or not the writing was in symbols unlike any known to the wise men, the text does not say. Certainly there is no indication that when the king asked Daniel to translate them, he did so from some unknown tongue, though the English reader may gain that impression. Later on Daniel read them off as Aramaic, the lingua franca of the capital. Perhaps the words, though written in standard Aramaic characters, simply did not convey any intelligible meaning. At any rate the diviners and cipher experts muttered among themselves, argued and debated, and finally came up with nothing (v.8)—and this in spite of great inducements for decoding the words: royal garments, a gold chain, and a top position in the government. (Belshazzar could offer nothing higher than the *third* highest rank in the government, since he himself was a viceroy under his father, Nabonidus.) But once again, as back in Nebuchadnezzar's day, even the most learned of the wise men were baffled (v.9; cf. 2:2–11; 4:7).

3. *The Queen Mother's Recommendation*

5:10–16

10The queen, hearing the voices of the king and his nobles, came into the banquet hall. "O king, live forever!" she said. "Don't be alarmed! Don't look so pale! 11There is a man in your kingdom who has the spirit of the holy gods in him. In the time of your father he was found to have insight and intelligence and wisdom like that of the gods. King Nebuchadnezzar your father—your father the king, I say—appointed him chief of the magicians, enchanters, astrologers and diviners. 12This man Daniel, whom the king called Belteshazzar, was found to have a keen mind and knowledge and understanding, and also the ability to interpret dreams, explain riddles and solve difficult problems. Call for Daniel, and he will tell you what the writing means."

13So Daniel was brought before the king, and the king said to him, "Are you Daniel, one of the exiles my father the king brought from Judah? 14I have heard that the spirit of the gods is in you and that you have insight, intelligence and outstanding wisdom. 15The wise men and enchanters were brought before me to read this writing and tell me what it means, but they could not explain it. 16Now I have heard that you are able to give interpretations and to solve difficult problems. If you can read this writing and tell me what it means, you will be clothed in purple and have a gold chain placed around your neck, and you will be made the third highest ruler in the kingdom."

10 The text does not indicate why the aged Daniel (Wood [in loc.] estimates Daniel's age as eighty-one by 539) was not included among those the king summoned. Perhaps he was in semiretirement; 8:27 implies that he had been in government service as recently as the third year of Belshazzar (cf. 8:1) but had not been enjoying good health. Apparently Belshazzar did not know him (cf. 5:13), except possibly by reputation. Evidently Belshazzar's administration had set him aside though he lived in Babylon. But the king's mother, who was in all probability a daughter of Nebuchadnezzar, thought of Daniel as soon as she heard about what had happened in the banquet hall. Although she had not been present as an invited guest, her quarters must have been nearby. So she came to the king with her recommendation and urged him to stop worrying.

11–12 The queen mother told Belshazzar that Daniel would be able to interpret the writing (v.11). Apparently she had not considered the possibility of its containing bad news. At any rate she commended the aged Jewish sage as a truly inspired seer: "There is a man in your kingdom who has the spirit of the holy gods" (echoing Nebuchadnezzar's own appraisal of him years before [4:8]). His credentials stemmed from his notable service to Nebuchadnezzar, who found him so far superior to all the rest of his wise men that he placed him in charge of them all: "magicians, enchanters, astrologers and diviners." Like no one else in the realm, Daniel could unravel mysteries and solve enigmas (v.12); surely, then, he was the right one for the king to turn to.

The queen mother referred to Nebuchadnezzar as Belshazzar's "father" (*'āḇ*). Strictly speaking Nabonidus was his true father; but on the reasonable supposition that Nabonidus had married a daughter of Nebuchadnezzar to legitimize his usurpation of the throne, Nebuchadnezzar would have been the grandfather of all his daughter's children (cf. Introduction, pp. 15–16).

13–16 Belshazzar sent for Daniel at once and met him, apparently for the first time, face to face (v.13). Having established Daniel's identity, Belshazzar proceeded to tell him the reason for his concern and to ask him to explain the mysterious writing (vv.14–15). He also enumerated the same rewards—including the position of "third highest ruler"—he had offered the other wise men (v.16).

4. *Daniel's Interpretation*

5:17–28

17Then Daniel answered the king, "You may keep your gifts for yourself and give your rewards to someone else. Nevertheless, I will read the writing for the king and tell him what it means.

18"O king, the Most High God gave your father Nebuchadnezzar sovereignty and greatness and glory and splendor. 19Because of the high position he gave him, all the peoples and nations and men of every language dreaded and feared him. Those the king wanted to put to death, he put to death; those he wanted to spare, he spared; those he wanted to promote, he promoted; and those he wanted to humble, he humbled. 20But when his heart became arrogant and hardened with pride, he was deposed from his royal throne and stripped of his glory. 21He was driven away from people and given the mind of an animal; he lived with the wild donkeys and ate grass like cattle; and his body was drenched with the dew of heaven, until he acknowledged that the Most High God is sovereign over the kingdoms of men and sets over them anyone he wishes.

22"But you his son, O Belshazzar, have not humbled yourself, though you knew all this. 23Instead, you have set yourself up against the Lord of heaven. You had the goblets from his temple brought to you, and you and your nobles, your wives and your concubines drank wine from them. You praised the gods of silver and

gold, of bronze, iron, wood and stone, which cannot see or hear or understand.
But you did not honor the God who holds in his hand your life and all your ways.
24 Therefore he sent the hand that wrote the inscription.
25 "This is the inscription that was written:

MENE, MENE, TEKEL, PARSIN

26 "This is what these words mean:

Mene: God has numbered the days of your reign and brought it to an end.
27 *Tekel*: You have been weighed on the scales and found wanting.
28 *Peres*: Your kingdom is divided and given to the Medes and Persians."

17 The aged Daniel may have realized that Belshazzar's honors would be short-lived, since his kingdom was about to collapse. Or else Daniel may simply have felt that after years of retirement he was too old to enter government service again (though later on he was used by the Persian government). At any rate, he disclaimed all promotions as he went on to answer the king's request.

18–24 Studying the inscription on the wall and understanding its message, Daniel prefaced his interpretation with a homily on the reason for the judgment it contained. He reviewed the experience of Nebuchadnezzar in being humbled by the decree of the Lord God Almighty (vv.18–22). These experiences of his grandfather were well known to the young king, and he should have remembered what they taught about humility and respect for Yahweh (v.22), the God of the Hebrews he had been mocking in this very banquet hall. He was guilty of blasphemy in using the Lord's holy vessels as common dishes for his drunken orgy (v.23). How could he hope to measure his puny human strength against the power of the Almighty, on whom his very life depended and who was completely sovereign over all his fortunes? This was the crime that led to the handwriting on the wall (v.24), with its proclamation of Belshazzar's doom.

25–28 Daniel then translated and interpreted the four words on the wall (v.25). The first two were identical: *m^{e}nē*, meaning "numbered," "counted out," "measured" (passive participle of *m^{e}nā'*, "to number"). This signified that the years of Belshazzar's reign had been counted out to their very last one, and it was about to terminate (v.26). Observe that even if the court diviners had been able to make out the three consonants *m-n-'* correctly, they still would not have known what vowel points to give them. For example, it could have been read as *m^{e}nâ'* or *mina*—a heavy weight equivalent to sixty Babylonian shekels.

The second word (v.27) was "Tekel" (*t^{e}qēl*, cognate with the Hebrew "shekel" [šeqel] and coming from *t^{e}qal*, "to weigh"). Following after a *m-n-'* (which might mean "mina" or "maneh"), "Tekel" would look like "shekel" (a weight of silver or gold slightly over eleven grams). But Daniel explained it as the passive participle *t^{e}qîl* ("weighed") and applied it to Belshazzar himself. God found him deficient in the scales and therefore rejected him.

The third word is *p^{e}rēs*, which is derived from a root *p^{e}ras*, meaning "to divide." Daniel read it as a passive participle (*p^{e}rîs*, "divided") and interpreted it to mean that Belshazzar's kingdom, the Babylonian Empire, had been divided or separated from him and given over to the Medes and Persians besieging the city. This word too might have been taken as meaning a monetary weight, like the two words preceding it; for the Akkadian *parsu* meant "half mina," and this may have been borrowed into Aramaic with that meaning. But more likely, as Eissfeldt and others have argued, it means "half shekel," since the root simply indicates division into two parts; and the usage in each individual language would determine what weight was being halved. In the descending scale of "mina," "shekel," the next weight to be expected would be something lighter than a shekel, namely "a half shekel." If, then, all that the diviners could make out of the strange inscription on the wall was "Mina, mina, shekel, and half-shekels" (reading *ûparsîn*), then they might well have concluded that this series of money weights (this was, of course, still prior to the introduction of coined money into the Middle East) made no sense and conveyed no intelligible message. Daniel, however, being inspired of God, was able to make very clear sense of these letters by giving them the passive participle vowel pattern in each case.

One very important aspect of this third word, *p-r-s*, has already been discussed in the Introduction (pp. 16–17, 25), but it will bear repeating at this point, since it has a direct bearing on chapter 6. The same radicals that spell out *p^e^rēs* ("half shekel") furnish the root for the word "has been divided," *p^e^rīsat*. But furthermore *p-r-s* also points to the word for "Persian," *Pārās*. This means that the author of this Book of Daniel believed that the kingdom that followed right after the Babylonian (over which Belshazzar reigned) was the Persian, without any intervening, independent Median Empire. Nothing could be plainer, in the light of this triple wordplay, than that the author understood the Persians to be the dominant element in empire number two, with the Medians being associated with them as a federated nation. The theory of a Median kingdom as empire number two is devoid of support in the text of Daniel itself. The important consequence of this identification of the combined Medo-Persian Empire as the second kingdom in Daniel's series of four (embodied in Nebuchadnezzar's four-part dream-image in ch. 2) is that the third kingdom must be the Greek one; therefore, the fourth empire must be the Roman Empire—which, of course, did not actually take over the Near East till 63 B.C., a century after the Maccabean uprisings. Therefore, this handwriting on the wall demolishes the Maccabean date hypothesis, which insists that nothing in Daniel prophesies any event later than the death of Antiochus Epiphanes in 164 B.C., a hundred years before Pompey annexed Palestine-Syria to the Roman Empire.

Notes

25 If the inscription was recorded in the contemporary Aramaic script, it would have looked like this:

(מנא מנא תקל ופרסין)

The Aramaic words are written from right to left; transcribed they are vocalized by Daniel as *m^e^nē' m^e^nē' t^e^qēl ûparsîn*. As explained in the text, the first two words seem to mean "a mina, a mina" (which was a unit of fifty or sixty shekels—the latter was the standard in Babylon). *T^e^qēl* was the same as the Hebrew שְׁקֶל (*šeqel*, "shekel," which weighed about four-tenths of a troy ounce). *Ûparsîn* would be "and halves ['divisions']," which probably indicated half shekels; the singular for this word is *p^eres*, as Daniel discusses it in v.28. The verb for "separate/divide" is פְּרַס (*p^eras*), of which פְּרִסַת (*p^erisat*) is the Pe'al passive third feminine singular form ("has been separated"). The word for "Persia" is *pārās*.

---

5. *Daniel's Honor and Belshazzar's Demise*

5:29–31

29Then at Belshazzar's command, Daniel was clothed in purple, a gold chain was placed around his neck, and he was proclaimed the third highest ruler in the kingdom.

30That very night Belshazzar, king of the Babylonians, was slain, 31and Darius the Mede took over the kingdom, at the age of sixty-two.

29 Daniel's interpretation must have greatly disturbed Belshazzar, for it spelled his imminent doom. His natural response would have been to have the prophet executed on the spot for his bold condemnation of the king in front of the court. But perhaps the God-given authority Daniel spoke with awed Belshazzar, and he was afraid of incurring still greater wrath if he laid a hand on God's spokesman. Whatever his motives, the king fulfilled his promises to the letter, bestowing the royal chain of gold on Daniel and having him proclaimed the third ruler in the kingdom. Possibly he thought that Yahweh might relent and not destroy Babylonia if his prophet became prime minister.

30–31 But the time for repentance had run out. Belshazzar had gone too far in profaning the holy vessels from God's temple. Destruction was closing in on him and all his drunken companions even while Daniel's investiture was taking place in the banquet hall. The Medo-Persian troops were stealthily moving along the exposed riverbed under cover of darkness and climbing the walls of the defenses while revelry was going on throughout the city. Some eighty years later, Herodotus (1.191) recorded the following:

> Hereupon the Persians who had been left for the purpose at Babylon by the river-side, entered the stream, which had now sunk so as to reach about midway up a man's thigh, and thus got into the town. Had the Babylonians been apprised of what Cyrus was about, or had they noticed their danger, they would never have allowed the Persians to enter the city, but would have destroyed them utterly; for they would have made fast all the street-gates which gave upon the river, and mounting upon the walls along both sides of the stream, would so have caught the enemy as it were in a trap. But, as it was, the Persians came upon them by surprise and took the city. Owing to the vast size of the place, the inhabitants of the central parts (as the residents at Babylon declare), long after the outer portions of the town were taken, knew nothing of what had chanced, but as they were engaged in a festival, continued dancing and revelling until they learnt the capture but too certainly.

Verse 30 tersely reports that Belshazzar was slain that same night. As translated in Barton (p. 483), the Nabonidus-Cyrus Chronicle states that after Cyrus had entered Babylon on 3 Marcheswan (Oct./Nov.), "in the month Marcheswan, on the night of the 11th, Gobryas into . . . the son of the king was killed." On the basis of this rendering, which was actually dependent on questionable conjectures filling in gaps in this fragmentary inscription, it could be argued that v.30 was in error when it stated that Belshazzar (who would presumably have been "the king's son") was killed the very night the city was taken. But the corrected translation in ANET 306 reads: "In the month Arahshamnu [Marcheswan] on the night of the 11th day, Gobryas [i.e., Ugbaru] died. In the month of (Arahshamnu, the . . . nth day, the wi)fe of the king died." In other words, the cuneiform traces of the word "of the king" suggest "wife" rather than "son." Hence the charge of inaccuracy cannot be sustained on the basis of this text.

Verse 31 (which MT quite justifiably takes as v.1 of ch. 6) indicates that the government of Babylon was entrusted to a Darius the Mede at the age of sixty-two. This marked the fulfillment of Daniel's prediction that the Babylonian Empire would pass under the yoke of the Medo-Persian Empire, as kingdom number two in the four-kingdom series. As explained in the Introduction (pp. 16–17), this "Darius the Mede" is in all probability to be identified with the Gobryas of Herodotus's account, though Herodotus seems to have confused two different generals bearing similar names: Ugbaru and Gubaru. The Nabonidus Chronicle clearly distinguishes between the two, as Whitcomb (p. 11) brings out:

> The 15th day (of Tashritu or Tishri), Sippar was seized without a battle. Nabonidus fled. The 16th day Ugbaru, the governor of Gutium, and the army of Cyrus entered Babylon without a battle. . . . In the month of Arahshamnu, the 3rd day, Cyrus entered Babylon, green twigs were spread in front of him—the state of peace was imposed upon the city. Cyrus sent greetings to all Babylon. Gubaru, his governor, installed sub-governors in Babylon. . . . In the month of Arahshamnu, on the night of the 11th day, Ugbaru died.

Because of the resemblance between Ugbaru and Gubaru, earlier Assyriologists supposed that they referred to the same man. But the syllable GU is written quite differently from UG in Akkadian cuneiform. Thus the passage just quoted makes it quite clear that while it was Ugbaru who engineered the capture of Babylon, he lost his life to a fatal illness less than a month later (Babylon was taken on 12 October 539, and Ugbaru died on 6 November). It was not Ugbaru, then, but Gubaru whom Cyrus appointed vice-regent of the Chaldean domains on 29 October. The Nabonidus Chronicle and other cuneiform texts of that era indicate that he continued on as governor of Babylonia for at least fourteen years, even though Cyrus may have taken over the royal title at a solemn public coronation service two years later. Presumably urgent military necessity drew Cyrus away from his newly subdued territories to face an enemy menacing some other frontier. Until he could get back and assume the Babylonian crown with appropriate pomp and ceremony, it was expedient for him to leave control of Babylonia in the hands of a trusted lieutenant like Gubaru. A.T. Olmstead (*The History of the Persian Empire* [Chicago: University of Chicago Press, 1948], p. 71) puts it thus: "In his dealings with his Babylonian subjects, Cyrus was 'king of Babylon, king of lands.' . . . But it was Gobryas the satrap who represented the royal authority after the king's departure."

As pointed out in the Introduction (pp. 18–19), the name "Darius" may have been a title of honor, somewhat as "Caesar" or "Augustus" became in the Roman Empire. It is apparently related to "dara" ("king" in Avestan Persian); thus the Old Persian

Darayavahush may have meant "The Royal One." It was only natural that this honorific title be used of the official viceroy of the Medo-Persian Empire in this account, rather than his personal name. Completely decisive objections stand in the way of interpreting the figure of Darius the Mede as a garbled confusion with Darius I, the son of Hystaspes, sometimes called "the Great," who began to reign in 522. Darius I was obviously a young man, under thirty, at the time he took over the throne (IDB, 4:769, indicates that he was about twenty-eight by 522, having been born in 550); Darius the Mede was sixty-two when he began his rule. Darius I was of a Persian royal line because his father, Hystaspes, was of the Achaemenid dynasty; the vicegerent Darius was a Mede, Ahasuerus. Darius I won the throne in a coup d'état; Darius the Mede "received" (Aram. *qabbēl*; NIV, "took over") the royal authority from one who was empowered to invest him with it—presumably Cyrus himself. Daniel 9:1 states that he "was made ruler" (Heb. *homlak*) over the realm of the Chaldeans—a term never applied to one who seizes the sovereignty by force of arms but rather to one who is appointed to kingship by a higher authority. All this fits Gubaru perfectly, and it is only reasonable to conclude that he was the one referred to in Daniel 5:31 as "Darius the Mede."

As Whitcomb (p. 35) points out, the statement in 6:28—"and the reign of Cyrus the Persian"—may very well imply that both of them ruled concurrently, with the one subordinate to the other (i.e., Darius subordinate to Cyrus). It would seem that after he had taken care of more pressing concerns elsewhere, Cyrus himself later returned to Babylon (perhaps a year or two afterward) and formally ascended the throne in an official coronation ceremony. It was in the third year of Cyrus's reign (presumably as king of Babylon) that Daniel received the revelations in chapters 10–12. Yet it is also evident from the cuneiform records referred to above that Gubaru continued to serve as governor of Babylon even after Cyrus's decease. The tablets dating from 535 to 525 contained warnings that committing specified offenses would entail "the guilt of a sin against Gubaru, the Governor of Babylon and of the District beyond the river [i.e., the regions west of the Euphrates]" (Whitcomb, p. 23).

VI. Daniel and the Lions' Den (6:1–28)

1. *The Conspiracy Against Daniel*

6:1–9

1It pleased Darius to appoint 120 satraps to rule throughout the kingdom, 2with three administrators over them, one of whom was Daniel. The satraps were made accountable to them so that the king might not suffer loss. 3Now Daniel so distinguished himself among the administrators and the satraps by his exceptional qualities that the king planned to set him over the whole kingdom. 4At this, the administrators and the satraps tried to find grounds for charges against Daniel in his conduct of government affairs, but they were unable to do so. They could find no corruption in him, because he was trustworthy and neither corrupt nor negligent. 5Finally these men said, "We will never find any basis for charges against this man Daniel unless it has something to do with the law of his God."

6So the administrators and the satraps went as a group to the king and said: "O King Darius, live forever! 7The royal administrators, prefects, satraps, advisers and governors have all agreed that the king should issue an edict and enforce the decree that anyone who prays to any god or man during the next thirty days, except to you, O king, shall be thrown into the lions' den. 8Now, O king, issue the decree and put it in writing so that it cannot be altered—in accordance with the laws of the Medes and Persians, which cannot be repealed." 9So King Darius put the decree in writing.

1–3 One of Darius's first responsibilities was to appoint administrators over the entire territory won from the Babylonians (v.1). The 120 "satraps" chosen by him must have been of lesser rank than the 20 satraps Herodotus mentioned (3.89–94) in listing major districts composed of several smaller regions (e.g., the fifth satrapy included Phoenicia, Palestine, Syria, and Cyprus). Here in Daniel the *'ᵃḥašdarpᵉnayyā'* ("satraps") must have been in charge of all the smaller subdivisions. But over these 120 there were three commissioners (*sārᵉḵîn*, v.2), of whom Daniel was chairman (v.3). In view of Daniel's successful prediction in Belshazzar's banquet hall, it was only natural for Darius to select him for so responsible a position, though he was neither a Mede nor a Persian. His long experience and wide acquaintance with Babylonian government made Daniel an exceptionally qualified candidate. But after he had assumed office and turned in a record of exceptional performance, it became obvious that he had superhuman knowledge and skill; and he became a likely choice for prime minister.

4 "The administrators" (*sārᵉkayyā'*, from *sārak*, "high official" [a possible cognate of Arab. *šārikun*, "partner," "companion," though etymologies from Persian and Hittite have also been suggested]) "and satraps tried to find grounds for charges against Daniel in his conduct of government affairs [lit., 'the kingdom']." Just as his three friends had become the target of envy many years before (ch. 3), so Daniel encountered hostility in the new Persian government. Undoubtedly the great majority of his enemies were race-conscious Medes or Persians, and they did not take kindly to the elevation of one of the Jewish captives. To be sure, King Cyrus was either looking favorably on the request of the Jews for release or had already promulgated the decree cited in Ezra 1:2–4 (which is dated in Ezra 1:1 as the "first year of Cyrus king of Persia," i.e., c. 539–538, if his rule as king of Babylon is meant). But even this improvement in the status of the exiled Jews did not erase the shame of their deportation in the days of Nebuchadnezzar. Though they were the objects of Cyrus's charity—perhaps in compliance with Isaiah's remarkable predictions (cf. Isa 44:28–45:4)—they were nevertheless considered an inferior race, especially by their conquerors. The elevation of a Jew to the place of prime minister was so disturbing that they made a thorough investigation of Daniel's management of public affairs. Surely there was some sort of chicanery they could accuse him of, some shady dealings that marred his past. But all their investigations proved fruitless. Daniel's integrity was beyond question. What were his rivals going to do?

5 The only way to get at Daniel was to place him in a position where he had to choose between obedience to his God and obedience to the government. Daniel was a strict monotheist and would never make any concessions to idolatry. But Persia had no law against monotheism. Somehow a new statute had to be devised that would seem merely political to Darius but would impose a religious issue for Daniel. So they proposed that for the period of one month all petitions and prayers throughout the realm had to be directed toward Darius alone. This not only flattered him personally but also served to impress on the whole population of his empire that they were no longer under the Chaldeans but the Persians.

6–9 The government overseers (v.6) came to the king "as a group" (*hargišû*, from *rᵉgaš*, presumably cognate with Heb. *rāgaš*, "be in commotion," "throng," and Arab. *raǧasa*, "to thunder"). As an official delegation, they presented their proposal, falsely implying that Daniel had concurred in their legislation. "The royal administrators [of whom Daniel was chief], prefects, satraps, advisers and governors have all agreed" (v.7)—i.e., in drawing up the decree. Darius should have noticed that Daniel was not there to speak for himself. Yet Darius had no reason to suspect that the other two royal administrators would misrepresent Daniel's position in this matter, and certainly the reported unanimity of all the lower echelons of government must have stilled any doubts Darius had about the decree. The suggested mode of compelling every subject in the former Babylonian domain to acknowledge the authority of Persia seemed a statesmanlike measure that would contribute to the unification of the Middle and Near East. The time limit of one month seemed reasonable. After it the people could resume their accustomed worship. So, without personally consulting Daniel himself, Darius went ahead and affixed his signature or seal to the decree (v.9).

2. *Daniel's Detection, Trial, and Sentence*

6:10–17

[10]Now when Daniel learned that the decree had been published, he went home to his upstairs room where the windows opened toward Jerusalem. Three times a day he got down on his knees and prayed, giving thanks to his God, just as he had done before. [11]Then these men went as a group and found Daniel praying and asking God for help. [12]So they went to the king and spoke to him about his royal decree: "Did you not publish a decree that during the next thirty days anyone who prays to any god or man except to you, O king, would be thrown into the lions' den?"

The king answered, "The decree stands—in accordance with the laws of the Medes and Persians, which cannot be repealed."

[13]Then they said to the king, "Daniel, who is one of the exiles from Judah, pays no attention to you, O king, or to the decree you put in writing. He still prays three times a day." [14]When the king heard this, he was greatly distressed; he was determined to rescue Daniel and made every effort until sundown to save him.

[15]Then the men went as a group to the king and said to him, "Remember, O king, that according to the law of the Medes and Persians no decree or edict that the king issues can be changed."

[16]So the king gave the order, and they brought Daniel and threw him into the lions' den. The king said to Daniel, "May your God, whom you serve continually, rescue you!"

[17]A stone was brought and placed over the mouth of the den, and the king sealed it with his own signet ring and with the rings of his nobles, so that Daniel's situation might not be changed.

10 The new ordinance mandated a very severe sanction: death by caged lions (v.12). When the aged Daniel received notice of this new law, which had been enacted without his knowledge, he was faced with a dilemma. It was this prayer-fellowship with Yahweh that had safeguarded Daniel from the corrupting influences of Babylonian culture. To be sure, he might have compromised his integrity by ceasing to pray to God during the month the decree was in effect—or by praying privately, perhaps in the night, when no one could see him worshiping at his window. To rationalize such compromises to preserve his role in government would have been easy. But Daniel could not compromise. For him the issue was whether he was going to please man or obey God. Daniel had to choose between loyalty to his Lord and obedience to a sinful government commanding him to perform idolatry. So he was willing to risk his life for the Lord, trusting him for deliverance even as Shadrach, Meshach, and Abednego had been delivered years before.

Daniel was in the habit of praying toward Jerusalem, for it was there in Solomon's temple that the glorious presence of Yahweh had come to reside (1 Kings 8:10–11). Even though this shekinah cloud had forsaken the temple prior to the Fall of Jerusalem in 587 (Ezek 11:23), Daniel knew that the Lord had promised to return there (cf. Ezek 43:2) and to restore Jerusalem (Jer 29:10, 14), even as he was then doing, for Cyrus's decree of restoration had probably been already promulgated. To what other direction should Daniel turn than to the Holy City, the place of his heart's desire, the focal point of his hopes and prayers for the progress of the kingdom of God? Chapter 9 tells us how earnestly Daniel was concerned about the return of the Jewish captives to Jerusalem and their land; 9:2 refers to his diligent study of the prophecies of Jeremiah concerning the seventy-year limit to the Exile—a study he undertook "in the first year of Darius son of Xerxes [Heb., 'Ahasuerus']" (9:1). This concern for the captives' return may have been on his prayer list as he knelt at his window.

11–12 Verse 11 indicates that a group of the hostile officials had waited for Daniel to pray and then had burst in on him to catch him violating the new decree. It is clear that the officials were in collusion to make a public test-case of Daniel's violation of the royal decree. They "found him praying and asking God for help." It is not clear whether they arrested him on the spot or first referred the matter to the king. In any event, they lost no time in reporting to Darius (v.12). They reminded him that he had forbidden all petitions to anyone but himself during the thirty-day period. Darius acknowledged that the decree was still in force and that the "laws of the Medes and Persians" could neither be changed nor revoked (v.12). This verse incidentally, proves that Darius the Mede was serving under the authority of the Medo-Persian Empire, for no independent Median ruler, reigning before the Persian regime, could possibly have been subject to the law of the Persians. Obviously the idea of a Median Empire ruling over Babylon before the Persian conquest was unknown to the author of the Book of Daniel and is merely an ill-founded hypothesis.

13–14 In reporting Daniel's disobedience to the king, the conspirators said, "Daniel . . . pays no attention to you, O king" (v.13; cf. the similar charge against Shadrach, Meshach, and Abednego in 3:12: "[They] pay no attention to you, O king"). They represented Daniel's praying thrice daily as willful disrespect to his king rather than as devotion to his God.

Darius's response (v.14) was not what the conspirators had expected. Indeed, he "was greatly distressed" (*śaggî' bᵉ'ēš 'ᵃlôhî*, lit., "It was greatly displeasing to him"), not because he resented Daniel's praying to Yahweh, but because for the first time the real reason for the decree dawned on him. He probably realized that he had been manipulated by Daniel's enemies, and he regretted his failure to consult Daniel before putting the decree in writing. Undoubtedly Darius respected Daniel for his consistent piety to his God. Throughout the day he tried his best to save Daniel's life. He may have thought of ways of protecting him from the lions, perhaps by overfeeding them or by covering Daniel with armor. Such schemes would have been interpreted as subterfuges undermining the king's own law. A miracle was Daniel's only hope. Darius undoubtedly respected Daniel's God—the God who had enabled him to interpret the letters on Belshazzar's wall and who had made Daniel the most able administrator in the court. Could it be that this God might save him? In all probability Darius had also heard of the deliverance of Daniel's three comrades from Nebuchadnezzar's furnace.

15–17 By sunset, therefore, the king had resigned himself to comply with the conspirators' desire; and when they again reminded him of his irrevocable decree (v.15), he was ready to go ahead with the penalty. Yet to show his personal concern for his cherished minister, Darius went with Daniel to the very mouth of the pit where the lions were kept. So Daniel, who must have been about eighty-three, was thrown into the pit (v.16). Apparently the lions took no notice of him as he stood among them. Before the pit was closed, Darius called down to Daniel: "May your God, whom you serve continually [*dî 'antâ* (Kethiv; Qere, *'ant*) *pālaḥ-lēh,* a present periphrastic, indicating continual action] rescue you [*y*^{e}*šêz*^{e}*binnāḵ*, from šêzîb, 'save,' 'deliver']!" For Darius these words voiced a tremulous hope (cf. v.20). Thereupon the king had a heavy stone put over the top of the den and had it sealed with clay tablets on which he pressed his royal seal and the seals of the nobles who had escorted Daniel to the place of execution—as they supposed (v.17). Undoubtedly this meant that each one rolled his own cylinder seal across the face of the moist tablets attached to the chains holding the stone in place. (Many examples of such cylinder seals are on display in museums specializing in ancient Near East artifacts. They were in constant use from the Sumerian period in the third millennium to the Persian era in the sixth to fourth centuries B.C.)

3. *Daniel's Deliverance and His Foes' Punishment*

6:18–24

18 Then the king returned to his palace and spent the night without eating and without any entertainment being brought to him. And he could not sleep.

19 At the first light of dawn, the king got up and hurried to the lions' den. 20 When he came near the den, he called to Daniel in an anguished voice, "Daniel, servant of the living God, has your God, whom you serve continually, been able to rescue you from the lions?"

21 Daniel answered, "O king, live forever! 22 My God sent his angel, and he shut the mouths of the lions. They have not hurt me, because I was found innocent in his sight. Nor have I ever done any wrong before you, O king."

23 The king was overjoyed and gave orders to lift Daniel out of the den. And when Daniel was lifted from the den, no wound was found on him, because he had trusted in his God.

24 At the king's command, the men who had falsely accused Daniel were brought in and thrown into the lions' den, along with their wives and children. And before they reached the floor of the den, the lions overpowered them and crushed all their bones.

18–20 Darius walked back to his palace a troubled man (v.18). Where could he find another minister of such integrity and judgment? The more he thought about Daniel's peril, the more anxious Darius became—so anxious, in fact, that he could eat nothing. Nor was he in any mood for entertainment—whatever diversions may be implied by the uncertain term *daḥ*[a]*wān*.

Darius tossed about on his bed, with anxious thoughts keeping him awake till the first gray light of dawn. Without eating breakfast, he hastened to the lion pit. He must already have ordered it to be unsealed, for on coming to it, he called, "Daniel, servant of the living God, has your God, whom you serve continually, been able to rescue you from the lions?" (v.20). Notice the emphasis on Yahweh as the "living" God; clearly the king regarded Daniel's fate as a test of whether his God was really alive or just an unproved supposition, like all the deities the non-Jews worshiped. If the Hebrew God really existed, he would preserve his faithful servant from death; and if anyone deserved well from his God, it was Daniel, who would not stop worshiping even on pain of death.

21–22 Then Darius heard Daniel's voice from the bottom of the pit, saying, "O king, live forever!" (*malkā' l*[e]*'āl*[e]*mîn ḥ*[e]*yî*, the Aram. equivalent of "Long live the king!"), and telling how God had sent his angel (presumably *the* Angel of the Lord; cf. 3:25) to shut the lions' mouths. Moreover, as Daniel said (v.22), the Lord had delivered him to prove him guiltless before God and man.

23 With great joy Darius had Daniel brought out of the lions' den and examined for any injuries. Not a scratch was found on him. The evidence was incontrovertible. The God Daniel had remained faithful to had kept him safe. So through his reliance on Yahweh, Daniel gained his place among the heroes of the faith listed in Hebrews 11—"who through faith . . . stopped the mouths of lions" (v.33).

24 Without any judicial hearing or trial, King Darius, absolute monarch that he was, ordered Daniel's accusers to be haled before him and then cast *with their families* into the pit they had conspired to have Daniel thrown into. Presumably Darius considered them guilty of devising the decree that could have deprived the king of his most able counselor. Furthermore, they had lied to the king when they had averred that "all agreed" (v.7) to recommend this decree, when Daniel (the foremost of the administrators) had not even been consulted in the matter. With a masterly touch of poetic justice, Daniel shows us the fate of the conspirators and their families: "And before they reached the floor of the den, the lions overpowered them and crushed all their bones."

What Darius did seems arbitrary and unjust. But ancient pagan despots had no regard for the provision in the Mosaic law (Deut 24:16): "Fathers shall not be put to death for their children, nor children put to death for their fathers; each is to die for his own sin." (Even in Israel this humanitarian rule had been flouted, as when Abimelech ben Gideon had nearly all his father's sons massacred, or when Queen Athaliah nearly exterminated the Davidic royal line and Jehu had all Ahab's sons decapitated.)

Perhaps Darius acted as he did to minimize the danger of revenge against the executioner by the family of those who were put to death. At any rate, Daniel's position as prime minister was now secure, and he apparently continued in it till his retirement a few years later.

Notes

18 דַּחֲוָן (*daḥ^a wān*) has been variously explained as "concubines," if related to the Arabic *daḥâ* ("sleep with"); "items of food," as the early versions suggest; "musical instruments," as Ibn Ezra proposed; "tables," according to Rashi; or "perfumes," if related to the Arabic *duḫânun* ("smoke," "vapor").

4. *Darius's Testimony to God's Sovereignty*

6:25–28

25Then King Darius wrote to all the peoples, nations and men of every language throughout the land:

"May you prosper greatly!

26"I issue a decree that in every part of my kingdom people must fear and reverence the God of Daniel.

"For he is the living God
and he endures forever;
his kingdom will not be destroyed,
his dominion will never end.
27He rescues and he saves;
he performs signs and wonders
in the heavens and on the earth.
He has rescued Daniel
from the power of the lions."

28So Daniel prospered during the reign of Darius and the reign of Cyrus the Persian.

25–27 As Nebuchadnezzar had done, Darius made a public proclamation giving glory to the God of the Hebrews, commanding all citizens of the realm to honor and respect him (v.25). The sense of vv.26–27 is like the last clause of 3:29 ("no other god can save in this way"—i.e., the way the three were saved from the fiery furnace) and like 4:34 ("His dominion is an eternal dominion; his kingdom endures from generation to generation"—words Nebuchadnezzar spoke on recovering from his madness).

Three emphases stand out in this passage: (1) Daniel's God is alive and shows that he lives by the way he acts in history, responding, like a real person, to the requirements of justice and the needs of his people; (2) God's rule is eternal and will never pass away (as do empires built by human power), even though the Hebrew monarchy did not survive its apostasy; (3) God miraculously delivers his true worshipers, performing wonders both in heaven and on earth. He has furnished objective proof of his eternal power and godhead, in contrast with all other deities, whose existence is at best conjectural and traditional.

Once again, during this time of Israel's helplessness with her survival in doubt, Yahweh of hosts acted redemptively to strengthen his people's faith in him. On the eve of their return to the Land of Promise under the leadership of Zerubbabel, God reassured them that he was still the same as in the days of Moses and was able to take them back to Canaan, where they could establish a new commonwealth in covenant fellowship with him.

28 The chapter ends with this notice to Daniel's continued usefulness throughout the rest of the reign of Darius (Gubaru) as king of Babylon and in the reign of Cyrus (cf. 1:21) as king of Babylon. After this Daniel apparently retired from public service and gave himself to Bible study and prayer. He received the revelations of chapters 10–12 in the third year of Cyrus (cf. 10:1). Apparently it was during his retirement that he revised his memoirs. A likely date for the publication of the Book of Daniel would seem to be about 532 B.C., judging from linguistic evidence (cf. Introduction).

VII. The Triumph of the Son of Man (7:1–28)

1. *The Four Beasts and the Succession of Empires*

7:1–8

[1]In the first year of Belshazzar king of Babylon, Daniel had a dream, and visions passed through his mind as he was lying on his bed. He wrote down the substance of his dream.

[2]Daniel said: "In my vision at night I looked, and there before me were the four winds of heaven churning up the great sea. [3]Four great beasts, each different from the others, came up out of the sea.

[4]"The first was like a lion, and it had the wings of an eagle. I watched until its wings were torn off and it was lifted from the ground so that it stood on two feet like a man, and the heart of a man was given to it.

[5]"And there before me was a second beast, which looked like a bear. It was raised up on one of its sides, and it had three ribs in its mouth between its teeth. It was told, 'Get up and eat your fill of flesh!'

[6]"After that, I looked, and there before me was another beast, one that looked like a leopard. And on its back it had four wings like those of a bird. This beast had four heads, and it was given authority to rule.

[7]"After that, in my vision at night I looked, and there before me was a fourth beast—terrifying and frightening and very powerful. It had large iron teeth; it crushed and devoured its victims and trampled underfoot whatever was left. It was different from all the former beasts, and it had ten horns.

[8]"While I was thinking about the horns, there before me was another horn, a little one, which came up among them; and three of the first horns were uprooted before it. This horn had eyes like the eyes of a man and a mouth that spoke boastfully.

1 The book now turns from episodes in Daniel's life to a series of visions and revelations granted him in the latter part of his career. The particular revelation in this chapter is dated "in the first year of Belshazzar king of Babylon." Nabonidus, his father, came to the throne in 556; but he apparently entrusted to Belshazzar the "army and the kingship" of Babylon while he himself campaigned in North and Central Arabia (so the Nabonidus Chronicle). Wiseman (NBD, p. 139) suggests that Daniel may have dated events from the time when this coregency began. Thus the "first year of Belshazzar" would have been 556 or 555. Wood (p. 179) inclines to a few years later (i.e., 553). But it is still uncertain whether the actual kingship of Babylon was immediately entrusted to Belshazzar at the commencement of his father's reign (though that would be a fair inference from the statement in the Nabonidus Chronicle), or whether his appointment as viceroy came somewhat later, as Nabonidus found himself unable to return from Arabia as soon as he had hoped. It is probably safer to say that the present state of the evidence hardly grants us precision on this matter.

Belshazzar's regnal years may have been reckoned from the 550s, but the usual procedure of kings in that period was not to appoint the crown prince to actual kingly status till after the father had reigned at least for a few years as sole monarch. Especially was this true in the kingdom of Judah, where Uzziah was not appointed junior king by his father, Amaziah, till six years after his accession in 790. Similarly, Jotham did not appoint Ahaz till eight years after he took over the government from his leprous father, Uzziah. Still, there seems to be nothing to militate against the supposition that Belshazzar's appointment as king of Babylon came three years after his father's accession in 556—unless, of course, Nabonidus did not marry till after he seized the throne. In that case, Belshazzar could not have been born till 554, which would have made him only fifteen in 539, a most unlikely supposition.

Verse 1 says that Daniel recorded only the "substance" (*rē'š*, rightly rendered in NIV, since the term for "beginning," as some suggest for this word, would more likely have been *rē'šîṯ*, in either Heb. or Aram.) of his memorable vision—even through twenty-six verses may seem to us a rather full report.

Chapter 7 parallels chapter 2; both set forth the four empires, followed by the complete overthrow of all ungodly resistance, as the final (fifth) kingdom is established on earth to enforce the standards of God's righteousness. The winged lion corresponds to the golden head of the dream image (ch. 2); the ravenous bear to its arms and chest; the swift leopard to its belly and thighs; the fearsome ten-horned beast to its legs and feet. Lastly, the stone cut out without hands that in chapter 2 demolishes the dream image has its counterpart in the glorified Son of Man, who is installed as Lord over all the earth. But chapter 7 tells us something chapter 2 does not—viz., that the Messiah himself will head the final kingdom of righteousness.

The sea (v.2) is symbolic of polluted, turbulent humanity (cf. Isa 57:20) as they try to exploit and govern in their own wisdom and strength. Revelation 7:1 portrays the four winds as under the control of four mighty angels; in Revelation 9:14, by the River Euphrates, they are bidden to release the winds on the earth, so that one-third of mankind will perish in war (Rev 9:15). From this we may conclude that the four winds represent God's judgments, hurling themselves on the ungodly nations from all four points of the compass. In the successive rise and fall of the four empires of Babylon, Medo-Persia, Greece, and Rome, these destructive forces will exert their power through the centuries to come, till the final triumph of the Son of Man.

2–3 The scene of action is "the great sea" (v.2), which possibly meant the Mediterranean. At any rate, it stood for the ever-changing Gentile world (cf. the similar symbolic usage in Rev 13:1 and also in 21:1, which predicts that in the new earth there will be no more "sea" [*thalassa*]). From the sea (Gentile nations) emerge in succession four fearsome beasts (v.3), which apparently go on shore to perform their roles.

4 The first of these beasts is a winged lion, whose eaglelike pinions are soon plucked, so that instead of flying it stands on the ground. A human heart (*lᵉḇaḇ*) is given to it. In the light of Nebuchadnezzar's career, it is clear that the plucking of the lion's wings symbolizes reduction of his pride and power at the time of his insanity (ch. 4). The lion symbol was characteristic of Babylon, especially in Nebuchadnezzar's time, when the Ishtar Gate entrance was adorned on either side with a long procession of yellow lions on blue-glazed brick, fashioned in high relief. As late as Alexander's conquest, the satrap Mazaeus used the lion as the reverse type on the Babylonian silver shekel—a practice continued for a time by Seleucus I. But too much should not be made of this fact, since none of the three succeeding beasts can be similarly connected with individual rulers, rather than with the empires that they represent. The final detail—"the heart of a man was given to it"—may refer to the restoration of Nebuchadnezzar's sanity after his seven-year dementia. In any event, the correspondence between the winged lion and the Babylonian Empire is acknowledged by biblical critics of every persuasion.

5 The second beast appears on the stage—a hulking bear, who apparently displaces the lion, though no mention is made of any conflict between the two. The bear is then described in a way that very clearly suggests that it is to involve the alliance of two powers, one of which will dominate the other. The Median Empire (with which the advocates of the Maccabean date theory associate this bear) did not do this. But the symbolic action was altogether appropriate for the federated Medo-Persian Empire, in which the Persian element dominated the Median. Moreover, one side of the bear was higher than the other, and Daniel saw it devouring three ribs from some other animal it had killed. Indeed, it was divinely encouraged to feast on the ribs. This corresponds perfectly to the three major conquests the Medes and Persians made under the leadership of King Cyrus and his son Cambyses: viz., the Lydian kingdom in Asia Minor (which fell to Cyrus in 546), the Chaldean Empire (which he annexed in 539), and the kingdom of Egypt (which Cambyses acquired in 525). Needless to say, nothing in the career of the Median Empire before Cyrus's time corresponds to the three ribs. In view of these things, it is hopeless to make out any plausible link between this bear and the earlier, separate Median Empire that preceded Cyrus's victory over Astyages.

6 This verse introduces the third symbolic beast—the four-winged leopard with four heads. This beast portrays the division of Alexander's swiftly won empire into four separate parts within a few years after his death in 323 B.C. The initial arrangement involved the area of Greece and Macedon (under Antipater and then Cassander), Thrace and Asia Minor (under Lysimachus), all of Asia except Asia Minor and Palestine (under Seleucus), and Egypt-Palestine (under Ptolemy). Even after the breakdown of Lysimachus's kingdom, a separate realm was maintained by Eumenes of Pergamum and others, so that the quadripartite character of the Greek Empire was maintained, despite the most determined efforts of the more aggressive Seleucids and Ptolemids to annex each other into a single realm. Very clearly, then, the four heads and four wings represent the Macedonian conquest and its subsequent divisions. But there is no way in which a quadripartite character can be made out for the Persian Empire either under Cyrus or under any of his successors. That empire remained unified till its end, when it suddenly collapsed under the onslaught of Alexander the Great in 334–331.

7 Verse 7 presents a fourth beast, unlike any predator known to natural history. The writer described it as "terrifying and frightening and very powerful" (implying that it would be even fiercer and stronger than any of the preceding empires). Its very teeth were of iron; and it would be more crushing in its military power, exploitation, and repression than the other three: "It . . . trampled underfoot whatever was left" (*šᵉʾārā'*, "that which remains as a residue"—i.e., whatever survived from the preceding empires). In one other way it differed from the first three: it had ten horns (conceivably two five-pronged antlers, rather than ten independently rooted horns). There is an unmistakable correspondence between these horns and the ten toes of the dream image (ch. 2), and the mention of iron in the teeth suggests the legs and toes of iron in that image. Thus the superior power of the colossus of Rome—as over against the less-unified or less-stable empires of Greece, Persia, and Babylon—is emphasized in the symbolism of this terrible fourth beast. Its ultimate form in a confederation of ten states is suggested by the horns, as it had been by the toes in chapter 2.

8 Verse 8 introduces a new feature concerning this latter-day ten-state federation—namely, the emergence of one of the smaller horns as the largest of them all. This "little horn" becomes dominant by uprooting and destroying three of its adjacent horns (resulting apparently in the survival of the remaining six as vassal powers under the overlordship of the enlarged horn). It should be observed that the contemporaneity of all ten of these states (or rulers, if that is what the horns refer to) is virtually demanded by these factors. Since six remain in subservience to the aggressive little horn, after he has destroyed the other three, a chronologically consecutive series of rulers (or states) is quite definitely precluded. Just as the ten toes of the dream image were contemporaneous, so are all the ten horns of this fourth beast. The victorious little horn is further described as possessing "eyes like the eyes of a man and a mouth that spoke boastfully." These features seem to imply that this little horn symbolizes an arrogant and vainglorious ruler, rather than an entire kingdom. (This is somewhat similar to the lion of v.4, which apparently symbolizes the Chaldean power in the personality of Nebuchadnezzar, whereas the bear and the leopard symbolize the Medo-Persian and Greek empires as entire realms rather than as individual leaders.)

The final clause of v.8 introduces us for the first time to the ruthless world-dictator of the last days who is referred to in 2 Thessalonians 2:3, 8, as "the man of lawlessness [*anomias*]" or "the lawless one [*anomos*]," who "exalts himself over everything that is called God or is worshiped, and even sets himself up in God's temple, proclaiming himself to be God" (2 Thess 2:4). It should be carefully noted that *this* little horn emerges from the fourth empire, in contrast to the little horn of chapter 8 (vv.9–11), which arises from the third empire. (See the exposition of ch. 8 for the relationship between the two.)

Notes

---

6 Roger H. Simpson (EBr, 14th ed., 14:485) says this concerning Lysimachus as king of Thrace and western Asia Minor:

> It was not until 302, on the occasion of the second alliance of the enemies of Antigonus, that he emerged as a power of the first rank. Then, reinforced by troops given him by Cassander, he entered the dominions of Antigonus in Asia Minor and bore the brunt of the campaign which ended in the overthrow of Antigonus at the battle of Ipsus (301;

> *q.v.*). The division of Antigonus' kingdom resulted in Lysimachus' acquiring the greater part of Asia Minor. This, with his European possessions, gave him a position of great strategic strength; his territory at its greatest extent embraced about 160,000 sq. mi. He had taken the title of king at the same time as the other Successors in 306/305, having already built himself a new capital, Lysimachia, in the Thracian Chersonese (Gallipoli peninsula) near the older city of Cardia (309).
>
> After 301 Lysimachus consolidated his power in both Asia and Europe in wars against Demetrius Poliorcetes. Only in 294 did he conclude peace, having by then annexed the cities in Ionia and Caria which Demetrius retained after Ipsus. An attempt to carry his power beyond the Danube ended in failure, but in 288 he joined hands with Pyrrhus, the king of Epirus, to drive Demetrius from Macedonia. Pyrrhus was at first allowed to remain in possession of half of Macedonia with the title of king, but in 285 Lysimachus seized the whole country for himself.

In view of these facts, it is hard to see how any legitimate question can be raised concerning the quadripartite division into which the Alexandrian Empire fell after the collapse of the final effort made to hold it together. Antigonus Monophthalmus and his son, Demetrius Poliorcetes, were the last contenders for the unity of the empire; and so when they were crushed, the fourfold division of the Alexandrian domain became official. While it is true that Lysimachus's kingdom did not long endure after his death in 281, there almost always was a buffer state (or several buffer states) between Macedon-Greece and the Seleucid domains. By 200 B.C. there was a complex of such independent kingdoms: Thrace, Pergamum, Bithynia, Galatia, Pontus, and Cappadocia (cf. W.R. Shepherd, *Historical Atlas* [New York: Barnes & Noble, 1929], whose map 19B shows these states as distinct from Macedonia on the west and from the Seleucid Empire on the east).

---

2. *The Kingdom of God and the Enthroned Messiah*

7:9–14

9"As I looked,

"thrones were set in place,
  and the Ancient of Days took his seat.
His clothing was as white as snow;
  the hair of his head was white like wool.
His throne was flaming with fire,
  and its wheels were all ablaze.
10A river of fire was flowing,
  coming out from before him.
Thousands upon thousands attended him;
  ten thousand times ten thousand stood before him.
The court was seated,
  and the books were opened.

11"Then I continued to watch because of the boastful words the horn was speaking. I kept looking until the beast was slain and its body destroyed and thrown into the blazing fire. 12(The other beasts had been stripped of their authority, but were allowed to live for a period of time.)

13"In my vision at night I looked, and there before me was one like a son of man, coming with the clouds of heaven. He approached the Ancient of Days and was led into his presence. 14He was given authority, glory and sovereign power; all peoples, nations and men of every language worshiped him. His dominion is an everlasting dominion that will not pass away, and his kingdom is one that will never be destroyed.

9–10 At this point the Aramaic text becomes poetical as the parallelism shows. Some modern EVs print vv.9–10 and vv.13–14 as poetry, with vv.11–12 left as prose. Verse 9 ushers in the fifth kingdom as the final form of world power, which is destined to overthrow and utterly destroy all the preceding empires erected by violence-worshiping men. The opening words present a plurality of "thrones" (*korsāwān*), but attention is immediately directed to one great throne, on which, symbolically, God himself takes his seat. He is described as "the Ancient of Days" (*'attîq yômîn*, lit., "advanced of days"), with pure white hair and attired in shining white robes. The throne he sat on blazed with fire, and the wheels on which it rested and moved about were ringed with flame. (Compare Ezekiel's description in 1:13 of the glory of the Lord, which literally says: "In the midst of the living beings, there was something that looked like burning coals of fire, like torches darting back and forth among the living beings. The fire was bright, and lightning was flashing from the fire.")

Quite clearly in this passage from Daniel, at least, the fire not only represents the blindingly brilliant manifestation of God's splendor but also the fierce heat of his judgment on sin and on all those opposed to his supreme authority. There is something almost lavalike in the way a "river of fire" (v.10) flows from his throne—a river of vast destructive power, at which the court of angels marvel. "Ten thousand times ten thousand" (*ribbô riḇwān*, i.e., "hundreds of millions") celestial beings stood by for the triumphant judgment of the rebellious little horn (in this case the "beast" or final world-dictator of the last days).

But apparently this scene is a court of judgment for more than the beast alone, for after the heavenly court convened for the examination and conviction of the guilty (*dînā' yᵉṯiḇ*, "the court was seated"), then an entire set of books of record was opened, presumably containing the sins of the little horn and his adherents (cf. Rev 20:12–13, which indicates the contents of these books, even though it depicts the later judgment at the end of the Millennium). So the stage is set for bringing the wicked and unrepentant to justice.

11 According to v.11, the blasphemous beast still spews out his boastings against both man and God till the very moment he is dragged before the heavenly tribunal. Then suddenly his mouth is stopped as his physical life is taken and his body consigned to the flames of judgment. This ends his loud-mouthed defiance of the almighty God. Great was Daniel's satisfaction as he witnessed the triumph of divine holiness and truth over the wickedness of unrepentant humanity. He would have exclaimed with John, "Hallelujah! For our Lord God Almighty reigns" (Rev 19:6).

12 The remnants of the world powers (i.e., "the other beasts") that will precede the final tribulation of the last days will likewise come under judgment. Then follow the intriguing words: "But [they] were allowed to live for a period of time" (*'aḏ-zᵉmān wᵉ'iddān*). It may be that the unbelieving adherents of the world powers that precede the rise of the little horn are simply reserved for a day of judgment by the returning Christ, when they will be sent to the outer darkness of hell. Or else it might be that these survivors of the judgment on the Beast will be moved to repentance and faith, and thus be permitted to go on living for some time into the Millennium, as obedient subjects of the King of Kings. *'Aḏ-zᵉmān wᵉ'iddān* would admit of either interpretation, but the former seems more likely.

13–14 At this point in his vision, Daniel saw the glorified Son of Man (v.13). This is the verse from Daniel that the NT quotes most frequently. The personage who now appears before God in the form of a human being is of heavenly origin. He has come to this place of coronation accompanied by the clouds of heaven and is clearly no mere human being in essence. The expression "like a son of man" (*k^{e}ḇar '^{e}nāš*) identifies the appearance of this final Ruler of the world not only as a man, in contrast to the beasts (the four world empires), but also as the heavenly Sovereign incarnate.

During his earthly ministry, the Lord Jesus Christ maintained this same emphasis on his incarnate nature, viz., that he was true man as well as true God. He constantly referred to himself as "*the* Son of Man" (i.e., that same one "like a son of man" foretold in Dan 7:13). Since Jesus had this particular passage in mind, he spoke of himself as *the* Son of Man, even though here the Aramaic text uses, by implication at least, an indefinite article. Moreover, v.13 is the only place in the OT where *bar '^{e}nāš* (or its Heb. equivalent *ben-'āḏām*) is used of a divine personage rather than a human being. (The principal use of *ben-'āḏām* is found in Ezekiel, where it is addressed to that prophet himself at least ninety times.) But it should also be noted that Christ himself emphasized his return to earth "in clouds with great power and glory" (Mark 13:26), or "on [*epi*] the clouds of the sky" (Matt 24:30), or "sitting at the right hand of the Mighty One and coming on the clouds of heaven" (Matt 26:64). See also Revelation 1:7: "Look, he is coming with [*meta*, closely corresponding with the Aramaic *'im* of the original] the clouds." Nothing could be clearer than that Jesus himself regarded Daniel 7:13 as predictive of himself and that the two elements "like a son of man" and "with the clouds of heaven" combined to constitute a messianic title. Frequently in the OT God is said to come from heaven in a chariot of clouds to execute judgment (Pss 18:10; 97:2–4; 104:3; Isa 19:1; Nah 1:3).

Many liberal scholars (e.g., Montgomery, p. 319) take this cloud-borne son of man to be mere personification of the Jewish people as a holy nation and point to vv.22, 27 (which speak of the "saints" or "the saints of the Most High" as taking possession of the kingdom). It is quite true that the "saints" (*qaddîšê 'elyônîn*, lit., "the holy ones of the Most High") are to share in the eternal triumph of their all-conquering Lord (v.22 says they "possessed the kingdom"), and that in the millennial kingdom they will have dominion over all the surviving nations on earth (v.27), as well as in the eternal phase that will ensue after the Millennium is over. But it is plain that this vision makes a clear difference between the Son of Man and his people. Verse 21 states that these same "saints" are locked in combat with the world dictator and are defeated by him on the earthly scene of battle; whereas the Son comes from heaven in a chariot of clouds before the presence of God himself, and there without any prior warfare he is crowned sovereign over all the earth (v.14). As Keil (KD, *Daniel*, p. 235) points out: "But the delivering of the kingdom to the people of God does not, according to the prophetic mode of contemplation, exclude the Messiah as its king, but much rather includes Him, inasmuch as Daniel, like the other prophets, knows nothing of a kingdom without a head, a Messianic kingdom without a King Messiah." Therefore it is out of the question to suppose that here only in the OT do we have a kingdom without a king, or that an earthly people could be represented as coming down from heaven in the clouds of the sky. Therefore the identification of the "son of man" as the entire nation of Israel is untenable, not only because it contradicts the teaching of Christ himself (who appropriated this title to himself alone), but also because it is exegetically wrong to assume an author guilty of self-contradiction when an easy harmonization is available.

The messianic Son of Man is brought before the throne of the Ancient of Days (v. 13) to be awarded the crown of universal dominion (v. 14). This refers, not to his inherent sovereignty over the universe as God the Son (as consubstantial and co-eternal with the Father and the Holy Spirit), but to his appointment as absolute Lord and Judge by virtue of his atoning ministry as God incarnate—the one who achieved a sinless life (Isa 53:9), paid the price for man's redemption (Isa 53:5–6), and was vindicated by his bodily resurrection as Judge of the entire human race (Acts 17:31; Rom 2:16). So also his ascension into heaven means that he will be enthroned in glory (Ps 110:1; Acts 2:34–36) till all his enemies have been subdued.

The universality of the rule of the Son of Man is emphasized in v. 14: "He was given authority [*šolṭān*], glory [*y*^{e}*qār*] and sovereign power [*malḵû*]; all the peoples, nations and men of every language worshiped him." Christ is to be the supreme source of political power on earth after his earthly kingdom is established; and all humans, whatever their race, nationality, ethnic origin, or language, will worship and serve him (*lēh yipl*^{e}*ḥûn*), *p*^{e}*laḥ* being equivalent to the cultic use of the Heb. *'āḇaḏ*). "His dominion" (in contrast to the ephemeral power of the first four kingdoms) "is an everlasting dominion that will not pass away, and his kingdom is one that will never be destroyed"—as, of course, all man-erected empires have been and ultimately will be. The final outcome of human history will be a return of Adam's race under the rule of the divine Son of Man to loving obedience and subjection to the sovereignty of God, never again to fall away from him. (Jesus probably had v. 14 in mind when he told his disciples at the Great Commission, "All authority in heaven and on earth has been given to me" [Matt 28:18].)

Notes

12 זְמַן (*z*^{e}*man*) points to time as an appointed or appropriate moment for something to happen; עִדָּן (*'iddān*), on the other hand, refers to time as duration, or as the interval between a temporal *terminus a quo* and the *terminus ad quem*. The LXX equivalent bears out this distinction, for it translates *z*^{e}*man* by καιρός (*kairos*, "time" as opportunity or occasion for something to happen), whereas *'iddān* is rendered χρόνος (*chronos*, the interval of time between two points of measurement, time as duration). In 2:21 Daniel glorified God as the one who changes the "times" (עִדָּנַיָּא, *'iddānayyā'*, times of opportunity or crisis) and the "seasons" (זִמְנַיָּא, *zimnayya'*, intervals or epochs of time). In this passage (7:12), the expression עַד־זְמַן וְעִדָּן (*'aḏ-z*^{e}*man w*^{e}*'iddān*) probably implies "up to the appointed length of time and to the appointed moment in time" when the four beasts (or kingdoms) will have lived out their various periods of supremacy and come to the time appointed for their destruction.

3. *The Vision Interpreted by the Angel*

7:15–28

15"I, Daniel, was troubled in spirit, and the visions that passed through my mind
disturbed me. 16I approached one of those standing there and asked him the true
meaning of all this.

"So he told me and gave me the interpretation of these things: [17]'The four great beasts are four kingdoms that will rise from the earth. [18]But the saints of the Most High will receive the kingdom and will possess it forever—yes, for ever and ever.'

[19]"Then I wanted to known the true meaning of the fourth beast, which was different from all the others and most terrifying, with its iron teeth and bronze claws—the beast that crushed and devoured its victims and trampled underfoot whatever was left. [20]I also wanted to know about the ten horns on its head and about the other horn that came up, before which three of them fell—the horn that looked more imposing than the others and that had eyes and a mouth that spoke boastfully. [21]As I watched, this horn was waging war against the saints and defeating them, [22]until the Ancient of Days came and pronounced judgment in favor of the saints of the Most High, and the time came when they possessed the kingdom.

[23]"He gave me this explanation: 'The fourth beast is a fourth kingdom that will appear on earth. It will be different from all the other kingdoms and will devour the whole earth, trampling it down and crushing it. [24]The ten horns are ten kings who will come from this kingdom. After them another king will arise, different from the earlier ones; he will subdue three kings. [25]He will speak against the Most High and oppress his saints and try to change the set times and the laws. The saints will be handed over to him for a time, times and half a time.

[26]" 'But the court will sit, and his power will be taken away and completely destroyed forever. [27]Then the sovereignty, power and greatness of the kingdoms under the whole heaven will be handed over to the saints, the people of the Most High. His kingdom will be an everlasting kingdom, and all rulers will worship and obey him.'

[28]"This is the end of the matter. I, Daniel, was deeply troubled by my thoughts, and my face turned pale, but I kept the matter to myself."

15–16 Despite the victorious conclusion of his dream, Daniel was distressed (v.15) about the suffering the future might hold for his people. Perhaps he was also distressed by his inability to understand the meaning of several features of his dream, particularly those relating to the fourth empire. Therefore, approaching the angels who were standing nearby—a detail he had not previously mentioned—he asked one of them to explain some of these puzzling details (v.16). Though the angel's name is not given, it could conceivably have been Gabriel, who speaks to him in chapter 9. (Note 9:21, which seems to imply that Gabriel had spoken to Daniel on an earlier occasion.)

17–18 Daniel first asked a general question (v.16), to which the angel gave a general reply (vv.17–18), indicating that the four beasts represented the successive world empires that would dominate the Near East till the last days. But he added (v.18) that the ultimate sovereignty over the world would be granted to "the saints of the Most High" (*qaddîšê 'elyônîn*, with the plural of majesty for "Most High"). Observe the prominence accorded to the Lord's true believers, who will share the responsibilities of government with him (so also in v.27: "The sovereignty . . . will be handed over to the saints, the people of the Most High"). But this no more means that the author of this passage identified the Son of Man with the latter-day Jewish people (as some critics have argued) than did the author of Revelation, where true believers occupy the kingdom, serving as priests to God the Father (1:6) and reigning with him for a thousand years (20:6). They sing a hymn of praise to God for making them a kingdom and priests who shall rule on the earth (5:10). Yet nothing could be clearer than that in Revelation Christ himself is regarded as the foundation and basis of all the kingly power conferred on his people (cf. 1:5: "the ruler of the kings of the earth"; 5:12–13; 11:15; 17:14; 19:11–16). The reason for emphasizing the participation of God's people in the final kingdom seems to be that it is a literal, earthly kingdom, replacing the previous empires of men, rather than a spiritual domain, a sort of ideal kingdom of God consisting only of the Lord himself.

19–22 Of all the beasts Daniel saw, he regarded the fourth with the greatest curiosity and dread (v.19), because it resembled no animal known to human experience. In particular he wondered about the ten horns from which the little horn emerged (v.20) and which was allowed to overcome God's holy people (v.21). Daniel perceived the sinister implications of this for the political welfare of true believers and cringed at the prospect of their being crushed by this reviler against God. Despite the assurance (v.22) that the ultimate victory would be the Lord's and that his people would finally prevail, Daniel was deeply concerned about their impending persecution.

23 The angel's answer (vv.23–27) centers on the career of the little horn (who is apparently the same person as the "lawless one" [2 Thess 2:8–9] and "the beast" [Rev 13:1–10]) and his rise and fall at the second coming of Christ to set up his kingdom. But in v.23 the angel refers to the Roman Empire in future history, with its widespread power. It will be "different from" the three preceding empires in many respects. Its difference will not be size; Alexander's empire, stretching from Yugoslavia to Pakistan, covered a substantially greater area than Trajan's empire, which in A.D. 110 extended from England to beyond the Tigris and included all North Africa and Rumania. But it will differ in organization and unity, which will enable it to endure for centuries beyond the lifetime of the preceding empires of the Near East. "The whole earth" (*kol-'ar'ā'*) refers, not to all known parts of the inhabited earth, but rather (as in general OT usage) to the entire territory of the Near and Middle East that in any way relates to the Holy Land. The word *'ar'ā'* (and its Heb. equivalent, *'ereṣ*) does not necessarily mean "earth" in the sense of "the entire inhabited globe" but—depending on context—might mean a single country (*'ereṣ yiśrā'ēl* is "the land of Israel") or a larger geographical unit, such as "territory" or "region." In almost every instance, the extent of the district involved is determinable from the context. Here it is clearly tantamount to the NT *oikoumenē* (the portion of the world included within the Roman Empire, or possibly the regions immediately adjacent to it). The Roman state is seen here as devouring all the surrounding nations bite by bite (i.e., by the picturesque term *'ᵃḵal*, "to eat," "devour") and thus acquiring an entire complex of subject kingdoms and nations.

24 The interpreting angel turned from the historic Roman Empire to its ultimate ten-horn phase (corresponding to the ten toes in Nebuchadnezzar's dream-image [2:41–43]) and the emergence of the final world-dictator. He arises after ten horns have been set up and subdues three of these ten to his own direct rule. He will then subject the other seven states to vassalage, somewhat as Hitler subjected Norway, Holland, Hungary, and the Balkan countries to a leader of their local Nazi party. In theory they were separate nations, but in practice they were subservient to Hitler. There is apparently to be a strong personality cult attached to this empire of the little horn (cf. the quasi-deification of Hitler).

25 The little horn will claim divine honors (even as he blasphemes the one true

God). He will abandon all pretense of permitting freedom of religion and will actually revile Yahweh, the Lord of heaven and earth, and will denounce as fools and rebels those who still retain biblical convictions. By cruel and systematic pressure, he will "oppress" (*yeballē'*, from *belā'*, which in the Pael means "wear away" or "wear out" as friction wears our clothes or sandals). Such continual and protracted persecution far more effectively breaks the human spirit than the single moment of crisis that calls for a heroic decision. It is easier to die for the Lord than to live for him under constant harassment and strain—as many a German Christian in Hitler's horror camps and some imprisoned missionaries found out during World War II. Revelation 13:16–17 suggests how economic pressure will be brought to bear on loyal Christians during the reign of the Beast, when "no one could buy or sell unless he had the mark, which is the name of the beast or the number of his name."

This dictator will impose a new legal system on all his subjects, doubtless based on totalitarian principles in which the service of the government or the state will be substituted for the absolute standards of God's moral law. All dissent or opposition to the decisions and policies of the little horn will be adjudged treasonable and punishable by death. His program will include a revision of the calendar; this seems to be implied by "to change the set times" (*zimnîn*, lengths or periods of time).

This kind of calendar reform was attempted during the French Revolution, when it was desired to replace the A.D. dating by the first year of the Republic, 1792. There was also an elaborate attempt to revise the months and weeks. For twelve years, from 1793 to 1805, this revolutionary calendar was made absolutely obligatory; and those who adhered to the Christian (Gregorian) calendar were subject to criminal prosecution (cf. EBr, 14th ed., 9:909).

It is also significant that this radical phase of the rule of the beast is to endure for "a time, times and half a time," or three and a half years (for *'iddān* ["time" as *kairos*] seems to be used as a term for "year" in the prophetic portions of Daniel; cf. 4:16, where the seven *'iddānîn* are clearly seven years). This, of course, is half of the seven years that mark the period of the little horn's career. Judging from 9:26–27, it would appear that at the beginning of this final heptad of years the "ruler who will come" will "confirm a covenant with many for one 'seven,' but in the middle of that 'seven' " will compel the offering of sacrifices to cease. We may therefore infer that after the first three and a half years of his career, the Beast will abrogate his "covenant" with the religious establishment (or possibly the Jewish hierarchy carrying on Mosaic sacrifices in a rebuilt temple on Mount Moriah; cf. 12:11; Matt 24:15; 2 Thess 2:4). This would leave three and a half years more for his program to be carried out without any rival ideology of a theistic sort to deal with. Presumably it will be during this second half of the final heptad of years that the progressive judgments of the wrath of God, described in Revelation 14–19, will be worked out, paving the way for the final conflict of the Battle of Armageddon and the return of Christ as conquering King over all the earth.

26–27 The last two verses of the angel's explanation make it clear that a great day of judgment and destruction on the Beast's empire and on the whole wicked world will usher in the seating of the Son of Man on the throne of absolute sovereignty and the commencement of the fifth kingdom (of ch. 2) administered by his faithful believers. No unsubdued, rebellious elements will be left among the surviving inhabitants of earth; "the sovereignty, power and greatness of the kingdoms under the whole heaven" will be granted Messiah's people. Observe that here the followers of the

Son of Man are spoken of (v.27) as "the saints, the people of the Most High" (*'am qaddîšê 'elyônîn*), indicating that the Son of Man (v.13) is to be equated with the Most High himself. Observe also that a clear difference is made between the plural "saints" and the singular "him" in the final clause ("and all rulers will worship and obey him [*lēh*]"), the one who is called "the Most High" (*'elyônîn* being a plural of majesty, like the Heb. *'elōhîm*, "God"), whose kingdom will be an everlasting kingdom—words not applicable to a finite human being. Hence no possibility remains of equating the nation of "saints" with the "Son of Man" in v.13, there being a definite distinction here in v.27 between the Most High and his people.

The final verse (28) suggests the tremendous emotional drain on Daniel resulting from his extended interview with Heaven; in the presence of God's supernatural messenger, this Hebrew seer felt most keenly his weakness and inadequacy as a mortal (cf. Isa 6:5), even though he walked in fellowship with God by faith. Daniel's face paled (*zîway yištannôn 'alay* literally means "my facial hue was changing on me") because of his inward concern about the severe trials and afflictions awaiting his people. Yet these solemn disclosures from God were not proper matters for him to divulge to anyone else, he felt; and so apart from writing them down, he kept them to himself. Thus he lacked the solace of a human confidant. No wonder he found the burden of this secret knowledge oppressive.

VIII. The Grecian Conquest of Persia and the Tyranny of Antiochus Epiphanes (8:1–27)

With chapter 8 there is a shift of language from Aramaic (used in chs. 2–7) to Hebrew, used throughout the remainder of the book. The choice between the two languages was apparently made on the basis of subject matter and the audience these various portions of Daniel's memoirs were intended for (cf. Introduction: Languages).

1. *The Vision of the Ram, the He-Goat, and the Little Horn*

8:1–12

[1]In the third year of King Belshazzar's reign, I, Daniel, had a vision, after the one that had already appeared to me. [2]In my vision I saw myself in the citadel of Susa in the province of Elam; in the vision I was beside the Ulai Canal. [3]I looked up, and there before me was a ram with two horns, standing beside the canal, and the horns were long. One of the horns was longer than the other but grew up later. [4]I watched the ram as he charged toward the west and the north and the south. No animal could stand against him, and none could rescue from his power. He did as he pleased and became great.

[5]As I was thinking about this, suddenly a goat with a prominent horn between his eyes came from the west, crossing the whole earth without touching the ground. [6]He came toward the two-horned ram I had seen standing beside the canal and charged at him in great rage. [7]I saw him attack the ram furiously, striking the ram and shattering his two horns. The ram was powerless to stand against him; the goat knocked him to the ground and trampled on him, and none could rescue the ram from his power. [8]The goat became very great, but at the height of his power his large horn was broken off, and in its place four prominent horns grew up toward the four winds of heaven.

[9]Out of one of them came another horn, which started small but grew in power to the south and to the east and toward the Beautiful Land. [10]It grew until it reached the host of the heavens, and it threw some of the starry host down to the earth and trampled on them. [11]It set itself up to be as great as the Prince of the

host; it took away the daily sacrifice from him, and the place of his sanctuary was brought low. [12]Because of rebellion, the host ⌞of the saints⌟ and the daily sacrifice were given over to it. It prospered in everything it did, and truth was thrown to the ground.

1 This revelation came in the "third year of King Belshazzar." This, however, does not yield us a firm basis for precise dating (cf. comment at 7:1). If Belshazzar was appointed viceroy in 553, the "third year" would have come out to 550; but we cannot be certain that his appointment did not come a few years later. At any rate, this vision was granted Daniel two years after the previous one (cf. 7:1). It somewhat resembles it in subject matter and in manner of presentation, for it too portrays successive world empires as fierce beasts; and it also culminates in a tyrant described as a "little horn." Yet there are significant differences in detail as between the two chapters, especially regarding the third and the fourth kingdoms.

2 Daniel received this new vision either at the Babylonian capital itself or else while on a diplomatic mission to Susa, the capital of Elam. It is not quite clear what the political status of Elam (or Susiana, as it later came to be called) was at this time. Evidently at one time it maintained its independence of both the Babylonian and the Median empires. But after Cyrus's victory over Astyages in 550 B.C., it is quite probable that Elam came under vassalage to Persia—if not immediate incorporation as one of its provinces. At this earlier period, Nabonidus's policy toward Cyrus was friendly and cooperative, since he gave promise of weakening the power of the Medes, the Persians' traditional rivals. But soon after the Persians had made a close merger with the Medes, the Babylonians had reason to fear them even more than before. Nabonidus therefore began to make secret overtures to Croesus of Lydia and the government of Egypt under Dynasty XXVI, hoping to forge a triple alliance against the dangerous aggressiveness of Cyrus the Great. A trusted old minister like Daniel might have been sent to Susa to carry on some delicate negotiations in the Babylonian interest. On the other hand, since Belshazzar seems to have been personally unacquainted with Daniel (cf. 5:13), it is less likely that he was an official envoy from the court of Babylon. Nabonidus would hardly have sent him in so responsible a capacity without prior concurrence on the part of Belshazzar, his son. If, therefore, Daniel was in Susa on state business of some sort, he would have been in a humbler capacity than that of ambassador. On the other hand, Daniel may well have had this vision in Babylon itself, even though the setting of the dream was in Susa.

Verse 2 goes on to state that the scene Daniel saw in the vision was not Susa proper but rather the Ulai, a wide artificial canal connecting the Choaspes (mod. Kerkha) River with the Coprates (mod. Abdizful) River, which flowed not too far from the city itself. He saw himself standing on the bank of this canal. Appropriately enough, this furnished the setting for the rise of the beast representing Persia.

3 This verse presents the Medo-Persian power in the form of a large, powerful ram with two formidable horns. Though one of the horns was larger than the other, the horn that "grew up later" outstripped the former in size. Obviously this refers to the domination of the Persian power over the Median in the federated Medo-Persian Empire that was even then being formed (cf. 7:5, the bear "raised up on one of its sides"). The larger horn came later, even as Cyrus and his Persians came later than Cyaxeres and Astyages of Media.

4 The three general areas of Medo-Persian expansion were westward (toward Lydia, Ionia, Thrace, and Macedon), northward (toward the Caspians of the Caucasus Range and the Scythians east of the Caspian Sea and the Oxus Valley all the way up to the Aral Sea), and southward (toward the Babylonian Empire and later to Egypt itself). During the initial phase of conquest, the Medo-Persian troops were nearly invincible (except for Cyrus's last campaign against Queen Tomyris of the Scythians); hence the various beasts representing the surrounding nations opposing Persian expansion are described as helpless to withstand the fierce charges of the mighty ram. Cyrus had everything his own way and became arrogant over his universal success, as did his successors till the debacle of Salamis (480 B.C.) and Plataea (479) in Xerxes' invasion of Greece. But the term *higdîl* ("he . . . became great") carries with it the sinister suggestion that his overweening pride was ripe for a fall.

5–7 Verse 5 foretells coming disaster for Cyrus in the figure of an amazingly swift, one-horned goat that with one mighty charge shatters the horns of the Medo-Persian ram. First, the goat is described as coming from the west, that is, from the region of Macedonia and Greece (as Alexander the Great did in 334 B.C., when he won the Battle of Granicus in Asia Minor). Second, he moves so fast that his hooves barely touch the ground as he charges all the way to the eastern limit of the Persian domain ("crossing the whole earth"). Third, this irresistible invading force is to be under the leadership of one man, rather than under a coalition of nations, as the Persians had been. In vain the ram attempts to withstand the charge of the goat (v.6), as the goat hurls himself against the ram—an implied prediction that the Macedonian-Greek forces would launch an unprovoked invasion such as took place in 334. The completeness of Alexander's victories at Granicus (334), Issus (333), and the final contest at Arbela (331) is fittingly prefigured by this crushing attack on the ram, who is unable to resist (v.7). Alexander's conquest of the entire Near and Middle East within three years stands unique in military history and is appropriately portrayed by the lightning speed of this one-horned goat. Despite the immense numerical superiority of the Persian imperial forces and their possession of military equipment like war elephants, the tactical genius of young Alexander, with his disciplined Macedonian phalanx, proved decisive.

8 This verse may suggest Alexander's thrust beyond the borders of the empire he had conquered—"the goat became very great"—even into Afghanistan and the Indus Valley, as he did in 327 B.C. Or else *higdîl* ("became great") may suggest the growth in arrogance that led him to assume the pretensions to divinity that distressed his Macedonian troops, who finally mutinied against any further advances into northwest India. In support of his pretensions to descend from Zeus-Ammon, which had been solemnly announced by the Egyptian priesthood after his liberation of Egypt from Persian tyranny, Alexander had required even his comrades-in-arms to prostrate themselves before him, in conformity with Oriental custom. In accord with his newly conceived imperial policy of granting equality to his Persian subjects along with his victorious Macedonian-Greek supporters, he went so far as to take the Persian princess Roxana as his queen and to designate his future son by her, Alexander IV, as his successor to the Greco-Persian Empire.

Yet, as v.8 goes on to predict, "at the height of his [the goat's] power his large horn was broken off"; i.e., he died of a sudden fever brought on by dissipation (though rumor had it that he was actually poisoned by Cassander, the son of Antipater, viceroy of Macedonia) at Babylon in 323, at the age of thirty-three. Although efforts were made to hold the empire together—first by Antipater himself as regent for little Alexander IV (and for Philip III Arrhidaeus, his half-witted uncle), and then, after Antipater's death in 319, by Antigonus Monopthalmus, another highly respected general—the ambitions of such regional commanders as Ptolemy in Egypt, Seleucus in Babylonia, Lysimachus in Thrace and Asia Minor, and Cassander in Macedonia-Greece made this impossible. By 311 Seleucus asserted his claim to independent rule in Babylon, and the other three followed suit about the same time. Despite the earnest efforts of Antigonus and his brilliant son, Demetrius Poliorcetes, to subdue these separatist leaders, the final conflict at Ipsus in 301 resulted in defeat and death for Antigonus and the validation of the claims of the four Diadochi to complete independence from all central authority.

Verse 8 goes on to say that "in its [the large horn's] place four prominent horns grew up toward the four winds of heaven." This was fulfilled when Cassander retained his hold on Macedonia and Greece; Lysimachus held Thrace and the western half of Asia Minor as far as Cappadocia and Phrygia; Ptolemy consolidated Palestine, Cilicia, and Cyprus with his Egyptian-Libyan domains; and Seleucus controlled the rest of Asia all the way to the Indus Valley. While it is true that various vicissitudes beset these four realms during the third century and after (Pergamum, Bithynia, and Pontus achieved local independence in Asia Minor after the death of Lysimachus; and the eastern provinces of the Seleucid Empire achieved sovereignty as the kingdoms of Bactria and Parthia), nevertheless the initial division of Alexander's empire was unquestionably fourfold, as this verse and also 7:6, with its reference to the four-winged leopard, indicate.

9–10 Verses 9–12 foretell the rise of a "small horn" (v.9) from the midst of these four horns of the Diadochi. It is described as attaining success in aggression against the "south" (*hannegeḇ*), or the domains of the Ptolemies in Egypt. This evidently refers to the career of Antiochus IV Epiphanes ("the Manifest/Conspicuous One"), who usurped the Seleucid throne from his nephew (son of his older brother, Seleucus IV) and succeeded in invading Egypt 170–169 B.C. His expeditions against rebellious elements in Parthia and Armenia were initially successful "to the east" as well, and his determination to impose religious and cultural uniformity on all his domains led to a brutal suppression of Jewish worship at Jerusalem and generally throughout Palestine (here referred to as "the Beautiful Land" [*haṣṣebî*, "glory," "adornment," "pride," apparently abbreviated from *'ereṣ-haṣṣᵉbî* (11:16, 41), "the land of adornment," or "of glory"]). This suppression came to a head in December 168 B.C., when Antiochus returned in frustration from Alexandria, where he had been turned back by the Roman commander Popilius Laenas, and vented his exasperation on the Jews. He sent his general, Apollonius, with twenty thousand troops under orders to seize Jerusalem on a Sabbath. There he erected an idol of Zeus and desecrated the altar by offering swine on it. This idol became known to the Jews as "the abomination of desolation" (*haššiqqûṣ mᵉšōmēm*, 11:31), which served as a type of a future abomination that will be set up in the Jerusalem sanctuary to be built in the last days (cf. Christ's prediction in Matt 24:15).

Excursus

At this point some observations are in order concerning the relationship between the "little horn" (*qeren-'aḥaṯ miṣṣᵉʿîrâ*, lit., "a horn from a small one") in this passage (8:9) and the "little horn" in the previous chapter (7:8). The horn in chapter 7 emerged from the ten horns of the fourth beast, whereas this horn in 8:9 arises from the four-horned beast that represents the third kingdom, the empire of Alexander and his Epigonoi (as critics of every persuasion agree). Now since the author of Daniel lays great emphasis on numbers and invests them with high significance, there is no possibility that he could have meant to equate a ten-horned beast with one bearing only four horns. The only really plausible explanation, therefore, is that the little horn arising from the third kingdom serves as a prototype of the little horn of the fourth kingdom. The crisis destined to confront God's people in the time of the earlier little horn, Antiochus Epiphanes, will bear a strong similarity to the crisis that will befall them in the eschatological or final phase of the fourth kingdom in the last days (as Christ himself foresaw in the Olivet Discourse [Matt 24:15]). In each case a determined effort will be made by a ruthless dictator to suppress completely the biblical faith and the worship of the one true God. Rather than concluding, as the Maccabean date hypothesis insists, that the little horn of chapter 7 is also intended as a prophecy of Antiochus Epiphanes (with a resultant identification of the fourth kingdom as the Greek or Seleucid Empire), we are to understand the relationship between the little horn of the Greek Empire and that of the latter-day fourth kingdom to be that of type and antitype similar to that between Joshua and Jesus (Heb 4:8) and Melchizedek and Christ (Heb 7). In Daniel 11, as we shall see, both the typical little horn (Antiochus) and the antitypical little horn appear in succession, the transition from the one to the other taking place at 11:40, after which are predicted the circumstances of the destined death of the antitype that were not at all true of Antiochus Epiphanes himself. Therefore, the two figures cannot be identical, nor can the Greek Empire be equated with the fourth kingdom of Daniel's prophetic scheme.

Continuing on with the predicted career of Antiochus (v.10), we encounter the remarkable statement that he will grow up to "the host of heaven" and will throw "some of the starry host down to the earth," where he will "trample on them." The "host" (*ṣāḇā'*) is a term most often used of the armies of angels in the service of God (esp. in the frequent title *YHWH ṣᵉḇā'ôṯ*, "Yahweh of hosts"), or else of the stars in heaven (cf. Jer 33:22). But it is also used of the people of God, who are to become as the stars in number (Gen 12:3; 15:5) and in Exodus 12:41 are spoken of as "the hosts of Yahweh" (NIV, "the LORD's divisions") who went out of the land of Egypt. Daniel 12:3 states that true believers (*hammaśkîlîm*, "those who are wise") "will shine like the brightness of the heavens [*kôḵāḇîm*, lit., 'stars'—the same term used here in v.10] for ever and ever." Now since the Greek tyrant can hardly affect either the angels of heaven or the literal stars in the sky, it is quite evident that the phrase "the host of the heavens" must refer to those Jewish believers that will join the Maccabees in defending their faith and liberty. It is then implied here that Antiochus will cut down and destroy many of the Jews during the time of tribulation he will bring on them, when he will have "trampled on them."

From 171 or 170 B.C. and thereafter, Antiochus pursued his evil policy of securing control of the high priesthood and bringing increasing pressure on the Jewish hierarchy to surrender their religious loyalties in the interests of conformity to Greek culture and idolatry. Already in 175, at the beginning of his reign, he had expelled the godly high priest Onias III from office and replaced him with his Hellenizing younger brother, Jason. But before long a certain Jew named Menelaus, who was apparently also of the high priestly family, bribed Antiochus to depose Jason and appoint him high priest in his place. But while Antiochus was successfully campaigning in Egypt against Ptolemy VII (181–145 B.C.), Jason laid siege to Jerusalem in the hope of ousting Menelaus. In the process of dealing subsequently with Jason, Antiochus took occasion to storm Jerusalem and pillage the temple itself. Reinstalling Menelaus as high priest, Antiochus gave him the mandate to continue an aggressive policy of Hellenization. But in December of 168 (cf. above), he had Jerusalem again seized by treachery and subjected it to prolonged looting and massacre, as he converted its sanctuary into a temple to Zeus. So it continued until that memorable day, three years later, when Judas Maccabaeus rededicated the sacred structure to the worship of God (25 Dec. 165 B.C.), an event celebrated as Hanukkah by the Jewish community ever since.

11 This verse describes how the megalomania of Antiochus will advance to such extremes that he will declare himself equal with God (who is here referred to as *śar-haṣṣāḇā'*, "Prince of the host," i.e., the Lord of the army of saints referred to in the previous verse). He will halt the regular morning and evening sacrifice (*hattāmîḏ*). (This *tāmîḏ*—or *'ōlaṯ-hattāmîḏ,* "the burnt offering of continuity"—was the standard daily burnt offering ordained in Num 28:3, consisting of one lamb presented at sunrise and one presented at sunset, together with a quantity of flour and oil [Num 28:5].) This offering presented the atonement of the believing nation, whether or not any other sacrifice was brought before the Lord on that particular day. But the Seleucid tyrant commanded these offerings to be suspended in 168 and substituted a heathen sacrifice presented to an idol of Zeus, after the altar of Yahweh had been destroyed and his temple pillaged and desecrated ("and the place of his sanctuary [*m*ᵉ*ḵôn miqdāšô*] was brought low").

12 Judah's three-year tribulation period, during which the temple would be defiled and prostituted to heathen use, is now described. The host of Jewish believers will be "given over" (*tinnāṯēn*)—viz., to the oppression of Antiochus—along with, or possibly on account of, the continual burnt offering because of transgression; and it (the little horn) will cast truth to the ground and perform its work and prosper. (NIV translates this as a simple past rather than as a prophetic perfect.) This indicates that Antiochus will be successful for that brief interval and will have everything his own way. The phrase *'al-hattāmîḏ* is somewhat ambiguous on account of the versatility of the preposition *'al* before *hattāmîḏ;* it may mean "concerning" (which clearly does not fit here) or "in addition to," "along with" the regular burnt offering (NIV, "daily sacrifice") or else "because of" (NIV). But since the preposition *b*ᵉ before *peša'* ("transgression," "rebellion") seems to indicate the cause of this dreadful humiliation of Israel, it seems best to render *'al* as "along with" (so NASB; Young has "together with," likewise Wood). Therefore the verse as a whole should be interpreted as follows:

> And on account of transgression [presumably the transgression of Jason and Menelaus and the pro-Syrian faction among the worldly minded Jews of the Maccabean period] the host [of God's people, the Jewish believers] will be given

up [to the persecuting power of Antiochus IV] along with the [suspended] continual burnt offering; and the horn [Antiochus] will fling the truth [of the scriptural faith and service of God] to the ground [by forbidding it on the pain of death], and he will perform [his will, or carry out his program of enforcing idolatry] and will [for the three-year period] prosper.

Notes

---

2 It is also possible that Daniel saw this vision in Babylonia, even though its setting was in Susa. Ezekiel had visions of scenes in Jerusalem (Ezek 8–10) even though he was a thousand miles away in Tel Abib. Nevertheless, it is hard to account for the setting by the Ulai unless Daniel was physically present in Susa or its environs.

3 Ford (p. 134) has this interesting sidelight on the symbolism of the ram: "In Ezek. 34:17–22; 39:18, the ram is a symbol of princely power, and ancient records declare that the king of Persia, when at the head of his army, bore in the place of a crown the head of a ram. The same figure is frequently found on Persian seals." This helps establish that rather than an earlier, separate Median Empire, as the Maccabean date hypothesis demands, it was the united Medo-Persian Empire that was represented by a ram during the Achaemenid dynasty.

10 In Zech 9:13 we find a clear reference to the coming victory of the Jewish patriots over their Greek overlords:

> I will bend Judah as I bend my bow
> and fill it with Ephraim [as the arrow
> fills the bow that shoots it].
> I will rouse your sons, O Zion,
> against your sons, O Greece,
> and make you like a warrior's sword.

The three following verses go on to indicate God's special intervention on their behalf, in terms reminiscent of his triumph over the allied Canaanites when Joshua fought the Battle of Gibeon. Verse 16 is particularly noteworthy:

> The LORD their God will save them on that day
> as the flock of his people.
> They will sparkle in his land
> like jewels in a crown.

This strongly suggests that God favored and blessed the Maccabean cause and highly esteemed their valiant leaders as "jewels" in his land. In the light of this passage, we are justified in regarding them as "the host of the heavens" referred to in Dan 8:10. Observe that מִן (*min*, "some") is used partitively before הַצָּבָא (*haṣṣāḇā'*, "host") and before הַכּוֹכָבִים (*hakkôḵāḇîm*, "the stars"; NIV, "starry host")—i.e., "some of the host, even some of the stars"; cf. 12:3.

12 An additional comment should be made about פֶּשַׁע (*peša'*). The basic idea of the root *pāša'* is "rebel against." We may legitimately infer that revolt against the authority of God is the fundamental thrust of this word. Nevertheless, there is no clear or undisputed case where the noun *peša'* (in contradistinction to the verb *pāša'*) actually means "rebellion." BDB defines it as "punishment for transgression" in this passage and nowhere else construes it to mean "rebellion," only "transgression." Gesenius-Buhl (*Hebräisches und aramaisches Handwörterbuch*) gives the rendering "transgression," "crime" and for this passage adds the comment: "the culmination of heathen sins." F. Zorell and L. Semkowski, edd.,

Lexicon Hebräicum et Aramaicum Veteris Testamenti (Rome, 1940), define it as "a sacrifice for sins" in this passage and in general as "sin," "crime," "offense," "legal violation"—none of which mean "rebellion." Only KB gives it as "rebellion," "revolt," which probably accounts for NIV's choice of "rebellion." But despite its etymology, it is highly dubious that it carries over the original idea in actual usage as a noun. KJV, RSV, ASV, NASB all translate it as "transgression"; Vulgate, LXX, and Theodotion understand it as meaning "sin" or "sins."

---

2. *Gabriel's Interpretation of the Vision*

8:13–27

13Then I heard a holy one speaking, and another holy one said to him, "How long will it take for the vision to be fulfilled—the vision concerning the daily sacrifice, the rebellion that causes desolation, and the surrender of the sanctuary and of the host that will be trampled underfoot?"

14He said to me, "It will take 2,300 evenings and mornings; then the sanctuary will be reconsecrated."

15While I, Daniel, was watching the vision and trying to understand it, there
before me stood one who looked like a man. 16And I heard a man's voice from the
Ulai calling, "Gabriel, tell this man the meaning of the vision."

17As he came near the place where I was standing, I was terrified and fell prostrate. "Son of man," he said to me, "understand that the vision concerns the time of the end."

18While he was speaking to me, I was in a deep sleep, with my face to the ground. Then he touched me and raised me to my feet.

19He said: "I am going to tell you what will happen later in the time of wrath,
because the vision concerns the appointed time of the end. 20The two-horned ram
that you saw represents the kings of Media and Persia. 21The shaggy goat is the
king of Greece, and the large horn between his eyes is the first king. 22The four
horns that replaced the one that was broken off represent four kingdoms that will emerge from his nation but will not have the same power.

23"In the latter part of their reign, when rebels have become completely wicked,
a stern-faced king, a master of intrigue, will arise. 24He will become very strong,
but not by his own power. He will cause astounding devastation and will succeed
in whatever he does. He will destroy the mighty men and the holy people. 25He
will cause deceit to prosper, and he will consider himself superior. When they feel secure, he will destroy many and take his stand against the Prince of princes. Yet he will be destroyed, but not by human power.

26"The vision of the evenings and mornings that has been given you is true, but seal up the vision, for it concerns the distant future."

27I, Daniel, was exhausted and lay ill for several days. Then I got up and went about the king's business. I was appalled by the vision; it was beyond understanding.

13–14 Verse 13 states that there were two or possibly even three "holy ones" (*qādôš*, "holy one," in this instance being clearly a heavenly being rather than a sanctified human believer) involved in a conversation about the prophetic meaning of the vision just described. Apparently it was the second angel ("another holy one") who posed the question to the third (*lappalmônî hamᵉdabbēr*, "that particular one who was speaking"; NIV, "to him") as to the duration of the terrible period during which the temple and altar of the Lord would be desecrated, as suggested by the words of v.11: "And it took away the daily sacrifice from him, and the place of his sanctuary was brought low." The answer given in v.14 by the third angel was that this condition would last for "2,300 evenings and mornings" (*'aḏ 'ereḇ bōqer 'alpayîm ûšᵉlōš mē'ôṯ*).

This apparently precise period of time has been understood by interpreters in two different ways, either as 2,300 twenty-four-hour days (understanding *'ereḇ bōqer,* "evening morning," as indicating an entire day from sunset to sunset, like the similar expression in Gen 1), or else as 1,150 days composed of 1,150 evenings and 1,150 mornings. In other words, the interval would either be 6 years and 111 days, or else half of that time: 3 years and 55 days. Both views have persuasive advocates, but the preponderance of evidence seems to favor the latter interpretation. The context speaks of the suspension of the *tāmîḏ* ("sacrifice"), a reference to the *'ōlaṯ tāmîḏ* ("continual burnt offering") that was offered regularly each morning and evening (or, as the Hebrews would reckon it, each evening, when the new day began, and each morning). Surely there could have been no other reason for the compound expression *'ereḇ bōqer* than the reference to the two sacrifices that marked each day in temple worship.

Wood's suggestion (p. 218) that *tāmîḏ* referred to *all* the ceremonial observances in general rather than to this one in particular is belied by the fact that the lexicons record no use of *tāmîḏ* alone in a cultic context except as an abbreviation for *'ōlaṯ tāmîḏ,* which is defined as a twice-a-day observance in Exodus 29:42, and is thus used at least sixteen times in Numbers alone (esp. chs. 28–29). Consequently we are to understand v.14 as predicting the rededication of the temple by Judas Maccabaeus on 25 Chislev (or 14 December) 164 B.C.; 1,150 days before that would point to a *terminus a quo* of three years, one month, and 25 days earlier, or in Tishri 167 B.C. While the actual erection of the idolatrous altar in the temple took place in Chislev 167, or one month and 15 days later, there is no reason to suppose that Antiochus Epiphanes' administrators may not have abolished the offering of the *tāmîḏ* itself at that earlier date. (Delitzsch [KD, *Daniel,* p. 302] favors this view; so also does Aalders, p. 165.)

Keil himself (KD, *Daniel,* p. 304) insists that the 2,300 evening-mornings would only be understood by the Hebrew reader as a locution for 2,300 days (likewise Wood, p. 219). But none of the scholars espousing this view can give any convincing explanation as to why this peculiar expression should have been used here for "day." Moreover, there is not the slightest historical ground for a *terminus a quo* beginning in 171 B.C. While it is true that the interloper Menelaus murdered the legitimate high priest Onias III in that year, there was no abridgement of temple services at that early date. It was not till the following year that Antiochus looted the temple of its treasure, and the abolition of the *tāmîḏ* (predicted here in v.12) did not take place till 167. Keil objects to the 165 date for the *terminus ad quem* and suggests that we should rather look for it in the defeat of Nicanor at Adasa in 161 B.C. (overlooking the fact that one month after that victory Judas fell in a disastrous conflict with Bacchides [1 Macc 9:1–22]). Verse 14 simply specifies that when the 2,300 evenings and mornings have elapsed, "then the sanctuary will be reconsecrated." That certainly is what happened when the first Hanukkah was celebrated on 25 Chislev 164.

15–18 These verses describe the awesome confrontation between Daniel and the angel Gabriel, who is here named for the first time (v.16). Some other heavenly being, not otherwise specified, commissioned Gabriel—who later appeared to the Virgin Mary to announce the coming of Jesus—to explain the meaning of the vision to the swooning prophet (v.17). Gabriel was instructed to identify the coming world empires and the climactic events of the "time of the end" (*'eṯ-qēṣ*). The overwhelming splendor of Gabriel's presence affected Daniel somewhat as John on Patmos was to be affected by the angelic appearance (Rev 22:8); Daniel was rendered completely helpless and unable even to speak (v.18). Yet the angel's transforming touch restored Daniel to consciousness.

19–22 This passage furnishes a general summary of the rise of the second kingdom (here explicitly named as Medo-Persian) and of the third kingdom (Greece). Gabriel gave no details about the Persian era beyond indicating its compound character as Medo-Persian (v.20). But he did identify the large single horn between the goat's eyes as the first king of the Greek Empire (v.21). This mighty conquerer was soon replaced by four other horns (v.22), which (cf. comment at 7:8) were the Diadochi who took over Macedon-Greece, Thrace-Asia Minor, Egypt-Palestine, and Syria-Persia. He added that none of these four would "have the same power" (i.e., of Alexander). History, of course, proved this true.

23–25 This passage depicts the rise of Antiochus Epiphanes, who is described (v.23) as a "stern-faced king, a master of intrigue" (*mēḇîn ḥîḏôṯ* literally means "understanding hidden things," i.e., craftiness; Charles [in loc.] suggests "skilled in double dealing"), who will at first enjoy much success (v.24). He will manage to crush "mighty men" (presumably nobles and regional commanders of his own realm who supported rival claimants to the throne) and also "the holy people," i.e., the believing Jews.

Two noteworthy traits will characterize Antiochus's rule: (1) his treachery and intrigue (v.25), in order to catch his victims unawares and unprepared (as he did in Jerusalem in 168–167 B.C.); (2) his overweening pride, which led him to claim divine honors (v.25). In fulfillment of this, the coins of Antiochus actually bore the title *theos epiphanēs* ("God manifest"). This clearly exhibited his character as the typical "little horn," a model for the antitypical "little horn" referred to in 7:8 ("this horn had eyes like the eyes of a man and a mouth that spoke boastfully"). We are reminded of 2 Thessalonians 2:3–4, which states that the Day of the Lord will not come "until the rebellion occurs and the man of lawlessness is revealed, the man doomed to destruction. He opposes and exalts himself over everything that is called God or is worshiped, and even sets himself up in God's temple, proclaiming himself to be God."

While we are not definitely told whether Antiochus made a formal claim to deity while enthroned in splendor in the court of the Jerusalem temple, he certainly did assume the right to determine what gods his subjects should worship, feeling that he was the earthly embodiment of the powers of heaven and that all rule and authority was given him. Like Nebuchadnezzar, he expected all his subjects to bow down to the great image he had set up. But he went even beyond Nebuchadnezzar in trying to abolish the ancestral religion of the Jews, forbidding them on pain of death to circumcise their children and making the possession of the Hebrew Scriptures a capital offense. By erecting the statue of Zeus Olympius (or Capitolinus) in the temple of Yahweh and sacrificing swine on the altar, he committed the greatest possible sacrilege and affront to the Jewish people.

Yet v.25 predicts Antiochus's sudden desruction, not by human means, but by God's intervention. As a condign penalty for having taken "his stand against the Prince of princes" (the Lord God Almighty), Antiochus would be removed from the scene. He was. After making an unsuccessful attempt to pillage Nanaea, a wealthy temple in Elymais, he died of a sudden malady.

Ancient sources have somewhat diverse accounts of Antiochus's fatal illness. First Maccabees 6:4, 8–16 says that he withdrew to Babylon after his repulse at Elymais, that he became deathly ill after hearing of the victories of Judas Maccabaeus, and that he died many days later. Second Maccabees 9:1–28, however, states that Antiochus had attempted to raid a temple in Persepolis (rather than Elymais), and that it was at Ecbatana that he heard the disturbing news of the Maccabean victories. Then, as he was uttering dire threats of reprisal against them, he was seized with severe abdominal pains that never left him; and thus he fell out of the chariot in which he was riding. Finally, as a result of his severe injuries from the fall and the attack of worms on his bowels, accompanied by a revolting stench, he finally died with vain petitions on his lips, imploring the God of Israel to spare his life. Josephus affirms that it was the temple of Artemis that Antiochus attacked in Elymais (as in 1 Macc 6) and then follows in general the description of 2 Maccabees 9 in regard to the fatal illness and the final admission of wrong in opposing the God of the Hebrews (cf. Antiq. XII, 354–59 [ix.1]). At all events, these accounts agree in stating that the tyrant met his end by a nonhuman agency, whether by a chariot fall, by abdominal cancer, or by some other illness. (Roger Simpson [EBr, 14th ed., 2:77] suggests that Antiochus died of "consumption" in Gabae, or Isfahan, in Persia.) This question of the place and manner of Antiochus's death becomes a matter of special importance in 11:45.

26–27 The close of chapter 8 contains Gabriel's command (v.26) for Daniel to keep confidential ("seal up") the predictions just revealed to him because they are related to "the distant future." Hence Daniel recorded them in Hebrew, rather than in the Aramaic of chapters 2–7. This may well have been the reason why the subsequent chapters of Daniel were also written in Hebrew. Certainly 12:9 contains the same injunction or principle of secrecy: "The words are closed up and sealed until the time of the end." It is also significant that Gabriel states that the vision refers to "many days" (*yāmîn rabbîm*), i.e., to many years in the future. (NIV's "distant future" is somewhat inexact; certainly it should not be pressed to refer to the last days just before the Lord's return. The "many days" in this case obviously refers to the crisis years of 167–164 B.C.) Verse 27 describes the emotional strain the prophet felt following this encounter with the angel Gabriel. It drained him to the point of illness for several days. Even after he went back to the king's service, he kept brooding over the vision and its fulfillment: "I was appalled by the vision; it was beyond understanding." Perhaps what most disturbed Daniel was the prediction of the time of great tribulation appointed for the true people of God under the tyranny of the "little horn." He may well have been puzzled about why Yahweh would permit even this brief time of brutal oppression under the little horn.

Notes

17 Wood (pp. 221–24) argues for a strong eschatological overtone in vv.17–26, interpreting עֶת־קֵץ (*'eṯ-qēṣ*, "time of the end") in v.17 and מוֹעֵד קֵץ (*mô'ēḏ qēṣ*, "appointed time of the end") in v.19 as referring to the Great Tribulation rather than to the persecutions of Antiochus Epiphanes. He urges that 167–164 B.C. could hardly be conceived of as "the

time of the end," when Christ had not yet been crucified and the church had not yet been established on a NT basis. He then moderates his interpretation constructively (p. 223): "An answer is called for which takes into account all of these questions. . . . It sees the angel Gabriel as now giving the meaning of the vision by showing, not only the significance involving Antiochus of ancient history, but also that of the one whom Antiochus foreshadowed, the Antichrist of future history. That is, Antiochus' oppression is seen to provide a partial fulfilment of the prophetic vision, but that of the Antichrist the complete fulfilment." This interpretation has much to commend it, for Daniel makes it clear through the assignment of the symbol of the "little horn" both to Antiochus of kingdom three and to Antichrist of the latter-day phase of kingdom four that they bear to each other the relationship of type-antitype. Insofar as Epiphanes prefigured the determined effort to be made by the Beast to destroy the biblical faith, that prophecy that described the career of Antiochus also pertained to "the time of the end." Every type has great relevance for its antitype. But the future dealings of Antichrist can only be conjectured or surmised. Therefore our discussion will be confined to the established deeds of Antiochus Epiphanes.

IX. The Vision of the Seventy Weeks (9:1–27)

1. *Daniel's Great Prayer*

9:1–19

1In the first year of Darius son of Xerxes (a Mede by descent), who was made
ruler over the Babylonian kingdom—2in the first year of his reign, I, Daniel, understood from the Scriptures, according to the word of the LORD given to Jeremiah the
prophet, that the desolation of Jerusalem would last seventy years. 3So I turned
to the Lord God and pleaded with him in prayer and petition, in fasting, and in
sackcloth and ashes.
4I prayed to the LORD my God and confessed:

"O Lord, the great and awesome God, who keeps his covenant of love with
all who love him and obey his commands, 5we have sinned and done wrong.
We have been wicked and have rebelled; we have turned away from your
commands and laws. 6We have not listened to your servants the prophets, who
spoke in your name to our kings, our princes and our fathers, and to all the
people of the land.
7"Lord, you are righteous, but this day we are covered with shame—the men
of Judah and people of Jerusalem and all Israel, both near and far, in all the
countries where you have scattered us because of our unfaithfulness to you. 8O
LORD, we and our kings, our princes and our fathers are covered with shame
because we have sinned against you. 9The Lord our God is merciful and forgiving, even though we have rebelled against him; 10we have not obeyed the LORD
our God or kept the laws he gave us through his servants the prophets. 11All
Israel has transgressed your law and turned away, refusing to obey you.
"Therefore the curses and sworn judgments written in the Law of Moses, the
servant of God, have been poured out on us, because we have sinned against
you. 12You have fulfilled the words spoken against us and against our rulers by
bringing upon us great disaster. Under the whole heaven nothing has ever
been done like what has been done to Jerusalem. 13Just as it is written in the
Law of Moses, all this disaster has come upon us, yet we have not sought the
favor of the LORD our God by turning from our sins and giving attention to your
truth. 14The LORD did not hesitate to bring the disaster upon us, for the LORD our
God is righteous in everything he does; yet we have not obeyed him.
15"Now, O Lord our God, who brought your people out of Egypt with a mighty
hand and who made for yourself a name that endures to this day, we have

sinned, we have done wrong. 16O Lord, in keeping with all your righteous acts, turn away your anger and your wrath from Jerusalem, your city, your holy hill. Our sins and the iniquities of our fathers have made Jerusalem and your people an object of scorn to all those around us.

17"Now, our God, hear the prayers and petitions of your servant. For your sake, O Lord, look with favor on your desolate sanctuary. 18Give ear, O God, and hear; open your eyes and see the desolation of the city that bears your Name. We do not make requests of you because we are righteous, but because of your great mercy. 19O Lord, listen! O Lord, forgive! O Lord, hear and act! For your sake, O my God, do not delay, because your city and your people bear your Name."

1–3 These verses show Daniel as a diligent student of Scripture who built his prayer life on the Word of God. It is significant that he included the written prophecies of Jeremiah as inspired Holy Scripture, even though Jeremiah had died only a few decades before (probably as a martyr in the Jewish refugee colony at Tahpanhes, Egypt). Even before any formal ecclesiastical endorsement had been accorded the Book of Jeremiah by an official council, Daniel recognized that Jeremiah's writings were inspired of God and therefore inherently trustworthy and dependable. As Daniel studied Jeremiah 25:11–13, he saw that God had appointed a period of seventy years for the captivity of Israel (v.2), at the end of which Babylon itself would be smitten by a God-directed stroke of judgment. Daniel was gripped by these words in Jeremiah 29:10: "When seventy years are completed for Babylon, I will come to you and fulfill my gracious promise to bring you back to this place [Jerusalem]."

"Seventy years?" Daniel asked himself, "When did those seventy years begin? How soon would they end?" Now since this episode (v.1) took place in 539 or 538 ("the first year of Darius son of Xerxes [Ahasuerus]"), less than fifty years had elapsed since the Fall of Jerusalem to Nebuchadnezzar (587 B.C.) or the destruction of the temple in 586. But for the earliest possible *terminus a quo* for the seventy years of exile, the year of Daniel's own captivity in Babylon (604 B.C.) would be the starting point for the seven decades. Now while 538 might be three or four years short of the full seventy, it was not too soon for Daniel to begin praying (v.3). In view of the recent collapse of the Chaldean Empire and the benevolent attitude of Cyrus the Great toward the religious preferences of his newly conquered subjects, Daniel was moved to claim the promise implied by the number seventy in the Jeremiah passages he had just read. So he implored the Lord God to reckon those years from the year of his own exile and to ensure the reestablishment of the Commonwealth of Israel in the Land of Promise by seventy years from the first Palestinian invasion of King Nebuchadnezzar.

Although this passage does not actually mention the predictions concerning King Cyrus that were revealed to Isaiah back in the early seventh century, during Manasseh's reign, it is fair to assume that Daniel knew about them. Isaiah 44:28 quotes Yahweh as saying:

> [I am the LORD,]
> who says of Cyrus [*kôreš*], "He is my shepherd
> and will accomplish all that I please;
> he will say of Jerusalem, 'Let it be rebuilt,'
> and of the temple, 'Let its foundations be laid.' "

Again, in 45:1–2, the Lord continues:

"This is what the LORD says to his anointed,
  to Cyrus, whose right hand I take hold of
to subdue nations before him
  and to strip kings of their armor,
to open doors before him
  so that gates will not be shut:
I will go before you."

Daniel must have been stirred when he first heard reports of the young king of Anshan, Persia, who brilliantly overthrew his uncle Astyages in battle and made himself master of the entire Medo-Persian domain. When Cyrus finally launched his invasion of Mesopotamia and laid siege to Babylon itself, Daniel's heart must have leaped at seeing prophecy being fulfilled. Now that Cyrus had indeed attained the success that the Lord had promised him years before, Daniel besought the Lord to move the conqueror's heart to let the Hebrew exiles return to their Promised Land. Isaiah had written (45:4):

"For the sake of Jacob my servant,
  of Israel my chosen,
I call you by name
  and bestow on you a title of honor,
  though you do not acknowledge me."

Isaiah then specified that Cyrus would set the captives free (45:13):

"I will raise up Cyrus in my righteousness:
  I will make all his ways straight.
He will rebuild my city
  and set my exiles free,
but not for a price or reward,
  says the LORD Almighty."

These were promises that Daniel could claim at this critical time in Israel's history.

4–6 Verses 4–19 teach us much about prayer and show how a true man of God should approach the Sovereign of the universe on behalf of his people. Striking is the spiritual preparation Daniel had made for this ministry of intercession: he had fasted, mourned, and clothed himself with sackcloth (v.3), so deep was his concern for the deliverance of his people and their restoration to God's favor. Daniel realized he could not urge on God any merit of his nation, for they had forfeited all claim to divine mercy. By their persistent transgression of their covenant with God, their embracing of heathen idolatry and immorality, and their martyrdom of the prophets sent to them by Yahweh (cf. 2 Chron 36:16), they had literally compelled him to bring on them the promised curses (i.e., Lev 26:39–45; Deut 28:45–63; 30:1–5). They had richly deserved the destruction of their cities and the loss of their property, freedom, and native land; and they lacked any ground of merit on which to entreat God's favor. The only basis for Daniel's approach to God was his earnest desire for God to glorify himself by displaying the riches of his mercy and grace in pardoning and restoring his guilty but repentant people to their land in fulfillment of his promise in Jeremiah 25 and 29.

With these convictions Daniel devoted himself to a prayer of adoration and confession (vv.4–6). It is significant that in this chapter Daniel for the first time used the sacred Tetragrammaton, the covenant name of Yahweh (tr. LORD, v.2 and the preamble of v.4). Even though he found himself exiled from the sacred soil of Israel, Daniel boldly claimed Yahweh's mercy as the covenant-keeping God of Israel. Although he addressed him as *'ᵃdōnāy* ("Lord") in the opening sentence of his prayer and in v.7, Daniel addressed him directly as Yahweh ("LORD") in v.8 and referred to him by the same covenant name in 10, 13, and 14.

In his first words (v.4), Daniel combined both aspects of God's nature, his sublime transcendence and his covenant-keeping grace. Daniel glorified him as the "great and awesome God" and yet also as the faithful, promise-keeping God who never forsakes those who love and obey him. Whatever may have been the grumbling and bitterness of the majority of the exiles over their terrible calamities, Daniel was clear on the holy love and absolute sovereignty of Yahweh. It was not because Yahweh did not care for his people that he allowed them to go down in utter defeat; nor was it because of his inability to withstand the power of the gods of Babylon. It was only because they had forced his hand by flagrant and shameless sin.

"We have sinned and done wrong" (v.5), Daniel confessed as the spokesman of his people. "We have been wicked [*hiršaʿ*nû implies a guilty, godless way of life] and have rebelled [*mārāḏnû*]; we have turned away from your commands and laws." Lured on by the rhetoric of those who had heaped scorn on the old taboos and outworn shibboleths of the past (as they considered the holy standards of the Torah), the Jews had succumbed to the pagan cultures by which they were surrounded. They were unwilling to repent at the rebuke and warning of God's prophets (v.6), like Isaiah and Jeremiah. The whole nation had become involved in rejecting the Lord; there remained such a small remnant of faithful believers that Judah was not worth saving from the coming destruction. Daniel could find no extenuation for their betrayal of their sacred trust.

7–11a This paragraph stresses the humiliation of the Hebrew people in the eyes of all the heathen. Back in the days of Moses, it was said of them: "For you are a people holy to the LORD your God. The LORD your God has chosen you out of all the peoples on the face of the earth to be his people, his treasured possession" (Deut 7:6). He had promised them military success so long as they remained faithful to him: "The LORD will grant that the enemies who rise up against you will be defeated before you" (Deut 28:7). They would enjoy the respect of all the nations around them: "Then all the peoples on earth will see that you are called by the name of the LORD, and they will fear you" (Deut 28:10). But now all that was reversed. From the time when King Josiah died at Megiddo (609 B.C.), the nation met with defeat by the Egyptians and the Babylonians. It was laid waste, and all its inhabitants were killed or exiled as slaves. Instead of respect from the pagan nations round about, the Jews became objects of scorn (vv.7–8), deprived of property and freedom, and derided for their claim to know the one true God. What made their disgrace even more shameful was their flagrant ingratitude toward their compassionate, forgiving God (v.9), whose pardon and mercy they ridiculed and rejected (vv.10–11a).

11b–14 In this paragraph Daniel exalted the justice of God in dealing with his people according to all his warnings and promises in the days of Moses (v.11b; cf. Deut 28–32). As Daniel put it: "You have fulfilled the words spoken against us and against our rulers by bringing upon us great disaster. . . . Just as it is written in the Law of Moses, all this disaster has come upon us, yet we have not sought the favor of the LORD our God by turning from our sins. . . . The LORD did not hesitate to bring the disaster upon us, for the LORD our God is righteous in everything that he does; yet we have not obeyed him" (vv.12–14).

To Daniel it was more important for the God of Israel to retain his integrity and uphold his moral law than for his guilty people to escape the consequences of their infidelity. Had God not fulfilled his word of judgment, little credence could be placed in his word of grace. If a nation like Judah, instructed so perfectly in the truth of God, could fall into idolatry and immorality and defy the Lord to punish them as he had promised to do, why should anyone obey the Almighty or believe in him? The Fall of Jerusalem, the destruction of the temple, and the removal of the nation from their ancestral soil—all this served to vindicate the holiness and righteousness of God and to demonstrate to all the world the sanctity of his moral law. As Israel's spokesman and intercessor, then, Daniel offered neither defense nor excuse for the guilt of his people. He freely admitted that they had only been punished as they deserved. He made no plea for a mitigation of their guilt and shame.

15–19 Daniel went on to appeal to God's pity on the exiled nation and her ruined city of Jerusalem (v.16). He based his appeal wholly on God's own honor and glory. "For your sake, O Lord, look with favor on your desolate sanctuary" (v.17). Like Moses in his prayer of intercession after the golden calf apostasy (Exod 32:12–13), Daniel was chiefly concerned about the tarnishing of God's reputation in the eyes of the world (vv.18–19). If Yahweh allowed his sanctuary and holy city to lie permanently in ruins and his people to remain in exile, then who among the surrounding nations would believe that the God of the Bible was the true and holy Sovereign over all the universe? "Give ear, O God, and hear. . . . For your sake, O my God, do not delay, because your city and your people bear your Name" (vv.18–19). That, in Daniel's mind, was the worst thing about the tragedy of Jerusalem's fall and the captivity of Judah—all the pagans would surely conclude that it was because of Yahweh's inability to protect his people against the might of Babylon's gods that Israel had fallen and had been driven out of her ancestral soil.

Certainly a deity who could not preserve his own temple from Nebuchadnezzar's troops was no match for Marduk or Nebo. It was this reproach that had befallen the name of Yahweh and had tarnished his glory before the idol-worshiping world that so distressed Daniel's heart. Moreover, since God had freely promised full pardon and restoration to his repentant people, the prophet felt emboldened to press the Lord as hard as he could for an early return of the Jewish captives to Palestine, that a new commonwealth of chastened believers might be established there and a testimony set up again for the one true God, the holy Sovereign of the universe. Because of the purity of his motives and the earnestness of his desire, Daniel was heard and soon received his answer through Gabriel, the same angel who had spoken to him before.

Notes

3 Cyrus's kindly attitude toward the oppressed peoples of the Chaldean Empire is confirmed in ANET (p. 316), where Cyrus is quoted as saying: "As to the region from . . . as far as Ashur and Susa, Agade, Eshnunna . . . as well as the region of the Gutians, I returned to [these] sacred cities on the other side of the Tigris, the sanctuaries of which have been in ruins for a long time, the images which [used to] live therein and established for them permanent sanctuaries. I [also] gathered all their [former] inhabitants and returned [to them] their habitations." The parallels with the decree of Cyrus recorded in 2 Chron 36:23 and Ezra 1:2–4 are also significant.

2. *The Divine Answer: Seventy Heptads of Years*

9:20–27

[20]While I was speaking and praying, confessing my sin and the sin of my people Israel and making my request to the LORD my God for his holy hill—[21]while I was still in prayer, Gabriel, the man I had seen in the earlier vision, came to me in swift flight about the time of the evening sacrifice. [22]He instructed me and said to me, "Daniel, I have now come to give you insight and understanding. [23]As soon as you began to pray, an answer was given, which I have come to tell you, for you are highly esteemed. Therefore, consider the message and understand the vision:

[24]"Seventy 'sevens' are decreed for your people and your holy city to finish transgression, to put an end to sin, to atone for wickedness, to bring in everlasting righteousness, to seal up vision and prophecy and to anoint the most holy.

[25]"Know and understand this: From the issuing of the decree to restore and rebuild Jerusalem until the Anointed One, the ruler, comes, there will be seven 'sevens,' and sixty-two 'sevens.' It will be rebuilt with streets and a trench, but in times of trouble. [26]After the sixty-two 'sevens,' the Anointed One will be cut off and will have nothing. The people of the ruler who will come will destroy the city and the sanctuary. The end will come like a flood: War will continue until the end, and desolations have been decreed. [27]He will confirm a covenant with many for one 'seven.' In the middle of the 'seven' he will put an end to sacrifice and offering. And on a wing ⌞of the temple⌟ he will set up an abomination that causes desolation, until the end that is decreed is poured out on him."

20–23 The Lord's response came swiftly. Verses 20–23 tell how Gabriel came back once again to reveal God's will to his faithful servant. Daniel had not even finished his time of prayer (v.20) before the angel made his appearance (v.21). Note that the term *hā'îš* ("the man") does not signify "man" in contradistinction to angels or other spiritual powers residing in heaven; that would have been *'ādām* or *'enôš* in Hebrew. It rather indicates that this mighty archangel had appeared in a humanlike form and had spoken to Daniel intelligibly as one man speaks to another. Similar terms are used of the angels who announced Christ's resurrection to the disciples who had come seeking to anoint his corpse: "Suddenly two men in clothes that gleamed like lightning stood beside them" (Luke 24:4). So also was it at the Ascension: "Suddenly two men dressed in white stood beside them" (Acts 1:10).

It is significant that Daniel saw Gabriel approaching in "swift flight" (which may or may not have involved visible wings) and that Gabriel responded to his prayer at the time of the evening sacrifice—i.e., at sunset (v.21). Evidently Daniel had protracted his prayer till late afternoon. Of course, no actual sacrifice could have been offered there in Babylon, or indeed even in Palestine, prior to the erection of a new altar on the site of the destroyed temple. But devout Jews in the Persian Empire would have observed both sunrise and sunset as appropriate times of the day for offering adoration and praise and also supplication—even though there was now no Yahweh altar.

Gabriel began his teaching (v.22) by encouraging Daniel (v.23): "As soon as you began to pray, an answer was given, which I have come to tell you, for you are highly esteemed [*ḥamûḏôṯ*, lit., 'precious things' or 'a precious treasure']." God had taken pleasure in this intercessor because his heart was wholly set on the will and glory of the Lord. His faith was precious in God's eyes (hence *ḥamûḏôṯ*, "things to be desired" or "a precious treasure"). Observe how ready the Lord was to answer Daniel's prayer of faith: "As soon as you began to pray, an answer was given [i.e., by God]." The Lord is more eager to answer than we are to ask, and in Daniel's case there were powerful grounds for a speedy reply, reassuring him of the Lord's intention to bring to an end the seventy years of discipline and hardship for captive Israel.

24 This verse sets forth the approach of "seventy 'sevens' " of years during which God would accomplish his plan of national and spiritual redemption for Israel. The seventy "weeks" or "heptads" (*šaḇu'îm* literally means "units of seven," whether days or years) are 490 years (divided, as we shall see, into three sections). This period was the time to elapse before the accomplishment of six great achievements for the Holy City and for God's covenant people. The first three relate to the removal of sin; the second three to the restoration of righteousness.

1. The first achievement is "to finish transgression." The culmination of the appointed years will witness the conclusion of man's "transgression" or "rebellion" (*peša'*) against God—a development most naturally entered into with the establishment of an entirely new order on earth. This seems to require nothing less than the inauguration of the kingdom of God on earth. Certainly the crucifixion of Christ in A.D. 30 did not put an end to man's iniquity or rebellion on earth, as the millennial kingdom of Christ promises to do.

2. The second achievement is very closely related to the first: "to put an end [*hāṯēm*, from *tāmam*, 'be complete'] to sins (*ḥaṭṭā'ôṯ*, or, according to the Qere reading, *ḥaṭṭā'ṯ*, 'sin']." This term refers to missing the mark or true goal of life and implies immorality of a more general sort, rather than the revolt against authority implied by the *peša'* ("transgression") of the previous clause. This second achievement suggests the bringing in of a new society in which righteousness will prevail in complete contrast to the present condition of mankind. Again we see indications pointing to the kingly rule of Christ on earth, rather than to the present world order.

3. The third achievement is "to atone for wickedness," which certainly points to the Crucifixion, an event that ushered in the final stage of human history before the establishment of the fifth kingdom (cf. 2:35, 44). As Peter affirmed at Pentecost, "This is what was spoken by the prophet Joel: 'In the last days, God says, I will pour out my Spirit on all people' " (Acts 2:16–17). This implies that the "last days" began at the inauguration of the NT church at Pentecost. The Feast of Pentecost occurred just seven weeks after the Resurrection, which followed the Crucifixion by three days. The Crucifixion was the atonement that made possible the establishment of

the new order, the church of the redeemed, and the establishment of the coming millennial kingdom.

4. The fourth achievement is "to bring in everlasting righteousness" (*ṣeḏeq ʿôlāmîm*, "righteousness of ages"). This clearly indicates an order of society in which righteousness, justice, and conformity to the standards of Scripture will prevail on earth, rather than the temporary periods of upright government that have occasionally occurred in world history till now.

5. The fifth achievement will be the fulfillment of the vision [*ḥāzôn*] and "the prophecy," which serves as the grand and central goal of God's plan for the ages—that final stage of human history when the Son of Man receives "authority, glory and sovereign power" (7:14) so that all nations and races will serve him. This fulfillment surely goes beyond the suffering, death, and resurrection of Christ; it must include his enthronement—on the throne of David—as supreme Ruler over all the earth.

6. The final goal to be achieved at the end of the seventy weeks is the anointing of "the most holy" (*qōḏeš qāḏāšîm*). This is not likely a reference to the anointing of Christ (as some writers have suggested) because *qōḏeš qāḏāšîm* nowhere else in Scripture refers to a person. Here the anointing of the "most holy" most likely refers to the consecration of the temple of the Lord, quite conceivably the millennial temple, to which so much attention is given in Ezekiel 40–44.

The reason for our detailed discussion of the six goals of v.24 is that the *terminus ad quem* of the seventy weeks must first be established before the question of the seventieth week can be properly handled. If all six goals were in fact attained by the crucifixion of Christ and the establishment of the early church seven years after his death, then it might be fair to assume that the entire 490 years of the seventy weeks were to be understood as running consecutively and coming to a close in A.D. 37. But since all or most of the six goals seem to be as yet unfulfilled, it follows that if the seventieth week finds fulfillment at all, it must be identified as the last seven years before Christ's return to earth as millennial King.

25–26 Verse 25 is crucial: "From the issuing of the decree to restore and rebuild Jerusalem until the Anointed One [*māšîaḥ*], the ruler, comes, there will be seven 'sevens,' and sixty-two 'sevens.' " It should be observed that only sixty-nine heptads are listed here, broken into two segments. The first segment of seven amounts to forty-nine years, during which the city of Jerusalem is to be "rebuilt with streets and a trench, but in times of trouble."

Verse 26 specifies the termination of the sixty-nine heptads: the cutting off of the Messiah. That is to say, *after* the appearance of Messiah as Ruler (*māšîaḥ nāgîḏ*)—483 years after the sixty-nine weeks have begun—he will be cut off. This accords very well with a three-year ministry of the Messiah prior to his crucifixion. Verse 26 goes on to say: "After the sixty-two 'sevens,' the Anointed One [Messiah] will be cut off and will have nothing [*wᵉʾên lô* can mean either 'nothing' or 'no one']." This indicates that when Messiah is cut off, he will be bereft of followers; all of them will flee from him at the time of his arrest, trial, and death. (Or else, if *ʾên* here means "nothing," it suggests that he will die without any material wealth or resources.)

As we turn our attention to the *terminus a quo,* we note that v.25 specifies the rebuilding of the city of Jerusalem with streets and moats, which will be completed within forty-nine years of the *terminus a quo*. The first possible fulfillment might be the first decree of Cyrus the Great (2 Chron 36:23; Ezra 1:2–4). Both versions of this decree stress just one undertaking: the rebuilding of the temple of Yahweh—a project in which Cyrus promised to cooperate with the Jewish leaders and the rank and file of all the Jewish returnees. This says nothing about the restoring and building of the city as such, though of course the rebuilding of the temple itself would imply the building up of a community of worshipers around it. It is most unlikely, then, that this decree can fulfill the specifications of v.25—"the decree [*dāḇār* literally means 'word' and may be rendered 'commission' or 'commandment'] to restore and rebuild Jerusalem."

The next possible fulfillment is the decree issued to Ezra in the seventh year of Artaxerxes I (464–424), that is, in 457 B.C. Its text is found in Ezra 7:12–26, which lays the chief emphasis on adorning and strengthening the temple at Jerusalem and enforcing the laws and regulations of the Mosaic code. Yet in his understanding of the implications of that decree, Ezra himself affirmed in his solemn, penitential prayer on behalf of Israel that "our God has not deserted us in our bondage. He has shown us kindness in the sight of the kings of Persia: He has granted us new life to rebuild the house of our God and repair its ruins, and he has given us a wall of protection in Judah and Jerusalem" (Ezra 9:9). To Ezra's mind, then, the commission he received from Artaxerxes included permission to rebuild the wall of Jerusalem. To be sure, he did not succeed in doing so; his attention was monopolized by the social and religious reforms the Jerusalem community so urgently needed. Certainly he lacked the manpower and financial resources to proceed with so ambitious an undertaking; so the rebuilding never went beyond the talking stage. If this led to a delay of thirteen years in working on the walls, Nehemiah's disappointment (Neh 1:4) when in 446 he heard from Hanani that no progress had been made seems all the more appropriate. Nehemiah no doubt had hoped for more tangible results from Ezra's leadership and expected him to have made some headway in fortifying the city during the twelve years he had been there.

If, then, the *terminus a quo* for the decree in v.25 be reckoned as 457 B.C. (the date of Ezra's return to Jerusalem), then we may compute the first seven heptads as running from 457 to 408, within which time the rebuilding of the walls, streets, and moats was completed. Then from 408 we count off the sixty–two heptads also mentioned in v.25 and come out to A.D. 26 (408 is 26 less than 434). But actually we come out to A.D. 27, since a year is gained in our reckoning as we pass directly from 1 B.C. to A.D. 1 (without any year zero in between). If Christ was crucified on 14 Abib A.D. 30, as is generally believed (cf. L.A. Foster, "The Chronology of the New Testament," EBC, 1:598–99, 607), this would come out to a remarkably exact fulfillment of the terms of v.25. Christ's public ministry, from the time of his baptism in the Jordan till his death and resurrection at Jerusalem, must have taken up about three years. The 483 years from the issuing of the decree of Artaxerxes came to an end in A.D. 27, the year of the "coming" of Messiah as Ruler (*nāśî'*). It was indeed "after the sixty-two 'sevens' "—three years after—that "the Anointed One" was "cut off."

The third possibility for the *terminus a quo* of the decree to restore and build Jerusalem is the commission granted by the same King Artaxerxes to his cupbearer, Nehemiah, in the twentieth year of his reign, i.e., in 446 B.C. The text of this decree is found in Nehemiah 2:5–8, which gives the tenor of Nehemiah's request to the king. The main object in view is the rebuilding of Jerusalem, with timber to be supplied from the royal forest, both for the gates of the fortress and for the walls in general. But the problem with this 445 date is that 483 solar years would come out to A.D. 38 or 39, which is wrong for the ministry and death of Jesus Christ. But proponents of this view urge that lunar years rather than solar years are intended in this particular passage.

Robert Anderson (pp. 67–75) calculated what he called "prophetic years" as consisting of 360 days each. The 360-day year was known, to be sure, in Egypt, Greece, Assyria, and Babylon, all of which made some use of a system of twelve months having 30 days each. All of them, however, used some sort of intercalary month in order to make an approximation to the 365 days of the solar year—whether 5 days added after the twelfth month or an additional month every six or seven years. In other words, they all used various devices to mark the phases of the moon (29½ days from one new moon to the next) and yet reconcile these twelve lunar units with the solar year of 365¼ days. The Assyrians usually alternated between 29-day months and 30-day months (which therefore totaled 354 days) and the needed 11 extra days were supplied by varying methods, depending on the decision of the local or national priests. The same was true with the Babylonians and Sumerians (cf. P. Van Der Meer, *Chronology of Ancient Western Asia and Egypt* [Leiden: Brill, 1963], p. 1).

As for Egypt, the 365-day year was followed—but without the insertion of an extra day every fourth year ("leap year") as was later done with the Julian calendar. The unhappy result for the Egyptians was that over a cycle of 1,460 years, their three seasons would gradually work their way around the calendar, till "winter" (p-r-t.) would occur during the summer, and so on. But even at that, the Egyptians never used a 360-day year, as Anderson supposed; they simply used the fraction 1/360 as a rough estimate for daily quotas (cf. A.H. Gardiner, *Egyptian Grammar*, 3d ed. [New York: Oxford University Press, 1957], pp. 203–5). It remains completely unsubstantiated that any of Israel's ancient neighbors ever used 360-day years in complete disregard for the solar cycle. Nor did they ever use long series of 360-day years without some form of intercalation. If, then, the Hebrews did this, they would be the only nation in world history ever to do so.

Anderson finds support for the 360-day year in the reference to 1,260 days in Revelation 12:6 as the period of persecution during the Great Tribulation; in 12:14 this interval is referred to as "a time, times and half a time or 3½ years. While it is perfectly true that 3½ times 12 times 30 comes out to 1,260, it seems most unlikely that the figure of 3½ years was intended in that context to be any more than approximate. Twelve hundred and sixty days is only 16 or 17 days short of 3½ solar years, and even in modern usage we would have no hesitation whatever in speaking of 1,260 days as "about three and a half years." This evidence from Revelation 12 therefore furnishes very slender support for the supposition that the Hebrews of the first millennium B.C. differed from all others in the ancient (or modern) world and used 360-day years rather than solar years in reckoning prophetic time. Certainly in their numerous chronological statements in Kings and Chronicles, the OT authors used nothing but true solar years. This consideration alone ought to be decisive against Anderson's theory.

The 445 B.C. date is intended with one further difficulty, that it comes out to A.D. 32 as the exact year of the Crucifixion. (H.W. Hoehner, "Chronological Aspects of the Life of Christ," BS 132 [January–March 1975]: 64, follows Anderson's method with minor corrections and contends for an A.D. 33 date for the Crucifixion.) Those who hold to this interpretation seem therefore to be committed to a deviation of two or three years from the generally accepted date of A.D. 30 as the year of Jesus' death. In view of the claim for great exactitude advanced by proponents of this view, a discrepancy of even two or three years would seem almost fatal to the tenability of their theory. That is to say, 360 days times 483 comes out to 173,880 days in all; and according to Hoehner's reckoning, 173,880 days is the exact interval of time between 5 March 444 B.C. (which he assigns as the correct date for the twentieth year of Artaxerxes, who began his reign in 465 or 464) and 30 March A.D. 33. Yet it seems rather irrelevant to establish what the exact date of the Crucifixion may have been in this connection since all that v.25 really says is that 483 years will elapse between the decree to rebuild Jerusalem and the appearance of "the Anointed One, the ruler." It says nothing about the time of his death. It is only v.26 that speaks of his being cut off, and it does so only in the words "after the sixty-two 'sevens.'" Three years later—or however long the interval between the beginning and the end of the Messiah's public ministry—fulfills the specification "after" perfectly.

The second sentence of v.26—"The people of the ruler who will come will destroy the city and the sanctuary"—perhaps would be more accurately rendered, "The people of a prince who shall come will destroy both the city and the sanctuary." (The reason for the ambiguity here is that the definite article is missing in front of *nāgîḏ* ["ruler"], which would be necessary for the rendering "the people of *the* ruler." There is only the definite article before "who is coming"; so this may be intended to convey the thought of the alternative rendering. In other words, *'am nāgîḏ habbā'* may mean "the people of a ruler who shall come.") From the standpoint of subsequent history, this would seem to be a very clear reference to the destruction of Jerusalem by the Romans under Titus in A.D. 70. It was then that the city and the sanctuary were completely destroyed. This event took place forty years after the event of Calvary, or forty-three years after the end of the sixty-ninth "week"—if the 457 B.C. theory is correct for the commencement of the seventy weeks.

The next sentence or two indicate what is to happen after the destruction of Jerusalem: "The end will come like a flood: War will continue until the end, and desolations have been decreed." (More literally this might be rendered thus: "And the end of it will be in the overflowing, and unto the end there will be war, a strict determination of desolations" or "the determined amount of desolations.") The general tenor of this sentence is in striking conformity with Christ's own prediction in the Olivet Discourse (Matt 24:7–22). There he stated that hardships, suffering, and war would continue right up to the end of the present age, culminating in a time of unparalleled tribulation. It is important to observe that this entire intervening period is referred to *before* the final or seventieth week is mentioned in v.27. It is difficult to explain why this is so, if in point of fact the entire seventy weeks are intended to run consecutively and without interruption. It seems far more reasonable to infer that a long period of time of war and desolation is to intervene between the sixty-ninth week (when Messiah appears at his first advent) and the seventieth week, which is to usher in his second advent.

27 This verse gives immediate rise to the question, Who will confirm the covenant with the many? The last eligible antecedent in the Hebrew text is the *nāgîḏ* of the construct phrase *'am nāgîḏ* ("the people of a [the] ruler") in v.26. Normally the last eligible antecedent is to be taken as the subject of the following verb. If, then, it was a ruler of the Roman people who was to destroy Jerusalem (viz., the event in A.D. 70), it would be reasonable to suppose that it will be a ruler of the Roman Empire—in its final phase, viz., the ten-toes phase of chapter 2 and the ten-horned-beast phase of chapter 7—who will be involved in concluding this covenant with the people of God during the final seven years before Christ's return. (Of course, it could not be the *same* ruler of the Roman people as was mentioned in v.26b, for a long process of war, suffering, and tribulation seems to be referred to in the last part of v.26; the earlier ruler [*nāgîḏ*] must therefore be a type or forerunner of the "Roman" ruler of the last days.)

Who are "the many" with whom this latter day ruler will confirm a covenant? The Masoretic vowel-pointing of *lārabbîm* clearly indicates "*the* many" rather than "many," which would have been *lᵉrabbîm*. Quite evidently—if the vowel-pointing is correct—this is a technical term referring to the true believers among the people of God, presumably Jewish believers in Christ (cf. Isa 53:11–12, where this meaning for "the many" is clearly established; *hārabbîm* stands in contrast to "the One" who gave up his life as an atonement for them). In the Qumran *Rule of the Congregation, hārabbîm* often occurs in reference to the sectarian community of "true believers"; therefore, G. Vermes (*The Dead Sea Scrolls in English* [London: Harmsworth, 1962]) often renders it "the Congregation."

From the foregoing we are led to infer that the latter day ruler over the "Roman" people will "confirm" (*higbîr*) a "covenant" (*bᵉrîṯ*) with the believing Jews for a stipulated period of seven years. Young's suggestion that here *higbîr* means "will cause to prevail" is not well supported and seems hard to fit into this context. The ruler will conclude a treaty or make some kind of binding commitment to permit the Jewish believers to carry on their religious practices in their newly built temple, including the offerings and sacrifices set forth in the Mosaic Law. (Since these Jewish believers trust in Jesus as their Messiah, it may well be that the sacrifices will be conducted as memorial services like the Lord's Supper, rather than for atonement purposes as in OT times. This will certainly be the case during the Millennium—if indeed Ezek 43 pertains to that age; see this commentary series, in loc.)

Verse 27 goes on to say that "in the middle of that 'seven' he will put an end to sacrifice and offering." After about three and one-half years, for reasons not here explained, the world dictator will see fit to break his own agreement with the Jews and prohibit the public exercise of their religion. Possibly he will feel secure enough in his autocratic position and the efficient operation of his secret police so that he can carry out all features of his original, secret plan to impose an absolute dictatorship on all the people of his empire, especially the Jews. All pretense of religious toleration will be dropped, for the *nāgîḏ* ("ruler") will aspire to absolute authority and complete control over the life and thought of all mankind. Then he will display himself as the incarnation of all divine authority on earth. As we learn from 2 Thessalonians 2:4, he will even go so far as to enthrone himself as the living embodiment of God on earth: "He opposes and exalts himself over everything that is called God or is worshiped, and even sets himself up in God's temple, proclaiming himself to be God." (In many ways this step-by-step progression of tyranny here described bears a remarkable resemblance to the development of the Nazi tyranny in Germany; those of strong religious convictions were at first lulled into a false sense of security till Hitler had consolidated his power through the whole security system of the German Reich.)

The final statement of v.27—"And on the wing [of the temple] he will set up an abomination that causes desolation, until the end that is decreed is poured out on him"—is difficult (cf. NIV mg. and the earlier rendering of NIV). And even this latest rendering of NIV is questionable. The MT has no word for "temple" or any verb for "set." A more literal translation is "And on the wing of abominations (he is going to) commit abominations, and towards the end [or else *'aḏ* may be rendered 'up until'] the predetermined (judgment) will be poured out upon him." In other words, the subject of the participle *mešōmēm* ("commit abominations") is the Antichrist himself, carried over from v.26; and what we have here is more likely a periphrastic construction of imminence (i.e., "he is about to commit abominations") rather than a noun of agency (i.e., "because of abominations"). It seems unjustified to imply a verb "to set" from the mere preposition *'al* ("on") when the obvious rendering is "on a wing." Since there is no word for "temple," it is more reasonable to understand "wing" (*kenap*) as a figure for the vulturelike role of the Antichrist as he swoops down on his beleaguered victims for the purposes of oppression and despoliation.

Apparently the difficult phrase "on the wing" involves some symbolism familiar to the author and his readers. In all probability it referred either to the outstretched wings of some bird to which the *nāgiḏ* ("ruler") is tacitly compared or else to the hawklike wings that adorned the royal insignia of the kings of Egypt and Assyria, as well as that of Rome.

The phrase "that causes desolation" (*šiqqûṣîm mešōmēm*, lit., "a desolator of abominations") bears an interesting resemblance to *haššiqqûṣ mešômēm* ("the abomination that causes desolation") in Daniel 11:31 and to *šiqqûṣ šōmēm* ("the abomination that causes desolation") in Daniel 12:11. Apparently these three passages were in Christ's mind when he predicted in his Olivet Discourse (cf. Matt 24:15) the final horrors of the Tribulation. Significantly the evangelist inserted the parenthetical exhortation "Let the reader understand." This might indicate that Matthew himself was not quite sure how the phrase should be interpreted, but he nevertheless included it as a statement from Christ's lips. It is important to observe that this reference to "the abomination that causes desolation," or "of desolation" (as the Greek actually puts it), conclusively proves that Jesus himself regarded the fulfillment of the prophecy in Daniel as yet future rather than as having been completely realized in the time of Antiochus Epiphanes, as the Maccabean date hypothesis supposes. This means that a genuine theological or doctrinal issue is at stake here; for if the hypothesis of complete fulfillment by Antiochus is correct, as many liberals insist, it raises a real question as to whether God the Son was mistaken in his understanding of prophecy and the theological interpretation of the OT.

As for the "desolator" himself, it is simplest to take him to be the world dictator of the last days, who will resort to violence to carry through his ruthless policy of despotism. The account in Revelation 13 indicates that the eschatological little horn will remain in control of world affairs down to the End, enforcing his will by violent means till the final conflict of Armageddon.

The phrase *we'aḏ-kālāh* may be rendered in two ways: either as "right up till the end" (modifying the preceding "that causes desolation") or else as "until the end that is decreed is poured out" (understanding the waw [*w*] before *neḥerāṣāh* ["the end that is decreed"] as some kind of waw apodosis; cf. GKC, par. 143 d). There are difficulties either way, but the general sense is beyond dispute. The dictator will hold sway till the wrath of God is poured out in fury on the God-defying world of the Beast (little horn or ruler). That which is poured out may include the vials or bowls of divine wrath mentioned in Revelation 16; but certainly what "is poured out on him" points to the climax at Armageddon, when the blasphemous world ruler will be crushed by the full weight of God's judgment.

Notes

24 Note that Daniel elsewhere (10:2) specified when he meant weekdays: שְׁלֹשָׁה שָׁבֻעִים יָמִים (šᵉlōšāh šābuᶜîm yāmîm, "three weeks"). No plausible argument has ever been raised against the deduction that the heptads here referred to consist of years rather than days, for 490 days would be meaningless in this context. Almost all the lexicons so define it in connection with this passage (BDB, p. 989; W. Gesenius, *Hebraisches und Aramaisches Handworterbuch*, 17th ed., ed. F. Buhl [Leipzig, 1921], p. 800; F. Zorell and L. Semkowski, eds., *Lexicon Hebräicum et Aramaicum Veteris Testamenti* [Rome, 1940], p. 815). KB (p. 940) alone adheres to "period of seven days," apparently on the ground that only symbolic value is involved rather than an actual time. But the preceding verses show that the subject under discussion is the seventy-year captivity predicted in Jer 25:11–12; 29:10. Gabriel's response to Daniel's prayer concerning the termination of the Exile must have had the year-unit in view, not the more usual day-unit. As for the purely symbolic use of "seventy 'sevens,' " there is not the slightest analogy for such usage in all Scripture. According to 2 Chron 36:21, the Jewish nation had been punished by this captivity so that the land might at last enjoy rest from cultivation for a period equivalent to all the seventh-year Sabbath rests that had been prescribed in the Law of Moses but that had been routinely neglected (Exod 23:10–11; Lev 25:15–11; Deut 15:1–11; 31:10–13). In this divine oracle, therefore, the multiplying of seventy by seven was analogous to Jesus' response to Peter about the number of times an offender should be forgiven (Matt 18:22).

The term "decreed" translates the Hebrew נֶחְתַּךְ (neḥtak, a Niphal perfect from חָתַךְ [ḥātak, "divide," "determine"]). This is the only occurrence in the Hebrew text of the OT, but in Aramaic the verb means "cut," "decide" (likewise in modern Hebrew). This suggests that the amount of years involved have been precisely and accurately determined —an implication clearly borne out by the fulfillment.

The verb כַּלֵּא (kalle᾽) is probably not to be connected with kālā᾽, which in the Qal stem means "restrain" but does not otherwise occur in the Piel. Rather, it comes from כָּלָה (kālāh), meaning "to bring to an end," "to finish" (NIV), as virtually all the lexicons construe it.

The Kethiv has לַחְתֹּם (laḥtōm, "to seal up"). But since laḥtōm actually appears in the line below (where it does mean "seal up"), the first occurrence is probably a scribal error for לְהָתֵם (lᵉhātēm), the Hiphil infinitive of תָּמַם (tāmam), meaning "to bring to an end," "complete." The Qere reading indicates this correction by its vowel pointing: lᵉhātēm.

Twice קֹדֶשׁ קָדָשִׁים (qōdeš qādāšîm, "the most holy") refers to the altar—Exod 29:37; 30:10; four times to the holy objects of the Holy Place or temple—Num 18:10; Ezek 43:12; 45:3; 48:12. Gesenius-Buhl (*Handworterbuch*, p. 704) suggests that in Dan 9:24 qōdeš qādāšîm refers to the temple. In Exod 30:36 it is used of holy incense; in Lev 24:9 of the memorial bread (showbread). Or it refers to the priestly portion of peace offerings ("fellowship offerings," NIV)—Lev 2:3, 10; 6:10; 10:12. In Lev 6:18, 22 it is used of sin offerings; in Num 18:9; Ezra 2:63; Neh 7:65 of offerings in general; likewise in Lev 21:22; 2 Chron 31:14; Ezek 42:13; 44:13. Ten times it is used of the Holy Place of the tabernacle or temple—Exod 26:33–34 (bis); 1 Kings 6:16; 7:50; 8:6; 2 Chron 3:8, 10; 4:22; 5:7; Ezek 41:4.

25 עַד־מָשִׁיחַ נָגִיד (ᶜad-māšiaḥ nāgîd, lit., "till an Anointed One, Ruler") could be translated "till an anointed one, a ruler." But since this pair of titles is hopelessly vague and indefinite, applying to almost any governor or priest-king in Israel's subsequent history, it could scarcely have furnished the definite *terminus ad quem* the context obviously demands. It is therefore necessary to understand each of these terms as exalted titles applying to some definite personage in future history. In Hebrew proper names do not take the definite article, and neither do titles that have become virtually proper nouns by usage. GKC (pars. 125 f–g) cites many examples of these: e.g., שַׁדַּי (*šadday*, "the Almighty"). שָׂטָן (*śāṭān*, "the Adversary"), תֵּבֵל (*tēḇēl*, "the world"), עֶלְיוֹן (*ʿelyôn*, "the Most High"). We therefore conclude that "Messiah the Ruler" was the meaning intended by the author. The word order precludes construing it as "an [or 'the'] anointed ruler," which would have to be נָגִיד מָשִׁיחַ (*nāgîḏ māšîaḥ*).

26 As for the Hebrews themselves, it is quite certain from the references to regularity of seasons throughout the OT books that they followed a solar year. If they had followed a 360-day year, with a loss of 5¼ days each successive year, it would not have taken very long for the seasons to shift all around the calendar. Thus it would have come about that within every eighteen years the whole season of fall would have shifted to winter (because of the deviation of ninety days that would have accumulated by then). Correspondingly, winter would have shifted to spring, and spring would sizzle with the heat of summer. There is no trace of this in the OT record, but the twelve months of the year fit into the same seasonal rhythm year after year throughout the recorded history of Israel. In Egypt, as we have just seen, that very thing did take place, though over a much slower cycle—1,460 years. That resulted from their using a year of 365 days, ignoring a portion of the additional time (approximately six hours) required by the sun to reach exactly the same position as it had occupied a year before.

The Muslim year, which is purely lunar, consists of 354 days. This means that every 33 years the twelve months have made their way completely around the four seasons, and there is the gain of one additional year, as compared with the solar calendar of the Christians. But nothing of this sort was ever practiced by the Jews during the OT period, and it is unlikely that they ever followed a 360-day year at any time in their history.

It is not to be wondered at that Bible scholars down through the centuries had difficulty dealing with the chronological factors involved in the prophecy of the seventy weeks. Jerome (A.D. 400) in his commentary (pp. 95–110) surveyed the opinions of Africanus (who dated the *terminus a quo* from Nehemiah's mission to Jerusalem), Eusebius (who proposed two dates, one from Cyrus's decree in 538, the other from the completion of the second temple in 516), Hippolytus (who reckoned from 49 years before the return from exile—and came out to a totally wrong date, as Jerome points out), Apollinarius (who started from the birth of Jesus and computed to his second coming, which he looked for in A.D. 482), Clement of Alexandria (who computed the time from the reign of Cyrus to the time of Vespasian to be only 490 years), Origen (who pointed to the accession of Darius son of Ahasuerus, i.e., 539 B.C., as the starting point but was uncertain as to whether 490 years would work out correctly to the coming of Christ), Tertullian (who computed from the beginning of the reign of Darius I in 522), and even one of the Jewish interpretations, which started from Darius the Mede (539 B.C.) and ended with the collapse of the second revolt (in A.D. 135).

As for Jerome himself, he leaves the question quite undecided, saying (p. 95): "I realize that this question has been argued over in various ways by men of greatest learning, and that each of them has expressed his views according to the capacity of his own genius. And so, because it is unsafe to pass judgment upon the opinions of the great teachers of the Church and set one above another, I shall simply repeat the view of each, and leave it to the reader's judgment as to whose explanation ought to be followed." But with the increasing precision achieved in biblical chronology in the nineteenth and twentieth centuries, it has become quite clear how the connection is to be made, from the issuance of the decree to rebuild the city of Jerusalem to the appearance of Messiah the Ruler—understanding this interval to be 69 sevens, or 483 years, and the final 7 years to be postponed till the last days of the Tribulation. Yet strangely enough, even in recent decades there has been considerable confusion even on the part of conservative scholars in regard to the seventy weeks.

Young (pp. 202–6) inclines to the 538 B.C. decree of Cyrus (with Calvin, Keil, Kliefoth, and Mauro) as the *terminus a quo* (p. 203) and feels that the *terminus ad quem* was the birth or ministry of Jesus Christ. Young even suggests (pp. 204–5) that if the *'atnāḥ* (a disjunctive accent) is wrongly placed under the numeral שִׁבְעָה (*šib'āh*, "sevens") in v.25, then we do not have to construe the first group of seven weeks as extending from Cyrus to Christ (as Keil and Kliefoth insist). Leupold (p. 421) falls into the same error of the infallibility of Masoretic accent marks, saying, "The first seven heptads, as we indicated, come to a culmination in one who is designated as 'an Anointed One, a Prince.' "

Young (p. 205) then goes on to remark: "It may be that the Mas. pointing is in error, as I think it certainly is in vs. 24. At any rate, this violent separation of the two periods [i.e., of the seven heptads and the sixty-two heptads] is out of harmony with the context. Furthermore, I question whether it is really in accord with the rules of Heb. syntax to render, '(for the space of) sixty-two sevens,' i.e., as an acc. of duration [as Keil and Kliefoth insist]. . . . It is best, therefore, to understand (although I am painfully aware of the difficulties) the text as stating that between the *terminus a quo* and the appearance of an anointed one, a prince, is a period of 69 sevens which is divided into two periods of unequal length, 7 sevens and 62 sevens."

Thus far Young stands on very firm ground; but since he insists on regarding 538 B.C., the decree of Cyrus, as the starting point, it becomes impossible to make out a satisfactory correlation with the facts of subsequent history, even as regards the first installment of forty-nine years. Having ruled out the correct starting point of 557/558 (Artaxerxes' commission to Ezra—and *dāḇār* ["word," "decree"] in v.25 really is better suited to an informal commission rather than an official decree, such as Cyrus issued), he is faced with an impasse of his own making. Young therefore ends up (p. 206) with this feeble conclusion: "The burden of proof rests with those who insist that sevens of years are intended. Of this I am not convinced. If the sevens be regarded merely as a symbolical number, the difficulty disappears."

In the view of this writer, however, the difficulty is greatly intensified. There is no analogy in Scripture for the use of symbolic numbers in connection with chronological predictions. From the standpoint of legal evidence, the burden of proof always rests on the litigant who wishes to show that terms are used in a special or unusual way, rather than in the plain, ordinary usage of the words involved. Since day-weeks could not have been intended (for Daniel would then have been discarded as false prophecy within two years after its composition, if that had been the meaning), it could only have been year-weeks the author had in mind. And in view of the fact that reckoning from Ezra's return to the appearance of Jesus Christ as "Messiah and Ruler" in A.D. 27 comes out to exactly 483 years (or sixty-two heptads), all motive for resorting to an unprecedented and unparalleled use of "symbolic" numbers is removed.

X. The Triumph of Persistent Prayer (10:1–21)

1. *Daniel's Disturbing Vision and Prayerful Concern*

10:1–3

1In the third year of Cyrus king of Persia, a revelation was given to Daniel (who was called Belteshazzar). Its message was true and it concerned a great war. The understanding of the message came to him in a vision.

[2]At that time I, Daniel, mourned for three weeks. [3]I ate no choice food; no meat or wine touched my lips; and I used no lotions at all until the three weeks were over.

1 The date of this revelation indicates that this was the latest of all the visions recorded in the Book of Daniel. It came in the "third year of Cyrus," which must refer to his official regnal year as the crowned and enthroned king of Babylon. (As king of Persia, Cyrus had begun his reign in 558, and the third year would have been 555/554; but this would have had no relevance for Daniel in Babylon, which was then ruled over by Nabonidus.) Since the reign of Gubaru (Darius the Mede) must have lasted until 538 or 537, the third year of Cyrus would have been 535/534, in all probability just a few years before Daniel's death. (If he was born around 620 B.C., he would have been ninety by 530.)

We are not told exactly in what form the first disclosure of this revelation came to Daniel, but presumably it was through a personal confrontation with an angel; all the other prophetic revelations granted to him personally had come in that form. Yet it had not been followed by an explanation of its meaning on the part of the angel himself. We are not given any hint as to what symbols may have appeared in the vision (statues, beasts, trees, or whatever). We are simply told that it related to "a great war" (*ṣāḇā'*). Since it is referred to simply as a *dāḇār* ("word," "message," "saying"), it may not even have come in a pictorial form at all. Its message, however, clearly portended times of testing and crisis for the people of God.

2–3 Assuming that v.2 chronologically preceded vv.4–21, we are to understand that Daniel was so deeply impressed by this revelation that he resorted to three weeks of mourning (*miṯ'abbēl*, a word often used in connection with lamenting the death of a loved one). From v.12 we know that this mourning and the semifast that accompanied it (v.3) marked a prolonged period of intense supplication and prayer. Daniel abstained altogether from meat, wine and delicacies so that he might give himself over to beseeching and waiting on God. Daniel even neglected the usual niceties of personal grooming, such as fragrant oil on his hair or body. His consuming desire was to intercede for his people and obtain assurance from Yahweh that the nation would survive and carry out with honor and faithfulness its holy mission as God's witness to the world. He wanted to be certain that the remnant of forty-two thousand that had already gone back to Jerusalem with Zerubbabel and Joshua and had reinstituted public worship at the site of the temple would not fail in their trust, and that the commonwealth they had established would carry on till the last days and the coming of Messiah, the Son of Man. Conceivably Daniel had heard of the halting of all construction on the temple in Jerusalem (cf. Ezra 4:5, 24) and was dismayed at this development.

Notes

1–3 A simpler way to handle these verses would be as a summary introduction or descriptive label of the vision that begins with the appearance of the angel presented in v.5 as "a man dressed in linen." The vision itself would then be the extended revelation granted him in chs. 11–12. In other words, after the general characterization of the vision (vv.1–3) and the description of Daniel's emotional response to it during the following three weeks, the author proceeds to fill in the details as to the date and location of this angelic interview. If this is the true intent of these verses, then vv.2–3 represent the latest episode in the entire Book of Daniel, even after the conclusion of ch. 12.

---

2. *God's Delayed Messenger*

10:4–14

4On the twenty-fourth day of the first month, as I was standing on the bank of the great river, the Tigris, 5I looked up and there before me was a man dressed in linen, with a belt of the finest gold around his waist. 6His body was like chrysolite, his face like lightning, his eyes like flaming torches, his arms and legs like the gleam of burnished bronze, and his voice like the sound of a multitude.

7I, Daniel, was the only one who saw the vision; the men with me did not see it, but such terror overwhelmed them that they fled and hid themselves. 8So I was left alone, gazing at this great vision; I had no strength left, my face turned deathly pale and I was helpless. 9Then I heard him speaking, and as I listened to him, I fell into a deep sleep, my face to the ground.

10A hand touched me and set me trembling on my hands and knees. 11He said, "Daniel, you who are highly esteemed, consider carefully the words I am about to speak to you, and stand up, for I have now been sent to you." And when he said this to me, I stood up trembling.

12Then he continued, "Do not be afraid, Daniel. Since the first day that you set your mind to gain understanding and to humble yourself before your God, your words were heard, and I have come in response to them. 13But the prince of the Persian kingdom resisted me twenty-one days. Then Michael, one of the chief princes, came to help me, because I was detained there with the king of Persia. 14Now I have come to explain to you what will happen to your people in the future, for the vision concerns a time yet to come."

4–6 It was in early spring, on 24 Nisan (just ten days after Passover), that Daniel received his answer from God. We are not told why Daniel was absent from Babylon and was standing on the bank of the Tigris River (v.4). Evidently he was on some kind of official business in the eastern part of Mesopotamia.

Verses 5–6 are probably the most-detailed description in Scripture of the appearance of an angel. In Judges 13:6, Samson's mother reported that the angel she saw was "very awesome" in appearance, but she did not go into further detail. The angels at Christ's tomb were described by the women who saw them as dressed "in clothes that gleamed like lightning" (Luke 24:4), much like "the two men dressed in white" who spoke to the Eleven at the Ascension (Acts 1:10). Here we read that (1) the angel was dressed in linen, which may well have been the dazzling white apparel referred to above; (2) the belt or sash (*ḥ^agurîm*, lit., "girded," "belted") around his waist was made of the "finest gold" (*keṯem*), in the form of chain-links, hinged panels, or gold thread embroidery; (3) his body glowed with a luminous color, "like chrysolite" (*taršîš* represents a yellow or golden shade of beryl); (4) his face flashed like lightning in its splendor; (5) his eyes blazed like torches (Rev 1:14 states that Christ appeared to John with "eyes . . . like blazing fire"); (6) his arms and legs (which evidently were exposed rather than covered) gleamed like burnished bronze (which supports *taršîš* as being yellow in color): (7) his voice was like the "sound of a multitude" (*qôl hāmôn*, which often is used of a crowd of people but also of rain or of chariot wheels). In Revelation 10:3, the angel is said to give "a loud shout like the roar of a lion." (Note Rev 10:1, where the angel is depicted as robed in a cloud, with a rainbow above his head, his face shining like the sun, and his legs like fiery pillars—a description with striking similarities to this one in Daniel.)

7–10 Verse 7 tells us that when Daniel received his vision, he was not alone. His companions, however, did not see the vision of the angel but sensed his presence. Overwhelmed with terror, they fled. Similarly, in 2 Kings 6 at first Elisha alone saw the angelic host encircling Dothan; only after intercessory prayer was his young assistant enabled to see them too. Also, in Acts 9:7 the companions of Saul saw something of the light but could not behold the vision of the risen Christ; they could only tell that there was a voice from heaven but could not distinguish its words (Acts 22:9). One who sees a heavenly being must be spiritually alert. And so Daniel was left to face this awesome messenger of God. Once again he found himself emotionally overwhelmed (v.8), just as he had been at the end of the vision in 8:27. His face paled and his strength left him. After hearing the angel speak to him—presumably some words of greeting—Daniel swooned (v.9). Yet he was soon aroused, for the angel reached out and actually touched him (v.10).

11 Daniel stood up, respectfully attentive to God's message. "You are highly esteemed" (*'îš ḥ^{a}mu̱dôṯ*) literally reads "man of preciousness" (cf. 9:23). This remarkable greeting reassured Daniel of the personal love and concern that the Almighty has for each one of his faithful servants. To Daniel this must have been even more incredible than it is for us who know the boundless love of God displayed in the sacrifice of his Son on Calvary. But observe that Daniel's privileged status as one especially precious to God resulted from his complete absorption in the will and glory of the Lord to whom he had yielded his heart. His was the whole-souled devotion of a Paul or a Moses.

The angel called on Daniel to give his careful attention so as to understand the details of the explanation he was about to give him of the vision he had received. Such attention was certainly needed; for chapter 11 is full of confusing detail couched in somewhat vague terms—from the standpoint of 535 B.C., at least—though the subsequent fulfillment in Hellenistic times is amazingly accurate. Incidentally, this furnishes an instructive analogy for prophecy students today, since they too (esp. in books like Isaiah, Ezekiel, and Revelation) have to deal with predictions that are capable of varying interpretations but that will someday be fulfilled with similar exactness to those in Daniel 11:1–39.

12–14 These verses give us a fascinating insight into the supernatural forces involved when a believer engages in protracted and earnest prayer. Though James 5:16 tells us that "prayer of a righteous man is powerful and effective," we may not realize the mighty forces that are unleashed when we really devote ourselves to intercession before the throne of grace. Daniel was told what happened in heaven when three weeks earlier he had begun to pray daily for an understanding of God's plan for Israel's future. Because Daniel had set his "mind to gain understanding and to humble [himself] before [his] God" (v.12), the Lord commissioned his angelic messenger with the answer to Daniel's petition. The powers of evil apparently have the capacity to bring about hindrances and delays, even of the delivery of the answers to believers whose requests God is minded to answer. God's response was immediate, so far as his intention was concerned. But "the prince of the Persian kingdom" (v.13)—apparently the satanic agent assigned to the sponsorship and control of the Persian realm—put up a determined opposition to the actual delivery of the divine answer.

While God can, of course, override the united resistance of all the forces of hell if he chooses to do so, he accords to demons certain limited powers of obstruction and rebellion somewhat like those he allows humans. In both cases the exercise of free will in opposition to the Lord of heaven is permitted by him when he sees fit. But as Job 1:12 and 2:6 indicate, the malignity of Satan is never allowed to go beyond the due limit set by God, who will not allow the believer to be tested beyond his limit (1 Cor 10:13).

Verse 13 shows that the angels of God have power to counteract and thwart the agents of the Devil. Here it was the archangel, Michael ("one of the chief princes"), who broke the hindrance put up by the demonic "king of Persia" and paved the way for the interpreting angel to deliver God's answer to Daniel. As Hebrews 1:14 asks, "Are not all angels ministering spirits sent to serve those who will inherit salvation?" So Michael came to help Daniel, not because he prayed directly to Michael or to any other angel—Scripture nowhere permits prayer to anyone other than God himself—but because Michael was a faithful "minister" to an "heir of salvation." We little know what loving and powerful heavenly agents are watching over our lives; nevertheless, they are always at hand to deliver and to protect us from Satan's malignity.

Observe also that one basic principle of prayer is set forth by this example of delayed response. It is the principle of undiscourageable persistence. Jesus taught his disciples that "they should always pray and not give up" (Luke 18:1). There may be hindering factors of which a praying Christian knows nothing as he wonders why the answers to his requests are delayed. Nevertheless, he is to keep on praying. It may be that he will not receive an answer because he has given up on the twentieth day when he should have persisted to the twenty-first day. If Daniel had become discouraged, as many Christians do, then he might not have received the words of chapter 11.

In v.14 the angel begins to explain to Daniel the destiny of the Hebrew people up to the last days. Observe that if the vision pertains to the last days, it is a mistake to try to interpret the *terminus ad quem* as being the time of Antiochus Epiphanes in the second century B.C. The vision goes beyond his age to the final period in world history before the Son of Man comes in great power to establish the kingdom of God on earth. Beyond the type (Antiochus IV) is projected the antitype, referred to in Revelation (chs. 13, 17) as "the beast"—as we shall see when we come to 11:40.

3. *The Angel's Encouragement*

10:15–21

[15]While he was saying this to me, I bowed with my face toward the ground and was speechless. [16]Then one who looked like a man touched my lips, and I opened my mouth and began to speak. I said to the one standing before me, "I am overcome with anguish because of the vision, my lord, and I am helpless. [17]How can I, your servant, talk with you, my lord? My strength is gone and I can hardly breathe."

[18]Again the one who looked like a man touched me and gave me strength. [19]"Do not be afraid, O man highly esteemed," he said. "Peace! Be strong now; be strong."

When he spoke to me, I was strengthened and said, "Speak, my lord, since you have given me strength."

[20]So he said, "Do you know why I have come to you? Soon I will return to fight against the prince of Persia, and when I go, the prince of Greece will come; [21]but first I will tell you what is written in the Book of Truth. (No one supports me against them except Michael, your prince.)

15–17 Although he was fully conscious, thanks to the restorative touch of the angel (vv.10–11), Daniel remained speechless—perhaps he was too emotionally overcome to form any words. According to v.15, his face bowed toward the ground (*nāṯattî pānay 'arṣāh,* lit., "I set my face earthward") as the angel spoke to him. But then some heavenly figure in human form (whether the interpreting angel himself or some other angel, we cannot tell) reached out and touched Daniel's lips, enabling him to say how he felt (v.16b). Daniel's response—"I am overcome with anguish because of the vision, . . . and I am helpless"—parallels the awe of young Isaiah in 740 B.C., after seeing the vision of God's throne. Isaiah could only exclaim, "Woe to me! . . . I am ruined! For I am a man of unclean lips, and my eyes have seen the king, the LORD Almighty" (Isa 6:5). A seraph put a live coal to Isaiah's lips, to grant his mouth new power to speak to Israel in God's name. Similarly here, the angel's touch was all Daniel needed to regain his speech. At first he could only speak of his utter weakness (vv.16b–17).

18–19 The same angel touched Daniel again, giving him renewed strength. Like Paul (2 Cor 12:9–10), Daniel found that God's strength was made perfect through his own weakness—once he had humbly faced his utter inadequacy and thrown himself on the grace and power of God. So the angel once more reassured Daniel, again addressing him as "O man highly esteemed" (*'îš ḥamuḏôṯ,* v.19; cf. v.11) and exhorting him as Joshua had been exhorted on the eve of his conquest of the Holy Land (Josh 1:9). In the presence of the mighty angel, Daniel felt certain that the Lord was with him and was ready to use him mightily. Reassured, the aged Daniel was then ready to give close attention to God's revelation of the future and to write it down with utmost care. "Speak, my lord," he said to the angel, "since you have given me strength."

20–21 In this paragraph of chapter 10, the interpreting angel indicated that he was still in combat for the Lord and would soon have to return to the battlefield and fight against renewed attacks from the demon assigned to Persia by the prince of hell ("the prince of Persia," *śar pārās,* v.20). This antagonist would be succeeded and perhaps aided by another satanic champion called the "prince of Greece"(*śar-yāwān*).

These references to contests of strength between the warriors of heaven and the warriors of hell raise interesting questions. Where do such battles take place? Revelation 12:7 suggests that they are waged up in "heaven," for we read: "There was war in heaven. Michael and his angels fought against the dragon, and the dragon and his angels fought back." The subsequent verses relate that in that future contest (which apparently will take place during the Great Tribulation), the dragon (i.e., Satan himself; cf. Rev 20:2) will be vanquished and cast out of heaven, compelled to confine his activities to the earth alone. At present he enjoys the status of "ruler of the kingdom of the air" (Eph 2:2). We have no way of knowing how bodiless spirits —heavenly or hellish—fight one another or what weapons they use. But the Bible tells us that they are organized into various provinces or domains, which are referred to in the NT as *archai* ("governments, " "rulers"), *exousiai* ("authorities"), and enjoy the status of *kosmokratores* ("world rulers," "powers of this world"). Without flesh and blood, they are evil spirit-beings who occupy assigned superterrestrial regions (cf. Eph 6:12: "the spiritual forces of evil in the heavenly realm"). It is encouraging for God's people to know that he has mighty champions among the holy angels whose task is to defend the saints against the attacks of the evil one.

XI. The Tribulation Under Antiochus and Under Antichrist (11:1–45)

1. *From the Persian Empire to the Death of Alexander*

11:1–4

1And in the first year of Darius the Mede, I took my stand to support and protect him.)
2"Now then, I tell you the truth: Three more kings will appear in Persia, and then a fourth, who will be far richer than all the others. When he has gained power by his wealth, he will stir up everyone against the kingdom of Greece. 3Then a mighty king will appear, who will rule with great power and do as he pleases.
4After he has appeared, his empire will be broken up and parceled out toward the four winds of heaven. It will not go to his descendants, nor will it have the power he exercised, because his empire will be uprooted and given to others.

1 For some reason not quite clear, the first verse of chapter 11 (as divided by both the MT and the LXX) has been linked to the predictions of the destinies of the world empires (ch. 11), rather than being assigned to the end of chapter 10. But as the Kittel edition of the OT indicates, the true connection is with what precedes. Clearly 11:1 points back to 10:21, which speaks of the angel's alliance with the archangel, Michael, against the demons of Persia and Greece and specifies the first year of Darius the Mede (539–538 B.C.) as the time when his contest with Satan's emissaries began. This suggests that the struggle had already been going on for four or five years (since the episode of chs. 10–12 takes place in the third year of Cyrus as king of Babylon).

The occasion for the spiritual warfare was the restoration of the believing remnant of Israel to the Holy Land and their survival there as a commonwealth of the faithful, living in obedience to Holy Scripture. Knowing that such a development could lead to the ultimate appearance of the Son of God as the Messiah for God's redeemed, Satan and all his hosts were determined to thwart the renewal of Israel and the deliverance of her people from destruction. The supreme effort to exterminate them altogether was to take place some fifty-five years later, in the reign of Ahasuerus (Xerxes), when Haman secured his consent to obliterate the entire Jewish race. The conflict between Michael and the "prince of Persia" (10:13) may have had some bearing on this event, and it may have been Michael's victory over his satanic foes that paved the way for Queen Esther to thwart this genocide. The second effort of Satan was to take place under Antiochus Epiphanes, who sought to obliterate the Jewish faith by forbidding its practice on pain of death. The momentous events of 167–164 B.C. may well have been profoundly affected by this supernatural warfare between the forces of heaven and hell. Though this is not explicitly stated here, in the light of subsequent events it is reasonable to assume that these were some of the issues over which Michael was locked in combat with Satan's deputies to Persia and Greece.

2 Michael began to detail what God ordained for the future of the second commonwealth up till the crisis reign of Antiochus Epiphanes. The Persian king who invaded Greece was, of course, Xerxes, who reigned 485–464 B.C. The three kings who preceded him after the death of Cyrus, the incumbent ruler, were (1) Cambyses, Cyrus's elder son, who in the six or seven years of his reign (529–523) succeeded in conquering Egypt; (2) then for a year or two an imposter named Gaumata or Bardiya (523–522), who passed himself off as Cyrus's younger son, Smerdis (even though the true Smerdis had been secretly murdered by his brother's agents); and (3) Darius the Persian (522–485), the son of Hystaspes, who in 522 assassinated the imposter and was elevated to the kingship in his place. Darius himself was of royal blood, since he was a cousin of Cyrus through his father, Hystaspes.

Darius had made an earlier attempt to conquer Athens in 490 B.C. to punish it for aiding the Ionian Greek cities in their abortive revolt against their Persian overlords. But Darius's naval expedition, commanded by Datis and Artaphernes, came to grief at the Battle of Marathon, fought near the north-central coast of Attica; and the battered survivors had to withdraw from the fierce onslaught of the Athenian militia. And so it was an inherited obligation that Xerxes, Darius's son, took over on his accession, to wreak vengeance on Athens. But there was the added factor of the momentum of empire building that would in any event have motivated the Persians to keep pushing westward, in order that Xerxes himself might win the personal glory of adding yet another realm to the vast domain he inherited from his father. As it turned out, however, Xerxes sustained an even more crushing defeat than his father had. After his great army (estimated by Herodotus at a million men) had subdued virtually all of Greece down to the Isthmus of Corinth and the city of Athens had been reduced to ashes, Xerxes' navy was thoroughly worsted by the united Greek fleet at the Battle of Salamis in 480 B.C. This unexpected setback prompted him to beat a hasty retreat to Asia. The one-hundred-thousand-man land army he left behind under the command of Mardonius was completely crushed in the following year by the allied forces of the Greeks at the battle of Plataea.

3–4 Verse 3 introduces us to the next phase in world empires: the rise of Alexander the Great. Although this verse does not make it altogether clear that this "mighty king" would inaugurate a new empire in place of the Persian one, v.4 leaves us in no doubt that he was the ruler predicted here.

"After he has appeared" (which might be better translated "As soon as he has appeared," a good rendering of the particle *k*ᵉ before the infinitive *ʿomdô* ["his standing up"]) clearly suggests that this mighty conqueror was going to have a comparatively brief reign. Alexander's first clash with the Persian troops came at the Battle of Granicus in 334, and his final overthrow of the Persian power took place in 331 at Gaugamela, seventy-five miles northwest of Arbela. After that he pushed all the way eastward to Afghanistan and the Indus River and Bahawalpur, beyond the farthest reaches of Persian conquest. There at last he was compelled by his battle-weary troops to return westward to Babylon in 327. Thus in seven or eight years he accomplished the most dazzling military conquest in human history. But he lived only four years more; and after one of his drunken bouts, he died of a fever in 323 in the imperial capital of Babylon.

Verse 4 foretells the division of Alexander's domains among four smaller and weaker empires. After a period of imperial regency under Perdiccas (murdered in 321) and Antigonus (who was finally crushed at the Battle of Ipsus in 301), the widespread domains of Alexander were parceled out into (1) Macedonia-Greece under Antipater and his son Cassander; (2) Thrace-Asia Minor under Lysimachus, who had been the principal leader in the Battle of Ipsus; (3) Seleucus Nicator, the ruler over all the rest of Asia except lower Syria and Palestine; and (4) Ptolemy, son of Lagus, the king of Egypt and Palestine. The infant son of Alexander III (the Great) was Alexander IV, born of the Persian princess Roxana. Kept under Cassander's custody, he was removed by murder in 310 B.C. His uncle, Philip Arrhidaeus, who was an illegitimate brother of Alexander III and mentally deranged, had already been assassinated in 317. Thus there were no descendants or blood relatives to succeed Alexander himself, and the prediction "not go to his descendants" found fulfillment. The four ruthless and powerful generals named above became the "Diadochi" ("Successors") who engineered the partition of the Macedonian Empire into four realms.

2. *The Wars Between the Ptolemies and the Seleucids*

11:5–20

5"The king of the South will become strong, but one of his commanders will become even stronger than he and will rule his own kingdom with great power. 6After some years, they will become allies. The daughter of the king of the South will go to the king of the North to make an alliance, but she will not retain her power, and he and his power will not last. In those days she will be handed over, together with her royal escort and her father and the one who supported her.

7"One from her family line will arise to take her place. He will attack the forces of the king of the North and enter his fortress; he will fight against them and be victorious. 8He will also seize their gods, their metal images and their valuable articles of silver and gold and carry them off to Egypt. For some years he will leave the king of the North alone. 9Then the king of the North will invade the realm of the king of the South but will retreat to his own country. 10His sons will prepare for war and assemble a great army, which will sweep on like an irresistible flood and carry the battle as far as his fortress.

11"Then the king of the South will march out in a rage and fight against the king of the North, who will raise a large army, but it will be defeated. 12When the army is carried off, the king of the South will be filled with pride and will slaughter many thousands, yet he will not remain triumphant. 13For the king of the North will muster another army, larger than the first; and after several years, he will advance with a huge army fully equipped.

14"In those times many will rise against the king of the South. The violent men among your own people will rebel in fulfillment of the vision, but without success. 15Then the king of the North will come and build up siege ramps and will capture a fortified city. The forces of the South will be powerless to resist; even their best troops will not have the strength to stand. 16The invader will do as he pleases; no one will be able to stand against him. He will establish himself in the Beautiful Land and will have the power to destroy it. 17He will determine to come with the might of his entire kingdom and will make an alliance with the king of the South. And he will give him a daughter in marriage in order to overthrow the kingdom, but his plans will not succeed or help him. 18Then he will turn his attention to the coastlands and will take many of them, but a commander will put an end to his insolence and will turn his insolence back upon him. 19After this, he will turn back toward the fortresses of his own country but will stumble and fall, to be seen no more.

[20]"His successor will send out a tax collector to maintain the royal splendor. In a few years, however, he will be destroyed, yet not in anger or in battle.

5–6 "The king of the South" (v.5) was to be Ptolemy I (Soter), son of Lagus, whose ambitions extended far beyond the borders of Egypt (over which Alexander had placed him in charge) to Palestine and the rest of Asia. Temporarily his naval forces captured Cyprus and important bases in Asia Minor, and there even were times when he wielded considerable influence over some of the city-states of the Greek mainland. But during the 280 years between Ptolemy I and Cleopatra VII (who met her end around 30 B.C.), the domain of the Ptolemies was pretty well restricted to Egypt and Cyprus; they lost Palestine to the Seleucid king Antiochus III shortly before 200 B.C.

The "one of his commanders [who] will become even stronger than he" was none other than Seleucus Nicator of the Seleucid Empire. Originally he had served under Perdiccas and Antigonus in Babylon but had had a falling out with the latter in 316. Thereafter he defected to Ptolemy; and, after the defeat of Antigonus, he made his way back to Babylon (where he was well liked) with Ptolemy's sponsorship in 312, two years after which he assumed the title of king, so that 310 became the official starting date for the Seleucid Era. Since Seleucus secured control of Alexander's old domains all the way to the Indus on the east and to Syria and Phoenicia on the west, his authority far surpassed that of his sponsor, Ptolemy. Seleucus's dynasty endured till 64 B.C., when Pompey delivered the coup de grâce to a truncated empire that had already lost Babylon and all its eastern dominions to the Parthians.

After the death of Ptolemy I in 285, his son Ptolemy II (Philadelphus) continued the contest with the Seleucids till 252, when a treaty of peace was finally arranged with Antiochus II (Theos), under the terms of which Antiochus was to marry Berenice, the daughter of Philadelphus. This furnished a serious complication, however, for Antiochus already had a wife, a powerful and influential woman named Laodice. She did not take kindly to being divorced, despite the obvious political advantages accruing from an alliance with Ptolemaic Egypt (v.6). She therefore organized a successful conspiracy, operating from her place of banishment, where she had been sent after the divorce; and she managed to have both Berenice and her infant son, whom she had borne to Antiochus, assassinated. Not long afterward the king himself was poisoned to death (247 B.C.), and the pro-Laodice party engineered a coup d'état that put her in power as queen regent during the minority of her son, Seleucus II (Callinicus). In this manner, then, the prophecy was fulfilled concerning Berenice, that she would be "handed over," along with the nobles who supported her in Antioch.

7–12 Verse 7 sets forth the subsequent reprisal. Ptolemy Philadelphus died in 247 B.C., soon after the tragedy that had overtaken his daughter Berenice. But his capable son Ptolemy III (Euergetes) organized a great expeditionary force against Syria, in order to avenge his sister's death. This war raged from 246 to 241, in the course of which Ptolemy captured and pillaged the Seleucid capital of Antioch and invaded its eastern domains as far as Bactria. Finally he returned to Egypt laden with spoil, but he did not see fit to add much of the Seleucid territory on a permanent basis. He did, however, shatter the Seleucid navy in the Aegean Sea and remained the foremost naval power in that region for the duration of his reign. He succeeded on other fronts as well, for he reunited Cyrenaica (at the western end of Libya) with the Ptolemaic domains, after it had enjoyed twelve years of independence. He also recovered all his father's conquests on the coasts of Asia Minor and temporarily gained control of some portions of Thrace.

Verse 8 calls attention to the recovery of the long-lost idols and sacred treasures from Persia taken as booty by Cambyses in 524 B.C. For this return of their cherished images, the native Egyptian populace received Ptolemy III with adulation as he returned to the Nile laden with spoil. It was for this restoration of their national honor as against the hated Persians that they acclaimed him as *Euergetes* ("Benefactor"). He then seized "their gods, their metal images and their valuable articles of silver and gold and [carried] them off to Egypt." Alluding to the treaty of peace that Ptolemy III made with Seleucus II in 240—for he was much occupied with his Aegean conquests after that time—the verse concludes: "For some years he will leave the king of the North alone."

Verse 9 records a subsequent foray of Seleucus II into Ptolemaic territory, referring to the successful attempt of the Seleucid forces to regain control of northern Syria and Phoenicia, probably in the 230s. There is no record of Seleucus II's attempting an invasion of Egypt proper.

Verse 10 foretells an important new development in the struggle between the two great powers, with the advent of Antiochus the Great and his conquest of the Holy Land. Seleucus II (Callinicus) died in 226 and was succeeded by his son Seleucus III (Soter), who reigned for only three years. His principal efforts were directed against Asia Minor, where he fought against King Attalus of Pergamum.

The second son of Callinicus and Antiochus III; because of his military successes, he received the surname of "the Great" (*Megas*). Coming to the throne in 223, he first had to suppress a revolt in the eastern provinces. His trusted governor, Molon, had turned against him and set himself up as an independent king. After defeating Molon in battle (220 B.C.), Antiochus III next launched an expedition against Phoenicia and Palestine (219–218) that ended in a serious setback at the Battle of Raphia, where he was soundly beaten by the smaller army of Ptolemy IV. Verses 11–12 tell the story: "Then the king of the South will march out in a rage and fight against the king of the North, who will raise a large army, but it will be defeated." This refers to that setback administered to the forces of Ptolemy IV at Raphia. Then comes the sequel: "When the army is carried off, the king of the South will be filled with pride and will slaughter many thousands, yet he will not remain triumphant."

In the peace that followed, Antiochus III was compelled to cede all Phoenicia and Palestine back to Ptolemy IV and leave him in undisturbed possession of them till some more convenient time. During the following years, Antiochus attained his most brilliant successes in subduing and subjugating the rebellious provinces in the Middle East all the way to the Caspian Sea in the north and the Indus River on the east. These invasions absorbed all his energies from 212 to 204. But finally in 203, Antiochus saw his opportunity to strike at Egypt again, since Ptolemy IV had just died and had been succeeded by Ptolemy V (Epiphanes), who was a mere boy of four.

13–19 Verse 13 tells us that "the king of the North will muster another army, larger than the first; and after several years, he will advance with a huge army fully equipped." In 202 Antiochus advanced once more against Phoenicia and Palestine with his battle-seasoned veterans and pushed all the way down to the fortress of

Gaza, which fell in 201. Verse 14 continues: "In those times many will rise against the king of the South [i.e., Ptolemy V]. The violent men among your own people [i.e., the pro-Seleucid Jews] will rebel in fulfillment of the vision [i.e., this prophecy now being revealed], but without success." This refers to the counteroffensive launched by the powerful General Scopas of the Egyptian forces, who was able to punish all the leaders in Jerusalem and Judah who favored the claims of Antiochus and were disaffected with the Ptolemaic government. But soon the war swept down from the north, and Scopas met with a severe loss at the Battle of Panium (near the NT Caesarea Philippi, now called Banias) in 200 B.C. From there he retreated to Sidon on the Phoenician coast. This set the stage for v.15: "Then the king of the North will come and build up siege ramps and will capture a fortified city [i.e., Sidon]. The forces of the South will be powerless to resist; even their best troops will not have the strength to stand."

When Scopas finally surrendered to Antiochus III at Sidon, the Holy Land was permanently acquired by the Antioch government, to the exclusion of Egypt. Verse 16 reads: "The invader will do as he pleases; no one will be able to stand against him. He will establish himself in the Beautiful Land [i.e., Palestine] and will have the power to destroy it." Antiochus did not pursue a general policy of destruction, once he had secured full possession of the land of Israel; he simply exacted reprisals from the pro-Egyptian party leaders he was able to capture. On his entrance into Jerusalem in 198 B.C., he was welcomed as a deliverer and benefactor.

Verse 17 may be more literally translated thus: "Then he will set his face to come with the power of all his kingdom, and equitable conditions [*y^e^šārîm*] shall be with him, and he will accomplish it. And he will give to him the daughter of women in order for her to corrupt (or 'destroy'] him [or possibly 'it,' referring to the kingdom of Egypt]." That is to say, the third feminine singular pronominal suffix *āh* appended to the Hiphil infinitive *hašḥîṯ* ("corrupt," "destroy") may be a subjective genitive (i.e., "for her to corrupt"), or else it may be the object and mean "in order to destroy her [or 'it']"—with no eligible antecedent in sight. Perhaps the implied antecedent would be "the kingdom of the South," but this is quite debatable. The NASB leaves the *āh* as the object "it"—which is accurate enough but leaves the antecedent completely ambiguous. Aalders (pp. 237–38) is inclined to equate the "it" with "the land of Egypt" and condemns the subjective genitive interpretation as "linguistically impossible." But actually this alleged impossibility seems much preferable to coping with an object pronoun for which there is no available antecedent whatever. And so it is better to take the *āh* as referring to Antiochus's daughter Cleopatra rather than construing it as an impersonal object, "it."

The clear intention of Antiochus himself was to bring the boy king Ptolemy V, who in 197 was no more than ten years old, under the influence of his daughter, with the expectation of her maintaining a strongly pro-Seleucid policy in Egypt. Then, of course, if Cleopatra should give birth to a son, that boy would become legal heir to both crowns. This in turn might create a situation favorable to intervention or strong control in Egypt on the part of Antiochus himself, as the maternal grandfather.

As it turned out, however, after the marriage finally took place in 195, Cleopatra became completely sympathetic to her husband, Ptolemy V, and the Ptolemaic cause, much to the disappointment of her father, Antiochus. Therefore when she gave birth to a royal heir, who became Ptolemy VI, this gave no particular advantage or political leverage to her father. When Ptolemy V died in 181, Cleopatra was appointed queen regent by the Egyptian government, because they all loved and appreciated her loyalty to their cause. But she herself died not long after, and this meant the end of all possible Seleucid influence on Egyptian affairs. Yet by that time Antiochus himself, who died in 187 B.C., was gone.

Verse 18 points to an important new development in the career of Antiochus the Great. "Then he will turn his attention to the coastlands and will take many of them, but a commander will put an end to his insolence and will turn his insolence back upon him." Soon after his victory over Scopas at Panium and Sidon, Antiochus became involved in a new war front, against the powerful principality of Pergamum and the Aegean coastline island of Rhodes. As Antiochus's forces closed in on them, the Rhodians sent urgent appeals for Rome to come to their aid. Another important development was the arrival of Hannibal from his exile in Macedonia to join the court of Antiochus as a military adviser. It was only natural for the Roman government to resent his offering asylum to their enemy. But Antiochus was not to be cowed, for he felt that he had the power to cope successfully with the military might of Rome. Therefore in 196 after capturing several cities in Aeolis and Ionia, he crossed the Hellespont and the Aegean with his powerful navy and conquered considerable territory in Thrace. The "coastlands" (*'Iyyîm*, which usually means "islands") included all areas contiguous to the seacoast, whether or not they were islands. It was used from earliest times as a term for the Mediterranean, with its large islands like Cyprus and Crete and its numerous smaller islands in the Aegean and the West.

About this time the west-central Greek confederacy of the Aetolian League sent a legation to Antiochus, asking for his assistance against Macedon and the Peloponnesians. He therefore sent a modest naval force in 192 to land on the coast of central Greece and cooperate with the Aetolians. But the latter proved to be militarily ineffective, and the Macedonians joined forces with the Achaean League to oppose Antiochus both from the north and from the south. The Romans were only too happy to jump into the fray at this point; so they joined their Greek allies to overwhelm the Seleucid command post at Thermopylae—the historic battle-site of the Persian War in 480 B.C. As a result of this setback, Antiochus had to withdraw to Asia Minor in 191, especially since his navy was beaten in several engagements with the Roman fleet. During the winter of 190–189, the Roman troops followed him across to Asia and finally met him in a pitched battle at Magnesia, west of Sardis. Although Antiochus had an army of seventy thousand at his disposal to confront the Roman force of thirty thousand, he was badly defeated. Thus his "insolence" (*ḥerpāh*, "reproach," "reviling," which may also be rendered "scorn" or even "defiance") met with disaster.

The Roman "commander" (*qāṣîn*) was none other than Lucius Cornelius Scipio Asiaticus, the brother of the Publius Cornelius Scipio Africanus, who had brilliantly defeated Hannibal at the Battle of Zama back in 202 B.C. After he compelled Antiochus to surrender, the commander dictated severe peace terms, which were included in the Treaty of Apamea, signed in 188. Antiochus was compelled to surrender not only all claims to Europe but also the greater part of Asia Minor as well; his boundary was to be the Taurus Range. Furthermore, he had to surrender his entire elephant brigade, all his navy, and twenty selected hostages. Finally he was obliged to pay an indemnity of fifteen thousand or twenty thousand talents over a period of several years. Antiochus's second son, who was named after him, was among the twenty hostages taken to Rome, where he spent the formative years of his life. He later became the dreaded persecutor of the Jews, Antiochus Epiphanes.

The end of the career of Antiochus the Great is briefly indicated in v.19: "After this, he will turn back toward the fortresses of his own country but will stumble and fall, to be seen no more." As a matter of fact, this erstwhile conqueror met an inglorious end in the following year (187). Unable to meet the required indemnity payments out of his exhausted treasury, he resorted to the sacrilege of pillaging—or attempting to pillage—the temple of Bel in Elymais. But the local inhabitants were so incensed that they stormed his modest armed force with desperate bravery and succeeded in killing him and defending their temple.

20 This verse sums up the uneventful reign of the elder son of Antiochus, Seleucus IV (Philopator). The rendering "His successor will send out a tax collector [*nôḡēś*] to maintain the royal splendor" assumes that *nôḡēś* is in construct (i.e., in a genitive relationship) with *heḏer malḵûṯ* ("of the glory of the kingdom"), which is taken to mean "to maintain the royal splendor." But another attractive possibility is to make *heḏer malḵûṯ* the second object after the participle *ma'ᵃḇîr* ("one who sends out"). Then *heḏer malḵûṯ* would refer to the land of Palestine, as the glorious adornment (from God's standpoint) of the Seleucid Empire. Thus NASB has "one will arise who will send an oppressor through the Jewel of his kingdom."

At all events, the oppressor or tax collector (*nôḡēś*) sent out by Seleucus IV was apparently his special fund-raiser, Heliodorus. According to 2 Maccabees 3:7–40, a certain traitorous Jew named Simon sent information to the king that the Jerusalem temple contained sufficient treasure to meet all the king's needs. Impoverished as his treasury was (partly through the yearly indemnity payments to Rome of one thousand talents), Seleucus eagerly grasped at the prospect of plundering the temple and sent off Heliodorus to carry out this assignment. It was only because of a frightful vision of mighty angels assaulting and flogging him that Heliodorus desisted from his invasion of the temple of Yahweh and returned home empty-handed. No other details are given in this verse of the twelve-year reign of this rather ineffectual king, except that he did not die in battle or in a mob action as had his father, Antiochus. Yet Seleucus IV met an untimely end through poison administered by Heliodorus.

Notes

7 Actually, the MT has כַּנּוֹ (*kannô* "his place"). Therefore NASB is better: "But one of the descendants of her line will arise in his place," i.e., in his own capital down in Egypt.

9 The principal ancient sources of information concerning this period are as follows: (1) Polybius of Megalopolis (203–111 B.C.), who composed the general history in forty volumes, comprising the history of the Roman world from 199–167 B.C.; (2) Titus Livius of the first century B.C., who in his monumental history of Rome (*Ab Urbe Condita Libri CLXII*) treats of the Roman contacts with the Near East up to the death of Philip V of Macedon in vols. 31–60: (3) Flavius Josephus, the Jewish historian of the late first century A.D., whose principal works (*Antiquities of the Jews* and *The Wars of the Jews*) were composed in Greek; (4) Appianus Historicus (his other names are not known), who composed most of his works in Greek, although *Bella Civilia* survives only in Latin. He came originally from Alexandria but transferred to Rome for his adult career during the reigns of Trajan, Hadrian, and Antoninus Pius. His Συριακή (*Syriakē*) relates particularly to the Seleucid and Ptolemaic period; (5) Lucius Annaeus Florus, likewise in the time of Trajan (early second cent. A.D.), composed *Epitome de Gestis Romanorum*; (6) Marcus Junianus Justinus (of the late second cent. A.D.) composed a summary of the work of an earlier historian named Trogus. It was entitled *Historiarum Philippicarum et Totius Mundi Originum . . . ex Trogo Pompeio Excerptarum Libri XLIV* and was dedicated to Marcus Aurelius.

10 וְשָׁטַף (*w^e^šāṭap*, "will sweep on") is cognate with בַשֶּׁטֶף (*baššeṭep*, "like a flood") in 9:26.

11–12 Concerning Ptolemy IV Philopator (221–203 B.C.), S.B. Hoenig (IDB, 3:965) contributes the following information: After the victory over Antiochus at the Battle of Raphia in 217 B.C., Ptolemy IV came to Jerusalem and wanted to enter the temple there, "considering everything as his realm and believing that he could not be denied admission. He had no mercenary motives. He was prevented, however, and . . . was smitten by divine agents. Returning to Egypt he vented his anger upon the Jews, and issued an edict to punish them and reduce them to slavery." Presumably the persecution was leveled particularly at the large Jewish colony in Alexandria. Ptolemy IV was a cruel debauchee who began his reign by murdering his own mother, Berenice of Cyrene, and then his wife, his sister, and his brother. He then gave himself over to a degenerate dissipation with male and female sex partners and finally succumbed to disease in 203.

---

3. *The Great Persecution Under Antiochus Epiphanes*

11:21–35

21"He will be succeeded by a contemptible person who has not been given the honor of royalty. He will invade the kingdom when its people feel secure, and he will seize it through intrigue. 22Then an overwhelming army will be swept away before him; both it and a prince of the covenant will be destroyed. 23After coming to an agreement with him, he will act deceitfully, and with only a few people he will rise to power. 24When the richest provinces feel secure, he will invade them and will achieve what neither his fathers nor his forefathers did. He will distribute plunder, loot and wealth among his followers. He will plot the overthrow of fortresses—but only for a time.

25"With a large army he will stir up his strength and courage against the king of the South. The king of the South will wage war with a large and very powerful army, but he will not be able to stand because of the plots devised against him. 26Those who eat from the king's provisions will try to destroy him; his army will be swept away, and many will fall in battle. 27The two kings, with their hearts bent on evil, will sit at the same table and lie to each other, but to no avail, because an end will still come at the appointed time. 28The king of the North will return to his own country with great wealth, but his heart will be set against the holy covenant. He will take action against it and then return to his own country.

29"At the appointed time he will invade the South again, but this time the outcome will be different from what it was before. 30Ships of the western coastlands will oppose him, and he will lose heart. Then he will turn back and vent his fury against the holy covenant. He will return and show favor to those who forsake the holy covenant.

31"His armed forces will rise up to desecrate the temple fortress and will abolish the daily sacrifice. Then they will set up the abomination that causes desolation. 32With flattery he will corrupt those who have violated the covenant, but the people who know their God will firmly resist him.

33"Those who are wise will instruct many, though for a time they will fall by the sword or be burned or captured or plundered. 34When they fall, they will receive a little help, and many who are not sincere will join them. 35Some of the wise will stumble, so that they may be refined, purified and made spotless until the time of the end, for it will still come at the appointed time.

21 Verses 21–35 are devoted to the career of the tyrannical oppressor who did his utmost to destroy the Jewish religion altogether. He previously appeared in 8:9–12, 23–25 as the sinister "little horn" who will suspend the worship of God in the Jerusalem temple. Now he is introduced as a despicable tyrant (*nibzeh*, "contemptible person") who will shed much blood and enjoy power for a time.

Verse 21 states that this tyrant "has not been given the honor of royalty." The young son of Seleucus IV, Demetrius I, was next in line to receive the crown. But since he was still held as a hostage in Rome, it was deemed best to put his uncle Antiochus IV—the second son of Antiochus the Great—in charge of the government as prince regent. But Antiochus was determined to set aside his nephew's claims altogether even though he was already in his twenties and quite competent to rule. So Antiochus curried favor with governmental leaders and, by promises of promotion and large favors in return for their support, managed to secure approval for succession to the throne vacated by his poisoned brother. Fortunately for Demetrius, he was still being held in Rome; so he was safe for the time being from assassination by his uncle's agents. Later on he was able to make good his claim to the throne, for he left Rome to lead an army against the son of Antiochus Epiphanes, Antiochus V (Eupator), in 162.

As for Epiphanes, that "contemptible person who has not been given the honor of royalty," he converted his regency into royalty soon after 175 and launched his own career as an ambitious and vigorous leader. It should be observed that the title "Epiphanes" ("the Illustrious One") also carries the meaning of "very evident" or "manifest." From his coins we know that he linked up this *Epiphanēs* with the added title *Theos* ("God"). Thus the two in combination meant "Illustrious God," or else "God Manifest." Bearing in mind his role as a type of the Antichrist, or Beast of the last days (who appears in ch. 7 as the "little horn," arising from the fourth kingdom), it becomes particularly meaningful to read of that future antitype in 2 Thessalonians 2:3–4: "The man of lawlessness . . . [who] opposes and exalts himself over everything that is called God or is worshiped, and even sets himself up in God's temple, proclaiming himself to be God." Not only did Antiochus enthrone himself for adoration by the Jews as he sat in the court of the desecrated Jerusalem temple (in 168 B.C.), but he also claimed divine honors for himself on every major coin that he minted. (Many of his detractors, however, referred to him as Epinanes ["madman"] rather than Epiphanes; cf. Polybius 26.1.1.)

22–24 Verse 22 introduces us to the brilliantly successful commencement of Antiochus Epiphanes' reign, as he took up anew the struggle with Ptolemaic Egypt. It was Epiphanes' policy to throw his intended victims off guard by offering them his friendship and alliance. Then he would maneuver for an advantageous position till he could catch them by surprise. So it was with Ptolemy VII (Philometor), who had ascended the throne in 181 B.C. at the age of six. His mother, Cleopatra (daughter of Antiochus the Great), governed as queen regent till her death. But after he assumed power as king, he determined to recapture the regions of Palestine and Phoenicia that had been lost to Antiochus III. At first Ptolemy VII's invasion met with considerable success, for he had challenged Antiochus with a large and well-equipped army. But eventually he encountered a serious reverse and became a prisoner of Antiochus Epiphanes.

At this turn of events, the Egyptians gave up hope of regaining their king and decided to appoint his young brother Physcon as king in his place. On learning of this, Epiphanes craftily intervened on behalf of Ptolemy Philometor, his royal prisoner, and mounted an expeditionary force against Physcon's government in order to reestablish Philometor on his throne—now as Antiochus's ally rather than as his adversary. So as the price of his help in expelling Physcon, Antiochus made a treaty of friendship and alliance with Philometor aimed at obtaining a foothold in Egypt itself and ultimately uniting the two kingdoms under his own authority. The seriousness of this aim is attested by the issue of coinage (in the large and medium-sized bronzes, at least) that bore the same types as the corresponding Ptolemaic coinage (the head of Zeus on the obverse and the Ptolemaic eagle on the reverse) but with the legend "King Antiochus, God Manifest" rather than the usual Egyptian "Ptolemy the King." Though these Egyptian-type coins were presumably used in the Seleucid territory rather than in Egypt itself, they at least served to suggest his potential claims to the Ptolemaic domains. In point of fact Antiochus had succeeded in penetrating Egypt itself all the way to Memphis, which he managed to capture, along with the person of Philometor himself.

Later on, however, Antiochus's alliance with Philometor wore so thin that his reestablished protégé decided to make peace with Ptolemy Physcon, his defeated brother, because he felt he needed his help in dislodging Antiochus's troops from the border fortress of Pelusium.

Having made Physcon his associate king, Ptolemy Philometor was able to raise a considerable armed force for the expulsion of the Seleucid army. But no sooner did Epiphanes learn of this development than he again marched against Egypt, intending to subdue it once and for all. But this effort was forestalled by the intervention of the Roman fleet, which had been hurriedly dispatched to Alexandria in response to the urgent request of the embattled Ptolemies. The aggressive Roman commander Popilius Laenas met Antiochus marshalling his hosts for a siege of Alexandria and informed him that the Roman government ordered him to quit Egypt immediately or face the consequences of war with Rome. Remembering what had happened to his father at the Battle of Magnesia and recalling also his years as a young hostage in Roman captivity, it did not take Antiochus very long to give way before this mandate—especially after Popilius drew a circle around him with his staff and ordered him to make his decision before he stepped outside it. Even though Antiochus had for a time succeeded in destroying the power of "the prince of the covenant" (v.22)—Ptolemy Philometor—the remaining verses predicting his eventual failure found their fulfillment in this humiliation that took place near Alexandria in 169 B.C.

Verses 23–24 describe the developments already set forth above: "After coming to an agreement with him [i.e., Philometor], he will act deceitfully, and with only a few people [his initial invasion had been made by a small force] he will rise to power." The phrase "richest provinces" (*mišmannê mᵉdînāh*) apparently refers not only to Egypt itself, as described above, but also to the eastern provinces all the way to Bactria, where successful campaigns were conducted by Eucratides, Antiochus's general. In 166, Antiochus conducted a full-scale muster of his armies at Daphnae, just outside Antioch, in celebration of the tenth anniversary of his rule—even after his expulsion from Egypt by Popilius Laenas.

25–28 Verses 25–26 refer more particularly to the earlier invasion of Egypt in 170, after Ptolemy had attempted an attack on Palestine. The king of the South's great army did not make him invincible beause "of the plots devised against him" by

Antiochus and his agents in Egypt. "Those who eat from the king's provisions will try to destroy him [i.e., Ptolemy Philometor]; his army will be swept away" probably refers to negotiations carried on by the two victors at the banquet table, apparently after Physcon had been defeated and expelled from Egypt, with the help of Antiochus's troops. At this stage these ostensibly cordial allies were already plotting against each other.

Quite clearly "the end" (v.27) pertained to the permanent suspension of Antiochus's campaign to annex Egypt to his domains; it is explained by v.28: "The king of the North will return to his own country [i.e., to his capital of Antioch] with great wealth [from plundering Physcon's army], but his heart will be set against the holy covenant [*b^e^rîṯ qōḏeš*]. He will take action against it and then return to his own country." The significant term here is "the holy covenant." Apparently this does not refer to the covenant between Antiochus and Ptolemy VII—as we have taken "prince of the covenant" in v.22 to mean, though some interpret that phrase as referring to the Jewish high priest. It rather seems to signify the religious establishment in Jerusalem, or even the monotheistic Jewish population as a whole. It is here that the clash between Antiochus and the faith of Israel begins on a serious level.

The original friction had arisen over the question of the high priesthood. It seems that early in his reign, Antiochus IV had been approached by a younger member of the high priestly family named Jason, who promised the king that if he would depose from office the current, legitimate high priest, Onias III, then he—Jason—would pay the king a handsome bribe for this service. Antiochus was happy to accede to this request; Onias was removed and Jason installed in his place. But once the precedent of imperial interference had been set, still another brother, Menelaus, offered Antiochus a bribe still larger than Jason's if he would be installed in place of Jason. Antiochus had no scruples about supplanting one rascal by another, so long as he himself was enriched in the process. So in 172 B.C. Menelaus took Jason's place and set about selling some of the votive offerings and golden utensils of the temple to raise the cash necessary for the bribe. At this sacrilege the godly high priest Onias, though deposed, earnestly protested and so angered Menelaus that he had Onias killed. But this murder so angered the populace of Jerusalem that they became bitter against Menelaus and sent representatives to Antiochus himself to accuse Menelaus and his wicked brother Lysimachus. Antiochus did execute Andronicus, the agent of Menelaus who had murdered Onias. But a little later a courtier Menelaus had bribed persuaded Antiochus to act against the Jerusalemites. So instead of punishing Menelaus as he deserved, the king had the Jerusalem representatives put to death in Tyre, where the whole matter was being adjudicated (cf. 2 Macc 4:30–50).

Later on (167 B.C.) Antiochus, following his bitter disappointment in Egypt, went and encamped near Jerusalem. He had a score to settle with Jason, who had taken the city in an effort to overthrow Menelaus. Acting on a false report that Antiochus had died in Egypt, Jason had organized a regiment of a thousand armed supporters for a coup d'état. He massacred a large number of citizens and shut Menelaus up in the Jerusalem citadel. Hearing of this, Antiochus decided to suppress the Jewish religion altogether and to exact stern reprisal from those who had taken up arms against his government. So he marched into Jerusalem with overwhelming forces, released Menelaus, and conducted a massacre in which eighty thousand men, women, and children were put to the sword (2 Macc 5:11–14). Then he profaned the temple, accompanied by the despicable Menelaus, and robbed it of its golden vessels and other sacred objects valued at eighteen hundred talents (vv. 15–21).

The date of this desecration and pillage of Jerusalem was 16 December 168—a day of special significance, in view of the fact that exactly three years later the patriot leader Judas Maccabaeus rededicated the temple to the worship of Yahweh, having cleansed it from all its pagan defilements. But the actual suspension of the regular morning and evening sacrifices had apparently taken place 55 or 54 days prior to the desecration of the temple itself (if our interpretation of Dan 8:14 is correct), because three years would total 1,095 or 1,096 days, and the 2,300 "evenings and mornings" (i.e., sacrifices—*'ōlaṯ-tāmîd*) come out to 1,150 days. It seems, therefore, that during the earlier disturbances between Jason and Menelaus, the regular daily offerings were suspended, since the incumbent high priest was shut up in the Acra (Citadel) by Jason's troops. This, then, was the fulfillment of the prediction of 11:28 regarding Antiochus's "action" taken "against the holy covenant." This verse actually sums up as a single process the entire series of measures taken by Antiochus in subduing and suppressing the religious liberties of Judah, from 172 to 168 B.C.

29–30 The more exact chronology of Antiochus's later act of desecration is set forth in these verses. The "outcome" (v. 29) was different this time because he was compelled by Popilius Laenas to withdraw from Egypt altogether. From the preceding discussion, it is evident that it was the followers of Menelaus, who made no protest as Antiochus removed the holy vessels from the Holy Place of the temple, who are referred to here as "those who forsake the holy covenant." Menelaus and his followers were willing to suppress all religious scruples rather than cross the will of the tyrant who had put them in power.

31 This verse gives further details about the momentous events of December 168 B.C. The desecration was, as already described, the rifling of the sanctuary and temple treasury and the removal of all the sacred vessels. The abolition of the daily sacrifices to the Lord was now made binding by the erection in the temple of Yahweh of "the abomination that causes desolation" (*šiqqûṣ mᵉšōmēm*). Apparently this was a statue of Jupiter or Zeus Olympius, if we may judge from the statement of 2 Maccabees 6:2 that the temple itself was to be renamed the Temple of Zeus Olympius. Pagans invariably installed an image in the inner sanctuary of any temple dedicated to the worship of that deity. Even if the actual statue was not installed in the Jerusalem temple as early as 16 December (25 Chislev) 168 B.C., we may be sure that an idolatrous altar was formally consecrated there at that time. Thus the same type of desecration overtook the second temple as befell the first temple in the evil days of Ahaz (735–715) and Manasseh (695–642), when they too had set up an idolatrous altar (by Ahaz—2 Kings 16:10–16) and images of heathen gods (by Manasseh—2 Kings 21:3–5).

Perhaps it should be added that Christ's only explicit reference to "the prophet Daniel" as being the author of the Book of Daniel occurs in the Olivet Discourse (cf. Matt 24:15; Mark 13:14). There our Lord refers to "the abomination that causes desolation" (*to bdelygma tēs erēmōseōs*)—which is the exact wording of the LXX for this verse (Theod. uses *ēphanismenon*, "done away with")—as a sinister sign of the approach of the final siege of Jerusalem in the last days. This phrase, incidentally, recurs in 12:11 (q.v.) in an end-time context as *šiqqûṣ šōmēm* (Qal participle instead of Polel participle) with substantially the same meaning: "a devastating abomination" or "an abomination of a devastation."

32 Verse 32 continues the narrative of Antiochus's machinations. This tyrant was a past master in manipulating Jewish leaders who were divided in their loyalties, winning them over to his cause by glowing promises of preferment and reward. As a matter of fact, Antiochus already had as partisans for his cause a considerable number of influential leaders in Jerusalem society and politics who were convinced of the expediency of a pro-Hellenic policy. These were doubtless the group referred to in the prophecy concerning "those who have violated the covenant"—that is, their covenant relation with the Lord.

First Maccabees 1:11–15 describes how certain "transgressors of the law" gathered about them a party of collaborators who were ready to throw off their Jewish loyalties and commitment to Yahweh in their zeal to be accepted and find approval with their Syrian-Greek overlords. They therefore built a Hellenic type of gymnasium in Jerusalem (which, of course, involved their exercising naked, as the Greeks did) and even attempted to conceal their circumcision by a surgical procedure. All this was intended to ingratiate themselves with Gentile society and please their foreign rulers. This led to a serious polarization that compelled the Jews to take definite sides either for or against the collaborationist party, which somewhat resembled the Herodians of Christ's day. In some ways this defection of the would-be "progressives" among the Jews themselves was an even more serious threat to the survival of Israel as a nation than the tyrannical measures of Antiochus. For it was the same kind of large-scale betrayal of their covenant obligations toward the Lord that had made inevitable the former destruction of Jerusalem and the Babylonian captivity in the days of Jeremiah.

But the hope of Israel lay with the completely committed believers who preferred to risk their lives rather than betray their honor. A band of heroic patriots was stirred to action by a certain priest named Mattathias in the town of Modein. He was the father of the valiant Maccabees: Judas, Jonathan, and Simon, each of whom later became *nāśî' yiśrā'ēl* ("prince of Israel") during the victorious war of independence against the Seleucid government. These patriots, sparked by the zeal of the Hasidim movement, were the mainstay of the resistance, which opposed the pro-Seleucid Jewish compromisers as well as Antiochus and his successors. They fulfilled the prediction of v.32: "The people who know their God will firmly resist him [i.e., Epiphanes]." Their uncompromising commitment to faithful adherence to the Mosaic covenant and law resulted in the spiritual survival of the nation till the first coming of the Lord Jesus.

In their later development, some of the Hasidim ("the godly, pious, loyal ones") became the sect of the Pharisees (*p^erûšîm*, "separated ones") who gave their earnest attention to obeying every regulation of the Law and every oral interpretation of it that had been handed down in previous generations. Later still a smaller group broke off from the same movement and became out-and-out separatists rather than attempting like the Pharisees to reform the religious establishment from within. These were the Essenes, one group of whom made their headquarters at Qumran under the leadership of the unnamed "Teacher of Righteousness," who figured so prominently in the Qumran sectarian literature. The Essenes believed in complete separation, abjuring the rationalistic theology of the Sadducees and the materialism of the Pharisees. Such, then, were the offshoots of "the people who know their God."

33 During the persecution by Antiochus, the patriot leaders would preach to their fearful and intimidated countrymen a stirring message of repentance and wholehearted commitment to the holy standards of Moses' law and of the prophets who upheld their sanctity during the ensuing centuries. They would summon their people to trust in the promises and power of the Lord instead of bowing to the demands of the pagan tyrant who would command them to turn to idols from the living God. Thus these *maśkîlîm* (lit., "men who show wisdom"; NIV, "those who are wise") would engage in a ministry of education and evangelism, as it were, among their own countrymen, urging them first to get back to God and to pattern their lives according to Scripture. Then they were to answer the call to arms and hazard their very lives for the liberation of their land from the yoke of their God-hating persecutor. Yet the patriot leaders would have to endure great hardships and danger, and many of them would lose their lives and property, as the tyrant's forces turned their swords against them and burned their fields and cities.

The fulfillment of these predictions came in 168 B.C., when the standard of revolt was raised by Mattathias, the leading priest in the city of Modein, located in the hills of the tribe of Ephraim. After killing the officer of Antiochus who had come to enforce the new decree concerning idolatrous worship, Mattathias and his five sons (John Gaddis, Simon Thassi, Judas Maccabaeus, Eleazar Avaran, and Jonathan Apphus) led a guerrilla band that fled to the hills (1 Macc 2:23–28) and attracted many adherents from various other cities in the Judean province. A large number of these original patriots died in their first engagement with the king's troops because they refused to fight in their own defense on the Sabbath, the day on which they were attacked (1 Macc 2:38). But revising their policy after this tragic slaughter, they decided they would fight even on the Sabbath, if compelled to do so. Then they engaged in vigorous attacks on all their fellow Jews who had bowed to Antiochus's ordinance and forsaken their God. Not long afterward Mattathias died, whether from illness or wounds, after entrusting the leadership of the Israelite forces to his own capable sons.

Judas Maccabaeus (for it was originally he alone that received this title of "Hammer," rather than the family as a whole) assumed the military leadership and gained a brilliant victory over the forces of Apollonius, whom he slew in battle. Judas's second triumph involved routing an even larger army under Seron. A third army of formidable proportions came down from Syria under Lysias, Antiochus's deputy, equipped with a fearsome elephant corps. Thanks to the heroism of Judas's brother Eleazer, who managed to plunge his sword into an elephant's chest before it fell on him and crushed him to death, even this mighty host was put to flight by the Maccabean forces. So the Maccabees fulfilled the predictions (cf. Mic 4:12–13 [Payne, *Biblical Prophecy*, p. 403] and Zech 9:13; 10:8–9 [Payne, *Biblical Prophecy*, p. 449).

34 This verse speaks in moderate terms of the successes achieved by these valiant warriors. Presumably the "little help" refers to the relatively small numbers of compatriots who joined the Maccabean troops after the early successes of the original guerrilla band. They saw how they kept on fighting with great courage against overwhelming odds, even though they soon lost Mattathias and many of their first leaders. And then, because one Seleucid army after another fell before their onslaught, the Maccabean troops were able to intimidate many of their fellow citizens who had previously held back from the conflict. Particularly when the Hasidim began to round up those who had collaborated with the Seleucids and put them to death (1 Macc 2:42) and Judas himself hunted out those in the various cities who had deserted scriptural standards ("the lawless," as Maccabees calls them), goodly numbers of insincere followers attached themselves to the patriot cause, hoping to save their own skins. Such supporters as these, however, proved to be of more help to the enemy than to the cause of freedom when later invasions were launched against them by the successors of Antiochus Epiphanes after his death in 164.

35 The account of the Maccabean uprising concludes with a strong emphasis on the spiritual meaning of this heroic struggle for those who risked their lives for the survival of the commonwealth of Israel. In the first instance, v.35 refers to the terrible reverse that overtook the pitifully outnumbered army of Judas himself at the battle of Mount Azotus in 161. He chose to die bravely in battle rather than save his life through a strategic retreat (1 Macc 9:1–19). After he had won this victory for King Demetrius I in 161, Bacchides followed it up with a systematic search for all Judas's leaders and supporters and did his best to wipe them out. But it was not long before the tide turned and Jonathan, Judas's brother, was able to defeat the Syrian forces and compel them to retreat to Antioch. Thus the cause of freedom was maintained through vicissitudes of defeat and success, till finally a strong Jewish kingdom was founded by John Hyrcanus, son of Simon Maccabaeus (135–105), and enlarged to its fullest extent by his warlike son Alexander Jannaeus (104–78 B.C.).

Notes

---

32 Only the earliest phase of the independence effort in the Jewish war of liberation is described here; therefore there is no mention of Judas Maccabaeus's ultimate success in recapturing Jerusalem and cleansing the temple of heathen pollution in 165 B.C. Nor is there mention of the rededication (Hanukkah) of the cleansed temple to the service of Yahweh. But the description of the earlier defeats and sufferings of the patriot forces—מַשְׂכִּילִים (*maśkîlîm*, "those who are wise")—can clearly be discovered in vv.33–35.

33 Virtually all the commentaries identify the מַשְׂכִּילֵי עָם (*maśkîlê ʿām*, lit., "those of the people who are wise") with the Maccabean warriors who exhibited unsurpassed courage and readiness to die in order to defend the true faith and the cause of the Lord. Keil (KD, *Daniel*, p. 459) remarks concerning *maśkîlê ʿām*: "The words point to a warlike rising up of the faithful members of the covenant people against the hostile king, and have their first historical fulfillment in the insurrection of the Maccabees against Antiochus Epiphanes." Young (p. 245) says, "In the book of Maccabees the ones who were true to the Law were called 'godly ones' (Hasidaeans)." Leupold (p. 505) observes: "There are ample implications in our historical sources to show that the sufferings predicted came to pass. The following passages from the first book of Maccabees illustrate our point: 1:56; 2:38; 3:41; 5:13; cf. also II Macc. 6:11." Wood (p. 302), in speaking of "those who are wise among the people," says: "This imparted understanding would give peace and strength, but not deliverance from the enemy. Indeed, those who took the strong stand against the regulations of Antiochus proved to be those in the greatest danger. Mattathias Maccabeus, father of five sons, refused to offer sacrifice in the Grecian way, etc."

As we pointed out in the commentary, the prophetic passage in Zech 9:13 predicts the astonishing victory of the Maccabean heroes over the Greek overlords in terms of divine approbation and appointment. Quite clearly God was promising to use the Jewish defense forces of a coming era against Hellenic armed might—which happened only during the second century B.C. As for Heb 11:33–35, the roster of the pre-Christian heroes of the faith shifts very clearly to martyrs and warriors of the exilic and postexilic periods. "Who shut the mouths of lions" refers to Daniel in the lions' den (Dan 6); "quenched the fury of the flames" points to the three who were thrown into Nebuchadnezzar's furnace (Dan 4). Right after these examples we read, "Who became powerful in battle and routed foreign armies." This last clause evidently relates to the Maccabean freedom fighters whose arms God so signally blessed as they resisted Gentile efforts to stamp out the biblical faith.

---

4. *The Latter-Day Counterpart Persecution*

11:36–39

[36]"The king will do as he pleases. He will exalt and magnify himself above every god and will say unheard-of things against the God of gods. He will be successful until the time of wrath is completed, for what has been determined must take place. [37]He will show no regard for the gods of his fathers or for the one desired by women, nor will he regard any god, but will exalt himself above them all. [38]Instead of them, he will honor a god of fortresses; a god unknown to his fathers he will honor with gold and silver, with precious stones and costly gifts. [39]He will attack the mightiest fortresses with the help of a foreign god and will greatly honor those who acknowledge him. He will make them rulers over many people and will distribute the land at a price.

36–39 With the conclusion of the preceding pericope at v.35, the predictive material that uncontestably applies to the Hellenistic empires and the contest between the Seleucids and the Jewish patriots ends. This present section (vv.36–39) contains some features that hardly apply to Antiochus IV, though most of the details could apply to him as well as to his latter-day antitype, "the beast." Both liberal and conservative scholars agree that all of chapter 11 up to this point contains strikingly accurate predictions of the whole sweep of events from the reign of Cyrus (during which Daniel brought his career to a close) to the unsuccessful effort of Antiochus Epiphanes to stamp out the Jewish faith. But the two schools of thought radically differ in the explanation for this phenomenon. Evangelicals find this pattern of prediction and fulfillment compelling evidence of the divine inspiration and authority of the Hebrew Scriptures, since only God could possibly foreknow the future and see to it that his announced plan would be precisely fulfilled. To the rationalists, however, who begin with the premise that there is no personal God and that whatever superior force may govern the affairs of men leaves the human race quite free to manage its own affairs without any supernatural interference, there is no possibility of a genuine fulfillment of prophecy. Therefore all biblical instances of fulfilled prophecy must be accounted for as pious fraud in which only after the event takes place has the fiction recording its prediction been devised. Since no man can truly foreknow the future, or even be sure of what will happen to him the next day—to say nothing of events to happen several centuries later—it follows that any and every record of a fulfilled prophecy is spurious—a *vaticinium ex eventu*. This is what rationalists have to say about all predictive portions anywhere in the Bible. For them there can be no such thing as divine revelation of events to come. Otherwise they must surrender their basic position and acknowledge the possibility of the supernatural, as demonstrated by detailed fulfillment of events foretold, as here in Daniel, by a prophet of God more than 360 years in advance.

As we come to the substance of vv.36–39, we must recognize a minor difference of opinion among evangelical commentators. Some (e.g., Wood, pp. 304–6) feel that the Antichrist is the only clear fulfillment of these verses; this follows Jerome (p. 136), who says of the king mentioned in v.36, "We too understand this to refer to the Antichrist." Leupold (p. 511) likewise feels that the fewest difficulties attach to the view that these verses point directly to the Antichrist. But Fausset (JFB, p. 646) feels that this is a transitional prophecy in which the willful king here described is "primarily Antiochus" but "antitypically and mainly Antichrist . . . of Rev. 13."

As for these options, observe first of all those features that can be applied to Antiochus IV and those that cannot. Verse 36 contains both types of material: "The king will do as he pleases [cf. 8:4; 11:3; 11:16—the latter two referring to Alexander the Great and Antiochus the Great, respectively]. He will exalt and magnify himself above every god [which is hardly demonstrable of Antiochus, as we shall see] and will say unheard-of things against the God of gods [as Antiochus blasphemed against Yahweh]. He will be successful until the time of wrath is completed [presumably referring to the wrath of God, who decreed this tribulation as a punishment for sin, possibly referring to the time between the desecration of the temple in 168 and its rededication in 164]." Yet as these words stand, they seem equally if not more appropriate to Christ's statement in Matt 24:21–22 predicting the Tribulation.

Some writers have argued that since Antiochus entitled himself "God Manifest" on his coins, this was tantamount to "magnifying himself above every god." But in point of fact he placed a statue, not of himself, but of Zeus Olympius (or possibly Jupiter Capitolinus) as the cult image in the Jerusalem temple, just as he represented Zeus enthroned on the reverse side of his coins, adorned with the title of *Nikēphoros* ("Victory-winner"). Antiochus was evidently loyal to the Greek religious tradition, which revered the entire Olympian pantheon; and so it is hardly justifiable to accuse him of such impiety as exalting himself above all the gods to whom he offered sacrifice on the altar.

The first clause of v.37—"He will show no regard for the gods of his fathers"—hardly fits Antiochus either. On the contrary, his deliberate policy was to compel his Jewish subjects to worship the god of his fathers on pain of death. It seems far more appropriate for a dictator of our modern age (like Stalin of Russia, who began as a candidate for the priesthood in the Russian Orthodox faith before defecting to Marxism and atheism) or some such dictator in the Last Days.

The next words of v.37—"He will show no regard . . . for the one desired by women"—are difficult. Some commentators have taken them to be an allusion to Tammuz or Adonis, the object of a special cult practiced by women from the second millennium B.C. and continued till the time of Antiochus. Yet there is no slightest evidence in the historical records that Antiochus ever opposed or forbade this ancient practice. But if the phrase *ḥemdaṯ nāšîm* is translated more literally, it means simply "the love of women" or, better, "the desire of women"; then perhaps it simply points to the cruelty Antiochus showed toward all women he was sexually involved with.

As for the reference to "the gods of his fathers" (v.37), this phrase might conceivably refer to the true God, who generally is referred to in the plural (though with a singular verb or adjective); the Hebrew *'ᵉlōhê 'ᵃḇōṯāyw* is susceptible of either meaning. Indeed, some commentators (especially those of dispensational persuasion) have taken this phrase to refer to the God of the Hebrews and therefore deduce that the Antichrist himself will be an apostate Jew. In favor of this, it is true that elsewhere in the OT the phrase *'ᵉlōhê 'ᵃḇôṯêḵem* ("the God of your fathers") does indeed refer to Yahweh himself. Here, however, it does not necessarily follow that the Antichrist is a Jew, unless it can be demonstrated (as it surely cannot be) that the pagans never worshiped the god or god*s* (the plural would be more likely than the singular in the case of the heathen) of their own fathers. In Joshua 24:14–15, Joshua makes reference to the false gods worshiped by some of the Israelites during the Egyptian sojourn and also by the ancestors of Abraham in Mesopotamia. While the actual formula "gods of their fathers" does not occur in that passage, the remarks made there certainly do add up to the concept of "the gods of your fathers."

Verse 37 goes on to emphasize that this little horn will have no regard for any god (*'al-kōl-'ᵉlôah lō' yāḇîn,* "will not give heed to [attend to] any god"). This hardly applies to Antiochus, who exalted Zeus on the reverse side of his coinage and did everything to compel his Jewish subjects to sacrifice and bow down to his heathen gods. This therefore could only apply to his eschatological antitype, the Beast of the last days—who apparently will be an atheistic or ungodly dictator, perhaps a Marxist totalitarian. At any rate, whether or not the Beast concedes the existence of gods in theory, he will certainly exalt himself above them all in conducting his government. He will represent himself as the incarnation of the power and the will of the gods, if such there be. Thus there will be no appeal from his will to the will of heavenly deities who might outrank him or sit in judgment over him.

That the Beast will not exclude all practice of religion, however, is clear from v.38: "Instead of them [i.e., the gods of his fathers], he will honor a god of fortresses ['ᵉlōah mā'uzzîm]; a god unknown to his fathers he will honor with gold and silver, with precious stones and costly gifts." There is little likelihood of this referring to the well-known devotion Antiochus showed toward Zeus Olympius (he contributed generously to the great temple of Zeus Olympius in Athens and purposed to build one of his own in Daphne, a suburb of Antioch), for Zeus Olympius was certainly a god of his fathers. Rather, if this prediction relates to Antiochus, it would apply to some Roman deity, whose cult he embraced as a youth while a hostage at Rome. Some have suggested that the reference is to Mars, the god of war. The more likely reference, however, is to Jupiter Capitolinus, the patron god of Rome itself, whose powerful protection Antiochus may have sought. In that case, he may have equated Zeus Olympius with Jupiter Capitolinus, as the deity to whom he dedicated the Jerusalem temple in 168 B.C. If so—and this is merely inferential—then this might furnish a historical basis for the later decision of the emperor Hadrian in A.D. 130 to rebuild the ruined site of Jerusalem as "Aelia Capitolina," the Aelia being derived from his own family name (Publius *Aelius* Hadrianus) and the Capitolina from Jupiter Capitolinus, whose temple stood on the Capitoline Hill in Rome. This, then, might possibly be construed as applying to Antiochus Epiphanes as the type of the latter-day Antichrist.

On the other hand, it must be conceded that "god of fortresses" does not clearly point to "Capitolinus," and so this whole interpretation is thoroughly conjectural. Yet it is worth pointing out that the offering of votive gifts of silver, gold, and precious stones sounds more like an ancient, pre-Christian setting than a religious practice of our modern age, except perhaps in the older traditions of medieval Christianity.

Verse 39 continues the account of the little horn and his conquests. Presumably this "foreign god" is the same one mentioned in the previous verse, even though the definite article is missing before *'ᵉlôah* ("god"). The application of this verse to Antiochus is hardly clear. Jerome (in loc.) inclines to an eschatological interpretation and suggests that it speaks of the Antichrist, who will "instruct the Jews to worship a strange god, which doubtless means Jupiter. And displaying the idol to them, he will persuade them that they should worship it. Then he will bestow upon the deluded both honor and very great glory, and he shall deal with the rest who have borne rule in Judaea, and apportion estates unto them in return for their falsehood, and shall distribute gifts." Clearly, then, Jerome takes this in a completely futuristic sense.

Notes

39 Walvoord (pp. 281–82) relates this entire passage to the end times:

> The entire section from Daniel 11:36 to 12:3 constitutes a revelation of the major factors of the time of the end, namely: (1) a world ruler, (2) a world religion, (3) a world war, (4) a time of great tribulation for Israel, (5) deliverance for the people of God at the end of the tribulation [by which Walvoord means those who become converted after the NT church has been removed by the Rapture at the beginning of the seventieth Week], (6) resurrection and judgment, and (7) reward of the righteous. All of these factors are introduced in this section. Added elsewhere in the Scriptures are the additional facts that this time of the end begins with the breaking of the covenant by "the prince that shall come" (Dan 9:26–27); that the "time of the end" will last for three and one-half years (Dan 7:25; 12:7; Rev 13:5); that the time of the end is the same as the time of Jacob's trouble and the great tribulation (Jer 30:7; Mt 24:21).

This interpretation has much to commend it.

5. *The Triumph and Fall of Antichrist*

11:40–45

40"At the time of the end the king of the South will engage him in battle, and the king of the North will storm out against him with chariots and cavalry and a great fleet of ships. He will invade many countries and sweep through them like a flood.
41He will also invade the Beautiful Land. Many countries will fall, but Edom, Moab and the leaders of Ammon will be delivered from his hand. 42He will extend his power over many countries; Egypt will not escape. 43He will gain control of the treasures of gold and silver and all the riches of Egypt, with the Libyans and Nubians in submission. 44But reports from the east and the north will alarm him, and he will set out in a great rage to destroy and annihilate many. 45He will pitch his royal tents between the seas at the beautiful holy mountain. Yet he will come to his end, and no one will help him.

40 As for the final paragraph of this chapter, the effort to tie its details into the known career of Antiochus Epiphanes becomes utterly hopeless. Verses 36–39 contain, as we have seen, important features irreconcilable with Antiochus. And from v.40 on there is the greatest contrast between his career and that of the little horn, whose end is here described. Furthermore, the shift of scene to the last days seems to be doubly emphasized by the introductory words "At the time of the end" (*ûḇeʿēṯ qēṣ*, lit., "And in the end time"). The transition between v.35 and v.36 is not so clearly indicated, for the latter verse is simply introduced with a waw connective (*weʿāśāh ḵirṣônô hammelek,* lit., "Then the king will do as he pleases").

On the analogy of the struggle between the Ptolemies of Egypt and the Seleucids of Syria, we might expect to see in the final Near Eastern struggle a contest between a bloc of nations allied with Egypt, including Libya and Nubia (or Sudan) referred to in v.43, and a Syrian coalition, comprising a league of Middle Eastern nations. Yet if the antitype of Antiochus Epiphanes is referred to by the title "king of the North," which was applied to the Seleucid kings in the earlier narrative, then we cannot be altogether certain that we are dealing with a ruler located in either Syrian Damascus or Antioch (a city now under Turkish control). It may be that the eschatological counterpart, the little horn emerging from the fourth or Roman Empire, is actually an Italian leader. The "ruler who will come" mentioned back in 9:26 will have to be a Roman, or be somehow connected with the latter-day revival of the Roman Empire. The historical Roman Empire was mainly centered around the Mediterranean, with its capital in Italy, and so there is a good possibility that "the ruler who will come" will be from Europe rather than from the Near East. This is not beyond dispute, however, since at least one emperor of Rome, Elegabalus, was a Syrian or Phoenician; he reigned A.D. 218–22 and was succeeded by his cousin Severus Alexander, who was also Syrian or Phoenician, having been born in Acre.

Wood (pp. 308–10) suggests that the title "king of the North" might rather point to a Russian leader, since Russia lies to the far north of Palestine, with Moscow situated at nearly the same longitude. But he bases this identification more on parallel prophecy (Ezek 38, which describes the future invasion of the Near East by Rosh, Meshech, and Tubal) than on any specific indications here in Daniel. Moreover, Wood's position becomes ambiguous when he deals with the latter part of v.40, with its reference to "chariots and cavalry"; for then he begins to speak (p. 310) of the Antichrist (whom he understands to be a different person from the Russian leader): "The Antichrist, the common antecedent, is the general subject of the passage. . . . The phrase, along with the two following verbs, indicates clearly that the Antichrist will emerge victorious in the battle with the two opposing kings." It seems much simpler and more convincing, however, to take the "king of the North" in this verse to be none other than the latter-day little horn, the Antichrist.

The political cause of the clash between the two superpowers and their allies is not suggested in any way, but the large amount of troops and armaments is clearly implied by the "chariots," "cavalry," and "fleet of ships." Presumably the warfare will be carried on by armored vehicles and missiles such as are used in modern warfare—though in order to communicate with Daniel's generation, ancient equivalents of these are used here. Likewise, the ancient names of the countries or states occupying the region where the final conflict will be carried on are used in the prediction, though most of those political units will no longer bear these names in the last days. Thus Edom, Moab, Ammon, Assyria, and Babylon, which are mentioned in eschatological passages, have long since ceased to exist as political entities, their places having been taken by later peoples occupying their territory.

"He will invade many countries and sweep through them like a flood" suggests the kind of spectacular success the Nazis had early in World War II. It also indicates that a large number of smaller, weaker nations will be drawn into the conflict between the two great powers of the North and the South and that Antichrist in particular will extend his authority with irresistible power.

41 This verse focuses on the Holy Land, which will furnish the focal point for this terrible war. The land of Israel will be ravaged by Antichrist's forces, as will many of the surrounding states, except for those in the area of the present-day kingdom of Jordan, which for some unexplained reason (possibly because of their willing collaboration against Israel) will be spared from invasion. The term *'ereṣ haṣṣᵉḇî* ("the Beautiful Land") refers to the Holy Land from the standpoint of its special favor in the eyes of God, rather than because of conspicuous natural beauty.

42–45 Verse 42 continues Antichrist's triumphant progress. Apparently the king of the South is going to suffer defeat at the hands of Antichrist ("the king of the North"), even though he had at first felt strong enough to initiate the conflict with the king of the North. Egypt will at last be defeated, whether or not it is completely and permanently added to Antichrist's realm. He will go on to capture all the reserves of silver and gold locked up in their vaults, for v.43 states: "He will gain control of the treasures of gold and silver and all the riches of Egypt." Their loyal allies, the Libyans to the west and the Nubians (or Sudanese) to the south, will also be subjugated by him. At last his triumph over the powerful antagonists to the south will be consummated. But his satisfaction over this will be short-lived because (v.44) news of trouble in the Middle East will bring him out of Egypt in a fury to crush his opponents in Palestine. There, perhaps in the vicinity of Megiddo, he will encamp ("between the seas" [v.45], indicating the Dead Sea and the Mediterranean), within easy striking distance of Jerusalem itself—"the beautiful holy mountain," i.e., Moriah, where the temple stood.

Verse 45 ends with this abrupt obituary: "Yet he will come to his end, and no one will help him." This comes with a jolt, just at the moment when Antichrist seems to be sweeping away all opposition. All at once crushing disaster overtakes him, like that which will overtake the pillaging and raping attackers of the Holy City, when suddenly "the LORD will go out and fight against those nations" (Zech 14:3) and the attackers will disappear. Similarly in Revelation 19:19–20, the "beast and the kings of the earth" gather against the Lord to make war on his people. In the next verse (20) we read: "But the beast was captured, and with him the false prophet. . . . The two of them were thrown alive into the fiery lake of burning sulphur." This seems to pick up Revelation 16:16: "Then they gathered the kings together to the place that in Hebrew is called Armageddon" (i.e., *har-Mᵉgiddō*, "the mountain of Megiddo"), which lies "between the seas."

Such will be the sudden end of the Antichrist of Daniel 11:36–45, and it will take place in the Holy Land. This prediction of the location of his death eliminates the figure of Antiochus Epiphanes, who met his end in Persia, after an unsuccessful raid on a temple in Elymais. There is no possibility of explaining *this* prediction as a *vaticinium ex eventu*, concocted by a Maccabean storyteller who wanted to stir up patriotic ardor by a set of spurious prophecies. Therefore the entire case for a rationalistic explanation for the composition of Daniel in the second century *after* the fulfillment of its predictions is logically untenable. There is no way the details of vv.40–45 can be fitted into the career of Antiochus Epiphanes. A rationalistic critic may label this paragraph unsuccessful or unfulfilled prophecy, but he cannot convincingly avoid the implication that the other predictions too may have been made before the time of their fulfillment. If the author of Daniel did not wait till the fulfillment of 11:40–45 before composing these verses as predictions, there is no valid reason for insisting that he devised the other predictions fulfilled in the fourth, third, and second centuries only after they had actually been fulfilled.

Notes

---

45 The preposition לְ (*l^e*) before הַר־צְבִי־קֹדֶשׁ (*har-ṣ^{e}ḇî-qōḏeš*, “the beautiful holy mountain”) is rendered “at” by NIV, but it may be better rendered “and” (cf. NIV mg.: “between the sea and the beautiful holy mountain”).

XII. The Tribulation and Final Triumph of God’s People (12:1–13)

1. *The Great Tribulation*

12:1

> 1 “At that time Michael, the great prince who protects your people, will arise. There will be a time of distress such as has not happened from the beginning of nations until then. But at that time your people—everyone whose name is found written in the book—will be delivered.

1 The opening words of this chapter—“At that time”—refer to the fortunes of God’s covenant people during this period of the career of Antichrist. The closing verses of chapter 11 deal exclusively with his military and political career, described in broad and general outline. But his internal policy toward the community of God’s people within his empire has not so far been referred to. Here we are told that it will be characterized by a policy of brutal oppression and persecution surpassing in severity any tribulation through which Israel—or perhaps any other nation—has ever passed. “Such as has not happened from the beginning of nations until then” sounds like a generalization of broadest scope, reaching all the way back to the beginnings of ordered society.

It is highly significant that our Lord Jesus in the Olivet Discourse (Matt 24:21) picks up and enlarges on this prediction, saying: “For then there will be great distress [*thlipsis*] unequaled from the beginning of the world [*hoia ou gegonen ap’ archēs kosmou*—which corresponds very closely to the Theodotion rendering of Dan 12:1: *thlipsis hoia ou gegonen aph’ hou gegenētai ethnos*, ‘distress such as has not happened from the beginning of a nation’] until now—and never to be equaled again.” Quite evidently Jesus took this prophecy in Daniel as relating to the Last Days and particularly to the Great Tribulation with which our present church age is destined to close. Jesus said that there would be great loss of life during this terrible period (Matt 24:22): “If those days had not been cut short, no one would survive, but for the sake of the elect those days will be shortened.” It is not altogether clear whether this large-scale slaughter will result from the direct persecution by the Beast himself, or whether it also includes the great numbers to be slain by the terrible plagues of God occasioned by the breaking of the seventh seal (Rev 8) and by the bowls of wrath (Rev 16). In these various stages of devastation described in the Book of Revelation, one-third of all the ships at sea will be destroyed (8:8), large numbers will die from drinking Wormwood-poisoned water (8:11), the remaining population will wish for death during the months of torment inflicted by satanic locusts (9:6), and another third of mankind will be destroyed by them (9:15). It would seem that after the armies themselves have been annihilated, the final denouement at Armageddon will suddenly terminate this mounting loss of life.

The agent of preservation for God's people through the time of horror is here specified to be the same archangel who had assisted Gabriel against the demonic "prince of the Persian kingdom" back in 10:13. Here Michael is described as "the great prince who protects your people [lit., 'who stands beside your people']." From Jude 9 we learn that Michael had disputed with Satan over the body of Moses, presumably at the time of Moses' death, though Jude does not give this detail (nor is it contained in the available fragments of the pseudepigraphal Acts of Moses; cf. IDB, 3:373). It would appear that God has assigned the special protection of Israel (as a covenant nation) to this mighty champion, the archangel Michael, and that he will have a key part in combating the attacks of the satanic Dragon against the people of Christ in the last days (Rev 17:6).

The last sentence in v.1 guarantees the preservation of all faithful believers through this harrowing ordeal. They are referred to as those whose names are "found written in the book." This is apparently "the Book of Life" first referred to in Exodus 32:33 as the roster of professing believers who stand in covenant relationship with God, though apostates among them may have their name removed from this list. In Psalm 69:28 the writer prays that the malevolent enemies of the Lord and of his true servants may be "blotted out of the book of life" and that their names may not be written down with the "righteous"—i.e., with those who walk with God in covenant-keeping faithfulness. Malachi 3:16 refers to the heavenly roster: "Then those who feared the LORD talked with each other, and the LORD listened and heard. A scroll of remembrance was written in his presence concerning those who feared the LORD and honored his name." Even in the Great White Throne judgment at the close of the Millennium (Rev 20:12), these books of record will be opened as the souls of the dead stand before the Lord for judgment; and all whose names are not found written in the Book of Life will be consigned to the second death and to the lake of fire (v.15). Jesus himself was very conscious of this heavenly register, for he said to his disciples, "However, do not rejoice that the spirits submit to you, but rejoice that your names are written in heaven" (Luke 10:20). As we compare these references, we find that the Book of Life contains the names of both the "elect" and those who profess faith in Christ but by their attitudes and actions deny the authority and will of God in their lives. These latter will be deleted from the list of the redeemed.

Verse 1 concludes with the assurance that all those whose names are "found written" in the Lord's book "will be delivered" (*yimmālēṭ*—which may also mean "will slip away," "will escape"). In what sense will they be delivered? Does this mean "delivered from the first death"? Will they be exempt from martyrdom at the hands of the Beast during the Great Tribulation? Probably not, since a great many of the true believers even back in the days of the Maccabean revolt were compelled to lay down their lives, such as the heroic Eliezer, brother of Judas Maccabaeus. The context of this passage seems to be definitely eschatological, referring to the end times; and v.2 clearly refers to those who have already died but attain to the resurrection from the dead. They are delivered from the power of Satan and the curse of the "second death" (Rev 21:8).

Notes

1 The MT has the singular גּוֹי (*gôy*, "a nation"). However, since in this context "from the beginning of a nation" implies "from the time that there ever was such a thing as a nation [in the sense of an organized ethnic unit—*gôy*], it is perhaps justifiable to render *gôy* as a plural—viz., "nations."

Walvoord (pp. 286–90) has an illuminating discussion of possible pretribulational implications in vv. 1–3. He points out that even though the Great Tribulation is actually mentioned first ("a time of distress"), the final clause reads, "But at that time your people . . . will be delivered." "At that time" points definitely to the time of the Tribulation. If they are to be delivered *from* this time of distress, this may well imply that they will be removed from the Antichrist-dominated world before the Tribulation begins. If so, this would definitely point to a pretribulation rapture of the church, as indicated in 1 Thess 4:13–17. Whether at the beginning of the seventieth week or at its midpoint (as could be inferred from Dan 9:27), the true believers would be taken up from earth to meet the Lord Jesus "in the clouds" before the time of divine wrath begins. The language of 12:1–3 can certainly be harmonized with this view. Nevertheless it is also possible to construe this deliverance from the time of distress in the sense of remaining steadfast in faith and triumphant in witness through it all, as Daniel and his three comrades did in the days of Nebuchadnezzar and Darius. In other words, deliverance *from* despair and fear could mean the ability to stand successfully in the face of adverse pressures.

Walvoord closes this part of his discussion with the following comment (p. 290):

> From the standpoint of the pretribulational interpretation of prophecy, which holds to a resurrection of the church before the tribulation and therefore as preceding this resurrection, this passage can be taken quite literally. As a matter of fact, if the pretribulationists are correct, there will be an extensive resurrection of the righteous at this point when Christ returns to reign. Although it would be too much to say that this confirms pretribulationism, it harmonizes with this interpretation precisely. At the same time, Young is probably correct that the hope of resurrection is especially extended to the martyred dead of the tribulation who are given special mention in Revelation 20:4.

2. *The Resurrection and Judgment*

12:2–3

> 2Multitudes who sleep in the dust of the earth will awake: some to everlasting life, others to shame and everlasting contempt. 3Those who are wise will shine like the brightness of the heavens, and those who lead many to righteousness, like the stars for ever and ever.

2 This verse refers to the inclusion of all the dead believers in the victory of the Resurrection. They will be "many," though the text does not say that they will necessarily be the majority of the human race, as some scholars have suggested. Those involved in this raising of the dead are said to "sleep in the dust of the earth"—i.e., they have experienced physical death (the "first death") and have been buried. Yet they do not experience annihilation or a permanent imprisonment in the bonds of death—even so far as their body is concerned. They will be awakened from "the dust of the earth"—a promise that definitely points to *bodily* resurrection, not simply a renewal of the soul. They will then enter the next phase of their existence according to their faith or unbelief in their earthly life.

"Some to everlasting life, others to shame and everlasting contempt" shows that resurrection will come universally to all men, whether believers or unbelievers, whether saved or lost. But the resurrection of the unsaved will be neither a blessing nor a deliverance, as it will be for the saved. Rather, as Jesus said in John 5:28–29, it will bring them public judgment and condemnation before almighty God. They will be exposed to "shame" (*ḥ^{a}rāpôṯ*) and "contempt" (*d^{e}rā'ôn*) before the whole tribunal of angels and men (as Rev 20:11–15 depicts with awesome grandeur), when all their sins will be exposed to view and they will be covered with utter confusion and disgrace as they are led off to their everlasting place of torment in the lake of fire.

The word for "everlasting" is *'ôlām* (which stands in a construct relationship with *d^{e}rā'ôn*). Originally *'ôlām* meant "lifetime" or "era," "age"; but when it is used of God and his life (without beginning or end), it takes on the connotation of endlessness, i.e., eternity. Thus in Psalm 90:2 we read, "From everlasting to everlasting [*mē'ôlām 'aḏ-'ôlām*] you are God." Those who argue simply on the basis of the concept of "lifetime" or "age" for only an age-long punishment in hell rather than one of endless duration must reckon with the many passages in the OT that apply *'ôlām* to the endless life and sovereignty of God himself. In other words, if hell is not eternal, neither is God; for the same Hebrew and Greek words are used for both in the Bible (cf. Rev 4:10; 20:10; 21:8). The corresponding Greek word *aiōn* exactly parallels the Hebrew *'ôlām* in connotation and semantic development.

3 Verse 3 lays additional emphasis on the reward of true believers in the day of resurrection-judgment. Before the judgment seat of Christ (cf. Isa 11:3 and Rom 2:16 for the identity of the Judge), those believers who have shown a true and living faith will be welcomed as true children of God and will be robed in the shining garments of their Redeemer's righteousness, not only that which is imputed to them by grace from the sinless perfection of Christ, but also that holiness of life and walk he has wrought in them by his Holy Spirit. True believers are here described as "those who are wise" and "those who lead many to righteousness." The term for "wise" is *maśkîlîm,* the participle of the Hiphil stem of *śāḵal* ("observe carefully," "be circumspect," "be prudent"). In the Hiphil (causative) stem it means either "make wise," "instruct," or else (as a Hiphil characteristic) "act circumspectly, prudently, intelligently." Perhaps it would be better to render *hammaśkilîm* as "those who act wisely" or "those who show intelligence," i.e., in the way they meet situations (cf. Ps 2:10 for this usage: "Therefore [i.e., in view of the irresistible power and judgment of the Messiah], you kings, be wise [*haśkîlû*]; be warned, you rulers of the earth." Thus the word connotes acting sensibly or appropriately in view of the holy will of God Almighty and of the final day of judgment awaiting us beyond the grave.

The parallel expression is "those who lead many to righteousness." The fruit of a Christ-centered, godly life is new believers, won to the Lord through God's servants. The Good Shepherd rejoices to see his sheep brought home to him through faithful soul winners. Such "will shine . . . like the stars for ever and ever." He who will come like "a star . . . out of Jacob" (Num 24:17) will see his glory reflected and displayed by all his agents who have devoted themselves to the winning of others to their divine Lord. And this glory of theirs will endure in heaven forever—not just for some limited time, but throughout eternity.

Verses 2–3, then, clearly affirm the doctrines of resurrection and of eternity beyond the grave. Even the most skeptical OT scholars concede the presence of these doctrines here, though they date the composition of Daniel in the second century B.C. and attribute much of its eschatology to some kind of Zoroastrian influence. But since they tend to deny the presence of this doctrine in the earlier parts of the OT, it may be appropriate to recall other books besides Daniel that embrace this expectation of resurrection glory. Even in what may well be the pre-Mosaic setting of Job, we find the exclamation: "And after my skin has been destroyed,/ yet in my flesh I will see God" (Job 19:26). In Psalm 17:15 David similarly affirmed: "And I—in righteousness I will see your face;/ when I awake [using the same verb, *hēqîṣ*, that is used here in Dan 12:2], I will be satisfied with seeing your likeness." Psalm 73:23–24 tells us:

> Yet I am always with you;
> you hold me by my right hand.
> You guide me with your counsel,
> and afterward you will take me into glory.

Note that the "afterward" (*'aḥar*) in this context can only refer to life beyond the grave. Isaiah 25:8 says: "He will swallow up death forever./ The Sovereign LORD will wipe away the tears from all faces." Even more clear is Isaiah 26:19:

> But your dead will live;
> their bodies will rise.
> You who dwell in the dust,
> wake up and shout for joy. . . .
> the earth will give birth to her dead.

This present passage is to be understood in the light of these many assurances of resurrection and life in heaven beyond (cf. also Ps 16:11). It is no late importation from some foreign religion but rather the capstone of OT revelation, going all the way back to the time of Job, David, and Isaiah.

3. *The Sealed Prophecies*

12:4

4But you, Daniel, close up and seal the words of the scroll until the time of the end. Many will go here and there to increase knowledge."

4 Here Daniel is told to "close up" (*s^e^ṯōm*) the scroll containing the text of this prophecy and to "seal" (*ḥ^a^ṯōm*) it till the end time, when all these predictions and promises will be fulfilled. In the ancient Near East, important documents such as contracts, promissory notes, and deeds of conveyance were written out in duplicate. The original document was kept in a secure repository, safe ("closed up") from later tampering, in order to conserve the interests and rights of all parties to the transaction. Though copies might be made from it, the original was to remain secure so that it might be consulted if any future challenge of its terms were made.

The practice of "sealing" was likewise derived from Near Eastern usage. In Mesopotamian cultures, it was usual to write out the terms of contractual promises on a clay tablet and then run the cylinder-seals of the attesting scribes over the bottom section. First of all came the seal of the recording scribe himself, who in this case was Daniel, and then the seals of the various witnesses who heard the exact words as they were dictated to the scribe. Once the document was thus sealed, it became the official and unchangeable text. It was usual to have the second tablet, the official copy, likewise witnessed by seal. Daniel, then, was to certify by his personal seal, as it were, to the faithfulness of the foregoing text as an exact transcript of what God had communicated to him through his angel. Thus this record would be preserved unaltered down to the day when all the predictions would be fulfilled.

"Will go here and there" translates *yᵉšōṭᵉṭû*, the Polel form of the verb *šûṭ*. It depicts back and forth movement, like the strokes of an oar or of a swimmer's arms. The verb is also used of gleaners gathering manna or grain. The Polel stem (*šôṭēṭ*) connotes an intensity that may imply eagerness in moving quickly and excitedly back and forth in searching for a desired object (Amos 8:12), or else of an observer searching for particular persons in a crowd or watching all the activities of a person under investigation (2 Chron 16:9; Zech 4:10). Here the meaning seems to be that many of God's people who pay heed to these prophetic sayings will eagerly seek to understand how they are presently being fulfilled or how they are going to be fulfilled in the future. Some commentators understand *yᵉšōṭᵉṭû* as simply referring to the movement of the eyes in the actual reading of the text. Such may be the case here, but usage elsewhere in the OT lends little support for this interpretation.

The purpose or consequence (the *wᵉ* of *wᵉṭirbeh* may mean either "that knowledge may increase" or "and knowledge will increase") of this eager investigation is to grow in understanding the significance of these mystifying prophecies. That is to say, with the passage of time, the predictions concerning the Persian and Greek kings will be carried out during the fourth, third, and second centuries B.C., and those referring to the Roman conquest in the first century. This will help clarify the distinction between the typical tribulation under Antiochus Epiphanes and the antitypical Great Tribulation awaiting the people of God in the end time. From this standpoint the knowledge of Bible students greatly increased between the time of Daniel's sixth century B.C. contemporaries and the period of Jerome, whose epoch-making commentary appeared around A.D. 400. Since Jerome's time, there has been a corresponding increase of knowledge, especially with the rise of archaeology and the knowledge of ancient linguistics, to say nothing of the amazing developments leading up to the return of the Jewish people in large numbers to their ancestral land since 1948.

4. *The Prediction of the Three and One-Half Years*

12:5–7

5Then I, Daniel, looked, and there before me stood two others, one on this bank of the river and one on the opposite bank. 6One of them said to the man clothed in linen, who was above the waters of the river, "How long will it be before these astonishing things are fulfilled?"

7The man clothed in linen, who was above the waters of the river, lifted his right hand and his left hand toward heaven, and I heard him swear by him who lives forever, saying, "It will be for a time, times and half a time. When the power of the holy people has been finally broken, all these things will be completed."

5–7 Here we have a striking scene. On either side of the Tigris River (mentioned at the beginning of this vision in 10:4), Daniel saw (v.5) two "others" (*'ᵃḥērîm*), that is, other angels besides the one who had been addressing him since 10:11, the "man clothed in linen" (v.6). The two angels were standing opposite each other on either side of the river. They were personally interested in coming events in God's program of redemption, somewhat as they were later on in Zechariah's time (cf. Zech 1:12–13; 2:3–4). First Peter 1:12 implies that even the angels are not fully informed as to how the prophetic promises of God are going to be fulfilled but are eager to find out how and when they will come to pass. In this instance, then, one angel asked the man in linen how long it would be till the remarkable prediction concerning the Antichrist (ch. 11) would be fulfilled. Literally his question was "Until when is the end of the marvels?" The man in linen furnished the information (v.7) through a solemn oath accompanied by the raising of both his hands heavenward and the assurance that the time interval would be "a time [*mō'ēḏ*], times [presumably two of them] and half a time" (viz., three and a half years). The word for "times" may originally have been intended as a dual (*mô'ᵃḏayîm*, "two years"). He then added that the power of the holy people—i.e., the true believers of the end time—would be broken. In other words (as in Zech 14:2), the brave defenders of Jerusalem will be overwhelmed by the irresistible forces of Antichrist; and they will appear doomed to utter defeat and extinction. Then it will be that God will intervene in a mighty judgment on all the invaders; and they will be utterly destroyed, though this passage does not specify this denouement as explicitly as Zechariah 14:3 does.

It should be observed, incidentally, that three and a half years is exactly one-half the full seven years of the seventieth week referred to in 9:27. It would be the second half that is intended by "a time, times and half a time," since it ends (in all probability) with the destruction of the Beast at the Battle of Armageddon.

5. *The Final Commission to Daniel*

12:8–13

8I heard, but I did not understand. So I asked, "My lord, what will the outcome of all this be?"

9He replied, "Go your way, Daniel, because the words are closed up and sealed until the time of the end. 10Many will be purified, made spotless and refined, but the wicked will continue to be wicked. None of the wicked will understand, but those who are wise will understand.

11"From the time that the daily sacrifice is abolished and the abomination that causes desolation is set up, there will be 1,290 days. 12Blessed is the one who waits for and reaches the end of the 1,335 days.

13"As for you, go your way till the end. You will rest, and then at the end of the days you will rise to receive your allotted inheritance."

8 This verse relates how confused and nonplused Daniel became as he tried to unravel and sort out all these predictions. It was only natural for him to ask for clearer details regarding these mystifying prophecies. His particular concern was doubtless directed toward the ultimate fortunes of the covenant people of God, especially in view of the intimidating language of v.7. Would they survive after their power was "broken," or would they go under as a nation in their futile struggle for truth?

9 The angel did not directly answer Daniel's question, despite its earnestness. Yet the implication of victorious survival comes through quite clearly at the close of v.13, the very last verse: "At the end of the days you will rise to receive your allotted inheritance." That is to say, after the resurrection, Daniel—as one of those who have died in the true faith—will rise from the grave to claim his heavenly inheritance.

The more immediate answer of the angel relates to the faithful completion and custody of the prophetic scroll itself: The words are "closed up" (*s^e^ṯûmîm,* the plural of the word used in v.4, where it means "keep close"or "preserve in a safe place"), as an official, validated document. The words are also to be "sealed" (*ḥ^a^ṯumîm*) by the recording scribe, Daniel himself, as a faithful transcript of God's revealed truth.

10 Verse 10 states that during this intervening period of time, the people of God will be refined in their faith and purified in their motivation through the testings they will endure. In all probability this higher quality of faith and life is viewed as the result of the indwelling of the believer's heart by the Holy Spirit in the NT age, granting to the believer all the resources of Christ in the battle against evil. Moreover, the unbelieving world will not improve as a result of the testimony of the faithful but will increase in wickedness. There will be no general movement of mankind toward the establishment of God's kingdom on earth through the efforts of an enlightened society; on the contrary, "evil men and imposters will go from bad to worse, deceiving and being deceived" (2 Tim 3:13). So we read here that "the wicked will continue to be wicked" and that "none of the wicked will understand," though those who are "wise" in the Scriptures will comprehend quite fully what is going on during these times.

11–12 These verses seem intended to furnish believers with a prophetic yardstick to measure the length of the second, more intense phase of the Great Tribulation. Verse 7 has supplied the approximate figure of three and a half years (for which the total number of days would be 1,278; see comments and note at 9:24–26). But it appears from v.11 that the interval between the setting up of the "abomination that causes desolation" (subsequent to the abrogation of the covenant between Antichrist and Israel) and the final deliverance of Jerusalem from his hosts will come out more exactly to 12 more days than that, or a total of 1,290 days. For beleaguered saints enduring the horrors of the catastrophic plagues and massacres of the end time, the precise knowledge of the exact day of deliverance (cf. Matt 24:22) will be of great reassurance. The horror will continue just 1,290 days from the time that the covenant was abrogated and the abominable image set up in the temple of the Lord in Jerusalem.

With v.12 we come to one of the most enigmatic statements in this chapter. Between 1,290 and 1,335 days there is an interval of 45 days, or a month and a half. What is destined to take place in that short period can only be conjectured. Quite possibly it may be the time when the thousand-year earth-rule of Christ will be officially inaugurated, as he takes his seat on David's throne. The intervening time may well be devoted to repairing the devastation and burying the bodies left by the Armageddon campaign (cf. Ezek 39:12, which seems to specify seven months as the time for a complete cleanup after Armageddon). The believers who survive to that day and share in the glory of Jesus' coronation on earth are here acclaimed as "blessed." They are about to become citizens of the most wonderful society governed by the most wonderful ruler in all human history—the millennial kingdom of our Lord Jesus Christ!

13 The final verse of the book contains an encouraging word for the aged Daniel: "Go your way till the end. You will rest [i.e., his body will rest in the grave], and then at the end of the days you will rise [on the day of resurrection] to receive your allotted inheritance." Revelation 20:4 states, "I saw thrones on which were seated those who had been given authority to judge," and then it goes on to say that those who have died as martyrs will at that time "come to life" and reign with Christ a thousand years. Surely Daniel will be outstanding among the galaxy of judges and kings. Yet it is also true that those of us who are sincere and obedient believers will have a part in this glory and will see Daniel on his throne. And far eclipsing such honors as these will be the supernatural glory of the Son of Man himself, the Son of God incarnate, who will assume supreme control over the entire earth. His dominion will stretch from sea to sea and from the Euphrates to the ends of the earth (Zech 9:10). And under his rule the earth shall be filled with righteousness, "as the waters cover the sea" (Isa 11:9).

HOSEA

Leon J. Wood

HOSEA

Introduction

1. Historical Background

Hosea, prophet to the northern kingdom of Israel, ministered in the stirring days just preceding the Fall of Assyria. When he began his work, one would not have thought the end was near. Jeroboam II (793–753 B.C.; cf. 2 Kings 14:23–29) was the ruler, and a strong one. He had established approximately the same boundaries on the east and north of his country that had been held in the empire days of David and Solomon. This success had given him a remarkable position of influence along the entire Mediterranean coastland. Similarly, Uzziah, king of Judah, a contemporary of Jeroboam for thirty-seven years, had expanded his territory to a size nearly that of the southern boundary in the earlier period. Together Israel and Judah had almost reduplicated the area held by Israel's two greatest rulers.

Before the accession of Jeroboam II, the situation had been quite a different one. Because of military attacks by Assyria, far to the east, and Syria, to the immediate north, Israel had been brought to abject humiliation. During the reign of Jehoahaz (Jeroboam's grandfather), the strength of Israel's army had fallen to only "fifty horsemen, ten chariots and ten thousand foot soldiers." The king of Syria had "destroyed the rest, and made them like the dust at threshing time" (2 Kings 13:7). Recovery from this low state had begun with Jeroboam's father, Jehoash. He had defeated the Syrians on three different occasions (2 Kings 13:25). Jeroboam had then been able to continue this resurgence and bring the country to the strong position already noted.

Because of this recovery, Hosea's generation, living at the close of Jeroboam's reign and following it, knew of humiliating defeat or foreign oppression only through the memories of their fathers. By this time there had been peace for many years, and with it had come economic prosperity. The land was again producing abundantly (2 Chron 26:10), and many people were becoming wealthy. Luxuries had once more become common. Building activity was flourishing on every hand (Hos 8:14), and this led to a widespread feeling of pride (Amos 3:15; 5:11; Isa 9:10). Though people are pleased with conditions of this kind, seldom does prosperity lead to behavior that pleases God. This was true at this time in Israel. Social and moral conditions developed that were wrong and degrading. Side by side with wealth, extreme poverty existed. Through dishonest gain and false balances, the strong took advantage of the weak (Hos 12:7; Isa 5:8; Amos 8:5–6). Those who had wealth felt free to oppress the orphans and widows, and even to buy and sell the destitute on the public markets (Amos 8:4, 8). Justice seemed at a premium, and the courts apparently did little to help.

Religious conditions were no better. Though the pagan cult of Baal, brought into the land during the dynasty of Omri (1 Kings 16:29–33), had been largely brought to an end (2 Kings 10:19–28), many of its offensive features continued under the guise of the calf worship at Bethel and Dan. For this reason, Hosea, speaking against this kind of idolatry, referred to it as a worship of Baal (2:8; 11:2; 13:1). Apparently sacred prostitution, common in the fertility rites of the Baal cult, was still practiced (4:10–18). Also, the people still built "high places" and set up images and Asherah poles "on every high hill and under every spreading tree" (2 Kings 17:7–12).

Amos had preceded Hosea in preaching against this idolatry and sin, but the people had clearly paid little attention. Now it was Hosea's turn, and the fact that Amos had not met with greater success did not make Hosea's task any easier. Yet he went on with it courageously and spoke out strongly against the evils of the day. He also warned of ruin and disaster if his message was not heeded.

After the reign of Jeroboam II, Israel's political fortunes declined rapidly. His son and successor, Zechariah (753 B.C.; cf. 2 Kings 15:8–12), was killed by Shallum after reigning only six months. Shallum was in turn killed by Menahem after a rule of only one month (2 Kings 15:13–15). Menahem (752–742 B.C.; cf. 2 Kings 15:17–22) then ruled for ten years. The series of brief reigns resumed when his son Pekahiah (742–740 B.C.; cf. 2 Kings 5:23–26) was killed by Pekah, one of his military leaders. Pekah was able to keep the throne for twenty years, until 732 B.C. (2 Kings 15:27).[1] His rule was marred by the crushing invasion of Tiglath-pileser III of Assyria in 733 B.C. The next Assyrian king, Shalmaneser V, marched into the region in 724 B.C. and put Samaria, its capital, under siege. The strong city held out for many months. Finally, however, when it capitulated in 722 B.C., many more Israelites were taken captive; and the sovereign days of Israel as a nation were over.

2. Authorship and Composition

The author of this first book of the Minor Prophets was Hosea, son of Beeri (Hos 1:1). The book assigns itself to him. A few critical scholars have, however, cast doubt on the authenticity of two classes of texts from the book.

The one class is constituted of passages that refer to Judah (e.g., 4:15; 5:5, 10, 12–14; 6:4, 11; et al.). The assumption is that Hosea, a citizen of Israel, would not have made such references to the southern neighbor country. Eissfeldt, however, notes that not every mention of Judah can be considered of later date, because "the removal of the name Judah" would destroy "the sense of the whole passage."[2] One

[1]Menahem and Pekah began to rule in the same year. Pekah may have confined his rule to Gilead in Transjordan, as a rival to Menahem and later Pekahiah, and then finally gained courage to strike into the land proper with the help of fifty Gileadites (2 Kings 15:25) and seize the entire country from Pekahiah (cf. E. Thiele, *The Mysterious Numbers of the Hebrew Kings* [Grand Rapids: Eerdmans, 1951], pp. 124–25; cf. also ZPEB, 4:669).

[2]Otto Eissfeldt, *The Old Testament, An Introduction* (New York: Harper & Row, 1965), p. 387.

may reason, then, that if some of these passages referring to Judah must be assigned to Hosea, there is little cause for denying any of them to him.

The other class is made up of the so-called salvation passages (e.g., 11:8–11; 14:2–9). Here the objection is that the tone of these passages is in unusual contrast with the remainder of the book. Admittedly, they are contrasting, but cannot an author include such material in this book? Furthermore, we should recognize that the same "salvation" note is already sounded in the first three chapters of the book (1:10–11; 2:14–23; 3:5); yet nearly all expositors consider these as having come from Hosea.

The book itself contains convincing evidence that Hosea was a prophet to the northern kingdom of Israel. His messages, while occasionally referring (as already noted) to Judah, were directed mainly to Israel. Moreover, Hosea referred to the ruler in Samaria as "our king" (7:5); and he used a number of Aramaisms, showing that the Aramaic-speaking state of Syria immediately to the north had a close influence on Israel.

In view of this, some have questioned Hosea's manner of dating his ministry. He did this by listing four kings of Judah (Uzziah, Jotham, Ahaz, Hezekiah) and only one of Israel (Jeroboam II). Why should he seem to identify himself more with Judah's rulers than with Israel's? The answer commonly given—and probably correct—is that Hosea was indicating his recognition that the Davidic line ruling in Judah was the only legitimate one. God had promised David that his posterity would reign continuously (2 Sam 7:12–13). Thus the kings of Israel, not being descendants of David, were not included in this promise.

There are few clues to the date of Hosea's prophecies. For one thing, they were doubtless not given at the same time. The words about Hosea's marriage and also the earliest prophecies must have been delivered prior to the death of Jeroboam II, because in 1:4 Hosea referred to the coming vengeance on the "house of Jehu" (of which Jeroboam was a member). This vengeance came with the assassination of Jeroboam's son Zechariah six months after Zechariah began to reign (2 Kings 15:8–12). Other passages refer to assassinations of other kings, as though they had already occurred (e.g., 7:3, 16; 8:4). This means that such portions must have been written after these assassinations had happened.

Besides this, there are the references to contact with Assyria (e.g., 5:13; 8:9; 12:1), which point to the time of Menahem, who did negotiate with Tiglath-pileser III (i.e., Pul; 2 Kings 15:19–20). Finally, in 7:11 there is the reference to Israel's dealing with Egypt and Assyria; and this suggests that it was written in the days of Hosea, when Egypt was pitted by Israel against Assyria.

Hosea himself lived till the reign of Hezekiah (728–686 B.C.). Because he did not specifically refer to Samaria's fall to the Assyrians in 722 B.C., he probably had completed his writing by that time. Certainly he witnessed the fall of the northern kingdom. As there is no indication that he was taken captive, he doubtless remained in the land. Of his subsequent experience and ministry, we have no record. His ministry was a long one, extending at least from 753 to 715 B.C.

Hosea's principal significance lies in his sounding the call for Israel to repent. Other prophets—Elijah and Elisha during the reign of Omri, and Amos early in that of Jeroboam II—had given earlier warnings. But Hosea's warning was the last one. The people would have to hear him or else suffer crushing punishment. Hosea's theme, therefore, was the seriousness of Israel's sin and the certainty of punishment if she did not repent.

3. Hosea's Marriage

The marriage of Hosea has occasioned much discussion.[3] It is recorded in 1:2–3—where the Lord addressed Hosea, who then went on to refer to himself in the third person—and in 3:1–3—where the Lord also addressed Hosea, who then went on to refer to himself in the first person. In chapter 1, the Lord commanded him to take "an adulterous wife and children of unfaithfulness." So he married Gomer, who bore three children: Jezreel, Lo-Ruhama, and Lo-Ammi. In chapter 3, the Lord told Hosea to love a woman though she was an adulteress and was cherished by another man. Hosea did this and, in doing so, made a payment of money and barley. The different views regarding the marriage may be divided into four principal types.

a. *Hypothetical marriage*

This view sees the marriage as never happening historically but understands it as either a vision or an allegory symbolic of the relation of God to unfaithful Israel. This view was held by medieval Jews and continued to be popular into the last half of the nineteenth century. E.J. Young was a recent exponent of the allegorical view.[4] Those who hold it say that God would not have commanded a prophet to marry an unchaste woman, especially since the priests had been expressly forbidden to do this (Lev 21:7, 14). They also point out that the significance of an act, as described in the book, is regularly given immediately after the description (e.g., 1:2, 4, 6, 9, et al.), which is a pattern in symbolic literature. Young advances two other arguments: first, Hosea's ministry would have been shattered had he married an unchaste woman; second, the messages given him to preach after the birth of each child (1:4–5; chs. 6–7; 9) would have been too far apart in time to be meaningful in relation to one another.[5]

Evidence against this view includes several points.

First of all, Hosea's straightforward narrative style gives little indication of symbolism being intended (despite Young's assertions). Also, some things of central importance to the narrative (e.g., the name of Hosea's wife, Gomer) are not presented symbolically at all. Furthermore, the narrative includes numerous details uncalled for were the intent only symbolical: viz., Gomer is called the daughter of Diblaim; the third child, Lo-Ammi, is said to have been born only after the second was weaned; the children are said specifically to have been two boys and one girl. Again, in chapter 3 the exact amount of payment for Gomer is stated, both in money and barley. Such details belong to history, not allegory. And, finally, it is difficult to understand why an allegory should be spread over two chapters (1 and 3) separated by the longest chapter in the whole book.

b. *Literal marriage—Gomer unchaste*

This view holds that the marriage did occur and that Gomer was already an unchaste person, possibly a temple prostitute. Arguments in favor of this view are mainly three.

---

[3]For a survey of problems and representative positions, see H.H. Rowley, "The Marriage of Hosea," BJRL 39 (1956): 200–233.

[4]E.J. Young, *Introduction to the Old Testament* (Grand Rapids: Eerdmans, 1949), pp. 245–46.

[5]Ibid.

1. This is the most natural meaning of God's command to Hosea, "Go, take to yourself an adulterous wife and children of unfaithfulness" (1:2).

2. The word of command "take" most likely goes with "children of unfaithfulness" as well as "an adulterous wife"; therefore Gomer must already have been a prostitute at this time in order to have had such children.

3. So far as the ethical impropriety of this command is concerned, it was only the priest that was forbidden by the law to marry an unchaste woman; Hosea was a prophet.

In respect to the first reason, however, it is questionable whether this view does take the command in its most "natural" meaning. One would hardly expect the descriptive term "an adulterous wife" (*'ēšeṯ zᵉnûnîm*) on this basis but merely the word "harlot" (*zōnāh*). Also, one would expect the terms "an adulterous wife" and "children of unfaithfulness" to carry parallel meanings; but if the first means a woman who already practiced prostitution, then the second should mean children who did the same—which is unlikely, considering their probable age. A more likely parallel meaning takes "an adulterous wife" to signify a woman of an adulterous character (but not necessarily having practiced adultery yet) and the children being born to have similar characters, a view supported by 2:4 (cf. 4:2; 5:4). Furthermore, the term "an adulterous wife" is exactly the type of designation one would expect for indicating the idea of a woman of this kind of character.

In respect to the second reason, that three children are said to have been born—each designated by name with a respective symbolic meaning—directly after the indication of the command to marry Gomer makes the conclusion all but necessary that they are the children in question. If so, they do not give reason to believe that Gomer was already an adulteress before marrying Hosea.

In respect to the third reason, it is true that the prohibition noted is given only to priests, but it is unthinkable that God therefore approved other religious leaders' marrying unchaste persons. It should be realized that regulations for prophets (which Hosea was)—unlike those for priests—are not prescribed in the law. If they had been, it is only reasonable to assume that a similar prohibition would have been given; for prophets were as much religious leaders (i.e., in places of influence) as priests. Moreover, this command to Hosea was given by God himself; it was not just something Hosea did or that some human told him to do. It is quite unthinkable that God would have commanded anyone—much less a religious leader—to marry such a person.

c. *Spiritual infidelity*

Another view, held less widely, is that the situation is one of spiritual rather than physical infidelity. Gomer became unchaste because, like the Israelites of Hosea's day, she became a worshiper of false gods. Thus this view obviates the ethical difficulty of marital unfaithfulness. Furthermore, Scripture often uses harlotry as a figure of spiritual unfaithfulness. But one must ask whether the difficulty of God's ordering Hosea to marry an unchaste woman is any greater than his ordering Hosea to marry one who worshiped false gods. Besides, the question arises how Hosea could have used this kind of infidelity by his wife as an illustration for people involved in the same type of sin.

d. *Literal marriage—Gomer chaste*

This view holds that the marriage did indeed occur but that Gomer was chaste when married and only became adulterous later. This is the preferred interpretation, in spite of Pfeiffer's calling it plain "sleight of hand."[6] The words "an adulterous wife" are to be understood proleptically. Gomer was not a harlot at the time Hosea married her; and if she was not, then the objections raised to the second view are removed. Such a marriage would have been difficult for Hosea to contemplate and carry out, knowing his bride would surely prove to be unfaithful; but the ethical problem of his marrying an acknowledged harlot would not have existed.

Some have objected that this view would take many years out of Hosea's life to allow for his marriage, the birth of three children, his separation from Gomer, then their reunion, and that all this would have unduly shortened Hosea's prophetic ministry. Yet for these events six or seven years would probably have sufficed—which is by no means excessive in comparison with a normal life span. Another point in favor of this view is that, as the book shows, Hosea genuinely loved Gomer.

Both of Young's objections to the preferred view can be answered. If Gomer was chaste when they married, there is no reason for the marriage to have shattered Hosea's ministry. People would have sympathized with a husband whose wife had been proved scandalously unfaithful. Indeed, they might well have listened more closely to his messages because of this. Nor is the objection valid that Hosea's messages would have been too far apart in time. While it is true that Hosea was given a new message each time a child was born, we need not think that these messages comprised everything Hosea preached.

Perhaps the most convincing reason in favor of the preferred view is that it implies a significant parallel between Hosea's marriage and God's experience with Israel (cf. 1:2, 6–7, 9; 2:2–13). In the OT Israel is presented as having been chaste when espoused by God in the wilderness (Jer 2:2–3), though God, of course, knew that she would become unfaithful. Also, the parallel requires that the woman loved by Hosea again (ch. 3) be the same Gomer as in chapter 1. And this is surely correct. Again and again God extended his love toward Israel, though she continually proved unfaithful to him. Problems concerned in the reunion of Hosea and Gomer (ch. 3) are dealt with in the commentary.

4. Theology of Hosea

The central thought of Hosea concerns God's covenant with Israel that the people had broken. The covenant had been made at Mount Sinai in the wilderness, at which time God found the people like "grapes in the desert" and "early fruit on the fig tree" (9:10). God "loved" the people and called them his "son" (11:1; cf. Exod 4:22). Through the passing years, however, they had wandered away from God; and the more he had called after them, the further they went from him (11:2). They fell into deep sin, breaking the covenant so graciously made with them.

Hosea repeatedly described this sin, committed by both people (4:1–2, 9–19; 6:4–11; et al.) and religious leaders (4:5–10). Because Israel's sin constituted the breaking of the covenant, Hosea gave more attention to this matter than any other.

---

[6]R.H. Pfeiffer, *Introduction to the Old Testament* (New York: Harper & Brothers, 1941), p. 568.

Along with these descriptions, however, he told also of God's love and patience with Israel in her sin (11:1–4; 14:1–9) in wanting Israel to return to him.

Hosea employed the forceful illustration of the unhappy marriage relationship he experienced with his own wife, Gomer (1:2–3), to impress these truths on the minds of his readers. She proved unfaithful to him, and he told Israel that the people had been unfaithful to God. Hosea's taking Gomer back after she had left him (3:1) further parallels God's frequent taking Israel back after her many occasions of waywardness.

Hosea not only described Israel's sin but also warned of the people's coming punishment. Israel's reprimand for breaking God's covenant was long deserved, but he had thus far been patient. The time would come, however, when patience would no longer be appropriate and punishment would be necessary. This punishment would come in the form of desolation for the land (4:3; 5:1–15) and exile for the people. The country of exile is sometimes identified as Assyria (9:3; 10:6) and sometimes symbolically as Egypt (9:3, 6). The reference to Egypt reminded the people of their father's experience there and thus dramatically foreshadowed the future exile in Assyria.

The prophet included a note of joy in this otherwise somber picture. Israel's future punishment would not spell the end; it would be followed by a glad time of restoration. Hosea characterized this time as one of true repentance on the part of the people (6:1–3) and of rich blessing at the hand of God. The people would be "like the sand on the seashore, which cannot be measured or counted," and would be called "sons of the living God" (1:10). At the time God would "speak tenderly" to the nation and "give her back her vineyards," she would "sing as in the days of her youth, as in the day she came up out of Egypt" (2:14–15).

5. Bibliography

Books

Andersen, Francis, and Freedman, David. *Hosea*. Anchor Bible. Garden City, N.Y.: Doubleday, 1980.

Brown, S.L. *The Book of Hosea*. Westminster Commentaries. London: Methuen & Co., 1932.

Cheyne, T.K. *Hosea*. Cambridge Bible for Schools and Colleges. Cambridge: Cambridge University Press, 1884.

Hailey, H. *A Commentary on the Minor Prophets*. Grand Rapids: Baker, 1972.

Harper, W.R. *Amos and Hosea*. International Critical Commentary. Edinburgh: T. & T. Clark, 1905.

Henderson, E. *The Book of the Twelve Minor Prophets*. Andover: Warren F. Draper, 1866.

Horton, R.F. *The Minor Prophets*. The Century Bible. London: Oliphants, 1972.

Hubbard, D.A. *With Bands of Love*. Grand Rapids: Eerdmans, 1968.

Keil, C.F. *The Twelve Minor Prophets*. KD. 2 vols. Grand Rapids: Eerdmans, 1949.

Kidner, Derek. *Love to the Loveless*. Bible Speaks Truly Today. Downers Grove, Ill.: Inter-Varsity, 1981.

Knight, G.A.F. *Hosea, Introduction and Commentary*. London: SCM, 1960.

Laetsch, T. *The Minor Prophets*. St. Louis: Concordia, 1956.

Morgan, G.C. *Hosea, The Heart and Holiness of God*. New York: Revell, 1934.

Pusey, E.B. *The Minor Prophets With a Commentary*. 1885. Reprint. Grand Rapids: Eerdmans, 1949.

Robinson, G.L. *The Twelve Minor Prophets*. New York: Harper & Brothers, 1926.
Robinson, W.H. *Two Hebrew Prophets*. London: Lutterworth, 1948.
Smith, G.A. *The Book of the Twelve Prophets*. Rev. ed. New York: Harper & Brothers, 1928.
Smith, N.H. *Mercy and Sacrifice*. London: SCM, 1953.
Vandermey, H. Ronald. *Hosea*. Everyman's Bible Commentary. Chicago: Moody, 1981.
Wolff, Hans Walther. *Hosea*. Hermenia. Philadelphia: Fortress, 1974.

6. Outline

- I. Israel's Infidelity Illustrated (1:1–3:5)
  - A. Historical Setting (1:1)
  - B. Marriage and Children of Hosea (1:2–9)
  - C. A Future Day of Hope (1:10–2:1)
  - D. Israel, the Adulterous Spouse (2:2–13)
  - E. The Blessing of Israel (2:14–23)
  - F. Gomer Loved Again (3:1–3)
  - G. Israel's Future Return to God (3:4–5)
- II. Israel's Indictment, Punishment, and Restoration (4:1–14:9)
  - A. Israel's Indictment (4:1–7:16)
    1. A general indictment of the people (4:1–4)
    2. Sins of the priests (4:5–11a)
    3. Sins of the people (4:11b–19)
    4. A warning to priest, people, and king (5:1–7)
    5. A warning to Ephraim and Judah (5:8–15)
    6. Words of repentant Israel (6:1–3)
    7. Continued indictment of the people (6:4–11)
    8. A ruinous domestic policy (7:1–7)
    9. A fatal foreign policy (7:8–16)
  - B. Israel's Punishment (8:1–10:15)
    1. Warning of approaching judgment (8:1–14)
    2. Assyrian captivity soon to come (9:1–9)
    3. The fleeting glory of Israel (9:10–17)
    4. Guilt and coming captivity (10:1–8)
    5. Sin and punishment (10:9–15)
  - C. Israel's Restoration (11:1–14:9)
    1. God's love and Israel's rebellion (11:1–7)
    2. Restoration in the last days (11:8–11)
    3. The folly of Israel (11:12–12:14)
    4. Israel's fall into sin (13:1–16)
    5. Israel's repentance and God's blessing (14:1–9)

Text and Exposition

I. Israel's Infidelity Illustrated (1:1–3:5)

A. *Historical Setting*

1:1

[1]The word of the LORD that came to Hosea son of Beeri during the reigns of Uzziah, Jotham, Ahaz and Hezekiah, kings of Judah, and during the reign of Jeroboam son of Joash king of Israel:

1 This verse concerns matters of background and introduction. For a discussion of them, see Introduction: Historical Background.

B. *Marriage and Children of Hosea*

1:2–9

[2]When the LORD began to speak through Hosea, the LORD said to him, "Go, take to yourself an adulterous wife and children of unfaithfulness, because the land is guilty of the vilest adultery in departing from the LORD." [3]So he married Gomer daughter of Diblaim, and she conceived and bore him a son.

[4]Then the LORD said to Hosea, "Call him Jezreel, because I will soon punish the house of Jehu for the massacre of Jezreel, and I will put an end to the kingdom of Israel. [5]In that day I will break Israel's bow in the Valley of Jezreel."

[6]Gomer conceived again and gave birth to a daughter. Then the LORD said to Hosea, "Call her Lo-Ruhamah, for I will no longer show love to the house of Israel, that I should at all forgive them. [7]Yet I will show love to the house of Judah; and I will save them—not by bow, sword or battle, or by horses and horsemen, but by the LORD their God."

[8]After she had weaned Lo-Ruhamah, Gomer had another son. [9]Then the LORD said, "Call him Lo-Ammi, for you are not my people, and I am not your God.

2 For a discussion of "an adulterous wife," see Introduction: Hosea's Marriage. "Children of unfaithfulness" translates *yaldê zᵉnûnîm*, which is exactly parallel with "an adulterous wife" (*'ēšeṯ zᵉnûnîm*). The phrases may be translated literally "children of harlotries" and "wife of harlotries." Because "harlotries" in "wife of harlotries" means immoral acts of the wife, the same word in "children of harlotries" could well mean the parallel thought—immoral acts of the children. "Children of harlotries," then, would mean children who would come to be like their mother (so Schmoller, CHS, in loc.). Often the influence of parents will have this kind of result in their children's lives. This interpretation finds support in 2:4 (q.v.), where the parallel term carries this meaning.

Keil believes the children were the result of adulterous acts of the wife, born before her marriage to Hosea; for Keil holds that Gomer was a prostitute before she married Hosea, a view already seen as unlikely. Harper believes that the first child was Hosea's but that the second and third were those of another man, since their names are of a different type from the first (as will be seen). This is possible. Yet we should realize that all three names were designated by God for their symbolic significance respecting his own relation to Israel. They may then have all been Hosea's own children.

That the nation was "guilty of the vilest adultery in departing from the LORD" sets forth the parallel, followed in much of the book, between Hosea's marriage and God's relation to Israel. The parallel is not well maintained by the assumption that Hosea's wife was a prostitute before he took her. But it is maintained if she became unfaithful after her marriage and if her children, in turn, followed her example; for Israel became unfaithful after God chose her, and her descendants then followed in the same pattern of life.

3 Nowhere else in the Bible is the name Gomer used of a person, though it is used for a people (Gen 10:2–3; Ezek 38:6). The name is best taken to mean "completion." Nor does "Diblaim," the name of Gomer's father, appear elsewhere of a person. Keil (1:38) believes that "Diblaim" means "fig-cakes." Neither name has symbolic significance in the text; so the meanings should not be pressed. We should observe that Hosea obeyed God's command, though this was certainly not easy, knowing what Gomer would become. The text makes clear that the son that was now born was a proper son of the new marriage.

4 Three children were born to Hosea and Gomer, and each was given a symbolic name. The first was called "Jezreel," after the name of the city where Jehu slaughtered the "house of Ahab" (2 Kings 9:7–10:28). The use of the name Jezreel here looks back to the time and also ahead to a future day, when "the blood" Jehu then shed would be avenged, as the next words indicate. This shows that Jehu was wrong in what he did—a seeming conflict with 2 Kings 10:30, where God is said to have commended Jehu. The difficulty may be resolved as follows: Although Jehu had done well in carrying out God's directive (2 Kings 9:1–10), he had sinned in killing more people than God had intended. Jehu had probably done this more out of a desire for personal advancement than obedience to God. The punishment for Jehu's sin is to be the cessation of the kingdom of Israel as a nation. This occurred in 722 B.C.—within Hosea's ministry (cf. Introduction: Historical Background).

5 The bow was a symbol of power in a day when it was a principal instrument of warfare. Thus a broken bow symbolized the loss of power. The "Valley of Jezreel," where Israel's bow would be broken, lay north of the city of Jezreel, between the ridges of Gilboa and Moreh. To the west, it merged into the Esdraelon Valley, and both have been scenes of major battles all down through history. The prediction here is that this valley would see a significant stage in Israel's final defeat. Its fulfillment came mainly in the campaign of Tiglath-pileser III, who in 733 B.C. seized the area (cf. Introduction).

6 The second child born, a daughter, was given the name "Lo-Ruhamah," meaning "not loved." The meaning is directly stated: God would no longer show love to Israel but would bring judgment on her. "No longer show love" translates a phrase meaning, literally, "no longer further to pursue with favor." God would not extend favor any longer toward this rebellious people. Thus the reason Israel had continued this long was that God had favored them. "I should at all forgive them" translates a phrase that may also be rendered "I will utterly take them away." The verb used (*nāśā'*) normally means "to lift up," "carry away." It can mean "forgive" (i.e., to carry away sin). Either thought fits here. Because of the intensive form of the verb used (cf. Notes), perhaps the more basic idea is preferable, supporting the paraphrase "I will no longer show love toward the nation of Israel, but will instead violently carry her away in judgment."

7 Now there is a direct contrast. God would no more show love to Israel; yet he would continue to show love to Judah. These words were probably written during the reign of Uzziah in Judah—a "good" king (2 Kings 15:3; 2 Chron 26:4), the third in a line of four "good" kings (Joash, Amaziah, Uzziah, Jotham). The favor of God here indicated would be an apparent result; and, as otherwise known, this favor did continue for a century and a half.

Since God was the speaker, he might have said that he would save Judah "by himself," rather than by "the LORD their God." That he referred to himself by name shows his desire to impress on the citizens of Israel the name of their true God, whom they had forgotten. The declaration that Judah would not be saved by "bow, sword or battle, or by horses and horsemen" implies that Israel's hope had been in these sources of strength rather than God. Judah's hope was fixed in God and therefore would be spared. God often uses physical means of strength to deliver his people. Yet he—not the physical means—is the one who really does this.

8 That Gomer had her third child after the second was weaned shows that the births of the children came fairly close together. A detail such as this, unexpected in an allegory, shows that the narrative is intended to be historical.

9 The name "Lo-Ammi" means "not my people." The significance of this is stated in the remainder of the verse. Israel was disowned by God as his people; he would no longer be their God. The reason is in v.2: The people had departed from the Lord in faithfulness, going after other gods. Lo-Ammi is harsher in meaning than the name of the second child. The name Lo-Ruhamah spoke of not being loved; Lo-Ammi speaks of being fully disowned.

Notes

2 "Guilty of the vilest adultery" translates זנה תזנה (*zānōh tizneh*), an infinitive absolute followed by an imperfect, giving reason for this forceful expression.

6 Though the Hebrew does not identify the Lord as speaker or Hosea as recipient of the message, the context makes the translation given very clear. The words "that I should at all forgive them" again reflect the intensification of an infinitive absolute followed by an imperfect.

C. *A Future Day of Hope*

1:10–2:1

10 "Yet the Israelites will be like the sand on the seashore, which cannot be measured or counted. In the place where it was said to them, 'You are not my people,' they will be called 'sons of the living God.' 11 The people of Judah and the people of Israel will be reunited, and they will appoint one leader and will come up out of the land, for great will be the day of Jezreel.

1 "Say of your brothers, 'My people,' and of your sisters, 'My loved one.'

10 In the Hebrew, this verse begins chapter 2. It relates closely, however, to v.9; and the same is true in respect to the section of the chapter it begins. A contrast is intended. Though in Hosea's day God was disclaiming the Israelites as his people, in a day to come God will make their number "like the sand on the seashore." God had a message of hope for his people along with a message of warning. God will still carry out his promise of an innumerable posterity for Abraham, in spite of the unfaithfulness of the people, which called for severe punishment.

The identification of "the place" is of little importance. Some have suggested Palestine; others Mesopotamia, the place of the coming captivity. The point is that, wherever the place, the contrasting declarations would cancel each other. Whereas in Hosea's day God would not call them his people, in the day to come they would be called "sons of the living God" (cf. Rom 9:26).

11 By speaking of both the "people of Judah and the people of Israel," Hosea makes clear that the time of future hope will involve both nations. His statement that the two peoples "will be reunited, and they will appoint one leader" is a clue to the identification of the hoped-for day.

The reunion between Israel and Judah was partially realized when the people returned from the Babylonian exile. No longer was there a division of the two nations. Then, however, they were unable to choose their head of government. They were under governors appointed by the Persian court and never attained true autonomy then, nor at any time before the dispersion following the Fall of Jerusalem in A.D. 70. In fact, not until May 1948 was it possible to speak of a truly autonomous, undivided nation of Israel.

Another clue to the hoped-for day is found in the words "they . . . will come up out of the land." While the identity of "the land" has been much discussed, it is best seen as Egypt (so Keil, 1:47, referring to Exod 1:10), symbolizing the nations throughout the world, among which the Israelites would in due time be dispersed (cf. Deut 28:68). This view is sustained by Hosea's reference in 2:14–15 to a time when Israel would go up out of Egypt, a time also symbolic of Israel's return to Palestine from her places of future dispersion. So this twentieth century has seen thousands of people returning to Palestine from this collective "land."

The statement "great will be that day of Jezreel" gives us a third clue. The day will in some sense be outstanding, and something about it will justify its being called "that day of Jezreel." This is a reference back to 1:4–5, where Israel's defeat in the Valley of Jezreel is predicted; but it is also a reference forward to 2:22–23, where Jezreel really stands for Israel, in the sense of the nation's being "sown" in the land by God for her rebirth and multiplication. This implies that, in contrast to the former day of Jezreel when Israel was brought down by Assyria, the coming day would be "great" because it would see the nation reborn for a time of glory.

The one period that fits all three clues is the thousand-year reign of Christ. The undivided, autonomous nation is already in the land, having "come up from the land" of her dispersions; and in the Millennium she will see a time of reborn glory, when her chosen leader will be Christ himself (cf. Isa 2:1–5; 11:1–12; Rev 20:1–6).

2:1 Though this verse begins chapter 2 in most EVs, it actually belongs with chapter 1. It sets forth the spiritual relation between God and Israel in the future day of hope, which contrasts so directly with Hosea's day. The relationship in his day was symbolized by the names Lo-Ruhamah and Lo-Ammi ("not loved" and "not my people"); but in the future day the appropriate names will be positive, not negative —viz., "my people" (*ammî*) and "my loved one" (*ruḥāmāh*). Apparently "my people" is related to "brothers" and "my loved one" to "sisters" only because Lo-Ammi was a son's name and Lo-Ruhamah a daughter's (1:8–9).

Notes

10 The context shows that all Israel, both the northern and southern kingdoms, is intended by בְּנֵי־יִשְׂרָאֵל (*bᵉnê yiśrā'ēl*, "children of Israel"). The phrase "sons of the living God" (instead of something like "you are my people") places the stress on אֵל־חָי (*'ēl ḥāy*, "living God"). It was not only that the future would see Israel as God's people, but it would see them as people of the *living* God in contrast to the dead and nonexistent deities Israel had worshiped in Hosea's day.

10–2:1 That this section belongs—though some (e.g., JB) place it elsewhere—here is evident in that the thoughts expressed in it correspond by contrast to thoughts in the preceding verses.

1. The promise of population increase contrasts to the termination of the "kingdom of Israel" (1:4; cf. 9:11–16).
2. The promise of return from captivity contrasts to the breaking of "Israel's bow" (1:5; cf. 8:8–10; 9:3, 6, 17).
3. The promise of the unity of the people under one leader contrasts to God's rejection as indicated by the names of the children (1:4, 6, 9; cf. 7:3–7; 8:4).

D. *Israel, the Adulterous Spouse*

2:2–13

2"Rebuke your mother, rebuke her,
for she is not my wife,
and I am not her husband.
Let her remove the adulterous look from her face
and the unfaithfulness from between her breasts.
3Otherwise I will strip her naked
and make her as bare as on the day she was born;
I will make her like a desert,
turn her into a parched land,
and slay her with thirst.
4I will not show my love to her children,
because they are the children of adultery.
5Their mother has been unfaithful
and has conceived them in disgrace.
She said, 'I will go after my lovers,
who give me my food and my water,
my wool and my linen, my oil and my drink,'
6Therefore I will block her path with thornbushes;
I will wall her in so that she cannot find her way.
7She will chase after her lovers but not catch them;
she will look for them but not find them.
Then she will say,
'I will go back to my husband as at first,
for then I was better off than now.'

8She has not acknowledged that I was the one
who gave her the grain, the new wine and oil
who lavished on her the silver and gold—
which they used for Baal.

9"Therefore I will take away my grain when it ripens,
and my new wine when it is ready.
I will take back my wool and my linen,
intended to cover her nakedness.
10So now I will expose her lewdness
before the eyes of her lovers;
no one will take her out of my hands.
11I will stop all her celebrations:
her yearly festivals, her New Moons,
her Sabbath days—all her appointed feasts.
12I will ruin her vines and her fig trees,
which she said were her pay from her lovers;
I will make them a thicket,
and wild animals will devour them.
13I will punish her for the days
she burned incense to the Baals;
she decked herself with rings and jewelry,
and went after her lovers,
but me she forgot,"

declares the LORD.

2 Although the language of this section (especially in the earlier verses) applies in good part to Hosea's unfaithful wife, it is primarily intended for Israel. The entire passage is based on the parallel between God's relation to Israel and Hosea's relation to Gomer.

The verb translated "rebuke" (*rîḇ*) means basically "to contend or strive." Here the meaning is to "strive with your mother in rebuke" for her life of sin. The mother is Israel as a nation, and the children are individual Israelites. Thus Israelites were being urged to call for their nation to return to faithful living before God. The repetition of "rebuke" is for emphasis. The statement "she is not my wife" implies that Hosea had disowned his wife (see 3:1, where the Lord directs him to take her back). Likewise God had disowned Israel, a thought already expressed in the symbolic name Lo-Ammi (1:9) of Hosea's third child. The remainder of v.2 is a stark portrayal of Gomer's unfaithfulness. The reference to her "breasts" may imply that she had laid bare her bosom to entice her lovers. So Israel, having turned from her own true God, Yahweh, was guilty of unblushing idolatry and voluptuous service to false gods.

3 Israel was next told the consequences of her sinful ways. If she did not change, she would be stripped naked—a thought that may be related to her having bared her breasts. The fuller meaning, however, is that she would be made as she was at birth—a naked, helpless child. The time of infancy was Israel's experience in the wilderness after the Exodus. It was a barren, desert area. God protected Israel at that time, but she herself would be like that parched and desolate land unless she returned to him.

4 Again there is a distinction between mother and children, even though both are really the same. In this case the guilt is particularized. Israel, as a nation, was guilty and deserving of punishment, but so too were individual Israelites. "Love," therefore, would not be shown to individuals any more than to the nation as a whole. "Children of adultery" should be seen as parallel to the similar words in 1:2 (even though the word for "children" is different: *yaldê* in 1:2 and *b^enê* here). Here, however, the words must refer to those who are called children because they practiced the sins of their mother (cf. 1:2, where the meaning is the same).

5 In the Hebrew this verse begins with *kî*, used in a causal sense. Its force, however, is directed forward in the text to the "therefore" of v.6 rather than backward. It shows that reasons are to be given for the punishment the following verses will specify. "Mother" again refers to the nation as a whole; "them" refers to the children of v.4. The direct quotation attributed to Israel, as Yahweh's unfaithful wife, applies equally to Gomer, Hosea's wife. As she was running after "lovers" who would give gifts to her, so Israel was running after the false gods of the surrounding nations. From these nations Israel was receiving gifts of food, water, wool, linen, oil, and drink. Although these were no doubt the result of trade agreements, Israel thought of them as coming from the gods of the nations, who attributed what they had to their gods. So the implication is that the desire for trading benefits led Israel into going after these other gods.

6 This verse begins a vivid portrayal of God's judgment on unfaithful Israel. He will keep her lovers from her by blocking "her path with thornbushes." In fact, he will use them to wall her in. The participle *śāḵ* (from *śûḵ*, "to hedge, wall") implies that God's activity in blocking Israel's path will be continuous. The figure of the thornbushes found its historical embodiment in all the warfare and hardship that God permitted to come on Israel in the following years and that cut her off from contact with many foreign nations (cf. Introduction: Historial Background; cf. also Job 3:23; 19:8 for a parallel idea).

7 Though Israel's path will be blocked, she will still try to "chase after her lovers"; but her pursuit of them will be futile. That she will go on pursuing them all the more intently is suggested by the use of the Piel (intensive) form of the verb *rāḏap* ("to pursue, chase"). "My husband as at first" is a reference to God. Israel, frustrated in chasing false gods, will finally recognize the supremacy of her own God, as she realizes that she was better off when following him than when pursuing strange gods. Verses 14–20 show how Israel was to be brought to a recognition of her God. This happened in part after the Exile, when the people were more faithful to God than before. Yet even then they fell short. Only in the last days (cf. comments at 1:10–11) will Israel fully return to her "first husband."

8 Here is the reason for Israel's unfaithfulness: The people did not recognize God as the source of their benefits—grain, wine, oil (the staple food products), and silver and gold (the precious metals used in trade). They had used much silver and gold for idols of Baal. The name "Baal" probably stands for all the false gods, of which Baal himself was the most popular one. Jehu had done much to eliminate Baal worship (2 Kings 10:19–28), but it still persisted.

9 As a result of Israel's idolatry, God would punish her by taking away the "grain when it ripens" and the "new wine when it is ready." The third staple mentioned in v.8, "oil," is not listed here, though it too would doubtless become scarce. Both wool from the sheep and linen (*pištāh*, "flax") are included. Because of their sin, the people would lack food and clothing. Each of these products has the possessive pronominal suffix "my" in the Hebrew, showing that in God's sight they belonged to him. Presumably they would be withheld by lack of rain.

10 In the Hebrew "expose her lewdness" is literally "uncover her shame." The word for "shame" (*naḇlûṯ*) means "withered state." Israel would be withered because God would withhold his bounty. God also would uncover this condition by revealing it before the neighboring nations. Israel's "lovers" thus would come to despise her, not wanting to have dealings with one so distressed. No one would "snatch" (*nāṣal*, lit., "deliver") her from God's control, both because they would not care to and because God would not permit it.

11 Israel will no longer enjoy her "celebrations" and "festivals." The annual festivals included the three main feasts—Passover, Pentecost, and Tabernacles—and the monthly festival, the feast of the new moon. The Sabbaths, of course, were weekly. The word translated "appointed feasts" is the plural of *mô'ēḏ* and means "set times," probably referring to regular celebrations not covered by the other terms.

12 The "vines" and "fig trees" represent the finest of the land's products. God would destroy them because Israel had regarded them as "pay for her lovers." These would now become merely "thickets" for wild beasts to roam and eat in. In other words, the protective hedges would be taken away and cultivation stopped. These things were fulfilled in various ways during Israel's last days. Her land was devastated by Assyrian forces (see Introduction: Historical Background); then, in 722 B.C., it was totally subjugated by them. God's warnings are never to be taken lightly.

13 The reason for these punishments now becomes more specific; it goes back to "the days" when Israel "burned offerings to the Baals." Such occurrences were mainly in the reign of Ahab and his sons; but even after Jehu had slaughtered the religious personnel of the Baals, idol worship continued to some degree. The plural "Baals" rather than the singular "Baal" of v.8 suggests many manifestations: Baal-Zephon, Baal-Hermon, Baal-gad, et al., which were all local Baals. The remainder of the verse depicts activities of Israel in following the Baals, activities characteristic of a prostitute in her attempt to lure men.

Notes

3 For an adulteress to be stripped naked was not uncommon in the Middle East; see J. Mauchline, IB, 6:577–78, for references.

6 The use of the second person in דרכך (*darkēḵ*, "your path"; NIV, NASB, et al., "her path") is probably for emphasis; suddenly God is depicted as talking to Israel rather than merely about her. The LXX and Syriac have smoothed the reading by changing to the third person.

E. *The Blessing of Israel*

2:14–23

14"Therefore I am now going to allure her;
I will lead her into the desert
and speak tenderly to her.
15There I will give her back her vineyards,
and will make the Valley of Achor a door of hope.
There she will sing as in the days of her youth,
as in the day she came up out of Egypt.

16"In that day," declares the LORD,
"you will call me 'my husband';
you will no longer call me 'my master.'
17I will remove the names of the Baals from her lips;
no longer will their names be invoked.
18In that day I will make a covenant for them
with the beasts of the field and the birds of the air
and the creatures that move along the ground.
Bow and sword and battle
I will abolish from the land,
so that all may lie down in safety.
19I will betroth you to me forever;
I will betroth you in righteousness and justice,
in love and compassion.
20I will betroth you in faithfulness,
and you will acknowledge the LORD.

21"In that day I will respond,"
declares the LORD—
"I will respond to the skies,
and they will respond to the earth;
22and the earth will respond to the grain,
the new wine and oil,
and they will respond to Jezreel.
23I will plant her for myself in the land;
I will show my love to the one I called 'Not my
loved one.'
I will say to those called 'Not my people,' 'You are
my people';
and they will say, 'You are my God.' "

This section develops a thought that corresponds to that of 1:10–11. This passage looks forward to when Israel will experience great blessings from God. A partial fulfillment occurred at the return from the Babylonian captivity, but the complete fulfillment can be only in the glorious millennial reign of the future. Numerous expositors (Calvin, Keil, et al.) find this fulfillment in terms of the church. The text, however, gives no hint of this. Normal principles of interpretation call for the blessings of Israel, here enumerated, to be taken just as literally as the punishments set forth in vv.6–13.

14 "Therefore" (*lāḵēn*), used in vv.6, 9 to introduce the punishments of Israel, now introduces the coming blessings. God, who has withheld the blessings, cannot bestow them till after Israel's sin has been punished. In the Hebrew the interjection *hinnēh* ("behold") stresses this marked change in subject. The word for "allure" (*pāṯāh*) connotes persuasion by means of attractive benefits. The word "desert" in this verse and "Egypt" in the next one point to a historical parallel with the time of Israel's journey from Egypt. As during that forty-year period God persuaded Israel to leave Egypt, go out into the desert, and move on finally to the Promised Land; so in the final day he will persuade her to leave the Egypt of spiritual declension, go out into the wilderness of fellowship alone with God, and move on to the Promised Land of blessed rest. In that day God will "speak tenderly to her" (lit., "speak on her heart"), rather than in harsh words as in vv.6–13.

15 God will not only speak consolingly; he will give Israel's vineyards back to her. In the historical parallel, this means that as soon as the future Israel has passed through her wilderness and entered her Canaan, she will receive again the vineyards that had been taken away (v.12). The Valley of Achor, a place of trouble and disgrace at the time of Israel's entrance into Canaan under Joshua (cf. Achan's sin and punishment—Josh 7:24–26), will in the future be "a door of hope." So Israel's future response in song-filled thanksgiving will be as when she entered Canaan the first time. In partial fulfillment, there was praise when Israel returned from the Babylonian captivity. But in the future day there will be even greater praise, when the people return to their land and Christ is their king.

16 "My husband" translates *'îšî*, the symbolic name the people of God were to give him on returning to him. In this future day, Israel will be spiritually revived so that she will recognize God to be her true husband and she his wife. No longer will she think of him as *Baali* (lit., "my Baal"; NIV, "my master"). It may be that Israel had substituted Baal for Yahweh and had tried to think of Yahweh as Baal, even calling him by his heathen name. If so, her sin had been great indeed.

17 In the coming day Yahweh will remove Baal worship and all remembrance of the names of the Baals from Israel. Then Yahweh will be truly worshiped.

18 Not only will Israel be reconciled with God, but in that day there will be peace on earth. Yahweh will make a covenant with the beasts, the birds, and the little creatures of the ground. These categories of living creatures are the same as in Genesis 9:2, where the context implies their separation from man through fear (cf. Isa 11:6–9). Also the bow and sword, the two main weapons of Hosea's day, will be abolished (lit., "broken," from *šāḇar*, "to break in pieces"). Thus war will be eliminated so that "all may lie down in safety." Since war has been a scourge throughout history, the day Hosea is speaking of must still be future (cf. Isa 2:4; Mic 4:3).

19 Here God promises Israel that she will be betrothed to him forever. In the future day there will be no period of estrangement, as in OT times. The betrothal involves several qualitative relationships, four being mentioned here: "righteousness and justice" (which indicate that all legal standards will be met in the betrothal) and "love and compassion" (which denote God's emotional concern for the new bride).

20 A fifth relationship—"faithfulness"—is also promised. While God's faithfulness to Israel is certainly in view, the emphasis is perhaps even more on Israel's faithfulness to God. In OT times God had also been faithful to Israel, but then there had to be a separation because of sin. The new relationship in the future day, which will do away with any further need for separation, will include Israel's faithfulness to God. This is no doubt the connotation of the statement that "you [Israel] will acknowledge the LORD."

21 As a result of this beautiful relationship between Yahweh and Israel in the future day, Yahweh will "respond" to the needs of the people. Verses 21–22 contain a series of metaphors, all progressively related. In v.21 the skies are seen as pleading with God to send rain (blessings) on the earth, to which God responds favorably; and the earth is seen as asking the heavens to send rain (blessings), and to this the heavens respond favorably.

22 Now the grain, the new wine, and the oil are viewed as asking the earth for its provisions—a request to which the earth responds favorably. Finally Jezreel is viewed as asking the grain, new wine, and oil to provide blessings, and these also respond favorably. Implicit in this reciprocity is the assurance that God will supply Israel's needs through the skies and the earth and its products. Here "Jezreel" almost certainly means all Israel. The Valley of Jezreel was a center for the production of food. Moreover, the name means "God plants" (cf. v.23, which clearly refers to all Israel).

23 The verb for "I will plant" (*zāraʿ*, "to sow, plant") is the basis of the name Jezreel. This underlying meaning shows the need for the grain, new wine, and oil. Israel (Jezreel), sown bountifully, will bring forth a large population (cf. 1:10–11). In contrast to the OT way, when the names "not loved" (Lo-Ruhama) and "not my people" (Lo-Ammi) were appropriate (1:6, 8), the future day will find the opposite true. Love will be shown toward "Not my loved one," and "Not my people" will be called "You are my people" (cf. Rom 9:25). The Israelites, in turn, will respond, "You are my God." Thus vv.22–23 give response to all three of Gomer's children: Jezreel, Lo-Ruhama, and Lo-Ammi. Further, in 1:4 Jezreel stood for the place of judgment and captivity that brought an end to Israel; here it stands for population growth, as the people of the future will be sown bountifully in the land. The millennial day will truly see a complete reversal of what Israel experienced in the OT time of Hosea.

Notes

15 The word translated "sing" (עָנָה, *ʿānāh*) commonly means "to answer, respond." The context, however, calls for a joyful manner of response, such as singing.

16, 19–20 All three verses have the same change of person as in v.6, third to second, with doubtless the same significance (see note at v.6).

F. *Gomer Loved Again*

3:1–3

[1]The LORD said to me, "Go, show your love to your wife again, though she is loved by another and is an adulteress. Love her as the LORD loves the Israelites, though they turn to other gods and love the sacred raisin cakes."
[2]So I bought her for fifteen shekels of silver and about a homer and a lethek of barley. [3]Then I told her, "You are to live with me many days; you must not be a prostitute or be intimate with any man, and I will live with you."

1 The narrative now returns to the relations between Hosea and Gomer (cf. Notes), after having dealt with the relations between God and Israel (1:9–2:23). It is clear that Gomer had left Hosea following the birth of their third child. There is no indication of the intervening time. God tells his servant to take back his unfaithful wife. The opening words read, literally, "Go yet, love a woman, loved by a friend, and one who commits adultery." Gomer is called merely *'iššāh* ("woman"), without a possessive suffix to indicate "your woman" or "your wife," apparently showing the degree of estrangement existing between the two. That Hosea may have come to think of her in this detached manner would have made God's command the more difficult to carry out.

The verse continues by giving the reason for Yahweh's difficult command. In taking Gomer back, Hosea would be illustrating God's continuing love for Israel, who had turned to "other gods" and lusted after "raisin cakes." These were among the delicacies of the day. Here they seem to represent the idolatrous worship to which the Israelites had given themselves. Or the raisin cakes may have been eaten as part of the false worship.

2 The price Hosea paid for Gomer was fifteen shekels in money and "a homer and a lethek of barley" (about ten bushels). It is unlikely that this was paid to Gomer's parents. As Keil (1:69) points out, there is no evidence that such a payment was customary in Israel. Moreover, though estranged, Gomer was still Hosea's wife; and no payment was officially due her. It probably was given to Gomer as a kind of bridal gift. The amount was actually not large; fifteen silver shekels was not a great sum, and barley was a more modest food than wheat. That the gift was given at all, as if for a new marriage, and its modest size show the emotional gap between Hosea and Gomer.

3 The Hebrew words translated "many years" (lit., "many days") point to an indefinite period of time. Hosea wanted Gomer to know that this time he intended their relationship to last indefinitely. Therefore she must resolve to live no longer as a prostitute or "be intimate with any man" (*wᵉlō' ṯihyî lᵉ'îš*). Keil (1:69–70) holds that these words imply that, in order to discipline her, Gomer was not even to have intimate relations with Hosea. So Keil takes the words *wᵉgam-'ᵃnî 'ēlāyiḵ* (lit., "and also I to you"; NIV "and I will live with you") to mean that Hosea would reciprocate by having no intimacy with her either.

Keil's interpretation should, however, be rejected on three grounds.

1. God had commanded Hosea to "love" (*'ᵉhaḇ*) Gomer again, and this surely implies more than merely letting her live in his house.

2. In the eschatological parallel implicit in the passage, God's restoration of Israel in the Millennium will be like restoring full marital rights to a beloved wife.

3. Little purpose is served by the addition of the words "and also I to you," for this is already implied in what precedes: Hosea could not have relations with Gomer if she could not have them with him.

The sense of the verse is best seen, then, as Hosea's urgent request that Gomer be faithful to him. She was not to have relations with other men but was to be faithful to Hosea alone as her proper husband.

Notes

---

1 Arguments that the woman of this chapter is Gomer are as follows:

1. Her character was the same as that of Gomer.

2. Hosea was told to "love" her, not "take" her (which would apply to a new marriage). Moreover, the command for Hosea to "love" Gomer fits the situation because Hosea had clearly lost the love he had once felt for her.

3. The word עוֹד (*'ôḏ*, "again") in the phrase "Go show your love to your wife again" indicates a repeated action. Admittedly, the repeated element could be merely that of loving some woman; but the word comes first in the command—in the place of emphasis—which strongly suggests that it is the same woman in view and not merely the same type of action. It should also be observed that the MT punctuation places *'ôḏ* with the idea of the command and not of God's saying something again, as some have understood it.

4. If the woman in this chapter were other than Gomer, then there would be the ethical problem of God's telling Hosea to marry an adulteress—a problem not relevant to the original marriage because at that time Gomer was pure.

5. The parallel between the relation of God and Israel and that of Hosea and Gomer stands only if the woman here in ch. 3 is Gomer. God had been taking Israel back just as Hosea should now take Gomer back.

רֵעַ (*rēa'*, "friend"; NIV, "another") is best understood as referring to a paramour with whom Gomer had perhaps been living, rather than to Hosea as her rightful husband. Though the word can mean "husband" (cf. Jer 3:29; S of Songs 5:16), it can also mean "paramour" (cf. Jer 3:1). The man referred to here loved her (אֲהֻבַת, *'ahuḇaṯ*, a participle meaning "one who loves"). That Hosea was told only now to do this implies that he had lost his previous love for Gomer. The subsequent participle מְנָאָפֶת (*menā'āpeṯ*, "one who is an adulteress"; NIV, "an adulteress"), then, is not antithetical (as Keil holds) but supplemental. Gomer was not only loved by her paramour but was living in adultery with him.

2 A "homer" (חֹמֶר, *ḥōmer*) equaled ten "ephahs" (אֵיפָה, *'êpāh;* Ezek 45:11). Since the "letek" (לֶתֶךְ, *leṯeḵ*) was half a homer, the total here was fifteen ephahs of barley. Keil (1:68–69) holds, on the basis of 2 Kings 7:1 (despite Schmoller's disagreement), that one ephah of barley was worth one shekel, thus making the total value of the silver and the barley thirty shekels. Because the price of a slave was thirty shekels (Exod 21:32), it is possible to infer that Hosea paid thirty shekels to a person (possibly the paramour) to whom Gomer, in her degraded state, had sold herself.

G. *Israel's Future Return to God*

3:4–5

4For the Israelites will live many days without king or prince, without sacrifice or sacred stones, without ephod or idol. 5Afterward the Israelites will return and seek the LORD their God and David their king. They will come trembling to the LORD and to his blessings in the last days.

For the third time in as many chapters, the future time of reconciliation between God and Israel is foreseen. The parallel between the relation of God to Israel and of Hosea to Gomer continues. Just as there was a time when Hosea and Gomer were separated, so Israel and God will be estranged. As Hosea was commanded to love Gomer again in spite of her unfaithfulness, so God will restore Israel to his favor in spite of her sin.

4 In this verse Israel's separation from God is portrayed by her loss of three pairs of things: "king or prince," "sacrifice or sacred stones," and "ephod or idol." The first pair shows that Israel will be without an autonomous rule. The second concerns religious ceremonies. The "sacred stones" (*maṣṣēḇāh*) represent idolatrous worship, adopted from Israel's neighbors (cf. 2 Kings 3:2; 10:26–28; 17:10). Thus the people will be without proper or improper means of worship. The third pair of things also represents worship, but in special reference to devices for searching into the future. The "ephod" contained the Urim and Thummim, a divinely appointed method by which the high priest could initiate an occasion of revelation (see 1 Sam 23:9; 30:7). The "idol" here in view (*t*[e]*rāp̄îm*) was a heathen import (cf. Gen 31:19–34) and was probably used for divination.

5 After the "many days" referred to in v.4, the Israelites "will return and seek the LORD their God." This will also involve seeking "David their king." The Israelites will come "trembling" (*pāḥaḏ*) to the Lord. All this will occur in the "last days" (*'aḥ*[a]*rîṯ hayyāmîm*). For the complete fulfillment of these things, we must look once more to the millennial reign of Christ. The extent to which the Israelites sought God after the Babylonian captivity was limited and surely not with "trembling." While the people did cease from following false gods, their worship was cold and formal; and there was much sin among them.

If the search for "David their king" is to be assigned to the day of Christ's first coming, there is a problem—viz., the Jews did not seek Christ at that time but definitely rejected him. In the Millennium, however, they will indeed seek Christ (the David of the time, ruling on David's throne). They will also truly seek after God in heaven (Isa 12:1–6; 66:23; Jer 33:11; Ezek 20:40; et al.).

Notes

4–5 Evidence that all Israel, rather than merely the northern kingdom, is intended here is found in the corresponding section in ch. 1, where in v.11 Judah and Israel are spoken of together.

II. Israel's Indictment, Punishment, and Restoration (4:1–14:9)

A. *Israel's Indictment* (4:1–7:16)

1. *A general indictment of the people*

4:1–4

[1]Hear the word of the LORD, you Israelites,
because the LORD has a charge to bring
against you who live in the land:
"There is no faithfulness, no love,
no acknowledgment of God in the land.
[2]There is only cursing, lying and murder,
stealing and adultery;
they break all bounds,
and bloodshed follows bloodshed.
[3]Because of this the land mourns,
and all who live in it waste away;
the beasts of the field and the birds of the air
and the fish of the sea are dying.

[4]"But let no man bring a charge,
let no man accuse another,
for your people are like those
who bring charges against a priest.

1 Hosea exhorted the citizens of the northern kingdom to listen because God was charging them with sinfulness. Here the charge is brought only in general terms; in the next two sections it becomes more specific. Verse 1 speaks of the people's threefold lack; they had no faithfulness (*'ᵉmeṯ*), kindness (*ḥeseḏ*), or knowledge (*da-'aṯ*) of God. They were untrustworthy, failed to show compassion toward others, and lacked a true knowledge of the being and nature of God.

2 A list of the people's overt sins follows: "cursing, lying and murder, stealing and adultery." Keil (1:75) says cursing "refers to the breach of the second commandment, stealing to that of the eighth" and the next three "enumerate the sins against the fifth, the seventh, and the sixth commandments." The phrase "bloodshed follows bloodshed" is literally "bloody deed touches bloody deed" in the Hebrew. Apparently violent crimes had become so common that one seemed immediately to follow another, as if touching it.

3 The sins named in v.2 resulted in drought that came as a judgment. As in the time of Elisha, the drought devastated the environment—the land, cattle, birds, and fish (cf. 1 Kings 17–18). It made the land dry up (*'āḇal*, lit., "mourn"); and "all who live in it"—meaning the beasts and the birds—"waste away" (*mālal*, lit., "wither"). It had even brought death to the fish through the drying up of the streams and ponds.

4 The first line literally reads "However [*'aḵ*] let no man bring a charge." Though conditions in Israel were shockingly bad, mutual charges and accusations could not remedy them. Accusing others only increases problems. The relation of the last two lines of this verse with the first two is perhaps best taken as a continuation of the jussive (i.e., a mild command) idea. So a paraphrase might read thus: "But your people should be as those who bring a charge against the priest." In other words, the people, though wrong in accusing one another, could well be accusing the priests, who, as the next section (vv.5–10) shows, were blameworthy.

Notes

2 The sins listed are all infinitive absolutes, a form that gives added emphasis.

4 For evidence that אַךְ (*'ak̲*) (untr. in NIV)—which normally means "surely," "certainly"—can mean "however," "yet," see Jer 34:4.

2. *Sins of the priests*

4:5–11a

5You stumble day and night,
   and the prophets stumble with you.
So I will destroy your mother—
6my people are destroyed from lack of knowledge.

"Because you have rejected knowledge,
   I also reject you as my priests;
because you have ignored the law of your God,
   I also will ignore your children.
7The more the priests increased,
   the more they sinned against me;
   they exchanged their Glory for something disgraceful.
8They feed on the sins of my people
   and relish their wickedness.
9And it will be: Like people, like priests.
   I will punish both of them for their ways
   and repay them for their deeds.

10"They will eat but not have enough;
   they will engage in prostitution but not increase,
because they have deserted the LORD
   to give themselves 11to prostitution,

5 Hosea next spoke directly to the priests (cf. shift to second person). The mention of prophets in the second line implies that they were included in the indictment. Both groups, instead of being leaders for the right, had been stumbling day and night, committing sin; while there may have been some exceptions, apparently a majority were sinning. Jeroboam I had made priests "from all sorts of people" (1 Kings 12:31; 13:33). Therefore, large numbers of true priests—and doubtless true prophets, also—had left the northern kingdom (2 Chron 11:13–16). In the last line of v.5, "mother" refers to Israel (cf. 2:2–5), as the mother of individual Israelites. The stumbling of the priests and prophets into sin led to the conditions that brought down destruction.

6 The priests had not been teaching the people about God and his law, though such

teaching was a prime responsibility of the priests and Levites (Deut 33:10; Ezek 44:23; Mal 2:7). So the people were "destroyed" (*dāmāh*, "ruined," same word as in the last line of v.5). Moreover, God removed the priests from their service because they themselves had rejected the knowledge of God and his law. The closing lines of v.6 describe the poetic justice that would overtake them: Since they had "ignored" (*šāḵaḥ*, "forgotten") the law, God would ignore their sons (descendants).

7 Though the pronouns now change back to the third person, the context shows that the priests were still in view. The greater their power became, the more they sinned. As a result God would turn their "Glory" (*kāḇôḏ*, "honor") into "something disgraceful" (*qālôn*, "shame").

8 So given over to iniquity were the priests that Hosea said they were feeding on (*'āḵal*, lit., "devouring") "the sins of" the people. This they did by enjoying the benefits of the people's sins, such as taking bribes and eating the sin offerings. So the priests actually relished Israel's wickedness.

9 The aphorism "Like people, like priests" shows that the priests were no better than the people they were called to lead. Despite their priestly office, they would share the punishment of the people.

10–11a Though the priests "eat" (same Heb. word as in v.8 [NIV, "feed on"]) the sins of the people, their appetite for evil remains insatiable (v.10). Though the people engage in ritual prostitution of the Canaanite fertility rites, they have no harvest. These rites were thought to enhance human and animal reproduction and to ensure good crops. Israel's indulgence in these rites is a shameless example of the depth to which the people had fallen in forsaking the true God for these detestable heathen rites.

Notes

8 Keil (1:78–79) takes **חַטָּאת** (*ḥaṭṭā't*) to mean "sin offering," which is possible. It is questionable, however, to what extent sin offerings were being made in the northern kingdom at this decadent time. Apparently the priests were well able to eat all the offerings, but they were probably enjoying even more the bribes and special favors brought by wealthy sinners. In the clause **יִשְׂאוּ נַפְשׁוֹ** (*yiś'û napšô*, lit., "they lift each his soul"; NIV, "relish"), the singular suffix on *napšô* stresses the involvement of each priest in the encouragement of sin.

10 The first word of v.11, **זְנוּת** (*zᵉnûṯ*, "prostitution"), is best taken as the concluding word of v.10, and so of this section of the chapter.

3. *Sins of the people*

4:11b–19

to old wine and new,
which take away the understanding
12 of my people.

They consult a wooden idol
and are answered by a stick of wood.
A spirit of prostitution leads them astray;
they are unfaithful to their God.
13They sacrifice on the mountaintops
and burn offerings on the hills,
under oak, poplar and terebinth,
where the shade is pleasant.
Therefore your daughters turn to prostitution
and your daughters-in-law to adultery.

14"I will not punish your daughters
when they turn to prostitution,
nor your daughters-in-law
when they commit adultery,
because the men themselves consort with harlots
and sacrifice with shrine prostitutes—
a people without understanding will come to ruin!

15"Though you commit adultery, O Israel,
let not Judah become guilty.

"Do not go to Gilgal;
do not go up to Beth Aven.
And do not swear, 'As surely as the LORD lives!'
16The Israelites are stubborn,
like a stubborn heifer.
How then can the LORD pasture them
like lambs in a meadow?
17Ephraim is joined to idols;
leave him alone!
18Even when their drinks are gone,
they continue their prostitution;
their rulers dearly love shameful ways.
19A whirlwind will sweep them away,
and their sacrifices will bring them shame.

11b Since the first word in the Hebrew text of v.11 (*z^enûṯ*, "prostitution") has been added to v.10, the first two lines here should read as follows: "Old wine and new take away the understanding of my people." Thus attention turns to Israel, here called "my people." The priests had been the leaders in wrongdoing, but the people had followed them all too closely. The mention of "old wine and new" implies intoxication, which steals away the people's "understanding" (*lēḇ*, lit., "heart," used here in the sense of "understanding")—a reason why drunkenness is a sin.

12 That the people had been bereft of understanding is seen in their appeal for guidance to a mere "stick of wood," a common practice among pagan peoples. The "spirit of prostitution" prevalent in the land included the people as well as the priests (v.10). The reference to being unfaithful to their God suggests that the prostitution is to be regarded primarily as spiritual, not physical. The people were worshiping and looking for leading from false gods rather than from their own true God.

13 Mountaintops, hills, and groves of oak, poplar, and terebinth trees were favorite places for idolatrous worship (see Deut 12:2; Jer 2:20; 3:6; Ezek 6:13). It was into such worship that Israel was slipping. Middle Eastern religion in Hosea's time made cultic prostitution an important part of its practice; and because the Israelites had adopted other aspects of this kind of religion, their daughters and daughters-in-law were prostituting themselves.

14 Yet even though the younger women were immoral, God would not punish them, because "the men" (*hēm*, lit., "them") were consorting with harlots, meaning the shrine prostitutes. In other words, even-handed justice forbade punishment of the young women while the men were enjoying the prostitutes! In such ways does a senseless people come to grief.

15 Though Hosea prophesied chiefly to the northern nation, he occasionally directed his warnings to Judah also. Here he warned the southern kingdom not to follow Israel, its northern neighbor, in this abominable kind of worship. Judah must not, he declared, go either to Gilgal or Beth Aven for this purpose. Under Elijah and Elisha (2 Kings 2:1; 4:38), Gilgal had been a center for prophetic instruction. Now, however, it had apparently become a center of false worship (Hos 9:15; 12:11; Amos 4:4; 5:5). Beth Aven is to be identified with Bethel (cf. Amos 4:4; 5:5) and means "house of deceit"—a deliberate substitution by Hosea for Bethel ("house of God").

Bethel was the southern center of calf worship established by Jeroboam I (1 Kings 12:28–29). Though God's people had been permitted to "swear" an oath in the name of Yahweh (Deut 6:13; 10:20), Hosea now warned the people of Judah not to do this, probably because at this time such oaths were being sworn in connection with the false worship at Gilgal and Bethel. Thus any taking of oaths at these places would appear to justify the false worship being conducted there.

16 Here the thought shifts to the people of the northern nation. Hosea told them, with vivid sarcasm, that if they acted like stubborn cows, they could not expect to be treated like obedient sheep.

17 The Ephraimites were the most influential tribe of the northern nation and were often referred to as representative of that nation. They were so far gone into idolatry as to have become incorrigible. They were, therefore, to be let alone till punishment came.

18 Furthermore, as evidence of the depths of the Israelites' sin, the people are said to have continued their prostitution even after they had finished their drinks (*sōḇe'*, "strong drink," with its lower inhibitions against sexual immorality). This is in part because "their rulers" (lit., "their shields," i.e., those who gave protection; cf. Ps 47:9 [NIV, "kings"]) influenced them through their love of shameful ways.

19 The literal meaning of this verse is vivid: "A whirlwind has wrapped her [Ephraim] up in her wings," i.e., for the purpose of destruction. When this happens, the people's "sacrifices will bring them shame." They will realize how ineffective their sacrifices have been, whether to false gods or to Yahweh, when made out of unbelieving hearts.

Notes

---

11 The first word of v.12, עַמִּי (*'ammî*, "my people"), is properly taken as the concluding element of v.11.

13 The oak tree has abundant shade; the poplar has little shade but has lovely white blossoms that give an attractive, sweet smell; the terebinth produces a fine crown, giving deep shade.

16 A more traditional interpretation takes the last line to say that God, as a result of Israel's stubbornness, will pasture her people as sheep in a large place, where they will be subject to attack by vicious animals. Against this, however, is the fact that מֶרְחָב (*merḥāḇ*, used here for "large place") regularly speaks of a place of blessing, not danger (cf. Pss 18:19; 31:8; 118:5).

18 The text follows Keil (1:84) in taking הֵבוּ (*hēḇû*) as a contraction of אָהֲבוּ (*'āhᵃḇû*), thus placing double stress ("dearly love") on the degree of love shown for shameful ways. This is preferable to the more common way of taking the word as the imperative "Give" from יָהַב (*yāhaḇ*).

---

4. *A warning to priest, people, and king*

5:1–7

1"Hear this, you priests!
  Pay attention, you Israelites!
Listen, O royal house!
  This judgment is against you:
You have been a snare at Mizpah,
  a net spread out on Tabor.
2The rebels are deep in slaughter.
  I will discipline all of them.
3I know all about Ephraim;
  Israel is not hidden from me.
Ephraim, you have now turned to prostitution;
  Israel is corrupt.

4"Their deeds do not permit them
  to return to their God.
A spirit of prostitution is in their heart;
  they do not acknowledge the LORD.
5Israel's arrogance testifies against them;
  the Israelites, even Ephraim, stumble in their sin;
  Judah also stumbles with them.
6When they go with their flocks and herds
  to seek the LORD,
they will not find him;
  he has withdrawn himself from them.
7They are unfaithful to the LORD;
  they give birth to illegitimate children.
Now their New Moon festivals
  will devour them and their fields.

1 The threefold call to attention in this verse is parallel to a similar one in 4:1. The general thought continues as before. Three imperatives demand attention; and three groups of people are alerted: the priests, already given special notice in chapter 4, the people of Israel, and the royal family (lit., "house of king"). The "judgment" referred to is no doubt the one cited in v.2. The "snare" (*paḥ*) and the "net" (*rešeṯ*) were used to trap prey; and "Mizpah" (likely of Gilead [Judg 10:17; 11:29] rather than of Benjamin [1 Sam 7:5; 10:1]) and "Tabor" (Mount Tabor) were likely places for hunting. The figure is that of people being hurt, as if hunted and trapped, by the religious and civil leaders of the day.

2 That rebels were "deep in slaughter" reflects the plight of a people not only hunted but slaughtered. But God would discipline those responsible for this.

3 Though Hosea often mentions Ephraim as representing all Israel (see 4:17), in this chapter the reference to those foremost in fornication is primarily to this tribe. The Bethel altar was in Ephraim, the center of a religion not only corrupt (see 4:10, 12) but corrupting all Israel, also. God knew the whole sad story; nothing was hidden.

4 "Deeds" are the product of the state of one's heart. Because the hearts of the people desired prostitution (probably both kinds—spiritual and physical), their subsequent deeds did not allow a return to God.

5 The Israelites, steeped in the sin of idolatry, had grown arrogant against God. Again Ephraim, presumably the worst-offending tribe, was singled out for censure. Judah, too, was indicted for wayward behavior, probably in anticipation of fuller treatment in the following section.

6 To go with "flocks and herds to seek the LORD" means to search after God's favor through sacrifice. But without the evidence of true faith, mere outward sacrifice will not do (cf. 6:6; 1 Sam 15:22–23). Thus the people find only that God "has withdrawn himself from them."

7 In being "unfaithful" (*bāgaḏ*, "to act treacherously or deceitfully," like an unfaithful wife, cf. Jer 3:20; Mal 2:14), the people had produced "illegitimate" (*zār*, lit., "strange") children. Parents had reared their children in their own sinful ways rather than in the fear of God. "New Moon festivals" (*ḥōḏeš*, "month") refers to the monthly sacrifices, which were debased by hypocritical worship and thus, devoid of God's blessing, would bring about the ruin of people and fields alike.

Notes

3 Contrary to Harper (p. 272), עַתָּה (*'attāh*, "now") is not to be changed to אַתָּה (*'attāh*, "you"; NIV has both). It stresses the seriousness of the sin—something happening at that very time—without ruling out past occurrence of it.

5 Keil (1:88) understands גְּאוֹן (*ge'ôn*, "arrogance," NIV) to mean "glory" and refers it to God as the one who bears witness against the people. Elsewhere in the context, however, God is not referred to by such a descriptive term but directly by name, making the text as translated probable.

5. *A warning to Ephraim and Judah*

5:8–15

8"Sound the trumpet in Gibeah,
the horn in Ramah.
Raise the battle cry in Beth Aven;
lead on, O Benjamin.
9Ephraim will be laid waste
on the day of reckoning.
Among the tribes of Israel
I proclaim what is certain.
10Judah's leaders are like those
who move boundary stones.
I will pour out my wrath on them
like a flood of water.
11Ephraim is oppressed,
trampled in judgment,
intent on pursuing idols.
12I am like a moth to Ephraim,
like rot to the people of Judah.

13"When Ephraim saw his sickness,
and Judah his sores,
then Ephraim turned to Assyria,
and sent to the great king for help.
But he is not able to cure you,
not able to heal your sores.
14For I will be like a lion to Ephraim,
like a great lion to Judah.
I will tear them to pieces and go away;
I will carry them off, with no one to rescue them.
15Then I will go back to my place
until they admit their guilt.
And they will seek my face;
in their misery they will earnestly seek me."

8 Hosea next warned Judah while continuing to warn Ephraim, the tribe nearest the southern kingdom. At that time a trumpet (*šôp̄ār*) was customarily used to sound a warning. Both Gibeah and Ramah were important cities of Benjamin, serving as strategic points on Judah's northern border. Beth Aven is probably another reference to Bethel (cf. 4:15; 10:5), which lay at the extreme south of Israel, near the border with Judah. Benjamin was summoned to "lead on" in the conflict. Because of its geographic proximity to Israel, Benjamin should have been especially watchful of Israel's influence on her.

9 Here a further reason is given why Benjamin was to be especially watchful. Punishment would soon descend on Ephraim, making it a "waste." When that happened, the way would be opened for similar judgment to descend on Benjamin. Being north of Judah, it would suffer first from an invader from the north, as Assyria eventually was. The last line shows the certainty of this.

10 Next Hosea turned to the reason for the coming punishment of Judah—viz., its leaders were "like those who move boundary stones," which was tantamount to stealing property from neighbors (cf. Deut 19:14; 27:17). Property lines, indicated often only by stone markers, could be easily moved in a night. Judah's leaders, however, were not shifting physical property lines but spiritual lines established by God, changing the boundary between right and wrong, between true and false religion, between the true God and the idols.

11 Here the prophet turned back to Ephraim and said that the tribe was "oppressed" and "trampled in judgment," looking on it as an accomplished fact. The LXX renders the passive participles *'āšûq* and *r^eṣûṣ* as "oppresses" and "tramples," actions being carried out by Ephraim and, thus, a further reason for her judgment (so Harper, p. 276). The reason is that the people had been intent on pursuing "idols." (On the use of "idols" instead of "command" [KJV, NASB] or "vanity" [RSV, cf. JB], see Notes.) What may be in view here is Jeroboam's institution of calf worship on substitute altars at Bethel and Dan (1 Kings 12:27–30), which so displeased God.

12–13 A bold figure of speech describes the judgment referred to in v.11. It was not future but already on them. The people were being eaten—as if by moths and decay—by problems and troubles.

On realizing the situation described in v.12, Ephraim sought help from Assyria rather than from God. The precise time when Ephraim did this is uncertain, though it may have been when Menahem paid tribute to Assyria (2 Kings 15:19–20). Later on there was a parallel case in Judah, when Ahaz sought assistance from Tiglath-pileser III (2 Kings 16:5–9). Ahaz's need, however, was for help when Judah was threatened from without, whereas here Ephraim's troubles were internal ones and indeed incurable (cf. the last line of the verse).

14 Help could not come from Assyria. A good reason for this is advanced. God, mightier than this foreign country, was "like a lion" in bringing destruction on both Ephraim and Judah. God's justice, like his love, works inevitably, irresistibly. His chastisement, already operating through the mothlike and decaying conditions indicated in v.12, would be greatly accentuated through the coming devastation by Assyria—the very country whose aid had been sought. Against Israel, Tiglath-pileser III would come in two crushing campaigns (743 and 734–732 B.C.); and later (722 B.C.) Shalmaneser V would do much to bring Israel's history to an end. Against Judah, Sennacherib would come (701 B.C.).

15 When the punishment has been inflicted, God will withdraw to await the desired results. The people will admit their guilt and will search out the presence of God. The Assyrian-Babylonian captivity, in fact, witnessed little of such a change of heart. The language would appear to reach into the Millennium, when the Israelites will indeed repent before God and seek his face (cf. 1:10–11; 2:14–23).

Notes

9 נֶאֱמָנָה (*ne'ᵉmānāh*, "certain") is taken by Keil (1:90) and others to mean "lasting" (cf. Deut 28:59), in the sense that God's punishment on Ephraim would be no temporary thing. This meaning is possible but not generally followed.

11 The word in question, צָו (*ṣāw*), is used only here and in Isa 28:10, 13, where it clearly has the idea "commandment" or "precept." NIV's "idols," an extension of "nonsense," "vanity," derives from שָׁוְא (*šāw'*, a word reflected in the Greek, Syriac, and Targum translations (cf. BDB, p. 996; KB, s.v.).

13 The MT pointing of מֶלֶךְ יָרֵב (*melek̲ yārēb̲*) gives the meaning "King Jareb." The pointing may be changed to give "great king," as in our text. Whether "King Jareb" or "great king" is followed, however, the meaning remains about the same; "Jareb" is not a known Assyrian's name but means "warrior," evidently in a descriptive sense.

---

6. *Words of repentant Israel*

6:1–3

1"Come, let us return to the LORD.
He has torn us to pieces
but he will heal us;
he has injured us
but he will bind up our wounds.
2After two days he will revive us;
on the third day he will restore us,
that we may live in his presence.
3Let us acknowledge the LORD;
let us press on to acknowledge him.
As surely as the sun rises,
he will appear;
he will come to us like the winter rains,
like the spring rains that water the earth."

For three verses Hosea gives the words of Israel in the day of her repentance. The section carries a close relationship in thought with 5:15, which notes that this time of repentance will come only with the beginning of Christ's millennial reign. Israel as a nation has never yet prayed like this.

1 Keil (1:94) sees Hosea praying in Israel's behalf here, but the words seem more appropriately to be coming from people who themselves desire to be right in God's sight. This verse depicts the people as urging one another to return truly to God, in the confidence that he who has punished them will heal them and bind up their wounds.

2 The reference to "two days" and "the third day" means only that the restoration mentioned in v.1 will come surely and quickly. A similar use of numbers occurs in Job 5:19; Proverbs 6:16; 30:15, 18; Amos 1:3, 6, 9; et al.

3 Again the people admonish themselves, this time to "acknowledge the LORD." True knowledge of God provides the basis for faith and obedience. The people exhort themselves to "press on" in obtaining this knowledge. And God, they are sure, will respond to their persistence in seeking him. He will come to them as surely "as the sun rises," a coming as delightfully welcome as the "winter rains" and the "spring rains."

Notes

---

3 At the end of the first line, NIV inserts "the LORD," which in the MT appears at the end of the second line but is needed here.

---

7. *Continued indictment of the people*

6:4–11

4"What can I do with you, Ephraim?
What can I do with you, Judah?
Your love is like the morning mist,
Like the early dew that disappears.
5Therefore I cut you in pieces with my prophets,
I killed you with the words of my mouth;
my judgments flashed like lightning upon you.
6For I desire mercy, not sacrifice,
and acknowledgment of God rather than burnt offerings.
7Like Adam, they have broken the covenant—
they were unfaithful to me there.
8Gilead is a city of wicked men,
stained with footprints of blood.
9As marauders lie in ambush for a man,
so do bands of priests;
they murder on the road to Shechem,
committing shameful crimes.
10I have seen a horrible thing
in the house of Israel
There Ephraim is given to prostitution
and Israel is defiled.

11"Also for you, Judah
a harvest is appointed.

After the inserted words of repentance, Hosea returned to his main theme of warning the people against their sin. He continued to address Ephraim and Judah, as in 5:8–15. Probably, however, Ephraim is here to be understood again as representing all Israel, unlike chapter 5, where the reference is specifically to the tribe.

4–5 Hosea first brought a strong indictment against both Ephraim and Judah, in the form of two rhetorical questions. Their force is indicated in the second pair of lines: the love of the people for God was as unstable as the "morning mist" and "the early dew that disappears." The word translated "love" is *ḥesed*, connoting continued faithful love; but the people fell lamentably short when it came to sustaining it. As a result, God had sent his prophets to speak words of warning, which included predictions of doom and death. These "judgments" came clear and ominously "like lightning" to the people.

6 The prophet sounded a note given also by the other eighth-century prophets (cf. Isa 1:11–17; Amos 5:21–24; Mic 6:6–8): God desires true faith rather than empty sacrifice (cf. Matt 9:13; 12:7). This was not a denial of sacrifice as such but only of improper, faithless sacrifice. God had commanded the people to sacrifice, but the ceremony had to be marked by a proper attitude of heart; otherwise it was meaningless and worthless (cf. 5:6). The word for "mercy" is again *ḥesed̠* (cf. v.4). The importance of "knowing God" is stressed as it had been in v.3.

7 Hosea listed a series of wrongdoings of the people, starting with the general sin of covenant breaking. The people were doing this knowingly, deliberately, just as Adam had eaten the forbidden fruit. "There" (*šām*) refers to Israel's land, covenanted to them by God, and perhaps especially to Bethel, where such flagrant sin occurred at the false altar.

8 More specific wrongs are now listed. Gilead is first noted as a "city of wicked men." Possibly a particular city of this name is in view (see Gen 31:47–48; Judg 10:17), though the name Gilead is normally applied to all the northern Transjordan area. Perhaps the prophet viewed the whole region as a unit, like a city, joined in wickedness of mind.

9 The prophet next thought of the priests, stating that they were acting in packs like highwaymen. Shechem lay on the road from the capital city, Samaria, to the religious center, Bethel. The thought is that the very priests, appointed by Jeroboam from "all sorts of people" (1 Kings 12:31), were robbing and murdering pilgrims. The word translated "shameful crimes" (*zimmāh*) often carries a sexual connotation (cf. Lev 18:17; 19:29), but probably it is more general here (cf. Prov 10:23; 21:27).

10 "House of Israel" no doubt stands for the Israelite nation. The idea of a special house of worship is unlikely, since Israel had no God-approved house, outside the temple in Jerusalem. The "horrible thing" singled out is the sin of prostitution.

11 Judah seems never to have been far from Hosea's mind. As with Israel, Judah's "harvest" was her time of coming punishment. "Harvest" elsewhere carries this sense (cf. Joel 3:13).

Notes

---

5 The second line has הֲרַגְתִּים (*hᵃragtîm*, "I have killed them"). The change to the second person in the text is supported, however, by the context. The translation of the third line is based largely on a pointing that appears justified from the LXX, Syriac, and Targum translations. The MT pointing is difficult to understand.

7 Henderson (in loc.) and Harper (p. 288) prefer the reading "like men" rather than "like Adam." The latter is to be preferred (so NIV), however, for the figure then is much more specific; Adam broke a definite prohibition of God.

9 The word כִּי (*kî*, untr. in NIV) is used as an asseverative, not a causative; e.g., "Surely they have committed crime" (NASB).

---

8. *A ruinous domestic policy*

7:1–7

[1]"Whenever I would restore the fortunes of my people,
whenever I would heal Israel,
the sins of Ephraim are exposed
and the crimes of Samaria revealed.
They practice deceit,
thieves break into houses,
bandits rob in the streets;
[2]but they do not realize
that I remember all their evil deeds.
Their sins engulf them;
they are always before me.

[3]"They delight the king with their wickedness,
the princes with their lies.
[4]They are all adulterers,
burning like an oven
whose fire the baker need not stir
from the kneading of the dough till it rises.
[5]On the day of the festival of our king
the princes become inflamed with wine,
and he joins hands with the mockers.
[6]Their hearts are like an oven;
they approach him with intrigue.
Their passion smolders all night;
in the morning it blazes like a flaming fire.
[7]All of them are hot as an oven;
they devour their rulers.
All their kings fall,
and none of them calls on me.

Hosea continued to speak of the people's sin, particularly in domestic matters. He would deal with sins in foreign relations later.

1–2 The chapter division (both MT and most EVs, e.g., NASB, JB, RSV, KJV) shows line 1 as part of chapter 6. Our text (NIV), however, properly places it with the present section. So taken, the first two lines speak of attempts by God to help and heal Israel—attempts that included sending prophets to warn and remonstrate. But the people's sins had thereby become more evident and exposed. The prophets' efforts had brought more sin to light, thus compounding the people's guilt.

Ephraim continues to be mentioned as representative of the northern kingdom; and Samaria, the capital city, is cited as the center of crime. This verse goes on to specify some of the sins: deceit, burglary, and street robbery by gangs. God knew about all this sin and saw it as engulfing the people, who themselves are depicted as unaware that God knew of their wrong deeds.

3–4 An important reason for this sad situation is now noted: the king and his princes were pleased with it. The sin of adultery was singled out for special mention. This adultery was no doubt primarily spiritual, though there would be a physical aspect inasmuch as it involved the licentious worship of Baal. The people in their zeal for this sin were compared to a heated oven—a striking illustration of lust. The oven was so hot that a baker could cease tending the fire during an entire night—while the dough he had mixed was rising—and then, with a fresh tending of the fire in the morning, have sufficient heat for baking at that time.

5–7 In these verses the prophet gave an example of the kind of sin that resulted from such inflamed passion: the assassination of the king. Hosea saw it happening on a special day, a festival day, for the king. During the festivities the ringleaders planning the crime became drunk, and the king with them. Keeping the figure of the oven, the prophet stated that the hearts of the plotters were hot with desire to perform their treacherous deed. Each time they were near the king, their hearts flamed up, as they contemplated their deed. They waited during the night, however, with their passion smoldering like the baker's fire, anticipating the morning.

With morning the blaze of passion was stirred anew. The terrible deed was done. "Rulers" (pl.) (v.7) were mentioned because Hosea was not describing an isolated incident but one repeated several times in Israel's history. During Hosea's time alone, Zechariah was killed by Shallum, Shallum by Menahem, Pekahiah by Pekah, and Pekah by Hoshea (2 Kings 15:10, 14, 25, 30). The last two lines of v.7 recall that, though so many kings fell in this way, still no one in the land called to God for help, so far were the people from him in their attitude and actions.

Notes

---

1 Some translate בְּשׁוּבִי שְׁבוּת (*b^{e}šûḇî š^{e}ḇûṯ*) as "in my returning the captivity." This does not fit the context, however, which speaks only of adversity in general. It says, literally, "in my turning the adversity," which means, positively, "in my restoring the fortunes" (so Harper, p. 292).

רָפָא (*rāpā'*, "to heal") is Hosea's only word for the idea "to forgive."

5 The first line reads יוֹם מַלְכֵּנוּ (*yôm malkēnû*), which means "the day of our king"; the added thought "festival" is implied, however, for such a day would be a festive occasion.

The word חֲמַת (*h^{a}maṯ*) is an example of a construct followed by a preposition, which may carry the thought "heat of" (NIV, "inflamed with") all that is connected with drinking "from wine."

6 "Their passion" translates אֹפֵהֶם (*'ōpēhem*), meaning literally "their bakers." As in the prior figure, the baker could sleep all night without further stirring his fire, since the fire had been so hot the evening before. Similarly, the "passion" of these plotters could smolder all night and still be sufficiently intense to do the evil deed the next morning.

---

9. *A fatal foreign policy*

7:8–16

8 "Ephraim mixes with the nations;
 Ephraim is a flat cake not turned over.
9 Foreigners sap his strength,
 but he does not realize it.
His hair is sprinkled with gray,
 but he does not notice.
10 Israel's arrogance testifies against him,
 but despite all this

he does not return to the LORD his God
  or search for him.

11"Ephraim is like a dove,
  easily deceived and senseless—
now calling to Egypt,
  now turning to Assyria.
12When they go, I will throw my net over them;
  I will pull them down like birds of the air.
When I hear them flocking together,
  I will catch them.
13Woe to them,
  because they have strayed from me!
Destruction to them,
  because they have rebelled against me!
I long to redeem them
  but they speak lies against me.
14They do not cry out to me from their hearts
  but wail upon their beds.
They gather together for grain and new wine
  but turn away from me.
15I trained them and strengthened them,
  but they plot evil against me.
16They do not turn to the Most High;
  they are like a faulty bow.
Their leaders will fall by the sword
  because of their insolent words.
For this they will be ridiculed
  in the land of Egypt.

Having noted the weaknesses in Israel's internal affairs, Hosea next spoke of foreign relations, which he found equally wanting.

8 Outsiders were living among the Israelites. "Mixed in" translates a reflexive form (Hithpolel), showing that the Israelites themselves had encouraged this mixed population. As the context implies, heathen gods and pagan ways of worship were imported into the country. "A flat cake not turned over" is one that is overdone on one side and not baked on the other, thus being completely worthless. Verse 9 gives the significance of the figure.

9 The debilitating inroads of the foreigners, through their licentious cultic practices, were not recognized by Israel. As hair turning gray symbolizes aging, so Israel was becoming old and feeble without noticing it. All in all, the nation was becoming as worthless as a half-baked cake.

10 The first line repeats 5:5 (q.v.). "All this" refers to the things described in vv.8–9. Yet in spite of them, Israel had no thought of turning back to God and had no desire to seek him.

11 Hosea compared the people to "doves," which are proverbial for their naiveté (cf. Matt 10:16). As doves, "easily deceived and senseless," may be lured by food into snares, so Israel was lured by both Egypt and Assyria as sources of assistance, only to be entrapped by them—especially by Assyria, which ultimately brought her down.

12 Here the figure is extended as God is portrayed as a fowler throwing his net over Israel and pulling her down for correction. "Flocking together" may refer to the efforts of Israel's leaders to unite in seeking aid from Egypt and Assyria. The word translated "catch" (*yāsar*) means literally "to chastise." This chastisement from God is to come in full measure when he permits Assyria to devastate Israel.

13 Here the prophet characterized the impending punishment as "woe" (*'ôy*) and "destruction" (*šōḏ*) about to come on the people, doubtless by Assyria. God wanted to redeem the people, but they told lies about him, probably saying that he would not help them.

14 Though they were bewailing their plight, the people were not truly turning their hearts to the Lord. They were gathering together in an attempt to get "grain and new wine," which had evidently become scarce under the divine correction. But instead of seeking them from God, they persisted in turning away from him.

15 In their apostasy the people even went so far as to "plot evil" against God, though he was the one who had actually trained and strengthened them. By "plot evil" the prophet meant their practice of foreign cultic ceremonies and, in particular, their worship of the golden calves at Bethel and Dan.

16 "Most High" translates (*'āl,* which simply means "upwards," though it implies God, who is "the Most High." The people were turning everywhere but "upwards" to him who alone could help them. So they were like a warped bow, which sends its arrows awry. The mention of the leaders who "fall by the sword" points to such men as Zechariah, Shallum, Pekahiah, and Pekah, all victims of assassination (cf. v.7), typical of "the broken years [when] one party monarch was lifted after another to the brief tenancy of a blood-stained throne" (G.A. Smith, in loc.).

"Insolent words" is *za'am lešônām* in Hebrew and literally means "defiance of their tongue." In the prosperous days of Jeroboam II, Israel had boasted of her strength to Egypt. Now she would be ridiculed in Egypt because of the downfall of her leaders.

Notes

13 The personal pronoun אָנֹכִי (*'ānōḵî,* "I") is used for emphasis in "I want to redeem them." God wanted to do this, but the people would not have it.

14 Some twenty MSS and the LXX favor the reading יִתְגּוֹדָדוּ (*yiṯgôḏāḏû,* "they slash themselves"). The MT reading יִתְגּוֹרָרוּ (*yiṯgôrārû,* "they assemble themselves") is, however, followed by NIV and preferred by most.

15 The use of the personal pronoun אֲנִי ('ănî, "I") in the opening words "I trained them" again shows emphasis on God. It was he himself who trained and strengthened Israel.

B. *Israel's Punishment* (8:1–10:15)

1. *Warning of approaching judgment*

8:1–14

1"Put the trumpet to your lips!
  An eagle is over the house of the LORD
because the people have broken my covenant
  and rebelled against my law.
2Israel cries out to me,
  'O our God, we acknowledge you!'
3But Israel has rejected what is good;
  an enemy will pursue him.
4They set up kings without any consent;
  they choose princes without my approval.
With their silver and gold
  they make idols for themselves
  to their own destruction.
5Throw out your calf-idol, O Samaria!
  My anger burns against them.
How long will they be incapable of purity?
6 They are from Israel!
This calf—a craftsman has made it;
  it is not God.
It will be broken in pieces,
  that calf of Samaria.

7"They sow the wind
  and reap the whirlwind.
The stalk has no head;
  it will produce no flour.
Were it to yield grain,
  foreigners would swallow it up.
8Israel is swallowed up;
  now she is among the nations
  like a worthless thing.
9For they have gone up to Assyria
  like a wild donkey wandering alone.
  Ephraim has sold herself to lovers.
10Although they have sold themselves among the nations,
  I will now gather them together.
They will begin to waste away
  under the oppression of the mighty king.

11"Though Ephraim built many altars for sin offerings,
  these have become altars for sinning.
12I wrote for them the many things of my law,
  but they regarded them as something alien.
13They offer sacrifices given to me
  and they eat the meat,
  but the LORD is not pleased with them.
Now he will remember their wickedness
  and punish their sins:
  They will return to Egypt.
14Israel has forgotten his Maker
  and built palaces;
  Judah has fortified many towns.
But I will send fire upon their cities
  that will consume their fortresses."

Here Hosea began to speak primarily about punishment. He had been describing Israel's sin, but here he moved on to tell of its awful consequences. Yet intermixed with all this are further examples of their sin.

1 God bid Hosea to trumpet a warning (cf. comment at 5:8). An eagle (Assyria) was ready to descend on "the house of the LORD." As there was no temple in the northern kingdom to which it could refer, "house of the LORD" must refer to Israel as the people among whom God should and would dwell (cf. 9:15; Num 12:7; Jer 12:7; Zech 9:8). The last two lines of v.1 show why God would permit this "eagle" of punishment to come.

2–3 Though Israel would cry out that she knew God, this would be a cry of desperation rather than the cry of a believing heart. The people had rejected the "good" of truly knowing and serving God. Therefore their enemy would be permitted to pursue them.

4 The people had chosen their leaders, including their kings, without seeking guidance from God. Hence there was no continuing dynasty; in fact, nine different dynasties came to power in Israel. Furthermore, the people had made idols of silver and gold, a reference especially to the golden calves at Bethel and Dan. It is significant, however, that excavations in Palestine have revealed no images of Yahweh but only images of false gods. The last two lines of this verse reemphasize the note of warning in v.1 by linking idol-making to destruction. Israel's destruction would come as a result of this sin.

5 "Throw out your calf-idol" is literally "your calf stinks" (*zānaḥ ʿeglēḵ*). Here again the golden calves at Bethel and Dan, which were so odious to God, are in view. The word *zānaḥ*, used here of God's attitude toward the calves, was used in v.3 of Israel's attitude toward "good," where it is rendered "rejected." The rhetorical question at the close of the verse implies that there would never be a time when the idolatry of Israel would not be sinful.

6 The reason the calves were a stench before God was that they were manmade (1 Kings 12:28). Therefore God would see that they were demolished. The calf idol is linked to Samaria only in the sense that Samaria, which was the capital city, represents the whole northern kingdom. Actually the calves stood at Bethel, in the extreme south, and at Dan, in the extreme north.

7 The figure of sowing and reaping, here put in proverbial form, is common in the Bible (cf. 10:12–13; Job 4:8; Prov 22:8; Gal 6:7). The "wind" speaks of the emptiness of Israel's sin; the "whirlwind" speaks of God's impending destruction. Israel's punishment had already begun: the stalks were not producing grain that could be milled into flour. God had apparently withheld the rain. Furthermore, if any stalks did produce grain, it was only for foreigners to snatch it up.

8 So Israel was, like the grain itself, being swallowed up. This meant the loss of her national identity and independence. So she was despised like worthless pottery (lit., "a vessel for which there is no desire").

9 The context shows that the Assyrian captivity was not in view here. Israel had "gone up to Assyria" in the sense of asking for aid there. Hosea compared this to the solitary wandering of the wild donkey (cf. Jer 2:24). Wild donkeys are intractable; so Israel was stubborn in having her own way and repudiating God's guidance. Like a prostitute, she was selling herself to the heathen nations (cf. 2:5).

10 In this verse Hosea anticipated the full force of the Assyrian captivity on Israel. "Although" (or possibly "because" [*kî*]) the people had looked to the nations for help, God would "gather them together" for the purpose of inflicting this punishment. As a result, their numbers would diminish under the oppression of the "mighty king" (lit., "king of princes"). This most likely refers to the Assyrian ruler through whom God would bring the punishment (cf. Isa 10:8).

11 God had ordained the one altar at his central sanctuary as the place for the people to worship. With the division of the kingdom, Jeroboam had set up false altars at Bethel and Dan (and perhaps others of less importance elsewhere) as a show of religious devotion. Hosea made it clear that these were in no way a religious help to Israel but that God considered them only as altars for committing sin.

12 In the Pentateuch God had given the people "the many things" of his law so that they could know his will. But they had thought of his law as something "alien" or strange. "Many things" translates *ribbô* (Kethiv reading, favored by both Harper and Keil), which means "ten thousand" or "myriad." Thus God had given his law in abundant detail so that the people were wholly without excuse.

13 With the altars still in mind, Hosea said that God charged the people using these false altars to offer sacrifices that belonged to him (and therefore should have been offered in the proper place and manner). Though God permitted certain parts of various sacrificial animals to be eaten, these people were apparently eating whatever they desired, and so compounding their sin. For emphasis the word for "meat" (*bāśār*) is placed ahead of its verb: the force is that in God's sight such offerings were only meat and had no sacrificial value at all. Of course, God was not pleased with them. So punishment would come in the form of a forced return to "Egypt," which is here used representatively for Assyria, where Israel would actually be taken. The people, knowing what Egypt had meant to Israel in the past, should have realized that Assyria would be their "Egypt" in the future.

14 Here Hosea noted an additional ground of Israel's punishment—the people had forgotten their Maker and had instead put their confidence in fine palaces. Judah, too, had come to rely on fortified cities. Therefore God would hurl fire on the cities and burn up the fortresses. This would come—and did come—with the Assyrian invasion not many years after Hosea's writing.

Notes

---

1 The "eagle" (נֶשֶׁר, *nešer*) is swift (2 Sam 1:23; Jer 4:13; Lam 4:19) and voracious (Job 9:26; Prov 30:17 [NIV, "vultures"]; Hab 1:8 ["vulture"]).

2 "Israel" appears last in the verse in the MT, the place of appositional stress, showing Israel as saying boastfully, "We, Israel, know God."

4 In the last line of this verse, NIV makes Israel the object of the destruction in view. However, the MT, the context, and the history involved make it possible to make the "idols" (taken collectively) the objects. A choice is difficult.

8 The use of the perfect נִבְלַע (*niḇla'*, "swallowed up") shows that this condition already existed as Hosea wrote.

11 NIV renders לַחֲטֹא (*laḥaṭō'*) "for sin offerings," which could well mean simply "to sin." Keil (1:116) translates it "for sinning," meaning that Ephraim multiplied altars for the purpose of sinful idolatry. This seems forced, however, and the NIV rendering is to be preferred.

13 Most authorities, including NIV, derive the noun הַבְהָבַי (*haḇhāḇay*) from the verb יָהַב (*yāhaḇ*, "to give"), yielding, literally, "sacrifices of my gifts." Schmoller (CHS, in loc.) follows Furst in deriving it from הוּב (*hûḇ*, "to roast"), yielding "sacrifices of my burnt offerings." The first appears preferable, though the meaning does not greatly differ whatever derivation is followed.

---

2. *Assyrian captivity soon to come*

9:1–9

1 Do not rejoice, O Israel;
do not be jubilant like the other nations.
For you have been unfaithful to your God;
you love the wages of a prostitute
at every threshing floor.
2 Threshing floors and winepresses will not feed the people;
the new wine will fail them.
3 They will not remain in the LORD's land;
Ephraim will return to Egypt
and eat unclean food in Assyria.
4 They will not pour out wine offerings to the LORD,
nor will their sacrifices please him.
Such sacrifices will be to them like the bread of mourners;
all who eat them will be unclean.
This food will be for themselves;
it will not come into the temple of the LORD.

5 What will you do on the day of your appointed feasts,
on the festival days of the LORD?
6 Even if they escape from destruction,
Egypt will gather them,
and Memphis will bury them,
Their treasures of silver will be taken over by briers,
and thorns will overrun their tents.
7 The days of punishment are coming,
the days of reckoning are at hand.
Let Israel know this.
Because your sins are so many
and your hostility so great,
the prophet is considered a fool,
the inspired man a maniac.
8 The prophet, along with my God,
is the watchman over Ephraim,
yet snares await him on all his paths,
and hostility in the house of his God,
9 They have sunk deep into corruption,
as in the days of Gibeah.

God will remember their wickedness
and punish them for their sins.

The message of warning continues, as it goes on to speak more specifically about the coming captivity in Assyria.

1–2 The people of Israel were not to rejoice; neither were they to celebrate like other nations. This solemn word was necessary. Though the neighboring nations might celebrate in their heathen fashion, Israel was appointed to be the people of God, with standards much higher than those of the heathen with their false gods. The shame of Israel was that the people were denying their own supreme God and attributing their blessings to the heathen gods. This was spiritual adultery, analogous to the physical adultery practiced by prostitutes. The mention of threshing floors probably carries through the figure of prostitution, for the Canaanites frequently used threshing floors and winepresses as places for carrying out their fertility rites. In v.2 the implication is that, because of insufficient rainfall, the threshing floors and winepresses would fail to produce enough food for the people.

3 The people of Israel were soon to be taken as captives from the land. The place of their captivity was first called "Egypt" (cf. 8:13) in order to show its general character; then Assyria was named as the actual place the people would be taken to (cf. 11:5). The food they were to eat there would be "unclean" because it would not be selected and prepared according to the Mosaic Law nor sanctified by presenting its firstfruits (cf. Exod 22:29; Lev 23:10–12).

4–5 Moreover, the captive Israelites would not be able to present "wine offerings" (*yayin*, "wine," but here standing for the offerings) or "sacrifices," because there would be no temple of the Lord in Assyria (Deut 12:5–14). Therefore, if they tried to sacrifice, their sacrifices would be like "the bread of mourners" (cf. Deut 26:14)—unclean and unacceptable, like food touched by a mourner defiled by a dead body (Num 19:22). Anyone eating the meat from such sacrifices would also be unclean. The rhetorical question in v.5 puts vividly the plight of Israel: captive in Assyria, without temple or sacrifices, and so unable to celebrate the holy days. The "day of your appointed feasts" and "festival days of the LORD" are synonymous and thus emphatic.

6 "Even if they escape" renders ***kî-hinnēh hālᵉḵû***, which means, literally, "because, indeed, they will have gone." The thought is that even if Israel is not utterly destroyed, the people will be taken captive; they will be gathered by Egypt (again used typically for Assyria; cf. v.3) and buried by Memphis (another typical usage), an ancient capital of Egypt and a celebrated place of burial. Meanwhile their own fine land (symbolized by "treasures of silver") would revert to briars and thorns.

7–8 With an eloquent power, Hosea announced the days of punishment that were coming on Israel and called for understanding of it. Yet Israel had sunk so deep into sin that the people considered the prophet who warned them a madman and a fool (cf. note at v.7). Verse 8 carries on the thought regarding the thinking of sinful Israelites in respect to God's prophets. As the prophets stood with God over

Ephraim (the northern nation), the people motivated by animosity sought to entrap them. Hosea called this "hostility in the house of his God" (the latter phrase being a reference to Israel; cf. 8:1).

9 Here the sin of Israel is likened to that of the men of Gibeah, who committed a heinous crime against the concubine of a Levite who was their guest (Judg 19–20). This incident, which is one of the most shocking examples of sin in the OT, led to civil war and brought the tribe of Benjamin to the brink of annihilation.

Notes

---

6 The last two lines of this verse in the NIV give a rather free translation of the difficult Hebrew, which more literally reads, "With respect to their delightful things of silver, the thistle shall possess them; the thorn shall be in their tents."

7 Some authorities (Keil, 1:222; Laetsch, pp. 72, 74) believe that the last two lines of this verse refer to a false prophet, who was truly a fool and a maniac for resisting the truth of God. But this is unlikely for several reasons: the man is called אִישׁ הָרוּחַ (*'îš hārûaḥ*, "a man of the spirit"; NIV, "the inspired man"); in v.8 he is called "the watchman over Ephraim . . . with my God"; the context does not otherwise present the idea of a false prophet; and the idea of unbelievers calling a true prophet a מְשֻׁגָּע (*mešuggā'*, "a maniac") is not strange in the OT (see 2 Kings 9:11; Jer 29:26).

8 The same authorities take the prophet of this verse as false also, using the possible translation "The prophet is the snare of the bird catcher." This view, however, leads Keil (1:122), for instance, to translate the first part of the verse "A spy is Ephraim with my God," which certainly is strange. Keil sees Ephraim as an ally of God, opposed to such prophets, but this is out of keeping with the context.

Because the Hebrew of line 1 is difficult, some authorities emend the MT to read "people of God" rather than "with my God." The MT, however, as translated in NIV makes good sense and fits the context and is therefore preferable.

---

3. *The fleeting glory of Israel*

9:10–17

10"When I found Israel,
it was like finding grapes in the desert;
when I saw your fathers,
it was like seeing the early fruit on the fig tree.
But when they came to Baal Peor,
they consecrated themselves to that shameful idol
and became as vile as the thing they loved.
11Ephraim's glory will fly away like a bird—
no birth, no pregnancy, no conception.
12Even if they rear children,
I will bereave them of every one.
Woe to them
when I turn away from them!
13I have seen Ephraim, like Tyre,
planted in a pleasant place.
But Ephraim will bring out
their children to the slayer."

> 14Give them, O LORD—
> what will you give them?
> Give them wombs that miscarry
> and breasts that are dry.
>
> 15"Because of all their wickedness in Gilgal,
> I hated them there.
> Because of their sinful deeds,
> I will drive them out of my house.
> I will no longer love them;
> all their leaders are rebellious.
> 16Ephraim is blighted,
> their root is withered,
> they yield no fruit.
> Even if they bear children,
> I will slay their cherished offspring."
>
> 17My God will reject them
> because they have not obeyed him;
> they will be wanderers among the nations.

The warning now turns to more general matters as it speaks of punishments that would apparently take place prior to the Assyrian captivity.

10 This is a poignant reference to Israel's earliest days as a nation, when God found her and chose her. Then she was like "grapes in the desert" and "the early fruit on the fig tree." Grapes, unusual in the desert, are a special delight when found there; the early figs are considered especially delicious. When God first found Israel in the desert (Deut 32:10), it was like finding such delicacies. Things soon changed, however. Already at Baal-peor, before even entering the Promised Land (Num 25:3–18), the people slipped into the worship of the local Baal. "Shameful idol" renders the word *bōšeṯ*, ("shame"). This was not Israel's only time of sin, but it is singled out here because it was the first instance of their worship of Baal—worship they persisted in till it became their besetting sin.

11 The "glory" God gave Ephraim (Israel), through making her a fine nation after he had found her in the wilderness, was to take wings like a bird because of her recurring sin. "No birth, no pregnancy, no conception" is a terse way of saying that Israel's population would decrease.

12 Even if children were born they would die young before reaching adulthood (cf. Deut 32:25). So God would turn his favor from Israel because of her unfaithfulness. The implication is that punishment of this kind was to precede the captivity to Assyria and that the captivity itself would climax it.

13–14 God had given Israel a pleasant and advantageous location. All caravan trade between Egypt and countries to the north had to pass through her land, because the Mediterranean Sea was to the west and the desert to the east. She was like Tyre, for Tyre also had a situation highly advantageous for her maritime activities. Israel failed, however, to realize her potential because of her sin. Instead, her children would be led out to the "slayer"—a further factor in the diminishing of population. The use of the word "slayer" connotes frequent murders, civil strife, and also warfare. Hosea's irony in v.14 is as unmistakable as it is powerful. In its terse vigor, it is reminiscent of the imprecatory psalms.

15 God said the severe treatment of Israel was because of "all their wickedness in Gilgal." By this time Gilgal had clearly become a center of false worship (cf. 4:15). Here they represent the worst elements in the land. The meaning of "hate" (*śānē'*) in this context is defined by the words "I will no longer love them." It was not that God had a positive animosity toward Israel, but he had nothing favorable to say of them. Because of their "sinful deeds" and the rebellion of their leaders, God would expell them from his "house" (the congregation of Israel; cf. 8:1; 9:8).

16 Hosea returned to the warning that Israel would be diminished in population, using again the figure of a plant (cf. 10:1; 14:8). The people would be withered even to the root (cf. Mal 4:1), and thus rendered fruitless and therefore hopeless.

17 In summary, God would reject the people because of their persistent disobedience. As a result they would become "wanderers among the nations"—another allusion to their coming captivity.

Notes

---

12 NIV follows the reading of the Vulgate and Targum (besides other authorities) in taking שׂוּר (*śûr* "turn away") as another spelling for סוּר (*sûr*, "turn aside"). Harper (p. 341) argues for שׁוּר (*šûr*, "to wander"), but not convincingly.

13 Some authorities consider the Hebrew word order of line 1 to be impossible. "Ephraim," however, is placed first for emphasis. Rendered literally the thought is "Ephraim, as I have seen it, in comparison with Tyre, is planted. . . ."

---

4. *Guilt and coming captivity*

10:1–8

1 Israel was a spreading vine;
he brought forth fruit for himself.
As his fruit increased,
he built more altars;
as his land prospered,
he adorned his sacred stones.
2 Their heart is deceitful,
and now they must bear their guilt.
The LORD will demolish their altars
and destroy their sacred stones.

3 Then they will say, "We have no king
because we did not revere the LORD.
But even if we had a king,
what could he do for us?"
4 They make many promises,
take false oaths
and make agreements;

therefore lawsuits spring up
  like poisonous weeds in a plowed field.
5The people who live in Samaria fear
  for the calf-idol of Beth Aven.
Its people will mourn over it,
  and so will its idolatrous priests,
those who had rejoiced over its splendor,
  because it is taken from them into exile.
6It will be carried to Assyria
  as tribute for the great king.
Ephraim will be disgraced;
  Israel will be ashamed of its wooden idols.
7Samaria and its king will float away
  like a twig on the surface of the waters.
8The high places of wickedness will be destroyed—
  it is the sin of Israel.
Thorns and thistles will grow up.
  and cover their altars.
Then they will say to the mountains, "Cover us!"
  and to the hills, "Fall on us!"

Here Hosea spoke still more explicitly of the impending captivity of Israel.

1 Hosea began by referring once more (as in 9:10) to Israel's early history, when the people were like a luxuriant vine. But as the "fruit" of prosperity "increased," there was a sad spiritual deterioration. Pagan "altars" were built and "sacred stones" (or "pillars") adorned. The people thus turned from the worship of the true God.

2 The word translated "deceitful" is *ḥālaq* ("smooth," "flattering"). The OT elsewhere speaks of lips or tongues as "smooth" in the sense of being insincere (cf. Pss 5:9; 12:3[4 MT]; Prov 5:3). Because the same is true here of the heart of a guilty people, God would destroy both the altars and the sacred stones they had erected.

3 As a result, the people would be brought to admit that they had no king worthy of the name but rather one chosen by them without due reverence for the Lord. The time referred to can only have been just before the captivity, when Israel's kings showed themselves ineffectual both in tackling Israel's problems and in coping with the Assyrian menace. The last two lines note despairingly that even if the land did have a truly capable king, things were so bad that he would be powerless to help.

4 Hosea here enlarged on the idea of deceitfulness of heart (cf. v.2): promises had been made, false oaths taken, and contracts signed. Though such treaties were being made with other countries (especially Assyria), the thought here mainly concerns agreements among the people themselves. With the denial of people's legal rights, "lawsuits" (*mišpāṭ*, "judgment," "right") were springing up like "poisonous weeds" (*rō'š;* cf. Deut 29:17) in a "plowed field" (lit., "furrows of a field").

5 In this verse the people of Samaria (representative of all Israel), seeing the ominous signs of the soon-coming punishment, are said to be anxious about their "calf-idol" at Beth Aven (Bethel; cf. 4:15) rather than about their own sin. "Its people" (*'ammô*, lit., "his people," thus identifying Israelites as the people of this calf!)

mourn concerning the matter, along with the idolatrous priests (*k*^{e}*mārîm;* cf. 2 Kings 23:5) that serve it. The Hebrew of the last line allows for the translation of our text (which sees the antecedent of "it" as the calf-idol) or for the translation "because it is departed from it" (which sees the antecedent as "splendor"). Either idea fits the context, and a decision between the two translations is difficult.

6–7 Verse 6 clearly speaks of the Assyrian captivity. The antecedent of "it" is the calf-idol. This shameful but materially valuable object would be carried to the victorious king of Assyria as tribute. And Israel would smart under feelings of disgrace and humiliation. The word for "its wooden idols" is often translated "its counsel" (NIV mg.). Either is possible with no change in the Hebrew. The given translation refers disdainfully to the calf as mere wood; the other translation to the "counsel" given by Jeroboam I when he had first established calf worship. Not only the calf-idol but also Samaria and its king would be taken captive (v.7), borne away to foreign Assyria, helpless as a twig on a river.

8 "The high places of wickedness" translates *bāmôṯ 'āwen* ("high places of Aven"), signifying the calf temple at Bethel (Aven; cf. 4:15; 5:8; 10:5). Destruction there by the Assyrians would be so complete that thorns and thistles would replace the buildings containing the altars. In Genesis 3:18, referring to the ground being cursed as a result of Adam's sin, there is a similar biblical combination of thorns and thistles. Also, the people would cry in despair for the mountains and hills to fall on them, apparently to terminate their time of disgrace. Christ used similar words about people in the last days (cf. Luke 23:30; Rev 6:16).

Notes

---

2 Line 3 reads literally "will break the neck [עָרַף, (*'ārap̱*]" of their altars. This may refer to breaking the horns off from the altars (cf. Amos 3:14) or to a serious breaking, as when one breaks the neck of a living animal or a human.

3 "But even if we have a king" translates וְהַמֶּלֶךְ (*w*^{e}*hammeleḵ*), which literally means "and the king." The idea intended, however, is well expressed in the translation.

5 The fact that the word for "calf-idol" is feminine plural does not indicate that the Bethel calf was female or that several existed. The following suffixes are all masculine single. Most authorities agree that the word is an abstract noun, carrying such an idea as "calfhood."

In regard to the last line, one argument in favor of taking the antecedent of "it" as "splendor" rather than "calf-idol" is that the verb tense is perfect (גָּלָה, *gālāh*) whereas the verb tense in the next verse, which clearly speaks of the Assyrian captivity, is imperfect.

6 In the Hebrew, according to the MT pointing, "the great king" should be translated "King Jareb," as in 5:13 (q.v.).

7 "Float away like" translates נִדְמֶה (*niḏmeh*), which literally means "will be like."

---

5. *Sin and punishment*

10:9–15

9 "Since the days of Gibeah, you have sinned, O Israel,
and there you have remained.

Did not war overtake
  the evildoers in Gibeah?
10 When I please, I will punish them;
  nations will be gathered against them
  to put them in bonds for their double sin.
11 Ephraim is a trained heifer
  that loves to thresh;
so I will put a yoke
  on her fair neck.
I will drive Ephraim,
  Judah must plow,
  and Jacob must break up the ground.
12 Sow for yourselves righteousness,
  reap the fruit of unfailing love,
and break up your unplowed ground;
  for it is time to seek the LORD,
until he comes
  and showers righteousness on you.
13 But you have planted wickedness,
  you have reaped evil,
  you have eaten the fruit of deception.
Because you have depended on your own strength
  and on your many warriors,
14 the roar of battle will rise against your people;
  so that all your fortresses will be devastated—
as Shalman devastated Beth Arbel on the day of battle,
  when mothers were dashed to the ground
    with their children.
15 Thus will it happen to you, O Bethel,
  because your wickedness is great.
When that day dawns,
  the king of Israel will be completely destroyed.

Hosea here spoke more generally again, referring to both Israel's sin and her resulting punishment. He also gave a word of instruction. Mention of the Assyrian captivity reappears at the close of the section.

9 Once more the prophet reverted to an incident from Israel's early history: the sin at Gibeah (cf. Judg 19–20 and comments at 9:9). The thought is that Israel, since that tragic occurrence, has defiantly continued in the same basic sin and that the appropriate punishment—such as was meted out to the original offenders—has not been experienced but is now due.

10 This punishment, at God's pleasure, would see nations gathering against Israel—a passing reference to the captivity. The "double sin" (*šᵉttê ʿᵃwōnôṯām,* lit., "their two sins") is probably not a reference to the sin of worshiping calves at both Bethel and Dan—for this was really only one sin—but of forsaking God and of departing from the rule of David's house (so Keil, 1:133).

11 Ephraim (Israel) had been well trained in past days, like a heifer broken to the yoke. She had come, however, to enjoy only the work of threshing grain (pleasant to the heifer because she could then eat her fill of grain). But God would put a yoke of true work on her "fair neck" so that she would have to work hard in plowing and breaking up the hard soil. Judah was included once more (cf. 6:11; 8:14 et al.) as meriting the same treatment. "Jacob" may be a reference to all twelve tribes.

12 Hosea paused in the use of the figure to give advice. The people should sow righteousness, and then they would reap kindness in return. Thereby unplowed ground would be plowed (cf. v. 11). Just as plowing is hard work, so it would be hard for the people to change their lifestyle; but they must do so. Only by searching for the Lord and his righteousness would they be delivered from the coming punishment. The first admonition—sowing righteousness—concerned the relation of people to people, and the second—searching for God—the relation of people to God.

13 Instead of doing this, however, the people were planting (*ḥāraš*, "plowing") wickedness and reaping evil. Deceit and its baneful results therefore abounded. Most authorities relate the "because" (*kî*) of line 4 to the earlier part of the verse, but this does not make good sense. Our text relates it more aptly to v. 14. It was because Israel had depended on her own strength and her many warriors that God would permit the roar of battle to come against the people.

14 The outcome would be the destruction of all Israel's fortifications—obviously an allusion to the Assyrian attack. To illustrate how bad the time would be, it is compared with another, no doubt well known to the people of Hosea's day, but difficult now to identify. Harper (p. 358) cites several possibilities. Perhaps Shalman is Shalmaneser V, who played such a decisive part in the Assyrian action leading to Israel's captivity (2 Kings 17:3–6). The identity of Beth Arbel, however, remains a pure guess. The context shows that it was an occasion of tragic slaughter.

15 So, concluded Hosea, Bethel, the calf-idol center, representative of all that was wicked in Israel, would experience the same as this Beth Arbel. In that day even the "king of Israel" would be "completely destroyed." Israel was facing a most foreboding future. Since her destruction would occur "when that day dawns" (meaning the very beginning of the day of battle), it is noteworthy that Israel's final king, Hoshea, was taken captive by the Assyrian conqueror Shalmaneser V before the actual siege of Samaria began.

Notes

10 The translation "double sin" comes from the Qere reading, observed in the LXX, Syriac, and Vulgate.

11 "I will put a yoke on her fair neck" renders the Hebrew that literally says, "I will pass over on her fair neck," using the verb עָבַר (*'āḇar*, "to pass over"). NIV is fully in keeping with the context when it takes this as referring to the passing of the yoke over the animal's neck so that it could do useful work.

C. *Israel's Restoration* (11:1–14:9)

1. *God's love and Israel's rebellion*

11:1–7

> [1]"When Israel was a child, I loved him,
> and out of Egypt I called my son.
> [2]But the more I called Israel,
> the further they went from me.
> They sacrificed to the Baals
> and they burned incense to images.
> [3]It was I who taught Ephraim to walk,
> taking them by the arms;
> but they did not realize
> it was I who healed them.
> [4]I led them with cords of human kindness,
> with ties of love;
> I lifted the yoke from their neck
> and bent down to feed them.
>
> [5]"Will they not return to Egypt
> and will not Assyria rule over them
> because they refuse to repent?
> [6]Swords will flash in their cities,
> will destroy the bars of their gates
> and put an end to their plans.
> [7]My people are determined to turn from me.
> Even if they call to the Most High,
> he will by no means exalt them.

The theme now changes from Israel's punishment to Israel's restoration. It is introduced by a moving contrast between God's steadfast love and Israel's persistent apostasy.

1 Once more (cf. 9:10; 10:1, 9) Hosea reverted to the earlier history of Israel, this time looking back to the Lord's words in Exodus 4:22–23: "Israel is my firstborn son. . . . 'Let my son go, so he may worship me.' " The reason Israel was God's son is that God had especially chosen him as his own (cf. Gen 12:2–3). (For the NT fulfillment of the words "Out of Egypt I called my son," see Matt 2:13–15.)

2 God had multiplied the people of Israel and had shown his power in bringing them into the land of Canaan. Yet despite these evidences of his love, Israel forsook him and worshiped other gods (Judg 2:11–13). So God disciplined them through six times of foreign oppression in order to call them back; but the more he did so, the more they apostatized.

3–4 Here the tender figure of a parent teaching an infant to walk shows the Lord's compassion in disciplining Israel (Ephraim). But they were blind to his healing purpose in dealing with them. The poetic language continues in v.4. God had "led" (*māšak̲*, lit., "drawn") them with cords of "human kindness" (*'ād̲ām*, lit., "man") and "ties of love." He also had lifted "the yoke from their neck" (*l^e^ḥêhem*, lit., "their cheeks"). The yoke was sometimes lifted away from the face of the ox so that it might eat more comfortably. So God had dealt gently with his people, in spite of their sin. The Hebrew text gives no ground for taking "the yoke" as symbolic of God's law, as some do. "Bent down to feed them" presents a beautiful picture of God's gracious condescension in his loving provision for his undeserving people.

5 A rhetorical question that implies an affirmative answer points to the impending captivity—the consequence of Israel's sin, which had been compounded because the people persisted in it despite God's continuing grace. (For the sense in which Egypt and Assyria are used in this verse, see comments at 8:13 and 9:3.)

6 When Assyria attacked, swords would bring death in the cities, the gate bars (i.e., the cities' defenses) would be broken, and all the plans for survival would be frustrated.

7 In their apostasy the people of Israel were obdurate—"determined to turn from [God]." The remainder of this verse is difficult but may best be taken to mean "Even if together they [the prophets] call him [Israel] unto upwards [the Most High], he [God] will not exalt them." The people would not harken to the prophets who called them to return to God but were choosing to remain in the mire of sin.

Notes

2 NIV reflects the LXX reading. The MT has "As they [the prophets] called to them [Israel], so they [Israel] went from them [the prophets]." The basic idea remains the same, for the prophets were God's representatives.

3 The use of the personal pronoun "I" stresses God (as against "the Baals" just mentioned) as the one who had "taught" Israel. The unusual form תִּרְגַּלְתִּי (*ṯirgaltî*) is basically a Hiphil but formed as a Tiphel. Also, קָחָם (*qāḥām*, "taking them") is an abbreviated form of לְקָחָם (*l^{e}qāḥām*).

4 "And bent down" translates וָאַט (*wā'aṭ*, first person pl. impf. Hiphil) from נָטָה (*nāṭāh*), a reading favored by the Syriac. The MT has *w^e'aṭ* ("and gently"), which also fits the context.

5 The LXX takes לֹא, (*lō'*, "not"), as לוֹ (*lô*, "to him") and places it with the last phrase of v.4. This gives the reading for the first line of v.5 as "They will return to Egypt," much as in 8:13 and 9:3.

6 "Gate bars" translates בַּד (*baḏ*, "a part"). Some authorities see it as referring to a part of the people, such as "the priests," or "the leaders." The NIV reading, however, finds support in Job 17:16 and Jer 51:30.

2. *Restoration in the last days*

11:8–11

8"How can I give you up, Ephraim?
  How can I hand you over, Israel?
How can I treat you like Admah?
  How can I make you like Zeboiim?
My heart is changed within me;
  all my compassion is aroused.

9I will not carry out my fierce anger,
nor will I turn and devastate Ephraim again.
For I am God, and not man—
the Holy One among you.
I will not come in wrath.
10They will follow the LORD;
he will roar like a lion.
When he roars,
his children will come trembling from the west.
11They will come trembling
like birds from Egypt,
like doves from Assyria.
I will settle them in their homes,"
declares the LORD.

These verses are like a window into the heart of God. They show that his love for his people is a love that will never let them go. Like the beautiful final chapter of the book, these verses look forward, beyond the chastisement of the immediate future, to the time, still distant, when Israel will truly return to her God and he will bless her once more. Ultimately it must be the millennial kingdom that is finally in view here. No other period in Israel's history, past or prospective, fits the picture.

8 Two poignant questions reveal the depth of God's love for his people. Despite the sure judgment that was soon to come on unfaithful Israel, he could not bear to give up his chosen people (here called Ephraim and Israel) forever. His enduring love precluded his treating them as he did Admah and Zeboiim, two cities that had been utterly destroyed along with Sodom and Gomorrah (cf. Deut 29:23).

9 In that future day God would not devastate Ephraim (Israel) again, as he was about to do through the Assyrians. He is "God, and not man"—that is to say, he is one whose ways transcend those of sinful humanity. Because he is holy, he does not let passion or bitterness govern his decisions. He promised wondrous blessing on the people, if they would follow him (cf. Deut 28:1–14). But in that future day of restoration, he would not come against any city or land "in wrath," as he was about to do in Hosea's day.

10 Here Hosea states God's reason for carrying out his promise of restoration in the coming day: The people "will follow the LORD." The metaphor of the lion's roar means that God's call to his people would sound so clearly throughout the earth that they would come "trembling" (i.e., "humbly") "from the west" (*miyyām*). The return of Judah from the Babylonian captivity was from the east. But this mention of "the west" sets off the future return from the earlier one (cf. Isa 11:11–12).

11 Hosea next compared the swiftness (i.e., the readiness and responsiveness) of the future return of his people to the flight of birds and doves. Egypt and Assyria were named because of Israel's years of bondage in Egypt and their impending captivity in Assyria. In this context Egypt and Assyria typify the many nations from which God's people will return in the future day. Then he will settle them "in their homes"—an assurance of their permanent residence in their land (cf. 2:19).

Notes

9 Keil (1:142) et al. understand בְּעִיר (b^e'îr), as meaning "in the heat of wrath" (NIV, "in wrath"), from עוּר ('ûr, "to rouse, stir up"), rather than "in the city" (NIV mg., KJV). This gives the thought that God would not come in the Last Day in the heat of his wrath. Either thought is possible and fits the context.

3. *The folly of Israel*

11:12–12:14

12Ephraim has surrounded me with lies,
the house of Israel with deceit.
And Judah is unruly against God,
even against the faithful Holy One.
1Ephraim feeds on the wind;
he pursues the east wind all day
and multiplies lies and violence.
He makes a treaty with Assyria
and sends olive oil to Egypt.
2The LORD has a charge to bring against Judah;
he will punish Jacob according to his ways
and repay him according to his deeds.
3In the womb he grasped his brother's heel;
as a man he struggled with God.
4He struggled with the angel and overcame him;
he wept and begged for his favor.
He found him at Bethel
and talked with him there—
5the LORD God Almighty,
the LORD is his name of renown!
6But you must return to your God;
maintain love and justice,
and wait for your God always.

7The merchant uses dishonest scales;
he loves to defraud.
8Ephraim boasts,
"I am very rich, I have become wealthy.
With all my wealth they will not find in me
any iniquity or sin."
9"I am the LORD your God,
who brought you out of Egypt;
I will make you live in tents again,
as in the days of your appointed feasts.
10I spoke to the prophets,
gave them many visions
and told parables through them."

11Is Gilead wicked?
Its people are worthless!
Do they sacrifice bulls in Gilgal?
Their altars will be like piles of stones
on a plowed field.
12Jacob fled to the country of Aram;
Israel served to get a wife,
and to pay for her he tended sheep.

> [13]The LORD used a prophet to bring Israel up from Egypt,
> by a prophet he cared for him.
> [14]But Ephraim has bitterly provoked him to anger;
> his Lord will leave upon him the guilt of his bloodshed
> and will repay him for his contempt.

This section, along with chapter 3, reverts to the main theme of the book—Israel's unfaithfulness to her God. The book, however, will end on the contrasting note of Israel's future restoration.

12 In most EVs the chapter division places this verse with the preceding one. But in the Hebrew it goes with what follows it. This is logical, for the verse accuses the Israelites of surrounding God with deceit and dishonesty, as though attacking him. Once more Israel's sin is paralleled by Judah's rebellion against God, who is their "faithful Holy One."

1 Ephraim (Israel) is now said to feed on the wind, meaning that her efforts were to no worthwhile purpose. Harper (p. 377) makes the striking comment that "Ephraim herds the wind, and hunts the sirocco." One aspect of this effort was the treaties they made with Assyria and Egypt (cf. 2 Kings 17:4; 18:21; Isa 30:7). But such were seldom of benefit to Israel. "Lies and violence" were often involved in making them. Indeed, Israel while making a treaty with Assyria might at the same time be sending olive oil to Egypt in an effort to enlist her support against Assyria (cf. 2 Kings 17:4).

2 Once more Judah is referred to as being accused by God and facing retribution. "Jacob" is probably a reference to both Judah and Israel combined; he was the ancestor of all the Israelites and so becomes the subject of vv.3–4. All his descendants, the people of both the northern and the southern kingdoms, were guilty before God.

3 Here the patriarch Jacob, who while being born seized his brother's heel and when a man struggled with God himself, is mentioned as an example for the people of Hosea's day to follow (so Keil, 1:146). (Harper, however, says that Jacob is a bad example and that his treatment of his brother before birth "indicates that fatal characteristic of the nation which, as exhibited again and again in its history, has now reached the point at which punishment must be administered" [p. 379].)

Jacob's struggling with God was a time of triumph, which means that the first occasion should be understood in the same way. Jacob's act in "the womb" of his mother (Gen 25:26) was one in which the providential direction of God symbolized Jacob's desire for the birthright and blessing. Years later, when he had become a man, Jacob struggled all night at the brook Jabbok (Gen 32:25–29) so that he might receive God's blessing. Similarly, Israel in Hosea's time should be striving for God's favor and blessing rather than chasing the wind.

4 Hosea enlarged on Jacob's struggle at Jabbok, pointing out that Jacob overcame the angel because he wanted the blessing so much that he even "wept and begged" for it. Then the prophet shifted to Jacob's encounter with God at Bethel (Gen 35:1–15), when God confirmed the blessing already promised him. The implication is that God would do the same thing for Israel if she desired God's blessing as much as Jacob had.

5 Here the thought turns to God himself, the one who had blessed Jacob and wanted to do the same thing for Israel in Hosea's day. His great name is given—the name that stands for him in all his excellency: "LORD God Almighty," or, more literally, "The LORD, the God of hosts." The phrase "name of renown" suggests that Israel was always to think of God in this way. Because he was all that this name implied, the people could be sure that he would keep every promise he had ever made to them.

6 In this verse the people are exhorted to repent. They are to "return" to God, to "maintain love and justice" in respect to one another, and to "wait" in expectancy for God to bring them the same kind of blessing he had brought Jacob. All this they were to do with the help of God. We work for God as God enables us; so only is God's work done.

7 Hosea next turned to a specific area of sin in Israel. "The merchant" (lit., "Canaan," used here for Israel and connoting the people as merchants) used dishonest scales and loved "to defraud" (*'āšaq,* "to oppress"). What a way to be remembered! Much of Israel's dealing with the nations of the day had involved trading and had been contaminated by deceit.

8 As a result of these shady practices, Ephraim had been boasting of her wealth and declaring that no one could find her guilty of any sin. So the people did not see themselves as deserving any punishment. Apparently they had devised loopholes in the law to justify what they had been doing. As a result they thought they were innocent. Perhaps the reign of Jeroboam II, when Israel prospered greatly, was the time Hosea was speaking of here.

9 While the people were thinking themselves self-sufficient, God countered this thinking. He reminded them that he had been the Lord their God "from the land of Egypt." The words "who brought you" are not in the MT and could be omitted here, for God simply stated that he had been Israel's God since the days of Egypt. But now, because of their sin, he would drive them out of their "wealthy" circumstances and make them "live in tents again," as they did in the days of their "appointed feasts" (*mô'ēḏ,* here likely the Feast of Tabernacles, which commemorated the wilderness dwelling). This is clearly a reference to the coming days of captivity. Because the Feast of Tabernacles was also a joyous occasion, reminding the people of God's blessing in the wilderness, the implication may be that even in this transient time of captivity God would again graciously provide for them—as indeed he did.

10 Here Hosea resumed his general theme. God, he recalled, had communicated his will to Israel through prophets, visions, and parables. The people therefore could not plead ignorance and were without excuse.

11 Gilead on the east of the Jordan and Gilgal on the west are here made representative of all the land. Rhetorical questions concerning both serve to underline their wickedness. The very idea of bulls being sacrificed at Gilgal indicates one of the ways in which wickedness was involved there, for it was the wrong place for such sacrifice (cf. 4:15; 9:15). As a result God would reduce the altars there to mere piles of stones on a "plowed field" (lit., "the furrows of a field"). In other words, they would be useless and in the way.

12 Once more Hosea spoke of Jacob (cf. vv.3–4). Earlier he had mentioned the blessing Jacob received; here he spoke of the hardship Jacob endured. The point is that God had blessed this ancestor, even though things had happened at the time—the long years served for Rachel, the flight from Esau—that had not seemed like blessings.

13 Hosea said that God had similarly provided for Israel when he had brought the people by a "prophet" (presumably Moses; cf. Deut 18:18) from Egypt and cared for them. Israel, too, had experienced hardship while in the foreign land.

14 This past history should have led Israel to a state of humility and submission before God, but it had not. Instead, said Hosea, Ephraim (Israel) had "bitterly provoked him to anger" through her extensive sinning. Therefore Ephraim's "Lord" (*'ᵃḏōnay,* "master") would leave the people in their "guilt of . . . bloodshed" (cf. Lev 20:9; Deut 19:10) and "repay" (*šûḇ,* "return") them for the insults rendered. Punishment would indeed come.

Notes

11: 12 [12:1 MT] The participle רָד (*rāḏ*) is best taken from רוּד (*rûḏ,* "to wander about, act unruly"; cf. Gen 27:40; Jer 2:31). Some take it from רָדָה (*rāḏāh,* "to rule"), giving the translation "Judah rules with God," meaning "Judah is still known with God" (so Harper, p. 376).

4 [5 MT] In line 4 "with him" in Hebrew is עִמָּנוּ (*'immānû,* "with us"). There is reason for the plural: though God was speaking primarily to Jacob, Hosea wanted the people of his day to recognize that in a secondary sense he was speaking also to them.

6 [7 MT] The prepositional prefix on "your God" (בֵּאלֹהֶיךָ, *bē'lōheyḵā*) is taken instrumentally in our translation. It may also be translated "in respect to," which gives good sense as well.

4. *Israel's fall into sin*

13:1–16

1 When Ephraim spoke, men trembled;
he was exalted in Israel.
But he became guilty of Baal worship and died.
2 Now they sin more and more;
they make idols for themselves from their silver,
cleverly fashioned images,
all of them the work of craftsmen.
It is said of these people,
"They offer human sacrifice
and kiss the calf-idols."

3Therefore they will be like the morning mist,
like the early dew that disappears,
like chaff swirling from a threshing floor,
like smoke escaping through a window.

4"But I am the LORD your God,
⌞who brought you⌟ out of Egypt.
You shall acknowledge no God but me,
no Savior except me.
5I cared for you in the desert,
in the land of burning heat.
6When I fed them, they were satisfied;
when they were satisfied, they became proud;
then they forgot me.
7So I will come upon them like a lion,
like a leopard I will lurk by the path.
8Like a bear robbed of her cubs,
I will attack them and rip them open.
Like a lion I will devour them;
a wild animal will tear them apart.

9"You are destroyed, O Israel,
because you are against me, against your helper.
10Where is your king, that he may save you?
Where are your rulers in all your towns,
of whom you said,
'Give me a king and princes'?
11So in my anger I gave you a king,
and in my wrath I took him away.
12The guilt of Ephraim is stored up,
his sins are kept on record.
13Pains as of a woman in childbirth come to him,
but he is a child without wisdom;
when the time arrives,
he does not come to the opening of the womb.

14"I will ransom them from the power of the grave;
I will redeem them from death.
Where, O death, are your plagues?
Where, O grave, is your destruction?

"I will have no compassion,
15even though he thrives among his brothers.
An east wind from the LORD will come,
blowing in from the desert;
his spring will fail
and his well dry up.
His storehouse will be plundered
of all its treasures.
16The people of Samaria must bear their guilt,
because they have rebelled against their God.
They will fall by the sword;
their little ones will be dashed to the ground,
their pregnant women ripped open."

Hosea continued to speak of Israel's unfaithfulness to God, but here he took on a more historical note.

1 Hosea has frequently referred to the whole northern nation as Ephraim, but in this verse the tribe was intended. In former years when Ephraim had spoken, the

other tribes had listened with deference and respect. Ephraim had often asserted leadership in prior days, sometimes in improper ways (see Judg 8:1–3; 12:1–6; 1 Kings 12:25; cf. 11:26). Things had changed for Ephraim, however, since Baal worship had crept in. In view of v.2, this Baal worship must be primarily the calf worship at Bethel, though Jeroboam I had instituted it as the worship of Israel's God (1 Kings 12:26–33). Doubtless elements of the Baal cult had come to be practiced there.

2–3 Spiritual death was the result of Baal worship. The people heaped sin on sin, owning and worshiping idols made from silver by clever craftsmen (cf. 8:4). The last two lines admit of two renderings (cf. Notes). Our translation takes them to refer to "human sacrifice." This, however, seems unlikely since no other indication is given that human sacrifice was practiced at Bethel or Dan. The other and more likely rendering may be expressed as follows: "In respect to the images [of the calves], they [leaders in this form of worship] are saying, 'Let the sacrificers among men [i.e., those who would sacrifice] do so by kissing the calf-idols.'" To kiss an image was to do homage to it (see 1 Kings 19:18; cf. Ps 2:12). Jeroboam I had first bidden the people to give this homage, and leaders in the worship were continuing the practice. Persistence in this sin, answered Hosea, would have but one outcome. This he traced in four striking figures (v.3) that reiterate how surely and speedily the offending people would disappear and perish.

4 This verse begins with the same words as 12:9 (q.v.). The last two lines of this verse are probably best translated as in NIV, as an admonition to people of Hosea's day to acknowledge God alone as their God and Savior. The admonition tallies with the tenor of the book. Another possible translation is "You acknowledged no God but me, no Savior except me." This takes the thought as a historical comment. Such is not easily related, however, to the rebellion and sin Israel displayed during the wilderness travel.

5–6 Hosea reverted to history in reminding the people how God had cared for them during those arduous desert days, a reminder that should have stirred them to observe the admonition. God's care for the people involved his feeding them (v.6), which thought is probably intended here to cover generally all of God's provisions; but one aspect was the miraculous feeding by manna. This satisfied the people, but then they "became proud" (lit., "their heart was lifted up") and forgot God (cf. Deut 8:11–20). This had happened in the wilderness; it had been happening during the intervening centuries.

7 This brings Hosea again to his theme of coming judgment. God would pounce on the rebellious people like a lion and like a leopard, to bring punishment (cf. 5:14). The figure is apt, for in v.6 the people have been pictured as a flock under God's care. The change was not in God but in the relation of the people to God, due to sin.

8 To intensify this theme of punishment, the figure of a bear, crazed by the loss of her cubs, is also used, followed once more by the figure of a lion. The "wild animal" of line 4 is not a fourth beast but refers to the others as beasts of the field (*ḥayyaṯ* *haśśāḏeh*). The three mentioned—lion, leopard, and bear—were all native to Palestine and known for their relentless manner of killing prey.

9 A literal translation of the MT is "It destroys you, O Israel, that you are against me, against your helper." The thought is that Israel would suffer destruction because she lived in opposition to God's will. This anticipates the lines that follow.

10 The thought of this verse is not to say that Israel was kingless but that she did not have one who could deliver the people from the Assyrian threat. Only God, their true "helper" (v.9), whom they rejected, could do this. "Your rulers" (lit., "your judges") could be the king's assistants. The people had asked for "a king and princes" in the days of Samuel (1 Sam 8:4–6); but this reference evidently marked the occasion when the northern tribes—and Hosea was now addressing the northern kingdom—wanted their own king after rebelling under Rehoboam (1 Kings 12:16–20).

11 Because of the imperfect tense of the two verbs here, the translation could well be "I have been giving" you a king and "I have been taking him away." No one king, apparently, was in view here but the series of kings that had occupied Israel's throne since the kingdom's division. God had been allowing them to rule; but because of their unfaithfulness to him, he had also been setting them aside. Many had come to a violent end (cf. 7:7).

12 Thus was the guilt of Ephraim "stored up" (participle from *ṣārar*, "to bind in a bundle" for preservation) and "kept on record" (participle from *ṣāpan*, "to hide" for safekeeping) against the day of reckoning.

13 An unusual illustration is pressed into service as Hosea further delineated the punishment of Israel. First he likened Israel to a mother in labor (line 1) and then to a son being born to the mother (lines 3–4). This son, he said, was without wisdom because he did not come to the "opening of the womb" (*mišbar bānîm*, lit., "breaking of sons"; cf. 2 Kings 19:3; Isa 37:3) at the proper time for the birth. God, in other words, was bringing punishment on Israel so that the people might be reborn to follow him as he desired; but they were foolish in not grasping the opportunity. God had been using various disciplinary measures against Israel for years, but to no avail.

14 Like 11:8–11, this verse is parenthetical to the context, which runs smoothly from v.13 to v.15. God broke in to sound a note of encouragement and promise to the people. They had severe punishment ahead of them in Hosea's time, but there would come a day when wondrous blessing would be their portion. Paul quoted (in a form related to the LXX) v.14b at the triumphant climax of his great chapter on resurrection (1 Cor 15:55: "Where, O death, is your victory?/Where, O sin, is your sting?"). One aspect of its fulfillment (that relating to the resurrection of the believer in a spiritual body) is to be found there. But since the context of Hosea 13 relates to the earthly punishment of Israel, another aspect of v.14b must still be future—i.e., at the time of Christ's reign on earth during the Millennium (cf. 11:8–11).

Verse 14a speaks of the people being ransomed "from the power of the grave" (*miyyaḏ šᵉʾôl*, "from the hand of Sheol") and from death. These dreaded enemies will be shorn of their power against God's redeemed people; these are glorious thoughts! The last line of v.14 literally reads, "Repentance is hidden from my eyes," which is best taken as meaning that God will not change his mind about doing what this verse declares.

15–16 Though in NIV the first line of this verse is syntactically linked to v.14, this rendering is problematic. It is better to understand v.15 as related to v.13 and so continuing to speak of punishment. So, though the people of Israel may thrive among their neighbors, eventually they will be dried up by an east wind from the desert. Because of this, springs and wells will fail. For Israel the time of thriving must in particular be the time of Jeroboam II, when prosperity was marked. The destroying east wind must be Assyria—a power that came from the east and effected Israel's fall in 722 B.C. Moreover, Assyria did indeed plunder Israel's "storehouse" at that time. When the Assyrians conquered them, the people bore the guilt of their rebellion against their God. The shocking brutalities described in v.16 are in keeping with the character of the Assyrians as revealed by archaeology. Here "Samaria," as the capital of the northern kingdom, represents all Israel.

Notes

---

1 The word רְתֵת (*r^e ṯēṯ*, "trembled"), used only here, corresponds in meaning to רְטֵט (*r^e ṭēṭ*) in Jer 49:24.

2 The key words in the last two lines are זֹבְחֵי אָדָם (*zōḇ^e ḥê ʾāḏām*), which can mean either "sacrifices of men" (i.e., "human sacrifices") or "sacrificers among men" (i.e., "men who sacrifice"); here the second meaning is preferable.

4 The verb תֵּדָע (*tēḏāʿ*, "you shall acknowledge") is an imperfect and can be understood either as a continuing act of knowledge or acknowledgement in Israel's past history or an admonition to be observed in Hosea's day.

7 Harper (p. 398) et al. point אַשּׁוּר as *ʾaššûr*, in keeping with the LXX, Syriac, and Vulgate, and read the noun "Assyria" instead of the verb *ʾāšûr* ("I will lurk"). The context, however, in no way calls for the country of Assyria to be mentioned in this verse.

10 The word for "where" (אֱהִי, *ʾ^e hî*) occurs only here and in v.14 (*bis*), a variation from אַי (*ʾay*) or אַיֵּה (*ʾayyēh*), and is also strengthened by the use of אֵפוֹא (*ʾēpôʾ*, "then"; untr. in NIV).

14 The word שְׁאוֹל (*š^e ʾôl*) occurs sixty-five times in the OT and is translated in KJV thirty-one times as "grave," thirty-one times as "hell," and three times as "pit."

The two uses of אֱהִי (*ʾ^e hî*) in this verse are best taken to mean "where," as in v.10, even though not strengthened here by the use of אֵפוֹא (*ʾēpôʾ*, "then").

---

5. *Israel's repentance and God's blessing*

14:1–9

1 Return, O Israel, to the LORD your God.
  Your sins have been your downfall!
2 Take words with you
  and return to the LORD.
Say to him:
  "Forgive all our sins
and receive us graciously,
  that we may offer the fruit of our lips.

3Assyria cannot save us;
we will not mount war-horses.
We will never again say 'Our gods'
to what our own hands have made,
for in you the fatherless find compassion."
4"I will heal their waywardness
and love them freely,
for my anger has turned away from them.
5I will be like the dew to Israel;
he will blossom like a lily.
Like a cedar of Lebanon
he will send down his roots;
6his young shoots will grow.
His splendor will be like an olive tree,
his fragrance like a cedar of Lebanon.
7Men will dwell again in his shade.
He will flourish like the grain.
He will blossom like a vine,
and his fame will be like the wine from Lebanon.
8O Ephraim, what more have I to do with idols?
I will answer him and care for him.
I am like a green pine tree;
your fruitfulness comes from me."

9Who is wise? He will realize these things.
Who is discerning? He will understand them.
The ways of the LORD are right;
the righteous walk in them,
but the rebellious stumble in them.

In beauty of expression these final words of Hosea rank with the memorable chapters of the OT. Like the rainbow after a storm, they promise Israel's final restoration. Here is the full flowering of God's unfailing love for his faithless people, the triumph of his grace, the assurance of his healing—all described in imagery that reveals the loving heart of God.

1 In the Hebrew text, this is v.2. The English chapter division, however, is more logical. The verse not only invites Israel to return to her God; it also reminds her of her sins. God's forgiveness is to be accompanied by awareness of sin.

2 The people are not to return to the Lord without bringing something; they are to come to him with words that he puts, as it were, in their mouths. When they ask for forgiveness, the Lord will graciously receive them. Here the Hebrew *weqaḥ-ṭôḇ* literally means "and take good." This is best understood as asking God to receive what "good" they can bring. This "good" is described as offering as sacrifices "the fruit of our lips." In the Hebrew this is "that we offer our lips as bullocks"—i.e., "that instead of bullocks we offer as our sacrifice our lips that utter prayer and praise to God" (cf. Notes).

3 The offering of words—all of them words of repentance—continues. Israel was to admit that neither Assyria nor any military might (symbolized by "warhorses") could save her. Once and for all, she was to renounce manmade images as her "gods." Moreover, since God has compassion on the orphans (cf. Exod 22:22; Deut 10:18), Israel could expect him to have compassion also on her.

4 In response to Israel's penitent words, the Lord described the wondrous blessings that he would bestow on them. Since they had not repented and would not repent nationally in the way Hosea described till the future Great Tribulation, and since the blessings from God described in vv.4–8 would not be fully bestowed till the Millennium, the ultimate meaning of this passage must be eschatolgoical—i.e., in it the last days are again in view (cf. 1:10–11; 2:14–23 et al.). Here (v.4) we have God's grace in action—his healing of their "waywardness" (*m*^{e}*šûḇāh*, "turning away," "defection") and loving them unconditionally. For he had indeed turned his anger away from them.

5–6 Among the great biblical figures of speech are those that relate to trees and flowers—figures especially meaningful to dwellers in semiarid lands like Palestine. Here Hosea likened Israel in her time of future blessing to a lily, a cedar of Lebanon, and that most essential of all trees, the olive tree.

NIV rightly makes the first line of v.6, with its reference to the growth of the young shoots, part of the second sentence of v.5. Cheyne (in loc.) says, "The roots will produce an abundance of fresh plants, so that Israel will be like not only a tree, but a garden." The second and third lines of v.6 show the result of this healthy growth: the cedar will have the "splendor" (*hôḏ*, "majesty") of the all-important olive tree and the "fragrance" (*rêaḥ*, "smell") of the cedar of Lebanon itself. So the nation of Israel will be admired throughout the world.

7 In the Hebrew the first two lines of this verse may literally (and awkwardly) be rendered, "They who dwell in his shadow shall again make grain to live." The antecedent of "his" is the tree (representative of Israel nationally); and the antecedent of "they," individual Israelites. It is a promise that the people of Israel in the future day will also flourish and blossom like a vine, with their fame (*ziḵrô*, "his remembrance") spreading abroad like the fame of Lebanese wine. How different from the situation of Israel in Hosea's day!

8 Here the rhetorical question relates to the idolatry that had been Israel's besetting sin. In God's sight idols are absolutely nothing, and so shall they be for Ephraim (Israel). God (line 2), not the idols, is the one who will answer and "care for" (*šûr*, "look on") Israel in her time of need. He is like a "green pine tree"; all Israel's fruitfulness comes from him.

9 This verse is like a noble epilogue. The balance between the rhetorical questions with their answers and the dignity of the last sentence with its concise parallelism closes Hosea's unique book on a note of solemn authority.

Notes

2 (3 MT) In choosing the reading פְּרִי (*p*^{e}*rî*, "fruit"), NIV follows the LXX and Syriac versions. The MT reads פָּרִים (*pārîm*, "bullocks"). But since the more difficult reading makes good sense, there seems to be no adequate reason for rejecting the MT.

7 (8 MT) Normally שׁוּב (*šûḇ*) means "return," but here it denotes repetition with the force of "again." In using the singular "he" in the last two lines, NIV makes the antecedent to be the tree (representing Israel as a nation); the Hebrew, however, uses a plural, making the antecedent those who dwell in the tree's shade (i.e., individual Israelites).

8 (9 MT) The use twice of the first person pronoun אֲנִי (*'anî*, "I") is to say that God alone, among those worshiped, can and will answer the people and that he alone can and will be their "green pine tree."

JOEL

Richard D. Patterson

JOEL

Introduction

1. Background

Joel prophesied in Judah in the exciting and pivotal days of Uzziah (792–740 B.C.), the tenth king of the southern kingdom (see Date). Those were days of unparalleled prosperity for Israel and Judah. Together the twin kingdoms acquired nearly the same territorial dimensions as in the days of the united monarchy. To the south Uzziah continued the control over Edom that Amaziah had effected, while reorganizing the work at Ezion-Geber and reactivating the port of Elath (2 Kings 14:22; 2 Chron 26:2). The seal of Jotham used in official transactions indicates that Ezion-Geber was an important center in the time of Uzziah and Jotham.[1] Uzziah also seized the caravan routes that led from Arabia (2 Chron 26:7). To the east he seems to have imposed tribute on the Transjordanian regions (v.8). To the west he moved with great success against the Philistines, taking Gath and the coastal plain, thus controlling the important trade routes there (vv.6–7) and eliminating the slave-gathering raids into western Judah (3:4–8).

A great military strategist, Uzziah improved the fortifications of Jerusalem and Judah, introducing antisiege machines into the weaponry of the armed forces (2 Chron 26:9, 15). His military preparedness included a total reorganization of the structure and equipment of the army (vv.11–15).

About 750 B.C., Uzziah contracted leprosy, because of his intrusion into the priest's office, and appointed Jotham, his son, as coregent and public officiator. Nevertheless, Uzziah continued to be the real power of the throne, for when Tiglath-pileser III invaded Syria in his first western campaign (743 B.C.), Uzziah was singled out as the leader of the anti-Assyrian coalition.

Uzziah also turned his attention to the internal affairs of his country. Indeed, most of his military activity had economic goals. He led the way, moreover, in agricul-

[1]See N. Glueck, "The Third Season of Excavations at Tell el-Kheleifeh," BASOR 49 (1940): 13ff.

tural reorganization (2 Chron 26:10), a fact confirmed by the archaeological excavations of Glueck in the Negev.

In short, the era of the early eighth century B.C. was one of great expansion, militarily, administratively, commercially, and economically, a period the prosperity of which was second only to that of Solomon's. It is small wonder, then, that Uzziah's fame should endure long after his death (2 Chron 26:8b, 15b).

In such an era God raised up the great writing prophets, men of intense patriotism and deep spiritual concern. Their message, unlike that of their predecessors, was not limited to national affairs but took in the entire international scene from their own time to the culmination of God's teleological program.

2. Unity

Critical doubt as to the unity of Joel became standardized with the work of Duhm.[2] He denied that any of the apocalyptic sections were Joel's and left only the nonapocalyptic sections of chapters 1 and 2 to his authorship. Other scholars followed his reasoning, especially Bewer, who eliminated as insertions all references to the Day of the Lord, the apocalyptic portions, and the historical problem of 3:4–8. To Joel were ascribed the nonapocalyptic sections of chapters 1 and 2, along with 2:28–31a; 3:2a; and 3:9–14a.

The denial of the unity of the book is based on supposed literary differences and also differences in thought or outlook. A careful look at the literary form of the book, however, reveals a consistency of style and vocabulary. Supposed differences in outlook cannot be proved. On the contrary, the author has a single unifying theme: the terrible locust plague is a harbinger of awesome things to come. "The Day of the Lord," rather than betraying a different hand, serves to unite historical occurrence with spiritual lesson. Moreover, all the extant Hebrew MSS and the ancient versions attest to the unity of the book.

3. Authorship

Little is known of the personal circumstances of the author, Joel ("Yahweh is God"), except that which can be gleaned internally from the book. The son of Pethuel (LXX, Bethuel), Joel lived and prophesied in Judah (though Pseudo-Epiphanius indicates that his original home was in Reuben). Thus he often referred to Judah and Jerusalem (2:32; 3:1, 17–18, 20) and to their citizens (3:6, 8, 19), or to Zion (2:1, 15; 3:17, 21) and its children (2:23). He was thoroughly familiar with the temple and its ministry (1:9; 13:14, 16; 2:14, 17; 3:18). He was intimately acquainted with the geography and history of the land (1:2; 3:2–8, 12, 14, 18).

Joel was a man of vitality and spiritual maturity. A keen discerner of the times, he delivered God's message to the people of Judah in a vivid and impassioned style, with a precision and originality of thought that served as a veritable quarry out of which many subsequent prophetic building stones were to be hewn.

---

[2]B. Duhm, "Anmerkungen zu den zwölf Propheten," ZAW 31 (1911): 1–43, 184–88.

4. Date

Perhaps no other problem has occupied the attention of those who have studied the Book of Joel with such varying results as that of its date. Since no date is given in the heading of the book, nor is any stated explicitly within the body of the book, the conjectures of the expositors for the date of its composition have ranged from the ninth century B.C. to the Maccabean Period. They may be divided roughly into postexilic and preexilic theories.

Advocates of the postexilic theory find the internal data of the book most reconcilable with a time when both kingdoms had fallen and Assyria and Babylonia had passed off the scene. The concentration on Judah, while failing to mention the northern kingdom; the "rebuilt" temple of Jerusalem and the priesthood; and the reference to the elders (rather than any king) as the leaders of the people suggest to many of them a mid-fourth century B.C. date. Certain literary data and the apocalyptic nature of Joel's theological outlook are put forward as further evidence of a late date.

Three general positions have been advanced by those who assign a preexilic date to Joel. The early preexilic view holds to a ninth-century date. Advocates of this theory stress Joel's failure to mention a king and the prominence he gives to the priesthood and elders. They explain these facts as pointing to the time of the boy-king Joash (835–796 B.C.) who began his rule through the regency of the high priest Jehoiada. The mention of the shedding of innocent blood (3:19) indicates a closeness to the invasion of Sheshonq in the tenth century and to the revolt of Edom in the days of Jehoram, Joash's grandfather (2 Kings 8:20).

The late preexilic view takes a seventh-century date. Kapelrud attempts to harmonize the literary forms and religious outlook of Joel with Jeremiah. Kapelrud decides that all historical, lexical, and sociological data are inconclusive for precise dating of the book. He finds Joel highly receptive to the influence of Jeremiah; hence, Joel was probably Jeremiah's younger contemporary.

The mid-preexilic view places Joel's prophecy in the early eighth century. That this view is to be preferred is seen from the following data.

1. The failure to mention the great powers of Assyria, Babylonia, and Persia as enemies of Judah is significant and may be explained by the fact that Assyria was in severe decline in power from Adad-nirari III's death (782 B.C.) till the accession of Tiglath-pileser III (745 B.C.).

2. The position of Joel among the dated minor prophets Hosea, Amos, and Jonah argues for an eighth-century date.

3. The contextual juxtaposition of six foreign nations in chapter 3 points to an early eighth-century date. Thus after the campaign of Adad-nirari III (805 B.C.), Phoenicia and Philistia were not again faced with outside intervention till the western campaigns of Tiglath-pileser III in 743 B.C. and 732 B.C; and thereafter their destiny is linked with that of Assyria throughout the eighth and seventh centuries. Accordingly, the Philistines were free between 805 and 743 to harass their old enemies, necessitating a campaign against them in Uzziah's day (2 Chron 26:6–7). In that age of great prosperity, the Phoenicians were again the leading merchants of the day (cf. 3:4–7). The whole Mediterranean basin was exposed to their commercial leadership, resulting in the foundation of Carthage in the western Mediterranean. The reference to Tyre and Sidon together (v.4) may point to their brief political unity in the early eighth century B.C.

The mention of Greece does not demand a late date, though its presence in Joel's prophecy is more difficult for an early preexilic date than for a mid-preexilic one. The eighth century was a great age of awakened commercial and colonial expansion for the Greeks. A broad area from the Black Sea to Italy was exposed to their commercial ventures. The Hebrew text at 3:6 may point to the Ionian Greeks rather than to the Greeks of the mainland or of the Aegean world. If so, the eighth century is again an ideal time, for this is the precise period when the Ionians seized the mainland trade routes of Asia Minor. In either case the evidence harmonizes well with this era when the Greeks entered into the commercial arena long dominated by the Phoenicians. Reference to the commercially minded Phoenicians and Greeks fits very well the renewed commercial interests of Uzziah's day.

While the era of the Sabeans' great kingdom was to be centered in the fifth century B.C., recent studies have pushed Sabean commercial operations backward to a time considerably before this.[3] Certainly Joel's viewing the Sabeans as a "far off" people does not necessitate a postexilic date. Since Arabs are known to have been in contact with the Philistines in Uzziah's day (2 Chron 26:7), and since Uzziah reopened Ezion-Geber and the port of Elath, thereby reestablishing contact with the Arabs to the south, an eighth-century reference to the Sabeans is not improbable.

Although mention of Egypt and Edom is not conclusive of any date, there is no evidence to link Joel's denunciation of a weakened Egypt to early preexilic times. While Egypt was to regain some of her lost strength in late preexilic times, she was then Judah's ally—and Judah was condemned for it (Jer 2:16–18, 36; 42:15–22). Joel, however, condemned Egypt as Judah's enemy. This situation harmonizes well with the eighth-century prophets' denunciation of the Israelite reliance on an idolatrous and treacherous Egypt (Isa 19; 30:1–5; 31:1–3; Hos 7:11; 12:1). That Amos, moreover, associated Edom with the Philistines (1:6) and the Tyrians (v.9) in the slave trade and condemned their oppression of the Israelites (vv.11–12), and that Obadiah also devoted his whole prophecy to the Edomites, argues for the possibility of an eighth-century date for Joel. Additionally, Uzziah had to subdue Edom (2 Kings 14:7), a subjugation quickly lost after his time.

Mention of any one of these nations gives no specific date to Joel's prophecy, but that all six are mentioned in close connection in one context necessitates their historical juxtaposition. The early eighth century B.C. best harmonizes with the known data.

4. The internal emphases reflect well Uzziah's time. There is the importance of agriculture (1:4–20; 2:18–27), the ease and debauchery of society (1:5; cf. Hos 4:11; 7:5, 14; Amos 2:8; 6:1–7; see also the many references in Isaiah), the occurrence of the locust attack itself (cf. Amos 4:9; 7:1–3), and the sheer formalism of the established religion of the day (2:12–13; cf. Amos 5:21–24).

5. In contrast to those who arbitrarily ascribe a dependence of Joel on the other prophets, a survey of the data relative to literary dependence reveals that Joel faithfully reflects the prevailing events, attitudes, and literary themes of his contemporaries in the early eighth century B.C. An intensive examination of Joel shows over four dozen instances of linguistic formulas and special lexical emphases that

---

[3]See, for example, A.B. Lloyd, "Necho and the Red Sea," *Journal of Egyptian Archaeology* 63 (1977): 147–48.

Joel has in common with the other eighth-century prophets. Likewise a comparison of Joel's use of theological terminology with that of these prophets reveals numerous places in every section of his prophecy where his viewpoint is in harmony with the prevailing message and outlook of that era. All this adds cumulative weight to the mid-preexilic view.

6. Joel's prophecy that the Day of the Lord will be accompanied by a great earthquake and his statement that "the LORD will roar from Zion" (3:16) may be connected with Amos's dating of his prophecy as two years before the earthquake of Uzziah's time (1:2; cf. Zech 14:5), a historical notice that he followed by citing Joel's very words.

7. As the political scene shifted from national to international emphases, the mid-preexilic view provides a logical time for the beginning of the writing prophets, whose activity was thereafter continuous till the close of the canon.

5. Occasion and Purpose

A locust plague without parallel had descended on Judah, ruining all the crops. Not only was the basic economy of the country disrupted, but all levels of society were deeply affected. Worst of all, the agricultural loss threatened the continuance of the sacrificial offerings, the central feature of the religious ceremony.

In these catastrophic circumstances Joel saw the judgment of God on Judah. Although God had abundantly blessed the Judah of Uzziah's day, the people had taken God and his blessings for granted. Faith had degenerated into an empty formalism and their lives into moral decadence. Under divine inspiration Joel told the people that the locust plague was a warning of a greater judgment that was imminent unless they repented and returned to full fellowship with God. If they did, God would abundantly pardon them, restore the health of the land, and give them again the elements needed to offer the sacrifices. The ceremonial system was designed to express a heart relationship with God. By their sin they had forfeited any right to religious ceremony. What was needed was a repentant heart that would allow ceremony and spiritual condition to coincide. The thought of further judgment led Joel also to reveal God's intentions for eschatological times.

6. Literary Form

Joel's literary style is rich and vivid. He wrote with a pure classical yet logical style, distinguished by its clarity, flow of thought, and beauty of expression.

Joel's thought pattern is easily discernible. In 1:2–20; 2:1–27; and 3:9–17, he developed his prophetic argumentation in a warning-instructional literary genre. After 1:2–4, each section (1:5–7, 8–10, 11–12, 13, 14–18, 19–20; 2:1–11, 12–14, 15–27; 3:9–12, 13–17) is built around an imperative-volitional statement and a motive clause introduced by the particle *kî* ("because").[4] A content clause may follow the imperative-volitional statement and a descriptive clause containing additional

[4]See W.T. Classen, "Speaker-oriented Functions of *kî* in Biblical Hebrew," *Journal of Northwest Semitic Languages* 11 (1983): 24–46.

details may precede or follow the motive clause; both are optional. The eschatological sections (2:28–32; 3:1–8, 18–21) are marked structurally as follows: Introductory formula + principle statement + added details + closing formula. The latter two are optional. While the thought pattern is structurally predictable, it is never mechanical, the optional elements being used with great variety and vitality.

Joel's genius and originality can be seen in his use of data and literary features. He skillfully wove the objective facts of the events of history and of his day into the fabric of his prophetical warnings and pronouncements. Special attention must be called to the two most characteristic literary devices Joel used to give balance and unity to his prophecy: (1) simile and metaphor (1:6; 2:2–7, 9, 11, 20, 25; 3:13, 16) and (2) repetition and recapitulation (1:2–3, 4; 2:2; 3:14; cf. 1:4–20 with 2:19–25; 1:4 with 2:25; 1:5 with 3:18; 1:6 with 2:2, 5; 3:9; 1:8 with 1:13; 1:9 with 1:13; 2:14; 1:10 with 1:17; 2:19, 24; 1:14 with 2:12, 15–16; 1:15 with 2:1, 11; 2:31; 3:14; 1:19 with 1:20; 1:19–20 with 2:21–22; 2:1 with 2:15; 2:2 with 2:3, 10; 3:15; 2:3 with 2:7, 11; 2:7 with 2:8; 2:8 with 2:9; 2:10 with 3:15; 2:11 with 3:16; 2:21 with 2:22; 2:24 with 3:13, 18; 2:26 with 2:27; 2:27 with 3:17, 21; 2:28 with 2:29; 3:1 with 3:18; 3:2 with 3:11–12; 3:4 with 3:7; 3:6 with 3:8; 3:7 with 3:8; 3:9 with 3:12; 3:17 with 3:21; 3:19 with 3:21).

7. Theological Values

A man of implicit faith in God, Joel imparted that reliance on the sufficiency of God and his prior claim on the believer's life in every section of the book. Only the leading characteristics of Joel's theological outlook can be sketched here.

Perhaps the basic tenet is that God is sovereignly guiding the affairs of earth's history toward his preconceived final goal (1:15; 2:1–4, 18, 20, 25–27, 28–32; 3:1–21). He alone is God (2:27). A God of grace and mercy (2:13, 17), of loving kindness and patience (2:13), and of justice (1:15; 3:1–8, 12–13) and righteousness (2:23), he calls for true and vital worship on behalf of his followers (2:13) who have trusted him for salvation by grace through faith (2:32). While the formal worship services are an essential part of the Israelite's religious experience (1:9, 13–14, 16; 2:13–17, 26–27), a mere externalism is insufficient before God (2:13, 18–19, 23, 26–27, 32; 3:21). Accordingly, the place of prayer and repentance is emphasized (1:13–14, 19–20; 2:12–13, 17, 19).

Joel taught that when sin becomes the dominant condition of God's people, they must be judged (1:15; 2:1, 11–13). God may use natural disasters (ch. 1) or political means (2:1–11) to chastise his people. For a repentant people (2:12–13) there will be the blessing of restored fellowship (2:14, 19, 23) and restored blessings in nature also (2:23–27).

Joel's theology contributes greatly to the field of eschatology. Of central concern is God's role to his people, Israel (1:6, 13–14; 2:12–14, 17, 18–20, 23–27; 3:1–3, 16–18, 20–21). While he may allow other nations to chastise Israel for her sins (2:11; 3:1–8, 19), God has reserved a remnant to himself (2:28–32). On them he will pour out his Spirit (2:28–29), to them he will manifest himself with marvelous signs (2:30–31), and them he will regather and bring to the Promised Land (2:32–3:1). He will gather for judgment those nations that have dealt so severely with his people (3:2, 12–13) and bring them to a great final battle near Jerusalem (vv.9–16). On that awesome day (v.15), he himself (v.16) will lead his people in triumph (vv.16–17), thereby ushering in an era of unparalleled peace and prosperity (vv.17–18, 20–21).

Integral to all Joel's prophecy is his teaching about the Day of the Lord (see comments at 2:32). By the skillful use of this term, which gives cohesion to his entire message, Joel demonstrated that God is sovereignly operative in all that comes to pass, directing all things to their appointed end.

8. Canonicity and Text

There are no serious problems as to the canonicity and text of Joel. The LXX, Peshitta, and Latin Vulgate versions diverge only slightly from the MT and from one another. The recently found portion of Joel from Wadi Murabba'ât (notice that the twelve Minor Prophets are in the traditional order) stands in the tradition of the MT. The minor additions to the text in the LXX found at 1:5, 8, 18; 2:12; 3:1 are of questionable value. Supposed corruptions in the MT (1:7, 17–18; 2:11; 3:11) are of doubtful status.

9. Bibliography

Books

Allen, Leslie C. *The Books of Joel, Obadiah, Jonah and Micah*. Grand Rapids: Eerdmans, 1976.

Bewer, J.A. et al. *A Critical and Exegetical Commentary on Micah, Zephaniah, Nahum, Habakkuk, Obadiah, Joel, and Jonah*. ICC. Edinburgh: T. & T. Clark, 1912.

Driver, S.R. *The Books of Joel and Amos*. Cambridge: Cambridge University Press, 1915.

Eiselen, F.C. *The Minor Prophets*. New York: Eaton and Mains, 1907.

Gaebelein, A.C. *The Prophet Joel*. New York: Our Hope, 1909.

Kapelrud, A.S. *Joel Studies*. Uppsala: Almquist and Wiksells, 1948.

Keil, C.F. *The Twelve Minor Prophets*. KD. 2 vols. Grand Rapids: Eerdmans, 1949.

Pusey, E.B. *The Minor Prophets*. 2 vols. New York: Funk and Wagnalls, 1886.

Rudolph, Wilhelm. "Ein Beitrag zum hebräischen Lexicon aus dem Joelbuch." *Hebräische Wortforschung*. Edited by G.W. Anderson et al., Leiden: E.J. Brill, 1967, pp. 244–50.

Thompson, John A. *Joel*. IB. New York: Abingdon, 1956.

Wade, G.W. *The Books of the Prophets Micah, Obadiah, Joel, and Jonah*. London: Methuen, 1925.

Wolff, H.W. *Joel and Amos*. Philadelphia, Fortress, 1977.

Periodicals

Driver, G.R. "Linguistic and Textual Problems: Minor Prophets, III. Joel." *Journal of Theological Studies* 15 (1972): 400–402.

Hosch, H. "The Concept of Prophetic Time in the Book of Joel." *Journal of Evangelical Theological Society* (1972): 31–38.

Sellers, O.R. "Stages of Locust in Joel." *American Journal of Semitic Languages and Literatures* 52 (1936): 81–85.

Thompson, John A. "Joel's Locusts in the Light of Near Eastern Parallels." *Journal of Near Eastern Studies* 14 (1955): 52–55.

10. Outline

- I. Joel's Present Instructions: Based on the Locust Plague (1:1–2:27)
  - A. The Occasion: the Locust Plague (1:1–4)
  - B. The Instructions: Based on the Locust Plague (1:5–2:27)
    - 1. Warnings in the light of the present crisis (1:5–20)
      - a. Joel's plea for penitence (1:5–13)
        - 1) A warning to the pleasure seekers (1:5–10)
        - 2) A warning to the farmers (1:11–12)
        - 3) A warning to the priests (1:13)
      - b. Joel's plea for prayer (1:14–20)
        - 1) The call for an assembly (1:14–18)
        - 2) The example to the assembly (1:19–20)
    - 2. Warnings in the light of the coming conflict (2:1–27)
      - a. Joel's plea for preparation (2:1–11)
        - 1) The general conditions (2:1–2a)
        - 2) The coming army (2:2b–11)
      - b. Joel's plea and prescription (2:12–27)
        - 1) The plea to turn to the God of mercy (2:12–14)
        - 2) The call to implore the God of grace (2:15–27)
          - a) The cry of the faithful (2:15–17)
          - b) The response of God (2:18–27)
- II. God's Future Intentions: the Eschatological Program (2:28–3:21)
  - A. The Promise of His Personal Provision (2:28–32)
    - 1. The outpouring of the Spirit (2:28–31)
    - 2. The outworking of salvation (2:32)
  - B. The Prediction of His Final Triumph (3:1–21)
    - 1. The tribulation program (3:1–17)
      - a. The coming of judgment (3:1–8)
        - 1) Its basis (3:1–3)
        - 2) Its execution (3:4–8)
      - b. The challenge in judgment (3:9–17)
        - 1) The call to judgment (3:9–12)
        - 2) The course of judgment (3:13–17)
    - 2. The millennial prosperity (3:18–21)

Text and Exposition

I. Joel's Present Instructions: Based on the Locust Plague (1:1–2:27)

A. *The Occasion: the Locust Plague*

1:1–4

1The word of the LORD that came to Joel son of Pethuel.

2Hear this, you elders;
listen, all who live in the land.
Has anything like this ever happened in your days
or in the days of your forefathers?
3Tell it to your children.
and let your children tell it to their children,
and their children to the next generation.
4What the locust swarm has left
the great locusts have eaten;
what the great locusts have left
the young locusts have eaten;
what the young locusts have left
other locusts have eaten.

1–4 Joel began his prophecy, as did his contemporary Hosea and his later contemporary Micah (and as did Zephaniah in the seventh century), by identifying himself and his lineage. More important, he clearly declared the divine source of his prophecy and the resultant need for readers to heed his utterance. Since the message was God's, not man's, it was to be followed implicitly.

Joel therefore commanded his people—from the eldest citizen downward—to give careful attention to what he had to say. None could recall such an intense and devastating calamity as the locust plague that had fallen on them. For this reason Joel's message and instructions based on the locust plague deserved to be handed down successively to the generations that followed.

Several theories have tried to account for the four different Hebrew words for locusts that appear in v.4. Probably the point is that the various Hebrew words are used to indicate the intensity of the locust plague. There had been a successive series of locusts that had made a thorough devastation of the land, a destruction indicated rhetorically by four distinct names. That there were four successive invasions may bear some relationship to the concept of thorough judgment (notice the four kinds of punishment mentioned in Jer 15:3 and the four types of judgment in Ezek 14:21). Amos, Joel's contemporary, mentioned the utter destruction left behind by a locust plague (Amos 4:9); but he noted that there had been no turning to God by the people of the northern kingdom. Joel recognized the seriousness of the situation. The locusts were God's army in judgment on Judah (cf. 2:25).

Notes

4 All eyewitnesses stress the utter devastation inflicted on the land by locusts—their penetration into every nook and cranny of a field, house, or town—and the helplessness of men to stop them. See the useful excursus in S.R. Driver, pp. 84–92, and J.D. Whiting, "Jerusalem's Locust Plague," *National Geographic Magazine* 28 (1915): 511–50.

B. *The Instructions: Based on the Locust Plague* (1:5–2:27)

1. *Warnings in the light of the present crisis* (1:5–20)

a. *Joel's plea for penitence* (1:5–13)

1) *A warning to the pleasure seekers*

1:5–10

5Wake up, you drunkards, and weep!
Wail, all you drinkers of wine;
wail because of the new wine,
for it has been snatched from your lips.
6A nation has invaded my land,
powerful and without number;
it has the teeth of a lion,
the fangs of a lioness.
7It has laid waste my vines
and ruined my fig trees.
It has stripped off their bark
and thrown it away,
leaving their branches white.

8Mourn like a virgin in sackcloth
grieving for the husband of her youth.
9Grain offerings and drink offerings
are cut off from the house of the LORD.
The priests are in mourning.
those who minister before the LORD.
10The fields are ruined,
the ground is dried up;

the grain is destroyed,
the new wine is dried up,
the oil fails.

5–7 With v.5 begins the first major section of Joel's prophecy. It is marked structurally by the characteristic use of an instructional genre (see Introduction: Literary Form). Thematically it reflects Joel's deep concern that the people of Judah understand the underlying reasons for the locust plague (vv.5–13) and its relation to the future purposes of God for his people (vv.14–20). In the light of the present crisis, Joel called the people to penitence; this unprecedented plague was nothing else but a display of God's judgment (vv.5–13) and a harbinger and dire warning of a still further judgment; therefore, they should pray earnestly (vv.14–20).

Joel began his call for penitence with a solemn warning to the pleasure seekers of his day. Three classes of society were singled out for consideration: the general citizenry (vv.5–10), the husbandmen (vv.11–12), and the priests (v.13). As in the northern kingdom, so in Judah, prosperity had disastrous effects. Despite a basic concern for spiritual things (2 Chron 26:4–5), Uzziah's spiritual progress was not consistent (2 Kings 15:4); and his varied successes were to lead to his downfall (2 Chron 26:2, 6–21). The citizenry, too, no doubt felt the influence of the king. The call for their repentance falls into two sections: vv.5–7 and vv.8–10.

Joel told the populace to awaken from their sleep of drunkenness (cf. Prov 23:35b). In so doing he called attention not only to the debased nature of society but to the people's insensitivity to their own condition, a moral decadence that if unchecked would bring on national disaster. Times of ease too often result in dissipation. The first half of the eighth century B.C. was one of great economic prosperity for both Israel and Judah (see Introduction: Background), but one also of spiritual, moral, and social corruption. The lavish splendor of the northern kingdom has been confirmed by archaeological excavations, particularly at Samaria and Megiddo. Many of the Samaria ostraca deal with receipts of wine, oil, and barley; and the names involved confirm the loss of vital religion.

Joel's contemporaries in the northern kingdom decried the free flow of wine. Hosea complained that wine and fornication had led to spiritual harlotry throughout society (4:11–19; 7:13–14); even the king was addicted to debauchery (7:5). Amos also placed wine among the lists of social evils (2:6–8), calling it the mark of an indolent and selfish luxury that had choked out spiritual concern (6:6). Joel demonstated that the southern kingdom was not much better off, despite its better spiritual heritage.

The fruit of the vine was not itself evil, for it could be a sign of God's blessing (cf. 2:23–24) and was to be used in that high expression of the joy of a life willingly poured out to God, the drink offering (cf. Lev 23:12–13; Num 6:17). What these prophets condemned was the misuse of wine, which led to drunkenness, debauchery, and the resultant loss of spiritual vitality. Their later contemporaries Isaiah and Micah also continued to denounce the wine-drinking habits of the people, complaining that this evil practice had infected every area of life and all levels of society and had led to gross spiritual failure (cf. Isa 5:11–12, 22; 22:13; 28:1, 7; 56:12; Mic 2:11).

Joel pleaded with his hearers to weep and wail with uncontrolled grief concerning the sweet wine that had been cut off from their mouths. The locusts, here likened to a great nation with a powerful and invincible army, had stripped bare the vines and fruit trees of the land. Joel amplified his hearers' need to cry out by describing the voracious locusts as having teeth like those of a lion. The accuracy of Joel's description of the great cutting power of the locusts has often been recorded. Pliny (*Natural History* 1.2.12) reported that they could even gnaw through doors.

All the land lay waste before that hostile army. The vine and the fig tree, symbols of God's blessing on his people (cf. Hos 2:12; Amos 4:9, Mic 4:4 with 1 Kings 4:25 [5:5 MT]; 2 Kings 18:31; cf. also Ps 105:33; Isa 36:16; Jer 5:17; 8:13; Hag 2:19; Zech 3:10), lay stripped even of their bark. All this greatly alarmed the prophet of the Lord. The conditions that necessitated the divine judgment must have grieved even more the Lord himself who still viewed Judah as "my land" (v.6; cf. 2:18; 3:2; Hos 9:1–3).

8–10 Joel had emphasized the seriousness of the cutting off of the source of wine and the attendant economic crisis (vv.5–7; cf. vv.11–12). He reminded them that there were greater issues at stake. Far worse was what the locust plague meant to their spiritual lives. The very worship of God was compromised. This should be a deeper cause of grief. They would no doubt howl over being deprived of their luxuries; far better would it be to imagine the consequences of the disaster from God's point of view.

Joel instructed the citizenry to mourn like an espoused virgin whose intended husband was taken from her before the wedding. How great would be her tragedy and sorrow! So also the people of Judah and Jerusalem should weep over the loss of vital religious experience through the devastation of the land.

The loss of agricultural produce meant the early cessation of the meal and drink offerings. Both were offered in connection with the daily burnt offerings (Exod 29:38–42; Lev 2; 6:14–18; 9:16–17; 23:18, 37; Num 15:5; 28:3–8). These offerings spoke of the very heart of the believer's daily walk before God: the burnt offering, of a complete dedication of life; the meal offering, of the believer's service that should naturally follow; and the drink offering, of the conscious joy in the heart of the believer whose life is poured out in consecrated service to his God.

The observance of these offerings had degenerated in Joel's day into merely routine ritual (cf. Hos 6:6; Amos 4:4–5; cf. also Isa 1:11; Mic 6:6–7). Still worse, the Israelites had made these times an occasion for drunkenness or had even offered the sacrifices to pagan gods (Hos 2:5; Amos 2:8). Therefore, as he had warned, God had taken away the privilege of offering that which symbolized purity of devotion (Hos 2:9–13; 9:1–4). The cutting off of the sacrifices was a severe step of chastisement, but it should have been a warning to the people of their grave condition. The loss of opportunity even to offer the sacrifices should have symbolized to them their breaking of the terms of the covenant bond between themselves and the Lord. Nothing could be more serious!

Joel continued the description of this tragedy by noting that the priests, the ministers of the Lord, were mourning; the once productive fields were utterly laid waste (cf. Mic 2:4); and the very ground, the custodian of the elements necessary for the sacrifice, grieved like the priests (cf. Amos 1:2; cf. also Isa 33:9; Jer 12:4, 11; 23:10).

Grain (i.e., wheat after threshing and separation from the husk), wine (i.e., the freshly squeezed fruit of the vine), and oil (i.e., the fresh juice of the olive) were all chief products in Israel and considered objects of God's blessing (note esp. Num 18:12; Deut 7:13; 11:14; 28:51; 2 Kings 18:32; Jer 31:12; Joel 2:19; Hag 1:11). These blessings, however, could be withdrawn as punishment for their sins (Hos 2:8–13).

Notes

---

8 For בְּתוּלָה (*b*ᵉ*ṯûlāh*, "virgin") as a figure of God's chosen people, see 2 Kings 19:21; Isa 37:22; 62:5; Jer 2:32; 14:17; 18:13; 31:4, 21; Lam 1:15 (cf. 1:18; 2:21); Amos 5:2. For its use with foreign nations, see Isa 23:12; 47:1; Jer 46:11.

בַּעַל נְעוּרֶיהָ (*ba'al n*ᵉ*'ûreyha*, "the possession of her youth") is a picture of the state of betrothal where both bride to be and bridegroom to be were under the same restrictions as husband and wife (cf. Deut 22:23–24; Matt 1:18–19).

10 הוֹבִישׁ (*hôḇîš*, "destroyed") could be from בּוֹשׁ (*bôš*, "to be ashamed," [cf. Lat. *confusum*], as in v.11). But more than likely it is from יָבֵשׁ (*yāḇaš*, "to dry up," as in v.12; cf. LXX *ἐξηράνθη* [exēranthē, "was withered"]). Keil (1:185) suggests that the form is written defectively where the root *bôš* is intended. If so, there is a conscious wordplay in vv.10–12, *bôš* being found in vv.11–12 (second instance) and *yāḇaš* in vv.10, 12 (first instance).

---

2) *A warning to the farmers*

1:11–12

[11]Despair, you farmers,
  wail, you vine growers;
grieve for the wheat and the barley,
  because the harvest of the field is destroyed.
[12]The vine is dried up
  and the fig tree is withered;
the pomegranate, the palm and the apple tree—
  all the trees of the field—are dried up.
Surely the joy of people
  is withered away.

11–12 Joel next turned to the ones who were most directly affected, those who cared for the yield. He called on the farmers and keepers of the vineyard to "despair" (cf. Job 6:20 [NIV, "disappointed"]; Isa 1:29; 20:5) and to "wail" (cf. v.5). The words Joel used signify an intense disappointment that is revealed in a terrified look and a cry of despair (cf. Amos 5:16–17). They were to lament the loss of the products of the field (v.11) and of the vineyard and orchard (v.12).

The vine and the fig tree are first singled out for notice. These were often used to symbolize the blessings of the relationship between God and Israel (see Ps 80:8–15 [9–16 MT]; Isa 5:2–6; Jer 2:21; Mic 4:3–4; Zech 3:10; cf. Matt 21:18–21, 28–46). Joel also mentioned the pomegranate, the palm, and the apple (or apricot) trees, all of which were not only important to the economy but were symbols of spiritual nourishment and refreshment and of the resultant joy and fruitfulness of life in the trusting believer (cf. Deut 8:6–10; Ps 92:12 [13 MT]; S of Songs 2:3). All these trees, so vital to the economy and so expressive of Judah's relation to her God, were withered up. The full joy of life that should have been theirs as God's children had been put to open shame.

Notes

---

12 כִּי (*kî*) is asseverative here; "yea," "surely" (cf. 2:1, 11). For details, see R. Gordis, "Asseverative Kaph in Ugaritic and Hebrew," JAOS 62 (1943): 76–78; M. Dahood, *Psalms III*, AB, pp. 400–406.

---

3) *A warning to the priests*

1:13

[13]Put on sackcloth O priests, and mourn;
  wail, you who minister before the altar.
Come, spend the night in sackcloth,
  you who minister before my God;

for the grain offerings and drink offerings
  are withheld from the house of your God.

13 Joel closed this section with a special plea to the second specially affected segment of society—the priests. They were bidden to gird themselves with sackcloth and to mourn and wail. The prophet had noted their sorrow (cf. vv.8–9). He now demonstrated the urgency of the situation by pleading with them to spend the whole night in their garments of sackcloth in deep contrition and penitence (cf. Esth 4:1–4), because of the loss of the daily sacrifices, the implications of which they should know full well.

b. *Joel's plea for prayer* (1:14–20)

Because the locust plague warned of a still further and more drastic judgment, Joel called for a solemn assembly to meet for prayer (vv.14–18) and then gave an example of a proper heart condition before God (vv.19–20).

1) *The call for an assembly*

1:14–18

14 Declare a holy fast;
  call a sacred assembly.
Summon the elders
  and all who live in the land
to the house of the LORD your God,
  and cry out to the LORD.

15 Alas for that day!
  For the day of the LORD is near;
  it will come like a destruction from the Almighty.

16 Has not the food been cut off
  before our very eyes—
joy and gladness
  from the house of our God?
17 The seeds are shriveled
  beneath the clods.
The storehouses are in ruins,
  the granaries have been broken down,
  for the grain has dried up.
8 How the cattle moan!
  The herds mill about
because they have no pasture;
  even the flocks of sheep are suffering.

14–18 Joel began his plea for prayer by continuing his address to the priests. These spiritual leaders were called on to convene the entire assembly of people at the temple for a solemn fast and a season of heartfelt prayer. The call for national fasting was an extraordinary event (Neh 9:1–3; Jer 36:9). But dreadful times called for decisive measures. It was to be a holy fast, on the part of a solemn assembly. Led by the elders (cf. 1 Kings 21:8–12), all were to come and cry to the Lord (cf. Ezek 30:2–3).

Hosea (7:14) lamented that the people of the northern kingdom did not cry to the

Lord from the heart in their assemblies but gathered themselves together only for the sake of their grain and new wine. Joel's observation was the same. The prophet was concerned that the people give a fervent cry of repentance and call on God for forgiveness, lest a greater judgment descend on them soon.

Joel then proceeded to the reasons for the repentant cry. He warned his hearers most strongly that all the available evidence pointed to the fact that the Day of the Lord stood near at hand. Joel's use of the term here seems clearly related to the historical situation. The locust plague was a dire warning that the day of the Lord's judgment for Judah was imminent.

Amos, Joel's contemporary, viewed the situation in similar terms. He reported that certain "prophets" were under a strange misconception. The Day of the Lord was not to be one of vindication for Israel but was to signal its demise (Amos 5:16–20). Like Joel, Amos warned of judgment due to sin and moral decay (3:1–5:13), a condition that necessitated thorough repentance (5:17). Likewise Hosea's constant message was one of rebuke for Israel's spiritual and moral corruption and of warning of judgment for her spiritual infidelity and sins. Joel's message was in accord with this same picture of life found in the early eighth century B.C.—a scene of spiritual bankruptcy, despite great political and economic assets.

Not only was the Day of the Lord imminent, but it was certain—"like destruction from the Almighty." Joel intended a play on words here. The words "destruction" and "Almighty" are from the same Hebrew root. The verb is also in an unusual position. One might paraphrase thus: "Like a shattering from Shaddai, it will surely come!"

In vv.16–18 Joel gave some added reasons for the call to assemble for penitence and prayer. Their need ought to have been obvious from the terrible conditions that were right before their eyes! Their food had been cut off so that there could be no feasts or offerings of gladness (the words are in emphatic order in the Hebrew sentence). Surely they could see it! Worst of all, it had affected the worship in the house of "our God."

Joel turned from the spiritual realm to the physical world. It, too, was a shambles. The unfructified grains lay shriveled under their hoes, the barns were desolate, and the granaries were trampled down. All the cattle were without pasturage and therefore groaned agonizingly.

Notes

14 By "elders" Joel may have intended those of advanced age (as in v.2) or "elders" in their official capacity (cf. Lev 4:15; 9:1; Deut 21:3–6; 1 Kings 21:8–12) or both.

15 For the Day of the Lord (i.e., God's active judgment against sin and spiritual degradation), see the remarks at 2:28–31.

Several etymologies have been proposed for the divine name אֵל שַׁדַּי (*'ēl šadday*). The older view that derives the second word from a root *šdd* ("to devastate," "to overpower") is perhaps still as good as any. The text here—and in Isa 13:6—demands a relationship between šadday and šdd. The idea behind the root in Akkadian and in Hebrew seems to be that of impelling force, hence, the sovereign, "Almighty God" (cf. LXX *παντοκράτωρ* [*pantokratōr*, Lat. *omnipotens*], "almighty").

17 עָבַשׁ (*'āḇaš*), פְּרֻדָה (*p^eruddāh*), and מֶגְרָפָה (*megrāp̄āh*) are all *hapax legomena* (i.e., they appear only here in the MT). *'Ābaš* appears to be related to the Arabic word for "to shrivel up" (*'abisa*); *p^eruddāh* is possibly related to the Syriac word for "grain" or "parted things" (*perdā'*), though the root bears several meanings in the various Semitic languages. Even a relation with the Egyptian word for "fruit," "seed" (*prt*) is not impossible. *Megrāp āh* is probably related to the Arabic word for "shovel," "rake" (*mijrafatun*), which comes from the Semitic root that means "to sweep away" (*grf*).

מַמְּגֻרוֹת (*mamm^egurôṯ*, "barns") is another seeming *hapax legomenon*. However, the word is probably מְגוּרָה (*m^egûrāh*) as in Hag 2:19, the first mem being either a case of prefixed מִן (*min*, "from," i.e., a partitive use) or an instance of enclitic m (i.e., to be read with the previous word), as H.D. Hummel ("Enclitic *Mem* in early Northwest Semitic," JBL 76 [1957]: 95) has suggested.

18 The three terms for cattle move from cattle in general (בְּהֵמָה, *b^ehēmāh*) to the herds of large (בָּקָר, *bāqār*) and small (צֹאן, *ṣō'n*) cattle. The Semitic inscriptions commonly mention large and small cattle together when meaning all kinds of cattle.

The Hebrew verb נֶאֶנְחָה (*ne'en^eḥāh*, "moan") is related to the Akkadian *ahāḫu* ("to be utterly exhausted from toil"; see A.L. Oppenheim et al., eds., *The Assyrian Dictionary of The Oriental Institute of the University of Chicago* [Chicago: University Press, 1956], pp. 101–5).

נָבֹכוּ (*nāḇōḵû*) is from בּךְ (*bûk*, "to wander aimlessly"). The cattle wander listlessly and frustratedly to and fro (NIV, "mill about") in search of food because there is no pasturage for them.

נֶאְשָׁמוּ (*ne'šāmû*, "suffering") is probably Niphal from אָשַׁם (*'āšam*, "suffer punishment"; see W. Baumgartner, ed., *Hebräisches und aramäisches Lexikon zum Alten Testament*, 3d ed. [Leiden: E.J. Brill, 1967], p. 92), not as mistakenly in KJV from שָׁמֵם (*šāmam*, "be desolate"). All creation is seen as sharing in the results of man's sin (cf. Gen 3:17–18; Jer 12:4; Zeph 1:2–3; Rom 8:19–22).

---

2) *The example to the assembly*

1:19–20

19 To you, O LORD, I call,
for fire has devoured the open pastures
and flames have burned up all the trees of the field.
20 Even the wild animals pant for you;
the streams of water have dried up
and fire has devoured the open pastures.

19–20 The first major section concludes with two examples for the populace: one from the prophet himself (v.19) and the other from the animal creation (v.20). As an example to the people and yet in sincere identification with his own people to whom he had been called to deliver God's message, Joel broke forth in a cry to the Lord who alone could forgive and deliver his people and all creation from this calamity and the still greater one that seemed certain to follow. The prophet spoke of the loss of pasturage as well as of the trees. What the locusts had not destroyed, a severe summer's heat and drought ruined.

Likewise, the beasts of the field made their ascent with longing desire to God. They had to seek higher ground because of the loss of pasture land and because the channels of water had dried up. Joel also intimated that they were more sensitive to the basic issues at hand than were God's own people (cf. Isa 1:3).

The conditions of the land were desperate. In the midst of seemingly unending prosperity, all the land had suffered an unprecedented locust invasion accompanied by a great drought, with the subsequent loss of all harvests. To Joel, God's message was plain. The barrenness of the land reflected the dryness and decay of the hearts of the people. Accordingly, God had judged them. Even the animal world seemed to sense this. How much more should the people! If, however, the hearts of God's people remained unmoved and unrepentant, a worse judgment loomed ahead.

Notes

20 עָרַג (*ʿārag*, "to pant," "to ascend") occurs in the OT only here and twice in Ps 42:1 [2 MT], where also the idea of "ascending" is probably to be understood. This rare word is related to the Ethiopic word for "to ascend" (*ʿärägä*). The full idea in the OT seems to be that of ascending with longing desire and strong impulse.

For the term "streams of water," see W. Leslau, "Observations on Semitic Cognates in Ugaritic," *Orientalia* 37 (1961): 350, who calls it "the innermost part of a valley flowing with water." Thus, because all the water courses—to their very center—had dried up, the beasts of the field had to ascend to the higher lands and reach out in longing desire to God their Provider.

2. Warnings in the light of the coming conflict (2:1–27)

a. *Joel's plea for preparation* (2:1–11)

1) *The general conditions*

2:1–2a

1 Blow the trumpet in Zion;
sound the alarm on my holy hill.
Let all who live in the land tremble,
for the day of the LORD is coming.
It is close at hand—
2 a day of darkness and gloom,
a day of clouds and blackness.

1–2a Several views have been held as to the identification of the locusts of 2:1–11 and their relation to the locust plague of chapter 1. The position taken here is that with the picture of the historical locust plague that he had just experienced vividly before him, and with the warning of judgment firmly in mind (1:15), Joel portrayed a coming army, in particular, that of the Assyrian armies of the eighth and seventh centuries B.C. The appearance and martial activities of the locusts were analogous to those of a real army. In describing throughout the next verses that coming contingent of invaders, Joel maintained the double figure of the locusts and the invading armies: their appearance (vv.2b–5), their operation (vv.6–8), and their effectiveness (vv.9–11). The locust plague of chapter 1 was a precursor of the locustlike plague of the Assyrian armies of chapter 2. The judgment effected by the Assyrian armies was in turn to be a harbinger of a still greater eschatological judgment (2:28–3:21).

That the near historical situation is in view under a double figure is understood from several data. For one thing, the ancient world abounded with examples of likening armies to locusts or vice versa. Indeed, the locust was a common figure of the armies of the Neo-Assyrian kings (see Oppenheim, *Assyrian Dictionary*, "E," pp. 257–58). The fitness of the image is further seen in Joel's account: in the darkening of the day (vv.2, 10), in the suddenness of the locusts' arrival (v.2), in their horselike appearance (v.4), in the orderliness of the battle (vv.7–8), and in the ubiquitous nature of their devastation (vv.3, 9).

Both locusts and armies are known to be the instruments of God's chastening (e.g., Deut 28:38–39; 1 Kings 8:35–39; Isa 45:1; Amos 4:9). Yet, while similar terms are used in connection with both (cf. 1:2 with 2:1; 1:6 with 2:2, 5), the imagery goes beyond a literal locust plague in 2:1–11 (e.g., vv.3, 6, 10), especially as amplified in the details contained in the spiritual challenge based on this event in 2:12–27 (cf. particularly vv.17, 20, 26–27).

Furthermore, the time of 2:1–27 is future to that of chapter 1 but anterior to 2:28–3:21. This is evident from the following:

1. The warning of 2:1 concerning things about to happen and the events of 2:1–27 provide the bases for the further eschatological formulas of 2:28; 3:1; and 3:18.
2. The promised blessings of 2:12–27 are related to the past events of chapter 1 but not to 2:28–32.
3. The terms of 2:2 speak of futurity but not of eternality.
4. The army of chapter 2 is called the "LORD's army" (vv.10–11), but the Assyrian host of a future time stands against the armies of the Lord.
5. Structural considerations also support the time difference.

There is a fundamental difference in the mood and tense of the verbs and in literary structure between the two major sections: 1:1–2:27 and 2:28–3:21 (excluding 3:9–17). All the leading verbs of the sections in 1:1–2:27 are imperative-jussive, while in 2:28–3:21 (excluding 3:9–17) they are both indicative and futuristic. Although there is a closeness in terminology and subject matter in 1:1–2:27 (cf. 1:2, 14 with 2:1; 1:4 with 2:25; 1:5, 10 with 2:19, 24; 1:8 with 2:16; 1:9 with 2:14; 1:9, 13 with 2:17; 1:13–14 with 2:12; 1:14 with 2:15–16; 1:15 with 2:1, 11; 1:19–20 with 2:21–22), an analysis of the verbal usage shows that there is a distinction in time perspective between 1:2–20 and 2:1–27. Thus while only three prefix conjugation verbs occur in chapter 1, none of which is distinctly future, twenty-nine occur in 2:1–27, all of which are futuristic. Accordingly, the weight of evidence, structurally and thematically, would seem to indicate that chapter 1 and 2:1–27 are to be distinguished from 2:28–3:21, yet also from each other. Therefore 2:1–27 is transitional; it builds on and is future to chapter 1 but anterior to 2:28–3:21.

In 2:1–2a Joel saw the invaders spread out before the walls of the city. Therefore he cried, "Blow the trumpet . . . sound the alarm!" The trumpet involved was the *šôpār*, the ceremonial horn. Made from a ram's horn, it was used from earliest times as a signal to battle (e.g., Judg 3:27; 6:34), or (as here) a signal of imminent danger (e.g., Hos 5:8; 8:1; Amos 3:6). The *šôpār* had both sacred and secular uses; its combination with "my holy hill" here stresses the spiritual basis of the war situation.

At the sound of the alarm, all would tremble because of the fearfulness of the events that were to take place. It was the Day of the Lord! That which was viewed as impending (1:15) is now seen as having arrived in all its frightful consequences.

Notes

2 Of the four words used here for the idea of darkness, the first, third, and fourth were used to describe the scene when the children of Israel were encamped at Mount Sinai (Deut 4:11); the first and second portrayed the ninth plague against Egypt (Exod 10:21–22). Zephaniah repeated all four in his description of that future "Day of the LORD" (1:15) as being one of impenetrable darkness.

2) *The coming army*

2:2b–11

Like dawn spreading across the mountains
a large and mighty army comes,
such as never was of old
nor ever will be in ages to come.

3 Before them fire devours,
behind them a flame blazes.
Before them the land is like the garden of Eden,
behind them, a desert waste—
nothing escapes them.
4 They have the appearance of horses;
they gallop along like cavalry.
5 With a noise like that of chariots
they leap over the mountaintops,
like a crackling fire consuming stubble,
like a mighty army drawn up for battle.
6 At the sight of them, nations are in anguish;
every face turns pale.
7 They charge like warriors;
they scale walls like soldiers.
They all march in line,
not swerving from their course.
8 They do not jostle each other;
each marches straight ahead.
They plunge through defenses
without breaking ranks.
9 They rush upon the city;
they run along the wall.
They climb into the houses;
like thieves they enter through the windows.
10 Before them the earth shakes,
the sky trembles,
the sun and moon are darkened,
and the stars no longer shine.
11 The LORD thunders
at the head of his army;
his forces are beyond number,
and mighty are those who obey his command.

The day of the LORD is great;
it is dreadful.
Who can endure it?

2b–3a Having given the characteristic feature of that "day" as one of darkness and gloominess, of clouds and thick darkness (v.2a; cf. Amos 5:18–20), Joel next utilized a series of comparative clauses to describe the enemy army in its arrival and advance (vv.2b–3a), its effect on the land (v.3b), its awesome appearance (vv.4–6), and its sure success (vv.7–11).

With the suddenness of dawn spreading over the tops of the mountains, a mighty army has appeared, which in its terrible battle array cast its shadow over the entire face of the land. Qualitatively and quantitatively this army was unparalleled in the records of the time prior to Joel's day. It would remain unrivaled for more than a century, and even then Assyria's fall would be due as much to inner stresses as to the combined efforts of the Scythians, Medes, and Babylonians.

3b The effect of the invaders' advance was then detailed. That which had been a scene of beauty would become a picture of utter desolation. Nothing in the land would escape.

4–6 A description of the appearance of the locustlike army follows. The double figure of locusts and armies must be kept in mind in reading these words. On the one hand, the locusts had appeared like horses (cf. Job 39:19–20; Rev 9:7). Not only had their swiftness and orderly charge been like that of a well-disciplined cavalry unit, but their very form was horselike. The clamor of the locusts' flight had been like the din of the dreaded war chariot or like the crackling of blazing stubble ignited by a wild fire. The regularity of their advance had been like that of men set in battle array. The awesomeness of their approach had caused great anguish of heart; all in their wake had been terror-stricken and in great fear.

On the other hand, Joel intended his readers to apply the dreadfulness of that past scene a fortiori to the coming devastation to be wrought by the Assyrian army. He noted first the approach of the war horses, then the frightful war chariots as they crested over the mountain passes above the cities of Judah. He compared the swiftness and noise of their advance to wild fire. He noted the uniformity of the charge of the finely trained and unstoppable host. If the locusts had caused terror, how much more the human invaders in their savage and irresistible onslaught!

7–9 The attack of that mighty army was then compared to the ubiquitous nature of a locust swarm. They performed as heroic warriors; keeping their appointed place of service without deviation, they climbed the walls of the city, rushed through its streets, and reached the innermost recesses of every place.

Verse 7 describes the onrush of the mighty men of war, first against, then over the walls. All the while each moved straightforward (cf. Josh 6:5), holding his rank and course. Having reiterated the unity and harmony of action among the soldiers, Joel next depicted (v.8) the invincibility of the invading soldiers as they unswervingly continued through the city's defenses.

Verse 9 describes the power and swiftness of their attack: they rushed unrestrictedly to and fro through the city; they ran along the tops of its walls; and they scaled up the house walls and entered in at the open or latticed windows in search of their prey with the speed and daring of a thief in search of that which is not his.

10–11 Joel brought this section to a close by explaining this army's sure success. Its leader was none other than the omnipotent and sovereign God himself. Utilizing epithets that were well-known to every Israelite since the days of the Exodus experience, Joel depicted God as moving with great might before the Assyrian host, "his army." There were signs on earth—a great shaking—and heaven—the luminaries darkened. Before the advancing army the thunderstorm raged. The sight of the Assyrian host ought to have been enough to strike terror into the hearts of men. The accompanying signs of God's visible presence leading that powerful battle array would melt the stoniest of hearts. It was nothing else than the day of the Lord's judgment against his own. Who could endure his visitation?

Notes

2b עַד־שְׁנֵי דּוֹר וָדוֹר (*'ad-šᵉnê dôr wāḏôr,* "in ages to come") is probably deliberately used to differentiate it from the usual דֹּר וָדֹר (*dōr wāḏōr,* "forever"). Like the Akkadian (*ana*) *dār(iš) šatti,* the primary emphasis is probably on continuance or permanence, not necessarily on eternality. Pusey is on the right track in translating the term "For the years of many generations."

4 That Sennacherib failed to take Jerusalem in his third campaign (the inevitable coup de grâce was left to the Neo-Babylonian Nebuchadnezzar) is beside the point. Sennacherib reported that he had thoroughly devastated the land, though admitting that he had failed to take Jerusalem: "He himself [i.e., Hezekiah], like a caged bird, I enclosed him in Jerusalem, his royal city" (*Assyrian Annals* 3.18–49, in R. Borger, *Babylonish-Assyrische Lesestücke* [Rome: Pontificum Institutum Biblicum, 1963], 3, table 46). The resemblance of locusts to horses has occasioned both the Italian (*cavalletta,* "little horse") and German (*heupferd,* "hay horse") terms for locusts.

5 The Assyrian war chariot was a dreaded item. Sennacherib's own special war chariot was named *sāpinat raggi u ṣēni* ("The Vanquisher of the Wicked and Evil") and *sāpinat zāiri* ("The Vanquisher of the Enemy") (*Assyrian Annals* 5.70).

6 The word translated "anguish" (חוּל, *ḥûl*) is a strong one. It is used of the anguish of a woman in travail (Isa 13:8; 26:17; Mic 4:9–10), of the Canaanites who trembled before the Israelites (Deut 2:25), of the dread of the Egyptians before the Babylonian invasion (Ezek 30:16), and of the fear of the Babylonians before the oncoming assault of the Medes and Persians (Jer 51:29). The terrifying aspects of the approach of the Assyrian army are often mentioned in the *Assyrian Annals*.

קִבְּצוּ פָארוּר (*qibbᵉṣû pā'rûr,* "turns pale") is a rare (only here and Nah 2:11 in the OT) and difficult phrase. Nearly every etymology for the Hebrew consonants involved in the word *pā'rûr* has been conjectured. In the light of current research, the possibility of dividing the word into the conjunction "p" and some understanding of the Semitic root *'ārar* cannot be ruled out a priori. The translation suggested here for this commentary has followed the lead of most modern expositors in deriving the word from the root *p'r* ("to beautify," "to glorify").

7 יְעַבְּטוּן (*yᵉ'abbᵉṭûn,* "swerving") has proven to be troublesome. Two possibilities commend themselves. (1) A. Guillaume, *Hebrew and Arabic Lexicography* (Leiden: E.J. Brill, 1965), 2:27, suggests a relation to the Arabic *'abaṭa* ("to go off the middle of the road"); or (2) the Hebrew word may be understood in the sense of "to hold to." Thus taking the Hebrew לֹא (*lō',* "not"), not as a negative, but as the asseverative particle לוּ (*lû,* "yea," "indeed"), the whole line would read "And each marches on his own way; yea, they hold to their own paths." That *lō'* occurs in the next verse as the regular negative particle is no argument against its being an asseverative particle here; for in 2 Sam 18:12 it occurs twice, once with asseverative emphasis and once as a negative. For an excellent discussion of the verb involved, see J.C. Greenfield, "Studies in Aramaic Lexicography I,"

JAOS 82 (1962): 295–96. On the problem of *lō'*, see D. Rudolf Meyer, *Hebräische Grammatik*, 2 vols. (Berlin: de Gruyter, 1969), 2:173.

8 The Hebrew word שֶׁלַח (*šelaḥ*, "defense") poses still another knotty problem. While it occurs in six other places in the OT (2 Chron 23:9–10; 32:5; Neh 4:17 [11 MT], 23 [17 MT]; Job 33:18; 36:12), the exact meaning has eluded exegetes in all ages. Either some weapon, such as the lance, or a watercourse or a defensive wall makes good sense here; perhaps the former is preferable in the light of the verbs that follow. For details see S. Yeivin, "שֶׁלַח," *Leshonenu* 15 (1947): 134–44; S.E. Lowenstamm, "וּבְעַד הַשֶּׁלַח," *Leshonenu* 28 (1961): 62.

10 The motif of shaking the physical world was a familiar one to the Jews (cf. Judg 5:4–5; Ps 18:7 [8 MT]=2 Sam 22:8; Isa 13:13; Amos 8:8; Nah 1:5). It was no doubt part of an early Hebrew epic, singing God's redemptive work in the movement from Egypt to the Jordan River, that is reflected not only in the extended accounts in Exod 15:1–18 and Hab 3:2b–15 but in remembrance scattered throughout the OT (e.g., Num 23:22; 24:8; Deut 33:1–2a; Judg 5:4–5; Ps 18:7–15[8–16 MT]=2 Sam 22:8–16; 68:7[8 MT]; 77:16–18[17–19 MT]; 144:5–6). For the darkened celestial luminaries, see also Isa 13:10; Ezek 32:7; Amos 8:9.

11 Assyria's prominence at the time of the Jews' spiritual decay also stands prophetically as a type of the powers that will oppose the Lord and his army in the last days and which Christ will destroy at his coming (see Isa 10:27–34; 14:24–27; 30:31–33; 31:8–9[?]; Mic 5:5–6; Zeph 2:13–15; cf. Zech 12:2–3; 14:1–4; Rev 19:17–21).

---

b. *Joel's plea and prescription* (2:12–27)

1) *The plea to turn to the God of mercy*

2:12–14

12 "Even now," declares the LORD,
"return to me with all your heart,
with fasting and weeping and mourning."

13 Rend your heart
and not your garments.
Return to the LORD your God,
for he is gracious and compassionate,
slow to anger and abounding in love,
and he relents from sending calamity.
14 Who knows but that he may turn and have pity
and leave behind a blessing—
grain offerings and drink offerings
for the LORD your God.

12–14 In the light of the impending day of the Lord, Joel turned to admonish the people to pray. He first pled with each Israelite to come with a repentant heart to the God of all mercy (vv.12–14). He then renewed his call for a holy assembly to implore fervently the God of grace to have mercy on his repentant people (vv.15–27).

By means of the introductory phrase " 'Even now,' declares the LORD," Joel presented God's own deep concern for his people. Like his contemporaries, Joel emphasized the need to turn to God in true repentance and in total reliance on the God of all mercies, turning from their past inequities, recognizing that the repentant heart is the only soil in which the regenerated soul can grow.

Joel pled with the people for broken and contrite hearts (cf. Ps 51:17 [19 MT]). Important as outward conformity to worship form might be, the heart condition is still more important to God (cf. Isa 1:11–17; 58:3b–12; Amos 5:21–24; Mic 6:6–8).

After reiterating his plea, Joel gave the grounds for its acceptance: God is a God of grace and mercy. Not only does God have compassion for all in their need (cf. Jonah 4:2), but he is a God of love who has revealed himself to man in redemptive grace (cf. Exod 34:6). This is the height of God's compassion; it ascends to himself. The length of that compassion is given next: he is slow to anger. The breadth of that compassion follows: he is abundant in his righteous concern for man's spiritual welfare. The depth of his compassion is seen in his willingness to reach down in forgiveness to man in his evil condition: "He relents from sending calamity."

Since the promise of judgment is conditioned on man's failure to meet God's standards, for man to repent and meet God in his gracious provision for him is to avert the just judgment of God. From man's point of view, God would seem to have "changed his mind" or "feelings" or "repented concerning the evil" (cf. KJV, i.e., the punishment for man's guilt; cf. Exod 32:14; 2 Sam 24:16). God might even restore the forfeited blessings and the fertility of the land so that the discontinued sacrifices might again be offered, this time out of a pure heart.

2) *The call to implore the God of grace* (2:15–27)

a) *The cry of the faithful*

2:15–17

15Blow the trumpet in Zion,
declare a holy fast,
call a sacred assembly.
16Gather the people,
consecrate the assembly;
bring together the elders,
gather the children,
those nursing at the breast.
Let the bridegroom leave his room
and the bride her chamber.
17Let the priests, who minister before the LORD,
weep between the temple porch and the altar.
Let them say, "Spare your people, O LORD.
Do not make your inheritance an object of scorn,
a byword among the nations.
Why should they say among the peoples,
'Where is their God?' "

15–17 Joel issued another call for a solemn assembly (cf. 1:14). Once again the *šô-pār* was to sound (cf. 2:1), this time to convene the assembly in the light of the revealed invasion that stood so near. All were to come, from the elders with their wise counsel (cf. 1:14), to the youngest suckling. All must meet with God and listen to his commandments and act on them, as was their privilege and responsibility as members of the assembly. Even the newlyweds, who might otherwise be legitimately exempted from such duties (Deut 24:5), were to be in attendance.

The priests were to be the first to experience repentance in their lives. Then they were to lead the people, standing between the vestibule on the east side of the temple (1 Kings 6:3) that separated the inner or priests' court (1 Kings 6:36) from the great court of the laity (2 Chron 4:9) and the brazen altar of burnt offering that lay within the inner court. The main business was to implore the God of all grace to spare his people, not only for their good, but, more important, that his inheritance be not a reproach before the world or his name be brought into disrepute because of what they had done.

b) *The response of God*

2:18–27

18Then the LORD will be jealous for his land
and take pity on his people.
19The LORD will reply to them:
"I am sending you grain, new wine and oil,
enough to satisfy you fully;
never again will I make you
an object of scorn to the nations.

20"I will drive the northern army far from you,
pushing it into a parched and barren land,
with its front columns going into the eastern sea
and those in the rear into the western sea.
And its stench will go up;
its smell will rise."

Surely he has done great things.
21 Be not afraid, O land;
be glad and rejoice.
Surely the LORD has done great things.
22 Be not afraid, O wild animals,
for the open pastures are becoming green.
The trees are bearing their fruit;
the fig tree and the vine yield their riches.
23Be glad, O people of Zion,
rejoice in the LORD your God,
for he has given you
the autumn rains in righteousness.
He sends you abundant showers,
both autumn and spring rains, as before.
24The threshing floors will be filled with grain;
the vats will overflow with new wine and oil.

25"I will repay you for the years the locusts have eaten—
the great locust and the young locust,
the other locusts and the locust swarm—
my great army that I sent among you.
26You will have plenty to eat, until you are full,
and you will praise the name of the LORD your God,
who has worked wonders for you;
never again will my people be shamed.
27Then you will know that I am in Israel,
that I am the LORD your God,
and that there is no other;
never again will my people be shamed.

18–19 Based on the fulfillment of his previous instructions regarding repentance and worship (vv. 12–17), God promised that he would have pity on his people (v. 18), would restore that which they had lost (v.19), and would take away the invading army from them (v.20) so that neither land nor cattle nor Zion herself need again have any fear (vv.21–22). Rather, they would be given righteousness (v.23a), refreshment (v.23b), and regular provision (vv.24–25), and thus experience satiety (v.26a) so that they could praise the Lord (v.26b) and know the security that he alone can give (v.27).

God promised to the repentant heart that his godly jealous love (as a husband for his wife) would move him to have pity on his people. His first promise was twofold: he would immediately restore all that had been lost in the locust plague, so necessary for their daily lives, physically (1:11–12) and spiritually (1:9); and they would be fully satisfied (cf. Deut 6:10–11; 8:7–10; 11:13–15). His second promise was that they would no longer be a reproach among the nations.

20 As the third of his promises, God pledged that he would take away from the people "the northern army" (lit., "the northerner"), a term that has been understood variously. When the term is interpreted in the light of the context and structure of chapter 2, the most adequate view sees it as referring to a foreign invader (i.e., the Assyrians) descending from the north. This prediction is built on the incident of the locust plague.

God promised through Joel that he would drive that enemy far away, if only the people would turn to him in genuine repentance. He would drive that army into a dry and desolate land, no doubt primarily the desert west of the Dead Sea and south and southeast of Judah.

A further reason for this turned-about condition, despite her being the Lord's army, would be that Assyria's haughty pride would cause her to leave her proper bounds (cf. Pss 35:26; 38:16 [17 MT]; cf. also Lam 1:9), thus bragging and assuming that the great destruction she would effect would be her own doing (similarly, cf. Ezek 35:13; Dan 8:4, 8, 11; 11:36–37).

21–27 Joel continued to give God's response. Should the people truly repent, not only would God's promises of restoration, rest, and protection be theirs, but certain additional benefits would accrue. The message was one of comfort: "Be not afraid."

The first object of God's consoling words was the ground—that which had directly suffered so much. It was not to fear but to rejoice and be glad (cf. 1:16); for God himself, the one who truly does great things (2:20; cf. 1 Sam 12:24; Ps 126:2–5), would undertake for it.

Next, God's comfort was directed to beasts of the field (cf. 1:18–20). They would have an abundance of tender grass. Furthermore, the fig tree and the vine (cf. 1:7, 12), the symbols of Israel's restored relation with her sovereign Lord, would bear again in full strength. This thought led Joel to the third and central object of divine solace: Israel herself (v.23). The "people of Zion" (i.e., all true Israelites; cf. Ps 149:2) were to rejoice and be glad in the Lord their God, for he would restore them in righteousness. He would send again the refreshing former and latter rains, thus speaking to them of his renewed care for his people.

The careful play on words in the Hebrew text has caused a great deal of discussion. The twice-occurring Hebrew word *môreh* can be translated "rains" (as in NIV). It may also be translated "teacher" (NIV mg.); and with the *liṣḏāqāh* (lit., "for righteousness") that follows, the first *môreh* has been understood by some to refer to God's righteous prophets or to the Messiah himself.

However, there is another alternative. One may take the first *môreh* (lit., *hammôreh,* i.e., with the definite article) in accordance with its basic construction as a participle, rather than as a noun, and view the construction impersonally. The verse would then be translated thus: "For he [God] will give to you that which gives instruction in righteousness, that is, he will send down to you the early and latter rain, as before." That this is the proper interpretation may be seen from the following reasons.

1. A wordplay is clearly intended. The correct reading of the second *môreh* may actually be *yôreh,* as is read in some thirty-four MSS; this seems to be the proper word for "early rain" (cf. Deut 11:14). The wordplay would thus be between *hammôreh,* "that which gives instruction" and *yôreh,* "early rain."

2. The conjunction that follows *hammôreh* is to be understood pleonastically, "yea," "for," or as an explicative, "that is." Thus that which follows identifies that which gives instruction in righteousness, namely, the renewed sending of the early and latter rains.

3. The renewed rain thus becomes another outward symbol of an inward reality, a restored fellowship with God. Since the signs of the covenant—the offerings—had been cut off in God's judgment through the locust plague, repentance of heart would bring restoration of fellowship, hence restoration of the covenant privileges. The rains would serve as the sign of God's forgiveness and provision, not only for their daily necessities, but of the revitalized earth that would enable the forfeited right to offer sacrifices to be regained (cf. Deut 6:24–25; 2 Chron 6:26–27; 7:14; Mal 3:3).

The "autumn rain" comes at the beginning of the rainy season in October-November; the "spring rain" is that of March-April. The arrival of these rains on proper schedule as in prior times would demonstrate the blessing of God on the heart that was now properly prepared before him (cf. Deut 11:13–17; Jer 5:24–25; Hos 6:1–3).

Joel next mentioned God's supplying the people's third need. Not only would he give renewed fellowship (v.23a) and renewed rain (v.23b) but also renewed provisions (vv.24–25). Their threshing floors would be filled with grain, their collecting vats would overflow with fresh wine and oil, and God would thoroughly restore to them the years that the devastating plague had caused them to lose (cf. 1:4, 10, 17; 2:19). Whereas the locust plague had brought on famine, the people would now experience the full satisfaction of an abundance of food (cf. 2:19). Therefore they could praise God in the full knowledge of all that his revealed name signifies (cf. Exod 6:3; Deut 12:7; Pss 8:1–2; 66:8–15; 67:5–7; Amos 5:8–9; 9:5–6).

The restored fellowship would be attested by God's renewed designation of them as "my people." They need never again "be humiliated," whether by locusts (1:11), among the heathen (2:17), or before the whole world (cf. Isa 29:22; 49:22–23; 54:4). No, never again! Best of all, his people would know experientially the abiding presence of God himself, dwelling in their midst (cf. 2:17; 3:17, 21; Hos 11:9; cf. also Ezek 48:35).

Notes

---

23 The only other occurrence of מורה (*môreh*) in the sense of "autumn and spring rains" is in a difficult text (Ps 84:6 [7 MT]) and is by no means certain. Rudolph also takes the term impersonally but points the preceding אֶת (*'eṯ*), the mark of the definite direct object, as *'ôṯ*, ("sign") and translates the phrase "The sign that points to salvation."

24 The יֶקֶב (*yeqeḇ*, "wine vat"; i.e., the place in which the juice collected) is to be contrasted with the גַּת (*gaṯ*, "vat"—cf. 3:13[4:13 MT]—i.e., the place where the fruit was trodden). The *yeqeḇ* was usually hewn out of rock and stood below the *gaṯ* to which it was connected by a channel.

26 By שֵׁם (*šēm*, "name") is intended the revealed character and reputation of God. The term came to be substituted for God himself (Dan 9:18–19; Amos 2:7; 9:12) and became applied to Christ in the NT (e.g., Acts 4:12; 5:41; 3 John 7) and was so used by the apostolic fathers.

II. God's Future Intentions: the Eschatological Program (2:28–3:21)

A. *The Promise of His Personal Provision* (2:28–32)

1. *The outpouring of the Spirit*

2:28–31

28"And afterward,
I will pour out my Spirit on all people.
Your sons and daughters will prophesy,
your old men will dream dreams,
your young men will see visions.
29Even on my servants, both men and women,
I will pour out my Spirit in those days.
30I will show wonders in the heavens
and on the earth,
blood and fire and billows of smoke.
31The sun will be turned to darkness
and the moon to blood
before the coming of the great and dreadful day
of the LORD.

28–31 The introductory formula with which this section begins clearly places the events that follow it after those detailed in 2:1–27. Since the previous section dealt with the near future, it may be safely presumed that the events prophesied here lay still farther beyond. Indeed, these chapters disclose the Lord's eschatological intentions. Two primary thoughts are included: the Lord's promise of personal provision in the lives of his own (2:28–32) and the prediction of his final triumph on behalf of his own at the culmination of the history of mankind (ch. 3).

The Lord first promised that he would pour out his Spirit in full abundance and complete refreshment. Hosea, Joel's contemporary, prophesied that the Lord must pour out his fury on an idolatrous Israel (5:10); Joel saw beyond this chastisement to the chastisement in the distant future (cf. Ezek 36:16–38), when in a measure far more abundant than the promised rain (cf. 2:22–26) God would pour out his Holy Spirit in power. In those days (cf. Jer 33:15) that power would rest on all (i.e., human) flesh (cf. Isa 40:5–6; 66:23; Zech 2:12–13 [16–17 MT]).

God's covenant people were primarily in view. Joel went on to point out that what the Lord intended is that his Holy Spirit would be poured out, not on selected individuals for a particular task, but on all believers, young and old, male and female alike, regardless of their status. It would be a time of renewed spiritual activity: of prophesying, of dreams, and of visions (cf. Num 12:6).

Accompanying the outpouring of the Holy Spirit in those days and as visible signs of his supernatural and overseeing intervention in the history of mankind, God will cause extraordinary phenomena to be seen in nature. Thus the totality of man's experience will be affected. Although the heavens are mentioned first (v.30a), the order that follows (vv.30b–31) is one of ascending emphasis, beginning with events on earth (blood, fire, and smoke) and moving to signs in the sky (the sun and the moon).

The earthly phenomena are no doubt principally concerned with the sociopolitical upheaval in that day: the blood and fire referring to warfare (cf. Num 21:28; Ps 78:63; Isa 10:16; 26:11; Zech 11:1; cf. also Rev 8:8–9; 14:14–20; 16:4–9; 19:1–18) and the rising smoke to gutted cities (cf. Judg 20:38–40)—though God's activity in the natural world may also play a part (cf. Exod 19:9, 16–18; Rev 6:12–17). These, it should be noted, are to be recognized as well-known signs of the presence of a holy God in his superintending activity (for blood, cf. Exod 7:17; 12:22–23; for fire, cf. Exod 3:2–3; 13:21–22; 19:18; Isa 4:4; Ezek 1:27; Dan 7:9; Zech 2:5; Acts 2:3; Heb 12:18; Rev 1:14; for smoke, cf. Exod 19:16–18; Isa 4:4–5; 6:4; Rev 15:8). The very signs speak of a redeemed and refined people eager to do God's will and to carry his message to a needy generation standing under his just judgment.

The heavenly phenomena are also portents of a miraculous nature. There will be a full eclipse of the sun by day (cf. 3:15; Amos 5:18–20; 8:9; Zeph 1:15); by night the moon will appear to be blood red, perhaps due to conditions caused by an accompanying earthquake (cf. Jer 4:23–24; Rev 6:12–13). All these will signal the advent of that great and terrible Day of the Lord. If the Day of the Lord in the Assyrian invasion would be "great" and "dreadful" (2:11), how much more the eschatological time designated "the great and dreadful day of the LORD"?

As was pointed out in the discussion at 1:15, the term "the Day of the Lord" deals with judgment. This is particularly true in the case of the enemies of Israel, whether Babylon (Isa 13:6, 9), Egypt (Jer 46:10; Ezek 30:2–4), Edom (Obad 15), or all nations (Joel 3:14–15; Obad 15; Zeph 1:14–18; Zech 14:3–15; Mal 4:5–6 [3:23–24 MT]; 1 Thess 5:2; 2 Thess 2:2; 2 Peter 3:10). It can also be true for Israel-Judah (Isa 2:12–22; Ezek 13:5; Joel 1:15; 2:1, 11; Amos 5:18–20; Zeph 1:7; Zech 14:1–2).

As to the time of judgment, it could be present (Joel 1:15), lie in the near future (Isa 2:12–22; Jer 46:10; Ezek 13:5; Joel 2:1, 11; Amos 5:18–20), be future-eschatological (Isa 13:6, 9; Ezek 30:2–3; Obad 15; Zeph 1:7, 14–18; Mal 4:1–6 [3:19–24 MT]), or be purely eschatological (Joel 3:14–15; Zech 14:1–21; 1 Thess 5:1–11; 2 Thess 2:2; 2 Peter 3:10–13).

The Day of the Lord, eschatologically speaking, also deals with deliverance for a regathered, repentant Israel (Joel 2:31–32; 3:16–21; Zech 14:3; Mal 4:5–6).

Theologically, the scope of these passages makes it clear that the eschatological Day of the Lord begins with the seventieth week of Daniel (Dan 9:24–27)—that great tribulational period of Israel's affliction (Deut 4:30; Isa 24–27; Dan 12:1; Matt 24:15–28; Rev 12) and of earth's judgment (Isa 13:9, 13; 26:20–21; Rev 6; 8–11; 14:14–16:21)—and closes with the return of the Lord in glory (Rev 19:11–16) and the Battle of Armageddon (Rev 16:16; 19:17–21; cf. Ezek 38–39). That day continues through the Millennium and its related events (e.g., Isa 2:1–4; 11:1–12:6; Mic 4:1–5; Rev 20) and culminates in the eternal state (2 Peter 3:10–13; Rev 21–22).

Joel's use of the term, then, is in harmony with the totality of Scripture. By "the day of the LORD" is meant that time when, for his glory and their good, God actively intervenes in the affairs of men in judgment against sin and in connection with his determined will for his own.

2. *The outworking of salvation*

2:32

> 32And everyone who calls
> on the name of the LORD will be saved;
> for on Mount Zion and in Jerusalem
> there will be deliverance,
> as the LORD has said,
> among the survivors
> whom the LORD calls.

32 Along with the outpouring of the Holy Spirit, there will be the outworking of salvation for him who truly trusts God as his Redeemer. To "call on the name of the LORD" is to invoke his name in approaching him (cf. Gen 4:26; 12:8), but especially to call on him in believing faith (Pss 99:6; 145:18; Rom 10:13). For such a one there will be not only physical deliverance but a spiritual transformation and an abundant entrance into that great millennial period of peace and prosperity, when a repentant Judah and Jerusalem are once again spiritual centers for a redeemed Israel (cf. Hos 3:5; Mic 4:6–8).

Joel closed the chapter by balancing this thought with another truth. While salvation-deliverance will be the experience of the one who truly "calls on the name of the LORD" (cf. 2:26) in that day, it is God himself who will summon that remnant.

Before leaving this chapter, we must briefly examine the problem of the citation of these words by Peter in his famous address at Pentecost (Acts 2:17–21). While several theories have been advanced as to the relation between these two passages of Scripture, the position taken here attempts to strike a balance between the extreme views of a total fulfillment at Pentecost and the complete lack of any relationship at all.

Although the full context of Acts 2 does not exhaust the larger context of Joel 2:28–3:21 [3:1–4:21 MT], we can scarcely doubt that Peter viewed Joel's prophecy as applicable to Pentecost because he plainly said that such was the case (Acts 2:16). Moreover, both his sermon and subsequent remarks are intimately intertwined with Joel's message (e.g., cf. Joel 2:30–31 [3:3–4 MT] with Acts 2:22–24; Joel 2:32 [3:5 MT] with Acts 2:38–40).

The precise applicability of Joel's prophecy to Pentecost can be gleaned from some of the Petrine interpretative changes and additions to Joel's text. Thus under divine inspiration Peter added to Joel's words relative to the outpouring of the Holy Spirit *kai prophēteusousin* ("and they will prophesy"; cf. Joel 2:29 [3:2 MT] with Acts 2:18). The intent of Joel's prophecy was not only the restoration of prophecy but that such a gift was open to all classes of mankind. The spirit-empowered words of the apostles on Pentecost were, therefore, evidence of the accuracy of Joel's prediction. (They were also a direct fulfillment of Christ's promise to send the Holy Spirit; see Luke 24:49; John 14:16–18; 15:26–27; 16:7–15; Acts 1:4–5, 8; 2:33.)

Again, Peter affirmed that Joel's more general term *'aḥᵃrê-kēn* ("afterward") is to be understood as *en tais eschatais hēmerais* ("in the last days"; cf. Joel 2:28 [3:1 MT] with Acts 2:17). The NT writers made it clear that both Israel's future age and the church age are designated by the same terms: "The Last [Latter] Days [Times]" (1 Tim 4:1; 2 Tim 3:1–8; Heb 1:1–2; James 5:3; 1 Peter 1:5, 20; 4:7; 2 Peter 3:1–9; 1 John 2:18; Jude 18). Accordingly, the point of Peter's remark in Acts 2:16 must be that Pentecost, as the initial day of that period known as "The Last [Latter] Days," which will culminate in those events surrounding the return of Jesus the Messiah, partakes of the character of those final events and so is a herald and earnest of what surely must come. Pentecost, then, forms a corroborative pledge in the series of fulfillments that will culminate in the ultimate fulfillment of Joel's prophecy in the eschatological complex.

It must also be noted that the outpouring of the Spirit is an accompanying feature of that underlying basic divine promise given to Abraham and the patriarchs, ratified through David, reaffirmed in the terms of the new covenant, and guaranteed in the person and work of Jesus the Messiah (cf. Gen 12:1–3; 15; 17; 2 Sam 7:11–29; Ps 89:3–4, 27–29 [4–5, 28–30 MT]; Jer 31:31–34; Acts 2:29–36; 26:6–7; Gal 3:5–14; Eph 1:10–14; Heb 6:13–20; 9:15).

At Pentecost, then, two tributary streams of prophecy met and blended together: Christ's prophetic promise was directly fulfilled; Joel's prophecy was fulfilled but not consummated. It awaits its ultimate fulfillment but was provisionally applicable to Pentecost and the ages of the Spirit as the initial step in those last days that will culminate in the prophesied miraculous signs heralding the Day of the Lord and the events distinctive to the nation of Israel. (For the concept of "fulfillment without consummation," see R.T. France, *Jesus and the Old Testament* [London: Tyndale, 1971], pp. 160–62.) Meanwhile, like an ever-rolling river, the central current of God's basic promise sweeps steadily onward toward that final shore where the Great Controller of the flow of earth's history shall gather up all the various waves of prophecy to himself in complete fulfillment. (See further, W. Kaiser, "The Old Promise and the New Covenant: Jeremiah 31:31–34," JETS 15 [1972]: 11–23.)

Notes

32 The "survivors" are God's elect remnant of Jews whom he will regather to his land and who will turn to their Messiah and enter into the millennial kingdom (Isa 10:20–23; 11:11–16; Jer 23:1–18; 31:1–14, 27–37; Ezek 11:13–20; Amos 5:15; Mic 2:12–13; 4:1–8; 5:7–8 [6–7 MT]; 7:18–20; Zeph 2:7–9; 3:9–20; Zech 8:6–8; cf. Rom 11:4–5). On the remnant, see the interesting discussion of R. de Vaux, "The 'Remnant of Israel' according to the Prophets," *The Bible and the Ancient Near East* (Garden City: Doubleday, 1971), p. 28.

B. *The Prediction of His Final Triumph* (3:1–21)

1. *The tribulation program* (3:1–17)

a. *The coming of judgment* (3:1–8)

1) *Its basis*

3:1–3

1"In those days and at that time,
when I restore the fortunes of Judah and Jerusalem,
2I will gather all nations
and bring them down to the Valley of Jehoshaphat.
There I will enter into judgment against them
concerning my inheritance, my people Israel,
for they scattered my people among the nations
and divided up my land.
3They cast lots for my people
and traded boys for prostitutes;
they sold girls for wine
that they might drink.

1–3 Chapter 2 ends with blessings and safety for the believer of the future. The third chapter begins with a warning of judgment. The basis of that judgment is stated first (vv. 1–3); the sure execution of that judgment follows (vv. 4–8).

In contrast with what has gone before, Joel now has a new and important announcement. In those future times (cf. 2:29) in which God deals kindly with his covenant people (cf. Jer 33:15–18), he will gather all nations together (cf. Zeph 3:8) and enter into judgment with them in the Valley of Jehoshaphat concerning the treatment of his own (cf. Rom 11:25–26).

The words "I restore the fortunes" lend themselves to two basic meanings.

1. The translation of the KJV—"I shall bring again the captivity"—is supported by the ancient versions (LXX, Syr.) and by such texts as Deuteronomy 30:3; Jeremiah 29:14; 30:3; 33:7, 11, 26 mg.; Zephaniah 3:20 (cf. Pss 14:7; 53:6 [7 MT]).

2. The rendering adopted here (cf. NASB) appears to be appropriate also in Hosea (6:11) and Amos (9:14 mg.). The latter idea includes the former and also involves the idea of Israel's renewed prosperity and felicitude. Since Joel's contemporaries seem to have used the term in this way, and because many of the passages in Jeremiah (e.g., 30:18; 31:23 mg.; 32:44) can also bear this more comprehensive idea, it seems to be the better understanding of the words involved.

Judah and Jerusalem will once again be the center of God's attention. The time involved in vv. 1–17 is that of the Great Tribulation, that period of Jacob's trouble (cf. Jer 30:7 with Matt 24:21; Mark 13:19, 24) and of great affliction for Israel (Deut 4:30; Dan 12:1), a period culminated by God's outpoured wrath against the sinful nations of earth (Isa 13:9, 13; 26:20–21; Zeph 1:15–18; Rom 2:5–10; 1 Thess 1:10; 5:10–11; 2 Thess 1:6–7; Rev 6:16–17; 11:18; 14:10; 16:19; 19:15) and the return of Christ in glory and to judgment (Matt 24:27–31; Mark 13:24–27; Rev 19:11–21).

Joel's words are those of assurance: even in those dire times, the immutable God is still on the throne, directing all things to their appointed end (cf. Mic 4:11–12).

While several views exist as to the words of the Hebrew text of "The Valley of

Jehoshaphat," one must conclude that the primary idea here has to do with a place where God enters into judgment with the nations, not a known valley, as the wordplay makes clear (i.e., "The valley of judgment," "I will judge," cf. v.12). Joel subsequently called it "the valley of decision" (v.14).

Kapelrud is no doubt correct in pointing out that there was a valley tradition in Israel with regard to battles of judgment. Nothing could be more natural in the light of the topography of the land of Canaan. Jeremiah told of the "Valley of Ben [Sons of] Hinnom" (7:30–34; 19:1–7) that became the "Valley of Slaughter." Isaiah spoke of the "Valley of Vision" in a message of judgment against Israel (Isa 22:1–13). Ezekiel (39:11) prophesied against the valley of the *'ob̠erîm* ("those who travel"), which will form the burial ground for the defeated northern foes and will become the "Valley of Hamon Gog."

Zechariah's valley (14:3–5), too, is connected with the Lord's judgment against the nations in a great battle. However, as the prophecy in Zechariah makes clear, the motif of a valley tradition can be utilized by the prophets precisely because there will be a literal valley involved. The broad valley in the Jerusalem area formed in connection with a cataclysmic earthquake will either be the scene of earth's final battles or will be the climactic stroke in them. No doubt the memory of the great earthquake in Uzziah's time (Amos 1:1) would form a vivid picture of what would occur in the last days (cf. Isa 13:9; 29:6; Ezek 38:19 with Joel 3:16; Zech 14:5). Thus, while Joel's primary intent was a play on words, a literal valley would also be involved in the final battle(s).

God rehearsed the charges against the heathen nations for which he would have to enter into judgment with them (vv.2b–3). First, they had scattered his people among the nations. God in his infinite wisdom and divine perspective looked back from eschatological times to call attention to the scattering of his own among the nations, not only after the Fall of Jerusalem, but their continued dispersion and persecution up to the end times. God himself, therefore, would have to call his people back to his land (cf. Jer 50:17–26).

Second, though the people had divided God's land (cf. Amos 7:17), he had not renounced his claim to his people or to his land. (See further W.C. Kaiser, Jr., "The Promised Land: A Biblical-Historical View," *BS* 138 (1981): 302–12.)

Third, so cheaply were his people valued that the heathen had cast lots for them and, even worse, had sold a boy for a harlot's hire (so Pesh.) and a girl so that they might drink a flask of wine.

2) *Its execution*

3:4–8

4"Now what have you against me, O Tyre and Sidon and all you regions of Philistia? Are you repaying me for something I have done? If you are paying me back, I will swiftly and speedily return on your own heads what you have done. 5For you took my silver and my gold and carried off my finest treasures to your temples. 6You sold the people of Judah and Jerusalem to the Greeks, that you might send them far from their homeland.

7"See, I am going to rouse them out of the places to which you sold them, and I will return on your own heads what you have done. 8I will sell your sons and daughters to the people of Judah, and they will sell them to the Sabeans, a nation far away." The LORD has spoken.

4–8 Joel went on to record God's solemn promise of the sure execution of his judgment on them. He began with God's question as to their purposes regarding himself. The districts of western Canaan, Tyre, and Sidon (well-known slave dealers in the ancient world) and the Philistine coast (often condemned with the Phoenicians by the prophets) were singled out as the chief representatives of Judah's enemies. Theirs had been the most inhuman of all crimes—that of dealing in human merchandise. God warned them that, having done despite to his people, if they would now add insult to injury by taking vengeance without cause against the Lord himself, they could be assured that God would most swiftly repay them in just kind.

The charges against the nations are detailed (vv.5–6). They had taken the silver and gold of God's people. The reference is probably to the continual plundering of their houses that were so handsomely furnished in this period of great prosperity. Again, they had taken Judah's valuables to their palaces (or temples). Furthermore, they had sold the Jewish children into the hands of the Greek slave-traders so as to send them far away from the borders of their homeland.

No doubt more than commercial gain motivated these hostile neighbors. There appears to be the deeper design of systematically reducing the number of God's children from the land of their promised inheritance. As such these powers of Joel's day stood as representatives of that great socio-religio-political system that would oppose God's people in a future day (cf. Dan 2:44–45; 7:9–14; 8:23–27; 11:36–45; 2 Thess 2:3–4; Rev 13; 14:8–11; 17–18).

God warned these enemies that for their oppression he would righteously repay them in kind (vv.7–8; cf. Isa 24:14–23; 2 Thess 1:6–8), while arousing his dispersed and captive people from the distant lands of their bondage. As he had warned them (v.4), he would give those slave dealers a taste of their own medicine. Their people would in turn be sold into captivity by the children of Judah to the Sabeans who would send them afar off.

Joel's prophecy, though intended for the eschatological situation, is also made historically applicable by being based on the current situation of his day. Not only would the great coalition of the future surely fall, but Uzziah's recapture of Ezion-Geber and his successes against the Philistines would serve as a warning of the dangerous position in which these allied commercial enemies of Joel's day stood.

Notes

1 The details of the final conflict in earth's history are found in several places in the Word of God. The following are those that demand the most careful attention: Ezek 38:39; Dan 11:36–45; Zech 12:1–14:7; Rev 9:13–19; 16:12–16; 19:11–21.

2 On the valley problem, see further C.L. Feinberg, "The Nations in the Valley of Decision," *Prophecy and the Seventies* (Chicago: Moody, 1971), p. 218.

3 For the selling of captives to foreign people, see Gen 37:36; Obad 11; Nah 3:10. This practice was common among the ancients (see Thucydides *History of the Peloponnesian War* 3.50) as the Jews themselves were to experience (1 Macc 3:41; 2 Macc 8:11, 25; Jos. Antiq. XII, 298–99 [vii.3]; id., War VI, 414–19 [ix.2]). Lamentably, it was a charge also brought against the Jews in the northern kingdom by Amos (2:6).

For the casting of lots for captives, see Nah 3:10 and Thucydides (*History of the Pel-*

oponnesian War 3:50). One is also reminded of the casting of lots for Messiah's garments (cf. Ps 22:18 [19 MT] with Matt 27:35).

4 The slave trading of the Phoenicians is described in Homer *Odyssey* 15.403–84; see also Herodotus *Persian Wars* 1.1; 2.54, 56.

---

b. *The challenge in judgment* (3:9–17)

1) *The call to judgment*

3:9–12

9Proclaim this among the nations:
  Prepare for war!
Rouse the warriors!
  Let all the fighting men draw near and attack.
10Beat your plowshares into swords
  and your pruning hooks into spears.
Let the weakling say,
  "I am strong!"
11Come quickly, all you nations from every side,
  and assemble there.
"Bring down your warriors, O LORD!

12"Let the nations be roused;
  let them advance into the Valley of Jehoshaphat,
for there I will sit
  to judge all the nations on every side.

9–12 In the light of the prophecy of certain judgment, a warning challenge is issued, constituting a call to judgment (vv.9–12) and announcing the cause and course of that judgment (vv.13–17).

The proclamation of the Lord's message is to be circulated among the nations (cf. Amos 3:6–11). All the men of war are to assemble and prepare themselves in accordance with the proper spiritual rites before battle (cf. 1 Sam 7:5–9), for in the final analysis theirs was to be the culmination of all holy warfare. The mighty men of battle were to be called up for duty (cf. 2:7). All segments of society and the economy were to be on a wartime footing. The basic agricultural tools were to be fashioned into weapons; weak and cowardly men were to count themselves as mighty men of war (v.10). The nations were soon to learn that the Lord, too, was mighty in battle (cf. Exod 15:3; Ps 24:8).

All the surrounding nations are next commanded to come quickly and gather themselves together (v.11; cf. Pss 2:1–2; 110:1–3, 5–6) to that great final struggle that will culminate earth's present history (cf. Isa 17:12; 24:21–23; Mic 4:11–13; Zech 12:2–3; 14:1–3; Rev 16:14–16; 19:17–19). The thought of this climactic event, when God and his people will be vindicated before a godless assemblage of nations, caused the prophet to exclaim, "Bring down your warriors, O LORD!" The reference is to the angelic host (cf. Deut 33:2b–3; Pss 68:17 [18 MT]; 103:19–20; Zech 14:5) of him who is the "Mighty God" (Isa 9:6 [5 MT]). Whereas God's mighty ones had been the Gentile armies (ch. 2), God was now against those forces. Joel, overcome by emotion, cried out for their just destruction.

The nations are bidden to deploy themselves in the Valley of Jehoshaphat (v.12;

cf. v.2). The Lord had warned that he would enter into litigation with the enemies of his people (cf. v.2 with Isa 50:8); now he sits as judge to impose sentence on them (cf. Isa 28:5–6; Matt 25:31–46).

2) *The course of judgment*

3:13–17

13 Swing the sickle,
  for the harvest is ripe.
Come, trample the grapes,
  for the winepress is full
  and the vats overflow—
so great is their wickedness!"

14 Multitudes, multitudes
  in the valley of decision!
For the day of the LORD is near
  in the valley of decision.
15 The sun and moon will be darkened,
  and the stars no longer shine.
16 The LORD will roar from Zion
  and thunder from Jerusalem;
  the earth and the sky will tremble.
But the LORD will be a refuge for his people,
  a stronghold for the people of Israel.

17 "Then you will know that I, the LORD your God,
  dwell in Zion, my holy hill.
Jerusalem will be holy;
  never again will foreigners invade her.

13–17 In v.13 God is pictured as sending his reapers into the harvest field (cf. Rev 14:14–20) and to the winepress of judgment (Isa 63:3), for the nations are ripe for judgment; their wickedness is great and filled to overflowing.

Then the reader is taken to the very scene of that awesome event. The confused and clamoring throng of nations and the tumultuous uproar and din of battle in this great day of reckoning are vividly portrayed (v.14; cf. Ezek 38:21–23; Zech 14:13; cf. also Judg 7:22). The valley named Jehoshaphat (3:2, 12), in accordance with its purpose of being the place of final accomplishment, is now called "the valley of decision" (cf. Ezek 39:17–29; Zech 14:12–15; Rev 19:17–21).

The accompanying signs in the natural world are depicted (vv.15–16). That which was applicable to the local scene of impending battle in the day of the Assyrian invasion (2:10b) is now seen in all its final intensity. The Lord comes forth out of Zion as a roaring lion (cf. Amos 1:2). Because the nations had roared insolently against God's people (Isa 5:25–30), the Lord would be as a lion roaring after its prey in behalf of the returned remnant (cf. Hos 11:10–11 with Jer 25:30–33). Heaven and earth will tremble at his presence here among the nations (cf. Ps 29; Isa 29:6–8; 30:30–31; Zech 14:3–7; Rev 16:16–18).

But the very manifestation of his coming, so fearful for the unbelieving nations (cf. Rev 6:12–17), gives assurance of protection and strength for God's own (v.17; cf. Isa 26:20–21). As Israel had learned of God's sovereign concern for his people through judgment (cf. Ezek 6:7), now as his restored wife (cf. Isa 54; Hos 2) she would know of his eternal compassion through her deliverance and his abiding presence with her (cf. 2:27). In contrast to the nations that would learn who God really is (cf. Ezek 36:36–38; 39:6–7), Israel would know the redeeming power and the continuous enjoyment of his glorious presence with her (cf. Isa 49:22–26; 60:16; Jer 24:7; Ezek 34:27–30; 36:11, 23; 39:22, 27–29; Joel 3:21; Zech 2:8–9 [12–13 MT]) forever (Jer 31:33–34; Heb 8:10–11). Because the Lord himself is there (cf. 2:32; 3:21), Jerusalem will be everlastingly holy (cf. Isa 52:1; 60:14, 21; Zech 14:21; cf. also Rev 21:2). None but his own shall again set foot in it.

Notes

---

9 The sense of the Hebrew idiom here is that of the Akkadian *gimilla turru* ("to return an act in kind"). That the Phoenicians were not above duplicity and double-dealing in their business relations may be seen in Homer *Odyssey* 14.290–97.

For the regulations about holy warfare at Qumran, see Y. Yadin, *The Scroll of the War of the Sons of Light Against the Sons of Darkness* (Oxford: Oxford University Press, 1962), pp. 141–228.

10 For the mustering of all the populace for war, see *Krt* A.2.85–105, 176–94, in UT, pp. 250–51.

רֹמַח (*rōmaḥ*, "spear") is probably better translated "lance." It may be related to the Egyptian word *mrḥ*, Coptic *mereḥ*, which is found also in Ugaritic. See W. Spiegelberg, *Koptisches Handwörterbuch* (Heidelberg: Carl Winters, 1921), p. 64. If so, it may be an example of consonant metathesis for lexical differentiation as in Ugaritic *mdl* = Semitic *lmd* (see J.C. Greenfield, "Ugaritic *Mdl* and its cognates," *Biblica* 45 [1964]: 527–34).

11 The Hebrew עוּשׁ (*ʿûš*) is a *hapax legomenon*. Rudolph (in loc.) is probably right in relating it to an Arabic root *ʿgšš* ("to hasten," "to hurry"). If so, the verb is probably to be taken with the following verb as hendiadys, i.e., "come quickly."

---

2. *The millennial prosperity*

3:18–21

18"In that day the mountains will drip new wine,
and the hills will flow with milk;
all the ravines of Judah will run with water.
A fountain will flow out of the LORD's house
and will water the valley of acacias.
19But Egypt will be desolate;
Edom a desert waste,
because of violence done to the people of Judah,
in whose land they shed innocent blood.
20Judah will be inhabited forever
and Jerusalem through all generations.
21Their bloodguilt, which I have not pardoned,
I will pardon."

The LORD dwells in Zion!

18–21 Joel looked beyond the great battle to the resultant millennial scene. He concluded his prophecy by contrasting the judgment of the nations—typified by Israel's most protracted antagonist, Edom, and by her most persistent source of spiritual defeat, Egypt—with the blessings that will rest on the repentant, restored, and revitalized people of God.

In glowing and hyperbolic terms, Joel described the great fertility of soil of the coming Millennial Age. That which was cut off in the locust plague of Joel's day due to sin (1:5) will be commonplace in that era permeated by the presence of the Holy One (cf. 2:19–27; Isa 55:1). The formerly barren hills will flourish again with vegetation. The wadis, dried by the drought of God's judgment, will flow again, giving renewed vitality to the land, as God pours out his blessing to people of renewed spiritual vitality (cf. Isa 30:25–26; Ezek 34:13–14).

In Jerusalem a fountain shall issue forth from the house of the Lord. Ezekiel (47:1–12) reported that it will terminate in the Dead Sea, transforming it from salt water to fresh water. Zechariah (14:8) spoke of a great flow of water from Jerusalem emptying into both the Dead Sea and the Mediterranean Sea, a prophecy that, once incredible, now stands authenticated by recent geological discoveries.

Joel went on to say that these waters will gush through the Wadi Shittim. The exact location of this place is uncertain and has occasioned many suggestions. Perhaps the best solution is to identify it with a barren valley east of Judah, where the Israelites suffered spiritual failure before making the last encampment prior to their entrance into the Promised Land (cf. Num 25:1; 33:49; Josh 3:1).

Shittim is also the plural form of the word for the acacia tree, which was prized for its strength and durability. Accordingly, it was extensively used in the construction of the tabernacle.

Physically, the waters from the temple will flow to the area of the Vale of Shittim. Spiritually, as the name of the place that for Israel was one of spiritual failure and then of spiritual triumph when the Israelites were led in redemptive strength into the Land of Promise, and as the name of the material from which the tabernacle was fashioned, it may have served as a symbol among the eighth-century prophets of the need of renewed spiritual vitality. It thus spoke of full redemption from past sin on the part of a people who would claim God as their king (cf. Mic 6:1–5).

Joel next contrasted the future condition of Judah and Jerusalem with that of Egypt and Edom, longtime adversaries of Israel. In contrast with their desolation, Judah and Jerusalem will be inhabited forever. All Judah's sins will be forgiven, and the Lord himself will abide in her midst forever (cf. Ezek 48:35).

Joel's last prophetic view is a picture of Israel's everlasting felicity. The reason for this state of unending happiness is apparent. The Lord himself will tabernacle in her midst in all his glory (cf. 3:17; Zech 8:3–8). Based on the basic idea of the Hebrew root (*škn*), theologians have spoken of the Lord's shekinah glory. Throughout the OT, from Sinai to Solomon's temple, "the shekinah glory" designates the active presence *now* of the invisible God who transcends the universe he created. However, due to the spiritual and moral decay that had led to religious formalism and open idolatry, the shekinah glory left the temple and Jerusalem (Ezek 10; 11:22–25) to return not at all till that day of God's future temple (Ezek 43:1–12), when God would again redeem his people and dwell among a repentant, regenerated, and grateful people (Zech 2:10–13 [14–17 MT]).

Before that millennial scene, the NT writers reveal that God has another "tabernacling" with men. The unique Son became flesh, dwelling among men (John 1:14) as the promised Immanuel (Isa 7:14). Having redeemed a lost mankind through his death and resurrection, and being ascended into heaven, he now dwells in his own whom he has taken into union with himself (Eph 1:15–2:21; Col 1:15–22, 27; 2:9–

10). As the triumphant Redeemer, he has given to the church, his body, gifts that it is to steward (Eph 4:8–10).

The believer's destiny is to enjoy God's presence forever (Rev 21:2–3). Yet even now he is to partake of that blessing through the indwelling Christ (John 17:20–22) and the Holy Spirit (John 16:7–14), who is the earnest of that eternal happiness and well-being that lies before him (2 Cor 1:22; Eph 1:14; 5:5), and let Christ's glory be seen through him (Gal 1:16).

May the reality of Christ be for the Christian—as for the millennial saint of Joel's prophecy—a conscious, ever-abiding presence that allows Christ's glory to be seen in all his life!

Notes

21 The technical term "shekinah" stresses the immanence of God in distinction to his transcendence (for which יָשַׁב [*yāšaḇ*, "he dwelled"] was used), somewhat as כָּבוֹד (*kāḇôḏ*, "glory") came to be a technical term for God in his visible and active presence among men.

AMOS

Thomas Edward McComiskey

AMOS

Introduction

1. **Background**
2. **Unity**
3. **Authorship**
4. **Date**
5. **Theological Values**
6. **Bibliography**
7. **Outline**

1. Background

In many ways the eighth century B.C. was unique in the history of Judah and Israel. It witnessed the toppling of the northern kingdom from the glory of economic prosperity and international influence to virtual subjugation by a foreign power. It also witnessed the near collapse of Judah, averted only by the steadying hand of King Hezekiah, who could do no more than slow Judah's progress toward certain ruin.

At the same time, however, the eighth century witnessed the rise of one of the most potent moral forces the world has ever known—the writing prophets. These men, from widely separated backgrounds, shared an overwhelming conviction that God had called them. They had various styles of writing, but all wrote with the authority of the Almighty. They denounced the sins of their contemporaries and also looked far into the future as they spoke of deliverance for both Jew and Gentile.

The dawn of the eighth century brought new hope to Israel and Judah. Israel's subjugation to Damascus ended abruptly when the Assyrians under Adad-nirari III crushed Damascus in 802 B.C. The internal difficulties that had plagued Judah also ended with Uzziah's accession to the throne (792–740 B.C.). He built up a powerful army and increased Judah's mercantile activities.

In the northern kingdom, Jeroboam II (793–753 B.C.) came to the throne at roughly the same time as Uzziah. Jeroboam restored much of the territory that had fallen to Damascus (2 Kings 14:28).

The conquest of Damascus and the attendant quiescence of Assyria, coupled with the brilliant leadership of Uzziah and Jeroboam, brought Judah and Israel to heights of prominence second only to Solomon's golden age. The kingdoms prospered financially and at the same time expanded their borders. But as their economic well-being and national strength continued to foster their security, an internal decay was eating at their vitals. It was primarily moral because it involved a basic violation of the covenant established by God at Sinai.

The covenantal stipulations required loyalty to God and love toward one's fellowman. Yet the idolatrous worship of their pagan neighbors had infiltrated the two kingdoms, producing a strange syncretistic worship. While pagan high places dotted the countryside and idols stood within the cities, the people continued to trust in such Yahwistic concepts as the "day of the LORD" (5:18) and aspects of Levitical worship (4:4–5).

Not only did the people disobey by worshiping idols, but they also violated the social legislation of the covenant. Amos is particularly vehement in denouncing the lack of social concern in his time. Archaeology has illuminated this period through a number of discoveries. Excavations at Samaria, the capital of the northern kingdom, have yielded hundreds of ivory inlays attesting to Amos's description of the luxury enjoyed by these people (6:4).[1] The nature of Canaanite Baal-worship, which so damaged the social structure of Israel and Judah, is now well-known from the Ugaritic epic material. The cult of Baal was primarily a fertility cult. It involved ritual prostitution as a means of exciting the lusty Baal, who was worshiped as the source of fecundity. Anat, one of the most prominent goddesses of the Canaanite pantheon, is pictured in the Ugaritic epic material as a brutal warrior. In one passage she wades in blood and beneath her roll the heads of her victims (UT, *'nt*, 2:5–31). Unbridled lust characterized the Canaanite observances. The intrusion of similar observances into Israel and Judah could lead only to a rending of the social fabric. The ethical concerns of the law were no longer necessary in a cult that required only external ritual.

The erosion of Israel's social structure showed itself primarily in a cleavage between the rich and the poor. The improved economic situation in Israel led to an increase of the wealthy, who not only neglected the poor but used them to increase their own wealth. The social concern inherent in the very structure of the law was forgotten. God's will, as it applied to the nation of Israel, was ignored; and this spurred the eighth-century prophets to action. Though their protest was largely ignored (2 Kings 17:13–14), it contributed to the establishment of a believing remnant. The prophets preserved faith by assuring the people that God had not forsaken his promise. They saw emerging from their fallen society a kingdom different from any other, an ideal kingdom headed by the messianic King whose rule would be completely just.

2. Unity

Almost all scholars agree that the prophecy of Amos is, at least in essence, an authentic production of the man whose name it bears. The consonance of Amos's message with the eighth-century milieu and his vividly forthright style of writing make it difficult to think otherwise.

Some, however, have thought the book to be the end product of a structural development with certain redactive intrusions. Weiser held that the oracles of chapters 1–6 and the section containing the visions existed separately for a time till they were united in the exilic or postexilic times.[2] The redactor revealed the union of

[1]For a discussion of the ivories found at Samaria, see *Encyclopedia of Archaeological Excavations in the Holy Land*, ed. by M. Avi-Yonah and E. Stern (Englewood Cliffs, N.J.: Prentice-Hall, 1978), 4:1044–46. See also "Nimrud," *Archaeology and Old Testament Study*, ed. D.W. Thomas (Oxford: Clarendon, 1967), pp. 69–70.

[2]A. Weiser and K. Elliger, *Das Buch der zwölf Kleinen Propheten*, 4 vols. (Göttingen: Vandenhoeck

these sections in the superscription to the book (1:1), which cites both the words and the visions of Amos. Weiser dated the oracles after Amos's mission to the northern kingdom and held that the visions preceded that mission. Yet the evidence for such a view is purely speculative. There is no reason Amos or an amanuensis could not have arranged the prophecies in their present order.

The early date cited for the vision section by Weiser seems somewhat artificial in view of its direct connection with the encounter between Amos and Amaziah during the northern ministry (7:10–17). The prediction of the destruction of the northern kingdom and the house of Jeroboam, an important element in the vision section (7:9), appears to have been the direct cause of Amaziah's protest (7:10–11).

An examination of the oracle section and the vision section reveals similar concerns. Both predict God's punishment of the northern kingdom (3:13–15; cf. 7:7–9), both foresee the captivity (4:1–3; cf. 7:17; 9:4), and both set forth the same denunciation of Israel's social crimes (3:10; cf. 8:4–6).

Some scholars think that the encounter at Bethel (7:10–17) is the product of another author, possibly an eyewitness (so Mays). Their major reason for this supposition is the use of the third person throughout 7:10–17. In other accounts where there is a personal reference, the prophet Amos characteristically used the first person (7:1–9; 8:1–2; 9:1). While it is possible that biblical authors reverted to the third person as a literary device, it seems unlikely that this device would be used by Amos only in this brief segment of the prophecy.

The detailed nature of the report of the Bethel encounter with its direct quotations seems to point strongly to the possibility of its having been written by an eyewitness. This could have been a disciple of Amos, or the prophet himself. The use of the third person may be an indication that the account was reported by Amos to a disciple who recorded it. This need not affect the authenticity of the account, nor need it be regarded as strong evidence for a complex process of redaction.

Some critical scholars regard the oracles against Tyre (1:9–10), Edom (1:11–12), and Judah (2:4–5) as later intrusions because they seem to reflect conditions in the exilic period or because they are similar to exilic or postexilic prophetic oracles.

Some scholars also deny the authenticity of these sections on internal literary grounds. The concluding formula "says the LORD," which ends the other oracles, is lacking in these three oracles. And the intrusive nature of the oracle against Tyre seems to be supported by the fact that the crime cited in it is like the one cited in the oracle against the Philistines, which immediately precedes it.

While it is true that similar oracles against Tyre and Edom exist in later books (Lam 4:21–22; Ezek 27:13; Joel 3:6; Obad 10–12), this is not necessarily an indication of the origin of these two oracles in Amos. As for Edom, the Edomites showed their hostility against Israel very early in Israel's history and continued it up to the destruction of Jerusalem (see commentary at 1:11–12). It is this long hostility against Israel that is emphasized in the oracle against Edom.

The internal differences do not provide a compelling reason for positing a later date for the three oracles. S. Paul ("Amos 1:3–23," pp. 397–403) observes a stairlike pattern in the first six oracles, in which certain phrases are repeated, thus creating a unified whole—*hikratti̇̂* ("I will destroy"; lit., "cut off"), 1:5, 8; *gālûṯ šᵉlēmāh*

& Ruprecht, 1949), 1:110–13; A. Weiser, *Die Profetie des Amos* (Giessen: Alfred Topelmann, 1929), pp. 249ff.

("whole communities"), 1:6, 9; *'aḥ* ("brotherhood," "brother"), 1:9, 11; *biṯrû'āh* ("war cries"), 1:14; 2:2. He does not conclude that this pattern necessarily indicates that the disputed oracles were written by Amos. However, these oracles are so closely woven into the structure of this section that it is not unreasonable to assume that Amos did write them. Paul also notes that a later writer would probably not accuse the people of Tyre of violating the covenant of brotherhood (1:9) since they remained loyal to the rebels during the invasion of Nebuchadnezzar.

The three disputed oracles possess the common concluding formula "consume the fortresses," while the other oracles conclude with the words "says the LORD." Some scholars allege that this departure supports the intrusive nature of these oracles and points to the presence of another hand in the composition of the book.

The dating of literary forms based on criteria that allow no room for creativity on the part of the author is rigid and artificial. The vivid forthrightness and vigor of Amos's style certainly argues for originality on his part. Amos seemed to make a studied attempt to avoid the tedious repetition of certain literary formulas. The formula "says the LORD" (*'āmar YHWH*) is used with great frequency in the book, but on occasion Amos used the expression "declares the LORD" (*n^e'um YHWH*); cf. 2:11, 16; 3:10, 15; et al.). On the whole there appears to be no compelling reason for assigning these disputed oracles to a later time.

One of the most difficult critical questions relating to the Book of Amos is the authenticity of its hymnic elements. These great doxologies, praising God in highly exalted language, occur at 4:13; 5:8–9; 9:5–6.

Among the first to express doubt about the authenticity of the doxologies was Duhm (1875).[3] Since then other scholars have questioned them. The doxologies have been assumed to be late additions for several reasons. They seem to interrupt the narrative flow and apparently do not logically fit the sequence of thought. They seem to reflect a sophisticated theology (i.e., the use of later language). And a similar doxology in the LXX text of Hosea 13:4 seems to establish a precedent for such doxological insertions.

Several things may be said about these contentions. As for the interruption of the narrative flow of the book, only the doxology of 5:8–9 poses serious difficulties. The first doxology (4:13) occurs at the end of a logical section and provides an appropriate meditation on the nature of God. The last doxology (9:5–6) occurs in a section in which the prophet sets forth the inevitability of Israel's downfall. The hymn it includes describes God's judgment in vivid, cosmic terms and is in no sense conceptually intrusive.

The second doxology (5:8–9) seems to interrupt the flow of Amos's condemnation of those who pervert justice. Yet it may have been included at this point because of the awesome confirmation it gives of the preceding statement (vv. 6–7). Verses 6–7 begin with a reference to the threat of destruction, while v.9 confirms Yahweh's ability to destroy the mighty. Intrusiveness is not necessarily an indication of lateness. The pericope at 6:9–10, for example, is clearly intrusive, differing from the surrounding context in content and literary style. But it contains several literary characteristics that are also peculiarities of Amos's style. For example, the second major clause of the pericope (the first line of v.10) contains several suffixes, all of

[3]Bernhard Duhm, *Die Zwölf Propheten in den Versmassen der Urschrift übersetzt* (Tubingen: J.C.B. Mohr, 1910); id., "Anmerkungen zu den Zwölf Propheten: III. Buch Micha," ZAW 31 (1911): 81–93.

them unreferred. That is, the referents are implicit, not stated. This phenomenon may be found in the suffix *nû* ("him") on *'ᵃšîḇennû* (lit., "I will turn back him [NIV, 'my wrath']") in 1:3, 6, 9, 11, 13; 2:1, 4, 6, which also has no clearly stated referent. The pericope is also characterized by the quick succession of dependent clauses that may be observed elsewhere in undisputed portions of Amos (cf. the oracles of 1:1–2:16; cf. also 5:14–15; 6:1–7; 8:4–6). There is thus strong likelihood that 6:9–10 was written by Amos. In the light of this, the argument that a pericope is late because it is conceptually or structurally intrusive must be tempered by a consideration of the author's style.

The sophisticated theology attributed to the doxologies relates mainly to the concept of Yahweh as the one who "creates" (*bōrē'*; 4:13) a concept that closely parallels the thought of the alleged Second Isaiah. Since Second Isaiah is placed in an exilic milieu by critics, the consonance between it and the theology of the doxologies is assumed to strongly favor an exilic origin for the doxologies. But the sovereignty of Yahweh that Amos sees extending to all nations and that is evident in the realm of nature (4:7–8) is difficult to comprehend apart from the role of Yahweh as Creator.

While it is true that Yahweh is not called *bōrē'* in undisputed passages earlier than Second Isaiah, it must be noted that Isaiah 37:16 and Jeremiah 27:5 attribute the role of fashioner of the universe to Yahweh. The word *ᶜāśāh* is used in these passages, not *bārā'*, but the idea that Yahweh is the architect of the universe is clearly there. Neither passage has escaped critical examination, however, and the authenticity of both are questioned by some scholars. In recent years the prose material of Jeremiah has been studied very closely, and many modern scholars affirm the Jeremaic authorship of 27:5. Thus, it is possible that the concept of Yahweh as the maker of the universe existed much earlier than the late exilic or postexilic periods.

The later language attributed to the doxologies consists mainly in the word "creates" and the expression "the LORD God Almighty is his name" (*YHWH 'ᵉlōhê ṣᵉḇā'ôṯ šᵉmô*).[4] Since the concept of creator was considered above, it is necessary to consider only the latter expression. The refrain "LORD Almighty is his name" occurs four times in the section of the Book of Isaiah generally regarded as exilic (47:4; 48:2; 51:15; 54:5). For this reason many critics regard the expression itself as belonging to the period of the Exile. But Amos used expressions similar to this throughout the book (3:13; 5:14, 15, 16; 6:8, 14). It is, however, the occurrence of the word "name" in the doxological expression that provides the correspondence with the second half of Isaiah and hence allegedly warrants a later date. One should, however, be cautious about using such an approach as this. We have only a small amount of written material from this vast historical period, and it is very difficult to make conclusive statements on such limited evidence. To confine a given expression to one historial period may be assuming too much. Moreover, one may wonder why "Second Isaiah" could not have depended on Amos.

A divine title containing the word "name" can be found in Exodus 15:3. It is "Yahweh is his name" (*YHWH šᵉmô*). The poem in which this name is found is dated by F.M. Cross and D.N. Freedman ("The Song of Miriam," JNES 14 [1955]: 240) as "scarcely later than the twelfth century in its original form." This date is based on

[4]For a thorough discussion of this expression from a form-critical standpoint, see J. Crenshaw, *Hymnic Affirmation of Divine Justice: The Doxologies of Amos and Related Texts in the Old Testament* (Missoula: Scholars, 1975), pp. 75–114.

philological evidence, not critical assumptions, and thus rests on objective data. The possibility that a divine title containing the word "name" existed in Israelite tradition long before Amos's time deserves careful consideration.

Some scholars approach the question of the authenticity of the doxologies on the basis of the usage of words within narrow chronological limits, such as that the expression *YHWH 'ᵉlōhê ṣᵉḇā'ôṯ šᵉmô* was dominant in the period of the Exile. This can lead to dubious conclusions because of the limited amount of Hebrew material. It is best to allow the context to govern our understanding of the hymnic elements.[5]

The presence of a doxological statement in the LXX text of Hosea 13:4, if not a witness to the original Hebrew text, may establish a precedent for such insertions. But this in itself is not proof that the doxologies in Amos are intrusive material.

Scholars differ widely regarding the doxologies. No conclusive evidence has been given as to their genre or origin. If one posits the role of Creator for Yahweh in the time of Amos, there is no compelling reason why the doxologies must be assigned to the late exilic period. If the doxological material is not original with Amos, it may well be that he drew on a common bank of prophetic material or quoted stanzas of familiar hymns.

As for the section dealing with the downfall of the Davidic monarchy (9:8–15), some scholars assume it was written after that event because it shows a knowledge of the end of the Judahite monarchy, an event that did not happen till much later (Mays, pp. 13–14; McKeating, p. 70). The Hebrew word *hannōpeleṯ* (v.11) is a participle and may connote continuing action; i.e., "crumbling." It need not be translated "fallen," as in some versions (NIV, NASB, RSV, et al.). Amos was well aware of the progressive dissolution of both kingdoms. His prophetic spirit gave him a perspective others did not have. He saw the monarchy already toppling; but out of the rubble of its collapse, he saw a new and greater kingdom emerging. The theology of this section is quite consonant with eighth-century prophetic theology.

Some (e.g., Cripps, p. 67) also argue that the distinction between the righteous and the wicked (9:8–10) is foreign to the thought of Amos because he predicted the doom of the entire nation. But if Amos expected the entire destruction of the nation, one may wonder why he appealed for repentance (5:14). Micah, another eighth-century prophet, set forth a full-orbed doctrine of a redeemed remnant (4:6–7; 5:4, 7–9) in language as denunciatory as that of Amos (Mic 1:6–7; 2:4; cf. also Isa 6:13). Amos predicted the demise of the nation as a political entity; he did not teach that the whole house of Israel would come to an end.

Those who deny the authenticity of this section (e.g., Cripps, pp. 72–73) also appeal to the fact that in Amos the promise of the restoration is not based on ethical response, something that goes counter to the prophet's strongly ethical message. But does not Amos 9:10 imply that only the righteous will inherit the kingdom because of the expulsion of sinners from it? To deny a message of hope in Amos removes him from the mainstream of eighth-century prophetic thought, where the concept of doom is often followed by hope (Isa 3:1–4:1; cf. 4:2–6; 8:16–22; cf. 9:1–7; Mic 2:1–11; cf. 2:12–13; 5:1; cf. 5:2–4. See also Lam 3, where the themes of judgment and hope are intertwined within the one chapter).

---

[5]Story says on this, "To analyse words, to determine place and time when words were in vogue, and to add together the sum total of these facts as the basis for interpretation, fails to do justice to the interpretative structure of text and context" (C. Story, "Amos—Prophet of Praise," VetTest 30 (January 1980): 79.

3. Authorship

The superscription of the book (1:1) attributes the work to Amos. Little is known of him apart from the sketchy references in the superscription and the body of the prophecy. Amos lived and worked in Tekoa (1:1), a town ten miles south of Jerusalem in the Judean range. The town was situated on a height commanding a magnificent view of the rugged wilderness below and of distant landmarks like the Mount of Olives. The eastern slopes of the Judean range around Tekoa are mostly arid, rock-strewn wastes. The western slopes, however, provide some pasture land and shelter in caves for shepherds who graze their flocks.

Amos was a shepherd (1:1) who also tended sycamore trees (7:14). He was an outdoor man; for he said, "I was a shepherd, . . . tending the flock" (vv.14–15).

Amos's natural surroundings apparently had a profound effect on him; his book is full of references to them (1:2; 2:9; 3:4–5; 5:19–20, 24; 6:12; 7:1–6; 8:1; 9:3–15).

Above all, Amos was a prophet. The dark days in which he lived called for a man of sturdy moral fiber and fearlessness. Such was Amos. His character, molded in the harsh terrain of the wilderness of Tekoa, enabled him to stand before the priest and the people, proclaiming the word God had given him.

4. Date

We may best place the prophetic activity of Amos in the latter half of the reign of Jeroboam II (793–753 B.C.). It would certainly have taken some time for the affluence during Jeroboam's reign to lead to the social decay that was so widespread when Amos carried out his mission to the northern kingdom.

Some scholars (Cripps, pp.734–41) have placed Amos's prophetic ministry after 745 B.C. to allow for the rise of Assyria under Tiglath-Pileser III. But it is significant that Amos did not mention Assyria by name, though he did affirm that Israel would go into exile "beyond Damascus." The mood of careless confidence pervading the nation at the time of Amos seems to fit best the period before the Syro-Palestinian incursions of Assyria.

The phrase "two years before the earthquake" (1:1) limits the date of the prophecy to a narrow period, perhaps no more than a year and probably much shorter than that. It is difficult to find an exact time in which Amos's mission would fit. Several possibilities may, however, be noted. Jotham, Uzziah's son, acceded to the regency of Judah when Uzziah was stricken with leprosy (c. 750 B.C.). That 1:1 mentions only Uzziah and not Jotham may point to a time before Jotham's accession. This would support a date before 750 B.C. for the northern ministry of Amos. If the superscription reflects this, Amos would have delivered his oracles before 750 B.C. The earthquake referred to in 1:1 may have occurred around 760 B.C., according to excavations at Hazor.[6]

In the light of these things, it seems best to place the prophetic ministry of Amos sometime before 760 B.C. This is consonant with the narrow scope of the superscription (1:1).

---

[6]Y. Yadin et al, *Hazor II: An Account of the Second Season of Excavations, 1956* (Jerusalem: Magnes, 1960), pp. 24, 26, 36–37).

5. Theological Values

a. *The doctrine of God*

Central in Amos's teaching about God is his divine sovereignty. Yahweh is the God of history. He effects the migrations of peoples (9:7) and controls the orderly progression of natural phenomena (4:13; 5:8). He is in no way a mere automaton controlled by the religious rituals of his creatures. Yet within that sovereign domain, mankind has freedom to bow in submission to Yahweh or to reject him.

b. *The doctrine of election*

Amos affirmed the historical election of Israel (3:2). But he inveighed against the perverted concept of election popularly held in his day—that is, the irrevocable commitment of Yahweh to the nation. Their election alone did not guarantee national blessing, for the sovereign Lord had promised that they would be his "treasured possession" if they obeyed him and kept his covenant (Exod 19:5). Amos, more than any other prophet, urged the responsibility of elective privilege.

c. *Eschatology*

The unique contribution of Amos to the eschatology of the OT is his teaching about the Day of the Lord. He stressed that it is a time when the Lord will judge all sin, even in his own people. The gloomy portrayal of that day in the prophecy of Amos reflects the fact that Amos's hearers were for the most part guilty of transgression. For them that day would hold no ray of light (5:18–20).

Another day is coming, however, when hope will shine with glorious promise (9:13–15). The Davidic promise will be realized in the restoration of David's kingdom, and Jews and Gentiles will be united in the kingdom of David's greater Son.

6. Bibliography

Books

Cripps, R. *A Critical and Exegetical Commentary on the Book of Amos*. London: Macmillan, 1929.

Hammershaimb, E. *The Book of Amos, A Commentary*. Translated by J. Sturdy. New York: Schocken Books, 1970.

Harper, W.R. *A Critical and Exegetical Study on Amos and Hosea*. ICC. Edinburgh: T. & T. Clark, 1955.

Mays, J. *Amos: A Commentary*. Philadelphia: Westminster, 1969.

McKeating, H. *The Books of Amos, Hosea and Micah*. Cambridge: University Press, 1971.

Motyer, J. *The Day of the Lion*. Downers Grove, Ill.: InterVarsity, 1974.

Rowley, H.H. "Was Amos a Nabi?" *Festschrift Otto Eissfeldt*. Dargebracht von Freunden und Verehrern. Herasugegeben von Johann Fück. Halle an der Saale: Max Niemeyer, 1947, pp. 191–98.

Wolff, H. *Joel and Amos*. Translated by W. Janzen, D. McBridge, Jr., and C. Muenchow. Philadelphia: Fortress, 1977.

Periodicals

Boyle, M. "The Covenant Lawsuit of the Prophet Amos: III 1–IV 13." *Vetus Testamentum* 21 (1971): 388–62.
Brueggemann, W. "Amos IV 4–13 and Israel's Covenant Worship" *Vetus Testamentum* 15 (1965): 1–15.
Christensen, D. "The Prosodic Structure of Amos 1–2." *Harvard Theological Review* 67 (1974): 427–36.
Heicksen, M. "Tekoa: Historical and Cultural Profile." *Journal of the Evangelical Theological Society* 13 (1970): 81–89.
Paul, S. "Amos 1:3–2:3. A Concatenous Literary Pattern." *Journal of Biblical Literature* 90 (1971): 397–403.
______. "Fishing Imagery in Amos 4:2." *Journal of Biblical Literature* 97 (1978): 183–90.
Weiss, M. "Pattern of Numerical Sequence in Amos 1–2." *Journal of Biblical Literature* 86 (1967): 416–23.

7. Outline

I. Superscription (1:1)
II. Introduction to the Prophecy (1:2)
III. The Prophetic Oracles (1:3–6:14)
   A. Oracles of Judgment Against the Surrounding Nations (1:3–2:5)
      1. The oracle against Syria (1:3–5)
      2. The oracle against the Philistines (1:6–8)
      3. The oracle against Tyre (1:9–10)
      4. The oracle against Edom (1:11–12)
      5. The oracle against Ammon (1:13–15)
      6. The oracle against Moab (2:1–3)
      7. The oracle against Judah (2:4–5)
   B. Oracles of Judgment Against Israel (2:6–6:14)
      1. A lesson from history (2:6–16)
      2. A lesson based on cause and effect (3:1–12)
      3. An oracle against the house of Jacob (3:13–15)
      4. The pampered women of Samaria (4:1–3)
      5. Sinful worship (4:4–5)
      6. A look to the past (4:6–13)
      7. A lament for fallen Israel (5:1–3)
      8. Seeking true values (5:4–17)
      9. The Day of the Lord (5:18–20)
      10. Unacceptable worship (5:21–27)
      11. A warning to the complacent (6:1–7)
      12. Pride before a fall (6:8–11)
      13. A grim paradox (6:12–14)
IV. The Prophetic Visions (7:1–9:15)
   A. The Vision of the Locusts, Fire, and the Plumb Line (7:1–9)
   B. A Historical Interlude (7:10–17)
   C. The Vision of the Summer Fruit (8:1–14)
   D. The Vision of the Lord Standing by the Altar (9:1–15)
      1. The destruction of the temple (9:1–6)
      2. Israel and the other nations (9:7)
      3. The restoration of the Davidic kingdom (9:8–12)
      4. The blessings of the restored kingdom (9:13–15)

Text and Exposition

I. Superscription

1:1

[1]The words of Amos, one of the shepherds of Tekoa—what he saw concerning Israel two years before the earthquake, when Uzziah was king of Judah and Jeroboam son of Jehoash was king of Israel.

1 The prophecy is introduced by the formula "the words of Amos." Frequently this expression is used for collections of sayings, as in the case of the prophecy of Jeremiah (1:1), various collections of proverbs (Prov 30:1; 31:1), and Ecclesiastes (1:1). Here it connotes the collection of prophetic oracles spoken by Amos during the northern ministry.

"Shepherd" (*nōqēḏ*) is not the usual word for shepherd. It is used of Mesha, king of Moab, where it implies that he was a breeder and supplier of sheep (2 Kings 3:4).

In Amos 7:14 the word *bôqēr* is used to describe Amos's occupation. This word occurs only once in the OT; thus its precise meaning is difficult to determine. While *bôqēr* may have been a general term that denoted a herdsman of any type, its linguistic connection with *bāqār* ("cattle") suggests the possibility that Amos kept cattle as well as sheep. The word *ṣō'n* (7:15) connotes smaller animals like sheep and goats; thus it is likely that Amos was a breeder of various types of animals besides sheep.

That Amos described himself in 7:15 as "tending the flock" (*mē'aḥ^{a}rê haṣṣō'n*) shows that he personally cared for the herds, rather than necessarily being a wealthy animal breeder who left the care of the flocks to others. The use of the term *nōqēḏ* of the king of Moab does not demand the conclusion that Amos was a wealthy and powerful person. It may simply show that Amos was a supplier of small animals.

Amos's character and ideals were shaped by the wilderness. There is no evidence that he was part of a prophetic movement in Judah; he denied that possibility by affirming that he was "neither a prophet nor a prophet's son" (7:14). Undoubtedly his simple life in the Judean wilderness led him to see more clearly the evils of city life that would be less apparent to the affluent who lived within the city walls, confined by their heartless greed.

The word "saw" (*ḥāzāh*) is in a relative clause logically dependent on "the words of Amos." *Ḥāzāh* is not the common word for "see." Although it is used in poetic literature as a synonym for it, *ḥāzāh* has a more distinctive meaning and includes the idea of mental apprehension as well as visual observation. So it lends itself well to the process of prophetic reception. Several noun forms meaning "vision" are based on this root. *Ḥāzāh* implies the words of Amos were perceived mentally—that is, by divine revelation—before they were communicated orally or in writing.

The prophetic word of Amos concerned Israel. While "Israel" may have included both kingdoms (6:1; 9:14), it is best to take the term as referring to the northern kingdom. The numerous references to localities in the north as well as the encounter with Amaziah support this. The reference to Judah in 2:4 need not indicate that the prophecy was directed to Judah as well. The Judah oracle is simply one of seven dealing with the nations surrounding Israel and leading up to the classic denunciation of Israel in the eighth oracle.

Uzziah (or Azariah), king of Judah, reigned 790–740 B.C. He was an energetic king whose policies contributed to the resurgence of Judah in the eighth century. He rebuilt the city of Elath and strengthened the defenses of Jerusalem.

Jeroboam II, king of Israel, reigned 793–753 B.C. He also was a vigorous leader. His greatest accomplishment was the expansion of Israelite territorial holdings into the Transjordan (2 Kings 14:23–29).

Notes

---

1 In Akkadian the cognate to the Hebrew נֹקֵד (*nōqēḏ*, "shepherd") is *nāqidu*. This word sometimes reflects a hierarchical value, with the *re'û* below the *nāqidu*. In some texts the *nāqidu* is described as working for the state administration and as being in charge of herds that were used for state and cultic functions. In Ugaritic the word *nqd* occurs in several lists with little descriptive context. However, in UT, 62:55, the word occurs in the honorific title *rb nqdm* ("chief of the herdsmen"). The bearer of this title is also called *rb khnm* ("chief of the priests"). This attests to his role as a cultic functionary.

חָזָה (*ḥāzāh*, "see") is used mainly in the poetic and prophetic literature of the OT. It is used in the narrative material on only four occasions. In Exod 18:21 it has the sense of active choice, that is, the act of selecting (*ḥāzāh*) involves a mental seeing of the qualities of the men chosen. In Exod 24:11 *ḥāzāh* is used of the Israelite leaders who "saw God"; and, in Num 24:4, 16, it is used of seeing a מַחֲזֶה (*maḥ^{a}zeh*, "vision"). The range of meaning in poetic and prophetic material involves apprehension of visions (Isa 1:1; Ezek 12:27) as well as mental perception and understanding (Job 15:17; 34:32; Prov 24:32). The emphasis on mental apprehension makes this word suitable for describing the process by which the prophets understood their revelations.

II. Introduction to the Prophecy

1:2

[2]He said:

"The LORD roars from Zion
  and thunders from Jerusalem;
the pastures of the shepherds dry up,
  and the top of Carmel withers."

2 The name "LORD" (*YHWH*, "Yahweh") introduces the prophecy; its initial position in the sentence gives it a certain emphasis. "Yahweh," one of several names that reveal aspects of God's character, connotes God's redemptive and covenantal concerns.

In the events associated with the Exodus from Egypt, the name Yahweh was given its greatest revelational content. Moses' first impression of God's character as revealed in "Yahweh" was that of his inviolable holiness (Exod 3:5). The awesome phenomena accompanying Yahweh's appearance on Sinai (Exod 19:16–25) and the restrictions he placed on the people (Exod 19:10–15) enforced the concept of his holiness. His mighty power that delivered the Hebrew people from Egyptian bondage manifested his sovereignty and his redemptive concern.

The prophet introduced a shocking note in depicting Yahweh as roaring from Zion. Though "roar" (*šā'ag*) is frequently used in the OT of a lion's roar, it need not always connote this (Job 37:4; Pss 38:8 [9 MT]; 74:4). Amos's words in the Hebrew here are identical to those of Joel 3:16, where *šā'ag* occurs with no apparent reference to a lion's roar. The cosmic effects of the roar of the Lord in Joel may connote the crashing of thunder. In Job 37:4 *šā'ag* is used in this way.

The parallel expression "thunders" (*yittēn qôlô*, lit., "gives his voice") appears in a number of passages depicting God's intervention in history. This intervention may involve personal deliverance (Ps 18:13 [14 MT]; cf. v.6 [7 MT]) or deliverance on a national scale effected by awesome judgment (Ps 46:6–11). It may be manifested in the continuing processes of nature (Jer 10:13; 51:16) or presage a mighty act of God (Joel 2:11). In each instance there is some manifestation of God's power expressed in natural phenomena, most frequently in a violent thunderstorm.

The roar of the Lord in Amos 1:2 is also accompanied by cosmic changes. Instead of a storm, however, the prophet saw God's wrath causing a withering drought to destroy the green hills of Mount Carmel—a landmark of the northern kingdom. So in this vivid way, Amos pictured the impending judgment of God on that kingdom.

The roar of the Lord also points to his divine intervention in history and presages his dire judgment on the nations dealt with in the subsequent oracles. The roar of the Lord, however, need not always be seen as heralding judgment; for in Hosea 11:10–11 it points to the restoration of God's people.

Verse 2 forms an appropriate introduction to the entire prophecy; its scope need not be limited only to the oracles of 1:3–3:8.

Notes

2 Zion in parallel with Jerusalem shows that Amos understood God as roaring from that city. The origin of God's judgment is not his heavenly abode but the city of Jerusalem. This reflects the Israelite belief that God was resident in Jerusalem, specifically in the temple (Pss 20:2 [3 MT]; 48:2–3 [3–4 MT]; 135:21; Isa 31:9). This statement no doubt angered the citizens of the northern kingdom, for it impugned the validity of their religious sites. The voice of the Lord from Jerusalem effected its results in the northern kingdom (Carmel). This parallels Amos's mission from Judah to Israel.

I. The Prophetic Oracles (1:3–6:14)

A. *Oracles of Judgment Against the Surrounding Nations* (1:3–2:5)

A striking pattern runs through these oracles. The prophet began with the distant city of Damascus and, like a hawk circling its prey, moved in ever-tightening circles, from one country to another, till at last he pounced on Israel. One can imagine Amos's hearers approving the denunciation of these heathen nations. They could even applaud God's denunciation of Judah because of the deep-seated hostility between the two kingdoms that went as far back as the dissolution of the united kingdom after Solomon. But Amos played no favorites; he swooped down on the unsuspecting Israelites as well in the severest language and condemned them for their crimes.

1. *The oracle against Syria*

1:3–5

3This is what the LORD says:

"For three sins of Damascus,
even for four, I will not turn back ⌞my wrath⌟.
Because she threshed Gilead
with sledges having iron teeth,
4I will send fire upon the house of Hazael
that will consume the fortresses of Ben-Hadad.
5I will break down the gate of Damascus;
I will destroy the king who is in the Valley of Aven
and the one who holds the scepter in Beth Eden.
The people of Aram will go into exile to Kir,"

says the LORD.

3 Damascus represented the entire nation of Syria (Aram). As the capital city it represented the nation and was its center of culture and influence. From the time of Ahab till the dawn of the eighth century, there were eruptions of hostilities between Israel and Damascus. Particularly embarrassing had been the incursion of Syria into Israelite territory during the reign of Jehu, in the latter half of the ninth century (2 Kings 10:32–33).

The numerical motif—viz., "for three sins . . . even for four"—is common in Semitic literature. It occurs mainly in the wisdom literature (e.g., Job 5:19; 33:29; Prov 6:16; 30:15–31; Eccl 11:2) but is used by the prophet Micah as well (5:5–6). In some instances the sequence is evidently to be taken literally with the final number equaling the number of elements cited by the author (e.g., Prov 6:16–19). In other cases it is more general and denotes an indefinite number (Mic 5:5–6). The latter usage seems to be intended in Amos 1:3 because Amos cited only one crime of Damascus in this oracle. He had in mind, however, the whole history of Aramean provocation of Israel.

Some have suggested that the masculine pronominal suffix *nû* ("him") on *'ašîḇennû* (lit., "I will turn back him [NIV, 'my wrath']") refers to Assyria, which would not be turned back in its progress toward the ultimate conquest of Israel. But this is unlikely because Assyria is not mentioned in the immediate context, and Amos never specifically spoke of it as the instrument of God's wrath. A reference to Assyria in the oracle concerning Judah (2:4–5) would be inappropriate since Judah fell to the Babylonians. The nearest possible referent of the suffix is *qôl* ("voice"; NIV, "thunders"), the voice of the Lord that presages the impending judgment. If the suffix finds its referent in "voice," the implication is that the Lord will not cause his voice to return—viz., the judgment it heralds is final.

This solution, however, entails certain difficulties. The word *qôl* is not in the immediate context of *'ašîḇennû*, and this makes the suggestion somewhat tenuous. The concept of recalling one's voice is unattested in the OT. The absolute identification of the voice of God with the threatened judgment is also foreign to the OT. The voice of the Lord heralds divine judgment; it is never one with it. In Jeremiah 25:30–31, for example, the roar of the Lord presages punishment by the sword. And the formula "This is what the Lord says" introduces a new logical unit that makes the possibility of a syntactical connection between *qôl* and *nû* questionable.

On the whole it is best to see the suffix *nû* as referring to the judgment that is to come on each of these nations. In this case the suffix would not have a syntactical referent but one implicit in the clause, for one naturally expects the phrase "for three sins of" to be followed by some reference to punishment. The lack of reference to a specific punishment following the statement "for three sins of" creates a feeling of dread uncertainty at the outset of the oracle. Thus the attention of the hearers would have been riveted on the prophet's words as they waited for the explicit description of the judgment that comes in the last section of each oracle.

The crime that provoked the judgment against Damascus was that the people had threshed Gilead with iron threshing sledges. Gilead, an extensive region east of the Jordan River, was known for its rich forests (Jer 22:6–7) and the balm produced there (Jer 8:22). The richness of the area, coupled with its being a frontier region, made it the object of numerous attacks by the nearby countries of Ammon and Syria.

The incident Amos referred to here is most probably the one recorded in 2 Kings 13:1–9. There an incursion of the Syrians into Israel during the reign of Jehoahaz is described as making the army of Jehoahaz "like the dust at threshing time" (v.7). The metaphor Amos used is that of a threshing sledge, an agricultural implement made of parallel boards fitted with sharp points of iron or stone. We do not, of course, need to understand the metaphor as a literal act in which the bodies of Israelites were torn apart by sledges. The use of the somewhat similar expression in 2 Kings 13:7 seems also to be metaphorical. The intensity of the metaphor, however, implies the most extreme decimation and may hint at especially cruel or inhuman treatment.

4 The judgment the Lord decrees for Syria is "fire upon the house of Hazael." Hazael ruled Syria about 841 to 806 B.C. His accession to the throne of Syria was revealed by the Lord to the prophet Elisha (2 Kings 8:13). The Lord also revealed that Hazael would commit monstrous crimes against the Israelites (2 Kings 8:12). When Hazael came to the throne, he fought against Joram and Ahaziah at Ramoth Gilead, an encounter in which Joram was seriously wounded (2 Kings 8:28–29).

Ben-Hadad ("son of Hadad," an ancient storm god) is the name of two or possibly three kings of Syria. It may be a dynastic name. Ben-Hadad I, a contemporary of Baasha, king of Israel (909–886 B.C.), and Asa, king of Judah (911–870 B.C.), took large territorial holdings from Baasha (1 Kings 15:20). Each of the kings named "Ben-Hadad" carried on continual hostilities against Israel. The name Ben-Hadad in Amos 1:4 could well stand for all the kings who bore that name; yet since only one Hazael is known, it may be that Amos had only one of the kings named Ben-Hadad in mind. It is likely that this was the son of Hazael (2 Kings 13:3). The names of Hazael and Ben-Hadad would be synonymous with the long history of Syrian conflict and oppression.

The fire mentioned in v.4 is not a description of an isolated occurrence relating only to Damascus, for it appears in all but one of the oracles. Only the oracle against Israel lacks it (2:6–16). It is best understood as a metaphorical representation of God's judgment (cf. 7:4).

5 The destruction of Damascus will involve the breaking of the "gate of Damascus" (lit., "the bar of Damascus"). The gates of ancient cities were equipped with massive bars, sometimes of iron or bronze (1 Kings 4:13). The breaking of the bar implies that the enemies had gained entrance to the city.

The "Valley of Aven" (*biq'aṯ 'āwen*) has not been positively identified. Since this valley was associated with Syria, it is quite likely that it was the plain between the Lebanon and Anti-Lebanon ranges, the most prominent landmark of its kind in the area of Damascus. Today this plain is called *Beqa'a*. The LXX renders the name *'āwen* ("Aven") as *'ōn*, adopting a vocalic tradition that differs from the MT. The name *'ōn* was the name of the ancient Egyptian city of Heliopolis, a city dedicated to the worship of the sun-god Re. One of the most prominent cities in the *Beqa'a* in ancient times was also called Heliopolis by the Greeks. It is the site of the modern city of Baalbek. While there is no solid evidence that the Aramean Heliopolis was also called *'ōn*, this is not impossible, particularly if there was interaction between Syria and Egypt before this time. The vocalic reading of the MT may be a deliberate distortion changing *'ōn* to *'āwen* ("evil") to make a derogatory pun on the name. The same type of pun on the name Bethel may be found in Hosea 4:15; 5:8; 10:5, where Beth Aven ("house of wickedness") is substituted for Bethel ("house of God").

Beth Eden is also difficult to identify. It seems best, however, to identify it with the Bit-adini of the Akkadian texts. This Aramean city-state, located on the banks of the Euphrates River, was an important city in the time of Amos. It was conquered by the Assyrians in 855 B.C. and thus was not under Syrian control when Amos was carrying on his prophetic ministry. Amos, however, seemed to be referring to the past history of Syria. Since Bit-adini was a flourishing city of that country for many years, it is quite likely that this is the city named by him.

The name Beth Aven may mean "house of evil" according to the MT tradition, and Beth Eden may mean "house of delight." Some commentators have thus understood the names to be surrogates for Damascus, expressive of the idolatrous practices associated with that city. This would, however, be the only instance where this occurs in the oracles. All the other places cited are referred to by their proper names, not symbolic ones.

The identification of Kir is also difficult. Amos understood Kir to be the place of the national origin of the Syrians (9:7) and predicted their return to that place. His prophecy was fulfilled when Tiglath-pileser took the people of Damascus captive, transporting them to Kir (2 Kings 16:9). The crimes attributed to Syria by Amos are of a social nature. They are crimes of unmitigated cruelty perpetrated on the Israelites in the numerous attacks waged by the Syrians.

Notes

3 Not only did Israel lose much of the Transjordan region during the reign of Jehu, but Jehoahaz, his son (814–798 B.C.), was conquered by Hazael and was allowed to retain only a token military force (2 Kings 13:7).

Examples of the numerical motif in Ugaritic may be found in UT, 8:2–3:51, III, 17–18; 52:19–20, 66–67; 128: II, 23–24. For a discussion of numerical sequence in the OT, see W. Roth, "The Numerical Sequence $x/x+1$ in the Old Testament," VetTest 12 (1962): 300–311.

While the feminine suffix seems more appropriate for expressing the abstract idea of punishment, the masculine was also used in this way, probably reflecting colloquial usage (cf. GKC, par. 135o). In Amos's usage of the suffix, the gender is not always precise. Note 4:1 where the masculine suffix הֶם *(hem)* on אֲדֹנֵיהֶם (*'ᵃḏōnêhem*) "their husbands" has a feminine referent. In 4:12 there is another instance of a threat followed by an unspecified judgment. See the discussion at that point.

4 Ben-Hadad was the name of two or possibly three kings of Syria. Several scholars posit only two kings with this name because the biblical accounts in 1 Kings and 2 Chron are not precise in this regard (F. Bruce, *Israel and the Nations* [Grand Rapids: Eerdmans, 1963], pp. 42–50).

Since Ben-Hadad, the son of Hazael, figured prominently in the events surrounding the reign of Jehoahaz (814–798 B.C.), it is probable that Amos had this Ben-Hadad in mind. Many of Amos's hearers in Israel would recall the oppressions under Hazael and his son Ben-Hadad (2 Kings 13:1–3).

5 For further discussion of the identification of Beth Eden with Bit-adini, see A. Malamat, "Amos 1:5 in the Light of the Til Barsip Inscriptions," BASOR 129 (February 1953): 25–26.

---

2. *The oracle against the Philistines*

1:6–8

6This is what the LORD says:

"For three sins of Gaza,
even for four, I will not turn back ⌞my wrath⌟.
Because she took captive whole communities
and sold them to Edom,
7I will send fire upon the walls of Gaza
that will consume her fortresses.
8I will destroy the king of Ashdod
and the one who holds the scepter in Ashkelon.
I will turn my hand against Ekron,
till the last of the Philistines is dead,"

says the Sovereign LORD.

6–8 The prophet next turned his attention to the Philistines. These perennial enemies of the Israelites were a non-Semitic people who may have had their national origin in the Aegean area, probably Crete, or whose migrations took them through that area. They occupied the coastal plain in southwest Palestine and conducted numerous raids on the Israelites till their power was broken by King David. The Philistines lived in five cities (Ashdod, Ashkelon, Ekron, Gath, Gaza; cf. Josh 13:3; 1 Sam 6:16–17) on the coastal plain, each ruled by a separate lord.

Amos mentioned four of the cities of the Philistine pentapolis in this oracle. Only Gath is excluded. It is suggested by some that the exclusion of this city reflects its destruction by Sargon in 711 B.C., thus the oracle is viewed as a later insertion. But perhaps Gath never fully recovered from Uzziah's successful military campaign described in 2 Chronicles 26:6. Uzziah reigned about 790 to 740 B.C., with a coregency with his father, Amaziah, from about 790 to 767 B.C. Uzziah's Philistine campaign may have taken place shortly after the death of Amaziah, because it is the first event to follow the historical summary in vv.1–5. It is quite likely that Uzziah's sacking of Gath occurred sometime in the period between Amaziah's death (767

B.C.) and Amos's ministry (760 B.C.). The destruction of the wall of the city would thus be well-known to Amos's hearers and would lend a sense of authenticity to his message predicting the doom of the other cities of the pentapolis.

There is a difficulty, however, with the latter view, for Ashdod is cited in 2 Chronicles 26:6 along with Gath. Both cities were sacked by Uzziah in the Philistine wars. The view does not explain why Ashdod is cited by Amos in the oracle of 1:6–8 and Gath alone is omitted. Perhaps Gath had not recovered sufficiently to be included among the five cities of Philistia in the time of Amos.

Others have suggested that Gath is not cited in Amos 1:6–8 because of its peculiar ethnic structure. Kassis argues that Gath was a Canaanite city, "ruled by a Canaanite king who was a vassal of Philistine overlords" (H. Kassis, "Gath and the Structure of 'Philistine' Society, JBL 84 [1965]: 259–71).

Another possibility why Gath is not mentioned is that it had never fully recovered from an attack by Hazael (2 Kings 12:17) during the reign of Jehoash of Judah (835–796 B.C.). But the later campaign of Uzziah against Gath indicates that the Philistines had regained control of the city and had sufficient strength to be a threat to Judah.

We cannot be certain of the reason for the exclusion of Gath, but its omission is insufficient evidence to impugn the authenticity of this oracle. Gath is excluded from all the lists of the Philistine cities cited after Amos (Jer 25:20; Zeph 2:4; Zech 9:5–6).

The Philistines are denounced for the crime of enslavement (v.6)—again, a social crime. Though the event referred to here cannot be identified, it was probably a series of border raids in which slaves were secured and sold to the Edomites. Amos indicates that whole communities were taken in this way, thus underscoring the enormity of the crime. It is likely that the crime was committed against Israelites. But it is impossible to be certain of this. The punishment to be inflicted on the Philistines was their absolute destruction (vv.7–8).

Notes

7–8 Gaza and Ashdod were conquered by Nebuchadnezzar (605–562 B.C.) and their kings transported to Babylon (ANET, pp. 307–8). Ashkelon was conquered by Tiglath-pileser III in 734 B.C. Later, in 701 B.C., Sennacherib conquered the city and carried off the king of Ashkelon to Assyria. In later years the city was overrun by the Scythians, Chaldeans, and Persians. Esarhaddon and Ashur-banipal required tribute of Ekron (ANET, pp. 291, 294). The city continued to exist till the time of the Crusades.

3. *The oracle against Tyre*

1:9–10

9 This is what the LORD says:

"For three sins of Tyre,
even for four, I will not turn back ⌊my wrath⌋.
Because she sold whole communities of captives to Edom,
disregarding a treaty of brotherhood,

> [10]I will send fire upon the walls of Tyre
> that will consume her fortresses."

9–10 So far Amos has moved from Damascus in the northeast to the Philistine territory in the southwest. He moved next to Tyre to the north of Israel and southwest of Damascus, thus closer to Israel than Damascus and the Philistine cities. Tyre was the most important city of Phoenicia at that time.

The crime of Tyre also involved the enslavement of whole communities (v.9), but to this Amos added a reference to its "disregarding a treaty of brotherhood." The treaty (*bᵉrîṯ*) that this slave commerce violated may refer to the pact made between Hiram, king of Tyre, and Solomon (1 Kings 5:12; cf. "brother" in 1 Kings 9:13). This relationship was strengthened further by the marriage of Jezebel, daughter of Ethbaal, king of the Sidonians, to King Ahab (1 Kings 16:31). While Jehu's purge of the family of Ahab (2 Kings 10) interrupted the good relationship between the two states, Amos may have been referring to the generally amicable relations that characterized these nations over their long histories.

Tyre's security, however, was only temporary (v.10). It came under Assyrian hegemony during the long period of that empire's dominance but emerged from Assyrian control to enter a period of power and affluence. Tyre was later besieged by the forces of Nebuchadnezzar and never fully recovered. The massive efforts required for its defense greatly weakened the city, and it entered a period of decline. In 332 Alexander besieged Tyre and conquered it.

Notes

9 Homer referred to the Phoenician practice of slave trading in *Odyssey* 4.288ff.; 15.473ff. See also "Contest of Homer and Hesiod," *Hesiod: The Homeric Hymns and Homerica*, translated by H. Evelyn-White (Cambridge: Harvard University Press, 1950), p. 569.

4. *The oracle against Edom*

1:11–12

[11]This is what the LORD says:

> "For three sins of Edom,
> even for four, I will not turn back ⌊my wrath⌋.
> Because he pursued his brother with a sword,
> stifling all compassion,
> because his anger raged continually
> and his fury flamed unchecked,
> [12]I will send fire upon Teman
> that will consume the fortresses of Bozrah."

11 The extensive, mountainous region of Edom lay to the southeast of the southern tip of the Dead Sea, east of the Arabah. It was one of the three Transjordanian kingdoms that included Ammon and Moab. Edom's crime was that "he pursued his brother with a sword" and "his anger raged continually"—a reference to the long-standing animosity of Edom toward the Israelites.

Edom was another name for Esau, the twin brother of Jacob. The Edomites and Israelites thus had close ethnic ties. These are reflected in the use of the word "brother" in reference to the Israelites (cf. Num 20:14; Obad 12; cf. Deut 23:7, where the Israelites were commanded not to hate an Edomite, "for he is your brother"). The bitter relations between Jacob and Esau were perpetuated in the affairs of the two countries. In their wilderness journey the Israelites sought access to the king's highway that ran through Edom. But the Edomites refused passage and even sent a military force to block them (Num 20:14–21). In 1 Samuel 14:47, the Edomites are mentioned as one of the enemies of Saul. David placed military garrisons in Edom (2 Sam 8:14), and an Edomite rebellion against Judah during the reign of Jehoram is recorded in 2 Kings 8:20–22. Their greatest act of hostility against Israel occurred during the sack of Jerusalem by Nebuchadnezzar in 587 B.C. At that time the Edomites gloated over the destruction of their enemies and hindered the fugitives' escape, delivering many over to their captors (Obad 10–14).

12 For these crimes the cities of Teman and Bozrah were to be destroyed. Teman was one of the largest cities of Edom, and Bozrah was a strong fortress city in the north of Edom. These cities represent the whole country. Both were denounced in several prophetic oracles (Isa 34:6; 63:1; Jer 49:13, 20; Ezek 25:13; Obad 9).

Edom became tributary to Tiglath-pileser III in 732 B.C. and was overrun by the Nabataeans later in its history. The crime of Edom was in many ways similar to that of the other nations Amos spoke against—viz., violence against one's fellow man. In this oracle Amos emphasized that the Edomites stifled "all compassion" (cf. the NT warning against failure to show love to one's "brother" [James 4:11; 1 John 2:9]).

Notes

11 Remnants of Edom's past glory may be seen today in the ruins of Petra, an ancient Edomite city. The ruins probably date from Nabataean times.

The reference to Edom in Obad 10–14 assumes a date of 450 B.C. for that book.

5. *The oracle against Ammon*

1:13–15

13 This is what the LORD says:

"For three sins of Ammon,
even for four, I will not turn back ⌞my wrath⌟.
Because he ripped open the pregnant women of Gilead
in order to extend his borders,
14 I will set fire to the walls of Rabbah
that will consume her fortresses
amid war cries on the day of battle,
amid violent winds on a stormy day.

[15]Her king will go into exile,
he and his officials together,"
says the LORD.

13 Ammon lay northeast of the Dead Sea and north of Moab. The area was dominated by a vast expanse of desert, though the valley of the upper Jabbok in the north of Ammon was fertile. The Ammonites frequently sought to enlarge their territory, sometimes with the help of Moab and Syria, their neighbors. In the time of the Judges, the Ammonites crossed the Jordan and went deep into Israelite territory (Judg 10:6–9). A serious threat to Israel by the Ammonites was quelled by the strong, personal leadership of Saul (1 Sam 11:1–11). They were finally subdued in David's time (2 Sam 12:26–31).

The account in Genesis 19:30–38 attributes the national origin of the Ammonites and Moabites to an incestual relationship between Lot and his two daughters. The crime Amos accused the Ammonites of was like that of the other nations, a crime against humanity. The Ammonites "ripped open the pregnant women of Gilead." This evidently took place in one of their attempts to expand their territorial holdings at Israel's expense. While we do not know the particular circumstances of this monstrous crime, it may have occurred during the campaigns of Hazael against Israel toward the end of the ninth century B.C. (cf. 2 Kings 8:12). At this time all Israel's territory in the Transjordan fell into the hands of the Arameans. The Ammonites may have taken advantage of this opportunity to exploit Israel's weakness. Apparently it was a notorious event, and its mention would stir feelings of revulsion in Amos's hearers.

Gilead was a mountainous region east of the Jordan, in the tribal territories of Gad and the half-tribe of Manasseh. It is easy to understand how this fertile frontier region would suffer when Israel was attacked by her enemies to the east. Certainly the crime Amos accused the Ammonites of went far beyond necessary acts of war and is attributed to the Ammonites' insatiable desire for Israelite territory.

14 Rabbah was the capital of ancient Ammon. Today it is the site of the modern city of Amman. As its punishment Ammon was to be destroyed by fire, to the accompaniment of the shouts of battle and "violent winds." The word translated "war cries" (*t^erû'āh*) may connote shouting for joy (Ezra 3:12), a trumpet signal (Num 10:5), or the shout of battle (Josh 6:5). In this instance it is the shout of the enemy "on the day of battle," a sound that would terrify the people as the enemy rushed to take the city.

The word "winds" (*sa'ar*) is used of a wind storm on three occasions (Ps 55:8 [9 MT]; Jonah 1:4, 12) but occurs most frequently as a metaphor of God's wrath (Ps 83:15 [16 MT]; Jer 23:19: 25:32; 30:23). Here, however, it need not connote a theophany. Its parallel member *t^erû'āh* ("war cries") does not. It simply describes the great force with which the enemy will sweep over the city.

15 The king of Ammon was to go into exile along with his officials. In an oracle against the Ammonites, Ezekiel berated them for rejoicing at the Fall of Jerusalem (Ezek 25:1–7). Yet their rejoicing was to last only a little while; for they were to be caught up in the same turmoil that affected Israel, and they passed from history for good.

Ammon's dominion came to an end when Nebuchadnezzar sacked the city of Rabbah and took large numbers of its citizens captive. This opened the way for Arab invaders to occupy the territory of Ammon.

Notes

14 For a discussion of the possibility of a "Yahweh theophany" here, see Mays, pp. 37–38.

15 In the parallel passage in Jer 49:1–3 [30:17–20 LXX], the word מַלְכָּם (*malkām*, "their king," NIV mg.) is rendered *milkōm* in the RSV. Milcom was the name of the national deity of the Ammonites. NASB renders the word "Malcam" and NIV "Molech." The LXX translates the word by Μελχομ (*Melchom*). The passage in Jeremiah (49:1–3) shows dependence on Amos 1:13–15 (cf. v.3), but the Jeremiah passage does not necessarily warrant reading Milcom in Amos 1:15. The use of the word שָׂרָיו (*śārāyw*, "his officials") in the parallel line of v.15 favors the reading "their king" rather than a reference to the Ammonite deity. Also, Jeremiah may have used a play on words in his oracle about Ammon, for in 49:3 the parallel line has כֹּהֲנָיו (*kōhanāyw*, "his priests") besides *śārāyw*. Amos 1:15 has הוּא (*hû'*, "he") at that point.

6. *The oracle against Moab*

2:1–3

1 This is what the LORD says:

"For three sins of Moab,
even for four, I will not turn back ⌊my wrath⌋.
Because he burned, as if to lime,
the bones of Edom's king,
2 I will send fire upon Moab
that will consume the fortresses of Kerioth.
Moab will go down in great tumult
amid war cries and the blast of the trumpet.
3 I will destroy her ruler
and kill all her officials with him,"

says the LORD.

1 Moab lay to the east of the Dead Sea, between Ammon to the north and Edom to the south. The northern boundary was the Wadi Arnon, though the Moabites extended their territory north of the Arnon in times of their strength.

Antipathy between the Hebrews and Moabites developed early when the king of Moab would not grant them permission to use the king's highway (Judg 11:17). As a result the Moabites were excluded from the assembly of Israel (Deut 23:3–4).

The Israelites camped in the plains of Moab before entering Canaan (Num 22:1). The king of Moab, concerned over the strength of the Israelites, engaged Baalam, the enigmatic seer, to curse them (Num 22:4–6). It was in the plains of Moab that the Moabite women seduced the Israelites to join in their idolatrous worship (Num 25:1–3). During a period of Israelite weakness in the time of the Judges, a coalition of Moabites, Ammonites, and Amalekites invaded Israel and subjugated them for eighteen years (Judg 3:13–14).

Saul defeated the Moabites (1 Sam 14:47), as did David (2 Sam 8:2). During Solomon's reign Moab seems to have remained under Israelite dominion, for Solomon included Moabite women among his many wives (1 Kings 11:1). But Mesha, king of Moab, rebelled against Israel after the death of Ahab (2 Kings 1:1). Joram of Israel and Jehoshaphat of Judah, along with the king of Edom, made an abortive attempt to subdue them (2 Kings 3). The Moabite stone, one of the few Moabite sources available to scholars, commemorates this event. Later on Hazael, an Aramean king, wrested from Jehu the disputed Moabite territory north of the Arnon (2 Kings 10:32–33).

The crime with which Amos charged the Moabites was their burning of the bones of the king of Edom. While this is not mentioned specifically in the OT, it may have taken place during the attempt of the coalition of the kings of Israel, Judah, and Edom to suppress the Moabite rebellion (2 Kings 3; cf. Notes). The expression "burn the bones" (*śārᵉpô ʿaṣmôṯ*) never refers to the burning of an individual as punishment for a crime. Except for two metaphorical uses where it connotes extreme suffering (Job 30:30; Ps 102:3[4 MT]), the expression refers to the burning of the skeletal remains of a corpse (2 Kings 23:20; cf. v.16; cf. also 1 Kings 13:2; Ezek 24:10) or the burning of the corpse itself (Amos 6:9–10). Thus the crime of Moab involved the desecration of the body of an Edomite king. How long after his death this happened is unknown.

2–3 The punishment of Moab was to be by fire that would consume Kerioth (v.2). Though Kerioth may be translated "cities," it is likely a proper noun referring to a major city in Moab—a city referred to in Jeremiah 48:24.

Amos used vivid language to describe the conflict that would overthrow Moab. One can almost hear the "war cries" and "the blast of the trumpet." Clearly the "fire" that would come on Moab symbolizes war.

Moab became subject to Tiglath-pileser III in 734 B.C. Later, Moab was involved in a rebellion against Assyrian domination that was quelled by Sennacherib. During the period of Babylonian supremacy, Moab was forced to pay tribute to Babylon. The Moabites rebelled against Babylon shortly after 598 B.C. and, according to Josephus (Antiq. X, 181–82 [ix.7]), were conquered by Nebuchadnezzar. This opened the way for Arab tribes to occupy Moabite territory.

Highly significant is the fact that Amos here pronounced the punishment of Yahweh on a social crime involving a non-Israelite. In his other oracles the crimes were, for the most part, against the covenant people. Amos understood that an aspect of God's law transcended Israel. He affirmed a moral law that extended to noncovenant nations, a law that would surely bring punishment if violated.

It is not the complex legal code of Sinai for which the Moabites were held liable but the law of social responsibility, respect for human dignity and for the rights of all people. This, of course, is also an aspect of the Mosaic law; and Amos's oracle against Moab eloquently attests to God's demand that the human rights of all people be respected, regardless of their relationship to the covenant. Christians must not limit their sphere of concern only to those within the church. Christians have an inescapable responsibility to call for obedience to the moral law. When anybody—Christian or otherwise—spurns that law, the judgment of the Lord inevitably follows.

Notes

1 While burning the bones of the king of Edom is not clearly cited elsewhere in the OT, it is possible that Amos alluded to the event recorded in 2 Kings 3:21–27. The eldest son who was offered for a burnt offering (v.27) may have been the son of the king of Edom rather than the son of the king of Moab. The object of the military tactic described in 2 Kings 3:26 was to "break through to the king of Edom." When this failed, the king of Moab may have captured the son of the king of Edom, who was heir to the throne (v.27), and ordered him burned. For a full discussion of this, see E. Pusey, *The Minor Prophets*, 2 vols. (Grand Rapids: Baker, 1950), 1:257.

7. *The oracle against Judah*

2:4–5

4 This is what the LORD says:

"For three sins of Judah,
even for four, I will not turn back ⌞my wrath⌟.
Because they have rejected the law of the LORD
and have not kept his decrees,
because they have been led astray by false gods,
the gods their ancestors followed,
5 I will send fire upon Judah
that will consume the fortresses of Jerusalem."

4–5 Having pronounced judgment on various pagan nations, Amos next turned to Judah. God plays no favorites and cannot condone the sins of his people. While both Israel and Judah had a common religious heritage, the cleavage of the two kingdoms after the death of Solomon left wounds that never healed. Deep-rooted antipathies existed between the two kingdoms. Amos's denunciation of Judah would fall on sympathetic ears in Israel.

Judah is condemned for rejecting the "law of the LORD" (*tôraṯ YHWH*) (v.4). This is the first time this expression occurs in these oracles, and its significance is obvious. This is an oracle against those who stood in relationship to the covenant. Hence they were judged on the basis of the light they possessed, not on the basis of a common moral consciousness, but on the statutes of Yahweh himself.

The word translated "led astray" (*tā'āh*) means basically "to wander around." It is used of straying animals and intoxicated persons, as well as moral aberration. Judah had been led astray by "false gods" (*kāzāḇ*, "lies"). The Hebrew expression "walked after them" (NIV, "followed") frequently relates to following false gods. The use of "lie" in conjunction with this expression shows that for Amos these deities were false in their very essence. The sin of idolatry has caused Judah to violate the law of Yahweh. Like their fathers of old, they continued to bow down to the false gods of the pagans and spurn the Creator of heaven and earth.

Judah's punishment was to be similar to that of the other nations—destruction by the fire of war (v.5). It was inflicted when Jerusalem fell to the Babylonians.

B. *Oracles of Judgment Against Israel* (2:6–6:14)

1. *A lesson from history*

2:6–16

6This is what the LORD says:

"For three sins of Israel,
even for four, I will not turn back ⌊my wrath⌋.
They sell the righteous for silver,
and the needy for a pair of sandals.
7They trample on the heads of the poor
as upon the dust of the ground
and deny justice to the oppressed.
Father and son use the same girl
and so profane my holy name.
8They lie down beside every altar
on garments taken in pledge.
In the house of their god
they drink wine taken as fines.

9"I destroyed the Amorite before them,
though he was tall as the cedars
and strong as the oaks.
I destroyed his fruit above
and his roots below.

10"I brought you up out of Egypt,
and I led you forty years in the desert
to give you the land of the Amorites.
11I also raised up prophets from among your sons
and Nazirites from among your young men.
Is this not true, people of Israel?"
declares the LORD.
12"But you made the Nazirites drink wine
and commanded the prophets not to prophesy.

13"Now then, I will crush you
as a cart crushes when loaded with grain.
14The swift will not escape,
the strong will not muster their strength,
and the warrior will not save his life.
15The archer will not stand his ground,
the fleet-footed soldier will not get away,
and the horseman will not save his life.
16Even the bravest warriors
will flee naked on that day,"
declares the LORD.

Though they may have rejoiced in the denunciation of their brothers in Judah, the Israelites themselves were to feel the lash of Amos's words. The same formula that introduces the condemnation of their pagan enemies begins this powerful oracle. It is the most extensive of all the oracles. Verses 6–8 set forth Israel's crimes, vv.9–11 appeal to God's past activity in their behalf, and vv.12–16 conclude the oracle with a vivid portrayal of their punishment.

6 The Israelites were accused of selling "the righteous for silver." The word "righteous" (*ṣaddîq*) is parallel to "needy" (*'eḇyôn*), establishing a connection between them. The word *ṣaddîq* connotes "righteousness," not necessarily in the sense of blamelessness, but rather in the basic sense of "rightness" or "justice." The needy are seen as being in the right, or having a just cause. The word *ṣaddîq* is used in this sense in Exodus 23:7, where in a context of litigation it is coupled with "innocent" (*nāqî*). In Deuteronomy 25:1 *ṣaddîq* is the antithesis of "guilty" (*rāšā'*). On a number of occasions (e.g., Isa 32:7; Jer 5:28) the prophets spoke of the "needy" as being in litigious situations. This shows us something of the social conditions of that time, when the poor had to fight for their just rights, which were all too frequently ignored.

The pronoun "they" applies to the oppressing classes, especially the judges and creditors who "sell the righteous." These people of power and influence were guilty of accepting bribes of money and apparel. They regarded the oppressed classes so lightly that they accepted such paltry bribes as a pair of sandals. Amos characterized their corruption as "selling."

7 Amos further described the oppression of the poor as trampling "on the heads of the poor." The word translated "trample" (*šā'ap*) may also mean "gasp" or "pant." Here the text presents certain difficulties; but if one follows the MT literally, the most favorable rendering is "who pant after the dust of the earth on the head of the poor." This would mean either that the oppressing classes longed to see the poor brought to extreme anguish or that they were so avaricious that they craved the dust that the poor had cast on their heads. In the ancient culture dust on the head was a sign of sorrow (e.g., 2 Sam 1:2; Job 2:12).

Israel's decadence was marked by sexual promiscuity. Whether or not this refers to ritual prostitution is not clear. The word for "girl" (*na'ᵃrāh*) is a general one and has no specific connotations. It is possible that the act described here refers to misuse of a legal aspect of concubinage such as described in Exodus 21:7–11. More likely, however, it relates to the ancient laws against incest. An indication of this may be found in the words "profane my holy name." These words occur in Leviticus 22:32, where they culminate a lengthy section dealing with personal and social purity. Leviticus 18:6–18; 20:17–21 are sections that specifically prohibit incest. In 18:7 intercourse with one's mother is forbidden, which reflects the fact that husband and wife are one flesh. Thus an incestuous relationship with one's mother also dishonored one's father. Similarly, sexual intercourse with one's stepmother was incestuous in that it also dishonored one's father (18:8; 20:11), and intercourse with an aunt by marriage was incestuous because it uncovered the nakedness of one's uncle (18:14; 20:20).

While these laws do not specify that the prohibition extended to intercourse with women outside the family, the principle may still apply. The use of one girl by both a father and a son was tantamount to incest in that the son uncovered the nakedness of his father, and vice versa, through their union with the same girl.

Even though the particular practice Amos condemned is difficult to determine, v.7 provides an insight into the social conditions of the time. The marital purity and faithfulness expected in a godly father were lacking, as both father and son engaged in deliberate acts of disobedience to God.

8 Amos also pictured members of his society as sleeping by the altars on "garments taken in pledge." Clothing was regarded as valid collateral for securing debts. Hebrew law, however, required that garments taken in pledge be restored to the owner each evening (Exod 22:26–27) as a covering during sleep. But many obviously disregarded this law by sleeping in the garments of others.

The placing of this practice in the prevailing cultus ("every altar") emphasizes the great disparity between religion and practice in Israel. This is further illustrated by the people's drinking in the "house of their god" the wine paid as fines.

9 Amos next recounted God's gracious acts during Israel's past. "Amorite" is an OT term sometimes used for the preconquest population of Canaan (Gen 15:16). The prophet reminded the people of God's destruction of the Canaanites in the conquest. The great height and strength of the Canaanites reflect a tradition begun at the return of the spies from their reconnaissance of Canaan (Num 13:22–33). It points to their apparent invincibility and contrasts it with the might of the Lord. Amos's vivid metaphor of the fruit and the roots portrays the destruction of the Canaanites when the Israelites took the Promised Land.

10 Amos saw the Exodus and the forty years of wandering in the desert solely as expressions of the gracious power of Yahweh. Thus there was no need for him to mention Israel's disobedience in the wilderness. He simply pointed out that the Lord gave them "the land of the Amorites."

11 The raising up of prophets and Nazirites was another of God's gracious acts. The parallel reference to these two groups does not imply that they were one and the same, or that one was derived from the other. They were simply two groups who ministered God's word to Israel and showed the Lord's care for their spiritual welfare.

12 The word "Nazirite" (*nāzîr*) means "separate." Thus it denotes the consecration to God practiced by this group. The Nazirites took a special vow of separation (cf. Num 6:1–12). They abstained from partaking of any product of the vine and from all fermented drinks. They vowed neither to cut the hair nor to touch a dead body. Like the Rechabites (Jer 35) and the prophets, they were an influence for good in Israel. They seemed to have protested non-Yahwistic practices and the religious decay that accompanied the urbanization of Palestine after the conquest. In mentioning these groups Amos rounded out his brief reference to Israel's history.

Verse 12 tells how Israel treated the Nazirites and the prophets. They forced the former to drink wine and violate their vows, and they muzzled the prophets. This was a more heinous crime than simply opposing these religious groups; it was tantamount to rejecting the word of Yahweh and the dedication to Yahweh that found expression among them.

Israel's rejection of the God who acted on their behalf—from Egypt to the present—is implicit in v.12. This rejection leads to the statement of doom that follows (vv.13–16). The coming judgment is vividly expressed in a series of images rapidly moving from one familiar realm to another.

13–16 First, Amos pictured the nation's being crushed like an object under the wheels of a heavily laden cart (v.13). This picture, drawn from the agricultural world, reflects Amos's familiarity with that life.

The other images include a swift runner, a strong man, and a warrior (v.14). These figures depict Israel's inability to escape the impending destruction. The archer cannot stand (v. 15). The brave warriors will flee with nothing left (v. 16), their weapons and armor scattered behind as on a battlefield.

The Israelites had experienced Yahweh's leading in the Exodus and in the wilderness, his sword hewing the way for them to the Promised Land. Now that sword would be turned against them, because they spurned the Holy One of Israel. The oracle closes with an awesome note of finality—"declares the LORD."

Notes

---

6 Several commentators (e.g., Wolff) understand the words "sell the righteous for silver" to refer to the Israelite practice of debt-slavery to aid those who were insolvent (Exod 21:7–8; Lev 25:39–55; 2 Kings 4:1; Neh 5:8; Isa 50:1). It is not always easy to distinguish the types of slavery legislated in the OT. However, where debt-slavery is clearly in view, the debtor initiates his servitude or that of a member of his family. This is not the emphasis in Amos 2:6, unless one understands the wealthy classes to have created the conditions under which the poor must enter debt-slavery; but this is not consonant with the active and direct involvement that Amos attributed to the oppressing classes. The point is that the innocent were being accused of crimes they did not commit. The magistrates were being bribed for paltry sums to punish the innocent. These dishonest practices were a direct violation of the law (Deut 16:18–20).

7 The word שָׁאַף (*šā'ap*, "trample") may also mean "gasp" or "pant." If understood as "trample," the בְּ (*b*[e], "with") prefix on רֹאשׁ (*rō'š*, "head") is difficult to construe as a preposition. Hammershaimb (p. 48) suggests that *b*[e] serves to introduce an object, observing the similar function of *b*[e] with the verbs פָּגַע (*pāga'*) and פָּגַשׁ (*pāgaš*). But these verbs, meaning "to meet, encounter," may prefer *b*[e] because the concept of motion or direction inherent in them is consonant with the basic meaning of that preposition. Thus the translation "those who trample to the dust of the earth, the head of the poor" is difficult. The translation that most accurately renders the MT is "who pant after the dust of the earth on the head of the poor."

BDB cites two roots שָׁאַף (*šā'ap*). One means to "crush, trample upon," the other is a parallel form of שׁוּף (*šûp*, "to bruise"). It is under the latter that Amos 2:7 is placed, along with Amos 8:4; Pss 56:2–3; 57:4; Ezek 36:3. KB and GKC cite the latter references under *šā'ap* as "to pant" or "to snap at." The LXX reads "sandals, with which to tread on the dust of the earth, and they have smitten upon the heads of the poor." This attests to a verb not present in the MT ("smitten"). The question is difficult, but the MT makes sense as it stands and best fits with the charge of greed in v. 6.

8 The so-called Yabneh-yam letter records an incident that reflects the biblical law of Exod 22:26–27 (25–26 MT) regarding seizure of one's garment for nonpayment of a debt (cf. ANET, p. 568; F. Cross, "Epigraphic Notes on Hebrew Documents of the Eighth-Sixth Centuries B.C., II. The Murabba'at Papyrus and the Letter Found Near Yabneh-Yam" BASOR 165 [February 1962]: 34–46).

11 The word נָזִיר (*nāzîr*, "Nazirite") is based on the root נָזַר (*nāzar*, "to separate"), which shows that the Nazirite was a separated or consecrated person. *Nāzîr* is translated "prince" in a number of EVs (Gen 49:26, NEB, NIV; Deut 33:16, RSV, NEB, NIV; Lam 4:7, RSV, NIV, NEB). However, this is best understood as a secondary meaning derived from *nēzer*, sometimes translated "crown." The long hair of a Nazirite was his "separation [*nēzer*] to God . . . on his head" (Num 6:7). The use of *nēzer* to connote the headgear of the priest (Exod 29:6) and a royal crown (2 Sam 1:10) seems to denote that the headgear is a sign of consecration to one's office.

13 The meaning of מֵעִיק (*mēʿîq*, "crush") is uncertain. It occurs only here. However, the meaning "press down" is supported by the related root עָקָה (*ʿāqāh*), which connotes the idea of "pressure" in Ps 55:4. The ambiguity of the Hebrew is reflected in various EVs: NASB, "I am weighted down beneath you"; RSV, "I will press you down." While the Masoretic tradition is admittedly difficult, it need not be rejected out of hand. The Hebrew says literally, "Behold I am pressing down under you as a cart loaded with sheaves presses down." Gese suggests that the wording עוּק (*ʿûq*) means "to cleave," "to furrow" (H. Gese, "Kleine Beiträge zum Verständuis des Amosbuches," VetTest 12 [1962]: 417–24). If this is correct, the picture is that of God cleaving the ground before Israel as a heavily loaded cart digs into the ground. Israel is thus impeded in its attempt to flee from the impending doom.

---

2. *A lesson based on cause and effect*

3:1–12

1 Hear this word the LORD has spoken against you, O people of Israel—against the whole family I brought up out of Egypt:

2 "You only have I chosen
of all the families of the earth;
therefore I will punish you
for all your sins."

3 Do two walk together
unless they have agreed to do so?
4 Does a lion roar in the thicket
when he has no prey?
Does he growl in his den
when he has caught nothing?
5 Does a bird fall into a trap on the ground
where no snare has been set?
Does a trap spring up from the earth
when there is nothing to catch?
6 When a trumpet sounds in a city,
do not the people tremble?
When disaster comes to a city,
has not the LORD caused it?

7 Surely the Sovereign LORD does nothing
without revealing his plan
to his servants the prophets.

8 The lion has roared—
who will not fear?
The Sovereign LORD has spoken—
who can but prophesy?

9 Proclaim to the fortresses of Ashdod
and to the fortresses of Egypt:
"Assemble yourselves on the mountains of Samaria;
see the great unrest within her
and the oppression among her people."

10 "They do not know how to do right," declares the LORD,
"who hoard plunder and loot in their fortresses."

11 Therefore this is what the Sovereign LORD says:

"An enemy will overrun the land;
he will pull down your strongholds
and plunder your fortresses."

12 This is what the LORD says:

"As a shepherd saves from the lion's mouth
only two leg bones or a piece of an ear,
so will the Israelites be saved,
those who sit in Samaria
on the edge of their beds
and in Damascus on their couches."

1 A summons to hear the "word of the LORD" introduces this oracle. The summons is directed against "the whole family I brought up out of Egypt" and thus seems to include Judah as well as Israel. It is certain that Amos did not have high hopes for Judah (2:5), and he would never have exempted them from divine wrath for their disobedience. The pronouncement of judgment, addressed primarily to the northern kingdom, warned Judah and Israel that their election by Yahweh in itself was insufficient ground for thinking they were nationally secure; for God demanded personal obedience as well.

2 The statement "you only have I chosen [*yāḏa'*, 'known'] of all the families of the earth" establishes Israel's elective privilege. The word *yāḏa'* bears a special sense of intimacy. Jeremiah 1:5 uses *yāḏa'* in a similar way, describing God's knowing and consecrating Jeremiah even before his birth. Thus the word connotes more than simple awareness or acknowledgment. It includes the idea of God's sovereign activity whereby the object of that knowledge is set apart or chosen for a divine purpose. Such was the case with Israel.

Israel's privilege, however, incurred her punishment. Verse 2 sets forth a foundational principle of Amos's message and of Scripture in general: Elective privilege entails responsibility. The two stichs of this verse are connected by "therefore" (*'al kēn*), establishing a logical relationship between them. Because Israel failed to live up to her holy calling, she was punished.

God's choice of Israel as the vehicle of his redemptive purposes is, from the human standpoint, strange. The people were slaves, possessing no homeland; and Israel was the weakest of the nations of the world (cf. Deut 7:7). The calling of Christians is quite similar, for Paul reminded us that God calls the weak so that human boasting may be excluded (1 Cor 1:26–29).

3–5 The pronouncement of the judgment predicted in v.2 does not appear till v.11. It is preceded by a series of questions that culminate in an affirmation of Amos's prophetic authority. Only then does he depict the desperate plight of the nation soon to be surrounded by an adversary.

The first question (v.3) asks whether two can walk together if they have not agreed to do so. The word "walk" is in the imperfect tense in Hebrew, denoting incompleted action. The question is, Is it customary for two to walk together without agreeing to do so? Certainly two people walking side by side would not be doing so only by sheer coincidence.

Verse 4 states that a lion does not roar when it is stalking its prey. When a bird is ensnared, it is because someone has set a trap (v.5); and a snare is not sprung unless something triggers it.

6 To this point each question has begun with the effect followed by the cause. But now the order is reversed. Amos's style is far from stereotyped. His writing is marked by variety and vigor. The prophets did not follow the mechanical, poetical style of the Ugaritic epic material. By rejecting it, they brought an element into their words that disturbed their smug hearers. Here the cause is the blast of the trumpet and the effect is the fear it brings to the city dwellers. The sound of the trumpet from a city wall warned of invaders, or the trumpet in the square heralded bad news. Ultimately the cause of the "disaster" coming to a city is "the Lord." We should not conclude, however, that "disaster" (*rā'āh*) implies "evil" in the ethical sense here. The word has that meaning in Hebrew, but the emphasis in this context on the city warrants only the meaning "disaster."

It is not necessary to see the figures in these questions as representations of Israel or her enemies. They are simply vivid analogies from life intended to illustrate the forthcoming conclusion (v.8).

7 The relationship of the first clause of this verse to the preceding clause is uncertain. Because there is no apparent logical connection between the sections, it is difficult to understand the particle *kî* in the sense of "for." It seems best to understand *kî* as an asseverative ("surely"). But this causes v.7 to interrupt the sequence of thought in vv.2–8 and has led some to see it as an intrusive element, possibly coming from the hand of the alleged "Deuteronomist." But v.7 seems to be an essential part of the narrative because the word "prophets" refers to "prophesy" in v.8. The words "lion" and "fear" in v.8 refer to "lion" in v.4 and "tremble" (*ḥāraḏ*) in v.6. Without v.7 the idea of prophecy in v.8 would stand alone, with no logical relation to the preceding argument (cf. 6:11 for a similar sentence).

Verse 7 is important for understanding Amos's concept of the prophetic office. "Plan" (*sôd*) has as its basic meaning the thought of "intimacy." This has several shades of meaning. It may connote a close relationship (Gen 49:6; Job 29:4; Ps 111:1; Jer 6:11) or the scheming of those united against others (Pss 64:2[3 MT]; 83:3[4 MT]) as well as the positive counsel derived from a close relationship (Prov 15:22). It may refer to something as intimate as a secret (Prov 11:13; 25:9) or close fellowship with a friend (Ps 55:14[15 MT]). When used of God, it refers to his secret council (Job 15:8). It also may denote the intimate relationship the righteous have with God in which he "makes his covenant known to them" (Ps 25:14) and takes them "into his confidence" (Prov 3:32). Jeremiah uses the word to describe a prophet's relationship to God through which he receives God's truth (Jer 23:18, 22); for the prophet stood in an intimate relationship to God in which he shared God's counsel and his words for the people.

8 "The lion has roared" sounds an alarm. There is indeed cause for fear—not from any lion or blast of a trumpet—it is Yahweh's voice through his prophet that should strike fear in people's hearts. Yahweh has spoken, and no one can contravene his word. So Amos pronounced judgment on the people.

9 Amos summoned the Egyptians and the Philistines of Ashdod to witness the oppression going on within Samaria. Amos may have chosen these nations because of their past oppression of Israel. The Egyptian bondage and recurrent Philistine oppressions in Israel's early history were not forgotten. It is as though Amos were summoning these nations to view the violence being done by the rich and powerful against their poor neighbors in Samaria, a kind of oppression that even the pagan nations had never seen. In addition Amos's rhetoric showed that Israel was as violent as they.

The word "fortress" (*'armôn*) generally connotes a fortified building such as a citadel (Ps 48:3[4 MT]; Isa 34:13) or the fortified section of a palace (1 Kings 16:18; 2 Kings 15:25). But it may also refer to large residential houses (Jer 9:21). The emphasis in vv.9–11 seems to be on "fortress" rather than residence because of the parallelism of *'armôn* with *'ōz* ("stronghold") in v.11 and the military motifs in the passage (cf. "oppression" and the reference to the two warlike peoples of Philistia and Egypt in v.9 and "plunder" and "loot" in v.10).

10 The Israelites, however, were different from aggressors because they plundered and looted in their *own* fortresses rather than in enemy territory. Through oppressing the poorer classes, they had been plundering their own people; and Ashdod and Egypt were called to witness this evil.

"They do not know how to do right," Amos declared of the Israelites. The word "right" (*n^ekōḥāh*) has the basic meaning of "straightness." Their moral sense had become so warped that the concepts of right and wrong were totally blurred.

11 "Therefore" logically connects the judgment segment of the oracle with the accusation stated in v.10. The following section of doom is a warning for those who flagrantly violated the covenant by treating a holy God lightly. Though the enemy who would overrun the land was not identified by Amos, historically it was Assyria.

12 Amos concluded the oracle with the analogy of a shepherd who retrieves the remains of an animal from the mouth of a lion. This reflects the Mosaic law, for a shepherd was required to produce the remains of an animal killed while in his care as proof that he did not steal it (Exod 22:13).

The remainder of the verse is textually problematic, and there have been various suggestions for its interpretation. The lack of cohesiveness within the lines may be an example of the way some prophets of great literary skill like Amos departed from poetical symmetry in order to achieve a powerful effect.

The word *d^emešeq* may, by a slight alteration in the pointing of the MT, be read "Damascus," in keeping with the ancient versions. The lines would then describe how the Israelites would be "saved"; i.e., "those who sit in Samaria, on the edge of their beds, and in Damascus on their couches." The broken nature of the line might have been intended to elicit images of the broken remains of Israel's wealth in the minds of Amos's hearers. As the remaining parts of the slaughtered animal attest to its destruction, so the broken remains of the wealth of Israel would be a pathetic witness to the complete destruction of that kingdom.

The reference to Damascus may seem anomalous to the passage because the oracle is specifically addressed to Israelites. Yet it is not impossible that an Israelite colony was in Damascus at this time; for, in all probability, the territory had been annexed by Israel during the reign of Jeroboam (2 Kings 14:28). Both Damascus and Israel were ultimately crushed in their futile attempt to take a stand against the Assyrian king Tiglath-pileser III. Amos had predicted in 1:3–5 the downfall of Syria.

Notes

2 For a discussion of “know” as a covenantal term, see H. Huffman, “The Treaty Background of Hebrew *yāda‘*,” BASOR 181 (1966): 31–37.

7 The particle כִּי (*kî*) functions as an element of emphasis in Ugaritic, somewhat like the Hebrew asseverative. However, it always occurs in an intraclausal structure (UT, 9.17).

9 The LXX reads “Assyria” for Ashdod. But this is most probably not representative of the original reading. It is easy to see how the great nation of Assyria could be paired with Egypt. But Amos did not mention Assyria anywhere in his prophecy, and Assyrian oppression of Israel was yet to reach its zenith.

12 The Code of Hammurapi has a law similar to Exod 22:13—“If a visitation of god has occurred in a sheepfold or a lion has made a kill, the shepherd shall prove himself innocent in the presence of god, but the owner of the sheepfold shall receive from him the animal stricken in the fold” (Law 266, ANET, p. 177).

In Hebrew “Damascus” is דַּמֶּשֶׂק (*dammeśeq*), while the word in the text is spelled *d^emeśeq;* only slight alterations in the Masoretic pointing are necessary to render the reading “Damascus.” The reading “damask” suggested by a number of commentators, is based on the Arabic *dimaqs*. But this is speculative and requires a change in radicals. The reading “Damascus” seems to be the simplest solution, but one must admit that the passage is extremely difficult.

3. *An oracle against the house of Jacob*

3:13–15

13 “Hear this and testify against the house of Jacob,” declares the Lord, the LORD God Almighty.

14 “On the day I punish Israel for her sins,
I will destroy the altars of Bethel;
the horns of the altar will be cut off
and fall to the ground.
15 I will tear down the winter house
along with the summer house;
the houses adorned with ivory will be destroyed
and the mansions will be demolished,”
declares the LORD.

13 The threat of the preceding oracle gains renewed solemnity from the declaration of the Lord that precedes the next section. The command to hear is not addressed to Israel, for it goes on to say, “and testify against the house of Jacob.” But this is best understood as a rhetorical statement, similar to 3:9 (“proclaim”), where Amos addressed imaginary witnesses either for dramatic effect or to establish a legal atmosphere with Yahweh and Israel as adversaries (Isa 1:2; cf. Deut 32:1).

“House of Jacob” recalls Israel’s heritage, especially the promise to the patriarchs that established the ground on which the Lord would deal with his people. The covenant became the external structure of the eternal promise (Gen 15:12–20), providing the vehicle for obedience. Obedience to the covenantal stipulations marked one’s participation in the promise. Israel as a nation had betrayed the covenant and so had forfeited every right to its promised blessing.

14–15 As a result of Israel's disobedience, the "altars of Bethel" would be destroyed (v.14) as well as the expensive homes of the people (v.15). Amos focused here on the two major aspects of Israel's disobedience: false religion and misuse of wealth and power. According to Israelite law a fugitive could find refuge at the altar by grasping its horns (1 Kings 1:50), but even this last refuge would be lost (v.14).

Notes

14 The altars of Bethel were mentioned by Amos because they were the focal point of Israel's rebellion (cf. 1 Kings 12:32; 13:2; 2 Kings 23:15–16).

15 The winter house and the summer house were either separate houses or two dwelling places in the same building. Many houses had an upper story that would be cool in summer (cf. Judg 3:20). Jeremiah 36:22 refers to a winter house that was heated by a brazier. Amos's reference is best understood to apply to separate houses because of the use of עַל (*'al*, "along with"). While this preposition may mean "on," Amos hardly used it in this sense, for that would mean that the winter house would be struck down on top of the summer house—the reverse of what is expected. It is best to understand *'al* in the sense of "together with" (BDB, p.755), thus indicating separate houses. The winter house would be destroyed along with the summer house. The inscription of Barrākib refers to summer and winter houses as separate buildings (H. Donner and W. Röllig, *Kanaanäische und Aramäische Inschriften* [Weisbaden: Otto Harrassowitz, 1966], p. 40). The inscription states that the kings of Sam'al had only one palace, which served as quarters for winter and summer. Another house was built to remedy the situation.

The reference to the "houses adorned with ivory" underscores the affluence of Amos's society. Similar decorations have been found in Assyrian sites (K. Schoville, *Biblical Archaeology in Focus* [Grand Rapids: Baker, 1978], pp. 468–69).

4. *The pampered women of Samaria*

4:1–3

1 Hear this word, you cows of Bashan on Mount Samaria,
you women who oppress the poor and crush the needy
and say to your husbands, "Bring us some drinks!"
2 The Sovereign LORD has sworn by his holiness:
"The time will surely come
when you will be taken away with hooks,
the last of you with fishhooks.
3 You will each go straight out
through breaks in the wall,
and you will be cast out toward Harmon,"
declares the LORD.

1 The region of Bashan was known for its excellent cattle (Ps 22:12; Ezek 39:18), and Amos sarcastically likened the women of Samaria to these sleek cattle that grazed in the rich uplands of Bashan. Amos accused these rich women of oppressing the poor, just as he had accused the male leaders of his society. These women may not have been directly involved in mistreating the poor. But their incessant demands for luxuries drove their husbands to greater injustices. Their demand "Bring us some drinks" creates a vivid picture of their indolence.

2–3 An oath in which Yahweh swore by his holiness introduces the judgment section of this oracle. The element in the oath formula by which one swears forms an external guarantee of the thing being affirmed (cf. Heb 6:16). When God takes an oath, that element usually relates to the nature of the thing sworn. For example, in Isaiah 62:8 the Lord swore by his right hand and his mighty arm—metaphors of his strength—that he would do what he had promised. In Jeremiah 44:26 it is said that the Lord swore by his great name. The "name" signifies his reputation achieved by his mighty deeds, demonstrating the power and authority by which the oath is guaranteed.

The holiness of God is not a transferable divine energy but the absolute separation of God from anything that is secular or profane. When God swore by his holiness in Psalm 89:35, it was the guarantee that he would not lie, because that would be a violation of holiness. When he swore by his holiness in Amos 4:2, he guaranteed that the judgment would become a reality, because the holy God does not lie, nor can his holiness allow sin to go unpunished.

The Hebrew words used to describe Israel's judgment (v.2) are obscure. "Hooks" (*ṣinnôṯ*) is generally understood as being derived from *ṣēn*, which may mean "thorn," though this meaning is dubious. The word *ṣēn* occurs only in the masculine plural whereas *ṣinnôṯ* is feminine plural. "Fishhooks" is *sîr*, which means "thorn" but does not have an attested feminine plural. In the only other occurrence of *sîr* in the plural (Hos 2:8), it is masculine. Here in Amos it is feminine plural (*sîrôṯ*). The common element of "thorns" in these two words underlies the suggestion that they refer to some kind of hook.

The feminine plural *ṣinnôṯ*, however, is attested in Hebrew as meaning "shields." Thus it may picture these indolent women, who lay on beds of luxury, being carried away on the enemies' shields. If *sîr* is taken in its more common meaning of "pot" or "receptacle," its association with "fish" (*dûgāh*) may mean a receptacle for carrying fish or a cauldron for boiling fish. At any rate, these women would be led in humiliating fashion through the breached wall of Jerusalem.

The meaning of Harmon is uncertain. If it is a locality, as it certainly seems to be, its location remains unknown.

Notes

2 The verb קָדַשׁ (*qāḏaš*, "holy") connotes that which is separate from the secular or common (Exod 29:21, 37; 30:29; Num 16:38). Because God is holy, he is not subject to human imperfection and will thus be faithful to his word.

צִנּוֹת (*ṣinnôṯ*, "shields"), the feminine plural form of צִנָּה (*ṣinnāh*), is attested in 2 Chron 11:12. סִירוֹת (*sîrôṯ*, "pots"), the feminine form of סִיר (*sîr*), is attested in 1 Kings 7:45. A possible Akkadian cognate of *ṣinnāh* is *ṣinnatu*, meaning "halter," which is appropriate to the context. However, it occurs only once in text materials and is associated with the word *ṣerretu* in the vocabularies. It is possible that *ṣinnatu* is a phonetic variant of *ṣerretu*, a musical instrument, in which case it would not offer a solution to the problem here (I.J. Gelb et al., eds., *The Assyrian Dictionary* [Chicago: The Oriental Institute, 1968], p. 201).

5. *Sinful worship*

4:4–5

> [4]"Go to Bethel and sin;
> go to Gilgal and sin yet more.
> Bring your sacrifices every morning,
> your tithes every three years.
> [5]Burn leavened bread as a thank offering
> and brag about your freewill offerings—
> boast about them, you Israelites,
> for this is what you love to do,"
> declares the Sovereign LORD.

4 Amos addressed all the people in this shocking command: "Go to Bethel and sin." Bethel was the chief religious sanctuary of the northern kingdom. It once housed the ark of the covenant and was one of the locations in the circuit followed by Samuel in his work as judge (1 Sam 7:16). Shortly after the division of the two kingdoms, Bethel was established as a sanctuary by Jeroboam I to provide an alternative center to Jerusalem. In the time of Amos, Bethel was known as "the king's sanctuary" (7:13). It thus may have been the scene of royal as well as religious pomp.

The cultic worship practiced at Bethel in Amos's time combined concepts common to Canaanite religion, resulting in a syncretistic Yahwism devoid of real allegiance to the covenant of the Lord. Certainly, elements of Yahwistic religion were observed there (4:4–5; 5:21–23). But the idolatrous influences had left their mark: external allegiance to cultic requirements fulfilled one's obligation to God. The heart—indeed, the very life of Yahwism—had been destroyed; and the covenantal obligation of a heart response to God and a caring love for one's fellow man were forgotten.

Gilgal was another Israelite sanctuary in Amos's time (5:5; cf. Hos 4:15; 9:15; 12:11). Lest the people think that Bethel, with its pagan heritage, should be the only sanctuary that bore an onus, the prophet included Gilgal.

The word "sin" (*pešaʿ*) connotes the basic concept of "rebellion." Little did these worshipers know that as they participated in the cult to maintain their relationship to Yahweh, they were in rebellion against him. The sacrifices are those offered with respect to (*l*ᵉ) "the morning." The preposition *l*ᵉ is distributive and implies "every morning." Symmetry favors a distributive function for *l*ᵉ in the next clause also—viz., "every three years." The sacrifices are probably not the continual burnt offering presented each morning and evening (Exod 29:38–41; Lev 6:8–13; Num 28:3–4). These were offered daily at the door of the tabernacle, while the context of Amos 4:4–5 deals with the individual sacrifices of pilgrims to the cultic centers. The other aspects of worship mentioned—the tithe, the thank offering, the freewill offering—are also individual obligations.

The practice of bringing tithes every three days does not appear in the law. A tithe was to be brought every three years (Deut 14:28). Yet the word *yāmîm* may mean "days" (cf. Notes).

5 It is possible that Amos represented the cultic practices prescribed for the pilgrimage to the cult centers that were current in his time, but it is also possible that he was using hyperbole to show the futility of offering many sacrifices and tithes. This seems to reflect the intent of the passage, because Amos said, "This is what you love to do." It is as though he was telling them that even if they sacrificed every morning and tithed every three days so that they had something to boast about, in the end they were only engaging in acts of rebellion against God.

Notes

4 יָמִים (*yāmîm*, "days") may be used to refer to the full cycle of days in a given period and thus mean a year (Exod 13:10; Judg 11:40; 1 Sam 1:3). It also has an indefinite sense and may mean "a few days" (Gen 40:4) or "sometime" (1 Kings 17:7; 18:1). In Deut 14:28 the tithe was commanded to be given every three years, but the word used there is not *yāmim* but שָׁנִים (*šānîm*). Since *yāmîm* may mean "years,"it is possible that it is used here with that meaning. The view adopted here, however, is that Amos meant "every three days," since he encouraged the sacrifices to be offered much more frequently than the law required ("every morning"). Thus Amos ironically called for them to go beyond the demands of the law. So the presentation of the tithe every three days is consonant with the preceding statement in this view.

6. *A look to the past*

4:6–13

6"I gave you empty stomachs in every city
and lack of bread in every town,
yet you have not returned to me,"
declares the LORD.

7"I also withheld rain from you
when the harvest was still three months away.
I sent rain on one town,
but withheld it from another.
One field had rain;
another had none and dried up.
8People staggered from town to town for water
but did not get enough to drink,
yet you have not returned to me,"
declares the LORD.

9"Many times I struck your gardens and vineyards,
I struck them with blight and mildew.
Locusts devoured your fig and olive trees,
yet you have not returned to me,"
declares the LORD.

10"I sent plagues among you
as I did to Egypt.
I killed your young men with the sword,
along with your captured horses.
I filled your nostrils with the stench of your camps,
yet you have not returned to me,"
declares the LORD.

11"I overthrew some of you
as I overthrew Sodom and Gomorrah.
You were like a burning stick snatched from the fire,
yet you have not returned to me,"
declares the LORD.

12"Therefore this is what I will do to you, Israel,
and because I will do this to you,
prepare to meet your God, O Israel."
13He who forms the mountains,
creates the wind,
and reveals his thoughts to man,
he who turns dawn to darkness,
and treads the high places of the earth—
the LORD God Almighty is his name.

This section expresses one of the most fundamental aspects of prophetic thought, the immanence of God in history. Amos related a series of events from Israel's past that he interpreted as God's intervention on her behalf. Terrible as these catastrophes were, they were designed by a loving God to alert Israel to her sin and to the certainty of judgment; yet the nation did not return to him (v.11). This section vividly illustrates God's permissive will that brings suffering so that his own may be brought closer to him (Heb 12:6).

6 The Hebrew of this verse is literally "I gave you cleanness of teeth" (NIV mg.), an expression describing complete lack of food. The catastrophes mentioned are difficult to identify historically. They were neither necessarily recent nor specific. They reflect God's continuing activity in history on Israel's behalf.

7–8 The "withheld rain" (v.7) is the latter rain, so important to the full development of the crops. That rain fell on some towns and not on others might show that God's hand was in the catastrophe. Nevertheless, the suffering (v.8) that resulted did not lead to repentance.

9–10 Even the blighted gardens and dying trees did not remind the people of their spiritual responsibility (v.9); neither did God's judgment on individuals (v.10). The reference to plague and sword recalls the curse of Leviticus 26:25, which was to come on the nation if the people walked contrary to God. The "sword" refers to war and was a reminder of the long period of warfare with Syria (2 Kings 13:3).

11 Here Amos compared the overthrow of certain Israelite cities to the fall of Sodom and Gomorrah. Some expositors suggest that Amos was referring to earthquakes that occurred in the past, because Sodom and Gomorrah were apparently destroyed by an earthquake (Gen 19). But Sodom and Gomorrah are used as analogies of destruction in a number of passages without reference to the means of destruction (Isa 1:9; 13:19; Jer 50:40; Zeph 2:9). It is best, therefore, to see this verse as referring to violence suffered by certain Israelite cities during the Syrian incursions. The account of them in 2 Kings 13:1–9 refers to a "deliverer" (v.5) who restored the conquered people to their homes. The analogy of the stick snatched from the fire aptly describes the conquered towns that might have been lost forever to Israel but were "snatched" from the fire of conflict and restored to their inhabitants because of the intervention of this unnamed "deliverer."

This section throws light on the chastisement of the Lord. Chastisement is that aspect of his dealing with his children in which he uses punishment to bring them back to him. This was emphasized by Elihu in the Book of Job (33:19–33). It is found in Proverbs (3:11; cf. Heb 12:5–11). Of course, suffering does not always have this purpose. There are many reasons why God disciplines his people.

The point of vv.6–11 is that the Israelites had become spiritually hardened. Because Amos did not want his hearers to forget this, he stated five times, "Yet you have not returned to me" (vv.6, 8, 9, 10, 11).

The preceding verses contain a number of connections with Deuteronomy 28–29, where Moses set forth the blessings of obedience and the curses of disobedience. Thus Amos showed Israel that the catastrophes mentioned are evidence that God has chastised Israel in the past for her sins. The curses of Deuteronomy have been realized. Soon the ultimate curse will follow: "Then the Lord will scatter you among all nations from one end of the earth to the other" (Deut 28:64).

12 Judgment is impending, but Amos does not state what the judgment will be. It is difficult to see the intended judgment in the catastrophes of vv.6–11 because the word "this" (*kōh*) in v.12 normally refers to what follows. Also, the calamities cited in vv.6–11 are broader in scope than the captivity Amos elsewhere envisions as the impending judgment.

Some commentators assume a redactive intrusion here. Wolff, for example, understands vv.6–13 as the work of an editor who depicts the destruction of "the sanctuary of Bethel by king Josiah" (p. 220). Others assume a corrupt text.

It is possible, however, to explain the passage on the basis of Amos's literary style. If the interpretation of the significance of the pronominal suffix *nû* ("his") on *'ašîḇennû* ("turn back") in 1:3 is correct (q.v.), there is precedent in the book for the similar phenomenon in 4:12. The veiled reference to judgment in 1:3 adds force to the prophetic statement because of its enigmatic quality. The same thing may be true here. The haunting uncertainty in Amos's words makes the threat of judgment even more ominous.

The yet unspecified judgment is to come when Israel meets her God, and she is told to prepare for that awful moment. Israel is to meet her God, not in a face-to-face sense, but in her encounter with him as he intervenes in history to effect her destruction. The Israelites had already learned of God's intervention. (See vv.6–11, where Amos described repeated events that were meant to bring Israel to repentance.) But the imperative "Prepare to meet your God, O Israel" has an aura of finality. When Israel meets her God, she will finally learn the nature of the coming judgment.

The command "Prepare" should not be understood as a plea for the people to repent. The die was cast. They did not turn to God when he chastised them (vv.6–11), and now Amos held out no hope for their full-scale repentance. The words seem nothing more than an imperative for the people to get ready for the national calamity about to befall them.

13 A hymnic element, portraying some aspects of the nature of the God the Israelites are to face in judgment, closes this section. "For" (*kî*, untr. in NIV) connects v.13 to the preceding reference to God. The word "forms" (*yôṣer*) refers to God's activity in creation and is paralleled by "creates" (*bōrē'*). These words are participles in Hebrew. The use of participles is typical of these hymnic elements. This is often used as an argument for their lateness because participial constructions may be found in other poetic celebrations of God's creative power, especially in "Second Isaiah" (40:22–23, 26–29; 42:5; 44:24; 45:7, 18). This phenomenon also occurs in Jeremiah (10:12–16; 51:15–19) and certain Psalms (94, 104). While the passages in Jeremiah arc considered late additions by some scholars, there is good reason to believe that both psalms cited are of preexilic origin (Dahood, AB), thus placing the tradition much earlier than "Second Isaiah." The reason for the participial structure is difficult to determine. It may be that the Hebrew theology assumed a role for God both in creating and in sustaining his universe. It is also possible that the participial construction may be simply a stylistic device.

The word "form" (*yāṣar*) has as its basic emphasis the shaping of the object involved, whereas "create" (*bārā'*) emphasizes the initiation of the object. Not only does God form the mountains and create the wind, but he reveals to man "his thoughts" (*śēḥô*). The word for "thoughts" is never used of God in Hebrew; and, in the light of 3:7, it is unlikely that Amos believed that God revealed his thoughts to all people. It is best to apply the suffix *ô* ("his") to man and understand the verse to speak of God's activity in searching the hearts of all mankind and revealing their thoughts and motives.

In describing God's treading the high places of the earth, the hymn takes on a theophanic tone. The Hebrew word for "high places" (*bāmāh*) basically means "height." It may refer to pagan religious sanctuaries (Jer 7:31); but in the cosmic atmosphere of this hymn, it must refer to the mountains and hills. In ancient times possession of the heights of enemy territory meant that the enemy was virtually brought into subjection (Deut 33:29; Ezek 36:2). The majestic metaphor of God striding over the hills and mountains shows his sovereignty over the earth. A similar theophany occurs at the beginning of Micah, where it precedes the description of God's judgment in Samaria and Jerusalem (1:3–7; 3:9–12). The theophany presages judgment, as God steps into history and treads the heights of the earth. The prophets' theophanic language, depicting God's presence in the events of history and in natural phenomena, shows their belief in his immanence.

The awe this picture brings is heightened by the last line: "the LORD God Almighty" (*YHWH 'ᵉlōhê-ṣᵉḇa'ôṯ*, lit., "LORD God of Hosts"). The "hosts" are generally taken to be either the heavenly bodies or the armies of heaven. While the latter is probably the best alternative, *YHWH 'ᵉlōhê-ṣᵉḇa'ôṯ* certainly connotes the vast power of the God of heaven and earth.

In one bold sweep, this hymn shows the sovereignty of God—from his creation of the world to his daily summoning of the dawn, from his intervention in history to his revelation of mankind's thoughts. Every believer can take comfort in the fact that, while sometimes it seems that God does not interfere in human affairs, the world is never out of his control. His sovereignty extends to every aspect of human experience.

This brief but sublime hymn is so in keeping with Amos's preceding words and lends such a note of finality to his message that its authenticity should be given fairer consideration. It implies the right of the Creator to judge his people and points to the divine judgment that is so vital a part of Amos's prophecy.

Notes

8 The Hebrew of the first clause says literally, "Two, three cities wandered to one city to drink water." The implication is that the citizens of cities that were suffering drought sought water in localities where it was available but could not get sufficient water for their needs. Hence NIV's translation: "People staggered from town to town."

6–11 The connection of this section with Deut 28–29 is established by "rain" (v.7; cf. Deut 28:21, 24); "blight and mildew" (v.9; cf. Deut 28:22); "I sent plagues among you as I did to Egypt" (v.10; cf. Deut 28:27 ["boils of Egypt"] and v.60 ["diseases of Egypt"]); "Sodom and Gomorrah" (v.11; cf. Deut 29:23).

11 The metaphor of a stick snatched from the fire is also applied to Israel in Zech 3:2, where Joshua is symbolic of the nation.

The fact that Israel did not return to God even after he had punished her as a nation is reechoed in Isa 9:13; Jer 5:3; Hos 7:10.

12 The adverb כֹּה (*kōh*, "therefore") usually refers to what follows and כֵּן (*kēn*) to what precedes (BDB, p. 462).

7. *A lament for fallen Israel*

5:1–3

[1]Hear this word, O house of Israel, this lament I take up concerning you:

[2]"Fallen is Virgin Israel,
never to rise again,
deserted in her own land,
with no one to lift her up."

[3]This is what the Sovereign Lord says:

"The city that marches out a thousand strong for Israel
will have only a hundred left;
the town that marches out a hundred strong
will have only ten left."

1–2 Amos next took up a lament (v.1). The lament (*qînāh*) was a song or poem mourning the death of a relative, friend, or national hero. In this one Amos mourned the fall of Israel (v.2). The main verbs are in the perfect tense, expressing completed action. It is as if Amos was so certain that what he said would happen that he treated it as an accomplished fact. He saw Israel as a virgin whose life had been ended in the bloom of youth. He described her hopelessness in the words "never to rise again" and her desolation in the words "deserted in her own land with no one to lift her up."

Israel's predicted fate stands in stark contrast to the promise God gave Abraham. Abraham's descendants would be as numerous as the "dust of the earth" and as the stars in the sky (cf. Gen 12:15; 15:15). But Amos said that Israel was cut off as a virgin who had never borne children, and the enemy was soon to carry her off to his own land.

This passage illustrates the principle that the blessings of God's promise—which was irrevocable and eternal (Gen 13:15; 17:19; cf. Heb 6:13, 17–18)—were conditioned on the obedience of its recipients. Its eternality was guaranteed by God's sovereign activity in history and the existence of a believing remnant in Israel, whose obedience to the covenant stipulations marked them as the vehicle through whom God would keep the promises.

3 This verse depicts the finality of Israel's demise. As the cities send out their defending armies to face the invader, they shall be cut down. Only a handful of ragged, war-weary men will be left of Israel's proud army.

Notes

2 "Never to rise again" need not mean that God had no future role for Israel in his redemptive program. This seems to be precluded by Zech 12:10. Amos was referring here to the nation. The northern kingdom would never be reestablished, but there would be a believing remnant through whom the promises would continue (9:9–12).

8. *Seeking true values*

5:4–17

4This is what the LORD says to the house of Israel:

"Seek me and live;
5 do not seek Bethel,
do not go to Gilgal,
do not journey to Beersheba.
For Gilgal will surely go into exile,
and Bethel will be reduced to nothing."
6Seek the LORD and live,
or he will sweep through the house of Joseph like a fire;
it will devour,
and Bethel will have no one to quench it.

7You who turn justice into bitterness
and cast righteousness to the ground
8(he who made the Pleiades and Orion,
who turns blackness into dawn
and darkens day into night,
who calls for the waters of the sea
and pours them out over the face of the land—
the LORD is his name—
9he flashes destruction on the stronghold
and brings the fortified city to ruin),
10you hate the one who reproves in court
and despise him who tells the truth.
11You trample on the poor
and force him to give you grain.
Therefore, though you have built stone mansions,
you will not live in them;
though you have planted lush vineyards,
you will not drink their wine.
12For I know how many are your offenses
and how great your sins.

You oppress the righteous and take bribes
and you deprive the poor of justice in the courts.
13Therefore the prudent man keeps quiet in such times,
for the times are evil.

14Seek good, not evil,
that you may live.
Then the LORD God Almighty will be with you,
just as you say he is.
15Hate evil, love good;
maintain justice in the courts.
Perhaps the LORD God Almighty will have mercy
on the remnant of Joseph.

16Therefore this is what the Lord, the LORD God Almighty, says:

"There will be wailing in all the streets
and cries of anguish in every public square.
The farmers will be summoned to weep
and the mourners to wail.
17There will be wailing in all the vineyards,
for I will pass through your midst,"
says the LORD.

4 The word "seek" (*dāraš*), when referring to the Lord, means to turn to him in trust and confidence (Pss 34:4[5 MT]; 77:2[3 MT]; Jer 10:21). The word "live" (*ḥāyāh*), like "seek," is imperative, connected by waw ("and") with the preceding imperative. It shows the result of the condition implied in the first imperative. Though the concept of "life" in the OT often relates to spiritual life, that does not seem to be the meaning here; for Amos uses "live" (*ḥāyāh*) in a context of national collapse. Since he has spoken of Israel as a fallen nation, the meaning of national life or restoration for *ḥāyāh* seems appropriate. When a similar command is given in v.14, *ḥāyāh* apparently refers to national welfare.

In the light of this, it is hardly right to say that Amos confronted the people only with doom. He held out a gracious invitation to them, but he looked only for calamity because he knew they would not repent. His invitation may have been instrumental in leading some to seek the Lord. Thus it contributed to the establishment of the remnant.

5 The people were warned not to keep relying for help on the centers of cultic worship. These could offer no help; for when the invader came, the centers would fall just like all the cities of Israel. Bethel, Gilgal, and Beersheba were not the objects of God's favor but of his judgment.

Bethel, in Amos's time a center of religious externalism, was the place where Jacob met the Lord (Gen 28:10–15). It was there that God reiterated the promise to him. How the religious significance of Bethel had deteriorated! The promise, first made to Abraham, had a covenant structure requiring a heart response to God. In Amos's day, however, Bethel stood for mere external religion that did not require a true heart attitude toward God. So Bethel no longer represented the true promise. The idolatry practiced there could only lead to continued separation from God and the ultimate destruction of the nation. So the promise of Bethel became a promise of doom.

The reference to Beersheba shows that Israelites continued to cross the border with the southern kingdom to worship at the sanctuary in Judah.

6 The name "house of Joseph" stands for the northern kingdom and reflects the descent of its largest tribe, Ephraim, from Joseph. The fire Amos spoke of is reminiscent of the judgment in the oracles of 1:3–2:11 and symbolizes the coming captivity.

A clear alternative is offered to the people in the word "or" (*pen*). The choice is to "seek the LORD," with all the blessing and favor this will bring, or experience ultimate doom. One wonders at the spiritual blindness that led the people to the second choice.

7 In vv.7–12 Amos set forth the reason for the coming judgment. "Justice (*mišpāṭ*) connotes the fair and impartial administration of the requirements of the law. The Mosaic law required concern for others (Exod 23:4–5; Deut 24:17–22). Jeremiah defines "justice" as defending the rights of the poor (5:28). These concepts were being violated in Amos's day, for justice was being turned into "bitterness." The word translated "bitterness" (*la'ᵃnāh*) is literally "wormwood," one of the bitterest of plants. Elsewhere the word is used metaphorically of bitter experiences (Jer 9:15; Lam 3:15, 19). The perversion of justice in Amos's day was causing deep bitterness for the wretched people whose causes were being subverted in the legal system of that time.

8–9 Some have felt the hymnic element in v.8 to be intrusive, as has already been noted (cf. Introduction: Unity). But the logical sequence of 6:8–13 is also broken by vv.9–10. This may simply be Amos's style. The content of the doxology is certainly appropriate here.

In sublime words Amos depicted Yahweh's creative power in making the constellations, establishing the succession of day and night, and summoning the vast oceans to cover so much of the land. But then he turned from the sovereignty of God in creation to his sovereignty in human history, as seen by his overthrowing military strongholds (v.9). This fits perfectly with the reference to judgment in v.6. Also, the use of the verb *hāpaḵ* ("turns") in v.8 contrasts with its use in v.7.

10 The accusation continues with Amos's description of his contemporaries' hating the one who reproves in the "court" (*ša'ar*, lit., "gate"). The city gate was the place where the legal proceedings were carried on (5:15; cf. Deut 21:19; Josh 20:4; Ruth 4:1). The "one who approves" (*môḵîaḥ*) was any individual who protested the injustices of the courts. The "reprovers" were hated, as were those who spoke the truth during the proceedings. The very fabric of justice had been destroyed.

11 Amos next spoke vividly of the oppressive measures that exploited the poor and made the rich richer. "Therefore" introduces the judgment. The grand homes, built at the expense of the needy, will one day stand empty; and the vineyards will go untended. These symbols of Israel's wealth and greed, her houses and lands, are to become the objects of God's wrath. A terrible calamity was to befall the nation. As yet, it has not been fully described; but each of Amos's allusions to it builds on the other till in chapter 9 it attains its fullest statement.

12–13 All these judgments result from the people's many sins (v.12)—sins that entailed rebellion and failure to live up to God's standards. In the light of the corruption of the times, the prudent man said nothing, because anything he might have said would have been unavailing (v.13). The reprovers were despised (v.10). Protest would only have made the situation worse and brought greater woe. Amos, as a prophet, would hardly have condemned protest. He understood, however, that the innocent could find no justice in the corrupt court system. Therefore, it was best to avoid any reproof that could lead to even greater injustices.

14 Amos exhorted the people to seek good and not evil as the way to life. In the similar exhortation in v.4, he urged them to seek Yahweh as the *object* of their trust and confidence, as opposed to the pagan sanctuaries. Here he urged them to seek good as the *means* of receiving the Lord's help.

The practice of "good," that is, the social ethic of the law, would not only establish the ground on which the Lord would be able to mediate the benefits of his promise to Israel but would reverse the trend toward social disintegration that was rending the nation's fabric. To seek "good" was the only way the nation could be restored to "life."

To "seek good, not evil," then, means to concern oneself with good, to practice good and to reject evil. As a result the Lord of Hosts (see comment at 4:13) would be with them. This expression "the LORD . . . will be with you" connotes the Lord's presence, not only to dispense national and individual blessing, but to defend and fight for his people (cf. Deut 31:8; Judg 6:12).

Amos made the ironic observation that the people thought that the Lord was with them. They thought their privilege as Yahweh's elect and their lip service to him guaranteed them protection.

15 The people were not only to stop seeking evil (v.14) but were to hate evil and love good. The imperatives in this section are progressive. The people were exhorted to seek the Lord (v.4), not just in external allegiance to him, but in ethical obedience that involved commitment to him (v.14). Therefore Amos stated that they were to hate evil and love good. The will, along with the emotive powers, was to be devoted to the love of good and the hatred of evil. This alone would bring "life." If the people fulfilled these conditions, it was possible that the Lord would have mercy on the remnant of Joseph (see comment at v.6).

The term "remnant" (*šᵉʾērîṯ*) connotes a portion of something. This has led several commentators to apply "remnant of Joseph" to those Israelites who would survive the Assyrian decimations (KD, Mays). Verse 3 certainly supports that interpretation. Yet, if Amos's exhortation in v.14 holds open the possibility of the nation's restoration based on their repentance, it is difficult to see why the similar appeal in v.15 is thrust far into the future to find fulfillment only in the remnant who would survive the impending destruction. If Amos's appeal to the northern kingdom for repentance in v.6 carries with it the possibility of escape from God's judgment, it is likely that the appeal of v.15 does also.

The people of God through whom the terms of the promise are guaranteed were hardly the "remnant," for the word "perhaps" implies that God's promise could be invalidated. If the term "remnant of Joseph" is understood as a surrogate for the northern kingdom, the appeals of vv.14–15 are consonant with each other. One difficulty with this view is that Israel had extensive territorial holdings and was hardly a remnant. Also, "remnant" implies a part of something. Yet, in spite of the fact that the northern kingdom was enjoying the glory of the "Silver Age," Amos saw it as small and weak. He interceded for the kingdom in 7:2 thus: "How can Jacob survive? He is so small!" The prophet saw Israel as God saw it, not mighty and powerful, but vulnerable and on the verge of destruction. "Remnant" may connote Israel's insignificance in the world of her day. In answer to the objection that the word connotes a part of something, Micah 4:7 uses the word to refer to the whole nation in the restoration. It is parallel to "strong nation" in the couplet.

If these appeals for repentance seem not to be in accord with Amos's pronouncements of inevitable doom elsewhere, it may be that while he saw no hope for the nation, he continued to hold out the gracious offer of deliverance, even though only a few would respond.

16 "Therefore" relates back to the accusation in vv.7–12 and introduces the judgment of the Lord. Amos pictured the people weeping as the Lord passed through their midst, judging the sin that he had so severely condemned.

Notes

---

5 The alliteration in this verse is impossible to duplicate in English. The words "Gilgal will surely go into exile" appear in Hebrew as הַגִּלְגָּל גָּלֹה יִגְלֶה (*haggilgāl galōh yigleh*).

The call to come to Bethel in 4:4 and the warning not to seek Bethel in 5:5 are not incompatible. In 5:5 Amos warned the people that Bethel, which is used as a surrogate for their false worship, would not give life. In 4:4 his summons was given in a spirit of irony.

8 The word צַלְמָוֶת (*ṣalmāwet̠*, "blackness") is sometimes regarded as a word compounded from the roots צֵל (*ṣēl*, "shadow") and מָוֶת (*māwet̠*, "death"). The likelihood of this is diminished by the paucity of compounded words in Hebrew and the root *ṣlm* that is attested in Akkadian. The Akkadian root *ṣalmu* means "black" or "dark" (Gelb, *Assyrian Dictionary*, pp. 77–78). The Hebrew word may be understood as a form of this root with the abstract ending וּת (*ût̠*), thus meaning "blackness" or "deep darkness."

11 A number of allusions to Deut 28–29 may be present in the lament of vv.1–11. Note the concept of "going out" (v.3; cf. Deut 28:6, 19). The small number remaining to Israel in the same verse may be reflective of Deut 28:62. The reference to building houses and not living in them (v.11) is paralleled in Deut 28:30. Planting vineyards but not enjoying them finds a parallel in Deut 28:30, 39.

The reference to "stone mansions" reflects the great wealth of the time. The houses of the wealthy were not made of the usual kiln-dried brick (cf. Isa 9:10).

---

9. *The Day of the Lord*

5:18–20

18Woe to you who long
 for the day of the LORD!
Why do you long for the day of the LORD?
 That day will be darkness, not light.
19It will be as though a man fled from a lion
 only to meet a bear,

as though he entered his house
and rested his hand on the wall
only to have a snake bite him.
20Will not the day of the LORD be darkness, not light—
pitch-dark, without a ray of brightness?

18 This verse affords an insight into the popular theology in Amos's time. The Day of the Lord is an important eschatological concept that runs through the prophetic writings. It refers to the complex of events surrounding the coming of the Lord in judgment to conquer his foes and to establish his sovereign rule over the world. The people were looking forward to that day. Apparently they understood it as the time when Yahweh would act on their behalf to conquer their foes and establish Israel as his people forever. They regarded their election as the guarantee of the Lord's favor. But their moral vision was blurred. They failed to see the Day of the Lord as the time when God will judge all sin—even theirs. They named the name of Yahweh but did not obey his precepts. For these people, Amos said, that coming day will be one of darkness.

19–20 Amos used two metaphors to show the error of the popular concept of the Day of the Lord (v.19). A man flees from a lion only to meet a bear. Another enters his home, his place of security, but is bitten by a snake. The meaning is both clear and powerful. The Israelites saw the Day of the Lord as a comforting concept. It was to them their ultimate salvation. But like the false security of the one who thinks he has escaped the lion and the one who is falsely secure in his home, the faithless Israelites will find that day to be a time of judgment for them. As a matter of fact, there is no hope for them in that day, for the Day of the Lord will bring not one ray of light (v.20).

10. *Unacceptable worship*

5:21–27

21"I hate, I despise your religious feasts;
I cannot stand your assemblies.
22Even though you bring me burnt offerings and
grain offerings,
I will not accept them.
Though you bring choice fellowship offerings,
I will have no regard for them.
23Away with the noise of your songs!
I will not listen to the music of your harps.
24But let justice roll on like a river,
righteousness like a never-failing stream!

25"Did you bring me sacrifices and offerings
forty years in the desert, O house of Israel?
26You have lifted up the shrine of your king,
the pedestal of your idols,
the star of your god—
which you made for yourselves.
27Therefore I will send you into exile beyond Damascus,"
says the LORD, whose name is God Almighty.

21 The shock felt by the people when Amos so vehemently attacked their comforting eschatology was immediately followed by another shock. The prophet turned to their worship and in words of burning eloquence proclaimed Yahweh's hatred of their religious observances. Amos used the same word (*śānē'*, "hate") earlier to describe the attitude Israel should have toward evil (v.15). He applied that word here to the very things they thought pleased the Lord. The routine observance of the Levitical ritual was empty because the people lacked the love, concern, and humble obedience to God that marks sincere profession of faith. Their religion was a mockery of true religion. Every aspect of their ritual was an act of disobedience because it ignored the heart of the law—love for God and concern for others.

22–23 The people may, Amos said, continue to bring sacrifices, but the Lord would not accept them (v.22). The "burnt offering" (*'ōlāh*) is the offering that was entirely consumed. The "grain offering" (*minḥāh*) was any offering given as a gift to the Lord. However, sometimes the term specifies only the grain offering. The "fellowship offering" (*šelem*) was offered in part to the Lord and the rest shared with the offerer, his family, and his friends. Even their songs were a source of revulsion to the Lord. God says they were to be put away from him (*mē'ālay*, v.23).

24 The element that will transform the people's sterile worship into worship acceptable to God is "justice." The interpretation that the verse speaks of the Lord's judgment and righteousness that is to fill the land is inadequate because Amos addressed only the people. "Justice" and "righteousness" relate to the social order. Only when the personal concern of the law is incorporated into their social structure and "rightness" characterizes their dealings with others will their worship be acceptable. A token practice of justice and righteousness will not do.

Like the full commitment to "good" called for in v.15, justice and righteousness are to "roll on like a river, . . . like a never-failing stream." This is one of the great metaphors in the OT and one the church needs to ponder. A momentary flow of justice and righteousness will not do; these virtues are to keep on in the social order like a stream that does not dry up with summer heat.

25–27 Verses 25–26 are difficult. Many commentators hold that because the question of v.25 expects a negative answer, Amos was affirming that sacrifice was unknown during the wilderness period, or that it was not regarded as necessary for a proper relationship with Yahweh, obedience being the sole requirement. But this interpretation does not do justice to the continuity of vv.25–26 called for by the Hebrew particle waw (untr. in NIV) that begins v.26; nor does it adequately explain why a statement denying the efficacy of sacrifice was placed in the judgment section of the oracle.

The question (v.25) calls for a negative answer: no, the Israelites did not sacrifice then. Evidently the forty-year period was a time when obedience to the Levitical institutions had declined (Josh 5:5–6). This period began with the defection of the Israelites at Kadesh (Num 14:33–34; cf. Josh 5:6). The defection to idolatry in this wilderness period is emphasized in the prophetic tradition (Ezek 20:10–26; Hos 9:10; 13:5–6).

Verse 26 begins with a waw that is best understood as adversative: "But you have lifted." Israel disobeyed God and by her neglect of sacrifice turned to idolatry.

The words "shrine" (*sikkûṯ*) and "pedestal" (*kîyûn*) need not be altered to read

"Sakkut" and "Kaiwan," names of the god Saturn, though that view is attractive. It is not certain that Amos knew of this deity, and the MT makes sense as it stands. The verse refers to the implements of idolatrous worship of an unknown astral deity. Seen in this way, v.26 fits the formal structure well, for Amos, like Ezekiel and Hosea, traced the disobedience of God's people far back into their history. Verse 24 calls for obedience, the judgment section in vv.25–27 affirms their disobedience and bases the predicted judgment (v.27) on their long history of unfaithfulness to God.

Notes

25 For a discussion of the function of הֲ (*h^a*) in questions expecting a negative answer, see GKC, par. 150d.

26 The LXX renders the reference to the deities in this verse as *τὴν σκηνὴν τοῦ* Μολοχ, *καὶ τὸ ἄστρον τοῦ θεοῦ ὑμῶν* Ραιφαν (*tēn skēnēn tou Moloch, kai to astron tou theou hymōn Raiphan,* "the tabernacle of Moloch and the star of your god Raiphan"). This is quoted somewhat similarly in the NT, in Acts 7:43; but Raiphan appears in some EVs as Rephan. It is not known why the LXX reads Raiphan for the Hebrew כִּיּוּן (*kîyûn*). Possibly it is a form of Repa, the Egyptian deity of the planet Saturn.

11. *A warning to the complacent*

6:1–7

[1]Woe to you who are complacent in Zion,
 and to you who feel secure on Mount Samaria,
you notable men of the foremost nation,
 to whom the people of Israel come!
[2]Go to Calneh and look at it;
 go from there to great Hamath,
 and then go down to Gath in Philistia.
Are they better off than your two kingdoms?
 Was their land larger than yours?
[3]You put off the evil day
 and bring near a reign of terror.
[4]You lie on beds inlaid with ivory
 and lounge on your couches.
You dine on choice lambs
 and fattened calves.
[5]You strum away on your harps like David
 and improvise on musical instruments.
[6]You drink wine by the bowlful
 and use the finest lotions,
 but you do not grieve over the ruin of Joseph.
[7]Therefore you will be among the first to go into exile;
 your feasting and lounging will end.

1–2 With masterly irony, Amos addressed the self-satisfied rich, secure in their affluence (v.1; cf. Luke 6:24–25; 12:13–21). The cities he mentioned in v.2 have not necessarily met their doom, for this cannot be proved. Rather, the question has a sarcastic note: "Go to [these cities] and look. . . . Are they better off than your two kingdoms [i.e., Judah and Israel]?" It is as though he were echoing what the people of Israel were saying—"Look at the other countries: there is none greater than we." This is supported by the words "notable men of the foremost nation" (v.1), which also has a note of sarcasm. Evidently the people of Amos's day were boasting of their national security and power. The prophet proclaimed woe to those who felt secure in the strength of their nation. His parroting of their affirmations of self-assurance and national pride underscored their complacency and placed their false pride in stark contrast to the doom he predicted in the subsequent context.

3 The people were unwilling to hear of the "evil day," the day of their demise predicted by Amos. Yet they were all too willing to make the poor miserable.

4–7 Verses 4–6 describe the opulence of that society. To Amos their luxuries were symbols of the oppression by which they aggrandized themselves. So those who amassed all this wealth would be the first to go into exile (v.7).

Notes

1 רֵאשִׁית (*rē'šîṯ*, "foremost") and ראשׁ (*rō'š*, "first") in v.7 are from the same root. This may be an intended wordplay. The leaders of the "first and foremost nation," with all its wealth, would be the "first" to go into captivity.

2 The location of Calneh is uncertain. The name may appear in Gen 10:10 in association with Shinar, but the consonants may also be read "all of them" (RSV). Other occurrences of the name favor a location in the North. It is associated with Carchemish in Isa 10:9. Ezekiel 27:23 speaks of Canneh (evidently Calneh with an assimilation of the *l*) in association with Haran and Eden. This points to a location somewhere in the North as well (cf. Y. Aharoni and M. Avi-Yonah, *The Macmillan Bible Atlas* [New York: Macmillan, 1968], p. 93).

Hamath was a city in Syria, north of Damascus. Besides Amos 6:14, Hamath is cited also in 1 Macc 12:25.

Gath was one of the Philistine cities. It was located in southern Palestine near the coast of the Mediterranean.

12. *Pride before a fall*

6:8–11

8 The Sovereign LORD has sworn by himself—the LORD God Almighty declares:

"I abhor the pride of Jacob
and detest his fortresses;
I will deliver up the city
and everything in it."

9 If ten men are left in one house, they too will die. 10 And if a relative who is to
burn the bodies comes to carry them out of the house and asks anyone still hiding
there, "Is anyone with you?" and he says, "No," then he will say, "Hush! We must
not mention the name of the LORD."

11 For the LORD has given the command,
and he will smash the great house into pieces
and the small house into bits.

8 The Lord swore by himself in the preface to the oracle of doom. The guarantee of this oath is the trustworthiness of Yahweh himself, and it was secured by his holiness and power. The parallelism of the oracle indicates that the "pride of Jacob" has to do with Israel's vaunted "fortresses" (*'armᵉnôṯ*). Here the word "fortress" may refer to the great houses of the people (i.e., "mansions"), symbols of their misguided affluence (cf. 3:10, 15). The "city," evidently Samaria, and all its wealth was to be delivered up to a conquerer.

9–11 The continuity of the passage is broken by vv.9–10 because v.11 is connected conceptually and syntactically by the word "for" (*kî*) to v.8. The judgment (v.8) is vividly illustrated in vv.9–10. If ten men are in a house or fortress, they will die (v.9). When a relative of one of the dead comes to burn the corpses, should he find one person still alive, that person will not permit his mentioning the name of the Lord for fear that the Lord will turn his wrath on him (v.10).

Verses 9–10 reflect the responsibility of an individual for the burial of members of his family. Since cremation was not acceptable in ancient Israel, the reference is probably to the burning of corpses during a plague. Verse 11 is a powerful picture of the destruction that will surely come on oppressing Israel.

Notes

10 In this interpretation the word מְסָרְפוֹ (*mᵉsārᵉpô*) is understood as a participle of שָׂרַף (*śārap*, "burn"). In most instances in the OT, corpses were buried (Gen 25:9; 35:29; Judg 16:31). The bodies of Saul and his son may have been burned because they had been badly mutilated (1 Sam 31:12); but more likely it was necessary to dispose of the bodies in haste before the Philistines could mutilate them further (KD).

13. *A grim paradox*

6:12–14

12Do horses run on the rocky crags?
Does one plow there with oxen?
But you have turned justice into poison
and the fruit of righteousness into bitterness—
13you who rejoice in the conquest of Lo Debar
and say, "Did we not take Karnaim by our
own strength?"

14For the LORD God Almighty declares,
"I will stir up a nation against you, O house of Israel,
that will oppress you all the way
from Lebo Hamath to the valley of the Arabah."

12–13 By the patently absurd questions (v.12), Amos introduced the scathing rebuke that follows. One expected the courts to dispense justice, but the rich and powerful dispensed poison instead of justice and made bitter the fruit of righteousness. Those who did this are described as rejoicing in "Lo Debar" and "Karnaim"

(v. 13). These were evidently the sites of recent victories in Jeroboam's incursion into Aramean territory. But Amos pronounced Lo Debar so that it means "no thing." Through this biting sarcasm he proclaimed the utter futility of their burgeoning national influence.

Karnaim means "horns" and, by extension, "strength." The people's proud self-confidence was reflected in their boast that they took Karnaim by their own strength.

14 This verse specifies the judgment that would overtake the Israelites; a nation, not identified here by Amos, would oppress them from their northern border "from the entrance to [*l^{e}ḇô*, NIV mg., or 'Lebo'] Hamath" (cf. 2 Kings 14:25) on their northern border all the way to their southern border at the Wadi Arabah.

Notes

---

13 Lo Debar, spelled לוֹ דְבָר (*lô d^{e}ḇār*) in 2 Sam 9:4 and לֹא דְבָר (*lō' d^{e}ḇār*) in 2 Sam 17:27, is probably the city of Debir. In the MT of Amos 6:13, the word is spelled לֹא דָבָר (*lō' dāḇār*), which means "no thing."

IV. The Prophetic Visions (7:1–9:15)

A. *The Vision of the Locusts, Fire, and the Plumb Line*

7:1–9

[1]This is what the Sovereign LORD showed me: He was preparing swarms of locusts after the king's share had been harvested and just as the second crop was coming up. [2]When they had stripped the land clean, I cried out, "Sovereign LORD, forgive! How can Jacob survive? He is so small!"

[3]So the LORD relented.

"This will not happen," the LORD said.

[4]This is what the Sovereign LORD showed me: The Sovereign LORD was calling for judgment by fire; it dried up the great deep and devoured the land. [5]Then I cried out, "Sovereign LORD, I beg you, stop! How can Jacob survive? He is so small!"

[6]So the LORD relented.

"This will not happen either," the Sovereign LORD said.

[7]This is what he showed me: The LORD was standing by a wall that had been built true to plumb, with a plumb line in his hand. [8]And the LORD asked me, "What do you see, Amos?"

"A plumb line," I replied.

Then the LORD said, "Look, I am setting a plumb line among my people Israel; I will spare them no longer.

[9]"The high places of Isaac will be destroyed
and the sanctuaries of Israel will be ruined;
with my sword I will rise against the house
of Jeroboam."

1 The first of the series of visions that largely occupy the rest of the book consists of three dramatic elements. The first is the threat of a locust invasion "as the second crop was coming." This would place the event just before the dry season. If the threat materialized, the people would be left without food till the next harvest. Apparently the king had the privilege of claiming the first mowing. The needs of the government were great, and the large military establishment had to be supported.

2–3 When Amos saw in his vision that the locusts had finished the devastation, he prayed that what he had seen would not happen, because Israel would not be able to survive it. "Jacob [Israel]," he said, "is so small." This appeal seems strange in view of Israel's extensive territory and economic prosperity. But Amos had seen an awesome display of Yahweh's might in this vision; and, in comparison to that, the nation seemed small and helpless. Amos's prayer was answered. The Lord relented and the threat was revoked (v.3).

4–6 The second aspect of the vision involved the threat of fire (v.4)—an all-consuming fire, lapping up the sea and land. Again Amos's prayer was answered (v.5) and the Lord relented (v.6), as he had done in the first part of the vision.

7–9 The third aspect of the vision is climactic and contains the didactic element of the vision. The Lord was seen standing by a plumb wall with a plumb line in his hand (v.7). The word "standing" (*niṣṣāḇ*, a Niphal reflexive, i.e., "station oneself") connotes a posture of firmness and determination, thus providing a contrast to the change of heart attributed to Yahweh in the first two parts of the vision.

A plumb line is a standard by which a wall's vertical trueness is tested. So the Lord was testing the people by a standard. In the first two visions, no standard was given. Therefore, the threatened judgment could be withdrawn. But after the plumb line vision, the Lord could not be accused of arbitrariness if he carried out the threats. The people had failed to live up to their privilege as Yahweh's people. They had been called to be holy (Exod 19:6). But their repressive society violated the very standards of holiness itself. They gave lip service to the covenant of Yahweh but ignored the social concerns woven into its fabric. When the test came, they were found wanting. The plumb line showed that the Lord was not an arbitrary judge.

The coming judgment was to fall on the pagan sanctuaries of Israel and on the dynasty of Jeroboam (v.9). Thus the two major influences in Israelite life would perish.

Notes

7 The construct relationship חוֹמַת אֲנָךְ (*ḥômaṯ 'ᵃnāḵ*, "built true to plumb") functions adjectivally in this verse. The wall is plumb; hence, it does not represent Israel in the vision.

B. *A Historical Interlude*

7:10–17

[10]Then Amaziah the priest of Bethel sent a message to Jeroboam king of Israel: "Amos is raising a conspiracy against you in the very heart of Israel. The land cannot bear all his words. [11]For this is what Amos is saying:

" 'Jeroboam will die by the sword,
and Israel will surely go into exile,
away from their native land.' "

[12]Then Amaziah said to Amos, "Get out, you seer! Go back to the land of Judah. Earn your bread there and do your prophesying there. [13]Don't prophesy anymore at Bethel, because this is the king's sanctuary and the temple of the kingdom."

[14]Amos answered Amaziah, "I was neither a prophet nor a prophet's son, but I was a shepherd, and I also took care of sycamore-fig trees. [15]But the LORD took me from tending the flock and said to me, 'Go, prophesy to my people Israel.' [16]Now then, hear the word of the LORD. You say,

" 'Do not prophesy against Israel,
and stop preaching against the house of Isaac.'

[17]"Therefore this is what the LORD says:

" 'Your wife will become a prostitute in the city,
and your sons and daughters will fall by the sword.
Your land will be measured and divided up.
and you yourself will die in a pagan country.
And Israel will certainly go into exile,
away from their native land.' "

Amos's visions are momentarily interrupted by a passage that give us important information about Amos himself. It may have been placed here because it actually followed Amos's public report of the preceding vision. At any rate, the consonance between the two sections is apparent (see Introduction: Unity).

10–13 Amaziah, the priest of the sanctuary at Bethel, accused Amos of conspiracy (v.10). The words reported by Amaziah (v.11) seem to be based on the threat recorded in v.9. Jeroboam's reaction is not given, but it is likely that it is reflected in Amaziah's order to Amos (vv.12–13). The word "seer" (*ḥōzeh*) is associated with "prophet" (*nāḇî'*) in 2 Kings 17:13, affirming the legitimacy of the seer. Amaziah did not use "seer" in a derogatory sense. Indeed, since Amos had just received a vision, the term was quite appropriate.

14–15 Amos's reply to Amaziah's order is not without its interpretive problems. Did Amos say, "I am not a prophet," or, "I was not a prophet"? Most commentators have opted for the former because of the sequence of verbless clauses in Amos's reply, which connote most naturally the present tense. On the other hand, a number of commentators have followed the rendering of the RV: "I was no prophet." If the tense is present, Amos may have been denying that he was a *nāḇî'* ("prophet") in the sense that Amaziah understood him to be—viz., a professional prophet ("Earn your bread there," v.12).

There are, however, certain difficulties with the present-tense view. First, Amos used the term *nāḇî'* ("prophet") of true prophets in 3:7. To use it otherwise here would be unusual. Second, Amos claimed the function of a *nāḇî'* in 7:15 (*hinnāḇē'*, "prophesy").

The view that understands the affirmation of Amos in the past tense ("I was no prophet") seems to have the fewest problems. It retains the meaning of *nāḇî'* inherent in the noun form in 3:7 and the verbal form in 7:15. Also, that the Lord took Amos from being a shepherd (*mē'aḥᵃrê haṣṣō'n*, "from tending the flock," v. 15) may mean that the noun clauses in v. 15 describing his profession as a "shepherd" (*bôqēr*) and a "caretaker of sycamore-fig trees" (*bôlēm šiqmîm*) should be understood to describe his past status.

Regardless of one's understanding of Amos's denial, he certainly denied any connection with professional prophetism and affirmed that he was a prophet by divine vocation. (The occupations of Amos referred to here are discussed in the Introduction under Authorship.)

16–17 Amos's encounter with Amaziah ended with a prediction of dire judgment, despite his insistence that Amos desist in his preaching against Israel (v. 16). The judgment Amos pronounced against Amaziah and his family was personal in nature. Amaziah's wife would be violated, perhaps by the invading soldiers, and his children killed. He would lose all he had and would die in a "pagan" (*ṭom'āh*, "unclean") country. So the priest, whose task it was to maintain the purity of the cult, would die in a Gentile land.

Notes

10 Amaziah's report of Amos's threat, while essentially accurate, moved the emphasis from the house of Jeroboam to Jeroboam himself. This may have inflamed the situation and thus served Amaziah's cause. Jeroboam himself was not overthrown, but his dynasty fell a very short while after his death.

14 The question of tense cannot be decided by the fact that the verbless clauses are followed (v. 15) by the imperfect with waw consecutive וַיִּקָּחֵנִי (*wayyiqqāḥēnî*, "[the Lord] took me"). This grammatical construction connotes the past tense here, but that no more determines the tense of the verbless clauses than the imperfect with waw consecutive does in Exod 6:2–3. There the verbless clause אֲנִי יהוה (*ᵃnî YHWH*) must be understood in the present tense—"I am the LORD"—even though it is followed by the imperfect with waw consecutive וָאֵרָא (*wā'ērā'*, "I appeared") in v. 3. Generally, the tense of a verbless clause describes a state contemporaneous with the principal action (cf. GKC, par. 141e); yet one may question whether a verbless clause that precedes a verb in the past tense is also past tense. In Zech 13:5, the verbless clause לֹא נָבִיא אָנֹכִי (*lō' nāḇî' 'ānōḵî*, "I am not a prophet") precedes the verbless clause כִּי־אָדָם הִקְנַנִי (*kî-'āḏām hiqnanî*, "for the land has been my possession") and is clearly present in tense. The solution must be sought on other grounds.

Zevit translated Amos's denial as "No! I am a *nāḇi'*, I am not even a *ben nāḇi'*" (Z. Zevit, "A Misunderstanding at Bethel, Amos VII 12–17," VetTest 25, Fac. 4 [1975]: 783–90). Y. Hoffmann ("Did Amos Regard Himself as a Nabi'?" VetTest 27 [1977]: 209–12) countered this translation, observing that the "absolute denial" was never expressed by לֹא (*lō'*, "not").

The LXX translates the words of Amos in the past tense, Οὐκ ἤμην προφήτης ἐγῴ (*ouk ēmēn prophētēs egō*, "I was not a prophet), as well as the Peshitta-Syriac version.

Amos's occupation, described here as a בּוֹקֵר (*bôqēr*), may be that of a herdsman in general. The apparent linguistic connection with בָּקָר (*bāqār*, "cattle") does not demand the conclusion that Amos tended cattle. The LXX translates the term in the more general sense of αἰπόλος (*aipolos*, "goatherd"). There is no need to emend the word to נֹקֵד (*nōqēd*, "shepherd," BH). Zaleman proposed the reading דּוֹקֵר (*dôqēr*, "piercer"): "But I am a piercer and tender of sycamore figs" (L. Zaleman, "Piercing the Darkness at *Bôqēr* [Amos VII 14]," VetTest 30, Fasc. 2 [1980]: 252–53).

C. *The Vision of the Summer Fruit*

8:1–14

1 This is what the Sovereign LORD showed me: a basket of ripe fruit. 2 "What do
you see, Amos?" he asked.
"A basket of ripe fruit," I answered.
Then the LORD said to me, "The time is ripe for my people Israel; I will spare
them no longer.
3 "In that day," declares the Sovereign LORD, "the songs in the temple will turn
to wailing. Many, many bodies—flung everywhere! Silence!"

4 Hear this, you who trample the needy
and do away with the poor of the land,

5 saying,

"When will the New Moon be over
that we may sell grain,
and the Sabbath be ended
that we may market wheat?"—
skimping the measure,
boosting the price
and cheating with dishonest scales,
6 buying the poor with silver
and the needy for a pair of sandals,
selling even the sweepings with the wheat.

7 The LORD has sworn by the Pride of Jacob: "I will never forget anything they
have done.

8 "Will not the land tremble for this,
and all who live in it mourn?
The whole land will rise like the Nile;
it will be stirred up and then sink
like the river of Egypt.

9 "In that day," declares the Sovereign LORD,

"I will make the sun go down at noon
and darken the earth in broad daylight.
10 I will turn your religious feasts into mourning
and all your singing into weeping.
I will make all of you wear sackcloth
and shave your heads.
I will make that time like mourning for an only son
and the end of it like a bitter day.

11 "The days are coming," declares the Sovereign LORD,
"when I will send a famine through the land—
not a famine of food or a thirst for water,
but a famine of hearing the words of the LORD.

[12]Men will stagger from sea to sea
and wander from north to east,
searching for the word of the LORD,
but they will not find it.

[13]"In that day

"the lovely young women and strong young men
will faint because of thirst.
[14]They who swear by the shame of Samaria,
or say, 'As surely as your god lives, O Dan,'
or, 'As surely as the god of Beersheba lives'—
they will fall,
never to rise again."

1–2 While it is possible that Amos saw an actual basket of fruit (v.1) and that the Lord used it as a means of revelation, its inclusion in this section of the book makes it likely that it was another vision. There is a striking wordplay here (v.2). The word for summer fruit is *qāyiṣ*, similar in sound to the word *qēṣ*, which means "end" and is used in the response of the Lord: "The end has come for my people" (NIV, "The time is ripe for my people").

The basket of summer fruit, ordinarily associated with the joys and provisions of the harvest, becomes a mockery. The pleasant memories of past harvest festivals it might recall were shattered by the decisive words "the time is ripe" (*bā' haqqēṣ*, lit., "the end has come").

3 Just as the apparent promise of the summer fruit was turned into the assurance of Israel's destruction, so the joyous temple hymns (cf. 6:5) would give way to the wailing of the populace of Israel when the wrath of Yahweh fell on them. The last clause of v.3, though somewhat desultory, is typical of the vivid staccato style Amos had used earlier in describing calamity (3:12). The text may be translated: "Many are the corpses—they are flung everywhere—Silence!" The translation of *hišlîḵ* as "flung" understands it as an indefinite singular—"one flings," or "they are flung" (cf. Notes). The word "silence" calls for the reverence this appalling scene warrants.

4–6 This scene is followed by a recital (v.4) of the crimes of those whose disobedience to the Lord was responsible for the carnage. The words of v.4 are reminiscent of 5:11. The merchants could not wait for the end of the holy days so that they could increase their wealth by giving short measure and raising prices (v.5). They even sold the sweepings to increase the weight (v.6)! Yet these exploiters were careful to observe the Sabbath. Though the marketplace was deserted on the holy days, in the bustle of commerce their god was quite in evidence. Their god was Mammon; their true religious credo; gain at any cost.

7–8 In the oath formula, the "Pride of Jacob" (v.7) is best understood as an appellation for God (cf. 4:2; 6:8; cf. also Hos 5:5; 7:10). "Glory is used as a surrogate for God in Jeremiah 2:11. It is the pride of Jacob—i.e., the Lord, Jacob's glory—that guarantees this oath. The judgment to follow (v.8) would surely come because God does not allow his glory to be sullied. Verse 8 describes the convulsions the land would suffer. The striking metaphor of an earthquake represents the calamity Amos has referred to throughout the book.

9 "In that day" refers to the day of calamity and need not be understood as eschatological. It introduces a section that continues to describe the impending judgment in metaphorical language. The setting of the sun at noon describes an interruption of the natural order that would cause terror and panic among earth's inhabitants. The upheaval predicted by Amos would be a disruption of the national life on such a scale that the fear and dread in the hearts of the people would be similar to the terror a celestial cataclysm would cause.

10–12 The destruction to come on Samaria will be the cause of bitter mourning. Amos described the event in terms of a funeral for an only son (v.10). He continued the use of metaphorical language as he depicted a coming famine. It was no ordinary famine but one of the words of the Lord (v.11). He pictured men searching for the word as starving people seek food or water (vv.12–13). But they received no word from the Lord. They had rejected the word, not realizing its great value, and had lost it forever (cf. Luke 17:22; John 7:34).

The church must realize the preciousness of the Word of God. We must obey and honor it, because it points to the source of life.

14 The word "shame" (*'ašmāh*) has the primary meaning of "guilt." Sometimes it is used of the guilt incurred from idol worship (2 Chron 24:18; 33:23). Dan was the site of the worship of the golden calf under Jeroboam, and the "way to Beersheba" (*dereḵ bᵉ'er šāḇa'*; NIV, "god of Beersheba") apparently refers to the pilgrimage to that site (see comment at 5:5). The various shrines Amos referred to may indicate that a geographical split in the concept of Yahweh was taking place. A similar split related to the Canaanite god Baal. Thus the worship of Yahweh became idolatrous. Those whose confidence was in their distorted, pagan view of Yahweh would fall.

Notes

3 For a discussion of the indefinite singular, see GKC, par. 144d.

D. *The Vision of the Lord Standing by the Altar* (9:1–15)

1. *The destruction of the temple*

9:1–6

1 I saw the Lord standing by the altar, and he said:

"Smash the tops of the pillars
  so that the thresholds shake.
Bring them down on the heads of all the people;
  those who are left I will kill with the sword.
Not one will get away,
  none will escape.
2 Though they dig down to the depths of the grave,
  from there my hand will take them.
Though they climb up to the heavens,
  from there I will bring them down.

[3]Though they hide themselves on the top of Carmel,
there I will hunt them down and seize them.
Though they hide from me at the bottom of the sea,
there I will command the serpent to bite them.
[4]Though they are driven into exile by their enemies,
there I will command the sword to slay them.
I will fix my eyes upon them
for evil and not for good."

[5]The Lord, the LORD Almighty,
he who touches the earth and it melts,
and all who live in it mourn—
the whole land rises like the Nile,
then sinks like the river of Egypt—
[6]he who builds his lofty palace in the heavens
and sets its foundation on the earth,
who calls for the waters of the sea
and pours them out over the face of the land—
the LORD is his name.

1–4 Amos saw the Lord standing by the temple altar (v.1a). The Lord commanded the temple to crumble, and it collapsed on the people, destroying the whole nation (vv.1b–4). The temple was not a literal temple, for the collapse of such a building would affect only a few. Rather it represents the religion of the northern kingdom, which, in the end, brought about the destruction of its adherents. The decay of the social structure that resulted from their cold externalism could lead only to national ruin. The gross sin of idolatry could lead only to judgment. The god of "greed" is no respecter of persons and often turns his voraciousness on those who are his own. Amos allowed no escape for the nation.

5–6 The hymnic element is appropriate to the context because it sets forth the power of the Lord to carry out his threat. This hymn contains several elements common to other prophetic hymns, such as the reference to the heavens and the calling forth of the waters (5:8).

2. *Israel and the other nations*

9:7

[7]"Are not you Israelites
the same to me as the Cushites?"

declares the LORD.

"Did I not bring Israel up from Egypt,
the Philistines from Caphtor
and the Arameans from Kir?

7 Cush was a territory roughly corresponding to Ethiopia and Nubia. It is infrequently mentioned in the OT. This country seems to have been chosen because of its great distance from Israel. It lay at the outer extremities of the important nations of the ancient Near East. At the time of Amos, it was probably considered an insignificant region. Thus it would be shocking to the Israelites, who boasted of their election, to learn that in the eyes of the Lord they were no better than those obscure Cushites.

Israel was no different from the Philistines or Arameans, because the Lord governed the migrations of these people just as he led the Israelites from Egypt. The Exodus had led the Israelites to assume that the Lord was unalterably committed to them as a nation and that no other nation counted as far as he was concerned. But here Amos destroyed that false assumption by affirming the sovereignty of Yahweh over all the nations. The Exodus did not give them license to presume on the holiness and mercy of God.

3. *The restoration of the Davidic kingdom*

9:8–12

8"Surely the eyes of the Sovereign LORD
are on the sinful kingdom.
I will destroy it
from the face of the earth—
yet I will not totally destroy
the house of Jacob,"
declares the LORD.

9"For I will give the command,
and I will shake the house of Israel
among all the nations
as grain is shaken in a sieve,
and not a pebble will reach to the ground.
10All the sinners among my people
will die by the sword,
all those who say,
'Disaster will not overtake or meet us.'
11"In that day I will restore
David's fallen tent.
I will repair its broken places,
restore its ruins,
and build it as it used to be,
12so that they may possess the remnant of Edom
and all the nations that bear my name,"
declares the LORD, who will do these things.

8–10 The nation was to be destroyed, but not totally (v.8). Thus an element of hope is introduced at this point. Many scholars deny the words of vv.8–15 to Amos because the message of hope is not consonant with the gloomy message of total destruction presented to this point. But it is precisely this element of hope that places Amos in the mainstream of classical eighth-century prophetism. The concept of hope in vv.8–15 is quite unlike the eschatological hope of the post-exilic period, and the eighth-century prophets placed their hope of the future in a kingdom portrayed with obvious Davidic motifs (Isa 9:7; Mic 5:2). It is true that Amos held no hope for the nation of Israel. But that is not to say that he held out no hope for a preserved remnant. One of the important elements of Amos's message was that the nation was not to be equated with the remnant; it was precisely that false hope that he attacked. The sifting process (v.9) would produce a true remnant from Israel (v.10; cf. Jer 30:11). (For a study of the remnant in the OT, see G. Hasel, *The Remnant* [Berrien Springs, Mich.: Andrews University Press, 1972].)

Amos's denial of the popular belief that the nation was automatically the remnant raises serious questions. Did he deny the remnant concept altogether? Did he see no continuation of the promise to Abraham? It is difficult to answer such questions in the affirmative, for to do so would exclude Amos from the current of OT thought. Without the remnant passage of vv.9–15, the Book of Amos is incomplete. Amos was not a prophet who pronounced only doom. There are rays of hope not only here but even in undisputed passages such as 5:4, 6, 15.

Some commentators deny that the figure of "sifting" in v.9 implies a process of separation. They see the "pebbles" as representing the wicked, who are not allowed to escape and who are destined for judgment. But v.9 is logically connected to v.8 by the word "for" (*kî*), where a separation between the destroyed kingdom and the remnant is implicit in the statement affirming that the nation will not be totally destroyed. Verse 9 thus explains v.8 by analogy.

The concept of separation is inherent in the figure of sifting. Failure to see separation in the sieve motif leaves unexplained the shaking of Israel "among all the nations" (v.9). Amos decreed that the nation was doomed to exile (7:17). The consonance of this with the "shaking" of v.9 is apparent. The process of winnowing, whereby the grain falls to the ground and the larger refuse remains in the sieve, thus representing the sinners, is not necessarily in view here. The word "grain" does not appear in the Hebrew. It is simply "as one shakes with a sieve."

The word "pebble" (*ṣᵉrôr*) in v.9 need not be understood as "grain." It connotes anything that is compacted and refers to anything that will not pass through a sieve. In 2 Samuel 17:13 ("a piece," NIV) and Proverbs 26:8, *ṣᵉrôr* is used of a pebble, but never specifically of grain. There is no need to see a reference to good or evil in *ṣᵉrôr.* Amos simply stated that while the smaller pebbles pass through, the larger ones remain in the sieve. This material is analogous to the remnant.

11 "In that day" refers to the time when the sifting activity will be initiated, that is, the period of the Exile (vv.9–10). This period was seen by the prophets as continuing till the coming of Messiah (cf. Notes) and so includes the Christian Era.

The word "tent" (*sukkāh*) refers to a rude shelter (a "hut") and pictures the "house" of David that was becoming a dilapidated shack; in Amos's time the Davidic dynasty had fallen so low that it could no longer be called a house.

The continuation of the Davidic dynasty is envisioned in prophecy as continuing in the Messiah, who is often referred to in Davidic motifs (Isa 9:6–7; Jer 33:15, 17; Mic 5:2). Amos thus affirmed what other prophets affirmed, the perpetuity of the Davidic house. The national upheaval that ultimately led to the fall of Judah and Israel and the overthrow of the Judahite monarchy could not vitiate God's promise. The royal offspring would yet come. David's dynasty would be perpetuated in David's greater Son. He would uphold God's gracious promise.

The promise to David in 2 Samuel also carried with it the promise of an eternal kingdom (vv.12–13). While the Davidic dynasty is most prominent in Amos's prophecy, it is difficult to separate that concept from the concept of regnal authority or kingdom. Both are probably in view.

The word *nōpeleṯ*, an active participle, may be translated "fallen"; but there is no reason why it may not be given a continuing sense—viz., "is falling." The dynasty had not yet collapsed in Amos's time, but the seeds of its dissolution were present.

The Lord declared that he would restore that "tent." He would restore "their" (fem. pl.) broken places. The plural pronoun apparently refers to the divided kingdom. He would restore "his" (masc. sing.)—i.e., David's—ruins and rebuild "it" (fem. sing.), referring to "the tent" (*sukkāh*, fem.). The Davidic dynasty, represented by the tent, was, according to Amos, to be restored.

12 The NT follows the LXX here, reading "that the remnant of men may seek the Lord" (Acts 15:17) instead of "possess the remnant of Edom." The word "Edom" is almost identical to "man" in Hebrew. The subject of Acts 15:12–21, where this passage is quoted, is Gentile inclusion in the early church. James quoted the Amos passage to support the rightness of Gentile inclusion in the church. The textual question cited does not invalidate James's usage of the passage because the phrase "that bear my name" (*'ᵃšer niqrā' šᵉmî 'ᵃlêhem*) always connotes that which is God's peculiar possession (Deut 28:10; 2 Chron 7:14; Jer 14:9; 15:16). This is precisely James's argument. He saw Gentile inclusion in the redemptive program of God predicted in Amos 9:11–12.

Since the inclusion of Gentiles takes place, according to Amos, in the kingdom of the scion of David, one may assume that that kingdom has been established in some way. It is invisible now but will appear in glorious power when Christ, David's greater Son, returns. If this passage in Amos predicted only a future inclusion of Gentiles in the millennial kingdom, it is difficult to understand why James would have appealed to it for support of Gentile admission to the first-century church. It seems to be clearly relevant to the issues facing the early church. If this is so, then James understood the restored Davidic monarchy to be represented, at least in its invisible sense, in the church in his time.

The inclusion of Gentiles in the divine promise is a concept attributed to the Servant of Isaiah (Isa 49:6). Amos echoes the same truth. The ancient promise that Gentiles as well as Jews (Gen 12:3) would experience divine blessing is fulfilled in the Offspring of David.

Notes

11 With regard to the suggestion that the OT prophets saw the period of exile continuing to the coming of Messiah, note Hos 3:1–5, where the period of estrangement continues till the people seek "David their king." See also Isa 11:11; Mic 5:2–6; Zech 10:10, where Assyria, the nation that initiated the Exile, functions as a surrogate of the oppressing nations in end-time events.

The NT (Acts 15:16) paraphrases בַּיּוֹם הַהוּא (*bayyôm hahû'*, "in that day") in the words *μετὰ ταῦτα* (*meta tauta*, "after these things"). This is not the translation of the LXX, which reads *ἐν τῇ ἡμέρᾳ ἐκείνῃ* (*en tē hemera ekeinē*, "in that day"). James may have been interpreting "in that day" so as to better communicate the fact that the prophecy of Amos did not find its fulfillment in the Babylonian captivity. This supports the suggestion that the captivity was understood as continuing throughout history.

סֻכָּה (*sukkāh*, "tent," "shelter") connotes a "shelter" for animals (Gen 33:17), a "shelter" from the sun (Jonah 4:5), and the "booths" the Israelites occupied in observance of the wilderness experience (Lev 23:42).

4. *The blessings of the restored kingdom*

9:13–15

13"The days are coming, declares the LORD,

"when the reaper will be overtaken by
the plowman
and the planter by the one treading grapes.

New wine will drip from the mountains
and flow from all the hills.
14 I will bring back my exiled people Israel;
they will rebuild the ruined cities and live in them.
They will plant vineyards and drink their wine;
they will make gardens and eat their fruit.
15 I will plant Israel in their own land,
never again to be uprooted
from the land I have given them,"
says the LORD your God.

A time is coming when there will be a superabundance of agricultural produce and wine (v.13). In this time Israel will be restored to the land forever (v.15).

13 The fact that the reaper will be overtaken by the plowman in this time implies a great abundance of the produce of the field. Scarcely can the grape vines be planted than the grapes are ready for pressing. The great amount of wine in this time is pictured in the metaphor of new wine flowing from the hills. Amos saw here a radical reversal of Israel's fortunes. He depicted a time when God's blessing would be poured out in unimaginable abundance.

14–15 The period when this abundance will be manifested will witness the restoration of Israel to her land. Ruined cities will be rebuilt (v.14), and Israel will again flourish as a nation. Amos saw this restoration as being permanent. He said that Israel would be planted in her own land "never again to be uprooted" (v.15). It is difficult to understand his words as finding fulfillment in the postexilic period. Not only were the economic conditions of that time not consonant with Amos's prediction, but its impermanency makes the identification doubly difficult.

Other OT prophets used somewhat similar language to describe this period. Like Amos, they associated the abundance of blessing with the Davidic King (Isa 9:2–7; 11:1–9; Mic 4:1–5; 5:2–5).

It is difficult to apply the concept of universal peace to the invisible kingdom, the church, unless the meaning of the prophet's language is severely restricted. If one understands the kingdom to have a present aspect as well as a future aspect, the problem becomes less difficult. The NT teaches a present, invisible aspect of the kingdom, which is the church. The millennial kingdom is that aspect of the kingdom in which God's reign will be realized within the sphere of human history and natural order. It is in this aspect of the kingdom that Amos's prediction of the blessings of the kingdom may be placed.

The hope of Amos is not an isolated one that finds expression only in his book. Nor is it a purely prophetic tradition without relation to other OT traditions. It is an expression of one of the most important themes of OT theology—viz., the promise. This promise, given to Abraham, reiterated to the patriarchs, reaffirmed to David, and expressed throughout the OT, affirms that God will mediate his redemptive blessings to Jews and Gentiles in a promised offspring or "seed." In the prophets, this offspring is clearly the Davidic Messiah, who in the NT is Christ. Amos affirmed that God's promise has not ceased. In spite of the internal turmoil in the kingdom of his day, God would establish the Davidic monarchy; and through that monarchy God's blessing would come to "all peoples on earth" (Gen 12:3).

OBADIAH

Carl E. Armerding

OBADIAH

Introduction

1. Background
2. Unity
3. Authorship
4. Date and Occasion
5. Literary Form
6. Geography
7. Special Problems
8. Bibliography
9. Outline

1. Background

Edom, established in the region around Mount Seir (see Geography) as far back as patriarchal times (cf. Gen 36), was one of the small kingdoms that inhabited the Transjordanian highlands throughout the entire monarchical period. From the Exodus and wandering narratives, as well as from Egyptian records, we know that Edom was well-established in the area south and east of the Dead Sea by the thirteenth century B.C. In the period of the monarchy, it was David's lot to bring Edom under subjection; and relations were often hostile from then onward. The full history of the country may be found in a variety of sources (cf. ZPEB, 2:202–4). Of particular interest in the context of Obadiah's work are two questions relating to Edom: (1) When might the hostility between Edom and Judah have produced the kind of Edomite perfidy expressed in vv.10–14? and (2) When in Edom's history were Obadiah's words fulfilled? The first question will be dealt with in the commentary at v.14, while the latter question is addressed here.

Despite periods of subjugation to Judah, there is clear evidence that Edom still constituted an independent monarchy about 594–593 B.C. (cf. Jer 27:3), and it provided at least partial refuge to Judah's fugitives then (cf. Jer 40:11). Although Ammon and Moab, like Judah, were subsequently subjugated by Nebuchadnezzar (c. 582, Jos. Antiq. X, 180–82 [ix.7]; cf. Ezek 21:18–20, 28), no reference is made to Edom, which may therefore have followed Jeremiah's counsel to submit (Jer 27:6–7). Edom's continued existence in the sixth century is also attested by excavations at Ezion-geber (Tell el-Kheleifeh): in particular, a seal dating from around 600–550 B.C. was discovered bearing a typical Edomite name ("belonging to *Qws'nl* servant of the king"; cf. Allen, p. 131; Bartlett, p. 53), and an ostracon from the latter half of the sixth century B.C. lists four names of similar Edomite origin (Allen, p. 131). Edom also figures in OT writings from the Exile, which bear witness to its continued existence, albeit guilty and threatened (e.g., Lam 4:21–22; Ezek 25:12–14; 35; Dan 11:41).

By 312 B.C., however, it is certain that Petra was occupied by the Nabataeans (e.g., *Diodorus Siculus* 19, 95.2, 98.1), a nomadic Arabic tribe that had infiltrated the land. There is evidence that this transition to Arabic influence was already established in the fifth century. Ammon and Moab are cited as enemies of Judah's interests in the time of Nehemiah (c. 444–432; Neh 2:10, 19; 4:3, 7; 6:1–15; 13:1–2, 23); Edom, however, is not named among Judah's traditional opponents, being replaced by the Arabs who played a dominant role under Geshem (Neh 2:19; 4:7; 6:1–2; cf. 2 Chron 17:11; 21:16; 22:1; 26:7). A similar transition is evident at Ezion-geber, where Arabic names replace Edomite names on the fifth-century site, which was controlled by the Arabs during the Persian period (late sixth to the fourth centuries; cf. "The Moabites and Edomites" in Wiseman).

The destruction of Edom may therefore be located tentatively in the latter half of the sixth century. This dating is corroborated by Malachi, who described as past history the reduction of Esau's "mountains into a wasteland" and "his inheritance of the desert jackals" (c. 450, Mal 1:3–4; cf. Ezek 32:29), though the prophet envisaged a continuing identity and national striving by Edom, even in exile (Mal 1:4–5).

It has been suggested that Nabonidus (556–539), the last of the Babylonian rulers, was responsible for Edom's destruction and eventual displacement into the Negev. He campaigned in southern Transjordan in 552, in the interests of policing the major trade routes of western Arabia to which he devoted the greater part of his reign. Such a campaign could explain the overthrow of traditional Edomite control of the caravan routes leading to Egypt and the Mediterranean; and it would also have provided incentive for the Nabataeans to abandon their brigandry along the trade routes, now protected by Nabonidus's military colonies, and to adopt a more settled existence in the land of the crippled Edomites (Lindsay, pp. 23–39).

This reconstruction is still regarded as conjectural. Martin Noth (*History of Israel* [London: Black, 1959], p. 294) concurs with the opinion of Bartlett in writing, "The final fate of the Edomite kingdom remains completely shrouded in darkness." It is certain, however, that Edom's mountains were the scene of invasion and destruction in the sixth century, leading to the decease of Edom as a monarchy and as a stable culture.

2. Unity

The Book of Obadiah is structured around two interrelated themes: the destruction of "Edom" (vv.1, 8), referred to also as "Esau" (vv.6, 8–9, 18 [*bis*], 19, 21) and "Teman" (v.9), and the vindication of "Judah" (v.12), referred to by the names "Jacob" (vv.10, 17–18), "Jerusalem" (vv.11, 20), "Mount Zion" (vv.17, 21; cf. v.16), within the broader context of Israel as a whole (cf. vv.18–20). The prophecy abounds with these geographical and ethnic terms, which is one of the unifying factors of the book. These terms also vividly express the dynamics of these few, intense verses: the juxtaposition of "Jacob" and "Esau," in particular, draws attention to the blood relationship uniting the two nations—it is defined explicitly at the center of the book (cf. "your brother," vv.10, 12); and it is the violation of these ties that occasion both Obadiah's denunciation of Edom and the necessity for Judah's restoration. The book is similarly unified by the related concept of the "day" (*yôm*) of God's judgment (vv.8, 11 [*bis*], 12 [*quad*], 13 [*ter*], 14, 15) and by the principle of reversal that informs that judgment, stated throughout but most clearly in vv.15–16.

3. Authorship

Nothing is known of the author of Obadiah. The name, which means "servant of Yahweh," is given to at least twelve other OT characters, none of whom seem obviously to be the author named in the book. Most attempts at correlation founder on the inability of scholars to date the book with certainty (see below).

4. Date and Occasion

The date and occasion for the Book of Obadiah continue to be much debated. The prophecy is clearly a response to a time when Jerusalem was overrun by foreign armies, a sack in which the Edomites were understood to have some way collaborated (see commentary at v.15). If it was, as argued below, the 586 B.C. destruction under Nebuchadnezzar, and if Edom itself came under Nabataean control by the fifth century B.C., the date of the book is best left sometime after the 586 invasion of Zion.

5. Literary Form

The prophecy is composed of three major sections—vv.1–9, 10–14, 15–21—which portray the contrasting relations of Jacob, Esau, and the nations in past and future history. Verses 1–9 anticipate a "day" (v.8) of the "LORD" (vv.1, 4, 8) in which "Esau" (vv.6, 8–9) will be "cut down" in battle (v.9) by the "nations" (vv.1–2). Verses 10–14 recollect a corresponding "day" of calamity (vv.11–14) in which "Jacob" (v.10) has been "cut down" (*kāraṯ*, v.14) by Esau ("you," "your," vv.11–14) in collaboration with "foreigners" (v.11).

This reversal of roles is completed in vv.15–21, which correspond closely to vv. 10–14, as does that section to vv.1–9. A "day" (v.15) of the "LORD" (vv.15, 18, 21) is coming in which the house of "Jacob" (vv.17–18) will "possess" its inheritance (vv.17, 19–20), consuming the house of "Esau" (vv.18–19, 21) along with the "nations" (v.15; cf. vv.19–20).

This tripartite structure revolves around the book's central section, vv.10–14, to which both vv.1–9 and vv.15–21 correspond closely in different ways: vv.1–9 substitute Esau for Jacob in a fate that is outwardly identical; and vv.15–21 completely reverse the roles pictured in vv.10–14. There are thus two distinct facets to the theology of judgment set forth in Obadiah: the aggressor will reap what he has sown (vv.1–14; cf. vv.15–16), and the innocent victim will be exalted over his aggressors (vv.10–12). No theory of justice can be complete without this two-edge principle, which ensures both punishment and restoration (cf. Rom 13:3–4). Verses 10–14 thus state the evidence from which the sentences are derived in vv.1–9, 15–21. Their centrality is stressed conspicuously by the absence of any reference to the Lord. The adjacent sections are framed and punctuated symmetrically by the sovereign decree of the Lord (vv.1, 4, 8, and vv.15, 18, 21); but the events of vv.10–14 find no origin or ratification in his will. In this context the destruction of Jerusalem is not envisaged as a visitation from God; and Edom cannot claim exoneration as an instrument of such judgment (cf. Isa 10:5–15; Jer 49:12; Zech 1:15).

6. Geography

The land of Edom lay adjacent to Judah, on its southeastern boundaries (Num 34:3; Josh 15:1, 21; cf. Josh 11:17; 12:7; 15:10). It extended for about a hundred miles southward, from the Dead Sea to Elath on the Gulf of Aqaba (Num 21:4). It was bounded by desert to the east and by the Arabah to the west; to the north the Zered Valley at the southern end of the Dead Sea formed a natural boundary with Moab (Num 21:12; Deut 2:12–13). The main center of Edomite population comprised an area extending some seventy miles south from the Zered River, a narrow strip of mountainous country averaging no more than fifteen miles across, in which were located the main Edomite cities such as Bozrah (cf. vv.3, 9). The regions to the south and particularly those west of the Arabah were controlled loosely by Edom in periods of national strength (cf. Num 20:14; IDB, 2:24ff.). Edom was known as the land of Seir, Seir having been the ancestor of the Horites who occupied Edom before being displaced and assimilated by the Edomites (cf. Gen 32:3; 36:20–30; Deut 2:4–5, 8; 2:12, 22, 29).

The name "Edom" (*'ᵉdōm*) is associated with the adjective "red" (*'ādōm*), being derived from the color of the pottage Esau sold his birthright for (Gen 25:30). The same color characterized Esau himself at birth (Gen 25:25); it is also evident in the varied hues of Edom's sandstone cliffs.

7. Special Problems

A striking similarity exists between Obadiah and one or more of Jeremiah's oracles against Edom in chapter 49. Specifically, Obadiah 1b–5 and Jeremiah 49:9, 14–16 exhibit such clear parallels that we are forced to conclude either a dependence one on the other or a mutual dependence on a common source. Since the prophetic activity of Jeremiah is unambiguously datable to the late seventh and early sixth centuries B.C. (prior to or immediately following the Fall of Jerusalem), and since we have placed Obadiah some time after that destruction, it should follow that Obadiah drew from Jeremiah. Many scholars contend, however, that textual comparisons argue, not for simple copying (the common materials contain identical phraseology as well as less-exact parallels), but for a common source. For this reason it is often claimed that Jeremiah's material was secondary (see the useful summary in Allen, pp. 131f.), though that conclusion hardly seems necessary. Admittedly, the question is a complicated one. Differences will be treated in the body of the commentary, but in general one may concur with Watts (p. 33), who quoted with approval T.H. Robinson's 1916 judgment that "the material is more original in Obadiah, but better preserved in Jeremiah."

8. Bibliography

Books

Allen, Leslie C. *The Books of Joel, Obadiah, Jonah and Micah*. New International Commentary on the Old Testament. Grand Rapids: Eerdmans, 1976.

Baly, Denis. *The Geography of the Bible*. New York: Harper & Row, 1974.

Bewer, Julius A., et al. *A Critical and Exegetical Commentary on the Books of Micah,*

Zephaniah, Nahum, Habakkuk, Obadiah, Joel and Jonah. ICC. Edinburgh: T. & T. Clark, 1912.

Beck, Madeline H., and Williamson, Lamar, Jr. *Mastering Old Testament Facts: Book 4: Prophetic Writings*. Atlanta: John Knox, 1981.

Ellison, H.L. *The Old Testament Prophets*. 1958 Reprint. Grand Rapids: Zondervan, 1966.

Feinberg, Charles L. *The Minor Prophets*. Chicago: Moody, 1976.

Gaebelein, Frank E. *Four Minor Prophets*. Chicago: Moody, 1970.

Gelston, A., ed. *Dodekapropheton*. Leiden Peshitta. Vol. 3:4. Leiden: E.J. Brill, 1980.

Henderson, E. *The Twelve Minor Prophets*. Grand Rapids: Baker, 1980.

Keil, Carl F. *The Twelve Minor Prophets*. KD. Grand Rapids: Eerdmans, 1949.

Laetsch, Theodore. *The Minor Prophets*. St. Louis: Concordia, 1956.

Lurie, Benzion. *Sepher Obadya and the Prophetic Oracles About Edom*. Jerusalem: Kiryath Sepher, 1972.

Pusey, E.B. *The Minor Prophets*. Vol. 1. Reprint. Grand Rapids: Baker, 1950.

Schneider, D. *The Unity of the Book of the Twelve*. New Haven: Yale, 1979.

Smith, George A. *The Book of the Twelve Prophets*. Vol. 2. ExB. Garden City: Doubleday, Doran & Co.

Sperber, Alexander. *The Latter Prophets*. Vol. 3. The Bible in Aramaic. Leiden: E.J. Brill, 1962.

Vegas Montaner, Luis. *Biblia Del Mar Muerto: Profetas Menores*. Madrid: Instituto "Arias Montano" CSIC, 1980.

Watts, John D.W. *Obadiah: A Critical Exegetical Commentary*. Grand Rapids: Eerdmans, 1969.

Wiseman, D.J., ed. *Peoples of Old Testament Times*. Oxford: Oxford University Press, 1973.

Ziegler, Joseph. *Septuaginta: Duodecim Prophetae*. Vol. 13. Goettingen: Vandenhoeck & Ruprecht, 1967.

Periodicals

Bartlett, J.R. "From Edomites to Nabataeans: A Study in Continuity." *Palestinian Exploration Quarterly* 111 (1979): 53.

Lillie, J.R. "Obadiah—A Celebration of God's Kingdom." *Currents in Theology & Mission* 6 (1979): 18–22.

Lindsay, J. "Babylonian Kings and Edom, 605–550." *Palestinian Exploration Quarterly* 108 (1976): 23–39.

9. Outline

- I. The Message From the Lord (v.1)
- II. The Abasement of Edom (vv.2–9)
  - A. Edom's Character (vv.2–4)
    - 1. Edom's future smallness (v.2)
    - 2. Edom's present pride (vv.3–4)
  - B. Edom's Calamity (vv.5–9)
    - 1. Edom's ransacking (vv.5–6)
    - 2. Edom's entrapment (v.7)
    - 3. God's initiative (vv.8–9)
- III. The Charge Against Edom (vv.10–14)
  - A. The Reason for the Charge (v.10)
  - B. The Explanation of the Charge (vv.11–14)
    - 1. The charge defined (v.11)
    - 2. The charge repeated and amplified (vv.12–14)
- IV. The Day of the Lord (vv.15–21)
  - A. The Judgment of Esau (vv.15–18)
  - B. The Occupation of Edom (vv.19–21)

Text and Exposition

I. The Message From the Lord

Verse 1

[1]The vision of Obadiah.

This is what the Sovereign LORD says about Edom—
We have heard a message from the LORD:
An envoy was sent to the nations to say,
"Rise, and let us go against her for battle"—

Verse 1 summarizes the intent of vv.1–9, announcing the Lord's decree against "Edom," which is to be overthrown in "battle" by the "nations." This is reiterated and amplified in vv.2–9: the Lord's decrees (vv.4, 8) against "Edom"/"Esau" (vv.6, 8–9), who will be humbled, plundered, and devastated in battle (vv.2–9) by the nations (v.7; cf. v.2). Verses 2–9 are divided into three interdependent sections (vv.2–4, 5–7, 8–9) by the repeated phrase "declares the LORD" (*neʾum YHWH*, vv.4, 8). Each section describes the abasement of Esau and the deception that precipitates his downfall; as in the prophecy as a whole, there is no reference to the Lord in the central section, which describes the human agencies of treachery and greed by which this abasement is accomplished.

1 Obadiah's prophecy opens with the formal announcement of a message from the Lord "about" or "against" (*le*; cf. Ps 137:7) Edom, a pattern repeated in the following lines. Although the verse constitutes an unusual opening to a prophecy, through the sudden change of speaker, the passage is unified by the parallelism noted above.

"Edom" represents an alternative name of "Esau," the brother of Jacob (Gen 36:1, 8, 43; cf. Obad 6, 8–9, 18–19, 21). It also denotes the descendants of Esau (Gen 36:9, 16–17; cf. 36:31, 43), whose blood relationship with Israel is invoked repeatedly in the OT (Num 20:14; Deut 23:7; Amos 1:11; Mal 1:2; cf. Obad 10, 12); and it describes the land inhabited by them (Num 20:23; 21:4; 34:3; cf. Obad 18–21).

The "message" (*šemûʿāh;* cf. Isa 28:9, 19; 53:1) is evidently a supernatural revelation, being "from the LORD," as in the preceding line, a conclusion corroborated by the prophecy's description as a "vision" (*ḥāzôn;* cf. Hab 1:1; 2:2–3). Such revelation was mediated primarily through the prophets, and the plural "we" might indicate a prophetic group; by extension it would certainly include the believing community to which the revelation was to be mediated.

The intent of this message is encapsulated in the following lines, which define the measures initiated by the Lord against Edom. An "envoy" (*ṣîr*) is normally a human ambassador, "sent" (*šālaḥ*) to represent the authority of those he served. Verse 1 even more than its parallel in Jeremiah 49:14 points to an envoy who represents one of the combatants ("let us").

The dual thrust of v.1 indicates two levels at which human history moves. The Lord is the ultimate mover, but there is also an international political alliance, motivated only by callous self-seeking (cf. vv.5–7). Even nations raised up by such base motives serve the overriding purposes of a God who sovereignly shapes human affairs through countless envoys of his own (cf. Ps 104:4). The "nations" are deaf to this realm, in which they serve unconsciously (cf. Isa 45:4–7); but it is the privilege and responsibility of Israel to walk in the knowledge of what it hears from the courts of the Great King.

II. The Abasement of Edom (vv.2–9)

A. *Edom's Character* (vv.2–4)

1. *Edom's future smallness*

Verse 2

2 "See, I will make you small among the nations;
you will be utterly despised.

2 Verse 2 introduces the central motif of vv.2–9, anticipating Edom's abasement. This is stressed by the introductory exclamation "See" and by the parallel adjectives "small" and "despised," which both stand emphatically at the beginning of their clauses in the MT. The second adjective defines the first: Edom's smallness is qualitative, corresponding to its despicable and debased character.

2. *Edom's present pride*

Verses 3–4

3 The pride of your heart has deceived you,
you who live in the clefts of the rocks
and make your home on the heights,
you who say to yourself,
'Who can bring me down to the ground?'
4 Though you soar like the eagle
and make your nest among the stars,
from there I will bring you down,"
declares the LORD.

3–4 These verses reiterate the sentence of abasement in the final, climactic line ("I will bring you down"), analyzing its causes in terms of pride and deception, the concomitant of pride. "Pride" (*zāḏôn;* cf. *zēḏ*, "proud") is derived from a verb meaning "to boil up, seethe" (*zîḏ*; cf. Gen 25:29; Ps 124:5). A cognate noun denotes food that has been boiled (*nāzîḏ*); the root occurs three times in the account of Esau's squandered birthright. In its literal usage, the root thus describes food or water that boils up under pressure, from which the figurative application of inflated self-exaltation logically follows. The essence of this "pride" is insubordination, rooted in an inordinate self-estimation: the proud man rejects authority, whether from God or man, and arrogates it to himself.

Edom's pride is grounded in its geographical location "on the heights," from which it draws its sense of security and self-sufficiency: it can flaunt external control, having the physical resources to evade it. And, indeed, Edom's natural defenses were imposing. Its main centers of civilization were situated in a narrow ridge of mountainous land southeast of the Dead Sea (cf. v.1). This ridge exceeded a height of 4,000 feet throughout its northern sector, and it rose in places to 5,700 feet in the south. Its height was rendered more inaccessible by the gorges radiating from it toward the Arabah on the west and the desert eastwards. Baly (p. 235) describes travel along this ridge, the route of the ancient King's Highway: "The road, of course, keeps to the more level ridgeland, but from time to time it approaches the rim and the traveler peers dizzily down into a bizarre world of dark, gigantic cliffs and deep, terrifying gorges. Here is a region altogether apart, forbidding, and inaccessible, the home still of the leopard and such other animals as man in his ferocity has not yet succeeded in destroying" (cf. Num 20:17).

The frontiers of this lofty plateau were formed on the west by the Arabah, to which the land dropped over 4,000 feet within the space of a few miles. The northern border was similarly defended by the deep canyon of the Wadi Zered, and to the south the precipitous walls of the Wadi Hismeh mark the abrupt descent of the tableland to the desert. In addition to these natural fortifications, Edom was strongly defended by a series of Iron Age fortresses, particularly on the eastern frontier where the land descended more gradually to the desert.

Such was Edom's refuge "in the clefts of the rocks" (*b̲ᵉḥag̲wê-sela'*; so S of Songs 2:14; Jer 49:16), whose austere environment might well foster thoughts of invulnerability. The term "rocks" (*sela'*) is used of large rock strata; and here it describes the sandstone and granite cliffs Edom drew its security from. "Sela" is also the name of an Edomite settlement captured by Amaziah (c. 800–783, 2 Kings 14:7; cf. NIV mg., "Sela"). It is commonly associated with the subsequent Nabataean capital, Petra, whose name also signifies "rock" (cf. Matt 16:18)—an identification now disputed on the basis of excavations at the site. It is in any case preferable to follow NIV in omitting the geographical allusion from the text.

Edom's sense of security has "deceived" it (*nāšā'*; cf. Jer 49:16). Although virtually impregnable to human forces, Edom is still utterly vulnerable before the wisdom and power of God. Edom's deceived pride has been expressed in the confident question "Who can bring me down?" It is echoed in the unanticipated answer; "I will bring you down" (both from *yārad̲*), a blunt statement of a single Hebrew word that embodies the heart of the prophecy. All that follows develops and amplifies the reversal of conditions heralded in this message from the Lord (cf. Jer 49:21).

B. *Edom's Calamity* (vv.5–9)

1. *Edom's ransacking*

Verses 5–6

5"If thieves came to you,
if robbers in the night—
Oh, what a disaster awaits you—
would they not steal only as much as they wanted?
If grape pickers came to you,
would they not leave a few grapes?
6But how Esau will be ransacked,
his hidden treasures pillaged!

5–6 Verse 5 picks up and repeats the clause of v.4 (*'im . . . 'im*, lit., "If . . . if"; NIV, "Though . . . and") and its consequence ("would they not," *hᵃlô'*), contrasted abruptly with the impending fate of Esau ("Oh, what," *'êk̲*). The same pattern is repeated in a slightly revised order (cf. Notes) in the following lines of vv.5–6: conditional clause ("If," *'im*), consequence ("would they not," *h^alô'*), contrast ("But how," *'êḵ*). The first contrast is thus an integral part of the two verses: its insertion between the condition and its apodosis effectively communicates the intent of the analogy and the urgency that motivates it. The structural features that unify these verses also integrate them into the adjacent sections: v.4 is similarly constructed as a double conditional sentence ("though . . . and," *'im . . . 'im);* and v.8 opens with the words "will I not" (*h^alô'*), echoing both the consequences of vv.5–6 and the initial rhetorical question of v.3 that it counters.

As "thieves" plunder a household, so "grape pickers" strip a vineyard. Yet in both cases they "leave" at least a pittance that escapes detection and despoliation. By contrast Esau will be "ransacked" with a terrible thoroughness that leaves nothing (cf. vv.8–9; Jer 49:9–10). This will be the work, not of thieves who come furtively and in haste "in the night," nor of vintagers who are restricted by law or by the urgency of their own greed from removing all the grapes (cf. Lev 19:9–10; Deut 24:19–21; Isa 17:6; Jer 6:9): it will represent the Lord's own judgment, from which nothing can remain "hidden." The repeated exclamation "what . . . how" (*'êḵ*) is characteristic of mourning in the presence of death, and it anticipates Edom's decease. Whereas the Lord consistently promised to "leave" a remnant for Jacob, no such promise is extended to Edom.

Notes

---

5 Most commentators maintain that a transposition of lines has occurred here. For example, Allen would move אֵיךְ נִדְמֵיתָה (*'êḵ niḏmêṯāh*, "what a disaster awaits you") to follow דַּיָּם (*dayyām*, "only as much as they wanted"), thereby creating parallel structure to v.5b. Watts takes his cue from Jer 49:9 and reverses the order of lines 1 and 2. However, the present order, as followed in NIV and NASB, makes reasonable sense and is retained here.

---

2. *Edom's entrapment*

Verse 7

> [7]All your allies will force you to the border;
> your friends will deceive and overpower you;
> those who eat your bread will set a trap for you,
> but you will not detect it.

7 The second line of this verse is relatively clear-cut in its meaning, and it forms a basis from which the adjacent lines may be understood. It threatens Edom with deception by its "friends"; the noun "friends" translates a phrase implying not merely coexistence but communal commitment (lit., "the men of your peace" [*'anšê š^elōmeḵā*]; so Ps 41:9; Jer 20:10; 38:22). This deception is the expression of calculated hostility, as indicated by the verb "overpower" (*yāḵōl l^e*). The keynote of the line is the verb "deceived" (*hiššî'ûḵā*, from *nāšā'*): it epitomizes the treachery evoked by its juxtaposition to the subject, "friends"; and it gains emphasis from v.3 where it is foreshadowed by almost the same form (*hiššî'ek̲ā*). Thus Edom's self-deception is now accompanied by deception from allies, belying its vaunted claim to independence.

The first line is clearly parallel to the second. The noun "friends" is echoed by "allies," in which the existence of covenant loyalty is explicitly presupposed (*'anšê b^{e}rîṯek̲ā*, lit., "the men of your covenant"). It follows that the verbs are parallel also. When followed by a personal object, the form "force" or "send away" (*šillaḥ*) is almost always used of authoritative dismissal, away from the subject's point of reference. The "border" would therefore be viewed from the perspective of anonymous "allies" and would represent their own frontiers to whose limits (*'aḏ*) the Edomites are expelled (but cf. Jer 49:19–20); and Edom is pictured as being rejected and betrayed by those allies when seeking help or refuge with them. Edom's fate in vv. 1–9 is proportioned exactly to that of Judah in vv. 10–14 (see introduction to v. 1); it is therefore appropriate that Edom should be denied help and refuge as it had done to its brother Jacob's "survivors" (vv. 10, 12, 14).

The third line is obscure in Hebrew, but this obscurity is mitigated by its parallelism with the preceding couplet (cf. Notes).

Notes

7 Line three is rendered obscure by its opening word לַחְמְךָ (*laḥm^{e}k̲ā*, "your bread"), translated by NIV as "those who eat your bread," and by the noun מָזוֹר (*māzôr*, "a trap"), which does not occur elsewhere in the OT with this meaning. As it stands the singular noun "your bread" represents a second object to the plural verb יָשִׂימוּ (*yāśîmû*, "they will set, place"). This suggests the meaning "they will make your bread a trap." It yields good sense if "your bread" is interpreted as a synecdoche (i.e., a part for the whole): they make the friendship expressed and ratified when they ate your bread a trap (since their commitment was illusory). A similar meaning is suggested by the structure of the verse:

B	*A*
כֹּל אַנְשֵׁי בְרִיתֶךָ	עַד־הַגְּבוּל שִׁלְּחוּךָ—
אַנְשֵׁי שְׁלֹמֶךָ	הִשִּׁיאוּךָ יָכְלוּ לְךָ—
יָשִׂימוּ מָזוֹר תַּחְתֶּיךָ	לַחְמְךָ—
(i.e., *'aḏ⁻hagg^{e}ḇûl šill^{e}ḥûk̲ā*	—*kōl 'anšê b̲^{e}rîṯek̲ā*
hiššî'ûk̲ā yāk^{e}lû l^{e}k̲ā	—*'anšê š^{e}lōmek̲ā*
laḥm^{e}k̲ā	—*yāśîmû māzôr taḥteyk̲ā*)

This may be translated literally:

"To the borders they will force you" (A)—"all the men in covenant with you" (B).
"They will deceive you and overpower you" (A)—"the men at peace with you" (B).
"[The men of] your bread" (B)—"they will make a trap under you" (A).

The predicate (A) and subject (B) of the first line both end with the second masculine singular pronominal form ךָ (*k̲ā*, "you"). The predicate (A) and subject (B) of the second line also end with this suffix; this correspondence between the two lines is strengthened by the repeated noun אַנְשֵׁי, (*'anšê*, "men") and by the shared theme of commitment-treachery. The third line is similarly divided into two sections by the same suffix. The second section forms an unambiguous predicate (A), which further corresponds to its predecessors in reiterating the motif of treachery (see further, below). It follows that the initial word לַחְמְךָ (*laḥm^{e}k̲ā*, "your bread") corresponds to the preceding subjects. This parallelism is corroborated by the consonance of "bread" with the covenantal associations of the preceding subjects, and particularly by its correlation with the phrase אִישׁ שְׁלוֹמִי (*'îš šᵉlômî*, lit., "the man at peace with me"; NIV, "my close friend") in Ps 41:9 [10 MT]. In view of these correspondences, *laḥmᵉḵā* will function as subject (B) of the following clause: like the preceding forms with which it rhymes, it will be a genitive dependent on the noun *'anšê*, repeated in the first two lines and implied in the third by the plural verb. Although this is an unusual example of incomplete parallelism, it is well established by its context. A similar understanding is shown by the LXX, Symmachus, the Vulgate, and the Targums, which appear to read it as a participial form: לֹחֲמֶיךָ (*lōḥᵃmêḵā*, "those who eat [with] you"). In view of the conspicuous parallelism established by the pronominal suffixes, *laḥmᵉḵā* should therefore be regarded as an elliptical subject rather than as a second object. This yields a chiastic pattern that defines a self-contained unit of thought (ABABBA); it is summarized in the fourth line, which forms a transition to v.8: תְּבוּנָה (*tᵉḇûnāh*, "detect," v.7; "understanding," v.8).

The noun מָזוֹר (*māzôr*, "trap") has the meaning "sore," "wound" in Jer 30:13; Hos 5:13. This translation is appropriate to the overall context of unexpected aggression, but not to the following prepositional form תַּחְתֶּיךָ (*taḥteyḵā*, lit., "under you"; NIV, "for you," but cf. Jer 49:17). It may also be derived from the root מזר (*mzr*), meaning "to twist, weave, cover with a web" in postbiblical Hebrew (M. Jastrow, *A Dictionary of the Targumim, the Talmud Babli and Yerushalmi, and the Midrashic Literature* [London: Pardes, 1950], p. 756) and "to stretch out" in a cognate root in Syriac (KB, p. 510; cf. also Arabic and Old Babylonian). As such it would denote a "trap," "snare," or "net," spread out stealthily by a hunter, and therefore a recurrent symbol of deception. A similar interpretation is evidenced in the early versions (LXX, Syr., Vul. ["ambush"]; Targ. ["stumbling-block"]; Ag., Theod. ["bond," "fetter"]).

---

3. *God's initiative*

Verses 8–9

8"In that day," declares the LORD,
"will I not destroy the wise men of Edom,
men of understanding in the mountains of Esau?
9Your warriors, O Teman, will be terrified,
and everyone in Esau's mountains
will be cut down in the slaughter.

8–9 "Declares the LORD" marks the opening of a new section (vv.8–9) as it closes vv.2–4, thereby reverting to the perspective of God's initiative in the impending destruction of Edom. The oracle signaled by this formula commences with the words "In that day." The expression, very familiar in the prophetic literature, frequently looks forward to a specific time appointed by God in his sovereignty, when he will intervene in human history in judgment and salvation.

The parallel lines of v.8 are dominated by the references to Edom's noted "wise men" and their "understanding," both of which the Lord would destroy. Verse 8 thus echoes the intent of v.7, to which it is related explicitly by the noun "understanding" (*tᵉḇûnāh;* so "detect," v.7). Verse 8 emphasizes the failure of Edom's traditional wisdom (cf. 1 Kings 4:30; Job 1:1; Job 2:11; 4:1; Jer 49:7; Lam 4:21; Obad 8; Baruch 3:22–23), thereby amplifying further the theme of deception. Ultimately, Edom was deceived because the Lord gave it up to deception; and v.8 anticipates the violent slaughter that would accompany this failure.

Verses 8–9 are further related by their geographical references. The "mountains of Esau" (*har 'ēśāw*, v.8; so vv.9, 19, 21; cf. Ezek 35:2) constitutes a further correspondence to vv.2–4, where Edom's mountainous terrain is first described (cf. v.3).

The term "Teman" is generally taken to describe a region in the northern sector of Edom, though it is identified by some scholars as a city on the site of modern Tawilan, near Petra (cf. Hab 3:3; Allen, p. 153; Baly, p. 235). In the present context the term clearly speaks of the population of "Edom" as a whole, with which it is correlated in vv.8–9.

As noted in v.7, no certainty exists regarding the historical outcome of this prophecy concerning Edom's demise at the hands of the "nations" (cf. Introduction: Background).

III. The Charge Against Edom (vv.10–14)

Verse 10 forms a brief statement of the charges against Edom, as v.1 summarizes the sentence developed in vv.2–9. This charge is defined as one of "violence" against "your brother Jacob" (cf. Joel 3:19); and it is reiterated in detail in vv.11–14, where Edom is accused of participating in the "destruction" of "your brother" (v.12).

A. *The Reason for the Charge*

Verse 10

10Because of the violence against your brother Jacob,
you will be covered with shame;
you will be destroyed forever.

10 The noun "violence" (*ḥāmās*) denotes both moral wrong and overt physical brutality (cf. Hab 1:2), both of which had characterized the course of Edom's relations with Israel. The OT traces this pattern to the very origins of the two nations, in the hatred of Esau for his brother Jacob (Gen 27:40–41). This hatred emerged again in Edom's hostility to Israel after the Exodus (Exod 15:15; Num 20:14–21; Deut 2:4; Judg 11:17–18); and Edom is numbered among Israel's "enemies . . . who had plundered them" before they were defeated by Saul (1 Sam 14:47–48). It is against this background of aggression that David's later campaigns are also to be understood (2 Sam 8:13–14; 1 Kings 11:15–16; 1 Chron 18:11–13; Ps 60). All this culminated in Edom's exultation over the destruction of Jerusalem (Ps 137:7; Lam 4:21–22; Ezek 25:12; 35:5, 15; 36:5; Joel 3:19).

Verse 10 also summarizes the content of vv.2–9, resuming the key concepts that section opens and terminates with; it thus forms a pivotal verse within the prophecy, in its terse juxtaposition of crime ("violence") and corresponding punishment ("destroyed"). It defines the principle of retaliation by which the judgments in both vv.1–9 and vv.15–21 are balanced against the wrong in vv.10–14 (cf. introduction to v.1).

B. *The Explanation of the Charge (vv.11–14)*

Like vv.2–9, this passage consists of two sections—a precise definition of the charge (v.11; cf. v.2) and the reiteration and amplification of its main details in vv.12–14 (cf. vv.3–9). It is framed by the word "day," with which it opens and closes, and which reverberates with tragic insistence throughout vv.12–14. Edom's action (vv.12–14) is precisely equated with that of the invading foreigners (v.11) and is therefore liable to the same judgment.

1. *The charge defined*

Verse 11

> [11]On the day you stood aloof
> while strangers carried off his wealth
> and foreigners entered his gates
> and cast lots for Jerusalem,
> you were like one of them.

11 The equating of Edom with the "foreigners" is intimated in the first two lines, which are structurally parallel. Both open with the phrase "on that day" (*b^{e}yôm . . . b^{e}yôm;* NIV, "On the day . . . while; cf. NASB, RSV), which is followed in each case by an infinitive, a subject, and an adverbial qualification. The equation becomes explicit in the final line ("you were like one of them").

The correlation of these subjects in the opening lines involves a definite contrast, based on the word "aloof." It is derived from a substantive used as an adverb or preposition with the meaning "in front of," "opposite to," "in the sight of" (*neged̲*); such usage normally implies the juxtaposition of one entity to another. In the specific prepositional phrase represented here (*minneged̲*, lit., *min-neged̲*, "from in front of"), this idea of juxtaposition signifies a definite detachment in virtually all its occurrences, as suggested by the preposition "from" (Gen 21:16; 2 Kings 2:7, 15; et al.). The intent of this phrase is therefore well represented by NIV's "aloof" (so RSV, NASB), which thereby differentiates sharply between the actual conduct of Edom and that of the rapacious "strangers": whereas the latter actually "entered" Jerusalem, casting "lots" for its conquered property and probably for its citizens (cf. Joel 3:3; Nah 3:10).

It should be noted that most commentators perceive a progression in v.11, from detachment (line 1) to active involvement on the side of the enemy (line 5). The main weakness of such an interpretation is its failure to give sufficient weight to the opening contrast in v.11: Edom is specifically dissociated from the factual account of invasion and looting, which are then attributed to it in v.13 only in terms of prohibitions that do not necessarily purport to describe actual events (cf. v.13). However, the same point emerges with compelling clarity from both interpretations of v.11. In the sight of God, who looks not on the outward appearance but on the heart, there is little distinction in moral accountability between overt sin and an inner bias toward that sin that permits it to go unchecked (cf. Matt 5:21–32).

2. *The charge repeated and amplified*

Verses 12–14

> [12]You should not look down on your brother
> in the day of his misfortune,
> nor rejoice over the people of Judah
> in the day of their destruction,
> nor boast so much
> in the day of their trouble.

13You should not march through the gates of my people
in the day of their disaster,
nor look down on them in their calamity
in the day of their disaster,
nor seize their wealth
in the day of their disaster.
14You should not wait at the crossroads
to cut down their fugitives,
nor hand over their survivors
in the day of their trouble.

This passage is united by a remarkable series of eight negatives ("You should not, . . . nor . . ." *'al;* cf. RSV), corresponding to eight descriptions of a "day" of Judah's calamity (*yôm;* NIV omits the first reference, before "your brother," v.12; cf. NASB, RSV). It consists of two distinct subsections, v.12 and vv.13–14. Verse 12 is unified by its three clauses describing Edom's malicious exultation (cf. at v.12). Its opening and closing words recur near the beginning and end of vv.13–14 ("not look [down]," *'al-tēre',* vv.12–13; "in the day of their trouble," *beyôm ṣārāh,* vv.12, 14), thereby framing the two sections and defining their limits. Both v.13 and v.14, in turn, form individual units within vv.13–14; v.13 is unified by the refrain "in the day of their disaster" (*beyôm 'ēḏām/'ēḏô,* 13 [*ter*]); the couplet in v.14 describes Edom's treatment of Judah's "fugitives"/"survivors."

These repetitions suggest that v.12 is the focal verse, being amplified in vv.13–14. Its emphasis on Edom's cruel role as a spectator lies at the heart of v.13 ("look down"); and it is repeated in the verb "wait" of v.14, which corresponds to the indictment in v.11 that Edom "stood" aloof. As in v.11, therefore, the main emphasis of these verses is on Edom's hostile attitudes, rather than on its physical violence at Jerusalem.

12 The initial Hebrew verb is the common root *r'h,* meaning to "look on" or "see." Its connotations are varied, and either the sense of contempt (NIV, "look down on") or exultation (NASB, "gloat") is drawn from the context and parallel verbs. The following verbs betray the perverted and reprehensible values of this typical enemy of Israel (e.g., "rejoice," *śāmaḥ;* and "boast," lit., "enlarge your mouth"), for whom covenant loyalty to a brother meant nothing.

13 Verse 13 echoes the description of the "foreigners" in v.11, attributing their conduct directly to Edom (see below). However, v.11 has identified Edom with the foreigners in intent but not explicitly in action; and it is at the level of intent that Edom is accused of active participation in the sack of Jerusalem. Even in these verses any inferences about its conduct must be qualified both by the jussive forms of prohibition and by the preceding narrative on which they are based; while moving closer to participant status, Edom's historical role was still primarily an attitudinal one ("look down").

14 The distinction between action and intent is virtually obliterated in v.14, since the verb "wait" echoes the one action predicated clearly of Edom in v.11—"stood" (*'āmaḏ*). The verse describes Edom's treatment of Judah's "survivors." It thereby corroborates the impression of detachment from the main scene of action, since the "fugitives" would be fleeing away from the city. However, it also qualifies this detachment sharply, for it is shown to be accompanied by outright aggression, whose venom is in keeping with Edom's gloating over its fallen adversary.

The verb "cut down" (*kārat̠*) echoes its usage in vv.9–10 ("cut down," "destroyed"): Edom's fate is in no way arbitrary but corresponds to the measure it has itself used (cf. Luke 6:37–38). The word "destruction" (*'āḇad̠*, v.12; so "destroy," v.8) implies a similar application of the lex talionis, which is defined clearly in vv.15–16.

The central concern of these verses is with the "day" that befell the people of Judah. This is portrayed as a major tragedy by the foreboding epithets that are applied to it and repeated with the crushing weight of a death knell (cf. Zeph 1:14–16). The nouns "distress" (*ṣārāh*, vv.12, 14) and "destruction" (*'āḇad̠*, v.12) both point to a national catastrophe of major proportion. It remains to ask whether this catastrophe can be identified with a specific historical occasion: that occasion will be characterized by the invasion of Jerusalem, wholesale plundering of its property, and probably enslavement of its people; by widespread slaughter both within Jerusalem and in the outlying regions; and by the participation of Edom in this disaster as a mocking bystander and as a collaborator with the foreign invaders, so betraying an existing bond of loyalty with Judah. Six periods in the history of Jerusalem and Judah present themselves for consideration, of which the last corresponds to these criteria most closely.

1. Jerusalem surrendered to Shishak in the fifth year of Rehoboam (931–913), after her fortified cities had fallen to the Egyptian ruler with his allied foreign troops. He then exacted heavy tribute, and his conquest was attributed to the Lord's judgment (1 Kings 14:25–28; 2 Chron 12:2–10). Moreover, Edom is identified explicitly as an adversary in this era, after its incomplete suppression by David; and Edom's hereditary ruler is represented as a protegé of Egypt in the time of Solomon (cf. 1 Kings 11:14–22). However, Rehoboam's submission to Shishak averted the enslavement, devastation, and flight described by Obadiah; this incident, therefore, does not provide a suitable background for Obadiah's prophecy.

2. The second-recorded invasion of Jerusalem occurred in the reign of Jehoram (853–841), when a coalition of Arabs and Philistines invaded Judah, carrying off both the property and family of the king, which would have been located in Jerusalem (2 Chron 21:16–17; 22:1). This occurred at a time of sharp conflict with Edom (2 Kings 8:20–22; 2 Chron 21:8–10; cf. 20:1–2; 22–23); however, this judgment was aimed specifically at the king, who experienced the main impact of the invasion (2 Chron 21:14, 17). It is also unlikely that help would be anticipated from Edom in view of its aggression against Jehoshaphat, culminating in open rebellion during Jehoram's own reign.

3. A third invasion of Judah is implied during the reign of Joash (835–796). The Syrians caused widespread destruction among Judah's leaders, taking considerable spoil and defeating a large Judean army as a consequence of the Lord's judgment on the king (2 Chron 24:23–24). Edom's continued hostility is evidenced in the following reign of Amaziah, whose drastic measures against the Edomites may be associated with his reprisals for the murder of his father, Joash (2 Kings 14:5–7, 2 Chron 25:1–12). The account's reconstruction, however, is largely inferential, particularly with regard to Edom's role; in addition, it is unlikely that the Syrians' small expeditionary force would have crushed Jerusalem so completely as intimated by Obadiah (cf. 2 Chron 24:24).

4. Jerusalem was clearly captured in the time of Amaziah (796–767), with seizure

of its treasure and hostages at a period of open conflict with Edom (2 Kings 14:7–14). This incident is scarcely consistent with Obadiah's prophecy, however, since the invaders were not foreigners but Israelites.

5. The eighth century provides further evidence of Edomite aggression at a time when Judah was increasingly threatened by foreign powers, most notably during the reign of Ahaz (735–715). As a consequence of his faithlessness to the Lord, this king suffered the catastrophic depredations of Syria, Israel, the Philistines, Assyria, and Edom itself (2 Chron 28:17): Judah and Jerusalem became "an object of dread and horror and scorn," experiencing widespread bloodshed and captivity (2 Chron 29:8–9; cf. 2 Kings 16:1–20). The city was similarly threatened by Assyria in the following reign of Hezekiah (c. 701; 2 Kings 18–19; 2 Chron 32). It was in this century, moreover, that the first clear notes of judgment and conquest were sounded against Edom among Israel's prophets (Isa 11:14; 21:11; 34:5–15; 63:1–6; Amos 1:6, 9, 11; cf. Num 24:18; Joel 3:19). However, no record exists of Jerusalem actually being captured. Again, therefore, no conclusive identification can be made between Obadiah and this era.

6. The final invasion of Jerusalem during Edom's existence as an independent nation took place when the city fell to the Babylonians in 586, following Jehoiachin's previous capitulation to Nebuchadnezzar in 597. On both occasions the city suffered seizure of its "wealth" and wholesale deportation of its population (2 Kings 24:13–16; 25:4–17; 2 Chron 36:18, 20). In 586 the city was virtually burned to the ground, including the temple (2 Kings 25:9–10; 2 Chron 36:19), and many of its inhabitants were massacred (2 Kings 25:8–21; 2 Chron 36:17; cf. Jer 6:1–9:22; Ezek 4:1–7:27). There is specific reference to unsuccessful "fugitives" in the account of the king's escape with his retinue (2 Kings 25:4–5). Of particular significance are the accounts of Edom's conduct at this time. There is evidence for its participation as an ally in a coalition of Palestinian states against Nebuchadnezzar (Jer 27:3; 40:11); yet it was later accused of taking vengeance on Judah (Ezek 25:12), and of delivering the Israelites "over to the sword at the time of their calamity, at the time their punishment reached its climax" (Ezek 35:5–6; cf. Lam 1:17). Edom was equally guilty at this time of rejoicing in Jerusalem's destruction (Ps 137:7; Lam 2:15–17; 4:21; Ezek 35:11–15; 36:2–6); and it is therefore at this time that the prophetic announcements of Edom's annihilation reached a climax (Jer 9:26; 25:21; Lam 4:21–22; Ezek 25:13; 32:29; 35:3–4; 7–9, 11, 14–15; 36:7). Specific correlations include numerous points of contact in Jeremiah 49:7–22 and in Ezekiel 35–36.

The balance of evidence therefore suggests that Obadiah was looking back to the Fall of Jerusalem in 586, in which Edom was clearly implicated. This conclusion falls short of proven certainty. In particular, it assumes that the position of Obadiah and Joel among the Minor Prophets is not of chronological significance; and it does not necessarily account for Obadiah's relationship to Jeremiah 49 (though Jer 49:14–22, dated c. 600 B.C., would clearly corroborate this argument), Ezekiel 35, and Joel. In the absence of other, compelling evidence against this interpretation, however, it provides a satisfactory context for Obadiah unmatched by any other period of Judah's political and religious history.

IV. The Day of the Lord (vv.15–21)

The concluding oracular formula in v.18 divides this passage into two main sections: vv.15–18 and vv.19–21. The first section (vv.15–18) is framed by its references to the Lord as the initiator of word and event ("day of the Lord. . . . The Lord has spoken"). The sequence of themes follows the now-familiar reversal of roles—with destruction and deliverance; survivors and no survivors; possessors and dispossessed; Joseph-Jacob and Esau, juxtaposed in a stark antithesis.

This sequence is repeated in vv.19–21, amplifying the central concept of "possession" (*yāraš;* so "occupy," "possess," or "dispossess," cf. vv.19–20). As in v.18, "Esau" is singled out from among the nations as the object of conquest, the passage being framed by the phrase "mountains of Esau" (vv.19, 21); this phrase is also contrasted with the role of "Mount" Zion, as the "house" of Jacob is opposed to the "house" of Esau in v.18. The prophecy concludes with the ringing affirmation: "The kingdom will be the LORD's" (v.21).

A. *The Judgment of Esau*

Verses 15–18

15"The day of the LORD is near
for all nations.
As you have done, it will be done to you;
your deeds will return upon your own head.
16Just as you drank on my holy hill,
so all the nations will drink continually;
they will drink and drink
and be as if they had never been.
17But on Mount Zion will be deliverance;
it will be holy,
And the house of Jacob
will possess its inheritance.
18The house of Jacob will be a fire
and the house of Joseph a flame;
the house of Esau will be stubble,
and they will set it on fire and consume it.
There will be no survivors
from the house of Esau."

The LORD has spoken.

15–16 These verses are both introduced by the conjunction "for" (*kî;* cf. NASB, RSV), and they are parallel in structure. They exhibit a complex, alternating, thematic arrangement that is typical of Obadiah's style and that revolves around the central concept of retaliation that shapes this prophecy as it does the entire OT view of moral order in a world ruled by God's justice.

The "day of the LORD" is a theme of great significance in Israel's eschatology (cf. ZPEB, 2:46f.), and it gives final definition to the preceding references to a "day" in Obadiah: Edom's and Judah's downfall both constitute elements in the pattern of this "great and dreadful day of the LORD" (Joel 2:31). It signals the climactic establishment of God's rule in human history and, as such, brings judgment on all those enemies who oppose his dominion. Such a judgment engulfed apostate and rebellious Israel, most notably in the fall of Samaria and of Jerusalem—so confounding the popular theology of the eighth and seventh centuries—and descended subsequently on "the Gentile," those foreign nations not bowing to God's sovereignty. This "day," then, with its eschatological overtones, defines the destiny of Edom and the nations in both vv.1–9 and vv.15–21. After the nations have had their "day" on the Lord's holy mountain, his "day" will come in power and great glory, with none to oppose its thrust. This "day" is, in the first instance, promised in terms that admit a preliminary fulfillment within history for the faithful remnant of Israel; and it is from this hope of restoration and blessing for a "holy" people that Obadiah derives his promise of "deliverance" and conquest for the "house of Jacob" (vv.17–21). Above all it is purged and restored Israel, whether in historical or eschatological terms, that serves as the instrument by which the Lord introduces and establishes his reign.

The opening line of v.15 therefore constitutes the core of Obadiah's prophecy. It provides a theological framework for the preceding verses: the localized disasters befalling Edom and Jerusalem are not merely isolated incidents in a remote and insignificant theater of war, for they mark the footsteps of the Lord himself as he approaches to set up a "kingdom that will never be destroyed" (Dan 2:44). And the following verses are essentially a commentary on the implications of that impending "day."

Verse 15 accordingly sets forth its guiding principle of retaliation: "As you have done, it will be done to you." The actions perpetrated by the nation addressed will correspond precisely to those perpetrated on her, as indicated by the repetition of the same verb ("done," *'āśāh*) with different subjects; the final line reiterates the consequences of this law, so emphasizing the certainty of its application.

Verse 16 demonstrates the same equivalence of past and future action ("drank," "drink," both from *šāṯāh*), attributed to different subjects; and the certainty of this equivalence is again emphasized by repetition of the consequences in the final lines. The repeated verb clearly has the same meaning in both clauses of v.15. In view of this clear-cut parallelism, it follows that the same is true of the verb "drink" in each clause of v.16; and since it evidently implies the future experience of judgment in the final three lines, it will have the same connotations of judgment in the past in the first line. These connotations are suitable only to Judah, whose suffering on God's "holy hill" in Jerusalem has been described in vv.10–14; for Edom and the nations, any such suffering is still future at the time of Obadiah's prophecy.

The transition from active to passive in both verses is signaled by the second person pronominal forms in each verse. In v.15 they are singular: every other such second person form (thirty-three of them) is applied to Edom, which by implication is addressed here also—for the last time. The second person plural pronoun in v.16 is without precise parallel in the prophecy (cf. v.1: "Rise," *qûmû*); and it is therefore appropriate for this isolated address to Judah that elsewhere constitutes a silent and humbled third party in the Lord's proceedings against her adversaries.

The metaphor of drinking is commonly used of the experience of judgment and humiliation (cf. Hab 2:15–16). It recurs in the parallel passage of Jeremiah, which again alludes to Judah as the prior victim of such judgment (Jer 49:12–13; cf. 25:17–18, 28–29). Drinking may also be a sign of carousing and debauchery (e.g., Exod 32:6; 1 Sam 30:16), and some commentators (e.g., Watts) attribute this meaning to the first reference in v.16: by an ironic twist, those who "drank" in celebration of their conquest over God's "holy hill" would subsequently "drink" a very different cup. These implications are somewhat muted by the structural relations of vv.15–16 (cf. above).

17–18 "Mount Zion" (v.17) denotes the place of God's rule in Jerusalem. It is therefore rendered "holy" by his presence, localized in the temple (e.g., Pss 5:7; 11:4;

74:2; Joel 3:17, 21); and it demands of its inhabitants a corresponding holiness. As the visible expression of God's sovereign holiness, Mount Zion becomes the source of judgment on man's sin (e.g., Isa 31:9; Joel 3:16; Amos 1:2–2:16); and it is the final locus of God's judgment on the citizens of Judah (e.g., Isa 10:12; Lam 2:1–8; 4:2–16; Mic 3:12; cf. Obad 11–14, 16). However, the Lord's kingly rule is expressed equally by his salvation, which also emanates from Mount Zion (e.g., Pss 20:2; 53:6), and which restores to it the "holy" character consonant with his presence there. Obadiah's announcement of salvation in v.17 belongs to this tradition.

The root underlying "deliverance" (*plṭ*) implies escape from danger and widespread destruction, being used, for instance, of fugitives from military disasters (e.g., Gen 14:13; Judg 12:4–5; Obad 14). It is applied most consistently to God's gracious preservation and purification of a remnant in Israel, particularly after the Fall of Jerusalem (cf. Ezra 9:8–13; Isa 4:2; 10:20; 37:31–32; Jer 50:28; 51:50; Ezek 6:8–9; 7:16; 14:22; 24:26–27; 33:21–22). The promise given here is repeated in similar terms in Joel 2:32, and both verses correspond closely to Isaiah 4:2–3; 37:31–32.

The final line expresses the outworking of this restoration. The verb "possess" (*yāraš*) and its cognate noun "possessions" are associated preeminently with Israel's conquest of the Promised Land, to which they are applied over one hundred times (e.g., Exod 6:8; Deut 3:8; 4:1, 22; cf. TWOT, 1:420ff.). Israel succeeded in this conquest because she obeyed the Lord, who entered the battle on behalf of his people and dispossessed the enemy before them. Israel therefore forfeited her control of the land through her subsequent disobedience; the prophets, however, held out to the nation the hope of repossessing the land on the same condition of an obedient and militant faith (e.g., Isa 54:3; 57:13; 60:21; 61:7; Ezek 36:12; Amos 9:12; cf. Gal 3:29; 1 Peter 1:4); and it is to this hope that Obadiah appealed in expectation of a "holy" community that would be able to appropriate it (cf. vv.19–21).

In keeping with the military associations of v.17, the "house of Jacob" (v.18) is to annihilate the "house of Esau," as the Israelites were to wipe out the Canaanites whom they displaced. The destructiveness of "fire" consuming "stubble" forms a repeated image of the relentless judgment predicted here (e.g., Exod 15:7; Isa 10:17; Joel 2:5; Mal 4:1). This prophecy will revive an earlier subjugation of Edom under Saul, David, and their successors, a yoke Edom later threw off. Edom's final submission is therefore still anticipated by the prophets, in accordance with the oracle pronounced by Balaam (Num 24:18; Isa 11:14; Ezek 25:13–14; Amos 9:12); as in Isaiah 11:13–14, it will be accomplished by a reunited Israel—intimated by the parallel terms "Jacob" and "Joseph" (cf. Pss 77:15; 80:1; 81:4–5; Jer 3:18). Unlike the house of Jacob, the house of Esau can expect no "deliverance," no remnant; as the Edomites had thought to plunder and possess the land of Israel, cutting off its "survivors," so it will happen to them.

A progression in the judgment of Edom is marked by v.18. The Lord had enlisted the heathen nations to eradicate Edom from its homeland in "Esau's mountains" (cf. vv.8–9); now, however, his own people were to cooperate with him in destroying the "house of Esau" altogether. Historical events support this progression. Edom was displaced from its country east of the Arabah in the sixth and fifth centuries, in a period of Judah's weakness; this was therefore executed by foreigners, culminating in Nabataean possession of that territory. In the same period the surviving Edomites were settling west of the Arabah, in the Negev—a process reflected in the charges of Ezekiel (Ezek 35:10, 12; 36:2, 5). Thus the postexilic region of Judah extended no further south than Beth-zur, north of Hebron. Hebron itself and the neighboring towns were all occupied by Edomite populations (cf. 1 Esdra 4:50; 1 Macc 4:61; 5:65; Jub 38:8–9; Jos. Antiq. XIII, 257–58 [ix.1], 395–96 [xv.4]; War I, 62–63 [ii.6]); and, by the end of the fourth century, their territory had acquired the Hellenistic name for Edom: Idumaea (i.e., Edom-aea). However, the fortunes of Judah were revived under the Maccabees, or Hasmoneans (c. 168–63 B.C.; ZPEB, 4:2–8), and this era saw a resurgence of Jewish aspirations to possess its former lands.

The Idumaeans were defeated in 166 B.C. by Judas Maccabaeus (died 160 B.C.), who recovered the cities of southern Palestine ceded to them (cf. 1 Macc 5:3, 65). Under John Hyrcanus (135–104 B.C.) this conquest of the Idumaeans was completed (c. 125 B.C.), and they were compelled to submit to circumcision and to full observance of the Jewish law. They continued to haunt the Jews, however, for the family of Herod the Great was of Idumaean descent; but after the second century B.C., they had virtually been consumed by the house of Jacob, to which they lost their national identity and autonomy.

B. *The Occupation of Edom*

Verses 19–21

19 People from the Negev will occupy
the mountains of Esau,
and people from the foothills will possess
the land of the Philistines.
They will occupy the fields of Ephraim and Samaria,
and Benjamin will possess Gilead.
20 This company of Israelite exiles who are in Canaan
will possess ⌞the land⌟ as far as Zarephath;
the exiles from Jerusalem who are in Sepharad
will possess the towns of the Negev.
21 Deliverers will go up on Mount Zion
to govern the mountains of Esau.
And the kingdom will be the LORD's.

19–20 Verses 19–20 form a distinct section after the concluding oracular formula in v.18, being unified by the keyword "possess," "occupy" (*yaraš*, vv.19 [*bis*], 20; cf. v.17). These verses are written in an elliptical style, containing considerable difficulties in syntax and vocabulary; however, the MT is clearly reflected in the early versions (Targ., LXX, Symm., Theod., Aq., Vul.), and NIV's adherence to it is therefore to be followed. In particular, both occurrences of the verb "possess" in v.19 and the first in v.20 are absent from the MT; but they are clearly implied by the structure of the adjacent clauses and by the centrality of that verb in vv.17–20.

Not only the term "possess," but also the ethnic and geographical references resonate with the recollection of Israel's conquest of Canaan (cf. below). These references are virtually all specified or implied in the commission given to Israel in Deuteronomy 1:7. The "Negev" was not always to be the home of the Edomites, dispossessed as they were from their own "portion," the "mountains of Esau" (cf. Deut 2:4–5); rather the reverse would be true. The "foothills" (*š*^{e}*pēlāh,* lit., "Shephelah"), the low-lying region separating the Judean hills from Philistia, would extend itself westward. Even the northern territories of Ephraim and Samaria, lost to

Assyria during the preexilic period, would again be part of Israel. Benjamin, the small tribe virtually absorbed by Judah in historic times, was to move east and north into Transjordan and possess the lush highlands of Gilead, while exiles in Canaan (v.20; or, "who are Canaanites"; note the antiquated name with its Exodus and conquest overtones) and from Jerusalem would expand north to the Lebanese coast at Zarephath and south to the Negev.

"Sepharad" (v.20) is not definitely identified but may refer to Sardis in distant Lydia (near modern Izmir, Turkey); if so, it reflects an early colony of Jewish exiles (ZPEB, 5:342) who, with more local refugees, were expected to inherit portions of the Holy Land. (Medieval Jewry mistakenly identified Sepharad as Spain; cf. ibid.). In short, the land seen by Obadiah as promised to a reunited Israel in "the day of the LORD" is the land originally given to the Twelve Tribes. It was the inalienable bequest of the Lord to Abraham and his descendants (Gen 13:14–17; 26:2–5; 28:13–15), and neither Edomite treachery nor Assyrian–Babylonian dispersion could keep God's promises from their fulfillment.

Reference to "exiles" (*gālûṯ*) in v.20 further corroborates the historical background discussed earlier (cf. at v.14). The term is applied predominantly to the deported population of Judah after 586 (e.g., 2 Kings 25:27; Isa 45:13 et al.). Such an application is clearly appropriate to the qualification "from Jerusalem": no other major deportation from that city is known, and that background is most suitable to the events described in vv.10–14. The "Israelite exiles" would therefore be the survivors from the northern kingdom of Israel, from which they were deported after the Fall of Samaria (cf. 2 Kings 17:6, 18, 20, 23; 18:11). On this evidence, not only Israel, but also Judah had been destroyed as an independent nation; and Obadiah's prophecy is proclaimed with heroic faith to "the poorest people of the land" (2 Kings 24:14; 25;12, 22–24; Jer 40–44), during an era of destitution and weakness in the exilic or postexilic period.

21 Verse 21 corresponds to vv.19–20, which it summarizes with special reference to Edom, the three verses being framed by the phrase "mountains of Esau" (vv.19, 21). It reiterates the theme of conquest, expressed in the verb "govern" or "judge" (*šāpaṭ*). The noun "deliverers" (from *yāšā'*) has similar connotations of military victory (cf. Hab 1:2; 3:13, 18): significantly, the name "Joshua" (*yᵉhôšûa'*) is derived from the same root (*yš'*), as is that of Jesus whose conquest procured a better inheritance "that can never perish, spoil or fade" (1 Peter 1:4). As in vv.19–20, this conquest finds its source in Judah and specifically in its capital, "Mount Zion." The ultimate goal of the conquest had been to unite Israel, with centralized worship in the temple (Deut 12:1–28), and with centralized rule in dynastic monarchy (Deut 17:14–20; 2 Sam 7). These were not to have autonomous functions, for they were the visible institutions of the theocracy through which the Lord himself was to rule as "king over Jeshurun" (Deut 33:5). Obadiah's vision of Mount Zion restored to its destined leadership of nations is grounded in these promises. It presupposes the existence of a nation obedient to its theocratic calling, which will "serve him without fear, in holiness and righteousness before him" (Luke 1:74–75; cf. v.17). And it finds its consummation in the true realization of that theocracy.

The Lord is indeed Israel's "king from of old" (Ps 74:12). He is in reality "the living God, the eternal King" (Jer 10:10), "the great King over all the earth" (Ps 47:2, 7). But the day is coming when that kingdom will be acknowledged universally, when every knee shall bow. It will be said to Zion, "The LORD, the King of Israel, is with you" (Zeph 3:15; cf. Isa 24:23; 33:20–22; 40:9–10; 62:3; Mic 4:7–8; Zech 9:9); and they will say among the nations, "The LORD reigns" (Ps 96:10). Edom will be set aside, with "every pretension that sets itself up against the knowledge of God" (2 Cor 10:5); "And the kingdom will be the LORD's" (cf. 1 Cor 15:24–28; Rev 11:15; 12:10; 22:1–5).

JONAH

H. L. Ellison

JONAH

Introduction

1. Background

The Book of Jonah is the fifth of the Minor Prophets (the Book of the Twelve). It is unique among the "Latter Prophets" in being almost completely narrative. Jonah, the son of Amittai, from Gath Hepher in Galilee (cf. 2 Kings 14:25; Josh 19:13), prophesied during or shortly before the reign of Jeroboam II (793–753 B.C.). This makes it virtually certain that we should place the story of the book in the period of Assyrian weakness between the death of Adad-nirari III in 782 B.C. and the seizing of the Assyrian throne by Tiglath-pileser III in 745 B.C. During this time, Assyria was engaged in a life and death struggle with the mountain tribes of Urartu and its associates of Mannai and Madai in the north, who had been able to push their frontier to within less than a hundred miles of Nineveh. The consciousness of weakness and possible defeat would go far to explain the readiness of Nineveh to accept the prophet's message.

2. Unity

The majority of modern scholars accept the book as a unity, though most of those who regard it as nonhistorical consider that the psalm (2:2–9) is a later interpolation. In 5 below and in the commentary on chapter 2, it is argued that there are no adequate grounds for the theory of interpolation. In addition some would find a few later glosses, but they are so insignificant that they need not be mentioned.

3. Date and Authorship

Most modern introductions and commentaries argue for a postexilic date—the time of Ezra and Nehemiah being especially preferred. They refer to the past tense in 3:3 (see commentary), the allegedly exaggerated picture of Nineveh (see commentary at 3:3), and the differences in style between Hosea and Jonah, especially to the considerable element of Aramaisms in the latter. Apart from the unprovable assumption that a certain unity of style existed among the northern prophets, this argument overlooks that Jonah was from Galilee, that we have no other literary composition from there, and that Aramaic influence must have been much stronger there. It is claimed that 3:9 and 4:2 reflect Joel 2:14 and 2:13—in fact, both are almost certainly using traditional material—but if Joel is dated around 803 B.C., the argument is valueless.

Unless the historicity of the book is denied (see 4a below), the information in the book clearly must have come from Jonah himself. Since he is nowhere claimed as author, and since he is constantly referred to in the third person, the possibility cannot be dismissed that its present form comes from another hand. There is much to suggest that a story originally intended for the northern tribes appeared in a revised version in Judah—the chief change being a generalizing of the background —in the time when the shadows of coming judgment had grown very long.

4. Purpose

Our views on the purpose of the book will depend partly on our views on its nature, partly on our exegesis. So only a provisional answer can be given here. Two main theories are held today about Jonah. It is either (a) historical or (b) allegorical or parabolic. With few exceptions, to be noted in the commentary, the main purpose of the book is almost universally found in chapter 4, though its application may vary widely, depending partly on how the book as a whole is taken.

a. *Historical*

Until the nineteenth century, Jonah was regarded as history. Before that there had been skeptics who had denied much of its truth and regarded its miracles as mere folklore; but the first significant voice was that of J.G. Eichhorn (1823). Now it is normally taken for granted that the historical truth of the book cannot be defended and that it is no more than a beautiful allegory or parable. Such a view, however, faces almost insuperable difficulties.

If, as alleged, the story was written in the time of Ezra and Nehemiah as a protest against narrow-minded nationalism and exclusivism, its effect would have depended almost entirely on its being regarded as truth. There is no evidence that any rabbi doubted its truth. Though Philo (first century A.D.,) was such a master and lover of allegory, in *De Jonae Oratione* (16.21) he was at pains to explain the marvel of the fish literally. This argument must not be pressed, for this has come down to us only in an Armenian version regarded by many as spurious. It is, however, unlikely that this was the work of a forger, if Philo was known to have taken it allegorically.

Our Lord referred to the story of Jonah as something obviously historical (Matt 12:38–41; Luke 11:29–30, 32). Even if it were true that his knowledge had been restricted in the way demanded by the kenosis theory, it is impossible to think that, filled with the Holy Spirit as he was, he would not have been able to distinguish between history and allegory or parable. So much is this argument felt by some that there is a growing tendency, based on modern criticism of the synoptic Gospels, to deny that Jesus mentioned Jonah at all.

The arguments based on the language used about Nineveh are dealt with in their proper place in the commentary. The main argument against the historicity of the book is, of course, the alleged impossibility of Jonah's surviving three days and three nights in the belly of the fish (1:17). There are sufficient well-attested occurrences to show that a man could survive under these circumstances (cf. R.K. Harrison, IOT, pp. 907–8); but none of them seems to be strictly parallel, and they were certainly of shorter duration. On the other hand, various ingenious explanations have been given of how it could have happened with somewhat less discomfort for the prophet; but these cannot be deduced with any certainty from the narrative. As the type of fish is not identified and the story is told in the most general terms, we should avoid making the incident, which in itself is physically possible, more difficult by our interpretations. Jesus placed it alongside the even greater miracle of his own resurrection. What we must do, however, is find an adequate spiritual reason for so great a miracle.

In spite of a widely held belief, Jonah was not sent to preach monotheism, the knowledge of the God of Israel, or even a higher ethic to the people of Nineveh. Therefore the repentance of the Ninevites was not so great a miracle as is often maintained, for it did not involve any real change in their religion. The purpose of Jonah's proclamation was to bring them to repentance. The declaration of God's loving care was made, not to Nineveh, but to Jonah (4:11), and so to Israel. Taking the book as a whole, it is a revelation to God's people of God's all-sovereign power and care. It had a special relevance to Israel over which the shadow of Assyria was falling, and later to Judah, as it faced destruction at the hands of Babylon.

b. *Allegorical or parabolic*

For our purpose there is no need to make any sharp-cut distinction between these two interpretations. Allegorical interpretation seeks to find spiritual lessons in the various details of the story; parabolic interpretation concentrates on the story as a whole. The latter arose largely because of the obvious defects of the former, when it became increasingly clear that so many details would not bear the interpretation put on them. Such an approach can give us very satisfactory spiritual results, but the great divergencies among the lessons deduced suggest that they have very largely been read into the narrative. When G.A. Smith (2:494) says, "The truth which we find in the Book of Jonah is as full and fresh a revelation of God's will as prophecy anywhere achieves: that God has *granted to the Gentiles also repentance unto life* is nowhere else in the Old Testament so vividly illustrated" (emphasis his), this is written from the NT standpoint and does not explain why God later allowed Assyria to descend with all its pomp to the shades of Sheol. Further, no real reason has been suggested for the link with Jonah. If the book contains an allegorical picture of Israel (i.e., Judah, disappearing in exile and then returning to its land), surely some Judean prophet would have been chosen.

5. Literary Form

With the exception of 2:2–9, the book is straightforward narrative that is remarkable for its lack of background and unnecessary detail. This is generally explained by its being a postexilic invention, but anyone capable of inventing the story could easily have added further fictional detail and background color. It is more likely that further detail was omitted so as not to weaken the main impact of the story, and that the sixth-century Judean editor reduced the local color to make the story equally appropriate for the new Babylonian situation.

The main feature of the psalm (2:2–9) is that, along with much that is unique, there is an unusually large number of quotations or reminiscences from other psalms. The main ones are as follows:

Jonah	Psalms
2:2a	3:4; 120:1
2:2b	18:4–5; 30:3
2:3a	88:6–7
2:3b	42:7
2:4a	31:22
2:4b	5:7
2:5a	69:1–2
2:6b	49:15; 56:13; 103:4
2:7a	107:5; 142:3
2:8a	31:6
2:9a	50:14; 69:30; 107:22
2:9c	3:8; 37:39

This combination calls for explanation. Even the assumption of a late date for the book does not exclude its being an original composition. While earlier it was assumed that many of the psalms apparently being quoted were of a postexilic date, this can no longer be maintained since the studies of Gunkel and Mowinckel on the relationship of the Psalter to Israel's worship (cf. H. Gunkel, *Ausgewählte Psalmen* [1904]; id., *Einleitung in die Psalmen* [Göttingen: Vandenhoeck & Ruprecht, 1933]; S. Mowinckel, *Psalmenstudien I–IV* [Kristiania: Dybwad, 1921–24]; id., *The Psalms in Israel's Worship*, tr. D.R. Ap-Thomas [Oxford: Basil Blackwell, 1962]). The concept of the Psalter as postprophetic, as H. Wheeler Robinson (*The Old Testament, Its Making and Its Meaning* [Oxford: Clarendon, 1937], p. 133) expressed it, is largely a relic of the past. If Jonah, like many prophets, was linked with the worship of the sanctuary, not merely would the Psalms have been very familiar to him, but he would probably have composed many for special occasions by adapting those in general use. Most of us, if we were called on to produce a hymn of thanksgiving on the spur of the moment, would show our knowledge of the hymnbook by quotation and reminiscence; this is what we may assume of Jonah with some degree of probability. That Jonah gave a later polish to his psalm cannot be excluded.

6. Canonicity

It seems clear from Ecclesiasticus 49:10 that Ben Sira (not later than 190 B.C.) knew Jonah as a constituent part of the Book of the Twelve. There is no rabbinic tradition that its canonicity was ever challenged.

7. Text

The text is very well preserved, and there is probably only one case—i.e., 3:4—where the reading of LXX may be preferable.

8. Bibliography

Books

Aalders, G.Ch. *The Problem of the Book of Jonah*. London: Tyndale, 1948.

Allen, L.C. *The Books of Joel, Obadiah, Jonah and Micah*. Grand Rapids: Eerdmans, 1976, pp. 175–235.

Bewer, J.A. *Haggai, Zechariah, Malachi and Jonah*. ICC. Edinburgh: T. & T. Clark, 1912.

Ellison, H.L. *The Prophets of Israel*. Grand Rapids: Eerdmans, 1969.

Ellul, J. *The Judgment of Jonah*. Translated by G.W. Bromiley. Grand Rapids: Eerdmans, 1971.

Fairbairn, P. *Jonah: His Life, Character and Mission*. Edinburgh: John Johnstone, 1849.

Gaebelein, F.E. *Four Minor Prophets*. Chicago: Moody, 1970.

Gretheim, T.E. *The Message of Jonah*. Minneapolis, Minn.: Augsburg, 1977.

Hart-Davies, D.E. *Jonah: Prophet and Patriot*. London: Thynne and Jarvis, 1931.

Jeremias, J. "Iōnas." *Theological Dictionary of the New Testament*. Edited by G. Kittel. Translated by G.W. Bromiley. 10 vols. Grand Rapids: Eerdmans, 1964–76, 3:406–10.

König, E. "Jonah." *Hastings Dictionary of the Bible*. Vol. 2. Edited by J. Hastings. New York: Charles Scribner's Sons, 1963.

Lanchester, H.C.O. *Obadiah and Jonah*. CBSC. Cambridge: Cambridge University Press, 1915.

Parrot, André. *Nineveh and the Old Testament*. London: SCM, 1953.

Robinson, G.L. *The Twelve Minor Prophets*. Grand Rapids: Baker, 1952.

Sampey, J.R. "Jonah." *The International Standard Bible Encyclopedia*. Vol. 3. Edited by James Orr. Grand Rapids: Eerdmans, 1939, pp. 1727–29.

Smith, G.A. *The Book of the Twelve Prophets*. 2 vols. ExB. London: Hodder & Stoughton, 1898.

Periodicals

Ben-Yosef, I.A. "Jonas and the Fish as a Folk Motif." *Semitics* 7 (1980): 102–17.

Blank, S.H. " 'Doest Thou Well To Be Angry?' A Study in Self-Pity." *Hebrew Union College Annual* 26 (1955): 29–41.

Brenner, A. "The Language of Jonah as an Index of its Date." *Beth Midra* 24 (1979): 396–405 (Hebrew).

Childs, B.S. "Jonah: A Study in Old Testament Hermeneutics." *Scottish Journal of Theology* 11 (1958): 53–61.

Clements, R.E. "The Purpose of the Book of Jonah." *Supplements to Vetus Testamentum* 28 (1975): 16–28.

Feuilet, A. "Les sources du livre de Jonas." *Revue Biblique* 54 (1947): 161–86.

———. "Le sens du livre de Jonas." *Revue Biblique* 54 (1947): 340–61.

Gevaryahu, H. "The Universalism of the Book of Jonah." *Dor leDor* 10 (1981): 20–27.

Holbert, J.C. "Deliverance Belongs to Yahweh! Satire in the Book of Jonah." *Journal for the Study of the Old Testament* 21 (1981): 57–81.

Payne, D.P. "Jonah From the Perspective of its Audience." *Journal for the Study of the Old Testament* 13 (1979): 3–12.

Kidner, F.E. "The Distribution of Divine Names in Jonah." *Tyndale Bulletin* 21 (1970): 126–28.

Qimran, E. "The Language of Jonah and the Date of Its Composition." *Beth Mikra* 25 (1980): 181–82.
Scott, R.B.Y. "The Sign of Jonah." *Interpretation* 19 (1965): 16–25.
Stek, J.H. "The Message of the Book of Jonah." *Concordia Theological Journal* 4 (1969): 23–50.
Trumbull, H. Clay. "Jonah in Nineveh." *Journal of Biblical Literature* 11 (1892): 53–60.
Wilson, A.J. "The Sign of the Prophet Jonah and Its Modern Confirmations. *Princeton Theological Review* 25 (1927): 630–42.
Wilson, R.D. "The Authenticity of Jonah." *Princeton Theological Review* 16 (1918): 280–98, 430–56.
______. " 'To Appoint' in the Old Testament." *Princeton Theological Review* 16 (1918): 645–54.

9. Outline

- I. The Disobedient Prophet (1:1–2:10)
  - 1. Jonah's Flight (1:1–3)
  - 2. The Storm (1:4–6)
  - 3. Jonah's Responsibility (1:7–10)
  - 4. Jonah's Rejection (1:11–16)
  - 5. Jonah's Protection (1:17–2:1)
  - 6. Jonah's Psalm of Thanksgiving (2:2–9)
  - 7. Jonah's Deliverance (2:10)
- II. The Obedient Prophet (3:1–4:11)
  - 1. Jonah's Proclamation (3:1–4)
  - 2. Nineveh's Repentance (3:5–10)
  - 3. Jonah's Displeasure (4:1–4)
  - 4. God's Rebuke of Jonah (4:5–9)
  - 5. God's Mercy (4:10–11)

Text and Exposition

I. The Disobedient Prophet (1:1–2:10)

1. *Jonah's Flight*

1:1–3

> [1]The word of the LORD came to Jonah son of Amittai: [2]"Go to the great city of Nineveh and preach against it, because its wickedness has come up before me."
> [3]But Jonah ran away from the LORD and headed for Tarshish. He went down to Joppa, where he found a ship bound for that port. After paying the fare, he went aboard and sailed for Tarshish to flee from the LORD.

1 Our story begins without preparation, with the conjunction *wa* (untr. in NIV), which is so common in Hebrew narrative (KJV, RV, RSV, "now"). We have a similar beginning to Judges, 1 Samuel, and Ruth. It may be merely the storyteller's natural style; but it could possibly indicate that our narrative was taken from a larger collection of stories about Jonah or about prophets generally. For our understanding, however, this is immaterial. Even with a prophet, not everything he did or said had revelatory meaning for posterity.

"The word of the LORD came to Jonah" literally means the word of the Lord "was" or "became" to Jonah. There is no indication how God communicated his will to Jonah. In fact, it is rare for prophets to relate how any particular message was received. In many cases there must have been the overwhelming certainty of the divine message without any consciousness of how it had come.

"Jonah son of Amittai" is the only prophetic name recorded for the North in the nearly forty years between the death of Elisha and the ministry of Amos (2 Kings 14:25). It would be illegitimate, however, to argue from silence that he was the only prophet available. Later rabbinic tradition tried to fill the gap in our knowledge. Relying on a wordplay, it claimed that Jonah was the widow's son brought back to life by Elijah (1 Kings 17:17–24). Jonah was also credited with a successful mission to Jerusalem similar to that to Nineveh. Both rabbinic tradition and many Christian commentators assume he had some relationship with the Jerusalem temple. (Did this exist for Elijah and Elisha, too? Scripture does not tell us.) The modern tendency, not necessarily to be rejected, is for the expositor to fit the prophet into his background. Here we are not dealing with revelation in the normal prophetic sense, for it is God's actions that are the real message. So the instrument is not more closely defined or described. So far as we know, Jonah was not picked because he was particularly suited to the task. When Jonah fled, God could have turned to someone else; but since it is the sovereignty of God that is being particularly stressed, God held to his choice (cf. 1 Cor 9:16).

2 "The great city of Nineveh" goes back to early postdiluvian days (Gen 10:11); archaeologists date the oldest of the discovered remains about 4500 B.C. Though it was not always the capital city of Assyria, Nineveh was always one of its principal towns. (For further information, see note at 3:3.) In the light of 4:11, it might be better to translate "great city" as "big city"; for it is the number of its inhabitants that is being stressed.

"Preach against it" has a shade of meaning that is not justified by the Hebrew. Probably JB has caught the sense best by "inform them that their wickedness has become known to me." We may infer from the Assyrians' own inscriptions that God was particularly concerned with their self-confident pride (Isa 10:13) and cruelty (Nah 3:1, 10, 19) (cf. comment at 3:8). It is often unwise for the stranger and outsider to put his finger on the faults of others. Resentment may stifle the voice of conscience; so Jonah had merely to announce imminent judgment, leaving it to his hearers' conscience to judge why it was coming.

3 Apparently "Tarshish" comes from a Semitic root meaning "to smelt"; so there were a number of places involved in the mineral trade with this name on the Mediterranean coast. It is highly probable that the most distant of them, Tartessus in Spain, at the mouth of the Guadalquivir, is intended. However, nothing depends on our identification. We need not go beyond Jonah's own words (4:2) to find his motive for not wanting to go to Nineveh, but this does not explain why he tried to run away.

There is nowhere a suggestion that Jonah considered himself to be the Lord's only representative. He knew that if he refused to go, there were others who could be sent in his place. The Bible gives no support to the common modern superstition that a Christian is indispensable or irreplaceable. It is equally baseless to suggest that Jonah thought that the Lord's writ did not extend to Tarshish. If he was convinced that God could and would bring destruction on Nineveh in the east, he knew that God could do it equally in Tarshish to the west, even if it was farther away. Jonah's words to the sailors (1:10) can hardly be quoted against this, for it is unlikely that he discussed his theological motivations with them in detail. Even less can we build on the statement that he "ran away from the LORD"; for it is characteristic of the Scriptures—as of Oriental storytelling generally—to describe actions objectively, allowing the underlying motives to show themselves in the course of the story.

Jonah knew full well that his commission showed God's desire to spare Assyria, something that as "Judge of all the earth" (Gen 18:25) he could not do unless it repented of its sins. With typical human shortsightedness, the prophet could see only one reason for this—that penitent and spared Assyria should be God's scourge for Israel, which had been threatened by its power at least three times in the past (under Ashurnasirpal II and Shalmaneser III). Israel was involved in the battle of Qarqar in 853 B.C. and under Jehu paid tribute to Assyria in 841 B.C. If Assyria were to be spared now, it could only be that the doom pronounced at Horeb to Elijah (1 Kings 19:15–18) should go into full effect. Sick at heart from the foreshortened view of the future, so common to the prophets in foretelling the coming judgments of God, Jonah wished to escape, not beyond the power of God, but away from the stage on which God was working out his purposes and judgments. The Christian worker anxious to avoid the full impact of modern problems should have no difficulty in understanding Jonah's action. "To flee from the LORD" is here probably the equivalent of "to flee from the LORD's land."

Notes

1 Jonah means "dove." Some supporters of the allegorical school make it refer to Israel.
3 "The fare" is literally "her fare." The rabbis interpreted this to mean that Jonah bought the ship.

2. *The Storm*

1:4–6

4Then the LORD sent a great wind on the sea, and such a violent storm arose
that the ship threatened to break up. 5All the sailors were afraid and each cried
out to his own god. And they threw the cargo into the sea to lighten the ship.
But Jonah had gone below deck, where he lay down and fell into a deep sleep.
6The captain went to him and said, "How can you sleep? Get up and call on
your god! Maybe he will take notice of us, and we will not perish."

4 For the ancient Near East, the gods had created order by defeating the powers of chaos; but these had been tamed, not abolished, and so remained a constant threat. The embodiment of these lawless and chaotic forces was the sea, which men could not control or tame. In Greek mythology Poseidon (Neptune), the god of the sea, was also the god of the earthquake. Frequently God's control of the sea is used to stress his complete lordship over creation (cf. Pss 24:2; 33:7; 65:7; 74:13; 77:19; 89:9; 114:3, 5; Isa 27:1; 51:10; 63:11; Jer 5:22; 31:35; et al.).

5–6 RSV's "each cried to his god" expresses the Hebrew better. The crew were probably all Phoenicians, whose language differed only slightly from Jonah's; so the crew would have shared in a common religion and pantheon. In a developed polytheism, however, individuals tended to concentrate on favorite deities; in addition, all sorts of attractive foreign deities tended to be adopted by sailors. A rabbinic idea is that the seventy nations of men were represented in the crew, and so the inadequacy of all heathen gods was being demonstrated.

There are no grounds for attributing Jonah's sound sleep either to his reaction after his hurried flight to Joppa, though this might have played a part, or to an easy conscience. The storm that can terrify the sailor can reduce the landsman to physical impotence and unconsciousness, as indeed the verb *rāḏam* ("deep sleep") suggests (cf. Gen 2:21; 15:12; Judg 4:21). The captain's command to Jonah that he pray (v.6) reflects both the heathen concept that the amount of prayer is of importance (Matt 6:7) and the fact that under a polytheistic system one could seldom be sure which god had been displeased and had, therefore, to be appeased.

Notes

4 The Hebrew is most vivid, literally reading "the ship thought she would be broken in pieces."

5 The Hebrew word כֵּלִים (*kēlîm,* "cargo") is indeterminate. Bewer (in loc.) renders it "tackle and utensils," leaving it open whether we are to include the cargo. NEB has the excellent vagueness of "they threw things overboard."

---

3. *Jonah's Responsibility*

1:7–10

7Then the sailors said to each other, "Come, let us cast lots to find out who is responsible for this calamity." They cast lots and the lot fell on Jonah.
8So they asked him, "Tell us, who is responsible for making all this trouble for us? What do you do? Where do you come from? What is your country? From what people are you?"
9He answered, "I am Hebrew and I worship the LORD, the God of heaven, who made the sea and the land."
10This terrified them and they asked, "What have you done?" (They knew he was running away from the LORD, because he had already told them so.)

7 "Come, let us cast lots" assumes that Jonah had joined in the chorus of prayer. Some assume also that because he had a guilty conscience—if indeed he did—he would not have prayed. It was probably the first time in Jonah's life that he had been on the sea. Though he may well have been terrified, he would hardly have realized, as did the sailors, that anything exceptional was happening. The lack of result from prayer and the rarity of such storms in the sailing season (cf. Acts 27:9) made the sailors conclude that someone on board must be responsible for their plight. In 1 Samuel 14:36–42 we have an example within Israel where it was assumed that a failure of God to answer the oracle must be due to someone's breach of divine law.

8 When the lot pointed to Jonah, the sailors' flood of questions was essentially an outcome of their heathen polytheism. Their gods were basically nonmoral; so their anger might equally be directed against the moral outcast, the one who had accidentally and even unknowingly sinned against them, or the one against whom the gods had taken a dislike as the result of a whim. With the generosity of men who constantly risked their lives in their daily work, they wanted to know whether Jonah was one who fully deserved his fate (cf. Acts 28:4), or whether there were extenuating circumstances that would justify their taking risks to try to save him.

9 Jonah's answer was simple. In saying "I am a Hebrew," he was using the term by which the Israelite was known to his neighbors (cf. 1 Sam 4:6, 9; 14:11). We may be sure that the earlier note of contempt in the term had by this time disappeared. In exactly the same way in NT times, the Israelite was an Israelite at home and a Jew among strangers. It may be that Israel's special relationship with Yahweh was felt to be something not to be flaunted in the face of strangers.

It is widely suggested that the title "the God of heaven," frequently used in postexilic books (e.g., Ezra 1:2; 7:12; Neh 1:4; Dan 2:8), is evidence that Jonah is postexilic. But it is far more likely that Israel deliberately chose the title to express the sovereignty of Yahweh in the contrast to Baal, who was himself a sky god. (See the conflict on Mount Carmel, where Elijah challenged Baal to bring down fire from heaven [1 Kings 18:24]. Note also the very much earlier use of the title in Gen 24:3, 7.) In a polytheistic society, it was difficult to find a title that would more perfectly express the supremacy of Yahweh. What terrified the sailors was the addition of "who made the sea and the land." They knew that Jonah was running away from Yahweh (v. 10), whom they knew to be the God of Israel. They had evidently regarded his action as reasonable, possibly amusing. As Phoenicians they did not take seriously Jonah's claim that Yahweh was superior to Baal. But now Jonah had claimed that Yahweh was the Creator of the sea. Terrified they said (not "asked"), "What have you done!" It is an exclamation, not a question (cf. Gen 4:10).

Notes

---

7 גּוֹרָלוֹת (*gôrālôṯ*, "lots") were little stones; we need not suppose either that there was a cultic person to handle them or that they had any special sanctity. The word is used equally in settings where the use of Urim and Thummim may be presumed, and in others where they may with certainty be excluded.

8 "What do you do?" may well not be a question about Jonah's occupation. Perhaps it is better expressed as "What are you doing [on this ship]?"

---

4. *Jonah's Rejection*

1:11–16

11The sea was getting rougher and rougher. So they asked him, "What should we do to you to make the sea calm down for us?"

12"Pick me up and throw me into the sea," he replied, "and it will become calm. I know that it is my fault that this great storm has come upon you."

13Instead, the men did their best to row back to land. But they could not, for the sea grew even wilder than before. 14Then they cried to the LORD, "O LORD, please do not let us die for taking this man's life. Do not hold us accountable for killing an innocent man, for you, O LORD, have done as you pleased."

15Then they took Jonah and threw him overboard, and the raging sea grew calm. 16At this the men greatly feared the LORD, and they offered a sacrifice to the LORD and made vows to him.

11 The sailors found themselves in a new and unexpected position. They realized that they were not dealing with a heinous criminal, or even with someone who had accidentally transgressed the regulations of some deity. Here was a god's servant who had fallen out with his lord. In a culture in which correct procedure in the service of the gods was essential, they had not merely to do the will of Yahweh but also to do it correctly. Only Jonah could guide them. "What should we do to you?" they asked.

12 Jonah's answer to the distraught sailors was, in essence, "Hand me over to my God." It is easy to overlook Jonah's spiritual greatness. Once the lot had pointed to him, he accepted that the storm was not simply "a natural phenomenon." So on the one hand, Jonah was willing to be handed over to his God, whom he had offended, though without realizing the seriousness of his act. On the other hand, he knew that the God of 4:2 would not make the sailors pay for what had been an innocent act on their part. Yahweh was not a nonmoral god like Baal, making them suffer out of sheer pique. So Jonah was confident that the sea would calm down once he was no longer in the ship. This shows that he had a far deeper understanding of God than he is often given credit for.

13–14 Since the sailors' religious outlook could make no sense of a god of heaven's creating and controlling the sea—they probably did not even think of the sea as created but rather as a remnant of the original chaos—to throw Jonah overboard was equivalent to murdering him. (After all, even Christians do not always take God's complete control of his creation seriously.) They could not know for certain whether they were doing Yahweh's will, and they feared that he might punish them for the death of his servant. So they tried hard to set him ashore, even though it involved great risk to the ship. That they were near enough to the coast to make the attempt shows that it was an on-shore wind, which could so easily have wrecked them on a lee shore. When the increasing storm made this impossible, they prayed that they should not be held guilty of Jonah's death (v. 14); for clearly the Lord had done as he pleased. When they called Jonah "innocent" (*nāqî*), they were not impugning God's actions; they were merely stating that no human tribunal had passed sentence on him.

15–16 So far as the sailors knew, Jonah had been dealt with by his angry god and master. Even had they seen him swallowed by the fish, which is highly improbable and not suggested by the story, they would never have guessed that it was the instrument of God's mercy. But the immediate cessation of the storm after they threw Jonah overboard showed them that Yahweh really had control of the sea. So "they offered a sacrifice to the LORD and made vows to him." It is quite likely that the Targum gives the sense in the rendering "They promised to offer sacrifices" as soon as they reached the shore. The Midrash understands this to mean that they threw their idols into the sea, returned to Joppa, went up to Jerusalem, and became proselytes. This is as fanciful as the modern idea that Jonah had become a missionary, even against his will. Certainly there was a new respect for the God of Israel, a new understanding of his power; but there is no suggestion that these Phoenician sailors renounced their ancestral religion or made any efforts to discover what, apart from power, distinguished Yahweh from Baal and Ashtoreth. In other words, they had been brought to the position envisaged by Paul in Romans 1:19–20, and that was not inconsiderable. But there is no evidence that their spiritual apprehension went further.

Polytheism and syncretism have always gone hand in hand. (Jesus is reverenced by millions in India today, but all too often it is as one divine figure among many.) In the action of the sailors, we find nothing of the concept of the "jealous God" who tolerates no division of loyalty. Because Jonah believed implicitly and wholly in the sovereignty of God, the sailors were brought to a realization of his power. So when such faith is sincerely held, it should affect others. In the book as a whole, however, the sailors' faith plays a very minor part. In accordance with its terse style, the story does not tell us what the vows were, nor the size and number of the sacrifices.

5. *Jonah's Protection*

1:17–2:1

[17]But the LORD provided a great fish to swallow Jonah, and Jonah was inside the fish three days and three nights.
[1]From inside the fish Jonah prayed to the LORD his God.

17 The sea did not change its nature when Jonah splashed into it, for God respects the qualities he has given his creation. Jonah did not suddenly develop into a champion swimmer, for normally God expects the abilities he has given to be suitably trained. But the necessary protection was there for all that. There is no suggestion that the fish was a special creation for the purpose, or that Jonah's preservation within it was miraculous. The power of God ensured that the fish was there at exactly the right time.

If it were more widely realized that the miraculous is probably always achieved by God's control over nature, not by contravention of the laws he has placed in nature, we might be able to recognize miracles more easily in our own experience. This is not meant, however, to be a theological definition of miracles. What has been said does not apply to God's creating *ex nihilo* (i.e., "out of nothing"), and the same is almost certainly the case with the other examples of "create" in Genesis 1. Similarly, it would be hazardous to suggest that God was merely adapting the laws of nature in the Virgin Birth or the resurrection of Christ.

In our ignorance of the nature of the fish, all discussion about where Jonah lay in it and how he was preserved is no more than interesting speculation (cf. Introduction 4.a). We should, however, ask ourselves why God chose this means of preserving Jonah's life. As we have already seen, the ship was not far from the shore; and God could easily have provided a piece of floating wreckage to which Jonah could have clung, till he washed up on the beach half-drowned. Miracle is not the gratuitous display of God's omnipotence, nor is it called out merely because of human need. Taken in its setting, it is probable that every miracle has a spiritual significance—hence the use of "sign" to describe it in John. This must surely be the case here, and all the more so when we remember that Jesus was prepared to use Jonah's experience as a picture of his resurrection (Matt 12:39–40). So we should ask ourselves what the fish meant to Jonah and to those who first heard the story.

For the sailors the raising of the storm and its subsequent quieting were indubitable evidence of Yahweh's control of chaos. This lesson had to be brought home to Jonah also. Yet he did not experience the sudden stilling of the storm, nor was he sufficiently versed in the ways of the sea to appreciate the miracle involved. In the ancient Near-Eastern mythology, which finds numerous reflections in OT poetic language, chaos is pictured by the sea monster Leviathan (*loṯan* in Ugar.). This is reflected in Psalm 74:13–14, where Leviathan refers both to God's rule over chaos and to the destruction of the Egyptians at the Red Sea. The concept is given another twist, however, in Psalm 104:26, where Leviathan, the dreaded sea monster, is merely God's plaything (NEB).

To Jonah and those familiar with the old mythological imagery, the fish represented Leviathan. The mythology that occurs periodically in the poetic and prophetic books of the OT is a dead mythology (i.e., there is no question of the old concepts of their neighbors having the slightest validity in Israel, but the pictorial image they conveyed was still alive). Just as we may still refer to fairies and even have a mental picture of them, though we know that they do not exist, so it was with Leviathan and similar monsters in Israel.

Since Leviathan was at God's disposal, it meant that every force in the world, however potentially dangerous, is completely under God's dominance and control. This finds its clearest expression in Daniel and Revelation, but it is a lesson hard to learn for the child of God placed in the midst of the world's hostility. So while in one way the fish is secondary in the revelation to Jonah, it was needed for the prophet to grasp that God's love is operative in a world that is entirely under divine control, however hostile it may be to him (cf. Rom 8:28).

Once Jonah was on dry land again, he could make some kind of estimate of how long he had been in the fish. Yet to make any exact measure of the number of hours would have been impossible for him. Roused suddenly from a deep slumber, stupefied by the violence of the storm, and in all probability seasick, Jonah would have been in no position to know at what hour he was thrown overboard. Furthermore, on reaching the shore he would have needed time to collect his wits. Clearly, then, the term "three days and three nights" is intended as an approximation, not a precise period of seventy-two hours. The use by Jesus (Matt 12:40) should almost certainly be understood in the same way (see Notes).

1 Some would object that Jonah would not have waited so long before he prayed. The popular idea that Jonah went straight from the deck of the ship into the fish's open mouth has no support from either the narrative or Jonah's prayer. He was half-drowned before he was swallowed. If he was still conscious, sheer dread would have caused him to faint—notice that there is no mention of the fish in his prayer. He can hardly have known what caused the change from wet darkness to an even greater dry darkness. When he did regain consciousness, it would have taken some time to realize that the all-enveloping darkness was not that of Sheol but of a mysterious safety.

Notes

---

17 On "three days and three nights," Rabbi Eleazar ben Azariah (c. A.D. 100) said, "A day and a night make an *'onah* [i.e., a twenty-four-hour period], and the portion of an *'onah* is reckoned as a complete *'onah*" (j *Shabbath* 9.12a). This shows how these terms were used in Jesus' time, and there is no reason for thinking that this had not been the understanding of the phrase "a day and night" all along. The difficulty some find in reconciling the expression "three days and three nights" with the time Jesus' body was in the grave comes from undue concern with clock time.

---

6. *Jonah's Psalm of Thanksgiving*

2:2–9

2He said:
"In my distress I called to the LORD,
and he answered me.
From the depths of the grave I called for help,
and you listened to my cry.

3You hurled me into the deep,
  into the very heart of the seas,
  and the currents swirled about me;
 all your waves and breakers
  swept over me.
4I said, 'I have been banished
  from your sight;
 yet I will look again
  toward your holy temple.'
5The engulfing waters threatened me,
  the deep surrounded me;
  seaweed was wrapped around my head.
6To the roots of the mountains I sank down;
  the earth beneath barred me in forever.
 But you brought my life up from the pit,
  O LORD my God.

7"When my life was ebbing away,
  I remembered you, LORD,
 and my prayer rose to you,
  to your holy temple.

8"Those who cling to worthless idols
  forfeit the grace that could be theirs.
9But I, with a song of thanksgiving,
  will sacrifice to you.
 What I have vowed I will make good.
  Salvation comes from the LORD."

Most modern scholars maintain that (1) this psalm is misplaced, for it should come after 2:10, and (2) it is entirely unsuited to the position in which Jonah found himself.

1. While there are phrases, sentences, and short passages in the OT that seem undoubtedly misplaced textually, they are rare; and the misplacements can normally be explained by the general principles governing scribal errors. Here, however, no adequate reasons for misplacement have been suggested. Indeed, G.A. Smith (p. 512), though not accepting the historicity of the book, argues that this is the correct position for the psalm: "From the standpoint of the writer, Jonah was already saved, when he was taken up by the fish—saved from the deep into which he had been cast by the sailors, and the dangers of which the Psalm so vividly describes."

2. It is claimed that the psalm is unsuited to its setting because it is a psalm of thanksgiving, not a prayer (2:1), and because it praises God for rescue from drowning. To be sure the statement that someone prayed to the Lord seems everywhere else in Scripture to be followed by a petition, even if the prayer includes thanksgiving. But is this psalm purely thanksgiving? There is a sudden change in v.9 to the future, or more accurately to the cohortative. It is questionable whether the rendering "But I . . . will sacrifice . . . I will make good" is adequate. Nearer the meaning is probably "may I sacrifice . . . may I make good." In other words, the petition is there, though in the light of God's mercy already shown it is expressed in a veiled manner. As for praising God for rescue from drowning, that is exactly what the psalm does. What else should it praise him for? Jonah desired to bring a thank offering and pay his vows because of God's mercies already shown. Though Jonah

did not tell us what he had vowed, the context leaves little doubt that it was complete obedience. This is also mirrored in the closing cry of confidence: "Salvation comes from the LORD," which in Jonah's mouth was equivalent to a recognition of God's absolute sovereignty.

A discussion of the psalm's peculiar nature and its many parallels to other psalms may be found in the Introduction (Literary Form).

2–4 "From the depths of the grave" in the Hebrew is literally "from the belly of Sheol," and this should be retained. It is true that Sheol is often no more than a synonym for the grave; Jonah was not saying, however, that he thought he was buried but that he had gone to join the dead. The terrifying experience described in v.3 brought Jonah to the realization of his plight and elicited the confession in v.4. "Yet I will look again," though a legitimate rendering, is open to misunderstanding. It is not a statement of salvation but of Jonah's determination to pray in spite of his banishment; probably "but" would suit the sense better.

5–6 Jonah continued the description begun in v.3 of his downward plunge into the deep. These verses vividly illustrate the hopelessness of his situation. He was, as it were, beyond human help. The "earth beneath" should probably be rendered the "land beneath," since it is in parallel to "pit," which is a synonym for Sheol. The reference is to the place of the dead, pictured as being within the earth, and once again points to Jonah's expectation of certain death.

7–8 As he plummeted through the waters, Jonah realized that "his life was ebbing away." In these fleeting moments his thought turned to the Lord and his "holy temple." Remarkably, in spite of the position in which he found himself, Jonah had a mental picture of the despairing sailors calling in vain on their gods, while he, whom they thought had been lost, was awaiting the demonstration of his God's salvation.

Notes

---

4 In the commentary, it was suggested that an optimistic interpretation, such as NIV's "yet I will look again," was not to be read into Jonah's words at this point (contra Keil, Laetsch). Bewer, G.A. Smith, JB, and RSV all render the Hebrew as "How shall I again look?" and this seems implied by NEB, too. This is based on the reading אֵיךְ (*'êḵ*, "how") in Theodotion instead of MT's אַךְ (*'aḵ*, "yet"). This latter reading is certainly more attractive; but on the criterion that the more difficult reading is to be preferred, we must hesitate before accepting it.

5 The Hebrew for the word rendered "me" in NIV is נֶפֶשׁ (*nepeš*), which is normally translated "soul" in KJV. Today, however, it is recognized that *nepeš* has a very wide range of meanings. But our text's rendering of "me" hardly suits the Hebrew. The marginal reading rightly links *nepeš* with one of its two primitive meanings, i.e., "throat," the other being "breath" (so JB, NEB). There seems to be a completely analogous case in Ps 69:1 (so JB, NEB, RSV).

6 "The earth beneath barred me in" translates הָאָרֶץ בְּרִחֶיהָ בַעֲדִי (*hā'āreṣ b^eriḥeyhā ḇa'^aḏî*, lit., "the earth, her bars against me"). The "bars of Sheol" (בַּדֵּי שְׁאֹל, *baddê š^e'ōl*; NIV, "gates of death") are mentioned in Job 17:16; its "gates" in Job 38:17; Ps 9:13; Isa 38:10;

Wisd Sol 16:13; Matt 16:18. It need hardly be said that such language is merely a poetic and metaphorical way of saying that no man returns from the realm of death.

7 "Your holy temple" presumably, though not certainly, refers to the heavenly sanctuary, while it is the earthly sanctuary that is meant in v.4.

8 "Grace" here renders חֶסֶד (*ḥesed*). This is a covenant word (cf. comments at 4:2). We may therefore question the translation. If Jonah was thinking of idolaters among his own people, "steadfast love" or some similar rendering is called for. If, as is more probable, he was thinking of the sailors, then we should choose between "forsake their true loyalty" (RSV) and "may abandon their loyalty" (NEB).

---

7. *Jonah's Deliverance*

2:10

10 And the LORD commanded the fish, and it vomited Jonah onto dry land.

10 The literal Hebrew reads, "And the Lord spoke to the fish" (JB, KJV, NEB, RSV). Unlike the prophet, the fish responded promptly, as soon as it knew God's will, and did not need any express command (NAB, NASB, NIV).

At what point, presumably on the Palestinian coast, the fish spewed out Jonah is not indicated; for it is completely immaterial to the story. Unfortunately some, whether they have or have not defended the historicity of the story, have allowed their fancy full scope here. P. Haupt, ("Jonah's Whale," *Proceedings of the American Philosophical Society* 46 [1907]: 151–64), for example, saw the fish as God's means for transporting the prophet to Alexandretta, the Mediterranean terminus of the shortest route from the sea to Nineveh. Trumbull suggested that Jonah came out of the fish "on the coast of Phoenicia, where the fish-god was a favourite object of worship." From this he deduced that "a multitude would be ready to follow the seemingly new avatar of the fish-god, proclaiming the story of his uprising from the sea, as he went on his mission to the city where the fish-god had its very centre of worship." A more acceptable form of this was advanced by Hart-Davies. He suggested that the effect of the fish's gastric juices on Jonah's face and other exposed parts of his body must have been terrible. Since the story of his miraculous deliverance had preceded him, Jonah was immediately recognized when he arrived in Nineveh.

All such theories suffer from two major and insurmountable objections. They demand that we interpret Scripture by something that cannot legitimately be deduced from it. What is worse, they make the miracle of the fish a necessary ingredient in Nineveh's repentance. What would have happened if Jonah had gone there when first commanded? The suggestion that the fish acted as a kind of submarine transport for the prophet is less objectionable, but it does detract from Jonah's obedience when the second call came.

Probably the majority of those who support an allegorical or parabolic interpretation of the book see in Jonah a personification of Israel and in the fish a type of the Exile. Provided we do not thereby deny the truth of the story, there is no reason why we should not at least in a measure, accept this. There is a typological purpose in many of God's OT actions. Israel's downfall and exile are clearly linked with chaos, directly as in Jeremiah 4:23–26, or through the picture of the wilderness (Jer

31:2; Ezek 20:35; Hos 2:14) or of a sea monster (Jer 51:34, 44). If the book is preexilic, Jonah's experience should have been a real consolation to those godly men who found themselves swallowed up by exile. At the same time we may not place this typology in the foreground and infer that Israel went into exile because it had failed to carry God's message to the nations. Here too the fish is secondary to the main message of the book.

Far more acceptable is the view given by E.J. Young (*An Introduction to the Old Testament* [Grand Rapids; Eerdmans, 1960], p. 263): "The fundamental purpose of the book of Jonah is not found in its missionary or universalistic teaching. It is rather to show that Jonah being cast into the depths of Sheol and yet brought up alive is an illustration of the death of the Messiah for sins not His own and of the Messiah's resurrection. Jonah was an Israelite and the servant of the Lord, and his experience was brought about because of the sins of the nations (Nineveh)."

While Young's view does full justice to Jesus' use of the story, it faces the objection that this meaning was not even remotely accessible to the pious Israelite till the fulfillment. It also lays the stress in the wrong place, for once again it forgets that there would have been no fish had Jonah not been disobedient. It is true that Jonah had to suffer because of Nineveh and for its salvation, but the suffering was caused by his own disobedience. In Scripture God deals with human disobedience and sin in a manner that teaches both the sinner and the future generations, but there is never any suggestion that the sin occurred in order to make the lesson or type possible.

II. The Obedient Prophet (3:1–4:11)

1. *Jonah's Proclamation*

3:1–4

1Then the word of the LORD came to Jonah a second time: 2"Go to the great city of Nineveh and proclaim to it the message I give you."

3Jonah obeyed the word of the LORD and went to Nineveh. Now Nineveh was an important city—a visit required three days. 4On the first day, Jonah started into the city. He proclaimed: "Forty more days and Nineveh will be destroyed."

1 The expression "a second time" is completely vague. There are no grounds for thinking with Bewer (p. 50) that "the command came to Jonah immediately after his deliverance." Alienation from life as it is really lived is always a major risk in biblical exposition. After the experience he had passed through, we can be sure that Jonah as God's servant was given some short time for physical recuperation and even more for digesting the spiritual lessons to be learned from his experiences. Nor should we take the "second time" for granted, as we are all too ready to do. There are many examples in the Scriptures of no second chance. Indeed, we should rather ask ourselves why the second call came to Jonah, for we must rule out typological motivations. The answer seems to be that the sovereignty of God is one of the main themes of the book. It is demonstrated not only in God's control of nature but also of his prophet. In another setting God might well have used someone else. It would be very rash for the Christian worker to presume, basing himself on Jonah, that his disobedience will be overlooked.

2 Since the Hebrew word *gāḏôl* ("great," "large") is used of Nineveh here and in v.3, it would be well to retain the same rendering: "large" would seem to be indicated in both verses, the more so as 4:11 suggests that it is the number of inhabitants that is being stressed. God does not lay weight on Nineveh's political importance or on the magnificence of its buildings. "The message I give you" does not necessarily suggest that Jonah would have said otherwise. It is merely one more indication that we are dealing with the sovereignty of God. It is strange, however, that many Christian preachers who take pride in proclaiming that sovereignty seem, at times, to spend much time in proclaiming their own views.

3 "Now Nineveh was a very large city" (NIV mg.) most probably is the correct reading. "A city important to God" not only does not suit the context but, worse still, introduces a note of particularity into a book where universality is constantly being implied. True enough, Jonah went to Nineveh, but the principle would have been the same had it been some other large city, e.g., Babylon, which was a major threat to Israel.

The use of the perfect (*hāyᵉṯāh*) in the clause "Nineveh *was* an important city" has been held by some to imply that the city had been overthrown, and this is one of the chief arguments relied on by those who uphold a late date for the book. Even if this interpretation is correct, it proves no more than that the book *in its present form* is late (see Introduction: Date and Authorship). However, it may be questioned whether this sense is demanded by the syntax. The structure would rather indicate a situation that had already come into being at the time referred to than one that had ceased to obtain at the time of writing. We may therefore be justified in translating, "Now Nineveh *had* (already) *become* a great city." Assyria had yet to become the rod of God's anger against his people, but already the sheer size of her teeming metropolis was fraught with impending menace in the prophet's intuitive vision, and deepened the feelings of dread foreboding for his beloved land and people, and this foreboding oppressed his subconscious mind and underlay his profound unwillingness that Nineveh should repent and be spared.

The stress on the importance and size of Nineveh is entirely justified. Its population was at least 120,000 (4:10), while Samaria, almost certainly larger than Jerusalem, had about 30,000 (R. de Vaux, *Ancient Israel* [New York: McGraw-Hill, 1961], p. 66). In addition, the Israelite cities, built in naturally defensive positions, normally on hilltops and tells, were cramped and crowded; but the royal cities in the Mesopotamian plain had room to expand.

"A visit required three days" renders the Hebrew phrase that literally says "a distance of three days." This could mean that it took three days to go either across it or around it; but it certainly does not mean what the English rendering might be taken to imply, viz., that it would take three days to visit every part of it. Diodorus Siculus (first century B.C.) gave the circumference of the city as approximately sixty miles (cf. Notes), and thus many have maintained that the three days referred to the journey around the walls. Modern archaeology has shown, however, that the inner wall had a length of almost eight miles (cf. Notes). Today defenders of the historicity of the book interpret the statement as referring to "Greater Nineveh," i.e., the administrative district of Nineveh, which Parrot (p. 17) calls "the Assyrian triangle." This interpretation receives strong support from Genesis 10:11–12, where "that is the great city" seems to refer to the whole area covered by Nineveh, Rehoboth Ir, Calah (Nimrud), and Resen.

4 Jonah was not necessarily proclaiming God's message as he went into the city. But sometime "on the first day," Jonah "proclaimed" his message. There may well have been something about Jonah, his bearing, his dress, or something else, as he strode toward the center of the city, looking neither to the right nor to the left, that drew many after him. When he finally stood and shouted, "Forty more days and Nineveh will be destroyed," the news spread like wildfire. The LXX has "three days" instead of forty. There is no doubt that this suits the setting far better and helps explain the urgency of Nineveh's repentance. In addition it does not ask us to see Jonah camping outside the city for over a month, while he waited to see the outcome. Yet, in variations of this type, which can hardly be merely the result of scribal corruptions, one has to be suspicious of the highly attractive reading (cf. note at 2:4). For all that, the LXX reading should have found a place in the margin.

The credibility of the message was underscored by the fact that at the time Assyria stood in considerable danger from its northern neighbors (cf. Introduction: Background). We are not told whether Jonah repeated his message—he probably did—or whether he was interrogated by those who heard him, and, if so, what he told them. But the word of the Lord worked the miracle, not Jonah or his commentary.

Notes

3 NIV's "an important city" translates עִיר־גְּדוֹלָה לֵאלֹהִים (*'îr-g^e^dôlāh l^e'lōhîm*, lit., "a city great for God"). We find a similar expression in Gen 10:9, where the sense is "a very mighty hunter." Other examples may be found in Gen 23:6; 30:8; Exod 9:28; 1 Sam 14:15; et al. For a discussion of this usage, see D. Winton Thomas, "Consideration of Some Unusual Ways of Expressing the Superlative in Hebrew," VetTest 3 (1953): 209–24.

Concerning Nineveh, Diodorus said: "It was well-walled, of unequal lengths. Each of the longer sides was 150 stadia; each of the shorter 90. The whole circuit then being 480 stadia" (cited in Bewer, p. 31). F. Jones, who surveyed the ruins in 1853, gave the length of the walls as follows: east wall, 16,000 feet; north wall, 7,000 feet; west wall, 13,600 feet; and south wall, 3,000 feet—i.e., 39,000 feet in all ("Topography of Nineveh," *Journal of the Royal Asiatic Society* [1855]: 324). Bewer (p. 51) quotes an inscription by Sennacherib that gives general support to these measurements.

2. *Nineveh's Repentance*

3:5–10

5 The Ninevites believed God. They declared a fast, and all of them, from the greatest to the least, put on sackcloth.

6 When the news reached the king of Nineveh, he rose from his throne, took off his royal robes, covered himself with sackcloth and sat down in the dust. 7 Then he issued a proclamation in Nineveh:

"By the decree of the king and his nobles:

Do not let any man or beast, herd or flock, taste anything; do not let them eat or drink. 8 But let man and beast be covered with sackcloth. Let everyone call urgently on God. Let them give up their evil ways and their violence. 9 Who knows? God may yet relent and with compassion turn from his fierce anger so that we will not perish."

10 When God saw what they did and how they turned from their evil ways, he had compassion and did not bring upon them the destruction he had threatened.

There now begins a subtle interplay on the two divine names. Up to this point, with the obvious exception of the sailors before the Lord's power had been revealed to them, we consistently find the name "the LORD" (Yahweh), i.e., the name of the covenant-making God of Israel. Now alongside it we find the name "God" (Elohim), the all-powerful One, the Creator, the Lord of nature. The obvious purpose is to bring home that Jonah had not been proclaiming Yahweh to those that did not know him but that the supreme God, whatever his name, was about to show his power in judgment. Behind all polytheism with its many gods and many lords, there was always the concept of one God who could enforce his will on the others, if he chose. There is not the slightest indication that Jonah had mentioned the God of Israel or had said that he came in his name. The Ninevites, however, recognized the voice of the supreme God, whatever name they may have given him, and repented. That Elohim ("God") is retained in v.10 shows that the sparing of Nineveh had nothing to do with an improved faith. Correct faith, in this sense, need not lead to salvation (James 2:19).

5 The hypercritical have found a contradiction between a fast that had already been declared (v.5) and the king's subsequent proclamation (v.7). A very common feature of Hebrew narrative is to mention the outcome first and the way it came to pass afterwards. This could easily be the case here. The fact, however, is that "they declared" is far too narrow a translation for *qārā'*, which simply means "to call" in the widest sense. We are intended to picture the people, both those who hear Jonah and those to whom his words are reported, as saying spontaneously, "Let us fast!" That they put on sackcloth does not invalidate this interpretation, for it was a standard, virtually obligatory accompaniment of fasting at the time (cf. 2 Sam 3:31, 35; Isa 58:5; Dan 9:3). Indeed, in many cases where sackcloth is mentioned, we can assume that there was fasting as well, and vice versa.

Sackcloth, the coarsest of cloth, often made of goat's hair, was the normal dress of the poor, prisoners, and slaves; it was worn by those who mourned (Ezek 7:18). Prophets wore it (2 Kings 1:8; Zech 13:4; Mark 1:6), partly to associate themselves with the poor, partly perhaps as a sign of mourning for the sins of the people. When used in mourning, it covered no more of the body than was demanded by decency. When used by the Ninevites, it expressed their complete inability to contend with the divine decree and that they were the slaves of the supreme God.

6 There is no suggestion that Jonah made any effort to reach the royal presence; hence the news would have reached the king later than it did many of his subjects. He not only came down from his throne and sat on the ground—a feature of mourning rites—dressed in sackcloth like the meanest slave, but he sat in the dust (cf. Notes), which means, presumably, in the open air, where he could be seen by his subjects. All this was done completely spontaneously. Then, however, as he sat with his courtiers ("nobles"), there came the realization that this concerned everyone; and the decree was issued (v.7).

There seems to be no doubt that the title "king of Nineveh" means the king of Assyria; and since the Assyrians did not use such a title, some point to this as one more proof of the unhistorical nature of the book. Those who take up this position are under obligation to explain why the alleged postexilic author should have invented the title—the more so as he had numerous names of Assyrian kings to choose from, and he would have known who was king of Assyria. The real explanation is not so difficult to find. Our attention has been fixed on one spot. Jonah's message was not to Assyria in general but to Nineveh in particular. Especially, if we accept that the doom was to fall in *three* days' time (cf. comments at v.4), this is not hard to understand. So it is irrelevant that the king of the doomed city is also king of a wider area; it is even irrelevant that this wider area would inevitably be involved in the destruction of Nineveh.

Equally, the name, titles, and achievements of Nineveh's king are irrelevant. He and the city are linked together and share in the same fate. We call it today an existential position, a moment of crisis; neither what went before nor what might follow after has any real bearing on the story. A city and its king have to act, and according to their action so will be their fate.

7 We are intended to picture the king's courtiers and counselors sitting in the dust around him and rapidly agreeing on a decree that makes the spontaneous response official. With the mourners were to be linked the domestic animals (*b^ehēmāh*), a touch suggesting that it was indeed "Greater Nineveh" that was involved. Though we have no records from Mesopotamia of animals being so involved in mourning rites, there is nothing alien to the Oriental mind in it. Herodotus (*Histories* 9.24) tells us of an analogous act by the Persians after the death of Masistius, in which they "shaved their heads, cut the manes of their horses and mules and abandoned themselves to such cries of grief that the whole of Boeotia was loud with the noise of them." Israel seems to have regarded it as natural (cf. Jud 4:10, a book written shortly before 100 B.C., and also Joel 1:10). The concept of a common Creator, today so often replaced by an impersonal idea of evolution, saw man and animal far more closely linked than does the modern concept of a purely biological link.

8 "Let them give up their evil ways and their violence" is the typically Hebrew way of joining the general and the specific. Anything and everything condemned by law and conscience is included under "evil ways." "Violence" (*ḥāmās*) means a defiance of the law by one too strong to be brought to account. Its use in Genesis 16:5, where this word is usually translated by "wrong," shows that no actual force need be involved; Sarai was complaining that Abram's protection of Hagar prevented her from obtaining justice.

If we think purely of the situation in Nineveh, only a relatively small section of the population would come within its scope. We should think rather of the Assyrian attitude toward others. Amos 1:3–2:3 shows that, while there was no written code of international law at the time, there was a generally accepted code of conduct. The Assyrian assumed that in virtue of his conquests he had been placed above lesser breeds and was entitled to ignore the dictates of conscience and compassion in his behavior to his neighbors. It is interesting that Habakkuk applies this same word "violence" (*ḥāmās*) to the Chaldeans (Hab 1:9; 2:8, 17). It is very easy to slip into the concept that our position gives us the right to dominate others. Much racial prejudice and discrimination come from this.

9–10 The operative phrase in these two verses is that God "had compassion" (*niḥam, wayyinnāḥem*), in a setting where KJV, RSV, RV have "repent." NIV's rendering is preferable because it avoids the possible misunderstanding linked with the traditional one; but that it is inadequate is shown by its being changed to "a God who relents" in 4:2, which in fact is nearer the sense here also. We may know the character of God only from what he does and the words he uses to explain his actions. When he does not do what he said he would, we as finite men can say only that he has changed his mind or repented, even though we should recognize, as Jonah did (4:2), that he had intended or desired this all along. Since, more often than not, it is the removal of threatened evil, punishment, and death that we experience—the opposite, however, is also true (cf. Jer 18:9–10)—we realize that the change of mind, the "repentance," is due to divine compassion for frail and mortal man.

Despite all this, "compassion" is an inadequate rendering because it does not bring out the concept of a change. Thus "relent" is better. Paul could stress that the work of Christ was God reconciling the world to himself (2 Cor 5:18), for in Christ we see the unchangeable character of God in all its loving compassion. Here God's change was due to the change in the Ninevites. Because of our almost incorrigible identification of faith with right belief, we fail to sufficiently realize that true faith must be bound up with true repentance. Notice that the name Elohim continues to be used of God. There is no suggestion that God's mercy was accompanied by any revelation of his nature and character. We are always inclined to underestimate God's "uncovenanted mercies," to use a term much loved by an earlier generation.

Notes

6 The word "dust" (אֵפֶר, *'ēper*) is traditionally rendered "ashes" (so BDB, p. 68), "dust" being reserved for עָפָר (*'āpār*); KB (s.v.), however, considers them to be variants distinguished purely by pronunciation but not meaning, which is in both cases "dust."

9 In all uses of the root נחם (*nḥm*, "to regret," "to be sorry"), some element of emotion is always present.

2. *Jonah's Displeasure*

4:1–4

[1]But Jonah was greatly displeased and became angry. [2]He prayed to the LORD, "O LORD, is this not what I said when I was still at home? That is why I was so quick to flee to Tarshish. I knew that you are a gracious and compassionate God, slow to anger and abounding in love, a God who relents from sending calamity. [3]Now, O LORD, take away my life, for it is better for me to die than to live."

[4]But the LORD replied, "Have you any right to be angry?"

1 We are so obsessed with pure doctrine that we are not satisfied when we meet obvious repentance but seek to ensure that it is accompanied by right doctrine. In circles where the doctrine is too rarefied to be understood by the ordinary man, which are more common than the trained theologian realizes, stress may well be laid on charismatic gifts and other outward manifestations of God's grace to act as a divine Amen to the repentance. Jonah, however, knew God well enough to understand that the man who really said, "God be merciful to me a sinner," i.e., a failure (Luke 18:14), would be justified in God's sight. While it remains a matter for debate how far we should attempt to bring out the play on words that occur so frequently in Hebrew, here the effort should have been made. The literal translation is "But it was evil to Jonah with great evil." In other words, the term "evil" (*rā'āh*), which has been repeatedly applied to the Ninevites, now characterizes the prophet. By objecting to the character and actions of God, Jonah as effectively put himself out of fellowship with God as the evil and ignorant heathen (cf. Rom. 2:1). But God showed him the same compassion as he had shown Nineveh.

Why was Jonah so angry? Rabbinic literature contains the idea, which is still very popular, that on the basis of Deuteronomy 18:21–22 he would be regarded as a false prophet. True enough, once the first wave of terror had passed and destruction did not come, many in Nineveh must have asked themselves whether Jonah had really been a messenger of the gods. That was an unavoidable result of divine mercy. But the attitude of the Ninevites and also incidents such as those recorded of David in 2 Samuel 12:14–23, of Ahab in 1 Kings 21:27–29, and of Hezekiah in 2 Kings 20:1–6 show that it was recognized universally that a pronouncement of divine punishment might be averted by suitable penitence. Jeremiah 18:1–11 is the formal statement of this. The fact is that, with minor but most important exceptions, prophecy is conditional. So even if this motive played a part in Jonah's thinking, it must have been a minor one; and it does not explain why he ran away. After all, he could simply have remained in Israel (see comment at 1:3).

2 Jonah told God exactly why he was angry. He objected to God's sparing Nineveh. Since nowhere else in Scripture do we have any trace of such hatred of the foreigner —despising him, yes, but not hating him—Jonah's motive could only stem from what Nineveh had meant in Israel's past and what he expected it to be in the future. (Compare the savage exultation over its fall in Nahum 2–3 and similar rejoicing over the Fall of Babylon [Isa 47] and of its king [Isa 14:4–20].)

"A gracious and compassionate God, slow to anger and abounding in love, a God who relents from sending calamity" is essentially a quotation of Exodus 34:6–7, which is a central expression of God's character in the OT. It is quoted in Numbers 14:18; Nehemiah 9:17; Psalms 86:15; 103:8; 145:8; Joel 2:13; and frequent reminiscences of it appear elsewhere. It also plays a major role in the worship of the synagogue. In the descriptive phrase "a gracious and compassionate God" (*'ēl ḥannûn weraḥûm*), the abbreviated form *'ēl* ("God") shows that we are dealing with a very early formulation of God's character, doubtless going back to the patriarchs. The word "gracious" is linked with *ḥēn* ("grace") and expresses God's attitude toward those who have no claim on him, since they are outside any and every covenant relationship.

Though the Hebrew term translated "compassionate" may originally have come from another root, in practice it came to be linked with *reḥem* ("the womb") and expressed the understanding and loving compassion of the mother to her child. Though no sexual connotation is involved, we have here the male and female aspects of understanding, compassion, and favor united in the one God. "Love" translates *ḥesed̠*, the word that expresses God's behavior in the covenant relationship. It is generally recognized that there is no one term in English that adequately expresses the wide and rich range of meaning of *ḥesed̠*. Certainly "kindness," "mercy," "loyalty," "loving kindness," and "unfailing love" (cf. TWOT, 1:305) contain elements that "love" alone does not express. What is clear is that Jonah was finding fault with God as he really is, not as he imagined him to be. This trait is more common among godly men than we sometimes realize. It explains why those who pride themselves on their loyalty to Scripture hold doctrines that stand in plain contradiction to the revealed character of God.

3 There can be little doubt that when Jonah asked God to take away his life, he was consciously echoing Elijah's words when he fled from Jezebel (1 Kings 19:4). If that is so, there is much more in what Jonah said than lies on the surface. He was virtually saying to God, "I have devoted my life to your service as your servant, as your prophet. But what I have experienced of you just does not make sense of the world order in which I find myself. Why should I go on living, for to leave your service would make my life purposeless. Once, in the past, you showed Elijah that there was a deeper purpose in life than he realized. Have you perhaps a similar message for me?"

4 "Are you right to be angry?" (JB) is preferable to "Have you any right to be angry?" God was not rebuking Jonah; God was not even asking him what right he, a man, had to criticize God. Rather he was suggesting to him that he might not be correct in his estimate of the position. Scripture has many examples—Job and Jeremiah being the most obvious—of men in agony who, as they tried to understand the ways of God, used language others might consider blasphemous (cf. Jer 15:15–18; 20:7–18). God shows his compassion with all such, Jonah not excepted.

Notes

2 חֶסֶד (*ḥeseḏ*, "love") is found 247 times in the OT, mainly in contexts involving God. In KJV it is translated by "mercy," "kindness," "loving kindness" and also by eight other words of similar meaning. Though in many cases the rendering expresses its meaning closely enough, none of these is adequate. *Ḥeseḏ* is a covenant word that expresses the behavior expected from those linked together in a covenant relationship. In a purely human relationship, "loyalty" is probably always adequate (cf. 2 Sam 3:8). When *ḥeseḏ* is applied to God, it does mean "mercy" and "love"; but it is always loyal love and covenanted mercy. There is much to be said for RSV's "steadfast love," but it is too wooden when used regularly. NEB was probably wise in reverting to a range of renderings, including "constant love."

4. *God's Rebuke of Jonah*

4:5–9

[5]Jonah went out and sat down at a place east of the city. There he made himself a shelter, sat in its shade and waited to see what would happen to the city. [6]Then the LORD God provided a vine and made it grow up over Jonah to give shade for his head to ease his discomfort, and Jonah was very happy about the vine. [7]But at dawn the next day God provided a worm, which chewed the vine so that it withered. [8]When the sun rose, God provided a scorching east wind, and the sun blazed on Jonah's head so that he grew faint. He wanted to die, and said, "It would be better for me to die than to live."

[9]But God said to Jonah, "Do you have a right to be angry about the vine?" "I do," he said. "I am angry enough to die."

5 The usual view is that Jonah, hoping against hope, was waiting to see whether God might not change his mind once again. Unless we are prepared to maintain that Jonah thought that Nineveh's repentance was merely superficial and transient—it probably did not last very long anyway, though there are signs that Assyria's extreme cruelty diminished—and therefore God might change his mind, any such concept is alien to the picture of the prophet we have been slowly building up. It is far more probable that Jonah was expecting something to happen that would explain God's ways with man a little more clearly to him.

6 In the rest of this section, the divine name Elohim ("God"), which has been used consistently for God's dealings with Nineveh, is now used for his dealings with Jonah. The use of "LORD God" (Yahweh Elohim) in this verse forms a link between the two usages, even as it does in Genesis 2:4b–3:24, linking the God of creation in Genesis 1 and the God of revelation in Genesis 4. Otherwise the reader or hearer might have been in danger of missing the subtle shift.

Even though Jerome's change of the traditional rendering of *qîqāyôn* from "gourd" to identify it with the castor oil plant caused a riot in Carthage when the Vulgate was introduced there, absolutely nothing depends on the word's botanical identification. The Palestinian Jewish tradition identified it with the castor oil plant (so JB). LXX, Syriac, and OL rendered it "gourd" (so KJV, Mof, NEB, RV). There is little to be said for "ivy" (so Knox, Vul.). It may well be that RSV was wise in its simple rendering of "plant," suggesting the castor oil plant in the margin. NIV's "vine" is also a safe rendering. Though not expressly stated, it is clear that the action Jonah took to "ease his discomfort" occurred in the hot season, when the mean daily maximum temperature in Mesopotamia is about 110 degrees Fahrenheit.

7 One of the characteristics of the Book of Jonah is its use of the verb *mānāh* ("to appoint," "to provide," "to prepare"). It is used of the fish (1:17), the vine (4:6), the worm (4:7), and the wind (4:8). This is not due to lack of stylistic ability but is intended to stress the divine initiative and sovereignty. This element is brought out in NIV by the consistent use of the verb "provided." The word *tola'at̲* ("worm") appears in a number of differing contexts, but in every case it implies something very small. It may well be that we should regard it here as a collective, but this is not necessary. God uses both the great fish and the insignificant worm equally as instruments of his purpose.

8 "A scorching east wind" is normally called a "sirocco," which means "east wind," though in various areas other terms are found. Dennis Baly (*The Geography of the Bible* [London: Lutterworth, 1957], pp. 67–68) describes it thus: "During the period of a sirocco the temperature rises steeply, sometimes even climbing during the night, and it remains high, about 16–22°F. above the average . . . at times every scrap of moisture seems to have been extracted from the air, so that one has the curious feeling that one's skin has been drawn much tighter than usual. Sirocco days are peculiarly trying to the temper and tend to make even the mildest people irritable and fretful and to snap at one another for apparently no reason at all." Obviously such a wind desiccates and withers all green growth (Isa 40:7).

When a sirocco comes, all who can, hasten to find shelter. But for Jonah there was no shelter, unless he was willing to reenter Nineveh. The booth he had made for himself (4:5) would not exclude the wind and only partially broke the force of the sun's rays. Completely dispirited he in essence said, "I would be better off dead than alive." Earlier he had wished to die, or said he did, because his activity as God's prophet seemed to have been emptied of all meaning. Now, when he had been robbed of all that seemed to make life worth living, he was speaking on the basis of common humanity.

9 As in v.4, it would be better to translate God's question by "Are you right to be angry about the vine?" and Jonah's answer by "I am." Modern Arabic usage suggests that we should understand the question as "Are you right to be grieved for the vine?" for the anger of pity is meant. Though "angry enough to die" seems to express the literal meaning of the Hebrew, we may question its accuracy. D. Winton Thomas ("The Superlative in Hebrew," p. 220) takes it, probably correctly, as a strong superlative, i.e., "exceedingly angry" (see note at 3:3).

Why was Jonah so angry, or why did he feel such grief for the vine? Many commentators, including Bewer, omit "shelter" (*sukkāh*) in v.5, thus making the *qîqāyôn* the only giver of shade that Jonah had. This would make the cause of Jonah's displeasure the fact that he had been deprived of his one bit of physical comfort. Such an interpretation overlooks that once the rains were over, anyone remaining out in the open overnight would normally build himself such a shelter or booth. In addition the sirocco is as vicious in Palestine as in Mesopotamia, and so its effects would come as no surprise to him.

God's answer in v.10 suggests that we take "Jonah was very happy about the vine" (v.6) to mean that sitting there in the burnt-up Tigris plain, shimmering in the heat, Jonah felt real joy in the sight of the fresh, green plant. True enough, it increased his comfort, but that was secondary. While there may seem to be comparatively little appreciation of the beauty of nature in the OT, there is sufficient to show that it was a real factor in Israelite life.

5. *God's Mercy*

4:10–11

> [10]But the LORD said, "You have been concerned about this vine, though you did not tend it or make it grow. It sprang up overnight and died overnight. [11]But Nineveh has more than a hundred and twenty thousand people who cannot tell their right hand from their left, and many cattle as well. Should I not be concerned about that great city?"

10 "You have been concerned . . . Should I not be concerned?" is an inadequate rendering, for it does not bring out the emotional connotation of *ḥûs*. It is remarkable that the same word is used for God's attitude and Jonah's, something that is missed by KJV and JB. Probably we should choose between "be sorry for" (NEB) and "pity" (RSV, RV).

One of the greatest dangers besetting men is that they should become such a part of their environment that they miss the pathos that pervades the universe. Paul described it as a "groaning as in the pains of childbirth" (Rom 8:22), which comes from the futility caused by its bondage to decay. The "Teacher" (*Qōheleṯ*) expressed it by "Utterly meaningless! Everything is meaningless" (Eccl 1:2). The Teacher was not, as is thought by so many, a cynic or a pessimist. He was moved to virtual despair by that element of transitoriness and lack of final achievement that seems to pervade all that a man does and experiences. This is seen in growing insensibility to beauty and pain in nature around them on the part of many who have allowed the natural world to dominate. On the other hand, a man can so immerse himself in things of the spirit, in philosophy, in the sciences and arts, in religion and theology, that he almost forgets that he has a body and becomes insensible to the pathos in the natural world as being outside the interests that dominate him. Jonah in the self-confidence of one who knew God's character (4:2) had apparently grown completely indifferent to the fate of God's creation outside Israel. We need hardly be surprised, for this attitude has been all too common within the church, and indeed within some small local churches. Even today we meet with the restricted outlook that called forth Jonathan Swift's scathing lines:

> We are God's chosen few,
> All others will be damned;
> There is no place in heaven for you,
> We can't have heaven crammed.

So God placed his prophet on the level of the ordinary man. The discomforts of the summer heat, the attractiveness of the vine, and the destructiveness and energy-sapping effects of the sirocco had nothing to do with Jonah's theology. He reacted to them as an ordinary man in the setting of nature.

So once again the narrative changes to Yahweh (the LORD). That which Jonah had learned as an ordinary man he was now to express in revelation and in theology. Once Jonah had realized his link with the rest of God's creation, God could declare the link between himself, the Creator, and his creation—not only man, made in the image and likeness of God, but also the animal creation.

11 The interpretation of "more than a hundred and twenty thousand people" is far from easy. The two main views are that it refers either to the whole population of Nineveh or to the small children, for the ability to tell the right hand from the left is seldom found in very early childhood. The former has been supported by archaeological considerations, because it has been estimated that the maximum population of Nineveh cannot have exceeded 175,000. Thus it is argued that if only children were intended, far too high a population would be involved. If, however, the great city of Nineveh was in fact "Greater Nineveh" in 3:2–3, it should be so here also. If we make it refer exclusively to young children, it could possibly be too large even for "Greater Nineveh." Since the more usual expression for the young child was one who did not know "enough to reject the wrong and choose the right" (Isa 7:16), we may well enlarge its scope to include all on whom a moral judgment could not well be passed. Against the view that the whole population is intended may be urged that Scripture nowhere suggests that separation from the community of Israel deprives men and women of all knowledge of right and wrong.

We do not find in Scripture the sentimentalism about animals found in many classes of society today. Yet the biblical position on animals is much sounder than that normally met among modern man, who assumes that his control of the animal world reflects his intrinsic superiority. God has subjected the animal creation to man (Gen 1:26, 28; Ps 8:6–8) because man, having been made in the image and likeness of God, is God's representative. A point often overlooked in the story of Noah's flood is that, theoretically at least, God could have arranged some other means for the preservation of animal life. Noah and his sons had to grasp their relationship with the rest of living beings by being the means of their preservation.

Even so, Jonah had to understand that the fulfillment of his wishes about Nineveh would have involved not only the destruction of innocent human beings but also of "many cattle as well" that had become especially dependent on man.

The curtain falls, and we are granted no answer to the question that all must surely ask, What, finally, did Jonah do or say? Indeed, unless we credit the highest degree of literary skill to the alleged postexilic writer, this sudden ending is one of the strongest arguments against the suggestion of a parabolic purpose; for it leaves entirely open what the application of the story is.

There is much to be said for the Jewish midrashic suggestion that "in that hour Jonah fell on his face and said, 'Govern your world according to the measure of mercy [in contrast to that of judgment], as it is said, To the Lord our God belong mercy and forgiveness' (Dan. 9:9)." This amounts to saying that Jonah thankfully welcomed the rule of divine mercy in the world, a rule he had formerly rejected so far as the enemies of Israel were concerned. But this does not answer the question as to what practical deductions and consequences should be drawn from it. If we suggest, however, that no further deductions have been made from it, we are probably not being unfair to Judaism.

In the light of the NT, many have read the missionary call into the Book of Jonah. We have already seen that the prophet had not tried to make the God of Israel known to Nineveh. Perhaps the feeling that he should have done so is responsible for the existence of "Jonah's tomb" on the site of ancient Nineveh. But those who know something of the fraudulent holy sites of the Bible lands do not take it seriously.

Not only did the story give no motivation for further missionary action by Jonah or the prophets who followed him (even in Ezekiel and Daniel we find no trace of it), but it probably raises as many questions as it answers. Why was Jonah sent only to Nineveh? Why in the fullness of time was not Jeremiah or Nahum sent there a century and a half later to save its being wiped off the face of the earth? Are we to deduce that men are given one chance and one alone? Though the divine warning came to Nebuchadnezzar through the dream interpreted by Daniel (Dan 4), why was there no prophetic call to Babylon to repent? For that matter, why did no one until much later, probably after 200 B.C., conceive of Israel's having a missionary task to the nations (cf. Matt 23:15)?

Quite simply, the book contains no call to action. It is, rather, a revelation of God's character and attitude toward his creation given to Jonah and through Jonah to Israel and to us. How we react to it is likely to depend largely on the position in which we find ourselves. There can be little doubt that for the godly in the northern kingdom, when inner corruption made any hope of resisting the remorseless pressure of Assyria a vain dream, the revelation of God's all-embracing love and pity must have brought a ray of hope; and the same must have been true in Judah in the dark days following the death of Josiah.

For the Christian, the Son of man's three days and three nights in the heart of the earth have assured him of a love that embraces all, even in the darkest hour. He knows that in Christ, God was reconciling the world to himself (2 Cor 5:18–19). He will then look with new eyes on those who have been thus reconciled, even though they know it not. Those whom God refuses to regard as his enemies the Christian cannot regard as enemies. This does not mean that the Christian is entitled to anticipate the final judgment. All he can do is insist that apart from Christ none can be or will be saved. The fact that God loves all men does not entitle the Christian to draw the illogical conclusion that all men will be saved. Over against Jonah we have to place the triumphal song of judgment in Nahum 2–3.

It would be perilous on the basis of Matthew 12:39–41 to try to draw too close an analogy between Jonah and Jesus. Yet there are certain striking similarities. There can be no doubt that John the Baptist moved Israel deeply, and the teaching and miracles of Jesus that followed must have caused what we would have called a revival of religion. But only in a few did it go deeply enough. So the day came when the King lamented over his city, "If you, even you, had only known on this day what would bring you peace—but now it is hidden from your eyes" (Luke 19:42). So a generation later temple and city were leveled to the ground, with no stone left on another, as a manifest sign of God's judgment. Nineveh's waiting time was longer, but it too was razed to the ground as a sign that God's love and forbearance do not defer judgment forever.

MICAH

Thomas Edward McComiskey

MICAH

Introduction

1. Background

Micah, like his great contemporaries Isaiah and Amos, prophesied during the eighth century B.C., a time when Israel and Judah had risen to heights of economic affluence but had fallen to depths of spiritual decadence. Under the able leadership of Jeroboam II of Israel (786–746) and Uzziah of Judah (783–742), the territories of both kingdoms became almost as extensive as they were during the reign of Solomon. It was a time of great economic prosperity, fostered, for a time, by the absence of international crises and by the mutual cooperation of both kingdoms. Excavations at the site of the ancient city of Samaria have yielded ivory inlays that attest to the accuracy of Amos's description of the luxurious life enjoyed by the prosperous citizens of this city (Amos 6:4).

While Israel and Judah appeared to be strong externally, an internal decay was sapping their strength and threatening to destroy the social fabric of these two kingdoms. A burgeoning wealthy class was becoming richer at the expense of the poorer classes. The prophets saw this as a violation of the covenantal requirements and thus a hindrance to God's blessing and a guarantee of the dissolution of the nation.

But the internal sickness of Israel involved more than social wrongs. Canaanite religion also had extended its influence among some of the people. And while Micah attacked the idolatry that accompanied the acceptance of Canaanite worship, it was not this aspect of Israel's condition that he emphasized most. It was rather the social injustices of the ruling classes to which Micah gave the greatest attention. (The extent of the intrusion of Canaanite influence at this time may be seen in the Samaria ostraca that contain many Hebrew names compounded with the name "Baal," a Canaanite fertility god.)

The halcyon days of peace were destined to come to an end, however, as Assyria arose from a state of quiescence to occupy a threatening posture on the national scene. Under Tiglath-pileser III (745–727), Assyria experienced a remarkable resurgence of power. At the same time Israel was being torn by internal strife and dissension. Finally, under the leadership of Shalmaneser V, Israel, the northern kingdom, was occupied; and several years later the city of Samaria fell to Sargon II (721).

In Judah, Ahaz's pro-Assyrian policies made Judah little more than a satellite of Assyria. Not till Hezekiah came to the throne (715) were sweeping religious—and most probably social—reforms instituted. Assyria continued to threaten Judah under Hezekiah's reign, but an attempt by Sennacherib to take Jerusalem was frustrated (2 Kings 19:32–36; 2 Chron 32:21; Isa 37:33–37). It was about a century after the death of Hezekiah that Jerusalem would finally fall to the Babylonians.

2. Unity

The unity of Micah was first questioned by Ewald in 1867, when he suggested that chapters 4 and 5 might have been written by someone other than Micah, possibly a contemporary of the prophet. And he suggested also that chapters 6 and 7 were written in the reign of Manasseh. In 1871, Oort alleged that Micah 4:1–7, 11–13 was inserted by a later prophet who was in disagreement with Micah's ideology.[1] Kuenen promptly challenged Oort's view and defended Micah's authorship of the disputed verses.[2]

The most seriously questioned chapters of Micah are 4 through 7. The literary-historical school, under the influence of Wellhausen, generally assigned portions of these chapters to post-Micah dates. Renaud and Robinson are more recent representatives of a similar approach.[3]

The form-critical approach, established by Gunkel, sought to establish the compass of each pericope and place it in its historical situation in the life of Israel (*Sitz im Leben*). Lindblom failed to find a literary coherence in the book but did affirm Micah's authorship of several pericopes, including portions of chapters 6 and 7.[4] Weiser revised the form-critical approach to Micah by assigning many of the pericopes to a cultic *Sitz im Leben*.[5] Supporting the latter, Kapelrud, like Weiser, nonetheless affirmed the authenticity of the eschatological sections of the book.[6]

A more recent discussion of the process of development of the book may be found in Mays (pp. 21–33).

Central to the problem of the unity of Micah is an alleged lack of coherence in the book, a factor that leads some to see certain portions as later insertions. This problem can be resolved only on exegetical grounds. It will be considered thoroughly in the commentary.

It seems difficult, however, to assign Micah 4:1–4, which is also found in Isaiah 2:2–4, to a date after Micah's time since it is rooted in the eighth-century tradition. The reference to Babylon in Micah 4:10 may well be a figure of speech for the world

---

[1]H. Oort, "Het Beth Efraat van Micha V:I," *Theologisch Tijdschrift* 5 (1871): 501–11.

[2]A. Kuenen, "De Koning uit Beth-Ephrath," *Theologisch Tijdschrift* 6 (1872): 45–66.

[3]B. Renaud, *Structure et Attaches littéraires de Michée IV–V* (Paris: J. Gabalda et Cie, 1964), pp. 82–88, 111; T.H. Robinson, *Die zwölf Kleinen Propheten* (Tübingen: J.C.B. Mohr, 1964), p. 127.

[4]J. Lindblom, *Micha literarisch untersucht* (Ǎbo: Ǎbo Akademi, 1929), pp. 6–9, 67, 124, 136, 149, 153.

[5]A. Weiser, *Das Buch der zwölf Kleinen Propheten* (Göttingen: Vandenhoeck & Ruprecht, 1963), pp. 236–89.

[6]A.S. Kapelrud, "Eschatology in the Book of Micah," VetTest 11 (1961):392–405.

powers. The predictive material in the immediate context is consonant with predictions in Isaiah 1–39.

Micah 4–5 is regarded by Mays (p. 26) as a complex consisting of independent oracles "assembled to form the counterpart of the prophecies of judgment in chaps. 1–3." For example, 5:2, 4, the promise of a king from Bethlehem, is regarded by Mays (p. 27) as "an independent unit, juxtaposed to 5:1 to fill out the pattern"; and he concludes (p. 113) that "5:1–4 is not an original unit of speech." It was probably added in "exilic times" (ibid.). This conclusion is based in part on the similar beginning of 5:1 with 4:8 (*wᵉ'attāh*), also considered late because it assumes the demise of Israel's king. The setting of 5:1 is the siege of Jerusalem by the Babylonians and is similar to Jeremiah's language and style. However, it is not certain that 4:8 assumes the loss of the realm of which Jerusalem was the capital. It is certain that it predicts a Deliverer-King. In this regard it is no different from Isaiah 9:6–7 [5–6 MT], which belongs to a generally undisputed portion of Isaiah (but cf. Mays, p. 113) and which predicts a future Davidic kingdom. The Davidic theology did not emerge full-blown in the eighth century. Its roots go back to 2 Samuel 7. Chapters 1–3 of Micah are generally considered to be authentic; yet there we can find statements of Jerusalem's demise (1:9, 12; 3:12) that do not demand the assumption that they were written later than the time of Micah. Also, comparisons of brief sayings with the language of other literary works is a tenuous procedure since it utilizes such a limited body of material.

Micah's charge in 6:1–8 and the theology of chapter 7 are quite in keeping with other eighth-century prophets.

The book exhibits an internal coherence in its basic structure. Three distinct sections may be discerned (1:1–2:13; 3:1–5:15; 6:1–7:20). Each begins with a summons to hear, followed by an oracle of doom, and ends with a statement of hope. While this strikingly symmetrical pattern may have come about as the speeches of Micah were arranged after his death, the inner coherence, the logical sequence of argument, and the general prophetic propensity for symmetrical arrangement of thought support the originality of the literary pattern.

The first oracle anticipates the Fall of Jerusalem and thus may have been written sometime before 721 B.C. The second oracle does not mention Samaria, an indication that it may have been written after the fall of that city. Jeremiah 26:18–19 places a portion of this oracle (3:12) in the time of Hezekiah (715–686 B.C.). If the oracles are regarded as independent literary units, the whole oracle may be placed sometime in the reign of Hezekiah. The third oracle is difficult to place chronologically. The social wrongs cited in the second oracle were also prevalent when the third was written. This may indicate that the second and third oracles were written in the same general period of time.

3. Authorship

The superscription to the prophecy (1:1) asserts the authorship of Micah. The prophet who bore that name was from Moresheth (probably Moresheth Gath) in Judah. This was a town in the general proximity of Isaiah's home, a factor that may explain certain similarities between the prophecies of both men. Little is known about Micah apart from what may be inferred from his prophecy. The book eloquently affirms his sensitivity to the social and religious wrongs of his time.

4. Date

The superscription (1:1) places Micah in the milieu of eighth-century prophetism. The reference to the destruction of Samaria (v.6) places the beginning of his prophetic career sometime before the capture of that city (722/721 B.C.); and this is in agreement with the superscription that fixes the beginning of his ministry in the reign of Jotham (750–731). The prophetic indictments of social and religious corruption fit well the time of Ahaz and could even be appropriate to the prereformation period of Hezekiah, who reigned 715–686 B.C. The reference to Micah's prophecy in Jeremiah 26:18–19 fixes at least a portion of Micah's message in the time of Hezekiah. There is no convincing reason for rejecting the period of time delineated in the superscription.

5. Literary Form

The Book of Micah, like most of the other prophetic writings, is written in the style of Hebrew poetry and is thus marked by a characteristic parallelism of expression. While his style does not attain to that of Isaiah, Micah's use of wordplays and contrast imparts a distinctive vividness to the book. As for the somewhat free form of the book, it need not indicate the hand of a later redactor; on the contrary, it may reflect the author's purpose to use a variety of literary devices to stir in the reader's mind emotions in accord with the message of the oracles.

6. Theological Values

Crystallizing the theology of the OT prophets is a difficult task, since they did not set out to write systematic theologies of eighth-century prophetic thought. Micah's prophecy, for example, is a collection of sermons that came about as a result of his deep emotional involvement in his nation's desperate plight. In Micah's case we have a collection of oracles that, in themselves, do not appear to present a consistent, unified development of theological themes. As a matter of fact, the prophet appears to jump from one theme to another, often without apparent connection (2:6–11; cf. 12–13; 3:5–8; cf. 9–12). While Micah may not have written a theology, he certainly based his pleas to the people on a consistent theology of God. The desultory nature of the oracles help us understand Micah's concept of God. Each appeal to the nature of God and each application of the word of God by Micah to his people give us greater insight into the theology that lies at his heart, which he made known in colorful phraseology, urgent pleas, and formal oracles.

The first theological emphasis we meet in the Book of Micah is the sovereignty of God (1:2). The Lord was no mere tribal deity to Micah but acted within the sphere of the nations to effect their destiny as well as the destiny of his own people. The divine intervention of God in history was not limited only to the Eschaton by Micah, for he understood the destruction of Samaria and Jerusalem to be the result of the Lord's punishing these centers of wickedness for their rebellion against him. However, it will be in the Eschaton that God's activity regarding the nations will reach its climax. Then the ultimate triumph and vindication of God's people will take place (4:11–13), and the nations will become subject to the rule of the Lord.

Another theological emphasis of Micah is the self-consistency of the Lord. He is immutably committed to his covenantal obligations. It is this theme, coupled with that of divine sovereignty, that gives such urgency to Micah's words. The Lord's consistency with the revelation of his will in the Mosaic covenant is not set forth in absolute terms by Micah but is seen in the Lord's condemnation of idolatry (1:5–7) and the social crimes of Micah's day (2:2; 3:1–3; 9–12; 6:8), an important aspect of the covenant (Exod 20:3–6; 23:1–9; et al.). While the word "covenant" (*b^e^rîṯ*) is not mentioned by Micah, the terms of the covenant ratified at Sinai are unmistakably present.

That God seems austere and unbending is only a partial picture of his self-consistency. He is consistent also with his nature, and that nature is to forgive. We must not forget the statement of 7:18–20, which is at once a theological statement and a heartfelt response. God will not give up his people altogether; he will forgive the sins of the believing remnant.

Micah's doctrine of the remnant is unique among the Prophets and is perhaps his most significant contribution to the prophetic theology of hope. The remnant is a force in the world, not simply a residue of people, as the word "remnant" (*š^e^'ērîṯ*) may seem to imply. It is a force that will ultimately conquer the world (4:11–13). This triumph, while presented in apparently militaristic terminology (4:13; 5:5–6), is actually accomplished by other than physical force. By removing everything that robs his people of complete trust in him (5:10–15), the Ruler from Bethlehem will effect the deliverance of his people. The source of power for God's people in the world is their absolute trust in him and his resources.

The messianic King in Micah is not a redemptive figure as is Isaiah's Servant. We are not told by Micah how God can be consistent with his law and at the same time be consistent with his forgiving nature. The basis of the divine redemptive activity lies within the nature of God according to Micah. We must look to Isaiah (53:4–6) to see that these dual aspects of the divine nature meet in the vicarious suffering of the Servant. The absence of a vicarious role in the redemptive work of the messianic King in Micah underscores the prophet's theological perspective, which is to assure us of the future exaltation and glory of the remnant; and this is done against the background of the humiliation the nation would soon endure. We may state this aspect of Micah's theology thus: The nation will suffer the shame of defeat and exile. But that is not the end, for certain triumph and glory lay ahead, not for the whole nation, but only for the remnant. The people of God will be delivered from affliction and exile by their King and will return with him, secure in his power. Thus Micah's focus is on the kingdom of the Lord and its manifestation in the world.

The kingdom is an expression of divine power and sovereignty within the sphere of the nations according to Micah. The messianic King is depicted in close association with the Lord and embodies his might and authority. The work of the messianic King is presented by Micah almost entirely in terms of power. Even the tender act of caring for his own as a shepherd cares for his sheep is done in the strength of the Lord (5:4).

Micah spoke to a people whose disobedience had led them to ignominy and ruin. But he reminded them—and us—that the Lord is almighty; and, because he is consistent with his word and with his nature, the people of God will not fail to receive all he has promised them. Though we suffer shame now, there is glory and vindication ahead because the Lord will "be true to Jacob, and show mercy to Abraham" (7:20).

7. Bibliography

Books

Allen, L.C. *The Books of Joel, Obadiah, Jonah and Micah*. In the New International Commentary on the Old Testament. Grand Rapids: Eerdmans, 1976.
Hailey, H. *A Commentary on the Minor Prophets*. Grand Rapids: Baker, 1972.
Hillers, Delbert R., *Micah*. Philadelphia: Fortress, 1984.
Keil, C.F. *The Twelve Minor Prophets*. KD. Vol. 1. Grand Rapids: Eerdmans, 1949.
Mays, J. *Micah: A Commentary*. Philadelphia: Westminster, 1976.
Orelli, C. von. *The Twelve Minor Prophets*. Translated by J.S. Banks. Edinburgh: T. & T. Clark, 1897.
Smith, J.M.P. *A Critical and Exegetical Commentary on Micah*. New York: Charles Scribner's Sons, 1911.
Wolfe, R.E., and Bosley, H.A. "The Book of Micah." In *The Interpreter's Bible*. Vol. 6. Edited by George A. Buttrick. New York: Abingdon, 1956.
Wolff, H.W. *Micah the Prophet*. Translated by R.D. Gehrke. Philadelphia: Fortress, 1981.

Periodicals

Collen, M. "Recherches Sur L'histoire Textuelle du Prophet Michee." *Vetus Testamentum* 21 (1971): 281–97.
Crenshaw, J.L. "Wedōrēk ‘al-bamote ’āres." *Catholic Biblical Quarterly* 34 (1972): 39–53.
Jeppesen, K. "How the Book of Micah Lost its Integrity." *Studia Theologica* 33 (1979): 101–37.
Willis, J.T. "On the Text of Micah 2, 1a." *Biblica* 48 (1967): 534–41.
______. "Micah IV 14–V 5—a unit." *Vetus Testamentum* 18 (1968): 50–54.
______. "Some Suggestions on the Interpretation of Micah I 2." *Vetus Testamentum* 18 (1968): 372–79.

8. Outline

I. The Superscription (1:1)

II. The First Oracle: Israel's Impending Judgment and Her Future Restoration (1:2–2:13)
   A. The Impending Judgment (1:2–7)
   B. The Prophet's Reaction to the Pronouncement of Judgment (1:8–9a)
   C. The Prophet's Warning and Summons to the People (1:9b–16)
   D. The Prophet's Indictment of the Oppressing Classes (2:1–5)
   E. The True Prophet Versus the False Prophets (2:6–11)
   F. The Prophet's Statement of Hope (2:12–13)

III. The Second Oracle: The Prophet's Indictment of the Leaders of the House of Israel and Israel's Future Hope (3:1–5:15)
   A. The Prophet's Indictment of the Rulers of Israel (3:1–4)
   B. The Prophet's Indictment of the Religious Leaders of Israel (3:5–8)
   C. The Result of the Leaders' Corruption on the Nation (3:9–12)
   D. The Future Exaltation of Zion (4:1–8)
   E. The Future Might of Zion (4:9–13)
   F. The Future King of Zion (5:1–4)
   G. The Future Peace of Zion (5:5–6)
   H. The Future Vindication of Zion (5:7–9)
   I. The Future Purification of Zion (5:10–15)

IV. The Third Oracle: God's Lawsuit With Israel and the Ultimate Triumph of the Kingdom of God (6:1–7:20)
   A. God's Accusations Against His People (6:1–8)
   B. The Sentence of Judgment (6:9–16)
   C. The Prophet's Lament of the Lack of Godly Fellowship (7:1–2)
   D. The Prophet's Lament of the Corruption in His Society (7:3–6)
   E. The Godly Man's Attitude in the Midst of Discouragement (7:7–10)
   F. The Assurance of Victory for the Kingdom of God (7:11–20)
      1. Victory described in terms of the extension of the kingdom (7:11–13)
      2. Victory assured because of God's leadership (7:14–15)
      3. Victory assured over the nations (7:16–17)
      4. Victory assured because of God's nature (7:18–20)

Text and Exposition

I. The Superscription

1:1

[1]The word of the LORD that came to Micah of Moresheth during the reigns of Jotham, Ahaz and Hezekiah, kings of Judah—the vision he saw concering Samaria and Jerusalem.

1 According to the superscription, the prophetic activity of Micah spanned the reigns of three kings of Judah in the eighth century B.C. This period was one of great spiritual declension especially for the northern kingdom; and the messages of Micah and the other eighth-century prophets, with their emphases on social justice and obedience to the obligations of the Mosaic covenant, were like a refreshing breeze in the arid climate of spiritual ignorance and disobedience.

Many scholars hold that the superscription may not have been written by Micah but may rather have been appended to the prophecy by a later editor. It is quite possible, however, that it was affixed by Micah, or another responsible person, when Micah's prophecies were arranged in final written form. Similar superscriptions preface the works of other prophets (e.g., Isaiah, Hosea, Amos, and Zephaniah). The fact that these superscriptions are not rigid formulas may reflect the individuality of the various prophets involved. At any rate, if the superscriptions were appended by later editors, they may have been affixed at a very early time. The superscription to Isaiah, for example, is reflected in 2 Chronicles 32:32.

The prophecy of Micah was directed primarily toward Samaria and Jerusalem, the capital cities of the northern and southern kingdoms (Israel and Judah). While Micah's message was applicable to all the inhabitants of these kingdoms, he singled out the capitals because the leaders of these centers of influence were largely responsible for the social ills of that time (1:5–7; 3:9–12). In particular he singled out Jerusalem, not only because of the corruption of its leaders, but also because of its future glory—a central motif in the prophetic theology of hope.

II. The First Oracle: Israel's Impending Judgment and Her Future Restoration (1:2–2:13)

A. *The Impending Judgment*

1:2–7

[2]Hear, O peoples, all of you,
listen, O earth and all who are in it,
that the Sovereign LORD may witness against you,
the Lord from his holy temple.

[3]Look! The LORD is coming from his dwelling place;
he comes down and treads the high places of the earth.
[4]The mountains melt beneath him
and the valleys split apart,
like wax before the fire,
like water rushing down a slope.

5All this is because of Jacob's transgression,
  because of the sins of the house of Israel.
What is Jacob's transgression?
  Is it not Samaria?
What is Judah's high place?
  Is it not Jerusalem?

6"Therefore I will make Samaria a heap of rubble,
  a place for planting vineyards.
I will pour her stones into the valley
  and lay bare her foundations.
7All her idols will be broken to pieces;
  all her temple gifts will be burned with fire;
  I will destroy all her images.
Since she gathered her gifts from the wages of prostitutes,
  as the wages of prostitutes they will again be used."

2 The opening statement of the prophecy consists of a summons to the nations to attend to the cosmic judgment scene so vividly described by the prophet in the subsequent verses. That the summons is directed to the nations and not to Israel and Judah is clear from the parallel expression "earth and all who are in it."

In this anthropomorphic representation, Micah pictured God as coming from his dwelling place to witness against the nations. This witness was effected in the cataclysmic destruction of the cities of Samaria (1:6) and Jerusalem (1:5; 3:12). Thus there was in the destruction of these cities a didactic element that related directly to the future of the nations of the world.

Micah, like Isaiah, saw the destiny of the nations as integrally related to the destiny of God's people. He deftly developed this theme throughout the prophecy. In 4:11–13 he stated that the nations, while looking with pleasure on the misfortune of God's people, were blind to the fact that this suffering was the precursor to their own disaster. In 7:8–10 he affirmed that though God's people would be punished for their sin, they had a God who forgives sin. The nations that do not know God will not know deliverance from his judgment.

The phrase "witness against" seems to be used here in the same sense as in Deuteronomy 31:19–21, 26, where the Song of Moses and the Book of the Law were to function as witnesses against the people. This ongoing witness served as a reminder of future punishment should the terms of the covenant to which they witnessed be violated. It is in this sense that God's judgment of his own people was to be a witness against the nations. It is a guarantee that they will ultimately be judged for their sin; for if God does not fail to judge his own, he will certainly judge those who do not belong to him.

The burning timbers and ruined houses of Samaria and Jerusalem would be an eloquent sermon to the people of the world. From this destruction they were to learn that God does not allow sin to go unpunished—even in the case of his own people. As the Song of Moses and the Book of the Law had testified of the sin of the Israelites and had pledged future punishment for it, so God's destruction of Samaria and Jerusalem was to be a witness against the nations in that it would demonstrate God's hatred of sin and be the harbinger of their own eventual destruction.

3–4 The act by which God witnessed against the nations is depicted in a vivid anthropomorphic scene (vv.3–4) in which God comes forth from heaven to tread the high places of the earth and to bring about the destruction of Samaria and Jerusalem (1:6; 3:12). In this metaphorical representation, the prophet asserted one of the most basic concepts of OT theology—viz., that God is not only transcendent above the world but immanent in it, and that he intervenes in history to effect his will.

The term "high places" (*bāmôṯ*) (v.3) connotes several concepts. Aside from the basic meaning of "height" or "summit," it was used of pagan religious sanctuaries (Jer 7:31; Ezek 20:29), the place of security and protection (Deut 32:13; Hab 3:19), and the place of military advantage with its companion idea that the one who possessed the heights of the enemy's territory had brought the enemy into subjection (Deut 33:29; Ezek 36:2).

Whether Micah intended "high places" to be understood as the heights of the earth or the pagan shrines of the land is difficult to determine. The cosmic scope of this context and the reference to mountains in v.4 seem to favor the former; yet he did predict the destruction of the centers of idol worship as represented by Samaria and Jerusalem (1:5–7). It seems best, therefore, to see a double reference in this phrase in which Micah envisioned God as the majestic Sovereign who steps from heaven into the course of human events. Samaria and Jerusalem cannot stand before the might and power of the Conqueror who strides across the heights of the earth and before whom the pagan sanctuaries crumble as the mountains melt. The motif of double reference is not uncommon in the prophecy of Micah (cf. vv.10–16).

The cataclysm that accompanied God's intervention in history is described in terms of a violent storm or earthquake (v.4). The language is metaphorical and describes the intensity of the destruction of Samaria and Jerusalem.

5 With telling force the prophet asserted that the national upheaval would be caused by the sins of the people of Israel. Verse 5 is built on the structure of two couplets, each with parallel stichs. The reader is led to expect the words "transgression" and "sins" of the first couplet to be repeated in the second. In these rhetorical questions, however, only the word "transgression" is repeated; and the second question in the Hebrew is "What are the high places [*bāmôṯ*] of Judah?" Many scholars emend the text on the basis of the LXX to read "sins" in the second stich in keeping with the parallelism of the first couplet. But the most difficult reading should be seriously considered. Also we should remember that the prophets did not use a poetic style that was slavishly regular.

The word "transgression" in the first question assumes a previous referent and points back to the occurrence of that word in the first couplet. So too the second rhetorical question demands a previous referent because these questions clarify and lend continuity to the argument. Instead of utilizing the word the reader expects, the text departs from the usual parallel structure and repeats the word *bāmôṯ* ("high places") used in v.3, giving to the term a specific connotation of idolatry. This lends support to the view that a double reference obtains in the use of this word in v.2. The rules governing parallelism are not, however, really broken by the writer; for *bāmôṯ* is a suitable word for use in parallelism with "transgression" because it occurs in apposition with "sin" (*ḥaṭṭā'ṯ*) in Hosea 10:8.

This dramatic departure from the strict literary norm has the effect of identifying Samaria and Jerusalem as the chief objects of God's destructive activity described in v.3. Also, the close association between "high places" and "sin" in the mind of the prophet makes it clear that to him the incursion of non-Yahwist religious practices was at the heart of the crisis of the house of Israel. Because of the influence of

Canaanite religion, Israel was giving only lip service to Yahweh; and the ethical demands of the law, with their resultant benign effect on the social structure of the nation, were being disregarded. This was the sin that led to estrangement from God and eventual captivity.

Literally the Hebrew says, "*Who* is Jacob's transgression?" The prophet personified the cites of Samaria and Jerusalem, possibly because he wished to depict them as harlots, as he does in the subsequent context, or because the Hebrew word *mî* ("who") was used when the writer had persons in mind (cf. Notes).

6–7 Samaria was to become a ruin, a place with vineyards planted on her sloping sides amid the stones of her ruined buildings. The expression "lay bare her foundations" (v.6) may echo the use of the word *gālāh* ("lay bare") for uncovering one's nakedness (Lev 20:11, 17–18, 20–21), a term used in the OT of prostitution (Ezek 16:36; 23:18) and lewdness (2 Sam 6:20; Hos 2:10). The imagery of the harlot appears in v.7 where the wages Samaria received from the practice of prostitution would be burned. The prostitution referred to is idolatry, which the OT consistently regards as spiritual fornication (Exod 34:15; Judg 2:17; Ezek 23:30; et al.).

The word translated "temple gifts" (*'eṯnannêyāh*) (v.7) seems out of place in a sequence describing the destruction of idols and may reflect a Semitic root meaning "resemble"; hence it may refer to an image or idol (cf. Notes). But the same word in Hebrew also connotes payment to a harlot, and Micah used it in that sense in the latter part of this verse. This may be another example of Micah's use of the pun, by which in this case he deftly identified the idolatry of Samaria as spiritual harlotry.

The wealth that accrued to Samaria from her idolatry would be taken away from her to be used again for the wages of prostitution—i.e., the invading Assyrians would transfer the wealth of Samaria to their own temples where it would again be used for idolatrous worship.

Notes

---

2 The major difficulty inherent in the interpretation of the phrase עֵד בְּ (*'ēḏ b^e^*, "witness against") is that the burden of the prophecy is directed against Israel and Judah and not the nations (1:5–7; 3:12). It is difficult to see how the prophecy may be a witness against the nations when God proceeded to condemn his people alone. Aside from explanations that posit the influence of a redactor or that advocate transposition or deletion of verses, the difficulty is sometimes met by translating the preposition בְּ (*b^e^*) in a locative sense, i.e., "witness among." For a full survey of the interpretation of the preposition, see Willis, "Suggestions on Micah I 2," pp. 372–79. It is suggested that the LXX so understands the expression *ἔσται κύριος ἐν ὑμῖν εἰς μαρτύριον* (*estai kyrios en hymin eis martyrion*, "the Lord is among you for a witness"). The Greek phrase is used in the LXX, however, to translate the Hebrew expression in instances where it seems clearly to mean "witness against" (Jer 49:5); and Ignatius used the same Greek phrase to mean "witness against" (Willis, "Interpretation of Micah I 2," p. 376). That *'ēḏ b^e^* means "witness against" in many cases in the Hebrew is particularly clear from Jer 49:5 and Deut 31:26, where the Hebrew word order is identical with that of Mic 1:2.

The translation "witness among" would make the nations simply the sphere of God's judgmental activity and would curtail any directly didactic element in it as far as the nations are concerned. Micah clearly asserted, however, that God's devastation of Samaria and

Jerusalem had a direct bearing on the destiny of the nations; for the destruction of these cities was part of a plan that involved the ultimate subjugation of the nations (4:11–13; 7:3–10).

3 John Gray's suggestion (*The Legacy of Canaan: The Ras Shamra Texts and Their Relevance to the Old Testament,* Supplements to VetTest, vol. 5 [Leiden: E.J. Brill, 1965], p. 189) that בָּמוֹת (*bāmôṯ,* "high places") in Deut 33:29 should be translated "backs" in keeping with its meaning in Ugaritic deserves consideration. Deut 33:29 would then indicate that Israel would tread on the backs of her enemies, and *bāmôṯ* would not in that case connote the heights of the enemy territory.

5 The word פֶּשַׁע (*peša',* "transgression"), like many Hebrew words of theological significance, was used in a secular sense as well. (See its use of the rebellion of Israel in 1 Kings 12:19 and the rebellion of Moab in 2 Kings 3:7.) In an ethical sense it may connote rebellion against God. The word חַטָּאת (*ḥaṭṭā'ṯ*) comes from a root that means basically "to miss." It was used of warriors adept at using the sling (Judg 20:16). Ethically it pictures sin as failure to meet God's standards. Both words cover the positive and negative aspects of sin.

The suggestion that the reading בָּמוֹת (*bāmôṯ,* "high places") be retained because precise verbal parallelism is unnecessary to prophetic speech is supported by the fact that while "Israel" is the poetic complement to "Jacob" in line 1, the poetic complement to "Jacob" in line 3 is "Judah" in line 5.

For a full discussion of the use of מִי (*mî,* "who") when the writer had persons in mind, see GKC, par. 137.

7 The Arabic root *tnn* means "to resemble" and hence may witness to a Semitic root meaning "image" (B. Halper, "The Root TNN," AJSL 24 [1907–8]: 366–69).

B. *The Prophet's Reaction to the Pronouncement of Judgment*

1:8–9a

8Because of this I will weep and wail;
 I will go about barefoot and naked.
I will howl like a jackal
 and moan like an owl.
9For her wound is incurable;
 it has come to Judah.

8–9 The prophet next lamented the destruction of the great metropolis of Samaria by representing himself as wailing and going about unclothed as a sign of mourning (v.8; cf. 2 Sam 15:30). The judgment to come on Samaria was like an incurable wound; i.e., it was irreversible (v.9). But in its malignant course it had come to Jerusalem as well.

C. *The Prophet's Warning and Summons to the People*

1:9b–16

It has reached the very gate of my people,
 even to Jerusalem itself.
10Tell it not in Gath;
 weep not at all.
In Beth Ophrah
 roll in the dust.
11Pass on in nakedness and shame,
 you who live in Shaphir.
Those who live in Zaanan
 will not come out.

Beth Ezel is in mourning;
its protection is taken from you.
12Those who live in Maroth writhe in pain,
waiting for relief,
because disaster has come from the LORD,
even to the gate of Jerusalem.
13You who live in Lachish,
harness the team to the chariot.
You were the beginning of sin
to the Daughter of Zion,
for the transgressions of Israel
were found in you.
14Therefore you will give parting gifts
to Moresheth Gath.
The town of Aczib will prove deceptive
to the kings of Israel.
15I will bring a conqueror against you
who live in Mareshah.
He who is the glory of Israel
will come to Adullam.
16Shave your heads in mourning
for the children in whom you delight;
make yourselves as bald as the vulture,
for they will go from you into exile.

10 Micah intensified the prediction of Samaria's desperate plight in a poem in which his masterly use of the pun is again evident. The play on words begins in v.10 with Gath (*gaṯ*) which is somewhat similar in sound to the Hebrew word "tell" (*nāgaḏ*). The Hebrew of the second clause reads "do not weep at all." It is tempting to read "do not weep in Acco" (NIV mg.), for the word "weep" in Hebrew is similar in formation to "in Acco"; but this requires assuming the dropping or elision of the ayin (ʿ). The "dropping" is speculative and the "elision" unattested in this way. If "in Acco" is accepted, this would be the only line in which two towns are introduced in such narrow compass; and the Hebrew makes good sense as it stands. Since these towns appear to be clustered in the Shephelah (Y. Aharoni, *The Land of the Bible* [Philadelphia: Westminster, 1967], p. 339), the inclusion of Acco would also be geographically anomalous.

The phrase "Tell it not in Gath" is reflective of David's lament at Saul's death (2 Sam 1:20). It warns the people not to weep lest the inhabitants of Gath, a Philistine city, learn of their impending destruction. In Beth Ophrah ("house of dust") the inhabitants are to roll in the dust as a sign of mourning (Josh 7:6; Job 16:15; Isa 47:1).

11–12 The people of Shaphir ("beautiful," "fair," "pleasant") are to experience something quite the opposite of what the name of their town means; they are to be reduced to shame and dishonor. Those who live in Zaanan ("come out") will not be able to come out from their city. Beth Ezel (*bêṯ hā'ēṣel*) is unknown to us. The word *'ēṣel* means "beside," "contiguous to" (BDB, s.v.). It is difficult to be certain of what Micah intended in this wordplay, but it is likely that we have a clue in *'emdāṯô* ("standing place"). We may paraphrase the name Beth Ezel as "nearby house." Perhaps the town was in close proximity to Jerusalem. That its "standing place" was to be taken away may indicate that this town that stood nearby would cease to exist. Thus a buffer ("standing place") between Jerusalem and the invading armies would be removed. The wailing would signify the destruction of the town as its citizens mourn their fate. In the MT "Beth Ezel" is followed by the causative particle *kî*. The reason Beth Ezel will do this is "because" Maroth ("bitter") will also endure God's punishment (v. 12). The causal particle is again used. All this is because God will punish his people, including Jerusalem.

13–14 The inhabitants of Lachish (v. 13) are to harness the team to the chariot. Assonance is achieved by pairing Lachish with *reḵeš* ("steed"; NIV, "team"). The citizens of Lachish are to flee the coming destruction like steeds.

The significance of Moresheth is difficult to determine. Its name is somewhat similar in sound to *mᵉʾōrāśāh* ("betrothed") and, since "parting gifts" were given to brides as dowries (1 Kings 9:16), it is possible that it was intended to connote that the town of Moresheth Gath was soon to be parted from Judah as a bride parts from her family.

Aczib ("deception") will prove to be a deception (*ʾaḵzāḇ*) to Judah. The word is used of a stream that has dried up (Jer 15:18); so this city will cease to exist.

15–16 The name Mareshah (v. 15) is somewhat similar to noun forms based on the root *yāraš* ("to possess"). The wordplay is achieved by pairing this name with *yōrēš* (a participial form of *yāraš*), which occurs in the first part of the clause. The word *yōrēš* denotes a possessor or conqueror (Jer 8:10). Thus this town whose name might have engendered associations with the word "conqueror" would be conquered. The glory of Israel, i.e., the people (cf. Hos 9:11–13), will be forced to flee as David did to Adullam. This thought continues in v. 16, where the people are to mourn because of the depopulation of the country.

This section (vv. 10–16) begins with words that recall David's lament at the death of Saul and ends with the name of the cave where David hid from Saul. These dark moments in David's life form a gloomy backdrop to the description of the fall of the towns Micah spoke of. Though he is never directly mentioned, the figure of David appears hauntingly in the tapestry of destruction—not a David standing tall in triumph, but a David bowed down by humiliation. It is as if Micah saw in the fall of each town and the eventual captivity of the two kingdoms the final dissolution of the Davidic monarchy. Like David, the glory of Israel would come to Adullam.

Notes

---

10 Note the similarity of the consonantal sounds in אַל תַּגִּידוּ (*ʾal taggîḏû*, "Tell it not") to גַּת (*gaṯ*, "Gath").

11 The name Zaanan is somewhat similar in sound to the word יָצָא (*yāṣāʾ*, "come out").

D. *The Prophet's Indictment of the Oppressing Classes*

2:1–5

[1]Woe to those who plan iniquity,
  to those who plot evil on their beds!

At morning's light they carry it out
  because it is in their power to do it.
2They covet fields and seize them,
  and houses, and take them.
They defraud a man of his home,
  a fellowman of his inheritance.

3Therefore, the LORD says:

"I am planning disaster against this people,
  from which you cannot save yourselves.
You will no longer walk proudly,
  for it will be a time of calamity.
4In that day men will ridicule you;
  they will taunt you with this mournful song:
'We are utterly ruined;
  my people's possession is divided up.
He takes it from me!
  He assigns our fields to traitors.' "

5Therefore you will have no one in the assembly
    of the LORD
  to divide the land by lot.

1–2 The oracle continues with a denunciation of the corrupt practices of the affluent and influential classes whose hold on the structure of society was so strong in Micah's day. The oracle as a whole reflects a distinct pattern. There is the summons to hear (1:2) (an element in each of the oracles), the announcement of doom (1:3–7), the prophet's reaction to the announcement (1:8–9), the warning summons (1:10–16), and the basis for the judgment culminating in the statement of hope (2:1–13).

It is in 2:1–5 that the prophet establishes the basis for the national crisis and the future collapse of the nation. It was not the imperialism of Assyria or the fortunes of blind destiny that brought the house of Israel to this critical stage. It was her disobedience to her God. How different is the prophetic view of history from that of the secular mind! The prophets frequently recalled the terms of the Mosaic covenant that promised blessing for the people should they respond ethically to the terms of the covenant and cursing if they should not (Deut 29–32). The covenant demanded that God's people show social concern (Exod 22:26; 23:4–9). Failure to do so would not only weaken the nation by affecting the social fabric but, even more important, would seriously affect the nation's relationship to God. It would mean that the people had taken themselves away from the ground of the covenant that was the vehicle for national blessing.

The events of the eighth century had produced two main classes of people: a burgeoning affluent group and a poor class that suffered at the hands of the rich. Micah turned to the powerful ruling classes and vividly pictured the intensity with which they sought to defraud the poor and become richer at the expense of the less fortunate. He pictured them lying awake at night devising (*ḥāšaḇ*) their plans (v.1). At first light of day, they proceeded to put their schemes into action. They could do this because "it [was] in their power." They controlled the structure of society and had a free hand to perpetrate their deeds with impunity (cf. 7:3). They coveted the houses and lands of those who could not adequately defend themselves in this oppressive society (v.2).

3 Micah referred to the nation as a "people" (*mišpāḥāh*; KJV, RSV, "family"). Amos (3:1) used the same expression to refer to the whole nation (Israel and Judah). Verse 3 begins with the word "therefore" (*lāḵēn*), thus establishing the preceding catalog of wrongs as the basis for the disaster that Micah predicted in this verse. He pictured the disaster as a burden from which the people would be unable "to remove their necks" (Heb.) The Hebrew word (*mûš*) that Micah used here means "to remove" (NIV, "save"). He saw the Captivity as certain (1:9), and they would not be able to avoid it. The prospect of the Captivity was like a galling yoke or a heavy burden from which they could not remove their necks. Because of the national humiliation, they would be unable to hold their heads high among the nations.

4 This verse contains a lament song that is characteristic of the way the people would mourn the desolation of the land. The clauses that precede the lament are governed by verbs in the impersonal third person singular. The first verbal clause (*yiśśā' ʿalêḵem māšāl*) may be translated "one will take up a *māšāl* ("a lament song," "a proverbial song") or a *māšāl* will be taken up" (NIV, "men will ridicule you"). The preposition *ʿal* may be understood in the sense of "concerning," and the whole phrase may be taken as introducing the lament song recorded in this verse. Because it is entirely in the first person, the lament song is clearly uttered by the house of Israel itself and not by someone else.

The word *māšāl* is used of figurative prophetic accounts (e.g., Isa 14:4). In general, however, it is a "descriptive saying," "byword," or "proverb" that has popular appeal or significance.

The second clause ("they will taunt you with this mournful song") is a remarkable example of alliteration in the Hebrew (*wenāhāh nehî nihyāh*). Again the verb (*nāhāh*) is in the impersonal third person singular and can hardly refer to an enemy of Israel, for it means "to lament." Literally the clause reads "one will lament with great lamentation." Then follows a third verb (*'āmar*, "saying"; untr. in NIV) in the impersonal third person.

The lamentation concerns the fact that the land allotted (*ḥēleq*) to the people had changed hands (*mûr*). The land that had been Israel's exclusive possession had become the property of her enemies. This is amplified in the next phrase, where God is pictured as reassigning the land. The land was to be assigned to "traitors" or, better, "to a rebel." The singular substantive *šôḇēḇ* may be a collective for the people of the enemy who would occupy the land or may refer to the Assyrian king himself. At any rate, Micah described the enemy as a rebel. This is not out of keeping with Micah's view of the nations in their relationship to God; for Micah described them as "nations that have not obeyed" (5:15), thus imputing to them a rebellious nature.

5 As a result of the calamity, there would be "none to cast the line by lot in the assembly of the LORD" (RSV). This reference would bring to mind the method by which Joshua apportioned the land to the tribes (Josh 14:1–5). The word "assembly" (*qāhāl*) may mean a "multitude" in general; but when used with an adjunctive word (in this case "LORD"), the phrase containing it takes on distinct limitations. It connotes the assembly of people that is distinctly the Lord's, i.e., the covenantal community (Deut 23). Because of their blatant disregard for the obligations of the covenant, the oppressors had removed themselves from any inheritance in the congregation. The prophet was saying that the corrupt people of his day would have no further participation in the covenant community.

Notes

4 For a discussion of the impersonal third person, see A.B. Davidson, *Hebrew Syntax* (Edinburgh: T. & T. Clark, 1901), pp. 153–55.

Many scholars understand the preposition עַל (*'al*) to mean "against" in the expression יִשָּׂא עֲלֵיכֶם מָשָׁל (*yiśśā' 'ᵃlêkem māšāl*, "take up a proverb") and hence see the phrase as indicating that Israel is to be taunted by others in her misfortune. This interpretation presents some difficulty in that the two other verbs in this sequence of three could not refer to Israel's enemies; for one verb means "to lament" (נָהָה, *nāhāh*), and the other, "to speak" (אָמַר, *'āmar*), introduces the lament that is spoken in the first person. The preposition *'al* need not mean "against" here any more than it does in Ezek 18:2, where it occurs with *māšāl* in the sense of "concerning." It was the Hebrews themselves who uttered the *māšāl* concerning their own land in Ezek 18:2; and the use of this expression in Mic 2:4 may indicate that the proverbial saying would be current among the house of Israel after the Captivity had become a reality. Those who understand *māšāl* to mean "a taunt song" must regard it as uttered by someone other than an Israelite. Allen (p. 285) understands it as taken up on behalf of Israel, while Mays (p. 65) sees it as a dirge sung by "professional mourners." *Māšāl* is understood too narrowly when translated "taunt song." Mays (p. 65) observes, "*Masal* is a term applied to the broadest variety of sayings and songs."

The last word of the phrase וְנָהָה נְהִי נִהְיָה (*wᵉnāhāh nᵉhî nihyāh*) has been understood by some as a Niphal form of הָיָה (*hāyāh*, "it is all over") (KD). Others see it as dittography. The DSS, however, witness to the meaning "lamentation" (J. Carmignac, "Précisions Apportées au Vocabulaire de L'Hébreu Biblique par la Guerre des Fils de Lumière Contre les Fils de Ténèbres," VetTest 5 [1955]: 351). It seems best to translate the phrase thus: "They shall lament with great lamentation."

The translation of שׁוֹבֵב (*šôḇēḇ*) as "captors" (RSV) is attractive in view of the Hebrew root שָׁבָה (*šāḇāh*, "take captive"). The same root (*šby*) is attested in Ugaritic (UT, 68:29–30). This translation requires a textual emendation that has, however, little supportive evidence. The MT form of the word requires that it be derived from שׁוּב (*šûḇ*, "turn back"). In its feminine form the word is used of a faithless or rebellious daughter (Jer 31:22; 49:4). The connotation "rebellious" for the Assyrian king would not be inappropriate (see commentary).

E. *The True Prophet Versus the False Prophets*

2:6–11

6"Do not prophesy," their prophets say.
"Do not prophesy about these things;
disgrace will not overtake us."
7Should it be said, O house of Jacob:
"Is the Spirit of the LORD angry?
Does he do such things?"

"Do not my words do good
to him whose ways are upright?
8Lately my people have risen up
like an enemy.

You strip off the rich robe
  from those who pass by without a care,
  like men returning from battle.
9You drive the women of my people
  from their pleasant homes.
You take away my blessing
  from their children forever.
10Get up, go away!
  For this is not your resting place,
because it is defiled,
  it is ruined, beyond all remedy.
11If a liar and deceiver comes and says,
  'I will prophesy for you plenty of wine and beer,'
  he would be just the prophet for this people!"

6 Micah quoted the false prophets of his day. "Do not prophesy," they said. The word translated "prophesy" (*nāṭap̱*) means primarily "to drip," a figure for words issuing from the lips. Though used of ordinary speech (Job 29:22), it predominantly describes prophetic speech (cf. Amos 7:16). The prohibition against prophesying is immediately followed by another form of *nāṭap̱* ("they prophesy"; NIV, "their prophets say"), indicating that the injunction to discontinue prophesying is in itself uttered by prophets—evidently the false, self-serving prophets of Micah's time. In the MT the command is in the plural, thus including along with Micah those who share his convictions.

The somewhat desultory character of v.6 reflects the emotion of the moment and creates a difficult problem for the interpreter. The first of the two negative clauses following the initial prohibition is governed by the Hebrew negative *lō'* and seems logically to carry through the prohibition—i.e., "They must [will] not prophesy about these things." The change of persons from second to third is not uncommon in the OT and occurs in the prophecy of Micah (1:2). The third clause is also governed by *lō'* but cannot be a clause expressing command. It seems best to understand it as a clause connoting result, i.e., "disgrace will not leave us." The word translated "leave" is the Hebrew *sûg*, which never means "to overtake" but always "to leave" (but cf. BDB, pp. 690–91). Thus the prophets who opposed Micah appear to be saying: "Do not prophesy. They must not prophesy of these things; for as long as they do, disgrace will not leave us."

The true prophets were apparently considered troublemakers whose powerful sermons disgraced the privileged classes and embarrassed the false prophets. As long as their prophetic protest continued, so would the humiliation these corrupt leaders felt continue—thus the prohibition "Do not prophesy." This interpretation gains support from the subsequent verses.

7 Micah asked, "Should it be said, O house of Jacob?" (referring to the preceding statement of v.6). The sense of v.7 indicates that one should not blame the continuing disgrace on the prophetic pronouncements of Micah. The subsequent questions —"Is the Spirit of the LORD angry? Does he do such things?"—imply that it is not of the nature of God only to punish or to reproach because, the prophet continued, "my words [i.e., the words of the Lord through the prophet] do good to him whose ways are upright." If the ungodly people of his day would have lived according to the covenantal standards of the Lord, Micah's words would have had a benign effect on their lives as well as on the life of the nation; and the reproach and disgrace that they felt as he prophesied to them would have become a means of blessing.

8 But the people were not living according to the standards of the Lord, for Micah said, "Lately my people have risen up like an enemy." This statement does not indicate against whom the people had risen up, but the subsequent context shows that their hostile acts were directed against the less fortunate. By their blatant disregard for the social concern demanded by the covenant, however, they were really rebelling against the Lord and evoking his anger (Exod 22:21–27; Deut 27:19; Matt 25:37–40).

The acts of unbelievable hostility Micah cited describe the ways in which the poor were treated like an enemy. The people forcibly stripped off the outer garments of those who unsuspectingly passed by. Perhaps the reference is to debtors whose garments were confiscated in lieu of payment (Exod 22:26; Amos 2:8; but cf. Notes). The word "strip" (*pāšaṭ*) frequently has the sense of a "raid" that a marauding party would make against an enemy (Judg 9:33; 1 Sam 23:27), and it is used also of stripping for spoil (Hos 7:1). This word, with its military connotations, seems to have been deliberately chosen by Micah to illustrate how the poor were treated like enemies. In 3:5 Micah used a similar motif as he pictured the avaricious prophets declaring war against those who could not pay them.

The poor who were treated so cruelly are described as being averse (*šûḇ*) to war (cf. Ps 120:7). The peaceful and unsuspecting were suddenly bereft of some necessity of life by those who cared nothing for their victims' security or comfort.

9–10 The money hungry even treated the women cruelly. That only women are mentioned implies that they were probably widows forced from their homes. The children too were affected, for the Lord's blessing (*hāḏār*) was taken from them forever. The word *hāḏār* when used of God refers specifically to his glory or majesty. In Psalm 90:16, where the writer asked God to work on behalf of the people, *hāḏār* occurs in parallel with God's acts. In Psalm 149:9 the glory of God's faithful ones was the work of God on their behalf.

Because of the sin of the leaders of Micah's day, a whole generation would never see the glorious works of God but would live out their days in a strange land. Micah emphasized this as the intensity of his language rose to a sharp command (v.10). The people were to be banished because the land was irrevocably defiled. This statement echoes the pronouncement of doom spoken earlier in this first oracle (1:2–7). Here, however, the desolation of the land was a result of sin primarily against the covenant regulations and not the sin of idolatry that was so central to the denunciatory message of Micah 1:2–7. The prophet intertwined in this oracle the two basic manifestations of Israel's internal sickness—her idolatry, which had turned her from the purity of historic Yahwism to the worship of pagan deities, and her violation of the covenant stipulations.

11 The people of this time had an intense desire for the fruits of their affluent society, expressed in the terms "wine" and "beer." So if someone were to preach to them of greater affluence and prosperity, they would listen to him; and he would readily find acceptance among them. The implication is that Micah's message of doom was unacceptable to those who were basking in the affluence of the eighth century.

Notes

8 In each of its occurrences outside of Micah (Isa 44:26; 58:12; 61:4), יְקוֹמֵם (*yeqômēm,* "rise up") has the causative sense of the Polel and means "to set up." Several commentators have followed the lead of Ewald in translating the clause "they" (i.e., the oppressors) have "set up" or "treated" my people as an enemy (cited in KD). That the verb is in the singular, however, presents a major difficulty. The verb may be regarded simply as an intensive conjugation of the ע״ו verb and need not have any causative connotation of the Polel. The translation "rise up" is acceptable grammatically (cf. GKC, par. 55c). Allan (pp. 292–93, n.46) emends the text to read וְאַתֶּם לְעַמִּי . . . קָמִים (*we'attem lecammî . . . qāmîm,* "you attack my people"). The emendation is adopted because עַמִּי (*cammî,* "my people") is the object of oppression in v.9, and the subsequent verbs have a second plural subject. However, *cammî* is used flexibly by Micah to refer to the oppressed classes (3:3) as well as the nation as a whole (1:9; 2:4; 3:5; 6:3, 5). The abrupt change of persons is quite typical of Micah's style (1:2; 2:3, 12; 3:9–10; cf. v.11, et al.). Micah 2:4 is particularly notable in this regard, where the person changes from the first plural to third singular to first singular in the scope of three consecutive clauses. There is no versional evidence for the suggested emendation. Micah could easily have referred to the oppressors in his society as "my people" because the same term is used in 6:3, where he appeals to the rebellious to return to God.

The precise meaning of Micah's words in the second line of v.8 are difficult to understand. מִמּוּל שַׂלְמָה אֶדֶר תַּפְשִׁטוּן (*mimmûl śalmāh 'eder tapšiṭûn*) is literally "from the front of the garment you strip off the mantle (or glory)." The word *'eder* is unattested elsewhere in the OT as "mantle"; but it may be related to the feminine אַדֶּרֶת (*'adderet*), which has that meaning. Since Micah was describing the way in which the people were being treated like enemies, it is possible that he imagined the oppressors brazenly standing before the less fortunate and spoiling them of their outer garments. There may be a wordplay in the use of *'eder* that would signify that as the garments (*'eder*) were taken from the poor, they were also being stripped of their honor (*'eder*) because of the indignity they were forced to endure. The last line of the indictment (v.9) also speaks of the loss of honor or dignity: "You take away my blessing from their children forever." For a consideration of the options in the interpretation of this passage, see Allan, pp. 296–97.

11 A typical Hebrew play on words is evident in Micah's use of שֶׁקֶר (*šeqer,* "lie") and שֵׁכָר (*šēkār,* "beer").

F. *The Prophet's Statement of Hope*

2:12–13

12"I will surely gather all of you, O Jacob;
I will surely bring together the remnant of Israel.
I will bring them together like sheep in a pen,
like a flock in its pasture;
the place will throng with people.
13One who breaks open the way will go up before them;
they will break through the gate and go out.
Their king will pass through before them,
the LORD at their head."

12–13 The prophet turned abruptly to the statement of hope that ends the first oracle. In it he announced Israel's future restoration (v.12). The abruptness of the transition serves to place his message of hope in stark contrast to the message of the hypothetical preacher of v. 11, who falsely preached of continuing bright prospects for Israel. Micah's hope was not centered in his generation but in a remnant that would be led by their king from captivity to deliverance.

If studied in isolation from the total context of the prophecy, the passage may be understood simply as a prediction of the return from the Captivity. But this is inadequate in view of the broader background of Micah's concept of the future. Micah envisioned a kingdom of eternal duration with Yahweh as King (4:7). The Deliverer-King of 5:2–4 seems to be identical with the king of the present passage (v. 13); he plays an important role in the restoration of God's people (2:13; cf. 5:3). In both passages the motif of the "flock" is prominent (2:12; cf. 5:4). The fulfillment of the great prophecy in Micah 5:2–4 requires a ruler whose birthplace is Bethlehem and who will extend his influence to the ends of the earth and bring security to God's people (5:4). Micah's perspective of hope extends beyond a mere restoration from captivity to the messianic kingdom. It is then that Israel's hope will be finally and consummately realized.

Micah used vivid pictorial language to depict the restoration of the remnant. He likened them to a flock of sheep penned up in an enclosure (v. 12). In the next clause the figurative depiction of sheep gives place to the picture of a vast throng of people. The word translated "throng" (*tehîmenāh*) means "to murmur" (the root *hûm* is onomatopoetic). It depicts the murmuring of the members of a community (Ruth 1:19) and the resonating sound of the earth echoing to the noise of a loud shout (1 Sam 4:5; 1 Kings 1:45). The subject of *tehîmenāh* is difficult to determine. One is tempted to regard *ṣō'n* ("sheep") as the subject because it is feminine, but the parallel word *ᶜēḏer* ("flock") is masculine. It is true that rules of agreement are not precise in Hebrew, but we would do well to look for another possibility. Although Micah depicted the remnant as a flock, which is feminine in Hebrew, he used a masculine suffix to refer to the remnant in line 2. This use of the masculine makes it somewhat difficult to construe the remnant as the subject of the verb "murmur" since the verb is feminine. More likely the subject is to be found in the two feminine nouns *ṣārāh* ("pen") and *dōḇer* ("pasture"). If this is so, he may have used personification to picture the fenced pasture lands as murmuring, or perhaps the word is used as it is in 1 Samuel 4:5 and 1 Kings 1:45 to depict the pasture land as echoing the sound of the vast multitude.

We might expect Micah to have sustained the metaphor by using another word for sheep when he spoke of the cacophony of sound that emanated from the enclosure, but he did not; he depicted them as people. Literally he said that the pasture murmured "because of [*min*, 'from'] the men" (NIV, "with people"; i.e., because of the multitude of people). The prophet was not concerned with absolute precision in his use of figures of speech. Throughout his extended use of metaphorical language and his complex applications of gender, he did not lose sight of the fact that he was describing the destiny of people.

Suddenly a figure, called "the Breaker" (*happōrēṣ*; NIV, "One who breaks open the way"), appears in the narrative with no introduction (v. 13). He is described as going up before the multitude. Where can they go? After all, they are confined. But this is why his activity is described as "breaking." Led by the Breaker, the people burst through the gate of the enclosure to form a procession with their King at their head.

Micah envisioned a time when the kingdom of God would burst forth into sudden reality and the people of God would be manifested. Micah's theology of the kingdom was thus similar to that of Christ's, who in the parable of the wheat and the tares (Matt 13:24–30) affirmed that the true people of God would be manifested and gathered to him at the time of the harvest (v.30), an evident reference to the Eschaton. Micah affirmed that the strictures that now prevent the visible realization of the power and glory of God's kingdom and that blur the identity of God's people in the world would be shattered and the Breaker would lead his people to glory.

The Breaker will "go up before them." Then, according to the clausal structure, the multitude will burst through the gate. The Breaker must be one of the throng, because he goes before them to lead them out. His work is not done from outside the enclosure. Together they go forward with their King before them. The parallelism of the last clause establishes a close relationship between the work of the Breaker and the King of 5:2–4. Both arise from the people (5:2) and bring deliverance to the people (5:4); the people they lead are likened to a flock (5:4); and both are intimately associated with Yahweh (5:4). We may thus understand the Breaker to be Israel's King.

The last line of v.13 establishes a close connection between the Lord and the King. It is the Lord whose strength and power is manifested in the reign of the King. The King in v.13 reflects the strength and majesty of the Lord as does the figure of 5:4. The remnant, according to Micah, will receive its final glory and vindication only through the Messiah. He will arise from his people and lead them into the security of God's kingdom. This passage anticipates a later passage (4:7) in which Micah envisioned the remnant as a "strong nation" over which Yahweh reigns.

Notes

---

12 בָּצְרָה (*boṣrāh*) need not be understood to mean "Bozrah," the Edomite city (so KD). A root *bṣr* exists in Hebrew that means "to make inaccessible" (BDB, s.v.). בִּצָּרוֹן (*biṣārôn*, "stronghold") comes from this root, a well as מִבְצָר (*miḇṣār*, "fortification"). While the meaning "pen"or "enclosure" is not attested for *boṣrāh*, its parallelism with דֹּבֶר (*dōḇer*, "pasture") supports an affinity with *bṣr*.

13 The MT clearly identifies הַפֹּרֵץ (*happōrēṣ*, "the Breaker") as one who arises from the people. It literally reads, "The Breaker will go up before them; they will break through and pass on." The people do not break through till the Breaker, who goes before them, has broken through. The people break out of the enclosure as they follow the one who first makes the breach.

III. The Second Oracle: The Prophet's Indictment of the Leaders of the House of Israel and Israel's Future Hope (3:1–5:15)

A. *The Prophet's Indictment of the Rulers of Israel*

3:1–4

[1]Then I said,

"Listen, you leaders of Jacob,
you rulers of the house of Israel.

Should you not know justice,
2 you who hate good and love evil;
who tear the skin from my people
and the flesh from their bones;
3who eat my people's flesh,
strip off their skin
and break their bones in pieces;
who chop them up like meat for the pan,
like flesh for the pot?"

4Then they will cry out to the LORD,
but he will not answer them.
At that time he will hide his face from them
because of the evil they have done.

1 The second oracle begins, like the first, with a summons to hear the prophet's message. The summons was directed in this instance to the rulers of Judah and Israel. Micah began this oracle with a devastating question: "Should you not know justice?" If any should know the meaning of justice, it is those who have the awesome responsibility of leadership. Here "justice" is used in the sense of fairness and equity in governmental administration.

2–3 The language of the prophet became vividly emotive as he described the harsh treatment directed against the poor. He pictured the civil leaders as treating the exploited classes like animals being butchered and prepared for eating. The skin (*'ôr*, a word frequently used for the hide of animals) was torn from them and their flesh butchered.

4 Because they had so treated the poor, these merciless authorities would not be heard when they cried to the Lord. Those who violated the stipulation of God's covenant could not expect him to maintain the blessings of the covenant. It was disobedience that took the people from the ground of the covenant and marred their relationship to God (cf. Ps 18:41; Prov 1:28; cf. note at 6:8).

B. *The Prophet's Indictment of the Religious Leaders of Israel*

3:5–8

5This is what the LORD says:

"As for the prophets
who lead my people astray,
if one feeds them,
they proclaim 'peace';
if he does not,
they prepare to wage war against him.
6Therefore night will come over you, without visions,
and darkness, without divination,
The sun will set for the prophets,
and the day will go dark for them.
7The seers will be ashamed
and the diviners disgraced.
They will cover their faces
because there is no answer from God."

> [8]But as for me, I am filled with power,
> with the Spirit of the LORD,
> and with justice and might,
> to declare to Jacob his transgression,
> to Israel his sin.

5 Micah addressed another group of leaders in Israel, the false prophets of the time. The Hebrew of v.5 is crisp and powerful: "Who bite with their teeth and cry 'Peace!' " The word "bite" (*nāšak̠*) is always used in the OT for the bite of a serpent—except where the root reflects the secondary connotation of paying interest on loaned money. Its primary use of the bite of a serpent has led some to interpret the phrase as describing the harm inflicted on the people by the lying prophets—prophets whose false message of peace was as harmful as a serpent's bite.

The evident antitheses in this verse seem, however, to warrant a different interpretation (e.g., NIV). The Hebrew says, literally, "Who bite with their teeth and cry 'Peace'; and if one does not put something into their mouths, they declare war against him." In this structure bite is paralleled by "not put into their mouths," and "peace" by "war." The parallelism thus determines that the word "bite" (*nāšak̠*) has to do with the action of putting something into the mouth. While *nāšak̠* is never used for "eating" in the OT, there is no reason why Micah could not have used this forceful figure to express the voracity with which these greedy prophets accepted the bribes given them for the performance of their prophetic activity. The rudeness of the figure is appropriate to the language of the context (vv.2–3). The two connotations of *nāšak̠*—viz., "bite" and "exact" or "pay interest"—may be reflected here as a kind of pun.

The professional prophets continually cried "peace." They predicted a bright future for Israel while Micah predicted doom (cf. 2 Tim 4:3).

6–7 The end would come for these religious hucksters (v.6). While they then basked in the sunlight of power and affluence, the sun would go down on their prophesying and the resultant night would be devoid of vision or divination. It would be a time in which false predictions of peace (v.5) would be discredited by the reality of the Captivity. These prophets would "cover their faces" (lit., "cover the beard"), which is an expression connoting deep mourning (v.7; cf. Lev 13:45; Ezek 24:17, 22).

8 A strong adversative (*'ûlām*, "But"; NIV, "But as for me") introduces Micah's affirmation in which he contrasted his prophetic activity with that of the false prophets. He asserted that he was filled with power "with the [help of] the Spirit." The implication is that the false prophets were not empowered by the Spirit but, as the preceding context has shown, were motivated by greed.

The word "justice" (*mišpāṭ*) is used frequently in the OT prophetic books in the sense of true religion—i.e., the crystallization of the ethic of the law (cf. Notes). Because Micah was not violating the covenantal standards, he stood in sharp contrast to the religious leaders who participated in and encouraged the social exploitation of their time.

The word "might" is from the root *gāḇar*, from which the word *geḇer* ("man") is derived. Here the feminine form *g^eḇûrāh* is used, a word connoting "might," "valor," or "manly courage." Because Micah was guiltless of his compatriots' crimes against their fellowmen, he could stand before his adversaries with the power of moral courage and a clear conscience. Thus he could fearlessly cry out against the sin of the house of Israel.

Notes

---

8 The Hebrew particle אֵת (*'et̲*) in the expression אֵת רוּחַ יְהוָה (*'et̲ rûaḥ YHWH*, "the Spirit of the LORD") may refer to the concept of assistance or direct agency (cf. Gen 4:1; Judg 8:7; Esth 9:29; Job 26:4; cf. R.J. Williams, *Hebrew Syntax: An Outline* [Toronto: University of Toronto Press, 1967], p. 61).

The word מִשְׁפָּט (*mišpāṭ*, "justice") covers a wide range of meanings. It is used in legal contexts in the sense of "law" or "regulation" (Exod 24:3; Lev 5:10) and of the process of litigation (Num 27:5; 35:12). The word also means "manner" or "custom," a connotation that may have been derived from its use in legal contexts for a legal requirement. It occurs with this meaning in Gen 40:13; 1 Kings 18:28. Frequently the word has a distinctly religious and ethical usage that is never entirely divorced from the Mosaic law. The prophets, in particular, used it in this sense. The law required the expression of concern for others (Exod 23:4–5; Deut 24:17–22). To the prophets *mišpāṭ* was the fulfillment of God's will as expressed in the law and hence had definite ethical significance. Jeremiah defined *mišpāṭ* as caring for the needy (5:28; 7:5), and Isaiah gave a classic definition of the term in 1:17. James defined true religion in the traditional prophetic sense (1:26–27).

C. *The Result of the Leaders' Corruption on the Nation*

3:9–12

9Hear this, you leaders of the house of Jacob,
you rulers of the house of Israel,
who despise justice
and distort all that is right;
10who build Zion with bloodshed,
and Jerusalem with wickedness.
11Her leaders judge for a bribe,
her priests teach for a price,
and her prophets tell fortunes for money.
Yet they lean upon the LORD and say,
"Is not the LORD among us?
No disaster will come upon us."
12Therefore because of you,
Zion will be plowed like a field,
Jerusalem will become a heap of rubble,
the temple hill a mound overgrown with thickets.

9 The address to the leaders of the house of Jacob continued with a biting portrayal of their sins (vv.9–12). Micah accused them of despising justice (v.9). The Hebrew world *tā'ab̲* ("despise") is a strong one that means utter abhorrence of something. It is used of the disgust for him that Job saw in his detractors (Job 30:10) and of the psalmist's disgust for lying (Ps 119:163). Amos used it as Micah did (Amos 5:10).

10–11 As the leaders discharged their duties, they did so with bloodshed and greed (v.10), motivated by their desire for personal gain. Characterized by avarice and violence, their whole system of government inevitably led to corruption.

These leaders maintained a form of external religion based to some extent on the covenantal relationship. "Is not the LORD among us?" they asked (v.11). But they had lost sight of the ethical requirements of the covenant and, maintaining a mere shell of true worship of Yahweh, felt that their historical relationship to the Lord would prevent the onslaught of misfortune. Yet a clear body of prophetic tradition preceded this time and made clear that God desired obedience, not allegiance to externals (1 Sam 15:22; Ps 51:17). This optimistic but unfounded trust in Yahweh displayed by the leaders is described as "leaning on the LORD" (cf. v.11). It was a kind of trust, but one devoid of the fruits of real faith in obedience and ethical response to God (cf. Rom 6:1–4; Gal 5:16–26; James 2:18–26).

12 Because of the actions of the corrupt religious and civil leaders, the predicted doom would become a reality. The prediction begins with "therefore" (*lāḵēn*), establishing, as Micah has already done, that the cause of the Captivity was the disobedience of the people.

One wonders whether the words of Micah were ever in the minds of these leaders as they walked the bustling streets of Jerusalem and passed Solomon's magnificent temple: "Because of you, Zion will be plowed like a field." What a telling illustration of the corporate effect of individual disobedience!

While the name "Zion" originally referred to the Jebusite stronghold captured by David (2 Sam 5:7), which in Solomon's time was distinct from the site where the temple was actually built (1 Kings 8:1), it became a synonym for the city of Jerusalem in the prophetic and poetic literature (Ps 149:2; Isa 4:3; 40:9; Amos 6:1). That this later usage is its sense here in Micah 3:12 is clear, both from its forming a poetic complement to Jerusalem in the parallel structure and from its use in Jeremiah 26:18, where Jeremiah quoted Micah's words as analogous to his prediction of the destruction of Jerusalem (cf. Jer 26:11–12).

But like Jeremiah (Jer 26:11–12, 18), Micah also included the destruction of the temple in his prophecy. He pictured a wooded height, starkly bare. The temple, the visible sign of God's presence, was to be destroyed. As in the case of their forefathers at Shiloh (1 Sam 4:3–11), the symbol of the people's empty religion would perish.

D. *The Future Exaltation of Zion*

4:1–8

1In the last days

the mountain of the LORD's temple will be established
  as chief among the mountains;
it will be raised above the hills,
  and peoples will stream to it.

2Many nations will come and say,

"Come, let us go up to the mountain of the LORD,
  to the house of the God of Jacob.
He will teach us his ways,
  so that we may walk in his paths."

The law will go out from Zion,
  the word of the LORD from Jerusalem.
3He will judge between many peoples
  and will settle disputes for strong nations far and wide.
They will beat their swords into plowshares
  and their spears into pruning hooks.
Nation will not take up sword against nation,
  nor will they train for war anymore.
4Every man will sit under his own vine
  and under his own fig tree,
and no one will make them afraid,
  for the LORD Almighty has spoken.
5All the nations may walk
  in the name of their gods;
we will walk in the name of the LORD
  our God for ever and ever.

6"In that day," declares the LORD,

"I will gather the lame;
  I will assemble the exiles
  and those I have brought to grief.
7I will make the lame a remnant,
  those driven away a strong nation.
The LORD will rule over them in Mount Zion
  from that day and forever.
8As for you, O watchtower of the flock,
  O stronghold of the Daughter of Zion,
the former dominion will be restored to you;
  kingship will come to the Daughter of Jerusalem."

The chapter division at the end of chapter 3 is unfortunate because Micah continues to speak of Jerusalem. The mood changes, however, from gloom to sublime hope as Micah portrays the future glory of the city. The temple mount, soon to become a shrub-grown hill, would be exalted in the latter days; and the city of Jerusalem would become the center of God's gracious activity to the peoples of the earth.

This oracle forms the basis of a similar expression of hope in the prophecy of Isaiah (2:1–4), where it occurs with some variations. It is difficult to determine its origin. While it is possible that it was an independent oracle utilized by both Micah and Isaiah, it seems likely that Micah was the original author. It is an integral part of his entire prophecy and follows logically from the preceding description of Jerusalem's doom. That the oracle is longer in the prophecy of Micah than in Isaiah may indicate that Isaiah adapted it for his own purposes. The superscription to the oracle in Isaiah (2:1) may simply indicate that Isaiah was conscious of the controlling influence of the Holy Spirit in using the prophecy.

1 "In the last days" (*beʾ aḥarîṯ hayyāmîm*) always denotes a period of time that, from the writer's perspective, is in the indefinite future. It is not primarily an eschatological term. However, since the term is used in this context of the reign of the Lord, it is eschatological. The context must determine which future period is in view. That the prophet envisioned the exaltation of Jerusalem in association with the messianic kingdom is clear from such verses as 4:8 and 5:2–4, 7–9. And the phrase "in the last days" occurs in the prophetic writings in reference to the Messianic Age (cf. esp.

Dan 10:4; Hos 3:5). So it appears that Micah looked for the fulfillment of this prophecy, not specifically in the return from the Captivity, but rather in that time when the messianic King would effect the will of God for his people and would restore the fortunes of Israel. Micah's hope centered not in wild dreams of a utopian era immediately to follow the Exile—an era that never materialized—but rather in his faith in the word of God, specifically the messianic promise that finds its fulfillment in the saving work of Christ and the eventual fruition of God's eternal purposes in history. In *that* time Jerusalem will be exalted above all the cities of the world and will become a center to which people will stream.

2 The object of the people's attraction to Jerusalem is to be their desire for God's word that emanates from the city. Micah saw a change in the hearts of all peoples at this time when the law of the Lord would be received universally rather than by Israel and Judah alone.

3 The result of God's rule in this time will be that the nations of the world will experience peace. While the people of God who are the church have experienced peace in their hearts, it is difficult to limit this prediction only to Christians. The prophecy is national and even universal in scope and looks forward to a time when the nations will come so fully under the benign influence of God's Word that war will be no more.

There can be no war when it is Yahweh himself who arbitrates disputes among the nations and whose authority determines the resolutions to their problems. Because of this, weapons of war will be fashioned into agricultural implements. The pastoral motif reflects the peace that Micah saw as the ruling element of the messianic kingdom, a concept used also by other prophets to symbolize the tranquility of that time (Isa 11:6–10; Hos 2:15[17 MT]; Amos 9:13–15). The close identification between the Lord and the messianic King is evident in the prophecy of Micah. In the present passage Yahweh's rule is dominant, but in 5:2 that authority is vested in a king who, in certain ways, is distinct from God (v.4).

4 Here the peacefulness of this era is further described in pastoral imagery. It reflects the description of Solomon's kingdom in 1 Kings 4:25 and later became a description of conditions in the Messianic Age (Zech 3:10). The verse goes on to assert that the people will dwell in peace and safety, not because of their own strength, but because of the Lord of Hosts by whose word this will be effected. The certainty of this event is established in Micah's mind, not because of groundless optimism or a naive trust in human nature, but because God has sovereignly declared that such will happen: "The LORD Almighty has spoken."

5 The reason for the people's safety and security is that they will walk in the name of the Lord forever. "To walk in the name" means more than simply adhering to the religious requirements associated with the deity in question. It means to live in reliance on the strength of that deity. In the case of Yahweh, it involves reliance on the might of his power by which his attributes are manifested (cf. Notes).

The implication is that the nations were walking in the strength of their gods, but that would not continue. The placing of the word "forever" at the end of the line in the Hebrew text indicates its emphatic nature. Unlike the nations, God's people would enjoy his strength forever. It would be otherwise with the nations, for the dominion of their gods would come to an end when the people of the world submit to the rule of Yahweh and recognize the vanity of their false deities.

6–7 "In that day" (v.6) refers back to the era of Jerusalem's exaltation introduced in 4:1. The future regathering of Israel in the time of Zion's exaltation is described differently from the way Micah described it earlier (2:12–13). Here Micah depicts those who are regathered as lame, referring to their weakness as a result of God's afflicting them; and he further describes them as exiles, connoting the shame of expulsion from one's homeland. The emphasis is on the misery and helplessness of the exiles and forms a striking contrast to the "strong nation" (v.7) they are to become as a result of God's intervention on their behalf.

The returning people do not automatically comprise the remnant, according to Micah, but are to be made into a remnant. The idiom *śîm lᵉ* means "to make into" and is used similarly in 1:6. To Micah the remnant was more than simply a residue of people. It was the repository of God's grace and promise as well as the force that would ultimately conquer the godless nations at the end time (5:8–15). It is thus an act of grace that forms these poor exiles into a remnant and bestows on them the blessings of the Messianic Age (cf. Rom 11:1–6).

This distinct and profoundly theological use of the term "remnant" is developed further in the poetic structure where its corresponding member in the parallelism is "strong nation." Since the remnant was the beneficiary of God's promise, it could not fail to experience ultimate vindication and glory. To Micah, therefore, the remnant was synonymous with power and might; and, in keeping with his understanding, it forms an apt synonym to "strong nation" in the couplet.

The nation into which the remnant is transformed will have the Lord as its King forever (Isa 24:23; 52:7; et al.). The center of God's governmental activity will be restored and exalted Zion.

8 The climax of this representation of Jerusalem's future glory is described in terms of its restoration as the seat of the "former dominion." The dominion soon to be lost in the dark time just ahead will be restored.

The phrase "watchtower of the flock" is in apposition with "stronghold [*'ōpel*] of Zion" and synonymous with it. The *'ōpel* was a fortified section of Jerusalem on the east side in the immediate area of the temple mount and the Kidron Valley. It was probably the same general geographical area known earlier as Zion or the City of David; for later books, such as 1 and 2 Chronicles and Nehemiah, rarely use the name Zion and apply the name *'ōpel* to what might properly be termed Zion. From 2 Chronicles 33:14 it is clear that *'ōpel* was located in the immediate environs of the City of David. Micah seems to have used the term in the same fashion, for "watchtower of David" would apply fittingly to the "City of David." Nehemiah 3:25–27 places the *'ōpel* and the king's house closely together as well. The appositional structure of the terms "watchtower" and "Zion" seems to negate the possibility that the "watchtower of the flock" was a tower in the vicinity of Bethlehem (Gen 35:19–21).

Since the expressions used by Micah have such close ties with the location of David's dominion, the words "former dominion" can mean little else than that the Davidic kingdom will in some sense be restored to Jerusalem. By asserting this, Micah stands firmly in the tradition of the preexilic prophets (Isa 9:17; Hos 3:5; Amos 9:11).

Notes

1 That בְּאַחֲרִית הַיָּמִים (*bᵉʾaḥᵃrîṯ hayyāmîm*, "in the last days") does not always have an eschatological perspective may be seen in Gen 49:1 and Deut 31:29, where it denotes an indefinite period in Israel's future.

5 For the concept of "strength" inherent in the expression "walk in the name," see Zech 10:12, where the phrase is parallel to "strengthen them." It is expressed also in 1 Sam 17:45 (cf. 1 Chron 14:11; Pss 33:22; 118:10–13; Prov 18:10). The word שֵׁם (*šēm*, "name") covers the nature, attributes, and even reputation of God. To walk in the name is to enjoy the strength expressed in God's attributes. See comment at 5:4.

E. *The Future Might of Zion*

4:9–13

9Why do you now cry aloud—
have you no king?
Has your counselor perished,
that pain seizes you like that of a woman in labor?
10Writhe in agony, O Daughter of Zion,
like a woman in labor,
for now you must leave the city
to camp in the open field.
You will go to Babylon;
there you will be rescued.
There the LORD will redeem you
out of the hand of your enemies.

11But now many nations
are gathered against you.
They say, "Let her be defiled,
let our eyes gloat over Zion!"
12But they do not know
the thoughts of the LORD;
they do not understand his plan,
he who gathers them like sheaves to the threshing floor.

13"Rise and thresh, O Daughter of Zion,
for I will give you horns of iron;
I will give you hoofs of bronze
and you will break to pieces many nations."

You will devote their ill-gotten gains to the LORD,
their wealth to the Lord of all the earth.

9 The reader's attention is abruptly shifted from the graphic description of the future glory of Jerusalem to the realities of the current crisis. The section begins with the word "now" (*ʿattāh*) in Hebrew, a word that frequently bears a chronological connotation, i.e., "at this time." From the heights of the previous pronouncement, Micah descended to the present dismal situation; his hearers were not to develop a false sense of security. The rhetorical questions were intended as affirmations. Israel would have no king. She would be left without a counselor.

The loss of the king not only meant the dissolution of the government; in the context of Israel's theocratic structure, it meant much more than it would to other nations. The king was the Lord's anointed and stood as the vicegerent of the Lord, mediating God's law to the people. The loss of Israel's ruler would lead many to question the veracity of God's promises as they related to the future of the nation and to the Messiah who was to come from Israel. One can hardly imagine a harder blow than this, for it signified that God had vented his wrath against his people. The extreme anguish the nation was to endure through losing its national sovereignty is pictured as that of a woman in childbirth (Isa 13:8; Jer 6:24; Hos 13:13).

10 Micah's use of contrast is again evident, for in the scope of one verse he both affirmed Israel's doom and predicted her deliverance. A bright future and a glorious destiny may await her, but that does not diminish Israel's present responsibility for her disobedience.

The prophet saw the Captivity as taking place in three stages: leaving the city, sojourning in the stretches of the open country, and arriving at the land of captivity. The use of "Babylon" is not necessarily an indication that the verse is a later interpolation. "Babylon" may simply be a metonomy for Mesopotamia; or it may have been used in a pejorative sense of the world powers whose hostility to Israel was exhibited in so many ways and would continue to be shown until the time of Israel's restoration. The use of "Babylon" in this sense may go back to Genesis 10:10 and 11:4–9, where Babylon's function as the center of godless world power is established.

That the plural "enemies" is used (v.10) and that the subsequent verses (11–13) speak of "many nations" seem to indicate that "Babylon" had for Micah a broader significance than the empire that would soon replace Assyria as the dominant world power. On the contrary, he seems to be saying that God's people were to come under the dominion of godless nations, a dominion that would endure till the "Daughter of Zion," by the plan of God, would conquer the nations (v.13).

Any argument for a late date for this section must be based on more than simply the occurrence of the name "Babylon." The future tenses used in v.10, the correspondence of the dissolution of the monarchy of Judah to the events of the Captivity (vv.9–10), and the accord that exists between this prophecy of the impending Captivity and similar passages in the early chapters of Isaiah all support the placing of this passage in the period before the Captivity, when the great eighth-century prophets carried on their ministries. Micah may have used "Assyria" in a similar fashion (cf. comment at 5:5).

A positive unity pervades the entire chapter. The statement of hope that opened the chapter is reiterated and complemented by the truth that it is not a hope to be realized by an unrepentant people who have not paid for their sins. They are to suffer for their disobedience; but beyond that night of despair is the bright morning of Zion's glory, when God's people will be redeemed from the hand of their enemies. For those who accept the validity of biblical prophecy, the picture of present crisis and future hope finds an adequate situation in the critical days in which Micah ministered.

11–13 The nations that exhibit hostility (v.11) do this in ignorance (v.12); for as they gather to gloat over the misfortune of God's people, the nations do not know their part in God's plan for his people. The prophet pictures the nations as sheaves brought to the threshing floor; and only too late do they recognize that they are to be threshed and broken by Israel herself (v.13). While the atmosphere of this passage is different from the placid mood of 4:1–4, there is no more need to see a different author reflecting a more militant ideology here than there is in Isaiah 9:2–7, where the peace that is predicted follows the conquest of Israel's oppressors.

The horn (v.13) symbolizes strength (cf. Deut 33:17; 1 Sam 2:1). The wealth of the world is to be devoted to God, and all its might is to be under his dominion.

F. *The Future King of Zion*

5:1–4

1Marshal your troops, O city of troops,
for a siege is laid against us.
They will strike Israel's ruler
on the cheek with a rod.

2"But you, Bethlehem Ephrathah,
though you are small among the clans of Judah,
out of you will come for me
one who will be ruler over Israel,
whose origins are from of old,
from ancient times."

3Therefore Israel will be abandoned
until the time when she who is in labor gives birth
and the rest of his brothers return
to join the Israelites.

4He will stand and shepherd his flock
in the strength of the LORD,
in the majesty of the name of the LORD his God.
And they will live securely, for then his greatness
will reach to the ends of the earth.

1 Verse 1 of chapter 5 occurs at the end of chapter 4 in the MT and is thus understood to be a continuation of the preceding discussion. But Micah's characteristic pattern of doom followed by hope suggests a typical use of contrast to emphasize his message. It thus forms an apt introduction to the section dealing with the Deliverer-King. The versification of the Hebrew text of chapter 5 differs by one from that of the EVs. It is the latter that will be followed in the comments on this chapter.

"Marshal your troops" is a summons to the soon-to-be beleaguered city of Jerusalem to gather in troops for her defense against the siege. The word "troops" (*geḏûḏ*) in the phrase "city of troops" is a noun form derived from the verb *gāḏaḏ* and is used always in a military sense. The expression "daughter of troops" (lit. Heb.) forms a Hebrew grammatical function denoting character and depicts Jerusalem as a warlike city. Here perhaps is an echo of the social crimes so vividly described in warlike terminology elsewhere in the Book of Micah (2:8; 3:2–3, 9–10; 7:2–6). The implication of this expression would then be that Jerusalem, so renowned for its hostility toward the less fortunate, is to suffer siege because of its wrongdoing.

The striking of the king on the cheek represents the extremest of insults and marks the victory of Israel's enemies over her (1 Kings 22:24; Job 16:10; Ps 3:7 [8 MT]).

The king is called "judge" (*šōp̄ēṭ*; NIV, "ruler"), depicting the judicial aspect of his office. The word may have been chosen by Micah to form a play on words with "rod" (*šēḇeṭ*).

2 The statement of doom is followed by one of hope, as the preceding picture of Jerusalem's fate and the ignominy of her king is followed by the prediction of a king who will bring lasting security to Israel and whose influence will extend to the ends of the earth.

Ephrathah is the ancient name of Bethlehem (Gen 35:16, 19; 48:7; Ruth 4:11; cf. Josh 15:60 LXX) and distinguishes it from other towns named Bethlehem, such as the one in Zebulun (Josh 19:15). Its use identifies Bethlehem as the town in which David was born (1 Sam 17:12), thus establishing a connection between the messianic King and David.

The ruler is to come forth "to me" (*lî*), according to the Hebrew text. Yahweh is represented as speaking here, and the close identification of the king with the purposes of God is thus implied. Some commentators apply the phrase "from ancient times" to the remote beginnings of the monarchy, but this is unsatisfactory. The term applies grammatically to the ruler. It is he whose activities stem from the distant past, yet whose coming is still future.

The words "whose origins" is a translation of the Hebrew word *môṣā'ōṯāyw* (lit., "his goings forth"). The expression "to go forth" means primarily "to conduct one's activities" (cf. 2 Kings 19:27). Beyond that the phrase has a military connotation referring to the departure of an army for battle (2 Sam 3:25; cf. 3:22; 5:2; 10:16; Num 27:17; Isa 43:17) and may speak of the kingly activities of the Messiah in terms of his might and power, a fitting contrast to the weakness and subjugation of the Israelite monarchy pictured in the preceding verse.

The terms "old" (*qeḏem*) and "ancient times" (*yᵉmê 'ôlām*) may denote "great antiquity" as well as "eternity" in the strictest sense. The context must determine the expanse of time indicated by the expressions. In Micah 7:14, 20, for example, *yᵉmê 'ôlām* is used of Israel's earliest history. But the word *qeḏem* is used of God himself on occasion in the OT (Deut 33:27; Hab 1:12), of God's purposes (Isa 37:26; Lam 2:17), of God's declarations (Isa 45:21; 46:10), of the heavens (Ps 68:33 [34 MT], and of the time before the Creation (Prov 8:22–23). At any rate the word *qeḏem* can indicate only great antiquity, and its application to a future ruler—one yet to appear on the scene of Israel's history—is strong evidence that Micah expected a supernatural figure. This is in keeping with the expectation of Isaiah in 9:6, where the future King is called *'ēl* ("God"), an appellation used only of God by Isaiah. It is also in keeping with the common prophetic tradition of God's eventual rule over the house of Israel (Isa 24:23; Mic 4:7; et al.). Only in Christ does this prophecy find fulfillment.

3 This verse begins with the word "therefore" (*lāḵēn*), which introduces the logical result of the emergence of Israel's ruler. Because a ruler will eventually come to deliver Israel, God will give her up only temporarily. That is, Israel will enter a period of absolute abandonment by God because of her sin (1:5–6; 2:1–5; 3:4, 9–12; 4:10; 6:9–16), but a ruler will come who will end the period of Israel's estrangement; therefore Israel will be given up only till that time. Hosea also spoke of a period when Israel would not be God's people (*lō' ᶜammî*) and saw the state of separation from God continuing till the exiles returned and sought the Lord and the messianic King who is called "David" (Hos 1:9; 3:4–5).

Micah saw the period of abandonment continuing till "she who is in labor gives birth." Several Protestant interpreters have seen Mary the mother of Jesus in this prediction. But this interpretation requires that the word "she" refer to a figure not previously cited in the context, thus introducing into the text an abruptness and a syntactical harshness that are not necessary. Micah earlier (4:9–10) used the metaphor of a woman giving birth in reference to Jerusalem, which by metonomy may represent the whole nation. It is best to maintain the same meaning of the figure here and to understand it as speaking of the bringing forth of the Messiah by Bethlehem in Judah. Up to this point the theme of Jerusalem's suffering has been central to Micah's message, and the application of the figure in this way seems most natural.

The end of the period of Israel's estrangement from God is marked not only by the bringing forth of the ruler but also by the return to Israel of "the rest of his brothers." The pronoun "his" finds its nearest grammatical referent in the ruler of v.2. The brothers are those who share a common national heritage with him (cf. 2 Sam 19:13) and are thus under his regnal authority and protection. We observed a similar relationship of the King to his people in 2:13 where the Breaker-King is one with them and emerges from them. The word "return" (*šûḇ*) implies an original identification with Israel. The need for their return indicates that they have been dispersed. Micah has already spoken of these in his account of the remnant in 4:6–7. There the "exiles" (v.6), "those driven away" (v.7), will be assembled and brought under the rule of the Lord.

The gathering of those who comprise the remnant is an essential element in Micah's theology. This may be observed in 2:12–13 and 4:6–7. The depiction of the future gathering of the remnant in 5:3 is presented in a captivity motif; the brothers have been dispersed—they are in exile. This depiction is not unusual in the Prophets. Zechariah (10:10) said that God's people would return from Assyria, a nation that had brought Israel into captivity but which had long since disappeared from the world scene. Isaiah (11:12) pictured the remnant as outcasts whom the Lord would gather from the lands of their dispersion (v.11). The future deliverance of God's people is presented in this way because the prophets saw the Captivity as continuing, in a sense, till the coming of the messianic King (see comment at 5:5–6). Micah envisioned a time when the national solidarity that characterized the Davidic kingdom would be realized again.

4 The benign effect of the kingly reign of Messiah is described in pastoral terminology. Israel will be lovingly cared for by the messianic King who will carry out his regnal duties in the strength of God. In effect Yahweh will reign over the people —but in the person of the King.

The expression "in the name of" is parallel to "in the strength of," establishing a connection between the two concepts (see note at 4:5). The Deliverer is to be the embodiment of the strength and might of God, communicating that attribute to the people under his authority and thereby establishing their security eternally. The gracious benefits of his reign are to extend beyond national limitations, for the authority of the King is to be universal in scope because his greatness is to extend "to the ends of the earth." This description of his power goes perfectly with the description of universal peace seen earlier (4:1–4) and complements it by affirming that the peace described there will be effected by the Ruler born in the insignificant town of Bethlehem. Isaiah called him the "Prince of Peace" (9:6).

Notes

1 Both בַּת (*bat*, "daughter") and בֵּן (*bēn*, "son") may be used with an adjunct to connote character or quality. Thus בַּת־גְּדוּד (*bat gᵉdûd*, "daughter of troops") means "warlike city." Note also בַּת־בְּלִיָּעַל (*bat bᵉlîya'al*, "daughter of Belial") in 1 Sam 1:16, which means "a worthless woman." Other words as well may occur in this construct relationship to express character or quality.

3 Mays (p. 117) cites Deut 15:12 and 17:15 to show that אָח (*'āḥ*, "brother") means "member of the people." The eventual union of the northern and southern tribes was predicted by Ezekiel (37:15–23).

G. *The Future Peace of Zion*

5:5–6

5And he will be their peace.
When the Assyrian invades our land
and marches through our fortresses,
we will raise against him seven shepherds,
even eight leaders of men.
6They will rule the land of Assyria with the sword,
the land of Nimrod with drawn sword.
He will deliver us from the Assyrian
when he invades our land
and marches into our borders.

5–6 The placid picture vanishes for a moment, and the tramping boots of the invader are heard (v.5). The events described here are difficult to place historically. Those who place this pericope in the context of the conquests of Antiochus III have great difficulty with the term "Assyrian"; yet if the passage is understood to describe a coalition of leaders who would successfully withstand the Assyrian invasion, the difficulties remain because the Jews offered no successful resistance at that time.

If, however, "Assyria" is understood as a figure of speech for all the world powers that oppress Israel, both present and future, the problem disappears; and we may then understand the passage as a prophecy of Israel's ultimate victory over her foes. Such a concept is in keeping with the total scope of Micah's message, for he saw "many nations" oppressing Israel, not just Assyria (4:11–13; 7:16–17).

The prophet used the word "Assyria" typically in 7:12, where in the restoration people come to Israel from Assyria. If this is understood as a description of the millennial period, then "Assyria" designates the godless nations from which the final regathering is to take place. Hosea saw the period of oppression as existing till the Israelites would unite under the Messiah (Hos 3:1–5). Isaiah used the term "Assyria" in similar fashion in 11:11, where the Messianic Age is described (v.10). He saw the eschatological restoration as being from "Assyria," "Egypt," and beyond.

Zechariah also used "Assyria" and "Egypt" (10:10) to refer to the nations God's people will be gathered from when the kingdom is to be established. That the prophecy of Zechariah was written long after the Fall of the Assyrian Empire is significant because it indicates that, in the mind of Zechariah, Assyria (no longer a nation in his time) represented more than the empire that brought down the northern kingdom.

The "seven shepherds" and "eight leaders" are to be understood as an indefinite number of leaders. The figure stresses the abundance of manpower Israel will enjoy when God accomplishes the work of gathering his people from the godless nations to establish them in the land under the Messiah (v.6).

Notes

---

5 The sequence of seven to eight is used also in Eccl 11:2. The progression three to four is used in Prov 30:15, 18, 21, 29, and Amos 1:3, 6, 9, 11, 13; 2:1, 4, 6. The former numerical sequence occurs frequently in Ugaritic, however (cf. UT, 128:II:23–24; 8:2–3; 52:19–20, 66–67; et al.). The same sequence occurs in the Arslan Tash incantation text.

wsb' srty "and his seven concubines"
wsmnh 'st bˁl "and the eight wives of Baal"

(W.F. Albright, "An Aramaean Magical Text in Hebrew from the Seventh Century BC," BASOR 76 [1939]: 5–11). In most instances the numerical sequence is clearly not to be understood literally but may indicate an indefinite and probably much larger number.

H. *The Future Vindication of Zion*

5:7–9

7The remnant of Jacob will be
in the midst of many peoples
like dew from the LORD,
like showers on the grass,
which do not wait for man
or linger for mankind.
8The remnant of Jacob will be among the nations,
in the midst of many peoples,
like a lion among the beasts of the forest,
like a young lion among flocks of sheep,
which mauls and mangles as it goes,
and no one can rescue.
9Your hand will be lifted up in triumph over your enemies,
and all your foes will be destroyed.

7 The remnant, that group of believers trusting in the promises of God, is to be transformed from an insignificant group to one of absolute dominance in the world (vv.7–9). It is in this way that the faith and ideals of this believing community will be disseminated throughout the earth.

While the remnant is specifically faithful Israel, there is a sense in which the church forms a part of the remnant by its engrafting into the "olive tree" (Rom 11:17–24). The church, the body of true believers, also awaits the appearance of Christ and the conquest of her enemies.

That the remnant is likened to "dew" is not necessarily an indication that Micah had in mind the beneficial results of that natural phenomenon. The word "dew" is not always used in a good sense. Hosea, for example, used it of Israel's ephemeral love (6:4). The simile is explained in the next phrase where Micah stated that the dew and showers "do not wait for man." They come from the Lord and not at man's behest. So the remnant will not be lifted to its place of sovereignty by the nations of the world or by the will of mankind but solely by the power of God.

If v.7 is so understood, vv.7–8 need not have come from different authors. If we understand the "dew" and "showers" of v.7 to refer to fecundity and, hence, the benign effect of the remnant in the world, there is a sharp contrast between that concept and the very militant description of the remnant in v.8. That description has led many to see an intrusion by a later author who was more "militaristic" than the "pacifistic" author of v.7. Such a view, however, is not demanded by the text.

8–9 Micah next used metaphorical language, picturing the remnant as a lion overcoming its prey. Thus he described the inexorable way the remnant will achieve victory over the godless forces that oppose it. One should, of course, be careful to avoid pressing every detail of a metaphor. The vivid description of the stalking lion does not mean that the victory of the remnant will be achieved by bloodthirsty militaristic conquest. Micah rather pictured the relentless force with which a lion captures its prey—"and no one can rescue." In v.7 the prophet indicated that the exaltation of the remnant will not be by the power of the nations. Now in v.8 he indicates that the nations will not be able to withstand the burgeoning power of the remnant in the end time. Both metaphors depict the inexorable progress of the remnant toward its ultimate triumph in the world.

The theme of the destruction of Israel's foes (v.9) is prominent in the OT. In it many writers saw the course of history as a struggle in which the forces of evil oppose "the LORD and . . . his Anointed One" (Ps 2:2). Only when the world is conquered by the Prince of Peace and the will of man is subject to his Creator will there be lasting peace (Isa 63:1–6; Rev 19:11–16). Christ is called both the "Lamb of God" (John 1:29) and the "Lion of the Tribe of Judah" (Rev 5:5).

Notes

7–8 For a discussion of the alleged ideological differences between the metaphors of these verses, see Wolfe and Bosley, p. 934.

I. *The Future Purification of Zion*

5:10–15

10"In that day," declares the LORD,
"I will destroy your horses from among you
and demolish your chariots.
11I will destroy the cities of your land
and tear down all your strongholds.
12I will destroy your witchcraft
and you will no longer cast spells.
13I will destroy your carved images
and your sacred stones from among you;
you will no longer bow down
to the work of your hands.

> [14]I will uproot from among you your Asherah poles
> and demolish your cities.
> [15]I will take vengeance in anger and wrath
> upon the nations that have not obeyed me."

10–13 This section begins with the phrase "in that day" (*ḇayyôm hahû'*). If the referent of this phrase is the period described in the previous context in which the remnant will achieve victory over the nations (vv.7–9), then the prophet conceived of God as destroying the weaponry of the remnant and expunging their idolatrous practices after the conquest has been achieved. This might imply that the conquest was accomplished by military force.

The phrase "in that day" may find, however, its referent in the description of Zion's exaltation in 4:1–4. In this case the purification of the remnant would take place in the initial stages of the era of peace (4:1–4); and the present passage (5:10–15) would indicate that the inexorable conquest will not be accomplished by the sword but by the remnant's total dedication to God, brought about as God removes everything that would interfere with their total trust in him.

The phrase need not refer to the immediately preceding context but may refer to what follows. This would parallel the structure of the pericope that begins at 4:6, where an identical phrase roots that section in the era of peace introduced in 4:1. Even though 5:10 (9 MT) begins with the word *hāyāh* ("it shall be") and follows a succession of occurrences of the same word (vv.5, 7, 8 [EV]), it does not necessarily follow that the *hāyāh* of v.10 is in sequence with them and that the purification of vv.10–15 is subsequent to the conquest by the remnant described in vv.7–9. In each of the preceding occurrences of *hāyāh*, the word has a definite subject. But the subject of *hāyāh* at v.10 is indefinite, denoting a general condition—"It shall be in that day that. . . ." There is a definite break in the verbal sequence and, hence, a logical interruption of the thought.

That the purification of the remnant takes place in the initial stages of the era of peace seems to be clear from v.15, where the expression of God's wrath against the nations—an event contemporaneous with the purification of the remnant—would be anomalous in a period characterized by absolute peace. It is hardly conceivable that an eighth-century prophet would envision the remnant as being exalted by God and made the vehicle of God's activity in the world while guilty of trusting in their own strength (vv.10–11) and still practicing idolatry (vv.13–14). It was for these reasons that eighth-century prophets proclaimed Israel's eventual downfall.

The implication of vv.10–15 is that the instruments of war and the elements of idolatrous worship are wrong. That is why God removes them from the remnant. If the remnant is to use these means of achieving the ultimate goal of conquest, an inconsistency is introduced into the message of Micah; for it was Israel's idolatry and oppressive practices that he specifically condemned.

If the phrase "in that day" relates to the era of peace (4:1–4), then the prophet is to be understood as indicating that the remnant's rise to dominance over the nations is not to be by military might but by their total dedication to God. Spiritual renewal is to be the source of the remnant's power. It is comforting to know that the world will eventually be conquered, not by its own corrosive corruption or false or subversive ideologies, but by the gospel. The prophet foresaw the eventual vindication and triumph of the people of faith.

Horses and chariots are to be removed from Israel (v. 10). These would not only be anomalous during the reign of peace but would tend to undermine Israel's complete trust in God (Deut 17:16; Isa 2:7; Zech 9:10). The cities and defenses are to be destroyed (v. 11) as well as the elements of false religion (vv. 12–13). Witchcraft denotes the ways primitive people sought control of natural forces or power over individuals. The MT literally reads "witchcrafts of your hand," possibly referring to the acts of divination performed by hand. The phrase "cast spells" is a translation of the Hebrew word *'ānan,* the root of which is dubious. It connotes a type of sorcery and is always condemned in the OT (Deut 18:10; 2 Kings 21:6). The foretelling of the future was an aspect of this type of divination as it was of the "witchcraft" that Micah cited first (Jer 27:9).

Israel's images are to be destroyed as well (v. 13). The word "image" (*pesel*) means idols carved from some material. The root *psl* denotes a "sculptor" in Ugaritic as well as "craftsman" in a broader sense. The "sacred stones" (*maṣṣēbôṯ*) were standing pillars, usually of stone, that represented pagan deities. The word generally refers to anything that is piled up or set up, such as the monument erected by Joshua (Josh 4:9). Both terms used in this verse require manual structuring or fashioning; hence, Micah said, "You will no longer bow down to the work of your hands."

14–15 Asherah (v. 14) was a Canaanite goddess who is called in the mythological texts from Ugarit the "Creatress of the gods." She was associated with all aspects of sexual life and thus with fertility in general. She was also a goddess of war. Sacred prostitution was an integral part of her cult.

The second stich of v. 14 unexpectedly contains a reference to "cities" (cf. v. 11) rather than a continuing condemnation of idolatry. The symmetrical arrangement of parallel elements has been deliberate and exact throughout this section. But the structure here is characteristic of the modified parallelism noted in 1:5. To Micah the cities were the centers of pagan worship, particularly the cities of Samaria and Jerusalem, though others were not exempted (1:13). "Cities" would make a fitting parallel to "Asherim" in view of Micah's understanding of the idolatrous practices carried on in the cities. The repetition of "cities" throws into bold relief the fact of the inevitable captivity of the cities that were about to perish. It is also quite possible, however, that v. 14 functions as a summary statement for the catalog of destruction in vv. 10–13. In that case there would be no synonymous parallelism here.

The nations that do not yield to God will be subjugated (v. 15) so that the peace promised in 4:1–4 will never be threatened. This supports the translation "witness against" in 1:2.

Notes

---

10 Keil (KD, p. 490) argues, "Only when the people of God shall have gained the supremacy over all their enemies, will the time have arrived for all the instruments of war to be destroyed." This view is at variance with the one taken here and is based, in part, on the fact that וְהָיָה בַּיּוֹם־הַהוּא (*w^ehāyāh bayyôm-hahû',* "and it will be in that day") in v. 10 (9 MT), "when compared with *hāyāh* in verses 4 [5 EV] and 6 [7 EV] shows at once that these verses are intended to depict the last and greatest effect produced by the coming of the Prince of peace" (ibid.). But the *hāyāh* in vv.5, 7 is not the same idiom as that in v.10. Each has a stated subject ("this," v.5 [NIV, "he"], and "remnant," v.7) whereas *hāyāh* in v.10 is used in the idiomatic expression "It will be in that day." This expression finds its counterpart in the somewhat similar expression in 4:1 rather than the two preceding occurrences of *hāyāh*.

IV. The Third Oracle: God's Lawsuit With Israel and the Ultimate Triumph of the Kingdom of God (6:1–7:20)

A. *God's Accusations Against His People*

6:1–8

1Listen to what the LORD says:

"Stand up, plead your case before the mountains;
let the hills hear what you have to say.
2Hear, O mountains, the LORD's accusation;
listen, you everlasting foundations of the earth.
For the LORD has a case against his people;
he is lodging a charge against Israel.

3"My people, what have I done to you?
How have I burdened you? Answer me.
4I brought you up out of Egypt
and redeemed you from the land of slavery.
I sent Moses to lead you,
also Aaron and Miriam.
5My people, remember
what Balak king of Moab counseled
and what Balaam son of Beor answered.
Remember ⌊your journey⌋ from Shittim to Gilgal,
that you may know the righteous acts of the LORD."

6With what shall I come before the LORD
and bow down before the exalted God?
Shall I come before him with burnt offerings,
with calves a year old?
7Will the LORD be pleased with thousands of rams,
with ten thousand rivers of oil?
Shall I offer my firstborn for my transgression,
the fruit of my body for the sin of my soul?
8He has showed you, O man, what is good.
And what does the LORD require of you?
To act justly and to love mercy
and to walk humbly with your God.

1–2 The third oracle begins in the format of a legal controversy (v.1). The mountains are called as witnesses in the litigation (v.2). Micah uses the motif of other writers of the OT who called on inanimate objects to function as witnesses in a legal context (Deut 32:1; Isa 1:2). The enduring hills have mutely observed Israel's history from its very beginning; hence they are called "everlasting foundations" (v.2). If they could speak, they would witness to the truthfulness of the Creator's claims. The appeal to the mountains should be understood simply as an entreaty to witnesses that have been in existence throughout Israel's history.

3 Micah placed the classic disputation form of the prophets in a legal context as he pictured God's pleading with his people. The mood of the passage is at first foreboding as the opening words summon God to arise and state his case against Israel. But the passage takes on an atmosphere of pathos as God is pictured as asking his people how he has wearied them. The Creator of those mountains seeks the cause of Israel's estrangement from him.

The word "burden" (*lā'āh*, "to be weary") when used in the causative stem (Hiphil), as it is here, signifies to wear down (Job 16:7), to cause someone to become impatient (Isa 7:13), or to become physically tired (12:5). The Lord's question emphasizes the second nuance, asking how he has caused them to become so weary of him that they have ceased to obey him. Their impatience with God cannot be due to inactivity on his part, for he has done much for them. This recital of events from Israel's past is intended to challenge the possible objection that Israel's estrangement from God was the result of his failure to act for her in the sphere of history.

4 The deliverance from Egypt is frequently cited in the Prophets and represents one of the first acts of redemption in which God demonstrated his saving love for the people. The deliverance from Egypt is an important aspect of the prophetic "theology of history."

Moses, Aaron, and Miriam are cited as reminders to the people of the great leadership God gave them. Moses was God's great prophet, the prototype of the line of prophets yet to come (Deut 18:15–22). Miriam was a prophetess (Exod 15:20); and Aaron, the progenitor of the Aaronic priesthood, was the representative of the people before God.

5 Micah also cited the failure of Balaam to curse the people (Num 22–24) as evidence of God's activity among them. Besides the failure of Balak to frustrate the progress of the people, the journey from Shittim to Gilgal witnessed the defeat of Midian, the crossing of the Jordan, and the conquest of Jericho carried out from the base at Gilgal. The recital of events stops abruptly as though the intent is to depict in one great sweep the progress of the nation from slavery in a foreign land to settlement in its own country.

The word translated "righteous acts" (*ṣiḏqôṯ*) is a plural form of the Hebrew word for "righteous." The word righteous means basically "rightness" and could apply to the secular as well as religious spheres of life. Judges were to be "righteous" in a legal sense (Lev 19:15). In reference to God's activities, however, the word underlines God's faithfulness to his standard, i.e., the covenant obligations. God's great acts on behalf of Israel are seen as more than simply God's coming to the aid of his people. They are seen as manifestations of God's righteousness as he maintains his faithfulness to the covenant promise.

6–7 The recital of Israel's history suddenly ended, and the prophet was heard speaking—in terse, abrupt words that somehow created a feeling of rapid movement and tension. Micah spoke, but it was as though he spoke on behalf of the people as they asked what their responsibility was in the light of God's faithfulness to the covenant. There is irony here; the section is meant to contrast external religion (to which they clung) with true religion.

The prophet asked how one may come before the "exalted God." The word "exalted" represents the Hebrew word *mārôm*, which means "height." The expression is literally "God of the height" and speaks of God in his dwelling place in heaven (2 Sam 22:17; Isa 33:5). How can this high God be reached in the far off heavens? What is the proper way to worship him? With burnt offerings and calves a year old? Yearling calves were specifically cited on a number of occasions in the Pentateuchal legislation (Lev 9:2–3; cf. Exod 12:5) and seem to have been regarded as the choicest sacrifices.

"Thousands of rams" (v.7) suggests the large quantity of animals that one might offer to curry God's favor. The implication is that God is interested neither in the choicest animals nor in the number offered, factors belonging to a religion of works and externals. Even great quantities of oil will not bring the worshiper into fellowship with God. Oil was an important part of certain sacrifices, such as the cereal offering (Lev 2:1–16).

The list reached a shocking climax in the mention of the firstborn. Child sacrifice was a Canaanite practice carried out by certain Israelites on occasion (2 Kings 3:27; 16:3; Isa 57:5). In keeping with the preceding catalog, the firstborn represents the most precious thing one could give to God. Again the implication is that this was not what God wanted.

8 What God does want, Micah now tells us. He does so in a verse justly regarded as one of the memorable and timeless expressions of OT ethical religion (cf. James 1:27). It is a heart response to God demonstrated in the basic elements of true religion. This was shown to Israel in the social concerns reflected in the Mosaic legislation.

God has told the people what is good. The Mosaic law differentiated between good and bad and reflected God's will in many areas of their religious and social lives. It indicated what God required (*dāraš*, "sought") of them. They were to act justly (lit., "do justice," *mišpāṭ*). The word "justly" has here the sense of "true religion," i.e., the ethical response to God that has a manifestation in social concerns as well (cf. note at 3:8). "To love mercy" is to freely and willingly show kindness to others (cf. Notes). The expression "to walk humbly with your God" means to live in conscious fellowship with God, exercising a spirit of humility before him. These great words recall similar words of our Lord in Matthew 23:23.

The prophet was not indicating that sacrifice was completely ineffectual and that simply a proper heart attitude to God would suffice. In the preceding verse he painted a caricature, a purposefully exaggerated picture, of the sacrificial system to indicate that God has no interest in the multiplication of empty religious acts. Jeremiah 7:22–23 is often appealed to as evidence that the prophets rejected the Levitical system; yet Jeremiah promised that the offerings would be acceptable if the people were obedient (Jer 17:24–26). A similar attitude toward sacrifice is expressed in Psalm 51:16–17, but the succeeding verses show the author to be indicating that the Levitical sacrifices are acceptable to God only when acccompanied by a proper heart attitude toward him (vv.18–19).

The ethical requirements of v.8 do not comprise the way of salvation. Forgiveness of sin was received through the sacrifices. The standards of this verse are for those who are members of the covenantal community and delineate the areas of ethical response that God wants to see in those who share the covenantal obligations. These standards have not been abrogated for Christians, for the NT affirms their continuing validity. We are still called to the exercise of true religion, to kindness, and to humility (1 Cor 13:4; 2 Cor 6:6; Col 3:12; James 1:27; 1 Peter 1:2; 5:5). Christians are in a covenant relationship with God in which the law (*tôrāh*) has been placed within their hearts (Jer 31:33; cf. Heb 10:14–17), not abrogated. But obedience for Christians is to the indwelling Holy Spirit, not to the letter of the law (2 Cor 3:6).

Notes

---

2 For a discussion of the characteristic רִיב (*rîḇ*, "disputation"; NIV, "case," "charge") form of the prophets, see W. Westermann, *Basic Forms of Prophetic Speech*, tr. H.C. White (Philadelphia: Westminster, 1967); G.E. Wright, "The Lawsuit of God: A Form-Critical Study of Deuteromony 32," *Israel's Prophetic Heritage*, ed. by B.W. Anderson and W. Harrelson (London: SCM, 1962), pp. 26–67; G.W. Ramsay, "Speech Forms in Hebrew Law and Prophetic Oracles," JBL 96 (1977): 45–58; and G. Gemser, "The *Rîb* or Controversy Pattern in Hebrew Mentality," VetTest Supplements, 3:124–37.

8 חֶסֶד (*ḥeseḏ*; NIV, "mercy") has the basic meaning of "kindness" (Gen 19:19; 40:14; Ruth 3:10). On occasion it contains an element of reciprocity, for the recipient of kindness was expected to show kindness in return (Gen 21:22–24; Josh 2:12–14). Kindness was expected between partners in certain previously existing relationships such as marriage (Gen 20:13) and friendship (1 Sam 20:8). *Ḥeseḏ* is also an attribute of God and is basic to his acts of redemption, and the demonstrations of *ḥeseḏ* on God's part establish a *ḥeseḏ* relationship in which God expects an ethical response from man as man's reciprocal responsibility. The ethical aspects of *ḥeseḏ* are peculiarly evident in the prophets. They make clear that if one fails to show *ḥeseḏ*, he has broken the terms of the covenant; and since the covenant is the vehicle for obtaining God's *ḥeseḏ*, the covenant breaker has removed himself from any right to obtain it. This applies on a broader scale to nations as well.

B. *The Sentence of Judgment*

6:9–16

9Listen! The LORD is calling to the city—
   and to fear your name is wisdom—
   "Heed the rod and the One who appointed it.
10Am I still to forget, O wicked house,
   your ill-gotten treasures
   and the short ephah, which is accursed?
11Shall I acquit a man with dishonest scales,
   with a bag of false weights?

12Her rich men are violent;
   her people are liars
   and their tongues speak deceitfully.
13Therefore, I have begun to destroy you,
   to ruin you because of your sins.
14You will eat but not be satisfied;
   your stomach will still be empty.
 You will store up but save nothing,
   because what you save I will give to the sword.
15You will plant but not harvest;
   you will press olives but not use the oil on yourselves,
   you will crush grapes but not drink the wine.
16You have observed the statutes of Omri
   and all the practices of Ahab's house,
   and you have followed their traditions.

> Therefore I will give you over to ruin
> and your people to derision;
> you will bear the scorn of the nations."

9 Another dramatic element is introduced. The voice of the Lord is suddenly heard. The phrase "calling to the city" signifies the cry of alarm that is heard when disaster threatens a city. Micah adds the observation that it is wise to fear God's name. The word "fear" is spelled with the same consonants as the word "see" in Hebrew and, in the MT, the word is vocalized so as to read "see." It is best to follow the versions in reading "fear," however, since the expression "see the name" is somewhat anomalous and the identical phrase "fear the name" is witnessed to in Psalm 86:11.

Although several modern versions (NASB, NEB, RSV, et al.) have emended the text for the last clause of v.9, NIV follows the Hebrew, which makes good sense as it stands. The "rod" (*maṭṭeh*) is the punishment that Israel will endure, and she is told to "heed" it.

Isaiah uses the word *maṭṭeh* ("club") of the Assyrians (10:5, 24). In Isaiah 10:5 the nation of Assyria is pictured as the instrument of God's wrath. If Micah used *maṭṭeh* in the same way here, there is then a logical connection with the cry of alarm in v.9. That alarm would herald the coming of the Assyrians, and the one who "appointed" the rod would be God himself. The people were to "heed," i.e., attend to the fact that the invasion would come and that it was God who would effect it through the instrumentality of the Assyrians.

10–13 The MT begins (v.10) with the word *'ôḏ* ("yet"). It is in the place of emphasis in the clause. The Hebrew says, literally, "Are there yet in the house of the wicked treasures of wickedness and the short measure that is cursed?" The question, of course, is rhetorical and affirms that the oppressing classes are still getting gain from their mistreatment of the poor and that the oppression has not ended. Hence the punishment is deserved and now imminent.

Micah emphasized social sins more than sins of idolatry, though ultimately they were closely intertwined in his thinking. In the brief catalog of Israel's sins that follows (vv.11–13), God continued to present his case and defend the sentence he was pronouncing. The response to the question of v.11 was, of course, a resounding no!

The society of Micah's time was characterized not only by violence but by lying and deceit (v.12). False promises were uttered and claims made that were not fulfilled. In any society when leaders of government deceive the people by making promises that are not kept, the will of the people is silenced and ignored and the structure of government weakened.

The Hebrew of v.13 states, literally, "I have made sick your smiting," i.e., "I have struck you severely." It is because of the people's sin that God was to bring ruin on them. It was not simply for the fortunes of history. The word "sick" in Hebrew is very close in formation to the word "begin" (NIV, RSV); which meaning should be read here is uncertain. The use of "sick" in the idiom is acceptable; the past tense may have been intended to imply the certainty of the event.

14–15 The land was to fall under the devastation of the sword and be totally unproductive. The greed that motivated the rich in that day would no longer be gratified because of the desolation of the land.

16 The prophet departed from the social sins of his society and turned to the pagan religious practices of the people. They were no better than the generation of Omri, the notorious king who headed the dynasty that produced Ahab the husband of Jezebel and allowed Baal worship to gain a strong foothold in Israel. Other crimes of that time included the persecution of Elijah and the murder of Naboth. Even in Micah's day the spirit of Omri lived on.

The second line of v.16 begins with the word *l*e*ma'an* ("to the end that"; NIV, "therefore"). The meaning is that Israel's disobedience to God had brought the punishment that the prophet was about to describe. Three calamities were to fall on her. She was to become a "ruin." The word translated "ruin" is a noun form of the verb *šāmam*, which means both "to be desolated" and "to be appalled." It frequently signifies the reaction of people appalled at God's judgment (Lev 26:32; Job 17:8; Ezek 26:16); thus the noun form may connote that which is an object of horror. This meaning seems best in view of the nature of the two other descriptive terms. For they were to become as well an object of hissing and the scorn of other nations.

Notes

---

9 In the OT יָרֵא (*yārē'*, "fear") is a complex concept. It involves reverent awe (Job 37:23–24; Ps 33:8), knowledge of God (Prov 9:10), turning from evil (Job 28:28; Prov 8:13), humble obedience (Jer 26:19), genuine piety (Gen 22:12; Ps 34:11–15), and "fear" in the strict sense of the word (Exod 20:20). It is an attitude toward God that involves worshipful submission to him as well as a turning from evil. In short, it is similar to the conversion experience.

10 While עוֹד)('*ôḏ*, "yet") appears before the interrogative particle ה (*ḥ*), a somewhat rare grammatical function, it need not be understood as being connected with the preceding clause. The particle '*ôḏ* appears before the interrogative pronoun in Gen 19:12.

13 MT's הֶחֱלֵיתִי, (*heḥ*e*lêṯî*, "I have made sick") is sometimes revocalized to read הַחִלּוֹתִי (*haḥil-lôṯî*, "I have begun") along with the LXX, Theodotion, the Syriac, and the Vulgate. The statement "I have made sick your smiting" seems anomalous and may have led to the emendation. However, this function of the Hiphil is idiomatic (cf. GKC, par. 114n), and the association of the two words in Jer 30:12—נַחְלָה מַכָּתֵךְ (*naḥlāh makkāṯēḵ*, "your wound is incurable")—confirms the validity of the expression.

C. *The Prophet's Lament of the Lack of Godly Fellowship*

7:1–2

1What misery is mine!
I am like one who gathers summer fruit
at the gleaning of the vineyard;
there is no cluster of grapes to eat,
none of the early figs that I crave.
2The godly have been swept from the land;
not one upright man remains.

All men lie in wait to shed blood;
each hunts his brother with a net.

Like a day that begins with a dark, foreboding sky but ends in golden sunlight, this chapter begins in an atmosphere of gloom and ends in one of the greatest statements of hope in all the OT. Clouds of gloom have rolled in on the horizon of the prophet's life because of the disobedience of the people and the somber fate that awaited his nation. But rays of hope—such as the affirmations in v.7—shine through the gloom. It is in the great affirmation of faith that concludes the book (vv.18–20) that the darkness is completely dissipated. One may wonder why the prophet did not succumb to utter pessimism in view of the conditions of his day. The answer is in this chapter. It was because of the triumph of faith.

The developing optimism of this chapter is not due to the prophet's lack of concern for the poor. If any were concerned for the oppressed classes, it was the eighth-century prophets. Nor was it due to an optimistic humanism (vv.5–7). In the midst of a crumbling society, Micah could look beyond to a hope secure in the promises of God. Micah could be optimistic because he could see the hand of God working even in the midst of ruin and despair.

The prophet speaks here as a representative of the godly remnant. While most of the chapter is written in the first person, a corporate concept begins in v.8 that cannot be limited to the prophet alone.

1 This section begins with a lament as the prophet mourned the lack of godly fellowship in his time. The Hebrew reads, literally, "I have become like the fruit gathering." The metaphor pictures the remnant as seeking for grapes and choice figs to satisfy its hunger, but it is as though it were the time of harvest when these have been picked and the hunger must go unsatiated.

2 The fruit described in the metaphor represents godly persons. The feeling of utter disappointment that would be felt by one seeking food and finding none is meant to communicate the feelings of the godly as they observe the nation and its great lack of individuals who have remained faithful to God. This passage is a vivid representation of the believer's need for fellowship with others of like faith. By severing fellowship with another believer, one may rob him of something very precious. The language of v.2 does not describe actual murder but rather describes the excesses that characterized the treatment of the "have nots" by the "haves."

D. *The Prophet's Lament of the Corruption in His Society*

7:3–6

3 Both hands are skilled in doing evil;
the ruler demands gifts,
the judge accepts bribes,
the powerful dictate what they desire—
they all conspire together,
4 The best of them is like a brier,
the most upright worse than a thorn hedge.
The day of your watchmen has come,
the day God visits you.
Now is the time of their confusion.
5 Do not trust a neighbor;
put no confidence in a friend.

Even with her who lies in your embrace
be careful of your words.
6For a son dishonors his father,
a daughter rises up against her mother,
a daughter-in-law against her mother-in-law—
a man's enemies are the members of his own household.

3 The situation in Micah's day was desperate. He described the strong hold that those in responsible positions had on the throat of society. "The ruler demands gifts" means that the ruler insisted that justice be distorted for his gain. Or perhaps he did it with the misguided notion that it would ultimately benefit the nation. Power can corrupt if not guarded by the law of a higher Sovereign. The judicial system was corrupted by the lust for bribes. The controlling classes, i.e., the rich, simply dictated their desires; and the implication is that they received them.

The Hebrew of the last line of v.3 is literally "and so they weave it all together." This expression describes the conspiracy of the ruling classes just cited by Micah. The ruler sought, perhaps, for the indictment of an innocent person; the judge carried it out for a bribe; and the rich man was involved in the conspiracy by speaking "the desire of his soul" (*hawwaṯ napšô*; NIV, "what they desire"). The word "desire" (*hawwāh*) is always used in a bad sense and may mean "evil desire" but more commonly "calamity" or "destruction." The word occurs in a similar context in Psalm 38:12 (13 MT), where it refers to the speech of those who seek the psalmist's life. It thus denotes the harm or injury that the rich man desired to see carried out. This wicked scheme had the cooperation of those who occupied positions of responsibility in society.

4 As Micah continued to characterize the society he lived in, he described the best of the people as briers. If one should seek to find mercy or sympathy from any of them, even those who appear to be upright and respectable, they would prove to be hard and piercing. This description of his contemporaries is suddenly interrupted. And in keeping with his use of sudden almost jarring contrasts, Micah pointed to the coming judgment. Literally he said, "The day of your watchmen has come."

The watchmen were the prophets (Jer 6:17; Ezek 3:17). They watched the course of their nation, saw its internal decay and decline, and, like watchmen who guarded the cities of ancient times, warned of the danger inherent in the wrongs of the people. The day of the watchmen was the day of punishment predicted by the prophets, i.e., the Captivity.

5–6 Micah returned to the description of the wrongs of his society as he depicted the disruption in the family unit. In Micah's day a man could not trust his friends (v.5) or even his wife, and respect for one's parents had vanished (v.6).

E. *The Godly Man's Attitude in the Midst of Discouragement*

7:7–10

7But as for me, I keep watch in hope for the LORD,
I wait for God my Savior;
my God will hear me.

8Do not gloat over me, my enemy!
Though I have fallen, I will rise.
Though I sit in darkness,
the LORD will be my light.
9Because I have sinned against him,
I will bear the LORD's wrath,
until he pleads my case
and establishes my right.
He will bring me out into the light;
I will see his righteousness
10Then my enemy will see it
and will be covered with shame,
she who said to me,
"Where is the LORD your God?"
My eyes will see her downfall;
even now she will be trampled underfoot
like mire in the streets.

7 The clouds of gloom began to separate as the prophet, speaking as the representative of the remnant, described the attitude of the godly person amid such difficult circumstances. Micah did not succumb to despair or lethargy but rather said, "I watch in hope for the LORD." The word "watch" (*ṣāpāh*) means to "look" or "wait expectantly." It was used of blind Eli who waited for the news of battle (1 Sam 4:13; cf. v.15). It is the same word used for "watchmen" earlier in this chapter (v.4). The godly man will look expectantly for God. As a watchman observes every shadow and listens to every night sound, so the godly man looks for every evidence of God's working. To close one's eyes to the working of God, no matter how small the evidence may be, is to open the door to despair.

Micah also waited for God to act in his own time. By thus acquiescing to God's holy will, Micah found peace in the knowledge of God's sovereign activity in the world. But Micah also expressed confidence that God would answer prayer. One can well understand how the societal wrongs of Micah's day might lead one to doubt the wise economy of God. But it was faith in that economy that kept the prophet from utter despair. That faith was ultimately confirmed by the realization of the Captivity, an event that was at once a national catastrophe and an evidence of the justice and holiness of God in dealing with a corrupt society.

8 Not only did Micah trust God to act and to answer prayer, but he trusted him to vindicate the faithful (vv.8–10). The remnant is speaking in v.8. Though the faithful are subjected to difficult experiences, they will one day rise to receive their heritage. There is vivid contrast between the people of God sitting in darkness and the gladdening effect of the light of God that will shine among them. The remnant of believers in any age can be confident of God's help and their eventual triumph (Matt 16:18).

9 Now there is a return to the legal atmosphere of chapter 6 as the remnant affirm their determination to wait till God pleads their cause and decides in their favor. They freely confess their sin in the awareness that the temporal punishment to be endured is a just punishment for their disobedience. This punishment is only for a time, however, for the remnant will be vindicated as they see God's righteousness. They can be confident of God's favorable action on their behalf; for they, unlike their guilty compatriots, stand on the ground of the covenant. Their sensitivity to sin, as illustrated in the opening line of this verse, and their allegiance to the covenant stipulations mark them as those who participate in the promises that are such a vital element of the covenant between Israel and her God.

10 Ultimately the remnant will be exalted and the hostile nations of the world covered with shame and trampled like mud. This latter figure is used by Isaiah (10:6) of the invading Assyrians. Micah uses it of the conquest of the hostile powers in the day of Israel's exaltation.

F. *The Assurance of Victory for the Kingdom of God* (7:11–20)

1. *Victory described in terms of the extension of the kingdom*

7:11–13

> [11]The day for building your walls will come,
> the day for extending your boundaries.
> [12]In that day people will come to you
> from Assyria and the cities of Egypt,
> even from Egypt to the Euphrates
> and from sea to sea
> and from mountain to mountain.
> [13]The earth will become desolate because of its inhabitants,
> as the result of their deeds.

11–12 The clouds of gloom have completely gone, and the remainder of the chapter is an exultant description of the eventual triumph of the remnant (vv.11–20). The prophet envisioned a great extension of the remnant's influence as he saw a future day when the nation would grow in area and numbers (vv.11–12). In this terminology the prophet pictured the then despised and persecuted remnant as occupying a position of broadest influence in the kingdom age. The future nation, cleansed of her sin and ruled by the King born in Bethlehem, would be greatly increased in population by an influx of people from Gentile nations, symbolized by Assyria and Egypt. This complements the message of 4:1–4 in that it gives to the revived nation of Israel a prominent role in the era of universal peace.

That the Gentiles are to become partakers of the promise through faith is a cardinal doctrine of both testaments (Gen 12:3; Amos 9:11–12; Rom 9:30; Gal 3:6–9). The perspective of the present passage seems not to be primarily the church age but rather the kingdom age, when the Jewish remnant will obtain visible prominence in the world and the unbelieving nations will be subjugated. Thus the passage is similar to Amos 9:11–12, where the inclusion of Gentiles in the promise is rooted in the era of peace when Israel's fortunes will be restored (Amos 9:13–15).

13 At the same time, however, the judgment of God will fall on the sinful world; for "the earth will be desolate" (RSV). Like Micah, Isaiah saw a judgment on the earth in connection with the kingdom age (Isa 34–35). Out of the decay of a crumbling society, Micah perceived the emergence of the kingdom of God. The prophet could be optimistic, for he knew that his lot was not with the impermanent society in which he lived but with the kingdom of God.

2. *Victory assured because of God's leadership*

7:14–15

> [14]Shepherd your people with your staff,
> the flock of your inheritance,
> which lives by itself in a forest,
> in fertile pasturelands.
> Let them feed in Bashan and Gilead
> as in days long ago.
>
> [15]"As in the days when you came out of Egypt,
> I will show them my wonders."

14 The remnant will triumph because of their relationship to God. This section is the remnant's prayer for restoration to the former days when their leaders brought them into the land. The remnant are pictured as dwelling alone, i.e., apart from the nations in a forest "in the middle of Carmel" (mg.). Bashan and Gilead were agricultural areas of great fertility that became symbols of plenty (Ps 22:12; Jer 50:19; Ezek 39:18). The reference to them here is symbolic. It is a request that Israel's former years of blessing be restored by her Good Shepherd.

15 The answer that comes from God is a promise of the restoration of the days when God led the people from bondage to their inheritance in Canaan. The Exodus was the central event in the prophetic theology of history. It was an event that could be repeated, because to the prophets history was continually being fulfilled. The Exodus would occur again—but in a new and even greater way. To the prophets, the Exodus was an event of more than historical interest. It revealed such attributes of God as his might, his sovereignty over the nations, and his love for his own. Because God is unchanging and his attributes timeless, his people could expect his acts to be repeated again and again in history. For this reason Hosea could view the impending captivity as a repetition of the Egyptian bondage (9:3; 11:5) and the Exodus as a pattern of their release from the impending captivity (11:11; cf. 12:9). (For a discussion of the repetition of the acts of God and its implications, see F. Foulkes, *The Acts of God* [London: Tyndale, 1955].)

3. *Victory assured over the nations*

7:16–17

> [16]Nations will see and be ashamed,
> deprived of all their power.
> They will lay their hands on their mouths
> and their ears will become deaf.
>
> [17]They will lick dust like a snake,
> like creatures that crawl on the ground.
> They will come trembling out of their dens;
> they will turn in fear to the LORD our God
> and will be afraid of you.

16 As a result of God's intervention on behalf of Israel, the nations will be humbled before God and his remnant. The might of the nations, which brought Israel into captivity, will be as nothing before the great power of God. To lay the hand on the mouth is to indicate reverence and awe (Job 29:9–10; Isa 52:15). The deafness of the nations may be caused by the thunderous events that God brings about (Job 26:14).

17 The vindication of God and his remnant in the world is pictured in extremely descriptive terms. The nations are pictured as animals crawling from their dens and trembling before the Lord.

4. *Victory assured because of God's nature*

7:18–20

18Who is a God like you,
who pardons sin and forgives the transgression
of the remnant of his inheritance?
You do not stay angry forever
but delight to show mercy.
19You will again have compassion on us;
you will tread our sins underfoot
and hurl all our iniquities into the depths of the sea.
20You will be true to Jacob,
and show mercy to Abraham,
as you pledged on oath to our fathers
in days long ago.

The remnant of God's people could be optimistic, not only because of the future hope that was theirs, but also because of the nature of God. Here was the great resource on which the remnant could draw.

18 The question "Who is a God like you?" points to the uniqueness of Yahweh. The name "Micah" means "who is like the LORD?" Whether this is another characteristic play on words is hard to say. The words "sin" and "transgression" recall the affirmation of Exodus 34:6–7, wherein the Lord proclaimed an essential aspect of his nature to be his willingness to forgive sin.

19–20 Because God's anger does not continue forever, the believing remnant could know that an end would come to their humiliation. After the great statement of forgiveness of v.19, the prophet recalled the promise given to Abraham and reaffirmed to Jacob (v.20). The remnant's optimism was rooted in the promise sworn to Abraham and the fathers. The promise is eternal (Gen 13:15; 17:7–8, 13, 19; 48:4); and its elements are still applicable to Christians—though reinterpreted by the new covenant—because they are a spiritual people (1 Peter 2:5), not a national entity as were the Israelites. We hear the same promises ringing in the NT: the Lord's being God to his people (Gen 17:7; cf. 2 Cor 6:16; Heb 8:10; Rev 21:3, 7), the concept of a royal people (Gen 17:6, 16; cf. 1 Peter 2:9; Rev 1:6; 5:10), the land or place of rest (Rom 4:13; Heb 4:1–10), to name only a few. The promise is a continuum that guarantees an inheritance to all God's people. The church thus shares the same heritage and hope as God's people in the OT. We, too, expect to reign with the King from Bethlehem (5:2), our sins having been trodden underfoot (7:19). We, too, know the loving care of the Shepherd who feeds his flock in the strength of the Lord. Micah's concept of the remnant encompasses believers today.

NAHUM

Carl E. Armerding

NAHUM

Introduction

1. Background

Nahum's prophecy is rooted in the Lord's revelation of himself at Sinai as a God of judgment and mercy. This self-revelation is echoed in 1:2–6 and given increasingly specific application in the remaining verses of the book. Nahum thus stands firmly in Israel's prophetic tradition as one inspired to interpret the complexities of the present and future in the light of the past: the general truths of the law belonged to every member of the covenant (Deut 29:29); the details of its outworking in history were understood only by those called to stand in the Lord's council (Jer 23:18, 22; Amos 3:7).

The setting of the prophecy of Nahum is the long and painful oppression of Israel by Assyria—"Although I have afflicted you" (1:12)—and the divine prospect of its end—"I will afflict you no more" (ibid.). Although God was the ultimate author of Israel's affliction, Assyria, the rod of God's anger, was the agent of his wrath; and the cup in the Lord's right hand was now coming around to her.

Assyria had long been central in God's affliction of his people, Israel. As early as the ninth century, Shalmaneser III (858–824 B.C.) exacted tribute from Jehu in one of his western campaigns (c. 824): "The tribute of Jehu (*Ia-ú-a*), son of Omri (*Ḫu-um-ri*); I received from him silver, gold, a golden *saplu*-bowl, a golden vase with pointed bottom, golden tumblers, golden buckets, tin, a staff for a king" (ANET, p. 281).

Adad-nirari III (810–782) similarly claimed the submission of Israel ("Omri Land") among his Palestinian vassals (ANET, p. 281). However, Tiglath-pileser III (745–727) represents the first major scourge of Israel. He invaded that land during the reign of Menahem (752–732; cf. 2 Kings 15:29; 1 Chron 5:6, 26; 2 Chron 30:6, 10; Isa 9:1). Tiglath-pileser recorded this campaign: "Israel (lit.: "Omri-Land" *Bit Ḫumria*) . . . all its inhabitants (and) their possessions I led to Assyria. They overthrew their king Pekah (*Pa-qa-ḫa*) and I placed Hoshea (*A-ú-si-'*) as king over them. I received from them 10 talents of gold, 1,000 (?) talents of silver as their [tri]bute and brought them to Assyria" (ANET, p. 284).

Tiglath Pileser III extended his authority into Judah, where Ahaz (735–715) pursued a policy of submission to Assyria ("[I received] the tribute of . . . Jehoahaz (*Ia-ú-ḫa-zi*) of Judah" [ANET, p. 282]). Ahaz thereby incurred the opposition of both Pekah, king of Israel (c. 740–732), who favored the anti-Assyrian coalition of his predecessor Ahab, and Isaiah, who denounced his faithlessness in depending on Assyria, rather than on the Lord, when faced with Pekah's aggression (2 Kings 16:5–18; 2 Chron 28:16–25; Isa 7:1–25; 8:6–8; cf. Jer 2:36). During the reign of Ahaz, therefore, Judah was faced with the issue of submission or resistance to Assyria—an issue that confronted the nation for over a century and to which it responded in faith or fear according to its relationship to the Lord. Pekah was murdered by Hoshea (732–722), who adopted a vacillating pro-Assyrian policy. His fickle decision to rely on Egypt and repudiate his allegiance to Assyria provoked the invasion of Shalmaneser V (727–722).

Samaria fell after a long seige by Shalmaneser's successor, Sargon II (721–705; cf. ANET, p. 284); the northern kingdom was destroyed and its population deported (2 Kings 17:3–6; cf. 18:20–21; Isa 7:8; 8:4; 10:11; 36:20; Hos 9:3; 10:6, 14; 11:5). This catastrophe is explicitly attributed to the Lord's affliction of Israel for her sin (2 Kings 17:20; cf. 17:7–19, 21–23; 18:9–12; see also 1 Chron 5:26; 2 Chron 30:7; Neh 9:30), as were the misfortunes of Ahaz in the same era (2 Chron 28:19–20). Palestine experienced further depredations under Sargon II (Isa 20:1–6), before facing the full brunt of Assyria's hostility in the reign of Sennacherib (704–681). Hezekiah (728–687) had succeeded Ahaz and abandoned his pro-Assyrian policy (2 Kings 18:7–8, 19–20). Sennacherib thereupon invaded Judah (701), conquering its fortified cities and threatening Jerusalem, before the decimation of his army by "a wasting disease upon his sturdy warriors" (Isa 10:16; cf. 2 Kings 18:13–19:37; 2 Chron 32:1–31; Isa 36:1–37:38. See 1:11; cf. ANET, pp. 287–88). Again, the terrible distress preceding this deliverance was specifically attributed to the Lord as he chastened his unfaithful yet beloved people (cf. Isa 5:26; 7:17–18, 20; 8:7; 10:5–6, 11–12, 24–25; 29:1–4; 31:4, 8). In the following century both Esarhaddon (681–669) and his son Ashurbanipal (669–633) exercised dominion over Judah, to which Esarhaddon referred explicitly in a building inscription: "I called up . . . Manasseh (*Me-na-si-i*) king of Judah" (ANET, p. 291). This may correspond to the biblical incident of Manasseh's bondage, a further instance of the Lord's affliction mediated by the Assyrians (2 Chron 33:1–11).

The stability of Ashurbanipal's long reign was followed by dynastic instability, his sons Ashur-etil-ilani and Sinshumlishir (?) being succeeded after brief reigns by the former's son, Sin-shar-ishkun (621–612). During this period Nabopolassar established himself securely as king of Babylon (625–605), attacking and successively capturing the pro-Assyrian cities of Babylonia and achieving complete independence from Assyria by 616. In 614 Ashur was seized amid brutal massacre by the Medes under Cyaxares; and after this major Assyrian loss, an alliance was concluded between Nabopolassar and Cyaxares against Assyria. The siege and destruction of Nineveh, completed in 612, were the outcome of this alliance and of Assyria's failure to maintain its hold on the disparate and deeply hostile elements of its empire. Assyria could scarcely be regarded as unscathed after 639, indeed.

The final years of Ashurbanipal's reign are marked by obscurity (c. 638–633), being largely devoid of historical records; uncharacteristically, during this period no great conquests are attributed to the Assyrian monarch, who had apparently withdrawn to Haran, abandoning the government of the empire to his successors. These implications of growing weakness are substantiated by Judah's history under Josiah (640–609): religious reforms expressed his repudiation of Judah's subordination to Assyrian rule and even extended his influence into the neighboring Assyrian province to the north (2 King 23:1–25). This evidence for the slackening of Assyria's grip on the west is confirmed also by the resurgence of Egypt as an independent power; for under Psammetik I (664–609; cf. ZPEB, 2:231) it successfully challenged Assyria's control of the Palestinian coastal plain, capturing Gerar, Ashkelon, Ashdod, and other cities. The condition of Assyria at the time of Nahum's prophecy therefore suggests a date prior to 640 and gives considerable weight to the authority of that prophecy. The downfall of the Assyrian colossus has been characterized as one of the greatest riddles of world history. In a similar vein, A.L. Oppenheim (quoted in Maier, p. 108) writes: "A strong period of silence blacks out the last twenty years of the reign of Ashurbanipal. From the prosperity and the apogee of Assyrian power and prestige—two topics on which the scribes of Ashurbanipal do not tire of elaborating in glowing terms—the country seems to have fallen with appalling suddenness into obscurity."

The subjugation of Israel and Judah had involved political servitude, accompanied by severe demands for tribute or indemnities (cf. 2 Kings 15:19–20; 16:8; 17:3; 18:14–16; Hos 10:6). It also threatened Judah with the social disintegration that swept Israel into exile (cf. 2 Kings 15:29; 17:6; 18:11; 1 Chron 6:6, 26; 2 Chron 30:6, 10; Isa 36:16–17; Hos 9:3; 10:6; 11:5). And, most significantly, it disrupted the nation's worship, since Assyrian political hegemony was accompanied by the cult of its gods and promoted the intrusion of a debilitating religious syncretism (cf. 2 Kings 16:10–18; 17:24–41; 21:1–18; 2 Chron 28:23–25; 33:1–11; Ezra 4:2). For this reason Judah's willing dependence on foreign powers was castigated as spiritual adultery, constituting an abandonment of true allegiance to the Lord and of dependence on him (e.g., 2 Chron 28:16–25; Isa 3:6; 8:5–22; Jer 2:18, 36; Ezek 16:28; 23:5–12; Hos 1:2; 5:13; 7:11; 8:9; 12:1; 14:3). For the same reason political independence was a necessary corollary of religious reform (e.g., 2 Kings 18:1–18; 22:1–23:30; 2 Chron 29:3–32:1).

2. Unity

a. *Thematic*

The two sections—Nahum 1 and 2–3—are unified thematically by key words: "fire" (1:6; 2:4; 3:13, 15); "consume," "devour" (1:10; 2:13; 3:12–13, 15 [*bis*]); and "destroy," "cut down" (1:14–15; 2:13 [NIV, "leave no"]; 3:15)—a fitting anticipation of the conflagration and slaughter attending Nineveh's end. These motifs illustrate the most prominent thematic strands uniting the three chapters, namely, destruction by fire (1:6, 10; 2:3–4, 13; 3:3, 13, 15) and military disaster (1:12, 14–15; 2:1, 3–5, 13; 3:2–3, 8–11, 12–15, 19). Other principal strands are (1) Nineveh's wicked opposition to the Lord and his people (1:2–3, 8–9, 11, 13, 15), expressing its universal cruelty and rapacity (2:11–3:1, 4, 19); (2) The Lord's corresponding opposition to Nineveh (1:2–6, 8–9, 14; 2:13; 3:5); (3) its decadence typified by drunkenness (1:10; 3:12–13, 15–18; cf. 3:11); (4) its helplessness in the face of disaster (1:10; 2:9–10; 3:11, 13); (5) its exposure to shame (1:14; 3:5–7); (6) flooding by water (1:8; 2:6, 8; cf. 1:3; 3:8); (7) the destruction of the dynasty and of the idolatrous religion undergirding it (1:11, 14; 2:6, 11–13; 3:18–19; (8) the dispersal of the population (1:8; 2:1, 7–8; 3:7, 10–11, 16–18); (9) Nineveh's extinction (1:8–9, 12, 14–15; 2:13; 3:7, 19); (10) the vindication of Judah (1:3, 7, 12–13, 15; 2:2). The prophecy is structured around these intricately interwoven elements, which set forth the causes (nos. 1–4, 10) and manner (nos. 5–9) of Nineveh's downfall. The close-knit composition of the book firmly unites its two main sections, and no rigid division can be made between them. They may, however, be roughly characterized as representing the judicial decree against Nineveh (ch. 1) and its precise execution (chs. 2–3). This execution corresponds in remarkable detail to the actual course of events, corroborated by historical and archaeological evidence, and represents an outstanding example of fulfilled prophecy (a major contribution of Nahum to the OT, perhaps neglected or depreciated precisely because it is now so obvious). It is therefore appropriate to deal with details of its fulfillment in chapters 2–3, at the most appropriate point of reference (e.g., flood, 2:6; fire, 3:15); only where such a clear reference point is lacking are such details advanced to chapter 1 (e.g., idolatry, 1:14).

b. *Stylistic*

Stylistically, Nahum is unified by its vivid imagery (e.g., 1:3–8, 10; 2:3–4, 8, 11–13; 3:2–3, 4–6, 12–13, 15–17) and the rapid switches of speaker and perspective (e.g., 1:7–8, 11–2:3, 8–11, 13–3:1, 4–8, 11, 18–19). These features contribute powerfully to the dramatic quality of the prophecy, in its portrayal of a violent and fateful crossroads in history. This contrast of interlocked, conflicting destinies brilliantly illustrates this tumultuous time in political and social history, events of which are attested by ancient Near Eastern records. It is constructed, however, on a clear-cut dialectic of "good" (1:7; cf. vv.3, 12–13, 15; 2:2) and "evil" (1:11; cf. vv.3–6, 8–11, 12, 14–15; 2:1–10), whose simple polarity orders and interprets that succession of events as moral history. And it is based on the monolithic concept of God's sovereign justice, whose working in salvation history eludes the sociologist and philosopher and is perceived by prophetic eyes alone. Thus Nahum's prophecy moves at many levels. Its structure reflects this complexity and is by no means fully represented here.

3. Authorship

Little is known of Nahum himself, the author according to 1:1. He is identified as "the Elkoshite" (*hā'elqōšî*). Since the sixteenth century, an Arab tradition has identified Elkosh with Al Qosh, a village near modern Mosul in Iraq. Ancient writers—including Jerome and Eusebius—however, understood the prophet's home to be somewhere in Galilee. Many have speculated that NT Capernaum ("Town of Nahum") was home to him, but there is no proof of this.

4. Date

From internal data it is possible to date the major blocks of material in Nahum, though critics continue to debate small pericopes. As a message of judgment, the book makes no sense if it was proclaimed following the collapse of the Assyrian empire in 612 B.C. On the other hand, references to the destruction of Thebes (No-amon) by the Nile (3:8) demand that the prophecy postdate that city's fall to Ashurbanipal in 663 B.C. Further consideration of the still formidable state of Assyrian power reflected in the book itself requires that we date the prophecy prior to the decline of that kingdom after about 626 B.C. (cf. comment at 3:8). P.A. Verhoef (ZPEB, 4:357) believes that the prophecy was written sometime before 645 B.C., which would be consistent with Assyria's power as reflected in the book.

5. Literary Form

The prophecy of Nahum is in two main sections—chapter 1 and chapters 2 and 3, which correspond to each other as outlined below.

Chapter 1 describes God's judgment (vv.2–11) and the sentence underlying that judgment (vv.12–14), incorporating its proclamation and the response it elicits (v.15). The chapter is dominated by its prediction of a total end for Nineveh and the dispersion of its inhabitants (vv.3, 8–9, 12, 14–15).

Chapters 2–3 repeat this pattern, with detailed and explicit application to "Nineveh" (2:8; 3:7); this passage consists of a number of corresponding subsections.

OVERVIEW OF STRUCTURE

	Chapter 1	Chapters 2–3
	Judgment (A)	Judgment (A')
Executed on evil	1:11 (*rā'āh*)	3:19 (*rā'āh*)
By flood	1:8 (*šeṭep*)	2:6, 8 (gates opened)
By fire	1:6 (*'ēš*)	2:4; 3:13, 15 (*'ēš*)
That consumes	1:10 (*'āḵal*)	3:13, 15 (*bis*) (*'āḵal*)
By drunkenness	1:10 (*sāḇā'*)	3:11 (*tiškᵉrî*)
Exception	1:7 (those who trust)	2:2 (Jacob/Israel)
	Sentence (B)	Sentence (B')
Messenger formula	1:12 ("This is what the LORD says")	2:13; 3:5 ("declares the LORD Almighty")
Against	1:14 (*'āleyḵā*)	2:13; 3:5 (*'elayiḵ*)
Result: cut off	1:14–15 (*kāraṯ*)	2:13; 3:15 (*kāraṯ*)
No more	1:14–15 (*lō' 'ôḏ*)	2:13 (*lō' 'ôḏ*)
End: vileness, shame	1:14 (*qālal*)	3:5 (*qālāh*)
	Response (C)	Response (C')
On the mountains	1:15 (*'al-hehārîm*)	3:18 (*'al-hehārîm*)
Proclaim	1:15 (*mašmîa'*)	2:13; 3:19 (*bis*) (*šāma'*)

6. Literary Parallel

Nahum's prophecy has many affinities with the Book of Isaiah. These affinities are signaled most clearly by the words in 1:15: "on the mountains the feet of one who brings good news, who proclaims peace" (*'al-hehārîm, raglê m^e^bāśśēr mašmîa' šālôm*), which recur verbatim in Isaiah 52:7 and are without close parallel elsewhere in the OT. A further clear correspondence is between Nahum 1:15—"No more will the wicked invade you"—and Isaiah 52:1—"The uncircumcised . . . will not enter you again." The reversal promised in both clauses is heralded by the refrain "no more, not again" (*lō' 'ôḏ*); this phrase is a keynote of Nahum 1:12–15 (cf. vv. 12, 15) and occurs also in Isaiah 51:17–23, which anticipates the content of Isaiah 52 (51:22). Similarly the verb "invade" (*'āḇar*, Nah 1:15) is used in the same context of invasion in Isaiah 51:23, where it is twice translated "walk over." These evidences of literary dependence are reinforced by a common context. Both passages promise liberation (Nah 1:12–15; Isa 51:22; 52:1–5), specifically from "shackles" or "chains" (*môsēr*, Nah 1:13; Isa 52:2), and from being "afflicted" (*'ānāh*, Nah 1:12; Isa 51:21; cf. also *mākar*, "enslaved," Nah 3:4; "sold," Isa 52:3). This promise is addressed to "Judah" and to "Zion," its capital (Nah 1:15; Isa 52:1, 2, 7), in the wake of Assyrian oppression (Nah 1:12–15; Isa 52:4); and it is introduced in the same terms by the messenger formula ("This is what the LORD says," Nah 1:12; Isa 52:3) and by the phrase "(and) now" (*w^e'attāh*, Nah 1:13; Isa 52:5), announcing a transitional moment in history. Thus the language and imagery of redemption in Nahum 1:12–15 corresponds with remarkable exactitude to that of Isaiah 51:21–52:7.

Moreover, the correlation between the Book of Nahum and Isaiah 51–52 extends to the second theme of judgment on the oppressor. In Isaiah 51:23 the Lord promised to Zion's enemies the judgment she herself had suffered, and the same reversal of fortunes pervades Nahum (cf. 1:12–2:2, 11–13; 3:4–7, 16–17). In particular Nineveh would become "drunk" (*šāḵar*, Nah 3:11; Isa 51:21); her leaders would prove inadequate ("lie down" [*šāḵan*], Nah 3:18; cf. vv.16–17; "lie" [*šāḵaḇ*], Isa 51:20; cf. v.18); she would experience the fate ascribed to Zion in Isaiah 51:19: "ruin" (*šāḏaḏ*, Nah 3:7) and "destruction" (*šeḇer*, Nah 3:19), "famine" (cf. "locusts," Nah 3:15–17) and "sword" (*ḥereḇ*, Nah 2:13; 3:3, 15). She would, in fact, experience the same "wrath" of God (*ḥēmāh*, Nah 1:2, 6; Isa 51:17, 20, 22). Considered individually these correlations are not uniformly distinctive, though the recurrence of Isaiah 51:19 in Nahum 3 is striking. They gain significance collectively, in view of the established relation between Nahum and Isaiah 51–52. And they receive added corroboration from a further distinctive correspondence linking Isaiah 51:19 and Nahum 3:7. The clause "who can comfort you?" (*mî yānûḏ lāḵ*, Isa 51:19) is echoed in Nahum 3:7: "Who will mourn for her? (*mî yānûḏ lāh*) and elsewhere only in Jeremiah 15:5. The following compressed question—"Who can console you?" (*mî 'ănaḥămēḵ*, Isa 51:19; lit., "How can I console you?")—is expanded in Nahum 3:7: "Where can I find anyone to comfort you?" (*mē'ayin 'ăḇaqqēš m^enaḥămîm lāḵ*), with one approximate parallel in Lamentations 2:13.

In view of the precision, uniqueness, and frequency of these correspondences, it seems evident, then, that Nahum's relationship to Isaiah 51–52 extends beyond participation in a common stock of prophetic imagery and motif to one of specific literary interdependence. This conclusion is confirmed by further extensive points of contact between the two books. First, the image of God drying the sea (Nah 1:4) is preeminently Isaianic. Thus the terms "rebuke" (*gā'ar*), "sea" (*yām*), "rivers" (*n^ehārôṯ*), and "dry" (*ḥārēḇ*) all recur in Isaiah 50:2.

Second, the following couplet of Nahum 1:4 also finds a precise parallel in Isaiah 33:9: the terms "Lebanon . . . Bashan . . . Carmel" do not recur together in a single verse or passage outside those two locations; and they are used in the same context of drought and desolation, expressed by the shared verb "fade . . . wither," "wastes away" (*'umlal*).

The third motif shared conspicuously by Nahum and Isaiah is the Lord's anger. This is obviously a common theme throughout the OT; however, it is expressed distinctively in these books—particularly in terms of fire and other natural imagery, and with explicit reference to Assyria.

The evidence for literary interdependence between Isaiah and Nahum is thus founded on unique, multiple verbal repetitions linking specific passages (e.g., Nah 1:2 and Isa 59:17–19; 1:3–6 and 29:6; 1:4 and 33:9; 50:2; 1:4–5 and 42:15; 1:15 and 52:1, 7; 2:9–10 and 24:1, 3; 2:10 and 21:3–4; 3:5–7 and 47:2–3; 3:7 and 51:19). It is reinforced by the extensive continuity of imagery in other related passages (e.g., drought, earthquake, fire, stubble, burial, lions). And it is corroborated to the point of virtual certainty by the shared pattern of oppression, deliverance, and judgment experienced specifically in relation to Assyria (cf. Isa 5:26–30; 7:17–20; 8:4–8; 9:1; 10:5–34; 11:11, 15–16; 14:24–27; 19:23–25; 20:1–6; 27:13; 30:27–33; 31:1–9; 36:1–37:38; 38:6; 51:17–52:7). There are forty-four references to Assyria in Isaiah, exceeded only by 2 Kings (forty-nine); no other OT book approaches this preoccupation with Assyrian history apart from Nahum and, to a lesser extent, Hosea and Jonah.

Evidently these correlations are of considerable significance for the literary criticism of Isaiah. They cannot be pursued in detail here, but several points are readily apparent.

The cycle of Isaianic prophecies regarding Assyria are usually attributed without dispute to Isaiah ben Amoz, who prophesied in Jerusalem in the eighth century; this would include most, if not all, of Isaiah 5–11, 14:24–27; 19:23–25; 20:1–6; 27:13–30:33 (cf. A. Weiser, *The Old Testament: Its Formation and Development* [New York: Association, 1961], pp. 187–93). It follows that Nahum is dependent on Isaiah in his allusions to Isaiah 5:24–30; 10:5–27; 29:1–6; 30:27–33, since Nahum is to be dated after 663. Such dependency on previous witnesses is characteristic of the prophetic tradition, and it is logical in this case, in view of Nahum's preoccupation with the same issues as Isaiah.

This leaves numerous correspondences unexplained (particularly, Nah 1:2 and Isa 59:17–19; 1:4 and 33:9; 50:2; 1:4–5 and 42:15; 1:3, 6 and 66:15–16; 1:15 and 52:1, 7; 2:9–10 and 24:1, 3; 2:10 and 21:3; 3:5–7 and 47:2–3; 3:7 and 51:19). It is conceivable that a "Second Isaiah," prophesying in the sixth century, would have drawn on Nahum in this way; the Fall of Nineveh would then provide a suitable analogy for that of Babylon. However, it is remarkable that so original a prophet as the author(s) of Isaiah 40–66 should draw this heavily on a work of such restricted scope as Nahum.

Alternatively, Nahum was drawing on Isaiah 1–66 in its entirety. This explains the continuity of Nahum's imagery (e.g., fire, vengeance, drought) with passages distributed throughout Isaiah. It also explains Nahum's application of prophecies concerning Babylon (Isa 13–14, 47) to Assyria, since he prophesied before the emergence of Babylon from its status as an Assyrian vassal. It is appropriate to the clear-cut evidence, which reveals Nahum as drawing on Isaiah. And, finally, this provides a suitable interpretation of the outstanding correlation between Nahum 1:15 and Isaiah 52:7, where the concept of "peace"—an integral element of Isaiah's message (*šālôm,* cf. Isa 9:6–7; 26:3, 12; 27:5; 32:17–18; 39:8; 45:7; 48:18, 22; 53:5; 54:10, 13; 55:12; 57:2, 19, 21; 59:8; 60:17; 66:12)—appears as an undeveloped theme in Nahum, more organically connected with the content of Isaiah, from which it is most likely to have been transposed. This appears more plausible than that a "Second Isaiah" appropriated and largely developed a peripheral motif of Nahum.

These interrelationships indicate that in Nahum we have an outstanding example of OT prophetic interpretation and application within the OT itself. And they also hold out the possibility that this "minor" prophecy holds a key to the authentication of its great forerunner. "The eye cannot say to the hand, 'I don't need you!' And the head cannot say to the feet, 'I don't need you!' On the contrary, those parts of the body that seem to be weaker are indispensable" (1 Cor 12:21–22).

7. Theological Values

Theologically, Nahum stands as an eloquent testimony to the particularity of God's justice and salvation. To the suffering remnant, there was little question that God would and did punish his own covenant people; but whether he was equally able and willing to impart justice to the powerful heathen nations surrounding Israel was untested. Among those nations, none had dominated world affairs in the second millenium B.C. as had imperial Assyria. Arrogant, self-sufficient, cruel, and assertive, the Assyrians had dominated every small nation in the region at one time or another from the days of the first Tiglath-pileser (1115–1076) onward.

The righteous Israelite might well have asked, as did Habakkuk (1:2),

> How long, O LORD, must I call for help,
>   but you do not listen?
> Or cry out to you, "Violence!"
>   but you do not save?

The severity and kindness of God were both under scrutiny: the former as to whether it applied only selectively to his own people, and the latter in the context of God's ability and desire to bring about ultimate salvation for those who were faithful to him.

Between the divine plan for salvation history and the wretched condition of his oppressed people stood the power of a particular, powerful human foe—Assyria. Over four hundred years of Middle Eastern history pointed in the same direction: Assyria and her gods were in control, if there was in fact any control over universal, historical direction. Back in Jerusalem each brief fling at independence by a petty monarch ended in disaster. The temple on Zion had survived over the years, but the shadow of destruction already lay over it. The worship of Yahweh in the mid-seventh century had already disappeared in the north and was threatened by syncretistic forces in the south. Nineveh stood, with her gods, as the capital of the most powerful kingdom the world had ever seen. "Where, then, is your God?" the skeptic might rightly ask. "And if he exists, what kind of God is he?"

Into this situation came the word of the Lord: "The LORD is a jealous and avenging God. . . . slow to anger and great in power; the LORD will not leave the guilty unpunished" (Nah 1:2–3). Nineveh's day would come to an end; no power on earth can long endure when it sets itself against the Lord and his Anointed in Zion (cf. Ps 2). The vivid imagery of Nahum's pictured demise of Nineveh is eloquent testimony to the power of a God whose strength is never simply an abstraction. A theology of divine sovereignty and justice, applauded by all the nations, emerges from the specifics of Assyria's fall.

It is not merely divine retribution, however, that emerges from the picture. There is also good news to proclaim. "Look, there on the mountains, the feet of one who brings good news, who proclaims peace!" (1:15). Judah is called to celebration as God's people inevitably are, when the day of Yahweh's wrath is fully understood, and the remnant are prepared in righteousness. The corollary to the severity of God is his kindness (*ḥeseḏ*), a mercy that includes covenant keeping and justice. Here is the theme of every prayer of every true remnant through the years as they cry out, "How long, O Lord, how long?" "Thy will be done, on earth as it is in heaven" is the natural concomitant of the cry, "Thy kingdom come!"

To the Christian longing for the day of good tidings, the message is clearly set forth in the new covenant. Paul, in Romans 10:15, extolled the preaching of the gospel of salvation with a quotation from this ancient book of judgment: "As it is written, 'How beautiful are the feet of those who bring good news!' " In this age it is the preaching of the gospel that will ensure the ultimate triumph of God, even, as the same chapter (v.18) points out: "Their words [will go forth] to the ends of the world." This promise, not the Assyrian or even the Roman dominion, will be the final word on history.

When the forces opposing God are so firmly ensconced and the flickering lamp of God's people is at the point of extinction, however, it is easy for the remnant to forget. Nahum reminds us, as do the ruins of ancient Nineveh, that God himself is the ultimate Ruler. He will have the final word. There is good news for the people of God. Just as years later the aged Simeon could pray in confidence (Luke 2:29–32):

> "Sovereign Lord, as you have promised,
> you now dismiss your servant in peace.
> For my eyes have seen your salvation,
> which you have prepared in the sight of all people,
> a light for revelation to the Gentiles
> and for glory to your people Israel,"

so the waiting supplicant in Nahum's day could look ahead to such a day. It was then—and continues today—to be the hope of the people of God: our eyes shall see the salvation of the Lord.

8. Canonicity and Text

The canonicity and text of Nahum have never been seriously challenged. Some rationalist scholars (e.g., Pfeiffer) alleged that 1:2–10 was not originally a part of the prophecy but is a late, corrupted piece of acrostic poetry added by a redactor. The form and order of these verses have often been rearranged in the interests of restoring the acrostic. This arrangement is suggested by v.2, which opens with the first letter of the Hebrew alphabet, and by the presence of some of the subsequent letters at or near the beginning of succeeding lines. However, since only two letters occur in their expected position (vv.2a, 3b), there appears to be insufficient grounds for seeking an acrostic here, let alone for rearranging the text to conform to one. Archer (SOT, p. 341) says, "As the text stands, there is virtually nothing acrostic about it. . . . Only by the most radical emendations and reshuffling of verses can the acrostic theory be made out."

9. Bibliography

Books

Beck, Madeline H., and Williamson, Lamar, Jr. *Mastering Old Testament Facts: Book 4: Prophetic Writings*. Atlanta: John Knox, 1981.
Bernini, Giuseppe. *Osea, Michea, Nahum, Abacuc*. Roma: Paoline, 1977.
Boadt, Lawrence. *Jeremiah 26–52, Habakkuk, Zephaniah, Nahum (Old Testament Message)*. Vol. 10. Wilmington: Michael Glazier, 1982.
Cathcart, Kevin J. *Nahum in the Light of Northwest Semitic*. Rome: Biblical Institute Press, 1973.
Ellison, H.L. *The Old Testament Prophets*. Grand Rapids: Zondervan, 1966.
Feinberg, Charles L. *The Minor Prophets*. Chicago: Moody, 1976.
Gailey, James H. *The Layman's Bible Commentary*. Vol. 15. Atlanta: John Knox, 1977.
Gelston, A., editor. *Dodekapropheton*. Leiden Peshitta. Vol. 3:4. Leiden: E.J. Brill, 1980.
Henderson, E. *The Twelve Minor Prophets*. Grand Rapids: Baker, 1980.
Keil, Carl F. *The Twelve Minor Prophets*. Vol. 2. Grand Rapids: Eerdmans, 1949.
Laetsch, Theodore. *The Minor Prophets*. St. Louis: Concordia, 1956.
Maier, Walter A. *The Book of Nahum*. Grand Rapids: Baker, 1959.
Pusey, E.B. *The Minor Prophets*. Vol. 2. Reprint ed. Grand Rapids: Baker, 1950.
Rudolph, Wilhelm. *Kommentar zum Alten Testament*. Vol. 13/3. Guetersloh: Mohn, 1975.
Schneider, D. *The Unity of the Book of the Twelve*. New Haven: Yale, 1979.
Smith, George A. *The Book of the Twelve Prophets*. Vol. 2. ExB. London: Hodder & Stoughton, 1898.
Sperber, Alexander, editor. *The Bible in Aramaic: The Latter Prophets*. Vol. 3. Leiden: E.J. Brill, 1962.
Vegas Montaner, Luis. *Biblia Del Mar Muerto: Profetas Menores*. Madrid Instituto "Arias Montano" CSIC, 1980.
Woude, A.S. van der. *Jona, Nahum: Prediking O.T.* Nijkerk: Callenbach, 1978.
Ziegler, Joseph. *Septuaginta: Duodecim Prophetae*. Vol. 13. Goettingen: Vandenhoeck & Ruprecht, 1967.

Journals

Becking, Rob. "Bee's Dating Formula and the Rock of Nahum." *Journal for the Study of the Old Testament* 18 (1980): 100–104.
Cathcart, Kevin. "The Divine Warrior and the War of Yahweh in Nahum." Biblical Studies in Contemporary Thought. Burlington: *Vetus Testamentum* (1975): 68–76.
______. "More Philological Studies in Nahum." *Journal of Northwest Semitic Languages* 7 (1979): 1–12.
Delcor, Matthias. "Allusions a la deese Istar, Nahum 2:8." *Biblica* 58 (1977): 73–83.
Mihelic, J.L. "The Concept of God in the Book of Nahum." *Interpretation* 2 (1948): 199–207.
Weinfeld, Moshe. "Late Mesopotamian Prophecies." *Shnaton Mikra* (Tel Aviv) 3 (1978): 263–76.
Woude, A.S. van der. "The Book of Nahum: A Letter Written in Exile." *Oudtestamentische Studien* 20 (1977): 108–26.

10. Outline

- I. The Anger of the Lord (1:1–15)
  - A. The Judgment of the Lord (1:1–11)
    - 1. Awesome in power (1:1–6)
    - 2. Just in execution (1:7–11)
  - B. The Sentence of the Lord (1:12–14)
  - C. The Purpose of the Lord (1:15)
- II. The Fall of Nineveh (2:1–3:19)
  - A. Warning and Promise (2:1–2)
  - B. Nineveh's Destruction Detailed (2:3–3:7)
    - 1. First description of Nineveh's destruction (2:3–3:1)
      - a. Onslaught (2:3–5)
      - b. Failing defenses (2:6–10)
      - c. An interpretive analogy (2:11–12)
      - d. Judgment from the Lord (2:13)
      - e. The verdict announced (3:1)
    - 2. Second description of Nineveh's destruction (3:2–7)
      - a. Onslaught and failing defenses (3:2–3)
      - b. An interpretive analogy (3:4)
      - c. Judgment from the Lord (3:5–6)
      - d. The verdict announced (3:7)
    - 3. Third description of Nineveh's destruction (3:8–11)
    - 4. Fourth description of Nineveh's destruction (3:12–19)
      - a. Onslaught and failing defenses (3:12–14)
      - b. Interpretive analogy and judgment from the Lord (3:15–17)
      - c. The verdict announced (3:18–19)

Text and Exposition

I. The Anger of the Lord (1:1–15)

This chapter is structured as three units (cf. Introduction: Literary Form): the judgment of God (vv.1–11), the sentence to follow (vv.12–14), and the response elicited (v.15), each of which involves a counterpoint of contrast between the goodness and severity of God. Within the first section, vv.2–6 form a general statement of the Lord's patience (v.3) and of his devastating judgment of his enemies (v.2). Verses 7–11 echo these contrasts in the reference to his goodness (v.7), defined further as being extended to those who "trust" and as affording protection from "trouble." These verses similarly picture the complete "end" (vv.8–11) of those who in their "wickedness" plot against the Lord.

Verses 12–14 (possibly including v.15) embody the sovereign decree of God, based on the preceding evidence and amplifying it further. His protection brings deliverance from the "yoke" of oppression (v.13; cf. vv.12, 15); it is promised to "Judah," whose trust as his covenant people is expressed in true religious service (v.15). Conversely, his judgment overthrows the oppressive military, political, and dynastic power of his enemies (vv.12–15), whose wickedness is expressed in idolatry (v.14). Verse 15, whether as part of the preceding section or isolated, continues the counterpoint effect, in which the central theme of judgment is intertwined and contrasted with that of mercy.

The entire chapter is unified and dominated by its revelation of the character and activity of the Lord, being punctuated repeatedly by explicit mention of his name (passim). It thereby sets forth the intricate yet coherent complexity of God's dealings with his creation: his ways in judgment and mercy are as variegated as those of the nations he governs: his ways are as profound as the sovereign purpose of his own heart.

The antiphonal character of chapter 1 extends to chapters 2 and 3: the enemy, hitherto anonymous (NIV interpolates with the name "Nineveh" in 1:8, 11, 14, and 2:1), is finally identified as "Nineveh" and its "king" (2:8, 3:7, 18). The major structural break noted between 1:15 and 2:1 must therefore be qualified in light of the concurrent pattern, by which Nahum 2–3 merely extends the progressive specification of God's vengeance and mercy, initiated in the first chapter.

A. *The Judgment of the Lord* (1:1–11)

The opening verses of Nahum form a prologue dominated by the revelation of God's eternal power and divine nature in creation (cf. Rom 1:20). As in Romans 1:18–32, this revelation is characterized preeminently by God's justice, expressed in retribution (v.2) and wrath (vv.2–3, 6) that shake the entire creation (vv. 3–6). The mercy of God, for all its reality, is a fleeting counterpart to this awesome display of majesty.

The passage, framed by the word "wrath" (*ḥēmāh*, vv.2,6), consists of a forceful enunciation of the "vengeance" accomplished by God's "wrath" (vv.2–3), manifested in nature (vv.3–5) and in society (v.5). These three elements are repeated in a summary section (v.6).

This dramatic representation has numerous echoes of the Exodus and Sinai: in the representation of God's character (vv.2–3; cf. v.7) and in the natural imagery—

"storm" and "clouds" (v.3), the "sea" rebuked (v.4), earthquake and "fire" (vv.5–6; cf. Hab 3). It also echoes the language of Isaiah (esp. v.2; cf. Introduction: Literary Parallel), whose work draws heavily on the historical analogies formed by the events of the Exodus. Also, this prologue is reminiscent of Elijah's ministry in its evocation of storm (v.3; cf. 1 Kings 18:41–45) and drought (v.4; cf. 1 Kings 17:1–7); of wind, earthquake, and fire (vv.3, 5–6; cf. 1 Kings 18:38; 19:11–12; 2 Kings 1:10–14). As such it forms a fitting prelude to the ensuing prophecy—as he judged Baal's spurious power over nature by natural means, so the Lord would judge Assyria's spurious military power by military defeat. However, the present passage has no clearly unified background: as in Isaiah, past history and natural phenomena form an analogy for the future, revealing the measure of God's power as it will be exercised in a new context of deliverance and judgment.

1. *Awesome in power*

1:1–6

1An oracle concerning Nineveh. The book of the vision of Nahum the Elkoshite.

2The LORD is a jealous and avenging God;
  The LORD takes vengeance and is filled with wrath.
The LORD takes vengeance on his foes
  and maintains his wrath against his enemies.
3The LORD is slow to anger and great in power;
  the LORD will not leave the guilty unpunished.
His way is in the whirlwind and the storm,
  and clouds are the dust of his feet.
4He rebukes the sea and dries it up;
  he makes all the rivers run dry.
Bashan and Carmel wither
  and the blossoms of Lebanon fade.
5The mountains quake before him
  and the hills melt away.
The earth trembles at his presence,
  the world and all who live in it.
6Who can withstand his indignation?
  Who can endure his fierce anger?
His wrath is poured out like fire;
  the rocks are shattered before him.

1–2 On Nahum, see the Introduction (Authorship). The adjective "jealous" (*qannô'*; cf. TWOT, 2:802–3) is used solely of God, primarily in his self-revelation at Sinai (Exod 20:5; 34:14). Against this covenantal background it denotes the Lord's deep, indeed, fiercely protective commitment to his people and his exclusive claim to obedience and reciprocal commitment (cf. Deut 4:24; 5:9). Where this relationship of mutual commitment is threatened, either by Israel's unfaithfulness or by foreign oppression, the inevitable expressions of such jealousy are "vengeance" and "wrath," directed to restoring that relationship (e.g., Num 25:11; Heb 10:27).

"Avenging" and "vengeance" (both *nōqēm*; cf. TWOT, 2:598–99) are judicial in nature, expressing judgment and requital for infractions of law and morality, primarily those committed with presumption and impenitence. Such infractions are defined in this case by the terms of the covenant that they threaten to disrupt (cf. Lev 26:25; Deut 32:35, 41, 43). As a judicial function "vengeance" belongs supremely to

God, the Judge of the whole earth (e.g., Deut 32:35), and to the ordained representatives of his authority (e.g., Exod 21:20–21; Num 31:2–3; Josh 10:13; Esth 8:13). Consequently, man is forbidden to take the law into his own hands or to exercise his own vengeance on enemies. Nineveh—despite God's use of her violence—had done just that. Now, as she had devastated cities and populations, so it would happen to her: military invasion (2:1–10), seige (3:14), slaughter (3:3), destruction by fire (1:10; 2:13; 3:13, 15), humiliation (3:5–7), captivity (3:10), exile (2:7; 3:10–11), and utter devastation (2:10). She had sown the wind and in her impenitence would surely reap the whirlwind.

Like jealousy, "wrath" (*ḥēmāh*; TWOT, 1:374–75) denotes intense and passionate feeling; as noted above, it represents here the outworking of jealousy, which moves to eradicate every obstacle to its commitment. Utterly different, like the preceding terms, from the sinful self-will of man (cf. James 1:20), "wrath" constitutes a divine characteristic that man must face whenever he breaks the proper limits of his relationship to God; to deny God's "wrath" is to deny the reality of judgment and the necessity of atonement.

Verse 2 lays a foundation for the entire prophecy: all that follows is rooted in this revelation of the justice and burning zeal of the Lord exercised on behalf of his people. To wrest the following chapters from the context, seeing only the historical details of carnage and destruction, is to miss their significance as a demonstration of the terrible wrath and power of God (cf. Rev 6:16–17).

3 The Lord's anger is balanced by his forbearance ("slow to anger," a further attribute associated preeminently with Sinai (Exod 34:6; Num 14:18; cf. Neh 9:17). It represents a restraint born of meekness and not of weakness—as evidenced by the contrast with his great "power"; it is not to be misunderstood as passivity (cf. Isa 65:2–5; Acts 17:30; Rom 2:3–5; 2 Peter 3:9; Rev 2:21). Nor is it exercised indefinitely, for his "power" assures that "he will not leave the guilty unpunished," which translates the verb *niqqāh* ("to acquit, pronounce innocent"; cf. TWOT, 2:596ff.). This verb therefore extends the forensic connotations of "vengeance" (*nāqām*), which it also echoes phonetically; and in fact the subsequent prophecy unfolds with the formal solemnity of a judicial procedure. This characteristic of divine justice is equally a facet of the Lord's self-revelation to Moses at Sinai (Exod 20:7; 34:7; Num 14:18; Deut 5:11), asserting his maintenance of moral distinctions and accountability.

The theophany at Sinai forms the basis of Nahum's proclamation against Nineveh, as it did for Jonah (cf. Exod 34:6; Jonah 4:2), to which Nahum may well have been alluding. The forbearance of God had been extended to Nineveh a century earlier in response to her repentance (Jonah 3:10); but it was forfeited by her subsequent history of ruthless evil, making way for God's judgment instead.

Although without any complete analogy, the power and majesty of God are evidenced most dramatically in the forces of nature. "Whirlwind" and "storm" are often expressions of his judgment, the two terms recurring together in Psalm 83:15 and Isaiah 29:6; "clouds" also extend the preceding associations with Sinai (cf. Exod 19:9, 16). For all their grandeur, however, these mighty forces are dwarfed in the presence of the Lord, whom the highest heavens cannot contain; the tempest is but the disturbance caused as he marches by, and the dark storm clouds are merely dust stirred up by his feet (cf. 1 Kings 19:11–13; cf. Hab 3:8).

O tell of His might, O sing of his grace,
Whose robe is the light, whose canopy space;
His chariots of wrath the deep thunderclouds form,
And dark is His path on the wings of the storm.
(Robert Grant, "O Worship the King")

4 The preceding description of the Lord's power is extended in the image of drought, consuming the fertile highlands of Palestine and their sources of water. The language of the first couplet is reminiscent of references to the Exodus (cf. Ps 106:9; Isa 42:15; 44:27; 50:2), but as in Habakkuk 3:8 it is expanded by the following geographical terms to represent a scene of widespread desolation. "Bashan" in Transjordan, "Carmel" in northern Israel, and the "Lebanon" range on Israel's northern frontier are frequently represented together as the choicest forest and pasture regions of the Promised Land (cf. TWOT, 1:137, 455–56, 468). Nevertheless, all are revealed as vulnerable; like the pride and strength of man, they are devastated and "wither" before the burning anger of the Lord (cf. Isa 33:9; Joel 1:10–12; Amos 1:2; Zech 11:1–2). The drought depicted here is abnormally severe in its catastrophic effects on "sea" and "rivers"; it is more evocative of the drought commanded by Elijah, directed against the northern kingdom whose frontiers are defined by the geographical references in this verse (cf. 1 Kings 17:1–18:46).

5 Earthquake forms a third, and common, biblical manifestation of the Lord's power, causing the hills to "melt away" (*mûg*). Such melting may be brought on by intense heat (cf. Ps 97:3–5; Mic 1:3–4), a phenomenon associated with the earthquake at Sinai to which vv.2–3 allude. However, the verb "melt away" may also be applied to the effect of flooding (cf. comment at 2:6).

6 This verse summarizes vv.2–5, emphatically recapitulating the concept of anger, repeating the noun "wrath" that is stressed further by the kindred terms "indignation" (*zāʿam*) and "fierce [lit., "burning"] anger" (*ḥªrôn ʾappô*; cf. TWOT, 2:808), and again describing the irresistible manifestation of this anger, before which the entire created world is subdued.

The simile of "wrath" being poured out "like fire" recurs elsewhere (2 Chron 34:25; Jer 7:20; 44:6; Lam 2:4; cf. 2 Chron 12:7; 34:21; Jer 10:25; Lam 4:11; Ezek 14:19; 22:22; 30:15), fire being a common expression of the Lord's judgment. The verb "pour out" (*nāṯaḵ*) is used literally of poured (Exod 9:33; 2 Sam 21:10) or molten (Ezek 22:20) liquid. More common is the figurative sense of divine wrath "poured out" as here.

The section concluding with v.6 is deeply imbued with the recollection of God's covenant with Israel, also sharing with numerous poetic passages their various images of divine judgment and power (cf. Pss 11:6; 18:7–15; 29:3–9; 50:3; 83:13–15; 97:2–5; Jer 23:29; Ezek 38:19–22; Joel 2:1–11; Mic 1:4). However, the marked recurrence of all these features in the work of Isaiah suggest again that Nahum stands as an heir if not a disciple of Isaiah, interpreting God's covenant with Israel to his own time (cf. Isa 8:16).

2. *Just in execution*

1:7–11

[7]The LORD is good,
a refuge in times of trouble.
He cares for those who trust in him,
[8] but with an overwhelming flood
he will make an end of ⌊Nineveh⌋;
he will pursue his foes into darkness.

[9]Whatever they plot against the LORD
he will bring to an end;
trouble will not come a second time.
[10]They will be entangled among thorns
and drunk from their wine;
they will be consumed like dry stubble.
[11]From you, ⌊O Nineveh,⌋ has one come forth
who plots evil against the LORD
and counsels wickedness.

This passage also portrays "the kindness and sternness of God" (Rom 11:22). Its continuity with vv.2–6, which it amplifies, is marked by a corresponding emphasis on the Lord as the prime mover in all that ensues (cf. vv.7, 9, 11) and by the increasing definition of his adversaries (cf. "his enemies" [*'ōyᵉḇāyw*], vv.2, 8; "his foes" [*ṣārayw*], v.2; "trouble" [*ṣārāh*], vv.7, 9). The passages are linked also by their continuity of imagery: "flood" and "darkness" (v.8; cf. "storm," v.3); drought ("dry" [*yāḇēš*], vv.4, 10); and the consequent burning of "stubble" (v.10; cf. "fire," v.6). As in vv.2–6, the redemptive work of God is juxtaposed to and overshadowed by his irrevocable judgment. This is set forth in vv.8–11, composed of three corresponding sections. Verse 8 describes the Lord's foes and their annihilation ("make an end" [*kālāh 'āśāh*], v.8), in two parallel clauses that resume the natural imagery of vv.2–6 (see above). Verses 9–10 define these foes more precisely as those who "plot" (*ḥāšaḇ*, v.9) against the Lord; their fate is reaffirmed in identical terms ("bring to an end" [*kālāh 'ōśeh*], v.9) and in similar metaphorical language (v.10). Verse 11 resumes the charge of plotting (*ḥāšaḇ*), which it applies more precisely to "one" individual; his fate is clearly implied by the pattern of the preceding verses. Verses 7–11 are thus unified by repetitions of vocabulary in vv.8–11 and by the conjunction that relates and contrasts v.7 to them ("but"). They are distinguished from vv.2–6 and vv.11–15 by the inclusio framing of vv.2–6 ("wrath") and by the introductory formula in v.12.

These verses have the menacing ring of a judicial indictment, citing the evidence against the accused. It reveals a conspiracy against the Judge himself, the Lord whose justice and supreme authority have been announced in the preliminary proceedings of vv.2–6; the outcome of the trial is therefore in no doubt, and the sentence is already anticipated in the charge developed here.

7 The goodness of God forms a basic tenet of Israel's faith, particularly celebrated in the psalmic literature whose language is prominent throughout v.7 (e.g., 2 Chron 5:13; Pss 25:7–8; 69:16; 118:1, 29; 135:3; 136:1; 145:7–9; Jer 33:11). As here, also, it repeatedly forms the basis for man's faith, expressed in trusting obedience (e.g., Ezra 8:18, 22; Pss 34:8; 73:1; 100:4–5; 106:1–3; 107:1–2; 109:21; Lam 3:25); where the goodness of God is impugned, with success, faith soon crumbles (e.g., Gen

3:1–7; Num 14:3, 27). In this context, as an expression of covenant commitment to defend his people, the Lord himself is a "refuge" or stronghold of protection (*mā'ôz*, "strength"; cf. Neh 8:10; Pss 27:1; 31:2, 4; 37:39; Prov 10:29; Isa 25:4; Jer 16:19). He "cares for" (*yāḏa'*, lit., "knows"; e.g., Exod 33:12; Pss 31:7; 91:14; Jer 1:5; 12:3) the faithful, acknowledging their relationship to him and their claim on his goodness inherent in that relationship. The "trouble" from which he gives protection is graphically illustrated in Judah's sufferings at the hands of Assyria. It demanded a "trust" that was too often misplaced, but it afforded one of Scripture's most dramatic testimonies to the Lord as a "refuge" for those who indeed put their hope in him (Isa 33:2–4; 37:3, 6–7, 29–38; cf. Isa 12:2; 26:3–4). The note of grace sounded here, highlighted by its juxtaposition to the surrounding verses, is already implicit in v.3; and it foreshadows the theme of Judah's vindication in the following sections (vv.12–13, 14; 2:2).

8 The goodness of God, like his patience, does not obviate his judgment. As in the Psalms, his judgment is directed against those who refuse to submit to his rule and who are therefore both "his foes" (*'oyeḇayw*) and the oppressors of his loyal people; as long as evil exists, his judgment is an inevitable expression of his goodness on behalf of the victims of evil. It is expressed here in terms of "flood," which recalls the previous description of storm in v.3 (cf. 2:6); and in keeping with these associations, it banishes the enemy into "darkness" (i.e., death; cf. 1 Sam 2:9; Job 15:23, 30; Ps 88:12; Eccl 6:4). These drastic measures are directed against a shadowy antagonist specified by "her place" (*meqômāh*; cf. NASB). Both the feminine suffix and the noun denoting a locality confirm NIV's interpretation ("[Nineveh]," cities being feminine in Hebrew; cf. 2:1, 7, 10, 13; 3:5–8, 11–17); but the prophecy effectively withholds the adversary's identity till she is fully engulfed by the destruction that is still impending here (cf. 2:8; 3:7).

9 The utter finality of this sentence is stressed by the phrase "bring to an end," repeated from v.8. It is reinforced by the terse ambiguity of the final line: "trouble" (*ṣārāh*; cf. 7; TWOT, 2:778–79) will not arise again for God's people, for it will descend on those who trouble Israel (cf. "his foes" [ṣārāyw], 1:2) in so conclusive a way that it need not arise again. The crime of these enemies, who are addressed directly in the Hebrew text (cf. NIV mg.), is identified here as settled, premeditated antagonism: they do not stumble into sin but actively "plot" (*ḥāšaḇ*) against the Lord (cf. TWOT, 1:330).

The abrupt switch of subject evident in the Hebrew of this verse is typical of Nahum's prophecy (cf. vv.11–12, 15; 2:2, 8, 9–10, 13; 3:1, 5, 8); this stylistic feature effectively evokes the violent crosscurrents of history that intersect in the fate of Nineveh. In proclaiming a complete "end" to Nineveh, this verse identifies the central theme of the book, to which all others are related as either cause or effect (cf. vv.8, 12, 14–15; 2:13; 3:7, 19).

10 As in v.8, the means of judgment are portrayed here in metaphorical language. The syntax of the first two lines is very compressed and therefore somewhat obscure (cf. NIV mg.). The individual words, however, make good sense. They are clearly syntactically unified by a striking alliterative pattern involving repetition of the consonants *s*, *b*, ', *k*, *m*; and the two lines are linked by complete assonance in their concluding participial forms (*kî 'aḏ-sîrîm seḇuḵîm, ûḵesoḇ'ām seḇû'îm*; cf. Eccl 7:5–6). The verse should therefore be interpreted as it stands, without recourse to textual emendation; although virtually impossible to reproduce fully, its effect is rendered partially by the translation "Torn among thorns, Drunk from their drinking."

"Thorns" (*sîrîm*) is one of many terms describing the spiny or prickly vegetation that proliferated in the semiarid climate of Palestine (cf. ZPEB, 5:736). They often grew as a tangled, impenetrable mass (Hos 2:6); as such as they were good for little more than burning (Eccl 7:6). The Assyrians are portrayed as being "entangled" (*sāḇaḵ*, cf. Gen 22:13) "among" or "like" (*'aḏ*) such thorns, to which they correspond both in their worthless character and in their merited destruction.

The following, related image of drunkenness reiterates these varied associations: a drunkard is good for nothing useful, and drunkenness is both a cause and consequence of judgment. The keynote of both lines, however, is helplessness. Like Abraham's ram entangled in the thorns (Gen 22:13), a drunkard is incapacitated from defending himself (cf. 1 Sam 25:36; Isa 28:7); the Assyrians would be no less vulnerable before the wrath of God.

These ideas are resumed in the concluding line: like thorns, stubble is without intrinsic value and is subject to be burnt; being "dry," it is an easy prey for the flames by which it is "consumed." The concomitant themes are similarly expressive. Nineveh's destruction by fire is rooted in her helplessness to avert the disaster (cf. 2:9–10; 3:11–13); and this in turn is due to her decadence, characterized by drunkenness.

11 The enemy is again defined as one who "plots" (*ḥāšaḇ*) against the Lord, being specified further as a distinct individual from whom the rebellion emanates; such an individual is identified clearly in 3:18 as the "king of Assyria." The ruler envisaged here emerged from Nineveh in his opposition to the Lord ("from you": feminine singular), an opposition directed against the visible manifestation of God's rule in Jerusalem, the city of the Great King (Ps 48:1–3), and in the Davidic monarchy (cf. Ps 2). Sennacherib, perhaps more than any of his dynasty, stands out as the most powerful aggressor to emerge from Nineveh against Judah. According to the Assyrian annals describing his Judean campaign (c. 701), he cruelly devastated forty-seven fortified cities including Lachish, whose siege is graphically recorded in a series of reliefs discovered in his palace at Nineveh (cf. 2 Kings 18:13; 19:8; cf. ANEP, pp. 371–74). That Nahum was referring primarily to Sennacherib's invasion is supported by his repeated reminiscences of Isaiah's prophecies relating to that era (see above); in particular, the verb "plots" recalls its description of Assyrian arrogance in Isaiah 10:7 ("has in mind" [*ḥāšaḇ*]).

The intent of this plotting is "wickedness" (*bᵉlîya'al*; cf. also v.15), a noun often translated as "worthlessness" (KJV, "Belial") and implying a total lack of moral fiber and principle (e.g., Deut 13:13, et al.; cf. TWOT, 1:111). This term is translated as "lawlessness" in the LXX and as such became a fitting title in the intertestamental period for Satan, the father of lies and lawlessness (i.e., Belial; cf. John 8:44; 2 Cor 6:15; 2 Thess 2:3; 1 John 3:4–12).

B. *The Sentence of the Lord*

1:12–14

12This is what the LORD says:

"Although they have allies and are numerous,
  they will be cut off and pass away.

Although I have afflicted you, ⌞O Judah,⌟
I will afflict you no more.
[13]Now I will break their yoke from your neck
and tear your shackles away."

[14]The LORD has given a command concerning you, ⌞Nineveh⌟:
"You will have no descendants to bear your name.
I will destroy the carved images and cast idols
that are in the temple of your gods.
I will prepare your grave,
for you are vile."

The judicial sentence anticipated in the preceding unit is announced more formally in the introductory formulas of vv.12, 14, which distinguish vv.12–13, v.14, and v.15 as corresponding subunits. This sentence decrees a complete reversal in the destiny of the opposing parties: Assyria's political and military power would be shattered (v.12), whereas Judah's political and military bondage would be shattered (vv.12–13). Assyria's religious system and monarchy would be terminated (v.14), while Judah's religion would be revitalized (v.15). This pattern of reversal unites vv.12–15 and distinguishes them from 2:1, whose language links it closely to 2:3–13 and 3:12, 14. Nahum 1:15 is therefore associated with vv.12–14 in this analysis, though separated from them in MT. Although Assyria had destroyed and mutilated countless nations, including the schismatic northern kingdom, its fate was determined by its treatment of Judah and Zion.

12 The opening clause of this verse is typical of the formula by which a messenger received or transmitted a message from his lord. It occurs countless times to introduce a message from the Lord (e.g., Exod 3:14–15; Josh 7:13; et al.) and is especially characteristic of the prophets, who transmitted the decrees of the Lord, the Great King, to his obedient or disobedient subjects. The present decree is addressed to Judah ("you") and is essentially an oracle of salvation; it incorporates an announcement of judgment that is addressed directly to Assyria in v.14.

The decree reverses the fortunes of the Assyrians. Although they had "allies" (*šᵉlēmîm*; cf. D.J. Wiseman, VetTest 32 [1982]:311–26, for a discussion of this translation), they would be "cut off"(*gāzaz*, normally used of shearing sheep; cf. Isa 53:7). Although "numerous," the Assyrians would "pass away" (*'āḇar*, "dwindle," "perish"), as waters that dry up or as chaff driven before the wind (cf. Job 6:15; 30:15; Jer 13:24; Zeph 2:2).

A similar reversal is decreed for Judah, whose penalty is remitted as that of Assyria is pronounced (cf. Isa 40:2; 51:22–23). To be "afflicted" (*'ānāh*) is to be humbled and oppressed. As in this case, such affliction is repeatedly the agent of God's chastisement (e.g., Deut 8:2–3, 16; Ps 90:15; 119:71, 75), frequently being administered to his own people at the hands of foreign nations (cf. Hab 1:5–11); though Nahum's attention is directed primarily to Assyria's guilt, it is clear from this reference that Judah was equally subject to the jealous wrath of God, when unfaithful to the covenant. The brief statement "I have afflicted you" is therefore pregnant with the suffering of centuries, though expressed in a single Hebrew word. Only against such a background can one appreciate the profound implications of what follows: the phrase "no more" (*lō' 'ôḏ*), which punctuates vv.12–15, truly means "life from the dead" (Rom 11:15). As noted previously, the phrase also characterizes Isaiah 51:22–

52:1, whose promise of reversal and liberation from affliction is reproduced in this passage; and it balances the menacing refrain "still" (*'ôḏ*) in the earlier chapters of Isaiah (5:25; 9:12, 17, 21; 10:4; cf. 10:20).

13 The continuing existence of such servitude is implied by the emphatic "Now" and by the future orientation of the promised deliverance from the "yoke" and the "shackles." This further supports dating Nahum's prophecy before Josiah's reign and, consequently, its inspired origin. Despite the devious and tragic analogy of the northern kingdom, which might have shaped a rational prediction of Judah's future, the southern kingdom was still to experience political and religious revival in the reign of Josiah; and though its sins had made exile inevitable, this did not occur at Assyrian hands, as might well have been expected in the middle of the seventh century. The breaking of Assyria's yoke is strikingly affirmed by Nabopolassar, who, like the Assyrians themselves and Cyrus in later times, was an unwitting instrument of the Lord's purposes (cf. Isa 45:4–5): "As for the Assyrians, who since distant days had ruled over all the people and with heavy yoke had brought misery to the people of the land, from the land of Akkad I banished their feet and cast off their yoke" ("The Babylonian Chronicle," quoted by Maier, p. 111).

14 The Lord's decree of judgment and salvation is again introduced by a formal pronouncement: "The LORD has given a command." It is now addressed to the social and particularly the religious systems undergirding the political conditions that were rescinded in vv.12–13.

The "name" of a population represented its living identity, perpetuated in its "descendants"; to be destitute of descendants therefore represented obliteration of identity and of life itself (cf. Deut 7:24; 9:14; 1 Sam 24:21; et al.). The root underlying "descendants" (*zr'*, "seed," "sow") is used of physical and particularly dynastic succession. It implies the eradication of Nineveh's dynastic rule, therefore, and of the nation whose cohesion derived from the Neo-Assyrian monarchy now centered at Nineveh; a similar sentence is passed on Babylon and its king in Isaiah 14:4, 20–23. Nineveh's consignment to the grave reiterates the certainty of this extinction and also appears to allude to the imagery of Isaiah 14 (cf. vv.9–11, 15–20). This judgment is rooted in the charge that the city, for all its regal and religious grandeur, is "vile"or "contemptible," "of no account" (*qālal*); the charge echoes the intent of 1:10, being developed in 3:5–6.

The Assyrian kings claimed to rule by the favor and authority of their "gods," whom they honored accordingly. Ashurbanipal, on a single cylinder, paid profuse homage to seventeen of the principal gods of the Assyrian pantheon. Two gods received special reverence; Ashur was acknowledged as "the great god who begat me," being honored seventy-nine times on this cylinder; and ninety-five times he referred to Ishtar, "The Mistress, Lady of Ladies," "Goddess of War," "Queen of the Gods" (Maier, p. 107; cf. also ANET, pp. 289, 297).

The judgment of Nineveh's king therefore demanded the destruction of the idolatrous religion on which his authority was founded. This was centralized in the "temple," which housed the "carved images" and "cast idols" within which its particular deity resided. These idols were normally made of precious wood plated with gold or of molten metal such as gold that had been poured into a mold. They would be shaped in human form, even in the likeness of the reigning king such as Sennacherib (IDB, 1:299). An elaborate ritual was required to endow them with life, sight, and purity, after which they would be clothed in sumptuous garments and placed on a pedestal in their inner sanctuary, or cella. In keeping with their human likeness, they would be fed three times a day and their clothes would be changed periodically (IDB, 1:298–99).

The utter inefficacy of such "gods," against which Israel's prophets sustained a vehement polemic, was thus to be exposed in the destruction of their place of residence that they were powerless to protect. The sentence was duly fulfilled (cf. also 3:7). The temple of Nabu, a major deity at Nineveh, was razed to the ground and buried with ash from the blaze. The statue of Ishtar was discovered, prostrate and headless, amid the ruins of her temple, which had stood at Nineveh for almost fifteen centuries.

C. *The Purpose of the Lord*

1:15

15Look, there on the mountains,
the feet of one who brings good news,
who proclaims peace!
Celebrate your festivals, O Judah,
and fulfill your vows.
No more will the wicked invade you;
they will be completely destroyed.

15 The message heralded in vv.12–14 is concluded with a further messenger formula, already proclaiming the predicted "good news" of salvation (cf. Introduction: Theological Values) and disaster; the second section, 2:1–3:19, concludes on the same note (cf. 3:19). The proclamation of "peace" (*šālôm*) is replete with the promise of God's redemption and, as noted previously, constitutes the most precise correlation of Nahum with Isaiah (e.g., Isa 9:6–7; 32:17; 53:5; 54:10, 13; 55:12; 57:19). The picture is one of joyous and complete restoration of the Lord's people and their legitimate worship.

The reversal of fortunes apparent in vv.12–13 is thus completed in vv.14–15. As Nineveh's flourishing religion was to be buried, so the worship of oppressed Judah would be resurrected. By implication it was still suppressed, as a corollary of the existing political subjection to Assyria. Such suppression of Yahwistic worship was entirely characteristic of the reigns of Amon and, for the most part, of Manasseh, who abandoned the piety of his father Hezekiah (cf. 2 Kings 21; 2 Chron 33); this provides further eivdence for dating Nahum's prophecy toward the middle of the seventh century. The anticipated renewal of vital worship was accomplished in the reign of Josiah, after about 631 (2 Kings 22:3–23:27; 2 Chron 34–35; cf. comment at 1:13).

As in Hezekiah's reign, this assertion of religious independence demanded that the "wicked" (*b^eliyyā'al*; cf. 1:1) who opposed it be "destroyed." The verb "destroy" (*kārat*) is commonly used of cutting down an enemy in battle or of "cutting off" the name of the rebellious; it recurs with both these connotations in 1:14; 2:13 ("[leave] no"; and 3:15 ("cut . . . down"). It is also echoed in 1:12 ("cut off," *gāzaz*). The verb "invade" ('āḇar) is similarly used of warfare, as indicated by NIV's translation. It repeats, as a further irony or reversal, the verb translated as "pass away" in 1:12: the invader will be swept away, the destroyer destroyed.

II. The Fall of Nineveh (2:1–3:19)

The judgment of God is not merely an abstract principle or rhetorical threat, as evidenced already in the natural phenomena that display his power. The judgment decreed in chapter 1 is now worked out with terrifying actuality.

Nahum 2:1–2 is transitional. On the one hand, it extends the dual perspective of judgment (v.1) and mercy (v.2) evident in 1:2–15; and v.2 is clearly a development of 1:7, 12–13, and particularly of 1:15 ("Judah"—"Jacob . . . Israel"). On the other hand, the military language and urgent imperatives of v.1 clearly anticipate the following description of battle in 2:3–10; 3:2–3, 10–13; and, particularly, in 3:14.

Thereafter the prophecy is devoted exclusively to Nineveh, expanding the emphasis of 2:1 on the "attacker" as the instrument of divine vengeance; and on Nineveh's vain attempts at self-defense. Nahum 2:3–3:19 consists of three major sections, 2:3–3:7 (itself broken into two balanced subunits: 2:3–3:1 and 3:2–7), 3:8–11, and 3:12–19, which reiterate the emphases shown below. They coincide in describing the savage onslaught awaiting Nineveh (A), which she will be impotent to resist (B). This remarkable collapse of her defenses is then explained by an array of interpretive analogies (C). Ultimately, however, the judgment is from the Lord's hands (D), stated with terse finality in the focal points of the two chapters (2:13; 3:5). As in 1:2–15, this sentence and its execution have the ring of a judicial procedure; and its major sections are concluded by the promulgation of the verdict to both the accused and the victims (E).

The following charts illustrate both the structure and the stylized vocabulary, all building on the pattern set forth in 2:1.

NAHUM 2–3

	2:3–3:1	3:2–7	3:8–11	3:12–19
A. Attacker and onslaught	2:3–5	3:2–3	3:10–11	3:12–13
B. Mocking of failing defenses	2:6–10	3:3	3:8–11	3:12–14
C. Interpretive analogy	2:11–12	3:4	3:8–10	3:15–17
D. Judgment from the Lord	2:13	3:5–6	3:11	3:15–17
E. Verdict announced	3:1	3:7		3:18–19

A. *Warning and Promise*

2:1–2

1 An attacker advances against you, ⌊Nineveh⌋.
Guard the fortress,
watch the road,
brace yourselves,
marshal all your strength!

NAHUM 2–3: STYLIZED VOCABULARY

Section	2:1	2:3–3:1	3:2–7	3:8–11	3:12–19
A.	attacker (*mēp̱îṣ*)	soldiers (*gibbōrê*) 2:3			
		warriors (*'anšê-ḥayil*) 2:3			
		picked troop (*'addîr*) 2:5			
		streets (*ḥûṣôṯ*) 2:4		streets (*ḥûṣôṯ*) 3:10	
B.	Use of imperatives				Use of imperatives
	fortress (*mᵉṣurāh*)				siege (*māṣôr*) 3:14
	brace (*ḥazzēq*)				strengthen (*ḥazzēq*) 3:14 (*bis*)
	yourselves (*moṯnayim*)	bodies (*moṯnayim*) 2:10			
	strength (*kōaḥ*)			strength (*'osmāh*) 3:9	
		wall (*ḥômāh*) 2:5		wall (*ḥômāh*) 3:8	
		gates (*ša'ᵃrê*) 2:6			gates (*ša'ᵃrê*) 3:13
		open (*pāṯaḥ*) 2:6			wide (*pāṯaḥ*) 3:13
					open (*pāṯaḥ*) 3:13
		river (*nᵉhārôṯ*) 2:6		river (*yām*) 3:8	
				waters (*yām*) 3:8	
		water (*mayim*) 2:8		water (*mayim*) 3:8 (cf. Notes)	
		be exiled (*gālāh*) 2:7		take captive (*gālāh*) 3:10	
		endless (*'ên qēṣeh*) 2:9	without number (*'ên qēṣeh*) 3:3	boundless (*'ên qēṣeh*) 3:9	
		wealth (*kāḇōḏ*) 2:9	piles (*kōḇeḏ*) 3:3	nobles (*niḵbodim*) 3:10	
C.		lion	harlot	Thebes	locusts
D.	against you (*'al-pānayiḵ*)		over your face (*'al-pānāyiḵ*) 3:5		
		against you (*'ēlayiḵ*) 2:13	against you (*'ēlayiḵ*) 3:5		
		flashes (*'ēš*) 2:3			fire (*'ēš*) 3:13, 15
		devour (*tō'ḵal*) 2:13			devour (*tō'ḵal*) 3:15
		sword (*ḥereḇ*) 2:13			sword (*ḥereḇ*) 3:15
		leave you no (*kāraṯ*) 2:13			cut down (*kāraṯ*) 3:15
E.		Woe (*hôy*) 3:1	mourn (*yānûḏ*) 3:7		Rejoicing over fall 3:19

> [2]The LORD will restore the splendor of Jacob
> like the splendor of Israel,
> though destroyers have laid them waste
> and have ruined their vines.

1 Nineveh's "attacker" is more literally a "scatterer," a common figure for a victorious king (*pûṣ*; cf. Ps 68:1; Isa 24:1; Jer 52:8); the verb also describes the scattering of sheep, anticipating the final scene of 3:18 (with a different verb, *pûš*).

In fulfillment of this prophecy, Nineveh was attacked in 614 B.C. by Cyaraxes, king of the Medes (c.625–585; IDB, 3:320). A sector of the suburbs was captured, but the city was not taken, the Medes diverting their energies to the overthrow of Ashur. However, a subsequent alliance of Cyaxares with the Babylonian Nabopolassar led to their concerted attack on Nineveh in 612, apparently accompanied by the Scythians (Umman Manda?), a battle recorded in detail by the Babylonian Chronicle (see D. Winton Thomas, ed., *Documents From Old Testament Times* [Oxford: University Press, 1958], p. 76; ANET, pp. 304–5).

The Assyrians are mockingly called to action in military language, reminiscent of Isaiah's exhortation to another doomed city (Isa 21:5). The city had in fact been well equipped to withstand both siege (cf. 3:14) and invasion. Sennacherib had spent no less than six years building his armory, which occupied a terraced area of forty acres. It was enlarged further by Esarhaddon and contained all the weaponry required for the extension and maintenance of the Assyrian empire: bows, arrows, quivers, chariots, wagons, armor, horses, mules, and equipment (cf. Ezek 23:24; 39:9). The royal "road" had been enlarged by Sennacherib to a breadth of seventy-eight feet, facilitating the movement of troops. However, the material resources would be of little avail, if the "strength" of the defenders could not be marshaled; and by the end of the seventh century it had been dissipated beyond retrieval.

2 This verse introduces the final reference to the salvation of God's people, whose "splendor" he will "restore." The noun "splendor" (*gā'ôn*) implies elevation or exaltation (cf. Job 8:11; Ezek 47:5; TWOT, 1:143–44); it is used with negative connotations of pride or with positive associations of majesty expressed in power and dominion. Both usages are applied to Jacob, the latter being clearly intended here. The comparison "like . . . Israel" suggests restoration to the full stature promised to the nation and once occupied by it. The names "Jacob . . . Israel" are usually synonymous (Gen 32:28; 1 Kings 18:31; 2 Kings 17:34; 1 Chron 16:17; Ps 105:23; Hos 12:12), and they came to denote the Twelve Tribes descended from Jacob (e.g., Pss 22:23; 78:5, 21, 71; 105:10; 114:1; 135:4; 147:19; Ezek 20:5; Mic 1:1, 5, 13–14; 3:1, 9–12). After the division of the kingdom, usage varies; but the names are more commonly applied to the northern kingdom. Following the destruction of Samaria, the southern prophets reclaimed these names (Isa 14:1–4; et al.) and evidently "Judah" is envisaged here (cf. 1:12–13, 15), though it is possible that the resurrection of Israel as a whole is promised (cf. Isa 9:1–8; 11:10–16; et al.). Such restoration is necessitated by the devastation of the land's "vines"—a mainstay of its economy (cf. Hab 3:17), a source of its joy and fulfillment (cf. Isa 24:7–15) and, indeed, a symbol of the very life and identity of the nation (cf. Isa 5:1–7). All these facets of existence in the northern kingdom had been obliterated by the Assyrian "destroyers" (*bāqaq*), and they were as yet severely threatened in the south (cf. 1:12).

Notes

1 The forms of the final three verbs, translated as imperatives in NIV, are ambiguous in the MT. נָצוֹר (*nāṣôr*, "Guard"), the first, is clearly an infinitive absolute, functioning with imperatival force (cf. GKC, par. 113bb). The following forms—צַפֵּה (*ṣappēh*, "watch"), חַזֵּק (*ḥazzēq*, "brace")—appear to be Piel imperatives with masculine singular subjects; on this understanding, they could not be addressed to Nineveh, which is consistently treated as feminine (cf. עַל־פָּנַיִךְ [*ʿal-pānayik*, "against you"]), and they would be addressed instead to the masculine singular מֵפִיץ (*mēpîṣ*, "attacker"). This is plausible since the verbs could all be understood from the perspective of those beleaguering the city, restricting movement to and from it; for instance, the verb נָצַר (*nāṣar*, "guard") is applied to Jerusalem as a city "under siege" (Isa 1:8). However, the last three verbs also represent the more common form of the Piel infinitive absolute, corresponding to that of the Piel infinite construct (GKC, par. 52o); on this reading the subject of all four verbs must be determined from the context. The verb *ḥazzēq* recurs in 3:14—חַזְּקִי (*ḥazzeqî*, "strengthen")—in a very similar context of five urgent commands. In that location they are clearly spoken to Nineveh, both because they call for defensive measures and because they are uniformly second feminine singular imperatives. In view of the precise correspondence of 2:1 to 3:14, it is clearly preferable to interpret 2:1 with reference to Nineveh also. This conclusion is favored also by the ensuing tactics of the "attacker," depicted as an active onslaught on the city rather than as preliminary siege warfare.

B. *Nineveh's Destruction Detailed* (2:3–3:7)

Nahum 2:3–3:7 forms the heart of 2:1–3:19, describing the details of Nineveh's defeat and the express purpose of the Lord that motivates it. The onslaught that menaced Nineveh in 1:2–15 and overshadowed it in 2:1 now breaks with fury on the condemned city. The centrality of this section is marked by the precisely balanced structure that links its two units (2:3–3:1; 3:2–7) and that defines the outlines of the following sections.

The attack is described by identical terms in 2:3–10 and 3:2–3: "chariots" (*rekeḇ*, 2:3–4; *merkāḇāh*, 3:2); "lightning" (2:4), "glittering" (3:3; both *bārāq*); "spears" (*berōšîm*, 2:3; *ḥanîṯ*, 3:3); "stumble" (*kāšal*, 2:5; 3:3); "endless" (2:9), "without number" (3:3; both *'ên qēṣeh*); "wealth" (*kāḇōḏ*, 2:9), "piles" (*kōḇeḏ*, 3:3). In addition both accounts are characterized by wild movement (2:3–5; 3:2–3); the image of fire ("flashes" [*'ēš*] 2:3; "flaming torches" [*lappîḏîm*] 2:4; "flashing" [*lahaḇ*] 3:3); and the description of weaponry ("shields," 2:3; "protective shield," 2:5; "whips," "wheels," "horses," 3:2; "swords," 3:3) and troops (2:3, 5; 3:3).

The close correlation of 2:9 and 3:3 evidences further irony: the "endless . . . wealth" has been stolen at the cost of life itself, being transmuted into "piles (of dead) . . . without number" (cf. Luke 9:25). In both passages details of the attack are followed by a metaphor (2:11–12; 3:4), which is developed in the following indictment: the lions will be cut down (2:13), the harlot will be stripped (3:5–6). The indictments are expressed in identical terms, unparalleled in Nahum (" 'I am against you,' declares the LORD Almighty"). They produce corresponding penalties, reversing the condition of the offenders in keeping with the law of retaliation: the beast of prey becomes a prey; the mistress of allurement an object of revulsion.

The exclamation "Woe" (3:1) is closely related to 2:11–13 by its reference to "victims" or "prey" (*ṭrp*; cf. 2:12 [*ter*], 13), of which it is full (*mālē'*; cf. 2:12), and also by the association of "plunder" and "blood" with the preceding image of ravening animals. As such it corresponds well to 3:7, which is similarly linked to 3:5–6 by a key word: "see" (*rā'āh*; cf. "show," 3:5; "spectacle," 3:6). Both verses are addressed to the condemned party, specifically the "city" (3:1) of "Nineveh" (3:7), by anonymous witnesses of the proceedings; the final section concludes on a similar note (3:18–19). The two verses are also distinguished from what follows. The abrupt description of the attacker in 3:2 corresponds to 2:3, which marks the beginning of a new unit; by implication 3:2 does so likewise. The transition at 3:7–8 is less apparent, since vv.8, 11 extend the direct speech of v.7; however, v.7 perceives Nineveh as already in ruins, differing from the perspective of vv.8–11, which still anticipate the debacle. For these reasons it appears preferable to associate 3:1 with 2:3–13. The MT, however, separates 3:1 from 2:13 in its paragraph (cf. 1:15), as does NIV—a decision favored by the common function of the word "woe" to introduce a new accusation. It is therefore plausible that 3:1 is a transitional verse, like 2:1–2 (but see comment at 3:1).

1. *First description of Nineveh's destruction* (2:3–3:1)

a. *Onslaught*

2:3–5

3The shields of his soldiers are red;
the warriors are clad in scarlet.
The metal on the chariots flashes
on the day they are made ready;
the spears of pine are brandished.
4The chariots storm through the streets,
rushing back and forth through the squares.
They look like flaming torches;
they dart about like lightning.

5He summons his picked troops,
yet they stumble on their way.
They dash to the city wall;
the protective shield is put in place.

3–4 The antecedent of "his" (v.3) appears to be the "attacker" of 2:1, in view of the military language common to both verses. It is possible that the "Lord" (v.2) is also intended, summoning an enemy against Nineveh as he had summoned the Assyrians against Judah (Isa 5:26–30; 10:5–6, 15; cf. 13:2–5; Joel 2:11, 25; Hab 1:5–10). The attack is led by the invader's chariot forces, the most formidable wing of an army fighting in open terrain (cf. Josh 17:16, 18; Judg 1:19). The Neo-Assyrian "chariots" were built of various types of wood, for lightness and speed, with fittings of leather and of "metal" that would flash with reflected light (v.3). The chariots were fitted with a pole and yoke for the horses, normally a team of two, and with spoked wheels and a single axle, which permitted a high degree of maneuverability. Under Ashurbanipal a chariot crew comprised as many as four members: the driver, equipped with a long spear and round shield, an archer, and two shield bearers for protection of their fellow crew-members. The Assyrian shields were either round or rectangular in shape, the latter being designed to cover most of the body, particularly to defend archers or spearmen in siege warfare. The shields were made of wood or wickerwork covered with leather, which could have been dyed "red" (cf.

Exod 25:5). Doubtless the enemy's chariots were similar in design, and they could account for all the features described in vv.3–4 (cf. "shields," "soldiers," "spears"). However, it is evident from the parallel passage in 3:2–3 that cavalry accompanied the chariots, a typical feature of Assyrian warfare; and both "shields" and "spears" might also be carried by the infantry who penetrated the defenses in 2:5 (cf. Yigael Yadin, *The Art of Warfare in Biblical Lands* [New York: McGraw, 1963], pp. 4–5, 294–95, 297ff., 452).

The conflict was located in the "streets" (v.4) of Nineveh, denoting its suburbs outside the inner defensive "wall" that had not yet been reached (cf. v.5). According to the fragmentary information of the Babylonian Chronicle, three battles may have been fought during the three months of intense siege before the city fell (ANET, pp. 303ff.; Maier, pp. 112–13). Indeed, the historian Diodorus Siculus (c. 20 B.C.), quoting earlier sources of varying authenticity, claimed that the Assyrians were victorious in the early stages of the conflict; as a result they became overconfident and were decisively defeated while their soldiers were feasting and drinking (cf. 1:10; Dan 5) (Maier, pp. 109–10, 192).

5 This verse is rendered ambiguous by the verb translated "stumble" (*kāšal*), suggesting the weakness of the defenders rather than the ferocity of the attackers depicted in vv.3–4. Such an interpretation would indicate that the antecedent of "he" was the king of Assyria (cf. 3:18), whose troops were summoned to defend the "city walls." However, the final couplet is more appropriate to the rapid movement of the enemy ("dash," cf. vv.3–4), and the unusual term "protective shield" (*sōḵēḵ*, lit., "covering"; cf. Exod 25:20; Ezek 28:14, 16) appears to be used as a technical term describing the besiegers' defensive equipment (see below). It is therefore preferable to view v.5 as a further stage in the enemy's advance, like v.6.

On this understanding the "picked troops" represent the shock troops directed to breach the "wall." The "protective covering" would describe the screen set up to protect the troops engaged in undermining and penetrating the wall (Yadin, *Art of Warfare*, p. 316). The verb "stumble" retains an enigmatic ring. It is best explained in 3:3: the stumbling of the "picked troops" is due, not to their weakness, but to the "corpses" of their victims, obstructing their advance; the conjunction "yet," which appears to conflict with this interpretation, is not present in the Hebrew.

b. *Failing defenses*

2:6–10

6 The river gates are thrown open
  and the palace collapses.
7 It is decreed that ⌞the city⌟
  be exiled and carried away.
Its slave girls moan like doves
  and beat upon their breasts.
8 Nineveh is like a pool,
  and its water is draining away.
"Stop! Stop!" they cry,
  but no one turns back.
9 Plunder the silver!
  Plunder the gold!
The supply is endless,
  the wealth from all its treasures!

10 She is pillaged, plundered, stripped!
Hearts melt, knees give way,
bodies tremble, every face grows pale.

6 This brief verse (five Hebrew words) marks a decisive turning point in the campaign, as the main line of defense was broken and the heart of the city destroyed. The noun "river" is plural in Hebrew, and in fact Nineveh lay at the confluence of three rivers. The Tigris flowed close to its walls, and two tributaries, the Khosr and the Tebiltu, passed through the city itself. Virtually all of Nineveh's fifteen gates gave access also to one of these rivers or to a canal derived from them, thus being designated "gates of the rivers." Alternatively, the "gates" were those controlling the flow of the rivers rather than those giving access to the city. All three rivers were capable of rising to flood proportions when swollen by rain, and the inscriptions of Sennacherib repeatedly describe both the undermining effects of flood on the walls and buildings and the extensive damage or sluicing operations required to correct the problems.

It is very possible, therefore, that the "river gates" envisaged are those regulating the flow of water through one or more of these dams; indeed, the Akkadian term "gate of the river" (*bab-nari*) was applied to a canal gate by Sennacherib. When "thrown open" by the enemy, who already controlled the suburbs where they were situated, the gates would have released a deluge of water, as a result of which the palace "collapses." The Assyrians had flooded other cities themselves; it was fitting that their own city, corrupt and full of violence, should perish in the same manner. The verb *mûg* means "to melt" (NIV, "collapses"). Its literal usage is primarily of dissolution by water, providing further corroboration for the preceding interpretation.

Nineveh's principal palaces in the seventh century included Sennacherib's residence, the alleged "Palace with No Rival." Adorned with cedar and cypress wood, bronze lions (cf. vv.11–13), bull colossi of white marble, and many sculptured reliefs, the palace's main hall alone measured forty by one hundred and fifty feet. It had been built in place of a smaller structure, whose foundations had been eroded by flooding of the Tebiltu (u.s.). Now the same fate threatened its successors; and fire swept away all that survived the flood. The term "palace" (*hêḵāl*) can also be translated "temple"; and the major temples of Ishtar and Nabu, restored by Ashurbanipal, were also ravaged in the Fall of Nineveh. The judgment decreed for the idolatrous monarchy was fully accomplished.

7–8 These verses delineate (with some notorious translation difficulties; cf. Notes) the aftermath of this decisive turning point in v.6. The survivors are "exiled" (v.7) amid the mourning of the "slave girls" (cf. Ezek 7:16)—a recurrent feature of ancient Near Eastern literature (cf. the "Curse of Agade," ANET, Supplement, p. 650) and a not uncommon scene in Assyrian wall carvings depicting the agonies of their captives.

The image of water depicts Nineveh's fate with vivid irony (v.8). Nineveh was a place of watered parks and orchards. As at the Flood, however, "water" became a source of death, overflowing its boundaries and bringing chaos to the inundated city. Unlike the Flood, this "pool" promised no respite as its waters "drained away" ("fled," cf. Notes). Although the first stich of the verse is difficult (cf. NASB and Notes), the second line is clear; like water ebbing quickly away when the dams are breached, the defenders of Nineveh heeded no cry to remain at their posts.

9 The exaction of plunder had characterized the Neo-Assyrian Empire throughout its history. From the days of the first Tiglath-pileser (1115–1076) down to the destruction of the empire, Assyrian monarchs boasted of the booty taken in war (cf. ANET, pp. 274–301, especially the list of Ashurnasirpal II and Sennacherib). Those that submitted were drained of their resources more methodically by the exaction of tribute, a fate suffered by Israel and Judah at various times (cf. ANET, pp. 281, 283, 288 for tribute recorded sent from Jehu, Menahem, and Hezekiah). Thus Nineveh became in the seventh century the richest city throughout the ancient Near East, as the seat of the Sargonide Dynasty to which its kings returned with their prey. Now it was to suffer the same fate: its own people were to be led away (cf. 2:7; 3:10–11), its "wealth" in "gold," "silver," and valuables was to be seized. The fulfillment of this sentence is confirmed by the Babylonian Chronicle, which states that "they carried off much spoil from the city and the temple-area" (Gailey, p. 1000).

Nahum's emphatic phrase *'ên qēṣeh* ("no end") recurs in 3:3 (NIV, "without number"), 3:9 (NIV, "boundless"), and elsewhere only twice in Isaiah 2:7.

10 The defeat of the city is summarized forcefully in the initial line, expressed by the rhyme and alliteration joining its first three words (*bûqāh ûmᵉḇûqāh umᵉḇullāqāh*). NIV's terse phrases capture the mood. The inhabitants had failed to "brace" themselves (v.1, *ḥazzēq moṯnayim*, lit., "strengthen the loins") and instead "bodies tremble" (*ḥalḥālāh bᵉkol-moṯnayim*, lit., "writhing in loins"). The verb underlying "tremble" (*ḥûl*) is often applied to labor pains and may foreshadow the charge of effeminacy in 3:13. It recurs in an identical context of disabling fear in Isaiah 13:8, and the noun form is used similarly in Isaiah 21:3. The expression of psychological states in terms of their physical manifestations is a common and vivid characteristic of Hebrew, particularly in poetry.

Notes

7–8 These verses contain several difficult expressions, particularly "it is decreed" (v.7) and "its water" (v.8). The first translates a Hophal form derived from the verb נָצַב (*nāṣaḇ*, "to stand") and literally means "it is caused to stand." A Hophal participle is clearly used in Gen 28:12, describing the stairway "set up," "erected," from earth to heaven (cf. Judg 9:6 MT). No extant parallel to Nahum's nonliteral usage of this form occurs in the OT. However, a similar verb, קוּם (*qûm*, "to arise, stand"), is often used of establishing a covenant or decree (e.g., Gen 6:18; 9:11, 17; Num 30:14; et al.). Another verb, כוּן (*kûn*, "to stand, be firm"), is similarly used of establishing a throne or matter (e.g., 1 Sam 20:31; 2 Sam 7:13; 1 Kings 2:12, 46). The same connotation of establishing a matter is evident in 1 Chron 18:3, and particularly in the use of the Niphal participle referring to "officers," i.e., those appointed to stand in an office, in 1 Kings 4:5, 7, 27; 5:16; 9:23; 22:47. The present usage, therefore, has adequate support and may be taken to express the certainty of Nineveh's exile, with undertones of the divine purpose that establishes it.

The initial couplet of v.8 appears to read in the MT as follows: "Nineveh (is) as a pool of water, since the days of it (existing), and/but they are fleeing." NIV reads מִימֵי הִיא (*mîmê hî'*, "since the days of it") as *mêmê hî'* or *mêmeyhā* ("its water"), which it transposes into the second clause after the conjunction ו (*w^e*, "and/but"), in place of the pronoun הֵמָּה (*hēmmāh*, "they"). The MT reading is admittedly obscure; in particular it provides an awkward antecedent for the following clause: "they are fleeing." Alternatively, the form *mîmê* can be interpreted as the construct plural of מַיִם (*māyîm*, "water"), if read with sere (*ê*) in place of hireq (*î*) as its initial vowel (*mêmê*). The use of an independent genitive pronoun is not attested by grammarians of biblical Hebrew (i.e., הִיא [*hî'*, "of it"]; cf. GKC, par. 130d, n. 3); but it is found in Ugaritic (Gordon, UT, 6:4). It yields the approximate translation: "Nineveh, its waters are like a pool," i.e., Nineveh is like a pool with all its water. Such a reading of the noun is supported by the LXX and the Vulgate and is well suited to the context (cf. 1:8; 2:6). In addition this provides a suitable antecedent for the following clause: "they are fleeing, draining away" (נָסִים, *nāsîm*; cf. Deut 34:7; Ps 114:3, 5, where waters or moisture "flee"), extending the compressed ambivalence of the image. The waters that came in like a flood drained away like the very life blood of the city as its inhabitants forsook it. By contrast the reading "from the days of it" is unquestionably more difficult but makes too little sense to be accepted here.

---

c. *An interpretive analogy*

2:11–12

11Where now is the lions' den,
the place where they fed their young,
where the lion and lioness went,
and the cubs, with nothing to fear?
12The lion killed enough for his cubs
and strangled the prey for his mate,
filling his lairs with the kill
and his dens with the prey.

11 The mocking rhetorical question introduces an extended metaphor that interprets the horror of the preceding verses: Nineveh has ravaged Mesopotamia like a savage beast of prey and must be judged accordingly. The metaphor is particularly appropriate as a designation of Nineveh: its kings compared themselves to lions in their terrible power (e.g., Sennacherib: "Like a lion I raged"); and its game parks sheltered such lions. Like a pride of such lions, Nineveh has been free to terrorize the land "with nothing to fear." The "lion" is a typical image of destruction in the OT, as in Assyrian literature; and Assyria had been represented in such terms as an agent of the Lord's judgment on Judah (Isa 5:29–30; Jer 50:17; et al.). Now, however, an accounting was due for the ruthless spirit in which that judgment was executed (cf. Isa 10:5–19).

12 The intent of the metaphor emerges clearly here. The verse is dominated by the root "killed" (*ṭrp*), recurring in the nouns "kill" (*ṭerep*) and "prey" (*ṭ^erēpāh*); it is normally used of wild beasts that hunt and tear open their prey. The verb "strangle" is equally apt to the image, and lions are represented as killing their prey in this manner in ancient Near Eastern art. Assyrian brutality matched and surpassed such displays of violence; and it is extensively chronicled, with sickening detail, with references to flaying, walling up, and impaling of captives (cf. ANET, p. 285; ANEP, p. 373, Lachish Relief). The goal of the lion's violence was prey "for his cubs"; as the lion filled its "lairs with the kill," so Nineveh had been filled with foreign plunder, recounted in numerous military reports (cf. 2:9).

d. *Judgment from the Lord*

2:13

13"I am against you,"
  declares the LORD Almighty.
"I will burn up your chariots in smoke,
  and the sword will devour your young lions.
  I will leave you no prey on the earth.
The voices of your messengers
  will no longer be heard."

13 The climax is announced in the verdict of condemnation passed on this seemingly unrestricted tyranny; it is introduced by a common phrase reserved exclusively for utterances of the LORD. The condemnation ("against you") further extends the previous metaphor in the two clauses referring to "young lions" (*kᵉpîr*; so "young," v.11) and "prey" (*ṭᵉrēpāh*, so v.12). The threat of leaving "no prey" (lit., "I will cut off your prey"; cf. NASB) is a metonomy of effect: the taking of prey will be cut off with the extermination of the predator. These clauses are framed chiastically by a corresponding sentence against Assyria's "chariots" and "messengers": the predator is identified unambiguously as Nineveh, whose military power and political control over its empire were to be eradicated. The reference both to "chariots" and to "messengers" again recalls Sennacherib's "evil," plotted against the Lord (cf. Isa 37:9, 14, 24; cf. Nah 1:11).

This verse draws together the major motifs and vocabulary of Nahum's prophecy: the Lord's inexorable opposition to Nineveh; the destruction of its military resources; the role of "sword" and "fire" that "consume" the enemy; the cutting off of Nineveh and its "prey"; the termination of its cruelty, symbolized by the "young lions"; and the reversal of fortunes that awaits Assyria and Judah, exemplified in the fate of the "heralds."

e. *The verdict announced*

3:1

1Woe to the city of blood,
  full of lies,
full of plunder,
  never without victims!

1 The relation of this verse to its context is rendered uncertain by the interjection "Woe" (*hôy*; cf. TWOT, 1:212). Normally "woe" introduces a new section, suggesting here that v.1 belongs with 3:2–7; and MT indicates a break after 2:13. However, 3:1 is related thematically to 2:11–13 much more closely than to 3:4; it repeats the focal concept of killing (*ṭrp*; 2:12 [ter] 13) in the noun "victims" (*ṭerep*; so "kill," 2:12; "prey," 2:13)—an association reinforced by the parallel nouns "plunder" (*pereq*) and "blood." And it also represents the city as "full (of plunder)" (*mᵉlē'āh*), like the lion's den (cf. *yᵉmallē'* ["filling"], 2:12).

In addition the introductory function of the expression "Woe" is by no means clear-cut here. It is usually linked explicitly to what follows when introducing a new section, whereas no clear transition is apparent between vv. 1–2. Nor is it consistently used at the beginning of an extended section; thus it may occur in virtual isolation (Isa 33:1) or in close dependence on what precedes (Isa 1:4; 5:8–23; Zeph 2:5; 3:1; Zech 2:6–7) or at the conclusion of a passage (Jer 30:7; 47:6; 50:27). The latter function predominates in contexts of mourning, and the following parallel section concludes on precisely this note (v.7). Thus the proposed association of 3:1 with 2:11–13 is validated by OT usage, and moreover it completes the distinctive parallel structure uniting 2:3–3:1 and 3:2–7 (cf. introduction to 2:3–3:7): both open abruptly with a battle scene (2:3–5; 3:2–3), and both close with the decease and "mourning" of the condemned criminal. As such v.1 summarizes vv.3–13, linking cause (vv.11–13) to effect (vv.3–10), crime to punishment.

2. *Second description of Nineveh's destruction* (3:2–7)

a. *Onslaught and failing defenses*

3:2–3

2The crack of whips,
the clatter of wheels,
galloping horses
and jolting chariots!
3Charging cavalry,
flashing swords
and glittering spears!
Many casualties,
piles of dead,
bodies without number,
people stumbling over the corpses—

2–3 These verses resume the battle scene of 2:3–5, evoking the rapid movement and particularly the sound of the onslaught led by the chariots. This evocation is enhanced through the guttural consonants by which it is expressed, especially in the alliteration of the final phrase (*merkāḇāh meraqqēḏāh*, "jolting chariots"). The visual element of this imagery is developed in v.3, in terms of light and fire as in 2:3–4 (cf. "flashing," lit., "flame"; "glittering," lit., "lightning"). The term "cavalry" may denote the mounted horsemen that are depicted accompanying chariots in Assyrian reliefs, or it may refer to the horses of the chariot corps (cf. TWOT, 2:740: *pārāš*). "Swords" were characteristic weapons of footsoldiers, being used in hand-to-hand combat; they did not form part of the regular equipment of horsemen or chariot crews, at least among the Assyrians (Yadin, *Art of Warfare*, p. 294). The "spears" also formed an integral part of the infantry's weapons, without being restricted to them.

As in 2:3–10, the defenders are annihilated by the attack: four times—using three different words—the verse refers to the corpses left in the wake of the invading army. Possibly the "people stumbling" are the fugitives; in view of the repetition of this verb (*kāšal*) in 2:5, they are more likely to be the victors, impeded by the sheer mass of bodies.

The allusions to 2:3–3:1 reveal a grotesque irony in the catastrophe: in place of "wealth [*kāḇōḏ*, 2:9] from all its treasures," Nineveh shall possess "piles" [*kōḇeḏ*, 3:3] of "dead"; "bodies without number" (*w*e*'ên qēṣeh lagg*e*wîyāh*, 3:3) are the consequence of its "endless" supply (*w*e*'ên qēṣeh latt*e*ḵûnāh*, 2:9). So terrible was the slaughter that even the Babylonian Chronicle refers to the evil manner in which a suburb of Nineveh had been butchered.

b. *An interpretive analogy*

3:4

> 4all because of the wanton lust of a harlot,
> alluring, the mistress of sorceries,
> who enslaved nations by her prostitution
> and peoples by her witchcraft.

4 The defeat of Nineveh is again followed by a metaphor, whose interpretive function is here made explicit ("all because of," cf. 2:11–12). The root underlying the word "harlot" (*znh*) occurs three times in this verse, which it dominates (cf. "wanton lust," "prostitution"), as 2:11–12 is dominated by the figure of the lions. The biblical references to "prostitution" have varied connotations. They imply treachery and infidelity (Judg 2:17; 8:33–34), pollution (Lev 20:3–5; Jer 13:27), and lust (Ezek 23:5–21). All are appropriate to this city that sacrificed any semblance of morality to personal interest. Of primary significance in this context, however, is the prostitute's motive of personal gain and the ominous attraction that she exercises to attain it, with fatal consequences for the victims (cf. Prov 7:5–27; though the "adulteress" is not offering her favors for hire, the result is the same). Nineveh's attraction is specified by the word "alluring," for her iniquity was overlaid with the splendor of her wealth and power. As Ahaz had been lured into unholy relations with Assyria formerly (cf. 2 Kings 16:7–18), so Nineveh had drained the life of those enticed by her smooth ways (cf. Isa 36:16–17). Both her quest for personal gain and the fate of the one attracted is evoked by the word "enslaved" (*māḵar*, lit., "sold"; cf. NASB).

The harlot's practice of allurement and manipulation is abetted by the second major metaphorical characteristic of v.4: "sorceries, . . . witchcraft" (*k*e*šāp̄îm*). Both sorcery and harlotry suggest a control that is exercised by illicit, surreptitious yet deadly means, and they recur together elsewhere (2 Kings 9:22; Isa 57:3; Gal 5:19–20; Rev 21:8; 22:15); they correspond to the stealth of the hunting lion and, though less overt in their bloodshed, they are equally destructive. Nineveh is here seen as using both immoral attractions (the city was a center of the cult of Ishtar—herself represented as a harlot) and sorcery (Assyrian society was dominated by magic arts; IDB, 1:283–87) as a means to enslave others. The metaphor is very close to the reality.

c. *Judgment from the Lord*

3:5–6

> 5"I am against you," declares the LORD Almighty.
> "I will lift your skirts over your face.
> I will show the nations your nakedness
> and the kingdoms your shame.

[6]I will pelt you with filth,
I will treat you with contempt
and make you a spectacle.

5–6 As the Lord's condemnation overthrows the city's brutality (2:13), so it annuls the demonic power that promotes that brutality. The preceding metaphor is extended in vv.5–6, which portray the humiliation and disgrace of the woman indicted in v.4 (cf. 2:11–13); the second person pronominal forms throughout vv. 5–7 are feminine, as suggested by the removal of her "skirts." The same principle of reversal is effected: violence has been requited with violence (2:13); Nineveh's hidden arts are destroyed by exposure; as she enslaved "nations," so she will be bared to the "nations." Such exposure is emphasized by the repeated root "to see" (*r'h:* "show," v.5; "spectacle," v.6; cf. "see," v.7). This form of punishment for harlotry recurs in Scripture (Jer 13:26–27; Ezek 16:37–41; Hos 2:3–5; Rev 17:15–16).

d. *The verdict announced*

3:7

[7]All who see you will flee from you and say,
'Nineveh is in ruins—who will mourn for her?'
Where can I find anyone to comfort you?"

7 As in v.1, this section concludes a note of mourning in response to the Lord's verdict—mourning occasioned, not by grief, but merely by the presence of death. In v.1 death is foreshadowed in the city's sin; in v.7 it is an accomplished fact, and the witnesses respond in revulsion and amazement to the humiliated prostitute. The "ruins" of Nineveh reflect the Lord's determination to make a full "end" of it (1:8–9), and the fulfillment of this purpose is amply attested both inscriptionally and archaeologically. The Babylonian Chronicle merely summarizes a variety of contemporary records in its comment concerning the sack of Nineveh: "They . . . turned the city into a ruin mound and a heap of debris" (Thomas, *Documents*, p. 76).

The debacle is still regarded as one of the greatest riddles of world history. Within a span of eighty years, Nineveh, which had been raised to unrivaled prominence by Sennacherib and his successors, was obliterated from living memory. Sennacherib had boasted of his city: "Nineveh, the noble metropolis, the city beloved of Ishtar, wherein are all the meeting-places of gods and goddesses; the everlasting substructure, the eternal foundation; whose plan had been designed from of old, and whose structure had been made beautiful along with the firmament of heaven" (Maier, p. 318).

But the Lord had purposed Nineveh's end, and the imperial city was never rebuilt; trouble did not come "a second time" from that quarter.

For the next three hundred years at least, there is no evidence that the site of Nineveh was even occupied. Xenophon passed the ruins without recognizing them (c. 400 B.C.) (Maier, p. 135). Lucian stated: "Nineveh has perished, and there is no trace left where it once was" (ibid.). Layard, one of Nineveh's excavators, wrote as follows:

> We have been fortunate enough to acquire the most convincing and lasting evidence of that magnificence and power, which made Nineveh the wonder of the

> ancient world, and her fall the theme of the prophets, as the most signal instance of divine vengeance. Without the evidence that these monuments afford, we might also have doubted that the great Nineveh ever existed, so completely has she become "a desolation and a waste" (ibid., pp. 135–36).

According to the Cambridge Ancient History (3:130–31) "no other land seems to have been sacked and pillaged so completely as was Assyria."

The references to "mourning" and "comfort" are parallel to those in Isaiah 51:19, regarding Jerusalem, and the humiliation of Nineveh corresponds to that of Babylon in Isaiah 47 (cf. vv.2–3, 9, 12). The other major prophecy regarding Nineveh, in Zephaniah, shows similar affinities with Isaiah's oracles against Babylon and Edom in its prediction of utter desolation (Zeph 2:13–15; Isa 13:19–22; 14:22–23; 34:10–17; 47:8, 10; cf. Rev. 18:2, 7). Thus ended the life of imperial Assyria, unmourned and virtually forgotten!

3. *Third description of Nineveh's destruction*

3:8–11

8Are you better than Thebes,
situated on the Nile,
with water around her?
The river was her defense,
the waters her wall.
9Cush and Egypt were her boundless strength;
Put and Libya were among her allies.
10Yet she was taken captive
and went into exile.
Her infants were dashed to pieces
at the head of every street.
Lots were cast for her nobles,
and all her great men were put in chains.
11You too will become drunk;
you will go into hiding
and seek refuge from the enemy.

The clear structure uniting 2:3–3:7 is abandoned after 3:7. Nahum 3:8–11 is linked to both 3:5–7 and 3:12–17 by the second singular feminine pronominal forms ("you," "your") and might be considered an extension of the Lord's indictment of the harlot. However, the characteristic imagery of 3:5–7 is abandoned in these verses, which are distinguished by a different analogy in the comparison to Thebes. This analogy corresponds to that of the lion and the harlot, being introduced by a rhetorical question as in 2:11 (cf. 3:7). It is followed by an implicit sentence of judgment (3:11), corresponding to those in 2:13; 3:5–6; and the direct address that frames this section (vv.8, 11) is also distinctive in the preceding judicial verdicts (cf. 1:9, 11, 14; 2:1). In addition 3:8–11 repeats from 2:3–3:7 the central themes of Nineveh's defense and defeat signaled by specific repetitions of vocabulary (see charts at introduction to 2:1–3:19). It is therefore treated as a complex and abbreviated correspondent to the previous sections, on which it depends for its structural and thematic identity.

8 In the "Thebes" is "No Amon" ("the city of Amon"; cf. NIV mg.; Jer 46:25; Ezek 30:14–16). "Amon" was the chief god of the Theban pantheon and one of the principal deities of Egypt since the New Kingdom (c. 1580–1090); the term "No" is derived from Egyptian "city" (*nwt*; cf. Akkadian *ni'u*). Thebes, which lay on the Nile about four hundred miles south of modern Cairo, constituted the chief city of Upper, or southern, Egypt and was a leading center of Egyptian civilization. A place of temples, obelisks, sphinxes, and palaces, it has been described as the "world's first great monumental city" (IDB, 4:616). It was dominated by the mighty temples of Amon at Luxor and Karnak on the east bank of the Nile, opposite the funerary temples of the kings to the west. Its temples and palaces are said to have found no equal in antiquity, and they are still regarded by some as the mightiest ruins of ancient civilization to be found anywhere in the world.

As intimated above, the city lay on both banks of the Nile. The river was divided into the principle channels by the islands that interrupted its flow. There is also evidence of an embankment, built by Amenhotep III, to retain the waters of an artificial lake a mile long and one thousand feet wide (ZPEB, 2:231). Thebes could truly be described, therefore, as a city "with water around her." The term "river" (*yām*) is normally translated "sea" (cf. NASB); it is applied elsewhere to the Nile (Isa 18:2; 19:5; cf. Jer 51:36), and indeed the Nile is known as "the sea" (*al-bahr*) to this day. The strategic location of Thebes made the river its natural or "outer" wall, a normal meaning of the noun *ḥêl*, here translated "defense." In addition, it enjoyed the protection of a main, inner "wall" (*ḥômāh*), visualized again here as constituted by the surrounding waters or extending from them (cf. Notes). It is thus equated with Nineveh, similarly defended by a "wall" and by water through its location on a great river (2:5–6, 8).

9 Thebes had intermittent periods of great glory as the capital of Egypt from Middle Kingdom times (c. 2160–1580) onward, reigning especially supreme in the Eighteenth to Twentieth dynasties of the New Kingdom (c. 1580–1090) and in the Twenty-First Dynasty as well (c. 1085–950). After some indifferent periods, the establishment of an Ethiopian dynasty (biblical "Cush") in the seventh century assured a continuing place for Thebes, with access to the strength of both Egypt and Ethiopia. The adjective "boundless" corresponds to "endless" (2:9—*'ên qēṣēh*), evoking the vast resources shared by the two cities and foreshadowing the "bodies without number" (v.3) that they were destined to share also.

"Libya" (lûḇîm) lay to the west of Egypt, with which it possessed similar ties: the long-lived Twenty-Second Dynasty had originated from Libya (c. 950–730), exemplified in the ruler Sheshonk I (Shishak; cf. 1 Kings 14:25–26). "Put" is also to be located in North Africa on the basis of biblical references that associate it with Egypt and Ethiopia (cf. Gen 10:6; 1 Chron 1:8; Jer 46:9; et al.). It is now commonly identified with the same area as Libya, on the basis of Old Persian inscriptions referring to Libya as "Putaya" (IDB, 3:971). Like Nineveh, Thebes was surrounded not only by natural defenses but by the confederate resources of a vast and ancient empire.

10–11 For all her strength, Thebes fell to the Assyrians (c. 664). The Ethiopian kings of the Twenty-Fifth Dynasty had provoked this attack by their policy of intrigue in Palestine. Rather than confront Assyria directly, they tended to incite the minor states to rebel against their Assyrian overlords, with a view to reestablishing Palestine as an Egyptian sphere of influence (cf. Isa 30:1–7; 31:1–3; 36:6; 37:9). As a result of such intrigue by Tarhaka (689–664; cf. Isa 37:9) with the prince of Tyre,

Egypt was invaded by Esarhaddon in 675/674; the campaign was launched in earnest in 671, when the Egyptians were routed before the Assyrians who captured Memphis. Upper Egypt, including Thebes, surrendered; Tarhaka fled south to Ethiopia, and his rule was abrogated in Lower Egypt, which Esarhaddon fragmented under the rule of minor princes.

Esarhaddon died in 669 as he was marching to suppress further insurrection in Egypt, and Tarhaka immediately moved north into Egypt again: Thebes resumed its traditional allegiance to him, Memphis was seized, and Lower Egypt was again overrun. In 667 Ashurbanipal was in a position to take Egypt in hand, reversing the previous sequence of events. Memphis fell to his troops; Thebes surrendered with the rest of Egypt; Tarhaka fled south to Napata where he died. He was succeeded as king of Ethiopia by Tanutamon, who renewed the attempt to control Egypt. Again, Thebes reversed its allegiance, receiving him with acclaim. Memphis was taken, its Assyrian representatives were slaughtered, and Tanutamon gained temporary sovereignty over Egypt. The Egyptians were no match for the Assyrian army, which returned under Ashurbanipal in 664/663. Tanutamon fled south like his predecessors, the Delta was reconquered, and Thebes fell. Both Ashurbanipal and Esarhaddon had exercised restraint in their Egyptian foreign policy, as a means of securing loyalty in a distant country they could only with difficulty garrison effectively. Now, however, Ashurbanipal's patience was exhausted. Thebes was razed to the ground, in vengeance on its vacillating allegiance to Ethiopia (cf. 2 Kings 17:3–6). His enraged and vehement attack on the city—and on "Egypt" and "Ethiopia" (Kusi) on which it relied—is documented in his annals (cf. CAH, 3:285), a report corroborated by the subsequent history of Thebes: from that time onward it has been largely a place of monuments to a glory and dominance now long departed. Both the Egyptian and the Assyrian sources therefore validate Nahum's description of a city scattered to the winds, its posterity cut off, its trained "nobles" plundered, and its leaders fleeing for refuge.

The account of this verse echoes the preceding announcement of judgment on Nineveh, in the threat of "exile" (*gālāh*; cf. 2:7) and of destruction in the "streets" (*ḥûṣôṯ*, 2:4); the human resources represented by its "nobles" (*niḵ bāḏîm*) suffered the same fate as Nineveh's "wealth" (*kāḇōḏ*, 2:9; cf. 3:3). And in v. 11 this correlation is made explicit. Its first and third lines open with the emphatic "You too . . . you too" (*gam-'at*; cf. NASB, KJV), echoing the same adverb repeated twice in v. 10 ("Yet she" [*gam-hî'*]; "[also] her infants" [*gam 'ōlāleyhā*; cf. NASB, KJV). Nineveh has been equated with Thebes in its defenses (v. 8); it would surely be equated with Thebes in its downfall. The finality of this sentence is sealed by its further correspondence to 1:2–15. Nineveh would be "drunk" as decreed by the Lord (1:10). She would seek "refuge" in vain (*mā'ôz*, so 1:7), for she trusted in carved images and idols.

Notes

8 NIV appears to point מִיָּם, *mîyām* ("from the sea, river") as *mayim* ("waters"), in which it is supported by the LXX, Syriac, Vulgate, and RSV. MT is fully intelligible as it stands and may be translated either "her wall (consisted) of the river" or "her wall (extended) from the

river." The repetition of a word within a verse is characteristic of Nahum's style, giving grounds for MT's reading (e.g., 1:2, 4; 2:2, 8, 9, 11; 3:2, 3, 4 [*bis*], 15 [*ter*]; cf. many other repetitions between verses). It also serves to explain the variants, effected by translators who would have found the repetition awkward, or who overlooked it in reading the consonants *mym* for the common noun "water." Of the two options noted for MT, the first is preferable, in view of the parallelism "river"= "defense"; "river" = "wall," and of the strong emphasis on the role of water in v.8. That Thebes was also protected by a conventional wall is attested by Homer, however, who wrote of its hundred gates (Maier, p. 315).

---

4. *Fourth description of Nineveh's destruction*

3:12–19

Verses 12–19 are related to vv.8–11 by the direct address that extends from v.12 to the end of the chapter. However, they abandon the analogy of Thebes and are unified by the distinct image of the city being "consumed." The verb "to eat" (*'āḵal*) occurs four times ("eater," v.12; "consumed," v.13; "devour," "consume," v.15; cf. 1:10; 2:13); and the motif pervades the section, being evidenced in the images of devouring "fire" (3:13, 15), and particularly of the voracious "locusts" (vv. 15, 16, 17 [bis]; cf. "grasshoppers," v.15 [bis]; "strip," v.16). It yields two composite images that reiterate and amplify the destruction depicted in previous sections: Nineveh and her "fortresses" will be consumed from without by "fire," as fig trees stripped of their fruit (vv.12–15); but she is also consumed from within by her own officials, who strip her like parasitical "locusts" (vv.15–18).

A pattern corresponding to that of previous sections underlies this imagery, which is developed with great artistry. Verse 15 corresponds closely to 2:13 in pronouncing the sentence on Nineveh. The two verses share the words "fire," "devour," "sword," "leave no . . . ," "cut down." Verse 14 likewise corresponds closely to the call to defense in 2:1; the series of five taunting imperatives echoes the four admonitions in 2:1, without other parallels in Nahum, and similarly are directed to Nineveh's fortifications. The remaining elements of the preceding structures emerge clearly in the light of these precise correlations, though the focus is predominantly on Nineveh's destruction and no longer on its agents (cf. 2:1; 3–5; 3:2–3). The failure of the defenses and the impotence of her "troops" is a recurring feature (vv.12–13; cf. 2:6–10; 3:3, 8 11); and the section is again characterized by a vivid metaphor (vv.16–17), elucidating her downfall and developed in the accompanying sentence (v.15; cf. 2:13; 3:5–6, 11). And it concludes with a final response to this judgment, addressed directly to its victim (vv.18–19; cf. vv.1, 7).

a. *Onslaught and failing defenses*

3:12–14

12 All your fortresses are like fig trees
with their first ripe fruit;
when they are shaken,
the figs fall into the mouth of the eater.
13 Look at your troops—
they are all women!
The gates of your land
are wide open to your enemies;
fire has consumed their bars.

[14]Draw water for the siege,
strengthen your defenses!
Work the clay,
tread the mortar,
repair the brickwork!

12–13 For Nineveh no "refuge" would be forthcoming (cf. v.11). Her "fortresses" (v.12, probably walled cities [*miḇṣār*] ; cf. Num 32:17; 2 Kings 3:19; et al.) guarding the approach to Nineveh were ripe for destruction, being dislodged with as little effort as "figs" ready for harvesting. As the "gates" (v.13) guarding entrance to the land, they were "open" to the enemy like those of Nineveh herself (cf. 2:6). This collapse is explained by the effeminate, weakened condition of her "troops" (cf. Isa 19:16; Jer 50:37). Such debility is developed in vv.15–18 as a major cause of Nineveh's fall, with reference to the self-interested decadence of her officials.

14 The impending condition of "siege" demanded an independent supply of "water," since the enemy would cut off all external sources provided by the rivers flowing into the city (cf. 2:6). The Babylonian Chronicle corroborates this anticipation of siege, referring to a campaign that lasted three months (Thomas, *Documents*, p. 76; ZPEB, 1:688, 690). It also intimates that operations against the city had begun in 614 under Cyaxeres (cf. 2:1), so that Nineveh was subject to intermittent siege for more than two years.

For "defenses" (*miḇṣār*), see comment at v.12. The word can also mean "fortifications" or walls of the city. "Clay" was the principal building material of Mesopotamia, which lacked adequate resources in stone (cf. Gen 11:3). The walls of Nineveh, which were built of such "worked clay" bricks (IDB, 1:465–661), averaged fifty feet in breadth, extending to over one hundred feet at the gates; they therefore demanded an enormous effort for their maintenance, as indicated here by the urgent and repeated references to the processes involved. Evidence of the Ninevites' ill-fated attempts at self-defense is still apparent in the rubble of a counterwall, erected hastily within the city after the main fortifications were breached (Maier, pp. 116–17, 340–41).

b. *Interpretive analogy and judgment from the Lord*

3:15–17

[15]There the fire will devour you;
the sword will cut you down
and, like grasshoppers, consume you.
Multiply like grasshoppers,
multiply like locusts!
[16]You have increased the number of your merchants
till they are more than the stars of the sky,
but like locusts they strip the land
and then fly away.
[17]Your guards are like locusts,
your officials like swarms of locusts
that settle in the walls on a cold day—
but when the sun appears they fly away,
and no one knows where.

15 Nineveh's conquest by fire, together with sword, is amply revealed in the ruins. Maier (pp. 125–26), quoting A.H. Layard, writes: "The palace (Sennacherib's) had been destroyed by fire. The alabaster slabs were almost reduced to lime, and many of them fell to pieces as soon as uncovered. The palaces, which others had occupied, could only be traced by a thin white deposit, like a coat of plaster, left by the burnt alabaster upon the wall of sun-dried bricks." Greek tradition in fact records that the king himself set fire to his palace, perishing by his own hand in its flames (Maier, pp. 109–10).

The devouring (*'āḵal*) fire evokes the destruction inflicted by "grasshoppers" or locusts, which similarly "consume" (*'āḵal*) all that lies in their path. Verses 15–17 develop this image of "locusts" with intricate detail, which may be schematised as follows:

v. 15 fire	devour		
locusts	consume	multiply	
v. 16 merchants, like locusts	strip	increased	fly away
v. 17 guards, like locusts	(settle)	swarms	fly away

NIV normally translates the noun "grasshopper" (*yeleq*) as "locusts" (cf. Jer 51:14, 27; Joel 1:4; 2:25), which is preferable. The term is used in Psalm 105:34 with reference to the Egyptian plague that was clearly the work of locusts (cf. Exod 10:4–15; NIV, "grasshoppers," Ps 105:34); and the initial emphasis of v. 15 is on their omnivorous behavior, typical of locusts rather than of grasshoppers.

The following word, "locusts" (*'arbeh*), denotes a different species or stage of development in the same type of insect (ZPEB, 3:948–50). This word is related phonetically, and possibly etymologically, to the Hebrew *rāḇāh* ("to increase, be many"; cf. NASB, "swarming locust"). The association determines another abrupt transition in the repeated verb "multiply," becoming explicit in the following statement: "you have increased" (*hirbêṯ*). The ability of the locust to proliferate in vast numbers underlies its menace to vegetation, and this characteristic is also reflected in the OT (cf. Exod 10:5–6, 14–15; Judg 6:5; 7:12; Jer 46:23; 51:14).

16 The significance of the startling comparison emerges in this verse: like locusts, Nineveh's "merchants" proliferated beyond measure; and they likewise "strip" (*pāšaṭ*) the land. The comparison to locusts is thus arranged chiastically, correlating the verbs "consume" and "strip": "consume . . . multiply" (v. 15); "increased . . . strip." It introduces a further element to the analogy in the second panel: like locusts, these "merchants" also "fly away," unconcerned for the region they have exploited.

17 This verse repeats the preceding comparison with emphasis on this final element: Nineveh's "officials," like her "merchants," are multitudinous as "swarms of locusts"; they "settle" within her boundaries for shelter and food, but they abandon her and "fly away" when tribulation comes.

With remarkable artistry and use of word association, Nahum transformed the perspective of the prophecy. The sentence of judgment is now executed from within, by those claiming to serve Nineveh's interests as they flock to her (v. 15); and her fall is explained in terms of the disloyalty of her own people (vv. 16–17). The Assyrians had based their empire on expediency and self-interest, multiplying power, wealth, and personnel like locusts for their own gratification. Now their empire was to succumb as a victim of the self-interest it had promoted—eaten away from within no less than it was devoured by the sword from without.

c. *The verdict announced*

3:18–19

18O king of Assyria, your shepherds slumber;
  your nobles lie down to rest.
Your people are scattered on the mountains
  with no one to gather them.
19Nothing can heal your wound;
  your injury is fatal.
Everyone who hears the news about you
  claps his hands at your fall,
for who has not felt
  your endless cruelty?

18–19 The collapse of effective loyalty penetrated even Assyria's aristocracy, represented by its "nobles" and "shepherds," or "rulers" (*rō'eh,* v.18; cf. Isa 44:28; Jer 23:1; Ezek 34:2–23; 37:24). Their destiny is expressed with ironic ambiguity that is typical of Nahum; although the vocabulary is unusual, their "slumber" (*nāmû*) and "rest" (*yiškᵉnû*—many scholars follow the LXX, which reflects *yāšnû* ["their sleep, death"] for *šāḵan* ["rest"]) foreshadow both their death (Jer 51:39) and the inertia that occasions it (Isa 56:10).

The corollary of this failure is the scattering of the people, "with no one to gather them," a phrase used elsewhere of sheep without "shepherds" (Isa 13:14; cf. Isa 40:11; Jer 23:3; 31:10; Ezek 34:13; 37:21; Mic 2:12). Such scattering duly accompanied Nineveh's end (cf. 2:8), on which the following comment is made:

> The disappearance of the Assyrian people will always remain an unique and striking phenomenon in ancient history. Other, similar, kingdoms and empires have indeed passed away, but the people have lived on. Recent discoveries have, it is true, shown that poverty-striken communities perpetuated the old Assyrian names and various places, for instance on the ruined site of Ashur, for many centuries, but the essential truth remains the same. A nation which had existed two thousand years and had ruled a wide area, lost its independent character (CAH, 3:130).

The "king of Assyria" is addressed directly throughout vv.18–19, and ultimately it was his fatal injury that accounted for his breakdown in authoritative government and military leadership. As anticipated by Nahum, the dynasty fell with the city. The "wound" (v.19) could not be healed; the brief attempt by Ashur-uballit to keep the dynasty alive in Haran failed two years later. The injury was indeed fatal.

The book closes (cf. 1:15) with the response of witnesses who heard of these events ("hears . . . news" [*šōmʿê . . . šēmaʿ*], v.19; "proclaims" [*mašmîaʿ*], 1:15); the "endless cruelty" (*rāʿāh*; so "evil," 1:11) was ended!

> For his anger lasts only a moment,
>   but his favor lasts a lifetime;
> weeping may remain for a night,
>   but rejoicing comes in the morning.
> (Ps 30:5)

HABAKKUK

Carl E. Armerding

HABAKKUK

Introduction

1. Historical Background and Date

Habakkuk's prophecy is set against a background of the decline and fall of the Judean kingdom (c.626–586 B.C.). Although nothing is known of the prophet himself apart from the book bearing his name—the book is not dated in the usual manner (cf. Amos 1:1; Zeph 1:1; et al.)—the general background of Habakkuk is clear from the internal data. Verses 5–11 represent a period before 605, the year the Babylonians (the Chaldeans [*kaśdîm*], 1:6) rose to power (cf. v.5: "you would not believe, even if you were told"), and probably prior to the 612 destruction of Nineveh. By contrast it is sometimes argued that 1:12–17 and 2:6–20 must reflect a period after 612 B.C. (so Ellison et al.), when the power and rapacity of the Babylonians had become common knowledge to the prophet. Various solutions have been proposed, but the best seems to be found in taking the sections of the dialogue as representative of Habakkuk's spiritual struggles over a long period of time, possibly beginning as early as 626 and continuing as late as 590 or after.

During this period Judah enjoyed its last bit of prosperity under Josiah (died 609 B.C.); Assyria's wound was revealed as fatal with the ultimate fall of Nineveh in 612; and the short-lived Babylonian Empire established its dominance over Palestine, with Jerusalem a casualty and its people taken into exile in 586 B.C. Conditions during the life of the prophet would have progressed from excellent—with considerable material prosperity and even promise of spiritual revival—to the height of desperation as the net was drawn closer and closer around the hapless capital. There is no direct evidence from the book that Habakkuk lived past the destruction of Jerusalem, though some find such evidence in 3:16–19 (cf. commentary).

2. Unity

The major challenge to unity comes with chapter 3, the psalm. Stylistic shifts from the narrative portions and the older critical tendency to date psalmic material in the postexilic period have combined to call the authenticity of chapter 3 in question. The failure of the Qumran "commentary" to include an exposition of the psalm has, for some scholars, added weight to the denial of Habakkuk's authorship. Against this is the clear note of continuity of theme in all three chapters and, in general, the lack of any compelling reasons not to accept the book's attribution of the psalm to Habakkuk.

3. Authorship

Nothing is known of Habakkuk except his name, which does not lend itself to attempts at finding a Hebrew meaning (contra Luther et al.). Of his temperament and personal situation, we know only what may be inferred from the book. Literary dependences and early canonical reception leave no doubt that Habakkuk's work was circulated and accepted early, but the details remain lost.

4. Occasion and Purpose

Prophecy is a result of revelation given to a person who then proclaims the inspired message to the people. Often such revelation and inspiration are occasioned by conditions in the nation (with the exception of Jonah and Jer 27, prophecy is always proclaimed to Israel, even when about other nations) about which the prophet has been burdened.

Habakkuk was unique among the prophets because he did not speak for God to the people but rather spoke to God about his people and nation. The similarity with the other prophets is in the setting: the people of God, covenantally bound to him since the days of the Exodus, had sharply fallen away from those covenant standards (1:2–4). Violence and law-breaking (covenant violations) abounded, and the wicked seemed at least superficially to triumph. According to all that Habakkuk knew about God's holiness and covenant (cf. Deut 26–33, on which Habakkuk seemed dependent), Yahweh should have arisen to correct the situation, particularly in response to believing prayer for change by such as Habakkuk. Such correction had not been forthcoming, and the prayers of the righteous and the struggle for justice in the land seemed in vain, with the result that God's program of redemptive history was threatened.

The early part of the prophecy of Habakkuk is a dialogue in which the prophet's questions receive divine answers. Externally, the Assyrians would naturally have been a threat to Judah; and apart from the problem of the future of God's covenant promises, the prophet would have expected Assyria to be "the rod of God's anger." The new element externally is the introduction of Babylonian power, with such awful potential consequences and with no clear vision of when and how Yahweh would continue his commitments to the chosen line. But initially Habakkuk was more concerned with internal injustices and Yahweh's apparent complacency toward the evil generation. It was God's reply (1:5–11) that catapulted the prophecy onto the international and eschatological level.

Larger questions quickly engulf the local concerns, and chapters 2–3 carry us well beyond the last days of Judah to the future. Habakkuk himself was never told when or exactly how it would end, but 2:14, 20 assured him of the ultimate triumph of

Yahweh; and the psalm in chapter 3 shows that Habakkuk learned to live in the light of this fact.

5. Structure

Habakkuk 1:1–2:5 clearly is a dialogue between God and the prophet in which two stylized complaints are answered by two penetrating replies. The opening complaint (1:2–4) has to do with Judah's moral and spiritual decline and the apparent unwillingness of Yahweh to intervene. The first reply (1:5–11) sets forth the coming destruction of Judah by Babylon as Yahweh's discipline for errant Judah. For the patriotic and nationalistic covenant Israelite, this was hardly a solution: 1:12–17 sets forth the complaint that such a solution would only aggravate the problem of God's working in history and the apparent compounding of injustice. Habakkuk 2:1 leaves the prophet sitting on his spiritual tower awaiting an answer; and vv.2–5, the central message of the prophecy, foresee ultimate justice for the arrogant Chaldean and call for the righteous man, in the intervening years, to live by his faith (or "faithfulness," mg.).

Habakkuk 2:6–20 is a taunt or mocking song put in the mouths of the nations that had suffered at the hand of Babylon. It consists of five "woes," punctuated by a vision of the universal knowledge of God's glory (v.14) and climaxed by a call for reverent submission to the Lord of history, who through all the vicissitudes of history remains seated in his holy temple (v.20). In typical prophetic form the taunt moves from the third to the second person, and the subject matter—with the exception of the fifth woe, which opposes idolatry—deals with a nation arrogantly building its own power at the expense of its less-able neighbors.

Habakkuk 3:1–19 is a psalm, replete with musical directions (v.1: *šigyōnôṯ*, ["*shigionoth*"]; cf. Ps 7:1, and v.19: *negînôṯ* ["stringed instruments"]). Because of its unique features, we have left fuller discussion to the commentary.

6. Theological Values

Habakkuk's message, the core of which is found in 2:4, forms a basic point in three NT books. Paul, in Romans 1:17, introduced his gospel as one of salvation by faith, as opposed to salvation by works, and cited Habakkuk 2:4—"the righteous will live by his faith"—as OT support for his argument. Galatians 3:11–12 sets forth faith as the antithesis of law or legal salvation, and again Habakkuk 2:4 serves as a prooftext. Finally, in an intriguing passage from Hebrews 10:37–38, Habakkuk 2:3–4 is again quoted; but the context focuses on the pending arrival of the fulfillment of the vision and the identification of the Hebrews with those who have faith and thus persevere under pressure.

The theological value of Habakkuk, however, cannot be limited to a few, though crucial, NT quotations. The prophet asked some of the most penetrating questions in all literature, and the answers are basic to a proper view of God and his relation to history. If God's initial response sounded the death knell for any strictly nationalistic covenant theology of Judah, his second reply outlined in a positive sense the fact that all history was hastening to a conclusion that was certain as it was satisfying.

In the interim, while history is still awaiting its conclusion (and Habakkuk was not told when the end would come, apparently for him prefigured by Babylon's destruction), the righteous ones are to live by faith. The faith prescribed—or "faithfulness," as many have argued that *'ᵉmûnāh* should be translated—is still called for as a basic response to the unanswered questions in today's universe; and it is this, a theology for life both then and now, that stands as Habakkuk's most basic contribution.

7. Canonicity

Habakkuk was early grouped with the other so-called Minor Prophets in the Book of the Twelve (attested as such in Ecclus 49:10 [c. 190 B.C.]), the acceptance of which is never questioned, either in Jewish or Christian circles. Questions of the unity of the book do not seem to have affected its acceptance, and in fact there is no ancient record of a dispute over chapter 3.

8. Bibliography

Books

Armerding, C.E. "Habakkuk." *International Standard Bible Encyclopedia*. Revised edition. Edited by G.W. Bromiley et al. 5 vols. Grand Rapids: Eerdmans, 1979—, 2:583–86.
Beck, Madeline H., and Williamson, Lamar, Jr. *Mastering Old Testament Facts: Book 4: Prophetic Writings*. Atlanta: John Knox, 1981.
Boadt, Lawrence. *Jeremiah 26–52, Habakkuk, Zephaniah, Nahum (Old Testament Message)*. Vol. 10. Wilmington: Michael Glazier, 1982.
Brownlee, W.H. *The Text of Habakkuk in the Ancient Commentary from Qumran*. JBL Monograph XI. Philadelphia: Society of Biblical Literature, 1959.
______. *The Midrash Pesher of Habakkuk*. Missoula, Mont.: Scholars, 1979.
Calvin, John. *Commentaries on the Twelve Minor Prophets*. Grand Rapids: Eerdmans, n.d.
Ellison, H.L. *The Old Testament Prophets*. Grand Rapids: Zondervan, 1966.
Feinberg, Charles L. *The Minor Prophets*. Chicago: Moody. 1976.
Gaebelein, Frank E. *Four Minor Prophets*. Chicago: Moody, 1970.
Gelston, A., editor. *Dodekapropheton*. Leiden Peshitta. Vol. 3:4. Leiden: E.J. Brill, 1980.
Gowan, Donald E. *The Triumph of Faith in Habakkuk*. Atlanta: John Knox, 1979.
Harris, J.G. *The Qumran Commentary on Habakkuk*. London: A.R. Mowbray, 1966.
Henderson, E. *The Twelve Minor Prophets*. Grand Rapids: Baker, 1980.
Keil, Carl F. *The Twelve Minor Prophets*. Vol. 2. Grand Rapids: Eerdmans, 1949.
Laetsch, Theodore. *The Minor Prophets*. St. Louis: Concordia, 1956.
Lloyd-Jones, M. *From Fear to Faith*. London: Inter-Varsity, 1953.
Marbury, Edward. *Obadiah and Habakkuk*. Minneapolis: Klock, 1979.
Monloubou, L. *Les Prophetes de l'Ancien Testament*. Paris: Cahiers Evangile, 1983.
Poovey, William A. *Six Prophets for Today*. Minneapolis: Augsburg, 1977.
Pusey, E.B. *The Minor Prophets*. Vol. 2. Grand Rapids: Baker, 1950.
Rudolph, Wilhelm. *Kommentar zum Alten Testament*. Vol. 13:3. Guetersloh: Mohn, 1975.
Schneider, D. *The Unity of the Book of the Twelve*. New Haven: Yale, 1979.
Smith, George A. *The Book of the Twelve Prophets*. Vol. 2. ExB. Garden City, N.Y.: Doubleday, Doran & Co., 1929.
Vegas Montaner, Luis. *Biblia Del Mar Muerto: Profetas Menores*. Madrid: Instituto "Arias Montano," 1980.
Ward, W.H. *A Critical and Exegetical Commentary on Habakkuk*. ICC. Edinburgh: T. & T. Clark, 1911.

Periodicals

Brownlee, W.H. "The Historical Allusions of the Dead Sea Habakkuk Midrash." *Bulletin of the American Schools of Oriental Research* 126 (1952): 10–20.

Eaton, J.H. "The Origen and Meaning of Habakkuk 3." *Zeitschrift fur die alttestamentliche Wissenschaft* 76 (1964): 144–71.

Irwin, W.A. "The Mythological Background of Hab 3." *Journal of Near Eastern Studies* 1 (1942): 10–40.

Janzen, J. "Habakkuk 2:2–4 in the Light of Recent Philological Advances." *Harvard Theological Review* 73 (1980): 53–78.

———. "Eschatological Symbol and Existence in Habakkuk." *Catholic Biblical Quarterly* 44 (1982): 394–414.

O'Connell, K.G. "Habakkuk, Spokesman to God." *Currents in Theology and Mission* 6 (1979): 227–31.

Tsumura, D.T. "Hab 2:2 in the Light of Akkadian Legal Practice." *Zeitschrift fur die alttestamentliche Wissenschaft* 94 (1982): 294–95.

Zemek, George J., Jr. "Interpretive Challenges Relating to Habakkuk 2:4b." *Grace Theological Journal* 1 (1980): 43–69.

9. Outline

I. Habakkuk's Initial Lament (1:1–4)
II. God's First Response (1:5–11)
III. Habakkuk's Second Lament (1:12–2:1)
IV. God's Second Response (2:2–20)
  1. Prologue (2:2–3)
  2. Indictment (2:4–5)
  3. Sentence (2:6–20)
V. The Prayer of Habakkuk (3:1–19)
  1. Introduction (3:1)
  2. Prayer (3:2)
  3. Theophany (3:3–15)
  4. Response (3:16–19a)
  5. Epilogue (3:19b)

Text and Exposition

I. Habakkuk's Initial Lament

1:1–4

1The oracle that Habakkuk the prophet received.

2How long, O Lord, must I call for help,
but you do not listen?
Or cry out to you, "Violence!"
but you do not save?
3Why do you make me look at injustice?
Why do you tolerate wrong?
Destruction and violence are before me;
there is strife, and conflict abounds.
4Therefore the law is paralyzed,
and justice never prevails.
The wicked hem in the righteous,
so that justice is perverted.

These verses correspond closely to the psalms of lament, or "complaint": prominent features of this form in vv.2–4 include the questions addressed to the Lord, the urgent description of dire need, and the sustained petition for deliverance (cf. Pss 10:1–13; 13:1–4; 22:1–21; 74:1–11; 80; 88). Habakkuk's prophecy is thus located clearly within the community of faith, exposed to many tribulations, yet oriented to the Lord as its help in trouble. The structure of the passage is defined by prominent repetitions within it, which emerge more clearly in RSV. Twice Habakkuk emphasized the opposing principles of evil and justice, thereby revealing his dominant concern: not only is the lawlessness of "violence" rampant, but it has mastered the very mechanisms of law by which it should be curbed. In such circumstances it is clear that only divine intervention can correct the imbalance (cf. "save," v.2); when this intervention is not forthcoming, faith is stretched beyond its limits. Habakkuk personally confronted the situation he described: it was "before" him, he had to "look at" (v.3) it, and the wicked were at close quarters, hemming in the righteous (v.4). It is also evident that this occurred in Palestine among God's people, which was the proper sphere of the "law" and the social justice flowing from its observance (infra.; cf. Deut 4:8; Isa 2:3; Amos 2:4). The "wicked" themselves are not defined precisely, however, and they have been identified either as fellow Judeans or as members of a foreign nation. Normally where "justice" and social "violence" are opposed, the "wicked" are Israelites unless clearly identified in other terms (e.g., Exod 23:1–9; Isa 5:7–15). Here, in a similar context, they may be assumed to be Judeans in accord with this pattern.

1–2 For comments on the prophet, see the Introduction. The question "How long" (v.2) is typical of a lament (Ps 13:1–2; cf. Pss 6:3; 80:4; 89:46; Jer 12:4; Zech 1:12). It implies a situation of crisis from which the speaker seeks deliverance, as does the following verb (*šiwwa'*, "call for help"). The verb "listen" (*šāma'*) normally carries connotations of an active response to what is heard (e.g., Judg 13:9; Ps 4:1; Ezek 8:18); where that response is lacking, the righteousness of either the petitioner or the one addressed is called in question (cf. Job 19:7; 30:20; Ps 18:41). The crisis in which Habakkuk called for help was "violence"; the response expected from the Lord was that he should "save."

"Violence" (*ḥāmās*) denotes flagrant violation of moral law by which man injures primarily his fellowman (e.g., Gen 6:11). Its underlying meaning is one of ethical wrong, of which physical brutality is only one possible expression (e.g., Judg 9:24; cf. TWOT, 1:297). *Ḥāmās* occurs six times in Habakkuk (1:2, 3, 9, 2:8, 17 [*bis*]), a frequency exceeded only in the longer Book of Psalms (fourteen times) and Proverbs (seven times); it is therefore a key word in this prophecy.

To "save" (*yāša'*) means to deliver from what oppresses or restricts. Such salvation is to be found ultimately only in the Lord, by those who are righteous toward him (e.g., Pss 18:27, 41; 33:16–19; Isa 59:1–2). This opening verse (2) of Habakkuk's dialogue with the Lord sets the tone of chapter 1, which is fraught with the tension of unanswered prayer. The faith underlying it will be only partially vindicated in chapter 2; it is affirmed more fully in chapter 3 (vv.17–19), where it is vindicated by repeated assurances of the Lord's "salvation" (v.18; cf. vv.8, 13).

3 Like the question in v.2, the interrogative "why" is typical in psalms of lament (e.g., Pss 10:1; 44:23–24; 74:1, 11; 80:12; 88:14, where the question is probably more rhetorical than here). Three word-pairs follow. The concepts of "injustice" (*'āwen*) and "wrong" (*'āmāl*) are correlated in ten other verses; NIV usually translates them as "evil" and "trouble." This word-pair is also used predominantly in contexts of perverted justice and social oppression (cf. Job 15:35; Ps 7:14 [15 MT]). "Destruction" (*šōḏ*) and "violence" (*ḥāmās;* cf. comment at v.2) are similarly correlated repeatedly in Scripture, associated with unjust oppression of the weaker members within a community (Jer 6:7; 20:8; Ezek 45:9; Amos 3:10). The two clauses *'āwen* and *'āmāl* allude to Numbers 23:21, where the same verbs and objects occur with the same subject, Yahweh. In this allusion to God's blessing in old times, as in the preceding question, the prophet's sense of a chasm between past revelation and present reality (cf. 3:2) emerges. A third word-pair, "strife" (*rîḇ*) and "conflict" (*māḏôn*), evoke the anger and dissension born of conflicting and uncompromising wills (cf. Prov 15:18; 17:14; 26:20–21; Jer 15:10).

4 The disintegration of a society into such factions is bound up with its rejection of the forces that bring it unity—"law" and "justice." The "law" (*tôrāh*) may refer to any form of authoritative "teaching" (e.g., Prov 3:1; 4:2); almost invariably it refers to God's "law," by which he reveals his will and directs the life of man. When used in the singular without clear definition, as here, "law" signifies God's covenantal code established with Israel, given through Moses and set forth particularly in the Book of Deuteronomy (e.g., Deut 1:5; 4:8; 17:18–19; 31:9; 33:4; Josh 8:31–32). The "law" was mediated primarily through the Levitical priesthood (e.g., Lev 10:11; Deut 33:10), in close conjunction with the king or other governing authorities (e.g., Deut 17:8–11). Its effectiveness was therefore "paralyzed" most extensively by corruption of the religious and civil leadership of the nation—a condition appropriate to the oppression described in v.3. Such a paralysis is very seldom attributed to foreign powers, who in the OT function instead as God's instruments of judgment.

"Justice" (*mišpāṭ*) has broad and varied connotations in the OT, implying the exercise not merely of legal processes but of all the functions of government; it is through "justice" and the act of "judging" (*šāpaṭ*) that law and order are represented, legislated, interpreted, and enforced (cf. TWOT, 2:947–49). Within Israel this order is based on *tôrāh* ("law"), of which "justice" is the application (e.g., Exod 18:16; Num 15:16; Deut 17:11; 33:10).

Notes

---

3 "Abounds" translates נָשָׂא (*nāśā'*, "to lift up"). The verb appears to be used intransitively here, requiring an unusual reflexive translation: "it lifts up (itself)" (cf. Ps 89:9 [10 MT]; Hos 13:1; Nah 1:5). This reading is corroborated by LXX's λαμβάνει (*lambanei*, "he takes") used absolutely, and its difficulty explains the variants in certain other versions. It should therefore be retained, despite the unfamiliar grammatical usage. The verb may also be interpreted as having an impersonal subject, i.e., "one raises, exalts conflict" (cf. GKC, par. 144d; Isa 8:4).

II. God's First Response

1:5–11

5"Look at the nations and watch—
and be utterly amazed.
For I am going to do something in your days
that you would not believe,
even if you were told.
6I am raising up the Babylonians,
that ruthless and impetuous people,
who sweep across the whole earth
to seize dwelling places not their own.
7They are a feared and dreaded people;
they are a law to themselves
and promote their own honor.
8Their horses are swifter than leopards,
fiercer than wolves at dusk.
Their cavalry gallops headlong;
their horsemen come from afar.
They fly like a vulture swooping to devour;
9 they all come bent on violence.
Their hordes advance like a desert wind
and gather prisoners like sand.
10They deride kings
and scoff at rulers.
They laugh at all fortified cities;
they build earthen ramps and capture them.
11Then they sweep past like the wind and go on—
guilty men, whose own strength is their god."

This passage is distinguished from vv.2–4 by a transition to the Lord as speaker. In form these verses resemble an oracle, yet scarcely the oracle of salvation that forms the turning point, explicitly or otherwise, in certain other laments (e.g., Pss 12:5; 13:5–6; 22:23–24; 28:6–7; 31:21–22). They correspond more closely to an expanded announcement of judgment on God's people, the prophet's lament serving now as the accusation on which this is based. This announcement is structured as, first, an introductory reference to the "nations" (*gôyīm*) who will be the source of the impending judgment (v.5; cf. Deut 28:65); second, a portrayal of the Babylonians, the specific "people" (*gôy*) from whom it will arise (vv.6–11a; cf. Deut 28:49–57); and, finally, a brief but pungent verdict on this instrument of judgment (v.11b). Within the second section v.6 sets forth the character of the Babylonians ("ruthless"), their conduct ("who sweep"), and their motivation ("to seize"), each element being elaborated in vv.7–11.

These seven verses echo focal concepts from vv.2–4, in the references to "violence" (*ḥāmās,* v.9; cf. vv.2–3) and to the "law" (*mišpaṭ,* v.7; cf. vv.3–4). This balance between the two passages is signaled in v.5, where the verbs "look at" and "watch" correspond to "look at" (*rā'āh*) and "tolerate" (*hibbîṭ*) in v.3, and in Numbers 23:21, to which v.3 appears to allude. In effect the Lord's answer to "violence" is "violence," as stipulated in the "law," whose paralysis with regard to injustice is only temporary (cf. Isa 55:11; 2 Tim 2:9).

The same principle (lex talionis) is applied subsequently to the Babylonians themselves (2:6–19). The Lord's sovereignty over the Babylonians, whom he raised up, is thus implied for the corresponding situation in Judah (vv.2–4). Evil and calamity do not exist independent of the sovereign rule and redemptive purposes of God (cf. Amos 3:6); but this truth is apprehended only by faith in God as he reveals himself (cf. Pss 37; 73; Eccl 8:11–13; Isa 51:12–16; Hab 2:4; 3:1–19). The truth applies equally to Judah or Babylon: the Lord's judgment of sin in his own people is thus extended to the same sin among the Babylonians, which is made explicit in v.11b and amplified in 2:6–19. The sovereignty of God does not eliminate human accountability; the time of the accounting merely varies (cf. Rom 2:4–11; 9:11–24; 1 Tim 5:24).

5 This verse is addressed to a plural audience. The hearers, by implication Judeans, are treated as distinct from the "nations" (or Gentiles), at whom they are to "look." To be "amazed" is man's response to an event that utterly confounds all previous expectations (cf. Gen 43:33; Ps 48:5; Isa 13:8; 29:9; Jer 4:9); it runs counter to what the listeners "believe." The destruction of Jerusalem was such an event, creating both a national crisis and a theological crisis among God's people.

6 This verse, linked to v.5 by the repeated conjunction "for" (*kî;* untr. in NIV but cf. RSV), identifies both the speaker and the amazing work introduced in v.5. The work entails Babylonia's rise to power; and the speaker is evidently the Lord, who alone rules the destiny of nations as described here. Conceivably the mere fact of Babylon's dramatic resurgence under Nabopolassar and Nebuchadnezzar is seen as the source of amazement. More likely, however, Babylon's impending domination of Judah is implied. This ran counter to popular theology (cf. Jer 5:12; 6:14; 7:1–34; 8:11; Lam 4:12; Amos 6 but was fully in accord with the Lord's chastisement of his sinning people (cf. Deut 28:49–50; 1 Kings 11:14, 23; Jer 4; 5:14–17; 6:22–30; Amos 6:14), and it is clearly anticipated in 3:16. The description of the Babylonians as "ruthless and impetuous" provides a faint echo of the rhyming word pair in Hebrew (*hammar wᵉhannimhār*). Character produces conduct, and this Babylonian character is expressed by unprincipled rapacity. The phrase "the whole earth" suggests unrestricted scope for such behavior, which by implication would engulf Palestine also. However, the verse concludes with a wordplay—"not their own" (*lō'-lô*)—whose sound and meaning undermine the imposing threat of the Babylonians: their conduct had no moral basis; so their achievements were without substance.

7 Verses 7–11 develop the description of the oppressors. Their character was rooted in a self-sufficiency that acknowledged no superior authority and no dependency, which was tantamount to self-deification (cf. v.11). Thus they were "feared" (*'āyōm*) and "dreaded" (*nôrā'*), usurping the place of God. If God's people refuse to fear him, they will ultimately be compelled to fear those less worthy of fear (cf. Deut 28:47–48; 58–68; Jer 5:15–22). In the final sentence the source of Babylonian law (*mišpaṭ*, "justice"; cf. vv.3–4) and "honor" ("dignity," RSV) is exposed—it is self-generated. Contrast the true God-fearer whose dignity derives from the Lord.

8 The Babylonian "cavalry" are compared to three predators whose speed and power brought violent death to their prey. The "leopard" and the "wolf" recur, together with the lion, in Jeremiah 5:6 as symbols of divine judgment on Judah (cf. Hos 13:7–8). The "vulture" translates an ambiguous term (*nešer*), which may also denote an eagle (cf. ZPEB 2:175–76; 5:891). The vulture is primarily a scavenger, feeding off carrion, whereas the eagle hunts and kills its prey. The imagery of the hunter better fits the historical context; in any case the reference constitutes a clear allusion to Deuteronomy 28:49–50.

9 As "law" (*mišpaṭ*) recurs in v.7 from vv.3–4, so "violence" (*ḥāmās*) recurs from vv.2–3: those who live by violence shall die by the violence of others (e.g., Ps 7:16; Prov 1:18–19; cf. Gen 9:6; Lev 24:20; Matt 7:2; Rev 16:5–6). NIV's final two lines embody a doubtful parallelism. "Like a desert wind," describing the Babylonian advance, pictures the hot, scorching wind from the Eastern desert; but the translation rests more on the parallel passage in Jeremiah 4:11–13 than on the Hebrew text. NASB preserves a more traditional reading. The parallel in line three—"like sand" (cf. Gen 22:17; Isa 10:22)—modifies the object "captives," creating a vivid portrait of numberless prisoners helplessly collected for deportation.

10 The corollary of Babylonian autonomy (v.7) is contempt for all other authority, which is evaluated in purely military terms. The Babylonians "deride kings" and "scoff at rulers," since they can "laugh" at their defenses. The "ramps," constructed primarily of earth, were a graded incline along which the cumbersome battering rams could be moved in besieging city walls (Y. Yadin, *The Art of Warfare in Biblical Lands* [New York: McGraw-Hill, 1963], pp. 17, 20, 315; cf. 2 Sam 20:15; Ezek 4:2; 21:22; 26:8–9). The "wicked" who "hem in" the "righteous" (v.4) would themselves be hemmed in by the horrors of siege (cf. Deut 28:52–57; Jer 39:1).

11 The onrushing cavalry (vv.8–9) was checked by the siege warfare, in which it would not have participated (v.10; cf. Yadin, *Art of Warfare*, p. 297). As the fortified cities fell and resistance crumbled, the cavalry's pent-up energy was released and its progress resumed.

In an abrupt shift, the final words of v.11 entirely undermine the dramatic account of the Babylonians, developed at length at vv.5–11a. "Sweep past" they may, but the final verdict was already in, though the perplexed prophet might indeed have been forgiven for wondering how it would make any difference. "Guilty men" (lit., "and [so] he is guilty") is followed immediately by the reason for the guilt: "his strength is his god." As in the verses above, the Babylonian horde is personified in the singular forms; and ruthless arrogance is rightly epitomized as a form of self-deification. Such people acknowledge no accountability, seek no repentance, and offer no reparations, while violating the most fundamental order of created life. For such the verdict of "guilty" can mean only the sentence of radical destruction (cf. 2:6–20; 3:13–16).

Notes

A number of textual variants occur in this passage that will not be handled in detail here. For a more extended treatment of these and subsequent variants, see the relevant passages in Brownlee, *Text of Habakkuk*, and id., *Pesher of Habakkuk*.

5 The DSS (1QpHab), LXX, and Syriac all imply the reading בֹּגְדִים (*bōgᵉḏîm*, "treacherous") for בַּגּוֹיִם (*baggôyim*, "among the nations"); the variant is supported also by Acts 13:41, quoting this verse according to the LXX tradition. The two readings involve the confusion of a single letter: וֹ (*ô*) for ד (*ḏ*). Both words are suitable to their context and recur repeatedly in Habakkuk. In the absence of decisive evidence favoring one reading, the MT should be followed, despite the strength of the variant tradition.

8 1QpHab, supported by the LXX, omits the verb יָבֹאוּ (*yāḇō'û*, "come"). These two texts also differ from the MT and from each other in their vocalization of the repeated word פָּרָשָׁיו וּפָרָשָׁיו (*pārāšāyw ûpārāsāyw*, "their cavalry . . . their horsemen"; NIV renders the same Hebrew word by two English words). LXX treats the second noun as a verb, whereas 1QpHab treats the first as a verb. LXX suggests an attractive alternative to MT, embodying an extended wordplay in the sequence וּפָשׁוּ פָּרָשָׁו וּפָרְשׁוּ (*ûpāšû pārāšāw upārᵉšû*, lit., "their cavalry careers and cavaliers"), reminiscent of v.6: הַמַּר וְהַנִּמְהָר (*hammar wᵉhannimhār*, "ruthless and impetuous"). However, MT makes good sense as it stands, and this repetition of vocabulary has numerous parallels within Habakkuk (e.g., *mišpaṭ*, 1:4).

9 The noun מְגַמַּת (*mᵉgammaṯ*, NIV, "hordes") is without parallel in the OT. NIV and many commentators derive it from גָּמַם (*gāmam*), whose Arabic cognates denote "abundance." A less-plausible derivation is from גָּמָא (*gāmā'*, "to swallow"; cf. Gen 24:17; Job 39:24). "Desert wind" translates the Hebrew קָדִימָה (*qāḏîmāh*), which occurs twenty times in Ezekiel with the meaning "east" or "eastward" (e.g., Ezek 11:1; 40:6; 45:7; 48:10). The "east wind" or "desert wind" is normally represented by רוּחַ קָדִים (*rûaḥ qāḏîm*) or simply *qāḏim*, without the suffix ָה (*āh*). However, *qāḏim* and *qāḏimāh* are used interchangeably in Ezekiel, with the meanings "east," "eastward" (e.g., 40:6, 10; 47:1, 18; 48:8). It is therefore not impossible that they also share the meaning "east wind," possessed by *qāḏim* in Gen 41:6, 23, 27; Job 15:2; 27:21; 38:24; Ps 78:26; Isa 27:8; Hos 12:2 (cf. Ezek 17:10; 19:12; 27:26). This interpretation is supported by the readings in 1QpHab, the Targums, Symmachus, Theodotion, the Vulgate, and the Palestinian recension of the LXX. It also has some claim to grammatical validity in that the directive *āh* may have a separative sense, i.e., "from the east" (cf. R.J. Williams, *Hebrew Syntax: An Outline* [Toronto: University of Toronto Press, 1967], p. 16).

III. Habakkuk's Second Lament

1:12–2:1

12O LORD, are you not from everlasting?
My God, my Holy One, we will not die.
O LORD, you have appointed them to execute judgment;
O Rock, you have ordained them to punish.

13 Your eyes are too pure to look on evil;
you cannot tolerate wrong.
Why then do you tolerate the treacherous?
Why are you silent while the wicked
swallow up those more righteous than themselves?
14 You have made men like fish in the sea,
like sea creatures that have no ruler.
15 The wicked foe pulls all of them up with hooks,
he catches them in his net,
he gathers them up in his dragnet;
and so he rejoices and is glad.
16 Therefore he sacrifices to his net
and burns incense to his dragnet,
for by his net he lives in luxury
and enjoys the choicest food.
17 Is he to keep on emptying his net,
destroying nations without mercy?

2:1 I will stand at my watch
and station myself on the ramparts;
I will look to see what he will say to me,
and what answer I am to give to this complaint.

This section has characteristics of a second lament, having many points of contact with 1:2–4 (q.v.). These include the invocation of the Lord's name (vv.2, 12); the urgent questions addressed to him (vv.13, 17); the description of the wicked oppressing the righteous (vv.13–17); and the issue of unrequited injustice that this raises, expressed in vocabulary echoing that of vv.2–4 (e.g., "righteous," "wicked," "tolerate," "look," "wrong," v.13). The note of confidence expressed in 1:12 is also typical of most laments—an attitude implicit in vv.2–4 in the prophet's perseverance and his insistence that his answers come from the Lord. As in many of the Psalms, the hard issues of God's goodness are set in a context, not of philosophical speculation or cynical debate, but of reverent worship and communion.

Verses 1:12–2:1 are structured on an A–B–A pattern: (A) a statement of faith in the Lord's covenantal justice (v.12); (B) an extended question on the existence of injustice (vv.13–17); and (A) a concluding statement of faith (2:1), in expectation of the Lord's answer to this dilemma. The dilemma is a classical biblical one. In section A the Lord's universal justice is affirmed as the source of this specific exercise of judgment; in contrast, section B questions that justice because of God's use of the wicked Babylonians. Section A calls for the answer—a further divine revelation to give faith its proper response to the apparent moral contradiction. The entire passage (1:12–2:1) represents the prophet's response to a divine revelation of the future (cf. vv.5–6); and it follows that his response has the same futuristic orientation. The justice of God will be seen in a further revelation of what he will do beyond the present limited circumstances.

12 This verse offers a typical example of the intricate parallelism in Habakkuk. Line one is paralleled by line two; similarly line four parallels line three, and finally lines three and four parallel lines one and two, a parallelism both preserved and heightened in NIV. The first line addressed the "LORD" by his covenant name (Exod 6:2–8), with reference to his involvement in covenant history. Although the word "everlasting" (*qeḏem*) may refer to eternity (e.g., Deut 33:27; Ps 55:19), it more often denotes an unspecified point in past history (Isa 46:10; cf. Isa 37:26; Lam 2:17); and it is applied repeatedly to God's former preservation of Israel, supremely in the nation's preservation from Egypt (Pss 44:1; 77:5, 11; et al.); when used with the preposition "from" (*min*), as here, it normally carries these historical connotations. Such a recollection of Yahweh's role in covenant history is borne out by the remainder of the verse and by the prophecy as a whole (e.g., 1:6–8; 3:2–3).

The second line reiterates and personalizes the content of the first. The address to God is repeated in covenantal terms, evidenced by the adjective "my" (cf. Ps 71:22); the holiness of God is associated with his transcendent sovereignty and power, manifested in the past redemption of his people (3:3; cf. Ps 71:22–23; TWOT, 2:788), and Habakkuk's confidence of survival ("we will not die") reflects his knowledge of God's future commitment to his people in salvation history (3:13; cf. Lev 26:44–45; Deut 4:29–31).

The third and fourth lines are similarly parallel. The name "Rock" evokes the strength and reliability of the "LORD" as Israel's God (TWOT, 2:762); and the concepts of "judgment" and "punishment" are correlated repeatedly (cf. Isa 11:3–4). The verb "punish" (*yāḵaḥ*) has a varied usage, with the underlying judicial meaning of "establishing what is just or right." Frequently it signifies correction, verbal or otherwise, of an offender (e.g., Lev 19:17; Job 5:17; Ps 6:1). In these contexts "punish" generally implies a chastening that is redemptive rather than destructive; and the same overtones are appropriate to the present clause, with its address of confidence to Israel's "Rock." The same nuance is therefore inherent in the parallel noun "judgment" (*mišpāṭ*), previously translated "justice" (1:4 [*bis*]) and "law" (1:7); in keeping with its broad definition in v.4, it here implies the restoration of rule and authority through removal of the causes of disorder. As intimated already in vv.7–8, the Israelites' rejection of God's authority mediated through the law merely exposed them to the harsher experience of his authority mediated through an alien people. Man may determine by his conduct how he will encounter God's sovereignty, but he cannot escape it!

13 The verbs "look on" (*rā'āh*) and "tolerate" (*hibbîṭ*) are repeated from vv.3, 5, marking a further development in this dialogue on justice. To "look" at a matter can imply that it is viewed with acceptance (cf. Pss 66:18; 138:6). That the Lord refused to view "evil" (*ra'*) and "wrong" (*'āmāl;* cf. v.3) in this manner was a basic tenet of Israel's faith (e.g.; Pss 5:4; 34:16, 21). As in v.3, the violent discrepancy between this premise and the prophet's perception of reality provokes the question "why?"—a question founded, nevertheless, on the obedient faith expressed in v.12. The evil apparently tolerated was that of the "treacherous" (*bôgᵉḏîm*), namely, those who are unreliable and break faith in relationship (cf. Jer 3:8, 11; Hos 5:7); the term is applied again to the Babylonians in Isaiah 21:2 (cf. Isa 39). The Lord's tolerance is implied because he was "silent," or uninvolved (cf. Ps 50:21; Isa 42:14); the treachery was typically that of the wicked who "swallow up" (cf. Exod 7:12; Pss 35:25; 124:3; Lam 2:16) the righteous as a wolf devours its prey.

The identity of the "wicked" has been disputed. Evidently they correspond to the fisherman in vv.15–17. NIV's transition between vv.12–13 and vv.15–17 from a plural to a singular third-person subject is not present in the MT, where singular third-person forms predominate throughout. These verses are also linked by a continuity of theme, the image of devouring food pervading the passage. In turn, vv.12–17 show extensive continuity with vv.5–11. The image of fishing corresponds to that of hunting (v.8; cf. Jer 16:16). The express purpose is to consume the prey (vv.8, 16; the root *'kl* ["eat"] occurs in each verse). This is motivated by a boundless greed, gratified without principle and pursued by means of a far-flung, international aggression (vv.6–10, 13–17; the root *'sp* ["gather"] occurs in vv.9, 15, and the noun *gôyīm* ["nations"] in vv.5, 17). This greed entails the overthrow of all opposing human authority (vv.10, 14) and the deification of the aggressor's own power (vv.7, 11, 16). Both passages attribute this tyrannical imperialism to God's initiative in judgment (vv.5–6, 12, 14), yet without condoning it (vv.11, 13).

In view of these detailed correlations, it may be concluded that the "wicked" in v.13 correspond to the Babylonians in v.6. They are thus distinct from the "wicked" in v.4, just as the "violence" and perverted justice in vv.7, 9 differ from that in vv.2–4; and they represent a further dramatic embodiment of the lex talionis, the "wicked" being judged through the "wicked" (cf. Ezek 7:23–24).

As the "wicked" in v.13 correspond to the fisherman in vv.15–17, so the "righteous" correspond to the "nations," likened to fish (vv.14–17), as their respective prey. The designation therefore includes Judah, whose sin caused her to be numbered among the nations of vv.14–17 in judgment (cf. Lev 26:33, 38; Deut 28:64–65; Jer 9:16; Ezek 4:13). Habakkuk's concern was, of course, his own people, both as the perpetrators and victims of injustice; and the dramatic exchange of vv.5–17 serves primarily to set his initial local concern in an international context of God's unfolding patterns of justice. For the prophet this only heightened the dilemma.

14 As in v.13, the presence of calamity and evil in the world is related without hesitation to God's sovereign control of human destiny (cf. Isa 45:7; Lam 3:37–38; Amos 3:6; Rom 9–11). The comparison to "fish" implies a condition that is subhuman and vulnerable (cf. Gen 1:26, 28; 9:2; Ps 8:8; Eccl 9:12). The "sea creatures" (*remeś*, "creeping things") in the second line are seen as equally helpless, lacking the organization or leadership normally expected in human society (cf. ZPEB, 1:1029, for the translation "sea creature").

15 NIV's rendering "the wicked foe" is not present in the MT, but it signals the continuity of vv.15–17 with the "wicked" in v.13. The "hook" (*hakkāh*) and line was an ancient, widely used device for fishing (cf. Isa 19:8; Matt 17:27). The "net" (*ḥerem*) was used for hunting and fishing and so had a diversity of application. It recurs figuratively as a symbol of aggression (Eccl 7:26; Mic 7:2) and divine judgment (Eccl 7:26; Ezek 32:3), as here. The "dragnet" (*mik̲meret̲*) is mentioned again as a fishing implement in Isaiah 19:8; two cognate nouns are used of hunting, again in figurative contexts of sin and judgment (Ps 141:10; Isa 51:20). The precise identification of these nets is not certain, owing to their infrequent occurrence and their varied, overlapping functions. However, they appear to correspond to the two main types of net, the throw-net and the seine, used in NT times and up to the present in Palestine (cf. also ZPEB, 2:541–44; ANEP, pp. 33–34).

The verbs "rejoice" (*śāmaḥ*) and "be glad" (*gîl*) are used with great frequency in religious contexts of worship and praise (cf. 3:18), and almost uniformly so when they are parallel as here (cf. 1 Chron 16:31; Pss 14:7; 16:9; Joel 2:21, 23; Zech 10:7). They thus indicate not merely pleasure or merriment but a response affirming what is valued and honored. As in v.11, the Babylonians are here exposed as exalting the images of their own power and dominance; their value system is utterly self-promoting.

16 The undertones of worship in v.15 become explicit in v.16, the two verses being linked also by the repeated adverb "therefore" (*'al kēn;* cf. KJV, NASB). The verb "sacrifice" (*zabaḥ*) denotes the slaughter of living creatures, usually in a context of worship and service offered to deity. The form of the verb occurring here normally has connotations of false, idolatrous worship (i.e., *zibbēaḥ;* e.g., 2 Chron 28:4; 33:22; Ps 106:38; Hos 4:13–14; 11:2). To "burn incense" (*qāṭar*) has the broad meaning of "burning," causing a sacrifice to smoke." The verb is used with various animal sacrifices (e.g., Exod 29:13, 18, 25; Lev 1:9, 13, 15, 17) and specifically with incense as its direct object (e.g., Exod 30:7; Num 16:40). More frequently it is used without an object, as here. Like the preceding verb, *qāṭar* occurs here in a form usually applied to illegitimate worship (i.e., *qiṭṭēr;* e.g., 2 Kings 17:11; 23:8; Isa 65:7; Jer 19:13; 32:29; 44:21); together the two verbs always have these connotations (cf. 1 Kings 22:43 [44 MT]; 2 Kings 12:3 [4 MT]; 14:4; 15:4, 35; 16:4; 2 Chron 28:4). The prophet was complaining that the Babylonians were clearly guilty of according to their own power the honor and strength due to God alone (cf. v.11).

The "hook" is present in v.15, suggesting skills of restraint and deception in the strategy for conquest and depredation. Here, however, it recedes from view. The Babylonians' full-blown delusion of greatness is depicted better by the swift violence of the "net" and the unyielding, wholesale spoliation of the dragnet (cf. vv.8–11). The second reference in v.16 to "his net" translates the pronoun "them," referring to both nets mentioned in the verse. The vast catch they procured had the one purpose of providing "food" for the Babylonian lifestyle. The adjectives underlying "luxury" (*šāmēn*) and "choicest" (*b^eri'āh*) both have the meaning of "fat," suggesting prosperity (well rendered in NIV). The root *šmn* is associated elsewhere with the prosperity of the wicked, whose well-being made them immune to any feeling of dependency or accountability (Deut 32:15; Neh 9:25 [rendered "fertile"]; Jer 5:28; cf. Deut 8:10–17; Matt 19:23–24). The same associations are present here, where the metaphorical language barely veils the fact that the food consumed by the Babylonians consisted of nations and individual lives (cf. v.13).

17 This verse reverts to the question posed in v.13: Can injustice, now defined more vividly by the intervening verses, be tolerated indefinitely by a God of justice? The phrase "empty his net" is virtually identical with "draw his sword" (cf. Notes). Possibly a double entendre is intended here, since the sword symbolizes the military power of which the net has been the image in vv.15–16, and since this anticipates the transition from metaphor to literal counterpart, completed in the following clause. This transition reverses and balances that in v.14, bringing the extended metaphor back to the ugly reality it portrays. A further double entendre is implicit in the phrase "without mercy." The verb underlying this translation (*ḥāmal*) has the basic meaning of "sparing," "removing from a situation" (cf. TWOT, 1:296). It is used of holding back or refraining from an action, and commonly of pity as the attitude that causes one to hold back or remove from harm. Both ideas are appropriate here. As in vv.6–7, the Babylonians' unrestrained self-will produced in them a hard insensitivity, making them a pitiless threat to other nations (cf. Deut 28:50; Jer 6:23).

2:1 The noun "watch" (*mišmereṯ*) has a varied meaning, denoting either the duty or act of watching, or a place of observation where such a responsibility is fulfilled. The present usage corresponds closely to Isaiah 21:8, where the noun and also the verb "watch," "look" (*ṣāpāh*) occur. Habakkuk's "watch" is evidently portrayed as being on the city walls, as indicated by the parallel noun "ramparts" (*māṣôr*). We do not know Habakkuk's home, but Mizpah represents a typical fortified city of this preexilic period. Yadin describes it as having had a solid wall 600 yards long, 4 yards thick on average, and perhaps 12 yards high, thus posing a considerable obstacle to both battering rams and attackers scaling it (cf. 1:10). It was built of stone with salients and recesses, being buttressed at its weak points with a total of ten towers; and it would have been crowned by a balcony with a crenelated parapet. The gate was also guarded by two towers, being carefully designed and fortified in keeping with its strategic function (Yadin, *Art of Warfare*, pp. 18–23, 323–24, 378–79, 391, 398; cf. 1 Kings 15:22; 2 Chron 26:15).

It was therefore at some point on such defenses as these that Habakkuk saw himself on duty (cf. Neh 11:19; 13:19–22; Ps 127:1; Isa 62:6). This setting is corroborated by the following verb, "look" (*ṣāpāh*) used literally of keeping watch for some event. It is applied particularly to sentries or watchmen on city walls (2 Sam 18:24–27; 2 Kings 9:17–18, 20), who were to warn the citizens of danger or other happenings outside (Isa 21:6; 52:8; Ezek 33:2–6). The verb is applied figuratively to the prophets, who as Israel's watchmen were to see the Lord's purposes and communicate them to their people (Hos 9:8; cf. Isa 56:10–11; Jer 6:17; Ezek 3:17; Mic 7:4, 7)—a fitting title for those called to be seers and visionaries. Such figurative usage undergirds the imagery of this verse, where Habakkuk the prophet (1:1; 3:1) looked to God for revelation concerning the nations (cf. 2:2–3). His "ramparts" and "watch" were the place of responsibility assigned to him, to stand in the council of the Lord and to see his word (cf. Num 12:6–8; 1 Kings 22:14–23; Jer 23:18, 22; Amos 3:7)—a role discharged in attentive, reverent prayer by the same conscientious watchfulness and persistence demanded of the literal watchman.

The noun "complaint" (*tôḵaḥaṯ;* cf. *yaḵaḥ* ["punish"], 1:12) denotes an argument by which one seeks to establish what is right (Job 13:6; 23:4) and a rebuke or correction by which right is restored (e.g., Ps 39:11; Prov 1:23, 25, 30; 3:11; Ezek 5:15). It occurs here with the possessive suffix "my" (cf. RSV), indicating either the agent of the noun, meaning "the argument that I have offered" (so Job 13:6), or its object, meaning "the correction that I receive" (so Ps 73:14; cf. NASB mg.). Both interpretations are apposite here, since Habakkuk was expecting a reply to his argument concerning God's justice (1:12–17), and since that argument was precipitated by the announcement of a judgment that would overtake him with his nation (1:5–17). The second alternative—a rebuke or correction by which right is restored—is preferable, since it balances the use of the same verbal root (*ykḥ*) in v.12, so completing the concentric structure of 1:12–2:1: judgment, v.12; injustice, v.13; developed image of injustice, vv.14–17; response to judgment, 2:1 (cf. introduction to 1:12–2:1).

Underlying both interpretations was Habakkuk's need to know how to respond to God's ways, both in his assessment of injustice and in his conduct amid the consequences of injustice. He revealed a mature wisdom in his determination that this response be shaped by what God himself would say. It is a wise man who takes his questions about God to God for the answers.

Notes

12 The reading "we will not die" represents one of eighteen alleged scribal emendations, the *tiqqûnê sôperîm* (cf. E. Würthwein, *The Text of the Old Testament* [Oxford: Basil Blackwell, 1957], pp. 14–15), the original reading being supposedly "you will not die." The intent of these emendations was to guard the divine name and character from unworthy associations—in this case, from the mention of death. The origin and value of these alterations is, however, doubtful; and since the MT is supported here by the LXX and Symmachus and implicity by 1QpHab, there are no good grounds for abandoning its reading.

17 Several textual variants occur in this verse. The question, indicated by a single consonant ה (*ha*) is lacking in 1QpHab, the LXX, and the Syriac; but it is supported by the Talmud and the Palestinian Recension of LXX. Since both readings are explicable and make sense, MT may be retained, particularly as the question it attests balances that in 1:13 and provides a suitable basis for 2:1.

חֶרְמוֹ (*ḥermô*, "his net") is supported by the LXX; 1QpHab and the Palestinian Recension read חַרְבּוֹ (*ḥarbô*, "his sword"), resulting from confusing מ (*m*) and ב (*b*). Both words are appropriate to their immediate context, since both imply the slaughter of nations, and since חֶרֶב (*ḥereḇ*, "sword") recurs repeatedly with the present verb ריק (*rîq*, "to empty"; cf. Exod 15:9; Lev 26:33; Ezek 5:2, 12; 12:14; 28:7; 30:11). The MT is preferable here, since it offers the more unusual reading while being more appropriate to its context: the transition from the imagery of fishing to that of the victimized nations in v.17 corresponds to that in v.14 and is consistent with the metaphor developed in vv.15–16.

"Keep on" translates the force of both the imperfect tense of יָרִיק (*yārîq*, "he empties") and the noun וְתָמִיד (*w^etāmîḏ*, "and continually"). The conjunction וְ (*w^e*, "and") is omitted by 1QpHab, the Talmud, and the Syriac but is retained in the LXX and the Vulgate. Either reading may be derived from the other, and both make sense. MT is to be retained as the harder reading, since it appears to associate *w^eṯāmîḏ* with the following clause (cf. MT accentuation), thus disturbing the obvious balance between them. NIV in fact relates *w^eṯāmîḏ* to the preceding clause, but the syntax of MT is preferable here. It serves to coordinate more closely the two clauses, both as questions and as continuous actions; and it heightens the emphasis on the first question, ending at חֶרְמוֹ (*ḥermô*, "his net").

IV. God's Second Response (2:2–20)

Verses 2–20 have often been regarded as containing a number of disjointed passages, a judgment applied particularly to vv.2–6. However, there is much in the form and content of these verses to show that they constitute a unity, and they are treated as such here. Verses 2–3 form a prologue, establishing the context as a "revelation" (or "vision") concerning the Babylonian oppressor; vv.4–5 clearly refer to the Babylonians, likewise, and form a summary of the preceding indictments (1:5–17); while vv.6–20 amplify those indictments, embodying them in an emphatic sentence of judgment on the tyrant. It is evident, then, that the content of the "revelation" of v.2 is given in vv.4–20—a conclusion supported by the clear break at 3:1 and by the length of this unified passage, which makes it suitable for preservation on a number of "tablets." In their form, vv.2–20 are cast as a judicial procedure, the alternation between accusation and announcement of judgment being most apparent in vv.6–20 (cf. Isa 5:1–30; Mic 2:1–5).

1. *Prologue*

2:2–3

[2]Then the Lord replied:

"Write down the revelation
and make it plain on tablets
so that a herald may run with it.
[3]For the revelation awaits an appointed time;
it speaks of the end
and will not prove false.
Though it linger, wait for it;
it will certainly come and will not delay.

2 The noun "revelation" (*ḥāzôn*) denotes vision that is almost invariably supersensory in nature, as do the cognate words derived from the same root (*ḥzh;* cf. RSV, TWOT, 1:274–75), and it is attributed especially to the prophets (e.g., 1 Chron 7:15; 2 Chron 32:32; Isa 1:1; Ezek 7:26; Obad 1; Nah 1:1). The cognate verb (*ḥāzāh*) is used to introduce Habakkuk's prophecy (i.e., "received," 1:1); in echoing 1:1, the present verse therefore serves to announce the central content of what he "received," or saw, as the outcome of his disciplined watchfulness (2:1).

The "revelation" was to be written down to preserve it for the future (cf. Exod 17:14; Ps 102:18; Jer 30:2; 36:2)—a motif explained in v.3. To "make plain" (*bē'ēr*) may refer to clarity either in form—e.g., by engraving the words (Deut 27:8)—or in content (Deut 1:5). The reference to the writing material and consequent similarity to Deuteronomy 27:1–8 slightly favors the former. Like the Lord's revelation to Moses, this prophecy has a lasting relevance and is to be guarded accordingly. The "tablets" may have been composed of stone, clay, or even metal (cf. IDB, 4:915–19); a similar means for preserving prophetic revelation occurs in Isaiah 30:8. The purpose of this procedure is given in the final clause. "Herald" (*qôrē'*) is literally "the one who reads." Such reading might plausibly be done by a herald, whose role would then be to "run" with the message (cf. 1 Sam 4:12; 2 Sam 18:19–27; Esth 3:13, 15; 8:10, 14; Jer 51:31). Alternatively, the idiom "run with" may refer specially to prophetic activity (Jer 23:21). The context is concerned in any case primarily with preservation of the revelation as a source of encouragement for the future (cf. v.3), rather than with its geographical proclamation.

3 The reasons underlying the directive of v.2 are made clear in v.3. First, the directive to "write" is given because the revelation "awaits" a future fulfillment, at "the end"; its impact extends beyond the present and must therefore be transmitted by means of a permanent record. Indeed, this fulfillment may appear to "linger," suggesting a delay beyond what is expected or intended (cf. Gen 19:16; 43:10; Exod 12:39; Judg 3:26; 19:8; 2 Sam 15:28): as in 1:2–4, the Lord's timetable and agenda are liable to differ from man's (cf. 1 Sam 13:8–15; Isa 55:8–9; John 11:5–21; 2 Peter 3:1–10). The verb "speaks" (*pûaḥ*) has the meaning "to breathe, blow" (cf. Pss 10:5; 12:5; S of Songs 4:6; Ezek 21:31), from which certain versions translate it here as "pant," "hasten" (e.g., ASV, RSV, NEB, NASB).

"The end" referred to (*qēṣ*) is definite in Hebrew, but it is not clearly specified; its usage implies the termination of a certain object, activity, or period of time (cf. Lam 4:18; Ezek 7:2–3; 21:25, 29). The immediate context of the "revelation" is the end of the Babylonian oppression (vv.4–20; cf. Jer 51:13), for which the prophet must "wait" (cf. 3:16). The noun "end" recurs frequently in Daniel (8:17, 19; 9:26; 11:6, 13, 27, 35, 40, 45; 12:4, 6, 9, 13), closely associated with the term "appointed time" (*môʿēḏ*, Dan 8:19; 11:27, 29, 35; 12:7), as here. In Daniel, however, the time of the end refers to the eschatological termination of Israel's oppression by wickedness (i.e., chs. 7–12).

Second, the purpose of v.2—that the reader may "run"—is based on the certainty of the "revelation." There is an "appointed time" for its fulfillment, determined by Yahweh; and it will not "prove false" or disappoint (cf. Isa 58:11) but "will certainly come." In consequence of this assurance, the reader may run with confidence and perseverance the race marked out for him (cf. 1 Cor 15:58; Heb 11:1; 12:1). The eschatological vision is further personalized by the LXX, which reads "(the) coming one will come" (*erchomenos hēxei*), in place of the MT's "he/it will certainly come" (cf. Mal 3:1; Matt 11:3; Heb 10:37). The logical outcome of this "revelation" is that one should "wait" (cf. Pss 33:20; 106:13; Isa 8:17; 30:18; 64:4; Dan 12:12; Zeph 3:8). Verses 2–3 thus provide a suggestive and compressed view of salvation history. Its future development is perfectly determined by God, and he allows man to glimpse this future as a basis for faith and hope (cf. Rom 8:18–25; 1 Cor 15:51–58). However, man never sees the entire pattern of salvation, so that events may seem delayed and disappointing from his perspective. For this reason man must lay hold of the future that God has revealed, waiting for it with an eager faith and hope that surpass the apparent obstacles to its realization (3:17–19; cf. Rom 4:16–23; Heb 6:11–12, 18–19; 10:32–11:1; 12:1–29).

2. *Indictment*

2:4–5

4"See, he is puffed up;
his desires are not upright—
but the righteous will live by his faith—
5indeed, wine betrays him;
he is arrogant and never at rest.
Because he is as greedy as the grave
and like death is never satisfied,
he gathers to himself all the nations
and takes captive all the peoples.

4 The verb "puffed up" (*ʿāpal*) carries the basic meaning of "swelling." The same root recurs in Numbers 14:44, where the idea of arrogance and presumption is again evident. "His desires" translates *napšô* ("soul," "life"; cf. KJV, RSV), whose meaning includes also the idea of desire or appetite (e.g., Gen 23:8 ["willing"]; cf. TWOT, 2:587–91). The suffix "his" evidently refers to the Babylonians in continuity with 1:2–2:1: v.4 introduces the Lord's answer to Habakkuk's lament concerning the devouring Babylonians. The verb "to be upright" (*yāšar*) denotes what is straight (e.g., 1 Sam 6:12; cf. Ezek 1:7) or level (e.g., Pss 32:11; 33:1). As in 1:4, the "righteous" (there *haṣṣaddîq*) may be defined by his commitment to the demands of *tôrāh* ("law"); as in 1:13 (also *ṣaddîq*), he is set within a context broader than Hebrew religion alone.

The noun "faith" (*'ᵉmûnāh*) implies fairness, stability, certainty, permanence, as do its numerous cognate terms (e.g., Exod 17:12 ["steady"]; Isa 33:6 ["sure foundation"]; cf. TWOT, 1:51–53). Hence it is commonly used of "fairness" applied to personal character and conduct, which is evidenced especially as reliability; thus in Deuteronomy 32:4 God's reliability ("faithfulness") is parallel to his name "Rock," with its connotations of stability and security as a basis for reliance (cf. 1:12).

The nature of the reliability is defined by the context. In the present context, this quality of reliability and stability is predicated of the "righteous," the only plausible antecedent of "his." It signifies that his commitment to righteousness is genuine and steadfast, the concepts of "faith" and righteousness often being coordinated in this way (e.g., 1 Sam 26:23; Pss 33:4–5; 40:10; 96:13; 119:75, 138; 143:1). The clause is thus expressing the Lord's demand for a righteousness that is pursued steadfastly from the heart, without vacillation, doublemindedness, or hypocrisy—its outcome being life (cf. Deut 6:1–25; 8:1–20; Ezek 18:1–32; 33:12–20; Heb 6:9–12; Rev 2:10; 14:12). Such a meaning is conveyed more precisely by the noun "faithfulness," by which NIV normally translates *'ᵉmûnāh* (e.g., Deut 32:4; 1 Sam 26:23; Ps 33:4; Hab 2:4 mg.; cf. Gordon Wenham, "Faith in the Old Testament," *Theological Students' Fellowship Annual* [1975–76]: 11–17). NIV's rendering here reflects that of the LXX —i.e., "faith" (*pistis*)—and of Romans 1:17, Galatians 3:11, and Hebrews 10:38, which are quoted from this verse.

The discrepancy between "faith" and "faithfulness" is more apparent than real, however. For man to be faithful in righteousness entails dependent trust in relation to God (e.g., 1 Sam 26:23–24); such an attitude is clearly demanded in the present context of waiting for deliverance (2:3; 3:16–19). And "faith" (*pistis*) implies obedient commitment no less than trust (e.g., Rom 1:5; 10:3, 16–17; 15:18–19; 16:26; Heb 3:18–19; cf. TDNT, 6:174ff.). This brief clause of three Hebrew words thus epitomizes the response of steadfast commitment demanded in vv.2–3; and it thereby answers Habakkuk's concern for the righteous in Judah, imperiled by the judgment intended for the wicked (cf. 1:13). Contrary to appearances, the judgment of God is selective and awe-inspiring in its precision: in the midst of disaster, his grace overshadows the righteous and causes them to "live" (Ps 91). Both Paul and a later rabbinic tradition found in this pregnant statement a summary of the OT way of salvation; they diverged radically, however, in their beliefs concerning the attainment of such a saving righteousness.

5 "Betrays" translates the same verb (*bôḡēḏ*) as "treacherous" in 1:13. "Wine," like the Babylonians, is deceptive and unreliable; although drunk to enhance one's life, wine impoverishes, confuses, and destroys (cf. Prov 20:1; 23:20–21, 29–35; Isa 28:7). The reference to "wine" is unexpected (cf. Notes). However, it is appropriate to the present verse, being associated with arrogance, unfulfilled greed, and social injustice elsewhere in the OT (e.g., 1 Sam 30:16; 1 Kings 20:12, 16; Prov 31:4–7; Isa 5:11–12, 22–23; Amos 6:6). Isaiah 5:8–30—with its six woes directed against human drunkenness, greed, rapacity, and pride—offers a close parallel to Habakkuk 2:4–20. The object of this betrayal is implicit in v.5, the pronoun "him" being absent in the Hebrew. His identity is clarified by the references to arrogance (*yāhîr*; cf. Prov 21:24) and restless ambition, clearly referring to the Babylonians (cf. 1:6–11, 13), as do the following clauses of this verse. And, indeed, the Babylonian regime was to be overthrown in just the circumstances of drunken pride portrayed here (cf. Dan 5:1–31)—such drunkenness being attested among ancient historians as characteristic of the Babylonians.

Napšô ("greedy") is also translated "his desire, throat, appetite" (cf. KJV, ASV, NEB, and TWOT, 2:587–91). The following figures develop the image further, describing the extent of this greed: it is insatiable (cf. Prov 27:20; 30:15–16; Isa 5:14), as demonstrated already in 1:5–17. "Grave" (*šeʾôl*, "Sheol") is perhaps better translated "underworld," "hell" (cf. KJV, ASV, RSV), a place depicted repeatedly as devouring its prey (Num 16:30–34; Prov 1:12).

The concluding couplet of v.5 describes in figurative terms the expression of this insatiable greed: political conquest. The verb "gathers" is repeated from 1:9, 15. The dominant metaphor, however, relates to the treachery of an addiction to wine, which, like political and military ambition, is an addiction that knows no limit of fulfillment and to which all other interests are sacrificed. Verses 4–5 thus recapitulate the preceding account of the Babylonians' character, in which pride, greed, and naked aggression prosper and overshadow the moral consequences of their conduct. In the following five woes (vv.6–19), however, those consequences break with fury on their unstable edifice, and it is overthrown. The brief intimations of guilt and false ideals (1:7, 11, 13, 17; 2:4–5) are more potent in their implications than the entire grandiose achievement by which they are incurred (cf. Ps 37:1–2, 7, 9–10, 35–36; Eccl 10:1).

Notes

---

4 The etymology of עֻפְּלָה (*ʿuppelāh*, "puffed up") is not entirely certain. It is cognate with either the Arabic *ʿaflun* ("a tumor") or *gafala* ("be heedless, neglectful"); some philologists derive both OT occurrences of the roots עפל (*ʿpl*) from the second alternative (cf. TWOT, 2:686–87). Both derivations are appropriate to the sinfulness exposed in vv.4–19. The versions differ widely from the MT in their reading of this verb. The LXX, Aquilla, the Palestinian Recension, and the Vulgate all refer to some form of timidity or unbelief and apparently read עלף (*ʿlp*), with the derived meaning "to faint" (cf. Isa 51:20; Amos 8:13; Jonah 4:8); this reading is attested in two Hebrew MSS and is quoted from the LXX in Heb 10:38. The Targum and Syriac both refer to wickedness and would have read עַוָּל (*ʿawwāl*, "wicked") or עַוְלָה (*ʿawlah*, "wickedness"). The MT remains the preferable reading here. The difficulty of its rare verbal form and the lack of clear parallelism with v.4b explain the variants, whose renderings are suggested by the interchange of a single root consonant. In addition the MT is corroborated by the same reading in 1QpHab, and it is well suited to the preceding and ensuing descriptions of the Babylonians. (For a more-detailed treatment of the text of vv.4–5, cf. J.A. Emerton, "Textual and Linguistic Problems of Habakkuk 2:4–5," JTS 28 [1977]: 1–18.)

5 The reading הַיַּיִן (*hayyayin*, "wine") is represented by the MT, Targum, and Vulgate. 1QpHab reads הוֹן (*hôn*, "wealth"). The Syriac, LXX, and OL all refer to some form of arrogance and may have read *hawwān* or הַיָּן (*hayyān*, "arrogant one"); the root *hwn* ("to be easy") is applied to the Israelites' presumption in Deut 1:41. The LXX text edited by Rahlfs reads κατοινωμένος (*katoinōmenos*, "drunk with wine"), but this corroboration of the MT is based on a conjectural emendation. The variants thus involve dittography or haplography of the consonant י (*y*), with confusion of י/ו (*y*/*w*). Of these readings the MT presents the greatest difficulty, in its sudden switch to "wine" as the subject. The alternatives are best explained as easier, more "appropriate" readings, facilitated by their similarity to the consonantal form of the MT and suggested by the moral terminology in 2:4 and by the Babylonian rapacity described in 1:5–17; 2:6–14. The Masoretic reading is suitable to its context, however, since it accords with the imagery of 1:8, 14–17; 2:4–5 (cf. comments at 2:5); and

it foreshadows the references to drunkenness in 2:15–16. Its reading may therefore be followed, particularly as it is well supported by the versions.

"At rest" translates the verb יִנְוֶה (*yinweh*), which has no precise parallel in the OT. It is commonly treated as a denominative verb derived from נָוֶה (*nāweh*, "an abode," "a habitation"; e.g., Exod 15:13; 2 Sam 7:8; Job 5:3; Prov 21:20; Isa 27:10; 65:10; Jer 23:3). From this derivation it would acquire the meaning "to be at home," i.e., "be settled, at rest" (cf. BDB, p. 627)—a meaning followed by the NIV and appropriate to the Babylonians' character (cf. 1:6, 8–11, 17). It also appears to underlie the interpretation in 1QpHab that applies it to apostasy, as forsaking the fold of the Lord (cf. Jer 50:7). Alternatively, the verb may signify "to aim at, attain a goal," i.e., "to succeed," since the Arabic root cognate with *nwh* has this meaning (cf. KB, p. 601). This translation is supported by LXX's περάνῃ (*peranē*, "he completes, effects his purpose") and possibly by the Targum. It is also suitable to the following woes introduced by v.5 and to the judgment implied in 1:11–12; 2:4. Underlying these two main options is the idea of instability and failure (cf. Deut 29:28; 1 Kings 14:15; Ps 37:10–11, 28–29; Prov 2:21–22; 10:30; Isa 13:20; Jer 1:10; 12:15–17). This forms a suitable parallel to בּוֹגֵד (*bôgēḏ*, "betrays"), in keeping with the more-developed parallelism of the following two couplets: for the Babylonian, his pursuit of conquest portends his exile as the victim of conquest.

---

3. *Sentence*

2:6–20

6"Will not all of them taunt him with ridicule and scorn, saying,

" 'Woe to him who piles up stolen goods
and makes himself wealthy by extortion!
How long must this go on?'
7Will not your debtors suddenly arise?
Will they not wake up and make you tremble?
Then you will become their victim.
8Because you have plundered many nations,
the peoples who are left will plunder you.
For you have shed man's blood;
you have destroyed lands and cities and everyone
in them.

9"Woe to him who builds his realm by unjust gain
to set his nest on high,
to escape the clutches of ruin!
10You have plotted the ruin of many peoples,
shaming your own house and forfeiting your life.
11The stones of the wall will cry out,
and the beams of the woodwork will echo it.

12"Woe to him who builds a city with bloodshed
and establishes a town by crime!
13Has not the LORD Almighty determined
that the people's labor is only fuel for the fire,
that the nations exhaust themselves for nothing?
14For the earth will be filled with the knowledge of the glory
of the LORD,
as the waters cover the sea.

15"Woe to him who gives drink to his neighbors,
pouring it from the wineskin till they are drunk,
so that he can gaze on their naked bodies.

16 You will be filled with shame instead of glory.
    Now it is your turn! Drink and be exposed!
  The cup from the LORD's right hand is coming around
      to you,
    and disgrace will cover your glory.
17 The violence you have done to Lebanon will
      overwhelm you,
    and your destruction of animals will terrify you.
  For you have shed man's blood;
    you have destroyed lands and cities and everyone
      in them.

18 "Of what value is an idol, since a man has carved it?
    Or an image that teaches lies?
  For he who makes it trusts in his own creation;
    he makes idols that cannot speak.
19 Woe to him who says to wood, 'Come to life!'
    Or to lifeless stone, 'Wake up!'
  Can it give guidance?
    It is covered wth gold and silver;
    there is no breath in it.
20 But the LORD is in his holy temple;
    let all the earth be silent before him."

The sentence of judgment implicit in 2:4–5 and 1:5–17 is stated with absolute finality in these verses, which form five sections structured around the accusatory cry "Woe." Their structure may be illustrated by the refrain linking 2:8, 17; by the pattern "woe"—retribution—"because"/"for" informing 2:6–17 (cf. KJV, ASV); and in the symmetrical juxtaposition of crime and punishment that pervades each of the five "woes."

6a The opening line introduces the oracle of woe (vv.6–20), characterized by three technical terms: (1) as a type of proverb, translated by the verb "taunt" (*māšāl,* cf. Num 23:7; 1 Kings 4:32; Prov 1:1; Ezek 24:3; TWOT, 1:533–34; (2) as an ambiguous, allusive saying that requires interpretation, translated "ridicule" (*mᵉlîṣāh,* cf. Prov 1:6; TWOT, 1:479); and (3), similarly, as a riddle or enigmatic saying, translated "scorn" (*ḥîḏôṯ,* cf. Num 12:8; Judg 14:12–18; 1 Kings 10:1; TWOT, 1:267). The first two terms have certain limited associations with mockery, but none are attested for the third. Moreover, all three terms recur together in Proverbs 1:6 without these overtones, as do *māšāl* and *ḥîḏāh* elsewhere (Pss 49:4; 78:2; Ezek 17:2). The dominant emphasis in these and other usages of the noun is not ridicule but didactic, as here verse 6a introduces an oration exposing the Babylonians as an object-lesson (*māšāl*) by means of compressed and allusive speech (*mᵉlîṣāh ḥîḏôṯ*).

6b–8 Verses 6–8 represent an extended oracle or judgment, signaled by the opening declamation of "woe"—an interjection commonly used in prophetic literature to introduce a judicial indictment (Isa 5:8, 11, 18, 20–22; Jer 22:13; 23:1; Amos 5:18; 6:1). The crime is specified, first, as unjust acquisition of wealth, achieved by "extortion" (v.6b) and plunder (v.8), and, more seriously, as the wholesale destruction of man and his environment in the pursuit of this wealth (v.8). The noun "extortion" (*ʿaḇṭîṭ*) denotes the accumulation of pledges taken as security by a creditor (cf. Deut 24:10–13; cf. also IDB, 1:809–10, ZPEB, 1:79ff., 3:295); such a procedure often accompanied the exploitation and even enslavement of the poor (cf. 2 Kings 4:1–7; Neh 5:1–13).

The noun *ʿabṭîṭ* can also be read as a phrase, meaning literally "a cloud of dirt" (*ʿab ṭîṭ*, cf. KJV). This use of double entendre has numerous parallels in vv.6–20 and signals the allusive quality of the oration introduced as a *meliṣāh* and as *ḥîḏôṯ;* in this instance the double meaning evokes the defilement accompanying such a path to wealth. The judgments announced in response to these accusations correspond precisely to the crimes, according to the law of retaliation that pervades the book. The word "debtors" (*nōšeḵîm*, v.7; also "creditors," NIV mg.) is a verbal form derived from a noun signifying monetary interest. These "creditors" are defined as "the peoples who are left" (v.8), that is, the survivors within the conquered nations; and the sentence announced here was indeed executed by former victims of Babylon, the Medes and Persians (cf. Jer 25:25; 49:34–39; Ezek 32:24–25; Isa 13:17–22; 21:2–10; Jer 51:11, 28; Dan 5:28).

9–11 This passage echoes the preceding charges of rapacity (cf. vv.6, 8) and bloodshed (cf. v.8): the noun "gain" (*beṣaʿ*, v.9) is generally associated with rapacity and wrongdoing (cf. 1 Sam 8:3; Prov 1:19; TWOT, 1:122–23), associations that are stressed by the adjective "unjust" (*rāʿ*, "evil"); and the verb translated as "plotted the ruin" (*qāṣāh*, v.10) implies the cutting off of life. The present section amplifies these accusations by exposing the self-interested purposes underlying such violence, namely, establishment of the Babylonian "realm" or dynastic house (*bayiṯ*, cf. ASV; RSV; TWOT, 1:105–6), by elevating it to the invulnerable security depicted by an eagle's "nest" (*qēn*, Num 24:21; Jer 49:16; Obad 4). However, this exercise of evil to escape "ruin" (*rāʿ*, "evil") is futile, for man reaps what he sows (cf. Eccl 8:8). As in vv.6–8, the sentence of judgment balances the crime: shame for self-exaltation, loss of life for destruction of life, a divided and discordant house (v.11) for a secure house. And, indeed, despite all its impregnable defenses, Babylon was to fall in precisely such circumstances of division and deluded pride (cf. Dan 5:1–30; IDB, 1:270–71, 335ff.; ZPEB, 1:440ff.).

12–14 The third "woe" reiterates from vv.6–11 the indictment of ruthless self-aggrandizement achieved by "bloodshed" (v.12; cf. v.8), applying it to the construction of the Babylonian capital, as it had been applied previously to Jerusalem (Mic 3:10). The judgment pronounced on such an enterprise is inevitable: a civilization built up by the destruction of other civilizations and by the conscription of their labor for its own ends will itself be destroyed (v.13; cf. Jer 22:13–14; 51:58). The divine origin of the judgments on the Babylonians becomes explicit in v.13. The mainspring of human history is to be found, not in its events themselves, but in the revealed purposes of the Lord who directs it. The title "LORD Almighty" may be translated more literally "LORD of armies" (*YHWH ṣeḇāʾôṯ;* cf. ASV; RSV; NIV Preface; TWOT, 2:750–51). It expresses the Lord's sovereign rule as king and commander over every created force, but primarily over Israel. It is associated repeatedly, as here, with his militant judgment of all that opposes his rule.

This new emphasis on the Lord is developed further in v.14, revealing the underlying purpose on which the preceding indictments are based. God's abiding intent is that his "glory" should fill the whole earth as it has filled his house (cf. Num 14:21; Pss 57:5, 11; 72:19; Exod 40:34–35; 1 Kings 8:11), and that man should know it fully—a "knowledge" (*daʿaṯ;* cf. TWOT, 1:336–37) that will be as the "sea" in its length, breadth, and depth. This entails the removal of all that rejects such "knowledge," of which the Babylonian character and aspirations are the very epitome. The phrase "glory of the LORD" (*k*[e]*ḇôḏ YHWH;* cf. IDB, 2:401ff.; TWOT, 1:426ff.; ZPEB, 2:730–35) is used of the visible presence of God, by which the preeminent value of his character and actions are revealed to men. It is associated most prominently with the tabernacle and temple, and especially with the cherubim above which the Lord is enthroned, ruling over Israel (e.g., Exod 29:43 Ezek 9:3; 10:4, 18–19), his sovereign majesty being of the essence of his "glory." To know the Lord in such "glory" is therefore to abandon the Babylonians' proud autonomy and to honor him as Lord, in submission and obedience, worship and praise (e.g., Lev 9:23–24; 2 Chron 7:3; Pss 72:19; 102:15; Isa 42:8; 59:19).

15–17 The fourth "woe" introduces a new accusation, expressed by the image of inducing drunkenness with its consequences of incapacitation, humiliation, and utter vulnerability. The figure is used repeatedly of God's judgment by which he prostrates man, confusing his faculties and thereby undermining his presumptuous claim to self-determination (e.g., Job 21:20; Ps 75:8; Isa 19:14; 29:9–10); and it is applied widely to the Babylonians as instruments of that judgment (cf. Isa 51:17–22; Jer 25:8–29; 51:7). However, the Babylonian motives in such judgment are entirely self-interested: they seek their own "glory" (*kāḇôḏ,* v.16; cf. v.14; John 5:44) through their malicious humiliation of their "neighbors," in which there is no acknowledgment of God's sovereign determination. Once again, therefore, their evil motivation and conduct reap a corresponding judgment: they will succumb to the same drunken humiliation that they have administered to others, a judgment now attributed explicitly to the Lord, as in vv.13–14.

The preceding crime is defined more literally as "destruction" and "violence" wrought on "Lebanon." Often associated with the territory of Israel (e.g., 1 Kings 9:19; S of Songs 4:8; 7:4; Isa 33:9; 35:2; Nah 1:4), to whose people it was allotted by the Lord (e.g., Deut 1:7–8; Josh 1:4), "Lebanon" is used as a symbol of Israel (2 Kings 14:9; cf. Jer 22:6, 23), and more specifically of Israel as a victim of Babylonian aggression (Ezek 17:3). In keeping with these connotations, the Babylonians' "violence" (*ḥāmās*) and "destruction" (*šōḏ*) refer to their rape and despoliation of the region of Israel—an injustice requiring Israel's own "destruction and violence" (cf. 1:3, 9) while incurring a corresponding retribution for the Babylonians themselves. The final accusation of v.17 repeats the refrain of v.8, surely again appropriate here.

18–20 A break in the pattern of the preceding accusations marks this concluding section of vv.6–20, the expression "woe" being transposed to the second verse (v.19) and there being no announcement of a specific judgment. The dominant motif of v.18 is its denunciation of "idols"; as artifacts made by man, idols are unable to "teach" (*yārāh*) truth to man, and they are therefore utterly unworthy of his "trust." This argument is stated in each couplet of v.18. It gains further emphasis by its development in the following "woe" (v.19), whose function as an accusation may be inferred from vv.6, 9, 12, 15. These artifacts of "wood" and "stone" are unable to "give guidance" (*yôreh*) because they are without "breath." It is therefore reprehensible folly for man to call on them (cf. 1 Kings 18:22–29). By contrast the Lord is in his holy "temple," or "palace" (*hêḵāl,* v.20; cf. TWOT, 1:214–15), ruling and judging in sovereign power (cf. Pss 11:4; 29:9–10; Isa 6:1–4; 66:1; Mic 1:2). Such a God is utterly worthy of man's reverent trust (Zeph 1:7; Zech 2:13).

This polemic against every form of "idol" (*pesel*) is typical of OT religion. The insidious futility of idols is contrasted repeatedly with the living God's unique claim to trust and obedience (e.g., Exod 20:4; Lev 26:1). As elsewhere, their futility is exposed here in ironic terms, for instance, in the phrase "idols that cannot speak": phonetically it evokes a nonsensical babble (*'ᵉlîlîm 'illᵉmîm;* cf. Isa 28:10, NIV mg.), and the noun "idols" (*'ᵉlîlîm*) is regularly applied to what is worthless and good for nothing (cf. TWOT, 1:46). Their insidiousness is suggested by their ability to usurp the place of God in men's lives, claiming a "trust" (*bāṭaḥ*) that belongs to him alone, and "giving guidance" (*môreh*) that can come from him alone (e.g., Exod 24:12; Ps 25:8, 12; Isa 2:3; cf. also the cognate *tôrāh*, "law"). In view of the Lord's implacable opposition to all such usurpers, the mere reference to his presence in v.20 constitutes an intimation of judgment—a judgment duly executed on Babylon (e.g., Isa 21:9; Jer 50:2, 38; 51:17, 47, 52) and still operative against man's bent toward idolatry (e.g., Rom 1:21–25; 1 Cor 5:11; 6:9; 10:7, 14; Gal 5:20; Eph 5:5; Col 3:5; 1 John 5:21; Rev 9:20–21; 21:8; 22:15).

Notes

15–17 חֲמָתְךָ (*ḥᵃmātᵉkā*), translated by NIV as "the wineskin," has a second masculine singular suffix in the MT ("your"; cf. KJV, ASV, RSV mg.), a difficult reading replaced by a third masculine singular pronominal form in 1QpHab, Symmachus, and the Vulgate but corroborated by Aquilla, Theodotion, and Quinta. The LXX, Syriac, and Targum omit the suffix entirely, which may reflect their evasion of MT's difficult reading or their omission of the consonant ו (*w*, "his") by haplography before the following word, וְאַף (*wᵉ'ap*, "till"). The MT presents a most-unexpected reading, the variants being easily explained as accommodations to the prevalent third singular forms following other "woes" in 2:6, 9, 12, 19. Moreover, such second singular forms are common in vv.6–20; indeed, they predominate in vv.16–17, whose direct address could be anticipated intelligibly by this reading (the pronoun "he" is supplied by NIV in v.15, being absent in Hebrew). In view of the additional evidence in the MT's favor among the Greek versions, its reading should be retained; such a break in a prevailing pattern is paralleled elsewhere in vv.6–20, particularly in the position of the final "woe" (cf. v.19). *Ḥᵃmātᵉkā*, the noun involved in this variant, is derived by NIV from the unusual noun חֵמֶת (*ḥēmet*), construct form *ḥēmat* ("a waterskin"; cf. Gen 21:14–15, 19). This interpretation is followed also by KJV and certain Jewish commentators. The noun may be derived more readily from חֵמָה (*ḥēmāh*), which means "heat," "venom," "wrath," all of which are appropriate here. "Heat" is associated with drunkenness in Hos 7:5–6; "venom" is associated with wine in Deut 32:33, and its destructive effects correspond to those of the "drink" given by the Babylonians (cf. Pss 58:5; 140:3). "Wrath" is represented repeatedly as being "poured out" (e.g., 2 Chron 12:7; 34:21; Ps 79:6; Jer 7:20; 42:18; Ezek 7:8; 9:8), and it is again related to the image of the "cup" in Isa 51:17, 22, and Jer 25:15; and the following word (*wᵉ'ap*) can be interpreted as a parallel noun in the accusative case, meaning "and (with) anger." It appears certain that these associations of *ḥēmāh* are intended here (cf. ASV, RSV); in view of Habakkuk's use of wordplay, particularly in vv.6–20, an allusion to a "wineskin" may also be implied.

Other examples of allusive double entendre in vv.15–17 include the imperative הֵעָרֵל (*hēʿārēl*, "be exposed"), which evokes הֵרָעֵל (*hērāʿēl*, "stagger"; cf. NIV mg.); and קִיקָלוֹן (*qîqālôn*, "disgrace"), which echoes קָלוֹן (*qālôn*, "shame") and evokes the phrase קִיא קָלוֹן (*qîʾ qālôn*, "shameful vomit"; cf. KJV, ASV).

V. The Prayer of Habakkuk (3:1–19)

Excursus

In its form and language, chapter 3 is closely related to the Psalms. The term "Selah" (cf. vv.3, 9, 13) recurs only in the Psalms, as does the musical subscript "On . . . stringed instruments" (v.19), while the phrase "For the director of music" (v.19) is seldom found elsewhere; all three elements recur together in Psalms 4, 54, 55, 61, 67, 76. Similarly, Habakkuk's recollection of Israel's past history (vv.2, 3–7, 8–15) is typical of the praises, instruction, and supplications in the Psalms (e.g., 42, 44, 68, 74, 78, 80, 83, 89, 105, 106, 135, 136). More specifically the passage resembles the psalms of lament. Its entitlement as a "prayer" related to "shigionoth" is typical of the lament form (v.1), as are the ensuing supplication for "mercy" in the midst of distress (v.2; cf. 1:2) and the subsequent statement of confidence and joy (vv.18–19). It shows particular affinities with Psalm 18, an acknowledgment of deliverance in response to David's lament (18:3–6): conspicuous points of contact include the dramatic theophany (18:7–15; cf. Hab 3:3–15); the deliverance from affliction (e.g., 18:2–3, 17–18, 46–50; cf. Hab 3:8, 13–14); and the assertion of praise and confidence in God (e.g., 18:1–33, 46–50; cf. Hab 3:18–19). An even closer relationship is apparent between Habakkuk 3 and the lament in Psalm 77. The two prayers demonstrate the same pervasive orientation to the past (Ps 77:3–12; cf. Hab 3:2–15), and specifically to the Exodus from Egypt (Ps 77:11–20; cf. Hab 3:8–15). Numerous words and motifs are common to these passages, including the language and imagery of earthquake and lightning. In keeping with these associations, Habakkuk's "prayer" extends the note of lament introduced in chapter 1, a lament that is now transformed, however, by acknowledgment of the Lord's anticipated intervention (cf. 2:1–20). In its final form it belongs in the setting of temple worship that characterizes the Psalms; but its origin is to be found in the inspiration of the individual "prophet," as with many of the Psalms. Beyond that, the original setting remains a matter of conjecture.

The remarkable power and enigmatic intensity of the "prayer" are due in part to the depth of allusion that informs it: its few, compressed verses draw on the entire spectrum of salvation history, from Creation and Exodus to the final revelation of God's rule and judgment still awaiting its fulfillment. This allusive quality is focused on certain primary passages, which form a background for the chapter and which, in turn, evoke the great "salvation history" events of Israel. First, as noted above, Habakkuk 3 is closely dependent on Psalm 77, which, second, has particular affinities to Exodus 15 (cf. 77:10–20): for instance, both passages, like Habakkuk 3, stress the redemptive power of God in a context of sea and water, using the common vocabulary of redemptive praise literature. It is the memory of God's past faithfulness and salvation as illuminated by his Spirit that provides a basis for faith in analogous circumstances.

Third, Habakkuk 3 draws on the language and imagery of Psalm 18, which evokes the Exodus in similar terms (cf. 18:4–19). Unlike Psalm 77, Psalm 18 explicitly recalls the Exodus as God's mighty victory over the enemy, foreshadowing Israel's subsequent conquests; and Habakkuk echoes the recollection of this psalm (cf. vv.8–11, 18–19). However, Psalm 18 fuses this revelation of God's power with a subsequent theophany, at Sinai (Ps 18:7–14; cf. Exod 19:9–19; Deut 5:22–27). As at Sinai, God's revelation is characterized by clouds and darkness (18:8–9, 11–12); by fire, thunder, and lightning (18:8, 12–14); and by devastating earthquake (18:7), as harbingers of the Lord's presence (cf. "came down," *yāraḏ*, 18:9; Exod 19:11, 18, 20). The background of Sinai may be similarly implicit in Psalm 77 (cf. esp. vv.3–7). The Lord's intervention both at the Red Sea and in later times is grounded in Sinaitic covenant history, by which he revealed his sovereign majesty and committed himself to Israel as his treasured possession; and this, rather than mere memory, was the anchor of Habakkuk's hope.

Fourth, the passage shows a conspicuous dependence on Deuteronomy 33, particularly v.2 (cf. Hab 3:3–4). Deuteronomy 33, like Psalm 18, perceives Sinai as the "deposit" of God's covenant commitment, guaranteeing Israel's future dominion (Deut 33:7, 11, 17, 21, 26–29; cf. Eph 1:14), a conviction at least echoed in Habakkuk 3.

Finally, Psalm 68 expresses a broad retrospect on Israel's prehistory and history and shows repeated points of contact with Habakkuk 3. As Psalms 77, 18, and 68 draw on the poetic traditions and historical backgrounds to Exodus 15 and Deuteronomy 32–33, so the hymnic passages of Habakkuk 3 echo earlier stages in Israel's history, most notably the parting of the Red Sea, which evokes both the Creation, when God divided the waters and imposed his will on them, and the Flood, when he again brought life and order out of chaos and destruction. In the Exodus, as in the beginning, God destroyed the powers of chaos and anarchy that threaten to engulf his creation; and the cosmic battle portrayed in Habakkuk 3:8–15 draws on this background.

This retrospective orientation of Habakkuk (cf. also Hosea) pervades the literature of Israel, for whom the past dealings and revelation of God constitute the seedbed of future revelation, the promise of subsequent dealings (e.g., Neh 9:6–38; Pss 77, 78, 83, 105, 106, 114; Isa 51:1–16; 63:1–64:12). Thus the covenant and theophany at Sinai embody a pattern for later revelations of God's power, culminating in the eschatological manifestation of his reign (e.g., Judg 5:4–31; Pss 18, 68, 97; Isa 64:1–4; Hag 2:6). These patterns culminate in the NT: in the institution of a new covenant on another mountain, amid darkness and earthquake, judgment and grace (cf. Matt 26:28; 27:45–51; Luke 9:28–36; Gal 4:24; Heb 10:16–31; 12:18–29); in the inauguration of another Exodus, through blood, water, and the wind of God's Spirit (cf. Luke 9:31; 1 Cor 10:2; 1 Peter 3:21); in a new creation (cf. John 3:3–8; 2 Cor 5:17; Gal 6:15). The vision of Habakkuk stands in a noble tradition.

The structure of this chapter is arranged chiastically: introduction, v.1 (A); prayer, v.2 (B); theophany, vv.3–15 (C); response, vv.16–19 (B^1); epilogue, v.19 (A^1). It is framed by the corresponding musical notations in v.1 and in the final line of v.19, which represent an editorial comment on the intervening "prayer"; such notations recur together frequently in the Psalms (e.g., Pss 4–12). Verse 2 is characterized by its first-person pronominal forms ("I," "our"), in which Habakkuk addressed his prayer to the "Lord." This prayer articulates the contrast between the past, awe-inspiring in its power ("I have heard," *šāmaʿtî*, and "I stand in awe," or "I fear," *yārēʾṯî*), and the present distress ("wrath," *rōgez*). Verses 16–19 echo this prayer: the first-person forms predominate again ("I," "my"); the Lord is again the focus of Habakkuk's attention (vv.18–19); his orientation to the past is signaled by the same introductory vocabulary ("I heard," *šāmaʿtî*); and this orientation is accompanied by the same awe and experience of present distress, amplified to portray its impact on the prophet himself ("quivered," *ṣālal*, "pounded . . . trembled," *rāgaz*, cf. v.2) and on his society (vv.16–17). However, this correspondence of vv.2, 16–19 contains a dramatic contrast. The content of Habakkuk's hearing in vv.16–19 is no longer derived from the remote past (cf. v.2) but from an overwhelming revelation of the past, as unleashed, invading the present (v.16; cf. vv.3–15); and, as in the case of Job (42:5), the new note of personal devastation mixed with faith is born of this revelation. Verses 3–15, consisting of two sections (vv.3–7, 8–15), constitute the central, focal passage of the chapter. They are closely linked to v.2, as the answer to Habakkuk's petition for a revelation of God's deeds and in their direct address to the "LORD" (i.e., "you," "your," vv.2, 8–15); and also to vv.16–19, as the basis for Habakkuk's response and in their third-person references to God (vv.3–7, 18–19). The three sections—vv.2, 3–15, 16–19—are further linked by the key word "to tremble" (*rāgaz*), which recurs in v.7 ("in anguish") and epitomizes the upheaval pervading vv.3–15: the "wrath" of God disrupts his entire creation, natural and human alike.

Verses 3–7 and 8–15 each have their own internal structure, with the former unified by poetic associations with Sinai as the place of divinely wrought upheaval (cf. Exod 15:13–18; 19:9–19; Judg 5:4–5; Ps 68:7–10). Verses 8–15 embody a consistent imagery of water, storm, and warfare, and are further unified by the introduction of direct speech in the transitional question of v.8 ("you," "your"), answered in the second-person affirmation of vv.13–14. Both use inclusios (vv.3, 7 are rhymed pairs of proper names having a common geographical association, while vv.8, 15 both speak of the "sea" [*yām*] and "your horses" [*sûseyḵā*]), and each is focused on a primary event in salvation-history (Sinai and Exodus/Conquest) with a common vocabulary associated with that event.

The climax of vv.3–15 is the new content in vv.13–14, which serves to answer, not only the question of v.8, but the theological dilemma posed by Habakkuk's initial cry. Although manifested in nature, the "wrath" of God is intensely personal, being exercised in the judgment and salvation of his people. Verses 3–7, 8–15 are thus defined as distinct units, with differing historical orientations but leading to the same conclusion. Just as Sinai and Exodus are intimately connected in history, in Israel's recollection of that history (e.g., Exod 19:4–5; Neh 9:9–14; Pss 18:7–16; 114; 144:5–7), and in their demonstration of God's sovereign control over the elements, so they are brought together here. And moving back from the center to the prayer as a whole, the verb "to tremble" (*rāgaz*) forms a central theme in vv.2–19, signaling the universal turmoil that is the hallmark of God's appearing in vv.3–15. His kingdom comes amid the shaking of all things (cf. Hag 2:6, 21–22; Matt 7:24–27; 24:1–8, 27–31; Heb 12:26–29).

The structure relating chapter 3 to chapters 1–2 cannot be elaborated here, but it is evident that in many respects they are parallel. Common features include their headings (1:1; 3:1); the lament form underlying their prayers (1:2–4, 12–2:1; 3:1–2); the preoccupation with salvation, triumphantly vindicated in the final chapter (*yāsa'*, 1:2; 3:8, 13 [*bis*], 18); the judgment on domestic sin through a foreign nation (1:2–11; 3:2, 14–17), the "wicked" (*rāšā'*, 1:13; 3:13) and their intent to "devour" (*'āḵal*, 1:8; 3:14); the concomitant disruption of the "nations" (1:5–17; 2:5–17; cf. 3:6–7, 12); the "revelation" that forms the turning point in the prophet's intercession (2:23; 3:3–15); the resultant promise of judgment ensuing on that nation (2:3–20; 3:12–16), as on a "house" destined to be razed to its foundations (*bayiṯ*, 2:9–10; 3:13; cf. 2:9–13; 3:13); the transformation effected by this promise, promoting both faith and patience (2:2–4; 3:16–19); the anticipation of God's universal reign (2:14; 3:3); and the common basis on the covenant, particularly Deuteronomy 28–32, that shapes the pattern outlined above. Habakkuk 1–2 appears to emphasize the human agents in the outworking of this pattern; chapter 3 reveals its inward dynamics in the sovereign agency of God, who implements the covenant through whatever earthly means he chooses. Together they form a compelling and tightly meshed testimony to the ways of God in judgment and in grace.

1. *Introduction*

3:1

> [1]A prayer of Habakkuk the prophet. On *shigionoth.*

1 The reference to "Habakkuk the prophet" marks a new section, distinct from chapters 1 and 2, which are similarly introduced (cf. 1:1). The following verses are characterized as a "prayer" (*tᵉpillāh;* cf. TWOT, 2:725–26), a title attributed elsewhere to five psalms of lament (Pss 17, 86, 90, 102, 142), and also to an early collection of Davidic psalms (cf. Ps 72:20); the term predominates in the Psalms, occurring most commonly in laments where intercession is made for divine intervention and vindication against oppression or injustice (e.g., Pss 4:1; 6:9; 17:1; 35:13; 54:2; 55:1; 69:13; 86:6; 88:2, 13; 102:1, 17 [*bis*]; 109:4, 7; cf. 1 Kings 8:28–54). These associations with the psalmic literature are reinforced by the phrase "On *shigionoth*": the corresponding "*shiggaion*" appears as the title of another lament (Ps 7), and the preposition "on," or "according to" (*ʿal,* is used in musical directions at the head of numerous psalms (e.g., 6, 8, 12, 22, 45, 46; cf. v.19). The precise etymology and meaning of the phrase are uncertain (cf. *šāgag/šāgāh;* TWOT, 2:903ff.; KB, p. 948; THAT, 2:869–72); its characteristics in Psalm 7 suggest that, as a musical genre, it constitutes a vehement cry for justice against sin. It is evident, then, that the heading that distinguishes chapter 3 also relates it to the preceding chapters, where a similar cry for justice is expressed in the same genre of a lament.

2. *Prayer*

3:2

> [2]LORD, I have heard of your fame;
> I stand in awe of your deeds, O LORD.
> Renew them in our day,
> in our time make them known;
> in wrath remember mercy.

2 The orientation of Habakkuk's "prayer" is to the past, as the basis for his appeal to God for present help (cf. Exod 32:13; Ps 77:11; Acts 4:25–28). The noun "fame" (*šēmaʿ*) is normally used of secondhand information (e.g., Job 28:22; Nah 3:19), suggesting a remoteness from the hearer's own experience to the persons or events referred to (cf. Job 42:5). The Lord's "deeds" envisaged here corroborate this sense of remoteness, being associated with his sovereign power and preeminently with his "work" (*pōʿal*) at the Exodus (e.g., Num 23:23; Pss 44:1; 68:28; 77:12; 90:16; 95:9; 111:3; cf. v.3)—a primary anchor-point of Israel's recollection, faith, and hope, as is the Cross to the Christian. Habakkuk's appeal for "mercy" (*rāḥam*) is thus grounded in God's covenantal commitment to Israel, displayed in the events of the Exodus as a whole and sealed at Sinai (cf. Deut 4:31); it is no wishful or manipulative plea for help, grounded merely in the desperation of the moment. However, it is also an admission of Israel's decline from the revelation of God's character and ways, made "known" at the Exodus: not only do the "deeds" of that epoch represent secondhand knowledge, but the need to "renew" (*hîyāh*) them implies that their impact in redemption and revelation was facing extinction. Moreover, the imminence of "wrath," or "turmoil" (*rōgez;* cf. v.7), betrays the presence of sin, which the Lord is committed to judge in his people—a judgment rooted in the covenant no less than "mercy" (e.g., Exod 32:10–12; Deut 6:15; 29:20–28; 31:17; 32:22). This appeal for God's covenanted "mercy" in the face of present distress and judgment echoes Psalm 77 (v.9), with which this chapter has much in common.

3. *Theophany*

3:3–15

3God came from Teman,
the Holy one from Mount Paran. *Selah*
His glory covered the heavens
and his praise filled the earth.
4His splendor was like the sunrise;
rays flashed from his hand,
where his power was hidden.
5Plague went before him;
pestilence followed his steps.
6He stood, and shook the earth;
he looked, and made the nations tremble.
The ancient mountains crumbled
and the age-old hills collapsed.
His ways are eternal.
7I saw the tents of Cushan in distress,
the dwellings of Midian in anguish.

8Were you angry with the rivers, O LORD?
Was your wrath against the streams?
Did you rage against the sea
when you rode with your horses
and your victorious chariots?
9You uncovered your bow,
you called for many arrows. *Selah*
You split the earth with rivers;
10the mountains saw you and writhed.
Torrents of water swept by;
the deep roared
and lifted its waves on high.

11Sun and moon stood still in the heavens
at the glint of your flying arrows,
at the lightning of your flashing spear.
12In wrath you strode through the earth
and in anger you threshed the nations.
13You came out to deliver your people,
to save your anointed one.
You crushed the leader of the land of wickedness,
you stripped him from head to foot. *Selah*
14With his own spear you pierced his head
when his warriors stormed out to scatter us,
gloating as though about to devour
the wretched who were in hiding.
15You trampled the sea with your horses,
churning the great waters.

3 "Teman" was located in Edom, or Seir, the land south and east of the Dead Sea traditionally occupied by the descendants of Esau (ZPEB, 5:624; cf. Jer 49:7, 20;

Ezek 25:13; Amos 1:11–12; Obad 8–9; cf. Gen 25:25, 30; 32:3; 36:1–9, 34). The wilderness of "Paran" was a large, relatively diffuse area, lying between Kadesh Barnea to the north and Mount Sinai to the south (cf. Num 10:11–12; 12:16; 13:3, 26; 1 Sam 25:1) and bounded by Edom to the northeast and Egypt to the southwest (cf. Gen 14:6; 21:21; 1 Kings 11:18). "Mount Paran" is generally thought to be situated to the east of this desert: either in the rugged granite mountains west of the Gulf of Aqabah, or among the desolate cliffs of the Plateau of Paran, northwest of the Gulf of Aqabah (E.M. Blaiklock, *The Zondervan Pictorial Bible Atlas* [Grand Rapids: Zondervan, 1969], p. 64). These geographical references constitute a clear allusion to Deuteronomy 33:2, "Mount Paran" being mentioned only in these two passages, and "Teman" corresponding to Seir (u.s.). Their primary function is thus to evoke the revelation of God's law at Sinai, to which Deuteronomy 33:2–4 refers explicitly (cf. Judg 5:4–5; Ps 68:7–8, 17; Isa 63:1–9) so corroborating the associations outlined in v.2 and setting the broad historical context for vv.3–15. However, Habakkuk's omission of the focal term "Sinai" admits a certain imprecision to the allusion: it recalls, not the exact details of a past event, but the dynamics of that event as an analogy for another revelation of God's presence and power.

The noun "glory" (*hôd*) is used primarily of kingly authority (e.g., Num 27:20; 1 Chron 29:25; Ps 45:3; Zech 6:13), revealed preeminently in the Lord's sovereignty over creation and history (cf. 1 Chron 16:27; 29:11–12; Job 40:10). The verb "covered" (*kissāh*) is used of extension over a surface, either to permeate or conceal, with the precise meaning here indicated by the parallel verb "filled" and by the allusion to 2:14 (see below). Thus God's "glory" covers "the heavens" in permeating them, being revealed in them as an expression of his majesty (e.g., Job 37:22; Pss 8:1; 104:1; 148:13; cf. Deut 33:26, 29; Ps 68:34). This thought is echoed in the following line; God's "praise" (*tᵉhillāh*) is a metonomy denoting the power of his character and works, for which he is to be praised (cf. Exod 15:11, ASV; Ps 78:4), and which similarly pervades his creation. This couplet clearly evokes the eschatological proclamation in 2:14 (cf. "glory" [*kābôḏ*], "earth," "filled," "cover"). Like the preceding couplet in v.3, it looks forward to a new and universal manifestation of God's rule, grounding it in his past breaking into history at Sinai—a brief moment in history, embodying repercussions for the whole of history; a remote event in the earth, destined to fill the whole earth (cf. Eph 4:10; Phil 2:7–11).

The expression "Selah" recurs in vv.9, 13, and also seventy-one times in thirty-nine of the Psalms (e.g., 3, 24, 46, 68, 77, 89, 140). Its meaning has been obscure to translators since early times; its exclusive association with psalmic literature suggests that it had a liturgical function, possibly relating to music or prayer in the temple worship.

4 God's "glory" is manifested as light, interpreted by NIV as a comparison with "the sunrise." The noun "splendor" (*nōgah*) denotes the shining of various sources of light, including the sun (2 Sam 23:4; Prov 4:18), while "sunrise" translates the common noun "light" (*'ôr*), often used of dawn and sunlight (e.g., Judg 16:2; 1 Sam 14:36; et al.). The noun "rays" (*qarnayim*) normally means "horns," with the derived meaning of "projections," such as beams or rays of light; an equivalent word is applied to the rays of the rising sun in Arabic poetry (Keil, p.99). These associations may validate NIV's rendering of v.4; and certainly the sun does form a fitting biblical symbol of God's "splendor." However, the vocabulary of v.4 is in fact in close harmony with the Sinaitic background developed in v.3, which points to a different context.

As noted above, "splendor" is used of light sources other than the sun. In particular, it recurs to describe the radiance of God's presence, in contexts that recall his theophanies at Sinai and in the wilderness (Ps 18:12; Isa 4:5; 60:1; Ezek 1:4, 13, 27–28; 10:4); as at Sinai, this radiance is generally manifested as intense fire, shrouded in clouds and darkness (e.g., Exod 19:16–19; Ps 18:8–12; Isa 4:5–6; 60:1–2; Ezek 1:4, 13, 27–28; 10:2–7)—an image very remote from that of the rising sun. In keeping with these associations, the noun "sunrise" is used of lightning (Job 36:32; 37:3, 11, 15), which is a prominent characteristic of Sinai and later theophanies (e.g., Exod 19:16; 20:18). On this understanding, the Lord is perceived as illuminating the world, not with the delicate light of sunrise, but with the awe-inspiring radiance that characterized his descent on Mount Sinai—a light as brilliant as the lightning that accompanied that event, incandescent with his glory.

This interpretation is confirmed, first, by the close connection of vv.3–4 with Sinai, to which the image of a sunrise is most inappropriate (cf. Exod 19:9–19; Deut 5:22–26; Judg 5:4–5; Ps 68:7–8). Second, this passage alludes specifically to Deuteronomy 33:2, in which God's glory is similarly portrayed. Third, the imagery of sunshine is equally remote from the ensuing vision. Instead, it is dominated by volcanic earthquake, storm, and specifically by lightning (v.11; cf. v.9), which again are consistent with Sinai. And, finally, in a passage that corresponds closely to vv.3–7 (cf. excursus), the two nouns for "splendor" and "sunrise" recur together in v.11—translated as "lightning" and "glint," respectively—in the unambiguous context of a lightning storm (cf. Ps 77:17–18). The final lines of v.4 are to be interpreted against this background. The "rays" (lit., "twin-rays," i.e., forked lightning) are flashes of light manifested at the Lord's presence. The "hand" is repeatedly a symbol of the Lord's power (e.g., Exod 13:14, 16; 14:31; Deut 3:24; 4:34; 32:41), to which the following line refers explicitly—a "power" manifested conspicuously in the forces of nature (e.g., Exod 15:13; Pss 68:33–35; 74:13; 77:14; 78:26; 150:1), which are "hidden" in his storehouses (cf. Deut 28:12; Job 38:22; Ps 135:7; Jer 10:13; 51:14; Ecclus 43:14). This imagery is clarified in the corresponding content of vv.9, 11, where "lightning" serves the Lord as the "arrows" and "spear" in his hand (cf. Deut 33:2, RSV—"flaming fire at his right hand").

5 God's "power" is here revealed in judgment: almost invariably "plague" (*deḇer*) and "pestilence" (*rešep*) are attributed directly to the sovereign agency and judgment of God. Accompanying him in the context of Sinai, they refer particularly to the plagues that devastated Egypt (Exod 9:3, 15; Ps 78:50) and which attended Israel's disobedience to the covenant given at Sinai (Exod 5:3; Lev 26:25; Num 14:12; Deut 28:21; 32:24; cf. 2 Sam 24:13, 15; 1 Kings 8:37; Jer 29:17–19; 34:12–20; Ezek 5:12, 17; 6:11–12; Amos 4:10).

6–7 The scope of this judgment embraces the "earth" as a whole (v.6; cf. v.3), which is convulsed by earthquake and volcanic upheaval. The verb "shook" (*yᵉmōḏeḏ*) is derived either from a root cognate with the Arabic "to be convulsed" (*mûḏ;* KB, p. 501; cf. LXX, Targ.) or from the Hebrew "to measure" (*māḏaḏ*, cf. Vul., KJV, ASV, RSV). The first etymology emphasizes the effects of God's action, whereas the second stresses the motive of judgment underlying it (cf. Isa 65:7; Dan 5:25–28). There seems to be little basis for choosing between them (cf. ASV, NASB). The repercussions of such judgment and physical upheaval are reflected among the "nations," the verb "tremble" (*nāṯar*) implying both emotional turmoil (cf. Job 37:1) and abrupt physical dislocation (e.g., Pss 105:20, "release"; 146:7, "sets free"). This shaking of all things is specified more precisely in the following two couplets of vv.6–7. The "mountains" and "hills" are symbols of grandeur, permanence, and security in the "earth" (e.g., Gen 49:26; Deut 33:15); yet they too are revealed as frail and impermanent. Before God's might they are shattered and prostrated (cf. Job 9:5; Pss 97:5; 104:42; Nah 1:5). Although they appear to be "age-old" (*ʿôlām*), in truth God alone is "eternal" (*ʿôlām*).

The "nations," in turn, are exemplified more specifically by the tribes of "Cushan" and "Midian" (v.7). The Midianites were localized in Transjordan, ranging southward from the regions of Moab and Edom (cf. Num 2:4, 7; 25:15; 31:1–12; Josh 13:21) and making incursions further west (cf. Gen 37:28; Exod 2:15; 3:1; Judg 6–8); the word "dwellings" (*yᵉrîʿôṯ*, lit., "curtains"; cf. Ps 104:2; S of Songs 1:5; Isa 54:2; Jer 4:20; 10:20; 49:29; ASV, RSV) typifies their nomadic existence. The phrase "in anguish" translates the verb "to be agitated, quake" (*rāgaz;* TWOT, 2:830–31; cf. *rōgez,* v.2); thus it echoes the verb "tremble" (v.6) in portraying the impact of God's "wrath" (v.8). The identity of "Cushan" is uncertain, but evidently it also denotes a nomadic group (cf. "tents") in similar "distress." This close parallelism suggests that "Cushan" was a nation related or even identical to "Midian"—an inference corroborated by the identification of Moses' wife as both Midianite and Cushite (Exod 2:18–22; 18:1–5; Num 12:1).

The imagery of vv.6–7 again recalls the earthquake and volcanic upheaval at Mount Sinai (e.g., Exod 19:18; Judg 5:4–5), thus echoing v.3 in its clear allusion to Sinai, and so framing the intervening verses and providing a specific context for their interpretation; this inclusio defining vv.3–7 as a unit is signaled more precisely by the names in vv.3, 7, which correspond to one another in their common geographical association with Sinai and in the rhyme linking their final syllables (i.e., *ān*).

8 The inclusio uniting vv.3–7 marks this verse as the introduction to a new section. This is corroborated by the emphatic switch to direct address, unparalleled in vv. 3–7 and extending to v.15; and also by the prominence of vocabulary denoting water and military conflict, similarly absent from vv.3–7. The Lord's "wrath" receives dramatic emphasis, being echoed by the words "angry" and "rage" (*ʿeḇrāh*). It is directed against the "sea" (*yām*), evoking his display of power at the Red Sea, a focal point in Israel's memory (e.g., Exod 14:2–15:22; Deut 11:4). The correlation of this verse with that event is substantiated by the reference to "chariots" and "horses" (cf. Exod 14:6–15:19; Deut 11:4; Josh 24:6) and to the Lord's victory, or salvation (*yᵉšûʿāh,* cf. Exod 14:13, 30; 15:2; Ps 106:8–10). It is also substantiated by the context. It is appropriate, first, to vv.3–7, Israel's deliverance at the Red Sea being the precondition for the covenant at Sinai. Second, the verse corresponds in content to vv.12–15 (cf. excursus; cf. "anger," v.12; "deliver," "save," v.13; "sea," "your horses," v.15), where the deliverance from the Egyptian enemy is echoed even more clearly (cf. vv.13–14).

The opening parallel lines of v.8 refer to the "rivers" and "streams" (both *nᵉhārîm;* cf. ASV, RSV) as witnessing the anger of the Lord. The waters of the Jordan may be envisaged (cf. Josh 3:13, 17; 4:7, 21–24; 5:1; Ps 66:6; 114:3, 5), but more likely the word "rivers" (normally plural, as here) is equivalent to "sea": the noun admits the meaning "currents," "watermass," and is not restricted to inland rivers. The Lord's dramatic conflict with the "sea" echoes his dominion over the waters of Creation and the Flood (cf. excursus and vv.9–11), a complex of events that pervades Israel's literature as a pattern of future salvation and judgment (e.g., Pss 18:4, 15–16; 29: 1–11; 65:7; 93:1–4; Isa 10:26; 11:15; 17:12–13; 43:16; 50:2; 51:10, 15; 63:11–12; Zech 10:11; Exodus and Sinai alike are the incarnation of events with universal significance.

God's "horses" and "chariots" evidence his power as Lord of hosts, or armies (NIV, "LORD Almighty," e.g., 2:13), and the martial imagery of v.8 permeates and unifies the following verses (vv.9–15). Elsewhere the clouds or the winged cherubim serve as his chariot or throne (Ps 104:3; cf. Ps 18:10–12; Isa 19:1, drawn by the wind and resplendent with the brightness of lightning. Thus the Lord's chariotry here represents both the power of wind and storm, driving back the sea and churning it up (cf. vv.9–11, 15; Gen 1:2; 8:1; Exod 14:21; 15:8, 10), and the cherubim and angelic hosts as executors of his sovereign will in such forces of nature (e.g., Gen 3:24; Deut 33:2; Ps 68:17; Rev 5:11; 7:1–2; 8:5–9:15). As in vv.3–7, therefore, Habakkuk's memory of Yahweh's "deeds" (v.2) reverts to the events surrounding the Exodus, in keeping with the Lord's repeated injunction to Israel (e.g., Exod 13:3). In keeping with the intent of this injunction, it is from those wellsprings of salvation that Habakkuk drew his joy, purified in the fires of adversity (vv.16–19): it was the revelation of God's faithfulness and justice in the past that empowered the prophet to face the future with the submissive yet exuberant confidence that it demanded of him.

9 All three Hebrew words in the second line of this verse are obscure, and they must be interpreted against the background of the first line. The noun "arrows" (*maṭṭôṯ*) normally means "staffs" or "tribes" (cf. TWOT, 2:574), but the first of these meanings can be applied to the shaft of a weapon (e.g., Isa 9:4; 10:5, 24; 14:5; 30:32; cf. "staff," *šēḇeṭ*). Such an application is appropriate to "bow." Moreover, the noun recurs in a context of warfare in v.14 ("spear"); and v.9 is related structurally to a similar context in v.11 (cf. excursus). A suitable parallel to "bow" is offered by either "arrows," or "spears"; both weapons are specified in v.11. In view of the connection with Deuteronomy 32:39–43 (see below), "arrows" is marginally preferable (cf. Deut 32:42). "Many" (*šᵉḇūʿôṯ;* cf. TWOT, 2:899ff.) translates a form derived from either the noun "heptad," "group of seven" (*šāḇûaʿ*), or the verb "to swear" (*šāḇaʿ*; cf. KJV, ASV). NIV follows the first alternative, its rendering apparently suggested in the sevenfold volleys of arrows used in Israelite warfare (Y. Yadin, *The Scroll of the War* [New York, McGraw, 1916], pp. 131–32, 140; cf. Eaton, commentary p. 152).

Although the issue is by no means clear-cut, "to swear" (*šāḇāʿ*) is preferable for the following reasons: vv.11–14 clearly echo Deuteronomy 32:39–43; v.9 is closely related to vv.11–14 by the imagery noted above, and also by the correspondence of "uncovered," v.9 (*ʿeryāh, ʿûr*) and "stripped," v.13 (*ʿeryāh*); it is therefore to be interpreted against the same Deuteronomic background, and this makes emphatic reference to the Lord's oath as underlying his judgment (Deut 32:40). Thus, his militant intervention is perceived as fulfilling the commitment sworn to Moses and Israel beyond the Jordan. This interpretation is substantiated further by the third word in the line—"called" (*ʾōmer*): the same root recurs in Deuteronomy 32:40 ("declare," *ʾāmartî*), and in the related contexts of Psalms 77 ("promise," v.8, *ōmer*) and 68 ("says," v.22, *ʾāmar*). A tentative though not very meaningful translation of the entire line would be "The arrows of the promise are sworn."

The final line is also obscure, since it could be translated "you split the rivers to the earth" (GKC, pars. 117 ll; 118 a, d, f, h; 142 f, g; R.J. Williams, *Hebrew Syntax* [Toronto: University of Toronto Press, 1967], pars. 54, 571–74). The noun "rivers" (*n^{e}hārôṯ*) echoes the form repeated in v.8 (*n^{e}hārîm*), suggesting that it has the same associations with the Exodus. These are reinforced by the verb "split" (*bāqaʿ*); it is often applied to the division of the Red Sea (cf. Exod 14:16, 21; Neh 9:11; Ps 78:13; Isa 63:12), which allowed God's people to walk securely on the dry "earth." However, the vision of the earth "split" by floods of water is appropriate to the following verses with their undertones of Creation and Flood (cf. Gen 7:11; Ps 74:15; Prov 3:20). The syntactical ambiguity is therefore effective and may be intentional, being a hallmark of Habakkuk's style. It is supported by the association of God's "bow" with the Flood (cf. Gen 9:13–14, 16) and by the similar juxtaposition of earthquake and flood in v.10. On this understanding "earth" (v.9) may correspond to "mountains" (v.10) at the center of the chiasmus in vv.9–11 (cf. excursus). Verse 8 would then deal with the Exodus and vv.9–11 more explicitly with the Flood, both motifs being integrated in vv.12–15.

10 The reference to "water" again evokes God's might revealed in driving back the Red Sea, as do the nouns "deep" (*t^{e}hôm;* cf. Exod 15:5, 8; Pss 77:16; 106:9; Isa 51:10; 63:13) and "torrents" (*zerem;* cf. Ps 77:17). This verse in particular draws on the language of Psalm 77, where the Exodus is the explicit focus of recollection (cf. excursus; e.g., 77:15, 20): additional correspondences to Psalm 77 are evident in the words "saw you" (*rā'ûḵā*, 77:16 [*bis*]); "writhed" (*yāḥîlû*, 77:16); and "roared" (*nāṯan qôlô;* cf. "resounded," 77:17). However, both passages envision that event in cosmic terms, as convulsing the "mountains" and the whole of nature (cf. v.6). They thereby portray the deliverance at the Red Sea as a reenactment of the Flood, itself a reversal and renewal of Creation when the Lord brought life and order out of the waters of the deep (*t^{e}hôm*, Gen 1:2). These precursors of the Exodus exhibit the same central imagery of sea and water, dominated by the Lord; and the upheaval of the mountains evokes the turmoil at the Flood (Gen 7:11, 19–20), as does the reference to "torrents" (*zerem*), which denotes both a downpour of rain and the resultant flooding (TWOT, 1:252; cf. Gen 7:12; 8:2). It is this awe-inspiring power of God, the Creator and Judge of all the earth, that is manifested in retribution and salvation at the Red Sea. As at the Cross, a universal cataclysm is compressed into a single, localized event in Israel's history; as at the Cross, that event is destined to shake the universe.

11 The "sun" and "moon" are prominent symbols of God's created order, and particularly of its permanence (cf. Pss 8:3; 72:5, 7; 89:37). Their inactivity indicates the interruption of that order (cf. Josh 10:12–13; Isa 38:8). Here the picture is probably of an eclipse; they stay in their place and cease to give light. Such an eclipse is suggested also by the noun "heavens," which denotes an exalted dwelling place (*z^{e}ḇulāh;* cf. 1 Kings 8:13; Ps 49:14, NIV: "princely mansion"): sun and moon remain hidden in their heavenly abode. Moreover, darkness is appropriate to the context of storm in vv.9–11; the cessation of sun and moon in Joshua 10:12–13, though often associated with this passage, seems less applicable in this context, unless the hailstorm of that passage also implies the darkness of a stormy eclipse (cf. Josh 10:11; TWOT, 2:674). And, finally, such an interruption of the created order typically accompanies the judgment of God, as here (vv.12–16); and this judgment, culminating in the eschatological Day of the Lord, is characterized consistently by darkness (e.g., Exod 10:21–22; 14:20; Eccl 12:2; Isa 13:10; 24:23; Jer 4:23, 28; Joel 2:2, 10, 31; 3:15; Amos 5:18–20; 8:9; Zeph 1:15; Matt 24:29; 27:45; Luke 23:45; Rev 6:12; 8:12; 9:2; 22:5). The following couplet corroborates this interpretation, in its portrayal of a lightning storm, which would be accompanied by clouds and obscurity. The noun "glint" is used of lightning (cf. comment at v.4; cf. Ps 77:18), and the Lord's "arrows" are equated with lightning in the parallel passages of Psalms 77 and 18 (77:17–18; 18:14; cf. 144:6; Zech 9:14). His "arrows" recur repeatedly as instruments of his judgment, most notably in Deuteronomy 32, which forms a background to vv.11–14 (Deut 32:23, 42; Job 6:4; Pss 7:13; 38:2; 64:7; Lam 3:12; Ezek 5:16). The correspondence to the Sinai imagery in vv.3–7 is clear.

12 This verse recapitulates the motif of God's wrath, the noun "anger" (*'ap*) being identical to "wrath" in v.8. It also recapitulates the military imagery of vv.8–9, 11: the verbs "strode" and "came out" (v.13) recur together in Judges 5:4 and Psalm 68:7, describing the Lord in his march to battle against the "nations"; and the same connotations are present here, in view of the close association between Habakkuk 3 and those passages in their dependence on Deuteronomy 32–33 (cf. excursus; cf. also Deut 33:2; Judg 5:4–5; Ps 68:7–8, 17; Hab 3:3). These connotations are present in other usages of the words "strode" (*ṣā'aḏ;* cf. 2 Sam 5:24; 6:13; Ps 18:36) and "came out" (*yāṣā';* cf. Judg 2:15; 4:14; 1 Sam 17:20; 2 Sam 5:24; Ps 108:11); and they were reinforced by those of "threshed" (*dûš;* cf. Judg 8:7; 2 Kings 13:7; Isa 21:10; 25:10; Dan 7:23; Amos 1:3; Mic 4:13) and by the content of vv.13–14.

Habakkuk's vision embraces the conquest of the "nations" as an integral part of the Exodus and of Israel's subsequent destiny (cf. Gen 24:60; 26:3–4; Exod 15:14–16; 34:24; Num 24:8; Deut 4:38; 7:1, 17–26; 32:43; 33:17, 29; 1 Chron 14:17; Pss 2; 9:5, 15–20; 18:43; 46:10; 77:14; Isa 34:1–3; 54:3; 60:12–14). The Lord may appoint the Babylonians to curse Israel, but they will surely inherit a curse themselves (cf. Gen 12:2–3; 27:29; Num 24:9; Deut 28; Ps 105:12–15). The common metaphor of threshing implies violent shaking and crushing, which also characterizes the effects on the "earth" and mountains as the Lord "strode" by (Judg 5:4–5; Ps 68:7–8; cf. 1 Kings 19:11–12; Ps 77:18–19). Thus v.12 also recapitulates the imagery of earthquake from v.10: in effect it resumes and integrates the content of both vv.3–7 and vv.8, 9–11 at the introduction to this concluding section (vv.12–15), in which the goal of the Lord's "wrath" and salvation becomes evident whether acting on the "earth" or the "nations."

13 The military associations of "came out" have been noted above. They are reiterated in the words "deliver" and "save" (both *yāša';* cf. Num 10:9; Deut 20:4; Judg 2:18; 1 Sam 9:16; Ps 33:16), derived from the same root as "victorious" (v.8) and "save" (1:2), and forming a part of names like Joshua, Isaiah, and Jesus. The third chapter emphatically speaks against the perspective of Habakkuk's initial prayer (1:2–4). This deliverance expresses the Lord's covenantal commitment to his "people" (*'am;* cf. Exod 3:7, 10, 12, et al.; Pss 68:7, 35; 77:15, 20) and to his "anointed one" (*māšîaḥ*, "Messiah"). The underlying root (*mšḥ*) is applied almost invariably to an individual; only in one doubtful instance might it refer to the people as a whole (Ps 28:8–9). Most commonly it designates a king (e.g., 1 Sam 2:10; 2 Sam 23:1; Pss 18:50; 89:38, 51); but it may also denote other individuals appointed to leadership, such as the high priest (e.g., Exod 40:13, 15; Lev 4:3; 6:22) and the patriarchs (1 Chron 16:22; Ps 105:15). In the present context of the Exodus, it appears to refer to

Moses, who, like King David, combined in himself the messianic functions of shepherd (e.g., Num 27:17; Ps 77:20), prophet (e.g., Deut 18:15; 34:10), servant of God (e.g., Exod 14:31; Num 12:7–8, and priest (Exod 6:16–26; Lev 8).

The context of the Exodus also throws light on the identity of the "leader" (or "head," *rō'š;* cf. TWOT, 2:825–26). Egypt represents an archetypal land of "wickedness" (*rāšā';* cf. Exod 9:27), and the Pharaoh of the Exodus figures prominently as an agent of Israel's oppression. This is suggested also by the verb "crushed" (or "pierced," *māḥaṣ*), which is applied to the destruction of Rahab at Creation (Job 26:12; cf. Ps 74:13–14)—Rahab being identified elsewhere with Egypt and specifically with the Exodus (cf. Ps 87:4; Isa 30:7; 51:9). This understanding is reinforced by the associations of the noun "land," normally translated "house" (*bayiṯ;* cf. below), since Egypt is characterized as Israel's "house of bondage" (NIV, "land of slavery"; cf. Exod 13:3, 14; Deut 5:6; Josh 24:17). However, this verse provides further evidence of the double perspective of the chapter: the oppression in Egypt foreshadows subsequent oppression, and the deliverance at the Red Sea embodies the promise of subsequent deliverance. The term "anointed one" lends itself more readily to later usage, both with reference to the preexilic kings and in anticipation of the eschatological Messiah (e.g., Dan 9:25–26; cf. 2 Sam 7:11–16; Isa 9:6–7; 11:1–5; Jer 23:5–6; Ezek 34:23–24; 37:22–25; Mic 5:2–5; Zech 6:9–14; 9:9–10). In the present chapter, set against the background of imminent danger preceding the Exile (vv.2, 16–17; cf. 1:5–11), and also fraught with eschatological undertones of judgment and salvation, the "anointed" will therefore represent both the king in Habakkuk's own time and the Christ whose sufferings and glory the prophets predicted (1 Peter 1:10–12). In the same way, the oppressive "leader" must be identified in terms of Israel's history both before and after the Exodus, as evidenced particularly by the words like "crushed" and "leader," vocabulary consistently applied to Israel's conquests from earlier times to the eschaton (Num 24:8, 17–19; Deut 33:11; Pss 18:38; 68:21, 23; 110:5–6; cf. Judg 5:26).

Despite the Exodus overtones in the chapter and the obvious contextual reference to Babylon (already identified as "wicked," 1:13), the "adversary" here cannot be limited historically any more than the one he opposes. The destruction of this enemy is specified in the final line by a complex metaphor, based on the image of a house razed to its "foundations"—this being the usual translation of "foot" (*yᵉsôḏ;* cf. Exod 29:12; 2 Chron 23:5; Job 4:19; Lam 4:11; Ezek 13:14; 30:4; Mic 1:6), anticipated already in the preceding noun "land," or "house." The metaphor establishes further associations with Babylon as with Egypt as the wicked house (cf. 2:9–13): the past devastation of Egypt and future destruction of Babylon foreshadow that of Israel's final enemies.

14 This devastation is elaborated further here, the verb "pierced" echoing a meaning of "crushed," and the noun "head" being identical to "leader." It is accomplished by turning the enemy's "spear," or "weapons," against himself (*maṭṭāyw;* cf. v.9). This is reminiscent of the overthrow of Pharaoh's horses and chariots (cf. Exod 14:24–25, and it also represents a fitting judgment on the Babylonians. Indeed, Babylon fell to Cyrus without opposition, its "leader" being betrayed by factions among his own subjects (IDB, 1:335; 2:494–95; cf. Dan 5). The scene described in the following lines is similarly evocative of the Exodus, in the Egyptians' pursuit of the slaves whom they had afflicted (e.g., Exod 14:3–10). It also recalls the description of the Babylonians' rapacity in the preceding chapters (e.g., "stormed," 1:9, 11;

"gloating," 1:15–16; "devour," 1:8, 13–17; 2:5). This victory is wrought on behalf of the "wretched," or "humble," "afflicted" (*ʿānî;* cf. TWOT, 2:682ff.). The adjective denotes a condition of material or spiritual poverty; such affliction is caused predominantly by unjust oppression, but the cognate verb (*ʿānāh*) is also associated with chastening for sin. Both associations—of oppression and sin—are appropriate to the Israel of Habakkuk's time (cf. 1:2–4, 12–17; 2:4–5): the salvation promised by the covenant presupposed the judgment demanded by the covenant (Deut 28–32), and both would be worked out in the furnace of "affliction" (Isa 48:10).

15 Verse 15 reverts again to the language of v.8 (i.e., "sea," "your horses"), thereby defining vv.8–15 as a unit and establishing the historical context of the intervening verses; the phrase "great waters" represents a further allusion to the Exodus from Egypt (*mayim rabbîm;* cf. Ps 77:19; cf. Exod 15:10).

4. *Response*

3:16–19a

16 I heard and my heart pounded,
my lips quivered at the sound;
decay crept into my bones,
and my legs trembled.
Yet I will wait patiently for the day of calamity
to come on the nation invading us.
17 Though the fig tree does not bud
and there are no grapes on the vines,
though the olive crop fails
and the fields produce no food,
though there are no sheep in the pen
and no cattle in the stalls,
18 yet I will rejoice in the LORD,
I will be joyful in God my Savior.

19 The Sovereign LORD is my strength;
he makes my feet like the feet of a deer,
he enables me to go on the heights.

16 As noted in the excursus, this verse corresponds closely to v.2. The term "heart" (*beṭen*) is applied in literal usage to the lower abdomen, particularly the womb or belly (e.g., Gen 25:23–24; Num 5:21–22, 27; Judg 3:21–22; Hos 12:3); as the seat of conception, it is used figuratively of the innermost thoughts and motives of man (e.g., Job 15:2, 35; 32:18–19; Prov 18:8; 20:27, 30; 22:18). As evidenced by the additional anatomical terms, the prophet was shaken and disabled throughout his being—he was not exempted from the turmoil that pervades and characterizes the chapter.

The verb "pounded" echoes the same root in vv.2, 7 (*rgz*), and it occurs again in the following line ("trembled"). The conspicuous repetitions of this root indicate the cause of Habakkuk's inward upheaval: it was occasioned by the imminence of God's "wrath" on Israel (v.2) and, more acutely, by the uncertainty of any time-frame that accompanies the subsequent judgment on the enemy. This is corroborated by the final, explanatory lines, whose introductory words might be translated more plausibly "because I must wait" (so ASV). These lines anticipate a "nation invading us" as instruments of that "wrath" (cf. Deut 32:15–33)—"a ruthless and impetuous people, . . . bent on violence" (1:6, 9), with fearful consequences for Israel (so ASV; cf. 1:5–11). They also anticipate for that nation its own "day of calamity" (cf. Deut 32:34–43). The phrase implies great pressure and distress from which only the living God can give effective deliverance; for Babylon whose own strength was its god (1:11), no such deliverance would be forthcoming (cf. Ps 18:41). For Habakkuk to see such things that were veiled to his contemporaries was to experience distress (cf. 1:5). To see beyond them, to the Holy One who appointed them, was to demonstrate the greatness of faith and to find strength to "wait quietly" (cf. 1:12; 2:2–4; 3:18–19).

17 The nouns used in this verse represent the bases of Israel's agricultural economy. Her prosperity was dependent on the nation's obedience to the covenant and on the Lord's consequent blessing (Lev 26:3–5, 10; Deut 28:2–14). Such prosperity was forfeited by disobedience and disloyalty to the covenant, which incurred the Lord's chastening through natural and military disasters (Lev 26:14–33; Deut 28:16–17, 22–24, 30–31, 38–42; cf. Deut 11:16–17; Isa 7:23–25; Hos 2:12; Joel 1:7–12; Amos 4:6–9; Hag 1:6–11; 2:16–19). In this vision of a devastated economy, Habakkuk acknowledged his nation's apostasy and the inevitability of judgment (cf. 1:2–4, 12; 3:2, 16).

18 The faith demonstrated in v.16 reaches full expression in this verse. The parallel verbs affirming Habakkuk's joy frequently reveal the psalmists' confidence and assurance of things hoped for (*'ālaz*, "rejoice"; *gîl*, "be joyful"; e.g., Pss 13:5; 16:8–10; 21:1, 6–7; 31:6–7; 32:10–11; cf. Isa 25:9; Joel 2:21, 23)—a confidence characteristic even in the lament form underlying this chapter (cf. Pss 6:8–10; 7:17; 28:6–7; 31:7; 35:9; 42:5, 11; 55:23; 56:3–4, 10–13; 61:8; 130:5–8; 140:12–13). For Habakkuk as for the psalmists, it was "God" himself and his intervention as "Savior" (*yēša'*) that motivated his longing and his joyful attaining. The Babylonians, by contrast, "gloat" (*'ālaṣ*, v.14) to "devour the wretched" (v.14) and "rejoice" (*gîl*, 1:15) over their prey: their god was, in truth, their stomach; and their destiny was destruction. The basis of Habakkuk's faith, as of Paul's, was the revealed word of God (cf. Rom 10:17). The covenant that promised the invasion and devastation of vv.16–17 also gave assurance of restoration to God's favor and presence (cf. Deut 30:1–10; 32:34–43); it was for this joy set before him that Habakkuk could set his face to confront and endure the intervening affliction.

19a This verse is clearly dependent on Psalm 18, in its affirmation of God-given "strength" (*ḥayil;* cf. Ps 18:32, 39) and most notably in the following two lines (cf. Ps 18:33): the image of "the feet of a deer, . . . on the heights" is found only in these two passages and in 2 Samuel 22 (v.34), which is parallel to Psalm 18. However, the phrase "go on the heights" (*dārak 'al bāmôṯ*) is anticipated in Deuteronomy 33:29, which itself echoes Deuteronomy 32:13 (cf. Isa 58:14; Amos 4:13; Mic 1:3). Both passages envisage Israel's conquest and possession of the Promised Land; the same background clearly informs this verse, in view of the extensive correlations in theme and language of Habakkuk 3 and Psalm 18 with Deuteronomy 32–33 (cf. excursus). Similarly, the reference to "strength" echoes the Song of Moses underlying this chapter (*ʿōz,* Exod 15:2, 13). These allusions to Exodus 15 and particularly to Deuteronomy 33:29 are corroborated by the note of praise and the reference to God as "Savior" in v. 18 (cf. Exod 15:1–2; Deut 33:26, 29), so emphasizing the covenantal framework to Habakkuk's faith. Like the "deer" in its resilience, grace, and vigor, that faith draws its life from God's providence; like the armies of Israel on the "high places" or "heights" (*bāmôṯ;* cf. Deut 33:29; TWOT, 1:113), it lives only by its settled hostility to every enemy and counterfeit of that providence. This chapter is thus framed by the same initial and concluding emphases as Deuteronomy 33 (cf. Hab 3:3; Deut 33:2). It thereby constitutes a remarkable statement of faith in God's "blessing" (Deut 33:1), in the very midst of disaster; Habakkuk himself stands as a noble example of the prophetic witness to a God who puts to death and who brings to life.

5. *Epilogue*

3:19b

For the director of music. On my stringed instruments.

19b The final line of the prophecy forms an editorial conclusion to chapter 3, expressed in the language of the Psalms. The word "director of music" (*m^enaṣṣēah;* cf. TWOT, 2:593) is associated with supervisory authority, particularly of the Levites in relation to the music of the temple service (1 Chron 15:21; 23:4; 2 Chron 2:2, 18; 34:12–13; Ezra 3:8–9). It is therefore translated in these terms in the Psalms, where it predominates (fifty-five times; e.g., Pss 4–6, 8–9, 11–14, 18–22, 39–42, 44–47, 51–62, 64–70). These musical connotations are reinforced by the following noun, "stringed instruments" (*n^egînôṯ*), which is translated "song" or "music" in common usage (cf. Job 30:9; Pss 69:12; 77:6; Lam 3:14; 5:14). The phrase recurs as a technical term, with minor variations, in the title of Psalms 4, 6, 54–55, 61, 67, 76; and it resembles similar notations in the Psalms introduced by the preposition "on" (*ʿal;* cf. 3:1).

ZEPHANIAH

Larry Lee Walker

ZEPHANIAH

Introduction

1. Author

As far back as the early church fathers, the etymology of Zephaniah's name was disputed. One explanation understood the name to contain the root *ṣāpan* ("to hide, shelter"). This etymology plus the common theophoric suffix *yāh* (for Yahweh) gives the meaning "Yah(weh) has hidden." This root is also linked with the theophoric element *El* ("God") in Elizaphan (Num 34:25) and Elzaphan (Exod 6:22; Lev 10:4).

Another suggestion derives the name "Zephaniah" from the root *ṣāpāh* ("to watch") plus the common theophoric suffix *yāh*; thus the name signifies something like "Watchman for the LORD." In this case the Hebrew letter nun (*n*) is explained as a paragogic nun, such as in the name "Samson" (*šimšôn*), from the root *šemeš* ("sun").

In unusual fashion the author traced his ancestry back four generations to Hezekiah (KJV, "Hizkiah"; variations in the spelling of this Hebrew name pose no problem). It has been commonly accepted that this Hezekiah was no less than the famous Judean king. This is not at all certain, however; and we have no other proof of any royal status for Zephaniah, despite the unusual mention of his great-great-grandfather. Although genealogies are frequent in the OT, only Zephaniah among the prophetic books exhibits a lengthy genealogical note about the author. On the other hand, some scholars argue that since the words "king of Judah" are not added to Hezekiah's name, the reference is not to King Hezekiah. Others explain this omission on the ground that "king of Judah" follows immediately after Josiah's name. We simply lack conclusive evidence to this interesting question.

Three other men bore the name Zephaniah in the OT: a Levite descended from Kohath (1 Chron 6:36–38); the second priest under the high priest Seraiah during the reign of King Zedekiah (2 Kings 25:18–21; Jer 52:24–27); and the father of Josiah, an exile who returned from Babylon (Zech 6:10, 14).

2. Date

The opening statement of the book indicates that Zephaniah prophesied "during the reign of Josiah son of Amon king of Judah" (640–609 B.C.). Zephaniah predicted the destruction of Nineveh (2:13–15), which took place in 612 B.C. The only point open for discussion is whether his prophecy belonged to the earlier or to the later part of Josiah's reign. Some commentators suppose that Zephaniah wrote at a time prior to any reformation attempted by Josiah; others assume that the predominance of idolatry had already been broken by the time of Zephaniah's ministry.

The reference to the "remnant of Baal" (1:4) is a key passage for many commentators in dating the book. They assume this statement reflects a time when Baalism had already been generally destroyed and only a "remnant" yet remained. But others respond that this is assuming too much. They argue that the point the prophet made was only that eventually all Baalism would be exterminated and that this had nothing to do with the amount of Baal worship during Zephaniah's ministry.

Another reference used to argue for the later date is 1:12: "those who are complacent, who are like wine left on its dregs." Hyatt believes this indicates the disappointment in the reformation of Josiah. The people who had endeavored to live up to the demands of the reforms had seen their dream of a reunited state crushed. But this interpretation is by no means certain.

Those who argue for a prereformation date (e.g., Eissfeldt) point out references to the star worship (from Assyria?) and vestiges of Canaanite worship (1:4–5), foreign dress (1:8), false prophets and priests (3:4), and the widespread injustice and violence among the civic leaders (3:2–3). But it is possible that Josiah's reforms were more superficial than we realize, and perhaps much idolatry remained. Moreover, Zephaniah seems to represent the condition of the people as a final one—doomed to judgment.

Another line of reasoning (cf. Kleinert and Elliot) finds frequent allusions to Deuteronomy (1:13, 15, 17; 2:2, 5, 7, 11; 3:5, 19–20). This could take place, it is argued, only after the rediscovery of the Book of the Law. This law seems to have come already into public use, and it was violated by the priests (3:4). Zephaniah apparently made no explicit reference to Josiah's reforms, and we can only make certain assumptions concerning the relationship of Zephaniah to the reforms of Josiah.

3. Political Background

After the wicked reigns of Manasseh (695–642 B.C.) and Amon (642–640 B.C.), the reformer king Josiah (640–609 B.C.) ascended the throne. For more than a half-century, during the reigns of his predecessors, apostate conditions had prevailed. It was during Josiah's reign that Zephaniah began warning the people of impending judgment. The Fall of Samaria in 722 B.C. had been a solemn reminder of God's justice and power.

Manasseh and Amon had remained loyal vassals to Assyria, but under Josiah independence was experienced. The death of Ashurbanipal, king of Assyria (669–633 B.C.), probably coincided with Josiah's eighth year (2 Chron 34:30), a time perhaps of Assyrian policy change. At any rate, by the time Josiah was of age (628 B.C.),

Ashurbanipal's son, the short-lived Ashur-etil-ilani (633–622 B.C.), had died; and Assyria was facing problems with Babylon at home and was no longer able to retain effective control in the west. Presumably it was about this time that Josiah launched sweeping reforms and moved to take possession of the provinces into which Assyria had divided the territory of northern Israel.

4. Religious Background

The message of Zephaniah, along with the early discourses of Jeremiah and the history recorded in 2 Kings 21–23, pictures the social, moral, and religious conditions in Judah at that time.

The reforms of Josiah certainly included a purge of foreign cults and practices. Undoubtedly heading the list for destruction were Assyrian religious practices, since Assyrian power was slipping. Various astral deities and old Canaanite practices were removed (2 Kings 23:4–25). Cult personnel—including prostitutes of both sexes—were done away with. The shrines of the north and their personnel—especially the rival temple of Bethel—were destroyed. Probably Josiah's most noteworthy reform policy was the centralization of worship in Jerusalem.

The precise relationship of Zephaniah to the reforms of Josiah has challenged commentators and students of this era. If Zephaniah preached after the reforms of Josiah, it appears that these reforms did not change society completely. Social injustice was widespread (3:1, 3, 7), and luxury was enjoyed by some through oppressing the poor (1:8–9). Remnants of Baalism were still present, and high places flourished (1:4–5). Duplicity and syncretism were reflected in the recognition of both the Lord and Molech (1:5).

5. Message

The focal point of Zephaniah's message is the "day of the LORD." Zephaniah used the expression more often than any other prophet. The day "is near" (1:7, 14); it is a day of "wrath, . . . distress and anguish, . . . trouble and ruin, . . . darkness and gloom, . . . clouds and blackness, . . . and battle cry" (1:15–16). The Day of the Lord is a day of doom! The prophet declared this was because "they have sinned against the LORD" (1:17), but he also held out a promise of shelter for those who sought the Lord (2:3).

In the first chapter Zephaniah centered this word of judgment on Judah; in the second chapter, after an exhortation to repentance, he predicted and pronounced judgment on Philistia, Moab, Ammon, Cush, and Assyria, neighbors of Judah; in the last chapter, after a word concerning judgment on Jerusalem, he promised future glory for Israel's remnant.

It has been observed that the Book of Zephaniah serves as a compendium of the oracles of the prophets. In many ways Zephaniah linked his prophecy to those of the earlier prophets, both in subject matter and in expression. In repeating and summarizing much of the judgment and salvation material common to all the prophets, he did not hesitate to use distinctive expressions found in his predecessors. "Be silent before the Sovereign LORD" (1:7) is found in Habakkuk 2:20; "the day of the LORD is near" (1:7) is found in Joel 1:15; and "the LORD has prepared a sacrifice" (1:7) is found in Isaiah 34:6. For additional examples compare 2:14 with Isaiah 13:21; 34:11, and 2:15 with Isaiah 47:8.

6. Style

Although not as majestic as Isaiah, the language of Zephaniah is graphic. The verses sometimes form a series of vivid sketches, as in chapter 1, where the peculiarities of Canaanite ritual are sharply delineated.

Zephaniah's style is chiefly characterized by a unity and harmony of composition plus energy of style. Rapid and effective alternations of threats and promises also characterize his style. As noted above, there are similarities of style between Zephaniah and other prophets; but we cannot be certain whether these are cases of borrowing or cases of coincidence due to common expressions or proverbial language. The prophets had much in common, including expressions, some of which—like the notable Hebrew parallelisms—can be traced back to Canaanite religious writings.

7. Special Problems

Criticism of the Book of Zephaniah is limited and of little weight. Some assume it was assembled piecemeal from various periods. Eissfeldt (p. 425) would deny to Zephaniah certain exilic or postexilic additions. Some critics would claim the oracle against Moab and Ammon (2:8–11) is late because its language reflects conditions of the Exile. Some take the account of the Fall of Nineveh (2:15) as being added after the event had taken place. But such negative assessments are very subjective.

Smith and Lacheman explain the whole book as a pseudepigraphon compiled about 200 B.C.! Hyatt places Zephaniah's activity two or three decades later under Jehoiakim (609–597). Generally speaking, however, critics have not labored over the authenticity and genuineness of this small book.

Some discussion has been evoked about whether Zephaniah has reference to a Scythian invasion of Palestine between 630 and 625. This is based on a reference in Herodotus (1.103–6) but is quite uncertain and has not been widely accepted.

Despite George Adam Smith's comment that "the text is very damaged" (p. 35), the text is in relatively good condition; and the LXX exhibits about the same general features as found with some of the other minor prophets.

8. Bibliography

Books

Calvin, John. *The Minor Prophets*. Vol. 6. Calvin's Commentaries. Grand Rapids: Associated Publishers and Authors, n.d.

Davidson, A.B. *The Books of Nahum, Habakkuk, and Zephaniah*. Cambridge: Cambridge University Press, 1899.

Driver, S.R. *Minor Prophets II*. NCB. London: Oliphants, 1906.

______. *An Introduction to the Literature of the Old Testament*. New York: Scribner's Sons, 1910.

Eiselen, F.C. "Zephaniah." Vol. 5. *International Standard Bible Encyclopedia*. Edited by J. Orr. Grand Rapids: Eerdmans, 1974, pp. 3144-46.
Ehrlich, A.B. *Randglossen zur hebräischen Bibel*. Bd. 5. Ezekiel und die kleinen Propheten. Hildeheim: Georg Olms Verlagsbuchhandlung, 1968.
Eissfeldt, Otto. *The Old Testament: An Introduction*. Translated by P.R. Ackroyd. New York: Harper and Row, 1965.
Feinberg, Charles L. *The Minor Prophets*. Chicago: Moody, 1976.
Foster, Luther. *Jehovah's Message According to Zephaniah*. Fort Worth, Tex.: Southwestern Baptist Theological Seminary, 1932.
Gerleman, G. *Zephania textkritisch und literaisch untersucht*. Lund: C.W.K. Gleerup, 1942.
Hailey, Homer. *A Commentary on the Minor Prophets*. Grand Rapids: Baker, 1972.
Johnson, Roy Lee. *The Message of Zephaniah*. Fort Worth, Tex.: Southwestern Baptist Theological Seminary, 1927.
Kapelrud, Arvid S. *The Message of the Prophet Zephaniah*. Oslo-Bergen-Troms: Universitetsforlaget, 1975.
Keil, C.F. *The Twelve Minor Prophets*. Vol. 2. Biblical Commentary on the Old Testament. KD. Grand Rapids: Eerdmans, 1949.
Kleinert, P. and Elliot, C. *Commentary on the Holy Scriptures: Minor Prophets*. Edited by John Peter Lange. Grand Rapids: Zondervan, n.d.
Laetsch, T. *The Minor Prophets*. St. Louis: Concordia, 1956.
Peiffer, R.F. *Introduction to the Old Testament*. New York: Harper and Brothers, 1941.
Pusey, E.B. *The Minor Prophets*. Vol. 2. *Barnes Notes on the Old Testament*. Edited by Albert Barnes et al. Grand Rapids: Baker, 1966.
Robert, A., and Feuillet, A. *Introduction to the Old Testament*. Translated by P.W. Skehan et al. New York: Desclee, 1968.
Sabottka, Lindger. *Zephania*. Rome: Biblical Institute Press, 1972.
Sellin, Ernest. *Introduction to the Old Testament*. Revised by Georg Fohrer and translated by David E. Green. Nashville: Abingdon, 1968.
Smith, George Adam. *The Twelve Prophets*. New York: A.C. Armstrong and Son, 1901.
Smith, J.M. Powis, and Fagnani, Charles B. *A Critical and Exegetical Commentary on Micah, Zephaniah, Nahum, Habakkuk, Obadiah and Joel*. ICC. Edited by S.R. Driver and C.A. Briggs. Edinburgh: T. & T. Clark, 1965.
Taylor, C.L. "The Book of Zephaniah." *Interpreter's Bible*. Vol. 6. New York: Abingdon, 1956, pp. 1005–34.
Zandstra, Sidney. *The Witness of the Vulgate, Peshitta, and Septuagint to the Text of Zephaniah*. New York: Columbia University Press, 1909.

Periodicals

Cazellelles, H. "Sophonie Jeremie, et les Scythes in Palestine." *Revue Biblique* 74 (1964): 24–44.
Heller, J. "Zephanjas Ahnenreihe." *Vetus Testamentum* 21 (1971):102–4.
Hyatt, J.P. "The Date and Background of Zephaniah." *Journal of Near Eastern Studies* 7 (1948):25–29.
Lipínski, E. "Recherches sur le livre de Zacharie." *Vetus Testamentum* 20 (1970):25–55.
Smith, L.P., and Lacheman, E.L. "The Authorship of the Book." *Journal of Near Eastern Studies* 9 (1950):137–42.
Stengel, M. "Zum Verständnis von Zeph. III 3b." *Vetus Testamentum* 1 (1951):303–5.
Thomas, Winton. "A Pun on the Name of Ashdod in Zephaniah 2:4." *Expository Times* 74 (1962–63):63.
Von Rad, G. "The Origin of the Concept of the Day of Yahweh." *Journal of Semitic Studies* 4 (1959):97–108.
Williams, D.L. "The Date of Zephaniah." *Journal of Biblical Literature* 82 (1963):77–78.

Unpublished Works

Edens, A. "A Study of the Book of Zephaniah as to the Date, Extent and Significance of the Genuine Writings with a Translation." Ph.D. dissertation, Vanderbilt University, 1954.

Williams, D.L. "Zephaniah: A Re-interpretation." Ph.D. dissertation, Duke University, 1961.

9. Outline

- I. Introduction (1:1)
- II. Day of Judgment (1:2–3:8)
  - A. Against Judah (1:2–2:3)
    - 1. General warning (1:2–3)
    - 2. Judgment for Judah (1:4–13)
    - 3. Description of that day (1:14–2:3)
  - B. Against Gentiles (2:4–15)
    - 1. Philistia (2:4–7)
    - 2. Moab and Ammon (2:8–11)
    - 3. Cush (2:12)
    - 4. Assyria (2:13–15)
  - C. Against Jerusalem (3:1–8)
- III. Day of Joy (3:9–20)
  - A. Return of a Scattered People (3:9–10)
  - B. Restoration of a Sinful People (3:11–13)
  - C. Rejoicing of a Saved People (3:14–20)

Text and Exposition

I. Introduction

1:1

> [1]The word of the LORD that came to Zephaniah son of Cushi, the son of Gedaliah, the son of Amariah, the son of Hezekiah, during the reign of Josiah son of Amon king of Judah:

1 For the meaning of the prophet's name, see the Introduction. The author gave us more information about his ancestry than any other prophet, tracing his pedigree back four generations. Perhaps this was because the good king Hezekiah was his great-great-grandfather. The time of the prophecy was during the reign of Josiah king of Judah (see Introduction).

II. Day of Judgment (1:2–3:8)

Like the other prophets, Zephaniah commenced with words of judgment and concluded with words of hope and salvation. The first part of his book (1:2–3:8) contains words of retribution and a description of desolation; the last part (3:9–20) contains words of redemption and a description of deliverance.

A. *Against Judah* (1:2–2:3)

1. *General warning*

1:2–3

> [2]"I will sweep away everything
> from the face of the earth,"
> declares the LORD.
>
> [3]"I will sweep away both men and animals;
> I will sweep away the birds of the air
> and the fish of the sea.
> The wicked will have only heaps of rubble
> when I cut off man from the face of the earth,"
> declares the LORD.

2 Before he focused attention on Judah, Zephaniah issued a general warning of coming destruction in broad terminology. God is judge of the whole world and especially of his people, Judah. The expression "face of the earth" (*pᵉnê hāʾăḏāmāh*), used of the great Deluge of Noah's time (Gen 6:7; 7:4), refers to more than just a local land, unless a specific limitation is added.

3 Language that pairs men and animals (sixth day of creation) and birds and fish (fifth day of creation) and prefaces each with "sweep away" vividly sets forth the totality and intensity of destruction.

"The wicked will have only heaps of rubble" is rendered "the stumbling-blocks with the wicked" in KJV and "overthrow the wicked" in RSV and NAB (cf. Notes). The general thrust of the passage, however, indicating thorough destruction, is clear enough.

Notes

2 "Sweep away" (also NEB, JB; cf. KJV, "utterly consume") translates אָסֹף אָסֵף (*'āsōp 'āsēp*). Instead of the expected אֶאֱסֹף (*'e'ᵉsōp*) with the infinitive absolute *'āsōp*, the author wrote *'āsēp*, which has generally been understood as a Hiphil form of סוּף (*sûp*), a root signifying "cease," "come to an end" (cf. CHS, KD, BDB). Keil argued that the two different roots are sufficiently similar in meaning to be used this way (cf. LXX's **ἐκλείψει ἐκλειπέτο** [*ekleipsei ekleipeto*] and Vul.'s *congregans congregabo*, which both reflect the use of cognate roots). Others have suggested various emendations to the text (cf. Sabottka, pp. 5–7) or different roots involved (Smith and Fagnani, p. 191).

3 "The wicked will have only heaps of rubble" translates וְהַמַּכְשֵׁלוֹת אֶת־הָרְשָׁעִים (*wᵉhammakšēlôṯ 'eṯ-hārᵉšā'îm*). LXX omits this phrase. NIV understands *hammakšēlôṯ*, a Hiphil participle of כָּשַׁל (*kāšal*, "stumble"), to mean that which is brought down ("heaps of rubble") and *'ēṯ* as the preposition "with." KJV understood the participle to mean that which causes downfall ("stumbling-blocks") and *'ēṯ* as the sign of the accusative. NIV's marginal note reflects the uncertainty of this phrase.

2. *Judgment for Judah*

1:4–13

4"I will stretch out my hand against Judah
and against all who live in Jerusalem.
I will cut off from this place every remnant of Baal,
the names of the pagan and the idolatrous priests—
5those who bow down on the roofs
to worship the starry host,
those who bow down and swear by the LORD
and who also swear by Molech,
6those who turn back from following the LORD
and neither seek the LORD nor inquire of him.
7Be silent before the Sovereign LORD,
for the day of the LORD is near.
The LORD has prepared a sacrifice;
he has consecrated those he has invited.
8On the day of the LORD's sacrifice
I will punish the princes
and the king's sons
and all those clad
in foreign clothes.
9On that day I will punish
all who avoid stepping on the threshold,
who fill the temple of their gods
with violence and deceit.
10"On that day," declares the LORD,
"a cry will go up from the Fish Gate,
wailing from the New Quarter,
and a loud crash from the hills.

[11]Wail, you who live in the market district;
all your merchants will be wiped out,
all who trade with silver will be ruined.
[12]At that time I will search Jerusalem with lamps
and punish those who are complacent,
who are like wine left on its dregs,
who think, 'The LORD will do nothing,
either good or bad.'
[13]Their wealth will be plundered,
their houses demolished.
They will build houses
but not live in them;
they will plant vineyards
but not drink the wine.

After the opening, universal depiction of judgment, the prophet narrowed his message to the small but special kingdom of Judah. Jerusalem and Judah had been recipients of the special revelation of God; now they would be recipients of his special judgment.

4 When the Lord said he would "stretch out his hand against," he was indicating a special work of punishment (cf. Isa 5:25; 9:12, 17, 21). If we assume that Josiah's reforms had already had some effect at this time, the reference to the "remnant of Baal" would be to the forms of Baal worship still left in the land from Manasseh's detestable institution of it (2 Kings 21:3, 5, 7; 2 Chron 33:3, 7). Josiah destroyed much of this (2 Chron 34:4); but pockets of Baalism still existed, necessitating judgment and eradication.

"Pagan and idolatrous priests" reflects the traces of idolatrous worship that yet remained despite official action against the cult. God intended a judgment that would totally eliminate Baalism. This was fulfilled in Judah by the Babylonian invasion.

5–6 These verses delineate and describe the persons involved in this pagan worship. Roof worship (v.5) provided a clear view of the sky and a good place for altars (cf. Jer 19:13; 32:29). Moses had spoken against worshiping the starry host much earlier (Deut 4:19), but Manasseh and his successors rebelled (2 Kings 21:3, 5; 23:5–6; Jer 7:17–18; 8:2; 44:17–19, 25). Josiah acted against this practice (2 Kings 23:5), but our reference suggests that the evil practice still persisted. The religious syncretism reflected in swearing by the Lord and also by Molech was not new. The deity called Molech is referred to in 1 Kings 11:33 (KJV, "Milcom") and possibly in Amos 5:26 (cf. NIV mg.; KJV, "Molech").

Finally listed are those simply and summarily described as the faithless and indifferent, those who "turn back" and "neither seek the LORD nor inquire of him" (v.6).

7 In view of the doom waiting, the prophet called all to silent attention before the Lord (cf. Hab 2:20). The reason: "The day of the LORD is near." The Day of the Lord in view here is the day of reckoning; it is a term used of God's judgment. Obadiah (v.15) says it is a time when "your deeds will return upon your own head."

"The LORD has prepared [his] sacrifice"—the people of Judah! "He has consecrated" (*hiqdîš*) the despised and dreaded Babylonians as his priests to slay this sacrifice. Isaiah (13:3) also called the Babylonians "holy ones" (*mᵉquddāšāy*) who were summoned by the Lord. Jeremiah (46:10) and Ezekiel (39:17) also referred to the Lord's offering sacrifice in his judgment. When the sinner will not repent and offer himself as a living sacrifice, then he himself becomes the sacrifice and victim of his own sins.

8 The royal leaders ("the princes and the king's sons") who bore chief responsibility were singled out for special notice. They should have led the people in righteousness instead of evil. Those of royal blood bore responsibility for the conditions in Jerusalem. Notice that the "king's sons" and "princes," not God-fearing Josiah, are mentioned—a typical Hebrew poetic parallelism.

"Foreign clothes" seems to refer to dress that imitated or reflected Egyptian or Babylonian styles, indicative of a foreign inclination of the heart. The Lord had made some stipulations about Israelite dress (Num 15:38; Deut 22:11–12). This was to remind the people of the Lord (Num 15:39–40) and to set them apart to him. Any departure was viewed as disobedience and sin, evidencing a wayward attitude.

9 "Stepping on the threshold" may reflect a cultic practice referred to in 1 Samuel 5:5, where we are told that the pagan priests avoided stepping on a defiled or sacrosanct threshold. This practice originated when the head and hands of the Philistine god Dagon broke off and lay there. But more probably this custom would only be observed in temples of Dagon. It appears unlikely that such practice would be transferred to Israelite worship.

A more likely interpretation understands this passage to refer to theft and plunder, which fits in nicely with the following couplet: "fill the temple of their gods with [the results of] violence and deceit." According to this interpretation, the verb should be translated "leap on" (or "over") the threshold, as in the RSV, NAB, and KJV.

10 "That day" refers to the Day of the Lord, the time of great wailing and outcry from the various sections of the city. The Fish Gate was in the north wall, probably near the present Damascus Gate. It is also mentioned in Nehemiah 3:3; 12:39; and 2 Chronicles 33:14. This is the direction the enemy would come from.

The "New Quarter" (lit., "second [town]") was probably near the Fish Gate. According to 2 Kings 22:14, Huldah the prophetess lived there. (The same Hebrew term is translated by the NIV as "Second District" in 2 Kings 22:14 [2 Chron 34:22] and Neh 11:9.)

"The hills" probably refers to those within Jerusalem (Zion, Opel, Moriah), not to the surrounding hills. The "loud crash" vividly depicts the city crashing down on the heads of its inhabitants.

11 "Market district" translates a Hebrew word that remains obscure. It is not clear whether it should be understood as a common noun or a proper noun. In view of the context, it seems to represent the area where merchants gathered. Most commentators identify the site somewhere in the depression of the Tyropean Valley. The choice of the Hebrew word that may mean "mortar" is especially appropriate since God was about to pound his people like grain in a mortar.

12 The older versions that rendered "lamps" as "candles" have inserted an anachronism into our text. The "lamps" were clay oil-lamps commonly used at that time. (Their use for close searching is also found in Luke 15:8.)

The vivid imagery of "wine left on its dregs," also used by Jeremiah (48:11), was proverbial for indifference and callousness, as shown by the parallel: "who are complacent." In making the best wine, the liquid is poured from vessel to vessel, separating the wine from its dregs. If allowed to remain too long on its lees, the wine becomes harsh. So evil men rested complacently on harsh and evil influences and were securely settled in their wicked society. They concluded that the Lord would do "nothing either good or bad," i.e., they denied God's providence, as though he brought about neither blessing nor judgment. The prophetic indictment of complacency is also found in Isaiah 32:9; Ezekiel 30:9; and Amos 6:1.

13 Because of their complacency and impudence, God would bring on the people the curses of the covenant: they would not enjoy their wealth, homes, and vineyards (cf. Lev 26:32–33; Deut 28:30, 39; Amos 5:11; Mic 6:15). The Lord would indeed demonstrate his activity and agency in the world. He would fulfill his promises to his people—for good or bad.

Notes

4 "Chemarim" is a KJV transliteration of the Hebrew כְּמָרִים (*kemārîm*), a term also found in 2 Kings 23:5 ("idolatrous priests," KJV; "pagan priests," NIV) and Hos 10:5 ("idolatrous priests," NIV, KJV). Some lexicons and commentators have suggested the term comes from a root for "black" (from the garments they wore) or from a root for "zealous" (for their fanaticism), but the precise meaning remains uncertain; it is left untranslated in the LXX. Usage in the Bible suggests the reference is to priests of foreign deities. The root seems to be preserved for us in some Canaanite personal names (Sabottka, p. 18). The suggestion that the use of כֹּהֵן (*kōhēn*), the other word for priest here, is a gloss to explain the enigmatic *kemārîm* (Kapelrud, p. 22; Smith and Fagnani, p. 187) is only a guess resulting from frustration over the precise nuance of *kemārîm*. The context indicates apostate or pagan priests are in view here.

5 Molech or Milcom, representing מַלְכָּם (*malkām*) may refer to a Canaanite deity mentioned in various Semitic texts, but the situation is complicated by the fact that מֶלֶךְ (*melek*, "king") is used as an epithet of other deities. Hence, "their king" (as our text could be translated) may refer to Baal (cf. Sabottka, p. 24), whom the Canaanites viewed as their (divine) king. The Lucianic version of the LXX, the Syriac, and the Vulgate support the reading Milkom, the detestable god of the Ammonites (1 Kings 11:5, 33; 2 Kings 23:13).

7 "Be silent" translates הַס (*has*), which is onomatopoetic for "hush!" Less graphic is KJV's "hold thy peace." This vivid interjection with imperative force is only used seven times in the Old Testament, always in noteworthy contexts (e.g., Amos 8:3).

9 The ancient versions do not help much with the difficult expression "stepping on the threshold." The Greek translators seem as much confused as modern translators. The Targum's "all those who walk in the laws of the Philistines" may tie in with the practice reflected in 1 Sam 5:5 (cf. Smith and Fagnani, p. 208).

NIV's rendering of אֲדֹנֵיהֶם (*'adōnêhem*) as "their gods" is a breaking-with-the-traditional rendering of "their masters" (KJV, RSV). The traditional understanding takes the context and terminology used to indicate the royal palace, not the temple. NIV understands the context as a continuing reference to pagan temples. אָדוֹן (*'ādôn*, "lord," "master") is frequently used in the Semitic inscriptions for deity (Sabottka, p. 43). LXX has *κυρίου τοῦ θεοῦ αὐτῶν* (*kyriou tou theou autōn*, "the Lord their God"), but with several variants in the MS witness.

10 "New Quarter" translates מִשְׁנֶה (*mišneh*, lit., "second" [KJV]). Keil understands this as a reference to the second part or district of the city, the lower area, i.e., the newer area.

11 "Market district" translates מַכְתֵּשׁ (*maktēš*). The versions vary: LXX has *τὴν κατακεκομμένην* (*tēn katakekommenēn*, "broken down"); Vulgate, *pilae;* Targum, "by the brook Kidron"; Aquila, Symmachus, and Theodotion have various translations (cf. Smith and Fagnani, p. 209). An educated guess would consider this some area of depression in the geography of Jerusalem, possibly an area noted for commerce. NIV presents the option of a proper noun ("the Mortar") in the margin.

12 הַקֹּפְאִים עַל־שִׁמְרֵיהֶם (*haqqōpeʾîm ʿal-šimrêhem*) is literally "the ones settled on their dregs [lees]," which is basically the way it is handled by the KJV. RSV's "[the men] who are thickening upon their lees" does not communicate much, and LB's "those who sit contented in their sins" captures the idea but misses the imagery. NIV tries to capture the best of both approaches with its somewhat expanded translation. קָפָא (*qāpāʾ*) means "to thicken, congeal, coagulate"; it is used of cheese in Job 10:10. שְׁמָרִים (*šemārîm*) is used of lees also in Ps 75:8; Isa 25:6; and Jer 48:11.

Smith and Fagnani's suggested reading (p. 209) הַשַּׁאֲנַנִּים (*haššaʾanannîm*, "the ones at ease") from the root שׁאן (*šʾn*) is presumptive and lacks textual support.

---

3. *Description of that day*

1:14–2:3

14"The great day of the LORD is near—
near and coming quickly.
Listen! The cry on the day of the LORD will be bitter,
the shouting of the warrior there.
15That day will be a day of wrath,
a day of distress and anguish,
a day of trouble and ruin,
a day of darkness and gloom,
a day of clouds and blackness,
16a day of trumpet and battle cry
against the fortified cities
and against the corner towers.
17I will bring distress on the people
and they will walk like blind men,
because they have sinned against the LORD.
Their blood will be poured out like dust
and their entrails like filth.
18Neither their silver nor their gold
will be able to save them
on the day of the LORD's wrath.
In the fire of his jealousy
the whole world will be consumed,
for he will make a sudden end
of all who live in the earth."

1Gather together, gather together,
O shameful nation,
2before the appointed time arrives
and that day sweeps on like chaff,
before the fierce anger of the LORD comes upon you,
before the day of the LORD's wrath comes upon you.

[3]Seek the LORD, all you humble of the land,
you who do what he commands.
Seek righteousness, seek humility;
perhaps you will be sheltered
on the day of the LORD's anger.

Verses 1:14–2:3 vividly describe the "great day of the LORD." First, the prophet indicated the imminence of that day: "near—near and coming quickly." It was much nearer than the people realized, and it sped toward full realization. Next, the prophet presented the horrors of that awesome day, horrors set forth in a series of typical Hebrew lines of poetic parallelism.

14 The Day of the Lord is called "great," as it is also described in Joel 2:11 ("the day of the LORD is great"). More significantly, this great day hung over the people like the famous sword of Damocles; it was right at hand, certain, and hastening to its goal.

The use of *qôl* ("Listen!") as an interjection is also found in Isaiah 13:4. "Listen!" implies a "sound" or "noise" to be heard, hence NIV's expansion: "Listen! the cry." RSV also captures the parallelism of the Hebrew, but without the double translation of *qôl*: "The sound of the day of the LORD is bitter, the mighty man cries aloud there."

15 The "stacking" of vividly descriptive lines is designed to drive home the dreadful character of the great day of the Lord. First, its stressful conditions are reflected in the words "distress," "anguish," "trouble," and "ruin." Then its ominous conditions are depicted by the use of such words as "darkness," "gloom," "clouds," and "blackness." Luther mentioned that the passage was often chanted by the Roman Catholic priests at funeral Masses. This passage in the Vulgate forms the first line of the medieval sequence *Dies irae* ("day of wrath").

16 The stark description continues so vividly that one feels he is present at the battle, seeing the clouds of smoke billowing upward and hearing the trumpet blasts from various parts of the city.

17 The prophet again brought in his cause-effect observation: this deep distress was "because they have sinned against the LORD." The judgment the people would experience would cause them to stagger and stumble like blind men (cf. Deut 28:29). In addition, their life and entrails would be spilled out like dust and refuse to be trampled underfoot by their enemy. God was against them.

18 To emphasize their desperate plight, the prophet warned the people that they could not buy their way out. Neither silver nor gold would protect them from the wrath of the Lord. This section closes with the universal terminology—"all who live in the earth." It started with v.3—"man from the face of the earth."

2:1 The prophet continued his description of the Day of the Lord (cf. v.2) but added an admonition to "seek the LORD" (v.3) and to "seek righteousness." Verse 1 opens with the invitation to "gather together" (emphasized by the double use of the verb *qāšaš*) and includes a derogatory note, as reflected in the term "shameful nation."

The verb *qāšaš* is used for the gathering of stubble or sticks for burning (cf. 1 Kings 17:10, 12).

2 The "appointed time" refers to the Day of the Lord, the time of his giving vent to his holy wrath. The gathering together (in repentance) must take place before the judgment if it is to be averted. The reference to "chaff" indicates that the wicked nation would be scattered before the fierce anger of the Lord, as chaff is scattered before the wind.

3 Repentance must be manifested in works: seeking the Lord and doing what he commands. The "humble" are to "seek the LORD," which is defined in the same verse as seeking righteousness and humility. Only the "humble of the land" are exhorted because nothing can be done with the rest. (The expression "humble of the earth" is also found in Job 24:4; Ps 76:9; Isa 11:4; Amos 8:4; though translated in a variety of ways by NIV.) "Seeking the LORD" is essential to escape from judgment, but even with this the prophet said only, "Perhaps you will be sheltered."

Notes

15 יוֹם שֹׁאָה וּמְשׁוֹאָה (*yôm šō'āh ûmešô'āh,* "a day of trouble and ruin") is an example of assonance in Hebrew (cf. the same combination in Job 38:27).

16 "Corner towers" translates הַפִּנּוֹת הַגְּבֹהוֹת (*happinnôṯ haggebōhôṯ*). KJV's "high towers" and RSV's "lofty battlements" understand *happinnôṯ* as a general word for a fortified and strategic tower. Although the first word literally means "corner," it probably referred to towers at various "angles" in the wall.

17 "People" (KJV, "men") for אָדָם (*'āḏām*) is not an unusual translation for this word that often means "mankind." For stylistic reasons NIV's "people" is a good parallel with the next line's "men."

"Entrails" for לְחֻם (*leḥum*) is uncertain. In other contexts it refers to "body" or "flesh." The parallel lines in this couplet support NIV's translation.

גְּלָלִים (*gelālîm,* "filth") is the common Hebrew term for "dung" (cf. KJV).

18 כָּל־הָאָרֶץ (*kol-hā'āreṣ*), properly translated "whole world," refers back to vv.2–3 "face of the earth"—where undoubtedly the whole world is intended.

2:1 הִתְקוֹשְׁשׁוּ וָקוֹשּׁוּ (*hiṯqôšešû wāqôššû*) is appropriately rendered "Gather together, gather together," even though two different stems are used; the repetition of the root is probably for emphasis.

"Shameful," a translation of לֹא נִכְסָף (*lō' niḵsāp*), is an old *crux interpretum*. KJV has "not desired" and RSV, "shameless." The ancient versions reflect confusion about the meaning: "undisciplined" (LXX, Syr.), "unlovable" (Vul.), "that does not desire to be connected to the law" (Targ.) (cf. Smith and Fagnani, p. 212).

2 "Before the appointed time arrives" translates בְּטֶרֶם לֶדֶת חֹק (*beṭerem leḏeṯ ḥōq*); KJV renders "before the decree bring forth," but RSV follows the Greek Syriac: "before you are driven away." The MT reads literally "before a decree is born," which means "before that which has been decreed takes place."

לֹא (*lō'*) as a strengthening particle was already noted by Keil (p. 139); Ugaritic used a prefixed ל (*l*) with the imperfect for emphasis.

אַף (*'ap,* "anger") is found twice in this couplet, as reflected in KJV. For stylistic reasons, apparently, the NIV translated it once as "anger" (when modified by "fierce") and once as "wrath."

B. *Against Gentiles* (2:4–15)

Representative nations from the four points of the compass were selected for indictment: Philistia (west), Moab and Ammon (east), Cush (south), and Assyria (north).

1. *Philistia*

2:4–7

> 4Gaza will be abandoned
> and Ashkelon left in ruins.
> At midday Ashdod will be emptied
> and Ekron uprooted.
> 5Woe to you who live by the sea,
> O Kerethite people;
> the word of the LORD is against you,
> O Canaan, land of the Philistines.
>
> "I will destroy you,
> and none will be left."
>
> 6The land by the sea, where the Kerethites dwell,
> will be a place for shepherds and sheep pens.
> 7It will belong to the remnant of the house of Judah;
> there they will find pleasure.
> In the evening they will lie down
> in the houses of Ashkelon.
> The LORD their God will care for them;
> he will restore their fortunes.

4 The four cities—Gaza, Ashkelon, Ashdod, Ekron—represented the entire area of Philistia. As in Amos 1:6–8 and Zechariah 9:5–7, Gath is not named among the group. Gaza and Ashkelon are summarily dismissed in judgment by a typical Hebrew synonymous couplet. Ashdod and Ekron are to be uprooted and emptied at midday—an unusual time since this hottest time is used for siesta in the Orient. Undoubtedly the point being made is that judgment will fall on them when they least expect it.

5 Kerethite is a term used of the Philistines, perhaps originally of one branch of them (cf. Ezek 25:16). David's bodyguard was made up of Kerethites and Pelethites (2 Sam 8:18), usually considered designations for sources or branches of the Philistines.

6–7 The once heavily settled seacoast of the Philistines would become a desolate place for shepherds and sheep pens (v.6). The lowly shepherd would be able to find a place for his sheep to graze where there was no sowing or reaping and where no civilization flourished. Eventually, however, it would be enjoyed and inhabited by the remnant of Judah. A note of hope for Judah is sounded: "The LORD their God will care for them; he will restore their fortunes" (v.7). They will occupy the sites of their former enemy the Philistines. (The alternate reading is "will bring back their captives" [NIV mg.].)

Notes

---

4 Paronomasia, a play on words, is involved with the threat against two cities of Philistia: עַזָּה עֲזוּבָה (*'azzāh 'ᵃzûḇāh*, "Gaza will be abandoned") and וְעֶקְרוֹן תֵּעָקֵר (*wᵉ'eqrôn tē 'āqēr*, "and Ekron uprooted").

5 חֶבֶל הַיָּם (*ḥeḇel hayyām*, "by the sea") occurs again in v.6, where the NIV translates "land by the sea." The word *ḥeḇel* meant "cord" or "measure," then was later applied to the tract of land measured out, or just a tract of land in general.

6 כְּרֹת (*kᵉrōṯ*, rendered "cottages" by KJV and "Kerethites" by NIV) is difficult. Keil (p. 141) suggested it referred to the excavations made by shepherds as they "dig themselves huts under the ground as a protection from the sun." This has been a view popular with many commentators and is based on the root (*krṯ*) meaning "to dig." Others prefer to find here another example of כַּר (*kar*), a word for "pasture" (cf. Isa 30:23, "broad meadow") but its plural form in Pss 37:20; 65:13 is כָּרִים (*kārîm*). RSV understands "meadows"; KJV's "cottages" is unwarranted. NIV's rendering of "Kerethites" is based on the general context—including the occurrence of this word in the preceding verse—and the fact that the LXX has the term in both verses. But this leaves the question of why the term is masculine plural in v.5 but feminine plural in v.6, hence the NIV mg. admitting uncertainty.

7 חֶבֶל (*ḥeḇel*) is reflected in NIV's "it" (NIV sometimes represents a noun—more often a proper noun—with a pronoun).

וְשָׁב שְׁבוּתָם (*wᵉšāḇ šᵉḇiwṯām*, "will restore their fortunes") is an expression in the NIV that normally has the margin giving the alternative reading: "will bring back their captives" (cf. Jer 29:14; Ezek 39:25; Amos 9:14).

---

2. *Moab and Ammon*

2:8–11

8 "I have heard the insults of Moab
and the taunts of the Ammonites,
who insulted my people
and made threats against their land.
9 Therefore, as surely as I live,"
declares the LORD Almighty, the God of Israel,
"surely Moab will become like Sodom,
the Ammonites like Gomorrah—
a place of weeds and salt pits,
a wasteland forever.
The remnant of my people will plunder them;
the survivors of my nation will inherit their land."

10 This is what they will get in return for their pride,
for insulting and mocking the people of the
LORD Almighty.
11 The LORD will be awesome to them
when he destroys all the gods of the land.
The nations on every shore will worship him,
every one in its own land.

8 The encounter with Philistines dates back to the time of the patriarchs (Gen 20–21; 26). The confrontation with Moab goes back to the time of Moses (Num

22–24), followed by later conflicts (Judg 3:12–30; 1 Sam 12:9; 2 Kings 3:5–27; 13:20). Conflicts with Ammon appear in Judges 10:6–11:33; 2 Samuel 10:1–11:1; and Nehemiah 2:10, 19; 4:3, 7. Moab and Ammon are mentioned together in conflict with Israel in Judges 3:13, and 2 Chronicles 24:26 mentions a conspiracy against King David that included an Ammonite and a Moabite. Later, because of the fall of the northern kingdom and the decline of the southern kingdom, the pride of the nations east of Israel increased greatly. They showed their enmity toward God's people on every opportunity. The insults and taunts mentioned here probably refer to the hostility assumed at various times and not to just one particular episode.

9 The comparison of Moab and Ammon to Sodom and Gomorrah is not surprising in view of their origin: Moab and Ammon were the offspring of the incestuous relations of Lot's daughters with their drunk father after he fled the destruction of Sodom and Gomorrah (Gen 19:30–38).

"'Weeds" and "salt pits" reflect desolation and sterility. To this day many rock-strewn ruins of ancient villages in the regions of ancient Moab and Ammon bear mute testimony to the truth of the prophet's words: "a wasteland forever."

Only a remnant of God's people would be needed to plunder these ancient enemies, and only the survivors of Israel would inherit the ancient sites of Moab and Ammon.

10 "Pride" is cited as the sin that led Moab and Ammon to insult and mock the people of God. The pride of Moab is also referred to by Isaiah (16:6) and Jeremiah (48:26).

11 The Lord destroys the gods by destroying the nations that depend on these gods; these deities have no real existence apart from the people who serve them (1 Cor 8:4–6). By revealing the unreal nature of these gods, he brings the nations to acknowledge him as the one true God.

Notes

---

8 וַיַּגְדִּילוּ (*wayyagdîlû*) is one of those graphic expressions in Hebrew: "enlarged (themselves)"; cf. KJV's "magnified" (themselves)." NIV's "made threats" captures the idea.

9 "A place of weeds" translates מִמְשַׁק חָרוּל (*mimšaq ḥārûl*). *Ḥārûl* ("weeds") is attested also in Job 30:7 and Prov 24:31, but *mimšaq* is found only here. The precise meaning remains elusive; some, out of desperation, attempt to find some help from מֶשֶׁק (*mešeq*) in Gen 15:2, but it also is found only once and is uncertain.

---

3. *Cush*

2:12

> 12 "You too, O Cushites,
> will be slain by my sword."

12 Having foretold God's judgment on nations east and west of Judah, Zephaniah next directed attention to nations south and north: Cush and Assyria. The "too" indicates that the Lord would bring Cush to an end just as he would Moab and Ammon.

Cush was located in the upper Nile region (cf. NIV mg.). "Ethiopia" (KJV) is somewhat misleading inasmuch as the boundaries of the two countries were not the same. It seems best, therefore, to transliterate Hebrew *kûš* for this ancient area. (NIV faced the same kind of issue with the terms Syria/Aram.) Since Egypt had been under the rule of Cushite kings for years, the prophet's words probably included Egypt as well.

Nebuchadnezzar was the Lord's sword that slew the Cushites: "I will strengthen the arms of the king of Babylon and put my sword in his hand" (Ezek 30:24–25).

3. *Assyria*

2:13–15

13He will stretch out his hand against the north
and destroy Assyria,
leaving Nineveh utterly desolate
and dry as the desert.
14Flocks and herds will lie down there,
creatures of every kind.
The desert owl and the screech owl
will roost on her columns.
Their calls will echo through the windows,
rubble will be in the doorways,
the beams of cedar will be exposed.
15This is the carefree city
that lived in safety.
She said to herself,
"I am, and there is none besides me."
What a ruin she has become,
a lair for wild beasts!
All who pass by her scoff
and shake their fists.

13 The prophecies against surrounding nations climax with Assyria, the strongest political factor and the most northerly nation of that time. The prediction of Nineveh's utter desolation while that Assyrian capital ruled the world testifies to the divine origin of Zephaniah's message. The prediction that God would leave Nineveh "dry as the desert" is remarkable in view of the fame of the city's great irrigation system.

14 Instead of marching armies and a prosperous population, the prophet predicted that flocks of sheep and goats and all kinds of creatures would be found at Nineveh (cf. v.6). The renowned city would become fit only for herds and wild animals. The "owls" are depicted in another picture of desolation in Isaiah 34:11 (cf. Ps 102:6 [7 MT]). Nineveh's once-magnificent buildings, tumbled into debris, would become dwelling places for various creatures. Only doleful sounds would emerge from the doorways.

15 The city—complacent and carefree at the time of Zephaniah's prediction—would become a lair for wild beasts and an object of contempt for every passerby. She boasted in her self-sufficiency, "I am, and there is none besides me." But the inspired prophet predicted that she would become a ruin and a habitat for the creatures of the fields. This same claim of self-sufficiency is found in reference to Babylon (Isa 47:8) and Laodicea (Rev 3:17).

Notes

14 "Creatures of every kind" translates כָּל־חַיְתוֹ־גוֹי (*kol-ḥayṯô-gôy*). RSV's "all the beasts of the field" is based on the LXX, as the margin indicates. In Joel 1:6 *gôy* is used of a swarm of locusts, a similar usage to what we have here where *gôy* is used of a swarm, pack, crowd of creatures (for other suggestions, see Sabottka, pp. 95–96).

The obvious uncertainty about קִפֹּד ... קָאַת (*qā'aṯ* . . . *qippōḏ*, "desert owl and screech owl," NIV, NAB; "cormorant and bittern," KJV; "pelicans and hedgehogs," Keil, p. 146; "vulture and hedgehog," RSV; "pelican and heron," JB) is reflected in both the ancient and the modern traditions, but the latest information suggests that they were terms for owls (cf. Sabottka, pp. 96–97).

15 אֵיךְ (*'êḵ*) is translated in NIV's "What . . . !" This particle is used to indicate reproach (Judg 16:15), amazement (Isa 44:4), and horror (Ps 73:19) (cf. TWOT, p. 35).

יָנִיעַ יָדוֹ (*yānîaʿ yāḏô*) is translated in various ways: "shake their fists" (NIV, JB; cf. NAB), "wag his hand" (KJV), "swing his hand" (Keil, p. 146). It is difficult to know exactly which emotion is reflected in this gesture. Keil (p. 149) suggests the idea "away with her, she has richly deserved her fate." Nahum 3:19 expresses another hand gesture at the Fall of Nineveh: תָּקְעוּ כַף עָלֶיךָ (*tāqᵉʿû ḵap ʿāleyḵā*, "claps his hands").

C. *Against Jerusalem*

3:1–8

1Woe to the city of oppressors,
  rebellious and defiled!
2She obeys no one,
  she accepts no correction.
She does not trust in the LORD,
  she does not draw near to her God.
3Her officials are roaring lions,
  her rulers are evening wolves,
  who leave nothing for the morning.
4Her prophets are arrogant;
  they are treacherous men.
Her priests profane the sanctuary
  and do violence to the law.
5The LORD within her is righteous;
  he does no wrong.
Morning by morning he dispenses his justice,
  and every new day he does not fail,
  yet the unrighteous know no shame.
6"I have cut off nations;
  their strongholds are demolished.
I have left their streets deserted,
  with no one passing through.
Their cities are destroyed;
  no one will be left—no one at all.

7I said to the city,
'Surely you will fear me
and accept correction!'
Then her dwelling would not be cut off,
nor all my punishments come upon her.
But they were still eager
to act corruptly in all they did.
8Therefore wait for me," declares the LORD,
"for the day I will stand up to testify.
I have decided to assemble the nations,
to gather the kingdoms
and to pour out my wrath on them—
all my fierce anger.
The whole world will be consumed
by the fire of my jealous anger.

1 After the series of judgments against various surrounding nations predicted in chapter 2, the prophet returned to focus on Jerusalem (cf. v.2) and Judah. The guilty city harbored oppressors (those who disregarded the rights of the poor, the orphans, and the widows), rebels (those who refused submission to God's will), and defiled people (those who were polluted by sinful practices). The defiled or polluted people often washed themselves with water and observed other ceremonies of external sanctity, outwardly appearing to be pure; but actually their whole life was defiled (cf. Calvin, p. 770).

2 The continuing indictment of Jerusalem contains three specific charges: (1) she obeyed no one—not even the Lord; (2) she did not trust in the Lord; and (3) she did not draw near to her God, who was the one who could provide direction and guidance for her. The text describes the Lord as "her God."

3–4 Four classes of leaders represent the total leadership of the whole people.

1. "Officials" (*śārîm;* KJV, "princes") possibly represented the royal leaders who should have been characterized by justice and equity rather than greed and avarice.
2. "Rulers" (*šōp^{e}ṭîm;* KJV, "judges") also represented those in places of leadership, probably civil magistrates, who should have set an example for the rest of the people; instead, they are tagged "evening wolves who leave nothing for the morning," a label suggesting predatory and ravenous beasts.
3. "Her prophets" (*n^{e}ḇî'eyhā*) are described as arrogant and treacherous. They are called "treacherous" (unfaithful) because they were unfaithful to the one they claimed to represent.
4. "Her priests" (*kōh^{a}neyha*) represents the other religious leaders; they were profaning the sanctuary and violating the law. Their ordained function was to interpret the law and officiate at the sanctuary with reverence; they had done just the opposite.

5 In contrast to her misleading leaders "within her" (*ḇ^{e}qirbāh,* lit., "in her midst"; so v.3 Heb., untr. in NIV), the Lord in Israel's midst was a righteous standard against which the people were measured. His holy and righteous presence demanded judgment for sin and corruption. He is never implicated with iniquity—"he does no wrong." Moreover, he continuously—"morning by morning"—manifested his justice and righteousness before the people (contrast the evening wolves of v.3) in his treatment of both Israel and the surrounding nations. Despite all this the people were so calloused that they recognized no wickedness or felt no shame for what they had done.

6 As an object lesson, God reminded his people—vividly expressed in the first person—what he did to other nations: They were "cut off" and their strongholds demolished; their streets were left deserted and their cities destroyed. The nations referred to are not specified; so commentators disagree and are left uncertain. Keil (p. 152) says the reference concerns "neither those nations who are threatened with ruin, ch. ii. 4–15, nor the Canaanites, who have been exterminated by Israel, but nations generally, which have succumbed to the judgments of God, without any more precise definition."

7 In view of the judgments mentioned in v.6, the Lord spoke imploringly to his people, "Surely you will fear me and accept correction!" The Lord declared that judgment and punishment could have been averted and avoided. But trapped in the grip of sin, the people "were still eager to act corruptly."

8 We expect the "therefore" (in view of the preceding!) to be followed by a promise to pour out deserved judgment on those wicked people. Instead, the punishment was veiled; they were admonished to "wait for me, . . . for the day I will stand up to testify." This verse also promises a purging and purifying action: The Lord promised "to pour out [his] wrath on them [the assembled nations]—all [his] fierce anger." He continued in strong language: "The whole world will be consumed by the fire of my jealous anger." This is the kind of universal judgment found in 1:2–3.

The last part of v.8 contains graphic words that portray a scene of great prophetic significance. The Lord had determined to gather the nations and kingdoms to pour out on them in great judgment his "wrath" and "fierce anger" and to consume them with "the fire of [his] jealous anger."

Notes

1 The position of the indeterminate predicates מֹרְאָה (*mōr*[e]*'āh*, "rebellious") and נִגְאָלָה (*nig'ālāh*, "defiled") before the subject ("oppressing city") gives them emphasis according to Keil (p. 149). For stylistic reasons NIV and NEB reverse the order. The analysis of *mōr*[e]*'āh* is uncertain (cf. Sabottka, pp. 102–3). The root מָרָא (*mārā'*) seems to refer to "fatness" of grazing. The root מָרַר (*mārar*) is used of "bitterness" or "despair," a meaning that could fit in this context. NIV ("rebellious") takes this as an example of a ל״ה (*l"h*) root treated as ל״א (*l"'*) (cf. GKC, par. 75rr). LXX's ἐπιφανής (*epiphanēs*, "glorious") shows an apparent understanding of the form as a Hophal of the root רָאָה (*rā'āh*, "to see").

3 Israel's leaders are called "lions" also by Ezekiel (19:1–7), who also called them "wolves" (22:27).

KJV's "they gnaw not the bones till the morrow" for לֹא גָרְמוּ לַבֹּקֶר (*lō' gār*[e]*mû labbōqēr*) is misleading, suggesting, not ravenous wolves, but patient wolves, waiting till the next morning to gnaw! This translation also assumes that the verb גָּרַם (*gāram*) is from the noun *gerem* ("bone") and therefore means to "gnaw" or "break" bones (Num 24:8). JB's "they have had nothing to gnaw that morning" follows the same meaning for the verb but also expresses the ravenous character surely intended in this context, a meaning brought out in the NIV rendering. The ancient versions already reflect difficulty with this passage (cf. Smith and Fagnani, pp. 244–45). Recent research has not produced any new light that is decisive (cf. Kapelrud, p. 35).

4 "Arrogant" translates פֹּחֲזִים (*pōḥᵃzîm*). KJV's translation as "light" presumably understands the verb in the sense of "wanton" (cf. RSV, "reckless"). C. Rabin (*Scripta Hierosolymitana* 8 [1961]:398) distinguishes פחז (*pḥz*) I—"to boast" (Judg 9:4 and this passage)—from *pḥz* II—"to scatter" (Gen 49:4; NIV, "turbulent"). The idea of boasting or arrogance is probably to be found in the cognate פַּחֲזוּת (*paḥᵃzûṯ*) in Jer 23:32, though NIV translates it "reckless lies"; NAB's "empty boasting" captures both idea. NIV's translation is based on the meaning of *pḥz* I.

"Treacherous," from the root בגד (*bgd*), is used often to express the idea of unfaithfulness or faithlessness (TWOT, 1:89).

5 "Dispenses" translates יִתֵּן לָאוֹר (*yittēn lā'ôr*). KJV's "bring . . . to light" is a literal translation.

6 "Strongholds" translates פִּנּוֹת (*pinnôṯ*), a word with a basic meaning of "corner" but with a wide range of meaning. Zephaniah earlier (1:16) used it of the tower strongholds.

7 מְעוֹנָהּ (*mᵉ'ônāh*, "her dwelling") was read by LXX as ἐξ ὀφθαλμῶν (*ex ophthalmōn*, "out of sight"), apparently reading the Hebrew as מֵעֵינֶיהָ (*mē 'êneyhā*). This is repeated in the Syriac and the NAB ("[she should not] fail to see") and the JB ("[she cannot] lose sight"); but the MT makes sense in this context, and there is no reason to depart from it.

אָכֵן (*'āḵēn*, "therefore") is sometimes used in a strongly contrastive sense, as here. Also, the eagerness to sin is vividly portrayed in הִשְׁכִּימוּ (*hiškîmû*, "they were still eager"), which KJV renders literally: "they rose early."

הִשְׁחִית (*hišḥîṯ*, "to act corruptly") is intensified by the addition of עֲלִילוֹתָם (*'ᵃlîlôṯām*, "they did"), which usually refers to evil deeds when used of the action of men (cf. TWOT, 2:671).

8 The Masoretes vocalized עד (*'ḏ*) as *'aḏ* ("plunder"); but the LXX, followed by the Syriac, read *'ēḏ* ("witness"). Most of the recent versions (NIV, NAB, NEB, JB) follow the LXX. The NIV margin renders the MT.

"I have decided" translates מִשְׁפָּטִי (*mišpāṭî*). KJV's "my determination" is the idea expressed in most new translations (cf. NAB, NEB, RSV, JB). But this expression is understood by some (e.g., Keil, p. 154) to mean "my justice" (cf. v.5); it is God's justice that is reflected in his treatment of the nations.

Notice the stacking of terms for God's holy justice and wrath in this verse: "wrath" (זַעַם, *za'am*); "fierce anger" (חֲרוֹן אַף, *ḥārôn 'ap*); "jealous anger" (קִנְאָה, *qin' āh*).

The Masoretes noted that this is the only verse in the OT that contains all the letters of the Hebrew alphabet (except for שׂ [*ś*]), including final forms.

III. Day of Joy (3:9–20)

"Then," after the judgment thus described, the Lord will turn to himself a people of "purified lip" and united heart ("shoulder to shoulder"). The following verses describe in glowing terms the promises of blessing and restoration for God's people and the nations.

A. *Return of a Scattered People*

3:9–10

9Then will I purify the lips of the peoples,
  that all of them may call on the name of the LORD
  and serve him shoulder to shoulder.

10 From beyond the rivers of Cush
my worshipers, my scattered people,
will bring me offerings.

9 The scattered people who return (v.10) will bring offerings and experience purification (v.9). They will together call on the name of the Lord and worship and serve him. "Then" refers to the time after the judgment just mentioned. Before the scattering of the people at the tower of Babel, the world was unified by one language; but it was a world of rebellious people. In contrast, the new purified language will characterize a responsive people. The lips or language that had become impure through use in idol worship will become purified so that all may in unison call on the name of the Lord. The reference to lips, the organ of speech, includes the heart behind the language; as Keil noted (p. 156): "Purity of the lips involves or presupposes the purification of the heart."

To "call on the name of the LORD" is to turn to the Lord out of a sense of need (TWOT, 2:810). Again, this kind of language may refer back to the pre-Flood period (cf. Gen 4:26).

"Shoulder to shoulder" is literally "one shoulder" (cf. KJV, NEB, "one consent"; NAB, "one accord"). The expression "one mouth" is ~~used to~~ indicate unanimity in 1 Kings 22:13.

10 Cush, the southern extremity of the known world, represented the southern limits of the judgments in 2:12. "The rivers" presumably indicates the Blue and the White branches of the Nile. (For the identification of Cush, see comment at 2:12.)

Keil (p. 155) translates the latter part of this verse "will they bring my worshippers, the daughter of my dispersed ones, as a meat-offering to me" (cf. also the alternate reading of the ASV). This indicates that the converted Gentiles would attempt to convert and bring wayward Israel as an offering to the Lord. But this is strained; both the old and the new translations understand "my worshipers . . . my scattered people" as the subject and not the object of "bring." Isaiah (11:11; 27:13) also speaks of a remnant returning from such distant places as Cush and Egypt.

Notes

9 "Purify the lips" translates שָׂפָה בְרוּרָה (*śāp̄āh ḇ^{e}rûrāh*), which is literally something like "purified lip," lip representing speech or language. The passive participle *ḇ^{e}rûrāh* suggests something that has become purified and would rule out Luther's interpretation that applied this to God's pure speech.

"Shoulder to shoulder" translates שְׁכֶם אֶחָד (*š^{e}ḵem '^{e}ḥāḏ*, "one shoulder"). Supposedly this expression is derived from the idea of bearers who carry a load with even shoulders. Although this figure does not appear elsewhere in Hebrew, it is attested in Syriac (cf. Smith and Fagnani, p. 248). The LXX, followed by the Syriac, translated *š^{e}ḵem* as "yoke," a translation repeated in JB. A similar expression—"one mouth"—is used to indicate unanimity in 1 Kings 22:13.

10 "My worshipers" represents עֲתָרַי (*ʿatāray*), which KJV rendered "my suppliants." The root עתר (*ʿtr*) is a rare word for prayer or worship, probably related to an Arabic cognate meaning "to sacrifice" (cf. TWOT, 2:708).

"My scattered people" translates בַּת־פּוּצַי (*bat-pûṣay*, lit., "daughter of my dispersed"), a typical Hebraism meaning "my scattered [people]." Of greater question is the syntax of the sentence: NIV (also AV, RSV, NEB, JB) took these two expressions ("my worshipers, my scattered people") as subjects of the verb; but Keil, Luther, Hengstenburg, et al. take them as objects and understand the passage to say that the remote heathen will eventually worship the Lord and be used to convert the scattered Jews (cf. Keil, p. 157).

B. *Restoration of a Sinful People*

3:11–13

11On that day you will not be put to shame
for all the wrongs you have done to me,
because I will remove from this city
those who rejoice in their pride.
Never again will you be haughty
on my holy hill.
12But I will leave within you
the meek and humble,
who trust in the name of the LORD.
13The remnant of Israel will do no wrong;
they will speak no lies,
nor will deceit be found in their mouths.
They will eat and lie down
and no one will make them afraid."

Verses 11–13 describe the future restoration of God's people. God's restoration program includes removal of the proud and haughty from the city (v.11), the presence of the "meek and humble" (v.12), and the promise that "no one will make them afraid" (v.13). This passage goes beyond the promise of return to the promise of glorious restoration. No more will shame, pride, or fear be in their midst. No more will deceit or lies be among them.

11 "That day" refers to the day fulfilling vv.9–10, the time when Israel will be gathered together from the dispersion, as the Daughter of Zion (cf. v.14). They will not be put to shame because the very source of pride and haughtiness will be abolished: intolerable attitudes on "God's holy hill." Mount Zion is made holy by the presence of God.

12 Instead of the haughty, there will be the meek and humble, those "who trust in the name of the LORD." Their confidence and strength is derived from God himself.

13 Further description of this remnant of Israel presents them as free from all deception, duplicity, and deceit, a probable allusion to their former idolatry. In such a spiritual condition, they are fit to experience physical prosperity. The last part of the verse has parallel terminology in Micah 4:4.

Notes

11 "Wrongs" translates עֲלִילוֹת (*ʿalîlôṯ*), a word usually in the plural and applied to both man and God. The deeds of God are good and right, but the *ʿalîlôṯ* of men are wicked (cf. TWOT, 2:671). In addition to this observation, it should be noted that our text uses the verb פָּשַׁע (*pāšaʿ*, "to rebel, sin") with the noun "wrongs." RSV captures the idea: "the deeds by which you have rebelled against me."

12 עָנִי וָדָל (*ʿānî wāḏāl*, "meek and humble") are paired elsewhere (Isa 26:6; Job 34:28) and suggest those who are oppressed or in need. Here they imply words denoting the opposite of proud and haughty (cf. v.11).

13 עַוְלָה (*ʿawlāh*, "wrong") is often used with verbs of action, as here, and indicates the opposite of צְדָקָה/צֶדֶק (*ṣeḏeq*/*ṣᵉḏāqāh*, "right"; cf. TWOT, 2:653).

רָעָה (*rāʿāh*, "eat") and רָבַץ (*rāḇaṣ*, "lie down") are pastoral terms used because of the comparison of the remnant of Israel to a flock.

C. *Rejoicing of a Saved People*

3:14–20

14Sing, O Daughter of Zion;
shout aloud, O Israel!
Be glad and rejoice with all your heart,
O Daughter of Jerusalem!
15The LORD has taken away your punishment,
he has turned back your enemy.
The LORD, the King of Israel, is with you;
never again will you fear any harm.
16On that day they will say to Jerusalem,
"Do not fear, O Zion;
do not let your hands hang limp.
17The LORD your God is with you,
he is mighty to save.
He will take great delight in you,
he will quiet you with his love,
he will rejoice over you with singing."

18"The sorrows for the appointed feasts
I will remove from you;
they are a burden and a reproach to you.
19At that time I will deal
with all who oppressed you;
I will rescue the lame
and gather those who have been scattered.
I will give them praise and honor
in every land where they were put to shame.
20At that time I will gather you;
at that time I will bring you home.
I will give you honor and praise
among all the peoples of the earth
when I restore your fortunes
before your very eyes,"
says the LORD.

The messianic era is described vividly in this concluding passage. It will be a time of great joy; the Lord will be in the midst of his people. Fear and sorrow will be removed, and the Lord will restore their fortunes. It will be a time for singing and rejoicing (v.14). The time of punishment will be passed, and the Lord will have turned back their enemy (v.15). Fear and apprehension will be gone (v.16). God's people will rest in his love (v.17), and he will take great delight in them (v.17).

Because they could not celebrate their holy feasts in exile, the Lord's people were burdened with sorrows (v.18); but he will remove this reproach and deal with those who oppressed his people (v.19). The concluding verse (20) reiterates the Lord's promise to gather and bring his people home, where their fortunes will be restored and they will enjoy honor and praise from "all the peoples of the earth."

14 An exhortation to sing and rejoice begins this conclusion to the prophet's message. "Daughter of Zion" refers here to the reassembled remnant of Israel; "Daughter of Jerusalem" is a parallel expression to Daughter of Zion (cf. Isa 37:22; also note the parallel of Jerusalem with Zion in v.16).

15 In typical hymnic style the prophet followed the call to praise with the cause for praise: "The LORD has taken away your punishment, . . . turned back your enemy. . . . [he] is with you; never again will you fear any harm." The fact that the Lord "is with" his people is stated also in vv.5, 17.

16 In that wonderful messianic day, the remnant's hands will not hang limp because there will be no despair that slack hands symbolize (cf. 2 Sam 4:1 [Heb.]; Isa 13:7; Jer 6:24; Heb 12:12).

17 Since the Lord "is with" (lit., "in the midst of") his people, they need no longer be in fear; he is a "hero" who delivers or saves. "Mighty to save" (cf. Jer 14:9) is an expression in Hebrew that can be understood in an active verbal sense (cf. NEB, "a warrior to keep you safe"; RSV, "a warrior who gives victory"), or as a noun with a modifier (JB, "victorious warrior"; NAB, "mighty savior"). Isaiah 10:21 mentions the remnant that would return to the "mighty God."

The Hebrew "he will quiet you with his love" was translated by the KJV "he will rest in his love" (KJV mg. is "he will be silent [in his love]"). This reading of the text has been understood and interpreted in various ways: (1) because of his love, the Lord will keep silent regarding his people's sins; (2) the Lord's love will be so strong and deep as to hush motion or speech; there will be silent ecstasy; and (3) the Lord's silence is due to his planning of good deeds toward Israel.

Some commentators and versions (NAB, NEB, RSV, JB), however, read the Hebrew form from the root *ḥdš* ("to renew") instead of *ḥrš* ("to quiet"); and this has yielded various ideas: (1) he will do new things; (2) he will renew his love; (3) he will renew himself in his love; (4) he will renew Israel through new life; and (5) he will show you his love. Luther caught the sense when he explained, "He will cause you to be silent so that you may have in the secret places of your heart a very quiet peace and a peaceful silence."

The prophet continued his description of this saving God as one who "will take great delight in you" and "rejoice over you with singing" (cf. Isa 62:5).

18 The scattering of the people in judgment brought on sorrows as they yearned for the old assembly experiences at the appointed feasts, the festive meetings (cf. Lam 2:6). Hebrew *mô'ēḏ* is not restricted to a particular "feast" but may be understood as relating to various feasts to which pilgrimages were made. Jack Lewis (TWOT, 1:389) correctly points out, "Appearing at times (Hos 9:5) with *ḥag* (which designates the three great annual festivals), *môʿēḏ* must be thought of in a wide usage for all religious assemblies."

19 The Lord promises "at that time" to deal with all who oppressed Israel (cf. Isa 60:14). The restoration is regularly represented in connection with the destruction of those nations that are hostile to the purpose of God (Isa 59:17–21; 66:15–16). The pathetic condition of God's people is reflected in the references to the "lame" (cf. Mic 4:7) and "scattered." This language uses the figure of a flock (cf. Ezek 34:4–6, 16). Undoubtedly these references apply to all in the Dispersion; all will be regathered and restored. But that is not the end of the story; also they will enjoy receiving praise (cf. Isa 62:7) and honor—even from the lands where they had been put to shame.

20 With a slight change in wording, the Lord repeats the promise just made, giving emphasis to it. It is also supplemented with the addition of the temporal clause "when I restore your fortunes [cf. 2:7] before your very eyes." (Additional emphasis is made by the repeated use of the personal pronoun "I" throughout vv.18–20.)

The work of redemption, as well as judgment, belongs to the Lord. He will accomplish his purposes with his people. This promise is the basis of their hope and joy.

Notes

14 Emphasis is manifested by the stacking of Hebrew words with similar meaning: רָנַן (*rānan*, "sing"), רוּעַ (*rûaʿ*, "shout aloud"), שָׂמַח (*śāmaḥ*, "be glad"), and עָלַז (*ʿālaz*, "rejoice").

15 The form תִּירְאִי (*tîr^{e}'î*) was understood to involve the root רָאָה (*rā'āh*, "see") by the KJV translators, but most translations (RSV, NEB, NAB, JB) understand the form to contain the root יָרֵא (*yārē'*, "fear"), though Kittel's note says two Hebrew MSS read תִּרְאִי (*tir'î*), which reflects the root *rā'āh*. Internal evidence also supports the term for "fear" here (cf. Sabottka, p. 128).

17 גִּבּוֹר (*gibbôr*, "mighty") probably is to be understood as the subject of the verb "save": so RSV, "a warrior who gives victory." This term is often used of the heroes and mighty men of Israel.

"He will take great delight in you" is rendered more literally by KJV as "he will rejoice over thee with love" and parallels the last stich: "he will rejoice over you with singing" (NIV).

"Quiet you" follows MT's חָרַשׁ (*ḥāraš*); some versions (RSV, NEB, NAB, JB) emend the text to read חָדַשׁ (*ḥādaš*, "renew"). This involves the change of one letter and changing the vowels to read a Piel form. The LXX and Syriac reflect "renew," but MT makes sense here and need not be emended.

18 NIV takes "sorrows" to be the subject of "they are a burden and a reproach to you"; the NIV margin understands "reproach" to be the "burden" the people bear. MT's accentuation is unexpected here; we expect the *'aṯnāḥ* to be on the preceding word, מִמֵּךְ (*mimmēḵ*, "from you"). Attempts to reflect the MT accentuation in translation are awkward (cf. KJV, "who are of thee"; Keil, "they are of thee"). Most new translations (e.g., NIV) take הָיוּ (*hāyû*) with the final clause.

19 "Will deal" translates עֹשֶׂה (*'ōśeh*), the common verb that means "to do" whatever is called for by context (so also NEB, NAB; cf. JB, "take action").

"Honor" translates שֵׁם (*šēm*), the Hebrew for "name." Even KJV translates the Hebrew word for "name" here with the term "fame."

20 The infinitive קַבְּצִי (*qabb^e ṣî*, "to bring, gather") may be unexpected here, but it is not necessary to adopt the suggested emendation אֲקַבֵּץ (*'^a qabbēṣ*, "I will bring"). Perhaps the temporal use of the infinitive is intended here, as RSV reflects: "At that time I will bring you home, at the time *when* I gather you together" (emphasis mine). (Home is supplied by both the NIV and the RSV; NIV supplies it with the second line, and RSV supplies it with the first line.)

HAGGAI

Robert L. Alden

HAGGAI

Introduction

1. Background

The Lord's words in Haggai 1:8—"Build the house, so that I may take pleasure in it and be honored"—frame the theme of the book. Everything else in this brief prophecy hangs on this one imperative—build God's house.

The setting of this command reflects much of the history of Israel—the days of the tabernacle, the beginning of the monarchy under Samuel, David's desire to build a dwelling for God, Solomon's building of the temple, its destruction by the forces of Nebuchadnezzar, and the returning exiles who began to rebuild the temple in Jerusalem in 538 B.C. More immediately the setting of Haggai 1:8 begins with the rise of Cyrus.

In 559 B.C. Cyrus was only the king of Anshan, a district in Elam. He joined with Nabonidus, one of the several weak successors of Nebuchadnezzar, to conquer Ecbatana, the capital of Media, in 550. Cyrus broke with Nabonidus and turned against him to capture Babylon in 539. Nabonidus had lost support because of his disinterest in Marduk and other traditional Babylonian deities. He failed also in his effort to secure Egyptian help against Cyrus. On the other hand, Cyrus, respectful of all deities, was probably welcomed to Babylon by the priests of the religion so unpopular with Nabonidus.

Nabonidus, the fourth king after the death of Nebuchadnezzar in 562 B.C., himself died in 539, after a seven-year reign.[1] Belshazzar, his son, had evidently been coregent; but in fulfillment of Daniel 5:25–28, he too died.

Cyrus, who had been king of Media and Persia since 549, now brought Babylon

[1]D. Wiseman, NBD, s.v., "Belshazzar," and J.H. Walton, *Chronological Charts of the Old Testament* (Grand Rapids: Zondervan, 1978), p. 65, believe it was seventeen years. The Nabonidus Chronicle is ambiguous.

under his control. In the following year he made his famous edict allowing all peoples to return to their native lands. The peaceful surrender of Babylon is recorded in both the so-called Nabonidus Chronicle[2] and the Cyrus Cylinder.[3] The latter document contains the additional feature of returning exiles: "I returned to (these) sacred cities on the other side of the Tigris, the sanctuaries of which have been ruins for a long time, the images which (used) to live therein and established for them permanent sanctuaries. I (also) gathered all their (former) inhabitants and returned (to them) their habitations."[4]

Ezra 5:13–4 describes the effect of this decree on God's people: "However, in the first year of Cyrus king of Babylon, King Cyrus issued a decree to rebuild this house of God. He even removed from the temple of Babylon the gold and silver articles of the house of God, which Nebuchadnezzar had taken from the temple in Jerusalem and brought to the temple in Babylon."

According to Ezra 5:16 the foundations of the temple were laid by Sheshbazzar and his company, and Ezra 3:2 tells how the leaders built the altar and began sacrificing burnt offerings. Obviously, however, the work was not completed eighteen years later. Otherwise Haggai would not have preached the sermons he recorded in his book.

Why did the enthusiasm of God's people wane? Several answers come to mind. For one thing, during the seventy years in Babylon, most of the exiles had come to consider it their home. Further, some Hebrews may have been doing so well financially that they were reluctant to return to Jerusalem and face the dangers involved in rebuilding the temple. Or perhaps they were preoccupied with the injunction of Jeremiah 29:5–7: "Build houses and settle down; plant gardens and eat what they produce. Marry and have sons and daughters; find wives for your sons and give your daughters in marriage, so that they too may have sons and daughters. Increase in number there; but do not decrease. Also, seek the peace and prosperity of the city to which I have carried you into exile. Pray to the LORD for it, because if it prospers, you too will prosper."

Ezra 1:2–4 leaves no doubt about the proper course of action, for Ezra recorded the specific decree relating to the Jews: "The LORD, the God of heaven, has given me all the kingdoms of the earth and he has appointed me to build a temple for him at Jerusalem in Judah. Anyone of his people among you—may his God be with him, and let him go up to Jerusalem in Judah and build the temple of the LORD, the God of Israel, the God who is in Jerusalem. And the people of any place where survivors may now be living are to provide him with silver and gold, with goods and livestock, and with freewill offerings for the temple of God in Jerusalem."

A more-detailed decree of Cyrus is found in Ezra 6:3b–5: "Let the temple be rebuilt as a place to present sacrifices, and let its foundations be laid. It is to be ninety feet high and ninety feet wide, with three courses of large stones and one of timbers. The costs are to be paid by the royal treasury. Also, the gold and silver articles of the house of God, which Nebuchadnezzar took from the temple in Jerusalem and brought to Babylon, are to be returned to their places in the temple in Jerusalem; they are to be deposited in the house of God."

---

[2]See ANET, pp. 305–7.
[3]Ibid., pp. 315–16.
[4]Ibid., p. 316.

Those who returned in 538 B.C were perhaps the poorer ones who had nothing to lose in such a venture.

The reconstruction project may have faltered also because of the unstable political situation that followed the death of Cyrus in 529 B.C. Cambyses came to the throne and reigned for seven years. His major accomplishment was his bringing Egypt under Persian control. The passage of his armies through the land of Israel may have worked a hardship on the native population. Demands for food, water, clothing, and shelter may have greatly diminished the meager resources of a people engaged on a building project well beyond their means.

When Cambyses died in 522, there were several contestants for the throne; and one of them actually ruled for two months. He was the Pseudo-Smerdis, the real brother of Cambyses. In any event, Darius I, or Darius the Great, the son of a general named Hystaspes, became king and ruled until 486.[5] He is the Darius of the Book of Haggai. With him came the stability the Jews thought necessary for continuing the work on the temple. Even then it was the second year of his reign before Haggai appeared on the scene to stir them to action.

The biggest problem the returned exiles faced was the opposition from the Samaritans and others who lived in the land. Ezra 4 details the course of events. At first the "enemies" offered to help build the temple, claiming that they had been sacrificing to God since the time of Esarhaddon, the Assyrian king whose exchange-of-population policy had brought them there. But Zerubbabel, Joshua ("Jeshua" in Ezra), and the other leaders declined the offer and insisted on doing the work themselves. This antagonized those who had offered to help, and they continued to hinder the reconstruction project. They even secured temporary restraining orders and in general frustrated the plans of the faithful Jews throughout the reign of Cyrus and down to the reign of Darius (Ezra 4:5).

At this point Haggai and Zechariah, who prophesied to the Jews in Judah and Jerusalem in the name of the God of Israel (Ezra 5:1), came on the scene.

2. Authorship

Haggai is unknown to us apart from his short book, the two isolated occurrences of his name in Ezra (5:1; 6:14), and an allusion in Zechariah 8:9. Linked with Zechariah as he usually was, Haggai's name appears in the apocryphal books of 1 Esdras (6:1; 7:3) and 2 Esdras (1:40). Ecclesiasticus (Sirach) 49:11 is a partial quotation of Haggai 2:23.

Various editions of the LXX attribute some psalms to Haggai and Zechariah. Adjusted to the numbering of the MT, these include 138, 146, 147, 147:12, and 148. The Latin Gallican Psalter, or Alcuin's Psalter, based on the LXX, has 111, 112, 146, and 147 credited to these two prophets. (The numbering has been adjusted to most EVs that follow the Hebrew.)

The word Haggai (*ḥaggay*) seems to be an adjective from the Hebrew word for "feast," and therefore the prophet's name may mean "festal." If the yod (*y*) on the end suggests a shortened form of Yahweh's name, the prophet's name would mean

---

[5]For greater detail, see John C. Whitcomb, Jr., *Darius the Mede* (Grand Rapids: Eerdmans, 1959), pp. 68–72; FLAP, pp. 192–205; R.A. Parker and W.H. Dubberstein, *Babylonian Chronology 626 B.C.—A.D. 45* (Chicago, University of Chicago Press, 1942), pp. 11–16.

"Feast of Yahweh." Many suppose he was born on a feast day. There is a Haggi (*ḥaggî*) mentioned in Genesis 46:16 and Numbers 26:15, a Haggith (*ḥaggîṯ*) in 2 Samuel 3:4, and a Haggiah (*ḥaggîyāh*) in 1 Chronicles 6:30 (v. 15 MT). This last one is the expected form for "Feast of Yahweh."

How old was Haggai when he wrote his book? If 2:3 indicates that he saw Solomon's temple before it was destroyed, then he must have been at least seventy years old at the time of his prophecy. Not all, however, agree with this view. Those who believe that he was a very old man say the shortness of the book suggests that death cut short an anticipated longer work. Since he was usually linked with Zechariah, and since his name comes first, Haggai was probably the older of the two. It is likely that he had returned to Jerusalem with Zerubbabel eighteen years earlier (in 538), but as to his age, there are no other clues.

The lists of returnees in the opening chapters of Ezra do not mention Haggai; and we know nothing of his parentage, tribal ancestry, or where his grandparents lived. Nor is there any information (within or without the Bible) about his occupation other than that he was a prophet.

The brief record of Haggai's ministry does, however, show him as a man of conviction. He has the unique place among the prophets of having been really listened to and his words obeyed. The people did what he preached, and in a mere four years the temple was complete. Though his words were plain and not poetic, he had one major point to make; and he made it forcefully and well.

3. Date and Place of Origin

A unique feature of Haggai is the precision with which the prophet dated his prophecies. Four specific days are mentioned in his book. According to 1:1 his first sermon was on the first day of the sixth month. That month was Elul and the date corresponds to 29 August. The year was the second of Darius Hystaspes (520 B.C.).

The second date is the twenty-fourth day of the same month (1:15) and corresponds to 21 September 520. At 2:1 we have the third date: the seventh month (Tishri) and the twenty-first day—17 October.

Both 2:10 and 2:20 have the ninth month (Chislev) and the twenty-fourth day. These last two paragraphs can then be 18 December 520 B.C.

Thus the recorded ministry of Haggai lasted less than four months, and we know nothing more about him. Zechariah also was prophesying at the same time, beginning in the eighth month (i.e., between the time of Hag 2:1 and 2:10).

Haggai obviously wrote in Jerusalem. The two chapters of his book contain references to the house of God (the temple in Jerusalem). The command to go to the nearby mountains to fetch wood for the construction of the temple clearly implies this setting (1:8). Since neither Babylonia nor the adjoining part of Assyria has mountains, references to them (again in 1:11) make sense best if understood as the mountains of Judea.

4. Destination

The first oracle was addressed to Zerubbabel, the governor of Judah, and to Joshua, the high priest, and indirectly to the people as a whole (1:1–2). The second oracle was for Zerubbabel, Joshua, and "the remnant of the people" (2:2). The third oracle was for the priest (2:11). And the fourth oracle was exclusively for Zerubbabel (2:21).

5. Occasion and Purpose

Depending on how one calculates them, the seventy years of captivity may or may not have been over in 520 B.C. The first exile was in 605 B.C. (2 Chron 36:6–7; Dan 1:1–3); and a seventy-year period would end in 535 B.C., or just two years after the first return under Zerubbabel. But the upper class was exiled in 597 according to 2 Kings 24:14. The largest exile and the one connected with the final destruction of Jerusalem was in 586 (2 Kings 25:8–11). Seventy years from that date would have been 516 B.C. Perhaps Haggai saw that date fast approaching and went to work to convince the people to get on with rebuilding the temple.

The prospect of returning to Palestine produced little response from the priests. Ezra 2:36–39 indicates that of the twenty-four orders, representatives of only four returned. Only 74 Levites and 392 temple servants came back (2:40, 58). Later it was no better. Compare Ezra 8:15–20, where no Levites came at first; but, with urging, about 37 answered the call, plus 220 temple servants.

Possibly there was initial enthusiasm, but it waned as the cost in materials and demands on time went higher. On the other hand, the people were able to find the resources to panel or "ciel" (KJV) their houses; so economics could not have been the primary reason for the lag in building the temple.

The constant oppression of hostile neighbors must have had a debilitating effect on the outlook of those trying to build for God. If, at every turn, they were confronted by unfriendly foes and opposed by people claiming that the law was on their side, they could easily have become discouraged.

Against these odds and in the midst of this despair, Haggai chided the people of God to resume the task enthusiastically taken up so many years ago and subsequently dropped. His message was simply "build God's house." To support his case he contended that recent crop failures (1:9) and drought (1:10–11) were God's way of reminding them of their dependence on him.

Another of Haggai's purposes was to remind his people of spiritual priorities: they were God's kingdom on earth, the only witness to divine truth. If they proved faithless, it would damage God's reputation. Haggai kept before them the fact that they were a unique people, a theocracy, God's representatives in the world, not merely another ethnic group enjoying newly restored freedom under Persian rule.

Interestingly, Haggai's message has none of the elements so characteristic of the other biblical prophets. For instance, he wrote no diatribe against idolatry. He said nothing of social ills and abuses of the legal system, nor did he preach against adultery or syncretism. His one theme was rebuilding God's temple.

6. Literary Form

The Book of Haggai is a mixture of prose and poetry. In general the frames or introductory passages are prose and the oracles or brief sermons are poetry. Opinions vary regarding some verses, but at least some of the sermonic passages have features of typical Semitic poetry. The antithetical parallelism of 1:6, for example, is clearly poetic. Verse 11 likewise has parallel lines. Other examples of this feature are 2:4, where the imperative "be strong" occurs in three successive stichs, and 2:16, where the two pictures of agricultural disaster are similar in several ways.

The oracles are generally considered to be 1:5–11; 2:3–9, 16–17, 19, and 21b–23. There are some questions on the nature of the middle of chapter 2 as to whether or not the "This is what the LORD Almighty says" of 2:11 introduces a sermon, NAB (mg.) calls 2:10–14 a torah, an instruction given the people by a priest. This version, *Young's Literal Translation of the Bible*,[6] and *The Holy Bible: An Improved Edition*[7] are the only EVs that print Haggai as poetry. *Biblia Hebraica* (edited by Kittel [BHK]) did not do this, but the new Stuttgart (BHS) edition of the Hebrew Bible does.

In addition to the parallelism noted above, Haggai used several other stylistic devices. In 1:6 he used antithesis. He also made use of rhyme in 1:6 (*hammiśtakkēr miśtakkēr*), 1:10 (*ʿal-kēn ʿᵃlêkem*), and 2:6 (*ʾaḥaṯ meʿaṭ*). His most obvious characteristic is repetition. He used the introductory form "This is what the LORD says" or the like twenty-six times in thirty-eight verses (1:1, 2, 3, 5, 7, 8, 9, 12, 13; 2:1, 4 [*ter*], 6, 7, 8, 9 [*bis*] 10, 11, 14, 17, 20, 23 [*ter*]). "Give careful thought" occurs five times (1:5, 7; 2:15, 18 [*bis*]—the two occurrences in chapter 1 being expanded to "Give careful thought to your ways"). Also notable are the threefold repetition of "spirit" in 1:14 and of "be strong" in 2:4. The little phrase "is mine" in 2:8 is another example of repetition, as are the two uses of "I will overthrow" in 2:22 (NIV, "overturn," "overthrow"). The expression "I am with you" occurs in 1:13 and 2:4.

There is no clear evidence that Haggai borrowed from another prophet. Some see allusions to Hosea 4:10 and 2:9 in Haggai 1:6 and 1:11, or perhaps 1:11 came from Micah 6:15. But these agricultural motifs were so common that they cannot actually be identified as borrowings.

7. Theological Values

Haggai is more a historical than a theological book. But if anything was central to his theology, it was the temple. In his time the temple was more significant than the palace, and his dealings were more with the priests than with the princes. The temple and Mount Zion on which it sat represented God's dwelling place on earth. The temple's destruction by Nebuchadnezzar amounted to the ultimate blasphemy. The only way to rectify this situation was to rebuild the temple.

Coupled with this concern for spiritual matters is Haggai's criticism of personal wealth and comfort. His opening charge is that the people of God had put their own concerns before God's. They had finished building their own houses but had let the program of reconstruction on God's house lapse.

On the basis of 2:10–19, one might charge Haggai with a commercial view of God's blessing; for it may appear that the observance of certain ritual details would

---

[6]Edinburgh, 1898; reprint ed., Grand Rapids: Baker, 1977.
[7]Philadelphia: American Baptist Publication Society, 1913.

lead to better crops. Behind this superficial observation, however, lies a conviction that God really wanted the sincere devotion and obedient service of his people. Some of them may indeed have had an eye to material gain, but Haggai had more insight into God's dealings than that. The whole matter of ceremonial uncleanness is very closely tied to the temple project, which was Haggai's chief concern.

In 2:11–14 Haggai asserted that sin was more contagious than righteousness. Although he was speaking directly to the priests, what he said applied not only to the priests and people of his time but also to all humanity.

Of theological importance is the prophecy in 2:9: " 'The glory of this present house will be greater than the glory of the former house,' says the LORD Almighty. 'And in this place I will grant peace,' declares the LORD Almighty." While these words are not quoted or alluded to in the NT, most interpreters take it as referring to the advent of the Messiah. The second temple was less sumptuous than Solomon's; but because it was to become the scene of some of Christ's ministry, it would actually have a greater glory than the first temple. The peace promised by the Lord in this prophecy would ultimately come through Christ.

8. Canonicity

Haggai is the first of three postexilic prophets and the tenth of the twelve minor prophets. Unlike many books of the Bible, it is placed in correct chronological order in the OT. His ministry came very near the end of God's revelation in the old dispensation.

Haggai's canonicity has never been questioned. If it is true that Ezra had a major role in establishing the canon, and if Ezra personally knew Haggai (and there is no certainty of this one way or the other), then that would have guaranteed him a place among the other sacred writers.

Haggai 2:23 is reflected in Ecclesiasticus 49:11. And Haggai 2:6 is quoted in Hebrews 12:26—a fact that places a kind of seal of acceptance on the whole of the prophet's writing.

9. Special Problems

There are a number of textual problems in Haggai. The commentary will deal with the most substantial of them, but not with the LXX's additions to the text. At 2:9 and 14 there are whole sentence additions (cf. JB mg.). Apart from these additions the LXX generally helps to solve textual problems rather than create them. In the commentary the alternate readings at 1:2, 9; 2:2, 5, 7, 9, 14, 16 will be noted.

Many students of Haggai desire to rearrange verses, a trend that began with J.W. Rothstein in 1908 (cf. Eissfeldt, p. 426). Placing 2:15–19 immediately after chapter 1 is the most common suggestion. (For more extensive juggling of verses, see margin at 1:13 in NEB.)

At 2:18 many would change the "ninth month" to the "sixth month." Others would eliminate the date formula altogether. All Hebrew MSS and ancient versions agree with the traditional reading.

Among the scrolls found at Wadi Murabb'at was the "Scroll of the Twelve"; in it is Haggai 1:12–2:10, 12–23, and these verses agree with the MT except for two quite insignificant places.[8]

10. Bibliography

Books

Ackroyd, Peter R. *Exile and Restoration*. Philadelphia: Westminster, 1968.
Baldwin, Joyce G. *Haggai, Zechariah and Malachi*. Downers Grove, Ill.: InterVarsity, 1972.
Barnes, William Emery. *Haggai*, Edinburgh: T. & T. Clark, 1936.
Calkins, Raymond. *The Modern Message of the Minor Prophets*. New York: Harper & Brothers, 1947.
Calvin, John. *Minor Prophets IV*. Grand Rapids: Eerdmans, 1950.
Dods, Marcus. *Haggai, Zechariah, Malachi*. Edinburgh: T. & T. Clark, 1879.
Dunning, H. Ray. "The Book of Haggai." *Beacon Bible Commentary*. Vol. 5. Kansas City: Beacon Hill, 1966.
Eiselen, Frederick Carl. *The Minor Prophets*. New York: Eaton & Maine, 1907.
Eissfeldt, Otto. *The Old Testament: An Introduction*. Translated by P.R. Ackroyd. New York: Harper and Row, 1965.
Ellison, Henry Leopold. *Men Spake From God*. Grand Rapids: Eerdmans, 1958.
Feinberg, Charles Lee. *Habakkuk, Zephaniah, Haggai, and Malachi*. New York: American Board of Missions to the Jews, 1951.
Freeman, Hobart E. *An Introduction to the Old Testament Prophets*. Chicago: Moody, 1968.
Gaebelein, Frank E. *Four Minor Prophets*. Chicago: Moody, 1970.
Hailey, Homer. *A Commentary on the Minor Prophets*. Grand Rapids: Baker, 1972.
Harrison, Roland K. "Haggai." *Zondervan Pictorial Encyclopedia of the Bible*. ZPEB. 5 vols. Edited by M.C. Tenney. Grand Rapids: Zondervan, 1975, 3:11–13.
Jones, Douglas R. *Haggai, Zechariah, Malachi*. London: SCM, 1972.
Keil, C.F. *The Twelve Minor Prophets*. KD. 2 vols. Grand Rapids: Eerdmans, 1949.
Laetsch, Theodore. *The Minor Prophets*. St. Louis: Concordia: 1956.
Lewis, Jack P. *The Minor Prophets*. Grand Rapids: Baker, 1966.
Mason, Rex. *The Books of Haggai, Zechariah, and Malachi*. The Cambridge Bible Commentary. Cambridge: Cambridge University Press, 1977.
Mitchell, Hinckley. *Haggai and Zechariah*. Edinburgh: T. & T. Clark, 1912.
Moore, T.V. *The Prophets of the Restoration: Haggai, Zechariah, Malachi*. 1856. Reprint. London: Banner of Truth Trust, 1960.
Perowne, T.T. *Haggai and Zechariah*. CBSC. Cambridge: Cambridge University Press, 1897.
Robinson, George. *The Twelve Minor Prophets*. Grand Rapids: Baker, 1952.
Smith, George Adam. *The Twelve Prophets Commonly Called Minor*. ExB. New York: Funk & Wagnalls, 1900.
Taylor, John B. *The Minor Prophets*. Grand Rapids: Eerdmans, 1970.
Thomas, D. Winton, and Sperry, Willard L. "Haggai." *Interpreters Bible*. IB. Vol. 6. Edited by G. Buttrick. New York: Abingdon, 1956.
Whedbee, J. William. "A Question-Answer Schema on Haggai 1: The Form and Function of Haggai 1:9–11." *Biblical and Near Eastern Studies in Honor of William Sanford LaSor*. Edited by Gary A. Tuttle. Grand Rapids: Eerdmans, 1978, pp. 184–94.
Wolf, Herbert. *Haggai/Malachi: Rededication and Renewal*. Chicago: Moody, 1976.

---

[8]P. Benoit, J.T. Milik, and R. deVaux, *Les Grottes de Murabba'at* (Oxford: Clarendon University Press, 1961), pp. 203–5.

———. "Haggai." *International Standard Bible Encyclopedia*. ISBE. Revised edition. Vol. 2. Edited by G.W. Bromiley. Grand Rapids: Eerdmans, 1982.

Wolff, Richard. *The Book of Haggai*. Grand Rapids: Baker, 1967.

Periodicals

Ackroyd, Peter R. "Studies in the Book of Haggai." *Journal of Jewish Studies* 2 (1951): 163–67.

———. "The Book of Haggai and Zechariah I–VIII." *Journal of Jewish Studies* 3 (1952): 151–56.

Bloomhardt, Paul F. "The Poems of Haggai." *Hebrew Union College Annual* 5 (1928): 153–95.

James, Fleming. "Thoughts on Haggai and Zechariah." *Journal of Biblical Literature* 53:1 (1934): 229–35.

Koch, Klaus. "Haggais unreines Volk." *Zeitschrift für die alttestamentliche Wissenschaft* 79:1 (1967): 52–66.

Mason, Rex. "The Purpose of the 'Editorial Framework' of the Book of Haggai." *Vetus Testamentum* 27 (October 1977): 413–21.

May, Herbert G. " 'This People' and 'This Nation' in Haggai." *Vetus Testamentum* 18 (1968): 190–97.

North, Francis S. "Critical Analysis of the Book of Haggai." *Zeitschrift für die alttestamentliche Wissenschaft* 68 (1956): 25–46.

Siebeneck, Robert T. "The Messianism of Aggeus and Proto-Zacharias." *Catholic Biblical Quarterly* 19 (1957): 312–28.

Steck, Odil Hannes. "Zu Haggai 1:2–11." *Zeitschrift für die alttestamentliche Wissenschaft* 83:3 (1971): 355–79.

Waterman, Leroy. "The Camouflaged Purge of Three Messianic Conspirators." *Journal of Near Eastern Studies* 13 (1954): 73–78.

11. Outline

I. A Call to Build the House of God (1:1–11)
   1. Introduction (1:1–3)
   2. Ordering Priorities (1:4–11)

II. The People's Positive Response (1:12–15)

III. The Promised Glory of the New House (2:1–9)
   1. Encouragement to Zerubbabel (2:1–5)
   2. The Glorious New House (2:6–9)

IV. Blessings on a Defiled People (2:10–19)
   1. The Past Defilement (2:10–14)
   2. The Future Blessing (2:15–19)

V. Zerubbabel, the Lord's Signet Ring (2:20–23)

Text and Exposition

I. A Call to Build the House of God (1:1–11)

1. *Introduction*

1:1–3

[1]In the second year of King Darius, on the first day of the sixth month, the word of the LORD came through the prophet Haggai to Zerubbabel son of Shealtiel, governor of Judah, and to Joshua son of Jehozadak, the high priest:
[2]This is what the LORD Almighty says: "These people say, 'The time has not yet come for the LORD's house to be built.' "
[3]Then the word of the LORD came through the prophet Haggai:

1–3 These three verses introduce the Book of Haggai; date the first sermon, or oracle; and identify the addressees. The second year of King Darius was 520 B.C. The sixth month was Elul, and the first day of that month would be 29 August by modern reckoning (cf. Introduction: Date).

The idiom translated "through the prophet" is typical. More literally the words are "by the hand of the prophet." By this point in the language's development, "hand" had become little more than a preposition, a figure of speech.

Unlike most of the other prophets, Haggai's father's name does not appear. In fact, we know very little about Haggai other than what can be deduced from the content of the messages. Neither his tribe nor his hometown is mentioned. Although we know the date of the prophecies with unusual precision, we have no certain facts about the prophet's age.

The first message is addressed to "Zerubbabel son of Shealtiel" and "Joshua son of Jehozadak." According to Ezra 2:2 and elsewhere, this is the Zerubbabel who led the exiles back to Judea. Haggai 1:1 (cf. Ezra 3:2, 8; 5:2; Neh 12:1; et al.) says he was the son of Shealtiel. In addition he was the grandson of Jehoiachin (Jeconiah in Matt 1:12). According to 1 Chronicles 3:19, Pedaiah was his father and Shealtiel his uncle; but this problem may be dealt with either through adoption or the levirate law. The identification of Zerubbabel with Sheshbazzar (Ezra 1:8, 11; 5:14, 16) raises more problems than it solves.

Zerubbabel was, then, an heir to the Davidic throne; and it is understandable that the magnanimous Cyrus and Darius should allow such a man to be the governor of the province of Judea. The term governor (*peḥāh*) appears only in the later parts of the OT and is a loan word from Persian, where it has the same basic meaning.

"Joshua son of Jehozadak" is spelled "Jeshua son of Jozadak" in Ezra (3:2, 8, et al.; cf. Neh 12:1, 8). Apparently he was a direct descendant of Aaron the Levite, the first high priest. That was Joshua's role here, the holder of the highest office in the religious hierarchy.

The formula of v.2 is typical of all the prophets and occurs proportionately more often in Haggai than in any other book. One gets the distinct impression from these two chapters that Haggai was speaking the very word of God with all possible authority and unction.

The actual message of Haggai begins with a quotation. The people were claiming that the time had not yet come for the Lord's house to be built. The Hebrew phrasing of the popular sentiment is somewhat cumbersome (cf. Notes). Exactly what lay behind this remark of the people is not certain. Perhaps they thought that the seventy years of predicted captivity were not yet up and that they would be out of God's will if they built the temple before those years were past. If they counted the captivity from 586 B.C, then only sixty-six years had passed. If, however, they counted from 605 B.C. (the first invasion of Nebuchadnezzar), then the time was well past.

A second explanation of their statement relates to the political situation of that time. From Ezra we learn of the opposition of the local population, mostly Samaritans. Perhaps the returnees were saying that it was better to wait for more propitious times, a more favorable climate.

In response to this, Haggai (and, indeed, any thoughtful Christian today) would have to say that the time was rarely just right to build the house of God—i.e., to do God's work. We can never expect the cooperation of the enemy in a truly spiritual task. Verse 3 is the introductory formula to Haggai's response to the people's claim that he had just quoted (cf. vv.5, 7).

Notes

---

2 NIV has rendered the participle בָּא (*bō'*, "coming") as a finite verb (*bā'*, "has come"), following the LXX. This is the best solution to the problem of the wordiness of the expression, which, according to the MT, literally reads "not time coming the time of the house of the LORD to be built." Another adjustment made by NIV is to render the first עֵת (*'et*, "time") as "yet" (*'attā*). Neither of these two changes involves the consonants Haggai wrote.

---

2. *Ordering Priorities*

1:4–11

4"Is it a time for you yourselves to be living in your paneled houses, while this house remains a ruin?"

5Now this is what the LORD Almighty says: "Give careful thought to your ways. 6You have planted much, but have harvested little. You eat, but never have enough. You drink, but never have your fill. You put on clothes, but are not warm. You earn wages, only to put them in a purse with holes in it."

7This is what the LORD Almighty says: "Give careful thought to your ways. 8Go up into the mountains and bring down timber and build the house, so that I may take pleasure in it and be honored," says the LORD. 9"You expected much, but see, it turned out to be little. What you brought home, I blew away. Why?" declares the LORD Almighty. "Because of my house, which remains a ruin, while each of you is busy with his own house. 10Therefore, because of you the heavens have withheld their dew and the earth its crops. 11I called for a drought on the fields and the mountains, on the grain, the new wine, the oil and whatever the ground produces, on men and cattle, and on the labor of your hands."

4 Verses 4–11 constitute the basic message of Haggai to the people. Undoubtedly he said much more than is recorded here, for this is an abridged version of his first sermon. A rhetorical question opens it (v.4). A spiritual man in his audience might have answered, "No, it is not right that we live in paneled houses, while this house remains a ruin." But the people had put their own comfort before the building of the temple.

Many Christians are like those ancient Hebrews, somehow convincing themselves that economy in constructing church buildings is all-important while at the same time sparing no expense in acquiring their personal luxuries. Contrast this with medieval Europe where peasants lived in squalid conditions while great cathedrals were being built.

The word translated "paneled" (*sāpan*) in v.4 raises some questions. The word occurs only five times elsewhere in the OT and apparently refers to an overlay of some kind, in some cases definitely wood. But it may be plaster as the KJV word "cieled" implies. In any case, it refers to an added measure of comfort the people thought they could not afford for the house of God. Some think that perhaps the temple was finished except for the "paneling." But the word "ruin" hardly describes a building completed except for some interior finishing.

5–7 Verses 5 and 7 are identical except that v.5 begins with "now." The Hebrew idiom "put your heart on your roads" is aptly phrased as NIV has it: "Give careful thought to your ways."

Verse 6 is a biting accusation. It may reflect a drought and consequent famine conditions. There is, however, no record of such a natural catastrophe apart from these inferences. Haggai broke into a kind of synonymous parallel poetry at this verse. There are five pairs, or stichs, that all say essentially the same thing—viz., "all your effort is in vain."

Pictured first is a lean harvest (cf. v.11). It is a vicious cycle if from the precious little harvest of one year one feels obligated to save even more of it for next year's seed. Then if that next year is unproductive, the loss is even greater. Such was the desperate situation of these returned exiles.

The next picture is of a person suffering from some disease where quantities of food fail to satisfy his needs. His metabolism somehow does not allow the food to be properly digested and turned into a healthy and strong body.

The third picture, referring to drink, is similar. The wine is so watery that it fails to provide the satisfaction and stimulus it ordinarily should. The Hebrew word for "full" (*šakrāh*) usually means inebriation. These people were unable to drown their sorrows because of the inadequate vintage. Additionally, their clothes were not sufficiently heavy to keep out the winter's damp chill. One is reminded of Isaiah 28:20: "The bed is too short to stretch out on, the blanket too narrow to wrap around you."

The last figure is one of economic distress. Somehow the people's income failed to meet their expenses; money seemed to disappear through holes in their pockets. It is possible that inflation was working against solvency, as in our day. The Hebrew expression is wordy: "The wage earner who earns wages." All these figures speak of the hardship that befalls people who have not included the Lord in their plans and who are preoccupied with their own interests.

8 With this verse the first positive part of Haggai's initial message begins, marked by three imperatives: "Go up into the mountains and bring down timber and build the house." The original temple was built with cedars from Lebanon (1 Kings 5:5–6). It is uncertain whether this verse refers to the mountains far to the north or the lower but rugged hills around Jerusalem. The limited financial resources of the people would point to the more modest forests of the nearby hills. The reference to wood rather than stones may further indicate that only the interior work was left to be done.

The two reasons the Lord gives for the people to obey and build the temple are that he may have pleasure and be honored in it. Proof of the people's devotion will come as they actually put their faith to work and finish the Lord's temple.

9 Verse 9 is in the same vein as v.6; agricultural and economic disaster result from God's withdrawal of his blessing because of their failure to do first of all what pleased him. Certain words are the same as in v.6: "much," "little," and the same word (*bû'*) lies behind "harvest" of v.6 and "brought" of v.9. The reference to God's blowing away what they brought home probably suggests that in the harvest was much chaff, which wind drives away (Ps 1:4). The kernels or grains of wheat were so insubstantial that they simply disappeared with the chaff in the winnowing process.

Unlike v.6, v.9 tells why the harvest was poor. On the one hand, each man was busy with his own house and no one cared for the house of God. Again we have an easy application of this message to the modern church. There may be a play on words between the "I may take pleasure" (*'erṣeh*) of v.8 and the "is busy," or, more literally, "runs" (*rāṣîm*) of v.9.

10–11 These verses, which conclude this first message of the prophet, pursue the theme of economic catastrophe as the price for unfaithfulness in regard to building God's house. First, the heavens withheld their dew, and consequently the earth withheld its crops. As long as the moisture came down, the crops came up; if the former failed, so did the latter. Through the long, dry summers of the Middle East, the only moisture apart from artificial irrigation was the dew. The moisture-laden air coming from the Mediterranean condenses through the cooler nights, and the thirsty plants absorb the dewdrops that have gathered on and around them. So while every summer is a limited drought, it is particularly severe if the weather is such that even the dew fails to meet the needs of the vegetable world.

Some of the affected areas of v.11 are arranged in pairs: fields and mountains, wine and oil, men and cattle. Though ordinarily receiving more dew than the fields, even the mountains are denied it. Thus not only the grain that grows in the fields but also the vineyards and olive orchards that normally grow on the mountains will be affected. Grain that supplies the staple bread, grapes that provide the basic beverage, and oil used for a number of things will all be in short supply. The people used oil for cooking, fuel, medicinal purposes, lotions, and tanning leathers. What a tragedy to have these three basic crops fail!

The cattle also would suffer as a result of the people's faithlessness. Throughout the Bible it is clear that the nonhuman creation suffers because of the sin of man. Ecology has biblical support. From the beginning, when thorns resulted from Adam's disobedience, to the end, when we read of a new heaven and a new earth with harmony between natural enemies in the animal world, it would appear that the happiness and productivity of the entire creation depends on the relationship of man to God and man to man.

Notes

---

8 LXX reads the second command הבאתם (*hăbē'tem*, "bring") as בראתם (*bērē'tem*) and translates it κοψατε (*kopsate*, "cut").

9 LXX, reflecting a minor variant reading, reads היה (*hāyāh*, "to be") for הנה (*hinnēh*, "behold"). If LXX is correct, the translation would read "You expected too much, but it was little."

II. The People's Positive Response

1:12–15

12Then Zerubbabel son of Shealtiel, Joshua son of Jehozadak, the high priest, and the whole remnant of the people obeyed the voice of the LORD their God and the message of the prophet Haggai, because the LORD their God had sent him. And the people feared the LORD.

13Then Haggai, the LORD's messenger, gave this message of the LORD to the people: "I am with you," declares the LORD. 14So the LORD stirred up the spirit of Zerubbabel son of Shealtiel, governor of Judah, and the spirit of Joshua son of Jehozadak, the high priest, and the spirit of the whole remnant of the people. They came and began to work on the house of the LORD Almighty, their God, 15on the twenty-fourth day of the sixth month in the second year of King Darius.

12 This verse records the positive reaction of the two leaders and the people to Haggai's initial sermon. The two verbs sum up their response—"obeyed" and "feared." Significantly the voice of the Lord and the message of the prophet are in apposition. Observe also that the reason for this wholesome response was that the Lord had sent Haggai. Exactly what Haggai did to authenticate his message is unknown. There must, however, have been some charisma or ring of authority that prompted this obedience and fear. A people who had been driven to their knees by the days of drought and famine would be all the more receptive to a word from God.

It is only in v.14 that we have the actual outworking of the people's obedience; v.12 does not specify it. Perhaps v.12 might be included with vv.1–11 because it is the response to that first message. In that case the second message would be v.13 alone and the response to it vv.14–15. The fact that the date formula is at the end of this pericope is a problem for some; yet their objection is without textual warrant. We are not told the date of the second message (v.13), only the date of the response (v.15).

13–15 In v.13 Haggai is named the messenger (Heb. *mal'āk;* Gr. *angelos*) and he brought the message (Heb. *mal'ākût*) of the Lord. The message itself is brief: "I am with you." Few though they are, these words were comforting and encouraging to a people oppressed by enemies and depressed by failing crops. The Hebrew words are different from "Immanuel," but their message is the same. Without God we can do nothing; with him all things are possible. By his divine aid this poor rabble could reconstruct a magnificent temple, repulse their enemies, seek and receive aid from an unbelieving monarch, and see dry ground bring forth food.

Verse 14 records the results of that brief but strong reassurance from the Lord through his prophet. The Lord stirred the spirits of the two leaders, Zerubbabel and Joshua, and of the people; and they began to work on the temple. The date (v.15) indicates that hardly three weeks had passed from Haggai's initial sermon to the people's obedience to his orders. Perhaps those intervening weeks were spent in taking inventory of their supplies, assessing and assigning jobs, and completing plans. Then the actual construction resumed on this twenty-fourth day of the sixth month of Darius's second year.

Notes

12 LXX reads אליהם (*'alêhem*, "to them") for the second occurrence of אלהיהם (*'elōhêhem*, "their God"). Still other MSS and ancient versions add the "to them" and also include both occurrences of "their God."

III. The Promised Glory of the New House (2:1–9)

1. *Encouragement to Zerubbabel*

2:1–5

1On the twenty-first day of the seventh month, the word of the LORD came through the prophet Haggai: 2"Speak to Zerubbabel son of Shealtiel, governor of Judah, to Joshua son of Jehozadak, the high priest, and to the remnant of the people. Ask them, 3'Who of you is left who saw this house in its former glory? How does it look to you now? Does it not seem to you like nothing? 4But now be strong, O Zerubbabel,' declares the LORD. 'Be strong, O Joshua son of Jehozadak, the high priest. Be strong, all you people of the land,' declares the LORD, 'and work. For I am with you,' declares the LORD Almighty. 5This is what I covenanted with you when you came out of Egypt. And my Spirit remains among you. Do not fear.'

1–2 The twenty-first day of Tishri (v.1) would correspond to 17 October. This is the third date-formula of the book and marks the beginning of the second major oracle. As in other places (e.g., 1:1), the Hebrew is, more literally, "by the hand of Haggai."

The addressees of this pericope are Zerubbabel, Joshua, and the "remnant of the people" (v.2). "Remnant" here merely means the population with the two leaders; there is no special emphasis on their status as the few survivors from a larger mass.

3–5 The third verse consists of three rhetorical questions. There may have been some present who could answer yes to the first question. They had seen the temple of Solomon in their childhood. They would have to be at least seventy years old because that temple was destroyed in 586 B.C., and Haggai was speaking some sixty-six years later (520 B.C.).

The next question was to those who might have remembered Jerusalem before Nebuchadnezzar destroyed it: "How does it look to you now?" If they did answer, it might have been something like this: "Well, it certainly does not compare in opulence; but it *is* the temple of the Lord, and we are happy to see it being built." There was no way these relatively poor exiles could have matched the extravagances of Solomon with his professional craftsmen working with imported woods and huge quantities of gold.

The third question virtually puts the discouraging sentiments into the mouths of the audience. They were all thinking it, and now Haggai has said it. The new is inferior to the old, and that fact along with the other discouraging circumstances had thoroughly depressed the people and stifled their initiative. One account of the effort Solomon put into his temple is recorded in 2 Chronicles 1–4. Compare this with the meager means of the returned exiles, whose temple must have looked small indeed.

Having brought the very problem of discouragement into focus, Haggai next offered the divine antidote: "Be strong . . . be strong . . . be strong . . . and work. For I am with you" (v.4). Notice the same imperative thrice repeated—to Zerubbabel, to Joshua, and to all the people. Notice also the threefold repetition of the formula "declares the LORD." The problem was essentially one of attitude. So the primary command was to take courage. When the people did that, the command to "work" would be fulfilled quite naturally. For the Lord to have only said "work" without giving assurances would have been inadequate motivation. These people did not need to be whipped but encouraged, not cudgeled but made optimistic. The most uplifting thing they or anyone could hear was that God was with them.

In v.5, the message continues with a reminder that this is what God covenanted with the people. (LXX omits the first half of v.5.) Perhaps Haggai had in mind the many references in Deuteronomy (12:5, 11, 21; 14:23; 16:6, 11; 26:2). After the reminder of this covenant, the prophet gave the people a promise and a command. The promise was that God's Spirit would remain with them, and the command, or prohibition, was simply "Do not fear." Of course, the promise was similar to the one in v.4. The thought must have passed through some minds that God was with them no longer. There must have been those who were theologically naive and doubted that God could be with them if the temple and the ark in particular were not intact.

Undoubtedly fear gripped many of the returnees—fear that God had written an eternal "Ichabod" over Jerusalem, fear that no amount of praying or piety would induce him to bless them again, fear that the whole endeavor was in vain, fear that the political enemies would in fact win, fear that all was lost. Therefore, the words of God through Haggai, which must have had a ring of authority to them, would have been of great comfort. And that encouraging word that shored up the sagging spirits of our spiritual forefathers should serve to bolster our spirits as well when we are spiritually discouraged.

2. *The Glorious New House*

2:6–9

> 6"This is what the LORD Almighty says: 'In a little while I will once more shake the heavens and the earth, the sea and the dry land. 7I will shake all nations, and the desired of all nations will come, and I will fill this house with glory,' says the LORD Almighty. 8'The silver is mine and the gold is mine,' declares the LORD Almighty. 9'The glory of this present house will be greater than the glory of the former house,' says the LORD Almighty. 'And in this place I will grant peace,' declares the LORD Almighty."

6–9 Verse 6 has the distinction of being the only verse in Haggai quoted in the NT. Hebrews 12:26 has a somewhat free quotation of it, and then the author of that epistle made some interpretative comments. The first "shaking" took place at Mount Sinai, when God gave the law to Moses (Exod 19:16); the second shaking will come at the end of the world. The NT author then went on to explain that we who are in Christ have an unshakable kingdom that will survive the cosmic earthquake yet to come (Heb 12:28–29).

The expression "In a little while . . . once more" is difficult in Hebrew. Word by word it reads "yet one time it." The translators of the LXX either skipped the last two words or paraphrased all four so that the Greek reads simply "once more," with no reference to the "little while." The question is not of much consequence, because "little while" could mean anything from days to millennia (cf. Ps 2:12, where the same word occurs in a similar context).

The thought of shaking continues into v.7. NIV makes v.7 a separate sentence from v.6 because of the repetition of the word "nations" in the first two elements of the verse. Verse 7 is perhaps the most difficult one in the book. KJV's "the desire of all nations" is beautifully messianic; most of the modern translations do not, however, support it. The problem centers on the words "the desired . . . will come." The noun (*ḥemdaṯ*, "desired") is singular, and the verb (*bā'û*, "will come") is plural (cf. Notes). Although this fact troubles many commentators, it is well known that such irregularities are common in OT Hebrew. Perhaps Haggai was thinking of the plural "nations" and so chose a verb to match it (cf. A.B. Davidson, *Hebrew Syntax* [Edinburgh: T. & T. Clark, 1894], pp. 159–61; GKC, par. 146).

Those who read *ḥemdaṯ* as plural do not, of course, take the verse messianically but say that the "desired things" are the wealth of other nations brought to Jerusalem. They may understand it to take place during the church age, but they do not see the "desired one" as the Messiah. Thus Isaiah 60:5 parallels Haggai 2:7. For specific instances of Gentile wealth coming to Israel, see Ezra 6:8–12 (from Darius), Ezra 7:12–26 (from Artaxerxes), and 2 Maccabees 3:3 (from Seleucus IV). Other interpreters even consider the gifts of the Magi (Matt 2:1–11) to be the fulfillment of this prophecy.

The messianic interpretation of v.7 began with the ancient rabbis and was passed on to the Christians through Jerome. The verse, however, is not quoted or alluded to in the NT. The reference to "glory" in the last clause tilts the interpretation toward a personal reference to the Messiah. Notice the use of "glory" in such acknowledged messianic passages as Isaiah 40:5 and 60:1. Notice also what Simeon said about Jesus in Luke 2:32: "A light for revelation to the Gentiles and for glory to your people Israel." But the messianic identification of "the desired of all nations" raises a different question: Were the Gentile nations desiring the Messiah? Certainly the Gentiles who receive Christ as Savior view him as desirable. Can that, however, be said of them before their salvation? Despite this and other problems, a messianic view of v.7 should not be wholly dismissed. NIV has left the question open by not capitalizing the word "desired" and by not rendering the word as a plural noun.

God's claim that the silver and the gold are his may be a response to the fears of the people—they were economically destitute. The drought and consequent famine had forced them to dip deeply into their meager resources. Subsequently they found no funds for the temple project.

A further note of assurance appears in v.9. To a people discouraged because the temple they were building was so inferior to the one the Babylonians had destroyed (cf. v.3), God promised that the glory of the present house would be greater than the glory of the former house. Certainly it would be a different kind of glory, for there was no way that the actual building was grander. And it is hard to see in this verse an allusion to the future improvements to be made by the unbelieving Herod the Great. Most Christian commentators see in this verse, too, a messianic reference. The second temple was to be honored by the presence of Christ, a divine presence quite different from the shekinah of the OT. The latter part of v.9 bears this out.

The second promise is that God will grant peace to the place. In fact, there were few periods of enduring political peace in Palestine from this time on. But since Christ is the Prince of Peace (Isa. 9:6), this too is probably a reference to his work and ministry (Matt 12:6). These people were plagued by enemies without and discouragement within. The promise of peace, which they thought of first in political terms, was a comforting one indeed. The phrase may also be a play on words since Jerusalem means "city of peace" ("salem" = *šālôm*).

Notes

7 The oldest and most common way to rectify the singular number of the subject and the plural of the predicate is to repoint the singular noun (*ḥemdaṯ*, "desire") so that it is plural (*ḥ*^{a}*mudoṯ*, "desires"), which involves no change to the consonants חמדת (*ḥmdṯ*; cf. GKC, par. 145e).

9 The LXX adds to this verse "and peace of soul, to save all those who laid the foundations for the rebuilding of this temple."

IV. Blessings on a Defiled People (2:10–19)

1. *The Past Defilement*

2:10–14

10 On the twenty-fourth day of the ninth month, in the second year of Darius, the word of the LORD came to the prophet Haggai: 11 "This is what the LORD Almighty says: 'Ask the priests what the law says: 12 If a person carries consecrated meat in the fold of his garment, and that fold touches some bread or stew, some wine, oil or other food, does it become consecrated?' "

The priests answered, "No."

13 Then Haggai said, "If a person defiled by contact with a dead body touches one of these things, does it become defiled?"

"Yes," the priests replied, "it becomes defiled."

14 Then Haggai said, " 'So it is with these people and this nation in my sight,' declares the LORD. 'Whatever they do and whatever they offer there is defiled.

10–12 The third sermon came two months after the second. Verse 10 states that it was on the twenty-fourth day of the ninth month: 18 December 520 B.C. The message is in didactic form. Haggai asked, on behalf of the Lord, the priests a question about the law. Verse 11 introduces the hypothetical problem. Verse 12 states the question. It concerns second-degree contact of sacred meat with other food via the fold of a garment in which the meat is carried. Exodus and Leviticus provide the background for this question. Exodus 29:37 speaks of the newly anointed altar's power to sanctify whatever touches it. Jesus alluded to this in Matthew 23:19. Leviticus 6:27 declares that the meat of the sin offering has the same power of contagiousness. Ezekiel 44:19 refers to the same question. The question Haggai posed is whether this holiness could be twice transmitted. Does the consecrated meat consecrate the garment? Can the garment in turn consecrate other foods such as bread, broth, wine, and oil?

The priests' answer was no (v.12). They did not believe that such consecration could be so passsed on. In short, holiness is not catching. This is the answer Haggai wanted, because he wished to show the people that it is easier to fall into sin than it is to fall into righteousness.

13–14 The opposite question is the substance of v.13. The question here is not, Is holiness infectious? but, Is defilement infectious? Leviticus 22:4–6 supplies the background: "If he touches something defiled by a corpse, . . . the one who touches any such thing will be unclean till evening." Numbers 19:11–16 is an expanded version of the same basic tenet; viz., uncleanness is contagious.

So the priests correctly answered yes to Haggai's question. With v.14 comes the interpretation of this little dialogue. The Lord declared, "So it is with this people and this nation." The dilatory attitude of what may have been only a few had infected and influenced the majority, and the temple rebuilding program had ground to a standstill. The selfish attitude of putting personal comforts first had spread throughout the repatriated community. The people had encouraged one another to build their own houses and to wait for more propitious times to work on rebuilding God's house.

When attitudes are wrong, nothing given to God is really acceptable. So the last part of v.14 charges that whatever these people offered was likewise defiled. From early times it was quite clear that God wanted sincere worship first and performance of the cult second. He basically wanted hearts, not hands. He desired obedience rather than sacrifice. That order of things was not changed in postexilic times, and it has not changed today. God still wants us to seek first the kingdom of God and his righteousness (Matt 6:33), and he still issues a solemn warning against deviation: "See to it that no one misses the grace of God and that no bitter root grows up to cause trouble and defile many" (Heb 12:15).

Haggai's sermons alternated between accusation and encouragement. (This is true of most of the prophets and in a sense should characterize all ministry.) The first sermon was basically negative. The second one aimed to encourage. This one is again essentially chiding and accusation. And, as we shall see, the last one is positive and uplifting.

Notes

14 The LXX adds to the end of this verse "because of their quickly won gains, they will suffer for their labors, and you hated those dispensing justice at the city gate."

2. *The Future Blessing*

2:15–19

[15]" 'Now give careful thought to this from this day on—consider how things were before one stone was laid on another in the LORD's temple. [16]When anyone came to a heap of twenty measures, there were only ten. When anyone went to a wine vat to draw fifty measures, there were only twenty. [17]I struck all the work of your hands with blight, mildew and hail, yet you did not turn to me,' declares the LORD. [18]'From this day on, from this twenty-fourth day of the ninth month, give careful thought to the day when the foundation of the LORD's temple was laid. Give careful thought: [19]Is there yet any seed left in the barn? Until now, the vine and the fig tree, the pomegranate and the olive tree have not borne fruit.

" 'From this day on I will bless you.' "

15–19 This third message of Haggai began with a twofold illustration: Is holiness or defilement contagious? Verse 14 is the interpretation of that illustration: the people are defiled. Verse 15 begins the other half of the message, the required response of the audience. The divine promise is at the end of v.19. Incidentally, these few verses are put by some commentators (e.g., D. Smith, *Haggai*, Broadman Bible Commentary, vol. 7, ed. C.J. Allen (Nashville: Broadman, 1972) at the close of chapter 1. This is done solely on the basis of content; there is no MS evidence for it.

The third use of "give careful thought" (cf. 1:5, 7; 2:18) opens this pericope. But there is a question with the word "on." The Hebrew reading is rather wooden: "from this day and upward" (so KJV). ASV translates the word "backward," while others translate it "onward" (e.g., RSV). The word can mean either, and either sense can fit into this sentence. If it means "backward," then a paraphrased translation would be thus: "Carefully remember how things *used to be* before the rebuilding of the temple began." If it means "onward," then the paraphrase might say, "*From now on* start thinking about the past." NIV takes it in this latter sense.

The building of the temple had begun twelve years earlier (Ezra 3:10), but the prophet urged the people to review what the situation was before their initial response to his first message to get to work. This, then, is a promise passage. There has been a marked contrast between the past and the future. The turning point was the start of the rebuilding project.

In the days of their disobedience, lethargy, discouragement, and concern with selfish comforts, the people never had enough in the pantry or the barn to meet their needs. Though there are some difficult words or missing words in v.16, the message is quite clear. It is the same as 1:6 or 9: "You expected much, but see, it turned out to be little." A person came to a silo or shed where he thought there was a pile of at least twenty "measures," but he found only ten. The same was true of the wine vat. He was sure there would be fifty; but before he drained off or dipped out only twenty, it was empty. These disastrous harvests and disappointing crops, the prophet was saying, were not mere freaks of nature, not just a happenstance series of droughts, but were the ways God was reminding his people of their duty to him.

Verse 17 continues the same theme. The natural catastrophes of blight, mildew, and hail were to effect a change in behavior. God intended through these hard lessons to have the people turn back to him. Alas, we know they did not. It took the preaching of the prophet to draw their attention to the connection between their behavior and the unproductivity of the soil. We might say that in this case general revelation was not enough. It required the oral interpretation of these events through the mouth of an inspired prophet to make clear to them exactly what the will of the Lord was.

The meaning of "from this day on," discussed under v.15, is again an issue in v.18. Here the date given is that of the message itself: the "twenty-fourth day of the ninth month" (cf. vv.10, 20). That means that work on the temple was recommenced three months earlier (cf. 1:15). The mention of laying the foundation, however, poses a problem. First, there is the record in Ezra (3:6, 10; 5:16) that the foundation was laid about 537 B.C. Second, Haggai 1:14–15 indicates that the building was started earlier. Regarded on the same basis as that used for 2:15, v.18 might be paraphrased thus: "From this day onward, the eighteenth of December, start thinking about how things have been for the last sixteen or eighteen years." On this interpretation the foundation was not laid a mere three months earlier, but the project was resumed after a delay of nearly two decades. This resumption was the real turning point; Haggai called attention to the marked difference in the productivity of the land and the general blessing of God on the people's efforts.

Like v.16, v.19 focuses on the barren years that had preceded, evidently attributing them to God's punishment for the people's nonconcern with the temple. There was, of course, no seed in the barn. All was gone. The investment in seed sown was a poor one; the returned exiles were on the brink of agricultural disaster. The word for "barn" (*m^egûrāh*) is unusual. Only Haggai used it in this sense and in this form.

In case the first half of v.19 was not clear, the second half restates the situation in different words. While "seed" implies the cereals and "vine" the basic beverage, the three trees mentioned indicate the fruits—figs, pomegranates, and olives. The olive, with its by-products of fuel, lotion, medicine, and cooking oil, is usually grouped with bread and wine to speak of the three most basic of foods for the ancient Palestinian (cf. Ps 104:15; Jer 31:12).

At the very end of this little sermon comes this promise: "From this day on I will bless you" (v.19). In the past it was touch and go; there was considerable uncertainty whether the supplies could be stretched to the next harvest. While the people were putting themselves first, they suffered the agonies of drought and consequent famine. But when they put the Lord first, they began to enjoy his blessing on the fruitfulness of the soil. Our view of God's economy must not degenerate into one of crass materialism. Many people do not hear God till he touches them where it hurts. This was merely one way God chose to remind the people of his sovereignty over them. He who was concerned with the temple was also in control of the rains. He insists on having first place.

V. Zerubbabel, the Lord's Signet Ring

2:20–23

20The word of the LORD came to Haggai a second time on the twenty-fourth day of the month: 21"Tell Zerubbabel governor of Judah that I will shake the heavens and the earth. 22I will overturn royal thrones and shatter the power of the foreign kingdoms. I will overthrow chariots and their drivers; horses and their riders will fall, each by the sword of his brother.

23" 'On that day,' declares the LORD Almighty, 'I will take you, my servant Zerubbabel son of Shealtiel,' declares the LORD, 'and I will make you like my signet ring, for I have chosen you,' declares the LORD Almighty."

20–23 These last four verses of the Book of Haggai constitute the fourth oracle and its introduction. Verse 20 indicates that it came on the same day as the preceding message, viz., 24 Chislev. The words are directed to Zerubbabel alone, and the opening statement is identical to the middle part of v.6. To make v.21 even more like v.6, the LXX adds "the sea and the land." Such apocalyptic language points to a day in the distant future. Verse 22 continues the theme: God promises to overthrow and destroy Gentile dominions. The description is in familiar terms: chariots and their drivers, horses and their riders and swords. Because of the cosmic language of vv.21–22a, many interpreters link these predictions to the final overthrow of all unregenerate nations at the end of the age, at the second advent of Christ. The infighting and mutual destruction among soldiers of the same army are reminiscent of how Gideon threw the Midianite camp into mass confusion (Judg 7:15–22). Isaiah characterized the advent of Christ as a time when "nation will not take up sword against nation" (Isa 2:4).

God's promise is expanded in v.23 to include Zerubbabel. Notice that he was not called by his title of "governor" (cf. 1:1, 14; 2:2, 21) but by the title "my servant." This was Isaiah's favorite designation of the Messiah (41:8; 42:1; 49:5–6; 50:10; 52:13; 53:11). Also, the word "chosen" recalls references to the chosen people and the chosen One from among those people (cf. 1 Kings 11:13; 1 Chron 28:4; Neh 9:7; Ps 135:4; Isa 42:1; Zech 1:17; et al.). This promise to Zerubbabel must be understood messianically, for the Persians simply would not tolerate a man laying claim to the promises here stated. Zerubbabel was no more the Messiah than Moses, Joshua, David, Solomon, or Isaiah. But Zerubbabel was in the genealogy of Christ (cf. Matt 1:12–13).

The mention of "signet ring" deserves special attention. In ancient times the signet ring corresponded to the crown, the throne, or the scepter. Ahab, the wicked king of Israel, had one that his even more wicked wife Jezebel used to seal a letter, framing the innocent Nabal (1 Kings 21:8). Darius used such a ring to seal the decree concerning the lions' den (Dan 6:17 [18 MT]). And King Ahasuerus (Xerxes) also used such a ring to seal his decrees (Esth 8:8). This token of authority would be granted to Zerubbabel much as it had been taken away from Jehoiachin king of Judah (cf. Jer 22:24, where he is called Coniah [mg.; cf. also vv.28; 37:1] and elsewhere Jeconiah [cf. Matt 1:11–12]). So Zerubbabel represents the resumption of the messianic line interrupted by the Exile, which in turn had been ushered in by the unfortunate reign of three of Josiah's sons.

So the Book of Haggai, which began on such a discouraging and depressing note, ends on an uplifting and promising one. Haggai's first message was one of indictment; his last one is of a great and blessed future for the people of God. As we now know, that future was much further away than either Haggai or Zerubbabel thought. But in the mind of God, it is as close and certain as tomorrow's rising sun.

ZECHARIAH

Kenneth L. Barker

ZECHARIAH

Introduction

1. Historical Background

Zechariah's prophetic ministry took place in the time of Israel's restoration from the Babylonian captivity, i.e., in the postexilic period. Approximately seventy-five years had elapsed since Habakkuk and Jeremiah had predicted the invasion of Judah by the Neo-Babylonian army of King Nebuchadnezzar. When their "hard service" (Isa 40:2) in Babylonia was completed, God influenced Cyrus, the Persian king, to allow the Hebrews to return to their homeland and rebuild their temple (Isa 44:28).

The historical circumstances and conditions Zechariah ministered under were, in general, those of Haggai's time, since their labors were contemporary (cf. 1:1 with Hag 1:1). In 520 B.C. Haggai preached four sermons in four months. Zechariah began his ministry two months after Haggai had begun his. Thus the immediate historical background for Zechariah's ministry began with Cyrus's capture of Babylon and included the completion of the restoration, or second, temple.

Babylon fell to Cyrus in 539 B.C.[1] Cyrus then signed the edict that permitted Israel to return and rebuild her temple (2 Chron 36:21–23; Ezra 1:1–4; 6:3–5). According to Ezra 2, a large group (about fifty thousand) did return in 538–537 B.C. under the civil leadership of Zerubbabel (the governor) and the religious leadership of Joshua (the high priest). This group completed the foundation of the temple early in 536 B.C. (Ezra 3:8–13). But several obstacles arose that slowed and finally halted the construction (Ezra 4:1–5, 24). During the years of inactivity, Cyrus died in battle (529 B.C.); and his son Cambyses II, who was coregent with Cyrus for one year, reigned (530–522 B.C.).

Political rebellion ultimately brought Darius Hystaspes to the throne in 522 B.C.

[1]Cf. ANET, p. 306, for the account of Babylon's fall according to the so-called Nabonidus Chronicle; see also pp. 314–16 of the same work for other historical accounts, including one by Cyrus.

(The Behistun Inscription pictures him putting down an insurrection.) His wise administration and religious toleration created a favorable climate for the Israelites to complete the rebuilding of their temple. He confirmed the decree of Cyrus and authorized resumption of the work (Ezra 6:6–12; Hag 1:1–2). The construction was resumed in 520 B.C., and the temple was finished in 516 B.C. For additional events in the history of the period, see the historical background of Ezra, Daniel, and Haggai.

2. Unity

One of the first to question the unity and authenticity of the Book of Zechariah was Joseph Mede in 1653. Because Matthew (27:9) apparently attributed Zechariah 11:12–13 to Jeremiah, Mede felt that Zechariah 9–11 should be placed in the preexilic period and assigned to Jeremiah. (For possible solutions to this problem, see comments at Zech 11:12–13.) In 1700, Richard Kidder maintained that chapters 12–14 also were written by Jeremiah. In 1785, William Newcome advanced the view that chapters 9–11 were written before the Fall of Samaria and chapters 12–14 at a later date but before Nebuchadnezzar's destruction of Jerusalem. This preexilic hypothesis was followed in general by Hitzig, Knobel, Ewald, Bleek, von Orelli, and Schultz.

Corrodi, however, in 1792 reasoned that chapters 9–14 ("Deutero-Zechariah") were composed long after the time of Zechariah (about the third century B.C.). Corrodi was followed, with modifications, by Paulus, Eichhorn, Stade, Cornill, Wellhausen, Eckardt, Cheyne, Kirkpatrick, Driver, Kraeling, Heller, and others.

The arguments against authorship of chapters 9–14 by Zechariah include (1) differences in style and other compositional features and (2) historical and chronological references that allegedly require a later date. For such objections there are satisfactory answers. For example, the differences in style may be adequately accounted for by the change in subject matter; the variation in literary form in the two major divisions of the book (see below); and the possibility that chapters 9–14, which are not dated, were written at a considerably later period in Zechariah's life, perhaps just before his death. Besides, as George L. Robinson has observed, there is "no mode of reasoning so treacherous as that from language and style."[2]

---

[2]ISBE, 5:3139. For a comprehensive list of vocabulary differences between the two parts of the book, see Mitchell's commentary, p. 236. One could just as easily draw up a list of the vocabulary that both parts share in common, thus offsetting the argument based on differences. Nothing determinative or conclusive is gained by such exercises. However, to demonstrate that the present writer's counterclaim is valid, it may be in order to present the following partial but suggestive list of words and expressions common to both major parts of the book: (1) "that no one could come or go" (7:14) and "*against marauding* forces (9:8, emphasis mine)—the Hebrew idiom is the same in both verses (it means literally "from crossing and from returning"), and the phrase occurs nowhere else in the MT; (2) "declares the LORD" (fourteen times in the first part of the book, but also in 10:12; 12:1, 4; 13:2, 7, 8); (3) "the LORD Almighty" (1:6, 12, 2:9; 9:15; 10:3; 12:5); (4) "will be" (2:4), "were at rest" and "were settled" (7:7), "will remain intact" (12:6), and "remain" (14:10)—the Hebrew verb (lit., "be inhabited, dwell") is the same for all these. One could also mention certain similarities of ideas: (1) joy because of the coming of the King (2:10; 9:9); (2) the necessity for repentance and cleansing (1:4; 3:4, 9; 9:7; 12:10; 13:1, 9); (3) the return and restoration of the theocratic nation (2:6; 8:7–8; 9:12; 10:6–10); (4) the exaltation of Jerusalem (1:16–17; 2:11–12; 12:6; 14:10–11); (5) the subjection and/or conversion of Israel's enemies (1:21; 2:11; 12:3–9; 14:12–19); (6) the picture of the Messiah as the true and ideal King of Israel (6:12–13; 9:9).

An example of a historical and chronological reference that purportedly calls for a post-Zecharian date is the mention in 9:13 of Greece rather than Persia as the dominant power. To this it may be answered that 9:13 is prophecy (probably of the conflict between the Maccabees and the Seleucids), not a description of the current situation. The verse constitutes a problem only to those who cannot accept prediction as a legitimate prophetic function. Besides, Greece was a considerable power even in Zechariah's time. After observing that where the time note is important the dates are given (Zech 1:1, 7; 7:1) but that the headings in 9:1 and 12:1 contain no date, Baldwin ("Pseudonymity," p. 9) asks, "May it not be that the author intends us to see that in what follows [ch. 9–14] he is no longer tied to historical time but is rather expressing theological truths related to God's future purpose?"

Later Baldwin (ibid.) writes:

> Moreover there is progression as the book moves from the establishment of the postexilic community, with its rebuilt temple and recommissioned leaders and its understanding of the role of God's people among the nations (chapters 1–8) to the more eschatological perspective of chapters 9–14. Here the prophet rings the changes on the themes of jubilation, rebuke, mourning for a suffering shepherd and cataclysmic judgment, but according to the recognizable pattern which occurs in its simplest form in part one. The final note, the universal kingship of the Lord of Hosts (14:16–21), picks up the same theme from 6:15, 8:22 and 14:9, bringing it to a climax by laying stress on the removal of every obstacle to wholehearted worship of the Lord as King over all. Thus the book is a unity that progresses from historic time to end time, from the local to the universal.

It is not unreasonable, then, to conclude that the Book of Zechariah, from beginning to end, is the work of the author whose name it bears. Further substantiation of this is given under "Structure" below and in various works in the bibliography, notably those by Archer, Baldwin, Harrison, and Perowne.

3. Author

An attempt has already been made to demonstrate the reasonableness of attributing all fourteen chapters to Zechariah (cf. 1:1, 7; 7:1). More may be added at this point about him personally. Like Jeremiah and Ezekiel, Zechariah was not only a prophet but also a priest. He was born in Babylonia and was among those who returned to Palestine in 538–537 B.C. under the leadership of Zerubbabel and Joshua (cf. Iddo, Neh 12:4).

At a later time, when Joiakim was high priest, Zechariah apparently succeeded his grandfather Iddo (Zech 1:1, 7) as head of that priestly family (Neh 12:10–16). Since it was the grandson (Zechariah) who in this instance succeeded the grandfather (Iddo), it has been conjectured that the father (Berekiah, Zech 1:1, 7) died at an early age, before he could succeed to family headship.

Though a contemporary of Haggai, Zechariah continued his ministry long after him (cf. Zech 1:1 and 7:1 with Hag 1:1; see also Neh 12:10–16). Considering his young age in the early period of his ministry (Zech 2:4, "young man"), it is possible that Zechariah continued into the reign of Artaxerxes I (465–424 B.C.).

4. Date

The dates of Zechariah's recorded messages may be correlated with those of Haggai and with other historical events as follows:

1. Haggai's first message (Hag 1:1–11; Ezra 5:1)—29 August 520 B.C.

2. Resumption of the building of the temple (Hag 1:12–15; Ezra 5:2)—21 September 520 (The rebuilding seems to have been hindered from 536 to about 530 [Ezra 4:1–5], and the work ceased altogether from about 530 to 520 [Ezra 4:24].)

3. Haggai's second message (Hag 2:1–9)—17 October 520

4. Beginning of Zechariah's preaching (Zech 1:1–6)—October/November 520

5. Haggai's third message (Hag 2:10–19)—18 December 520

6. Haggai's fourth message (Hag 2:20–23)—18 December 520

7. Tattenai's letter to Darius concerning the rebuilding of the temple (Ezra 5:3–6:14)—519–518 (There must have been a lapse of time between the resumption of the building and Tattenai's appearance.)

8. Zechariah's eight night visions (Zech 1:7–6:8)—15 February 519

9. Joshua's crowning (Zech 6:9–15)—16(?) February 519

10. Urging of repentance, promise of blessings (Zech 7–8)—7 December 518

11. Dedication of the temple (Ezra 6:15–18)—12 March 516

12. Zechariah's final prophecy (Zech 9–14)—after 480(?)[3]

5. Place of Composition

At the time of his prophesying and writing, Zechariah was clearly back in Palestine; and his ministry was to the returned exiles (Zech 4:8–10; 6:10, 14; 7:2–3, 9; Neh 12:1, 12, 16).

6. Occasion and Purpose

The occasion is the same as that of the Book of Haggai. Approximately fifty thousand former exiles had arrived in Jerusalem and the nearby towns in 538–537 B.C.,

---

[3]On the reason for the question mark, see discussion on Unity. For the dating system, see Baldwin, *Zechariah*, p. 29; also Parker and Dubberstein.

with high hopes of resettling the land and rebuilding the temple (Ezra 2). Their original zeal was evident; immediately they set up the altar of burnt offering (Ezra 3:1–6). They resumed worship and restored the sacrificial ritual that had been suspended during the seventy years of exile in Babylonia. The people then laid the foundation of the temple in the second month of the second year (536 B.C.) of their return (Ezra 3:8–13). But their fervor and activity soon met with opposition in various forms (Ezra 4:1–5; Hag 1:6–11). So the reconstruction of the temple ground to a halt and did not begin again till 520 B.C. (Ezra 4:24).

The chief purpose of Zechariah and Haggai was to rebuke the people and motivate and encourage them to complete the rebuilding of the temple (Zech 4:8–10; Hag 1–2), though Zechariah was clearly interested in spiritual renewal as well. Also, the purpose of the eight night visions is explained in Zechariah 1:3, 5–6: The Lord asked Israel to return to him; then he would return to them, and his word would continue to be fulfilled.

7. Theological Values

George L. Robinson calls Zechariah "the most Messianic, the most truly apocalyptic and eschatological, of all the writings of the OT."[4] Zechariah predicted Christ's first coming in lowliness (6:12), his humanity (6:12), his rejection and betrayal for thirty pieces of silver (11:12–13), his being struck by the sword of the Lord (13:7), his deity (3:4; 13:7), his priesthood (6:13), his kingship (6:13; 9:9; 14:9, 16), his second coming in glory (14:4), his building of the Lord's temple (6:12–13), his reign (9:10; 14), and his establishment of enduring peace and prosperity (3:10; 9:9–10). These messianic passages give added significance to Jesus' words in Luke 24:25–27, 44.

As for the apocalyptic and eschatological aspect, Zechariah predicted the final siege of Jerusalem (12:1–3; 14:1–2), the initial victory of Israel's enemies (14:2), the Lord's defense of Jerusalem (14:3–4), the judgment on the nations (12:9; 14:3), the topographical changes in Israel (14:4–5), the celebration of the Feast of Tabernacles in the messianic kingdom age (14:16–19), and the ultimate holiness of Jerusalem and her people (14:20–21).

The prophet's name itself has theological significance. It means "the LORD [Yahweh] remembers." "The LORD," the personal, covenant name of God, is a perpetual testimony to his faithfulness to his promises. He "remembers" his covenant promises and acts to fulfill them. In Zechariah, God's promised deliverance from Babylonian captivity, including a restored theocratic community and a functioning temple—the earthly seat of the divine sovereignty—leads into even grander pictures of the salvation and restoration to come through the Messiah.

Finally, the book as a whole teaches the sovereignty to God in history, over men and nations—past, present, and future.

---

[4]ISBE, 5:3136.

8. Literary Form and Hermeneutics

The Book of Zechariah is primarily a mixture of exhortation (call to repentance, 1:2–6), prophetic visions (1:7–6:8), and judgment and salvation oracles (chs. 9–14). The prophetic visions (or dream-visions) of 1:7–6:8 are apocalyptic ("revelatory") literature, which may be defined as "symbolic visionary prophetic literature, composed during oppressive conditions, consisting of visions whose events are recorded exactly as they were seen by the author and explained through a divine interpreter, and whose theological content is primarily eschatological" (Alexander, p. 45).

Apocalyptic literature is basically meant to encourage the people of God. When the apocalyptic section of Zechariah is added to the salvation oracles in chapters 9–14, it becomes clear that the dominant emphasis of the book is encouragement to God's people because of the glorious future.

A special problem created by the apocalyptic visions (1:7–6:8) and by the judgment and deliverance oracles (chs. 9–14) is how they are to be handled hermeneutically. As will become clear in the exposition, the writer's own approach is essentially that of Alexander.[5] A rather accurate and complete descriptive label of the approach would be the grammatical-literary-historical-theological method. Among other things, this basically means that even in prophetic literature one should interpret literally unless the context of the book itself or of the Bible elsewhere clearly suggests otherwise. Obviously, since certain literary genres—such as apocalyptic literature and poetry in general—abound in types, symbols, and other figures of speech, much of these types of literature must be interpreted typologically, symbolically, and figuratively. Fortunately, in most instances the text itself or the biblical context (the analogy of faith) furnishes the interpretation of such language.

9. Structure and Themes

a. *Structure*

While Zechariah may be divided into two parts (chs. 1–8 and chs. 9–14), it likewise falls rather naturally into five major divisions: (1) 1:1–6, introduction and call to repentance; (2) 1:7–6:8, eight night visions; (3) 6:9–15, the symbolic crowning of Joshua the high priest; (4) chapters 7–8, the question about fasting; and (5) chapters 9–14, two prophetic oracles (9–11 and 12–14).

For an excellent visual representation of the unified, chiastic plan of chapters 9–14 (based on Lamarche), see Baldwin (*Zechariah*, pp. 78–79), who then goes on to delineate a similar chiastic arrangement in chapters 1–8, thus arguing on structural grounds the unity of the entire book. Elsewhere ("Pseudonymity," pp. 9–10) Baldwin concludes, "So closely knit is the fabric of the book that one mind must be responsible for its construction, and the simplest explanation is that the prophet Zechariah himself is the author of the total work that bears his name."

---

[5]See his dissertation in the Bibliography. See also A. Berkeley Mickelsen, *Interpreting the Bible* (Grand Rapids: Eerdmans, 1963), pp. 265–305; Bernard Ramm, *Protestant Biblical Interpretation* (Boston: W.A. Wilde, 1956), pp. 220–53. See further the more theological discussion in S. Lewis Johnson, *The Old Testament in the New* (Grand Rapids: Zondervan, 1980), pp. 55–57, 69–71, 78–79, 93–94.

b. *Themes*

The central theme of Zechariah is encouragement—primarily encouragement to complete the rebuilding of the temple. In fact, Laetsch (p. 403) calls Zechariah "the prophet of hope and encouragement in troublous times." Various means are used to accomplish this end, and these function as subthemes. For example, great stress is laid on the coming of the Messiah and his overthrow of all antikingdom forces so that the theocracy can be finally and fully established on earth. The consideration of the current local scene thus becomes the basis for the eschatological, universal picture.

10. Canonicity and Text

a. *Canonicity*

The second division of the Hebrew canon (the Prophets) closes with the Twelve Minor Prophets, and Zechariah is placed next to last in the list. Neither Jew nor Christian has ever seriously challenged its right to be in the canon. Its value as Scripture is demonstrated by the frequency with which the NT quotes it and alludes to it.

b. *Text*

Text-critical problems in Zechariah are comparatively few. They are discussed in the "Notes" sections of this commentary.

11. Bibliography

Books

Baldwin, Joyce G. *Haggai, Zechariah, Malachi: An Introduction and Commentary*. Downers Grove, Ill.: InterVarsity, 1972.

Baron, David. *The Visions and Prophecies of Zechariah*. Reprint edition. Grand Rapids: Kregel, 1972.

Bullinger, E.W. *Figures of Speech Used in the Bible*. Reprint edition. Grand Rapids: Baker, 1968.

Childs, Brevard S. *Introduction to the Old Testament as Scripture*. Philadelphia: Fortress, 1979.

Davidson, A.B. *Hebrew Syntax*. 3rd edition. Edinburgh: T. & T. Clark, 1901.

Eichrodt, Walther. *Theology of the Old Testament*. Translated by J.A. Baker. 2 vols. Philadelphia: Westminster, 1961, 1967.

Feinberg, Charles L. *God Remembers: A Study of the Book of Zechariah*. New York: American Board of Missions to the Jews, 1965.

Freeman, Hobart E. *An Introduction to the Old Testament Prophets*. Chicago: Moody, 1968.

Hanson, Paul D. *The Dawn of Apocalyptic*. Philadelphia: Fortress, 1975.

Hengstenberg, E.W. *Christology of the Old Testament*. Reprint. Translated by Reuel Keith. Abridged by Thomas Kerchever Arnold. Grand Rapids: Kregel, 1970.

The Illustrated Family Encyclopedia of the Living Bible. 14 vols. Chicago: San Francisco Publications, 1967.

Jansma, T. *Inquiry into the Hebrew Text and the Ancient Versions of Zechariah IX–XIV*. Leiden: E.J. Brill, 1949.

Kaiser, Walter C. *Toward an Old Testament Theology*. Grand Rapids: Zondervan, 1978.
Laetsch, Theodore. *The Minor Prophets*. St. Louis: Concordia Publishing House, 1956.
Leupold, H.C. *Exposition of Zechariah*. Grand Rapids: Baker, 1965.
Luck, G. Coleman. *Zechariah*. Chicago: Moody, 1964.
Mason, Rex. *The Books of Haggai, Zechariah and Malachi*. Cambridge: Cambridge University Press, 1977.
Parker, Richard A., and Dubberstein, Waldo H. *Babylonian Chronology 626 B.C.–A.D. 75*. Providence: Brown University Press, 1956.
Perowne, T.T. *The Books of Haggai and Zechariah*. Cambridge: Cambridge University Press, 1886.
Pusey, E.B. *The Minor Prophets*. 2 vols. Reprint edition. Grand Rapids: Baker, 1950.
Smith, George Adam. *The Book of the Twelve Prophets*. 2 vols. New York: Harper & Brothers, n.d.
Snaith, Norman H. *The Distinctive Ideas of the Old Testament*. New York: Schocken Books, 1964.
Tatford, Frederick A. *Prophet of the Myrtle Grove*. Eastbourne: Prophetic Witness, 1974.
Unger, Merrill F. *Zechariah*. Grand Rapids: Zondervan, 1962.
Wood, Leon J. *The Prophets of Israel*. Grand Rapids: Baker, 1979.

Articles and Unpublished Works

Ackroyd, P.R. "Two Old Testament Historical Problems of the Early Persian Period." *Journal of Near Eastern Studies* 17 (1958): 15–27.
Alexander, Ralph Holland. "Hermeneutics of Old Testament Apocalyptic Literature." Th.D. dissertation, Dallas Theological Seminary, 1968.
Baldwin, Joyce G. "Is there Pseudonymity in the Old Testament?" *Themelios* 4 (September 1978): 6–12.
Barker, Kenneth L. "False Dichotomies Between the Testaments." *Journal of the Evangelical Theological Society* 25 (March 1982): 3–16.
______. "The Value of Ugaritic for Old Testament Studies." *Bibliotheca Sacra* 133 (April–June 1976): 119–29.
Bruce, F.F. "The Book of Zechariah and the Passion Narrative." *Bulletin of the John Rylands Library* 43 (1960–61): 167–90.
Cashdan, Eli. "Zechariah." *The Twelve Prophets*. Edited by A. Cohen. London: Soncino, 1948, pp. 266–332.
Ellis, David J. "Zechariah." *The New Layman's Bible Commentary*. Edited by G.C.D. Howley et al. Grand Rapids: Zondervan, 1979, pp. 1025–50.
Halpern, Baruch. "The Ritual Background of Zechariah's Temple Song." *Catholic Biblical Quarterly* 40 (1978): 167–90.
Johnson, S. Lewis. "The Triumphal Entry of Christ." *Bibliotheca Sacra* 124 (July–September 1967): 218–29.
Mitchell, Hinckley G. "Haggai and Zechariah." *A Critical and Exegetical Commentary on Haggai, Zechariah, Malachi and Jonah*. ICC. By Hinckley G. Mitchell et al. Edinburgh: T. & T. Clark, 1912, pp. 1–362.
North, Robert. "Zechariah's Seven-Spout Lampstand." *Biblica* 51 (1970): 183–206.
Reiner, Erica. "Thirty Pieces of Silver." *Journal of American Oriental Society* 88 (January–March 1968): 186–90.

12. Outline

Part I (chs. 1–8)

I. The Introduction to the Entire Book (1:1–6)
   A. The Date and the Author's Name (1:1)
   B. A Call to Repentance (1:2–6)
II. A Series of Eight Night Visions (1:7–6:8)
   A. The First Vision: The Horseman Among the Myrtle Trees (1:7–17)
   B. The Second Vision: The Four Horns and the Four Craftsmen (1:18–21)
   C. The Third Vision: The Surveyor (2:1–13)
   D. The Fourth Vision: The Cleansing and Restoration of Israel (3:1–10)
   E. The Fifth Vision: The Gold Lampstand and the Two Olive Trees (4:1–14)
   F. The Sixth Vision: The Flying Scroll (5:1–4)
   G. The Seventh Vision: The Woman in a Basket (5:5–11)
   H. The Eighth Vision: The Four Chariots (6:1–8)
III. The Symbolic Crowning of Joshua the High Priest (6:9–15)
IV. The Problem of Fasting and the Promise of the Future (7:1–8:23)
   A. The Question by the Delegation From Bethel (7:1–3)
   B. The Rebuke by the Lord (7:4–7)
   C. The Command to Repent (7:8–14)
   D. The Restoration of Israel to God's Favor (8:1–17)
   E. Kingdom Joy and Jewish Favor (8:18–23)

Part II (chs. 9–14)

V. Two Prophetic Oracles: The Great Messianic Future and the Full Realization of the Theocracy (9:1–14:21)
   A. The First Oracle: The Advent and Rejection of the Messiah (9:1–11:17)
      1. The advent of the messianic King (9:1–10:12)
         a. The destruction of nations and preservation of Zion (9:1–8)
         b. The advent of Zion's King (9:9–10)
         c. The deliverance and blessing of Zion's people (9:11–10:1)
         d. Warning and encouragement (10:2–4)
         e. Israel's victory over her enemies (10:5–7)
         f. Israel's complete deliverance and restoration (10:8–12)
      2. The rejection of the messianic Shepherd-King (11:1–17)
         a. The prologue (11:1–3)
         b. The prophecy of the rejection of the Good Shepherd (11:4–14)
         c. The worthless shepherd (11:15–17)

- B. The Second Oracle: The Advent and Reception of the Messiah (12:1–14:21)
    - 1. The deliverance and conversion of Israel (12:1–13:9)
        - a. The siege of Jerusalem (12:1–3)
        - b. The divine deliverance (12:4–9)
        - c. Israel's complete deliverance from sin (12:10–13:9)
    - 2. The Messiah's return and his kingdom (14:1–21)
        - a. The siege of Jerusalem (14:1–2)
        - b. The tokens of the Messiah's return (14:3–8)
        - c. The establishment of the Messiah's kingdom (14:9–11)
        - d. The punishment of Israel's enemies (14:12–15)
        - e. The universal worship of the King (14:16–19)
        - f. "HOLY TO THE LORD" (14:20–21)

Text and Exposition

Part I (chs. 1–8)

I. The Introduction to the Entire Book (1:1–6)

A. *The Date and the Author's Name*

1:1

[1]In the eighth month of the second year of Darius, the word of the LORD came to the prophet Zechariah son of Berekiah, the son of Iddo:

1 The eighth month of Darius's second year was October–November 520 B.C. According to Haggai 1:1, Haggai also began his prophetic ministry in the second year of King Darius, on the first day of the sixth month, i.e., on 29 August 520 B.C. (For a synchronization of the old lunar calendar with Julian-Gregorian calendar dates, see Baldwin, *Zechariah,* p. 29; also Parker and Dubberstein.) Zechariah was therefore a contemporary of Haggai. While it is clear that one of their purposes was to encourage the Israelites to rebuild the temple, it is equally clear that Zechariah was vitally interested in spiritual renewal as well (see, e.g., vv.2–6).

At the time of Israel's return from the Babylonian exile, she had no king of her own to date events by. So Zechariah's prophecy—as well as Haggai's—had to be dated by the reign of Darius, king of Persia and suzerain of Judah (see Introduction: Historical Background, on Darius and the Behistun Inscription, which greatly advanced the deciphering of Akkadian, the language of ancient Babylonia and Assyria). Thus the dating by a pagan king expresses that this is "the times of the Gentiles" (Luke 21:24).

"The word of the LORD" is a "technical term for the prophetic word of revelation" (Grether, TDOT, 3:111). That the word of the Lord "came" to Zechariah is indicative of the vitality of the divine word in the OT. This so-called word-event formula occurs approximately thirty times in Jeremiah and fifty times in Ezekiel (ibid., p. 113, n. 182). When reference is made to the coming of the word of the Lord, the historical character of the word of God is referred to—its character as an event (ibid.). But elsewhere God's word not only "comes," it also "comes true," or is fulfilled (v.6; cf. Isa 55:8–11).

In the ancient Near East, the word of a god was thought to possess inherent power, guaranteeing its effect. The Akkadian epic Enuma Elish (4:19–28) illustrates this (cf. ANET, p. 66). In this passage the destructive and creative or restorative power of the Babylonian god Marduk's word is related to his right to rule above all others. Similarly, the Lord's efficacious word, which can both destroy and deliver or restore, suggests his right to absolute sovereignty. He alone is the Great King, and he reigns supreme. One of the ways he demonstrates his sovereignty and superiority, then, is by speaking and fulfilling his dynamic word. The power of God's word, of course, resides in his will, not in magic. (For a discussion of the signification of "the LORD" as the personal name of God, see K.L. Barker, WBE, 2:1047–49.)

The recipient of the divine revelation is identified as "the prophet" Zechariah. A possible definition of Hebrew *nāḇî'* ("prophet"), based on both etymology and usage, is "one called by God to be his spokesman." This is one reason the prophets spoke with such authority (cf. v.3). The recipient is further identified as "son of Berekiah, the son of Iddo." The three names in the complete patronymic formula (Zechariah, Berekiah, Iddo) mean "the LORD remembers," "the LORD blesses," and "timely (?)." Feinberg (p. 17), combining the three names, believes they signify that "the LORD remembers," and "the LORD will bless" at "the set time," which, in a sense, is the theme of the book.

Iddo was among the priests who returned to Jerusalem with Zerubbabel and Joshua (or Jeshua; Neh 12:4, 16). Zechariah, who was born in exile, would have been quite young at the time of the return. Since Berekiah was his father, NIV correctly identifies Zechariah as a "descendant" (i.e., "grandson," not "son") of Iddo in Ezra 5:1 and 6:14. Semitic words for "son" can mean "grandson" or "descendant." Like Jeremiah and Ezekiel, then, Zechariah was a priest before God called him to the prophetic office and ministry.

Notes

1 The definition of נָבִיא (*nāḇî'*, "prophet") is based partly on an assumed etymological relationship to the Akkadian verb *nabû* ("to call"). Such an etymology was proposed originally by W.F. Albright (*From the Stone Age to Christianity*, 2d ed. [Garden City, N.Y.: Doubleday, Anchor Books, 1957], p. 303). The Hebrew substantive is either a verbal adjective or the alternative form of the Qal passive participle, thus giving the word a stative or passive sense.

A possible reference in Matt 23:35 and Luke 11:51 to the prophet Zechariah has created a problem. In the Matthean account Jesus used the expression "from the blood of righteous Abel to the blood of Zechariah son of Berekiah." It is possible that the prophet was martyred, but there is no independent record of this. Probably the reference is to the martyrdom of another Zechariah, the son of Jehoiada the priest, c. 800 B.C. (2 Chron 24:20–22). (See commentary of Donald A. Carson at note on Matt 23:35, EBC, 8:485). Regarding the problem of Jehoiada vs. Berekiah, the *New Scofield Reference Bible* (pp. 1032–33, n.3) explains: "This [Berekiah] was probably the actual father of this martyr, Zechariah, who is designated in 2 Chronicles as son of his famous grandfather, Jehoiada, who had died at the advanced age of 130 before Zechariah began his ministry. Cp. 2 Chr. 24:15, 20–22; 36:16; Lk. 11:51." In this case the term "son" is being used in the sense of "grandson" or "descendant" in the Chronicles passage (see above). If this is the correct resolution of the difficulty, our Lord is saying, in effect, "from the first murder in the Bible [Gen 4:8] to the last [2 Chron 24:20–21]"; for the last book in the Hebrew canon is Chronicles, not Malachi.

B. *A Call to Repentance*

1:2–6

2"The LORD was very angry with your forefathers. 3Therefore tell the people:
This is what the LORD Almighty says: 'Return to me,' declares the LORD Almighty,
'and I will return to you,' says the LORD Almighty. 4Do not be like your forefathers,
to whom the earlier prophets proclaimed: This is what the LORD Almighty says:
'Turn from your evil ways and your evil practices.' But they would not listen or pay

attention to me, declares the LORD. [5]Where are your forefathers now? And the prophets, do they live forever? [6]But did not my words and my decrees, which I commanded my servants the prophets, overtake your forefathers?

"Then they repented and said, 'The LORD Almighty has done to us what our ways and practices deserve, just as he determined to do.' "

2–3 Because a holy and just God must deal with sin, Zechariah began his message by reminding his people of how angry their faithful, covenant God had been with the covenant-breaking sins of their unfaithful preexilic forefathers (v.2). This reminder should have made a tremendous impact on Zechariah's hearers; they well knew that the exile they had recently returned from was the direct result of God's wrath against their ancestors, and that the temple they were now rebuilding had been destroyed because of the sins of their forefathers. "Forefathers" is more literally "fathers"; but Semitic words for "father" can mean "grandfather," "forefather," or "ancestor."

The divine wrath (v.2) is followed by the availability of divine grace (v.3). Verse 3 contains the main statement of the contemporary call to repentance, one of the conditions for the personal experience of God's full blessing. It begins with the inferential, or consequential, use of the Hebrew conjunction waw ("therefore"), as quite frequently with the waw consecutive perfect (BDB, p. 254, par. 4). The point may be stated thus: "Therefore, since the Lord was very angry with your forefathers because they refused to repent, do not make the same mistake they did; rather, return to me." Three times in v.3 for emphasis the words of the call to repentance are said to be the authoritative declaration of the Lord Almighty. The introductory clause, "This is what the LORD Almighty says" (NIV), or "Thus says the LORD of hosts" (NASB), contains the messenger formula, *kōh 'āmar* ("Thus says").

The literature of the ancient Near East contains references to messengers who carried a god's or king's words to a king or a people (cf. J.F. Ross, "The Prophet as Yahweh's Messenger," in *Israel's Prophetic Heritage*, ed. by B.W. Anderson and W. Harrelson [New York: Harper and Brothers, 1962], pp. 100–101). The messenger bore the authority of the one who sent him, appearing on the scene to deliver, not his own word, but the word of his sender. The messenger was the mediator of a word. The OT prophet is to be largely understood as the faithful conveyor of a message (cf. S. Wagner, TDOT, 1:339–40).

Zechariah, then, came with the message and authority of Israel's divine King, who is called "the LORD Almighty." The NIV preface explains the sense of this phrase as "he who is sovereign over all the 'hosts' (powers) in heaven and on earth, especially over the 'hosts' (armies) of Israel." Similarly, Eichrodt (1:193–94) concludes that "*ṣᵉbā'ōt* does not refer to any particular 'hosts,' but to all bodies, multitudes, masses in general, the content of all that exists in heaven and in earth. . . . [a] name expressive of the divine sovereignty." As "the LORD Almighty," Yahweh is the controller of history who musters all the powers of heaven and earth to accomplish his will. Patrick D. Miller, Jr. (*The Divine Warrior in Early Israel* [Cambridge: Harvard University Press, 1973], pp. 154–65), considers this epithet as part of the OT divine warrior motif. He isolates the activities of the divine warrior as salvation, judgment, and kingship (ibid., pp. 170–75). The messianic King will also be a divine warrior or strong ruler ("Mighty God" in Isa 9:6 [5 MT]; cf. Isa 10:21).

The content of the Lord Almighty's word through his prophetic messenger is, in brief, "Return to me, . . . and I will return to you" (cf. Mal 3:7). If the people of Zechariah's day would only return to the Lord or repent, i.e., change their course and go in the opposite direction from that of their forefathers, the Lord would return to them with a blessing instead of a curse. The Hebrew verb *šûḇ* ("return") can mean "repent" (as in v.6). One might expect "Return to my law, word, or covenant"; instead, the appeal is "Return to me, your covenant God and King." The emphasis is on personal relationship and allegiance.

4–6 The opening appeal (v.3) for repentance (change of mind and life) is now elaborated with a lesson from the past. History is replete with warnings, but people unfortunately do not often learn from the mistakes and successes of the past. "Forefathers" (v.4) refers to the preexilic forefathers (v.2); and "earlier prophets" refers to the preexilic prophets who had warned of the approaching Babylonian exile—prophets such as Isaiah, Habakkuk, and Jeremiah. Note that the oracles of the latter were already regarded as "canonical" by Zechariah. The following words in v.4 are not intended as a direct quotation from any particular prophet but as a general summary of the message of the preexilic prophets to God's erring people (but cf. Jer 35:15).

"Evil ways" and "evil practices" form a hendiadys, stressing the forefathers' wicked behavior in God's sight. In their failure to respond to the prophets, the people had not responded to God ("me"); for he is the one who had sent the prophets (cf. Jer 7:25–26). Instead of responding with repentance, faith, and obedience, the people "mocked God's messengers, despised his words and scoffed at his prophets until the wrath of the LORD was aroused against his people and there was no remedy" (2 Chron 36:16). Such brazen refusal to respond properly was the principal reason for the Fall of Jerusalem and the Babylonian exile (2 Chron 36:15–21).

Defiance of God and disobedience to his word are always dangerous. The result for Judah, as well as for the northern kingdom of Israel earlier, was disaster. The nature of that disaster is stated in vv.5–6. The answer to the rhetorical questions of v.5 is obvious: Both the forefathers and the prophets who warned them were dead. And some of those prophets died without seeing their predictions fulfilled. They went "the way of all the earth" (1 Kings 2:2).

Verse 6 reminds us that though the messengers may be gone, God's words live on to be fulfilled (cf. Isa 40:6–8). These words are further defined as "decrees"—the specific requirements of the law, including the threats and curses for breaking those laws. Although God's words were uttered by his servants the prophets, they were still his words ("my words"); for his Spirit inspired them (2 Peter 1:21).

The designation of the prophets as "my servants" is not a demeaning but an honorific title, for it is a rare privilege to serve the Lord, who is both Israel's King and the Sovereign of the universe. Indeed, man is exalted, not debased, in such service. As pointed out by W. Zimmerli (TDNT, 5:663–65), the meaning of this relationship is influenced by the usage of "servant" in the royal courts of the ancient Near East. In particular, Israel was Yahweh's kingdom, and the prophet was the messenger of the divine King's word. The office of messenger is also found in the secular royal courts. The messenger-servant-prophet belongs to King Yahweh's court and is assigned a specific, active mission to fulfill on earth.

In a bold personification God's words and decrees—including threats and curses for disobedience—are pictured as "overtaking" the disobedient forefathers (v.6). For a similar personification, see 5:3–4. The question, of course, anticipates an affirmative reply. God's curse did, in fact, pursue and catch up with the wrongdoers. "The exile, which involved the removal of leaders and the destruction of national institutions, was the death of the nation (Ezek 37:11)" (Baldwin, *Zechariah*, p. 91). This happened in direct fulfillment of the curse warnings in Deuteronomy 28:15, 45, where the same verb ("overtake") is used (cf. Isa 55:10–11 and Jer 1:12 for the principle). According to Deuteronomy 28:2, blessings, too, can "overtake" (NIV, "accompany"). The choice is to up to the subjects of the kingdom. The same situation obtained in Jesus' day. Destruction and dispersion again came because of the people's disobedience, unbelief, and rejection of him. The application is clear: Pay attention to God and his word, for even though his messengers die, his word lives on. The proof that it does is that its curses are fulfilled; they "overtake" the rebels.

"Then they repented" ("came to themselves," "changed their minds") is apparently a reference to what happened to the preexilic forefathers and/or to their offspring during the Exile and immediately afterward (cf. Ezra 9–10; Dan 9:1–19). They had to acknowledge that they had brought the divine discipline of the Exile on themselves because they had refused to "listen," or "pay attention," to the Lord and to his words of warning through his servants the prophets. They also had to acknowledge that the Lord was just and righteous in his judgment, for he had done to them what their ways and practices deserved, all in accord with what he had "determined to do" (cf. Lam 2:17). The result was forgiveness and restoration, likewise in accord with his promise (cf. Deut 30:1–3; Isa 55:6–7; Jer 3:12; Joel 2:12–13).

"To sum up this introductory message, Zechariah is making a plea for a wholehearted response to the Lord's invitation to return to him" (Baldwin, *Zechariah*, p. 92). "On exactly the same terms as had been offered to their fathers, young and old alike are invited to return to God. If they will do so the covenant relationship will be renewed, and spiritual restoration will accompany the material restoration of the Temple" (ibid.). (See also Feinberg, p. 21, for more principles and applications.)

Notes

---

2 קֶצֶף (*qeṣep*, "anger") following *qāṣap* ("he was angry") is an example of the cognate accusative, which stresses the verbal idea; hence the translation "was very angry" (cf. LXX; GKC, pars. 117 p, q; see also Davidson, par. 67b). Other examples of this syntactical phenomenon may be found in vv.14–15 and 7:9. Such anger on the part of God should not be classified as an anthropopathism. To deny real emotions to God is to deprive him of one of the clear marks of personality or personhood, which include intelligence, sensibility, and volition. The doctrine of impassibility—sometimes restricted in meaning to emotions, as though God had no emotions—in certain systematic theologies is without foundation in a truly biblical theology and so is unsound.

3 נְאֻם (*n*ᵉ'*um*, "declares") is probably the Qal passive participle construct, meaning "is the utterance of [the Lord]."

4 The Kethiv and the Qere have different noun forms for "practices," but there is no essential difference in meaning. The Qere overcomes a problem of gender in the Kethiv, but either reading is possible.

5 In Hebrew the first part of the verse, like the last part, features the *casus pendens* construction for emphasis (GKC, par. 143c): "Your forefathers, where are they?"

II. A Series of Eight Night Visions (1:7–6:8)

A. *The First Vision: The Horseman Among the Myrtle Trees*

1:7–17

7On the twenty-fourth day of the eleventh month, the month of Shebat, in the second year of Darius, the word of the LORD came to the prophet Zechariah son of Berekiah, the son of Iddo.

8During the night I had a vision—and there before me was a man riding a red horse! He was standing among the myrtle trees in a ravine. Behind him were red, brown and white horses.

9I asked, "What are these, my lord?"

The angel who was talking with me answered, "I will show you what they are."

10Then the man standing among the myrtle trees explained, "They are the ones the LORD has sent to go throughout the earth."

11And they reported to the angel of the LORD, who was standing among the myrtle trees, "We have gone throughout the earth and found the whole world at rest and in peace."

12Then the angel of the LORD said, "LORD Almighty, how long will you withhold mercy from Jerusalem and from the towns of Judah, which you have been angry
with these seventy years?"
13So the LORD spoke kind and comforting words to the angel who talked with me.

14Then the angel who was speaking to me said, "Proclaim this word: This is what the LORD Almighty says: 'I am very jealous for Jerusalem and Zion,
15but I am very angry with the nations that feel secure. I was only a little angry, but they added to the calamity.'

16"Therefore, this is what the LORD says: 'I will return to Jerusalem with mercy, and there my house will be rebuilt. And the measuring line will be stretched out over Jerusalem,' declares the LORD Almighty.

17"Proclaim further: This is what the LORD Almighty says: 'My towns will again overflow with prosperity, and the LORD will again comfort Zion and choose Jerusalem.' "

7 In a series of eight apocalyptic visions on a single night, God revealed his purpose for the future of Israel—Judah and Jerusalem in particular, since Jerusalem was the seat of the Davidic dynasty and the place of the Lord's throne, viz., in the temple. The revelations usually follow this pattern: introductory words, a depiction of what Zechariah saw, the prophet's request for the meaning of the vision, and the angel's explanation. An oracle accompanies four of the visions (1:14–17; 2:6–13; 4:6–10; 6:9–15; so Baldwin, *Zechariah*, pp. 92–93), making their message more specific. Each vision "contributes to the total picture of the role of Israel in the new era about to dawn" (ibid., p. 93). As an encouragement to the people to persevere in the work of rebuilding the temple, God disclosed to them through his prophet his gracious purposes.

The setting is the time of Darius, and the date is 15 February 519 B.C., about three months after the call to repentance (cf. 1:1). On this same day (24 Shebat), five months earlier, the rebuilding of the temple had been resumed (cf. Hag 1:14–15; see also 2:10, 18, 20). It was evidently a day in which God had special delight because of the obedience of his people.

The last half of the verse is identical with the last half of 1:1.

8 The basic teaching of the first vision (vv.8–17, including an oracle in vv.14–17, if Baldwin's analysis is correct) is that although God's covenant people are troubled while the oppressing nations are at ease, God is "jealous" for his people and will restore them, their towns, and the temple. The vision came during the night of the twenty-fourth day of the eleventh month (v.7). The Hebrew for "I had a vision" is simply "I saw," but the verb *rā'āh* ("to see") here means what NIV has (cf. Num 12:6; Isa 30:10; Hab 1:3). From this verb comes the participial noun "seer," another name for a prophet. The vision portrayed a man on a red horse, standing among myrtle trees in a ravine. The "man" is identified in v.11 as "the angel of the LORD." In Revelation 6:4 the red horse (see also Zech 6:2) is associated with a sword, the instrument of war and death, which may also be the significance of the color here (cf. Isa 63:1–6). Archaeology tells us that "representations of horsemen are known in Iranian [Persian] art from the third millennium B.C. onwards; and the cavalry was the mainstay of the Persian army at all times" (*Illustrated Family Encyclopedia*, 8:90).

In Nehemiah 8:15 myrtle trees, which are evergreen, are associated with the Feast of Tabernacles for making booths; and in Isaiah 41:19 and 55:13 they are included in a description of messianic kingdom blessing. Perhaps, then, they speak of the hope and promise of the future, the restoration from Babylonian exile being but the initial stage in the progressive fulfillment of that promise. The trees are situated in a ravine. At the foot of the Mount of Olives are myrtle groves in the lowest part of the Kidron Valley. The ravine may picture Judah's lowly condition at the time; but, as suggested above, there is a ray of light or hope for the future. Behind the horseman were red, brown, and white horses—presumably with riders on them, since they report to the angel of the Lord in v.11. These other riders or horses apparently represent angelic messengers (cf. v.10). White horses are associated with vengeance and triumph (cf. Rev 19:11, 14).

9–11 After Zechariah respectfully ("my lord") inquired about the meaning of the vision, the interpreting angel (mentioned also in vv.13, 14, 19; 2:3; 4:1, 4–5 [cf. Heb.]; 5:10; 6:4) indicated that he would explain the meaning (v.9). It was, however, the horseman among the myrtle trees who did the explaining (v.10). The explanation is that the other horsemen are angelic messengers sent by the Lord on missions throughout the earth. "Like the Persian monarchs who used messengers on swift steeds to keep them informed on all matters concerning their empire, so the Lord knew all about the countries of the earth, including the great Persian state" (Baldwin, *Zechariah*, p. 95). Such angels are part of the Lord's "hosts." The verb *šālaḥ* ("sent") seems to suggest that the horsemen are angelic messengers, for the Hebrew word for angel (*mal'āḵ*) literally means "sent one," "one sent with a message," "messenger." The root is *l'k*, which occurs in Ugaritic as a verb meaning "to send" (cf. UT, p. 426).

In v.11 the horseman among the myrtle trees in v.8 is identified as "the angel of the LORD." Here he served mainly as the captain of the Lord's host (the other horsemen). Elsewhere the angel of the Lord is identified quite often with the Lord himself (cf. Gen 16:11, 13; 18:1–2, 13, 17, 22; 22:11–12, 15–18; 31:11, 13; Exod 3:2, 4; Josh 5:13; 6:2; Judg 2:1–5; 6:11–12, 14; 13:3–23; Ezek 43:6–7; Zech 3:1–2). The other horsemen report to him that the whole world is at rest and in peace.

Such a description of the Persian Empire is confirmed by the inscription and bas-relief that Darius had incised on a rock at Behistun (or Bisitun), 328 feet above the highway connecting Ecbatana and Babylon. The bas-relief portrays the surrender of those who had rebelled against the king, while the inscription tells in Persian,

Elamite, and Babylonian the story of the political unrest in Persia during the first two years of Darius's reign, praising his feats of valor. Darius boasted that in nineteen battles he had defeated nine rebel leaders and had subdued all his enemies. So the empire was again virtually quiet by 520 B.C. Copies of the Behistun Inscription were sent to all the nations of the empire in their own languages. A fragment of the Babylonian copy survived in Babylon, and a piece of the Aramaic text was found in the Jewish colony at Elephantine (Yeb) in Egypt (cf. *Illustrated Family Encyclopedia*, 8:91). While the Persian Empire as a whole was secure and at ease by this time, the Israelites in Judah were oppressed and, of course, still under foreign domination, as the next verse makes clear.

12 The angel of the Lord was moved to intercede for the people of Judah. He desired the completion of the process of restoration, which required the reconstruction of the temple, Jerusalem, and the other towns of Judah. The report of the horsemen must have disappointed God's chosen people because it told of rest and peace among the nations, when, instead, they were expecting the "shaking of all nations" (Hag 2:6–9, 20–23) as the sign of returning favor and full blessing to Zion (cf. Perowne, p. 71). Through intercession suggestive of our Lord's high priestly prayer as our Mediator (John 17), the angel of the Lord prayed that in the mercy of God this situation would be rectified. The experience of God's disciplining anger for seventy years had been first predicted by Jeremiah (25:11–12; 29:10; cf. also 2 Chron 36:21; Ezra 1:1; Dan 9:2). This period may be calculated from 605 B.C. (the time of the first deportation from the land) to about 536 or 535 (the time when the first returnees were settled back in the land), or from 586 (when the temple was destroyed) to 516 (when the temple was rebuilt). Either way, the point is that the people wondered why God was still angry with them when the appointed time of their punishment had expired (or was almost over) (cf. Perowne, p. 71). The answer comes in the following verses.

13–15 Although it was the angel of the Lord who had interceded in v.12, the Lord's answer came directly to the interpreting angel and through him to Zechariah. Or "the LORD" (v.13) may refer to the angel of the Lord, who would then be giving the reply that he had received from the "LORD Almighty." The angel of the Lord is identified with the Lord elsewhere (see comment at v.11). The answer contained words that promised kindness (or "good things") and comfort (cf. Isa 40:1–2). The kind and comforting words (v.13) are those in the oracle of vv.14–17. In v.14 Zechariah was told to proclaim to the people that the Lord was "very jealous" for Jerusalem.

Attributing jealousy to the Lord poses no problem, for in OT usage jealousy is but the intolerance of rivalry or unfaithfulness. How one expresses that intolerance determines whether or not it is sin. When applied to the Lord, it usually concerns Israel and carries with it the notions of the marriage or covenant relationship and the Lord's right to exclusive possession of Israel. In this context the key idea is that of God's vindicating Israel for the violations against her, as v.15 indicates. Actually, jealousy is part of the vocabulary of love; through such language the Lord showed his love for Israel. Pusey paraphrases: "*I . . . am jealous* . . . with tender love which allows not what it loves to be injured" (2:344; emphasis his). The holy hill of Zion was particularly singled out as the Lord's special object of electing love (Ps 78:68; 132:13–14; cf. Zech 8:1–8).

In contrast to the Lord's jealous love for his people, he was "very angry" with the nations that treated them so harshly (v.15). The chiastic structure of v.15 (which, in Hebrew, begins with "great anger") in relation to v.14 (which, in Hebrew, ends with "great jealousy") emphasizes the Lord's anger; the participle *qōṣēp* ("angry") is probably intended to express the durative nature of that anger. The nations that God used to discipline his people included Assyria and Babylonia (cf. Isa 47:6, directed against the Babylonians; see also 52:4–5). They are characterized as "feeling secure" (cf. v.11). The sense is that the nations were arrogantly (or carelessly) at ease.

The reason for the divine displeasure is stated in the latter part of v.15. Since v.2 plainly says that the Lord was "very angry" with his sinning people, the clause "I was only a little angry" might be better rendered "I was angry only a little while." Such a nuance for *meʿāṭ* ("little") is possible (W.L. Holladay, *A Concise Hebrew and Aramaic Lexicon of the Old Testament* [Grand Rapids: Eerdmans, 1971], p. 206; see, e.g., Job 24:24). If this is correct, then in v.2 the stress is on the intensity of the anger, whereas in v.15 it is on the duration of the anger. This view is indirectly supported by Isaiah 54:7–8. The full charge against the nations, then, is that "they added to the calamity" of the divine discipline, not only by going too far and trying to annihilate the Jews, but also by prolonging the calamity. There is an implicit warning here against anti-Semitism (cf. Gen 12:3).

16–17 The Lord next presented the more positive aspect of the "kind and comforting words" (v.13). The word "therefore" shows the force: Because God had a jealous love for Israel and a jealous anger against her enemies, the following promises would be fulfilled. In response to the intercession of v.12, the Lord promised to return to Jerusalem with mercy (cf. Ezek 43:1–5; 48:35, which seem to reach to the end times for the final stage of the progressive fulfillment). The assurance that the temple ("my house") would be rebuilt expresses the divine mercy. The measuring line is that of those who were to reconstruct Jerusalem in a program of expansion (cf. 2:1–5). Halpern, comparing Jeremiah 31:38–40, correctly notes that the measuring line is "a symbol of restoration" (p. 178, n. 51). When one compares several other pertinent biblical references, it appears likely that the temple completed and dedicated in 516 B.C. (Ezra 6:15–16) was only the initial stage in the complete fulfillment (or in the "filling to the full") of vv.16–17 (note Isa 2:2–3; Jer 31:38–40; Ezek 40–42; Acts 15:14–18).

Verse 17 anticipates a time when the towns of Judah (also "my towns," says the Lord) will overflow (or "spread out") with prosperity. Thus the Lord would again comfort Zion and choose Jerusalem (cf. Isa 14:1). The temple, as the Lord's house, and Jerusalem, as the Lord's elect city in which his house and earthly throne were located, are inseparably linked in these verses. The "prosperity" in v.17 is to be connected with the "kind" words in v.13 and the "comfort" in v.17 with the "comforting" words in v.13, for the same Hebrew roots are involved in both places.

Feinberg (p. 38) has an excellent summary of the teaching and application of the first vision:

> The distinctive features of comfort for Israel in this first vision are: (1) the presence of the Angel of Jehovah in the midst of degraded and depressed Israel; (2) His loving and yearning intercession for them; (3) the promises of future blessings. We may say, then, that the import of the vision is this: although Israel

is not yet in her promised position, God is mindful of her, providing the means of His judgment on the persecuting nations, and reserving glory and prosperity for Israel in the benevolent and beneficent reign of the Messiah.

The series of visions carry us through God's dealings with Israel from the time of their chastisement by God under the Gentile powers until they are restored to their land with their rebuilt city and temple under their Messiah King. The first vision gives the general theme of the whole series; the others add the details. . . . When the world was busy with its own affairs, God's eyes and the heart of the Messiah were upon the lowly estate of Israel and upon the temple in Jerusalem.

Notes

10 Speiser (*Oriental and Biblical Studies: Collected Writings of E.A. Speiser,* ed. by J.J. Finkelstein and M. Greenberg [Philadelphia: University of Pennsylvania Press, 1967], pp. 506–14) has argued for a durative Hithpael of הָלַךְ (*hālak̲*, "to go"), going back originally to a *tan* form as in Akkadian. Such a sense would fit nicely in the context here: "They are the ones the Lord has sent to go continually throughout the earth."

11 עָנָה (*'ānāh*) does not always mean "to answer, reply." Sometimes it means "to respond, testify, speak, ask, report," as here (NIV). This was already recognized in BDB (pp. 772–73). The same is true of the Ugaritic *'ny*, which can mean simply "to say, speak up" (UT, p. 458). Other OT references that bear this out are Job 3:2 and Dan 2:26 (NIV).

13 נִחֻמִים (*niḥumîm*, "comforting") is not an adjective but a noun, functioning syntactically as a case of nominal apposition, with the collocation of the thing and the attribute (GKC, par. 131c; Davidson, par. 29e).

14 קִנְאָה (*qin'āh*, "jealousy") is the cognate accusative (see the note at v.2); so is קֶצֶף (*qeṣep̱*, "anger") in v.15.

15 אֲשֶׁר (*'ašer*) is here used in the sense of "for" (BDB, p. 83, par. 8c). NIV lets the juxtaposition of the clauses carry the force.

רָעָה (*rā'āh*, "calamity") can mean not only the "evil" that someone does but also the "disaster" he encounters as a consequence (G. Fohrer, "Twofold Aspects of Hebrew Words," in *Words and Meanings*, ed. by P.R. Ackroyd and B. Lindars [Cambridge: Cambridge University Press, 1968], p. 102).

16 רַחֲמִים (*raḥamîm*, "mercy" or "motherly compassion") is usually classified as the intensive plural (e.g., GKC, par. 124e), though it could also be simply the abstract plural (ibid., par. 124a).

B. *The Second Vision: The Four Horns and the Four Craftsmen*

1:18–21

18Then I looked up—and there before me were four horns! 19I asked the angel who was speaking to me, "What are these?"

He answered me, "These are the horns that scattered Judah, Israel and Jerusalem."

20Then the LORD showed me four craftsmen. 21I asked, "What are these coming to do?"

He answered, "These are the horns that scattered Judah so that no one could raise his head, but the craftsmen have come to terrify them and throw down these horns of the nations who lifted up their horns against the land of Judah to scatter its people."

18–19 The second and third visions build on the concept of the comfort promised in vv.13, 17: first, by presenting the manner in which God will execute his great anger against the nations that afflicted Israel (second vision), and second, by guaranteeing the prosperity and expansion promised Israel (third vision). The four horns (v.18) are identified as the nations (or their rulers) that attacked Judah, Israel, and Jerusalem to scatter their people (vv.19, 21). When used figuratively, "horn" usually symbolizes strength—either strength in general (Ps 18:2) or the strength of a country, i.e., its king (Ps 89:17; Dan 7:24; 8:20–21; Rev 17:12), or the power of a nation in general (here?). The horns are presumably on the heads of animals, since they are capable of being terrified (v.21).

The Targum translates "four horns" as "four kingdoms" (so Feinberg, p. 39). The kingdoms in question are claimed by some scholars to be the four world empires of Daniel 2 and 7 (namely, Babylonia, Medo-Persia, Greece, and Rome). Others suggest Assyria, Egypt, Babylonia, and Medo-Persia. Since the reference in vv.19, 21 is to nations that have already "scattered" God's people (though the Hebrew verb could also be translated "scatter" [present tense]), the latter view would seem preferable. God's people are referred to under the all-inclusive designation "Judah, Israel and Jerusalem," i.e., the whole nation scattered in exile. Jerusalem is mentioned because it was the capital of the united nation of Israel.

20 These craftsmen have been interpreted in at least two ways: (1) many of those who hold that the four horns symbolize the world empires of Daniel 2 and 7 (see discussion at vv.18–19) maintain that the craftsmen represent Medo-Persia, Greece, Rome, and the Messiah, since they are the destroyers of the preceding world empires (for the messianic role, see Dan 2:34–35, 44–45); (2) others (e.g., Charles Ryrie, *The Ryrie Study Bible* [Chicago: Moody, 1978], p. 1312n.) believe that the craftsmen denote the peoples and nations God used to overthrow Israel's past enemies—nations such as Egypt, Babylonia, Persia, and Greece, or perhaps Persia alone. In any event, it is clear in Scripture that all Israel's enemies—past, present, and potential—will ultimately be defeated.

21 The prophet's inquiry this time concerns, not identity or meaning, but function. The answer given (apparently by the interpreting angel) is that the horns came to scatter the people of Judah and render them helpless and powerless. This idea seems to be repeated from v.19 for emphasis. The horns that did this to Israel, Judah, and Jerusalem (v.19) have, by the time of Zechariah's prophecy, already been conquered and absorbed into the Persian Empire. The craftsmen are to be identified, then, at the very least with the world empire of Persia—and possibly with a few other nations as well (see remarks at v.20). Their function was to terrify and throw down the powers that, in arrogant defiance of God, went beyond all bounds in punishing and scattering God's covenant people. In v.15 the nations "feel secure" (or "are at ease"); now they are to be terrified and overthrown.

Notes

21 לְהַחֲרִיד (*lehaḥarîḏ*, "to terrify") and לְיַדּוֹת (*leyaddôṯ*, "to throw down") are good examples of the use of the infinitive construct with לְ (*le*, "to") to denote purpose (GKC, pars. 114f–g).

C. *The Third Vision: The Surveyor*

2:1–13

[1]Then I looked up—and there before me was a man with a measuring line in his hand! [2]I asked, "Where are you going?"

He answered me, "To measure Jerusalem, to find out how wide and how long it is."

[3]Then the angel who was speaking to me left, and another angel came to meet him [4]and said to him: "Run, tell that young man, 'Jerusalem will be a city without walls because of the great number of men and livestock in it. [5]And I myself will be a wall of fire around it,' declares the LORD, 'and I will be its glory within.'

[6]"Come! Come! Flee from the land of the north," declares the LORD, "for I have scattered you to the four winds of heaven," declares the LORD.

[7]"Come, O Zion! Escape, you who live in the Daughter of Babylon!" [8]For this is what the LORD Almighty says: "After he has honored me and has sent me against the nations that have plundered you—for whatever touches you touches the apple of his eye—[9]I will surely raise my hand against them so that their slaves will plunder them. Then you will know that the LORD Almighty has sent me.

[10]"Shout and be glad, O Daughter of Zion. For I am coming, and I will live among you," declares the LORD. [11]"Many nations will be joined with the LORD in that day and will become my people. I will live among you and you will know that the LORD Almighty has sent me to you. [12]The LORD will inherit Judah as his portion in the holy land and will again choose Jerusalem. [13]Be still before the LORD, all mankind, because he has roused himself from his holy dwelling."

1 The scope of the restoration and blessing promised in this vision is such that its fulfillment must extend beyond the historical restoration period to the messianic kingdom era. Perowne (p. 74) acknowledges this: "The [second] vision which describes the destruction of her enemies is followed by another, in which the consequent growth and prosperity of Jerusalem are depicted, and which in the largeness of its predictions extends into the more distant future." The persons connected with the introductory part of the vision are Zechariah, a surveyor, the interpreting angel, and an unidentified angel. Some have suggested that the surveyor ("a man") is the angel of the Lord (cf. 1:11; 6:12; Ezek 40:2–3). The "measuring line" is a symbol of preparation for rebuilding and restoring Jerusalem and the temple, ultimately in the messianic kingdom, as the following verses make plain. The restoration of the people, the temple, and the city immediately after the Babylonian exile was only the first stage in the progressive fulfillment of the promises that follow (see also Ezek 40:3, 5).

2–4a When Zechariah asked the surveyor where he was going, he replied that he was going to measure the width and length of Jerusalem, evidently to mark out its boundaries. This would be the first step toward the restoration of the city and the realization of the promised blessing (cf. 1:16; Ezek 40:5; Rev 11:1). At this point the interpreting angel started to leave; but as he did, he was met by another angel and was instructed to convey the message of vv.4–13 to Zechariah, who, in turn, would naturally declare it to his people. While some interpreters believe that the "young man" was the surveyor, it seems best and simplest to identify him with Zechariah.

4b The measuring was done with expansion in view; now that purpose is to be achieved. The promise is given that Jerusalem will become so large and prosperous that it will expand beyond its walls. Indeed, it will overflow so much that it will be as though it had no walls. Evidently many of its people and animals will have to live in the surrounding unwalled villages (cf. Ezek 38:11). Nothing like this has yet happened in the history of the city (certainly not in the time of Nehemiah, as is clear from Neh 7:4; 11:1–2). For this reason some commentators take the language of this and the following verses "spiritually" and apply it to the expansion of the church or the New (heavenly) Jerusalem. But Feinberg (p. 45) responds vigorously to such an approach:

> What baseless and unfounded hermeneutical alchemy is this which will take all the prophecies of judgment upon Israel at their face value, to be understood literally, but will transmute into indistinctness any blessing or promise of future glory for the same people? It is a sad state when men cannot see how kingdom conditions can exist alongside of spirituality. To many minds the introduction of literalness in kingdom promises does away with spirituality. What is so unspiritual about the personal, visible reign of the Messiah of Israel? Does not the same Word that predicts it also state clearly that from that Jerusalem, the seat of the government of the righteous King, will go forth the law and the Word of Jehovah (Isa. 2:1–4)? Wherein is the law lacking in spirituality? Paul declares the law to be holy, righteous, and good (Rom. 7:12). Again, we must maintain that literalness and a material kingdom with material conditions of prosperity *in no wise* exclude or militate against spirituality (emphasis his).

The realization of the full scope of this prophecy must therefore still be in a future earthly kingdom.

5 Although Jerusalem will become so large and prosperous that many of its inhabitants will spill over beyond the walls into the "suburbs," they will still be secure because of the divine protection ("a wall of fire around it") and the divine presence ("its glory"). "I" is emphatic in the original, hence NIV's "I myself." The "wall of fire" is reminiscent of the "pillar of fire" at the Exodus (Exod 13:21). Both are emblematic of God and his protection and guidance (Isa 4:5–6). In fact, both "fire" and "glory" recall the Exodus (Exod 13:22; 14:20; 40:34). Similarly, the future safety of Jerusalem and its people, including those living in the surrounding unwalled villages, is guaranteed. In addition, there is the promise of the Lord's glorious presence in regal holiness and majesty (cf. 1:16; Ps 24:7–10). The Lord's *kāḇôḏ* ("glory") is the "weight" of the impression of his self-manifestation. Here the manifestation is concerned with the final actualization of his rule (cf. G. von Rad, TDNT, 2:238–42). This anticipates the Lord's personal presence through the Messiah in his kingdom on earth (cf. 2:11–12; 14:9; Isa 60:19; Ezek 43:1–5; 48:35). So then the literal kingdom will be very spiritual.

6–7 According to Baldwin (*Zechariah*, pp. 93, 107–8), vv.6–13 constitute another prophetic oracle, not part of the vision proper. The land of the north (v.6) is Babylon (v.7), north being the direction from which the Neo-Babylonian army had invaded Judah (cf. Jer 1:14; 4:6; 6:1; 20:4–6; 31:8; et al.). The Jewish exiles who had not returned from Babylon in 538–537 B.C. were exhorted to do so at this time. The same Lord who had scattered them desired that they be restored and repatriated. The places of the Diaspora ("scattered") included not only Babylon ("the north") but also Assyria, Egypt, Persia, and the neighboring countries ("the four winds of heaven"; cf. Isa 43:5–6; 49:12). "Zion" (v.7) refers to the exiles from Zion in Babylon. "Flee" (v.6) and "escape" (v.7) imply that some imminent peril was coming on Babylon. Exactly what that peril was in the period immediately following 519 B.C. is historically uncertain. There is a similar exhortation to God's people to come out of the Babylon of Revelation 17–18, just prior to its final and complete destruction (cf. Rev 18:4–8).

"You who live in Daughter Babylon" would be a clearer rendering of the vocative at the end of v.7. The reference is to the Jews who had chosen to remain in Babylon. They were being called on to join the other returnees in Jerusalem, evidently to help them rebuild the temple and restore the city.

8 The opening words of the quotation ("After he has honored me and has sent me") are difficult and have given rise to several different translations and interpretations. For some of the possibilities, see Baldwin (*Zechariah*, p. 109). She prefers (with Théophane Chary, *Aggée-Zacharie Malachie* [Sources Bibliques, 1969], p. 70) "With insistence he sent me." All the Hebrew has is "After glory [or 'honor'; more literally, 'weight' or 'heaviness'] he has sent me." Some understand this to be saying "he has sent me to manifest my own glory" in judging the oppressing nations. Others take it to mean "he has sent me to glorify God [the Father]," arguing that God's glory is inseparably linked with the fortunes of his people (cf. Isa 61:3; John 17:4). NIV supplies a first-person singular pronoun ("me") with the word for "glory" or "honor," yielding the sense contained in its rendering.

Another problem is the identity of the referent in the pronominal suffix "me" both here and in v.9. While many think "me" refers to Zechariah, others maintain that, in the light of the language and the full scope of these verses, it looks toward the messianic Servant-Messenger, the Angel of the Lord (so Baron, Feinberg, Leupold, Unger). If the latter view is correct, as seems likely, the speaker, identified as the Lord Almighty at the beginning of the verse, is the Messiah himself, the Angel of the Lord. The mission of this person is directed against the nations that have plundered God's chosen people. Such treatment of the Jews is condemned because harming them is like striking the apple of God's eye, an obvious anthropomorphism. "Apple" is literally "gate," that is, the pupil, an extremely sensitive and vital part of the eye that must be carefully protected. God is so closely identified with his people that they are precious to him, and he is zealous to protect them and take care of them (cf. Deut 32:10; Ps 17:8; Matt 25:34–45; Acts 9:1, 4–5). Verse 9 gives proof of such care.

9 In a menacing gesture the Lord will raise his hand against Israel's enemies (cf. Isa 11:15; 19:16). The Hebrew for "raise" may also be rendered "wave." All it takes for God to punish his people's enemies is a wave of his hand, as it were. This is another evidence that the speaker here and in v.8 is deity (the Messiah or the Angel of the Lord). "My hand" refers to the display of divine omnipotence—God's infinite power. Here it is exerted in behalf of God's people and against their enemies. God brings about a reversal of the fortunes of his people; the tables are turned. The Jews, who were slaves of the nations that plundered them (v.8), will now plunder those nations (cf. Isa 14:2). Such reversals are quite common; the destroyed are often self-destroyed. Haman was hanged "on the gallows he had prepared for Mordecai" (Esth 7:10; cf. also Gal 6:7–8). When all this happens, the people "will know that the LORD Almighty has sent" his messenger. The fulfillment will authenticate the message and ministry of the messianic Servant-Messenger (or the Angel of the Lord or, possibly, Zechariah). These words also stress the certainty of the fulfillment.

10 In fulfillment of the great OT covenants, particularly the Abrahamic covenant, this section anticipates full kingdom blessing in the messianic era. Then many (Gentile) nations will become the people of God, but the Lord's special favor will continue to rest on "the holy land." The section begins with a call to joy, followed by the reason for such jubilation (cf. 9:9). The reason given is the personal coming of God himself to live among his people in Jerusalem (Zion). This language is ultimately messianic—indirectly or by extension from God in general to the Messiah in particular.

One of the four major categories of messianic prophecy is indirect messianic prophecy (the other three being direct, typical, and typical-prophetical). Indirect messianic prophecy refers to passages that can be literally and fully realized only through the person and work of the Messiah—e.g., passages that speak of a personal coming of God to his people, as in v.10 and 9:9 (cf. also Isa 40:9–11; Mal 3:1). The same is true of references to the expression "the LORD reigns" or "will reign," so characteristic of the so-called Enthronement Psalms (e.g., 93, 95–99). These "eschatologically Yahwistic" psalms are probably best labeled theocratic, "Rule-of-God" Psalms. The point is that all passages that speak of a future coming of the Lord to his people or to the earth, or that speak of a future rule of the Lord over Israel or over the whole earth, are ultimately messianic—indirectly or by extension—for to be fully and literally true, they require a future, literal messianic kingdom on the earth.

"The verb 'dwell' [NIV, 'live'] (*šāḵan*, from which is derived 'shekinah') recalls the making of the tabernacle (*miškān*) 'that I may dwell in their midst' (Ex. 25:8)" (Baldwin, *Zechariah*, p. 111). She continues: "This same purpose attached in turn to the Temple (1 Ki. 6:13), and when Ezekiel looked forward to the new Temple he saw the coming of the glory of the Lord (43:2, 4) and His acceptance of the Temple as the place of His throne (verse 7) for ever (verse 9)" (ibid.). For further biblical development of the theological theme of God's dwelling or living among his people, see vv.11–13 and 8:3 (cf. also John 1:14; 2 Cor 6:16; Rev 21:3).

11–12 In the great messianic future, many nations "will be joined with the LORD" (v.11) or "will join themselves to the LORD" (the Hebrew can be rendered either way). Such an ingathering of the nations to the Lord echoes the promise in the Abrahamic covenant: "All peoples on earth will be blessed through you" (Gen 12:3; cf. 18:18 and 22:18; see also Isa 2:2–4; 60:3; Zech 8:20–23). The result is that they, too, will become the people of God. All this will happen "in that day." "That day" is frequently an abbreviation of the Day of the Lord, which has both historical and eschatological applications and calls for special study. The context here concerns the eschatological fulfillment of the day. A few other key passages on the eschatological Day of the Lord are Isaiah 2:12–21, dealing with judgment; chapters 24–27, concerned with both judgment and blessing; Joel 1:15, stressing judgment; 2:28–3:21, emphasizing both judgment and blessing; Amos 5:18–20, on judgment, but 9:11–15, on blessing; Zephaniah, the early part of which refers to judgment but the latter part to blessing—all in connection with the prophet's theme, the Day of the Lord; and Zechariah 14, where reference is made at the beginning of the chapter to the coming invasion of Jerusalem by hostile nations and to the (second) coming of the Messiah (the Lord), followed by the blessing of the messianic kingdom—all under the heading of the "day of the LORD" (v.1). The Messiah's advent is the turning point between the judgment and the blessing aspects of "that day."

It seems clear, then, that the events of Daniel's seventieth "seven" (Dan 9:27)—i.e., the entire tribulation period (Rev 6–18), which is the judgment aspect of the Day of the Lord—the Messiah's second advent to the earth (Rev 19), and the messianic kingdom age (Rev 20)—which is the blessing aspect of "that day"—are all included in the scope of the Day of the Lord. In the light of biblical usage, the eschatological Day of the Lord may be defined as earth's final period of time. It commences with the judgment of Daniel's seventieth "week." It continues with the Messiah's (Christ's) return and reign on earth. And it extends to the appearance of the new heavens and the new earth (Rev 21:1), when the messianic kingdom will continue as (or, perhaps better, merge with) the eternal kingdom (1 Cor 15:24–28; Rev 21–22). Thus many supernatural, momentous events fall within the time span of the Day of the Lord. Man, so to speak, is having his day now. The Lord's day is yet to come. He will have his day at the time of the events of Daniel's seventieth "week" (the "time of trouble for Jacob," Jer 30:7) and of his own second coming and glorious reign on earth—a reign that will endure forever. Finally, since the text states that this conversion of many nations will take place "in that day" (the eschaton), the present ingathering (Acts 15:12–18) is but a stage in the complete fulfillment (cf. Matt 24:14; Rev 7:9; 21:24, 26).

If the person who said, "I will live among you" (v.10) was also the speaker of the same words in v.11, as seems certain, then the "me" at the end of v.11 must refer to the messianic Servant-Messenger (or Angel of the Lord), for the speaker in v.10 was clearly deity.

The conversion of many nations to the Lord does not abrogate the promise and purpose of God for Israel, his chosen and special covenant people (cf. Barker, "False Dichotomies," pp. 10–16). In keeping with that promise, v.12 indicates that the Lord will inherit Judah (both land and people) and will again choose Jerusalem (cf. 1:17), for many decisive events will yet take place there (e.g., 14:4). There is a similar emphasis on both Gentile and Jewish blessing in Isaiah 19:24–25: "In that day Israel will be the third, along with Egypt and Assyria, a blessing on the earth. The LORD Almighty will bless them, saying, 'Blessed be Egypt my people, Assyria my handiwork, and Israel my inheritance.' " Saints in the church are also said to be part of the glorious inheritance of Christ (Eph 1:18; see also Isa 52:15; 53:10–12).

The people of Judah are described as the Lord's portion in the "holy land" (v.12). This is the only occurrence of the epithet "holy land" in Scripture, though the following do occur: "holy hill" (Ps 2:6; 15:1; cf. Zech 8:3), "holy city" (Isa 48:2; Dan 9:24; Matt 27:53; Rev 21:2), and "holy nation" (Exod 19:6; cf. 1 Peter 2:9). The temple, as the place of God's earthly throne, was by definition "holy" (Ps 65:4; Jonah 2:4). But that holiness extended beyond the temple and beyond the holy city to the entire land (cf. also 14:20–21, where common things become holy because they are used for God's service; cf. Baldwin, *Zechariah*, p. 112). The root idea of the Hebrew word for "holy" is "separate" or "set apart" (here, in v.12, for God's use and glory; cf. Snaith, pp. 24–25—the full discussion is in pp. 21–50). Palestine is rendered holy (i.e., sacred, not common or ordinary) chiefly because it is the site of the earthly throne and sanctuary of the holy God, who dwells there among his covenant people.

In Isaiah 6:1–5 the ascription of "holiness" to the Lord begins with the Lord seated as King on a throne, high and exalted. Thus the Lord is "separated" spatially from his creation. Then, too, there is a close connection between the Lord's holiness and his kingship. Isaiah saw the Lord on his majestic throne in the year that Judah lost one of its better kings (Uzziah) after a long and prosperous reign (cf. 2 Chron 26). Thus the Lord is "separated" from the frailties of human rulers. Isaiah 6:3 closely associates the Lord's regal glory (his manifested character) with his "holiness." After seeing the vision, Isaiah's first utterance declared the Lord to be King (6:5; note the emphatic word order in the original). So the concept of the root *qdš* ("holy") in Isaiah 6 relates to the high, exalted, and "set apart" King of Israel. It is instructive to note that the remnant is a "holy" ("separated") seed (Isa 6:13). The Lord, the holy and all glorious King, will acquire a holy people who are to display and declare his holiness and glory (cf. further Exod 19:6; Lev 11:44–45; 19:1; Pss 24:3–10; 29:1–2, 10; 96:9; cf. 1 Peter 1:15–16; Rev 4:8). Finally, according to 3:9; 13:1; 14:20–21 (cf. Isa 35:8; 62:12), a time is coming when the land and the people will be "holy" (or "holier") in their experience.

13 All mankind was exhorted to be still (in awe) before the Lord because, in a threatening gesture (cf. v.9), he had roused himself from his holy dwelling (probably in heaven) and would judge the enemies of his people (cf. Hab 2:20; Zeph 1:7). He was about to break his apparent silence by acting in behalf of his elect (see, ultimately, 12:1–5; 14:1–5). With the opening of the scroll with seven seals in Revelation 5–6; 8, the present apparent silence of God will similarly be broken, unleashing the greatest judgments ever to strike the earth; yet once again his beleaguered people (or a remnant of them) will be delivered, restored, and blessed.

The first vision introduced the judgment (or curse) and blessing motif (1:15–17). That motif is then developed in the second and third visions in an alternating cycle: judgment for the nations (1:18–21) but blessing and glory for Israel (2:1–5); judgment for the nations (2:6–9) but blessing for Israel—and the nations (2:10–13).

Notes

4a רֻץ (*ruṣ*, "run") here means "run as a messenger," or "run with the message" (as in Jer 23:21), and so is appropriate for an "angel-messenger."

4b פְּרָזוֹת (*perāzôt*, "without walls") is an adverbial accusative of condition or manner (GKC, pars. 118 m, q, r; Davidson, pars. 70a; 71, rem. 1); hence, more literally, "Jerusalem will be inhabited [or 'will dwell'] as unwalled villages."

6 GKC (par. 154b) explains the prefixed ו (waw) in וְנֻסוּ (*wenusû*, "Flee") as the "waw copulativum" that joins a sentence apparently to what immediately precedes but, in reality, to a sentence that is suppressed. This is especially true when the waw is joined to an imperative. Sometimes the suppression of the protasis is due to passionate excitement or haste, which does not allow time for full expression, as in the instance before us.

7 בַּת (*bat*, "daughter") in phrases like "Daughter of Babylon" and "Daughter of Zion" (v.10; 9:9) is a form of personification, roughly equivalent to "city of . . ." or sometimes "people of . . ." (BDB, p. 123, par. 3).

8 עֵינוֹ (*ênô*, "his eye"), according to ancient Hebrew scribal tradition, is a *tiqqun sopherim* ("scribal emendation"). The Masorah informs us that the original reading was עֵינִי (*ênî*, "my eye"). The anthropomorphism was thought to be too bold; so the scribes changed

"my" to "his," intending that the antecedent be understood as "whoever" instead of God. If the correct text is "my eye," as seems probable, this strengthens the case for a messianic (or at least "Angel of the Lord") interpretation of the passage, for then the speaker throughout the oracle is even more clearly deity. For a full discussion of the problem of scribal emendations, see C.D. Ginsburg, *Introduction to the Massoretico-critical Edition of the Hebrew Bible* (New York: Ktav, 1966), pp. 347–63. The working principle for such textual changes was to alter all indecent, anthropomorphic, offensive expressions, particularly those that the scribes felt would detract from God in any way. The scribes were not consistent in the application of the principle, however, for some rather bold anthropomorphisms remain—even in the utterances of God himself.

9 "My hand" is not only an anthropomorphism but also a metonymy of the cause (hand) for the effect (power) (Bullinger, pp. 546–47). The suffix in לְעַבְדֵיהֶם (*le'abedêhem*, "their slaves") is best taken as objective genitive (cf. GKC, pars. 128h, 135m). This can be brought out clearly by translating the clause "so that they will be plunder for those who served them."

10 בָא (*bā'*, "coming") features the *futurum instans* or imminent action use of the participle (GKC, par. 116p).

וְשָׁכַנְתִּי (*wešākantî*, "and I will live") is the waw consecutive perfect, as the accent on the ultima indicates; it continues the *futurum instans* idea of the participle.

12 עוֹד (*'ôd*, "again"; perhaps better, "yet") "does not imply that God must choose Israel afresh, but that now, at long last, He will be able to manifest to the world the immutable character of His original choice and its practical outworking in renewed, restored, and resettled Israel" (Feinberg, p. 51).

13 הַס (*has*, "Be still" or "Be silent") is probably an example of onomatopoeia, i.e., a word formed by reproducing the sound one would frequently make in telling someone to be quiet, silent, or still. The similar word "hush" in English may also be onomatopoetic.

נֵעוֹר (*nē'ôr*, "he has roused himself") is the Niphal form of the verb, here used reflexively rather than passively, though either is possible.

D. *The Fourth Vision: The Cleansing and Restoration of Israel*

3:1–10

1Then he showed me Joshua the high priest standing before the angel of the LORD, and Satan standing at his right side to accuse him. 2The LORD said to Satan, "The LORD rebuke you, Satan! The LORD, who has chosen Jerusalem, rebuke you! Is not this man a burning stick snatched from the fire?"

3Now Joshua was dressed in filthy clothes as he stood before the angel. 4The angel said to those who were standing before him, "Take off his filthy clothes."

Then he said to Joshua, "See, I have taken away your sin, and I will put rich garments on you."

5Then I said, "Put a clean turban on his head." So they put a clean turban on his head and clothed him, while the angel of the LORD stood by.

6The angel of the LORD gave this charge to Joshua: 7"This is what the LORD Almighty says: 'If you will walk in my ways and keep my requirements, then you will govern my house and have charge of my courts, and I will give you a place among these standing here.

8" 'Listen, O high priest Joshua and your associates seated before you, who are men symbolic of things to come: I am going to bring my servant, the Branch. 9See, the stone I have set in front of Joshua! There are seven eyes on that one stone, and I will engrave an inscription on it,' says the LORD Almighty, 'and I will remove the sin of this land in a single day.

10" 'In that day each of you will invite his neighbor to sit under his vine and fig tree,' declares the LORD Almighty."

1 The fourth vision is different from the three previous ones in that there are no questions from the prophet and no explanations from the interpreting angel. The reasons for this are that the identity of Joshua is known from the beginning and the action is explained as the vision unfolds (cf. Baldwin, *Zechariah*, p. 113). As indicated by the NIV margin at v.1, Joshua is the same person as Jeshua in Ezra and Nehemiah. Both forms of the name mean "the Lord saves" (cf. NIV mg. at Matt 1:21).

This chapter presents the grand prophecy of Israel's restoration as a priestly nation. Regarding Israel's calling, Exodus 19:6 states, "You will be for me a kingdom of priests and a holy nation." Just as it was certain that there could be no failure in the restoration work on the temple that the remnant had taken up anew, so it is assured that God's future program for Israel will be consummated at the return of the Messiah to the earth (Zech 14). In this apocalyptic vision the high priest Joshua represents the sinful nation Israel (cf. comment at v.8). However, though Israel is presented in defilement, she is also cleansed and restored as a kingdom of priests for God—a condition that will be realized in the Messianic Age. This symbolic interpretation becomes progressively clearer as one moves through the chapter. Basically, visions four and five "concern Judah's standing before God and her spiritual resources" (Baldwin, *Zechariah*, p. 113).

The revealer of the vision is either the interpreting angel or, more likely, God himself (cf. 1:20). As has been said, Joshua represents Israel in her priestly character. The scope of this passage demands that interpretation. Then, too, in v.8 Joshua and his colleagues are definitely said to be symbolic of the future. The Angel of the Lord must be deity, for in v.2 he is specifically called "the LORD." Thus he clearly represents God. "Standing before the . . . LORD" is a technical designation for priestly ministry (metonymy of adjunct, Bullinger, p. 606; cf. Deut 10:8; 2 Chron 29:11; Ezek 44:15). Hence the scene is in the temple.

Although the scene is not basically a legal one, Satan's accusation invests it with a judicial character. The position of standing at the right side was the place of accusation under the law (Ps 109:6). Satan knows the purposes of God concerning Israel and therefore has always accused the Jews and accuses them still. The tool of his nefarious opposition to Israel has primarily been the Gentile nations—something that will be particularly true during the period of Daniel's seventieth "week." Satan is the accuser, not only of Joshua (i.e., Israel), but also of all believers (Job 1–2; Rev 12:10). Undoubtedly the accusation here relates to the sin of Joshua (cf. vv.3–4) and is made in the hope that God will reject his people irrevocably. But this we know he will never do, as the following verses assert (cf. also Lev 26:40–45; Jer 31:36–37; 32:40; Rom 3:1–4; 11:1–2). Regarding *wᵉhaśśāṭān . . . lᵉśiṭnô* ("and Satan . . . to accuse him"), Chambers (CHS, p. 35) says, "The force of this antanaclasis can hardly be expressed in a version—the *opposer to oppose him* fails to convey the force of the proper name Satan" (emphasis his). Other scholars, however, do not take *śāṭān* as a proper noun; they translate: "and the accuser . . . to accuse him." One cannot be dogmatic, as it is sometimes difficult to determine when (or if) a common noun also began to function as a personal name. With such nouns the presence or absence of the definite article does not finally settle the question. There is a similar problem with the Hebrew word for "man" and "Adam" in the early chapters of Genesis (cf. NIV mg. there).

2 Israel's denunciation (v.1) was followed by her defense. The defender was none other than the Lord himself. Since the speaker in this verse was quite clearly the Angel of the Lord (cf. v.1 and the quotation in v.2), this is but another evidence of the deity of the Angel of the Lord. That God chose Jerusalem further proves that Joshua portrayed Israel as a nation. The quotation contains a double rebuke of Satan ("the accuser"). The words are repeated for emphasis, "and with the repetition the motive which led Jehovah to reject the accuser is added. Because Jehovah has chosen Jerusalem, and maintains His choice in its integrity" (KD, *Minor Prophets*, 2:251–52; cf. 1:17; 2:12). God's sovereign choice of Jerusalem in grace shows the unreasonableness of Satan's attack (cf. Rom 8:33). The reference to the burning stick snatched from the fire is an additional indication that Israel, not Joshua, is ultimately in view. Israel was retrieved to carry out God's future purpose for her (cf. Amos 4:11). The "fire" refers to the Babylonian captivity. Metaphorically, Israel was snatched as a burning stick from that fire. However, this event may also look back to the deliverance from Egypt (cf. Deut 4:20; 7:7–8; Jer 11:4) and forward to the rescue from the coming tribulation period (cf. Jer 30:7; Zech 13:8–9; Rev 12:13–17).

3 The reason for Satan's accusation is given, namely, Israel's impurity. This verse raises the problem of how a holy God can bless a filthy nation like Israel. The answer is that he can do so only by his grace through the work of the Messiah. The Hebrew word *ṣô'îm* ("filthy") is "the strongest expression in the Hebrew language for filth of the most vile and loathesome character" (Feinberg, p. 58). Some interpreters maintain that Joshua was covered with excrement—only in the vision, of course! Such clothes represent the pollution of sin (cf. Isa 64:6). To compound the problem, Joshua (i.e., Israel), contaminated by sin, was ministering in this filthy condition before the Angel of the Lord.

4 NIV, probably correctly, identifies the unnamed speaker as the "angel" of the Lord. The removal of the filthy clothes (apparently by angels—"those who were standing before him") may connote that Joshua was thereby deprived of priestly office. If so, he is reinstated in v.5. Theologically, however, there also seems to be a picture here of the negative aspect of what God does when he saves a person. Negatively, he takes away sin. Positively, he adds or imputes to the sinner saved by grace his own divine righteousness (cf. v.5). The act of causing Joshua's sin to pass from him (cf. Heb.) represents justification, not sanctification. It is forensic forgiveness that is in view, as seen from v.9, which interprets Joshua's cleansing by applying it to the land (i.e., the people)—another evidence that more than Joshua himself is in view here.

Next, Joshua was to be clothed with rich garments—God's representative clothed in God's righteousness. God's servant went from filthy garments to festive garments. The festive garments (the Hebrew word is used only here and in Isa 3:22 speak of purity, joy, and glory; but their chief significance is that they symbolize the restoration of Israel to her original calling (Exod 19:16; Isa 61:6). There is a contrast here: Joshua in filthy garments—Israel as a priest but defiled and unclean; Joshua in festive garments—Israel's future glory in reconsecration to the priestly office. "I have taken away" emphasizes the agent of the forgiveness. It is God who causes sin to be removed, ultimately on the basis of the messianic Servant's substitutionary death. But note that here it was actually the Angel of the Lord who forgave sin, thus identifying him as deity (cf. Mark 2:7, 10).

5 As Zechariah contemplated the scene, he could not help but ask that the work be completed, hence his request. Joshua was crowned with a clean turban and clothed with rich garments, symbolic of divine righteousness. Previously Joshua had been filthy; now he received a clean turban. On the front of the turban were the words: "HOLY TO THE LORD" (Exod 28:36; 39:30). Once again this is a foreview of Israel's future purging and reinstatement to her priestly function. "While the angel of the LORD stood by" is a circumstantial clause. The thought is that he was standing by, approving and directing Joshua's purging, clothing, and crowning on the basis of the fact that God's righteousness and mercy were being bestowed.

6–7 Israel's originally intended position would finally be realized. The Angel of the Lord gave a charge to Joshua (v.6). In the charge (v.7) two conditions are stated, with three results following. The protasis is indicated by *'im* ("if"), the conditional particle. The apodosis or result is marked by *w^e* (*gam*), the waw being translated "then." "Walk in my ways" (the first condition) refers to the personal life and attitude toward the Lord. Personal or practical righteousness is in view (cf. 1 Thess 4:1; 1 Tim 4:16). "Keep my requirements" (the second condition) speaks of the diligent and faithful fulfillment of official, divinely appointed, priestly duties. Official faithfulness is in view.

An analysis of the three results of meeting the two conditions reveals Israel's earthly calling and her glory and ministry in the Messianic Age.

1. Israel will govern the house of God. This includes deciding disputed matters in connection with the sanctuary. Furthermore, from the temple the other nations will be ruled and judged by the Messiah of Israel, the Head of the nations (cf. Jer 31:7).

2. Israel will have charge of God's courts. This implies guarding the temple courts from pollution and idolatry. The temple will then be a house of prayer for all nations (Isa 56:7). Jeremiah 31:22 may well anticipate such a role for Israel in the future: "The LORD will create a new thing on earth—a woman will surround a man." The last line of the verse is probably a proverbial statement that Jeremiah applied to Israel's relation to God, the woman representing Israel and the man representing God in Jeremiah's usage. The meaning may be that Israel will at last protect God's interests rather than that God will protect Israel.

3. Israel will have ready and free access to God in the priestly function, just as the angels ("these standing here"—cf. v.4) have access to God. This may be regarded as a renewal of Israel's covenant of priesthood or as the reinstatement of the nation into her original calling, her priestly office and function (cf. Exod 19:6; Isa 61:6). Because of the work of Christ, Christians now enjoy free access to the presence of God (cf. Heb 4:16; 10:19–22).

8 The persons involved in this prediction were Joshua, his colleagues, and the Branch, the Servant of the Lord. They foreshadowed greater events in the future. Joshua and his fellow priests represented coming events and persons. They are said to be men of *môpēṯ* ("divine sign or wonder," "prophetic significance," or "token of a future event"; cf. Isa 8:18). They symbolized future events for Israel, as NIV correctly interprets it. They excited wonder because they were types of Israel in close association with someone to come. This coming one was called "my servant, the Branch"—two well-known OT appellations for the Messiah. As Servant, the Messiah came into the world to do the will of the Father. Through his work, Israel will yet be redeemed and restored as a priestly nation, which Joshua and his associate priests typified. (For a full development of the messianic Servant motif, see H. Blocher, *Songs of the Servant* [Downers Grove, Ill.: InterVarsity, 1975], and C.R. North, *The Suffering Servant in Deutero-Isaiah* [London: Oxford University Press, 1956]; see also the comments at 1:6.)

As Branch, the Messiah is presented in the OT in four different aspects of his character (King, Servant, Man, and God). These aspects are developed in the NT in the four Gospels: (1) in Matthew as the Branch of David, i.e., as the Davidic messianic King (Isa 11:1; Jer 23:5; 33:15); (2) in Mark as the Lord's Servant, the Branch (Isa 42:1; 49:6; 50:10; 52:13; Ezek 34:23–24; Zech 3:8); (3) in Luke as the Man whose name is the Branch (Zech 6:12); and (4) in John as the Branch of the Lord (Isa 4:2). The Aramaic Targum of Jonathan interprets the Branch as the Messiah, the King (so Feinberg, p. 63).

9 Here is a revelation of what the Messiah will accomplish in behalf of Israel. Some interpret the "stone" as Israel. It seems best and more consistent with the context, however, to take it as another figure of the Messiah (cf. Bullinger, pp. 896–97). To the Jews at his first advent, the Messiah (Christ) was the stumbling stone and rock of offense (Isa 8:13–15; cf. Ps 118:22–23; Matt 21:42; 1 Peter 2:7–8). But to those who trusted in him, he was a never-failing refuge (Isa 28:16; 1 Peter 2:6). Moreover, he is to be the smiting stone to the nations (Dan 2:35, 45). At present he is the foundation and chief cornerstone of the church (Eph 2:19–22). And to restored Israel in the Messianic Era, he will be the dependable rock of the trusting heart. While some understand the stone as a precious gem with seven facets (lit., "eyes"), typical of the Messiah's glory, it is probably better to interpret the figure in the light of biblical usage—in keeping with the above passage. The seven eyes would then speak of the fullness of the Holy Spirit or of the Godhead and would be symbolic of infinite intelligence and omniscience (cf. 4:10; Isa 11:2; Col 2:3, 9; Rev 5:6).

The engraving on the stone is difficult to interpret but is explained by the early church fathers as follows: "Beautiful beyond all beauty must be those glorious scars, with which He allowed His whole Body to be riven, that 'throughout the whole frame His love might be engraven' " (cited by Pusey, 2:359). Thus they refer these words to the wounds of Christ. The passage possibly connotes a sealing action by God, or perhaps a beautifying activity. Next, the Lord (the Angel of the Lord?) purged and cleansed Israel from sin. The sin of that land, not of Joshua, but of the people of the land of Palestine, was taken away in a single day, symbolized by the removal of the filthy clothes in v.4. Prophetically, the one day is the once-for-all deliverance potentially provided at Calvary—to be actually and finally realized in Israel's experience at the second advent of her Messiah, when there will be cleansing and forgiveness for the nation as a whole (Zech 12:10–13:1; Rom 11:26–27). Then will the benefits of the Day of Atonement and the provisions of the new covenant be fully applied to Israel. In 2:12 Palestine was called "the holy land." This appellation will be even more appropriate in the Messianic Age, after the action spoken of here in v.9. Thus the Messiah will accomplish the marvelous transformation from Israel's shame to her glory.

10 The result of the action of vv.8–9 is peace and security for God's people. God's purpose for Israel will be realized in the theocratic kingdom, when Israel will enjoy contentment, peace, and prosperity—similar to the peaceful and prosperous days of King Solomon (1 Kings 4:25). "That day" is the eschatological time of Israel's cleansing and restoration as a kingdom of priests—the Messianic Era (see on 2:11 and "the day of the LORD"). This closing verse pictures Israel's future condition under divine favor and blessing when there will be no more curse. The vine and the fig tree speak not only of spiritual blessing but also of the agricultural blessing of the land when the desert will blossom like the crocus and once again be fruitful (cf. Isa 11:1–9; 35; 65:17). There can be no such prosperity and peace for Israel till the messianic kingdom has fully come on earth, no such kingdom till Israel is restored, and no true restoration of Israel till the Lord returns to the earth with his saints (cf. Dan 7: 13–14, 27; Mic 4:1–4). Baron's summary (p. 122) is illuminating:

> And thus, in the last verse of this chapter, a picture is given of a day . . . when, on account of sin pardoned, free access to God's throne granted, and the Deliverer having come anointed with the plentitude of the Spirit and sealed by God the Father, each true Israelite would invite his friends as joyful guests to partake of festal cheer under his own vine and fig-tree. The days of peace once more are seen. The glorious era of the earthly Solomon has indeed returned in greater splendour under the reign of the Prince of Peace. "Paradise lost" has become "Paradise regained."

In this vision of the restoration of Israel as a kingdom of priests, Exodus 19:6 finds its fullest expression. The accomplishments of the Messiah in Israel's behalf are summarized in Romans 11:26–27, providing a fitting conclusion to this chapter:

> And so all Israel will be saved, as it is written:
> "The deliverer will come from Zion;
> he will turn godlessness away from Jacob.
> And this is my covenant with them
> when I take away their sins."

Notes

1 "And Satan standing at his right side" is a circumstantial clause introduced by the simple waw. The definite article in הַשָּׂטָן (*haśśāṭān*, "Satan" or "the accuser") is used to elevate into distinctive prominence a particular individual of the class (so Davidson, par. 21c).

ל (*l*ᵉ, "to") before the infinitive construct שִׂטְנוֹ (*śiṭnô*, "accuse him") expresses purpose.

2 מֻצָּל (*muṣṣāl*, "snatched") is a Hophal participle from the root *nṣl*, here used with adjectival significance.

3 The verb הָיָה (*hāyāh*, "was") with the participle לָבֻשׁ (*lābuš*, "dressed") is a periphrastic construction, stressing habitual condition (cf. Davidson, par. 100, rem. 2). The noun clause at the end of the verse describes a state contemporaneous with the preceding verb; NIV therefore translates the conjunction "as" (cf. GKC, par. 141e).

4 וְהַלְבֵּשׁ (*wᵉhalbēš*, "and I will put [or 'clothe']") is a Hiphil infinitive absolute, taking the place and having the force of a finite verb (cf. GKC, par. 113z; Davidson, par. 88a, rem. 1). This analysis, which continues the first person of the preceding verb, is to be preferred over the LXX reading ("and clothe him"), which changes the person of both the subject and the object.

5 The context dictates that יָשִׂימוּ (*yāśîmû*, "Let them put") be taken as a jussive.

The word for "turban" is צָנִיף (*ṣānîp*, from a verb meaning "to wind around").

8 הַכֹּהֵן הַגָּדוֹל (*hakkōhēn haggādôl*, "high priest") furnishes a good illustration of the vocative use of the definite article (GKC, par. 126e [e]; Davidson, pars. 21–22).

9 The correct etymology of מוּשׁ (*mûš*), the root behind the form rendered "and I will remove," is probably the Akkadian *mêšu*, "to forgive, disregard sins" (M. Civil et al., eds., *The Assyrian Dictionary* [Chicago: Oriental Institute, 1956—], X/2, pp. 41–42).

E. *The Fifth Vision: The Gold Lampstand and the Two Olive Trees*

4:1–14

[1]Then the angel who talked with me returned and wakened me, as a man is wakened from his sleep. [2]He asked me, "What do you see?"

I answered, "I see a solid gold lampstand with a bowl at the top and seven lights on it, with seven channels to the lights. [3]Also there are two olive trees by it, one on the right of the bowl and the other on its left."

[4]I asked the angel who talked with me, "What are these, my lord?"

[5]He answered, "Do you not know what these are?"

"No, my lord," I replied.

[6]So he said to me, "This is the word of the LORD to Zerubbabel: 'Not by might nor by power, but by my Spirit,' says the LORD Almighty.

[7]"What are you, O mighty mountain? Before Zerubbabel you will become level ground. Then he will bring out the capstone to shouts of 'God bless it! God bless it!' "

[8]Then the word of the LORD came to me: [9]"The hands of Zerubbabel have laid the foundation of this temple; his hands will also complete it. Then you will know that the LORD Almighty has sent me to you.

[10]"Who despises the day of small things? Men will rejoice when they see the plumb line in the hand of Zerubbabel.

"(These seven are the eyes of the LORD, which range throughout the earth.)"

[11]Then I asked the angel, "What are these two olive trees on the right and the left of the lampstand?"

[12]Again I asked him, "What are these two olive branches beside the two gold pipes that pour out golden oil?"

[13]He replied, "Do you not know what these are?"

"No, my lord," I said.

[14]So he said, "These are the two who are anointed to serve the Lord of all the earth."

1 The main purposes of the vision were (1) to encourage the two leaders, Joshua and Zerubbabel, in the work of rebuilding the temple by reminding them of their divine resources and (2) to vindicate them in the eyes of the community (so Baldwin, *Zechariah*, p. 119). In this chapter the lampstand probably represents the idea of testimony (light bearing; cf. Matt 5:16; Rev 1:20; 2:5). Zerubbabel and Joshua (the two olive branches testified to God's power in completing the temple. The whole nation of Israel was also intended to serve as God's witness to the other nations of the world. In the coming tribulation period, two special witnesses for God will again appear on the scene (Rev 11:3–12). All effective testifying must be done in the power of God's Spirit (the oil). By his Spirit, God provides the enablement to do his work—then and now (v.6).

In order to prepare Zechariah to receive the fifth vision, the interpreting angel woke him from his ecstatic sleep of wonder and astonishment over the previous vision. The wakening obviously took place on the same night, further corroborating the view that Zechariah received all the visions during one night.

2 If the lampstand of Zechariah's vision corresponds to those known from archaeology, probably the most accurate reconstruction is that of K. Galling. It is described by Baldwin (*Zechariah*, pp. 119–20): "Lamp pedestals excavated from Palestine . . . were cylindrical in shape, hollow, and looked rather like a tree trunk. . . . Zechariah's lampstand (*mᵉnôrâ*) was probably just a cylindrical column, tapering slightly towards the top, on which was *a bowl*. . . . Zechariah's large bowl . . . had *seven lamps on it, with seven lips on each of the lamps*. The picture is of seven small bowls, each with a place for seven wicks, arranged round the rim of the main bowl" (emphasis hers). An actual drawing of Galling's reconstruction is reproduced in IDB, 3:66, and in North's article (p. 189). North differs slightly from Galling and believes that each of the seven lamps had only one light instead of seven (see his reconstruction on p. 201 of his article). However, he essentially follows Galling in basic design and construction.

More important than how the lampstand looked is what it signified, and this has already been suggested in the introductory paragraph under v.1. The seven "channels" (or, more likely, "lips" or "spouts" for wicks) to each of the seven lamps (forty-nine spouts in all) would seem to stress the abundant supply of the oil, which in turn symbolizes the fullness of God's power through his Spirit (seven being the number of fullness or completion; cf. v.6).

3 Possibly the two olive trees stand for the priestly and royal offices in Israel. Undoubtedly the two olive branches (vv.12, 14) represent Joshua–Israel (ch. 3) and Zerubbabel (ch. 4; cf. v.14). According to v.12, each of the two olive trees has an olive branch beside a golden pipe that pours out golden oil. The olive oil is conducted directly from the trees to the bowl of oil at the top of the lampstand—without any human agency ("might" or "power," v.6). Similarly, Zerubbabel and Joshua are to bear continual testimony for God's glory and are to do God's work—e.g., on the temple and in the lives of the people—in the power of his Spirit (v.6). This combination of the priestly and royal lines and functions is apparently intended to point ultimately to the messianic King-Priest and his offices and functions (cf. 6:13).

4–6 The purpose of the vision was to encourage Zerubbabel to complete the rebuilding of the temple and to assure him of enablement of God's Spirit for the work. The answer to Zechariah's inquiry (v.4) was postponed (see vv.11–14) in order to emphasize the final verse of the chapter and, in the meantime, to focus attention on only one of the two olive branches, namely, Zerubbabel (v.6), and his special ministry. "These" (v.4) refers to the two olive trees of v.3, as v.11 makes clear.

Verse 6 interprets the symbolism of the oil ("by my Spirit"). Just as there was a constant and sufficient supply of oil without human agency, so Zerubbabel's work on the temple and in the lives of the people was to be completed, not by human might or power, but by divine power—constant and sufficient. The work was dependent on God; he would provide the oil or strength of his Spirit. Such enablement was solely needed because of the opposition and apathy hindering the rebuilding (Hag 2:1–9). "Looked at from a human point of view the manpower available was inadequate for the task. . . . Only if His Spirit governs every detail can service be glorifying to Him" (Baldwin, *Zechariah*, p. 121). Verses 6–10 are perhaps best regarded as an oracle within this vision.

7 Faith in the power of God's Spirit can overcome mountainous obstacles—indeed, can reduce them to "level ground." In a bold apostrophe ("you"; cf. Bullinger, pp. 901–5), a defiant challenge was laid down against whatever would hinder the rebuilding of the temple. The figurative mountain could include opposition (Ezra 4:1–5, 24) and the people's unwillingness to persevere (Hag 1:14; 2:1–9). (For a similar use of the word "mountain," see Isa 40:4; 41:15; 49:11; Matt 17:20; 21:21; Mark 11:23; 1 Cor 13:2.) That the project would ultimately succeed is indicated by the assurance that Zerubbabel will experience the joy of helping put the capstone in place, thus marking the completion of the restoration temple. The shouts at the end of the verse can be understood as either (1) an ejaculatory description of the finished structure ("How perfectly beautiful it is!") or (2) a prayerful desire for God's gracious blessing to rest on it (NIV). The latter seems more likely.

8–9 Verse 8 ("the word of the LORD came to me") would appear to support the notion of taking this section as an oracle within the vision. In contrast to chapter 3, which focused on Joshua, v.9 again focuses on Zerubbabel. The laying of the temple foundation refers back to what took place in 537–536 B.C. (Ezra 3:8–11; 5:16). The year was now 519, three years before the fulfillment of the prediction that Zerubbabel would complete the superstructure (Ezra 6:14–18). So then a delay in the execution of God's will need not end in ultimate defeat. Finally, the completely restored temple (in 516 B.C.) would prove the divine commission of the speaker.

On the difficulty of identifying the speaker in this formulaic expression, see the comment at 2:11. Here, as there, "me" apparently refers to the messianic Servant-Messenger (or the Angel of the Lord). Feinberg (pp. 76–77) maintains that just as chapter 3 had an immediate application to Joshua and then went on to speak of the messianic Branch and Stone, so this chapter has an immediate reference to Zerubbabel and then beyond him to the Messiah (cf. 6:12–13).

10 The opening question obviously implies that some of the people had a negative attitude toward the temple project and those involved in it. In the context "the day of small things" refers to the "day" of beginning the work on the temple and now continuing it. Some thought it was insignificant (Ezra 3:12; Hag 2:3), forgetting that little is much when God is in it. And God was definitely in this rebuilding program; by his Spirit (v.6) he was enabling Zerubbabel to finish the work. Perhaps the "despisers" were also discouraged because they were a relatively small group, forgetting that God's work is usually accomplished through a small, believing, righteous remnant. Yet their persevering faith and work would be rewarded when they joyfully would see the plumb line in the hand of Zerubbabel to complete the task.

The Hebrew for "plumb line" is difficult. The words may also be rendered "separated [i.e., chosen] stone," referring to the capstone of v.7. The parenthesis at the end of the verse is also difficult. As NIV renders it, it is perhaps best to understand it as a reminder to Zerubbabel and the people that God is omniscient ("seven eyes"). As such, he knows, sees, and governs all. Since he thus oversees the entire earth, he is in control of Israel's situation. So understood "eyes" is an anthropomorphism for God's all-knowing ("seven") observation (cf. Bullinger, p. 875), and "range" is a personification of the eyes. (See also the comment on "seven eyes" at 3:9.)

11–14 The question and response of vv.4–5 in the vision are now resumed after the intervening oracle of vv.6–10. In v.12 Zechariah repeated his question from v.11 in order to be more specific. He desired an explanation of what he saw in vv.2–3. In v.12 the Hebrew for "golden oil" is literally "gold," but NIV correctly represents the sense (the oil being described by its color).

The answer to the prophet's inquiry comes in v.14, where the two olive branches are implicitly identified as Zerubbabel, a member of the line of David, and Joshua. In the light of the context (chs. 3–4), they must be "the two who are anointed to serve the Lord." In the Hebrew text they are designated as "sons of oil," but NIV has accurately captured the sense ("anointed" as God's appointed leaders). Both priest and ruler were anointed for service to the Lord and the covenant community. The oil takes us back again to v.6 ("by my Spirit"). It has already been suggested in the comment at v.3 that this combination of ruler and priest is evidently intended to point ultimately to the messianic King-Priest (cf. 6:13; Ps 110; Heb 7). In keeping with one of the key ideas of the chapter (viz., bearing testimony), only the messianic King-Priest may be acknowledged as the perfectly "faithful and true witness" (Rev 3:14). Finally, since God was declared to be "the Lord of all the earth," he was master of all the circumstances in which Zerubbabel and the people found themselves.

Notes

---

2 The Qere reading, וָאֹמַר (*wā'ōmar*, "I answered"), is to be preferred over the Kethiv, which has the third person. The Qere is supported by many Hebrew MSS and the ancient versions.

וְגֻלָּה (*wegullā[h]*, "with a bowl") is probably a better reading than the suffixal form *wegullāh* ("with its bowl"). The former is supported by many Hebrew MSS, LXX, Syriac, and Targum.

The repetition in the construction שִׁבְעָה וְשִׁבְעָה (*šib̲'āh wešib̲'āh*, lit., "seven and seven") is best understood distributively (cf. GKC, par. 134q; Davidson, par. 38, rem. 4). Thus the sense would be "with seven channels [or 'spouts'] to *each* of the lights." The same syntactical idiom occurs in 2 Sam 21:20; 1 Chron 20:6.

6 The quotation at the end of the verse is unusually emphatic, with no subject or predicate.

7 Either אַתָּה הַר־הַגָּדוֹל (*'attāh har-haggād̲ôl*, "you, O mighty mountain" is an instance where the adjective is definite and the noun is anarthrous (Davidson, par. 32, rem. 2), or the first part of the expression is to be read אַתְּ הָהָר (*'attā hāhār*; so GKC, par. 126x).

The repetition of חֵן in חֵן חֵן לָהּ (*ḥēn ḥēn lāh*, "God bless it! God bless it!") is for emphasis: "May *all* [divine] favor rest on it!"

9 Baldwin (*Zechariah*, pp. 52–53) maintains that the temple foundation was not destroyed in 586 B.C. (2 Kings 25:9). Therefore it would not have been necessary to relay the foundation in 537. If she is correct, the first part of v.9 should be translated "The hands of Zerubbabel have begun to rebuild [or restore] this temple." Such a meaning for יָסַד (*yāsad̲*) seems attested in 2 Chron 24:27. (Baldwin argues for this meaning in order to remove certain apparent contradictions elsewhere.)

וְיָדַעְתָּ (*weyād̲a'tā*, "then you will know") is a waw consecutive perfect, as the accent on the ultima shows. Here it also introduces a temporal and/or logical consequence (cf. GKC, par. 112p.).

10 בַּז (*b̲az*, "despises") is probably a characteristic perfect, best rendered in English by the present tense. On the form itself, see GKC, par. 72dd. The NIV handling of אֶת־הָאֶבֶן הַבְּדִיל (*'et̲-hā'eb̲en habbed̲îl*, "the plumb line") is to be explained along the lines of GKC, par. 127h: "Of another kind are the instances in which a determinate noun is followed by a definition of the material *in apposition* . . . e.g. Zc 4[10] . . . *the weight, the lead,* i.e. *the leaden weight*" (emphasis theirs).

עֵינֵי יְהוָה (*'ênê YHWH*, "the eyes of the LORD") probably stands in apposition to "these seven," and הֵמָּה (*hēmmāh*, "are") functions as a copula (GKC, par. 141g–h). A somewhat literal translation reflecting such an understanding of the syntax would run like this: "These seven—viz., the eyes of the LORD—are ranging throughout the earth."

14 Based on Ugaritic etymological cognates, the meaning "lord," "sovereign" for אָדוֹן (*'āḏôn*) is apparently a semantic development from an original meaning of "father." There is also the form אֲדֹנָי (*'ᵃḏōnāy*), regarded by many as the plural of *'āḏôn* with the suffix "my"; hence, "my lord" (this is the word the Masoretes read in place of the ineffable, sacred Tetragrammaton, YHWH [Yahweh]). But the most probable explanation of *'ᵃḏōnāy* is that it contains a nominal afformative, which strengthens the meaning of the simple form *'āḏôn*, so that the meaning "Lord" (referring to God) comes from this. For the whole discussion, see Eissfeldt, TDOT, 1:59–72; also Barker, "Value of Ugaritic," pp. 124–25.

F. *The Sixth Vision: The Flying Scroll*

5:1–4

[1]I looked again—and there before me was a flying scroll!
[2]He asked me, "What do you see?"
I answered, "I see a flying scroll, thirty feet long and fifteen feet wide."
[3]And he said to me, "This is the curse that is going out over the whole land; for according to what it says on one side, every thief will be banished, and according to what it says on the other, everyone who swears falsely will be banished. [4]The LORD Almighty declares, 'I will send it out, and it will enter the house of the thief and the house of him who swears falsely by my name. It will remain in his house and destroy it, both its timbers and its stones.' "

1–2 The sixth and seventh visions are in harmony with one of Zechariah's concerns —namely, the promotion of spiritual renewal. In this vision, lawbreakers are condemned by the law they have broken; in the next one, the land is purged of wickedness. There is a movement from promise (ch. 4) to threat. In v.1 the scroll is not rolled up but flying (i.e., unrolled for all to read). Significantly, in the postexilic (restoration) period there was a renewed interest in the study and teaching of the law (Torah).

Not only was the scroll open for all to read, but it was also very large for all to see (v.2). Its message of judgment was not concealed from anyone. Such a bold, clear pronouncement of punishment for sin should have spurned the people on to repentance and righteousness. The dimensions of the scroll are calculated on the basis of a cubit equaling eighteen inches (cf. NIV mg. and table at back of NIV).

3 The message and meaning of the scroll are revealed. Those who persisted in breaking the covenant (Exod 20) would experience the curse (punishment) for disobedience and unfaithfulness (Deut 27:26). Since the scroll was apparently inscribed on both sides, like the two tablets of the law (Exod 32:15), one side must have contained the curse against those who violated the third commandment of the law while the other side contained the curse against those who broke the eighth commandment. The thief broke the eighth commandment, and whoever swore falsely violated the third commandment; it becomes clear from v.4 that the third commandment was in view rather than the ninth. We have here a form of synecdoche in which the species is put for the genus (cf. Bullinger, pp. 625–29). In other words, these two representative sins—perhaps theft and perjury were the most common ones at this time—stand for all kinds of sin. The point is that Israel was guilty of breaking the whole law.

According to James 2:10, one breaks the whole law if he "stumbles at just one point." Such lawbreakers are to be "banished." The precise meaning of the Hebrew verb so translated is difficult. Does it mean "cut off" (executed) or "banished"? Since either is lexically possible, one cannot be dogmatic. Either way it amounts to the more original etymological notion of "cleansing" or "purging" the land from chronic covenant-breakers. With exegetical insight Baldwin (*Zechariah*, p. 127) observes that "*every one who steals* is a pithy way of saying 'every one who wrongs his neighbour,' and *every one who swears falsely* (invoking the divine name) sums up blatant disregard for God's holiness" (emphasis hers). This is so because God has always required adherence, not only to the letter of the law, but also to the spirit of the law (cf. Barker, "False Dichotomies," pp. 5–6).

4 The pronoun "it" refers to the curse (v.3). There can be no hiding, no escape, from the judgment of that curse. God's word, whether promise or threat (as here), is efficacious (cf. Isa 55:10–11 and comments at 1:1, 6). "It" will enter and destroy the homes of the guilty. Even the privacy of their homes will afford them no refuge from divine judgment (cf. Num 32:23). The word "thief" recalls Exodus 20:15, and "him who swears falsely by my name" is a clear echo of Exodus 20:7—though both commandments are broader than the infractions singled out here. On "it will remain" Pusey (2:366) comments that it is "lit., 'lodge for the night,' until it has accomplished that for which it was sent, its utter destruction." To judge from the materials used in the houses (cf. Hag 1:3–9), it was primarily the wealthy and those in power who were guilty of committing these sins.

Notes

1 וָאָשׁוּב (*wāʾāšûḇ*, "again") is explained in GKC, par. 120d: "The principal idea is introduced only by the second verb, while the first . . . contains the definition of the manner of the action, e.g. Gn 26[18] וַיָּשָׁב וַיַּחְפֹּר [*wayyāšāḇ wayyaḥpōr*] *and he returned and digged*, i.e. he digged again" (emphasis theirs).

2 On בָּאַמָּה (*bāʾammāh*, lit., "by the cubit"), see GKC, par. 134n.

3 מִזֶּה . . . מִזֶּה (*mizzeh . . . mizzeh*) means "on one side . . . on the other side" (BDB, p. 262).

The Niphal, נִקָּה (*niqqāh*, "will be banished") is a prophetic perfect (cf. GKC, par. 106n).

4 הוֹצֵאתִיהָ (*hôṣēʾṯîhā*, "I will send it out") is also the prophetic perfect. On the other hand, וּבָאָה (*ûḇāʾāh*, "and it will enter") is the waw consecutive perfect but with the same force as the preceding prophetic perfect, on which it depends for its syntactical function. The same applies to וְלָנֶה (*w*ᵉ*lāneh*, "it will remain"); on the slightly anomalous form, cf. GKC, par. 73d.

וְכִלַּתּוּ (*w*ᵉ*ḵillattû*, "and it will destroy it") stands for וְכִלַּתְהוּ (*w*ᵉ*ḵillaṯhû*; GKC, par. 75mm).

G. *The Seventh Vision: The Woman in a Basket*

5:5–11

[5]Then the angel who was speaking to me came forward and said to me, "Look up and see what this is that is appearing."

[6]I asked, "What is it?"

He replied, "It is a measuring basket." And he added, "This is the iniquity of the people throughout the land."

[7]Then the cover of lead was raised, and there in the basket sat a woman! [8]He said, "This is wickedness," and he pushed her back into the basket and pushed the lead cover down over its mouth.

[9]Then I looked up—and there before me were two women, with the wind in their wings! They had wings like those of a stork, and they lifted up the basket between heaven and earth.

[10]"Where are they taking the basket?" I asked the angel who was speaking to me.

[11]He replied, "To the country of Babylonia to build a house for it. When it is ready, the basket will be set there in its place."

5–6 In 2:12 Palestine was called "the holy land." In 3:9 a future day was anticipated when the sin of that land would be taken away. The sixth vision has just dealt with the purging of flagrant, persistent sinners from the land. Now, in the seventh vision, this motif continues to be developed as the removal of wickedness is vividly depicted. Not only sinners, but also the whole sinful system must be removed—apparently to the place of its origin (Babylon).

What Zechariah saw this time was a measuring basket (v.6), literally, "an ephah"—here the measure stands for the container. An ephah would be less than a bushel; so a normal ephah measuring basket (or barrel) would not be large enough to hold a person. This one was undoubtedly enlarged—like the flying scroll—for the purpose of the vision. The end of v.6 indicates that the basket represents the people's iniquity or crookedness that pervades the land.

7–8 The import of the measuring basket is now fully revealed: When the cover of lead was lifted from the basket, wickedness was exposed, personified by a woman (cf. Rev 17:3–5). Like the basket itself (v.6), the woman in it represents the sin of the people in Palestine, whose measure or cup of evil was full. The whole evil system was to be destroyed. In v.8 the Hebrew word for "wickedness" is feminine. This may explain why the wickedness of the people is personified as a woman. "Wickedness"—a general word denoting moral, religious, and civil evil—is frequently used as an antonym of righteousness (e.g., Prov 13:6; Ezek 33:12). The woman (wickedness) "attempts to escape from captivity, but the angel with superior strength is able to confine her to the ephah, though the verbs indicate a struggle involved. The power of evil was to be taken seriously" (Baldwin, *Zechariah*, p. 129). For an analogous event, see 2 Thessalonians 2:6–8.

9 The fate of the woman (wickedness) is portrayed: She is to be removed from the land. Although some regard the two women as agents of evil (partly because the stork is an unclean bird, Lev 11:19), it seems preferable to regard them as divinely chosen agents. They, along with the wind (also an instrument of God, Ps 104:3–4), would thus demonstrate that the removal was the work of God alone. The simile "wings like those of a stork" is evidently intended to show that the winged women—carried along by the wind—were capable of supporting the woman in the basket over a great distance.

10–11 The destination of the women bearing the sin away was "Babylonia" (*šin'ār*, "Shinar"). As the present writer has pointed out elsewhere, Shinar "in Gen 10:10 apparently includes the area of both Sumer and Akkad" (WBE, 2:1631). It therefore roughly corresponded to ancient Babylonia (cf. also Gen 11:2; 14:1, 9). Ellis (p. 1034) notes: "Thus where Judah had been exiled was a fitting place for wickedness to be worshipped, but not in the land where God had placed *his* name. The idolatry of Babylon must once and for all be separated from the worship of the God of Israel" (emphasis his). Baldwin (*Zechariah*, p. 130), agreeing with Frey, suggests that if "the removal of Wickedness to Babylon is in preparation for the final onslaught between good and evil, the vision leaves no doubt about the outcome. God has evil in His power."

The evil will be put in a "house," perhaps referring to a temple or ziggurat. "Its place" may have in view a base or pedestal on which the basket and its contents are set up as an idol, "as Dagon or Ashtaroth, or Baal had their houses or temples, a great idol temple, in which the god of this world should be worshiped" (Pusey, 2:369). Feinberg (p. 93) concludes: "The two visions of our chapter thus bring before us God's twofold method of dealing with sin in His people. He pours out His wrath upon the transgressors who are impenitent, and then sees to the utter removal and banishment of sin from the land, that it may in truth be the holy land." Second Corinthians 7:1 provides an appropriate application for us: "Since we have these promises, dear friends, let us purify ourselves from everything that contaminates body and spirit, perfecting holiness out of reverence for God."

Notes

---

6 עֵינָם (*'ênām*) presents a text-critical problem. As it stands, it means "their eye" (i.e., their appearance), which does not yield a good sense (cf. the parallel in v.8, where the woman in the basket is interpreted as wickedness personified). NIV, probably correctly, follows one Hebrew MS, the LXX, and the Syriac in reading עֲוֺנָם (*'ᵃwōnām*, "their iniquity"). (The pronominal suffix refers to the people, perhaps with special reference to the godless rich.) The only significant variation between the two readings is the waw instead of the yod. Even here it should be borne in mind that in many ancient Hebrew MSS the only perceptible difference between the two letters is the length of the downward stroke. A long yod and a short waw are virtually indistinguishable. To further support the reading "their iniquity [or 'perversity']," Baldwin (*Zechariah*, p. 128) adds: "The ephah, named by Amos in his invective on short measure given by the merchants (Am. 8:5), symbolized injustice *in all the land*. The life of the community was vitiated by iniquity that infected it in every part (*cf*. Hg. 2:14). The meanness that prompted the making of false measures was a symptom of an underlying perversity that was at the root of perverse actions and relationships" (emphasis hers).

9 Syntactically וְרוּחַ בְּכַנְפֵיהֶם (*wᵉrûaḥ bᵉkanᵉpêhem*, "with the wind in their wings") is a circumstantial clause (cf. GKC, pars. 156a, c).

10 On הֵמָּה (*hēmmāh*, "they") instead of the expected feminine הֵנָּה (*hēnnāh*), see GKC, par. 32n.

11 לָה (*lāh*, "for it") is sometimes written with *rāphè* instead of *mappîq* (cf. GKC, pars. 23k, 103g. The feminine suffix refers to the measuring basket (or ephah). The subject of וְהוּכַן (*wᵉhûkan*, "when it is ready") is "house," and the subject of וְהֻנִּיחָה (*wᵉhunnîḥāh*, "it will be set") is "basket" (or "ephah"); this can be determined by correlating the genders of the nouns with those of the verbal forms. For the latter verb the LXX supports an active form: *wᵉhinnîḥuhā* ("they will set it"), but there is no sound reason to emend the MT.

H. *The Eighth Vision: The Four Chariots*

6:1–8

1 I looked up again—and there before me were four chariots coming out from between two mountains—mountains of bronze! 2 The first chariot had red horses, the second black, 3 the third white, and the fourth dappled—all of them powerful. 4 I asked the angel who was speaking to me, "What are these, my lord?"

5 The angel answered me, "These are the four spirits of heaven, going out from standing in the presence of the Lord of the whole world. 6 The one with the black horses is going toward the north country, the one with the white horses toward the west, and the one with the dappled horses toward the south."

7 When the powerful horses went out, they were straining to go throughout the earth. And he said, "Go throughout the earth!" So they went throughout the earth.

8 Then he called to me, "Look, those going toward the north country have given my Spirit rest in the land of the north."

1 This last vision obviously corresponds to the first, though there are differences in details, such as in the order and colors of the horses. (Regarding the latter problem, see the extended note in Baldwin, *Zechariah*, pp. 138–40.) As in the first vision, the Lord is again depicted as the one who controls the events of history. He will conquer the nations that oppress Israel. Since his war chariots claim victory in the north (v.8), total victory is certain. The chariots of v.1 must serve basically the same symbolic function—they are vehicles of God's judgment on the nations. Such judgment is probably also the symbolic significance of the "bronze" mountains (cf. the bronze snake [Num 21:9] and the bronze altar [Exod 27:2]). The two mountains would most naturally refer to Mount Zion and the Mount of Olives (so KD, Pusey et al.), with the Kidron Valley between them. The present writer has pointed out elsewhere (ZPEB, 2:84) the following:

> In Joel 3:14 this expression ["valley of decision"] refers to the valley of Jehoshaphat (Joel 3:2, 12). The latter in turn seems to be a symbolical name of a valley near Jerusalem which is to be the place of God's ultimate judgment on the nations gathered to attack Jerusalem. Significantly, Jehoshaphat had witnessed one of the Lord's historical victories over the nations (2 Chron 20). The valley has been traditionally identified with the Kidron, but the location remains a problem. Perhaps the solution is contained in Zechariah 14:4, which indicates that when the Lord returns to the Mount of Olives a great valley will be opened. Since Jehoshaphat's name means "The Lord judges," possibly this newly opened valley is so named because of the Lord's judgment there.

2–3 The chariots seem to represent angelic spirits (cf. v.5), while the variegated horses evidently signify divine judgments on the earth (cf. v.8). Unger (pp. 102–3), comparing Revelation 6:1–8, suggests that the red horses symbolize war and bloodshed; the black horses, famine and death; the white horses, victory and triumph; and the dappled horses, death by plagues and other judgments. White horses (cf. also 1:8) are clearly associated with vengeance and triumph in Revelation 19:11, 14. The fact that there are four chariots may indicate that the angelic spirits are ready to embark on universal judgments (cf. expressions like "the four winds of heaven" [2:6; Jer 49:36; Ezek 37:9], "the four quarters of the heavens" [Jer 49:36], and "the four corners of the earth" [Rev 7:1]).

4–6 "These" (v.4) refers to the chariots, with the horses harnessed to them. In v.5 the four chariots are identified as four spirits (i.e., angelic beings; cf. comment at 1:10). Although the same Hebrew word can also mean "winds" (cf. NIV mg.), angelic "spirits" as agents of divine judgment seems more appropriate, particularly since they stand before God here—but see Feinberg (p. 98), who argues for "winds." For "the Lord of the whole world," see comment at 4:14.

In v.6 the chariot with the black horses hitched to it goes toward the north country, primarily Babylonia, but also the direction from which most of Israel's formidable enemies invade Palestine. As the MT stands (cf. Notes and NIV mg.), the chariot with the black horses is followed northward by the one with the white horses. However, with a slight change in the Hebrew text (cf. Notes), the latter chariot would go toward the west (as in NIV), i.e., toward the islands and coastlands of the Mediterranean area. The south (at the end of v.6) is principally Egypt but also the other main direction (besides the north) from which Israel's foes invade Palestine. As the text now stands, nothing is said of the east, possibly because the Arabian Desert lay in that direction. Similarly, nothing is said of the chariot with the red horses, but the latter are undoubtedly included among "the powerful horses" of v.7.

7–8 As in v.3, "powerful" (v.7) describes all the horses. All were eager to take the chariots (angelic spirits) on the mission of bringing divine judgment on the peoples of the earth. But the horses cannot begin till authorized to do so. "From first to last (*cf.* 1:10) the affairs of the nations are under God's direction, not man's" (Baldwin, *Zechariah*, p. 132). "Those going toward the north country" (v.8) designates either the black horses and their chariots or both the black horses and the white horses (see comment at v.6).

The interpretation of the last part of v.8 depends on how "my Spirit" is to be understood. Under any view the pronoun "my" indicates that the speaker is ultimately deity, i.e., God or the messianic Servant-Messenger, i.e., the Angel of the Lord. If the NIV ("Spirit") is correct, the meaning is this: "Recent events had been the work of God's Spirit, but now that work is finished, and the messengers to the north have set God's *Spirit at rest*. No more remains to be done" (Baldwin, *Zechariah*, p. 132, emphasis hers). If, on the other hand, the NIV margin ("spirit") is correct, the meaning is this: The angelic beings dispatched to the north have triumphed and thus have pacified or appeased God's spirit (i.e., his anger). This interpretation receives some support from 1:15, where God's displeasure was aroused against oppressive nations. Either way, since conquest is announced in the north, victory is assured over all enemies.

Notes

1 On the syntactical function of וָאָשֻׁב (*wā'āšuḇ*, "again"), see the note at 5:1.

נְחֹשֶׁת (*neḥōšeṯ*) means "bronze" (sometimes "copper"), not "brass" (an alloy unknown in the biblical period).

3 אֲמֻצִּים (*'amuṣṣîm*, "powerful") probably describes all the horses (as in NIV; cf. v.7 for support), not just the dappled ones (as in KJV, NASB).

6 NIV fills in the ellipsis at the beginning of this verse: "The one [i.e., 'the chariot'] with."

As the text in the middle of the verse stands (MT), אַחֲרֵיהֶם (*'aḥarêhem*, "after them," NIV mg.) means that the white horses followed the black ones to the north. A slight emendation, however, yields אַחֲרֵי הַיָּם (*'aḥarê hayyām* "after [or 'behind'] the sea," i.e., "toward the west," NIV). Another factor to consider is that the MT itself may possibly mean "toward the west." After all, מֵאָחוֹר (*mē'āḥôr*) means "from the west" in Isa 9:12 (11 MT), and אַחֲרֹנִים (*'aḥarōnîm*) means "men of the west" in Job 18:20. Perhaps, then, such a nuance should be allowed for *'aḥarêhem;* thus "after [or 'behind'] them" = "their west." With the preposition אֶל (*'el*, "toward") added, the complete phrase would mean "toward the west."

7 For the significance of the Hithpael in לְהִתְהַלֵּךְ (*lehiṯhallēḵ*, "to go"), see note at 1:10. The speaker in וַיֹּאמֶר (*wayyō'mer*, "and he said") is either the interpreting angel or the Lord himself. Grammatically the feminine gender of וַתִּתְהַלַּכְנָה (*wattiṯhallaḵnāh*, "so they went") agrees with the chariots instead of the horses.

III. The Symbolic Crowning of Joshua the High Priest

6:9–15

[9]The word of the LORD came to me: [10]"Take ⌊silver and gold⌋ from the exiles Heldai, Tobijah and Jedaiah, who have arrived from Babylon. Go the same day to the house of Josiah son of Zephaniah. [11]Take the silver and gold and make a crown, and set it on the head of the high priest, Joshua son of Jehozadak. [12]Tell him this is what the LORD Almighty says: 'Here is the man whose name is the Branch, and he will branch out from his place and build the temple of the LORD. [13]It is he who will build the temple of the LORD, and he will be clothed with majesty and will sit and rule on his throne. And he will be a priest on his throne. And there will be harmony between the two.' [14]The crown will be given to Heldai, Tobijah, Jedaiah and Hen son of Zephaniah as a memorial in the temple of the LORD. [15]Those who are far away will come and help to build the temple of the LORD, and you will know that the LORD Almighty has sent me to you. This will happen if you diligently obey the LORD your God."

9–10 The position of this actual ceremony after the eight visions is significant. The fourth and fifth visions, at the center of the series, were concerned with the high priest and the civil governor in the Davidic line. Zechariah here linked the message of those two visions to the messianic King-Priest. In the fourth vision (ch. 3), Joshua was priest; here (v.13) the Branch was to officiate as priest. In the fifth vision (ch. 4), Zerubbabel was the governing civil official; here (v.13) the Branch was to rule the government. In 4:9 Zerubbabel was to complete the rebuilding of the temple; here (v.12) the Branch would build the temple. In 4:14 Zerubbabel and Joshua represented two separate offices; here the Branch was to hold both offices (v.13). Thus restored Israel is seen in the future under the glorious reign of the messianic King-

Priest. The passage is typical-prophetical. Joshua served as a type of the Messiah, but at certain points the language transcends the experience of the type and becomes more directly prophetical of the antitype.

Unger (*Zechariah*, pp. 109–10) stresses the importance of the context:

> Immediately following the overthrow of Gentile world power by the earth judgments symbolized by the horsed chariots (Zech. 6:1–8) occurs the manifestation of Christ in His kingdom glory (Zech. 6:9–15) typified by the crowning of Joshua the high priest. This is the usual prophetic order: first, the judgments of the day of the Lord; then full kingdom blessing (Ps. 2:5, cf. Ps. 2:6; Isa. 3:24–26, cf. 4:2–6; 10:33, 34, cf. 11:1–10; Rev. 19:19–21, cf. 20:4–6).
>
> The eight night visions have ended, but the coronation of Joshua is closely connected with these revelations which extend in scope from Zechariah's day to the full establishment of Israel in blessing. The crowning of King-Priest Messiah is thus set forth symbolically by the coronation of Joshua, which is not a vision, but an actual historical act, which evidently took place the day following the night of visions.
>
> The last thing the prophet saw was the horses galloping away with their war chariots. And in Jerusalem, what a sight meets his eyes, to demonstrate that the truth contained in his visions was already coming to pass!

Verse 9 introduces a prophetic oracle (for the formula, see also 4:8; 7:4; 8:1, 18). In the first part of v.10, representatives arrive from Babylon with gifts for the temple; and in the last part of the verse, Zechariah is told to meet them. The meeting takes place in the home of one Josiah, who was entertaining the returned exiles. In v.14 (q.v.) he is honored with the name "Hen."

11 In a coronation scene Zechariah was told to take the silver and gold brought from Babylon, to make a crown for royalty, and to put it on Joshua's head. The Hebrew word for "crown" is not *nēzer* (used for the high priest's crown or turban) but *ʿaṭārôṯ*, referring to an ornate crown with many diadems—a plural of extension (cf. Rev 19:12). From the verses that follow, it becomes obvious that the royal crowning of the high priest is a type of the goal and consummation of prophecy—the crowning and reign of the messianic King-Priest. Therefore Joshua, who was never a priest-king, was a type of the messianic Branch of v.12 (see comment at 3:8). According to v.13, the Branch would be a priest on his throne. Thus the fulfillment in the Messiah transcends Joshua's status and experience (cf. Ps 110:4 [also part of a coronation scene]; Heb 7:1–3). It was, in part, to keep this hope alive that this crown was made for Joshua's symbolic crowning and then placed in the temple as a reminder of this hope. How appropriate therefore that both the type (Joshua) and the antitype (Jesus) have a name meaning "the Lord saves" (cf. NIV mg. at Matt 1:21)!

Some interpreters argue that the original reading at the end of the verse was "Zerubbabel son of Shealtiel" instead of "Joshua son of Jehozadak." But Eichrodt (2:343, n.1) rightly considers "that the interpretation of this passage in terms of Zerubbabel, which can only be secured at the cost of hazardous conjecture, is mistaken and that a reference to a hoped-for messianic ruler after Zerubbabel's disappearance is more in accordance with the evidence." Furthermore, no Hebrew MSS or ancient versions have the Zerubbabel reading.

12 This verse predicts that the messianic Branch would appear as Joshua's antitype and would build the temple. The Aramaic Targum, the Jerusalem Talmud, and the Midrash all regard the verse as messianic. The words were addressed to Joshua; yet it is clear that the language refers to the messianic Branch. John 19:5—"Here is the man!"—may well be intended by John as an allusion to the statement "Here is the man whose name is the Branch." If so, Alan Richardson's comment (cited in Leon Morris, *The Gospel According to John*, NICNT [Grand Rapids: Eerdmans, 1971], p. 793, n. 10) is indirectly apropos: "Adam . . . was created by God to be a king over the whole created world; all creation was to be ruled by a son of man . . . (Ps. 8 . . .). In Christ, the Son of Man, God's original intention in the creation is fulfilled. He is the new Adam, the Messianic King. Thus, we have in Pilate's words a striking example of Johannine *double entendre;* whereas Pilate might merely have meant, 'Look, here is the fellow,' his words contain the deepest truth about the person of Christ." Indeed, Christ is pictured in Revelation 19:12 as the majestic Sovereign of the universe, with "many crowns" on his head—an ornate crown with many diadems, as in v.11 above.

For the Branch as a messianic appellation, see comment at 3:8. As the "Branch," he would "branch out" from his place (NIV here reflects the wordplay in the Hebrew text). "His place" (lit., "what is underneath") is most likely a reference to his humble and obscure origin, land, and people (cf. Isa 53:2; Mic 5:2).

Verse 12 closes with the prediction that the Branch will build the temple of the Lord. Since the rebuilding of the restoration temple is to be completed by Zerubbabel (4:9–10), it is difficult to see how this could refer to that temple. Instead, it must have in view the temple of the Messianic Age (cf. Isa 2:2–4; Ezek 40–43; Hag 2:6–9).

13 Not only will the messianic Branch build the temple, but he will also have regal splendor, will take his seat on his throne and rule, and will perfectly combine the two offices of king and priest. The clause at the end of v.12 is repeated at the beginning of v.13 for emphasis, particularly to stress the fact that "it is he" ("he" is also emphatic in the Hebrew; hence NIV's reading), namely, the Branch, not Joshua, who will build the temple. NIV has captured the sense of the idiom in the second clause of the verse, though "he will bear regal splendor" would be a more literal translation. As Perowne (p. 97) points out, the Branch will be clothed with "*royal* majesty, as the word is used [in] Dan. xi. 21; 1 Chron. xxix. 25" (emphasis his). "Will sit" means "will sit enthroned" (cf. BDB, p. 442, 1.a). "His throne" refers to the promised Davidic throne (2 Sam 7:16; Isa 9:7; Luke 1:32). As to the prediction that the Branch "will be a priest on his throne," Baldwin (*Zechariah*, p. 137) observes: "Nowhere else in the Old Testament is it made so plain that the coming Davidic king will also be a priest." One possible exception is Psalm 110.

The clause at the end of the verse means that the messianic Branch will combine the two offices of king and priest in full accord. As Ellis (p. 1035) puts it, the prophecy looks "forward to a time when kingly and priestly rule are combined in one." Apparently passages like this caused the priestly sect of Qumran to expect two messianic figures "at the end of the days": (1) the eschatological high priest-Messiah of the line of Phinehas (cf. Num 25:10–13) and (2) the eschatological son-of-David Messiah (2 Sam 7). Thus they were expecting a priestly Messiah and a kingly Messiah, with the priestly one ranked above the kingly one.

Since it seems clear that the sect at Qumran was priestly, it is not surprising that there the priestly Messiah was elevated over the kingly Messiah. Both Messiahs were to be God's instruments in the end time, when the true priesthood and the legitimate monarchy were to be restored in accordance with God's promise. The Qumran community also believed in the coming of an eschatological prophet, but there is some doubt as to whether or not they regarded him as messianic (cf. further TDNT, 9:511–20; F.F. Bruce, *Second Thoughts on the Dead Sea Scrolls* [Grand Rapids: Eerdmans, 1956], pp. 80–89). Of course, the point of the biblical passages is that the two offices and functions will be united in the one person of the Messiah, the Davidic king (see Ps 110; Heb 5; 7). See the excursus on the office and functions of ancient kingship immediately following the comment at 9:10.

14 It was to keep the messianic hope alive that the crown was made for Joshua's symbolic crowning and then placed in the temple as a reminder of this hope. Historically, however, it was a memorial to the devotion of the embassy that came all the way from Babylon with such rich gifts for the temple. They, in turn, are typical of the group in v.15. "Hen" (meaning "gracious one") is doubtless another name, and a very appropriate one, for Josiah, used on this occasion to honor him because he was so hospitable (v.10).

15 Gentiles will contribute materials for the construction of the messianic kingdom temple. When this happens, the people will know that the Lord sent his messenger (Messenger?) to them. All this will happen if the people render absolute obedience to the Lord's word. "Those who are far away" must refer to Gentiles and be paralleled with such passages as 2:11; 8:22; Isaiah 2:2–4; 56:6–7; 60:1–7. They will help build the temple by contributing their wealth (silver, gold, and other materials) to it, as was done for Solomon's temple and for the second temple (cf. the preceding verses). Isaiah 60:5–7 also predicts that this will happen. For the identification of the messenger ("me"), see comments at 2:8–11 and 4:9. Perowne (p. 98) gives the correct understanding of the conditional clause at the end of the verse: "The meaning is not, that the coming and work of Messiah, but that their share in it depended on their obedience." The conditional element—obedience—relates, then, to the people's participation individually (cf. Deut 28:1–2, 15; 30:1–10). In the new covenant (Jer 31:33–34; Ezek 36:26–27), God personally guarantees that the people will ultimately obey; his Spirit will enable them to do so.

Notes

10 לָקוֹחַ (*lāqôaḥ*, "take"), an infinitive absolute, is used here as a finite verb, in this case as an imperative (Davidson, par. 88, rem. 2). In the ellipsis after the verb, NIV correctly inserts the obvious object from v.11.

הַגּוֹלָה (*haggôlāh*) is a metonymy of adjunct in which the abstract ("exile") is put for the concrete ("[returned] exiles").

וּבָאתָ (*ûḇā'ṯā*, "Go") is a waw consecutive perfect, continuing the imperatival force of the preceding infinitive absolute, on which it depends for its syntactical function.

11 While there is some textual support for the singular עֲטֶרֶת (*ʿaṭereṯ*, "crown") instead of the plural עֲטָרוֹת (*ʿaṭārôṯ*), the preferred reading is given in the commentary. Note the singular verb in v.14, disputing KJV's "crowns." The purely conjectural emendation of Joshua to Zerubbabel has already been discussed and rejected.

12 צֶמַח שְׁמוֹ (*ṣemaḥ šᵉmô*, "whose name is the Branch") is explained in Davidson (par. 144, rem. 3) as a transposed descriptive sentence.

Perhaps as a signal that a new and different temple is in view, הֵיכָל (*hêkāl*, "temple") is now used for the first time in the book, though it is used later of the second temple. Etymologically the word is ultimately derived from Sumerian *é.gal*, literally, "great house" (cf. also Akkad *ekallu*, "royal palace," in *The Assyrian Dictionary* [Chicago: Oriental Institute, 1956–], 4:52–61).

14 On the reason for the singular תִּהְיֶה (*tihyeh*, "will be") in spite of a plural subject, see the comment at v.11.

"Helem" (NIV mg.) is either another name for Heldai or an unintentional scribal corruption of that name.

15 NIV has conveyed the nuance of the infinitive absolute, שָׁמוֹעַ (*šāmôa'*, "diligently").

The nun at the end of תִּשְׁמְעוּן (*tišmᵉ'ûn*, "obey") is either an old indicative plural ending or the so-called energetic nun. According to BDB (p. 1034, 1.m) the idiom שָׁמַע בְּקוֹל (*šāma' bᵉqôl*, "listen to the voice of") very often means "obey"; hence NIV's translation.

IV. The Problem of Fasting and the Promise of the Future (7:1–8:23)

A. *The Question by the Delegation From Bethel*

7:1–3

> [1]In the fourth year of King Darius, the word of the LORD came to Zechariah on the fourth day of the ninth month, the month of Kislev. [2]The people of Bethel had sent Sharezer and Regem-Melech, together with their men, to entreat the LORD [3]by asking the priests of the house of the LORD Almighty and the prophets, "Should I mourn and fast in the fifth month, as I have done for so many years?"

1 Perowne (p. 98) has a masterly synthesis of these two chapters:

> After the lapse of nearly two years, Zechariah is again called to prophesy, the occasion of his doing so being the arrival at Jerusalem of a deputation, sent from Bethel to enquire whether they ought still to observe a national fast, which had been instituted in the time of the captivity, vii. 1–3. The answer of Almighty God by the prophet falls into four sections . . . , each of which is introduced by the same formula, vii. 4, 8; viii. 1, 18. The return in the last of these sections (viii. 19) to the question out of which the whole arose, shews that the prophecy is really one. In the first section the people are reminded that their fasting and feasting had alike been observances terminating upon themselves and devoid of religious motive and spiritual aim, and consequently unacceptable to God; in accordance with the teaching of the earlier prophets, in the times of Jerusalem's prosperity, vii. 4–7. In the next section the substance of this teaching, as insisting on moral reformation and not on outward observances, is given; and to the neglect of it are traced the rejection by God of His people, and the calamities that had come upon them in their captivity and dispersion, vii. 8–14. Passing now to a happier strain of hope and promise, the prophetic word tells of the bright days of holiness and prosperity in store for Jerusalem, in contrast with her earlier condition of distress and discord, and urges the people, on the strength of these promises, to holy obedience, viii. 1–17. The concluding section predicts that the question from Bethel shall be solved, by the transformation of the fasts of their captivity into joyful feasts, to which willing multitudes shall throng from all parts of the land; heathen nations joining also in their celebration, and counting it an honour and protection to be associated with a Jew, viii. 18–23.

As early as 1:3–6 it was clear that Zechariah was interested in the spiritual renewal of the postexilic community. Here he deals further with this problem. The purpose of chapters 7 and 8 is to impress on the people their need to live righteously in response to their past judgment and future glory.

The date in v.1 is equivalent to 7 December 518 B.C., not quite two years after the eight night visions (1:7; cf. Introduction: Date, pars. h, j).

2–3 The occasion of the oracle is now given. Unfortunately that occasion is somewhat obscure, because the Hebrew in v.2 is open to several different interpretations. NIV's translation is as defensible as any; indeed, according to Feinberg (pp. 115–16) and Unger (*Zechariah*, pp. 120–21), this translation is most preferable. For the various possibilities see the EVs and commentaries (esp. Baldwin, *Zechariah*, pp. 141–43).

In the view adopted here, the occasion is a question about fasting raised by a delegation from Bethel (cf. Ezra 2:28; Neh 7:32; 11:31). To judge from the foreign names—Sharezer and Regem-Melech—the members of the delegation had probably been born in Babylonia. They directed their question to the temple priests and the divinely appointed prophets—the latter would have included Zechariah—at Jerusalem. Their inquiry was reasonable. The fasts had been observed in exile, but should they be continued in these better times back in the homeland? Now that the temple was nearly rebuilt, it would seem that they were no longer necessary. Thus the mission of these Jews concerned a fast day instituted by the Jews in exile in commemoration of the destruction of Jerusalem. (The OT itself required only one fast day—on Yom Kippur, the Day of Atonement.) In the beginning there was doubtless sincere contribution in the observance of the day; now it had become a mere form. According to 8:19, the question included all the fasts commemorating major events related to the fall and destruction of Jerusalem and the temple, namely, the "fasts of the fourth, fifth, seventh and tenth months." *The Illustrated Family Encyclopedia* (8:93) says:

> Counting the beginning of the year from the month of Nisan, the Jewish sages identified these dates as follows (in the Talmudical tractate *Rosh Hashanah* 18b): the fast of the fourth month fell on the ninth of Tammuz, the day when the city walls were breached (2 Kings 25:3–4; Jer. 39:2); the fast of the fifth month was on the ninth of Ab, when the house of God was destroyed by fire (2 Kings 25:8–10); the fast of the seventh month was on the third of Tishri, the anniversary of the assassination of Gedaliah the son of Ahikam (ibid. 25; Jer. 41:2); and the fast of the tenth month fell on the tenth of Tebeth, which was the day when the king of Babylon laid siege to Jerusalem (2 Kings 25:1, Ezek. 24:2). In Zechariah's day, sixty-eight years after the destruction, when the rebuilding of the Temple was almost complete, the question naturally arose whether the time had not come to annul these fasts, since Jeremiah's prophecy about the duration of the exile might well be thought to have been fulfilled.

Notes

2 וַיִּשְׁלַח (*wayyišlaḥ,* "had sent") is one of several instances where the waw consecutive preterite functions as a pluperfect (see also Gen 12:1 and Davidson, par. 48, rem. 2).

Bethel is apparently a metonymy of the subject in which the city is put for its inhabitants (Bullinger, pp. 579–80).

פְּנֵי (*pᵉnê*, lit., "face of") is an anthropomorphism, "used of the Divine presence in happiness and of Divine favour" (Bullinger, p. 873). The notion "to seek the face [i.e., favor] of the LORD" is contained in NIV's "to entreat the LORD."

3 The singular הַאֶבְכֶּה (*ha'eḇkeh*, "should I mourn") is used collectively for the people of Bethel, just as the whole nation of Israel is often construed in the OT as a corporate personality (or solidarity).

The Niphal infinitive absolute הִנָּזֵר (*hinnāzēr*, "should I . . . fast") in this context must mean "Should I separate [or 'consecrate'] myself by fasting?" (cf. BDB, p. 634); hence the NIV translation.

"So many years" is interpreted in v.5 as "the past seventy years."

B. *The Rebuke by the Lord*

7:4–7

4Then the word of the LORD Almighty came to me: 5"Ask all the people of the land and the priests, 'When you fasted and mourned in the fifth and seventh months for the past seventy years, was it really for me that you fasted? 6And when you were eating and drinking, were you not just feasting for yourselves? 7Are these not the words the LORD proclaimed through the earlier prophets when Jerusalem and its surrounding towns were at rest and prosperous, and the Negev and the western foothills were settled?' "

4–5 Through Zechariah the Lord strongly rebuked the attitude behind the question in v.3. Making an effective use of rhetorical questions, the Lord cast doubt on the people's sincerity when they previously had observed the fasts. They had turned a time that should have convicted them of their past and present sins into a rote ritual devoid of its divinely intended purpose—e.g., prayer and repentance. They had turned it into a time of self-pity for their physical condition, devoid of genuine repentance and moral implications. Since the question from the people of Bethel raised a larger issue touching the whole nation, the words of vv.5–7 were addressed, not just to the people in Bethel, but to "all the people of the land [primarily Jews living in or near Jerusalem and Judah] and the priests." Priests also had to listen to God's word that came through the prophets. For the significance of the fasts mentioned in v.5, see comments at vv.2–3. Since these fasts commemorated events related to the destruction of Jerusalem and the temple in 586 B.C., the "seventy years" are to be reckoned from that time. Strictly speaking, sixty-eight years had transpired; seventy is thus a round number.

"Me" (v.5) is set in obvious contrast with "yourselves" (v.6): Was it really for *me*? Was it not actually for *yourselves*? Their fasting had become a mere religious form, not supported by obedience to the word of God (cf. Isa 1:11–17; 58:1–7).

6–7 Ellis (p. 1037) suggests that "there is the strong inference in the prophet's words (v.6) that just as feasting was enjoyed in self-interest, so fasting could similarly be undertaken for motives other than those for which self-denial was originally designed." The reference to "the earlier prophets" (v.7; cf. Isa 58) shows that the problem is not lack of knowledge but lack of obedience. Without obedience and application, religious observance is meaningless. "At rest" and "prosperous" point to the preexilic situation when Jerusalem and the surrounding towns of Judah were bustling with life and the fields were being farmed—in contrast with their current condition resulting from disobedience, with only a partial restoration and without the full resumption of agriculture. The Negev (generally the area south of Beersheba down to the highlands of the Sinai Peninsula) and the western foothills (between the Judean hills and the Mediterranean coastal plain) were among the agricultural and grazing areas.

Notes

---

5 וְסָפוֹד (*w^e sāpôḏ*, "and mourned") is the infinitive absolute appearing as a substitute for the finite verb, in this case as a continuation of the preceding perfect (GKC, par. 113y–z). הֲצוֹם (*h^a ṣôm*, "really"), on the other hand, is the emphatic use of the infinitive absolute, stressing the idea in the accompanying finite verb (GKC, par. 113l–n).

On the somewhat rare connecting vowel (to the pronominal suffix) in צַמְתֻנִי (ṣamtunî, "Did you fast for me?"), see GKC, par. 59a (d). On the use of אָנִי (*'ānî*, "me") following this form, see GKC, pars. 117x, 135e; on the indirect object use of the suffix, see Davidson, par. 73, rem. 4.

6 תֹּאכְלוּ (*tō'ḵ^e lû*, "you were eating") is either the customary imperfect or the "historical" imperfect, much like the Greek customary imperfect or historical present.

C. *The Command to Repent*

7:8–14

[8]And the word of the LORD came again to Zechariah. [9]"This is what the LORD Almighty says: 'Administer true justice; show mercy and compassion to one another. [10]Do not oppress the widow or the fatherless, the alien or the poor. In your hearts do not think evil of each other.'

[11]"But they refused to pay attention; stubbornly they turned their backs and stopped up their ears. [12]They made their hearts as hard as flint and would not listen to the law or to the words that the LORD Almighty had sent by his Spirit through the earlier prophets. So the LORD Almighty was very angry.

[13]" 'When I called, they did not listen; so when they called, I would not listen,' says the LORD Almighty. [14]'I scattered them with a whirlwind among all the nations, where they were strangers. The land was left so desolate behind them that no one could come or go. This is how they made the pleasant land desolate.' "

8–9a With a solemn, authoritative message from God, the prophet focused on the covenantal unfaithfulness, disobedience, and unrighteousness that first led to the Babylonian exile. He did this, hoping that the restored community would perceive the moral implications of their fasting and would let their forefathers' disobedience and its consequences serve as a warning to them. This section also explains why the people's fasting meant nothing to God. They were guilty of legalism: an external adherence to the letter of the law while disregarding the internal spirit—the true divine intent—of the law (cf. Baker, "False Dichotomies," pp. 5–6).

9b–10 With a series of social, moral, and ethical commands, the Lord gave the people four tests of their spiritual reality.

1. "Administer true justice." While the Hebrew word *mišpāṭ* certainly includes the concept of "justice," Eichrodt (1:241) rightly asserts that it "is no abstract thing, but denotes the rights and duties of each party arising out of the particular relation of fellowship in which they find themselves. In this way everyone has his own special *mišpāṭ:* The king, the Deity, the priest, the firstborn son, the Israelites as a group, and so on. The task of righteousness is to render this justice, and the claims which it implies, effective in the proper way, so that the good of all those united in the one community of law may be safeguarded." There is a sense in which, at the broadest level, *mišpāṭ* ultimately has in view "the proper ordering of all society." It would seem that this more comprehensive meaning is definitely called for in Isaiah 42:1, 4, where it is presented as the mission of the messianic Servant of the Lord: He will establish "a proper order" on earth. F. Duane Lindsey ("The Career of the Servant in Isaiah 52:13–53:12," BS 139 [January–March 1982]:18) maintains that "any translation less comprehensive than 'a right order' or similar phrase, fails to take account of the far-reaching accomplishments purposed for Yahweh's servant. The servant's task is to make right within history all aspects and phases of human existence—whether moral, religious, spiritual, political, social, economic, and so forth." Again he notes that *mišpāṭ* "describes the totality of the just order which the servant will cause to prevail on the earth" (ibid., p. 21). Perhaps it is not amiss to suggest that as the Lord's servants today, we too are to strive to help bring about such a proper and just ordering of all society (cf. Mic 6:6–8).

2. "Show mercy and compassion." While *ḥeseḏ* includes "mercy," it is really stronger than that. "Faithful love" would be a better rendering (cf. Hos 10:12, where the same Hebrew word is translated "unfailing love," and Hos 12:6, where it is translated "love"). According to Snaith (p. 99), "the word represents a broad wedge of which the apex varies between 'love, mercy' at the one extreme, and 'loyalty, steadfastness, faithfulness' at the other." At the latter extreme it denotes "that attitude of loyalty and faithfulness which both parties to a covenant should observe towards each other" (ibid.). (For covenantal love applied to God, see Barker, "False Dichotomies," pp. 7–11.) Since *raḥ^a^mîm* ("compassion") is related to the Hebrew word for "womb," it focuses primarily on a tender, maternal kind of love. Faithful love and tender compassion were to govern all relationships among the covenant people of God.

3. "Do not oppress." Oppression is denounced so frequently in the OT that it is not necessary to multiply references (e.g., Amos 2:6–8; 4:1; 5:11–12, 21–24; 8:4–6). The most common victims of oppression are listed here as "the widow . . . the fatherless, the alien . . . the poor." These were the weakest, the neediest, the most defenseless, and the most disadvantaged members of their society—and the ones with the fewest legal rights.

Related to the Hebrew word for widow (*'almānāh*) is the Akkadian *almattu,* which Chayim Cohen defines as "a once married woman who has no means of financial support and who is thus in need of special legal protection" ("The 'Widowed' City," *The Journal of the Ancient Near Eastern Society of Columbia University* [The Gaster Festschrift] 5 [1973]: 76). He continues: "Finally, the statements made by Mesopotamian rulers to demonstrate their great concern with the plight of the *almattu* are best understood in the light of the above definition. Hammurabi's rationale for the writing of his laws is typical of such statements: . . . 'In order that the mighty shall not wrong the weak, in order to provide justice for the homeless girl, and the once married woman without financial support' " (ibid.). This concern is also seen in the Ugaritic text 2 Aqhat 5:7–8: "He [Danel] judges the case of the 'widow,' he adjudicates the cause of the 'orphan' " (for the text, see UT, p. 248; and for the biblical concern for such people, see Deut 10:18; Isa 1:17, 23; Jer 5:28; James 1:27; cf. 1 John 3:16–18).

Cohen goes on to suggest that the above definition for "widow" is "much more appropriate in [OT] contexts dealing with the protection of the rights of the socially disadvantaged classes in Israelite society. . . . Conversely, such widows as Abigail and Bath-Sheba are never called *'almānāh* because they probably did have some means of financial support ("The 'Widowed' City," p. 77). Richard D. Patterson adds: "Throughout the Babylonian legal stipulations and wisdom literature the care of the widow, the orphan, and the poor is enjoined, since the ideal king, as the living representative of the god of justice, the sun god Šamaš, is expected to care for the oppressed and needy elements of society" ("The Widow, the Orphan, and the Poor in the Old Testament and the Extra-Biblical Literature," BS 130 [July–September 1973]:226). (For a fuller treatment of these weak and helpless members of society, who were so easily victimized, see Patterson, ibid., pp. 223–34.)

4. "Do not think evil." Light is shed on this last part of v.10 by the opening part of 8:17, where the almost identical Hebrew is translated "do not plot evil against your neighbor." This certainly excludes a spirit of hatred, vindictiveness, and revenge that devises or plots wicked schemes for harming others. "Here, then, is a concise yet comprehensive range of ethical teaching condensed into four pithy utterances. Without attention to their importance any fasting becomes a mere parade of ritualism which, as the history of Judah had shown, can lead to moral and spiritual disaster" (Ellis, p. 1037). The clear inference is that the people of the restored community need to repent (change their way of thinking and living) and to begin practicing this ethical teaching; otherwise their fasting is mere formalism, legalism, and hypocrisy.

11–12a These verses stand in stark contrast with the previous ones: the Lord instructed the people to carry out the four commands of vv.9–10, *but* they refused ("they" referring to the preexilic forefathers, as the reference to "the earlier prophets" in v.12 shows). The lesson to the Jews of the restoration period is clear: Do not be like your unrepentant, unfaithful, disobedient, covenant-breaking forefathers, or you will suffer a similar fate. One indispensable ingredient in true spirituality is a dogged attentiveness to familiar truths, but they did not "pay attention." Deuteronomy 9:6, 13, 27 is echoed in "stubbornly they turned their backs," thus characterizing the Israelite ancestors as a stiff-necked and stubborn people. The fact that they "stopped up their ears" seems to reflect the disciplinary dulling of their ears in Isaiah 6:10 (cf. Acts 28:27).

In v.12 the people even "made their hearts [including their minds and wills] as hard as flint" (cf. Ezek 3:8–9). The precise meaning of the Hebrew word for "flint" is disputed. The NIV Preface states: "It should be noted that minerals, flora and fauna, architectural details, articles of clothing and jewelry, musical instruments and other articles cannot always be identified with precision. Also measures of capacity in the biblical period are particularly uncertain." In this instance the specific kind of mineral is uncertain.

Verses 11–12 involve the use of anabasis to stress the unseen cause of Israel's trouble: For the most part they were a recalcitrant, unresponsive, and obdurate people (cf. Bullinger, p. 431). Nor would they listen to the word of God in the law through the prophets (v.12). The latter were the secondary agents of divine revelation. The primary agent was the Spirit of God ("by his Spirit"). Thus the words of the prophets were inspired by God's Spirit. There are similar assertions in Nehemiah 9:20, 30 (cf. 2 Peter 1:21). "It was the spirit which gave rise to the word of God uttered in times past and now of normative significance in the present, and which is at the same time the power-giving life to the community" (Eichrodt, 2:64, n. 2).

12b–13 The result of the forefathers' rejection of the command to change—i.e., to reform their ways and actions (Jer 7:3)—was the terrible experience of God's wrath manifested in the destruction of Jerusalem and the temple in 586 B.C. and in the ensuing exile to Babylonia. The motif of God's wrath is reminiscent of 1:2, 15. Dispersion was part of the curse for disobedience to the Old (Mosaic) covenant (cf. v.14). The chiastic arrangement of v.13 is used to express just retribution (so Baldwin, *Zechariah*, p. 148). Jeremiah had warned of precisely this consequence (Jer 11:11–14).

14 The scattering was one of the curses for covenant disobedience (Deut 28:36–37, 64–68), as was the desolation of the land (Deut 28:41–42, 45–52). "The nations" refer primarily to Babylonia and Egypt, though "all" may at the same time anticipate a future, more widespread Diaspora—the principle of progressive fulfillment again. "Behind them" means "after they were removed from it." The Hebrew construction translated "that no one could come or go" occurs also in 9:8, where NIV has "*against marauding* forces" (emphasis mine). Unger (*Zechariah*, p. 131) believes that the use of this "peculiar expression" in Part II of the book "is one of the internal evidences binding together the first part of the prophecy (chapters 1–8) with the last part (chapters 9–14)" (cf. Introduction: Unity, esp. n. 2).

"This is how" means "by their sins" (e.g., unbelief and disobedience). Because of such sins, "they made the pleasant land [Palestine] desolate." How does all this relate to the question of fasting? Ellis (pp. 1037–38) answers: "Thus, whilst Zechariah may well not have answered the original enquiry directly, he had nevertheless taken up the very essence of ritual in the heart of the worshiper, which was that the outward form of religious activity was useless and lifeless without an accompanying spirit of obedience, confession and repentance." See 1:1–6.

Notes

---

9 מִשְׁפַּט (*mišpaṭ*, "justice") is a cognate accusative, here expressing a concrete instance of the effect or product of the action of the verb (Davidson, par. 67b), and אֱמֶת (*'emeṯ*, "true") is an attributive, adjectival, or descriptive genitive (GKC, par. 128p).

11 "Stopped up their ears" is literally "made their ears heavy that they might not hear," thus revealing the privative sense of the preposition מִן (*min*) in מִשְּׁמוֹעַ (*miššemôa'*); cf. Davidson, par. 101, rem. 1.c. (2). The same construction occurs in v.12.

13 The use of קָרָא (*qārā'*, third person, "he called") instead of the expected קָרָאתִי (*qārā'ṯî*, first person, "I called"), to agree with the following וְלֹא אֶשְׁמָע (*welō' 'ešmā'*, first person, "I would not listen"), is explained in the NIV Preface: "And though the Hebrew writers often shifted back and forth between first, second and third personal pronouns without change of antecedent, this translation often makes them uniform [as here], in accordance with English style and without the use of footnotes.

יִקְרְאוּ (*yiqreʾû*, "they called"), אֶשְׁמָע (*ʾešmāʿ*, "I would listen"), וְאֵסָעֲרֵם (*weʾēsāʿarēm*, "I scattered them," v.14) and לֹא־יְדָעוּם (*lōʾ-yedāʿûm*, "they were strangers," v.14) are either preterites without waw consecutive (as often in poetry) or are to be explained with Baldwin (*Zechariah*, p. 148): "The prophet has been using the third person in the previous verses and he continues to do so until suddenly he finds himself using the very words of the Lord, so vivid is the message in his mind. This also explains the future tense. . . . When the judgment was formulated the situation was still future." This expositor inclines toward the first option (classifying the forms as preterites).

14 "The idea of universality is sometimes expressed by the use of. . . . contrasted expressions, as Zech. 7:14" (Davidson, par. 17, rem. 5): מֵעֹבֵר וּמִשָּׁב (*mēʿōḇēr ûmiššāḇ*, "that no one could come or go"). The "contrasted expressions" are actually a form of merism, conveying the thought that "no one could go anywhere or do anything."

D. *The Restoration of Israel to God's Favor*

8:1–17

[1]Again the word of the LORD Almighty came to me. [2]This is what the LORD Almighty says: "I am very jealous for Zion; I am burning with jealousy for her."

[3]This is what the LORD says: "I will return to Zion and dwell in Jerusalem. Then Jerusalem will be called the City of Truth, and the mountain of the LORD Almighty will be called the Holy Mountain."

[4]This is what the LORD Almighty says: "Once again men and women of ripe old age will sit in the streets of Jerusalem, each with cane in hand because of his age. [5]The city streets will be filled with boys and girls playing there."

[6]This is what the LORD Almighty says: "It may seem marvelous to the remnant of this people at that time, but will it seem marvelous to me?" declares the LORD Almighty.

[7]This is what the LORD Almighty says: "I will save my people from the countries of the east and the west. [8]I will bring them back to live in Jerusalem; they will be my people, and I will be faithful and righteous to them as their God."

[9]This is what the LORD Almighty says: "You who now hear these words spoken by the prophets who were there when the foundation was laid for the house of the LORD Almighty, let your hands be strong so that the temple may be built. [10]Before that time there were no wages for man or beast. No one could go about his business safely because of his enemy, for I had turned every man against his neighbor. [11]But now I will not deal with the remnant of this people as I did in the past," declares the LORD Almighty.

[12]"The seed will grow well, the vine will yield its fruit, the ground will produce its crops, and the heavens will drop their dew. I will give all these things as an inheritance to the remnant of this people. [13]As you have been an object of cursing among the nations, O Judah and Israel, so will I save you, and you will be a blessing. Do not be afraid, but let your hands be strong."

[14]This is what the LORD Almighty says: "Just as I had determined to bring disaster upon you and showed no pity when your fathers angered me," says the LORD Almighty, [15]"so now I have determined to do good again to Jerusalem and Judah. Do not be afraid. [16]These are the things you are to do: Speak the truth to each other, and render true and sound judgment in your courts; [17]do not plot evil against your neighbor, and do not love to swear falsely. I hate all this," declares the LORD.

1–2 Zechariah here contrasted Israel's past judgment with her future restoration. The purpose of both sections is essentially the same: In the preceding section Israel was to repent and live righteously after the punishment of her captivity; here she is to repent and live righteously because of the promise of her future restoration. "God's strange work is judgment. His delight is to bless His people" (Unger, *Zechariah,* p. 133). This section is basically a salvation—for deliverance—oracle, the principal features of which are (1) the self-predication of God (cf. v.2), (2) the message of salvation (vv.3–8), (3) the direct address (vv.9–17), and (4) the "do not be afraid" phrase (vv.13, 15). It is "the LORD Almighty" (see comment at 1:3) who stands behind this glorious prophecy (vv.1–4, 6–7, 14, 19–20, 23). A more literal rendering of the chiastic structure of the quotation in v.2 would read thus: "I am jealous for Zion with great jealousy; with great burning, or ardor, I am jealous for her." For a resolution of the problem of God's jealousy, see comment at 1:14. Here the divine jealousy is directed toward the restoration of Israel.

3a On the Lord's returning to Zion and dwelling in Jerusalem, see the exposition at 1:16 and 2:10.

3b The blessed results of the Lord's return are now delineated. The first one is a new character for Jerusalem, resulting in new epithets. It is difficult to determine whether the first epithet should be translated "the City of Truth" or "the Faithful City" (cf. Isa 1:26). Either is possible, and both will be true. Verse 16, however, would seem to favor the former for this context. Furthermore, the temple mount will be called "the Holy Mountain" because of the Lord's holy presence there (cf. 14:20–21). "Jerusalem did not acquire this character in the period after the captivity, in which, though not defiled by gross idolatry, as in the times before the captivity, it was polluted by other moral abominations no less than it had been before. Jerusalem becomes a faithful city for the first time through the Messiah, and it is through Him that the temple mountain first really becomes the holy mountain" (KD, *Minor Prophets,* 2:312).

4–5 Other results of the Lord's return to dwell in Jerusalem are undisturbed tranquillity, long life, peace, prosperity, and security. That is the picture painted by these verses. There is a similar scene in Isaiah 65:20–25. The weakest and most defenseless members of society will be able to live securely. On these verses Perowne (p. 102) says: "We read, as a fulfillment of this prophecy, that in the days of Simon, in the times of the Maccabees, 'the ancient men sat all in the streets, communing together of good things' (1 Macc. xiv. 9); while our Lord alludes to the games of children in the market-place, as a familiar incident in His own days. Matt. xi. 16, 17." Although it may be possible to regard these historical references as stages in the progressive fulfillment of the passage, they certainly do not completely fulfill the scope of this grand prophecy as a whole. The final stage awaits the second advent of the Messiah.

6 Such things may have seemed too good to be true in the eyes of the Jewish remnant living "at that time," but the Lord Almighty did not so regard them. Nothing is too hard for him (see Gen 18:14; Jer 32:17, 27). Unger (*Zechariah,* p. 137) explains the thought of the verse thus: "If the remnant of the nation in that future day will scarcely be able to comprehend how such miraculous things just promised could become a reality, the divine reply is, 'Because they seem difficult to you, must they also seem hard to me?' " The answer is obvious.

7–8 Although God's action in v.7 is expressed in terms of saving, it is tantamount to regathering. "I will save my people" means "I will gather them from exile, bondage, and dispersion" (cf. Isa 11:11–12; 43:5–7; Jer 30:7–11; 31:7–8; cf. also K.L. Barker, "Deliver (Deliverance)," ZPEB, 2:89–90). "The east" and "the west" are best understood as a merism (where opposites are used to express totality), meaning "wherever the people are." Thus the regathering here will be universal. Perowne (p. 103) observes: "The promise is larger than has yet been fulfilled." In v.8 Israel's predicted complete restoration to covenant favor and blessing rests on nothing less than the faithfulness, veracity, and righteousness of God. "To live in Jerusalem" need mean no more than "to go there frequently to worship."

"They will be my people, and I will be . . . their God" is covenant terminology, pertaining to intimate fellowship in a covenant relationship (cf. Gen 17:7–8; Exod 6:7; 19:5–6; 29:45–46; Lev 11:45; 22:33; 25:38; 26:12, 44–45; Num 15:41; Deut 4:20; 29:12–13; Jer 31:33; 32:38; Ezek 37:27; 2 Cor 6:16; Rev 21:3). Although Israel may go through a Lo-Ammi ("Not My People") stage, she will be fully restored as Ammi ("My People"). So says God himself in Hosea 1:8–2:1; 2:23. It is true that Paul quoted Hosea in connection with Gentile salvation in Romans 9:25–26. But this is the application of a theological principle from the OT—the ultimate, complete, final fulfillment being yet future for Israel. The theological principle involved is that God is a saving, forgiving, delivering, restoring God—one who delights to take "Not My People" and make them "My People." In the case of Gentiles, as in the church, he does this in his sovereign grace by grafting them into covenant relationship and blessing (Rom 11). Hans Walter Wolff (*Hosea* [Philadelphia: Fortress, 1974], p. 29) acknowledges as much: "Since the people outside Israel—who are Not-My-People and Without-Pity—are to become a part of the blessed people of God (Rom 9:24f; 1 Pt 2:10), these words take on a meaning unforseen [*sic*] by the prophet. In this way the prophet's words are becoming fulfilled. But this is not yet completed with respect to Israel (Rom 10:1; 11:26) or the nations (Rev 7:9ff)." Israel's restoration depends on the dependable—"faithful and righteous"—God.

9 The immediate purpose of all this is to encourage Zechariah's audience to complete the rebuilding of the temple. The people addressed in the long vocative are those who had been listening to the preaching of, first, Haggai (1:1) and then Zechariah (1:1; cf. Ezra 5:1–2), since 520 B.C. (it was now 518). The laying of the temple foundation referred to in this verse is, accordingly, not the original one in 536. Rather, it is best understood as follows: "As a more precise definition of יוֹם יֻסַּד [*yôm yussaḏ*, 'when the foundation was laid'] the word לְהִבָּנוֹת [l^{e}*hibbānôṯ*, 'so that it may be built'] is added, to show that the time referred to is that in which the laying of the foundation of the temple in the time of Cyrus became an eventful fact through the continuation of the building" (KD, *Minor Prophets*, 2:315). To recapitulate the historical situation, although the foundation was restored in 536, the actual building of the superstructure was hindered from 536 to 530 (when it ground to a halt). Thus, in effect, the "founding" (almost in the sense of "building" or "rebuilding") of the temple did not begin in earnest till 520. "Let your hands be strong" is a way of saying "be encouraged" (Judg 7:11).

10 "This verse presents a contrast of the present, when they had begun to obey the Word of God, with the past, when they did not" (Unger, *Zechariah*, p. 140). The background for the verse appears to be the conditions described in Haggai 1:6–11;

2:15–19. "Before that time" refers to the period prior to 520 B.C. (at least 530–520, if not 536–520). "Before this work was started the commercial and civic situation was desperate" (Ellis, p. 1038). "No one could go about his business safely" is literally "No one could go out or come in safely." NIV has captured the sense of the merism ("go out or come in") by "go about his business." "Enemy" included the Samaritans (Ezra 4:1–5).

11–13 "But now" shows that the reasons for the people's discouragement have passed; God would now provide grounds for encouragement. Verse 12 stands in contrast to Haggai 1:10–11. In Haggai 2:19, God through his prophet had predicted just such a reversal as we have here. The fecundity described is part of the covenant blessings for obedience promised in the Pentateuch (Lev 26:3–10; Deut 28:11–12) and in Ezekiel 34:25–27. On the other hand, Israel's being an object of cursing among the nations (v.13) is part of the covenant curses for disobedience threatened in Deuteronomy 28:15–68 and predicted in Jeremiah 24:9; 25:18; 29:22. On the fact that both Judah and Israel are addressed in this message of salvation and blessing, Perowne (p. 105) comments: "Not only the two tribes but the ten. This has never yet been fulfilled." See also Jeremiah 31:1–31; Ezekiel 37:11–28. "As" God's old covenant people were an object of cursing, "so" God will save them (cf. vv.7–8); and they will be a blessing (cf. vv.20–23). Consequently they are not to fear but to be encouraged (cf. v.9 and the comment there).

14–15 These verses specify God's part in the people's restoration to favor and blessing; vv.16–17 delineate their part. In the past God had to bring disaster on them as covenantal discipline. On God's determination (v.14), see Jeremiah 4:28; 51:12. The Hebrew phrase *lᵉhāraʿ* here does not mean "to do evil" in a moral and ethical sense but "to bring disaster," just as *rāʿāh* "is the 'evil' which someone does and the 'disaster' which he encounters in consequence" (Fohrer, "Twofold Aspects," p. 102; cf. Isa 45:7). Strictly speaking the Hebrew for "showed no pity" does not mean "repented not" (KJV), as though God could repent (cf. 1 Sam 15:29; Ps 110:4). Rather it means something like what NIV has (cf. Jer 20:16). "So now" (v.15) answers to "just as" (v.14): "the very sorrows of the past became pledges for the hopes of the future" (Chambers, CHS, 14:64). As strong as was God's determination to bring disaster (v.14), so strong is his determination to do good (v.15). On the nature of this doing good, see vv.12–13. This is cause for not being afraid (repeated from v.13 because the fulfillment is certain).

16–17 Once again God's and Zechariah's interest in spiritual renewal comes to the fore (cf. 7:9–10). "The precepts that follow sum up the character of those who are in covenant relation with the Lord of hosts" (Baldwin, *Zechariah*, pp. 153–54). After the announcement of God's gracious action (v.15) came the stipulation of what he expected from his people in grateful response. Thus their obedience in the moral and ethical sphere had a gracious basis, just as the law itself did (cf. Barker, "False Dichotomies," pp. 6–8). Jerusalem will indeed be "the City of Truth" (v.3) when its inhabitants are truthful and when true judgment is rendered in its courts. As NIV indicates, Hebrew *šālôm* ("sound") is probably best understood as descriptive of "judgment." The root idea of the word seems to be "wholeness," "completeness," "soundness," though it is used principally of a state of "well-being," "health," "harmony," "peace," "security," and "prosperity."

The Hebrew for "courts" is literally "gates." The gates of cities in ancient Palestine often had built-in stone benches, where people could sit with friends, transact business, make legal contracts, hold "court," make public proclamations, etc. (Ruth 4:1–2; 2 Sam 18:24). At Tell en-Nasbeh (Mizpah), a gate lined with stone benches, which were seats for those conducting business there, has been found (WBE, 1:655–56).

The two positive injunctions (v.16) are balanced by two negative ones (v.17). On the first negative command, see comment at 7:10b. The second prohibition has to do with perjury (cf. comments at 5:3–4). "Do not love" perjury is another way of exhorting the people to hate it. The reason for the stipulations of v.17 comes next: God hates perjury and wicked schemes to harm others. Proverbs 6:16–19 designates seven things the Lord hates. Three of them relate directly to vv.16–17 here: "a lying tongue," "a heart that devises wicked schemes," and "a false witness who pours out lies." One theological rationale for ethics, then, is awareness that God hates attitudes and actions contrary to his character. We are to love what God loves and hate what he hates.

Notes

2 קִנְאָה (*qin'āh*, "jealousy") is a cognate accusative (GKC, par. 117p–q). A synonym is used in the parallel line instead of the expected cognate accusative—חֵמָה (ḥēmāh, "burning," "ardor"); cf. Davidson, par. 67, rem. 2.

3a שַׁבְתִּי (*šaḇtî*, "I will return") is a prophetic perfect. וְשָׁכַנְתִּי (*w^e šāḵantî*, "and I will dwell"), on the other hand, is a waw consecutive perfect but with the same force as the preceding prophetic perfect, on which it depends for its syntactical function.

5 "When an attribute qualifies several substantives of different genders, it agrees with the masculine, as being the *prior gender*" (GKC, par. 132d, emphasis theirs). This applies to מְשַׂחֲקִים (*m^e śaḥ^a qîm*, "playing").

6 "A question need not necessarily be introduced by a special interrogative pronoun or adverb. Frequently the natural emphasis upon the words is of itself sufficient to indicate an interrogative sentence as such" (GKC, par. 150a). This applies to גַּם־בְּעֵינַי יִפָּלֵא (*gam-b^e 'ênay yippālē'*, "but will it seem marvelous to me?")

10 If וַאֲשַׁלַּח (*wa'^a šallaḥ*, "for I had turned [lit., 'dispatched']") is not to be repointed *wā'^a šallaḥ*, the form is either a preterite without waw consecutive or a customary or historical imperfect (cf. the Greek customary imperfect and historical present; see *Davidson*, par. 51, rem. 6).

15 On the syntactical function of שַׁבְתִּי (*šaḇtî*, "again"), see note at 5:1; cf. Davidson, par. 83 (c).

17 רֵעֵהוּ (*rē'ēhû*, "your [lit., 'his'] neighbor") is an objective genitive; so "evil of your neighbor" means "evil against your neighbor."

"To the rule that את is used only before def. obj. there are apparent exceptions" (Davidson, par. 72, rem. 4). Here *'eṯ*, "seems merely to give emphasis or demonstrative distinctness to the subj., particularly the emph. which . . . is natural in *resuming* things already spoken of" (ibid., emphasis his). A more literal rendering of the end of the verse, to reflect the syntax, is "'For all these things are what I hate,' declares the LORD."

E. *Kingdom Joy and Jewish Favor*

8:18–23

18Again the word of the LORD Almighty came to me. 19This is what the LORD Almighty says: "The fasts of the fourth, fifth, seventh and tenth months will become joyful and glad occasions and happy festivals for Judah. Therefore love truth and peace."

20This is what the LORD Almighty says: "Many peoples and the inhabitants of many cities will yet come, 21and the inhabitants of one city will go to another and say, 'Let us go at once to entreat the LORD and seek the LORD Almighty. I myself am going.' 22And many peoples and powerful nations will come to Jerusalem to seek the LORD Almighty and to entreat him."

23This is what the LORD Almighty says: "In those days ten men from all languages and nations will take firm hold of one Jew by the hem of his robe and say, 'Let us go with you, because we have heard that God is with you.' "

18–19 In this closing section of the chapter and of Part I of the book, the Jews were told that there would be a reversal of their mourning and their position in the world. Returning at last to the question about fasting, the LORD announced through his prophetic messenger (v.18) that there will come a time when it would cease. The people's mourning (expressed in fasting) will be turned into joy, for their low position among the nations will be changed. And they will be a source of blessing to Gentiles, for all the peoples of the earth will join them on pilgrimages to worship the Lord at Jerusalem.

"The prophet has dealt with major ethical and spiritual principles which underlie all outward observances. From what he has said, as well as the way he has said it, it is evident that his 'digression' from the specific question put to him (cf. 7:3) was for a good purpose. Now he turns to answer that question" (Ellis, pp. 1038–39). He begins by announcing that a day is coming when their fasts and mourning will give way to festivals (cf. Isa 65:18–19; Jer 31:10–14). "The manifestation of the kingdom will be attended by such a fulness of salvation that Judah will forget to commemorate the former mournful events and will only have occasion to rejoice in the benefits of grace bestowed by God" (Unger, *Zechariah*, p. 148). (The four fasts mentioned in v.19 have already been discussed at 7:2–3, q.v.)

Verse 19 closes with an exhortation to Zechariah's contemporaries to "love truth and peace" (cf. vv.16–17). "Apart from the two great commandments (Lv. 19:18, 34; Dt. 6:5, and repeated elsewhere in Dt.), only in Amos 5:15 is there a command to love [in the OT], though in Psalm 31:23 there is an exhortation to love the Lord. The frequency or infrequency with which a truth occurs in Scripture is no guide to its importance" (Baldwin, *Zechariah*, p. 155, n. 1). Such love "underlies the whole covenant relationship and therefore also the ethics set out under the covenant as the condition of blessing" (ibid., p. 155).

20–22 For similar predictions, see 2:11; Isaiah 2:1–5; Micah 4:1–5. As v.22 indicates, the "peoples" of v.20 are Gentile nations. On the phrase "to entreat the LORD" (v.21), see the note at 7:2. For another example of the use of the singular "I" (v.21) for the inhabitants of a city, see the note at 7:3 (cf. 1 Sam 5:10, where the first person plural pronouns are singular in Hebrew). In v.22 the "response is in inverse order to the invitation, so forming a chiasmus, and avoiding monotony of style" (Baldwin, *Zechariah*, p. 155). In view of the parallelism with "many peoples," "powerful nations" is perhaps better translated "numerous nations." The Hebrew for "powerful" is rendered "numerous" in Exodus 1:9; Isaiah 53:12 (NIV mg.). Numerous Gentiles will make a pilgrimage to Jerusalem. "Jerusalem is no longer viewed simply as the heart of Judaism but as the centre of God's dealings with all nations, and as a glorious realization of the ancient promise given to Abraham (cf. Gen. 12:3)" (Ellis, p. 1039). The purpose of the pilgrimage is to seek and entreat the Lord. "With the Davidic kingdom established, Israel will be a medium of blessing to the entire globe" (Unger, *Zechariah*, p. 148). See also Isaiah 55:5; 56:6–7 (cf. Mark 11:17).

23 "In those days" is equivalent to "in that day" (see comment at 2:11). "Ten" is one way of indicating a large or complete number in Hebrew (e.g., Gen 31:7; Lev 26:26; Num 14:22; 1 Sam 1:8; Neh 4:12). Baldwin (*Zechariah*, p. 156) points out: "The word *Jew* . . . occurs first in Jeremiah 34:9, and only for the second time here. It is frequent in Ezra-Nehemiah." Feinberg (p. 146) says, "The prophecy teaches, then, that Israel will be the means of drawing the nations of the earth to the Lord in the time of the Messiah's reign of righteousness upon earth." The verse closes with the reason for the Gentiles' desire to accompany the Jews on pilgrimages to Jerusalem: "We have heard that God is with you." What better reason could there be? Ellis (p. 1039) puts it thus: "True spirituality is attractive to those who exercise genuine faith; but to others it may be a deterrent. The universalism with which the first part of the book ends is therefore not one of expediency, brought about by dialogue or conference. It is the work of God, initiated by him and mediated through his people." And Baldwin (p. 156) comments: "The renewed covenant of the post-exilic period (8:13) includes the nations, who, as Ezekiel saw (36:23), would recognize the Lord as God when, through the renewed Israel, He vindicated His holiness. True godliness draws others to Him (1 Cor. 14:25), and is a factor used of God in completing the number of His people."

Notes

21 The precise function of the infinitive absolute הָלוֹךְ (*hālôḵ*) is difficult to pinpoint. It may mean "at once" (NIV). On the other hand, since pilgrimages are involved, "regularly" may be the preferred nuance (cf. 14:16; cf. also GKC, par. 113u).

23 אֱלֹהִים עִמָּכֶם (*'elōhîm 'immāḵem*, "God is with you") is an example of asyndeton. The כִּי (*kî*, "that") that usually introduces an object clause is sometimes omitted (Davidson, par. 146, rem. 3; GKC, par. 157a).

Part II (chs. 9–14)

V. Two Prophetic Oracles: The Great Messianic Future and the Full Realization of the Theocracy (9:1–14:21)

A. *The First Oracle: The Advent and Rejection of the Messiah* (9:1–11:17)

1. *The advent of the messianic King (9:1–10:12)*

a. *The destruction of nations and preservation of Zion*

9:1–8

1The word of the LORD is against the land of Hadrach
and will rest upon Damascus—
for the eyes of men and all the tribes of Israel
are on the LORD—
2and upon Hamath too, which borders on it,
and upon Tyre and Sidon, though they are very skillful.
3Tyre has built herself a stronghold;
she has heaped up silver like dust,
and gold like the dirt of the streets.
4But the Lord will take away her possessions
and destroy her power on the sea,
and she will be consumed by fire.
5Ashkelon will see it and fear;
Gaza will writhe in agony,
and Ekron too, for her hope will wither.
Gaza will lose her king
and Ashkelon will be deserted.
6Foreigners will occupy Ashdod,
and I will cut off the pride of the Philistines.
7I will take the blood from their mouths,
the forbidden food from between their teeth.
Those who are left will belong to our God
and become leaders in Judah,
and Ekron will be like the Jebusites.
8But I will defend my house
against marauding forces.
Never again will an oppressor overrun my people,
for now I am keeping watch.

1–2a Part II of the Book of Zechariah contains two undated oracles, though they probably belong to Zechariah's old age (shortly after 480 B.C.). More important than the date are the wide scope of the prophecies and the frequent emphasis on the eschaton, particularly the arrival of the great Messianic Era. While chapters 1–8 contain occasional glimpses of future events, chapters 9–14 are almost exclusively eschatological. The future orientation is rendered more certain by the eighteen occurrences of the phrase "on that day."

The theme of Part II centers around the judgment and blessing that accompany the appearance of the messianic King. The mood of the first oracle is characterized by change. In the midst of judgment (9:1–7), Israel finds deliverance (9:8). Yet in the midst of blessing (9:9–10:12), Israel experiences sorrow (11:1–17). And when the messianic King comes, he is rejected! The judgment with which the first oracle begins commences north of Palestine and proceeds south down the west coast of Syro-Palestine (9:1–7). But Israel will be preserved for the advent of her Messiah (9:8). Thus this first section stands in sharp contrast with 1:11 and prepares the way for 9:9. Those interpreters are probably correct who understand 9:1–8 as a prophetic description of the Lord's march south to Jerusalem, destroying the traditional enemies of Israel.

As history shows, the agent of the Lord's judgment was Alexander the Great. After defeating the Persians (333 B.C.), Alexander moved swiftly toward Egypt. On his march he toppled the cities in the Aramean (Syrian) interior, as well as those on the Mediterranean coast. Yet, on coming to Jerusalem, he refused to destroy it. Verse 8 attributes this protection to the miraculous intervention of God. (For a different and less literal approach to 9:1–8, see Baldwin, *Zechariah*, p. 158.)

In v.1 syntactical and semantic problems are encountered immediately. First, how is *maśśā'* ("An Oracle") syntactically related to what follows? Is it a heading, as the NIV translators and the editors of the Hebrew Bible (critical editions) have construed it? Or is it to be joined with the rest of the verse ("The burden of the word"), as in NASB? The matter is uncertain; so one cannot be dogmatic about it. Either view is possible. Second, semantically or lexically, what is the meaning of *maśśā'*? Does it mean "oracle" or "burden" (as claimed by P.A.H. de Boer, *An Inquiry into the Meaning of the Term Maśśā'* [Leiden: E.J. Brill, 1948], and W.C. Kaiser, TWOT, 2:602)? Once again absolute certainty is not possible. Some, however, have insisted on the meaning "burden" and have consequently reached the hasty conclusion that chapters 9–14 consist of judgment oracles. Such a classification will not stand the test of literary analysis. When one examines the literary genres, or forms, in these chapters, it soon becomes evident that they contain not only judgment oracles but also salvation oracles and a mixed type (with both judgment and deliverance).

BDB (p. 672) defines *maśśā'* as meaning "utterance," "oracle," and Holladay (*Hebrew and Aramaic Lexicon*, p. 217) lists "pronouncement" as the definition. If, as many lexicographers and exegetes believe, the term is derived from *nāśā'* ("to lift up"), this may shed some light on its meaning. The verb is used of lifting up or uttering a *māšāl* ("oracle") in Numbers 23:7, 18; 24:3, 15, 20, 21, 23, and of lifting up the voice (NIV, "shouted") in Judges 9:7 ("voice" is omitted from the Hebrew idiom in Isa 3:7; 42:2). *Nāśā'*, then, means not only "to carry," hence the meaning "burden" for *maśśā'*, but also "to lift up" in a more general sense. Therefore *maśśā'* could refer to the "lifting up" of the voice—i.e., to utter an oracle, hence the meaning "oracle." The latter seems to fit the contents of these chapters.

On the dynamic activity of God's word in v.1, see comments at 1:1, 6. Hadrach is to be identified with Hatarikka, in the vicinity of Hamath (ANET, pp. 282–83; see also Merrill F. Unger, *Israel and the Aramaeans of Damascus* [1957; reprint ed., Grand Rapids: Baker, 1980], pp. 85–89, and the present writer's updated bibliography in the Introduction of that work). Damascus was the leading city-state of the Arameans. The last half of the verse may be rendered "For the eye of the LORD is on all mankind, as well as on the tribes of Israel" (as in NIV mg.). But the most natural translation of the Hebrew is that of NIV. The only question is What does it mean? Feinberg (p. 156) suggests that the picture is "one of terror at the visitation of God upon the then great world-powers." Unger (*Zechariah*, p. 153), however, declares: "What is meant is that when all civilized men at that time, as well as all the tribes of Israel, were fastening their gaze intently upon Alexander the Great and his phenomenal conquests, they were *actually fastening their eyes upon the Lord*. Alexander was simply God's servant of judgment and chastisement (cf. vs. 4 where the Lord Himself is said to have dispossessed Tyre, when Alexander is known to have done so)" (emphasis his). The parenthetical thought may also be that the eyes of men, *especially* all the tribes of Israel, are toward the Lord (for deliverance). Finally, in the Aramean sector, the judgment extends to Hamath (modern Hama), which Amos called "great Hamath" (6:2).

2b–4 The Lord's word of judgment next came on the great Phoenician cities Tyre and Sidon, particularly the former. The judgment of Tyre and Sidon was also foretold in greater detail in Ezekiel 26:3–14; 28:20–24. Ezekiel's prophecy against Tyre was remarkably fulfilled to the letter, first through Nebuchadnezzar, then through Alexander (see E.M. Blaiklock, ZPEB, 5:832–35). By building a mole out to this island bastion, Alexander accomplished what Nebuchadnezzar could not do in thirteen years.

The last clause of v.2 may be either concessive ("though they are very skillful"; cf. Ezek 28:5) or causal ("because they think they are so wise"; cf. Ezek 28:4). Either way, their skill or wisdom is explained in v.3, which describes Tyre's island fortress (Isa 23:4) and the great wealth she acquired through commerce. There is a wordplay (paronomasia) between "Tyre" ("rock") and "stronghold" (or "rampart") in the Hebrew (*ṣōr māṣôr*). "Stronghold" refers to the seemingly impregnable island defenses of offshore Tyre (New Tyre), which was surrounded by a wall 150 feet high. The similes in the rest of the verse underscore Tyre's proverbial wealth. Despite her abundance and power, she will be destroyed (v.4). (For an account of Tyre's fall [332 B.C.] and of Alexander's role in it, see George Willis Botsford and Charles Alexander Robinson, Jr., *Hellenic History*, 4th ed. [New York: Macmillan, 1956], pp. 314–20, and Albert A. Trever, *History of Ancient Civilization* [New York: Harcourt, Brace and World, 1936], 1:456–59.)

5–7 Verse 5 features two common stylistic devices. First, the names form a chiasm. Second, there is a wordplay between "see" and "fear" in the Hebrew (*tēre' . . . ṯîrā'*). Four of the five cities of the Philistine pentapolis are mentioned in vv.5–6. Gath is omitted, evidently because it had lost all significance by this time. The Philistine cities were greatly alarmed at Alexander's inexorable advance. This was particularly true of Ekron, the northernmost city and the one that would suffer first; her "hope" that Tyre would stem the tide would meet with disappointment.

In the Hebrew there is no "her" with "king," nor is there a definite article. Perowne (p. 110), then, may well be correct in his judgment: "The prediction is, not that the then reigning monarch should perish, but that monarchical government should cease. Such tributary monarchies were abolished by Alexander. "Foreigners" (v.6) probably refers to people of mixed nationality; they characterized the postexilic period (Neh 13:23–24). "In the middle of verse 6 there is a change from the third to the first person. Now the Lord explains what He will do. He is going to transform the Philistines by breaking down their stubborn pride, removing repulsive ritual, and making them part of the 'remnant' of His people" (Baldwin, *Zechariah*, p. 161).

The name "Palestine" is derived from the word "Philistines." Their arrogance is mentioned at the end of v.6. The Philistines' "repulsive ritual" is described in the first half of v.7. The "blood" is that of idolatrous sacrifices, and "forbidden food" refers to polluted or ceremonially unclean foods. Obviously, other idolatrous practices are also included. Yet a Philistine remnant will belong to God and will become leaders in Judah. "Leaders" in the LXX is literally "chiliarch," i.e., "leader of a thousand"; the Hebrew word (*'allup*) occurs also in 12:5–6. Perowne (p. 111) asserts, "The meaning is that the Philistine, the nation personified as before, shall take his place, ruler and people, as one of the divisions of the Jewish nation." This interpretation is confirmed by the prediction that Ekron (probably a synecdoche of a part for the whole) will be like the Jebusites in a good sense. When David conquered Jerusalem, he did not destroy the Jebusites; instead, they were absorbed into Judah (e.g., Araunah in 2 Sam 24:16; 1 Chron 21:18). So it will be with a remnant of the Philistines.

8 The verse begins with "But," setting it in contrast with the preceding judgments on the surrounding nations. "I" signals the fact that it was God who was speaking through Zechariah. Just as God was to be a "wall of fire" around Jerusalem (2:5), so here he will "defend" his chosen people and land. "House" is probably a metonymy for the land and people of Israel, among whom the Lord had his earthly throne, so to speak, in the temple at Jerusalem. The defense is against the marauding forces of Alexander. "Marauding" literally means "crossing and returning," and some have suggested that the reference is specifically to Alexander in going to and from Egypt. But the idiom is likely nothing more than a general way of describing Alexander's overrunning that area (cf. 7:14 where the same Hebrew expression occurs with a slightly different nuance). A fascinating story of Jerusalem's marvelous preservation on this occasion is told by Josephus (Jos. Antiq., XI, 317–39 [viii.3–5]). It may well be based on a historical incident (it also appears in the Midrash).

> And Alexander, coming to Syria, took Damascus, became master of Sidon and besieged Tyre; from there he dispatched a letter to the high priest of the Jews, requesting him to send him assistance and supply his army with provisions and give him the gifts which they had formerly sent as tribute to Darius, thus choosing the friendship of the Macedonians, for, he said, they would not regret this course. But the high priest replied to the bearers of the letter that he had given his oath to Darius not to take up arms against him, and said that he would never violate this oath so long as Darius remained alive. When Alexander heard this, he was roused to anger, and while deciding not to leave Tyre, which was on the point of being taken, threatened that when he had brought it to terms he would march against the high priest of the Jews and through him teach all men what people it was to whom they must keep their oaths, and for this reason continuing the siege with greater effort, he took Tyre. After he had settled affairs there, he advanced against the city of Gaza and besieged it together with the commander of its garrison, named Babēmēsis.
>
> Now Sanaballetēs, believing that he had a favourable opportunity for his design, abandoned the cause of Darius and came, along with eight thousand of the people under his rule, to Alexander, whom he found beginning the siege of Tyre, and said that he was giving up to him the places under his rule and gladly accepted him as his master in place of King Darius. As Alexander received him in friendly fashion, Sanaballetēs now felt confident about his plan and addressed him on that subject, explaining that he had a son-in-law Manassēs, who was the brother of Jaddūs, the high priest of the Jews, and that there were many others of his countrymen with him who now wished to build a temple in the territory subject to him. It was also an advantage to the king, he said, that the power of the Jews should be divided in two, in order that the nation might not, in the event of revolution, be of one mind and stand together and so give trouble to the kings as

it had formerly given to the Assyrian rulers. When, therefore, Alexander gave his consent, Sanaballetēs brought all his energy to bear and built the temple and appointed Manassēs high priest, considering this to be the greatest distinction which his daughter's descendants could have. But Sanaballetēs died after seven months had been spent on the siege of Tyre and two on that of Gaza, and Alexander, after taking Gaza, was in haste to go up to the city of Jerusalem. When the high priest Jaddūs heard this, he was in an agony of fear, not knowing how he could meet the Macedonians, whose king was angered by his former disobedience. He therefore ordered the people to make supplication, and, offering sacrifice to God together with them, besought Him to shield the nation and deliver them from the dangers that were hanging over them. But, when he had gone to sleep after the sacrifice, God spoke oracularly to him in his sleep, telling him to take courage and adorn the city with wreaths and open the gates and go out to meet them, and that the people should be in white garments, and he himself with the priests in the robes prescribed by law, and that they should not look to suffer any harm, for God was watching over them. Thereupon he rose from his sleep, greatly rejoicing to himself, and announced to all the revelation that had been made to him, and, after doing all the things that he had been told to do, awaited the coming of the king.

When he learned that Alexander was not far from the city, he went out with the priests and the body of citizens, and, making the reception sacred in character and different from that of other nations, met him at a certain place called Saphein. This name, translated into the Greek tongue, means "Lookout." For, as it happened, Jerusalem and the temple could be seen from there. Now the Phoenicians and the Chaldaeans who followed along thought to themselves that the king in his anger would naturally permit them to plunder the city and put the high priest to a shameful death, but the reverse of this happened. For when Alexander while still far off saw the multitude in white garments, the priests at their head clothed in linen, and the high priest in a robe of hyacinth-blue and gold, wearing on his head the mitre with the golden plate on it on which was inscribed the name of God, he approached alone and prostrated himself before the Name and first greeted the high priest. Then all the Jews together greeted Alexander with one voice and surrounded him, but the kings of Syria and the others were struck with amazement at his action and supposed that the king's mind was deranged. And Parmenion alone went up to him and asked why indeed, when all men prostrated themselves before him, he had prostrated himself before the high priest of the Jews, whereupon he replied, "It was not before him that I prostrated myself but the God of whom he has the honour to be high priest, for it was he whom I saw in my sleep dressed as he is now, when I was at Dium in Macedonia, and, as I was considering with myself how I might become master of Asia, he urged me not to hesitate but to cross over confidently, for he himself would lead my army and give over to me the empire of the Persians. Since, therefore, I have beheld no one else in such robes, and on seeing him now I am reminded of the vision and the exhortation, I believe that I have made this expedition under divine guidance and that I shall defeat Darius and destroy the power of the Persians and succeed in carrying out all the things which I have in mind." After saying these things to Parmenion, he gave his hand to the high priest and, with the Jews running beside him, entered the city. Then he went up to the temple, where he sacrificed to God under the direction of the high priest, and showed due honour to the priests and to the high priest himself. And, when the book of Daniel was shown to him, in which he had declared that one of the Greeks would destroy the empire of the Persians, he believed himself to be the one indicated; and in his joy he dismissed the multitude for the time being, but on the following day he summoned them again and told them to ask for any gifts

> which they might desire. When the priest asked that they might observe their country's laws and in the seventh year be exempt from tribute, he granted all this. Then they begged that he would permit the Jews in Babylon and Media also to have their own laws, and he gladly promised to do as they asked. And, when he said to the people that if any wished to join his army while still adhering to the customs of their country, he was ready to take them, many eagerly accepted service with him.

"Without denying that the story is in a legendary dress, we may admit the 'probability' of Alexander's visit to Jerusalem, and the certainty that the city was spared, and the people favoured by him, in accordance with the terms of Zechariah's prophecy" (Perowne, p. 113).

"Never again" (v.8) must anticipate the second advent of the Messiah for the final, complete fulfillment. "Oppressor" (*nōḡēś*) is translated "slave driver" in Exodus 3:7 et al.; thus it echoes the Egyptian bondage motif. On the divine providence at the end of the verse, see Exodus 3:7; Psalm 32:8. Unger (*Zechariah*, p. 160) put it well: "For their preservation at the time of Alexander and for their future deliverance from every oppressor, Israel is indebted to the providence of God which watched over them for good." Baldwin (*Zechariah*, p. 162) sums up 9:1–8: "The first section of this second part of the book establishes from the start two important facts: the Lord's victory is certain, and He intends to bring back to Himself peoples long alienated from Him. These truths underlie all that follows and culminate in the universal worship of the King, the Lord of hosts, in 14:16–19."

Notes

---

1 Some commentators to the contrary notwithstanding, the preposition בְּ (*b*^{e}) probably here means "against" (BDB, p. 89, II.4.a).

The conjunction וְ (*w*^{e}, "and") before Damascus apparently introduces a circumstantial clause, literally, "with Damascus as its resting place."

As it stands, עֵין (*'ên*, "eye[s]") is in the construct state, hence "eyes of men."

Several exegetes propose reading "Aram" instead of "men," an emendation involving only a minor change of one letter in the Hebrew. Unfortunately "Aram" is not attested in any Hebrew MSS or ancient versions; so there is no textual evidence to support the change.

The conjunction וְ (*w*^{e}, "and") prefixed to "all" may mean "especially" (BDB, p. 252, 1.a; GKC, par. 154, n. 1).

2a וְגַם (*w*^{e}*gam*, "and . . . too") resumes the thought prior to the dashes: The Lord's word will rest not only on Damascus but also on Hamath.

גָּבַל (*gāḇal*, "to border") is a denominative verb, from גְּבוּל (*g*^{e}*ḇûl*, "border").

2b חָכְמָה (*ḥāḵ*^{e}*māh*, "they are skilled") is singular (in spite of the compound subject), most likely because Zechariah was thinking primarily of Tyre, as the next verse indicates. Some (e.g., Baldwin, *Zechariah*, p. 159) suggest that there should be a full stop after "Sidon" and that the following clause should begin a new sentence that continues into v.3: "Because she is very skillful [or wise], Tyre has. . . ."

8 מִצָּבָה (*miṣṣāḇāh*, "forces," "army") stands for מִצָּבָא (*miṣṣāḇā'*) and is another of the numerous examples of orthographic confusion between final ה (*h*) and final א ('); see, e.g., GKC, par. 75nn–rr.

---

b. *The advent of Zion's King*

9:9–10

9Rejoice greatly, O Daughter of Zion!
Shout, Daughter of Jerusalem!
See, your king comes to you,
righteous and having salvation,
gentle and riding on a donkey,
on a colt, the foal of a donkey.
10I will take away the chariots from Ephraim
and the war-horses from Jerusalem,
and the battle bow will be broken.
He will proclaim peace to the nations.
His rule will extend from sea to sea
and from the River to the ends of the earth.

9a As has been seen, vv.1–8 predicted the military campaigns of Alexander the Great as he advanced on a war-horse south from Aram (Syria), subjugating city after city. The scene depicts intense battle and war; yet it is the implements of war that the messianic King is said to remove from Israel in v.10. Verses 7–8 in particular form a transition to vv.9–10, which the Talmud and the Midrashim take as messianic. The treatment here likewise classifies vv.9–10 as "direct" messianic prophecy, though some prefer the "typical" category. The language in the opening part of v.9 is an echo of Zephaniah 3:14. Zechariah first calls on Jerusalem's people to rejoice. "Daughter of Zion" and "Daughter of Jerusalem" (poetic ways of speaking of Zion and Jerusalem; cf. note at 2:7) involve several figures of speech: (1) personification ("Rejoice. . . . Shout"); (2) metonymy of the subject, in which the city is put for its inhabitants (Bullinger, pp. 579–80); and (3) synecdoche of the part (Jerusalem) for the value—the entire covenant nation.

9b The project now gives the reasons for the rejoicing. The jubilation is over a new Sovereign. The first reason for joy, then, is the coming of the messianic, Davidic (note the "your") King (see excursus below). Zechariah announces his coming in the opening line quoted above. "To you" may be alternatively rendered "for you," i.e., "for your benefit" (dative of advantage). After announcing the King's coming, the prophet describes the King's character: He is righteous and, therefore, saving; he is humble or gentle and, therefore, peaceful.

First, the King is righteous, conforming to the divine standard of morality and ethics, particularly as revealed in the Mosaic legislation. On this characteristic of the ideal king, see 2 Samuel 23:3–4; Psalm 72:1–3; Isaiah 9:7; 11:4–5; 53:11. Second, he is saving. The Niphal *nôšāʿ* may be either passive or reflexive. If it is passive, the probable meaning is "having salvation" (NIV). If it is reflexive, the likely meaning is "showing himself a Savior-Deliverer." "Saving" attempts to reconcile the two major possibilities. Third, in contrast to most kings (such as Alexander), he is humble or gentle (cf. Isa 53:2–3, 7; Matt 11:29). Fourth, he is peaceful, for this is the meaning of his riding on a colt, the foal of a donkey, though it possibly suggests both peace and humility. At any rate, he does not come on a war-horse (v.10).

Although Jesus was acclaimed Messiah at his Triumphal Entry into Jerusalem (Matt 21:1–9; Mark 11:1–10; Luke 19:28–38; John 12:12–15), his own people nonetheless rejected him and his peace (cf. Luke 19:39–44 and, later, his crucifixion). Johnson (pp. 228–29) captures the significance of the scene.

> Because they will have Him at His first coming in peace, peace shall flee from them. Seeing the future discipline and chastening of the nation, He wept. Walking headlong to ruin, they shall have to learn the sad lesson that the triumphal entry was not only the story of the nation's rejection of its King, but also of their King's rejection of them.
>
> Yet, all is not lost. The future holds a glorious hope. The promises, unconditioned in their ultimate fulfillment, shall be realized. Israel may deny Him, crucify Him, and attempt to forget Him; but His word is inviolable. Disobedience may thwart the enjoyment of the promises, but it cannot cancel title to them or the ultimate possession of them. The day is coming, as He Himself suggested a few days later, when Israel in full understanding shall shout the acclamation again, as they see Him coming the second time for deliverance: "Blessed is he that cometh in the name of the Lord" (cf. Matt. 23:37–39). Then shall take place the entry that is really triumphal (cf. Zech. 14:1–11). In the meantime, their house, as history has proved, is desolate.

10 The first reason for rejoicing is the coming of the King (v.9). The second reason is the establishment of his kingdom—a kingdom of universal peace in Israel and among the nations and universal sovereignty (v.10). Again in contrast with Alexander's empire, which was founded on bloodshed, the messianic King will establish a universal kingdom of peace. A shift begins from the foundation for peace (v.9) to the fact of peace (v.10). The progressive fulfillment of v.10 reaches to the Messiah's second advent, when weapons of warfare will be either removed or converted to peaceful pursuits (cf. Isa 2:4; 9:5–7; 11:1–10; Mic 5:10–15). The chariot is related to Ephraim because it was characteristic of the army of the northern kingdom of Israel. An impressive sidelight on the removal of war-horses from Jerusalem is Zechariah's statement that the messianic King would enter the city riding on a donkey, an animal symbolizing peace, not war (v.9).

The chariot, the war-horse, and the battle bow represent the whole arsenal used in ancient warfare; so the passage implies the destruction of this whole arsenal. Not only will there be disarmament and peace in Israel, but the messianic King will also proclaim "peace" (*šālôm*) to the nations—a fulfillment of the Abrahamic covenant (cf. 14:16; Gen 12:3; 18:18; 22:18). "From sea to sea" has been variously explained as "from the Nile to the Euphrates" (cf. Gen 15:18; Exod 23:31), "from the Mediterranean to the Red Sea," and "from the Mediterranean to the Dead Sea." The question is really not important because the context makes it clear that the expression is a merism, indicating that the extent of the Messiah's rule is to be universal. The same is true of the phrase "from the River [Euphrates] to the ends of the earth" (cf. Ps 72:8–11; Isa 66:18). "The only realistic hopes of world peace still centre in this king" (Baldwin, *Zechariah*, p. 167).

Notes

9b As NIV shows, the וְ (*w*[e]) prefixed to עַל (*'al*, "on") is to be construed as epexegetical (GKC, par. 154a, n. 1[b]).

On the problem of two donkeys in Matthew, Johnson (p. 222, n. 10) explains:

> Much ink has been spilt over the fact that Matthew mentions two animals while the other gospels mention only one. M'Neile, as others, feels that Matthew misunderstood the Hebrew synonymous parallelism of Zech. 9:9 and spoke 'mistakenly of two animals.' . . . The passage, then, becomes a shining example of a prophecy which, erroneously interpreted, creates a new and erroneous tradition. But this is not a necessary view at all, although many eminent interpreters have their names attached to it. It is more in accord with the context to have Matthew introduce the second animal to emphasize the fact that the colt was really unused, as the synoptics indicate. The mother animal was necessary since the unbroken young donkey would not have submitted to being ridden amid the tumultuous crowds unless she were along.

For a thorough treatment of this subject, see Donald A. Carson's exposition of Matt 21:5 (EBC, 8:438). See also Robert H. Gundry, *The Use of the Old Testament in St. Matthew's Gospel* (Leiden: E.J. Brill, 1967), pp. 197–99.

The plural **אֲתֹנוֹת** (*'ᵃṯōnôṯ*, "donkey") here denotes an indefinite singular (Davidson, par. 17, rem. 3; GKC, par. 124o).

10 The editors of *Biblia Hebraica Stuttgartensia* propose reading (with LXX) third person **הִכְרִית** (*hiḵrîṯ*, "he will take away") instead of first person **הִכְרַתִּי** (*hiḵrattî*, "I will take away"). But such shifts in person are common enough in prophetic literature (e.g., 12:10: "They will look on me . . . and they will mourn for him").

Excursus

Kingship in the Ancient Near East

In synthesizing all the available historical data, we discover that ancient Near Eastern kingship had at least six major functions: (1) the king represented the gods before the people (his role as mediator); (2) he represented the people before the gods (his role as priest); (3) he maintained justice (his role as judge); (4) he was the commander-in-chief of the military (his role as warrior); (5) he "tended" his people, which included protection, provision, and guidance (his role as shepherd); and (6) he guaranteed *šālôm*—well-being and harmony—in society and nature (one of his general roles as king).

Zechariah portrays the Messiah as the complete and perfect King by applying all six royal functions to him (see comments at the following verses): (1) mediating Servant (3:8); (2) Priest (6:13); (3) Judge (14:16–19); (4) Warrior (10:4; 14:3–4); (5) Shepherd (11:8–9; 13:7); and (6) "Peace"-bringing King (3:10; 9:9–10).

The Kingship of Yahweh

Some passages attributing kingship to Yahweh (the LORD) are 1 Samuel 12:12; Psalms 93, 95–99 ("theocratic" psalms); Isaiah 33:22; 43:15; Ezekiel 20:33. Regardless of mediatorial vice-regents, the Hebrew mind looked beyond the immediate mortal king to Yahweh's kingship (cf. Isa 6:1, 5). The divine *means* of rule was the theocracy, by which chosen agents represented Yahweh and did his divine will. The *basis* of Yahweh's kingship over Israel was their covenantal election and redemption; see Genesis 12:1–3, with the motifs of land (Deut 30: 1–10), seed (2 Sam 7:1–16), and blessing (Jer 31:31–40).

Kingship in Israel

Davidic kings served as a reflection of Yahweh's kingship and were typical of the ideal messianic King to come. They were divinely chosen, not elected by the nation. The relationship between the king and Yahweh was based on a personal covenant made with David and his royal progeny (2 Sam 7:12–16). The Davidic covenant established a father-son relationship between God and the king (2 Sam 7:14). This relationship was a kind of adoption, entailing discipline and direction. The "adoption" of David as "son" comes to the fore in Psalm 89:26–27. Among David's descendants will be the messianic King, who will be the accepted "Son" and a King above all kings (Ps 2:6–9). The messianic King in David's line will represent Yahweh perfectly, for he will be a wise Ruler ("Wonderful Counselor"), a strong Ruler or divine Warrior ("Mighty God"), a fatherly Ruler ("Everlasting Father"), and a peace-bringing Ruler ("Prince of Peace"). These are his "throne names" (Isa 9:6–7).

The king in Israel performed the same basic functions as ancient Near Eastern kings in general, except that he did not serve as priest. This significant lack in Davidic kingship, along with Israel's kings' failures even in the other functions, caused the people to look forward to one who would be the perfect, complete King and would establish the promised, ideal messianic kingdom. Significantly, the contemporary sepulcher inscription of King Tabnit of Sidon "is notable above all because of the priestly and royal titles given to the ruler of Sidon" (E. Lipínski, *Near Eastern Religious Texts Relating to the Old Testament*, ed. by Walter Beyerlin [Philadelphia: Westminster, 1978], p. 245); see Zechariah 6:11–13.

The ideal king portrayed in Psalm 72 exhibited four features: (1) righteousness and justice, (2) salvation, (3) humility, and (4) *šālôm* ("well-being," "harmony," "completeness," "balance," "security," "peace," "prosperity," etc.); see also Zechariah 9:9–10.

c. *The deliverance and blessing of Zion's people*

9:11–10:1

11 As for you, because of the blood of my covenant with you,
 I will free your prisoners from the waterless pit.
12 Return to your fortress, O prisoners of hope;
 even now I announce that I will restore twice as much
 to you.
13 I will bend Judah as I bend my bow
 and fill it with Ephraim.
I will rouse your sons, O Zion,
 against your sons, O Greece,
 and make you like a warrior's sword.
14 Then the LORD will appear over them;
 his arrow will flash like lightning.
The Sovereign LORD will sound the trumpet;
 he will march in the storms of the south,
15 and the LORD Almighty will shield them.
They will destroy
 and overcome with slingstones.
They will drink and roar as with wine;
 they will be full like a bowl
 used for sprinkling the corners of the altar.
16 The LORD their God will save them on that day
 as the flock of his people.
They will sparkle in his land
 like jewels in a crown.

> 17How attractive and beautiful they will be!
> Grain will make the young men thrive,
> and new wine the young women.
>
> 10:1Ask the LORD for rain in the springtime;
> it is the LORD who makes the storm clouds.
> He gives showers of rain to men,
> and plants of the field to everyone.

11–13 Although the Messiah's mission is to establish his kingdom of "peace" (*šālôm*), he must first conquer all enemies and deliver his people. This he sets out to do (vv.11–16; cf. Ps 110). Before he can reign in peace, he must fully deliver and restore Israel. The passage is filled with battle terminology: prisoners (v.11), fortress (v.12), bow (v.13), sword (v.13), arrow (v.14), trumpet (v.14), and slingstones (v.15). Here the Messiah is depicted as a conquering King (the divine Warrior motif).

"You" (v.11) is emphatic and refers to Zion (v.9). The "blood of my covenant with you" probably has in view the Mosaic covenant (Exod 24:3–8). "Prisoners" evidently refers to those still in the land of exile, Babylonia. The Lord will free them because he is bound to them by covenantal relationship. The "waterless pit" recalls Joseph's and Jeremiah's predicament (Gen 37:24; Jer 38:6–9). In v.12 those outside the land who have hope in the future, delivering King (vv.9–10) are exhorted to return. While "fortress" may refer initially to Jerusalem (Zion) and Judah, the ultimate reference may well be to God himself, the only source of real security. "Twice as much" is a metonymy of the subject (Bullinger, p. 585), indicating full or complete restoration (for the same figure but in a negative context indicative of full retribution, see Isa 40:2; 51:19; for a positive context, see Isa 61:7).

The basis for the hope is given in v.13, of which Laetsch (p. 458) says, "In a bold metaphor the Lord compares Himself to a warrior using Judah as His bow, Ephraim as His arrow." The verse is progressively fulfilled. The initial, partial fulfillment is apparently to be found in the conflict between the Maccabees ("Zion") and the Seleucids ("Greece"). But the final, complete fulfillment awaits the outworking of chapters 12 and 14 and 9:16–17. The point of the verse is that God's people will gain the victory over their enemies.

14–16 Verse 14 contains the language of theophany or epiphany (cf. Ps 18:7–15; Hab 3:3–15; see further Claus Westermann, *The Psalms: Structure, Content and Message* [Minneapolis: Augsburg, 1980], pp. 51–52). The language is also anthropomorphic ("will sound . . . will march"). Here the sound of the trumpet is evidently a reference to thunder. The words are reminiscent of Exodus 19:16–19. God will come down to aid, protect, and deliver his covenant people. The symbolism of v.14 "reminds one of Assur, the national god of Assyria, seen hovering protectingly over the embattled armies of his people, as appears on Assyrian reliefs" (Unger, *Zechariah*, p. 168). Perhaps the first stage in the progressive fulfillment of v.15 is to be found in 1 Maccabees 3:16–24; 4:6–16; 7:40–50. *The Illustrated Family Encyclopedia* (8:94) has this illuminating archaeological note on "slingstones":

> When the Messianic age dawns, the Israelites, with the Lord fighting at their side, will wreak vengeance on their foes (cf. Zech. 10:3–7). The prophet's description of this apocalyptic war is realistic in detail, the various weapons mentioned by him being amongst the most important used by the armies of the

> ancient East: the sword, the bow and arrow (ibid. 9:13–14), and also "slingstones"—large pebbles or smooth stones from the bed of a watercourse (1 Sam. 17:40) which were shaped to fit into the sling. . . . But all these will be of no avail against the Israelites.
>
> The sling was a long-range weapon, like the bow. Hence, in battle the units of slingers and archers were generally positioned side by side. The Dead Sea Scroll of "The War of the Sons of the Light Against The Sons of Darkness" also mentions "standards of slingers," each of the soldiers grouped beneath which was armed with seven slingstones (column 5, lines 1–2). The way in which the slinger operated his sling is well illustrated on the reliefs of Sennacherib (704–681 B.C.) portraying the capture of Lachish. . . . The artist has drawn the slingers in the act of hurling their slingstones, each with a pile of reserve ammunition at his feet. This weapon was a menace not only to the defenders who fought from the top of the wall to a besieged city, but also to the inhabitants inside, since its high trajectory made it possible for stones to be shot over the wall into the city's streets.

See also Yigael Yadin, *The Art of Warfare in Biblical Lands* (New York: McGraw-Hill, 1963), 2:296–97. In fact, Yadin's work on all the weapons of warfare mentioned in the Book of Zechariah is helpful.

On the bowl used for sprinkling the corners of the altar, see Leviticus 4:7. Unger (*Zechariah,* p. 169) maintains that this is a simile of Israel's warriors streaming with the blood of their conquered foes. For a less military and less gory view, see Baldwin (*Zechariah,* pp. 169–70). Verse 16 plainly declares the divine deliverance of Zion's people. "That day" is the time orientation "which always in chapters 9–14 embraces the final eschatological era of Israel's future reinstatement and deliverance" (Unger, *Zechariah,* p. 169).

"His people" is an appositional genitive; thus his people *are* the Lord's flock (cf. Ps 100:3). As for the rest of the verse, there is an apparent antithesis between the "slingstones" (v.15) used to subdue Israel's enemies and the precious stones, or "jewels" (the saved, victorious remnant), that will sparkle in the Lord's land. "The figure is evidently of the reward of the faithful martyrs and valiant saints of Israel who enter the kingdom of Messiah" (Unger, *Zechariah,* p. 170). The Hebrew for "crown" (*nēzer*) is often used of the crown of the high priest. How appropriate, then, for Israel, restored as a priestly nation (see ch. 3; also Exod 19:6; Isa 61:6)! Ellis (p. 1042) summarizes v.16: "Thus with a picture of the people restored and rejoicing without restraint in God's mighty deliverance, the prophet sees them as *jewels of a crown,* living emblems of all that the Lord has done for them" (emphasis his).

17 With Israel's deliverance comes blessing, including agricultural prosperity, because Israel's covenantal God controls the weather and the rain (10:1). The result is a land of peace, prosperity, and plenty. "They" is literally "he" (possibly the Lord), but the singular could be collective for the delivered remnant of the future; the context (v.16) seems to favor the collective understanding. "Grain" and "new wine" are signs of prosperity.

1 This verse probably contains a veiled polemic against Baal and Baalism, as do Jeremiah 14:22 and Amos 5:8 (see further Barker, "Value of Ugaritic," pp. 120–23).

Yahweh, not Baal, is the one who controls the weather and the rain, giving life and fertility to the land. Therefore the people of God are to pray to him and trust in him. Some scholars regard the spring rains as literal; others understand them as spiritual and typical. Perhaps both are in view, the literal rains being also typical of spiritual refreshment. Certainly in the grand consummation of the Messianic Era, both the physical and spiritual realms will flourish (cf. Isa 55:10–12; Hos 6:3; Joel 2:21–32).

Notes

---

11 שִׁלַּחְתִּי (*šillaḥtî*, "I will free") is a prophetic perfect, as are the first two perfects in v.13.

12 "The *personal pronoun* which would be expected as the subject of a participial clause is frequently omitted" (GKC, par. 116s; emphasis theirs). This applies to מַגִּיד (*maggîḏ*, "I announce").

13 אֶפְרַיִם (*'eprayim*, "with Ephraim") is adverbial accusative.

יָוָן (*yāwān*, "Greece") seems to be a transliteration of the Greek for "Ionia." Here, though, it refers primarily to the Seleucids, who sprang from Seleucus I Nicator, son of a Macedonian noble and one of Alexander's generals and founder of the Seleucid Dynasty, which held certain eastern portions of Alexander's short-lived empire—including Syria.

14 תֵּימָן (*têmān*, "south") is literally "what is on the right [hand]," i.e., as one faces east; hence "south" (cf. יָמִין [*yāmîn*, "right hand"]).

16 מִתְנוֹסְסוֹת (*miṯnôsᵉsôṯ*, "they will sparkle") is apparently a Hithpoel participle from נסס (*nss*), cf. BDB, p. 651.

17 יְנוֹבֵב (*yᵉnôḇēḇ*, "will make thrive") is a Polel imperfect from נוב (*nwb*); the verb does double duty for both "grain" and "new wine."

---

d. *Warning and encouragement*

10:2–4

2 The idols speak deceit,
diviners see visions that lie;
they tell dreams that are false,
they give comfort in vain.
Therefore the people wander like sheep
oppressed for lack of a shepherd.

3 "My anger burns against the shepherds,
and I will punish the leaders;
for the LORD Almighty will care
for his flock, the house of Judah,
and make them like a proud horse in battle.
4 From Judah will come the cornerstone,
from him the tent peg,
from him the battle bow,
from him every ruler.

2 Zechariah warned Israel's idolatrous leaders (vv.2–3a) but encouraged the people (vv.3b–4). There is also a clear contrast between v.1 and v.2: Prayer to God brings blessing (v.1), but trust in idols (or the false gods they represent) produces disappointment and sorrow (v.2). The Hebrew for "idols" is *t^erāpîm*, a reference to household gods (see Gen 31:19; cf. Moshe Greenberg, "Another Look at Rachel's Theft of the Teraphim," JBL 81 [1962]: 239–48). They were used for divination during the period of the "judges" (Judg 17:5; 18:5). "Diviners" were consulted to foretell the future. Since they "see visions" and "tell dreams," they would have been included among the false prophets ("deceit . . . lie . . . false . . . in vain"; cf. Jer 23:30–32; 27:9–10). Resorting to diviners for information and guidance is specifically proscribed in Deuteronomy 18:9–14, because God provided true prophets (and ultimately the messianic Prophet) for that purpose (Deut 18:15–22); see John 4:25; 6:14; Acts 3:22–23). (For an illuminating exposition of the passage in Deuteronomy 18, see Edward J. Young, *My Servants the Prophets* [Grand Rapids: Eerdmans, 1952], pp. 20–37.)

Because diviners are unreliable, "they give comfort in vain"—e.g., when they wrongly promise rain and fruitful seasons (cf. v.1 and Jer 14:22). Similarly, because diviners speak lies, "therefore" the people are led astray like sheep without a shepherd. What the people need is spiritual leadership, but it is lacking (cf. Mark 6:34). "The physical victory described in the previous section must be accompanied by a deeper and more fundamental spiritual battle" (Ellis, p. 1042).

Although "shepherd" can refer to any leader, it is primarily a royal motif, whether referring to human kings (Isa 44:28; Jer 23:2–4), to the divine King (Pss 23:1; 100:3), or to the messianic Davidic King (Ezek 34:23–24). "Shepherd" was a familiar metaphor in the ancient Near Eastern world; e.g., in the Prologue to the Code of Hammurabi, Hammurabi describes himself as "the shepherd, called by Enlil, . . . the one who makes affluence and plenty abound" (ANET, p. 164).

3–4 God threatened to judge the selfish, corrupt, unqualified leaders of the nation (cf. Ezek 34:1–10). Since the earthly leaders did not take proper care of the "flock," the Lord promised to care for them himself and to make them like a proud horse triumphant in battle. "Those who in their submission to the Lord are like sheep become invincible as war-horses in His service" (Baldwin, *Zechariah*, p. 174). Verse 3 contains an interesting wordplay on the Hebrew *pāqaḏ*: first "punish," then "care for." The word is susceptible of either negative or positive nuances (see BDB, p. 823, for references).

Verse 4 is variously interpreted. Those commentators are probably correct who, with the Targum, take it as messianic (the pronoun "him" referring to Judah, as in NIV). So understood, the Messiah will come from Judah (cf. Gen 49:10; Jer 30:21). He is called (1) "the cornerstone" (cf. comment at 3:9; cf. also esp. Ps 118:22; Isa 28:16); (2) "the tent peg," a figure of a ruler as the support of the state (so BDB, p. 450; cf. Isa 22:23–24; and (3) "the battle bow," part of the divine Warrior terminology (cf. Ps 45:5; Rev 19:11–16). From Judah will also come "every" divinely sanctioned king and ultimately the Messiah. Although the Hebrew *nôgēś* ("ruler") is used pejoratively in 9:8, it seems best to agree with BDB (p. 620) that here it is used in a good sense.

Notes

---

2 Apparently, the ן (*n*) at the end of יְנַחֵמוּן (*yᵉnaḥēmûn*, "they give comfort") was originally an ending of the indicative mood (cf. W.L. Moran, "New Evidence on Canaanite *taqtulū(na)*," *Journal of Cuneiform Studies* 5 [1951]: 33–35). In this article Moran advances the theory that Amarna Canaanite forms ending in *ūna* are indicative, while those ending in *ū* are jussive or otherwise volitive.

3 הָעַתּוּדִים (*hā'attûḏîm*, "the leaders") is literally "the he-goats," used figuratively of leaders (Isa 14:9; Ezek 34:17).

4 יֵצֵא (*yēṣē'*, "will come") is probably intended to serve as the verb for "cornerstone," "tent peg," "battle bow," and "every ruler" (NIV so renders it). As the alternative translation in the NIV margin indicates, יַחְדָּו (*yaṣdāw*, "together") can be translated either at the end of v.4 or at the beginning of v.5.

---

e. *Israel's victory over her enemies*

10:5–7

5Together they will be like mighty men
  trampling the muddy streets in battle.
Because the LORD is with them,
  they will fight and overthrow the horsemen.

6"I will strengthen the house of Judah
  and save the house of Joseph.
I will restore them
  because I have compassion on them.
They will be as though
  I had not rejected them,
for I am the LORD their God
  and I will answer them.
7The Ephraimites will become like mighty men,
  and their hearts will be glad as with wine.
Their children will see it and be joyful;
  their hearts will rejoice in the LORD.

5 The Lord promises to make Israel mighty and to reunite and restore the nation, causing the people to rejoice in him. Judah (v.4)—i.e., its people—is probably the antecedent of "they" (v.5). In the context "mighty men" has a military connotation: "valiant warriors." "Because" introduces the reason for their victory: supernatural help ("the LORD is with them"; cf. Josh 1:5; Jer 1:8). Because of divine aid the infantry overcomes the cavalry (a symbol of power). God's people win against superior odds. Although the final, complete fulfillment doubtless lies in the future, perhaps the first stage in the progressive fulfillment of the passage is to be found in the Maccabean victories.

6–7 The opening part of v.6 is chiastically arranged. The Hebrew order is "I will strengthen the house of Judah, and the house of Joseph I will save." There will be a reunification of south (Judah) and north (Joseph). The reason for their restoration is given as God's tender, motherly compassion. The reason for their not continuing in a state of rejection is that the Lord (Yahweh) is their covenantal God, bound to his people in a covenant relationship (cf. Rom 11). God's promise to answer them implies that they will pray to him for deliverance. Not only will Judah be like mighty men (v.5), but so also will Ephraim (v.7), resulting in great exuberance. For gladness associated with wine, see also Psalm 104:15. But here it is only a simile. The Lord is the secret, source, and sphere of this joy (as in Ps 32:11; Phil 4:4).

Notes

---

5 By analogy with בּוֹשִׁים (*bôšîm*), בּוֹסִים (*bôsîm*, "trampling") occurs here instead of the expected בָּסִים (*bāsîm*; cf. GKC, par. 72p).

6 וְהוֹשְׁבוֹתִים (*w*^{e}*hôš*^{e}*ḇôṯîm*, "I will restore them") is anomalous. According to some the form should be וַהֲשִׁיבוֹתִים (*wah*^{a}*šîḇôṯîm*) as in v.10, from שׁוּב (*šûḇ*); so GKC, par. 72x and NIV. Others propose וְהוֹשַׁבְתִּים (*w*^{e}*hôšaḇtîm*, "I will cause them to dwell"), from יָשַׁב (*yāšaḇ*), a reading supported by many Hebrew MSS and the LXX. Still others (including some Jewish writers of the past) suggest that the form is deliberately conflate in order to carry both sides: "I will bring them back and cause them to dwell." This last proposal has also been made for the troublesome form וְשַׁבְתִּי (*w*^{e}*šaḇtî*) in Ps 23:6. So understood, the sense there would be "and I will return and dwell." Probably, though, in Ps 23:6 the form is from *yāšaḇ*, and the *yā* has been lost through aph(a)eresis. NIV, probably correctly, assumes that the context of the Zechariah passage favors the same reading as in v.10 ("bring back" or "restore").

7 יָגֵל (*yāgēl*, "will rejoice") is a classic example of an apparently jussive form used as an ordinary imperfect (cf. GKC, par. 109k; Davidson, par. 65, rem. 6).

---

f. *Israel's complete deliverance and restoration*

10:8–12

8 I will signal for them
and gather them in.
Surely I will redeem them;
they will be as numerous as before.
9 Though I scatter them among the peoples,
yet in distant lands they will remember me.
They and their children will survive,
and they will return.
10 I will bring them back from Egypt
and gather them from Assyria.
I will bring them to Gilead and Lebanon,
and there will not be room enough for them.
11 They will pass through the sea of trouble;
the surging sea will be subdued
and all the depths of the Nile will dry up.
Assyria's pride will be brought down
and Egypt's scepter will pass away.
12 I will strengthen them in the Lord
and in his name they will walk,"
declares the Lord.

8–9 The Lord promises to regather his people from distant lands. He will strengthen them, but the power of their ancient and traditional oppressors will wane. Verse 8 begins with an anthropomorphism: "I will signal [lit., 'whistle'] for them." This is apparently a continuation of the shepherd metaphor (see Judg 5:16). "Now, as true shepherd of his flock, he calls the sheep and gathers them home" (Ellis, p. 1043). The Hebrew for "redeem" is often used for ransoming from slavery or captivity (see Isa 35:10; Mic 6:4; cf. 1 Peter 1:18–19). "Before" seems to recall the situation in Egypt (Exod 1:6–20). Even in the Diaspora the Jews will remember the Lord (v.9). According to the meaning of Zechariah's name, "The LORD [Yahweh] remembers" his covenant people and promises. Now the prediction is made that they will remember him. And they will also survive and return to the Promised Land. "Though in far-off lands, the people of Israel will not forget their God, and generation after generation will survive along with the expectation of a final homecoming" (Ellis, p. 1044). Kaiser (p. 255) underscores and clarifies the significance of the content of this promise (v.9):

> Yet even after Israel had been restored to the land after the Babylonian exile, the prospect of a regathered, reunified nation still appeared in Zechariah 10:9–12. The importance of this passage and its late postexilic date should not be lost by those who interpret the promise of the land spiritually or as a temporal blessing which has since been forfeited by a rebellious nation due to her failure to keep her part of the conditional (?) covenant. On the contrary, this hope burned brighter as Israel became more and more hopelessly scattered.

10–12 In vv.10–11 the names "Egypt . . . Assyria. . . . Assyria . . . Egypt" form a chiasm. These two ancient oppressors of God's chosen people are probably intended to represent all the countries where the Israelites are dispersed. They evoke memories of slavery and exile. The promise of regathering (v.10) is similar to that in Isaiah 11:11–16 (note "a second time" in Isa 11:11; Ezek 39:27–29). "Gilead" lies east of the Jordan and "Lebanon" west of the Jordan—both in the territory of the old northern kingdom. *The Illustrated Family Encyclopedia* (8:95) has this to say about Lebanon and Gilead:

> At the end of the apocalyptic war, the Lord will gather in the widely scattered exiles of His people. The house of Judah and the house of Joseph will be united as of old and they will all be mighty warriors (Zech. 10:6–7; cf. Isa. 11:11–16). In the prosperity that follows, the rapidly multiplying population will spread till it reaches the Lebanon and Gilead. The Lebanon . . . is referred to in the Old Testament as a symbol of strength, dignity and splendour (e.g., 2 Kings 19:23; Isa. 35:2), as are the mountains of Gilead. Hence the two are sometimes also mentioned together to denote power and pride . . . (Jer. 22:6). In our verse too this combination may be intended to demonstrate the future power and glory of the Messianic kingdom of Israel. The territory of Gilead in Trans-Jordan, with its good soil and abundant crops, was accounted one of the most fertile regions of Palestine, together with the Carmel, Bashan and the hills of Ephraim (Jer. 50: 19). North of the river Jabbok the soil of Gilead is of the type known as "terra rossa" which is very suitable for agriculture; while the land to the south of the river favours both cultivation and pasture alike (cf. Mic. 7:14; Song of Sol. 6:5).

On the statement that "there will not be room enough for them" (v.10), see v.8 and Isaiah 49:19–21; 54:2–3. Obstacles will be no barrier (v.11). The people "will pass through the sea of trouble" (v.11)—as at the Red Sea, or Sea of Reeds. The "scepter" (i.e., "rule") of other great powers over them will cease. If the Ephraimites (northern kingdom) are still in view (see v.7), God is promising in v.12 to do the same for them as he did for Judah (v.6), namely, strengthen them. The source of the strength is the Lord himself ("in the LORD"). Walking "in his name" is probably here equivalent to serving "as his representatives or ambassadors," though it may also mean that they will live "in keeping with his revealed character"—by divine enablement, of course.

Notes

---

8 אֶשְׁרְקָה (*’ešr^{e}qāh*, "I will signal") is a cohortative of resolve or determination, as in NIV.

On the emphatic use of כִּי (*kî*, "surely"), see BDB, p. 472, 1.e.; GKC, par. 159ee.

NIV, probably correctly for this context, construes פְּדִיתִים (*p^{e}ḏîṯîm*, "I will redeem them") as a prophetic perfect.

10 Something like "place" or "room" must be supplied in thought after יִמָּצֵא (*yimmāṣē’*, "there will [not] be found").

11 Although the subject of וְעָבַר (*w^e‘āḇar*, "will pass") could be the Lord, it seems preferable to take it as a collective reference to Israel (so NIV), echoing their "passing through" the Red Sea.

וְהִכָּה (*w^{e}hikkāh*, "will be subdued"; lit., "one will strike") is here used impersonally.

יְאֹר (*y^e’ōr*, "the Nile") is one of several Egyptian loan words in Hebrew.

A rather clear case of assonance appears at the end of the verse: אַשּׁוּר (*’aššûr*, "Assyria") and יָסוּר (*yāsûr*, "will pass away").

12 On the probable significance of the Hithpael יִתְהַלָּכוּ (*yiṯhallāḵû*, "they will walk"), see the note at 1:10. Applied here, it would mean "they will walk continually."

---

2. *The rejection of the messianic Shepherd-King* (11:1–17)

a. *The prologue*

11:1–3

1 Open your doors, O Lebanon,
  so that fire may devour your cedars!
2 Wail, O pine tree, for the cedar has fallen;
  the stately trees are ruined!
Wail, oaks of Bashan;
  the dense forest has been cut down!
3 Listen to the wail of the shepherds;
  their rich pastures are destroyed!
Listen to the roar of the lions;
  the lush thicket of the Jordan is ruined!

1–3 This little poem is beset with problems. For example, is it the conclusion of the previous section or a poetic introduction to the following section? Quite obviously the answer depends, in part at least, on one's interpretation of the piece. Some interpret it as a taunt song describing the lament over the destruction of the nations' power and arrogance (ch. 10), represented by the cedar, the pine, and the oak (vv.1–2). Their kings are represented by the shepherds and the lions (v.3). So understood, vv.1–3 provide the conclusion for the preceding section. Others, however, without denying the presence of figurative language, interpret the piece more literally as a description of the devastation of Syro-Palestine due to the rejection of the Messiah and Good Shepherd (vv.4–14). Verses 1–3 would then introduce the next section. The names in the text—Lebanon, Bashan, and Jordan—seem to favor this approach. Part of the fulfillment would be the destruction and further subjugation of that whole area by the Romans, including the fall of Jerusalem in A.D. 70 under Emperor Vespasian and General Titus, as well as the later fall of Masada. This action quelled one of several Jewish rebellions against Rome. Understood this way, the passage is in sharp contrast with what has just preceded in chapter 10, with its prediction of Israel's full deliverance and restoration to the covenant land. Now the scene is one of desolation for the land (vv.1–3), followed by the threat of judgment and disaster for both land and people (vv.4–6).

The picture that now unfolds is very vivid and graphic—"in words arranged with great rhetorical power, full of poetic imagery and lively dramatic movement" (Chambers, CHS, 14:83). Unger (*Zechariah*, p. 188) says: "One can feel the severity of the judgment visited upon the land (and inevitably upon the people also) which prepares the reader for the description of the heinous crime of Israel that provoked such severe visitation of wrath." Apostrophe (e.g., "open," v.1) and personification (e.g., "Wail," v.2) are among the figures of speech used.

Lebanon (cf. 10:10) was famous for its cedars (v.1), but they will be consumed. In the Talmud the Jewish rabbis identified Lebanon here with the second temple, "which was built with cedars from Lebanon, towering aloft upon a strong summit—the spiritual glory and eminence of Jerusalem, as the Lebanon was of the whole country" (Baron, pp. 378–79, esp. n. 2, where the reference in the Talmud is given). First Kings 6:15–18 and 2 Chronicles 2:8–9 may support such an interpretation of "Lebanon." The royal palace in Jerusalem was definitely referred to as "Lebanon" in Jeremiah 22:23 (see 1 Kings 7:2). But whether literal or figurative, the passage announces a judgment that would embrace both people and land, including Jerusalem and the temple. The pines and the oaks are to wail (v.2); for if the cedars do not survive the coming destruction, neither will they.

Bashan lay east of the Jordan and north of Mount Gilead. The Israelites took it from the Amorite king, Og, at the time of the conquest of Canaan (Num 21:32–35). It was allotted to the half-tribe of Manasseh (Num 32:33; Josh 13:30; 17:5). Bashan was renowned for its rich pastures and abundance of choice cattle (Deut 32:14; Ezek 39:18). The oaks of Bashan are to wail because the dense (or, perhaps better, "inaccessible") forest of Lebanon (vv.1–2a) has been felled. How, then, can the lesser and more accessible trees escape?

If v.3 is figurative, the shepherds and the lions would represent the rulers or leaders of the Jews (cf. v.5 and 10:3). The language is strikingly similar to Jeremiah 25:34–38. The Hebrew text is marked by an abbreviated literary style and elliptical construction (e.g., "Listen—the wail of the shepherds!"), as well as by the emphatic repetition of "Listen" and "destroyed" (though NIV has "ruined" for the second occurrence of the same Hebrew word); see also the repetition of "Wail" in v.2. The shepherds are wailing because the coming destruction will leave no pasture land for their flocks. Similarly, the lions are roaring because their lairs and food are gone, again because of the coming destruction.

Notes

2 הֵילִילוּ (*hêlîlû*, "Wail") is probably onomatopoeic, capturing the sound "of the wind wailing through the trees, fanning onward the fiery judgment sweeping over the land" (Unger, *Zechariah*, p. 189).

For "dense" (or "inaccessible"), the Kethiv reads הַבָּצוּר (*habbāṣûr*, Qal passive participle) while the Qere reads הַבָּצִיר (*habbāṣîr*, verbal adjective or alternate form of the Qal passive participle). Actually, either is possible—without altering the meaning. On its lack of agreement in definiteness with "forest," see GKC, par. 126w; Davidson, par. 32, rem. 2.

3 קוֹל (*qôl*, "Listen"), which usually means "voice," "sound," is here used as an interjection (BDB, p. 877, 1.f; GKC, par. 146b).

גְּאוֹן (*ge'ôn*, "the lush thicket of") is literally "the pride [or 'majesty'] of"; but, as BDB notes (p. 145, 1.c.), it here refers "to the green and shady banks, clothed with willows, tamarisks, and cane, in which the lions made their covert," hence NIV. For a thorough study of the Jordan River and the Jordan Valley, see Elmer B. Smick, *Archaeology of the Jordan Valley* (Grand Rapids: Baker, 1973).

b. *The prophecy of the rejection of the Good Shepherd*

11:4–14

4This is what the LORD my God says: "Pasture the flock marked for slaughter. 5Their buyers slaughter them and go unpunished. Those who sell them say, 'Praise the LORD, I am rich!' Their own shepherds do not spare them. 6For I will no longer have pity on the people of the land," declares the LORD. "I will hand everyone over to his neighbor and his king. They will oppress the land, and I will not rescue them from their hands."

7So I pastured the flock marked for slaughter, particularly the oppressed of the flock. Then I took two staffs and called one Favor and the other Union, and I pastured the flock. 8In one month I got rid of the three shepherds.

The flock detested me, and I grew weary of them 9and said, "I will not be your shepherd. Let the dying die, and the perishing perish. Let those who are left eat one another's flesh."

10Then I took my staff called Favor and broke it, revoking the covenant I had made with all the nations. 11It was revoked on that day, and so the afflicted of the flock who were watching me knew it was the word of the LORD.

12I told them, "If you think it best, give me my pay; but if not, keep it." So they paid me thirty pieces of silver.

13And the LORD said to me, "Throw it to the potter"—the handsome price at which they priced me! So I took the thirty pieces of silver and threw them into the house of the LORD to the potter.

14Then I broke my second staff called Union, breaking the brotherhood between Judah and Israel.

4–5 The reason for the calamity in vv.1–3 is now given, namely, the people's rejection of the messianic Shepherd-King (vv.4–14). Just as the Servant in the Servant Songs (found basically in Isa 42; 49; 50; 53) is rejected, so here the Good Shepherd (a royal figure) is rejected. The same messianic King is in view in both instances. The purpose of this section, then, is to dramatize the rejection of the coming messianic Shepherd-King and the resulting rejection of Israel, ending in their judgment.

"My God" (v.4) indicates Zechariah's personal, intimate relationship with the Lord. What follows is addressed to him. Evidently he is instructed to act out the role of a good shepherd for the flock, i.e., Israel. With this Cashdan (p. 314) agrees: "The prophet is directed by God to act the role of a shepherd (ruler) to the flock (Israel), since the earlier shepherds neglected the flock and led them to the brink of disaster. He thereupon enacts the part of a good shepherd, tending his flock with gentleness and loving care, but his efforts are spurned and in despair he leaves them to their fate. . . . Kimchi regards the prophecy as Messianic." The "slaughter" spoken of is explained in v.5, where the sheep (the Jews) are bought as slaves by outsiders. At least part of the fulfillment came in A.D. 70 and after. The sellers are their own shepherds—bad rulers or leaders.

6 "For" introduces the reason for the misery described in v.5, namely, the Lord's displeasure. The verse also interprets the parable of the flock. The "land" (not "earth") is Palestine. While the fulfillment may have been partially realized during the intertestamental period, it also seems to reach to Roman times; so one example of "king" would perhaps be the Roman emperor (cf. John 19:15), and those who "oppress the land" would include the Romans.

7–8 Zechariah carried out his divine instructions (v.4). The fact that he said he actually did this supports the notion that it was acted out. In doing so, he became a type of the messianic Shepherd-King. He gave special attention and care to the oppressed (or "afflicted," v.11) of the flock. He also took two staves to ensure divine "favor" on the flock and to ensure its "unity." Such unity (cf. Ezek 37:15–28) would be the result of the gracious leadership of the Good Shepherd. (For the significance of the breaking of the two staves, see vv.10, 14.)

Since so many interpretations have been given to the first part of v.8 (forty by one count), obviously no certainty is possible. "In one month" has been taken to refer to (1) a literal month, (2) a short period of time, and (3) a longer period of indefinite duration. One's conclusion on this matter will depend on his identification of "the three shepherds." Four of the more popular interpretations are (1) Eleazar, John, and Simon (the leaders of the three Jewish factions during the siege of Jerusalem by Titus in A.D. 70; see Baron, p. 396, n. 1); (2) Seleucus IV, Heliodorus, and Demetrius Soter (three Seleucid kings; see Mitchell, p. 307); (3) Jason, Menelaus, and Alcimus (high priests; see Ellis, p. 1045); and (4) three classes of leaders, such as prophet, priest, and king (or a lesser civil authority). This much is certain: The Good Shepherd will dispose of unfit leaders. Baldwin (*Zechariah*, p. 183) raises an interesting question: "Is the number three used in that way [symbolically] here . . . to signify completion? If so, the good shepherd would be removing from power all the unworthy leaders who frustrated his work."

8b–9 In spite of the ideal ministry of the Good Shepherd, the flock as a whole detested him. Similarly, he grew weary of them. (See the analogous reaction of God in Isa 1:13–14: "I cannot bear your evil assemblies. . . . your appointed feasts my soul hates. They have become a burden to me; I am weary of bearing them." Here Zechariah continues to be a type of the messianic Good Shepherd-King). In v.9 the Good Shepherd terminates his providential care of the sheep, so that they even "eat one another's flesh." According to Josephus, this actually happened during the siege of Jerusalem in A.D. 70 by the Romans (Jos. War VI, 193–213 [iii.3–4]). Baldwin

(*Zechariah*, p. 184) remarks: "By withholding his leadership the shepherd abandoned the people to the consequences of their rejection of him: death, and mutual destruction. He simply let things take their course."

10–11 A further consequence of the Shepherd's rejection is the cessation of his gracious favor. One indication of this is the revocation of his covenant of security and restraint, by which he had been apparently holding back the nations from his people (cf. Ezek 34:25; Hos 2:18). Now, however, the nations (e.g., the Romans) will be permitted to overrun them. Ellis (p. 1045) is probably correct in identifying "the afflicted of the flock" (v.11) with "the faithful few who recognize the word of the Lord, who know true authority when they see it in action." See also v.7, where the same Hebrew phrase is rendered "the oppressed of the flock." The last "it" in v.11 evidently refers to Israel's affliction by the nations. At least part of the fulfillment of these verses is to be found in Matthew 23 (note particularly vv.13, 23–24, 33–39). Faithful believers discern that what happens (e.g., the judgment on Jerusalem and the temple in A.D. 70) is a fulfillment of God's prophetic word—a result of such actions as those denounced in Matthew 23, which led to the rejection of the Good Shepherd.

12–13 Now comes the final, outright rejection of the Good Shepherd, including even "severance" pay (his death is predicted in 13:7). "Give me my pay" (v.12) speaks to the termination of the relationship; "keep it" is a more emphatic way of terminating the relationship. The "flock" (v.11) responds with thirty pieces of silver as the remuneration for the Shepherd's services. This sum was not only the price of a slave among the Israelites in ancient times (Exod 21:32) but also apparently a way of indicating "a trifling amount" (see Reiner, pp. 186–90, for this idea).

Next (v.13) the Lord instructed Zechariah: "Throw it to the potter"—possibly a proverb. NIV captures the irony and sarcasm in Zechariah's description of the thirty pieces as "the handsome price at which they priced me!" "So I took" indicates not only the prophet's obedience but also the fact that he was still "impersonating" the Good Shepherd by acting out this "parable." On the silver being thrown in the temple to the potter, Unger (*Zechariah*, p. 200) says: "The fulfillment of this prophecy in Matthew 27:3–10 is proof enough that the money was flung down in the temple and immediately taken up by the priests to purchase a field *of a potter* for a burying ground for the poor" (emphasis his).

For the NT use of vv.12–13, see Matthew 26:14–15; 27:3–10. For a list of the textual differences, see Gundry, *Old Testament in Matthew's Gospel*, pp. 126–27. The obvious textual differences are best accounted for by the fact that Matthew is apparently quoting Zechariah 11:12–13 and alluding to Jeremiah 19:1–13. William Hendriksen (*Exposition of the Gospel According to Matthew*, NTC [Grand Rapids: Baker, 1973], pp. 946–48), who basically follows Gundry, has a helpful treatment of the whole complex of problems involved (see also Gleason L. Archer, *Encyclopedia of Bible Difficulties* [Grand Rapids: Zondervan, 1982], p. 345, and Donald A. Carson, "Matthew," EBC, 8:528, 560–66).

Perowne (p. 127) has this summary: "Like the earlier prophecy of the King (ix. 9), the prophecy of the Shepherd is remarkable for its literal fulfillment. The 'thirty pieces of silver' were literally the 'goodly price' paid for Him, 'whom they of the children of Israel did value.' 'The potter' was literally the recipient of it, as the purchase money of his exhausted field for an unclean purpose (Matt. xxvii. 5–10)."

14 The first staff, called "Favor," was broken (v.10). Now the second one, called "Union," is broken. This signifies the destruction or dissolution of the covenant nation, particularly of the unity between the south and the north. Chambers (p. 86) rightly says: "The breaking up of the nation into parties bitterly hostile to each other, was one of the most marked peculiarities of the later Jewish history, and greatly accelerated the ruin of the popular cause in the Roman war." Feinberg (p. 211) has this observation:

> With real insight Dods notes the chronological sequence of the events: "It will be observed that the breaking of the first staff preceded, while the breaking of the second staff succeeded, the final and contemptuous rejection of the Shepherd by the people. This, too, is the historical order. The Jews had long been under foreign rule, Idumaean and Roman, before they were scattered and lost coherence as a nation." Now that we have concluded this section it will be all the more readily seen that the passage unquestionably speaks of the spiritual condition of Israel during the time of the Second Temple, and especially in the period of Christ's ministry, which eventuated in the catastrophic rejection by Israel of their Messiah and the subsequent breakup of the Jewish commonwealth. The Romans did come and take away both their place and nation. See John 11:48.

Yet even this new destruction and dispersion are not permanent; otherwise there would be no point in the promises of Israel's future deliverance, regathering, and restoration in the succeeding chapters.

Notes

---

4 הַהֲרֵגָה (*hah^a^regāh*, "slaughter") is a genitive of purpose or intention (cf. GKC, par. 128q), hence "marked for" (NIV).

5 The singular יֹאמַר (*yō'mar*, "say"), instead of the plural is explained in Davidson, par. 116, rem. 1: "General plurals are sometimes construed with sing. pred. from a tendency to individualize and distribute over every individual, or apply it to any individual supposed." Many examples are given in Davidson (q.v.). The same applies to יַחְמוֹל (*yaḥmôl*, "spare").

The Qere וָאעְשִׁר (*wa"šir*, "I am rich") is simply a reading of the Kethiv (*wā'a'šir* with syncope of the aleph (GKC, par. 19k). In such cases the aleph, though quiescent, is still usually retained as a historical spelling (as here).

Apparently the reason for the change from the feminine pronominal suffix in קֹנֵיהֶן (*qōnêhen*, "their buyers"), agreeing with צֹאן (*ṣō'n*, "flock"), to the masculine one in וְרֹעֵיהֶם (*w^e^rō'êhem*, "their own shepherds") is that the focus is now on the עַם (*'am*, "people"), represented by the "flock."

6 The pronominal suffix "them" must be supplied in thought after אַצִּיל (*'aṣṣîl*, "I will . . . rescue"). When the suffix to be supplied is obvious from the context, it is quite frequently omitted from the verbs in Hebrew.

7 Probably most modern interpreters follow the LXX and emend לָכֵן עֲנִיֵּי (*lāḵēn '^a^niyyê*, "particularly the oppressed of") to לִכְנַעֲנִיֵּי (*liḵna'^a^niyyê*, "for the traffickers of"), but the MT makes good sense (see also v.11).

10 For a reasonably reliable current study of בְּרִית (*b^e^rîṯ*, "covenant"), see Weinfeld, TDOT, 2:253–79, and the bibliography there; see also D.J. McCarthy, *Old Testament Covenant: A Survey of Current Opinions* (Richmond: John Knox, 1972); Moshe Weinfeld, *Deuteronomy and the Deuteronomic School* (London: Oxford University Press, 1972), pp.

75–81; id., "The Covenant Grant in the Old Testament and in the Ancient Near East," JAOS 90 (1970): 184–203.

11 On the text-critical problem in the Hebrew for "and so the afflicted of," see the note at v.7.

13 As it stands, "into the house" is an adverbial accusative of place (locative accusative); but it should not be overlooked that the preposition בְּ (*b*^{e}, "in," "into") is quite frequently omitted before a word beginning with *b*, as here.

---

c. *The worthless shepherd*

11:15–17

[15]Then the LORD said to me, "Take again the equipment of a foolish shepherd. [16]For I am going to raise up a shepherd over the land who will not care for the lost, or seek the young, or heal the injured, or feed the healthy, but will eat the meat of the choice sheep, tearing off their hoofs.

[17]"Woe to the worthless shepherd,
who deserts the flock!
May the sword strike his arm and his right eye!
May his arm be completely withered,
his right eye totally blinded!"

15–16 With the Shepherd of the Lord's choice removed from the scene, a foolish and worthless shepherd replaces him. Zechariah acted out the role of such a bad shepherd, thus signifying that a selfish, corrupt, and greedy leader would arise and afflict the flock—the people of Israel. So the first oracle of Part II ends on a note of sorrow. "Again" (v.15) doubtless refers to v.7, where Zechariah took two shepherd's staves as the equipment of the Good Shepherd. The "equipment" would also include a bag for food, a pipe or reed for calling the sheep, a knife, and a case for setting and binding up broken bones. The bad shepherd is here characterized as "foolish," a word denoting "one who is morally deficient" (NIV mg. to Prov 1:7).

The reason for Zechariah's impersonation of a foolish (and "worthless," v.17) shepherd is explained in v.16 ("For"): God is going to raise up a shepherd who will not do what a good shepherd should; instead he will destroy the sheep. When one removes "not" from the sentence, he has an enlightening description of a truly effective pastoral ministry in the church today. (1) "care for the lost [*hannikḥaḏôṯ*]," or, with BDB (p. 470, 2), "care for those in the process of being ruined or destroyed"; (2) "seek the young [*na'ar*]" (cf. Isa 40:11; on the other hand, if BDB [p. 654] is correct, the reference here is to "the scattered"); (3) "heal the injured," and (4) "feed the healthy." The bad shepherd will do none of these things. Instead of feeding the sheep, he will feed on them—preying on the unwary. He will even tear off their hoofs, apparently, as Unger suggests (*Zechariah*, p. 204), "in avaricious search for the last edible morsel."

17 This same sinister figure is now called "the worthless shepherd" because of his diabolical deeds, such as deserting the flock, in contrast to the Good Shepherd (John 10:11–13). For this reason judgment is pronounced against him. While this counterfeit shepherd may have found a partial, historical fulfillment in such leaders as Bar Kokhba, who led the Jewish revolt against the Romans in A.D. 132–35 and was hailed as the Messiah by Rabbi Akiba, it seems that the final stage of the progressive fulfillment of the complete prophecy awaits the rise of the final Antichrist (cf. Ezek 34:2–4; Dan 11:36–39; John 5:43; 2 Thess 2:3–10; Rev 13:1–8). The imprecation calls for his power ("arm") to be paralyzed ("completely withered") and his intelligence ("right eye") to be frustrated or nullified ("totally blinded"). For the fulfillment with respect to the Antichrist or "beast," see Revelation 19:19–21; 20:10. "With arm and right eye out of action the leader will be powerless to fight, or even to take aim, against his enemies" (Baldwin, *Zechariah*, p. 187). Feinberg (pp. 213–14) concludes the first oracle and introduces the second: "The judgment here (vs.17) brings to a close the cycle of prophecy which began with judgment (9:1). Judgment has gone from the circumference (the nations) to the center (Israel); Zechariah will yet reveal that in blessing the direction will be from the center (Israel) to the circumference (the nations) as in chapter 14."

Notes

---

16 יְכַלְכֵּל (*yᵉkalkēl*, "feed," "sustain," "support," "nourish") is a Pilpel imperfect from כּוּל (*kûl*, "to hold," "to measure").

17 רֹעִי (*rōʿî*, "shepherd") and עֹזְבִי (*ʿōzᵉbî*, "who deserts") feature the "*Ḥireq compaginis*" (GKC, par. 90 l–m), evidently owing its origin to an archaic ending of the construct state. This consruct ending is found also in certain words in Akkadian.

יָבוֹשׁ (*yābôš*, "completely") and כָּהֹה (*kāhōh*, "totally") are infinitives absolute, accentuating their respective verbal ideas. The accompanying finite verbs, in turn, are probably best construed as jussives (NIV).

B. *The Second Oracle: The Advent and Reception of the Messiah* (12:1–14:21)

1. *The deliverance and conversion of Israel (12:1–13:9)*

a. *The siege of Jerusalem*

12:1–3

An Oracle

1 This is the word of the LORD concerning Israel. The LORD, who stretches out the heavens, who lays the foundation of the earth, and who forms the spirit of man within him, declares: 2 "I am going to make Jerusalem a cup that sends all the surrounding peoples reeling. Judah will be besieged as well as Jerusalem. 3 On that day, when all the nations of the earth are gathered against her, I will make Jerusalem an immovable rock for all the nations. All who try to move it will injure themselves.

1 Zechariah next encouraged God's covenant people by contrasting initial judgment on them with their ultimate deliverance, restoration, and blessing. "In [or 'on'] that day" appears sixteen times in the second oracle, placing it, for the most part, in the eschaton. The oracle basically revolves around two scenes: the final siege of Jerusalem and the Messiah's return to defeat Israel's enemies and to establish his kingdom fully. Feinberg (p. 218) sets the stage for this last section of the book: "Says Dods, 'It is obvious that from the beginning of the twelfth chapter to the end of the book it is one period that is described.' In these chapters the city of Jerusalem holds a prominent place. . . . The Tetragrammaton is found with marked frequency. . . . The nations of the earth . . . play a major role in the events set forth."

For "An Oracle" (v.1), see comment at 9:1. It is surprising to be informed that the oracle concerns "Israel" instead of "Judah and Jerusalem," but it is clear that in chapters 12–14 "Israel" means the whole nation, not just the northern kingdom. The oracle begins by describing the Lord's creative power in the heavens, on the earth, and in man (Gen 2:7). He is "able therefore to accomplish what He predicts" (Perowne, p. 128). Perhaps this description is also a means of strengthening the royal and sovereign authority of the message (see comment on "the word of the LORD came" at 1:1).

2–3 Jerusalem is pictured as a cup "round which all nations gather, eager to swallow down its inviting contents" (Perowne, p. 129). But as they drink from her, they become intoxicated and reel. The end of v.2 indicates that the siege of Jerusalem will obviously affect Judah as well. In v.3 Jerusalem is compared to a heavy, "immovable rock" that the nations attempt to move but only hurt themselves in the process. This, of course, will be due to special divine intervention and protection (vv.4–5). On the invasion of Jerusalem (v.3), "when all the nations of the earth are gathered against her," see also 14:2; Joel 3:9–16; Revelation 16:16–21.

b. *The divine deliverance*

12:4–9

4On that day I will strike every horse with panic and its rider with madness," declares the LORD. "I will keep a watchful eye over the house of Judah, but I will blind all the horses of the nations. 5Then the leaders of Judah will say in their hearts, 'The people of Jerusalem are strong, because the LORD Almighty is their God.'

6"On that day I will make the leaders of Judah like a firepot in a woodpile, like a flaming torch among sheaves. They will consume right and left all the surrounding peoples, but Jerusalem will remain intact in her place.

7"The LORD will save the dwellings of Judah first, so that the honor of the house of David and of Jerusalem's inhabitants may not be greater than that of Judah. 8On that day the LORD will shield those who live in Jerusalem, so that the feeblest among them will be like David, and the house of David will be like God, like the Angel of the LORD going before them. 9On that day I will set out to destroy all the nations that attack Jerusalem.

4–6 In Deuteronomy 28:28, "panic [or 'confusion of mind']," "madness," and "blindness" (v.4) are listed among Israel's curses for disobeying the stipulations of the covenant. Now these curses are turned against Israel's enemies. Special emphasis is laid on the horses to exalt God's power. On God's "watchful eye" over his people, see Psalms 32:8 and 33:18. Feinberg (p. 223) observes: "In the same hour that God blinds the eyes of Israel's enemies [actually their horses], He will open His own upon the house of Judah in love and compassion to protect them." For the literal meaning of the Hebrew for "leaders" (v.5), see comment at 9:7. These wise leaders discern that the source of the people's strength is their God, the Lord Almighty. In v.6 these faithful leaders are compared to a fire destroying wood and sheaves of grain; thus will they consume their enemies (cf. Judg 15:3–5). By contrast Jerusalem and her people "will remain intact in her place."

7–9 In the coming deliverance there will be no superiority or inferiority complexes or ranking of some above others in honor. "The Lord will deliver the defenseless country before the fortified and well-defended capital, so that both may realize that the victory is of the Lord" (Feinberg, p. 225). For the principle of v.7, see Jeremiah 9:23–24; 1 Corinthians 1:29, 31; 12:22–26; 2 Corinthians 10:17. Ultimately the Lord is the one who does the saving (v.7), the shielding or protecting (v.8), and the destroying of enemies (v.9). He will make the "feeblest" (lit., "the one who stumbles") among them like David (v.8), who was celebrated as a great warrior. And the members of the Davidic dynasty will be "like God," which, in turn, is explained as being "like the Angel of the LORD going before them." God will be with them, will go before them, and will give them supernatural strength (cf. 4:6; and for the "Angel" motif referred to here, see Exod 14:19; 23:20; 32:34; 33:2, 14–15, 22).

Verse 9 is a summary of the previous verses. Perowne (p. 132) interacts with Wright's interpretation of the verse:

> It is true, as Mr. Wright points out, that in the only other passage in which this phrase ["I will set out," lit., "I will seek"] is used of Almighty God, the intention, though "manifested clearly and distinctly," was abandoned (Exod. iv. 24). But it does not follow that "this passage is not an absolute promise of the utter destruction of the nations," but only a promise conditional upon the future conduct of the Jews. The passage as a whole is quite against such a supposition. The verse would be a strange anti-climax, if after such promises as are contained in ver. 2–8 it only asserted, "My aim shall be to do all this that I have promised in glowing terms; but all may be frustrated and come to nought through the unfaithfulness of man."

Notes

---

5 According to Unger (*Zechariah*, p. 211), a "plausible and meritorious reading is *'emtsah leyoshebhey*. . . . This assumes a slight dittography." The resultant translation would be thus: "The strength of the people of Jerusalem is in the LORD Almighty, their God."

7 Conversely, יֹשֵׁב יְרוּשָׁלִַם (*yōšēḇ yerûšālaim*, "Jerusalem's inhabitants"), both here and in vv.8, 10, may be a case of haplography, so that the reading should be יֹשְׁבֵי (*yōšeḇê* . . .); this is supported by some Hebrew MSS and the ancient versions.

8 The use of אֱלֹהִים (*'elōhîm*, "God") here is similar to that in Exod 4:16; 7:1.

---

c. *Israel's complete deliverance from sin*

12:10–13:9

10"And I will pour out on the house of David and the inhabitants of Jerusalem a spirit of grace and supplication. They will look on me, the one they have pierced, and they will mourn for him as one mourns for an only child and grieve bitterly for him as one grieves for a firstborn son. 11On that day the weeping in Jerusalem will be great, like the weeping of Hadad Rimmon in the plain of Megiddo. 12The land will mourn, each clan by itself, with their wives by themselves: the clan of the

house of David and their wives, the clan of the house of Nathan and their wives,
13the clan of the house of Levi and their wives, the clan of Shimei and their wives,
14and all the rest of the clans and their wives.

1"On that day a fountain will be opened to the house of David and the inhabitants of Jerusalem, to cleanse them from sin and impurity.
2"On that day, I will banish the names of the idols from the land, and they will be remembered no more," declares the LORD Almighty. "I will remove both the prophets and the spirit of impurity from the land.
3And if anyone still prophesies, his father and mother, to whom he was born, will say to him, 'You must die, because you have told lies in the LORD's name.' When he prophesies, his own parents will stab him.
4"On that day every prophet will be ashamed of his prophetic vision. He will not put on a prophet's garment of hair in order to deceive.
5He will say, 'I am not a prophet. I am a farmer; the land has been my livelihood since my youth.
6If someone asks him, 'What are these wounds on your body?' he will answer, 'The wounds I was given at the house of my friends.'

7"Awake, O sword, against my shepherd,
against the man who is close to me!"
declares the LORD Almighty.
"Strike the shepherd,
and the sheep will be scattered,
and I will turn my hand against the little ones.
8In the whole land," declares the LORD,
"two-thirds will be struck down and perish;
yet one-third will be left in it.
9This third I will bring into the fire;
I will refine them like silver
and test them like gold.
They will call on my name
and I will answer them;
I will say, 'They are my people,'
and they will say, 'The LORD is our God.' "

10 Now there is movement from physical deliverance, just described, to spiritual deliverance (cf. the pattern of Deut 30:1–10). In anthropomorphic language the Lord promises an effusion of his Spirit on his covenant people. The imagery is doubtless that of water as an emblem of the Holy Spirit. The recipients are the royal leaders and people of Jerusalem, representative of the inhabitants of the whole land. The content of the effusion is "a spirit of grace and supplication," i.e., "the Spirit which conveys grace and calls forth supplications" (Perowne, pp. 132–33). While it is possible to construe "spirit" in the sense of "disposition," it seems preferable to follow the NIV margin (and Perowne above) and see here a reference to the Spirit of God. This would be more in keeping with what appear to be parallel passages (Isa 32:15; 44:3; 59:20–21; Jer 31:31, 33; Ezek 36:26–27; 39:29; Joel 2:28–29). Because of the convicting work of God's Spirit, Israel will turn to the Messiah with mourning.

The most common meaning of the Hebrew preposition translated "on" is "to" (NIV mg.), and there is no good contextual reason to depart from it here. The emphasis, then, is not on looking "on" (or "at") the Messiah literally but on looking "to" the Messiah in faith (cf. Num 21:9; Isa 45:22; John 3:14–15). According to some premillennialists, this will take place at the second coming of the Messiah (Christ) to the earth. According to others, it will happen just prior to his second advent. The object of the people's look of faith is identified as "the one they have pierced" (cf. Isa 53:5; John 19:34). John 19:37, which quotes this part of the verse, is but a stage in the progressive fulfillment of the whole. The final, complete fulfillment is yet future for Israel (Rom 11:25–27). Evidently the prospect of a "pierced" Messiah was such a stumbling block to the Jews that, according to C.C. Torrey ("The Messiah Son of Ephraim," JBL 66 [1947]: 273), the Babylonian Talmud (*Sukkah* 52a) presents two Messiahs; the one here in v.10 is identified as the Messiah son of Joseph. The similes at the end of the verse accentuate the people's mourning (see Jer 6:26 on mourning "for an only child" and Exod 11:5–6 on mourning "for a firstborn son"). (For the Jewish interpretations of the verse, see Baron, pp. 438–44, and Cashdan, pp. 321–22.)

11 The convicting work of the Spirit of God will produce national contrition or repentance, led by the civil (royal) and religious leaders. The future weeping ("on that day") in Jerusalem will be so great that it is compared with "the weeping of Hadad Rimmon in the plain of Megiddo." *The Illustrated Family Encyclopedia* (7:96) summarizes the major interpretations of this simile:

> The sound of weeping and wailing that fills the streets of the city will rise to the intensity of the cries of grief uttered for Hadad-Rimmon in the plain of Megiddo. This comparison is sometimes explained as a reference to a public mourning for some notable dignitary. Such, for example, is the rendering of the Targum Jonathan in 2 Chron. 35:25. Hieronymus [Jerome] (5th cent. A.D.), on the other hand, interpreted Hadad-Rimmon as the name of "a city close to Jezreel which is to-day called Maximianupolis," and which modern scholars locate at el-Lajjun near Megiddo. The modern Arabic name is derived from the Latin noun "legio", since it was here that the Sixth Legion (*Legio Ferrata*, the "Iron" Legion) had its camp from the revolt of Bar-Kokhba onwards. . . . Situated on the "Sea Road", the place had great strategic importance as guarding the passage from the valley of Jezreel to the coastal plain. Still a third interpretation would refer the words of our verse to Hadad-Rimmon the god of rain and fertility (perhaps to be identified with Baal, the Canaanite-Ugaritic god of fertility), whose death was annually bewailed at the end of the spring, with the coming of the summer's shrivelling heat. A similar ritualistic lament was also uttered for Tammuz (Ezek. 8:14). The fertile plain of Megiddo would indeed have made an appropriate setting for the mourning over Hadad-Rimmon, since in Palestine the success of the crops depends on an adequate seasonal rainfall.

Keith N. Schoville (*Biblical Archaeology in Focus* [Grand Rapids: Baker, 1978], p. 444) apparently agrees with the third view above, for he writes: "It is worth noting that a phenomenon common to all Israelite levels at Megiddo is an abundance of cult objects, especially ceramic figurines, along with objects for normal use bearing foreign cultic designs. The last reference in the Bible to Megiddo alludes to such religious syncretism (Zech. 12:11)." The present writer, however, prefers to take Hadad-Rimmon as a place name (containing the names of ancient Semitic fertility gods) near Megiddo. So understood, the simile in v.11 refers to the people of this town mourning the death of King Josiah (2 Chron 35:20–27; see v.22 there for the plain of Megiddo and vv.24–25 for the mourning).

12–14 The expressions "each clan by itself" and "their wives by themselves" (v.12) are doubtless intended to emphasize the sincerity of the mourning as true repentance. This is no purely emotional public spectacle. Nor are professional mourners involved. Individually and corporately, this is the experience of Leviticus 16 (the Day of Atonement) and Psalm 51 (a penitential psalm) on a national scale. As the colon in NIV indicates, this general statement of the mourning (v.12a) is followed by particulars (vv.12b–14). The mourning includes the royal house of David and the family of his son Nathan (2 Sam 5:14), also the house of Levi and the family of Shimei son of Gershon, the son of Levi (Num 3:17–18, 21), as well as "all the rest" (v.14). While the repentance is led by the civil (royal) and religious leaders, it extends to every clan in the nation. Isaiah 53:1–9 could well be their confession on the great occasion. Such true repentance, of course, "remains a gift of God's Spirit (verse 10)" (Baldwin, *Zechariah*, p. 194); and, in keeping with his covenantal promise, he will bestow that gift.

1 The repentance at the end of the previous chapter leads to what Perowne (p. 134) calls "worthy fruits of repentance" in vv.1–6. But v.1 also contains new-covenant terminology. In Jeremiah 31:33–34 God promised Israel these provisions: (1) enablement through his Spirit to obey his law (v.33a; Ezek 36:26–27); (2) an intimate personal relationship and fellowship (v.33b); (3) a saving knowledge of himself (v.34a); Rom 11:26a); and (4) the forgiveness of sins (v.34b; Ezek 36:25; Zech 3:4, 9). It is clear from the NT (e.g., Luke 22:20; 1 Cor 11:25; 8–10) that the church—Gentiles and the spiritual remnant of Israel (Rom 11:1–16)—is today the recipient of the benefits promised to Israel in the new covenant. This is made possible only by God's sovereign, gracious grafting of Gentiles into that place of blessing (Rom 11:17–24). These blessings will yet be experienced by ethnic Israel at the second advent of their Messiah (Rom 11:25–29), thus preparing the priestly nation for the Lord's service (ch. 3). The cleansing referred to in v.1 is related particularly to the fourth provision of the new covenant (see above) and is ultimately made possible through the atoning death of the pierced one (12:10).

2–3 Not only will there be personal internal cleansing—morally and spiritually—but also external cleansing, as the country is purged of idols and false prophets, both of which were such a constant snare and source of deception to Israel (10:2–3; Jer 23:30–32; 27:9–10; Ezek 13:1–14:11). God himself ("I") declares that he will rid the land of the names (i.e., the influence, fame, and even the very existence) of the idols. That false prophecy was still a problem in the postexilic period is clear from Nehemiah 6:12–14. That both idolatry and false prophecy would once again be a problem in the future is evident not only here but also in Matthew 24:4–5, 11, 15, 23–24; 2 Thessalonians 2:2–4; Revelation 9:20; 13:4–15. The "spirit of impurity" that inspired the false prophets to lie will also be removed. In that future day, if anyone dares to utter false prophecies ("lies," v.3), his own parents—in obedience to Deuteronomy 13:6–9—will take the lead in executing him. The Hebrew for "stab" is the same verb as "pierced" in 12:10, thus indicating that the feelings and actions shown in piercing the Messiah will be directed toward the false prophets.

4–6 Because of these stern measures, a false prophet will be reticent in identifying himself as such and will be evasive in responding to questioning. To help conceal his true identity, he will not wear "a prophet's garment of hair" (v.4), such as Elijah wore (2 Kings 1:8). Instead, to avoid the death penalty (v.3), he will deny being a prophet and will claim to have been a farmer from his youth (v.5). And if some suspicious person notices marks on his body and inquires about them (v.6), he will claim he received them in a scuffle with friends as discipline from his parents during childhood. Apparently the accuser suspects that the false prophet's wounds were self-inflicted to arouse his prophetic ecstasy in idolatrous rites (as in 1 Kings 18:28; cf. also Lev 19:28; 21:5; Deut 14:1; Jer 16:6; 41:5; 48:37).

A few expositors assign a messianic sense to v.6 (cf. Unger, *Zechariah*, pp. 228–30, for the best defense of such a position, though most of his arguments here are weak, forced, irrelevant, or debatable). The following observations, however, militate against any messianic import for the verse: (1) it presupposes an unnatural break between v.5 and v.6, with a complete change in subject matter; (2) in order to find a proper antecedent for "him," it reverts all the way back to 12:10, thus regarding 12:11–13:5 as parenthetical, which is neither obvious nor necessary; (3) the most natural antecedent for "him" (v.6) is "he" (v.5), since *wᵉ'āmar* ("if someone asks") at the beginning of v.6 certainly seems to be a response to *wᵉ'āmar* ("he will say") at the beginning of v.5; (4) there is a rather clear change in subject matter in v.7, indicating that the break is between v.6 and v.7, not between v.5 and v.6; (5) there is a change of person in v.7, indicating the same; (6) the verb changes to imperative in v.7, indicating the same; and (7) the literary form changes to poetry in v.7, indicating the same.

7 "This startling poem resumes the shepherd motif from chapter 11, though in chapters 12 and 13 the subject of leadership has never been far from the prophet's thoughts" (Baldwin, *Zechariah*, p. 197). Compared to the immediately preceding verses, the oracle now moves back to the time when Israel would be scattered because of her rejection of the true messianic Shepherd. Then, after the announcement of the dispersion, the oracle seems to advance to a future period when Israel will undergo a special, purifying discipline, as silver and gold are refined (vv.8–9). The surviving remnant will be the Lord's people (v.9).

Verse 7 begins with an apostrophe to a personified instrument of violent death. According to Bullinger (p. 548), "sword" (*ḥereḇ*) is sometimes a metonymy of cause for effect—sword is put for slaughter. Similarly, Edwin Yamauchi (TWOT, 1:320) notes: "In Ps 22:20 [H 21] *ḥereb* is used as a metaphor for a violent end." Death is announced against one whom God calls "my shepherd," i.e., the royal Good Shepherd—the true Shepherd of 11:4–14 in contrast with the foolish and worthless shepherd (11:15–17). God also identifies him as "the man who is close to me," on which Baldwin (*Zechariah*, pp. 197–98) comments: "The expression 'who stands next to me' is used elsewhere only in Leviticus (*e.g.* 6:2; 18:20) to mean 'near neighbour'; similarly the shepherd is one who dwells side by side with the Lord, His equal." The expression eventually leads to John 10:30: "I and the Father are one," and to John 14:9: "Anyone who has seen me has seen the Father" (cf. John 1:1–2).

In 11:17 it was the worthless shepherd who was to be struck; now (v.7) it is the Good Shepherd (cf. 12:10). Apparently the one who wields the "sword" is God himself. If so, this is perhaps the best explanation for the shift from the feminine gender of "Awake" (agreeing with "sword," which is also feminine) to the masculine gender of "Strike" (agreeing with God). In 12:10–14 the Messiah's death is presented as an act of Israel, but in v.7 it is the sovereign act of God (cf. Isa 53:10; Acts 2:23).

When the Shepherd is struck, the sheep (cf. 10:3, 9) are scattered, in fulfillment of the curses for covenant disobedience (Deut 28:64; 29:24–25). Keil (KD, *Minor Prophets*, 2:397–98) rightly maintains that the thought is that the Lord "will scatter

Israel or His nation by smiting the shepherd; that is to say, He will give it up to the misery and destruction to which a flock without a shepherd is exposed. . . . The flock, which will be dispersed in consequence of the slaying of the shepherd, is the covenant nation, *i.e.* neither the human race nor the Christian church as such, but the flock which the shepherd in ch. xi 4 sqq. had to feed." This part of v.7 is quoted by Jesus not long before his arrest (Matt 26:31; Mark 14:27) and applied to the scattering of the apostles (Matt 26:56; Mark 14:50), but they are probably intended to serve as a type of the Diaspora that occurred in A.D. 70 and following. Some take "I will turn my hand against [or 'on' or 'over']" in a negative sense, others in a positive one. Perowne (p. 140) strikes a balance: "For correction, but in mercy, ver. 8, 9. Comp. Is. i 25."

"The little ones" are the remnant (vv.8–9), "the oppressed" or "afflicted of the flock" (11:7, 11). Isaiah, too, spoke much of the remnant (e.g., Isa 6:13; 66:22–24).

8–9 These verses apparently precede vv.1–6 chronologically. They depict a refining process for Israel. While what happened in A.D. 70 at the hands of the Romans may have been an initial stage in the progressive fulfillment, the final and complete stage is yet future, for Israel as a whole is not in the proper covenant relationship with God described in v.9. The fact that a remnant will survive ("one-third," v.8) reveals God's mercy in the midst of judgment. *The Illustrated Family Encyclopedia* (8:97) elucidates the refining process mentioned in the first half of v.9:

> The process of refining metals, especially precious metals such as silver and gold, serves the prophets of Israel as a metaphor of the nation's spiritual purification (cf. Isa. 1:25 . . .). Thus, in our verse here, the remnant of Israel is compared to the small quantity of pure metal which is left after the smelting and refining: two thirds of the people will be cut off and perish, while the remaining third will be further reduced by being purified in the fire (Zech. 13:8–9). The method of extracting pure gold from the silver and other metals mixed with it by constantly repeated firing was known at an early period in human history, perhaps as early as the first half of the second millennium B.C. A Greek author gives a detailed description of the way in which gold was refined in a porous clay vessel. The vessel, containing lead, salt and zinc in addition to the gold ore, was tightly sealed and then placed in a fired kiln for five days. During this time the dross stuck to the sides of the container, while the pure gold collected in its centre. From many passages in the Old Testament (e.g. Ezek. 22:21–23; Ps. 12:6) it would seem that this method, or one similar to it, was also the one used in biblical times. The processes of metal-working employed in the classical world are illustrated by a bas-relief decoration on a Greek goblet of the Hellenistic period (4th cent. B.C.) . . . . It shows the bearded smith-god, Hephaestos, seated in a smithy beside a kiln . . . and holding in his hand the tools of his craft, a pair of tongs and a hammer.

The survivors (cf. Jer 30:7) are those of 12:10–13:1; they will constitute the Jewish nucleus of the messianic kingdom and will evidently include the 144,000 of Revelation 7:1–8 and 14:1–5. "The last four lines of the verse have an appropriate chiastic structure—*they, I, I, they*—reflecting that there are two sides to any relationship, even when it is between God and man" (Baldwin, *Zechariah*, p. 198, emphasis hers). The calling on the Lord's name includes the "supplication" of 12:10. The verse closes with the covenant formula: "I will say, 'They are my people,' and they will say, 'The LORD is our God.' " Thus the new covenant will be fulfilled for Israel, and they will be restored to proper covenant relationship with the Lord (cf. also Ezek 20:30–44, esp. v.37 for their restoration to "the bond of the covenant").

Notes

---

10 וְתַחֲנוּנִים (*w*[e]*ṯaḥ*[a]*nûnîm*, "supplication") is either the plural of intensification or simply the abstract plural.

The shift from first person in אֵלַי (*'ēlay*, "on me") to third person in עָלָיו (*'ālāyw*, "for him") is explained in the notes at 7:13 and 9:10.

The infinitive absolute וְהָמֵר (*w*[e]*hāmēr*, "and grieve bitterly") is here used as a substitute for the waw consecutive perfect (Davidson, par. 88, rem. 1).

12–14 Single words are sometimes repeated in order to express a distributive sense. This is true of לְבָד (*l*[e]*ḇāḏ*, "by itself" or "by themselves") throughout these verses (GKC, par. 123d).

1 The preposition לְ (*l*[e], "to") in לְבֵית (*l*[e]*ḇêṯ*, "to the house of") could just as easily be rendered "for [the benefit of]."

5 As the MT stands, the last clause of this verse should probably be rendered "a man sold me [as a slave] in my youth" (cf. NIV mg.). On the other hand, many Hebrew specialists propose that אָדָם הִקְנַנִי (*'āḏām hiqnanî*, "a man caused another to buy me,"i.e., "sold me") be slightly altered to אֲדָמָה קִנְיָנִי (*'*[a]*ḏāmāh qinyānî*, "the land has been my possession/livelihood"), yielding the rendering in the main text of the NIV.

6 בֵּין יָדֶיךָ (*bên yāḏeykā*, lit., "between your hands"—cf. NIV mg.) is an idiom meaning "on your back/chest," i.e., "on your body." The same idiom occurs in Ugaritic Text 68:14–15: *hlm ktp zbl ym bn ydm [ṯp]ṭ nhr*, "Strike the shoulder [i.e., 'back'] of Prince Yamm, between the hands/arms [i.e., on the back] of Judge Nahar" (see UT, p. 180, for the text, and ANET, p. 131, for Ginsberg's translation). Thus Ugaritic demonstrates that "between the hands" is parallel to "shoulder" or "back." Essentially the same idiom appears in 2 Kings 9:24, where the Hebrew literally has "between his arms" (NIV, "between the shoulders"). It is basically the same because "hand" in Hebrew can also mean "arm" (1 Kings 10:19; Jer 38:12; Ezek 13:18).

On the absence of the preposition בְּ (*b*[e], "in," "at") before בֵּית (*bêṯ*, "house"), see note at 11:13.

"My friends" is literally "those who love me [objective genitive]" and so is open to either of the ideas suggested in the commentary above ("friends" or "parents").

9 On the construction of the similes, see Davidson, par. 91, rems. 1, 3.

---

2. *The Messiah's return and his kingdom* (14:1–21)

a. *The siege of Jerusalem*

14:1–2

[1]A day of the LORD is coming when your plunder will be divided among you.

[2]I will gather all the nations to Jerusalem to fight against it; the city will be captured, the houses ransacked, and the women raped. Half of the city will go into exile, but the rest of the people will not be taken from the city.

1–2 The ultimate goal of all history is the Lord's personal appearance and reign. But before the literal and full manifestation of his kingdom, the earth must experience the throes of birth pangs. There is a return to the refining process of 13:8–9 as the nations gather at Jerusalem and ravish her (14:2). Baldwin (*Zechariah,* p. 199) describes the chiastic arrangement of the chapter:

> The dramatic reversal from defeat to victory is well expressed in the chiastic structure of this section. Verses 1–6 begin with Jerusalem crushed in defeat. 'The day of the Lord . . . is darkness, and not light' (Am. 5:18), but, though awesome events continue to overtake the city, there is progression towards one particular day, known to the Lord (verse 7). This is the turning-point. From that day Jerusalem becomes the source of light and life. There the Lord sets up His world government, and whereas at the beginning Jerusalem was being despoiled, at the end all the nations are financing God's kingdom. Whereas at the beginning God's people suffer, at the end His enemies suffer and die. Unity in the Lord is the only unity that endures. His kingship is very greatly stressed, hence the fall of those who oppose Him.

Unger (*Zechariah,* pp. 239–40) stresses the importance of normal, consistent hermeneutics in interpreting chapter 14. The chapter begins with an invasion of Jerusalem similar to that in the opening part of chapter 12. Verse 1 is a general statement; v.2 provides the particulars. Although "a day of the LORD" is not the usual construction for "the day of the LORD," it doubtless means the same thing; "that day" occurs throughout the context (chs. 12–14). Perhaps this particular construction is used here to emphasize the fact that the "day" is distinctively the Lord's. Man is having his day now; the Lord's day is yet to come (see comment at 2:11). "Your" refers to Jerusalem (v.2). Both "your" and "you" are an apostrophe in which Jerusalem is directly addressed.

"I" (v.2) is a reminder that the sovereign God is in complete control. As the Lord of history and nations, he is the Prime Mover. The scene depicted here (contingents from all nations gathered to fight against Jerusalem) is probably the same as the one in Revelation 16:16–21 (Armageddon). This eschatological verse alone—with its statement that "the city will be captured"—is sufficient to refute the notion popular in certain circles that "the times of the Gentiles" (Luke 21:24) were fulfilled as of the rebirth of the modern state of Israel. According to Lucan theology, after "the times of the Gentiles are fulfilled," Jerusalem will be trampled on no more. Since Zechariah 14:2 clearly indicates that Jerusalem will be "trampled on" again in the future, the "times of the Gentiles" would seem to extend to the Messiah's second advent, when those "times" will be replaced by the final, universal, everlasting kingdom of Daniel 2:35, 44–45.

The rest of v.2 delineates some of the horrors that still await Jerusalem and its people. Chambers (p. 110) correctly observes: "Only a part of the inhabitants are to be driven into exile, the rest remain. It was different at the Chaldaean conquest of Jerusalem, for then the greater portion were carried away, and afterwards even 'the remnant that was left' (2 Kings xxv. 11). The verse cannot therefore refer to that subjugation. Nor can it be applied to the overthrow of the holy city by Titus, who neither had all nations under his banner, nor left a half of the population in possession of their homes." The fulfillment, then, must still lie in the future. At that time all this will happen to fulfill the curses pronounced against covenant disobedience (Deut 28:30).

Notes

1 The pronominal suffix in שְׁלָלֵךְ (*šelālēḵ*, "your plunder") is best taken as objective genitive.
2 תִּשָּׁגַלְנָה (*tiššāgalnāh*, "will be raped") presents a Kethiv and Qere variation. The Masoretes apparently found the meaning of the Kethiv to be very obscene and proposed, instead, the euphemistic reading (in the margin of the Hebrew Bible) תִּשָּׁכַבְנָה (*tiššākabnāh*, "will be lain with").

b. *The tokens of the Messiah's return*

14:3–8

3Then the LORD will go out and fight against those nations, as he fights in the day of battle. 4On that day his feet will stand on the Mount of Olives, east of Jerusalem, and the Mount of Olives will be split in two from east to west, forming a great valley, with half of the mountain moving north and half moving south. 5You will flee by my mountain valley, for it will extend to Azel. You will flee as you fled from the earthquake in the days of Uzziah king of Judah. Then the LORD my God will come, and all the holy ones with him.

6On that day there will be no light, no cold or frost. 7It will be a unique day, without daytime or nighttime—a day known to the LORD. When evening comes, there will be light.

8On that day living water will flow out from Jerusalem, half to the eastern sea and half to the western sea, in summer and in winter.

3–5 Just when it seems that all hope is gone, "then the LORD" himself appears as "divine warrior" and delivers his beleaguered people (on the "divine warrior" motif, see comment at 1:3). But who is this "LORD"? When one compares this scene, including v.4, with Acts 1:9–12 and Revelation 19:11–16, it would appear certain that "the LORD" here is ultimately the Messiah. The passage, then, is indirectly messianic (see comment at 2:10). "The day of battle" is any occasion when the Lord supernaturally intervenes to deliver his people, such as at the Red Sea (Exod 14:13–14). Acts 1:11–12 may well allude to the prophecy that "his feet will stand on the Mount of Olives" (v.4), which is situated "east of Jerusalem." *The Illustrated Family Encyclopedia* (8:98) describes this mountain and its significance:

> The Day of the Lord, the day when God will take vengeance on the nations that have done harm to Israel, is a conception that first occurs in the utterances of the prophets of the Assyrian and Babylonian periods (Isa. 25:6–9 . . .), and is repeated in the visions of their post-destruction counterparts (Ezek. chaps. 38–39). On this day the Lord of Hosts will appear in His glory on the Mount of Olives, the mountain that rises high above Jerusalem, to war against the nations and mete out retribution to them. At this awe-inspiring theophany, the whole mountain will shake (cf. Judg. 5:4) and be cloven asunder, as the earth was convulsed in the great earthquake that occurred in the reign of Uzziah, king of Judah.
>
> The Mount of Olives—referred to by this name only here in the Old Testament (though a similar expression, "the Ascent of Olives", occurs in 2 Sam. 15:30)—is, in Ezekiel's words, "the mountain which is on the east side of the city" (Ezek. 11:23). The aura of sanctity which had enveloped it from the early days of Israelite history was in no way diminished in later times. Thus, in the period of the Geonim (8th–11th cent. A.D.), prayers were regularly offered up

> on the Mount of Olives, which faced the Temple Mount, and the Scrolls of the Law were carried round in circuit there on the festival of Hoshana Rabba, while its slopes were dotted with the tombs of the pious. The mountain rises to a height of 2710 ft. above sea-level, thus being as much as 330 ft. higher than the Temple Mount. Its soil—grey Rendzina—is well suited to the growth of olive-trees which thrust their roots down into the brittle rock. Hence, in the Mishna and Talmud it is called the Mount of Anointing.

In the eschaton, when the Lord will stand on this mountain, it will split in two (perhaps due to an earthquake, but not necessarily so), creating a great valley running east and west. Verse 5 states the purpose of the valley—viz., to afford an easy means of rapid escape from the final anti-Semitic onslaught detailed in v.2; the Mount of Olives has always constituted a serious obstacle to such an escape to the east.

Although some scholars construe the Hebrew for Azel as a preposition ("beside") or a common noun ("side"), it seems best to understand it as the name of a place east of Jerusalem, thus marking the eastern end of the newly formed valley. Some relate it to the Wadi Yasul, a tributary of the Kidron (cf. "Azal" in ISBE, 1979 rev. ed., 1:374). The future escape of God's people is compared with the time when their ancestors "fled from the earthquake in the days of Uzziah king of Judah"—an earthquake so devastating and memorable that it is mentioned also in Amos 1:1. Yohanan Aharoni (*The Land of the Bible*, tr. A.F. Rainey [London: Burns and Oates, 1966], p. 91) even suggests that it may have destroyed level VI at Hazor around 760 B.C. In announcing the Lord's coming, Zechariah expressed his own personal faith in him and relationship to him ("my God"). "All the holy ones" will be in the Lord's retinue when he comes. These apparently include both believers and unfallen angels (see Matt 25:31; Rev 19:14).

6–8 The precise meaning of these verses in Hebrew is admittedly uncertain, but the general picture is clear. The eschatological aspect of the Day of the Lord described here will be characterized by cataclysmic phenomena, including cosmic signs (cf. Isa 13:9–10; Joel 2:31; 3:15; Amos 5:18; Matt 24:29–30; Rev 6:12–14; 8:8–12; 9:1–18; 14:14–20; 16:4, 8–9). NIV at the end of v.6 ("no cold or frost") follows the interpretation of the ancient versions. Feinberg (pp. 254–55), however, probably correctly translates the verse this way (and then defends it):

> "And it shall come to pass in that day, that there shall not be light; the bright ones [i.e., luminaries] will be congealed" (v.6). The first portion of the verse has caused no difficulty, and is abundantly set forth in other prophetic passages. . . . But the last two words have called forth various views and differing interpretations. . . .
>
> The difficulties are several: (1) the verb (if we take the *Kethibh*), is masculine while the subject is feminine; (2) the word used for the lights of heaven is found nowhere else in that meaning; (3) if the second word is taken as a noun (so the *Qere*), no such noun is found. It is probably best . . . to understand that last clause as a reiteration in figurative language of that which is stated . . . in the first clause. The LXX and Vulgate with others (reading *weqaruth weqippa'on*) translate "cold and ice." But these are not opposites to light, as Keil has shown. . . . Gesenius-Robinson (1882) prefers the *Kethibh*, as does Keil. We have stated our preference in the translation above. Job 31:26 gives us a parallel use for the noun, while Exodus 15:8 and Job 10:10 furnish the same verb with the meaning

of "curdle, contract, congeal." That day will be characterized by absence of light, for the luminaries of heaven will be congealed to give forth no brilliance.

Because of the topographical, cosmic, and, indeed, even cataclysmic changes, that day will be "unique" (v.7). The situation will be such that it can be classified as neither day nor night—"a day known [only] to the LORD." But after the judgment and suffering (possibly the refining of 13:8–9) are past, "there will be light" again, possibly symbolizing the ushering in of the new order.

Is the "living water" (v.8) literal (physical) or figurative (spiritual)? Bullinger (p. 896) suggests that water can be emblematic of God, the gift of the Holy Spirit, or the blessings and merits of Christ. It is probably best to view the water as both literal and symbolic (cf. Pss 46:4; 65:9; Isa 8:6; Jer 2:13; Ezek 47:1–12; John 4:10–14; 7:38; Rev 22:1–2). As indicated by the NIV margin, "the eastern sea" is the Dead Sea and "the western sea" is the Mediterranean. Roland de Vaux (*Ancient Israel: Its Life and Institutions*, tr. John McHugh [London: Darton, Longman and Todd, 1961], pp. 189–90) explains why spring and autumn are not mentioned along with summer and winter: "The year was divided into two seasons, the winter, *ḥoreph*, and summer, *qayṣ*, corresponding roughly to the cold and hot seasons, to seedtime and harvest (Gn 8:22; cf. Ps 74:17; Is 18:6; Za 14:8). . . . This simple division corresponds to the climate of Palestine, where the hot, dry season and the cold, wet season succeed each other fairly quickly, leaving no distinct sensation of spring and autumn, as in more temperate countries." Perhaps the main point here is that "living" (fresh or running) water will not dry up in the summer, as most Palestinian streams do in the "hot, dry season."

Notes

4 גֵּיא (*gê'*, "valley"), in spite of the pointing, is probably absolute state (BDB, p. 161; GKC, par. 128w, n. 1).

5 The NIV margin offers this alternative: "My mountain valley will be blocked and will extend to Azel. It will be blocked as it was blocked because of the earthquake." This presupposes repointing the verbs to נִסְתַּם (*nistam*), from סתם (*stm*) and receives support from the LXX, Targum, and Symmachus. The MT, on the other hand, has *nastem*, from נוס (*nws*), and is supported by the Vulgate and Peshitta. Since the MT makes good sense (see the exposition) and there is no convincing reason to change it, the MT is to be preferred (as reflected in the main text of NIV).

The translation "by my mountain valley" is justified by analyzing גֵּיא (*gê'*, "valley") as an adverbial accusative of place (locative accusative) or perhaps as an adverbial accusative of manner. Apparently "mountain" is plural here (see Heb.) because it was "split in two" (v.4).

"With him" is literally "with you" (another apostrophe).

c. *The establishment of the Messiah's kingdom*

14:9–11

9 The LORD will be king over the whole earth. On that day there will be one LORD, and his name the only name.

[10]The whole land, from Geba to Rimmon, south of Jerusalem, will become like the Arabah. But Jerusalem will be raised up and remain in its place, from the Benjamin Gate to the site of the First Gate, to the Corner Gate, and from the Tower of Hananel to the royal winepresses. [11]It will be inhabited; never again will it be destroyed. Jerusalem will be secure.

9 Statements like "The LORD will be king over the whole earth" stand at the very center of a truly biblical theology (cf. Albert E. Glock, "Early Israel as the Kingdom of Yahweh: The Influence of Archaeological Evidence on the Reconstruction of Religion in Early Israel," *Concordia Theological Monthly* 41 [October 1970]: 558–605; Gary V. Smith, "The Concept of God/the Gods as King in the Ancient Near East and the Bible," *Trinity Journal* 3 [Spring 1982]: 1–38, esp. pp. 33–38). When this comes true in the fullest sense, the prayer of Matthew 6:9–10 will be answered:

Our Father in heaven,
hallowed be your name,
your kingdom come
your will be done
  on earth as it is in heaven.

While the Hebrew for "earth" could be rendered "land," Unger (*Zechariah*, p. 256) correctly argues for "earth" here: "*The Translation 'land,'* while certainly in line with the context outside of verse 9 (i.e., vss. 1–8 and 10), *is not consonant with the larger context of the verse itself*. That *the Lord will be one and his name one* only in Palestine is unthinkable. The scope of verse 9 demands the larger meaning of the Hebrew word 'earth,' and strikes the note of universality in its wording and thought pattern (emphasis his)."

According to the remainder of v.9, the time is coming when there will be no more idolatry, polytheism, or even henotheism, but only high, ethical monotheism. This theological statement recalls the Jewish Shema (Deut 6:4). "God's name Yahweh [the LORD] expressed all He had ever been and ever would be (Ex. 3:13–17)" (Baldwin, *Zechariah*, p. 204).

10–11 The land around Jerusalem is to be leveled while Jerusalem is to be elevated (see v.4 for the cause of these topographical changes). Geba ("height") was located almost six miles north of Jerusalem at the northern boundary of the kingdom of Judah (2 Kings 23:8). As the text indicates, the Rimmon mentioned here is the one situated "south of Jerusalem" (this distinguishes it from other OT towns of the same name). It is usually identified with En Rimmon ("spring of the pomegranate tree," Neh 11:29; cf. Josh 15:32), modern "Khirbet Umm et-Ramâmîm, about thirty-five miles south-west of Jerusalem, where the hill country of Judah slopes away into the *Negeb* or south" (Baldwin, *Zechariah*, p. 204).

The term "Arabah" (primarily rendered "plain" in KJV) "was applied specifically in part or wholly to the depression of the Jordan Valley, extending from Mt. Hermon, a 9100-ft. (2775-m.) elevation in the Anti-Lebanon Range, due S beyond the Sea of Chinnereth (Galilee), and including both sides of the river Jordan, the Dead

Sea, and the region slightly to the southwest as far as the head of the Gulf of Aqabah" (ISBE, 1979 rev. ed., s.v.). That Jerusalem will thus be elevated (probably both physically and in prominence) is in agreement with Isaiah 2:2. The Benjamin Gate, the First Gate, and the Tower of Hananel were all at the northeastern part of the city wall, the Corner Gate was at its northwest corner, and the royal winepresses were just south of the city (cf. Jer 31:38). "Thus the naming of landmarks on the east, west, north and south walls emphasizes that the whole city is included" (Baldwin, *Zechariah,* p. 204). Furthermore, the city will be densely populated ("inhabited," v.11; cf. 2:4), never again to be depopulated through destruction (as at the time of the exile to Babylonia—Isa 43:28). "In Zec. 14:11; Mal. 4:6 'curse' (Heb. *hērem,* RSV mg. 'ban of utter destruction') refers to a ban which was sometimes placed on a captured city, which meant that everything in the city was consecrated to the deity and offered as a holocaust (cf. Josh. 6:17–19, 24)" (see "curse" in ISBE, 1979 rev. ed., 1:837). (For further study of the Hebrew word translated "destroyed" [*ḥērem*], see TWOT, 1:324–25.) Finally, "Jerusalem will be secure" (see Jer 31:40).

Notes

10 The anomalous וְרָאֲמָה (*werā'amāh,* "will be raised up") is explained in GKC, par. 72p.

d. *The punishment of Israel's enemies*

14:12–15

12This is the plague with which the LORD will strike all the nations that fought against Jerusalem: Their flesh will rot while they are still standing on their feet, their eyes will rot in their sockets, and their tongues will rot in their mouths.

13On that day men will be stricken by the LORD with great panic. Each man will seize the hand of another, and they will attack each other. 14Judah too will fight at Jerusalem. The wealth of all the surrounding nations will be collected—great quantities of gold and silver and clothing. 15A similar plague will strike the horses and mules, the camels and donkeys, and all the animals in those camps.

12–15 The prophet next revealed how God will deal with the antikingdom forces of vv.1–3: First, he will strike them with a "plague" (v.12), just as he did the Assyrian army of King Sennacherib in 701 B.C. (Isa 37:36). Second, the Lord will strike the enemies of himself and his people with "great panic" (v.13), causing them to "attack each other" (cf. Judg 7:22; 1 Sam 14:15–20; 2 Chron 20:23). Third, the rest of the people of Judah will rally to defend the capital (v.14; cf. 12:2). The validity of this last point rests on the NIV rendering "at Jerusalem," not "against Jerusalem" (RSV).

Verse 14 ends with the Jews gathering the plunder, or spoils, of battle—a reversal of v.1. Verse 15 adds that a plague similar to that of vv.12–13 will strike the beasts of burden, thus preventing their use for escape.

Notes

12 The infinitive absolute הָמֵק (*hāmēq*, "will rot") is here used as a substitute for the finite verb. Davidson (par. 88c) states that "where the action in itself, apart from its circumstances, is to be stated, the inf. abs. is sufficient."

The singular pronominal suffix in בְּשָׂרוֹ (*b*[e]*śārô*, "their flesh"; lit., "his flesh") has the distributive or individualized use (Davidson, par. 116, rem. 1).

e. *The universal worship of the King*

14:16–19

> [16]Then the survivors from all the nations that have attacked Jerusalem will go up year after year to worship the King, the LORD Almighty, and to celebrate the Feast of Tabernacles. [17]If any of the peoples of the earth do not go up to Jerusalem to worship the King, the LORD Almighty, they will have no rain. [18]If the Egyptian people do not go up and take part, they will have no rain. The LORD will bring on them the plague he inflicts on the nations that do not go up to celebrate the Feast of Tabernacles. [19]This will be the punishment of Egypt and the punishment of all the nations that do not go up to celebrate the Feast of Tabernacles.

16 In spite of the awful decimation predicted in vv.12–15, there will be "survivors"—a converted remnant from those nations—who will make an annual pilgrimage to Jerusalem "to worship the King" (see Isa 2:2–4; also Ezek 40–48 for more on the nature of that worship). Two other passages also combine "the King" with "the LORD Almighty" (Ps 24:10; Isa 6:5). "The Feast of Tabernacles" marked the final harvest of the year's crops (Lev 23:34–43). Perowne (p. 147) suggests that, of the three great pilgrimage festivals (Passover, Pentecost, and Tabernacles), the reason Tabernacles (or Booths) will be selected as the festival for representatives of the various Gentile nations is that "it was the last and greatest festival of the Jewish year, gathering up into itself, as it were, the year's worship."

The Feast of Tabernacles was to be a time of grateful rejoicing (Lev 23:40; Deut 16:14–15; Neh 8:17). The people were to live in "booths" as a reminder that their ancestors lived in booths when the Lord brought them out of Egypt (Lev 23:42–43). Beginning with the period of Ezra and Nehemiah, the reading (and perhaps teaching) of "the Book of the Law of God" became an integral part of the festivities (Neh 8:18; cf. Isa 2:3). The festival seems to speak of the final, joyful regathering and restoration of Israel in full kingdom blessing, as well as of the ingathering of the nations. It may continue to have some significance (at least typically) in the eternal state (in the New Jerusalem on the new earth), since God will "tabernacle" (NIV, "live") with his people (Rev 21:3). Josephus (Jos. Antiq. VIII, 100 [iv.1]) says that Tabernacles was "especially sacred and important." For a more complete study of this festival, see de Vaux (*Ancient Israel*, pp. 495–502), who maintains (p. 506) that "the entire passage is devoted to the eschatological triumph, to that 'Day' when Yahweh will be king over the whole earth (v.9), and the feast of Tents is mentioned only because it was the main feast for pilgrimage to Jerusalem."

17–19 The prophet next unfolds what will happen to the recalcitrant nations that refuse to send delegations on this annual pilgrimage to worship the King in Jerusalem: The blessing of rain will be withheld from them (v.17; according to Deut 28:22–24, this was one of the curses for covenant disobedience). Baldwin (*Zechariah*, p. 206) relates v.17 to 9:11–10:1, "where an adequate rainfall is connected with the prosperity of the Messianic era." Unger (*Zechariah*, p. 268) observes: "In Ezekiel 34:26 the word ['rain'] is used figuratively of spiritual blessing, and Zechariah's usage, while literal, does not exclude the spiritual connotation." This principle is illustrated in v.18 with Egypt, but the Hebrew text may be read in different ways, as indicated by the NIV margin.

Ellis (p. 1050) suggests that "perhaps the Heb. is a rhetorical question: 'shall not the plague come upon them?' " Accepting the reading in the NIV margin, Baldwin (*Zechariah*, p. 207) points out that "Egypt was an exception among the nations because it depended for water not on rainfall but on the Nile. As Egypt had experienced plagues at the time of the Exodus, and through them had been brought to acknowledge God's sovereignty, so *plague* was a fitting symbol of disaster in the new era" (emphasis hers). Ultimately this, too, may include the withholding of rain, for drought would cause the Nile inundation to fail. Thus will all be punished who do not make the annual pilgrimage to Jerusalem to worship the King and to observe the thankful expressions associated with the Feast of Tabernacles (v.19), and thus will the King be universally worshiped.

Notes

---

16 לְהִשְׁתַּחֲוֹת (*l^ehištaḥ^awôṯ*, "to worship") is not to be derived from שׁחה (*šḥh*) or שׁחח (*šḥḥ*), as once thought; rather, it is the Hishtaphel stem of the root חוה (*ḥwh*, from an original *ḥwy*). (See Barker, "Value of Ugaritic," p. 125.)

19 חַטָּאת (*ḥaṭṭa'ṯ*) affords an excellent example of the meaning "punishment" for this word, instead of "sin," "guilt," etc. Thus what Fohrer ("Twofold Aspects," pp. 102–3) says of רָעָה (*rā'āh*, "evil") and עָוֹן (*'āwōn*, "sin") is likewise true of *ḥaṭṭa'ṯ*.

---

f. *"HOLY TO THE LORD"*

14:20–21

> 20On that day HOLY TO THE LORD will be inscribed on the bells of the horses, and the cooking pots in the LORD's house will be like the sacred bowls in front of the altar. 21Every pot in Jerusalem and Judah will be holy to the LORD Almighty, and all who come to sacrifice will take some of the pots and cook in them. And on that day there will no longer be a Canaanite in the house of the LORD Almighty.

20–21 Here the nature of the messianic kingdom is depicted: It will be characterized by "holiness" (for the meaning of this word, see comment at 2:12). Perowne (p. 148) gives an overview of these verses: "The ornaments of worldly pomp and warlike power shall be as truly consecrated as the very mitre of the High Priest, and every vessel used in the meanest service of the Temple as holy as the vessels of the altar itself, ver. 20. Nay every common vessel throughout the city and the whole land shall be so holy as to be meet for the service of the sanctuary, and every profane person shall be for ever banished from the house of the Lord, ver. 21." He adds (p. 149): "All distinction between sacred and secular shall be at an end, because all shall now be alike holy." The teaching of these verses may be summed up like this: There will be holiness in public life ("the bells of the horses," v.20), in religious life ("the cooking pots in the LORD's house," v.20), and in private life ("every pot in Jerusalem and Judah," v.21). Even common things become holy when they are used for God's service. So it is with our lives.

"*Holy to the Lord* was engraved on the plate of gold worn on the turban of the high priest (Ex. 28:36) as an expression and reminder of his consecration, but it was meant to be true of all Israel (Ex. 19:6; Je. 2:3)" (Baldwin, *Zechariah*, p. 207). So God's original purpose for Israel (Exod 19:6) will be fulfilled. "Cook" (v.21) means "cook the sacrifices." While the Hebrew for "Canaanite" can also mean "merchant" (cf. NIV mg.)—possibly referring either to 11:5 or to the kind of activity condemned by Jesus in Matthew 21:12–13 (cf. John 2:13–16)—"Canaanite" seems the better translation for this context. "Canaanite" would then represent anyone who is morally or spiritually unclean—anyone who is not included among the chosen people of God (cf. Isa 35:8; Ezek 43:7; 44:9; Rev 21:27).

The final scene of the Book of Zechariah anticipates Revelation 11:15, toward which all history is steadily moving—"the kingdom of the world has become the kingdom of our Lord and of his Christ, and he will reign for ever and ever"—and Revelation 19:16—"On his robe and on his thigh he has this name written: KING OF KINGS AND LORD OF LORDS." The only appropriate human response to all this is to heed Robert Grant's exhortation:

> O worship the King, all-glorious above,
> And gratefully sing His pow'r and His love;
> Our Shield and Defender, the Ancient of days,
> Pavilioned in splendor and girded with praise.

MALACHI

Robert L. Alden

MALACHI

Introduction

1. Background

Unlike most other prophets, Malachi mentioned no datable persons or events in his brief prophecy. Any clues to the origin and time of his book must come from the text and its implications. Tradition, however, gives us some information.

Malachi is and always has been placed last in the Minor Prophets, and there is an approximate chronological arrangement within the three major prophets and the twelve minor ones. In fact, the Talmud regularly classes Haggai, Zechariah, and Malachi together as the three postexilic prophets.[1]

From the contents of Malachi, we deduce that the prophet wrote sometime after Ezra. Zerubbabel, the first governor after the return from the Babylonian exile, had, with the aid of the prophets Haggai and Zechariah, encouraged the people to rebuild the temple. That was in 515 B.C. Ezra returned with another group of exiles in 458 B.C. That was also the seventh year of King Artaxerxes. In the twentieth year of that same king (445 B.C.), Nehemiah returned and led the people in rebuilding the walls of the city of Jerusalem. In the twelfth year of his governorship, Nehemiah returned to Persia for an unknown period of time (cf. Neh 5:14; 13:6). It was during this interim, perhaps in 434 B.C., that Malachi took the helm of spiritual affairs in Jerusalem.

Some of the exiles had returned, the temple had been rebuilt, and the sacrificial system had been reestablished. Indeed, it had been functioning long enough to develop certain abuses against which Malachi contended at some length in his book.

In 1:8 another hint appears: a Persian word for governor (*peḥāh*). Nehemiah had this title (Neh 5:14; 12:26). So did Zerubbabel (cf. Hag 1:1, 14; 2:2, 21). (Nehemiah

---

[1]*Yoma* 9b; *Sukkah* 44a; *Rosh Hashanah* 19b; *Megillah* 3a, 15a, et al.

is also called *tiršāṯā'*, another term for a governor; cf. Neh 8:9; 10:1.) Malachi 1:8 may very well not indicate Nehemiah because (1) his name is not there and its absence is hard to explain, and (2) the tone of the verse indicates a pagan ruler. Perhaps "the governor" is some interim public servant who filled the office during Nehemiah's absence (Neh 13:6). The other and more likely possibility is that Nehemiah had not yet arrived back on the scene, and Malachi's work preceded Nehemiah's second term as governor.

Many similarities exist between the thrust of Malachi's message and Nehemiah's reforms. This is why we connect the two. Among the points the two books have in common are the following: mixed marriages (Neh 10:30; 13:23–27; Mal 2:11; cf. Ezra 9–10); corrupt priesthood (Neh 13:4–9; Mal 1:6–2:9); financial abuses (Neh 13:10–13; Mal 3:5–10).

So the exiles had returned; the temple had been rebuilt; the city of Jerusalem had returned to a substantial degree of normalcy; and the inevitable lethargy, laxity, and leniency in spiritual matters had developed. A measure of comfort and security under Persian suzerainty encouraged the people of Judah to let their hands fall in their task of building their nation under God. To this declining state of affairs the last prophet of the OT addressed himself.

2. Authorship

Nothing is known of Malachi apart from his book. Even his name is in question. Some doubt that "Malachi" is a name and translate it as a title meaning, either "my messenger" or "the LORD's messenger." The *malach* part (or *mal'āḵ*, according to the transliteration scheme used in this work) means "messenger." The "i" (*î*) can be either the suffix "my" or an abbreviated form of the divine name Yahweh. The name-title appears again in 3:1 and without the suffix in 2:7 and 3:1. The suggestion that "Malachi" is not a proper name but a title has ancient support in the LXX, which reads "his messenger."[2]

To complicate the matter, the Targum of Jonathan added after "Malachi" the words "whose name was Ezra the scribe." Jerome concurred with this. In the Talmud (*Megillah* 15a) Mordecai is credited with writing the Book of Malachi.

Some scholars deny that Malachi is a separate book but affirm that it is actually only the last of three sections of Zechariah, which were cut off in order to make the Minor Prophets amount to the sacred number twelve.[3] Though Josephus mentioned all the major characters of this period, he failed to include Malachi among them.[4] The total obscurity of the author of the book is underlined by the absence of the name Malachi in all the rest of the Bible. Even where he is quoted in the NT, his name does not appear (Matt 11:10; Mark 1:2; Luke 7:27).

On the positive side, each of the other writing prophets is named in the opening verses of his book. If a man named Malachi did not write the book bearing this name, he would be the only exception. Moreover, Malachi is neither an unlikely name nor an unsuitable one for the author of this last book of the prophets. After all,

---

[2]The LXX also added to v.1 the exhortation "lay it on your hearts."

[3]See O. Eissfeldt, *The Old Testament: an Introduction*, trans. P.R. Ackroyd (New York: Harper and Row, 1965), p. 441.

[4]*Antiquities* XI, iv, i–v, 8.

Malachi was the Lord's messenger. His trumpet made no uncertain sound. Clearly and unmistakably he indicted his people and the priests for their sin and summoned them to righteousness.

3. Date

Malachi's book cannot be earlier than 515 B.C. because that was when the second temple was finished. Scholars have placed him anytime from then on through the administration of Nehemiah in Jerusalem. Ezra came to Jerusalem in 458 B.C. and Nehemiah in 445 (according to the traditional reckoning).

Based positively on the similarity of many of the themes in Malachi to those in Nehemiah and negatively on the nonmention of Nehemiah in Malachi, two popular views emerge. One is that Malachi the prophet preceded Nehemiah but followed Ezra. The other is that the Book of Malachi belongs to the interim of unknown length between the two terms of office Nehemiah had.

One can view Malachi's preaching as a precursor of the people's confessing, covenant making, and subsequent backsliding during Nehemiah's time. Or one can place him as more or less contemporary with Nehemiah and consider him as a charismatic voice expounding the same things as Nehemiah stood for.

Actually, it is of little moment whether Malachi's book is dated twenty-five or fifty years one way or the other. Today its timeless truths with the prophet's plea for sincerity and holiness are as relevant as they ever were.

4. Place of Origin and Destination

The opening verse tells us that this is "the word of the LORD to Israel." Ultimately, then, the origin of the book is in the mind of God and those addressed are the people of God.

More specifically, however, questions arise. For example, where were Malachi and Israel at the time of the writing of the book? We can assume that both were in Judah and, in particular, in Jerusalem (2:11). Malachi himself and most of the people he addressed were returned exiles or their children.

Among the returned Jews, the Levitical priests received special criticism and warning (1:6, 10; 2:1, 4, 7; 3:3). There is, however, no way of knowing whether Malachi was himself a priest; probably he was not.

The book contains several references to nations outside Israel. Although these nations were not in Malachi's immediate audience, they too must be considered ultimate recipients of his message (cf. 1:5, 11, 14; 3:12). It is possible that these are references to the Diaspora (i.e., the Jews still scattered throughout the nations of the ancient Near East).

5. Occasion

Apathy toward the temple ritual and especially toward the laws of Moses had reached such proportions in postexilic Judah that God raised up the prophet Malachi to reprimand the people. Apparently their goal of semi-independence and their hope of religious liberty had been realized. But the battle for truth and righteousness had waned because their obvious enemies were gone. Yet this left room for the not-so-obvious enemies—viz., smugness, pride, and compromise.

The people in general and the priests in particular had lost their sense of "chosenness" (1:2). Not respecting his codes and regulations (1:6) showed they had stopped honoring God. Among them intermarriage with unbelievers was rampant (2:11). The view of domestic commitment was low, and divorce was the result (2:16). In 3:5 there is a list of abuses and unacceptable practices: sorcery, adultery, perjury, fraud, oppression, and injustice. These were the things that occasioned Malachi's angry indictment. Judah's sins against both God and man were overt and numerous. No wonder Malachi saw a thorough purge by fire as the only sure cure (4:1).

6. Purpose

No prophet or preacher who loves his people really enjoys pointing out their sin or warning them of doom to come. So Malachi must have found his assignment, which was so packed with judgment of the people and the priests, a hard one. All the threats, warnings, challenges, encouragements, and promises were for the spiritual upbuilding of the repatriated exiles and their children. God and Malachi wanted a righteous nation, a pure and devoted priesthood, happy homes, God-fearing children, and a people characterized by truth, integrity, generosity, gratitude, fidelity, love, and hope.

Though Malachi's message was largely negative, here and there it offered a glimmer of hope or alluded to a brighter day as something the faithful of the land could take heart in. Statements like 3:10–12, 16–17, or 4:2 must have encouraged the returned exiles who truly loved and served God and their fellowmen.

7. Literary Form

Even a casual reading shows Malachi's use of rhetorical questions. Seven times he put them into the mouths of his audience (1:2, 6, 7; 2:17; 3:7, 8, 13, and perhaps 2:14). In addition he asked the people several rhetorical questions (e.g., 1:6, 8, 9; 2:10, 15; 3:2).

The format of 1:2 is typical of Malachi's style. First there is God's statement: "I have loved you." Then follows the popular objection that questions the truth of God's statement—viz., "How have you loved us?" Finally there is the justification for God's statement. In each case this is usually expanded and these expansions become the bulk of the prophet's message.

As he moved among the people, Malachi distilled these rhetorical questions from critical remarks he heard. Thus he used them as the basis for his message.

Here in Malachi we have an early example of an extended use of the question-and-answer method. Later it became quite popular and was, in fact, the usual format for the rabbis and scribes. The NT often used the rhetorical question to make a point (cf. Matt 3:7; 11:7–9; 12:26–27; Luke 14:5; John 18:38; Rom 3:1–4; 4:1–3; 6:21; 7:7; 1 Cor 9:7–13; Gal 3:21; Heb 1:14).

Otherwise Malachi's book consists of relatively short paragraphs on various themes. Malachi gave no oracles against foreign nations, no extended "burden" for Israel, and no personal experiences illustrating his message. His style cannot be called lofty. He had nothing apocalyptic unless it be the last few verses of the book. What he said was straightforward and easily understood. Only the use of the rhetorical question made his work unique among the prophets.

The Holy Bible: An Improved Edition (Philadelphia: American Baptist Publication Society, 1913) and AmT were the only English versions readily available that put Malachi into a poetic format till the appearance of the NAB. Since the most characteristic feature of Hebrew poetry is synonymous parallelism, a feature absent from Malachi, NIV and the majority of other translations are undoubtedly correct in understanding Malachi to be prose and not poetry.

8. Theology

Theologically Malachi stands within the tradition of the great writing prophets of the OT. The paramount theme of theology is the person and work of God himself. In this regard Malachi presents the sovereign Lord as both the God of Israel and the God of the whole world. In 3:6 not only is the immutability of God affirmed—"I the LORD do not change"—but the corollary of the impossibility of his promises being nullified is also stated: "So you, O descendants of Jacob, are not destroyed." God has determined to maintain a people for himself; and it will happen—if not in Malachi's day, then in a later age.

Malachi was in accord with the great OT prophets in reminding the people he was addressing of the universality of God. God was concerned with all nations, not just Israel (cf. 1:5).

It may seem that Malachi was overly concerned with the proper execution of the ritual parts of the Hebrew religion. Notice his remarks about blemished animals (1:8, 13) and tithing (3:8). But a careful and unprejudiced reading will show that Malachi was equally concerned with what Jesus called the "more important matters of the law—justice, mercy and faithfulness" (Matt 23:23). To these words Jesus added—and Malachi would certainly have agreed—"You should have practiced the latter, without neglecting the former."

The God Malachi preached was a God of justice. He would condemn sinners but would also reward the righteous. Tithing would produce blessing (3:10); the righteous would be spared on that "day" (v.17). Those who revered God's name would bask in the "sun of righteousness" (4:2). So Malachi was a prophet of both malediction and benediction, because he preached a God who was altogether fair in his dealings with people.

Malachi's most notable contribution to the OT's corpus of messianic prophecy was his reference to the forerunner. The first allusion is in 3:1. "My messenger" there cannot be Malachi (cf. Authorship) but rather some Elijah who would announce for the last time in the OT God's terms of repentance (4:5). We have Jesus' authoritative application of this office to John the Baptist in Matthew 11:14; 17:12–13 (cf. Mark 9:11–13; Luke 1:17).

9. Canonicity

Two sentences from Moore's commentary (p. 107) sum up the matter of canon: "The canonical authority of Malachi has never been called in question. It is found in all the authoritative enumerations of the canonical books, and is referred to repeatedly in the New Testament as an inspired prophecy. (See Matt. 11:10; 17:12; Mark 1:2; 9:11, 12; Luke 1:17; and Rom. 9:13.). In none of these NT passages, however, is Malachi mentioned by name. In fact the Mark 1:2 passage presents a problem because Malachi 3:1 is linked with Isaiah 40:3 and the whole composite quotation is attributed to Isaiah.

A tiny fragment containing Malachi 1:13–14 was found at Qumran.[5]

10. Text

Most scholars view Malachi's book as an indisputable unity. Some, however, have suggested that 1:11–14; 2:11–13a; 3:1b; and 4:4–6 are additions. Only the last of these suggestions has wide backing. Supposedly 4:4 was added by supporters of "the law of Moses," vv.5–6 being added because of the Elijah reference. Hence they form a conclusion to the whole prophetic collection rather than merely to Malachi. There is no textual support for viewing these verses as later additions.

The LXX and OL reflect both a high view of the book and the unity of it. Of these ancient versions Baldwin (p. 215) writes: "The LXX in general keeps so close to the Hebrew, even translating literally when the Greek had a more appropriate word, that it lends support to the Hebrew text, and where the Old Latin deviates from LXX it keeps even more closely to the Hebrew."

The most difficult verse in the book is perhaps 2:15, as differences in the English translations indicate. Even the editors of NIV changed the vowels on one word (*šᵉʾār*, "remnant") to produce the reading we are using (*šᵉʾēr* "flesh"; cf. Notes in loc.) This and other less significant variants are noted in the commentary.

11. Bibliography

Books

Baldwin, Joyce G. *Haggai, Zechariah, Malachi*. Downers Grove, Ill.: InterVarsity, 1972.

Bennett, T. Miles. "Malachi." *Broadman Bible Commentary*. Vol. 7. Nashville: Broadman, 1972.

Calvin, John. *Minor Prophets IV*. Grand Rapids: Eerdmans, 1950.

Dentan, Robert, and Sperry, Willard. "Malachi." *Interpreter's Bible*. IB. Vol. 6. New York: Abingdon, 1956.

Dods, Marcus. *Haggai, Zechariah, Malachi*. Edinburgh: T. & T. Clark, 1879.

Feinberg, Charles Lee. *Habbakuk, Zephaniah, Haggai, and Malachi*. New York: American Board of Missions to the Jews, 1951.

Freeman, Hobart E. *An Introduction to the Old Testament Prophets*. Chicago: Moody, 1968.

Hailey, Homer. *A Commentary on the Minor Prophets*. Grand Rapids: Baker, 1972.

---

[5]*Discoveries in the Judean Desert* 3:180.

Harrison, Roland K. "Malachi." *Zondervan Pictorial Encyclopedia of the Bible*. ZPEB. 5 vols. Edited by M.C. Tenney. Grand Rapids: Zondervan, 1975, 4:42–45.
Jones, Douglas R. *Haggai, Zechariah, Malachi*. London: SCM, 1972.
Keil, C.F. *The Minor Prophets*. KD. 2 vols. Grand Rapids: Eerdmans, 1949.
Laetsch, Theodore. *The Minor Prophets*. St. Louis: Concordia, 1956.
Lewis, Jack P. *The Minor Prophets*. Grand Rapids: Baker, 1966.
Mason, Rex. *The Books of Haggai, Zechariah, and Malachi*. The Cambridge Bible Commentary. Cambridge: Cambridge University Press, 1977.
Moore, T.V. *The Prophets of the Restoration: Haggai, Zechariah, Malachi*. 1856. Reprint. London: Banner of Truth Trust, 1968.
Packard, Joseph. "The Book of Malachi." *Commentary on the Holy Scriptures*. CHS. Edited by John Peter Lange. New York: Scribner's, 1887.
Pusey, E.B. *The Minor Prophets*. Vol. 2. New York: Funk & Wagnalls, 1885.
Robinson, George. *The Twelve Minor Prophets*. Grand Rapids: Baker, 1952.
Smith, George Adam. *The Twelve Prophets Commonly Called Minor*. ExB. New York: Funk & Wagnalls, 1900.
Smith, J.M. Powis. *A Critical and Exegetical Commentary on the Book of Malachi*. ICC. Edinburgh: T. & T. Clark, 1912.
Taylor, John B. *The Minor Prophets*. Grand Rapids: Eerdmans, 1970.
Wolf, Herbert. *Haggai/Malachi: Rededication and Renewal*. Chicago: Moody, 1976.

Periodicals

Althann, Robert. "Malachy 2.13–14 and UT 125, 12–13." *Biblica* 58 (1977): 418–21.
Boecker, H.J. "Bermerkugen Zur formgeschichtlichen Terminologie des Buches Maleachi." *Zeitschrift für die alttestamentliche Wissenschaft* 78, no. 1 (1966): 78–80.
Fischer, J.A. "Notes on the Literary Form and Message of Malachi." *Catholic Biblical Quarterly* 34 (July 1972): 315–20.
Freedman, David. "An Unnoted Support for a Variant to the M.T. of Mal. 3:5." *Journal of Biblical Literature* 98 (September 1979): 405–6.
Kaiser, Walter, Jr. "The Promise of the Arrival of Elijah in Malachi and the Gospels." *Grace Theological Journal* 3 (Fall 1982): 221–33.
Swetnam, J. "Malachi 1:11; An Interpretation." *Catholic Biblical Quarterly* 31 (April 1969): 200–209.
Waldman, N.M. "Some Notes on Malachi 3:9; 3:13 and Psalm 42:11." *Journal of Biblical Literature* 93 (December 1974): 543–49.

12. Outline

No unity of opinion prevails as to the outline of Malachi. The one below, like all outlines of this book, is not wholly precise. It is obvious that Malachi did not start with an outline. Instead he moved from topic to topic and occasionally went back and picked up an idea touched on earlier in the book.

I. The Favor of the Lord (1:1–5)
II. The Failure of the Priests (1:6–14)
   1. Disrespectful Service (1:6–7)
   2. Disqualified Sacrifices (1:8–9)
   3. Disdainful Attitudes (1:10–14)
III. The Rebuke of the Lord (2:1–9)
IV. The Unfaithfulness of the People (2:10–16)
V. The Coming Messenger of the Lord (2:17–3:5)
VI. The Robbery and Riches of God (3:6–12)
   1. The Neglect of the Tithe (3:6–9)
   2. The Promise of Blessing (3:10–12)
VII. The Servants of the Lord (3:13–18)
   1. The Faithless (3:13–15)
   2. The Faithful (3:16–18)
VIII. The Day of the Lord (4:1–6)

Text and Exposition

I. The Favor of the Lord

1:1–5

[1]An oracle: The word of the LORD to Israel through Malachi.
[2]"I have loved you," says the LORD.
"But you ask, 'How have you loved us?'
"Was not Esau Jacob's brother?" the LORD says. "Yet I have loved Jacob, [3]but
Esau I have hated, and I have turned his mountains into a wasteland and left his
inheritance to the desert jackals."
[4]Edom may say, "Though we have been crushed, we will rebuild the ruins."
But this is what the LORD Almighty says: "They may build, but I will demolish.
They will be called the Wicked Land, a people always under the wrath of the LORD.
[5]You will see it with your own eyes and say, 'Great is the LORD—even beyond the
borders of Israel!'

1 This verse is like the opening verses of other prophetic books or of chapters within such books (cf. Nah 1; Hab 1; Isa 13; 15; 17; 19; 21; 22; 23; Zech 9; 12; cf. also Prov 30; 31). It tells us the three barest minimum facts about the "oracle" (*maśśāʾ*; cf. Notes): (1) it is from the Lord, (2) it is for Israel, and (3) Malachi is its agent. Here in the first verse of his book, Malachi made unique use of "oracle" and "word." Other prophets used one or the other, never both together.

2–3 The prophecy itself begins with the beautiful words "I have loved you." This statement, with its challenge and elaboration, is the first of seven such dialogues between God and Israel in Malachi (cf. 1:6, 7; 2:14, 17; 3:7b–8, 13b–14). We do not know for certain whether the people actually put into specific words their doubt of God's love for them. In any event the popular attitude was that God had forsaken them. Though the Exile might have prompted such feelings, one would think that the near miraculous turn of events that led to the repatriation of many of the Hebrews would have given the people cause to think about God's faithfulness. These events, however, happened some half-century or more after the people returned from the Babylonian captivity. That return, though unaccompanied by the miracles of the Exodus from Egypt, was nevertheless viewed exultingly as the work of the hand of God. In the absence of any subsequent marvels, however, there came despair born of unfulfilled hopes.

The divine rejoinder to the people's question alludes to a crucial event in Isaac's family. While it is not baldly stated in Genesis 25:23, in his sovereignty God chose Jacob over Esau, a choice that was tantamount to "hating" Esau. In Romans 9:13 Paul quoted this and used it to illustrate the doctrine of election (cf. E.F. Harrison, "Romans," EBC, 10:97–126). Here in Malachi, v.3 describes the result of God's rejection of Esau; his territory, ancient Edom, became a wasteland inhabited by desert jackals. In the fourth century B.C., the Nabataeans moved through Edom—driving the Edomites westward out of their centuries-old homeland—to the southern part of Judah. This area later came to be known as Idumea (cf. Mark 3:8).

4–5 These verses elaborate God's rejection of Esau's land. This anti-Edom theme recurs in the prophets (cf. Isa 11:14; 34:5–6; Jer 49:7–22; Ezek 25:12–14; 35:15; Joel

3:19; Amos 1:11; and all of Obadiah). Of all the enemies of Israel, Edom was perhaps the most long-lived and consistent one. The enmity began with Amalek, an Edomite (Exod 17:8–16), and continued through the Exodus (Num 14:44–45), into the period of the Judges (3:12–13), and to the time of Saul (1 Sam 15:1–3) and David (1 Sam 27:8). Moreover, the enemies mentioned by Ezra (4:7) and Nehemiah (4:7) probably included Edomites (Amalakites), and this special curse directed at them would be an oblique kind of encouragement to the Israelites.

Though the Edomites in some small measure rebuilt their country, though never regaining its former territory or power, God spoke of his intention to see it perpetually cursed. This evidence of God's power beyond the borders of Israel will evoke from his people the doxology "Great is the LORD" (v.5). This is the first of three or four such phrases throughout the book that speak of God's plans going beyond the boundaries of Israel (cf. 1:11, 14; 3:12; and perhaps 4:6).

Notes

---

1 The opening word מַשָּׂא (*maśśā'*, "burden," "oracle") is commonly used for describing a prophecy. It is related to the verb נָשָׂא (*nāśā'*, "to bear"), hence implying a responsibility, duty, charge, or assignment from God. Most modern translations, including NIV, render it "oracle," which communicates better than "burden" but fails to bring out the onerous aspects the prophet's duty often entailed.

2 NIV uses the perfect tense "have loved" because of the nature of what follows. In Hebrew such a fine tense distinction is not possible.

5 Here a few MSS have no לְ (*l*, "l") prefixed to גְּבוּל (*g^e^bûl*, "border"), which indicates that there may have been dittography, since the preceding word מֵעַל (*mē'al*, "beyond") ends with an *l*. The presence or absence of the inseparable *l* makes no appreciable difference, since we already have a heavier independent preposition *l* in the *mē'al*.

II. The Failure of the Priests (1:6–14)

1. *Disrespectful Service*

1:6–7

> 6"A son honors his father, and a servant his master. If I am a father, where is the honor due me? If I am a master, where is the respect due me?" says the LORD Almighty. "It is you, O priests, who show contempt for my name.
> "But you ask, 'How have we shown contempt for your name?'
> 7"You place defiled food on my altar.
> "But you ask, 'How have we defiled you?'
> "By saying that the LORD's table is contemptible."

6–7 This first part of the indictment against the priests contains two more rhetorical questions. Malachi opened the section with an illustration reminiscent of the way Isaiah opened his book (Isa 1:3). The first rhetorical question is God's—viz., "Where is the respect due me?" The unwritten answer is that they had not been honoring the Lord. They, the servants at the temple who were the closest to sacred things, were the ones who had defaulted in the most central obligation of all—that of honoring God. And if the leadership failed, what could the people be expected to do? But spiritual leaders, both ancient and modern alike, have often run the risk of treating sacred things as ordinary. Intimate familiarity with holy matters conduces to treating them with indifference.

The vocative "O priests" occurs here and in 2:1. It can be assumed that all the "you"s throughout this section refer to the priests.

From the general charge of failing to honor the Lord, the prophet moved to this specific one: "You place defiled food on my altar" (v.7). The priests countered this charge with a question. Then the prophet responded with an explanation of the charge: the priests say "that the LORD's table is contemptible."

Notes

6–7 Three times in these verses, Malachi used the word בָּזָה (*bāzāh*, "show contempt"); and he used it again in v.12 and in 2:9.

7 The word גָּאַל (*gā'al*, "defiled") is somewhat characteristic of Malachi; his brief book contains three of its eleven occurrences (vv.7 [*bis*], 12).

---

2. *Disqualified Sacrifices*

1:8–9

8 "When you bring blind animals for sacrifice, is that not wrong? When you sacrifice crippled or diseased animals, is that not wrong? Try offering them to your governor! Would he be pleased with you? Would he accept you?" says the LORD Almighty.

9 "Now implore God to be gracious to us. With such offerings from your hands, will he accept you?"—says the LORD Almighty.

8 With four more questions, the prophet expanded the charge against the priests. Was it not wrong to sacrifice blind animals? Of course it was! Deuteronomy 15:21 forbade bringing any lame, blind, blemished, or sick animals to the altar. The priests should have been reminding the people of these ancient biblical regulations. Malachi's concern for the law of Moses is not confined to 4:4. On the contrary, the very fact that he dealt in this section with proper Levitical ceremony shows his knowledge of ritual details and his concern for them.

The second question in v.8 is like the first. The third and fourth ones clearly imply that such offerings would be unacceptable to the governor. The context probably implies that this governor was not Nehemiah but one of the Persian appointees who served before Nehemiah arrived in Jerusalem, or perhaps during his absence from it. Furthermore, animals were probably not brought to him as sacrifices but as a form of tax. Despite their generally favorable attitude toward the exiles, the Persians would not tolerate any cutting of corners by their subjects.

9 The closing verse of this section, where God spoke of himself in the third person, seems loaded with irony. Although some of the older commentators took it as a serious invitation to seek God, most modern translations and commentaries understand it as one more of Malachi's ways of charging the priests with sin. Moffatt's paraphrase makes it clear: "Try to pacify God and win his favour? How can he favour any one of you, says the LORD of hosts, when you offer him such sacrifices?" NAB puts it this way:

> So now if you implore God for mercy on us
> when you have done the like
> Will he welcome any of you?
> says the LORD of hosts.

The point is that God would not extend his favor when the gifts for thanksgiving and entreaty were given, because their shoddiness was an insult.

Notes

8–9 The expression יִשָּׂא פָּנֶיךָ (*yiśśā' pāneyḵā*, "accept you") is an interesting Hebrew idiom. Literally it reads, "He will lift up your face." The picture of Esther before Ahasuerus comes to mind. If he accepted her, he would extend the scepter, and she could lift her bowed head. Rejection meant she would back out the door with head bowed (Esth 4:10–11; 5:1–2).

3. *Disdainful Attitudes*

1:10–14

10"Oh, that one of you would shut the temple doors, so that you would not light useless fires on my altar! I am not pleased with you," says the LORD Almighty, "and I will accept no offerings from your hands. 11My name will be great among the nations, from the rising to the setting of the sun. In every place incense and pure offerings will be brought to my name, because my name will be great among the nations," says the LORD Almighty.

12"But you profane it by saying of the Lord's table, 'It is defiled,' and of its food, 'It is contemptible.' 13And you say, 'What a burden!' and you sniff at it contemptuously," says the LORD Almighty.

"When you bring injured, crippled or diseased animals and offer them as sacrifices, should I accept them from your hands?" says the LORD. 14"Cursed is the cheat who has an acceptable male in his flock and vows to give it, but then sacrifices a blemished animal to the LORD. For I am a great king," says the LORD Almighty, "and my name is to be feared among the nations.

The theme of these five verses is substantially the same as that of the preceding verses—viz., the behavior of the Levitical priests was unacceptable. God did not approve of them or their work; so he would find others who would serve him acceptably.

10 God, once again speaking of himself in the first person (cf. v.9), wished that the temple would go out of business. As long as it was not serving as a meeting place for God and man, why should any perfunctory and self-deceiving rituals go on in it? Not only were the sacrifices ineffective, but the priests and the people were lulled into thinking that their deeds were winning God's approval. So why not shut the temple doors and be done with what was for the priests merely a nuisance? The thought may be applied to present-day churches that have ceased to be places where people worship in spirit and in truth and are merely meeting places and nothing more. It would be better for them to close down than to continue misleading those who think that what they are doing pleases God. He could hardly have spoken his mind more clearly than he did in the last part of v.10: "I am not pleased with you, . . . and I will accept no offering from your hands."

11 God told his faithless priests that he had others who in different places and in later times would bring acceptable offerings and give him with love and devotion the worship he demanded. Of course, Christians do not bring incense and sacrificial animals to the Lord as ancient Israel did. But Revelation 5:8 reminds us that incense corresponds to prayer, and Hebrews 13:15–16 states that "a sacrifice of praise" is "the fruit of lips that confess his name." So Christians are among those spoken of in Malachi 1:11, those of the far-off nations living in the distant future, who in Malachi's day were thought to be without hope because they had no contact with the religion of Jerusalem and its priests (cf. 1 Peter 2:9).

12–13 Once more the altar of the temple was called a table (v.12; cf. v.7). The priests were charged with profaning the Lord's name when they declared that his table was defiled and its food contemptible. The food, of course, was the cereal and meat offerings the priests put on the Lord's table. It was true that certain species of animals and others that were blemished defiled the altar. But it was the priests' responsibility to keep such unacceptable offerings away from the altar. How strange that now they were the ones complaining of the defilement! Verse 13 is in the same vein. Malachi put into words the thoughts of the priests. For them the holy service of God had become a bore, a labor of duty rather than of love, a yoke around their necks. The very men who were the mediators between God and his people (Exod 28:1, 43), the teachers of Israel (Lev 10:11; Deut 33:10; 2 Chron 15:3), and the court of appeal (Deut 19:17–19) were, by their own choice, profaning their office and bringing shame on the name of Yahweh.

The question asked in v.13, like those in v.8, lists the things that make animals unacceptable for sacrifice. "Should I accept [such animals from you]?" God asked.

14 God spoke drastically but realistically: "Cursed is the cheat." The opposite of "blessed" is "cursed," and the opposite of an honest person is a cheat. And, as the writer of Ecclesiastes said, "It is better not to vow than to make a vow and not fulfill it" (5:5).

God will not tolerate such reneging. He is an absolute sovereign. If the people he chose reject him, he will choose others—Gentiles, foreigners—who will revere his holy name.

Notes

---

11 That NIV (like KJV, NASB, BV) has the future tense three times in this verse implies that the situation described here will probably happen in the future Messianic Age. Since the

Hebrew has no finite verbs here but only a-temporal participles, we have no sure way of knowing what Malachi meant temporally. Notice that at the end of v.14, NIV uses the present tense for a similar sentiment. It is hard to imagine that "incense and pure offerings" were brought to the Lord around the world in Malachi's day. So NIV's use of the future tense (contra RSV, NEB, JB, et al.) seems reasonable. Likewise, consistency would require the future tense to be used in v.14b, too.

12 One of the eighteen תִּקּוּנֵי סֹפְרִים (*tîqqûnê sōpᵉrîm,* "corrections of the scribes") occurs here (E. Würthwein, *The Text of the Old Testament* [Oxford: Basil Blackwell], pp. 14–15). Supposedly the scribes changed an original "me" to "it" to protect God from such a verb as "sniff." The change amounts to little in the interpretation of the verse.

14 The title "great king" was claimed by the Persian kings (but cf. Ps 47:2). It is possible that the prophet had this in mind when he recorded God as saying, "I am a great king."

III. The Rebuke of the Lord

2:1–9

1"And now this admonition is for you, O priests. 2If you do not listen, and if you do not set your heart to honor my name," says the LORD Almighty, "I will send a curse upon you, and I will curse your blessings. Yes, I have already cursed them, because you have not set your heart to honor me.

3"Because of you I will rebuke your descendants, I will spread on your faces the offal from your festival sacrifices, and you will be carried off with it. 4And you will know that I have sent you this admonition so that my covenant with Levi may continue," says the LORD Almighty. 5"My covenant was with him, a covenant of life and peace, and I gave them to him; this called for reverence and he revered me and stood in awe of my name. 6True instruction was in his mouth and nothing false was found on his lips. He walked with me in peace and uprightness, and turned many from sin.

7"For the lips of a priest ought to preserve knowledge, and from his mouth men should seek instruction—because he is the messenger of the LORD Almighty. 8But you have turned from the way and by your teaching have caused many to stumble; you have violated the covenant with Levi," says the LORD Almighty. 9"So I have caused you to be despised and humiliated before all the people, because you have not followed my ways but have shown partiality in matters of the law."

1–2 Very pointedly v.1 shows that the next eight verses (2–9) were aimed at the priests. In its repetitive nature, v.2 is typically Hebrew. The phrase "to set your heart" occurs twice and the word "curse" three times in different forms. The "curse" idea relates to 1:14. The "blessings" are probably the very things that ultimately benefited the priesthood. Two of them are named in 3:11—pest-free crops and fruitful vines. The Levites lived off the tithes the people brought. When the nation as a whole suffered from drought or any other calamity, the perquisites of the priests dropped off proportionately.

3–6 "Offal" (*pereš*) occurs twice in the MT of v.3, but NIV adequately carries the idea that is already very strong in itself. The "offal" was the internal waste of the sacrificial animal that normally was carried outside the camp. But here it is first used as a gross insult to the officiating priests, and then they and it would be carried away.

The word "covenant" appears six times in this little book. The first three (2:4–5, 8) refer to God's covenant with Levi; then come references to the "covenant of the fathers" (v.10), the marriage covenant (v.14), and the new covenant (3:1). The covenant with Levi must be the provisions of Numbers 3:45–48 and 18:21–24, while the "covenant of peace" of v.5 harks back to Numbers 25:12 and Phinehas the grandson of Aaron.

A change in the tone of the rebuke comes at v.4 and continues till v.8. It begins a historical reflection on what was and what should have been. That covenant arrangement with the Levites was to endure unaltered. Obviously they were not meeting their responsibilities.

The description in vv.5–6 of what a priest should be simply did not fit the priests of Malachi's day. "Life and peace," "reverence," "true instruction," and "uprightness" were to be the hallmarks of those serving in the temple. And in the old days such characteristics were found. There was the absence of falsehood on the lips and the ministry of turning many from sin. But in Malachi's day, instead of turning men *from* sin, the priests were, by their words and deeds, turning men *to* sin (v.8). It is inconceivable that those who should stand for righteousness actually practiced and promoted sin. How the unbelieving world delights to behold that spectacle! Hebrews 13:17 and James 3:1 both address this topic. The latter states: "Not many of you should presume to be teachers, my brothers, because you know that we who teach will be judged more strictly."

Throughout vv.4–6 Levi is spoken of ideally. What little we know of him is not so favorable; Jacob's "prophecy" regarding him in Genesis 49:5–7 tells us something of what Jacob felt. Much more positive is the "blessing" of Moses on the ideal Levite (Deut 33:8–11) that Malachi was speaking of in this section. And doubtless there were many who did their jobs conscientiously and with the required reverence and devotion.

7–8 Verse 7 begins with the conjunction "for" (*kî*). What the priests should have done (v.7) is then held up in stark contrast with what they had actually been doing (v.8). The priests were the custodians of learning, both the preservers and the pioneers of scholarship. But those who sought to drink at those wells found them either dry or poisoned. Instead of turning men into "the way," the priests did the opposite; they turned men from it. Such irresponsibility violated the covenant of Levi. Sins of omission were compounded with sins of commission. Malachi made it clear that God could tolerate the situation no longer. To have an ill-prepared minister, an incompetent pastor, a hireling for a shepherd was bad enough; much worse was it to have a deceiver, a schemer, a wolf in sheep's clothing for a leader.

9 The verdict came. Like v.3, the sentence on the priests involved shame and humiliation. The regrettable part was that all priests were painted with the same brush, even though there must have been some conscientious ones among them. An additional feature of the indictment comes right at the end of this verse; the offenders had shown partiality in matters of the law.

So ends the section charging the Levitical priests with various misdemeanors and failures. From these specific targets of his wrath, God next turned to the people as a whole.

Notes

---

3 NIV offers two alternative readings of v.3. The first problem is with the verb גֹּעֵר (*gō‘ēr*, “rebuke”). The translation follows the MT, but the relatively rare (thirteen times: once more in Mal 3:11) verb was read גֹּרֵעַ (*gōra‘*, with the last two consonants reversed [cf. K. Elliger, ed., *Biblia Hebraica Stuttgartensia* (Stuttgart: Deutsche Bibelstiftung, 1977)]) by the LXX and others. That change gives the reading “cut off.”

The word for “descendants,” זֶרַע (*zera‘*), can be rendered “seed.” If the vowel pointing is adjusted to *z*^{e}*roa‘*, the meaning is “arm” or “shoulder,” which the LXX has. NIV’s marginal reading—“will blight your grain”—does not come from an emended text but simply puts a different interpretation on the MT. Admittedly, “rebuke your descendants” is hard to explain in this context. What is clear is that the insult described in the following sentence would be remembered with everlasting shame on the house of Levi.

7 “Messenger” is (as noted in the Introduction: Authorship) the Hebrew word מַלְאָךְ (*mal’āk*), or the major element in the prophet’s name. Some see here an allusion to Malachi’s being a priest himself. The point is uncertain.

9 The idiom here is the same as that in the note on 1:8–9—“lifting up the face.”

IV. The Unfaithfulness of the People

2:10–16

10 Have we not all one Father? Did not one God create us? Why do we profane
the covenant of our fathers by breaking faith with one another?
11 Judah has broken faith. A detestable thing has been committed in Israel and
in Jerusalem: Judah has desecrated the sanctuary the Lord loves, by marrying
the daughter of a foreign god.
12 As for the man who does this, whoever he may
be, may the Lord cut him off from the tents of Jacob—even though he brings
offerings to the Lord Almighty.
13 Another thing you do: You flood the Lord’s altar with tears. You weep and wail
because he no longer pays attention to your offerings or accepts them with
pleasure from your hands.
14 You ask, “Why?” It is because the Lord is acting as
the witness between you and the wife of your youth, because you have broken
faith with her, though she is your partner, the wife of your marriage covenant.
15 Has not ⌊the Lord⌋ made them one? In flesh and spirit they are his. And
why one? Because he was seeking godly offspring. So guard yourself in your spirit,
and do not break faith with the wife of your youth.
16 “I hate divorce,” says the Lord God of Israel, “and I hate a man’s covering
himself with violence as well as with his garment,” says the Lord Almighty.
So guard yourself in your spirit, and do not break faith.”

The balance of chapter 2 deals with the same social evils Ezra and Nehemiah addressed themselves to: the problem of intermarriage with unbelievers and the subsequent divorces (Ezra 9:2; Neh 14:23–28). Hand in hand with this sin went a certain compromise of true religion. In fact, the interpretation of v.11b focuses on this problem. “The daughter of a foreign god” may mean that literally they married foreigners or that they adopted all or part of a pagan religion. Hosea often mixed the ideas of idolatry and adultery, or physical and spiritual intermarriage. Perhaps Malachi was touching on both points by his intentionally ambiguous remarks in this section.

10–12 This portion of the book begins with a broad introductory statement (v.10); but this is, of course, addressed to the people of Israel, not to the Moabites, Tyrians, Philistines, Syrians, or others with whom the intermarriage had taken place. NIV's marginal reading ("father," lower case) indicates a problem. Since Hebrew makes no proper-noun distinctions, the translators must decide whether "father" refers to God or to Abraham. In either case the point is clear: "We Jews should cooperate, work harmoniously, and marry within our own people." The implications of "breaking faith with one another" (cf. v.11) probably are broader than simply the matter of divorce. All betrayals, from the slightest unkindness to the grossest injustice, merit God's disapproval.

The mixture of the ideas of intermarriage and prostitution of the sanctuary is not unlike what Paul said in 2 Corinthians 6:14–16: "Do not be yoked together with unbelievers. For what do righteousness and wickedness have in common? Or what fellowship can light have with darkness? What harmony is there between Christ and Belial? What does a believer have in common with an unbeliever? What agreement is there between the temple of God and idols?" Not to distinguish between Israelite women and heathen women—or between Christian spouses and unbelievers—is to deny the difference between the God of the Bible and the pagan deities. Malachi said there would be no exceptions to the rule: Intermarriage meant excommunication (v.12).

13 Apparently the people made a great display of grief over their spiritual barrenness. How exactly the lay people could be in a position to weep over the altar is uncertain; but since the use of the word "flood" is hyperbole, then perhaps we should not be surprised to find figurative expressions in the rest of the verse either. The people's sorrow, however, was for the wrong reason; they should have been bemoaning their sins rather than their lack of divine acceptance and consequent blessing.

14 We might consider the "Why" as another of Malachi's rhetorical questions. Having put the question in their mouths, the prophet proceeded to answer it. The reference to "wife of your youth" in this verse suggests that the men were divorcing their aging wives in favor of younger women.

15 This is the most difficult verse in the book. NIV's rendering, though difficult, seems best to fit the Hebrew of this verse and its context in the chapter. In effect v.15 says that God made monogamous marriage and intends unions to last. Apparently the Israelites not only were marrying foreign women but were also divorcing their Israelite wives in the process. So they were really guilty of two sins—divorce and intermarriage with foreigners.

16 God succinctly gave his verdict: "I hate divorce." Many today would accuse Malachi of having a rigid view of marriage and divorce. But the covenant made between a man and a woman in the presence of a priest, the vicar of God, must be taken with utmost seriousness. "What God has joined together, let man not separate" was Jesus' way of saying it (Matt 19:6; Mark 10:9). Not even the man who is a part of that union may make such a separation.

Verse 16 presents some difficulties. The Hebrew is quite clipped, and several words must be supplied by any translation to make readable English. Hence the

NIV margin suggests the reading "his wife" instead of "himself," but neither is in the Hebrew text. Whether God is speaking of two distinct sins here is not clear. It may be that the divorce and the violence are the same thing. A man can, as Malachi strikingly suggested, wear violence like a garment. The closing two imperatives of v.16 are identical with the close of v.15.

Notes

---

11 בָּעַל (*bā'al*), the word for "marry," is the basis for the name of the pagan god Baal, whose sensual religion had been a temptation to the Israelites from the time of the Exodus (Num 25:3).

Malachi has a proportionately high number of occurrences of the word בָּגַד (*bāgad*, "break faith," vv.10, 11, 14, 15, 16). The noun from the same root letters (*bgd*) is "garment" because the idea of covering (i.e., "hiding," "deceiving") is in the verb. Even though the noun is not in v.16, the idea of covering is.

12 The Hebrew expression עֵר וְעֹנֶה (*'ēr wᵉ'ōneh*) is uncertain. KJV reads "the master and the scholar." Young's Literal Translation has "Tempter and tempted." NAB has "both witness and advocate." Moffatt translated it "kith and kin." NEB has "nomads or settlers." And Beck has "a participant or a witness." What variety and uncertainty! Obviously the Hebrew idiom is just another way of saying "everyone"—thus NIV's "whoever he may be."

15 A review of other translations of this verse shows, as in v.12, a wide variety of interpretations. NIV's marginal reading understands the second אֶחָד (*'eḥād*, "one") in the verse to be Abraham, which is an ancient Jewish interpretation. Then, too, the Hebrew word שְׁאָר (*šᵉ'ār*, "remain") is not emended to read "flesh" (*šᵉ'ēr*). The introduction of Abraham to illustrate the point does not seem the best, since the patriarch married and virtually divorced Hagar. It is true he did not divorce Sarah even though she had been barren. In support of the NIV text, see Gen 2:24 and Matt 19:4–5 (but the Genesis word for "flesh" is בָּשָׂר [*bāśār*], not the term used by Malachi).

V. The Coming Messenger of the Lord

2:17–3:5

17 You have wearied the LORD with your words.
"How have we wearied him?" you ask.
By saying, "All who do evil are good in the eyes of the LORD, and he is pleased with them" or "Where is the God of justice?"

1 "See, I will send my messenger, who will prepare the way before me. Then suddenly the LORD you are seeking will come to his temple; the messenger of the covenant, whom you desire, will come," says the LORD Almighty.

2 But who can endure the day of his coming? Who can stand when he appears?
For he will be like a refiner's fire or a launderer's soap. 3 He will sit as a refiner and
purifier of silver; he will purify the Levites and refine them like gold and silver.
Then the LORD will have men who will bring offerings in righteousness, 4 and the
offerings of Judah and Jerusalem will be acceptable to the LORD, as in days gone by, as in former years.

5 "So I will come near to you for judgment. I will be quick to testify against sorcerers, adulterers and perjurers, against those who defraud laborers of their wages, who oppress the widows and the fatherless, and deprive aliens of justice, but do not fear me," says the LORD Almighty.

17 This verse introduces chapter 3. Its closing question "Where is the God of justice?" points to the abuses in connection with worship and divorce. These have their roots in hearts destitute of the fear of God and culminate in avowed unbelief in the justice of almighty God and his moral government of the world. God himself will answer their question, for 3:1 has "the Lord you are seeking will come to his temple." And 3:5 reads, "So I will come near to you for judgment."

The first question in v.17 is "How have we wearied him [God]?" To this the prophet responded along now familiar lines. God was tired of hypocrisy, inverted morals, spiritual blindness, and obduracy.

1 This verse is quoted in the NT. Matthew (11:10), Mark (1:2), and Luke (7:27) include its first half. They all refer it to John the Baptist. Thus the NT settles the identity of the one called "my messenger." He is the forerunner of Christ, John the son of Zechariah and Elizabeth. The Lord who then follows is none other than Jesus Christ, the Son of God. The prophet's choice of the word "Lord" (*'aḏôn*) rather than LORD (YHWH) points to this (cf. Acts 2:36; 1 Cor 12:3; Phil 2:11). Notice, too, that the "me" establishes a significant identification between the First and Second persons of the Trinity. Christ came to the temple, first as a baby to be dedicated, then at least yearly for the festivals. Most notably he came the last week of his life.

The phrase "whom you desire" is interesting. Even in their sin, suggests 2:17, the people longed for deliverance through the Messiah. Amos, too, had people in his audience who "desired" the Day of the Lord; but he bluntly told them that the Day of the Lord would be darkness and not light (Amos 5:18–20). So, too, Malachi asked in 3:2, "Who can endure the day of his coming?" The coming Messiah would bring judgment—viz., vindication and exoneration for the righteous but condemnation and punishment for the wicked. Like most of the OT prophets, Malachi, in his picture of the coming Christ, mingled the two advents. So while the birth and earthly ministry of Christ are in view in v.1, we already have the returning Judge in v.2. It could be said that the latter days began with Bethlehem and continued through the present to be culminated in the eternal state. The Day of the Lord is any day God steps into history to do a special work, whether of judgment or deliverance. This passage speaks of purification and judgment.

2–4 Malachi continued his use of rhetorical questions as he asked in two ways, "Who will stand when he appears?" (v.2). Christ's judgment, a Second Advent function, is likened to two purifying agents: fire for metals and soap for clothing. Just as these remove impurities, he will purify the latter-day Levites so that they will gleam and endure like "gold and silver" (v.3). As a result of that process, God will have an approved and accepted priesthood to carry out the sacred ministry in a right spirit. Verse 4, of course, does not mean that descendants of Levi and Aaron will function in any NT temple; it is, rather, symbolic of a cleansed and sanctified church. See 1 Peter 2:5, 9 and Revelation 1:6; 5:10; and 20:6 for statements about Christians as priests. The soundest logical and theological reason for the abolition of the sacrificial system is found in Hebrews 9:23–10:14.

5 This is altogether judgmental. God simply said that he will at that time speedily bring to justice all sorts of malefactors. "Sorcerers" is a category that takes in practitioners of the occult. "Adulterers" includes any departure from God's ordained pattern of family life. Next come "perjurers," or, more literally, "false swearers" (KJV).

This covers everything from "white lies" to perjury in a high court. The indictment against oppressors of widows and orphans reflects Malachi's interest in social justice. Chapter 2 had been heavily weighted with liturgical concerns. But like all true ministers of God, Malachi could not divorce responsibilities toward God from those toward men. The number of laws in the Pentateuch and elsewhere for the protection of aliens suggests it must have been common or easy to exploit expatriates among the Israelites. Hospitality was a requirement, any breach of which would come under the rubric of depriving aliens. All the offenders listed in v.5 are categorized as those who "do not fear me." Their sin testified to a lamentable absence of that godly fear that is "the beginning of knowledge" (Prov 1:7).

VI. The Robbery and Riches of God (3:6–12)

1. *The Neglect of the Tithe*

3:6–9

6"I the LORD do not change. So you, O descendants of Jacob, are not destroyed. 7Ever since the time of your forefathers you have turned away from my decrees and have not kept them. Return to me, and I will return to you," says the LORD Almighty.

"But you ask, 'How are we to return?'

8"Will a man rob God? Yet you rob me.

"But you ask, 'How do we rob you?'

"In tithes and offerings. 9You are under a curse—the whole nation of you—because you are robbing me."

6–7 These verses provide a transition between the preceding sections and the one that follows. First there is a declaration of the immutability of God (v.6), the attribute of changlessness that ultimately preserves the nation from destruction. God keeps his promises to the patriarchs. He knows this evil generation will pass and that a God-fearing one will yet come to inherit the promises.

God next explained why he did not answer the people's prayers: "You have turned away from my decrees" (v.7). God is still pledged to give attention to those who earnestly seek him (cf. Jer 29:13). The invitation to return, which could as well have been translated "repent" or "convert," was met with a cynical question: "How are we to return?" Malachi did not answer this question; his whole book and ministry was basically one of telling people how to get right with God.

8 Tithing (being fiscally responsible before God) is introduced by the blunt question "Will a man rob God?" Stealing means not only taking what is not yours but keeping back for yourself what belongs to someone else. In this case one-tenth of a man's income was due God; failure to pay that debt amounted to robbery (cf. Ananias and Sapphira in Acts 5:1–11).

The tenth of all produce as well as of flocks and cattle belonged to the Lord and was by him assigned to the Levites for their services (Num 18:21, 24). It may be that the people's disobedience prompted some of the priestly grumbling Malachi had earlier referred to. Nehemiah dealt with the same problem (Neh 10:32–39; 13:10). If Malachi predated the events of Nehemiah 13, perhaps Malachi's words in v.8 had been heeded.

9 That God condemned the whole nation suggests that this "robbery" was a rather widespread abuse of his generosity. Most churches still fall under this indictment; their budgets are generally nowhere near 10 percent of the income of the members.

Notes

8 The Hebrew word for "rob" is קָבַע (*qāḇa'*), which is not the usual one, גָּנַב (*gānaḇ*), as found in the eighth commandment (Exod 20:15; Lev 19:11). Apart from its four occurrences here in vv.8–9, *qāḇa'* appears only two other times, both in Prov 22:23. Because the Greek word πτερνίζω (*pternizō*) translates *qāḇa'* and the similar sounding and much more common word עָקַב (*'āqaḇ*), some think *qāḇa'* is a metathesis (a transposition of letters). (*'Āqaḇ* means "circumvent," "overreach," and is the basis for the name "Jacob." If metathesis did occur, *'āqaḇ* still makes good sense in this context.

9 Malachi used the word גּוֹי (*gôy*, "nation") for Israel. Generally, however, this term was used of heathen nations, as Malachi himself did in 1:11 (*bis*), 14; 3:12.

2. *The Promise of Blessing*

3:10–12

[10] "Bring the whole tithe into the storehouse, that there may be food in my house. Test me in this," says the LORD Almighty, "and see if I will not throw open the floodgates of heaven and pour out so much blessing that you will not have room enough for it. [11] I will prevent pests from devouring your crops, and the vines in your fields will not cast their fruit," says the LORD Almighty. [12] "Then all the nations will call you blessed, for yours will be a delightful land," says the LORD Almighty.

10 The remedy for Israel was simply to start doing what was right—bring the whole tithe into the storehouse. The temple served as a warehouse for the produce the Israelites brought. The Levites then distributed it for sacrificial purposes, for their own domestic needs, and for whatever emergencies arose. So-called storehouse tithing does have a sound basis in this verse. Any private charity or gifts to Christian friends or institutions should be additional to the basic 10 percent demanded by God. The apostle Paul instructed NT believers on the necessity of regularly and proportionately setting aside support for the on-going work of the Lord (cf. 1 Cor 16:1–2). Moreover, the OT tithe is not the upper limit. Christians are urged to "excel in this grace of giving" (2 Cor 8:7), remembering that they owe everything to the one who for their sake "made himself nothing" (Phil 2:7; cf. 2 Cor 8:9).

In the latter half of v.10, God offered his people the challenge of testing him. By this offer he virtually guaranteed them a direct and abundant return on their investment. His "storehouse" of blessings was unlimited; so the only restriction on how much they received would be their ability to contain or use it.

11–12 From a general statement of blessing, Malachi next specified what form that blessing might take (v.11). Since he was dealing with an agrarian society, the "blessings" had to do with crops and the like. Then, as is always the case, there was a purpose for the blessing (v.12). Not merely would God's people be comfortable, healthy, and happy, but because of this the Lord's name would be honored. Whatever good happens to us should be turned into a testimony to the goodness of our God. Then unbelievers will note our blessedness and be drawn to our God.

Notes

12 The word for "delight" (חֵפֶץ, *ḥēpeṣ*) is the basis for the name (in Isa 62:4) God said he would give the land — *Hephzi-bah,* meaning "my delight is in her."

VII. The Servants of the Lord (3:13–18)

1. *The Faithless*

3:13–15

13"You have said harsh things against me," says the LORD.
"Yet you ask, 'What have we said against you?'
14"You have said, 'It is futile to serve God. What did we gain by carrying out his requirements and going about like mourners before the LORD Almighty? 15But now we call the arrogant blessed. Certainly the evildoers prosper, and even those who challenge God escape.' "

13–14 Once more, and for the last time, Malachi opened with a statement about what people said, followed by a question in which they implied that the charge was unfounded. The third element (v.14) then follows: an elaboration and explanation of the charge. The sin concerned essentially lack of trust in God. By innuendo, if not by outright statement, God was represented as unfair and the keeping of the law a useless exercise.

15 This verse is a restatement of the age-old question so prominent in the Book of Job: Why do the evil prosper and the righteous suffer? Malachi did not answer the complaint immediately.

Notes

14 The word for "mourners," קְדֹרַנִּים (*qᵉḏōrannayim*), is a hapax legomenon. Cognate words help us identify it with reasonable certainty as related to קָדַר (*qāḏar,* "to be dark").

2. *The Faithful*

3:16–18

16Then those who feared the LORD talked with each other, and the LORD listened and heard. A scroll of remembrance was written in his presence concerning those who feared the LORD and honored his name.

[17]"They will be mine," says the LORD Almighty, "in the day when I make up my treasured possession. I will spare them, just as in compassion a man spares his son who serves him. [18]And you will again see the distinction between the righteous and the wicked, between those who serve God and those who do not.

16 In this verse Malachi portrayed God as listening to those who feared him. What they were saying, we do not know; but we can assume it was an expression of love and worship. Then comes the remarkable statement that "a scroll . . . was written in his presence concerning those who feared the LORD." This idea of God's keeping written records appears occasionally in the OT (cf. Exod 32:32; Ps 69:28; Isa 4:3; Dan 12:1). The NT mentions it many times, especially in Revelation (cf. Luke 10:20; Phil 4:3; Heb 12:23; Rev 3:5; 13:8; 17:8; 20:12, 15; 21:27). Perhaps the most beautiful expression of the idea is in Isaiah 49:16: "See, I have engraved you on the palms of my hands."

17–18 Verse 17 says two things about God's people. They will be his very own, and he will spare them. On that day, when all wrongs are rectified and all wickedness punished, it will be apparent that God does judge justly and that he does make a distinction between those who serve him and those who do not (v.18).

Notes

---

17 The word for "treasured possession" is סְגֻלָּה (*s^egullāh*), which often appears as "peculiar" in the KJV (Exod 19:5; Deut 14:2; 26:18; Ps 135:4; cf. Titus 2:14; 1 Peter 2:9). Here "treasured possession" is an adequate rendering.

VIII. The Day of the Lord

4:1–6

[1]"Surely the day is coming; it will burn like a furnace. All the arrogant and every evildoer will be stubble, and that day that is coming will set them on fire," says the LORD Almighty. "Not a root or a branch will be left to them. [2]But for you who revere my name, the sun of righteousness will rise with healing in its wings. And you will go out and leap like calves released from the stall. [3]Then you will trample down the wicked; they will be ashes under the soles of your feet on the day when I do these things," says the LORD Almighty.

[4]"Remember the law of my servant Moses, the decrees and laws I gave him at Horeb for all Israel.

[5]"See, I will send you the prophet Elijah before that great and dreadful day of the LORD comes. [6]He will turn the hearts of the fathers to their children, and the hearts of the children to their fathers; or else I will come and strike the land with a curse."

1 The eschatological theme of the Day of the Lord bulks large in the OT prophets (cf. Isa 13:6; Jer 46:10; Joel 2:31; Zeph 1:14–2:3) and also appears in the NT (cf. Matt

24:3–25:46; Rom 2:5; 2 Peter 3:10; Rev 16:14). It continues into the second half of this somber verse in which Malachi alternately reproved and warned. The picture of it in v.1 is cosmological. Fire will be the agent of destruction on that day as was water in Noah's day.

The word for "arrogant" (*zēḏ*) is a relatively rare one, occurring in the Prophets only once in Isaiah (13:11) and once in Jeremiah (43:2). But Malachi used it also in 3:15. So those "blessed" arrogant ones of the former reference will now be burned as stubble. (Stubble, the unusable part of the grain, lasts only seconds when thrown into a blazing furnace.) Amos 2:9 uses the same figure for destruction—roots below and branches above. The mention of roots indicates the complete termination of growth. As with the two extremities of a plant, all the wicked—without exception—will be destroyed.

2–3 The fate of the wicked was described in v.1. Verse 2 focuses on the blessed future of the righteous. "Sun" is capitalized in the KJV (followed only by Mof, Amplified, and LB among modern versions). This capitalization has sustained the idea that the figure is a messianic one. No use is made of this figure, however, in the NT. For that reason most translations have not capitalized "sun."

The righteous, now enlightened and healed, will gambol like calves, frisking about in their new-found freedom. An added reward is described in v.3. The righteous will trample the wicked on that great judgment day. Compare Micah 2:12–13 for a similar picture.

4–6 These verses give us two somewhat unrelated "appendixes" to the book. The first (v.4) is an injunction to heed the law of Moses. This verse, in a sense, closes the entire book. Malachi began with an illustration from Genesis (Jacob and Esau) and spent most of the first half of the book reminding priests and people of the need to keep the Mosaic Law. Now, close to the end of his book, he gives another terse reminder of their continuing obligation to those laws.

The second "appendix" (vv.5–6) relates to Elijah's coming to announce the Messiah's arrival. Elijah, as has already been stated, was John the Baptist (Matt 11:14; 17:12; Mark 9:11–13; Luke 1:17). His ministry was to prepare for the Day of the Lord and to "turn the hearts of the fathers to their children" (v.6) and vice versa, "before that great and dreadful Day of the LORD" (v.5; cf. comment at v.1). The first Christmas was a day of the Lord. So were all the other days when God stepped into history and did something extraordinary. But all these are preparatory for "that great and dreadful day" when the curtain will drop on world history and the Lord, who came the first time as Savior and Friend, will come as King and Judge.

The mission of reconciling families has been successful insofar as people have come to Christ. Where this has not happened, God will "strike the land with a curse" (v.6). KJV reads this as "earth," giving more of a worldwide connotation; but "land" interprets Malachi's reference to be to the Promised Land, where his people were dwelling. Through the Exile the land had been denied them; now they had it back, but still only on probation. If they failed to honor that land and him who gave it to them, it would be permanently denied them. Since some of Malachi's remarks have dealt with the land (2:11; 3:11; and perhaps 2:3), it is altogether likely that is what he meant. What is not in doubt is that Malachi has set before Israel the age-old alternatives: respond to the God who loves them (1:2), or suffer the terrible consequences (4:1, 6).

Notes

---

1 In the Hebrew Bible, 4:1 is 3:19. And so the numbers go to the end of the book. There is no chapter 4.

2 The Hebrew word כְּנָפֶיהָ (*k^e^nāp̄eyhā,* "her wings") is unusual, since the word for "sun," שֶׁמֶשׁ (*šemeš*), appears as both a masculine and a feminine noun. Naturally the similarity between "son" and "sun" (a peculiarity of English and German) has contributed to the connection between them.

6 The word חֵרֶם (*ḥērem,* "curse"), as the standard NIV footnote in Num 18:14, Deut 2:34, 1 Sam 15:3, and elsewhere states, refers to the practice of devoting things or persons irrevocably to the Lord, often by total destruction. Here it would imply that God will make a whole burnt offering of the land. How different this is from the apostle's injunction in Rom 12:1, where believers are urged to present themselves voluntarily to God as a sacrifice!

Because Malachi ends with a curse, and particularly because his is the last book of the Prophets, there is a Jewish tradition to reread v.5 (3:23 MT) at the close of the book so that the entire corpus ends on a slightly more positive note.
